Learning Forensic Assessment

Major developments in the field since the publication of *Learning Forensic Assessment* are integrated in this revised edition, including revised editions of the DSM-5, HCR-20 scale, and child custody guidelines.

This textbook is designed for graduate students learning forensic assessment and psychologists coming to forensic practice later in their careers. It is organized around five broad areas: Professional and Practice Issues, Adult Forensic Assessment, Juvenile Forensic Assessment, Civil Forensic Assessment, and Communicating Your Findings.

Each chapter begins with a strong teaching and learning foundation. The latter part of each chapter is assessment specific, covering available assessment measures and approaches to assessment. The authors go well beyond simple descriptions of assessment measures and provide a conceptual discussion of the evaluation process that helps the reader understand how assessment measures fit into the overall evaluation process. The evaluation component is geared toward assessing the important aspects of the construct as laid out in the early part of each chapter. Each chapter then concludes with a case example to illustrate the measures and techniques described.

Rebecca Jackson, PhD, is the Clinical Director of the Florida Civil Commitment Center, a 720-bed sex offender civil commitment facility. Previously she was associate professor and director of the Forensic Certification Program in Psychology and Law at Palo Alto University, Palo Alto, CA.

Ronald Roesch, PhD, is Professor of Psychology at Simon Fraser University (SFU), and Director, Mental Health, Law, and Policy Institute, SFU, and Past President of the International Association of Forensic Mental Health Services (IAFMHS) and the American Psychology-Law Society (Div. 41 APA). He serves as editor of the International Perspectives on Forensic Mental Health Books Series.

International Perspectives on Forensic Mental Health
A Routledge Book Series
Edited by Ronald Roesch
Simon Fraser University

The goal of this series is to improve the quality of health care services in forensic settings by providing a forum for discussing issues related to policy, administration, clinical practice, and research. The series will cover topics such as mental health law; the organization and administration of forensic services for people with mental disorder; the development, implementation and evaluation of treatment programs for mental disorder in civil and criminal justice settings; the assessment and management of violence risk, including risk for sexual violence and family violence; and staff selection, training, and development in forensic systems. The book series will consider proposals for both monographs and edited works on these and similar topics, with special consideration given to proposals that promote best practice and are relevant to international audiences.

Published Titles

Learning Forensic Assessment
Edited by Rebecca Jackson

Handbook of Violence Risk Assessment
Edited by Randy K. Otto & Kevin S. Douglas

Dangerous People: Policy, Prediction, and Practice
Edited by Bernadette McSherry & Patrick Keyzer

Risk Markers for Sexual Victimization and Predation in Prison
Janet I. Warren & Shelly L. Jackson

How to Work With Sex Offenders: A Handbook for Criminal Justice, Human Service, and Mental Health Professionals, Second Edition
Rudy Flora & Michael L. Keohane

Managing Fear: The Law and Ethics of Preventive Detention and Risk Assessment
Bernadette McSherry

Case Studies in Sexual Deviance: Toward Evidence Based Practice
Edited by William T. O'Donohue

Forensic Psychological Assessment in Practice: Case Studies
Corine De Ruiter & Nancy Kaser-Boyd

Sexual Predators: Society, Risk and the Law
Robert A. Prentky, Howard E. Barbaree & Eric S. Janus

Forthcoming Titles

Learning Forensic Assessment, Second Edition
Edited by Rebecca Jackson and Ronald Roesch

Handbook of Forensic Social Work with Children
Edited by Viola Vaughan-Eden

Learning Forensic Assessment

Research and Practice

2nd Edition

Edited by
Rebecca Jackson and Ronald Roesch

Routledge
Taylor & Francis Group

NEW YORK AND LONDON

Second edition published 2016
by Routledge
711 Third Avenue, New York, NY 10017

and by Routledge
2 Park Square, Milton Park, Abingdon, Oxon OX14 4RN

Routledge is an imprint of the Taylor & Francis Group, an informa business

First edition published by Routledge 2007

Library of Congress Cataloging in Publication Data
Learning forensic assessment : research and practice / edited by Rebecca Jackson and
    Ronald Roesch. — 2nd edition.
        pages cm
    Includes bibliographical references and index.
  1. Forensic psychiatry.   2. Forensic psychology.   3. Personality assessment.   I. Jackson,
Rebecca (Rebecca L.)   II. Roesch, Ronald, 1947–
    RA1151.L43 2015
    614'.15—dc23
    2015030492

ISBN: 978-1-138-77617-3 (hbk)
ISBN: 978-1-138-77619-7 (pbk)
ISBN: 978-1-315-77337-7 (ebk)

Typeset in Times
by Apex CoVantage, LLC

Printed and bound in the United States of America by Publishers Graphics,
LLC on sustainably sourced paper.

Contents

About the Editors

Rebecca Jackson, PhD, is the Clinical Director of the Florida Civil Commitment Center, a 720-bed sex offender civil commitment facility. Previously she was associate professor and director of the Forensic Certification Program in Psychology and Law at Palo Alto University, Palo Alto, CA.

Ronald Roesch, PhD, is Professor of Psychology at Simon Fraser University (SFU), and Director, Mental Health, Law, and Policy Institute, SFU, and Past President of the International Association of Forensic Mental Health Services (IAFMHS) and the American Psychology-Law Society (Div. 41 APA). He serves as editor of the International Perspectives on Forensic Mental Health Books Series.

Contributors

Elizabeth W. Adams, MA
Psychology Department
Clinical Child Program
University of Alabama

Carmelina Barone, MA
Department of Psychology
Simon Fraser University

Marcus T. Boccaccini, PhD
Psychology Department
Sam Houston State University

Peter Buckley, MD
Dean
Georgia Regents University

Jeffrey Burl, PhD
Staff Psychologist
Bridgewater State Hospital

Abby Clark, BS
Department of Psychology
University of Alabama

Patricia I. Coburn, MA
Doctoral Student
Department of Psychology
Simon Fraser University

Mary A. Connell, EdD
Independent Practice
Fort Worth, TX

Deborah A. Connolly, PhD, LLB
Associate Professor
Department of Psychology
Simon Fraser University

Christmas N. Covell, PhD
Psychologist, Private Practice
Tacoma, WA

Mark D. Cunningham, PhD, ABPP
Clinical & Forensic Psychology
Austin, TX

Sara A. Debus-Sherrill
ICF International
Fairfax, VA

David DeMatteo, JD, PhD, ABPP (Forensic)
Associate Professor of Psychology and Law
Drexel University

Sarah Filone, MA
PhD Student (Forensic Concentration)
Drexel University

William E. Foote, PhD, ABPP
Private Practice
Albuquerque, NM

Geri Fuhrmann, PsyD
Massachusetts Dept. of Mental Health
Juvenile Forensic Services

Gregg J. Gagliardi, PhD
Clinical Associate Professor
University of Washington

Stephen L. Golding, PhD
Professor Emeritus
University of Utah

Andrew L. Gray, MA
Department of Psychology
Simon Fraser University

Ross D. Grimes, PhD
Brewer-Porch Children's Center
The University of Alabama

Michelle R. Guyton, PhD, ABPP
Northwest Forensic Institute
Portland, OR

Paige B. Harris, MA
Psychology Department
Sam Houston State University

Kirk Heilbrun, PhD
Professor and Head of Psychology Department
Drexel University

Phylissa P. Kwartner, PhD
Forensic Psychologist, Department of State Hospitals—Atascadero
Atascadero, CA

Emily A.M. MacDougall, MA
Graduate Student and Doctoral Candidate
Clinical Psychology
The University of Alabama

Kaitlyn McLachlan, PhD
Postdoctoral Fellow
Department of Pediatrics
University of Alberta

Audrey K. Miller, PhD
Department of Psychology and Philosophy
Sam Houston State University

Craig S. Neumann, PhD
Professor of Psychology
University of North Texas

Amy Phenix, PhD
Private Practice
Morro Bay, CA 93442

Richard Rogers, PhD, ABPP
Regents Professor of Psychology
Eminent Faculty
University of North Texas

Randall T. Salekin, PhD
Professor
The University of Alabama

Eric Strachan, MLS, PhD
Assistant Professor
University of Washington

Jodi L. Viljoen, PhD
Associate Professor
Simon Fraser University

Michael J. Vitacco, PhD
Assistant Professor of Psychiatry
Director of Forensic Psychology Training
Georgia Regents University

Lori T. Welch, PhD
Assistant Professor of Psychiatry
Georgia Regents University

Jennifer G. Wheeler, PhD
Psychologist, Private Practice
Pacific Evaluation, Consultation, & Treatment Services, PLLC
Seattle, WA

Patricia A. Zapf, PhD
Professor
John Jay College of Criminal Justice

Robert A. Zibbell, PhD
Private Practice
Framingham, MA

Preface

When *Learning Forensic Assessment* was first published, a clear need existed for a comprehensive, yet user-friendly textbook dedicated to forensic assessment. Existing titles tended to be either broad-based introductions to the field or in-depth treatments of specialized topics. As a result, they were less suitable for teaching of graduate level students or professionals coming to forensic evaluation later in their careers. That volume was created to "fill in the gap" that existed and provided both a foundation for teaching and learning about empirically-based forensic assessment as well as a wealth of practical, "how-to" information.

Feedback received about *Learning Forensic Assessment* indicated that instructors were adopting the text for their graduate level courses, but also that individual practitioners were turning to it as a resource. As was true in 2008, the field of Clinical Forensic Psychology continues to experience tremendous growth. I am grateful to Ron Roesch who convinced me that a second edition was warranted in light of the number of new studies, the publication of new or updated forensic assessment instruments, and recent developments in case law and statutes. I am more grateful that he volunteered to be my co-editor on this project and facilitated its timely completion.

Both Ron and I were extremely pleased that the majority of the original expert authors agreed to be part of this project. As noted in the first edition, one of the goals was to introduce readers to forensic experts. As teachers, each has his or her own style and each was free to adopt that personal style in teaching the reader about his or her subject matter. The aim was to create a forensic assessment course, in print form, in which each lecture was delivered by a different expert. At the same time, we also wanted the "lectures" to adopt a common structure to facilitate its usefulness as a learning tool. The authors in this volume have truly delivered—again.

Similar to the first edition, the chapters are explicitly designed to provide an overview of the topic, relevant case law, theory, and history of the construct in the legal system. Each chapter begins with a strong teaching and learning foundation. The latter part of each chapter is assessment specific, covering available assessment measures and approaches to assessment. The authors go well beyond simple descriptions of assessment measures and provide a conceptual discussion of the evaluation process that helps the reader understand how assessment measures fit into the overall evaluation process. The evaluation component is geared toward assessing the important aspects of the construct as laid out in the early part of each chapter. Each chapter then concludes with a case example to illustrate the measures and techniques described.

We hope you find these chapters informative, easy to read, and a valued updated resource for your training and practice.

Rebecca Jackson and Ron Roesch

Part I
Professional and Practice Issues

1 Training in Forensic Assessment and Intervention

Implications for Principle-Based Models

David DeMatteo, Jeffrey Burl, Sarah Filone, and Kirk Heilbrun

The field of forensic psychology as a distinct subdiscipline within professional psychology has emerged relatively recently but grown rapidly. There are several indicators of the field's growth and development. For example, there are a number of national and international professional organizations devoted to law and psychology/psychiatry, including the American Psychology-Law Society; the European Association of Psychology and Law; the Australian and New Zealand Association of Psychiatry, Psychology, and Law; the International Association for Correctional and Forensic Psychology; the American Academy of Psychiatry and the Law; and the International Academy of Law and Mental Health. The availability of psychological research and literature relating to forensic practice began to expand by the mid-1970s, and there are now numerous professional journals devoted to publishing empirical, theoretical, and practice articles relevant to law and psychology, including *Behavioral Sciences and the Law; Criminal Justice and Behavior; International Journal of Forensic Mental Health; Journal of the American Academy of Psychiatry and the Law; Law and Human Behavior;* and *Psychology, Public Policy, and Law*. A more recent indicator of the growth of forensic psychology is the publication of the *Best Practices for Forensic Mental Health Assessment* series by Oxford University Press (see Heilbrun, Grisso, & Goldstein, 2009), which serves as a collection of "best practice" books for various types of forensic mental health assessments.

The acceptance of psychologists in court proceedings represents another area of growth. Early court decisions rejected psychologists as testifying experts, holding that only physicians were qualified to offer testimony on mental health issues (Bartol & Bartol, 2014). Although psychologists occasionally were permitted to offer courtroom testimony in the early 20th century, it was not until 1962 that Judge David Bazelon, then a circuit judge for the U.S. Court of Appeals for the District of Columbia, wrote in *Jenkins v. United States* that psychologists who were appropriately qualified could testify in court as experts in mental disorders. *Jenkins* was a watershed moment for forensic psychologists, and a market for highly specialized forensic mental health assessments began to emerge shortly after the *Jenkins* decision. Based on practitioner estimates, it is reasonable to conclude that tens of thousands of forensic mental health assessments are conducted annually by psychologists and other mental health professionals (Melton, Petrila, Poythress, & Slobogin, 2007; Otto & Heilbrun, 2002).

This chapter focuses on another indicator of the growth of forensic psychology—the proliferation of specialized training programs. Formal law-psychology and forensic psychology training programs emerged in the early 1970s, and in recent years the number of specialized training programs has increased considerably. This chapter begins by defining forensic psychology and the role of forensic psychologists. Next, we discuss educational and training opportunities in forensic psychology, with a particular focus on (1) the practice, educational, and training opportunities available to students and practitioners in the field; (2) the diversity in training models employed in these various training programs; and (3) whether current training models adequately prepare students to become forensic practitioners. We then narrow the focus to training in forensic assessment and intervention, and in that section we compare forensic assessment and intervention and then explore best practice models for the delivery of such services. The discussion of best practice models highlights the role of existing principle-based approaches to forensic assessment, and how such models might be constructed in the area of forensic intervention. We conclude the chapter with a discussion of how principle-based approaches could enhance the quality of forensic training and practice.

The Role of Forensic Psychologists

Since the American Psychological Association (APA) formally recognized forensic psychology as a discrete specialization in 2001, forensic psychology has gained widespread acceptance as a freestanding practice specialty. There is, however, inconsistency in the terminology used to describe this discipline. For example, in place of *forensic psychology*, one may see the terms *psychology and law* (DeMatteo, Marczyk, Krauss, & Burl, 2009), *criminal justice psychology* (Olver, Preston, Camilleri, Helmus, & Starzomski, 2011; Simourd & Wormith, 1995), and *forensic/legal psychology* (Levine, Wilson, & Sales, 1980). One reason for the varying names given to this area of psychology is the differing meanings of the term *forensic*. Traditionally, *forensic* referred to matters relating to the court, but forensic psychology has also included any activity at the interface between psychology and the law (Levine et al., 1980). Therefore, depending on one's use of the term *forensic*, the activities of providing treatment in a correctional system, applying psychological principles to law enforcement selection, or conducting research on psycholegal topics have all fallen within the realm of forensic psychology. The use of differing names for the field is perhaps an effort to provide an inclusive umbrella for these diverse areas of research and practice.

Issues of nomenclature are further complicated by disagreement as to whether various domains of psychology and law fall within the professional ambit of forensic psychology. For example, police psychology is a specific application of psychology within the criminal justice system. Over its history, police psychology has developed into a specialized practice area within applied psychology (e.g., Scrivner, Corey, & Greene, 2014). However, despite its direct connection to the law, it typically is not considered within the sphere of forensic psychology (Bartol & Bartol, 2014). Correctional psychology has also often been identified as a domain of forensic psychology, but it too is often seen by its practitioners as a unique branch of psychological practice. It is defined by a core body of knowledge and clinical skills, and effective correctional psychology practice requires specific training and educational experiences to obtain these competencies (Gendreau & Goggin, 2014; Magaletta, Patry, Dietz, & Ax, 2007). Professionally, psychologists practicing within correctional settings appear primarily to identify themselves as correctional psychologists as opposed to forensic psychologists (Bartol & Bartol, 2014). In addition, forensic psychology graduate programs and professional conferences offer little exposure to correctional psychology in relation to other areas of the law (Burl, Shah, Filone, Foster & DeMatteo, 2012; Magaletta et al., 2013), although efforts have been made in recent years to address this gap (see American Psychology-Law Society, 2009).

There remains debate within the field of forensic psychology, therefore, over the definition and scope of the discipline. Although some definitions of forensic psychology are relatively narrow and restrictive, other definitions, particularly those offered more recently, are broad and inclusive. These broader definitions reflect the evolving and expanding role of forensic psychology. For contextual purposes, some of the definitions of forensic psychology, both narrow and broad, are discussed in this chapter.

The APA accepted a narrow approach to defining forensic psychology when it officially recognized the discipline as a specialty area in 2001. After much debate about the nature and definition of forensic psychology, the petition for recognition of forensic psychology as a specialty area, which was submitted to APA by the American Psychology-Law Society (Division 41 of APA) and the American Board of Forensic Psychology (ABFP), limited the field's scope primarily to the clinical aspects of forensic assessment, treatment, and consultation (Otto & Heilbrun, 2002). As such, those psychologists practicing within nonclinical areas of law and psychology (e.g., social, cognitive, developmental, experimental) were not included in the definition of forensic psychology.

In recent years, broader definitions of forensic psychology have been advanced. For example, the *Specialty Guidelines for Forensic Psychology* (APA, 2013b), which was jointly developed by the American Psychology-Law Society and the American Academy of Forensic Psychology (AAFP) and adopted as APA policy in August 2011, defines forensic psychology as "professional practice by any psychologist working within any subdiscipline of psychology (e.g., clinical, developmental, social, cognitive) when applying the scientific, technical, or specialized knowledge of psychology to the law to assist in addressing legal, contractual, and administrative matters" (p. 7). This is a broad definition that encompasses both clinical and nonclinical subdisciplines of psychology, and it recognizes that forensic psychologists can offer assistance to the legal system through both applied and nonapplied practice. A comparably broad definition of forensic psychology was adopted by the ABFP, which provides board certification in forensic psychology under the umbrella of the ABPP. The ABFP (2014) defines forensic psychology as the application of the science and profession of psychology to questions and issues relating to law and the legal system.

The broadest conceptualization of forensic psychology advocates using psychological knowledge and research not only to assist legal actors within the judicial system, but also to act as a therapeutic agent and evolutionary force within legal contexts. Under this definition, forensic psychology can act as a guide and advocate for making the law more therapeutic, thereby helping the legal system become more effective in achieving its aims. This approach is heavily influenced by the "theralaw" and therapeutic jurisprudence traditions, which assert that the legal system should seek to promote the health and emotional well-being of individuals in addition to ensuring justice and social order (e.g., Wexler & Winick, 1996). This conceptualization is sometimes referred to as *psycholegal*, and it frequently embraces a multidisciplinary, systemic approach to addressing psychological issues within a legal context (e.g., Elwork, 1984).

Although each of these conceptualizations posits a discrete breed of psychologist whose job is to interact with the legal system, many kinds of mental health professionals may find themselves drawn into contact with the law. Former APA President Donald Bersoff (2008) once stated that "every psychologist—whether clinician, scientist, or academician—is a potential expert witness . . . and each must be prepared to interact with the legal system" (p. 454). These are what Otto and Heilbrun (2002) referred to as "accidental experts" (p. 15). Although forensic psychologists may be specially qualified to understand and work in the legal system, they cannot and should not claim the whole of forensic practice as their exclusive domain.

Educational and Training Opportunities in Forensic Psychology

Prior to discussing the current training opportunities in forensic psychology, we consider a question from Sageman (2003): What is specific about forensic psychology education? Attempts to answer this question have been at the root of the field's efforts over the past 40 years to develop a system to train current and future forensic psychologists (Fenster, Litwack, & Symonds, 1975; Heilbrun & Brooks, 2010; Ogloff, Tomkins, & Bersoff, 1996). Before formal training programs were developed, any psychologist wishing to work in a forensic setting obtained specialized training "on the job." Indeed, it is likely that a sizeable portion of forensic psychologists did not attend formal forensic training programs, given the relatively recent development of those programs (Krauss & Sales, 2014).

Since the introduction of the first forensic psychology training programs in the 1970s, however, there has been a significant expansion in the educational opportunities available to students (Burl et al., 2012; Ogloff et al., 1996). There have been many important steps throughout this period of growth. For example, the 1995 National Invitational Conference on Education and Training in Law and Psychology at Villanova University identified the state of forensic education at that time and set a direction for the future development of training in psychology and law (Bersoff et al., 1997). More recently, Heilbrun and Brooks (2010) utilized recommendations set by the National Research Council (2009) to propose further meaningful planning in forensic psychology training.[1] Efforts to promote competent research and practice through formal training in forensic psychology have simultaneously occurred on an international level (Day & Tytler, 2012; Helmus, Babchishin, Camilleri, & Olver, 2011).

A variety of forces have shaped the current array of training options in forensic psychology. As discussed earlier, there is debate as to the scope of forensic practice, and different programs have therefore developed to meet these varied definitions. Some programs are developed or constrained by administrative limits, such as faculty lines (e.g., Krauss & Sales, 2014), while other programs are developed due to increased interest from students. Forensic psychology's development as a fast-growing specialty area has been propelled by the increasing student demand for training in this field (Brigham, 1999). Popular areas of study include both clinical/applied work (i.e., forensic mental health assessments and forensic-based interventions, such as restoration to competence) and forensic research (clinical and nonclinical).

The many efforts to purposely shape training programs in forensic psychology, in concert with the many other variables that have affected this process, have resulted in a diverse number of training programs in forensic psychology. These educational opportunities range from undergraduate survey courses that examine the broad intersection of law and psychology to joint-degree graduate programs that allow students to obtain terminal degrees in both law (JD) and psychology (PhD, PsyD). Forensic psychology graduate programs, or programs that offer a forensic psychology track or concentration, currently exist at both the master's and doctoral-level, and they offer a wide variety of educational and training opportunities in domains such as forensic assessment, specialized interventions, human development, legal policy, research, and program evaluation. In addition, opportunities for postdoctoral specialization in law and psychology are becoming increasingly more available and popular. Finally, anecdotal reports suggest that applications for admission to these forensic psychology training programs and tracks have increased considerably in recent years.

Despite this exceptional growth in educational and training opportunities for students and practitioners in forensic psychology, there is no consensus regarding the appropriate training models, curricula, and goals of these specialized training programs (see Bersoff et al., 1997, and Krauss & Sales, 2014, for descriptions of this debate). The field of forensic psychology continues to broaden in scope, encompassing a wide variety of knowledge and skills. Although forensic psychology training programs have increased in number, scope, and sophistication in recent years, important questions remain regarding the structure, focus, and goals of these programs.

The following sections discuss the educational and training opportunities available to students and practitioners in forensic psychology. As will be discussed, students and professionals in forensic psychology can now choose from a variety of educational and training experiences at several different levels. We also examine the diversity in training models employed in these various training programs, and consider whether current training models adequately prepare students to become forensic practitioners.

Educational, Training, and Credentialing Opportunities in Forensic Psychology

Over the past 40 years, the educational and training opportunities available to students and professionals interested in forensic psychology have increased considerably, and a variety of such opportunities currently exist at the undergraduate, graduate, and postdoctoral levels. There are also opportunities for advanced credentialing, including board certification, for forensic practitioners who wish to distinguish themselves as having advanced expertise in forensic psychology.

Undergraduate Training in Forensic Psychology

The number of colleges and universities that offer at least one undergraduate-level forensic psychology course continues to increase. Several surveys conducted in the 1990s indicated that the number of undergraduate law-psychology courses was rising (see Ogloff et al., 1996), and that many high-ranking psychology departments offered at least one course in law and psychology (see Bersoff et al., 1997, for a review of this research). Although no recent research has examined the availability of forensic psychology courses at the undergraduate level, other indicators suggest that this trend has become stronger. For example, the increasing number of students applying for admission to graduate programs in forensic psychology points to enhanced exposure to the discipline at the undergraduate level. Another example is the growing number of forensic psychology textbooks, some of which are targeted at undergraduates and have been published in multiple editions (Ogloff et al., 1996). Anecdotally, law-psychology courses, particularly courses that focus on forensic psychology, are often among the most popular undergraduate courses.

There has also been an increase in the diversity of the courses and training curricula being offered at the undergraduate level. Whereas historically most of the undergraduate courses offered were survey courses that focused broadly on the intersection between law and psychology, many of the newer courses take a more nuanced and sophisticated look at specific aspects of the field of law and psychology. (For a list of some undergraduate course offerings in law and psychology, refer to the "Undergraduate Course Syllabi in Psychology and Law" section on the Web site for the American Psychology-Law Society at www.apadivisions.org/division-41.) For example, in addition to broad law-psychology courses aimed at providing an overview of the field, undergraduate courses are now being offered in areas such as child witnesses, the role of psychology in the legal process, and forensic psychology (Burl et al., 2012). Some schools offer undergraduate degrees in forensic psychology. For example, John Jay College of Criminal Justice, which is part of the City University of New York, offers a Bachelor of Arts in Forensic Psychology that provides training in psychological theory, research methods, and the application of psychological principles to specific areas in the legal system.

Another recent effort at the undergraduate level has involved providing information for advisors who are not familiar with forensic psychology, but who nonetheless may mentor/advise students interested in pursuing graduate training in the field (Burl et al., 2012; Helms & Mayhew, 2006). Although articles describing research on forensic psychology training have appeared in several top-tier, mainstream journals that are read by a wide range of psychologists (e.g., Grisso, Sales, & Bayless, 1982; Otto & Heilbrun, 2002; Varela & Conroy, 2012), undergraduate advisors not immersed in the forensic psychology literature might miss trends in the field or have well-intentioned but misinformed ideas about forensic psychology education. Discussions in the literature that would be relevant for an undergraduate advisor include the wider range of forensic course work offered in master's programs relative to doctoral programs (Burl et al., 2012), a downward trend in correctional course work being offered in graduate programs (Magaletta et al., 2013), and a comparison of the benefits of joint-degree programs versus single-degree programs (Packer & Borum, 2003). To assist undergraduate faculty who advise students interested in graduate study in forensic psychology, several recent studies have been published in nonforensic journals geared towards educators. For example, relatively recent articles have identified the undergraduate course work most recommended for students interesting in pursuing a graduate degree in forensic psychology (Helms & Mayhew, 2006), described educational and training models in forensic psychology (DeMatteo et al., 2009), and surveyed the types of course work available to students in the various graduate degree options (Burl et al., 2012).

Graduate Training in Forensic Psychology

Despite the growing number of courses and curricula in forensic psychology at the undergraduate level, the educational and training opportunities for undergraduates interested in forensic psychology are still rather limited. There are far more educational and training opportunities in forensic psychology for students enrolled in graduate programs. Depending on one's academic and professional interests, various options are available at both the master's level and doctoral level, and there are also several clinical and nonclinical joint-degree programs for those who wish to obtain formal training in both law and psychology. For an informative discussion of graduate training opportunities available in forensic psychology, interested readers are referred to a recent chapter by Krauss and Sales (2014).

Graduate programs in forensic psychology can be broadly categorized by program focus (e.g., clinical forensic psychology, nonclinical legal psychology), training goals (e.g., clinical scientist-practitioner, nonclinical scientist-scholar), and degrees awarded (e.g., master's, doctorate, and joint degree) (see Krauss & Sales, 2014). Graduate programs in law and psychology, and forensic psychology programs more specifically, differ considerably in length of training, which can range from two to seven years after the bachelor's degree, and the degree of financial support provided to students. As will be discussed, students interested in forensic psychology have a wide variety of training programs from which to choose. (For an up-to-date listing [as of this writing] of available graduate programs that offer training in forensic psychology, interested readers should consult the Web site for the American Psychology-Law Society at www. apadivisions.org/division-41.)

At the master's level, rapid and recent growth is evident. In 1990, for example, a survey on forensic psychology training identified only one opportunity to obtain training in psychology and law at the master's level (i.e., the JD/MA program at the University of Denver; see Tomkins & Ogloff, 1990). Another significant review article in the same year did not address forensic training at the master's level (Otto, Heilbrun, & Grisso, 1990). However, a little over 20 years later, Burl et al. (2012) identified 17 master's-level training programs in the United States. As of this writing, the American Psychology-Law Society (2014c) Web site lists 26 master's programs.[2] Although these numbers reflect definite growth, a precise number of training programs is difficult to identify because programs may change names (e.g., the Pacific Graduate School of Psychology is now Palo Alto University) or may not admit students on a regular basis.

There is considerable variety among master's programs. Master's degree programs may be clinical or nonclinical in nature. These programs offer coverage of a wide range of topics in psychology and law and may therefore benefit students who are undecided about their forensic interests or who wish to obtain further education prior to pursuing doctoral-level training (Burl et al., 2012). Depending on the program's emphasis and the student's goals, master's degree programs may also prepare a student to assume research or clinical positions within various institutions and professional agencies. A master's degree may not provide the level of advanced training required to be fluent in forensic research or to provide the level of services that can be offered by a doctoral-level clinician, but there is a growing demand for master's-level clinicians in employment settings where psychology interfaces with the law (see Krauss & Sales, 2014; Zaitchik, Berman, Whitworth, & Platania, 2007).

There are a variety of educational and training opportunities available in forensic psychology at the doctoral level (PhD, PsyD) and joint-degree level (JD/PhD, JD/PsyD, JD/MA, PhD/MLS, "Master of Legal Studies"). The number of doctoral-level programs has increased considerably since 1990; in that year, 12 programs offering some form of doctoral-level training in psychology and law were identified in the United States (Tomkins & Ogloff, 1990). A more recent survey, however, identified 47 such programs (Burl et al., 2012).[3] Many schools have more than one program (e.g., Drexel University has two forensic training programs, one which culminates with a PhD and a joint-degree program in which a student earns a JD and a PhD).

Some students obtain doctoral training and experience in forensic psychology as part of a PhD or PsyD program in clinical psychology (or other applied area of psychology, such as counseling or school). In some of these programs, forensic psychology may not be a core component of the program, yet they may have faculty with forensic interests and students may be offered educational and practical experiences in forensic psychology. Other PhD and PsyD programs have a formal programmatic emphasis in an area of forensic psychology, and they may offer a specialty track or concentration in forensic psychology. Several graduate programs offer a PhD specifically in forensic psychology, also either with a clinical or nonclinical focus.[4]

Students interested in obtaining formal training in both law and psychology can choose from several joint-degree programs. The Guide to Graduate Programs in Forensic and Legal Psychology (Aderhold, Boulas, & Huss, 2011) lists eight programs that offer integrated joint-degree training in law and psychology: Arizona State University, Cornell University, Drexel University, Palo Alto/Golden Gate University School of Law, University of Florida, University of Minnesota, University of Nebraska, and Widener University. Some of these schools offer students the option of pursuing either clinical or nonclinical doctoral training in psychology, and some programs offer several different degree combinations. The University of Nebraska, for example, offers a variety of joint-degree options, including JD/PhD (clinical or nonclinical) or PhD/MLS. There are also several schools that permit students to pursue a JD and PhD concurrently but that offer no formal or coordinated/integrated curricula in law and psychology.

Clinically based doctoral programs emphasize practical training experiences that complement the education students receive in the classroom (Arrigo, 2000). The types of practica from which students may choose vary according to the type of degree (e.g., clinical or nonclinical) and the resources available in the community. Forensic practica opportunities have grown in conjunction with the overall increase in training opportunities in the discipline. A survey of APA-accredited graduate clinical psychology programs (i.e., not confined to forensic training programs) in 1997 found that most programs offered at least one practicum in forensic psychology (Bersoff et al., 1997). More recent research indicates that forensic sites are as common as other practicum settings (Morgan, Beer, Fitzgerald, & Mandracchia, 2007). The most common forensic settings include mental health centers, medical centers, medical schools, state forensic hospitals, and private practice settings (Bersoff et al., 1997; Morgan et al., 2007). University-based forensic clinics are another practicum opportunity in which students may gain training in assessment, intervention, and consultation under the supervision of faculty with specialized forensic training. Although fewer in number—currently there are only nine such clinics associated with graduate forensic psychology programs—such sites may increase given the role they play in providing high-quality forensic services to the community at a reasonable rate, and the significant research opportunities such clinics can provide (Heilbrun, Kelley, Koller, Giallella, & Peterson, 2013).

Students pursuing a PhD or PsyD in clinical, counseling, and school psychology are required to complete a one-year APA-accredited predoctoral internship prior to receiving their degree. Throughout the past 30 years, the percentage of predoctoral internships with either minor or major rotations in forensic psychology has remained close to 50% (see Levine et al., 1980; DeMatteo et al., 2009). Consistent with other areas of growth in forensic training, however, the number of internship sites that offer training and clinical/research experience in forensic psychology has risen dramatically (AP-LS, 2013).[5] These internships can be categorized as either providing a concentration in forensic psychology or providing a broader approach to clinical training; the latter internships assume that specialization occurs at the postdoctoral level (see Heilbrun, 1988, for a review of these two internship models). Both types of internship experiences are beneficial for students who are seeking to build upon an existing base of forensic knowledge, experience, and skills, and they often serve as an effective stepping stone for obtaining employment in a particular area of forensic psychology. A forensic-focused internship is also useful for those students without significant forensic experience who are seeking to specialize in forensic psychology.

One area in need of further study involves variability in student funding at the graduate level. In 1990, Tomkins and Ogloff stated, "One of the factors which often weighs heavily on students' minds when choosing a graduate program is the level of funding available" (p. 213). This remains true today. Although all of the universities surveyed by Tomkins and Ogloff (1990) indicated that funding was available for students, the rise of professional and master's degree programs in forensic psychology since that time suggests that funding is no longer a guarantee across all forensic psychology graduate programs. Given that one of the recent National Science Foundation recommendations was to increase funding in interdisciplinary forensic training, graduate funding in forensic psychology education and training may be a more prominent issue in future forensic training research (Heilbrun & Brooks, 2010; National Research Council, 2009).

Postdoctoral Training and Education in Forensic Psychology

There are several forensic psychology training opportunities available at the postdoctoral level, including formal postdoctoral fellowships in forensic psychology and forensically focused continuing education programs. A postdoctoral fellowship in forensic psychology offers the opportunity to obtain intensive, supervised research and/or practical experience (e.g., clinical, consulting). Postdoctoral fellowships are ideal for individuals with previous forensic training and experience who seek to specialize in a particular area of forensic psychology. For such individuals, a postdoctoral fellowship is an effective way to obtain highly intensive, specialized forensic experience (typically one or two years), and it often serves as a useful means of obtaining employment working with specific forensic populations. For those seeking licensure as a psychologist, these training opportunities are also useful because states typically require that licensure candidates obtain a specific amount of supervised experience after receiving their doctorate. Forensic postdoctoral fellowships are also ideal for individuals trained in nonclinical programs or nonforensic programs who are seeking to obtain respecialization training in clinical psychology with a forensic emphasis. Respecialization typically requires additional educational and experiential requirements, and it can take several additional years at the postdoctoral level.

Postdoctoral fellowships in forensic psychology have not increased as substantially as other types of forensic psychology training programs. A 1997 survey by Bersoff et al. identified 11 postdoctoral fellowships; more recent surveys report between 16 and 19 programs (AP-LS, 2014b; Proctor & Malesky, 2010). Although the total number of programs has increased, the number of such fellowships remains limited and cannot fill the needs of all students seeking specialization or the need of the legal system for qualified forensic practitioners (Packer, 2008).

Practitioners can also enhance their forensic knowledge and skills by attending Continuing Education (CE) training seminars. The AAFP, the educative branch of the ABFP, which is responsible for the board certification process in forensic psychology (see the next section), has driven much of the CE efforts in forensic psychology (Heilbrun & Brooks, 2010; Varela & Conroy, 2012). CE programs are available on a wide variety of topics within the field of forensic psychology, and they are appropriate for practitioners with varying levels of forensic skills and experience. Existing CE programs range from single three-hour sessions that provide an introduction to a certain topic area within forensic psychology to intensive three-day workshops that offer highly specific training on a particular assessment measure or intervention approach. Among other benefits, these programs effectively function to keep practitioners aware of recent developments in the field.

Credentialing in Forensic Psychology

Individuals wishing to distinguish themselves as having advanced expertise in forensic psychology can seek board certification. There are several organizations that offer board certification, but the most highly respected is the ABPP (Heilbrun & Brooks, 2010). Also, with the exception of a diplomate in hypnosis, board certification by ABPP is the only credential permitted by the APA in a member's listing in the APA directory (Packer & Borum, 2003). The ABPP offers certification in 15 specialty areas of psychology, including forensic psychology. The ABPP credential available for identifying the highest level of competence in forensic psychology is the Diplomate in Forensic Psychology (although ABPP titling terminology is shifting from Diplomate to Board Certified Specialist). Eligibility criteria to apply for the Diplomate in Forensic Psychology include the following: a doctoral degree from a program in professional psychology that is accredited by the APA or the Canadian Psychological Association, or listed in the *Doctoral Psychology Programs Meeting Designation Criteria*; licensure or certification at the independent practice level as a psychologist in the state, province, or territory in which the psychologist practices; a minimum of 100 hours of formal education, direct supervision, or continuing education in forensic psychology; and a minimum of 1,000 hours of experience in forensic psychology obtained by either the completion of a full-time (at least one-year) postdoctoral training program in forensic psychology (approved by the ABFP) or practice over a minimum period of five years, at least four of which were postdoctoral. The application process includes a credential review, written examination, practice sample review, and oral examination.

Many states also require by statute or administrative regulations state-level training and/or credentialing for forensic psychologists seeking to conduct court-ordered evaluations (i.e., evaluations referred and reimbursed by the state). In these states, practitioners must undergo a period of training and/or demonstrate competence in performing forensic mental health assessments (e.g., a five-day training program; review of practice reports by an expert committee) prior to being considered proficient in such evaluations (Heilbrun & Brooks, 2010).[6] About one-third of states currently utilize this type of training and/or credentialing system (Heilbrun & Brooks, 2010), and they have been demonstrated to improve the quality of forensic mental health assessments (Packer, 2008; Packer & Leavitt, 1998). These systems also help to protect the public from inadequately trained clinicians who seek to enter forensic practice, but do not engage in independent efforts to acquire needed knowledge and skills, such as by attending CE seminars or obtaining supervision from a forensic specialist (Krauss & Sales, 2014).

Basic Competencies and Training Models in Forensic Psychology

As forensic psychology training programs have increased in number and popularity, a variety of training models have emerged. Debate about the different approaches to forensic psychology training is not new (see Bersoff, 1999; Bersoff et al., 1997; Freeman & Roesch, 1992; Heilbrun, 1988; Otto et al., 1990; Poythress, 1979). The field has not reached a consensus on what is considered "the best" training model; rather, a theme in the forensic psychology training literature is that training programs will vary according to the resources of the program and the interests of the students. It is likely that the field will continue to take a critical look at existing training models and perhaps develop new ones as forensic psychology continues to develop as an area of specialization. Also, as forensic psychologists expand into new and often unforeseen areas of research and practice, it will be important for the field to consider the appropriate training models to properly prepare future researchers and practitioners by incorporating educational, training, and practical experiences that provide a solid foundation of forensic-related knowledge and skills.

The limited agreement regarding appropriate training models for forensic psychology may in part reflect the lack of consensus regarding the definition of forensic psychology and the roles that forensic psychologists are prepared to assume. As previously discussed, although some definitions of forensic psychology focus almost exclusively on the clinical aspects of the field, other definitions are broader and consider research into law-psychology and psycholegal issues to fall within the scope of forensic psychology. The evolving nature of forensic psychology provides a unique challenge to developing training programs. Given the expanding roles, functions, and skills of forensic psychologists, it would be very difficult (if not impossible) to design a single course of study that provides all of the educational and experiential components needed to properly prepare practitioners for a career in forensic psychology. This is particularly true given the time constraints of graduate training and the limited number of forensic psychology postdoctoral fellowships (Packer, 2008).

Nevertheless, several types of training or competency models have been proposed in recent years to address opportunities at various levels of training (e.g., Fernandez, Davis, Conroy, & Boccaccini, 2009; Varela & Conroy, 2012; Zaitchik et al., 2007). A core set of basic competencies that should be emphasized in forensic psychology training programs at the doctoral level has also been identified. For example, at a minimum, it would seem that forensic practitioners (again, referring to both researchers and clinicians) should obtain training and experience in the following areas: (1) substantive psychology (i.e., core knowledge of basic areas of psychology, such as developmental and abnormal); (2) research design/methodology and statistics; (3) conducting research (i.e., original research that culminates in a master's thesis or doctoral dissertation); (4) legal knowledge (i.e., judicial procedures, sources of law, substantive law in relevant areas); (5) integrative law-psychology knowledge (i.e., knowledge of research in legal psychology areas, such as eyewitness testimony, jury decision making, and admission of scientific/expert testimony); (6) ethics and professional issues (relating to both general clinical practice and forensic research and practice); and (7) clinical forensic training (i.e., forensic mental health assessments and interventions) (DeMatteo et al., 2009). A focus on these areas would seem to adequately prepare practitioners for basic forensic practice. The first three elements of this training model fall under the "broad and general" rubric identified by the APA's Committee on Accreditation (2008), which means they are foundational skills not specific to forensic psychology. As such, clinical forensic psychology training programs would need to focus on adding the latter four elements to their existing training curricula. Importantly, this training should be augmented through a forensic internship, postdoctoral experience, and continuing education (see DeMatteo et al., 2009, for more information about the development of these competency areas).

Recent reviews of curricula across doctoral and joint-degree programs that offer training in forensic psychology provide an estimate of how many programs incorporate the forensic elements (i.e., numbers 4 to 7) of the proposed curriculum (Burl et al., 2012; DeMatteo et al., 2009). According to Burl et al. (2012), roughly 40% of the programs reported offering one or more courses that would fall under the legal knowledge component, which includes courses on legal procedures, civil or criminal law, and mental health law. All of the programs reported offering courses that would fall under the integrated law-psychology knowledge component, which includes introductory/overview foundational courses on forensic psychology and courses on forensic assessment and intervention. Of note, however, is that most of these programs offered introductory courses, with roughly 60% offering a forensic assessment course and 30% offering a forensic intervention course. Although all programs reported offering a general ethics course, only three programs reported offering a course on ethics and professional issues specifically related to forensic psychology. Nearly all clinical PhD and PsyD programs reported offering practical experience in forensic psychology, which would satisfy the clinical forensic training component (Burl et al., 2012).

The results of the Burl et al. (2012) survey should be considered cautiously given study limitations (e.g., outdated posted curricula, ambiguous course titles), but the findings suggest that most programs offer course work that would satisfy the forensic components of the curriculum proposed by DeMatteo et al. (2009). However, less than half of the programs reported offering legal knowledge course work, and a large number of programs satisfy the integrated law-psychology component by offering an introductory course. Finally, the large majority of programs do not have curricula that satisfy all four forensic components of the proposed curriculum, although this is primarily a reflection of the small number of programs that reported offering ethics courses in forensic psychology.

There are several training goals that may be appropriate in graduate forensic psychology programs (see Krauss & Sales, 2014, for an informative discussion of training models and goals in forensic psychology). On the broadest level, students can be trained to become clinicians (i.e., applied forensic psychology), researchers (either clinical or nonclinical), or both. Using this broad distinction, we briefly summarize the three general training models used in forensic psychology programs. As noted, there is still considerable disagreement about how best to train forensic psychologists, and the following discussion of training models is not exhaustive.

Some programs train students to become scientist-practitioners using the Boulder Model. Students in these programs are trained in the science and practice of clinical and forensic psychology, and graduates from these programs are well prepared for careers in research, academics, and practice. Other programs follow a practitioner-scientist model of training. These programs focus less on research and more on the clinical/applied aspects of psychology. The curriculum in these programs focuses heavily on practice-focused course work and experiential training. Some forensic psychology programs prepare students to become scientists, with a clinical or nonclinical focus. Although some of these programs are clinical, others are in nonclinical areas, such as cognitive, developmental, social, and experimental psychology, and they train students to engage in empirical research designed to increase our forensic knowledge base. These three categories of training models are admittedly broad and not mutually exclusive, but they provide some indication of the types of training available in forensic psychology programs.

The Current State of Forensic Practice

As discussed in the introduction, the field of forensic psychology has undergone significant growth in the past 40 years. Examining a variety of indicators—development of professional organizations, increase in national and international conferences, publication of specialty journals and books, publication of a dedicated "best practices" book series, and increased opportunities for education and training—it becomes clear that forensic psychology is now a well-developed specialty area. Additionally, the jobs available to forensic psychologists are expanding in number and scope. Forensic psychologists are employed across a wide range of institutional and government settings, including state psychiatric centers, community mental health centers, federal and state law enforcement, universities and university-based clinics, court-sponsored clinics, and correctional facilities (e.g., jails, prisons, juvenile detention centers) (American Psychology-Law Society, 2014a). In addition, forensic practitioners can engage in private practice, with forensically oriented solo- and group-practice arrangements becoming more common.

Forensic psychologists are also conducting increasingly varied types of evaluations. Historically, forensic psychology has been most closely associated with the assessment of individuals involved with the criminal justice system, and such assessments have commonly included competency to stand trial and mental state at the time of the offense (Melton et al., 2007). Today, it is common for forensic psychologists to participate in other stages of criminal trials, such as the sentencing phase of a defendant's trial by evaluating whether the defendant's psychological state, cognitive capacity, or developmental background might provide mitigating circumstances upon which a sentence's severity may be reduced (Melton et al., 2007). Changes in constitutional law, such as the decision by the U.S. Supreme Court prohibiting the execution of offenders who are intellectually disabled (*Atkins v. Virginia*, 2002), make it likely that the demand for evaluations of offenders' intellectual functioning will increase (DeMatteo, Murrie, Anumba, & Keesler, 2011; Knauss & Kutinsky, 2004).

Forensic psychologists may also be called upon to evaluate individuals involved in civil disputes. Such evaluations occur across a range of legal contexts. For example, forensic psychologists frequently evaluate the mental health of plaintiffs in civil lawsuits who claim to have been harmed by the actions of a defendant, or they may assess whether an individual has the capacity to make important decisions (e.g., creating a will or contract, managing money, making health-care decisions) (Heilbrun, DeMatteo, Brooks Holliday, & LaDuke, 2014; Heilbrun, Marczyk, & DeMatteo, 2002; Melton et al., 2007). Forensic psychologists are also frequently called upon to evaluate both children and their parents in the family law context, especially where divorcing parents cannot agree on what type of custody arrangements are in their children's best interests, or where allegations of abuse or neglect have raised questions regarding parental fitness (Budd, Connell, & Clark, 2011; Fuhrman & Zibbell, 2012; Heilbrun et al., 2002, 2014; Melton et al., 2007).

In addition to forensic mental health assessments, forensic psychologists may be employed as treatment professionals working within adult correctional facilities, juvenile detention facilities, and other correctional institutions (Leschied, Bernfeld, & Farrington, 2001). Forensic psychologists also frequently provide treatment in state hospitals and psychiatric centers (American Psychology-Law Society, 2014a). In each of these settings, forensic psychologists may be called upon both to treat mental illness and possibly to restore emotionally or cognitively compromised individuals to a basic state of legal competence so that they may effectively participate in a legal process. Forensic psychologists employed in hospitals, mental health centers, or in private practice may also provide specialized treatment for individuals who are involved with the criminal justice system or remain at risk for future justice involvement (e.g., sex offenders, domestic violence perpetrators, drug offenders).

Finally, forensic psychological researchers work to better understand a range of issues at the intersection of psychology and the legal system. Such research includes the development and validation of psychological measures to be used with specific forensic populations (e.g., sex offenders, individuals with psychopathic characteristics, offenders who engage in domestic violence), and an examination of how forensic instruments are being used in practice (e.g., DeMatteo et al., 2014a, 2014b; McLaughlin & Kan, 2014). Others work to develop measures designed to assess specific legal questions that have psychological implications, such as assessment of competence to stand trial (Kruh & Grisso, 2009; Zapf & Roesch, 2009), or measures designed to assess psychological phenomena that often become important in the course of a legal proceeding, such as malingering. Still others examine the effectiveness of various treatments with specific forensic populations (e.g., efficacy of specialized treatment for sex offenders or domestic violence offenders). Some researchers study the ways in which crime and psychology interact, such as the impact of abuse or victimization on individual development, or identifying risk factors that make certain individuals prone to engaging in criminal behavior, violence, or drug use. Forensic psychologists will also increasingly be involved in the research and practice of legal interventions pre- and posttrial, such as interventions to reduce risk of recidivism (Heilbrun & Brooks, 2010).

Forensic Assessment and Treatment: Similarities, Differences, and Standards for Service Delivery

Forensic Assessment and Intervention Compared

The most common forms of forensic psychological service delivery are forensic mental health assessment (FMHA) and forensic intervention with individuals in the justice system. General practice directives for assessment and intervention were first articulated in the *Specialty Guidelines for Forensic Psychologists* in 1991 (Committee on Ethical Guidelines for Forensic Psychologists), and were subsequently revised and expanded in 2013 as the *Specialty Guidelines for*

Forensic Psychology (henceforth "2013 *Specialty Guidelines*"; APA, 2013b). The 2013 *Specialty Guidelines* provides aspirational recommendations for forensic psychologists in 11 areas: (1) responsibilities; (2) competence; (3) diligence; (4) relationships; (5) fees; (6) informed consent, notification, and assent; (7) conflicts in practice; (8) privacy, confidentiality, and privilege; (9) methods and procedures; (10) assessment; and (11) professional and other public communications. The 2013 *Specialty Guidelines* is notably broader than any other APA guidelines and it provides general parameters for developing and maintaining professionally competent service delivery; upholding the responsibilities inherent to the practice of forensic psychology (e.g., integrity, impartiality); communicating and interacting with the various parties in a case; resolving conflicts effectively; and identifying and protecting the privacy, confidentiality, and privileges associated with specific communications and services (APA, 2013b). As with all psychological services, relevant provisions of the APA's (2010a) *Ethical Principles of Psychologists and Code of Conduct* (henceforth "*Ethics Code*") also apply to forensic assessment and intervention activities. In addition, specific standards have been promulgated for evaluations involving divorce and child custody related issues (APA, 2010b), and evaluations pertaining to the abuse or neglect of children (APA, 2013a).

In addition to receiving guidance from the same professional ethics codes, FMHAs and forensic intervention share another similarity. Unlike their therapeutic counterparts, forensic assessment and intervention are driven by the legal constructs, competencies, and mandates they are designed to address. Thus, the ultimate goals of a forensic psychological service are defined primarily by legal considerations as opposed to an individual's clinical needs. Consequently, whereas a typical therapeutic assessment's goals may be to answer a question of clinical relevance to the patient (such as determining the cause of psychological distress, or determining what treatment strategies might be most effective in relieving that distress), the scope of a FMHA is typically limited to addressing a question relevant to a legal proceeding, such as whether a defendant is competent to stand trial, or addressing a defendant's mental state at the time of the offense.

Such legally derived capacities are context-specific functional abilities. Accordingly, the core tasks of any FMHA involve the measurement of those capacities (APA, 2013b). Similarly, forensic interventions or treatments derive their goals from the legal contexts in which they are being delivered. Thus, when an offender is adjudicated incompetent to stand trial, a forensic practitioner's treatment focus is on targeted remediation of those deficits that prevent the offender from having a factual and rational understanding of the proceedings, and being able to assist in his or her own defense. In this context, the goal is often limited to the restoration of those legal capacities and functional abilities that are directly relevant to the legal mandates driving the intervention, although other intermediary factors may require remediation to achieve that goal (Krauss & Sales, 2014).[7] This stands in contrast to more typical treatment goals, which are often broadly cast to include such patient-centered aims as psychological stabilization, symptom relief, and global improvement in functioning.

Various authors have highlighted the distinctions between assessments conducted in forensic contexts and assessments conducted in therapeutic contexts, and interested readers are referred to those resources (see, e.g., DeMatteo et al., 2011; Heilbrun, 2001; Melton et al., 2007). These factors, although designed to distinguish the two forms of assessment (forensic and therapeutic), can also serve to distinguish forensic interventions/treatments from their therapeutic counterparts. A critical feature of most forensic services is that, unlike their clinical counterparts, forensic psychologists are frequently working to assist the decision making of a third party (e.g., courts, attorneys) whose ultimate interests may be in conflict with those of the individual whom the psychologist is assessing or treating. As a result, professional objectivity and accuracy of findings are prioritized over the needs of the individual being examined or treated, especially in the context of legally mandated evaluation or treatment. Under these circumstances, the individual's confidentiality and privacy interests may not be protected in the same way that they would be in a therapeutic context. This may create an incentive for individuals to distort or omit critical information that would normally be imparted more freely. The inclination to be less than forthcoming may be further exacerbated because forensic practitioners should not give the impression, or any stated indication, that they are functioning in a helping capacity (APA, 2013b), thus potentially creating an additional barrier to open and effective collaboration between the patient and the psychologist. Finally, external time pressure imposed by courts, attorneys, and law enforcement often compress and disrupt evaluation and treatment timetables, which can hamper their effectiveness. As a result, opportunities to reexamine conclusions may be limited, while at the same time the need for accuracy and precision is enhanced (Melton et al., 2007).

Forensic Assessment: Best-Practice Models

Although forensic assessment and forensic intervention operate within similar contexts and receive guidance from the same professional ethics codes, they vary in the degree to which well-established standards of practice guide service delivery. In short, models for FMHA are far better established than for forensic intervention. As such, FMHA approaches are better represented in the literature and have been described in greater detail (e.g., Grisso, 1986, 2003; Heilbrun, 1995, 2001; Heilbrun et al., 2002, 2009, 2014; Melton et al., 2007).

FMHAs are conducted to assist a legal decision maker to make a better-informed decision about the individual being examined. These types of assessments often use approaches that are common to other types of psychological assessment, including clinical interview, psychological testing, and reviewing relevant records. Effective assessment of any kind requires sufficient objectivity and neutrality to ensure that personal biases and concerns for the examinee's well-being do not skew an assessor's methods or findings (APA, 2010a, at 9.02; APA, 2013b, at 1.02).

FMHAs, however, demand a level of scientific and methodological rigor beyond what is required in most other clinical realms. The sources of these demands are twofold. First, a court's procedural rules require the methodology and conclusions to meet legal admissibility standards, which in most jurisdictions involve a consideration of relevance, reliability, and validity. Although methodological rigor is always expected in any professional psychological assessment, the APA (2010a, at 9.06) *Ethics Code* allows for some leniency in the interpretation of assessment data.[8] By contrast, legal evidentiary standards in all jurisdictions require that a forensic examiner's methods and findings be directly relevant to the legal issue at hand, and the majority of states also require that the methods and findings satisfy the admissibility standard articulated by the U.S. Supreme Court in *Daubert v. Merrell Dow Pharmaceuticals* (1993).[9] Second, the 2013 *Specialty Guidelines* (APA, 2013b) creates a heightened standard regarding relevance of assessment procedures to the particular legal question at issue, overall procedural and methodological rigor, and validity of findings. In particular, the 2013 *Specialty Guidelines* (APA, 2013b) requires that forensic experts be able to (1) explain the psychometric underpinnings of any assessment instrument used, and identify any limitations on the instrument's use when used to evaluate a specific issue or individual; (2) identify the data and findings relied upon when drawing a particular conclusion, and explain how particular hypotheses were arrived at or rejected; (3) identify and explain factors unique to forensic contexts that may affect assessment results (e.g., response style, voluntariness, testing conditions); and (4) explain the relationship between their findings and the legal issues and facts of a case. These influences operate to create a heightened standard of professional accountability for forensic examiners.

Despite these enhanced obligations, a number of researchers and commentators have expressed concern that the practice of FMHA often falls short of meeting these stringent standards, and that there is significant variation in the practice and quality of FMHA across practitioners and referral questions (Borum & Grisso, 1995; DeMatteo & Edens, 2006; DeMatteo et al., 2011, 2014a, 2014b; Grisso, 2010; Heilbrun & Collins, 1995; Horvath, Logan, & Walker, 2002; Melton et al., 1997; Nicholson & Norwood, 2000; Otto & Heilbrun, 2002; Ryba, Cooper, & Zapf, 2003; Skeem & Golding 1998; Wettstein, 2005). Subsequently, a number of commentators called for the creation of issue-specific ethical and practice guidelines available to forensic practitioners (Elwork, 1992; Grisso, 1986, 2003; Otto & Heilbrun, 2002). These concerns prompted a relatively recent proliferation of guidance for forensic mental health practitioners, including the revision and expansion of the 2013 *Specialty Guidelines* (APA, 2013b), the delineation of principles for FMHA (Heilbrun, 2001; Heilbrun et al., 2002, 2014; Heilbrun, DeMatteo, Marczyk, & Goldstein, 2008), several books that provide substantial guidance for forensic practitioners (Ackerman, 2010; DeMatteo et al., 2011; Heilbrun et al., 2009, Melton et al., 2007; see also the *Best Practices for Forensic Mental Health Assessment* series by Oxford University Press), an enhanced focus on forensic ethics (Otto, Goldstein, & Heilbrun, in press), and guidelines for writing forensic reports (Conroy, 2006; Heilbrun et al., 2002, 2014; Melton et al., 2007; Otto, DeMeir, & Boccaccini, in press).

Concerns over the state of forensic practice, combined with a desire to improve service delivery, prompted the development of models for FMHAs. The earliest models were designed to provide guidance on how to effectively conduct FMHAs, particularly in the areas of data collection, data interpretation, and communication of results. The first such model was proposed by Morse (1978a, 1978b) and was based on the observation that the structures of many mental health laws are similar in that they focus on three broad questions: (1) the existence of a mental disorder; (2) the functional abilities related to the tasks that are part of the relevant legal question; and (3) the strength of the causal connection between the first and second areas. The resulting assessment model parallels these basic legal questions in that it requires the FMHA to address questions related to the existence of a mental disorder, whether the behavior in question was a product of the mental disorder, and how the examinee might behave in the future (Morse, 1978a, 1978b). These questions guide FMHA in that they highlight the importance of data collection in key areas such as mental health symptoms and deficits, capabilities and competencies that are directly related to the legal test, and how these characteristics affect functional capacities (Heilbrun, 2001; Morse, 1978a, 1978b).

Other commentators have noted that, although helpful, this relatively straightforward model might not account for other important influences that could affect the process of FMHA. In response to this concern, Grisso (1986) developed a model for forensic evaluations that consisted of six characteristics shared by legal competencies, which he later refined to five characteristics (Grisso, 2003). Grisso (2003) termed the five characteristics *functional, causal, interactive, judgmental*, and *dispositional. Functional* abilities refer to those that "an individual can do or accomplish, as well as the knowledge, understanding, or beliefs" that are relevant to the particular legal competency (Grisso, 2003, pp. 23–24). *Causal* inferences "explain an individual's functional abilities or deficits related to a legal competence" (Grisso, 2003, p. 29). The *interactive* component asks: "Does this person's level of ability meet the demands of the specific situation with which the person will be (was) faced" (Grisso, 2003, p. 32). The *judgmental* component addresses whether the "person-context incongruency is of a sufficient magnitude to warrant a finding of legal incompetence" (Grisso, 2003, p. 36). Finally, the *dispositional* component refers to the consequences of a finding of incompetence, which may authorize a "particular legal response to the individual, often including deprivation of fundamental rights" (Grisso, 2003, p. 40). Although there is overlap between the two models, Grisso's model emphasizes the importance of context and interaction in FMHA, which are aspects that were not accounted for in Morse's original model (Heilbrun, 2001).

Other efforts in this area focused on the differences between therapeutic and forensic assessment, and recommended FMHA procedures that were also relevant to psychological testing (Greenberg & Shuman, 1997; Heilbrun 1995, 2001; Heilbrun et al., 2002, 2009, 2014; Melton et al., 2007). Melton et al. (2007) offered four recommendations related to the application of psychological assessment in forensic settings. The first recommendation was that testing should be relevant to the legal inquiry, and should therefore provide accurate information related to the behavior or capacities inherent in the legal question being addressed. Evaluators should be aware of the research base regarding the link between the selected measure and relevant legal outcomes. The second recommendation highlighted the role of testing in hypothesis formulation and testing (Melton et al., 2007). This recommendation emphasized the importance of using collateral records and third-party interviews to test hypotheses generated by psychological testing, particularly given the limited time spent with examinees.

Melton et al.'s (2007) third recommendation highlighted the importance of collateral information and deemphasized the role of psychological testing in the context of reconstructive FMHAs. Specifically, they suggested that collateral approaches (e.g., interviews and document review) should be emphasized more strongly than present-state psychological testing when the evaluation requires reconstruction of the individual's functioning at an earlier time. The fourth recommendation emphasized the importance of selecting assessment tools and reporting results in a way that facilitates the understanding of the intended audience, and they suggested relying on idiographic rather than nomothetic data when possible (Melton et al., 2007).

Related recommendations offered by commentators and scholars include focusing on the psychometric properties of psychological tests used in forensic contexts to ensure they are valid and reliable for the purposes for which they are being used (Grisso, 2003; Otto & Heilbrun, 2002). Another recommendation highlights the importance of assessing the examinee's response style (Heilbrun et al., 2002). Given the legal context in which FMHAs are conducted, the possible exaggeration or fabrication of symptoms of mental illness and or cognitive impairment should be addressed (Heilbrun et al., 2002, 2014; Melton et al., 1997; Rogers, 2008).

Although several authorities have offered recommendations for conducting FMHAs, the recommendations tended to be circumscribed to a relatively narrow range of applications. For example, many practice recommendations target specific legal questions, including competence to stand trial (Grisso, 1988, 2014), criminal responsibility (Rogers, 1986; Rogers & Shuman, 2000; Shapiro, 1999), competence to consent to treatment (Grisso & Appelbaum, 1998), and child custody (Ackerman & Kane, 1998; Gould & Martindale, 2007). These recommendations and guidelines provide substantial guidance to practitioners who perform these types of FMHAs, but they are relatively narrow in scope.

In 2001, Heilbrun provided a detailed description of a set of principles that were designed to apply to all types of FMHAs. Heilbrun's (2001) original set of 29 principles of FMHA were organized sequentially around the four broad steps within FMHA: (1) preparation, (2) data collection, (3) data interpretation, and (4) communication. Heilbrun (2001) discussed each principle in terms of the support that it received from law (e.g., statutory law, case law, administrative regulations), ethics (professional ethics codes applicable to psychologists and psychiatrists), science (theory and empirical evidence), and practice (professional literature offering guidelines and recommendations for best practices). Based on these sources of authority, Heilbrun (2001) classified each of the 29 principles as either *established* (i.e., the principles are largely supported by research, accepted in practice, and consistent with ethical and legal standards) or *emerging* (i.e., the principles are supported in some areas, but with mixed or absent evidence from others, or supported by some evidence, but with continuing disagreement among professionals regarding their application).

After Heilbrun (2001) identified these principles, Heilbrun et al. (2002, 2014) published two casebooks illustrating how these principles could be applied to FMHAs in criminal, civil, juvenile, and family law contexts. Efforts were also made to demonstrate how these principles could be used to improve the overall quality of forensic practice (Heilbrun, DeMatteo, & Marczyk, 2004), and how they apply to specific offender populations (e.g., sexual offenders; Heilbrun, 2003) and to specific types of evaluations, including neuropsychological evaluations (Heilbrun et al., 2003) and death penalty evaluations (DeMatteo et al., 2011; Heilbrun et al., 2005).

More recently, Heilbrun slightly revised several of his original principles (see Heilbrun et al., 2009) and provided an integrated principle-based framework that combines his original principles with principles, guidelines, and maxims developed by other authorities (see Brodsky, 1991, 1999, 2004; Melton et al., 2007; Simon & Gold, 2004). As Table 1.1 indicates, the 38 integrated principles fall into the following categories (which expand upon Heilbrun's 2001 initial categories): general, preparation, data collection, data interpretation, written communication, and testimony.

Each of the FMHA models attempts to provide guidance for improving the overall quality of forensic assessment. The revised principles published by Heilbrun et al. in 2009 provide guidance for improving the overall quality of FMHA, but they also provide more substantive guidance that should translate across a wide variety of FMHA referral questions. Despite the obvious value of the approaches outlined by Heilbrun and others, research is necessary to validate the utility of these models for improving the overall quality of FMHA. In addition, although these models and principles provide useful guidance, most jurisdictions have not developed a standard of care (i.e., legally enforceable minimally acceptable standards of professional conduct) that applies specifically to forensic mental health professionals (Heilbrun et al., 2008). The absence of a standard of care further complicates the implementation and enforcement of best-practice guidelines.

Table 1.1 Principles of forensic mental health assessment

General

1. Be aware of the important differences between clinical and forensic domains.
2. Obtain appropriate education, training, and experience in one's area of forensic specialization.
3. Be familiar with the relevant legal, ethical, scientific, and practice literatures pertaining to forensic mental health assessment.
4. Be guided by honesty and striving for impartiality, actively disclosing the limitations on as well as the support for one's opinions.
5. Control potential evaluator bias in general through monitoring case selection, continuing education, and consultation with knowledgeable colleagues.
6. Be familiar with specific aspects of the legal system, particularly communication, discovery, deposition, and testimony.
7. Do not become adversarial, but present and defend your opinions effectively.

Preparation

8. Identify relevant forensic issues.
9. Accept referrals only within area of expertise.
10. Decline the referral when evaluator impartiality is unlikely.
11. Clarify the evaluator's role with the attorney.
12. Clarify financial arrangements.
13. Obtain appropriate authorization.
14. Avoid playing the dual roles of therapist and forensic evaluator.
15. Determine the particular role to be played within forensic assessment if the referral is accepted.
16. Select the most appropriate model to guide data gathering, interpretation, and communication

Data Collection

17. Use multiple sources of information for each area being assessed. Review the available background information and actively seek important missing elements.
18. Use relevance and reliability (validity) as guides for seeking information and selecting data sources.
19. Obtain relevant historical information.
20. Assess clinical characteristics in relevant, reliable, and valid ways.
21. Assess legally relevant behavior.

(Continued)

Table 1.1 Continued

22. Ensure that conditions for evaluation are quiet, private, and distraction-free.
23. Provide appropriate notification of purpose and/or obtain appropriate authorization before beginning.
24. Determine whether the individual understands the purpose of the evaluation and the associated limits on confidentiality.

Data Interpretation

25. Use third party information in assessing response style.
26. Use testing when indicated in assessing response style.
27. Use case-specific (idiographic) evidence in assessing clinical condition, functional abilities, and causal connection.
28. Use nomothetic evidence in assessing clinical condition, functional abilities, and causal connection.
29. Use scientific reasoning in assessing causal connection between clinical condition and functional abilities.
30. Carefully consider whether to answer the ultimate legal question. If it is answered, it should be in the context of a thorough evaluation clearly describing data and reasoning, and with the clear recognition that this question is in the domain of the legal decision maker.
31. Describe findings and limits so that they need change little under cross examination.

Written Communication

32. Attribute information to sources.
33. Use plain language; avoid technical jargon.
34. Write report in sections, according to model and procedures.

Testimony

35. Base testimony on the results of the properly performed FMHA.
36. Prepare.
37. Communicate effectively.
38. Control the message. Strive to obtain, retain, and regain control over the meaning and impact of what is presented in expert testimony.

Source: Heilbrun et al., 2009. By permission of Oxford University Press, U.S.

Forensic Treatment and Intervention: Constructing a Model Approach

In forensic contexts, psychological and behavioral treatments are often used to address cognitive deficits, behaviors, psychological symptoms, and personality factors that impact a person's functioning within a specific legal context. The goals of such treatments may include the acquisition or restoration of particular legal competencies (e.g., competency to stand trial or competency to make legal decisions), behavioral modification and offender rehabilitation (including interventions designed to reduce criminal recidivism), or fulfilling postsentence or diversion program requirements for those mandated or accepted into treatment in lieu of other legal sanctions (including problem-solving court interventions, court-ordered substance abuse treatment, and mandated anger management classes). Also relevant are treatments and interventions that have historically fallen under the purview of correctional psychology, including treatment offered within criminal justice contexts (e.g., prisons, jails, detention centers, juvenile justice facilities) and "wraparound" services (e.g., assertive community treatment) offered to offenders living in the community. Such programs often have multiple goals, including decreasing recidivism and preventing relapse to drug use, and they typically include psycho-educational training, sanctions for failing to comply with program requirements, offender rehabilitation, and supervision of those individuals who are on supervised release (Welsh & Farrington, 2001).

Unlike with FMHAs, forensic interventions have few agreed-upon conceptual models to guide their delivery. This is a significant gap in our profession. Although guidelines for treatment delivery must be specialized and specific to the particular population and needs being served, the field should pay attention to the shared features of various forensic interventions. A key question is whether forensic treatment is an activity that should be considered a collection of different services defined solely by legal issues or populations served, or whether there are common and identifiable principles that apply across various forensic treatments (Heilbrun et al., 2002, 2014).

Unfortunately, this question has received little attention. Despite the need for best-practice standards relating to forensic interventions, there is very little research and scholarship on the topic. An examination of several prominent textbooks canvassing the current state of forensic psychology revealed little discussion of general treatment standards and guiding principles for forensic intervention (e.g., O'Donohue & Levensky, 2004; Weiner & Otto, 2014).[10] The recently revised 2013 *Specialty Guidelines* includes only a brief section on therapeutic services; it cautions practitioners to consider the effects of any intervention on legal proceedings and to avoid providing both assessment and therapy services to a single client unless a therapeutic emergency arises during the course of an evaluation (APA, 2013b).

At least one author has offered a conceptual model for psychological intervention and treatment (Elwork, 1992). Elwork's (1992) model adapted Grisso's (1986) assessment model to therapeutic contexts. Consistent with Grisso's (1986) model, Elwork (1992) argued that any intervention provided in response to a legal mandate should be guided by attention to functional and interactive expectations, contextual characteristics, causal characteristics, and judgmental and dispositional considerations. Accordingly, this model asserts that the focus of any forensic intervention should be those functional abilities, behaviors, or capacities that the individual is legally expected to (re)gain or exhibit, and that treatment goals need to be concrete and specifically intended by law (Elwork, 1992).

Elwork's (1992) approach was an important contribution to the field in terms of standardizing forensic intervention practice, but it left several questions unanswered. A variety of other factors must be considered when describing an effective model for forensic intervention and treatment delivery. For example, forensic clinicians must be given guidance on how to proceed with forensic interventions when there is an apparent lack of established, well-validated, and effective treatments for the problem, population, and context in which the treatment is taking place. Further, at a minimum, a forensic intervention treatment model would need to provide guidance on how to approach the array of difficult-to-treat and often co-occurring disorders that may impair functional capacities, but that are of less interest to the law, such as antisocial personality disorder. Thus, protocols for effective discovery and dissemination of information on different treatment approaches and their outcome data are critical to any comprehensive model of forensic intervention (Leschied et al., 2001).

There is a relatively clear trend in modern psychology toward evidence-based practice throughout most specialties in professional psychology, even though there are still disagreements as to what constitutes best practices in many areas (Barlow, 2005, 2011; Barlow, Bullis, Comer, & Ametaj, 2013; Edwards, Dattilio, & Bromley, 2004; Hunsley & Mash, 2005; McCabe, 2004; Messer, 2004; Norcross, Beutler, & Levant, 2006). The primary driving forces behind the emphasis on evidence-based practice are cost containment, improving patient care, calls for professional accountability, and a gradually evolving empirical research base and applied literature (Barlow, 2005). There is pressure within psychology (from insurance companies, for example) to shift from theoretical treatment models to treatment models with empirical support.

Despite calls for using evidence-based practice, there is considerable variation in many areas related to the quality of forensic intervention. Moreover, there is little substantive or regulatory guidance for the vast majority of forensic pursuits in this area. As in the FMHA context, this situation suggests the need for the development of broad principles to guide forensic intervention.

In the absence of this guidance, the question becomes how such a set of principles would be developed.

Although there are similarities between assessments and interventions in forensic contexts, forensic interventions operate under different assumptions and conditions than forensic assessment. However, a set of preliminary guidelines could be established by adopting the approaches currently used to provide guidance for improving the quality of FMHA. As with FMHA, this approach would entail an examination of the available substantive guidance from relevant authorities, including ethics, law, science, and practice. For example, from an ethics standpoint, both the *Ethics Code* (APA, 2010a) and the 2013 *Specialty Guidelines* (APA, 2013b) address the issue of intervention in both a broad (*Ethics Code*) and specific (*Specialty Guidelines*) sense. In addition, there is a well-developed body of case law and statutory guidance that helps define the contours of intervention in criminal and civil contexts. The most common examples include the least restrictive alternative doctrine in the context of civil commitment, and the right to refuse and consent to psychiatric treatment in the context of competency determinations (see Slobogin, Rai, & Reisner, 2009). Information concerning the science and practice of intervention in both general therapeutic and forensic contexts would also contribute to a new intervention framework.

Although there is a relative lack of intervention data for some forensic interventions and populations, over the last decade several researchers have addressed the issue of treatment for forensic populations. Chandler, Peters, Field, and Juliano-Bult (2004) identified several emerging evidence-based practice approaches for the forensic treatment of individuals with co-occurring mental health and substance use disorders (COD), including pre- and postrelease intensive case management, specialized COD treatment programs, intermediate care programs with medication monitoring, community-based residential treatment, and telepsychiatry services. Chandler et al. (2004) also identified several challenges to widespread implementation of evidence-based practices throughout the criminal justice system, including the conflicting goals of treatment and the criminal justice system, providing a necessary range of treatment options, and limited resources for COD treatment.

Day and Howells (2002) provided a review of the extant literature and offered six key components of effective treatment programs for offenders. The identified features included treatment focus on criminogenic needs, behavioral and/or multimodal treatment approaches, the inclusion of a cognitive (attitudes and beliefs) component, treatments designed to engage high levels of participant responsivity, community-based programming, and high levels of treatment integrity (i.e., well-trained staff, program oversight). These broad features would seemingly apply to a wide range of offender populations.

More recently, Craig, Dixon, and Gannon (2013) highlighted evidence-based treatment approaches and outcomes for several types of forensic treatment programs (e.g., cognitive skills programs, secure settings) and offenders (e.g., individuals with personality disorders, juvenile offenders, individuals with histories of sexual offending). Although insightful, the available literature in this area focuses largely on system and policy-level variables, and there is little guidance for clinicians. Thus, empirically based outcome data and practice guidelines from the broader therapeutic forum may still need to be applied to a variety of forensic contexts and issues. It also seems likely that a distillation of guiding principles in a forensic intervention context will draw heavily from the developing literature surrounding evidence-based practice.

Despite recent heightened attention, the concept of evidence-based practice is not new to the field of psychological intervention (e.g., APA, 2006; Shakow et al., 1947; Sox & Wolf, 1993; Thorne, 1947). Although there is disagreement in the literature regarding the definition, the APA (2006) defines evidence-based practice as "the integration of the best available research with clinical expertise in the context of patient characteristics, culture, and preferences" (p. 273). Following from this definition, the purpose of evidence-based practice in the context of intervention is to promote effective psychological practice and enhance public health by applying empirically supported principles to case formulation, therapeutic relationships, and intervention (APA, 2006). The APA definition of evidence-based practice includes three components: (1) best available research; (2) clinical expertise; and (3) patient characteristics, cultures, and preferences.

The term *best available research* refers to the knowledge gained from a variety of research designs and approaches, including clinical observation, qualitative research, systematic case studies and single-case experimental designs, public health and ethnographic research, process outcome studies, randomized clinical trials, and meta-analysis (APA, 2006; McCabe, 2004; Messer, 2004). The data from these approaches are used to inform decisions regarding treatment efficacy (i.e., evaluation of whether a treatment works) and clinical utility (i.e., usefulness of the intervention in clinical settings). *Clinical expertise* refers to the competence attained by psychologists through education, training, and experience that results in effective practice (APA, 2006). Clinical expertise is essential for integrating the data obtained from group-based research (nomothetic) data with client-specific (idiographic) data. The construct of clinical expertise encompasses a number of competencies that contribute to effective practice, including assessment, diagnostic judgment, systematic case formulation, and treatment planning; clinical decision making, treatment implementation, and monitoring of patient progress; interpersonal expertise; continual self-reflection and acquisition of skills; appropriate evaluation and use of research evidence in both basic and applied psychological science; understanding the influence of individual and cultural differences on treatment; seeking available resources as needed; and having a cogent rationale for clinical strategies (APA, 2006). The final component, *patient characteristics, culture, and preferences*, reflects the belief that psychological services are most effective when they target the specific treatment needs of the individual being treated. In the criminal justice context, such tailoring of treatment is consistent with the Risk-Need-Responsivity model (Andrews & Bonta, 1998, 2010).

In essence, evidence-based practice provides a foundation for effective practice in all settings through the integration of nomothetic and idiographic data into a model that encourages ongoing professional development and training. This approach is consistent with the general framework of principle-based models. For example, two principles of FMHA emphasize the importance of using both idiographic and nomothetic data in FMHAs (Heilbrun, 2001; Heilbrun et al., 2009). A principle-driven model of forensic intervention would consider various sources of information or authority; most relevant would be intervention-based research and practice data. Evidence-based practice also emphasizes each of these areas. Given this overlap, a set of principles should provide more substantive guidance that should translate across a wide variety of forensic intervention referral questions. This supports the need for the development of broad practice guidelines to guide forensic practitioners in the context of intervention.

Conclusions and Implications for Training

As this chapter has discussed, training models in forensic psychology have increased in number and diversity in recent years, but there is little consensus regarding what training models are most appropriate or beneficial. Regardless of the training model, a movement toward principle-based models in forensic assessment (which has occurred) and intervention (which has not yet fully occurred) could have significant implications for research, training, practice, and policy. There is considerable variation in forensic assessment and intervention, both in terms of training models and how these activities are conducted, and there is little substantive guidance for most pursuits in forensic intervention. This lack of guidance may partially reflect disagreement among practitioners, but it may also reflect the limitations of the research base and practice guidelines that support such activities. We believe that this underscores the need for a principle-centered approach that is specific to *training* in forensic assessment and intervention.

We now describe how a principle-driven approach to intervention and assessment can improve the quality and consistency of forensic assessment, intervention, research, and policy. Incorporating such an approach might also have a significant impact on the quality of training in each of these areas. In addition to providing standardization in training programs, the application of these principles could help to minimize arbitrariness in the legal decision-making process by promoting thoroughness, consistency, clarity, and impartiality.

A principle-centered approach to training in FMHA and intervention holds promise for improving the quality of forensic practice because it has value at both broad and specific levels. At the broadest level, these principles could serve three important functions. First, this type of model could provide trainees with a broad-based and generalizable approach to FMHA and intervention that would foster the subsequent development of expertise with specific populations and legal issues. As such, this approach has implications for forensic training programs and related curricula and models. More specifically, it seems that broad-based exposure to principles would be an effective method of orienting graduate students and early career professionals to a guiding framework for assessment and intervention activities.

Second, the development and application of core principles should have a positive impact on research and theory development in forensic assessment and intervention. The sources of authority that would go into the development of guiding principles should reflect the current state of knowledge in the specialty, which would inform practice in both assessment and intervention contexts. Unfortunately, the literature is underdeveloped in some areas and virtually nonexistent in others. This reality should be integrated into a principles-based approach because it promotes awareness of the limitations in each area and highlights the need for ongoing research to address such shortcomings. This type of approach is demonstrated in Heilbrun's (2001) model, in which he identified principles as either *established* or *emerging*.

Principles-based approaches are only as good as the information that supports them. Accordingly, a principles-based approach, especially in the less-developed area of forensic intervention, might have limited empirical support because there is limited relevant research. Of note, though, such research could clarify the importance and appropriate application of model principles and contribute to theory development and refinement in forensic assessment and intervention. Of course, research might provide empirical support for some principles but not for others, and the principles should be modified as needed to reflect the most current empirical evidence. As was seen with Heilbrun's (2001) original principles, over time some principles might be amended, others might be retained intact, and new principles might emerge (see Heilbrun et al., 2009).

A principles-based approach might also be instrumental in addressing more narrowly focused research questions within the context of forensic assessment and intervention. For example, research could focus on how such principles are applied in the context of empirical descriptions of normative forensic assessment and intervention. This might be particularly important given the relative lack of empirical evidence on how assessment and intervention is actually performed across a variety of forensic settings. Similarly, principles-based approaches could be used to investigate and define empirical descriptions of desirable forensic practice, including approaches that have not yet been discussed in the literature (Heilbrun, 2001; Heilbrun et al., 2009).

Third, such principles would have relevance to policy. A broad set of principles could help to shape or interpret legislation, legal standards, or administrative or regulatory code relevant to forensic assessment and intervention. Similarly, a set of general principles could guide the development and implementation of policy intended to promote consistency and quality in forensic assessment and intervention.

Theoretically, such principle-driven models should improve the quality of forensic assessment and intervention when properly developed and applied. The issue of quality is an important one in an adversarial context. FMHAs that are poorly conducted are problematic given the importance and possible consequences of litigation (see Grisso, 2003). Examples of poorly conducted

FMHAs include those that fail to address the appropriate legal standard, exceed the scope of the evaluation and yield opinions that invade the province of the legal decision maker, or fail to provide sufficient credible information consistent with the conclusions drawn from the results of the evaluation (Grisso, 1986, 2003). Similar concerns can exist in the forensic intervention context. Interventions may fail to target legally relevant competencies, fail to take into account the value of evidence-based practice, and waste valuable clinical resources. Accordingly, a general set of principles in the context of forensic intervention should function to provide guidance for avoiding such problems and improve the overall quality of forensic services.

Notes

1   Under the Science, State, Justice, Commerce, and Related Agencies Appropriations Act of 2006, Congress authorized the National Academy of Sciences to conduct a study on the state of forensic science in the United States and make recommendations for improvement. "Forensic science" did not include psychology or psychiatry. However, Heilbrun and Brooks (2010) noted that the resulting report was highly relevant to the science and practice of forensic psychology.

2   Both Burl et al. (2012) and the Guide to Graduate Programs (Aderhold, Boulas, & Huss, 2011) identified one foreign program at Leicester University in the United Kingdom. The program at Leicester University, and other programs situated outside of the United States at the master's and doctoral levels, are beyond the scope of this chapter. Other countries have experienced significant growth in training opportunities in forensic psychology, each with their own particular developmental sequence, and interested readers are referred to other sources to learn more about international programs (e.g., Day & Tytler, 2011; Helmus et al., 2011).

3   To put this in context with two other specialty areas in psychology, Clinical Neuropsychology and Industrial and Organizational Psychology currently list 38 and 117 doctoral programs, respectively, on their division Web sites (Society for Clinical Neuropsychology, n.d.; Society for Industrial and Organizational Psychology, 2012).

4   Per APA policy, a "forensic psychology" program cannot be accredited by APA because the APA Committee on Accreditation (2008) does not recognize forensic psychology as an applied specialization for the purpose of accreditation. As such, some programs offer a clinical program with a forensic concentration, which avoids any issues relating to APA accreditation. APA will accredit programs only in clinical, counseling, or school psychology, or some combination of those three types of programs (see the APA's Accredited Programs Web page at www.apa.org/ed/accreditation/programs/).

5   An early survey conducted by Levine and colleagues (1980) identified 47 internship sites offering optional or regular experiences in forensic psychology. In contrast, the results of the most current survey of internship sites with either major or minor forensic rotations runs 95 pages and is divided by many site types (e.g., Correctional, Child Developmental, Community Mental Health).

6   State-level credentialing systems typically apply to both psychologists and psychiatrists conducting court-ordered forensic mental health assessments. See Heilbrun and Brooks (2010) for a comprehensive description of each program by state.

7   Of course, achievement of those goals may require addressing other cooccurring problems that indirectly impact the legal competency in question. Forensic treatment goals are discussed in greater detail later in this chapter.

8   Section 9.06 of the APA *Ethics Code* (2010a) reads: "When interpreting assessment results, including automated interpretations, psychologists take into account the purpose of the assessment as well as the various test factors, test-taking abilities, and other characteristics of the person being assessed, such as situational, personal, linguistic, and cultural differences, that might affect psychologists' judgments or reduce the accuracy of their interpretations. They indicate any significant limitations of their interpretations."

9   *Daubert* held that for scientific evidence to be admissible under Rule 702 of the Federal Rules of Evidence, that evidence must have been (1) derived from methodology that has or can be tested empirically, (2) subjected to peer review and publication, (3) have a known or documented potential rate of error, and (4) have achieved general acceptance in its relevant scientific community. A later decision held that *Daubert* applies to all forms of expert evidence (not just scientific) (*Kuhmo Tire Co. v. Carmichael*, 1999). This test has been adopted by a majority of states, although there remains considerable variation among state evidence rules.

10 These books contained some discussion of treatment-related issues involving specific populations (e.g., sex offenders, the elderly) or particular contexts (e.g., correctional settings), but the discussions were circumscribed.

References

Ackerman, M. J. (2010). *Essentials of forensic psychological assessment* (2nd ed.). Hoboken, NJ: Wiley.

Ackerman, M. J., & Kane, A. (1998). *Psychological experts in divorce actions* (3rd ed.). New York: Aspen Law & Business.

Aderhold, B., Boulas, J., & Huss, M. T. (2011). Guide to graduate programs in forensic and legal psychology, 2010–2011: A resource for prospective students. Retrieved February 26, 2014, from www.apadivisions.org/division-41/education/programs/guide.pdf.

American Board of Forensic Psychology. (2014). Forensic psychology. Retrieved March 1, 2014, from www.abfp.com/.

American Psychological Association. (2006). Evidence-based practice in psychology. *American Psychologist, 61*, 271–285. doi: 10.1037/0003–066X.61.4.271

American Psychological Association. (2010a). *Ethical principles of psychologists and code of conduct.* Washington, DC: Author. Retrieved May 6, 2014 from www.apa.org/ethics/code/principles.pdf.

American Psychological Association. (2010b). Guidelines for child custody evaluations in family law proceedings. *American Psychologist, 65*, 863–867. doi: 10.1037/a0021250

American Psychological Association. (2013a). Guidelines for psychological evaluations in child protection matters. *American Psychologist, 68*, 20–31. doi: 10.1037/a0029891

American Psychological Association. (2013b). Specialty guidelines for forensic psychology. *American Psychologist, 68*, 7–19. doi: 10.1037/a0029889

American Psychological Association Committee on Accreditation. (2008). *Guidelines and principles for accreditation of programs in professional psychology.* Washington, DC: Author.

American Psychology-Law Society. (2009, Summer). Division 41/American Psychology–Law Society executive committee meeting minutes. *American Psychology–Law News, 29*, 1–48.

American Psychology-Law Society. (2013). Resource directory of forensic psychology pre-doctoral internship training programs. Retrieved February 26, 2014 from www.apadivisions.org/division-41/education/programs/predoctoral-guide.pdf.

American Psychology-Law Society. (2014a). Careers in psychology and law: Subspecialties in psychology and law. Retrieved March 1, 2014 from www.apadivisions.org/division-41/education/students/careers.aspx?item=1

American Psychology-Law Society. (2014b). Forensic postdoctoral fellowship training programs. Retrieved February 28, 2014 from www.apadivisions.org/division-41/education/programs/postdoctoral.aspx.

American Psychology-Law Society (2014c). Masters programs. Retrieved March 1, 2014 from www.apadivisions.org/division-41/education/programs/masters.aspx

Andrews, D. A., & Bonta, J. (1998). *The psychology of criminal conduct* (2nd ed.). Cincinnati, OH: Anderson.

Andrews, D. A, & Bonta, J. (2010). Rehabilitating criminal justice policy and practice. *Psychology, Public Policy, and Law, 16*, 39–55. doi:10.1037/a0018362

Arrigo, B. A. (2000). Reviewing graduate training models in forensic psychology: Implications for practice. *Journal of Forensic Psychology Practice, 1*, 9–31. doi:10.1300/J158v01n01_02

Atkins v. Virginia, 536 U.S. 304 (2002).

Barlow, D. H. (2005). What's new about evidence-based assessment? *Psychological Assessment, 17*, 308–311. doi:10.1037/1040–3590.17.3.308

Barlow, D. H. (Ed.) (2011). *The Oxford handbook of clinical psychology.* New York: Oxford University Press.

Barlow, D. H., Bullis, J. R., Comer, J. S., & Ametaj, A. A. (2013). Evidence-based psychological treatments: An update and a way forward. *Annual Review of Clinical Psychology, 9*, 1–27. doi:10.1146/annurev-clinpsy-050212–185629

Bartol, C., & Bartol, A. (2014). History of forensic psychology. In R. B. Weiner & R. K. Otto (Eds.), *The handbook of forensic psychology* (4th ed., pp. 3–34). Hoboken, NJ: Wiley.

Bersoff, D. N. (1999). Preparing for two cultures: Education and training in law and psychology. In R. Roesch, S. D. Hart, & J. R. P. Ogloff (Eds.), *Psychology and law: The state of the discipline* (pp. 375–401). New York: Kluwer Academic/Plenum.

Bersoff, D. N. (2008). *Ethical conflicts in psychology* (4th ed.). Washington, DC: American Psychological Association.

Bersoff, D. N., Goodman-Delahunty, J., Grisso, T., Hans, V. P., Poythress, N. G., & Roesch, R. G. (1997). Training in law and psychology: Models from the Villanova conference. *American Psychologist, 52,* 1301–1310. doi:10.1037/0003–066X.52.12.1301

Borum, R., & Grisso, T. (1995). Psychological test use in criminal forensic evaluations. *Professional Psychology: Research and Practice, 26,* 465–473. doi:10.1037/0735–7028.26.5.465

Brigham, J. C. (1999). What is forensic psychology, anyway? *Law and Human Behavior, 23,* 273–298. doi:10.1023/A:1022304414537

Brodsky, S. (1991). *Testifying in court: Guidelines and maxims for the expert witness.* Washington, DC: American Psychological Association.

Brodsky, S. (1999). *The expert expert witness: More maxims and guidelines for testifying in court.* Washington, DC: American Psychological Association.

Brodsky, S. (2004). *Coping with cross-examination and other pathways to effective testimony.* Washington, DC: American Psychological Association. doi:10.1037/10748–000

Budd, K. S., Connell, M., & Clark, J. R. (2011). *Evaluation of parenting capacity in child protection.* New York: Oxford University Press.

Burl, J., Shah, S., Filone, S., Foster, E., & DeMatteo, D. (2012). A survey of graduate training programs and course work in forensic psychology. *Teaching of Psychology, 39,* 48–53. doi:10.1177/0098628311430313

Chandler, R. K., Peters, R. H., Field, G., & Juliano-Bult, D. (2004). Challenges in implementing evidence-based treatment practices for co-occurring disorders in the criminal justice system. *Behavioral Sciences & the Law, 22,* 431–448. doi:10.1002/bsl.598

Committee on Ethical Guidelines for Forensic Psychologists. (1991). Specialty guidelines for forensic psychologists. *Law and Human Behavior, 15,* 655–665. doi:10.1007/BF01065858

Conroy, M. A. (2006). Report writing and testimony. *Applied Psychology in Criminal Justice, 2,* 237–260.

Craig, L. A., Dixon, L., & Gannon, T. A. (Eds.) (2013). *What works in offender rehabilitation: An evidence-based approach to assessment and treatment.* Malden, MA: Wiley-Blackwell. doi:10.1002/9781118320655

Daubert v. Merrill Dow Pharmaceuticals, 509 U.S. 579 (1993).

Day, A., & Howells, K. (2002). Psychological treatments for rehabilitating offenders: Evidence-based practice comes of age. *Australian Psychologist, 37,* 39–47. doi:10.1080/00050060210001706656

Day, A., & Tytler, R. (2012). Professional training in applied psychology: Towards a signature pedagogy for forensic psychology training. *Australian Psychologist, 47,* 183–189. doi:10.1111/j.1742–9544.2011.00044.x

DeMatteo, D., & Edens, J. F. (2006). The role and relevance of the Psychopathy Checklist-Revised in court: A case law survey of U.S. courts (1991–2004). *Psychology, Public Policy, and Law, 12,* 214–241. doi:10.1037/1076–8971.12.2.214

DeMatteo, D., Edens, J. F., Galloway, M., Cox, J., Smith, S. T., & Formon, D. (2014a). The role and reliability of the Psychopathy Checklist-Revised in U.S. sexually violent predator evaluations: A case law survey. *Law and Human Behavior, 38,* 248–255. doi:10.1037/lhb0000059

DeMatteo, D., Edens, J. F., Galloway, M., Cox, J., Smith, S. T., Koller, J. P., & Bersoff, B. (2014b). Investigating the role of the Psychopathy Checklist-Revised in United States case law. *Psychology, Public Policy, and Law, 20,* 96–107. doi:10.1037/a0035452

DeMatteo, D., Marczyk, G., Krauss, D. A., & Burl, J. (2009). Educational and training models in forensic psychology. *Training and Education in Professional Psychology, 3,* 184–191. doi:10.1037/a0014582

DeMatteo, D., Murrie, D. C., Anumba, N. M., & Keesler, M. E. (2011). *Forensic mental health assessments in death penalty cases.* New York: Oxford University Press. doi:10.1093/acprof:oso/9780195385809.001.0001

Edwards, D. J. A., Dattilio, F. M., & Bromley, D. B. (2004). Developing evidence-based practice: The role of case-based research. *Professional Psychology: Research and Practice, 35,* 589–597. doi:10.1037/0735–7028.35.6.589

Elwork, A. (1984). Psycho-legal assessment, diagnosis and testimony. *Law and Human Behavior, 8,* 197–203. doi:10.1007/BF01044692

Elwork, A. (1992). Psycho-legal treatment and intervention: The next challenge. *Law and Human Behavior, 16,* 175–183. doi:10.1007/BF01044796

Fenster, C. A., Litwack, T. R., & Symonds, M. (1975). The making of a forensic psychologist: Needs and goals for doctoral training. *Professional Psychology, 6,* 457–467. doi:10.1037/0735–7028.6.4.457

Fernandez, K., Davis, K. M., Conroy, M. A., & Boccaccini, M. T. (2009). A model for training graduate psychology students to become legally informed clinicians. *Journal of Forensic Psychology Practice, 9*, 57–69. doi:10.1080/15228930802427072

Freeman, R. J., & Roesch, R. (1992). Psycho-legal education: Training for forum and function. In D. K. Kagehiro & W. S. Laufer (Eds.), *Handbook of psychology and law* (pp. 567–576). New York: Springer-Verlag. doi:10.1007/978–1–4757–4038–7_28

Fuhrman, G., & Zibbell, R. (2012). *Evaluation for child custody*. New York: Oxford University Press.

Gendreau, P., & Goggin, C. (2014). Practicing psychology in correctional settings. In R. B. Weiner & R. K. Otto (Eds.), *The handbook of forensic psychology* (4th ed., pp. 759–794). Hoboken, NJ: Wiley.

Gould, J. W., & Martindale, D. A. (2007). *The art and science of child custody evaluations*. New York: Guilford.

Greenberg, S., & Shuman, D. (1997). Irreconcilable conflict between therapeutic and forensic roles. *Professional Psychology: Research and Practice, 1*, 50–57. doi:10.1037/0735–7028.28.1.50

Grisso, T. (1986). *Evaluating competencies: Forensic assessments and instruments*. New York: Plenum Press. doi:10.1007/978–1–4899–5046–8

Grisso, T. (1988). *Competency to stand trial evaluations: A manual for practice*. Sarasota, FL: Professional Resource Exchange.

Grisso, T. (2003). *Evaluating competencies: Forensic assessments and instruments* (2nd ed.). New York: Kluwer Academic/Plenum.

Grisso, T. (2010). Guidance for improving forensic reports: A review of common errors. *Open Access Journal of Forensic Psychology, 2*, 102–115.

Grisso, T. (2014). *Competence to stand trial evaluations—Just the basics*. Sarasota, FL: Professional Resource Press.

Grisso, T., & Appelbaum, P. S. (1998). *Assessing competence to consent to treatment: A guide for physicians and other health professionals*. London, England: Oxford University Press.

Grisso, T., Sales, B., & Bayless, S. (1982). Law-related courses and programs in graduate psychology departments. *American Psychologist, 37*, 267–278. doi:10.1037/0003–066X.37.3.267

Heilbrun, K. (1988, August). *The role of the predoctoral clinical internship in forensic psychology training*. Paper presented at the Annual Convention of the American Psychological Association, Atlanta, GA.

Heilbrun, K. (1995). Child custody evaluation: Critically assessing mental health experts and psychology tests. *Family Law Quarterly, 29*, 63–78.

Heilbrun, K. (2001). *Principles of forensic mental health assessment*. New York: Klewer/Plenum.

Heilbrun, K. (2003). Principles of forensic mental health assessment: Implications for the forensic assessment of sexual offenders. *Annals of the New York Academy of Sciences, 89*, 1–18.

Heilbrun, K., & Brooks, S. (2010). Forensic psychology and forensic science: A proposed agenda for the next decade. *Psychology, Public Policy, and Law, 16*, 219–253. doi:10.1037/a0019138

Heilbrun, K., & Collins, S. (1995). Evaluations of trial competency and mental state at the time of the offense: Report characteristics. *Professional Psychology: Research and Practice, 26*, 61–67. doi:10.1037/0735–7028.26.1.61

Heilbrun, K., DeMatteo, D., Brooks Holliday, S., & LaDuke, C. (Eds.) (2014). *Forensic mental health assessment: A casebook* (2nd ed.). New York: Oxford University Press.

Heilbrun, K., DeMatteo, D., & Marczyk, G. (2004). Pragmatic psychology and forensic mental health assessment: Applying principles to promote quality. *Psychology, Public Policy, and Law, 10*, 31–70. doi:10.1037/1076–8971.10.1–2.31

Heilbrun, K., DeMatteo, D., Marczyk, G., Finello, C., Smith, R., & Mack-Allen, J. (2005). Applying principles of forensic mental health assessment to capital sentencing. *Widener Law Review, 11*, 93–118.

Heilbrun, K., DeMatteo, D., Marczyk, G., & Goldstein, A.M. (2008). Standards of practice and care in forensic mental health assessment: Legal, professional, and principles-based consideration. *Psychology, Public Policy, and Law, 14*, 1–26. doi:10.1037/1076–8971.14.1.1

Heilbrun, K., Grisso, T., & Goldstein, A. (2009). *Foundations of forensic mental health assessment*. New York: Oxford University Press.

Heilbrun, K., Kelley, S. M., Koller, J. P., Giallella, C., & Peterson, L. (2013). The role of university-based forensic clinics. *International Journal of Law and Psychiatry, 36*, 195–200. doi:10.1016/j.ijlp.2013.04.019

Heilbrun, K., Marczyk, G., & DeMatteo, D. (2002). *Forensic mental health assessment: A casebook.* New York: Oxford University Press.

Heilbrun, K., Marczyk, G. R., DeMatteo, D., Zillmer, E., Harris, J., & Jennings, T. (2003). Principles of forensic mental health assessment: Implications for neuropsychological assessment in forensic contexts. *Assessment, 10*, 329–343. doi:10.1177/1073191103258591

Helms, J. L., & Mayhew, L. L. (2006). Undergraduate preparation for graduate training in forensic psychology. Retrieved February 27, 2014 from http://citadel.sjfc.edu/faculty/tspitzer/forensics%20prep.htm.

Helmus, L., Babchishin, K. M., Camilleri, J. A., & Olver, M. E. (2011). Forensic psychology opportunities in Canadian graduate programs: An update of Simourd and Wormith's (1995) survey. *Canadian Psychology, 52*, 122. doi:10.1037/a0023176

Horvath, L. S., Logan, T. K., & Walker, R. (2002). Child custody cases: A content analysis of evaluations in practice. *Professional Psychology: Research and Practice, 33*, 557–565. doi:10.1037/0735-7028.33.6.557

Hunsley, J., & Mash, E. J. (2005). Introduction to the special section on developing guidelines for the evidence-based assessment of adult disorders. *Psychological Assessment, 17*, 251–255. doi:10.1037/1040-3590.17.3.251

Jenkins v. United States, 307 F.2d 637 (D.C. Cir. 1962).

Knauss, L., & Kutinsky, J. (2004). Into the briar patch: Ethical dilemmas facing psychologists following Atkins v. Virginia. *Widener Law Review, 11*, 121–135.

Krauss, D. A., & Sales, B. D. (2014). Training in forensic psychology In I. B. Weiner & R. K. Otto (Eds.), *The handbook of forensic psychology* (4th ed., pp. 111–134). New York: Wiley.

Kruh, I., & Grisso, T. (2009). *Evaluation of juveniles' competence to stand trial.* New York: Oxford University Press.

Kuhmo Tire Co. v. Carmichael, 526 U.S. 137 (1999).

Leschied, A., Bernfeld, G., & Farrington, D. (2001). Implementation issues. In G. Bernfeld, D. Farrington, & A. Leschied (Eds.), *Offender rehabilitation in practice* (pp. 3–24). Chichester, UK: Wiley.

Levine, D., Wilson, K., & Sales, D. (1980). An exploratory assessment of APA internships with legal/forensic experiences. *Professional Psychology, 11*, 64–71. doi:10.1037/0735-7028.11.1.64

Magaletta, P. R., Patry, M. W., Dietz, E. F., & Ax, R. (2007). What is correctional about clinical practice in corrections? *Criminal Justice and Behavior, 34*, 7–21. doi:10.1177/0093854806290024

Magaletta, P. R., Patry, M. W., Patterson, K. L., Gross, N. R., Morgan, R. D., & Norcross, J. C. (2013). Training opportunities for corrections practice: A national survey of doctoral psychology programs. *Training and Education in Professional Psychology, 7*, 291–299. doi:10.1037/a0033218

McCabe, O. L. (2004). Crossing the quality chasm in behavioral health care: The role of evidence-based practice. *Professional Psychology: Research and Practice, 35*, 571–579. doi:10.1037/0735-7028.35.6.571

McLaughlin, J. L., & Kan, L. Y. (2014). Test usage in four common types of forensic mental health assessment. *Professional Psychology: Research and Practice, 45*, 128–135. doi:10.1037/a0036318

Melton, G., Petrila, J., Poythress, N., & Slobogin, C. (2007). *Psychological evaluations for the courts: A handbook for mental health professionals and lawyers* (3rd ed.). New York: Guilford.

Messer, S. B. (2004). Evidence-based practice: Beyond empirically supported treatments. *Professional Psychology: Research and Practice, 35*, 580–588. doi:10.1037/0735-7028.35.6.580

Morgan, R. D., Beer, A. M., Fitzgerald, K. L., & Mandracchia, J. T. (2007). Graduate students' experiences, interests, and attitudes toward correctional/forensic psychology. *Criminal Justice and Behavior, 34*, 96–107. doi:10.1177/0093854806289831

Morse, S. J., (1978a). Crazy behavior, morals and science: An analysis of mental health law. *Southern California Law Review, 51*, 527–654.

Morse, S. J. (1978b). Law and mental health professionals: The limits of expertise. *Professional Psychology, 9*, 389–399. doi:10.1037/0735-7028.9.3.389

National Research Council. (2009). *Strengthening forensic science in the United States: A path forward.* Washington, DC: Author. Retrieved March 1, 2014, from www.ncjrs.gov/pdffiles1/nij/grants/228091.pdf

Nicholson, R., & Norwood, S. (2000). The quality of forensic psychological assessments, reports and testimony: Acknowledging the gap between promise and practice. *Law and Human Behavior, 24*, 9–44. doi:10.1023/A:1005422702678

Norcross, J. C., Beutler, L. E., & Levant, R. F. (2006). *Evidence-based practices in mental health: Debate and dialogue on fundamental questions.* Washington, DC: American Psychological Association.

O'Donohue, W., & Levensky, E. (2004). *Handbook of forensic psychology: Resource for mental health and legal professionals*. New York: Elsevier Science.

Ogloff, J. R. P., Tomkins, A. J., & Bersoff, D. N. (1996). Education and training in law/criminal justice: Historical foundations, present structures, and future developments. *Criminal Justice and Behavior, 23*, 200–235. doi:10.1177/0093854896023001012

Olver, M. E., Preston, D. L., Camilleri, J. A., Helmus, L., & Starzomski, A. (2011). A survey of clinical psychology training in Canadian federal corrections: Implications for psychologist recruitment and retention. *Canadian Psychology, 52*, 310–320. doi:10.1037/a0024586

Otto, R. K., DeMeir, R., & Boccaccini, M. (in press). *Forensic reports and testimony: A guide to effective community for psychologists and psychiatrists*. Hoboken, NJ: Wiley.

Otto, R. K., Goldstein, A. M., & Heilbrun, K. (in press). *Ethics in forensic psychology practice*. Hoboken, NJ: Wiley.

Otto, R. K., & Heilbrun, K. (2002). The practice of forensic psychology. *American Psychologist, 57*, 5–18. doi:10.1037/0003–066X.57.1.5

Otto, R. K., Heilbrun, K., & Grisso, T. (1990). Training and credentialing in forensic psychology. *Behavioral Sciences and the Law, 8*, 217–231. doi:10.1002/bsl.2370080305

Packer, I. K. (2008). Specialized practice in forensic psychology: Opportunities and obstacles. *Professional Psychology: Research and Practice, 39*, 245–249. doi:10.1037/0735–7028.39.2.245

Packer, I. K., & Borum, R. (2003). Forensic training and practice. In A. M. Goldstein & I. B. Weiner (Eds.), *Handbook of psychology, Vol. 11: Forensic psychology* (pp. 21–32). Hoboken, NJ: Wiley.

Packer, I. K., & Leavitt, M. (1998). *Designing and implementing a quality assurance process for forensic evaluations*. Paper presented at the biennial meeting of the American Psychology-Law Society, Redondo Beach, CA.

Poythress, N. G. (1979). A proposal for training in forensic psychology. *American Psychologist, 34*, 612–621. doi:10.1037/0003–066X.34.7.612

Proctor, S. L., & Malesky, L. A. (2010). Resource directory of forensic psychology postdoctoral fellowship training programs, 2009–2010. Retrieved February 28, 2014 from www.apadivisions.org/division-41/education/programs/postdoctoral-guide.pdf.

Rogers, R. (1986). *Conducting insanity evaluations*. New York: Van Nostrand-Reinhold.

Rogers, R. (2008). *Clinical assessment of malingering and deception* (3rd ed.). New York: Guilford Press.

Rogers, R., & Shuman, D. (2000). *Conducting insanity evaluations* (2nd ed.). New York: Guilford Press.

Ryba, N. L., Cooper, V. G., & Zapf, P. A. (2003). Juvenile competence to stand trial evaluations: A survey of current practices and test usage among psychologists. *Professional Psychology: Research and Practice, 34*, 499–507. doi:10.1037/0735–7028.34.5.499

Sageman, M. (2003). Three types of skills for effective forensic psychological assessments. *Assessment, 10*, 321–328. doi:10.1177/1073191103259533

Scrivner, E. M., Corey, D. M., & Greene, L. W. (2014). Psychology and law enforcement. In R. B. Weiner & R. K. Otto (Eds.), *The handbook of forensic psychology* (4th ed., pp. 443–468). Hoboken, NJ: Wiley.

Shakow, D., Hilgard, E. R., Kelly, E. L., Luckey, B., Sanford, R. N., & Shaffer, L. F. (1947). Recommended graduate training programs in clinical psychology. *American Psychologist, 2*, 539–558. doi:10.1037/h0058236

Shapiro, D. L. (1999). *Criminal responsibility evaluations: A manual for practice*. Sarasota, FL: Professional Resource Press.

Simon, R., & Gold, L. (Eds.). (2004). *Textbook of forensic psychiatry*. Washington, DC: American Psychiatric Publishing.

Simourd, D. J., & Wormith, J. S. (1995). Criminal justice education and training: A survey of Canadian graduate schools of psychology. *Canadian Psychology, 36*, 213–220. doi:10.1037/0708–5591.36.3.213

Skeem, J., & Golding, S. (1998). Community examiners' evaluations of competence to stand trial: Common problems and suggestions for improvement. *Professional Psychology: Research and Practice, 29*, 357–367. doi:10.1037/0735–7028.29.4.357

Slobogin, C., Rai, A., & Reisner, R. (2009). *Law and the mental health system: Civil and criminal aspects* (5th ed.). St. Paul, MN: Thomson/West.

Society for Clinical Neuropsychology. (n.d.). Training programs. Retrieved February 27, 2014 from www.div40.org/training/index.html

Society for Industrial and Organizational Psychology. (2012). View graduate training programs. Retrieved February 27, 2014 from www.siop.org/gtp/GtpLookup.asp.

Sox, H.C., Jr., & Wolf, S.H. (1993). Evidence-based practice guidelines from the U.S. Preventive Services Task Force. *Journal of the American Medical Association, 169*, 2678. doi:10.1001/jama.1993.03500200092041

Thorne, F.C. (1947). The clinical method in science. *American Psychologist, 2*, 159–166. doi:10.1037/h0060157

Tomkins, A.J., & Ogloff, J.R. (1990). Training and career options in psychology and law. *Behavioral Sciences and the Law, 8*, 205–216. doi:10.1002/bsl.2370080304

Varela, J.G., & Conroy, M.A. (2012). Professional competencies in forensic psychology. *Professional Psychology: Research and Practice, 43*, 410–421. doi:10.1037/a0026776

Weiner, I., & Otto, R. (2014). *The handbook of forensic psychology* (4th ed.). Hoboken, NJ: Wiley.

Welsh, B., & Farrington, D. (2001). Evaluating the economic efficiency of correctional intervention programs. In G. Bernfeld, D. Farrington, & A. Leschied (Eds.), *Offender rehabilitation in practice* (pp. 45–66). Chichester, UK: Wiley.

Wettstein, R.M. (2005). Quality and quality improvement in forensic mental health evaluations. *Journal of the American Academy of Psychiatry and the Law Online, 33*, 158–175.

Wexler, D.B., & Winick, B.J. (Eds.) (1996). *Law in a therapeutic key: Developments in therapeutic jurisprudence*. Durham, NC: Carolina Academic Press.

Zaitchik, M.C., Berman, G.L., Whitworth, D., & Platania, J. (2007). The time is now: The emerging need for master's-level training in forensic psychology. *Journal of Forensic Psychology Practice, 7*, 65–71. doi:10.1300/J158v07n02_05

Zapf, P.A., & Roesch, R. (2009). *Best practices in forensic mental health assessment: Evaluation of competence to stand trial*. New York: Oxford University Press.

2 Legal Theory and the Relationship Between Psychology and Law

Deborah A. Connolly and Patricia I. Coburn

Over 100 years ago, Hugo Münsterberg predicted that psychologists would begin to make important contributions to law. His book, *On the Witness Stand* (1908), which reported extensively on the contributions that psychology can make to interpretation and application of law, received several sharp critiques from the legal community. The most notorious rebuttal came from one of the most influential legal scholars and jurists of the time, John H. Wigmore (1909), who responded to Münsterberg's work with a satirical piece that put Münsterberg on trial and found his conclusion unsupportable. This exchange is often depicted as hostile and in a sense vividly illustrates the view that tensions existed between psychology and law. A very interesting alternative interpretation to the aforementioned debate between Münsterberg and Wigmore is provided by a Canadian psychologist J. Thomas Dalby (2014). He suggests that the exchange between the two is often distorted and exaggerated. The two, he argued, were somewhat collegial. Wigmore invited Münsterberg to publish in his journal and he contacted Münsterberg to give him advance warning of his intention to write a rebuttal. Why do we emphasize the tensions between Münsterberg and Wigmore? Perhaps it makes for a good story, it makes the history easy to remember, and it seems like a logical staring point.

An oft-cited article on tensions between psychology and law was written in 1980 by Craig Haney. We begin this chapter by revisiting Haney's "sources of tension" between psychology and law, with the clear advantage of about 35 years of advancements in our discipline. We use Haney's framework for two reasons. First, one would be hard pressed to find a member of the forensic psychology community who has not studied these sources of tension and, perhaps, accepted them as a reasonably complete explanation for the tepid relationship between psychology and law. Although Haney did not intend these issues to be conclusive, he would probably agree that once the genie (the message) is out of the bottle he has no control over what it does. Second, we use these sources to highlight similarities between psychology and law. Haney was quite clear that any attempt to dichotomize these inherently gray areas was bound to attract argument. It is not our intent to argue; in fact we agree that the disciplines of psychology and law differ in many ways. However, for those of us working at the intersection of psychology and law, it is as important to recognize the similarities between our disciplines as it is to understand how they are different. To do this we revisit the first six "tensions" discussed by Haney.

We don't deny that the relationship between psychology and law has been lukewarm. In this chapter, we explore an additional explanation. The second major section of this chapter focuses on legal theory. Our hypothesis is that legal theory has as much to do with the nature of the relationship between psychology and law (or any social science and law, for that matter) as differences in disciplinary details. To support our hypothesis, we review the history of legal theory from Confederation to the present day with an emphasis on how legal theory may impact processes from acceptance of nonlegal authority to final disposition of a case.

Tensions Between Psychology and Law

Tension #1: Conservative and Creative

Psychology and law are conservative. Legal professionals are bound by the principle of *stare decisis*. If there is a previous case that is "similar" to the current case and was decided by a higher court, the previous decision is binding. Psychologists are expected to conduct research that is grounded in theory, that naturally follows from previous empirical work, and that adheres to the scientific method. Although psychologists don't use the term *binding*, try, if you dare, to secure funds from a granting agency based on a research proposal that is void of theory, fails to address previous research, and uses untested methodology.

Psychology and law are creative. Legal professionals are creative, particularly if they are faced with a dispute that has no apparent precedent or, worse yet, they are on the side that will lose if a certain previous case is followed. Creativity is needed to successfully argue that the previous case that appears to be similar is actually quite dissimilar and of no value. If there is no apparent precedent, creative legal argument is needed to convince a court that the principles that are most likely to lead to success should apply and that principles most likely to lead to failure (the ones raised by the opponent) should not apply. Similarly, it is not uncommon for psychologists to find that the theory, methods, and/or statistical analyses that have been used, perhaps for a very long time, are no longer ideal. New data may be published that cannot be explained by an accepted theory. New questions may be asked that require more complex and sophisticated methodology and/or statistical techniques. Creative updating of psychological tools is constant.

Tension #2: Hierarchical and Empirical

Psychology and law are hierarchical, although this is more precisely stated in law than psychology. Legal practitioners are bound by previous decisions released by higher courts. In law, this principle would be very difficult to evade if two cases were *identical*. Of course, that is rarely, if ever, the case. A clever and creative lawyer may persuade a judge that the current case is different on at least one critical point and thereby be released from the authority of the precedent. Psychology is also hierarchical. Theory and prior research that are "like" the current research must be cited and can be dismissed only if the researcher can convince the grant review committee, the editor, and the peer reviewers that it does not apply, perhaps because the issue being studied is different in at least one important way from that which is explained by the theory or prior research. This is not precisely hierarchical because we don't speak about higher and lower authority. However, the outcome is the same: we, legal professionals and psychologists, are bound to attend to prior relevant data and either accept it or contest its relevance in the current circumstance.

Psychology and law are empirical, although this is more clearly stated and extensive in psychology than law. Before a legal argument is made, legal professionals are expected to gather data (that is, all relevant decisions and legislation), integrate them, and address each in argument. Most certainly, both sides will not cite all potentially relevant data; however, both sides should know all relevant data so each can respond to opposing counsel. Psychologists also are expected to gather and analyze all relevant literature, just like lawyers. However, we take the empirical method several steps further by employing the experimental method to arrive at a conclusion.

Tension #3: Argument and Experiment

This is a point on which our argument, that psychology and law are as similar as they are different, is more difficult to defend. An essential method used by legal professionals to arrive at the "truth" is argument while psychologists arrive at the "truth" through the scientific method. This need not be a point of "tension," however, if we understand the value and limitations of each method. Many questions that legal professions must answer are incompatible with the experimental method. Consider, for instance the case of *T.N.T. Management Pty. Ltd. v. Brooks* (1979), described by Jonathon Cohen (1981). Two employees were passengers in the cab of a truck that was driven by a third employee. Through the driver's negligence an accident resulted in such destruction that it was impossible to determine who was driving. The dependents of the two passengers were entitled to damages and the court had to identify the passengers and the driver. Because there were two passengers in the cab, each of the three sets of dependents had a 67% of being a plaintiff. This is not a question that could be answered with the scientific method. Argument, as a way to uncover all knowable relevant information (as well as a lot of irrelevant information) that will be heard and organized by an unbiased arbitrator (the judge) may not be flawless, but, we submit, is a valid way to approach the problems often faced by legal professionals.

Haney (1980) did not posit that the use of argument, per se, is fundamentally flawed. To state that argument is a poor way to discover the truth would be to say that much of what philosophers do and have done for centuries is invalid. The problem, as noted by Haney, is that arguments presented to judges are biased. This is true. Each side in the dispute will attempt to uncover all information to support their position. If both sides engage in this way, most (if not all) relevant and knowable information will be before the judge. We are not so naïve as to think that both sides will always engage all of their intellectual resources in all cases. However, that it is not executed precisely all the time does not mean that the system is fundamentally flawed.

Of course, bias can also creep in when professionals use the experimental method, beginning with the questions being asked, methods chosen to address the questions, participants selected to supply data, analyses used, and interpretations of the data (Haney, 1980). Humans, including psychologists, are vulnerable to a number of biases and use heuristics to make decisions (Tversky & Kahneman, 1974). All intellectual endeavors are vulnerable to biases such as anchoring and adjustment and confirmation bias. Forensic scientists are no less vulnerable than others (Dror, Kassin, & Kukucka, 2013). Instead of a stark contrast, there is a striking resemblance between the legal professionals and psychologists, all inherently human, vulnerable to employing heuristics, and potentially falling prey to bias regardless of how cautiously they proceed, and regardless of their epistemological or methodological approach.

Tension #4: Prescribe and Describe Human Behavior

Psychology and law describe human behavior. Law describes behaviors that are unacceptable, most notably through criminal codes. In legal argument, human behavior is first described and then compared to a legal standard. Psychology describes behaviors that are atypical (clinical psychology) and typical (academic psychology). Since Haney wrote his paper in 1980 there has been tremendous advancement in the area of forensic psychology and law. Psychologists are now able to describe behaviors and circumstances that are more and less likely to lead to undesirable outcomes including criminal recidivism, inaccurate eyewitness identification, and false confessions.

Psychology and law are prescriptive. Law is prescriptive in the sense that it describes and sanctions unacceptable behavior with an intent to change future behavior. Clinical psychology may also be defined as prescriptive. Although we wince at the choice of words, the objective, we submit, is similar. When a clinical psychologist and client enter into a therapeutic relationship their hope is to change that client's behavior; to prescribe a different behavior that will improve the quality of the client's life. When a risk assessment includes protective factors, the psychologist is recommending that the offender change his or her behavior to reduce the risk of recidivism. When recommendations are made to police officers to change the way they administer line-ups, interview suspects, or interview children, the objective is to change behavior to reduce miscarriages of justice. Although psychologists do not have (nor necessarily want) the power to sanction behavior that is contrary to recommendations, that is not the same as saying that psychologists do not prescribe behavior.

Tension #5: Idiographic and Nomothetic

Psychology and law use idiographic data, although this may define law more than psychology. Lawyers and judges are concerned with the particular parties in the dispute. Similarly, clinical psychologists are concerned with the individuals that are the subject of assessment and intervention. Academic psychologists are familiar with and use case studies in their research. In the area of memory we would be hard pressed to find a student who isn't familiar with HM, the man with no long-term memory.

Psychology and law use nomothetic data, although this may define psychology more than law. Psychological literature is a sea of statistics on central tendencies—means, medians, and modes—and statistical analyses. This point needs no further clarification. A more controversial position may be that legal professionals also rely on nomothetic data. A ubiquitous concept in law is "reasonableness": the reasonable person, a reasonable delay, reasonable compensation, reasonable evidence, a reasonable sentence, etc. If you look you will not find a single generally accepted definition of "reasonable." In spite of this, legal professionals often decide if a situation or an individual meets the criterion of reasonableness. What, then, is reasonable? We suspect that it is, at least in part, an average of the multitude of "similar" cases and life experience the legal professional has been exposed to over the years. It is hard to imagine that cases are not "combined" in some way to form a single coherent belief or attitude about relevant issues. Integration information theories suggest that judgments and decisions follow additive and multiplicative mathematical rules. These rules have been demonstrated to play a part in judges' bail-setting decisions, for instance (see Anderson, 2013).

Tension #6: Certainty and Probability

Neither law nor psychology can be certain, in fact. Law uses the rhetoric of certainty, not because there is no possibility of error, but, as Haney (1980) argued, because the consequences of legal decisions are grave. Imagine sentencing a convicted person to life in prison or to death because he or she is "most likely" guilty. Statements couched in probabilistic terms breed a lack of confidence and confidence in our legal system is essential to its legitimacy (Haney, 1980). Psychologists are subject to this same error: once we attain the $p < .05$ goal, we report effects without further reference to the probability of error.

Psychology and law are probabilistic. The argument for the probabilistic nature of psychology needs no further illustration than the following: if $p > .05$ it's not real! The important point is that law is also probabilistic. The probabilistic nature of law is quite clear when one looks at the standards of proof. In a criminal case, the prosecutor need not prove the case with absolute certainty; he or she must prove the case "beyond a reasonable doubt." In a civil action, the plaintiff must prove his or her case "on a balance of probabilities," not beyond all doubt. Legal professionals deal with margins of error all the time.

To this point we have argued that psychology and law share many similarities. We do not dispute that there are differences—of course there are. However, based on the same classification system used by Haney (1980), we have identified several points of similarity. This suggests that the reluctance of the law to embrace psychology may be rooted in some other source. In the next section we argue that the failure of the legal profession to accept psychology as a "coequal partner" has as much to do with prevailing legal theory as with the minutiae that separate or unite our disciplines. Our thesis does not rest exclusively on the relationship between psychology and law; rather, it rests on the relationship between social science authority and law.

Legal Theory

For many, the bond between legal theory and legal practice is akin to the relationship between basic research and applied research (e.g., Pattaro, 2005). Legal theory (basic research) is meant to explain and predict legal practice (applied research). In other words, legal theory attempts to articulate essential principles that guide legal decision making. A prevailing legal theory may not be plainly stated in a judgment or in legislation. However, we submit, that does not mean it is not operating in the background. Whether or not we are consciously aware of our implicit theories, they guide attention, comprehension, interpretation, memory, recall, and decisions (D'Amato, 1999; Gawronski & Payne, 2010, but see Fish, 1989; Soper, 2003).

Our thesis is that legal theories can help us to understand how legal practitioners view social science authority. The legal theories we discuss are foundational theories. That is, they are broad theories that attempt to answer the question "What is law?" Contrast this question with the question "What is a law?" The two questions are very different; the former being an abstract notion of what makes a law valid and the latter being a precise question about how courts may deal with a particular kind of dispute. In this section we address the former and not the latter.

The literature on legal theory is extensive and we do not purport to canvass it exhaustively, or even skate over the surface of many of the prevailing legal theories. Our goal is to provide an introduction to the foundational theories in legal thinking and to discuss particular theories if doing so will help to explain the broad theory from which it was derived. We take a very short jaunt through the story of America's development as it relates to changing legal theory.

To truly understand the development of legal theory, one must understand the political, social, and cultural milieu of the time. In this section we describe Feldman's (2000) interpretation of the events that initiated changes in legal theory. Legal theory and legal practice do not evolve in a void—whether the political, social, and cultural influences are acknowledged or not, their impact is unavoidable. This is not a new idea, of course. In 1881, the eminent jurist Oliver Wendell Holmes Jr. wrote the following in *The Common Law*:

> The life of the law has not been logic; it has been experience. The felt necessities of the time, the prevalent moral and political theories, institutions of public policy avowed or unconscious, even the prejudices which judges share with their fellow-men, have had a good deal more to do than the syllogism in determining the rules by which men should be governed. The law embodies the story of a nation's development through many centuries, and it cannot be dealt with as if it contained only the axioms and corollaries of a book of mathematics. In order to know what it is, we must know what it has been, and what it tends to become. We must alternately consult history and existing theories of legislation. (p. 1)

Much of the content for this section was taken from an excellent book by Feldman (2000) on legal thinking called *American Legal Thought from Premodernism to Postmodernism: An Intellectual Voyage*. This is an admirably accessible book on legal theory—a topic that is often mired in esoteric rhetoric. For pedagogical reasons, these theories are described separately and linked to the historical period during which each was dominant. The reader should not take this to mean that they are mutually exclusive; they can and do coexist. As Berman (2005) demonstrated, in today's legal landscape we see evidence of various theories operating together and in different spheres.

Natural Law in the United States

The basic tenet of natural law is that true law exists independent of humans: it can be revealed to or discovered by humans but not created or altered by them. The source of natural law could be for instance, God, human reason, or the order of nature itself, depending on the particular theory.

Whatever the source, it is beyond human creation. Natural law can and must be translated into requirements for particular behaviors, called *positive law*. Positive laws are only valid insofar as they were consistent with natural law.

Natural law described American legal thought from Confederation to the early to mid-1800s (Feldman, 2000). The Declaration of Independence unequivocally states the founding fathers' adherence to natural law: "We hold these truths to be self-evident, that they are endowed by their creator with certain unalienable Rights, that among these are Life, Liberty, and the pursuit of Happiness." America evolved in the first 100 years following the American Revolution and new positive laws were written to respond to the changing nation. As positive law developed, adherence to natural law remained. Consider arguments made in support of and contrary to slavery; both arguments appeal to natural law. Antislavery advocates argued that liberty is an inalienable right decreed by God Himself—a natural law that cannot be violated. Slavery advocates argued that natural law imposed an order on society and that slaves held their natural and appropriate place in that society. These contradictory conclusions, both "founded" in natural law, coexisted, uncomfortably, for a period of time, and their inevitable collision led to paradigmatic changes in legal thinking.

Positivism in the United States

Beginning around the mid-1800s positivism was beginning to creep into Western legal theory. According to positivism, law is what a valid authority says it is. Law is neither moral nor immoral; it simply is. If a rule is written by a person or a body with the authority to enforce the law and to sanction those who breach the law, it is law. The study and application of law, therefore, is the inductive process of discovering principles that reside in decided cases followed by the deductive process of applying the principle to a given case. "Analytical and logical soundness was the sole criterion for proper legal reasoning; a judge, therefore, was not to consider the justice or injustice likely to flow from a decision" (Feldman, 2000, p. 94).

Feldman (2000) argued that the American Civil War, the release of Darwin's *The Origin of Species* in 1859, unprecedented immigration, continued rapid industrialization, and technological advancement were the catalysts for the paradigmatic change in legal thinking from natural law to positivism. The Civil War destroyed the nation of relatively small rural communities; America was rebuilt and grew to become a more integrated nation. The population of the United States grew from 40 million in 1870 to 70 million in 1900—due in no small part to unprecedented immigration. Industrialization and the consequent movement of people from farms to factories were well under way. Finally, sparked, in part by Darwin's *The Origin of Species*, the secularization of law, science, and intellect was under way. The needs and wants of the nation changed—rapidly and profoundly. The stage was set for a new theory of law to take hold in the United States.

The rise of positivism did not mark the death of fundamental rights that were central to natural law. In Constitutional law, the notion of basic rights existed and continues to exist. However, the departure from natural law is that positivists held that the rights existed because they were enacted by duly appointed bodies; the rights did not exist independent of written law.

Modern Legal Thought in the United States

After World War I, modern legal thought began to emerge as a reasonable interpretation of how law develops and is applied. There are several theories that subscribe to this genre, but they share some basic principles (Feldman, 2000). Law is the behavior of judges, whose decisions are necessarily affected by their personal experiences and biases. Law affects social welfare and (given its inescapable connection to social welfare) it must promote social welfare. And, to accomplish the ultimate goal of promotion of social welfare, the legal system profits from a systematic examination of social reality. At least two fundamental premises separated positivists from modern legal theorists. First, modern legal theorists argued that the legal system is inherently value laden (although different schools argued different values) whereas positivists held that law and morality were independent. Second, on one hand, modern legal theorists searched for a foundation in law, something that legitimized it. Positivists, on the other, were not concerned with this; legitimacy derived from authority.

Feldman (2000) provided two reasons for this shift in legal thinking. First, the significance of the growing social sciences and the potential contributions social scientists could make to legal theory was becoming apparent. Perhaps law did not have to be isolated from history, economics, psychology, and sociology, to name a few. Second, there was political pressure for the government to be more proactive in social issues. Third, positivism was dealt a significant blow after World War II when the full extent of the Nazi atrocities became clear (Eskridge, 1993). Many Nazis defended their actions by saying that they were doing what the law commanded them to do—the morality of their actions was irrelevant. This, according to a strict interpretation of positivism, was true. However, the world was not prepared to allow perpetrators of these atrocities to find refuge behind the law.

Legal realism was one of the earliest modern legal theories. Legal realism held that law is what judges say it is. Some of the radical realists argued that judges make decisions intuitively and then find doctrine and precedent to support the decisions. Feldman (2000) reported that Abe Fortas, a legal realist and a Supreme Court justice, would occasionally write a draft decision without reference to law and have his law clerks "decorate" it with doctrine and precedent (p. 111). Factors as wholly irrelevant as the color of a witness' hair or what the judge had for breakfast could influence his or her decision, according to radical legal realists. If one accepts that judicial decision making is intuitive and based on each judge's biases and fleeting moods, the legal system is anarchy; yet, it has survived for centuries. How can an institution that is nothing more than the whims of its members survive? This brand of legal realism was mostly defeated by the mid-1900s. But its influence on new legal thinking was not.

Next in line were legal process theorists who focused on process. Around the time of World War II, political theorists turned their attention to why democracy exists and what conditions might lead to other forms of governance such as totalitarianism and communism. Political theory developed around a consensus model: democracy exists because there is consensus for it. Legal scholars turned their attention to consensus as a foundation for the rule of law. Consensus leading to legal legitimacy rests on the judiciary applying proper process. Issues that became significant under this theory included written decisions demonstrating reasoned and clear application of past law, deciding "like cases alike," and the application of neutral principles. This, argued the legal process theorists, would ensure consistency, transparency, and objectivity in law. Strict adherence to proper procedure results in consensus and therefore legitimacy.

According to Feldman (2000), legal process theorists were stymied by the decision in *Brown v. Board of Education* (1954). Chief Justice Warren, who wrote for the unanimous court, declared school segregation unconstitutional. The Warren court had not engaged in due process; all relevant case law had not been dealt with and the reasons were described as ad hoc, instrumental, and unprincipled. It is not up to the court to arrive at a decision based on its interpretation of what ought to be, according to legal process theorists. In fact, the Warren court was accused of being a "wayward realist," ignoring the rule of law. If legal process theorists could not find the right in *Brown*, legal process theorists must be wrong.

Postmodern Legal Thought in the United States

While there are many postmodern legal theories, Feldman (2000) argued that there are themes that are true across them. We report the themes that are most relevant to our discussion. First, postmodernists see law as ungrounded and shifting; law is interpretation and interpretation is inevitably and inescapably informed by prejudices, biases, and preconceived beliefs. Second, disciplinary boundaries are artifacts that restrict and constrain advancement. No single discipline has the tools or expertise to fully understand social events. An interdisciplinary approach is essential to reduce the inevitable bias that occurs when a single perspective or paradigm is used. A third theme in postmodern legal theory is the clever and helpful use of paradoxes: unlike previous theories that saw paradoxes as troublesome and anomalous, postmodernists view paradoxes as the essence of law; several "truths" collide to create an inescapable paradox. Finally, postmodern theorists hold that humans are not fully autonomous beings; they are social constructions who are influenced by, sometimes governed by, their legal, political, social, and cultural surroundings.

Unlike movements in legal theory discussed to this point, there does not appear to have been a single cataclysmic event that propelled legal theory to this next stage (Feldman, 2000). Rather, it was more likely the (relative) co-occurrence of many factors. This story starts with three seminal U.S. Supreme Court decisions. In all three cases the U.S. Supreme Court held that state law was unconstitutional. In *Engel v. Vitale* (1962) the court overturned a practice in New York that allowed for daily recitation in public schools of a nondenominational Christian prayer. In *Griswold v. Connecticut* (1965) a statute that banned contraceptives was overturned. In *Roe v. Wade* (1973), the Texas law that prohibited abortion, except if necessary to save the life of the mother, was ruled unconstitutional. Legal scholars scrambled, unsuccessfully, to find overriding principles of law to explain the *Engel, Griswold,* and *Wade* decisions. Second, by the 1960s and 1970s the United States could be characterized as a nation that had lost confidence in its legal and political institutions: the war in Vietnam, the civil rights movement, the women's movement, and environmental groups combined to reveal the failures of the American political and legal system. Third, in the legal academy, what was once homogenous became somewhat heterogeneous. The legal academy and the practice of law was no longer the exclusive domain of middle- to upper-class White heterosexual men: women, non-Caucasians, and persons with diverse sexual orientations were entering the profession. Fourth, Feldman argued, the introduction of computer-aided legal research had a substantial impact on legal practice and, perhaps, legal consensus. Before the late 1970s and into the 1980s and even 1990s, what legal professionals "knew" about law and particular legal issues was largely constrained by the index system of law reporters. When a legal issue arose, the legal professional would identify the index code and follow the research through the "relevant" cases and legislation. With computer-aided legal research, the manner in which legal research is done is constrained only by the imagination of the researcher. Fifth, there was a movement in the academy more generally to explore and embrace interdisciplinary study. Legal scholars began looking outside of their discipline to understand law. By about the early to mid-1970s, "without doubt, the disciplinary boundaries among different academic fields were beginning to show cracks" (Feldman, 2000, p. 131).

A Case Example: The Speluncean Explorers

To illustrate how different legal theories can lead to very different outcomes in a particular case we introduce Fuller's famous Speluncean Society case (Fuller, 1949). This is a fictional case that most law students study early in their legal education and legal scholars continue to discuss and extend. Fuller begins by explaining the facts of the case and then offers several "decisions" that are based on very different theories of what law is.

In the year 4300, five men from the Speluncean Society were exploring a cave when a landslide trapped them inside. The men settled near the blocked entrance and waited to be rescued. Due to radio contact with their rescuers, they knew they would be rescued from the cave, but it would take many days. It took 32 days, and the lives of ten rescuers, to release the trapped men. During their internment, radio communication between the trapped men and medical staff confirmed the trapped men's belief that they would all perish from lack of food before they could be rescued. To survive, one man was sacrificed—he was killed and his flesh was eaten. In the Speluncean Society, there was a law that stated, "if one man took the life of another, he would be put to death." There were no exceptions. Following their rescue, the four surviving men were charged and convicted of murder. They were sentenced to die. The case went to appeal. It is in the fictitious appeal that Fuller described how justices with different theoretical orientations would decide the appeal.

Justice Foster adhered to natural law. He found that the written laws of Speluncean Society do not apply. Although they were within the geographic confines of Speluncean, their captivity in the cave separated them from Speluncean as fully as if they were thousands of miles away. Natural law applies in this case. Based on natural law, the defendants did what was required to survive and so cannot be guilty of murder. In the alternative, Justice Foster reasoned, if Speluncean laws apply, the purpose of the law is to deter crime. It is not intended to remove self-defense or necessity as justifications for taking the life of another as one cannot be deterred from doing that. Moreover, if the law was intended to apply in cases of self-defense and necessity it would have been clearly expressed in the written law. It was not. Therefore, the men are not guilty of breaking the law and should be acquitted.

Chief Justice Truepenny was a positivist. For him the decision was clear, although unfortunate. The law prohibits willful murder and there are no exceptions. These men willfully killed another and for that they should be sentenced according to the laws of the land. However, this Justice called for mercy in the form of an executive clemency, a process that is separate from the courts. This would allow for justice with no impact on the law.

Justice Tatting lamented the fact that the case was brought to trial at all. The prosecution could have and should have declined to proceed. However, this did not happen and the Justice concluded that he could not decide; he recused himself.

Justice Keen began his decision by stating that it is not for him to decide "right" from "wrong" or "good" from "wicked." His role is to apply the law—full stop. To decide to acquit in this case would amount to discarding an unambiguous law duly instituted by an elected body. This constitutes an assault on democracy and would bring the administration of justice into disrepute.

Justice Handy based his decision on legal realism. He argued that the law exists for the people. To ignore their position will lead to social, political, and legal ruin. The vast majority of citizens of Speluncean (90%) felt that the men should not be put to death. Moreover, he knew that if the court did not acquit the men, they would die. Because it was the will of the vast majority of citizens, Justice Handy voted to acquit the men and to justify the decision with whatever argument was most expedient.

Social Sciences and Law

Under natural legal theory, specially trained minds are equipped to discover the natural laws and to translate those laws into practical (positive) restrictions on behavior. Social scientists had no role to play in the system. Under positivism, what mattered was the written law. If a rule was written down by a person or body with the power to restrict behavior and sanction breaches, it was law. Social scientists had no role to play in that system. It was not until modern legal theory and more significantly postmodern theory, around the middle of the 20th century that there was a sustained role for social scientists in the legal world. That "role" may have been fully occupied by economics.

Law and Economics

Some legal theorists embraced social sciences since the mid-1970s, when law and economics entered the theoretical world. In 1995, Richard Posner, a jurist, legal theorist, and economist who currently sits as a judge on the United States Court of Appeals for the Seventh Circuit in Chicago, said:

> Economic analysis of law has grown rapidly, has become the largest, most pervasive inter-disciplinary field of legal studies in the history of American law, has palpably influenced the practice of law and judicial decisions, has launched lucrative consulting spin-offs, has spawned courses and textbooks in economic analysis of law, has influenced legislation (economic analysis of law played an important role in the deregulation movement), has made it de rigueur for law schools of the first and second ranks to have one or more econo-mists on their faculty, has seeded a number of its practitioners in university administration and the federal judiciary, and has now crossed the Atlantic and begun making rapid gains in Europe. (p. 275)

Economics is a social science that employs methods similar to psychology. Economics relies on the scientific method to identify and explain relationship between variables. To do so it develops and tests hypotheses, explores causal and correlational relationships, and utilizes descriptive and inferential statistical analyses with *t*-tests and *f*-tests that require measures of central tendency and variability (Naghshpour, 2012). These methods are essentially the same as those used by psychologists. Why is it then that legal professionals have been more receptive to the ideas pro-posed in economics than psychology? Hanson (2012) argued that it is because economics posits a model that has rational choice at the core.

According to Hanson (2012), law and economics theorists describe individuals as having the power to make rational choices and the will and ability to execute those choices. According to this model, individuals are internally motivated to make choices that will maximize their personal well-being. In other words, individuals are motivated by internal desires and relatively immune to external forces. Toward the end of the 20th century, it became apparent to scholars in law and eco-nomics that a deeper understanding of the complexity of human behavior was necessary. A sig-nificant catalyst for this change was the work of Daniel Kahneman, arguably one of the world's most influential psychologists, who won a Nobel Memorial Prize in Economics in 2002 for his work on prospect theory (Kahneman & Tversky, 1979). This theory explains why individuals sometimes make choices that contradict strict principles of utility theory, the generally accepted rational choice model, popular in law and economics. Kahneman, Knetsch, and Thaler (1990) demonstrated that individuals sometimes expect to receive more for goods than they would be willing to pay for the same goods, which is called an *endowment effect*. In one experiment, partic-ipants were first given tokens and then were given mugs and instructed to exchange them. When exchanging tokens, participants performed in a predictable manner: the value of a token assigned by those with and without tokens was approximately equal and so exchange could proceed ratio-nally, resulting in about half of the tokens being traded (consistent with Coase Theorem). How-ever, when individuals were given mugs or some other good that became part of the individual's "endowment," the results differed. Emotional or subjective attachment to the possessions resulted in "sellers" wanting more than "buyers" were willing to spend. This research shows that the pure rational choice model offered by traditional economists has limits.

This promoted the development of behavioral law and economics. The basic principle behind this model is that human behavior has limits or boundaries: bounded rationality, bounded will-power, and bounded self-interest (e.g., Jolls, Sunstein, & Thaler, 1998). As Herbert Simon (1955) first argued, bounded rationality posits that we have limited cognitive processing capaci-ties. We are unable to identify and rationally weigh all possible outcomes of all decisions and so we rely on heuristics and other shortcuts when making decisions. Bounded willpower means that we sometimes behave in ways that are in conflict with our own best interests. For instance we sometimes make choices to maximize immediate gain at the cost of potential for long-term gain. Finally, individuals' self-interest is more bounded than classical utility theory would propose.

In some circumstances individuals will act in ways that promote the interests or well-being of others at the detriment of their own self-interest. These bounds result in human behavior being less predictable than posited by classic economic theories such as utility theory.

At least one social science, economics, has had a profound effect on legal theory and legal practice in the last 40 to 50 years. Details that separate the disciplines of economics and law are similar to the details that separate psychology and law. Why then, has psychology not had a similar impact? Benforado and Hanson (2012) and Hanson (2012) argue that psychological principles and theories make things messy. Economic legal theory is clear and easy to apply; people are rational and autonomous individuals who make choices based on dispositional motivations to maximize personal benefit and can be held personally accountable for those decisions.

Psychological theory, however, is not so tidy. Psychologists reject the "fundamental attribution error" subsumed in the law and economics model. Human behavior is a consequence of complex interactions between internal and external factors that cannot always be known to the external observer (or to the actor, for that matter), that are highly malleable, and may not be under the actor's full control. Not only is it messy, but it threatens the very core of legal beliefs—that we have the power to make decisions and the ability to behave in accordance with those decisions (see also Haney, 1980).

Over the last 35 years legal professionals have increasingly taken notice of psychologists and psychological theory and what it has to contribute to the law. To illustrate this point we return to Haney (1980) and his last tension.

Tension #8: Operational and Academic

Psychology and law are academic. As should be abundantly clear from the discussion of legal theory in this chapter, legal professionals turn their intellect to issues that may have no immediate "real world" catalyst but are inspired by curiosity and a desire to understand the practice of law. Similarly, basic psychological scientists are inspired to understand the psychology of emotion, thought, and behavior without a particular "real world" problem to solve.

Psychology and law are operational. That is, in both disciplines the issues under investigation are initiated by some external "real world" issue. For the most part, the catalyst for practicing lawyers and judges is a client or a case that is presented for resolution. Academics and practitioners of forensic psychology and law are also inspired by real-world legal problems that need resolution. "There are many instances of psychologically initiated and inspired—or at least aided and abetted—legal change" (Haney, 1993, p. 372).

According to Costanzo, Krauss, Schuller, and McLachlan (2014) the influence of psychology in the legal system has been mixed, from areas where we have had much success in making an impact to triers of fact and judges taking notice only of information that is consistent with what they originally felt about an issue. Judges are becoming more receptive to research, and are beginning to expect best practices that have been informed by empirical investigation (Costanzo et al., 2014). For example, procedures and practices such as recording interrogations have been undoubtedly informed by research regarding factors of social influence on the reliability of confession evidence. Heilbrun and Brooks (2010) illustrate several advancements made in the forensic psychology area over the last 30 years. For example, there is an increased number of journals, conferences, and training programs specifically related to psychology and law. In addition, the influence of psychologists can also be evidenced by an increase in specialized courts such as ones that deal with mental illness and with drug offences (Heilbrun & Brooks, 2010). With increasing development of risk assessment, there is growing emphasis on investigating the reliability and validity of these measures. Other advancements in the area of forensic psychology as pointed out by Heilbrun and Brooks are assessments that have been developed specifically to support legal decisions such as fitness to stand trial: Fitness Interview Test–Revised (Roesch, Zapf, & Eaves, 2006), and capacities to waive Miranda rights (Grisso, 1998), and Test of Memory Malingering (Tombaugh, 1996), just to name a few.

Conclusion

The relationship between psychology and law has not always been coequal, or even collegial. Haney (1980) proposed that the disciplines of psychology and law apply very different epistemologies and this may explain the tensions. In this chapter, we propose that prevailing legal theory may have as much to do with the nature of the relationship between legal professionals and nonlegal authority as details that differentiate our disciplines. We do not propose that this is a full explanation; however, it is a factor that must be considered in understanding the historical relationship between psychology and law. Until the middle of the 20th century, prevailing legal theory provided little opportunity for nonlegal authorities to affect legal thinking and practice. When the law was ready for social scientists, the field may have been fully occupied by economists. More recently, perhaps since the beginning of the 21st century (Hanson, 2012), the value of psychology to understanding and applying law has revealed itself. We have made many advances and, we are confident, there are more are to come. This is an exciting time to be a member of forensic psychology and law academy.

References

Anderson, N. H. (2013). Unified psychology based on three laws of information integration. *Review of General Psychology, 17*, 125–132. doi:10.1037/a0032921

Benforado, A., & Hanson, J. (2012). Backlash: The reaction to mind sciences in legal academia. In J. Hanson & J. Jost (Eds.), *Ideology, psychology, and law*. New York: Oxford University Press. doi:10.1093/acprof:oso/9780199737512.003.0020

Berman, H. J. (2005). The historical foundations of law. *Emory Law Journal, 54*, 13–24.

Brown v. Board of Education 347 U.S. 483 (1954).

Cohen, L. J. (1981). Subjective probability and the paradox of the gatecrasher. *Arizona State Law Journal*, 627–634.

Costanzo, M. A., Krauss, D., Schuller, R., & McLachlan, K. (2014). *Forensic and legal psychology: Psychological science applied to law* (Canadian ed.). Toronto: Worth Publishers.

Dalby, J. T. (2014). Forensic psychology in Canada a century after Münsterberg. *Canadian Psychology/ Psychologie canadienne, 55*, 27–33. doi:10.1037/a0035526

D'Amato, A. (1999) Symposium on talking legal argument: The effect of legal theories on judicial decisions. *Chicago-Kent Law Review, 74*, 517–528.

Darwin, C. R. (1859). *On the origin of species by natural selection*. London: J. Murray.

Dror, I. E., Kassin, S. M., & Kukucka, J. (2013). New application of psychology to law: improving forensic evidence and expert witness contributions. *Journal of Applied Research in Memory and Cognition, 2*(1), 78–81. doi:10.1016/j.jarmac.2013.02.003

Engel v. Vitale 370 U.S. 421 (1962).

Eskridge, W. N., Jr. (1993). The case of the Speluncean explorers: Twentieth century interpretation in a nutshell. *The George Washington Law Review, 61*, 1731–1753.

Feldman, S. M. (2000). *American legal thought from premodernism to postmodernism: An intellectual voyage*. Cary, NC: Oxford University Press.

Fish, S. (1989). *Doing what comes naturally: Change, rhetoric, and the practice of theory in literary and legal studies*. Durham, NC: Duke University Press.

Fuller, L. (1949). The case of the Speluncean explorers. *Harvard Law Review, 62*, 616–645. Retrieved on April 1, 2014 from www.nullapoena.de/stud/explorers.html.

Gawronski, B., & Payne, B. (2010). *Handbook of implicit social cognition: Measurement, theory, and applications*. New York: Guilford Press.

Griswold v. Connecticut 381 U.S. 479 (1965).

Grisso, T. (1998). *Instruments for assessing understanding and appreciation of Miranda rights*. Sarasota, FL: Professional Resource Press.

Haney, C. (1980). Psychology and legal change: On the limits of a factual jurisprudence. *Law and Human Behavior, 4*, 147–199. doi:10.1007/BF01040317

Haney, C. (1993). Psychology and legal change: The impact of a decade. *Law and Human Behavior, 17*, 371–398. doi:10.1007/BF01044374

Hanson. J. (2012). Ideology, psychology, and law. In J. Hanson & J. Jost (Eds.), *Ideology, psychology, and law*. New York: Oxford University Press. doi:10.1093/acprof:oso/9780199737512.003.0020

Heilbrun, K., & Brooks, S. (2010). Forensic psychology and forensic science: A proposed agenda for the next decade. *Psychology, Public Policy, and Law, 16*, 219–253. doi:10.1037/a0019138

Holmes, O.W., Jr. (1881). *The Common Law*. Retrieved on April 8, 2014 from www.gutenberg.org/files/2449/2449-h/2449-h-htm.

Jolls, C., Sunstein, C.R., & Thaler, R. (1998). A behavioral approach to law and economics. *Stanford Law Review, 50*(5), 1471–1550.

Kahneman, D., Knetsch, J., & Thaler, R. (1990). Experimental tests of the endowment effect and the Coase Theorem. *The Journal of Political Economy, 98*, 1325–1348.

Kahneman, D., & Tversky, A. (1979). Prospect theory: An analysis of decision under risk. *Econometrica, 47*, 263–291.

Münsterberg, H. (1908). *On the witness stand: Essays on psychology and crime*. New York: Doubleday.

Naghshpour, S. (2012). *Statistics for economics*. New York: Business Expert Press.

Pattaro, E. (2005). The law and the right: A reappraisal of the reality that ought to be. In E. Pattaro (Ed.), *A treatise of legal philosophy and general jurisprudence: Vol. 1*. The Netherlands: Springer.

Posner, R.A. (1995). The sociology of the sociology of law: A view from economics. *European Journal of Law and Economics, 2*, 265–284.

Roe v. Wade, 410 U.S. 113 (1973).

Roesch, R., Zapf, P., & Eaves, D. (2006). *Evaluation of competency to stand trial-revised: A structured interview for assessing competency to stand trial*. Sarasota, FL: Professional Resource Press.

Simon, H.A. (1955). A behavioral model of rational choice. *The Quarterly Journal of Economics, 69*(1), 99–118.

Soper, P. (2003). Justice White and the exercise of judicial power: Why theories of law have little or nothing to do with judicial restraint. *University of Colorado Law Review, 74*, 1379–1408.

T.N.T. Management Pty. Ltd. v. Brooks 23 A.L.R. 345 (1979).

Tombaugh, T. (1996). *Test of Memory Malingering (TOMM)*. Toronto, ON: Multi-Health Systems.

Tversky, A., & Kahneman, D. (1974). Judgment under uncertainty: Heuristics and biases. *Science, 185*, 1124–1131. doi:10.1126/science.185.4157.1124

Wigmore, J.H. (1909). Professor Muensterberg and pychology of testimony being a report of the case of Cokestone v. Muensterberg. *Illinois Law Review, 3*, 399–445.

3 Ethical Issues in Forensic Psychology

Mary A. Connell

Psychologists working in all settings strive to uphold general principles of ethical conduct. The American Psychological Association set forth, in its *Ethical Principles of Psychologists and Code of Conduct* (American Psychological Association, 2002, hereafter called the APA Ethics Code, 2002), the aspirational principles of psychologists. Psychologists are committed to the application of psychological knowledge and research in order to improve the situations of individuals, organizations, and society. The APA Ethics Code (2002) set forth the principle that psychologists respect the civil rights of others and strive to practice in a way reflective of the principles of beneficence and nonmalfeasance; fidelity and responsibility; integrity; justice; and respect for people's rights. Similarly, the *Canadian Code of Ethics for Psychologists, Third Edition* (Canadian Psychological Association, 2000, hereafter called the CPA Code of Ethics) identified four aspirational principles: respect for the dignity of the person; responsible caring; integrity in relationships; and responsibility to society.

In adhering to principles of beneficence and nonmalfeasance or responsible caring, psychologists attempt not only to avoid harming others, but also to benefit those with whom they work. Psychologists who work in the forensic arena, however, often provide services that, from the perspective of the examinee, may do harm or at least potentially thwart aims. For example, the forensic examination may contribute to the court's finding that a defense of insanity fails, or that a lengthy sentence is imposed, or that a defendant's claim of mental retardation is not supported. The consequences to the defendant may be dire—in the case of a capital offender unsuccessfully seeking to establish the existence of mental retardation as a mitigating factor, the consequence may be a sentence of death rather than life in prison. For the litigant in a family court matter, the forensic examination may result, at least indirectly, in the loss of a parent's contact with the child. How, in each of those cases, could the forensic psychologist assert that the principles of beneficence and nonmalfeasance were upheld?

In seeking to safeguard not only the welfare and rights of those with whom they interact professionally, but also other affected persons, forensic psychologists have loyalty to the system of justice within which they work. By doing their own work with rigorous honesty and integrity, they safeguard justice to the benefit of members of society. The client of the forensic psychologist is the court, or more generally, the system of justice for the society in which the psychologist works. The benefits from the work of forensic psychologists flow, ultimately, to the court or the justice system, although the examinee is accorded respect and consideration.

The practice of forensic psychology is unique in many respects and the very qualities that distinguish it also invoke particular ethical challenges. Forensic psychologists work with "involuntary" examinees. There is limited or no confidentiality afforded examinees, and their nonvoluntary participation may result in exposure of personal and sensitive information. The population of forensic examinees includes many vulnerable people, such as children or impaired adults, who lack the capacity to make independent judgments. Because of these unique aspects of their work, forensic practitioners regularly face situations in which they must be especially attuned to potential ethical risks. Since some ethical issues arise regularly in forensic work, it is possible to anticipate them and to develop plans for managing them. This ensures that the work proceeds as it should, with respect for the rights and needs of all involved and with an end product that is helpful to the court. Even with careful planning, the psychologist may encounter novel and complex circumstances where competing tensions exist and the "right thing to do" is not easily identified. In this chapter, an eight-step model for decision making in the face of those unanticipated ethical challenges will be described (Bush, Connell, & Denney, 2006), followed by an exploration of the ethical contours often encountered in the conduct of forensic assessment practice.

An Eight-Step Decision-Making Model

1. Identify the Problem

There are times when a proposed course of action is clearly appropriate and ethical, and times when matters are not so clear. Some professional activities are ambiguous or present complexities that must be untangled before the best course of action becomes clear. There is often a wide range of potentially appropriate courses of action. Further, the matter may hearken distinct ethical, legal, moral, and professional imperatives. A request made of the forensic psychologist, or a course of action considered, may be legally permitted but ethically questionable. Consider, for example, the court-appointed neutral evaluator meeting with one attorney outside the presence of the other at the outset of a case. While this may be legally permissible, it may be argued that it is ethically problematic because it gives one party the advantage of providing an unchallenged and self-serving introduction to the case. The contours of legal, ethical, moral, and professional perspectives require careful consideration, separately and together, to illuminate the full range of considerations.

2. Consider the Significance of the Context and Setting

A situation may call for one course of action in some settings, and a diametrically different course in another setting. Procedural rules in a specific setting may dictate how reports are constructed, for example, and may specifically limit the kinds of information that will be included. The social history information often included in a report of examination may be considered inappropriate in, for example, reports prepared in some fitness for duty examination contexts, because that information is not central to the issue of concern to the employer and its inclusion might be considered an unwarranted invasion of the examinee's privacy. Psychologists may be obligated, in one respect or another, to a number of entities at once including, for example, the referral source, the examinee, the guardian of the examinee, the employing institution, the profession of psychology, the trier of fact, the court, the legal system, and society at large. Sometimes these parties overlap, and in other situations they may be distinct. Sometimes their interests are parallel and at other times at cross-purposes. The demands or expectations placed on the psychologist by each of these potential "masters" must be considered.

3. Identify and Utilize Ethical and Legal Resources

There are a number of resources available to help the forensic psychologist sort out the potential ethical issues and best course of action. The APA Ethics Code (American Psychological Association, 2002) and the CPA Code of Ethics (Canadian Psychological Association, 2000) establish the principles and standards that guide psychologists in practice, and the standards established therein have enforcement mechanisms to ensure compliance. The State or Provincial rules of practice for psychologists are codified and have an enforcement mechanism as well. State and

Federal laws may also govern aspects of psychological service provision. The *Specialty Guidelines for Forensic Psychology* (hereafter called the SGFP, American Psychological Association, 2013a) offer guidelines to educate and assist the forensic practitioner, and are as such aspirational rather than mandated. Other useful guidelines and position papers ("white papers" or "best practice" papers) are promulgated by organizations including the American Psychological Association (2010, 2013a, 2013b), the Canadian Psychological Association (2000), other organizations of interest to psychologists practicing in various specialties, and the organizations of allied professions. Additionally, there exist many published resources that can assist the forensic psychologist who is anticipating or experiencing ethical challenges. Books and journal articles, both those specifically addressing professional ethics and those amplifying best practices in the field, offer substantial guidance. Last, consultation with colleagues is an invaluable resource, both in gaining perspective on a specific ethical issue and in generally raising awareness of case-specific and general forensic practice issues that may otherwise escape the forensic psychologist's awareness.

4. Consider Personal Beliefs and Values

Forensic psychologists are no different from others in that they individually hold beliefs, values, and moral positions on the issues that arise in forensic practice. Like all psychologists, they have a responsibility to evaluate the degree to which those personal beliefs or positions may bias them in their work. It is often difficult to anticipate the potential impact that one's values and biases may have on professional and ethical decision making. When working in an area that is particularly laden with special significance to the psychologist, it is important to find ways to correct for the insidious pull of personal biases on professional behavior. If it is not possible to negotiate the terrain in a way that reflects sound, fair, and even-handed professional behavior, the psychologist may have a duty to withdraw from work in that area of practice, particularly work that involves proving input or opinion to the courts. There, objectivity is an absolute requirement, while in some other areas, advocacy for a particular moral or values perspective may be acceptable. For example, the psychologist who has a strong commitment against the death penalty may be able to work in some capacity, such as with an advocacy organization, but should refrain from conducting assessments and offering opinions to the court regarding the factors in a specific case that argue for a lesser sentence than death. By knowing and anticipating the powerful effects of personal biases and beliefs, it is possible to find ways to attenuate their negative effects in forensic practice.

5. Develop Possible Solutions to the Problem

As the psychologist evaluates an arising ethical dilemma and seeks a solution, conflicting forces may be invoked. The psychologist's legal counsel or insurance representative may view the issue from a risk-management perspective. The psychologist may have a personal inclination to try to remedy or make right the potential ethical wrong. In the face of these conflicting tensions, the psychologist may quickly arrive at an impasse. Generating a list of possible solutions can be a helpful process. The psychologist may specifically focus on the significance of the context, information obtained from available resources, and personal beliefs and values, and then integrate the data garnered from these factors or sources, to generate the list of potential courses of action. Sometimes what emerges may be a clear solution, while in more complex situations with competing tensions a number of potential solutions may emerge.

6. Consider the Potential Consequences of Various Solutions

As the psychologist creates a list of potential courses of action to resolve the ethical dilemma, the likely benefits and consequences of each action can be considered. The timing of the action may be critical, in light of the potential ramifications, and should be carefully considered. Some situations may call for delaying action until a later time—after the case has been heard in court, for example. Other ethical dilemmas demand more immediate action. When the action is to be delayed, it is nevertheless important to document the nature of the dilemma, the efforts taken to develop a plan of action, the actual plan to be implemented, and the reasons for the delay, along with a timeline for implementation.

7. Choose and Implement a Course of Action

When the list of possible solutions to the ethical dilemma has been generated, the psychologist must select and implement the most appropriate course of action. In the careful consideration of possible positive and negative consequences, the right course of action may become apparent. When there is still ambiguity, the psychologist may choose to pursue the highest ethical option available. The chosen action may not represent a perfect solution—in situations where there are conflicting interests at stake, a perfect resolution may be unavailable. Nevertheless, the psychologist must strive to do the best thing possible to address the interests of those who will be affected and to whom an obligation is owed, to protect the interests of vulnerable individuals, to promote the interests of society, and to exercise integrity in carrying out the action.

8. Assess the Outcome and Implement Changes as Needed

When the psychologist has anticipated or faced an ethical dilemma and has engaged in a methodical search for resolution, the process should be carefully documented. That documentation may prove invaluable in later explaining the action taken and the rationale for it. The final step in the process is to assess the outcome and consider whether further action is needed. The experience may be viewed as a learning experience with consideration for whether a different approach might have been more effective. The conundrum may have illuminated an inherent set of tensions between interested persons or agents, or between the law and professional ethics. This newly gained perspective may call for further action to reduce likelihood of recurrence. For example, the record-keeping policies of an institution may differ from the psychologist's professional ethical obligations; working out a solution on one case when the difference first becomes known may be satisfactory for that case, but until there is some more global resolution, the dilemma is apt to occur again.

This model may provide the psychologist with a blueprint for resolving particularly complex ethical dilemmas. Some potential dilemmas can be avoided by anticipating them and adopting practices that protect against their occurrence. The remainder of this chapter will be devoted to exploring the circumstances that, for forensic psychologists, may call for special consideration in developing a professional practice. While the principles of practice discussed in this chapter are important to psychologists in general practice and to forensic psychologists in various forms of service delivery, for the purposes of this book the principles will be considered in light of their implications specifically for forensic assessment.

Forensic Practice Issues and Their Related Ethical Contours

The Referral

The Retaining Party–Examiner Relationship

The relationship between the retaining party and the examiner is clarified from the outset (American Psychological Association, 2002, Principle B, Fidelity and Responsibility). This clarification ensures that the examiner can competently and ethically respond to the request for services and reduces the likelihood of misunderstanding roles or purposes in the assessment (Melton, Petrila, Poythress, & Slobogin, 2007). When identifying one's role, it is essential to grasp the psycholegal question in play (Heilbrun, 2001; Heilbrun, Grisso, & Goldstein, 2009, 2013). The retaining party is generally the forensic psychologist's client, and it is first to the client that there is an obligation to provide sufficient information to allow the client to decide whether to retain the psychologist for the role being considered. A lack of clarity among involved parties regarding roles and responsibilities renders the working relationship vulnerable to subsequent misunderstanding and conflict and may, in itself, represent ethical misconduct on the part of the psychologist (American Psychological Association, 2002, Standard 3.07, Third-Party Requests for Services).

Consider the attorney who calls to request that the forensic examiner conduct an examination of the defendant and prepare a report that will form the basis for testimony to be offered at trial, and also to be available to assist with jury selection. The early discussion of the forensic psychologist's general commitment to assuming one role in a case, to avoid role conflicts, may assist the attorney in case planning. The attorney can then consider whether to retain the expert under those terms, and if so, to seek an additional expert for assistance with jury selection.

Competence

Psychologists work in areas in which they have competence (American Psychological Association, 2002, Standard 2.01, Boundaries of Competence). Forensic services must be performed competently to be useful, and it is the psychologist's affirmative obligation to develop competency before undertaking the independent provision of forensic services. Professional competence is obtained through a combination of education, formal practical training, and experience (Melton et al., 2007).

Competence in one area of psychology does not imply competence in other areas, and increasingly, specialization within forensic psychology is the rule rather than the exception. As the research base and practice standards evolve, and specialized instruments make their way into forensic practice, it is increasingly challenging to practice competently across multiple areas within forensic psychology. To develop competency in a new area, the psychologist may find it helpful to obtain continuing education, read in a new area, and to seek consultation and even shadow a practitioner who is experienced in that area of specialization. Furthermore, the psychologist who has strong clinical skills in a particular area should not assume that competence will translate to competent forensic practice in the area (Heilbrun, 2001; Heilbrun et al., 2009). Forensic practice in any specialty area calls for skills and knowledge that fall far outside the purview of clinical practice. The competent treatment of children traumatized by abuse or neglect, for example, does not serve as a sufficient basis for forensic assessment of children who are allegedly abused or neglected.

Financial Arrangements

Through management of fees for their services, forensic psychologists set the tone and, to some extent, define the terms of their relationship with the retaining attorney or the court-referred litigant. Poor fee management has the potential to significantly interfere, or appear to interfere, with objectivity. Fees should never be contingent upon the outcome of a legal case in which a psychologist is offering an opinion to be relied upon by the court (American Psychological Association, 2013a, 5.02). To hinge fee collection on success of the retaining party would render the psychologist vulnerable to intentionally or unintentionally producing a report or testimony that favors the retaining party.

Since impartiality is not a requirement of the trial consultant role, it is arguably acceptable to work as a trial consultant on a contingency agreement. Nevertheless, the psychologist working as a trial consultant may find that the decision to accept payment for services contingent upon the outcome of the case alters the manner in which services are delivered. If the consultant is willing to sacrifice any ethical principles in order to secure victory for the retaining party, then the contingency fee arrangement is ill advised.

A second area of fee management that raises potential ethical issues is charging higher fees for testimony (Heilbrun, 2001). Some psychologists charge a higher fee for deposition or court testimony on the basis that such work takes them out of the office, is more stressful than other work, or increases vulnerability to malpractice suits or board complaints. However, there are ways in which disparate fee setting may create ethical dilemmas.

First, the retaining attorney may be able to gain access to the forensic psychologist at a lower hourly fee than opposing counsel. When telephone consultation or in-office consultation is billed at the regular fee and deposition and testimony are billed at an inflated fee, opposing counsel may have to pay the higher fee to query the psychologist about the opinions to be offered, or challenge those opinions.

Second, it could be argued that the forensic psychologist who stands to be compensated a greater fee for deposition or testimony may have a vested interest in arranging matters so that a deposition or testimony is necessary in order to discover the opinions or their bases in a case. If the psychologist writes only a brief report or fails to disclose the data underlying an opinion to be offered to the court so that the only way counsel can discover and probe the basis of that opinion is through deposition or court testimony, it may be reasonably argued that the psychologist is purposely concealing data in order to increase the income from the case.

Preferable billing arrangements may include charging a flat fee for specific forensic services, or a fixed hourly fee regardless of activity. Flat fees or preset fees for specific services risk the possibility that a relatively more complex case generates less income per hour. The psychologist charging a flat fee for assessment in a particular area must be cautious not to give short shrift to the complex case in which the hourly pay is steadily decreasing because of the hours required by the case complexity. Since it may be difficult to control the natural resistance to providing additional hours of service without compensation, it may be more workable to charge an hourly fee. The paying party may justifiably wish to be provided with some estimate of the hours that will likely be required to complete the work.

Retainer arrangements are common in forensic service delivery in the private sector. The unused portion of the retainer may be fully refundable when service delivery is aborted for some reason or is completed, or some or the entire retainer may be deemed "nonrefundable" by the forensic psychologist, to guard against the loss of billable time. It is crucial to establish fee agreements ahead of time in sufficient detail to anticipate and reduce the likelihood of potential misunderstandings or conflicts (American Psychological Association, 2002, Standard 6.04 (a), Fees and Financial Arrangements). In considering billing options, the goals are to be adequately and fairly compensated for one's services, to charge fees that are a fair reflection of the value of the service being provided, and to establish procedures that limit the potential to have one's opinions or work product swayed by the possibility of increased revenue.

Collection and Review of Information

Bases for Opinions

Opinions offered in court are based on multiple data sources selected to address the referral question in as relevant and reliable way as possible (Grisso, 2003; Heilbrun et al., 2009). This includes not only the data collected directly from the examinee through interview and, where appropriate, testing, but also review of documents from, and potentially interviews with, third-party sources (Heilbrun, Warren, & Picarello, 2003). These collateral sources of information increase the examiner's certainty as opinions are formulated; divergent data generates new hypotheses to be explored, while convergent data increases reliability of findings. The information and techniques used in developing forensic opinions must be sufficient to substantiate those findings (American Psychological Association, 2002, Standard 9.01a, Bases for Assessments). It is a principle of forensic practice that the examiner considers and investigates rival hypotheses, looking at the matter from each plausible perspective and weighing the support found in the data for all possible interpretations of the data (American Psychological Association, 2013a, 1.02, Impartiality and Fairness).

Obtaining Information

In considering the data to be collected and reviewed, the psychologist may consider the possible sources of information about the examinee that would contribute to a full and accurate understanding of the examinee. The information gathered should provide incremental validity; yielding trustworthy or credible data. Information that is obtained from a source that lacks credibility, if given much weight, lessens the accuracy of the evaluation findings. Multiple sources of information can contribute (a) independent corroboration of essential aspects of the examinee's history; (b) relevant information about past mental states; and (c) observational data from a variety of contexts, thus increasing the likelihood that they are representative (Bush, Connell, & Denney, 2006).

Impartiality

Forensic examiners actively seek data that might be expected to support or refute each hypothesis, including those that are contrary to the retaining attorney's theory of the case (Shuman & Greenberg, 2003). For example, the psychologist retained by defense counsel to conduct an assessment for sentencing purposes may be assured by counsel, and by the defendant, that the defendant was never in trouble as a youngster and displayed exemplary behavior at school. Seeking further data to corroborate or refute this finding of good childhood behavior patterns, the psychologist may consider interviewing family members, obtaining school records, and seeking medical and mental health records from the period of the defendant's childhood. It is probable that family members will provide information they believe to be helpful to the defendant. School records may be limited to transcripts, but if more complete school records are available, they may contain some behavioral assessment data. Medical and mental health records, if available, may be the richest source of data about any reported behavioral difficulties. All three sources of data may be useful and provide convergent validity, but if variable information is obtained, the most reliable data may be data that was created contemporaneously, without the influence of litigation, by people with relatively little bias. An impartial search for reliable data calls for such discrimination (Heilbrun et al., 2003).

One's personal biases or wish to generate findings that may assist the retaining attorney can cloud this struggle to maintain impartiality. Boccaccini, Turner and Murrie (2008) found systematic differences in scoring a psychological instrument depending upon who retained the evaluator in sexually violent predator cases where evaluation was one prong for consideration for civil commitment following completion of confinement. There may be legitimate differences among evaluators in how a test result is interpreted, and there is no "gold standard" for determining the accuracy of assessment and opinion formulation in most cases (e.g., Mossman et al., 2010) The responsibility falls upon the evaluator to regularly monitor for personal bias while striving to be impartial in scoring and interpreting test results and arriving at opinions.

The Evaluation

The Psychologist–Examinee Relationship

The examinee or litigant is not the forensic examiner's client but rather is the client of an attorney—either the attorney who retained the forensic psychologist or the opposing attorney. No treatment relationship exists between the forensic examinee and the examiner. The nature of this relationship is in sharp contrast to that usually extant between psychologist and examinee, and should be clearly described to the examinee at the outset. It bears repeating when the examinee displays confusion, asking for advice or help with a current issue, for example, or reveals misconceptions by, for example, addressing the "helpfulness," of the examiner's work (Connell, 2006). Even absent the traditional treatment relationship, the forensic examiner has ethical obligations to the examinee. The examiner must try to ensure that the examinee understands the nature of the assessment, the limitations of confidentiality, the mechanisms for gaining feedback, and who is paying for the services (American Psychological Association, 2002, Standard 3.11[b], Psychological Services Delivered To or Through Organizations).

Informed Consent, Assent, and Notification of Purpose

The forensic examinee is almost always being examined at the request of someone else: the court, an agency, or counsel for one or the other side of the matter. This means that informed consent, which relies on voluntary, knowing participation, may not be altogether relevant. The forensic practitioner has certain ethical obligations to inform the service recipient of the procedure and the range of potential consequences, of who is paying for the services, and of any conflicts of interest the examiner may have (American Psychological Association, 2002, Standards 3.10, Informed Consent, & 9.03, Informed Consent in Assessments) but this may not be sufficient to protect the rights of the examinee.

In addition to this notification or informed consent process (or, if the examinee is a child, the assent process) that takes place with the examinee, other steps may also be required. The options available and their potential consequences need to be explored, and the examinee's legal representative can best do this. In order to fully comprehend what is about to occur, counsel requires information from the forensic practitioner as well (Connell, 2006; Cunningham, 2006; Foote & Shuman, 2006). Notification of Purpose or Informed Consent information, made available to the litigant and counsel before the assessment or services begin, can arm the legal representative with the necessary information to consider the ramifications and appropriately advise the client.

Procedures and Measures

The admissibility standards for expert testimony demand that opinions be based on techniques that are relevant to the matter before the court and that are reliable, and that enjoy general acceptance in the field (*Daubert v. Merrell Dow Pharmaceuticals, Inc., 1993*). In selecting procedures and measures, it is incumbent on the forensic examiner to focus on the psycholegal issue and select assessment techniques that may be expected to contribute to an understanding of that issue. Otto, Buffington-Vollum, and Edens (2002) posed a series of questions that examiners should consider when deciding the issue of testing in custody evaluation; however, these considerations also apply to psychological testing in other evaluation contexts (see Table 3.1).

Table 3.1 Considerations for selecting psychological tests

1. Is the test commercially published?
2. Is a comprehensive test manual available?
3. Are adequate levels of reliability demonstrated?
4. Have adequate levels of validity been demonstrated?
5. Is the test valid for the purpose for which it will be used?
6. Has the instrument been peer-reviewed?
7. Do I posses the qualifications necessary to use this instrument?
8. Does the test require an unacceptable level of inference from the construct it assesses to the psycholegal question(s) of relevance?

Source: Otto, Buffington-Vollum, and Edens (2002), p. 188.

Forensic psychologists are expected to be able to defend, on the basis of both general acceptance and scientific merit, the methods and procedures upon which they relied in reaching an opinion. The forensic expert must illuminate, in the report of findings and when testifying, the path that led from data to opinion (Grisso, 2003; Heilbrun, 2001; Heilbrun et al., 2009).

Procedures and measures are selected, additionally, with an eye to their potential to generate data that will fairly address the psycholegal construct, rather than to generate data that will predictably support the retaining attorney's theory of the case. For example, administration of a transparent or face-valid symptom checklist to a litigant seeking compensation for personal injury is likely to result in a positive finding. The utility of the instrument in fairly addressing the psycholegal question (whether the litigant suffered psychological injury) may be quite limited. By contrast, the issues may be addressed in a more balanced and fair way by using an instrument designed to assess not only the presence of psychological distress but also more general personality functioning and response style. Similarly, in evaluations of parenting capacity such as child custody evaluations, traditional clinical personality assessment instruments may offer some useful information but may also yield distracting, potentially prejudicial but irrelevant interpretative comments regarding personality style (Tippins & Wittman, 2005; Zimmerman, et al., 2009). Instruments should be carefully chosen and interpreted in a way that focuses on the referral issues.

Third-Party Observers

There are occasions when a party, usually the plaintiff in a civil matter, requests or demands to be accompanied during a forensic assessment. Generally this interest is to ensure that the examinee receives an appropriate and competently performed evaluation and to ensure that the examinee is not asked legally objectionable questions. In criminal matters, the defense attorney may want to observe an evaluation performed by the prosecution's expert. Sometimes, particularly with children or vulnerable adults, the interest is in the reassurance that might come from having a family member, therapist, or other trusted person present. Although these motives of ensuring adequacy of psychological evaluation and protecting the examinee's legal rights or emotional well-being are potentially legitimate interests, the presence of counsel or designees in the examination room does carry potential threats to the evaluation's validity.

For example, there may be unknowable effects on the performance of the examinee, particularly in the cognitive domain. While research into this area is thus far arguably equivocal, some studies have demonstrated negative effects on cognitive performance (e.g., Kehrer, Sanchez, Habif, Rosenbaum, & Townes, 2000; Lynch, 2003). The standardized administration for most of the commonly used assessment techniques, particularly those instruments that are administered "face to face" rather than in pencil/paper format, presumes the absence of observers or other potential distractions. For example, the WAIS-III Manual states, "As a rule, no one other than you and the examinee should be in the room during the testing" (p. 29). The potential effects of observers on a particular examinee's performance are simply not measurable, but some effect may be reasonably expected.

Similarly, effects on performance may also occur when the examination is being audio or video recorded (Constantinou, Ashendorf, & McCaffrey, 2002; Constantinou & McCaffrey, 2003). Again, research results are not robust and performance in various domains may be enhanced, depressed, or unaffected—what is known, at this point, is that the effects on the particular examinee are not known. This may not be of sufficient concern to outweigh the advantages of having an accurate record of forensic interviews, however. In each case, the relative risks and benefits may be assessed or the examiner may develop a routine practice of, for example, recording interview interactions but ceasing to record during test administration.

Finally, when recording occurs during verbal administration of instruments, or the administration of performance measures such as Block Design (a subtest on the Wechsler measures of intellectual functioning), test security may be significantly compromised. As a contracted user of these instruments, the examiner must resist disclosure that would reduce the effectiveness of the instrument (Pearson Assessments, 2006). Such influences pose a threat to the validity and reliability of subsequent interpretation of test results.

A potential solution to the dilemma that the forensic psychologist may face, particularly when the law clearly allows for observation, is to request a trained observer: a psychologist. This solution may satisfy the concerns of the litigant, provide reassurance in an adversarial process, and obviate the issues of test security. Although the presence of a psychologist observer would still be a departure from standardized test administration procedures, it may be a reasonable option in what is, in general, an aberrational assessment setting. The adversarial context of litigation itself may affect test performance in ways that are also not known. When it is necessary to have observers in the examining room, the psychologist should document the potential but unknowable impact this deviation from standardized procedures may have had on the examinee's performance.

Cultural Diversity Considerations

The forensic psychologist may regularly encounter circumstances in which a litigant's cultural background or characteristics differ significantly from those of the examiner. All psychologists have an obligation to strive to work effectively and sensitively with regard to cultural differences (American Psychological Association, 2002, Standard 2.01 [Boundaries of Competence], subsection [b] requires sensitivity to the impact of culture, disability, and other diversity factors on one's professional competency); however, the working alliance in a therapeutic context may mitigate the impact on services. Often, forensic assessments occur in an adversarial context and litigants may legitimately worry that their unique cultural heritage or other aspects of diversity may be unfamiliar or noxious to the examiner and may affect the examiner's view or opinions. Whereas within a working alliance, the individual may educate the psychologist about the diversity issue or openly explore its impact on the relationship, in a forensic context, the examinee may be less confident in being heard or understood.

Knapp and VandeCreek (2003) said, "It is not an ethical violation to provide less optimal treatment to members of . . . any groups; it is only a violation if the knowledge that is lacking is essential for providing services" (p. 303). For example, psychologists strive to use assessment instruments that have established validity and reliability for use with members of the population from which the examinee comes (American Psychological Association, 2002, Standard 9.02). When validity or reliability is not established for the population, psychologists must describe how this limitation should be considered in test interpretation. Sometimes the psychometric challenges faced in the assessment of racial or ethnic minorities are insurmountable (Iverson & Slick, 2003). When the use of an instrument, or an interpreter, would potentially have a profound effect on the outcome of the examination, or when there are so many potentially invalidating factors that the results are not likely to be of any use, it is preferable to note these limitations and forego attempting to develop an opinion about the matter before the court (Iverson & Slick, 2003).

Record/Peer Reviews

Sometimes rather than doing a direct examination of a litigant, the forensic psychologist reviews only the records or reviews the work of another examiner and then offers the limited observations or opinions that can be derived from that review. While it is rarely acceptable to offer an opinion about someone not directly evaluated, there are some potential exceptions. The APA Ethics Code (Standard 9.01, Bases for Assessment, section [b]) states:

> Except as noted in 9.01c, psychologists provide opinions of the psychological charac- teristics of individuals only after they have conducted an examination of the individuals adequate to support their statements or conclusions. When, despite reasonable efforts, such an examination is not practical, psychologists document the efforts they made and the result of those efforts, clarify the probable impact of their limited information on the reli- ability and validity of their opinions, and appropriately limit the nature and extent of their conclusions or recommendations.

The APA Ethics Code directly addresses the issue of record review and similar consultation: "When psychologists conduct a record review or provide consultation or supervision and an individual examination is not warranted or necessary for the opinion, psychologists explain this and the sources of information on which they based their conclusions and recommendations" (American Psychological Association, 2002, Standard 9.01, Bases for Assessments, section [c]).

It is the nature of the adversarial forum that evidence is scrutinized, and the expert witness's testimony is evidence. The forensic examiner should anticipate that it will be necessary to sub- ject one's own work to the scrutiny of an opposing expert and to scrutinize the opinions to be offered by an opposing expert. These reviews are not conducted with personal malice but are conducted methodically and dispassionately, much like a forensic assessment. The review may generate an account of the strengths and shortcomings or weaknesses of the assessment and some appraisal of how shortcomings may weaken the resultant opinion (Gould, Kirkpatrick, Austin, & Martindale, 2004).

Mandated Measures

There may be situations in which agency or institutional rules call for the administration of certain tests or measures. The psychologist is ultimately responsible for decisions about what instruments and techniques are utilized, and when institutional demands conflict with the psy- chologist's independent judgment, the psychologist seeks to reconcile the conflict by clarifying the issue and attempting to find a satisfactory solution (American Psychological Association, 2002, 1.03, Resolving Ethical Issues). When the psychologist believes that different, or addi- tional, measures should be used than those requested, an attempt should be made to reach an understanding with the retaining party of the importance of the psychologist making such test selection based upon professional expertise (Bush, Connell, & Denney, 2006).

A distinct but somewhat related issue arises when the psychologist is asked to provide a list of the examination measures in advance of the examination. To minimize the possibility of suc- cessful coaching of the examinee, the psychologist may elect to provide general categories of instruments to be used or a list of all measures from which selection will occur, without stating specifically which measures will be selected for the evaluation in question. Additionally, the psy- chologist may choose to identify the areas to be assessed, such as personality, verbal reasoning, memory, impression management, parenting style, or sexual violence risk potential, rather than the specific instruments that will be used.

Documentation of Findings and Opinions

Forensic Psychological Records

To enable review of the data underlying opinion, forensic psychologists have an ethical obliga- tion to appropriately document and maintain records of their work. In addition to the duty of all psychologists to document services and maintain records of those services (American Psychological Association, 2002, Standard 6.01, Documentation of Professional and Scientific Work and Maintenance of Records; Standard 5.01, Avoidance of False or Deceptive Statements, [b]), the SGFP states:

> Forensic practitioners are encouraged to recognize the importance of documenting all data they consider with enough detail and quality to allow for reasonable judicial scrutiny and adequate discovery by all parties. This documentation includes, but is not limited to, letters and consultations; notes, recordings, and transcriptions; assessment and test data, scoring reports and interpretations; and all other records in any form or medium that were created or exchanged in connection with a matter.
>
> When contemplating third party observation or audio/video-recording of examinations, forensic practitioners strive to consider any law that may control such matters, the need for transparency and documentation, and the potential impact of observation or recording on the validity of the examination and test security (cite omitted). (American Psychological Association, 2013a, 10.06, Documentation and Compilation of Data Considered)

This need to maintain documentation of services sufficiently to withstand judicial scrutiny means psychologists should keep track not only of the data generated in direct contact with the examinee, such as interview notes or recordings and test data, but also of other communications and activities regarding the matter. A reviewer should be able to see, from the record, what the forensic practitioner did and when it was done throughout the work on the case, from initial contact through completion of services. The expectation in the legal forum is that records reflect the sequence of events: when documents were received for review and from whom they were received, and when they were reviewed relative to other activities in the case; the content of telephone consultations; dates and times of all activities; and other relevant information such as, for example, who transported a child to appointments, who was present during interviews, and why appointments were canceled or changed. A detailed record helps to demonstrate that competent services were provided.

Scope of Interpretation

Forensic expertise is of value to the trier of fact when opinions are based on a combination of individualized (ideographic) and group referenced (nomothetic) approaches to data collection and interpretation (Heilbrun, 2001). Information specific to the examinee, or ideographic information, is collected and compared to relevant group data or nomothetic data. When the individual's performance on psychological measures or presentation upon interview differs from comparison groups, interpretations of the differences may incorporate the individual's unique life circumstances, with an emphasis on variables known to affect such performance. The APA Ethics Code states, "Psychologists' work is based upon established scientific and professional knowledge of the discipline" (American Psychological Association, 2002, Standard 2.04, Bases for Scientific and Professional Judgments). An opinion that is not grounded in objective data and scientific principles may be found to be inadmissible because its reliability cannot be demonstrated.

When there is pressure to make definitive statements to the court, psychologists may find that their academic inclination to qualify statements is anathema to the legal system's search for definitive opinion. It is important for psychologists to assert opinions as strongly as the data merits, but also to describe the limitations of those opinions (American Psychological Association, 2002, Standard 2.04, Bases for Scientific and Professional Judgments).

Diagnosis in Forensic Assessment

Often the legal question being addressed by the court invokes some consideration of psychological constructs such as cognitive capacities, intentionality of actions, competence to consult with counsel or to execute a will or to parent adequately, neurological consequences of head injuries, psychological suffering as a consequence of severe trauma or loss, and other such issues. To some extent these constructs are fairly clearly defined by statute or case law, and rarely does that definition include a specific diagnosis. Yet, the presence of a diagnosed condition may be relevant for consideration in legal matters. The task of the forensic psychologist may be to conduct an assessment, formulate an opinion about diagnosis, and then relate the diagnosis to the question before the court. The *Diagnostic and Statistical Manual-5* (American Psychiatric Association, 2013) addresses this relationship between diagnosis and the legal system in the Cautionary Statement for Forensic Use of the DSM-5:

> Although the DSM-5 diagnostic criteria and text are primarily designed to assist clinicians in conducting clinical assessment, case formulation, and treatment planning, DSM-5 is also used as a reference for the courts and attorneys in assessing the forensic consequences of mental disorders. As a result, it is important to note that the definition of mental disorder included in DSM-5 was developed to meet the needs of clinicians, public health professionals, and research investigators rather than all of the technical needs of the courts and legal professionals. It is also important to note that DSM-5 does not provide treatment guidelines for any given disorder. (p. 25)

The authors note that there are some appropriate uses of the DSM-5 to assist legal decision makers:

> When used appropriately, diagnoses and diagnostic information can assist decision makers in their determinations. For example, when the presence of a mental disorder is the predicate for a subsequent legal determination (e.g., involuntary civil commitment), the use of an established system of diagnosis enhances the value and reliability of the determination. By providing a compendium based on a review of the pertinent clinical and research literature, DSM-5 may facilitate the legal decision makers' understanding of the relevant characteristics of mental disorders. The literature related to diagnoses also serves as a check on ungrounded speculation about mental disorders and about the functioning of a particular individual. Finally, diagnostic information regarding longitudinal course may improve decision making when the legal issue concerns an individual's mental functioning at a past or future point in time. (p. 25)

The DSM-5 Cautionary Statement goes further in explicating the relationship between diagnosis and issues of concern to the courts:

> However, the use of DSM-5 should be informed by an awareness of the risks and limitations of its use in forensic settings. When DSM-5 categories, criteria, and textual descriptions are employed for forensic purposes, there is a risk that diagnostic information will be misused or misunderstood. These dangers arise because of the imperfect fit between the questions of ultimate concern to the law and the information contained in a clinical diagnosis. In most situations the clinical diagnosis of a DSM-5 mental disorder such as intellectual disability (intellectual developmental disorder), schizophrenia, major neurocognitive disorder, gambling disorder, or pedophilic disorder does not imply that an individual with such a condition meets legal criteria for the presence of a mental disorder or a specified legal standard (e.g., for competence, criminal responsibility, or disability). For

the latter, additional information is usually required beyond that contained in the DSM-5 diagnosis, which might include information about the individual's functional impairments and how these impairments affect the particular abilities in question. It is precisely because impairments, abilities, and disabilities vary widely within each diagnostic category that assignment of a particular diagnosis does not imply a specific level of impairment or disability. (p. 25)

Finally, the DSM-5 Cautionary Statement extends to apprise nonclinical decision makers that a diagnosis carries no necessary implications regarding etiology or causes of an individual's mental disorder or degree of control over behavior: "Even when diminished control over one's behavior is a feature of the disorder, having the diagnosis in itself does not demonstrate that a particular individual is (or was) unable to control his or her behavior at a particular time" (p. 25).

Ultimate Issue

Most issues to be decided by the court are legal issues that embrace society's values or moral judgments. Psychologists may be able to provide useful information to be considered along with other evidence and in light of the values and moral sensibilities of the trier of fact. Psychological training does not prepare psychologists to have expertise about moral issues. While, as individuals, they may have strong opinions, their testimony is being offered based on their psychological expertise, not on their own personal beliefs and values. However, attorneys and sometimes judges are quite interested in the psychologist's opinion regarding the legal question itself (Bow & Quinnell, 2004). Offering an opinion that embraces the ultimate legal question is not generally legally objectionable, but it does threaten to invade the province of the court, since it is specifically the task of the trier of fact to make this determination. Melton and colleagues (2007) noted that when forensic practitioners opine on the ultimate issue before the court, their overstepping of competency is sometimes egregious, particularly in matters of child custody. Psychologists who attempt to answer the legal question are vulnerable to exceeding the bounds of their expertise (Heilbrun, 2001). Grisso (2003) said, "An expert opinion that answers the ultimate legal question is not an 'expert' opinion, but a personal value judgment" (p. 477). Tippins and Wittman (2005) called for clinicians to assume a far more humble approach and resist inferential leaps that stretch the data to apply clinical formulations to legal issues.

There is vigorous debate within the forensic community about offering opinions on the ultimate issue. Those who argue in support of the offer of such testimony observe that the forensic psychologist's hesitancy to do so may be the exception, rather than the rule, among testifying experts (Bala, 2005; Erard, 2006). Experts from the fields of medicine, for example, regularly offer clinical judgments or professional opinions and courts presumably make use of their judgments in fact finding. Psychologists may be tying their hands behind their backs, critics argue, by holding themselves to a higher standard than do other experts and may make themselves less useful to the legal system in so doing (Bala, 2005; Erard, 2006).

Psychologists who practice in contexts in which it is expected or required that they answer the legal question may make special effort to temper their opinions by including cautionary language and caveats regarding the limitations of, and potential influences on, their opinions (American Psychological Association, 2010, 2013a, 2013b).

Release of Raw Data

The APA Ethics Code distinguishes test *materials*, including manuals, instruments, protocols, and test questions or stimuli from test *data* (American Psychological Association, 2002, Standard

9.11, Maintaining Test Security). In order to maintain test security (Standard 9.11) and thereby test utility, test materials are not widely disseminated. Test data, in contrast, includes "raw and scaled scores, client/patient responses to test questions or stimuli, and psychologists' notes and recordings concerning client/patient statements and behavior during an examination" (American Psychological Association, 2002, Standard 9.04[a], Release of Test Data). When test materials have responses written on them, they "convert" to test data.

Psychologists provide test data, with appropriate release, to anyone designated by the examinee or legal representative (American Psychological Association, 2002, Standard 9.04); in many forensic contexts, the attorney or court may determine to whom the data are released. Withholding test data on the grounds that releasing the data could result in substantial harm to the examinee is justifiable (American Psychological Association, 2002, Standard 9.03[a]); in most forensic contexts, this issue may not be relevant and the default assumption from the outset is that test data will be accessible as part of the foundation for the expert opinion that is to be proffered.

Feedback

Psychologists generally provide feedback to examinees about test results and interpretations. However, an exception may be made with forensic examinations where there is no ethical requirement to do so (American Psychological Association, 2002, Standard 9.10, Explaining Assessment Results). It is atypical, in fact, for forensic examiners to provide feedback directly to examinees in some forensic settings, such as examinations of plaintiffs by defense-retained experts (IMEs). Findings are instead released to the retaining party, who has control over their further release. Similarly, in court-ordered child custody evaluations, the evaluator may be directed by the court or may choose to release the report to the court and the attorneys without giving feedback directly to the parties. HIPAA does not seem to protect the examinee's right to access and amend psychological records in forensic contexts (Connell & Koocher, 2003; U.S. Department of Health and Human Services, 1996). The psychologist makes clear at the outset the manner in which findings will be released. When there are statutory requirements to provide feedback (for example, codified rules of practice), there may be no exemption from the requirement in forensic settings, and the psychologist would then need to comply with the regulation by providing feedback.

Testimony

Expert testimony generally involves the presentation of findings or opinions developed through forensic psychological services. It may be provided by way of affidavit, deposition, or court appearance. Often the thrust of testimony is an amplification of what is contained in the written report through direct examination and cross-examination. It reflects an assimilation of the data collected, the relevant research, and the link between that data and any opinions that have been formulated (Heilbrun, 2001). When testifying, psychologists should not, either actively or passively, engage in partisan distortion or misrepresentation (American Psychological Association, 2013a, 11.1). The SGFP (11.1) further states that forceful representation of the data and reasoning upon which one's opinion is based is not precluded, as long as the information is presented accurately. It is not acceptable, however, to omit important data or evidence that contradicts the opinions formulated; the SGFP states, "Forensic practitioners do not, by either commission or omission, participate in misrepresentation of their evidence, nor do they participate in partisan attempts to avoid, deny, or subvert the presentation of evidence contrary to their own position or opinion" (American Psychological Association, 2013a, 11.1). The attorney offering the psychologist as an expert should know the data that argue for or support the expert's opinion, as well as the countervailing data. The attorney can then decide whether to call the expert to testify. When the forensic psychologist testifies, it is with an affirmative ethical obligation to do so in a forthcoming, evenhanded way that fairly represents the data (American Psychological Association, 2013a, 11.1).

Summary

Forensic psychologists, practicing ethically and competently, make a valuable contribution to the justice system. Because they work in the public eye and their work is scrutinized through the workings of the adversarial process, they experience both a strong call for the highest ethical standards and the potential to be held accountable when their practice falls below acceptable standards or they engage in an unethical action. There are some potential inherent conflicts among the demands of the various entities the forensic psychologist encounters or serves, and there is at times seduction to ethical misconduct.

Forensic psychologists can make good ethical decisions by recognizing, from the outset, that in applying their psychological expertise in the legal arena, ethical dilemmas will arise for which there is no simple *yes* or *no* answer. There are vast resources available to the forensic practitioner to assist in the resolution of these problems, and a systematic approach to their application is useful. The psychologist works within a frame that respects the values of autonomy, nonmalfeasance, beneficence, and justice, and considers the inherent tensions between the civil rights of the parties in a legal action and the search for truth and justice. A systematic approach to the assimilation of information from all relevant sources, including professional standards and guidelines, the law, professional treatises, and collegial consultation may bring the practitioner nearer a satisfactory resolution, but other issues must also be considered. Also bearing consideration are personal biases and their effects, potential consequences to all involved parties, and timing of action. In many ethical dilemmas, a perfect resolution is not available and the psychologist must seek to find and employ the highest ethical action available.

Unintentional missteps may occur even for experienced practitioners, who may face novel ethical dilemmas in spite of careful forethought and planning. The standards for competent and ethical practice will continue to evolve with increasing sophistication in the specialty area and in the law's use of psychologists' input in matters at bar. Maintaining competent and ethical behavior in practice requires a lifelong commitment to ongoing professional development.

References

American Psychiatric Association. (2013). *Diagnostic and statistical manual of mental disorders* (5th ed.). Arlington, VA: American Psychiatric Publishing.

American Psychological Association (2002). Ethical principles of psychologists and code of conduct. *American Psychologist, 57*, 1060–1073. doi: 10.1037/0003–066X.57.12.1060

American Psychological Association (2010). Guidelines for child custody evaluations in family law proceedings. *American Psychologist, 65*, 863–867. doi: 10/1037/a0021250

American Psychological Association. (2013a). Specialty guidelines for forensic psychology. *American Psychologist, 68*, 7–19. doi: 10.1037/a0029889

American Psychological Association. (2013b). Guidelines for psychological evaluations in child protection matters. *American Psychologist, 68*, 20–31. doi: 10.1037/a0029891

Bala, N. (2005). Tippins and Wittman asked the wrong questions: Evaluators may not be "experts," but they can express best interests opinions. *Family Court Review, 43*, 554–562. doi: 10.1111/j.1744–1617.2005.00054.x

Boccaccini, M.T., Turner, D.B. & Murrie, D.C. (2008). Do some evaluators report consistently higher or lower PCL-R scores than others? Findings from a statewide sample of sexually violent predator evaluations. *Psychology, Public Policy, and Law, 14*, 262–283. doi: 10.1037/a0011452³

Bow, J.N., & Quinnell, F.A. (2004). Critique of child custody evaluations by the legal profession. *Family Court Review, 42*, 115–126. doi: 10.1177/1531244504421009

Bush, S.S., Connell, M. A., & Denney, R.L. (2006). *Ethical practice in forensic psychology: A systematic model for decision making*. Washington, DC: American Psychological Association.

Canadian Psychological Association. (2000). *Canadian code of ethics for psychologists* (3rd Ed.). Ottawa, ON: Author.

Connell, M. (2006). Notification of purpose in custody evaluation: Informing the parties and their counsel. *Professional Psychology: Research and Practice, 37*, 446–451. doi: 10.1037/0735–7028.37.5.446

Connell, M., & Koocher, G. (2003). HIPAA & forensic practice. *American Psychology Law Society News, 23*, 16–19.

Constantinou, M., Ashendorf, L., & McCaffrey, R. J. (2002). When the 3rd party observer of a neuropsychological evaluation is an audio-recorder. *The Clinical Neuropsychologist, 16*, 407–412. doi: 10.1076/clin.16.3.407.13853

Constantinou, M., & McCaffrey, R. J. (2003). The effects of 3rd party observation: When the observer is a video camera. *Archives of Clinical Neuropsychology, 18*, 788–789.

Cunningham, M. D. (2006). Informed consent in capital sentencing evaluations: Targets and content. *Professional Psychology: Research and Practice. 37*, 452–459. doi: dx.doi.org/10.1037/0735–7028.37.5.452

Daubert v. Merrell Dow Pharmaceuticals, Inc., 509 U.S. 579 (1993).

Erard, R. E. (2006). Tell it to the judge!: A counter-perspective to Wittman & Tippins (2005) on ultimate issue testimony in child custody matters. *National Psychologist, 15*, 1.

Foote, W. E., & Shuman, D. W. (2006). Consent, disclosure, and waiver for the forensic psychological evaluation: Rethinking the roles of psychologist and lawyer. *Professional Psychology: Research and Practice, 37*, 437–445. doi: 10.1037/0735–7028.37.5.437

Gould, J. W., Kirkpatrick, H. D., Austin, W. G., & Martindale, D. A. (2004). Critiquing a colleague's forensic work product: A suggested protocol for application to child custody evaluations. *Journal of Child Custody: Research, Issues, and Practices, 1*, 37–64. doi: 10.1300/J190v01n03_04

Grisso, T. (2003). *Evaluating competencies: Forensic assessments and instruments* (2nd ed.). New York: Kluwer Academic/Plenum.

Heilbrun, K. (2001). *Principles of forensic mental health assessment*. New York: Kluwer Academic/Plenum.

Heilbrun, K., Grisso, T., & Goldstein, A. M. (2009). *Foundations of forensic mental health assessment*. New York: Oxford University Press.

Heilbrun, K., Grisso, T., & Goldstein, A. M. (2013). Foundations of forensic mental health assessment. In R. Roesch & P. A. Zapf (Eds.), *Forensic assessments in criminal and civil law: A handbook for lawyers* (pp. 1–14). New York: Oxford University Press.

Heilbrun, K., Warren, J., & Picarello, K. (2003). Third party information in forensic assessment. In A. M. Goldstein (Ed.), *Handbook of forensic psychology* (pp. 69–86). Hoboken, NJ: Wiley.

Iverson, G. L., & Slick, D. J. (2003). Ethical issues associated with psychological and neuropsychological assessment of persons from different cultural and linguistic backgrounds. In I. Z. Schultz & D. O. Brady (Eds.), *Psychological injuries at trial* (pp. 2066–2087). Chicago: American Bar Association.

Kehrer, C. A., Sanchez, P. N., Habif, U., Rosenbaum, G, J. & Townes, B. D. (2000). Effects of a significant-other observer on neuropsychological test performance. *Neuropsychology, Development, and Cognition, 14*, 67–71.

Knapp, S., & VandeCreek, L. (2003). *A guide to the 2002 revision of the American Psychological Association's Ethics Code*. Sarasota, FL: Professional Resource Press.

Lynch, J. K. (2003). The effect of an observer on neuropsychological test performance following TBI. *Archives of Clinical Neuropsychology, 18*, 791.

Melton, G. B., Petrila, J., Poythress, N. G., & Slobogin, C. (2007). *Psychological evaluations for the courts* (3rd ed.). New York: Guilford Press.

Mossman, D., Bowen, M. D., Vanness, D. J., Bienefeld, D., Correll, T., Kay, J., Klykylo, W. M., & Lehrer, D. S. (2010). Quantifying the accuracy of forensic examiners in the absence of a "gold standard." *Law and Human Behavior, 34*, 402–417. doi: 10.1007/s10979–009–9197–5

Otto, R., Buffington-Vollum, J., & Edens, J. F. (2002). Child custody evaluation. In A. M. Goldstein (Ed.), *Comprehensive handbook of psychology, Volume 11: Forensic psychology* (pp. 179–208). New York: Wiley.

Pearson Assessments. (2006). Legal notice. Retrieved on July 17, 2014 from www.pearsonassessments.com/legal-notice.html#HIPPAA.

Shuman, D. W., & Greenberg, S. A. (2003). The expert witness, the adversary system, and the voice of reason: Reconciling impartiality and advocacy. *Professional Psychology: Research and Practice, 34*, 219–224. doi: 10.1037/0735–7028.34.3.219

Tippins, T. M., & Wittman, J. P. (2005). Empirical and ethical problems with custody recommendations: A call for clinical humility and judicial vigilance. *Family Court Review, 43*, 193–222. doi: 10.1111/j.1744–1617.2005.00019.x

U.S. Department of Health and Human Services (1996). Public Law 104–191: Health Insurance Portability and Accountability Act of 1996. Retrieved June 19, 2015 from www.hhs.gov/ocr/privacy/hipaa/administrative/statute/

Wechsler, D. (1997). *Wechsler Adult Intelligence Scale-III*. San Antonio, TX: The Psychological Corporation.

Zimmerman, J., Hess, A. K. McGarrah, N. A., Benjamin, G., A. H., Ally, G. A., Gollan, J. K. & Kaser-Boyd, N. (2009). Ethical and professional considerations in divorce and child custody cases. *Professional Psychology: Research and Practice, 40*, 539–549. doi: 10.1037/a0017853

Part II
Adult Forensic Assessment

4 Learning Forensic Examinations of Adjudicative Competency

Stephen L. Golding

The purpose of this chapter is to provide mental health professionals with an introduction to the assessment of *adult adjudicative competency*[1] as a forensic mental health professional. In doing so, I will attempt to outline the essential legal, ethical, professional assessment, and interpretational issues. However, individuals attempting to work in this area also need to obtain supervision and learn more about the overarching ethical, legal, and professional concepts and skills that are somewhat unique to forensic assessments. More comprehensive treatment of the broader forensic issues may be found in (a) *Specialty Guidelines for Forensic Psychology* (American Psychological Association, 2013); (b) *Principles of Forensic Mental Health Assessment* (Heilbrun, 2001); and (c) *Psychological Evaluations for the Courts: A Handbook for Mental Health Professionals and Lawyers* (Melton, Petrila, Poythress, & Slobogin, 2007). In addition, more detailed treatment of all of the issues raised in this chapter concerning adjudicative competency may be found in *Evaluating Competencies: Forensic Assessments and Instruments* (Grisso, 2003) and a series of essential reviews (Fogel, Schiffman, Mumley, Tillbrook, & Grisso, 2013; Pirelli, Gottdiener, & Zapf, 2011; Poythress, Bonnie, Monahan, Otto, & Hoge, 2002; Roesch, Zapf, Golding, & Skeem, 1999; Skeem, Golding, & Emke-Francis, 2004; Zapf, Roesch, & Pirelli, 2014), as well as the position statement of the American Academy of Psychiatry and Law (Mossman et al., 2007).

History and Significance of Adjudicative Competency

Adjudicative competency arose as an issue in 13th-century Anglo-Saxon jurisprudence. At that time, a number of modern rights, such as the assistance of counsel, did not exist. Many types of pleas existed and a trial could not proceed without a defendant's first entering a plea. If the defendant did not plead, the competency issue arose in the form of a query: Was he "mute by malice," i.e., not responding to the indictment in order to prevent a trial,[2] or "mute by visitation by God," i.e., unable to comprehend and respond to the charges because of mental retardation or disorder.

Conceptualizations of competency slowly changed as both the principles of jurisprudence and understanding of mental disorder matured. By the 17th century, Coke observed that allowing an incompetent defendant to proceed to trial compromised the moral authority of the court and would be "a miserable spectacle, both against the law, and of extreme inhumanity and cruelty, and can be no example to others" (see Roesch et al., 1999). A further core jurisprudential justification, that the trial of an incompetent defendant is like an unjust adversarial contest "in which the defendant, like a small boy being beaten by a bully, is unable to dodge or return the blows" also emerged (*Frith's Case*, 1790). In 1899, these conceptualizations were drawn into American case law in *Youtsey v. United States* (1899).[3]

The significance of adjudicative competency can be understood legally, procedurally, and economically. In our adversarial system, it is considered a fundamental violation of fairness and due process to proceed against an incompetent defendant (*Dusky v. United States*, 1960; *Drope v. Missouri*, 1975). The constitutional concern about proceeding against an incompetent defendant is both pragmatic and symbolic. Pragmatically, an individual who cannot participate vigorously and effectively in his defense is denied "fundamental fairness" and may be erroneously convicted. Symbolically, the moral authority of the judicial system is diminished, as was stated so eloquently in *Frith's Case* (1790).

Procedurally, adjudicative incompetency places a "hold" on all subsequent phases of adjudication. Thus, an issue of a defendant's competency is effectively an adjudicative bottleneck. Economically, competency evaluations, competency hearings, and competency restoration require the majority of forensic mental health dollars and account for approximately 10% of inpatient psychiatric beds in most jurisdictions (Golding, 1992; Mossman, 2007).

Adjudicative Competency as a Construct

I have long argued that competency is an "open-textured construct" in the precise sense set forth by Cronbach and Meehl (1955). Thus, competency cannot be reduced to a precise set of operational definitions (like a score of such-and-such on a test, or the presence of a given symptom or diagnosis), but is, by its nature, open-textured. As discussed subsequently, this is one of the main reasons why various proposals to operationalize competency, by means of nomothetic tests, often produce unsatisfactory or incomplete results. Nomothetic assessment devices, such as the MacArthur Competence Assessment Tool (MacCAT; Poythress, Nicholson, Otto et al., 1999) or the Evaluation of Competency to Stand Trial–Revised (ECST-R; Rogers, Tillbrook, & Sewell, 2004), are a useful supplement to other idiographic assessment techniques and integrative strategies that contextualize a defendant's competency in terms of the specific details of the case.[4] Being "open-textured" however, does not mean a conceptual free-for-all; careful review and understanding of relevant constitutional cases helps to reveal the possible contours of the adjudicative competency construct, and hence the contours of an assessment of adjudicative competency.

The Constitutional Structure of Adjudicative Competency

Relating Psychopathology or Intellective Functioning to Competency

All legal analyses of adjudicative competency are based upon the premise that competency does not have a precise relationship to either intelligence or level of psychopathological disturbance. The most common error made by inexperienced forensic examiners is *to equate either extreme psychopathology or significant retardation[5] with incompetency*. While incompetent defendants are often psychotic,[6] the converse is not true; that is psychotic defendants, in general, are not incompetent (Viljoen & Roesch, 2003). Significant cognitive deficits and psychopathology function in an "if-then" fashion in terms of their relationship to incompetency. Presence of either mental retardation or psychopathological disturbance is merely "a threshold issue that must be established in order to 'get one's foot in the incompetency door' " (Skeem et al., 2004). It is the "linkage" between "first base," (i.e., significant psychopathological or cognitive limitations) and functional impairment in critical psycholegal[7] abilities that is central to the competency construct (Skeem & Golding, 1998). Thus, the essence of a competency evaluation is not the assessment of pathology or cognitive functioning, but rather how and why this can be linked to deficits in specific psycholegal abilities that are required of a defendant in a particular case. Unfortunately, as Skeem and Golding (1998) have shown, this is most often the weakest part of competency evaluations and reports.

Defining Competency Constitutionally

The basic constitutional contours of adjudicative competency were set forth in *Dusky v. United States* (1960):

> It is not enough for (a) . . . judge to find that "the defendant is oriented to time and place and has some recollections of events," but that the test must be whether he has sufficient present ability to consult with his lawyer with a reasonable degree of rational understanding—and whether he has a rational[8] as well as factual understanding of the proceedings against him. (p. 402)

A fundamental skill for a forensic examiner is detailed knowledge of the competency statute and its case law and interpretation in their jurisdiction. From a legal perspective, this is best accomplished by "shepardizing"[9] *Dusky* within the jurisdiction. However, most jurisdictions simply adopt[10] the vague *Dusky* language. Professional levels of forensic competency are best achieved by study of those jurisdictions that have created articulated standards (e.g., Utah Annotated Code [2006], §77–15–5) and by knowledge of the professional literature.[11]

Even so, a forensic examiner must realize that the constitutional contours of competency prohibit an inflexible "list" of competency-related psycholegal abilities. Thus, in *Drope v. Missouri* (1975), the U.S. Supreme Court observed that, "there are, of course, no fixed or immutable signs which invariably indicate the need for further inquiry to determine fitness to proceed; the question is often a difficult one in which a wide range of manifestations and subtle nuances are implicated" (p. 180). In a subsequent section I discuss the more common psycholegal abilities usually evaluated in a standard competency evaluation, but one should realize that the specific psycholegal abilities "in play" are driven by the specific context of particular case and may involve other competencies not ordinarily evaluated when a defendant is represented by counsel (e.g., competency to waive counsel or waive an insanity defense recommended by counsel; competency to confess; competency to plead guilty or waive postconviction appeals; and competency to refuse psychotropic treatment aimed at competency restoration).

In the pivotal case of *Godinez v. Moran* (1993), the Supreme Court addressed the question of whether these other competencies (e.g., competency to proceed pro se, plead guilty, waive an insanity defense) should be judged according to the constitutionally mandated *Dusky* standard, or whether they should be judged by a higher standard because of the additional constitutional parameters of such decisions. The wisdom of the defendant's decision, whether the defendant is legally sophisticated, or whether the defendant's mental disorder compromises his or her ability to actually defend him- or herself (as in *Indiana v. Edwards*, 2008; discussed subsequently) is not the issue. Rather, the issue is whether or not mental disorder compromises the defendant's ability to make *rational* (though "stupid" or ill-advised) decisions. Many defendants who wish to proceed pro se or plead guilty (against the advice of counsel) do so because of depression or suicidal ideation, delusionally inspired thinking about religious issues, or extreme and idiosyncratic belief systems (usually of a political or social nature, as is the case with so-called "sovereign citizens"). These situations always pose difficult questions for courts and forensic examiners because distinguishing between delusionally influenced incompetent decision making and idiosyncratically inspired decisions pushes the boundaries of our scientific and social knowledge (Golding, Skeem, Roesch & Zapf, 1999; Litwack, 2003). While the issue legally framed in *Godinez* was whether a higher or different standard than *Dusky* applies, the more important legal and pragmatic issue is whether or not a full inquiry is made into a defendant's decisional capacities,[12] regardless of what standard is applied to that analysis. The *Godinez* court found that the standards were the same, but avoided the more troubling aspect of Moran's case. When Moran's competence was evaluated, the examination focused solely upon his capacity to stand trial with the assistance of counsel. At that time, he was cooperating with counsel. When he appeared at trial three months later, however, he sought to discharge his public defender and plead guilty to all three charges of capital murder, without any stipulation by the prosecution as to sentence. The trial judge relied upon the prior competency evaluations to accept his waiver of counsel and guilty plea. At his capital sentencing hearing, Moran presented no defense, and would not permit the introduction of any mitigation. He essentially "volunteered" for execution.

In *Indiana v. Edwards* (2008), the Supreme Court revisited the competency to proceed pro se issue, but again dodged the ambiguity in *Godinez*. It did so by asserting that the issue in *Godinez* was whether or not mental disorder influenced Moran's decision to represent himself (which was never evaluated!) from the influence of mental disorder on his ability to represent himself. In *Edwards*, therefore, the Supreme Court ruled that the influence of mental illness on a defendant's capacity to perform the task of self-representation was a different issue than that raised in *Godinez*.

The lack of conceptual clarity in Justice Thomas's opinion in *Godinez* continues to distort the judicial system's understanding of competency evaluations. The situation became even murkier after the Supreme Court's decision in *Edwards*. While scholars, attorneys, and forensic professionals continue to debate the "real" meaning of *Godinez* and *Edwards*, there is *no debate* as to the meaning of the essential holding in *Pate v. Robinson* (1966). (To be fair, there is debate about the meaning of how great a doubt constitutes a *bona fide* or *genuine* doubt, but that is a separate issue.) The uncontradicted core holding in *Pate* is that *any party* (defense, prosecution, or the court itself, *sua sponte*) has a constitutional obligation to raise the competency issue whenever a bona fide doubt exists. Translating this into real world considerations, the basic facts of *Godinez* would have led to an entirely different outcome, had *Godinez* been argued on the grounds of *Pate*, that is was there a *new and bona fide* doubt as to Moran's competency at Time Two, when he was refusing counsel and wanting to plead "straight up" to capital murder and not present any mitigation, despite his having been found competent at Time One, when he was cooperating with counsel and seeking to fight the capital murder charge.

To state this *Pate* principal in the abstract, prior competency evaluations in Context A (cooperating with counsel, wanting to defend oneself, accepting medication, etc.) have *some logical and empirical bearing* on competency in Context B (wanting to proceed pro se, "volunteering for execution," having worsening psychotic symptoms, refusing medication, etc.), but constitutionally, a new evaluation, in a distinguishable context, is mandated.

Thus, regardless of the jurisprudential issue of whether *the standard of competence* varies across contexts, the practical question is, *how does an evaluation in one context generalize to another very different context*? Clearly, Moran's mental state, like the change in context, may have changed. If so, a new inquiry into competency would be constitutionally required under *Pate*. Most courts and attorneys have interpreted (incorrectly, I believe) *Godinez* as standing for the proposition that competency assessed in a particular context and time frame generalizes across contexts.[13] A few courts have scrutinized the issue by the more appropriate *Pate* analysis and have not accepted the arguably erroneous interpretation of *Godinez*.[14] As discussed in the next section, any significant change in the context in which a defendant was evaluated may trigger the need for a reevaluation, and evaluators should stress this issue in their reports.[15]

Raising the competency issue

In *Pate v. Robinson* (1966), the U.S. Supreme Court recognized, given the constitutional imperatives involved, that an evaluation *must* take place when a *bona fide* doubt as to a defendant's competency exists. While usually raised in a preadjudication context, *Pate* requires that the issue be resolved whenever a genuine doubt exists, and thus it may arise as contexts change *before, during, and subsequent to*, the trial. This issue is particularly important with respect to defendants whose mental state fluctuates, even while medicated.[16]

Many inappropriate competency referrals are made because judges of the court are often hesitant to deny a *Pate* motion for fear of a conviction being overturned on grounds that an uninvestigated and unadjudicated *bona fide* doubt existed. A reasonable solution to the "does a genuine doubt" exist, or "is this a redundant or inappropriate *Pate* motion,"[17] is found in some jurisdictions that provide for hearing on the sufficiency of the *Pate* petition.[18] Regardless of statutory language, courts have the authority to reject inadequately founded, redundant, or frivolous motions (*United States v. Bradshaw*, 1982). Forensic examiners, as part of their evaluation procedure, should always ascertain the grounds for the petition from the moving party, because this provides an orientation to the particular psycholegal issues likely to be involved (Grisso, 1988; Melton et al., 2007).

There are other important practice implications of *Pate* and *Godinez*. First, since a mentally disordered defendant's competence can fluctuate dramatically and quickly, forensic examiners should emphasize this in their court reports, *especially when such fluctuations are part of the defendant's mental health history*. Second, forensic examiners should be cautious about relying upon "older" mental health records, again especially when there is reason to suspect fluctuation.[19] Third, forensic examiners should make the exact context of their evaluations clear to the court and state that their current opinions should not be taken as applicable to other, unevaluated contexts. Forensic examiners should write evaluative reports with this potential for misapplication in mind. A suggested boilerplate phrase would be something like, "Mr. X was evaluated in the following context [e.g., he was compliant with his medication, was cooperating with his attorney]. Should the context of his case change,[20] Mr. X would need to reevaluated in order to render a reliable and current opinion as to his competency."

Time Limits for Restoration

Once a defendant has been found incompetent, other constitutional issues arise in determining a defendant's restorability or progress towards restoration. In *Jackson v. Indiana* (1972), the Supreme Court addressed the issue of how long an incompetent pretrial defendant can be held by the state in an attempt to restore competency. The Court's holding, that a defendant "cannot be held more than the reasonable period of time necessary to determine whether there is a substantial probability that he will attain that capacity in the foreseeable future" (at 738), has given rise to wide jurisdictional disparities[21] because of its vagueness. Many jurisdictions do not have so-called Jackson limits (Morris & Meloy, 1993; Roesch & Golding, 1979) and similarly most jurisdictions[22] do not have a statutory scheme that dictates when and how often an incompetent defendant is reevaluated in terms of whether or not restoration progress has been made and whether or not restorability is still a "substantial probability." Further complicating the issue, many jurisdictions place no limits on the length of time a criminal charge may be maintained, even when the defendant has been found unrestorable and civilly committed.[23] Regardless of legal difficulties, *Jackson* poses a problem for forensic evaluators because it presupposes (a) effective restoration treatments and (b) an ability to predict restorability and response to treatment.

With respect to the prediction of restorability, Mossman (2007) has demonstrated that, while the overall base rate for restoration (approximately 75%) does not provide an individualized basis for prediction, there are two classes of defendants whose probability of restoration is considerably less. Both subgroups are entirely logical: (a) individuals whose incompetency stems from significant cognitive impairment (retardation, dementia, advanced age,[24] or brain damage) and (b) individuals with chronic psychotic conditions that have not responded to treatment and who have lengthy hospitalization histories. Morris and DeYoung (2012) studied prediction of restorability using changes in ratings of psycholegal deficits as measured by the original McGarry, Lelos, and Lipsitt (1973) criteria. They discovered that these criteria formed a continuum, conveniently described as deficits in "basic behavior and outlook" (managing courtroom behavior and appropriate motivation to cooperate), "factual understanding" (charges, court personnel, available defenses), and "rational attorney assistance" (with respect to strategy, testimony, etc.). Deficits across the continuum predicted difficulty in ultimate restoration, whereas fewer deficits, at lower levels of the continuum, predicted restorability. The finding that difficulties with the "rational assistance" prong may be the most difficult to restore is consistent with research that points to impairment in rational understanding as "taxonic" as opposed to continuous (Marcus, Poythress, Edens, & Lilienfeld, 2010).

Little systematic research exists on the issue of the ability of examiners to predict accurately restorability (Zapf & Roesch, 2011), even though *Jackson* and *Sell v. United States* (2003; see discussion later in this chapter) presume both. With respect to intervention effectiveness, a comprehensive review of the largely descriptive clinical and the scant empirical literature on psychosocial and psycho-educational restoration treatment programs[25] for both mentally disordered and mentally retarded defendants by Pinals (2005) led her to conclude that

> Overall, the competence restoration literature supports that between eighty and ninety percent of all defendants with mental illness[26] will be able to be restored to competence, and generally this restoration has been achieved in a period of less than six months. (p. 104)

Pinals further notes that almost all restoration programs utilize a combination of psychopharmacological and psycho-educational treatment programs. As Pinals appropriately points out, however, data on either the relative efficacy of psychopharmacological and psychosocial or psycho-educational programs, explicitly called for by the *Sell* court are mostly lacking (see also Roesch, Ogloff, & Golding, 1993). Nevertheless, the prevailing psychiatric status quo is that psychopharmacological interventions, when medically "appropriate" (i.e., almost always if the defendant has a mental disorder), are an essential component of competency restoration. This then leads to an analysis of the efficacy of psychotropic medications and medication refusal.

Constitutional Framework for Involuntary Medication and Restoration

Medication refusal and involuntary medication in the competency context have been addressed in three important U.S. Supreme Court cases. First, in *Washington v. Harper*, 494 U.S. 210 (1990), the Supreme Court ruled that individuals who have been lawfully convicted retain certain constitutional rights,[27] but authorized constitutionally acceptable procedures for the involuntary medication of prison inmates when such treatment was medically appropriate and necessary because of dangerousness to self or others. Second, in *Riggins v. Nevada* (1992), the Court extended its dangerousness justification to incompetent defendants, and also addressed the issue of whether an individual treated with psychotropic medications might be disadvantaged at trial because of those medications (what might be termed *iatrogenic incompetency*). On appeal to the Supreme Court, Riggins had argued that his medication altered his ability to assist his counsel and had affected his demeanor and mental state, thereby prejudicially affecting the jury's construal of his testimony and especially his constricted affect. The Supreme Court reversed Riggins's conviction on two principal grounds: the state had failed to demonstrate that Riggins's involuntary medication was justified under *Harper*, and the state had failed to show that, in order to adjudicate Riggins, he needed to be medicated to maintain his competency. The majority, therefore, believed that there was a substantial probability of trial prejudice. Thus, the Court held that due process *may* be violated if, absent a compelling state interest, a defendant is forced to stand trial while on antipsychotic drugs that may negatively affect his demeanor and ability to participate in proceedings.

The direct practice implication of *Riggins* (discussed in detail in the *Sell* section) is that competency examiners need to evaluate whether or not a particular defendant, on a given level of medication, will have difficulties tracking the proceedings, consulting with counsel, engaging in appropriate cognitive abilities, and displaying appropriate affect. While a few states have incorporated *Riggins* into their competency assessment criteria,[28] competency examiners in other jurisdictions should also include an assessment of these important issues in their evaluations.

The third and most problematic case is *Sell v. United States* (2003). Sell[29] was diagnosed as having persecutory delusional disorder and he was found incompetent, but he refused medication. He could not be medicated under a *Harper* rationale because he was not dangerous to self or others. The U.S. Supreme Court's decision in *Sell* was a multipronged and problematic test for resolving the issue. The Court ruled that trial courts should be encouraged to decide the issue on *Harper* grounds, but failing that, should consider a number of specific factors.

The first *Sell* prong is the state's showing that an important governmental interest is at stake in the forcible medication of the defendant. While apparently a purely legal issue, forensic examinations are implicated because the Court indicated that considerations in deciding the state's "interest" included the likelihood that Sell would remain in confinement (if untreated and unrestored) and the amount of time the defendant had already spent in confinement. Hence, examiners will be asked to assess the probability of nonrestoration given treatment refusal (see *United States v. Lindauer*, 2006).

The second *Sell* prong is that "administration of the drugs is *substantially likely* to render the defendant competent to stand trial." This prong has serious implications for forensic examinations, but it is very uncertain that a forensic examiner has much of a database upon which to base an opinion. Certainly, if the defendant has shown "good response" in the past without undesirable cognitive and affective side effects, one could opine on this basis. However, based upon the existing empirical literature on the effectiveness of psychotropic medications, on what basis could one render a "substantially likely" to respond opinion? The Supreme Court may have saddled lower courts and examiners with a scientifically unworkable standard given our current knowledge of the effectiveness of antipsychotic medications.

A careful critical analysis of the psychopharmacological outcome literature casts considerable doubt upon the oft-repeated mantra of the general effectiveness of psychotropic medications, particularly so-called second-generation antipsychotic medications. One must acknowledge from the outset that a critical analysis of this area has been complicated by the more recent deluge of information concerning the appropriateness of research designs mandated by drug-industry sponsored efficacy trials, the misreporting of data and/or authorship, and the statistical and research design assumptions of those efficacy studies (see Heres et al., 2006; Jørgensen, Hilden, & Gøtzsche, 2006; Tandon, 2006).

Additionally, the generalizability and external validity of most of the published psychopharmacological outcome literature is compromised because the most salient characteristics of forensic populations (e.g., frequent prior psychopharmacological failure, comorbid substance abuse disorders, and comorbid personality disorders) almost routinely lead to such individuals being excluded from efficacy trials. When one peers through the lens more carefully, being fully cognizant of the potentials for distortion, it is much less clear on what basis experts could opine about the likelihood of restoration given psychopharmacological interventions.

A reasonable read of the better psychopharmacological treatment outcome literature is that, on average, one-third of clients will show both clinically and statistically significant response, one-third will show a response pattern that is perhaps statistically significant but is meager clinically, and one-third will show little, if any, response.[30] In one of the most comprehensive and well-designed comparative outcome studies available, Lieberman et al. (2005) compared mainstream second-generation antipsychotic medications and a first-generation antipsychotic in a large national sample.[31] The principal outcome metric was "discontinuation for any reason."[32] Though there were some outcome differences between drugs, between 64% to 82% of the clients "discontinued." Thus, even in a general chronically psychotic population, the base rate for treatment ineffectiveness is quite high. While effectiveness in the special subpopulation of those adjudicated psychotic and incompetent has not been studied with randomized controlled trials (but, see discussion of Cochrane, Herbel, Reardon, & Lloyd, 2013, later in this chapter), on logical grounds the rate of ineffectiveness can be presumed even higher, because of prior treatment failure and lowered levels of therapeutic alliance attributable to prior involuntary treatment.

In an interesting study that contradicts this pessimistic conclusion, Cochrane et al. (2013) reviewed charts on a series of 287 federal prisoners for whom less-coercive attempts to obtain medication acceptance were unsuccessful. In 46% of the cases, a federal court ordered involuntary treatment under *Sell*. Cochrane reported that approximately 80% of those involuntarily treated were considered by treating staff to be sufficiently improved to be seen as restored to competency. The changes in level of psychopathology and psycholegal deficits were not independently assessed and standardized measures were not employed. Nevertheless, this report is of interest because it contradicts expectations based upon other empirical data.

Another pragmatic implication of the "substantial likelihood of treatment response" prong is the need to assess the defendant's medication refusal history, including the bases for that refusal (see Appelbaum, 1994, for an excellent review of treatment refusal). Treatment refusal is a longitudinal process that reflects not only a defendant's psychopathology (e.g., lack of insight into the need for treatment, refusal to acknowledge mental disorder), but also subjective reactions to prior treatments, therapeutic alliance and prior relationships with treating personnel, experience with adverse effects, and information or misinformation about medication (Ladds & Convit, 1994). In their recent review, Heilbrun and Kramer (2005) have stressed the importance of assessing the role of coercion in a patient's decision to accept or refuse the offered treatment, the importance of assessing the competence of the defendant to refuse treatment, and the critical role that concepts of procedural justice (Greer, O'Regan, & Traverso, 1996; Lidz et al., 1995) can have in facilitating the working relationship between the treatment team and the patient. Their argument can also be extended to the importance of examining the role of the alliance in predicting response to psychopharmacological as well as psychosocial interventions. A number of studies report relationships between poor therapeutic alliance, a prior history of coercive treatment, and low insight outcome for both psychosocial and psychopharmacological interventions (Day et al., 2005; Gaudiano & Miller, 2006; Krupnick et al., 1996).

A final part of the "substantial likelihood of response" prong is focusing on the nature of the defendant's insight into his disorder. A variety of specialized assessment instruments (Amador et al., 1993; McEvoy et al., 1989) can be used to guide inquiry into a defendant's insight. As part of this assessment, I would also recommend that an examiner consider using the MacArthur Competence Assessment Tool for Treatment (MacCAT-T), a semi-structured interview developed by Grisso and his colleagues (see Grisso & Appelbaum, 1998a, 1998b; Grisso, Appelbaum, Mulvey, & Fletcher, 1995). Their instrument follows the logic of the MacCAT (discussed later) and focuses upon the individual's understanding, reasoning, and appreciation with respect to grounds for treatment refusal. It is a well-designed approach to the assessment of competence to refuse treatment in a civil context and can be adapted to the *Sell* context.

The third *Sell* prong is a restatement of the Court's holding in *Riggins*. Essentially, there must be proof that the proposed medication "is substantially unlikely to have side effects that will interfere significantly with the defendant's ability to assist counsel in conducting the trial, thereby rendering the trial unfair" (*Sell* at 181). If testimony by the defendant is anticipated, examiners should attend to whether or not the defendant, on account of medication, appears to have constricted or hollow affect and whether or not he appears emotionally withdrawn. This is especially important if the defendant is going to testify in the mitigation phase of a death penalty case or in an insanity case (Eisenberg, Garvey, & Wells, 1998). Even if testimony is not anticipated, jurors carefully watch the emotional expressions of defendants. Therefore, forensic examiners need to evaluate the range and nature of a defendant's emotional expressiveness when psychotropic medications are involved. When defendants are medicated, the examiner should also attend carefully to the defendant's ability to concentrate and to attend to verbalizations since this could impair their ability to assist counsel at trial. Another issue that arises in medicated defendants is the degree to which the defendant is able to recall his or her mental state at the time of offense when unmedicated. Finally, when a forensic examiner has concerns about the impact of medications on *Riggins* factors, it is important to consult with the treatment team to investigate whether medications can be reduced or altered. It goes without saying that the examiner's report, with *Pate* in mind, should specify the exact medication profile at the time of examination and make clear that, if that profile has been significantly altered, a reexamination of the defendant in that new context would be needed. Informing the court about the nature and extent of *Riggins* concerns, stressed in both the original case and in *Sell* appears to be constitutionally mandated.[33]

The fourth *Sell* prong is the familiar "no less intrusive" interventions likely to achieve treatment response. Here again, there are implications for forensic examiners, but not much of a database upon which to rely. The fourth Sell prong is also familiar in that it stresses that the forced medication must be "medically appropriate," i.e., based upon knowledge that the particular drug anticipated to be used is "appropriate" for the treatment of the defendant's medical condition. This prong is based upon the myth that there exists a body of knowledge that finds a particular drug or drug class as uniquely suited to treatment of a particular diagnosis. Empirically, there is little scientific evidence for such associations and it is common practice to prescribe sequentially. That is, drug selection is not based upon scientific criteria, but rather pragmatics ("Let's try X1, if that doesn't work X2, if that doesn't work X3 if . . . well, let's try drug combinations"). This issue is likely to be a front-burner controversy for years to come, but as of now, most courts have paid only lip service to the *Sell* criteria, accepting unelaborated "yes, Zyprexa will be substantially likely to render the defendant competent without serious side effect" testimony without scrutiny.[34] Only a few courts have engaged in a serious *Sell* inquiry, and when they do, they get highly perplexing and contradictory testimony.[35]

The Assessment of Adjudicative Competency

Approaches to the assessment of adjudicative competency differ in their theoretical structures, though in practice they may lead to the same professional conclusion in all but the most difficult cases.[36] Some competency assessment instruments, like the Interdisciplinary Fitness Interview–Revised (IFI-R; Golding, 1993) and Fitness Interview Test–Revised (FIT-R; Roesch, Zapf, & Eaves, 2006) use an idiographic and structured clinical judgment approach. These instruments attempt to structure evaluations directly around an articulation of psycholegal abilities associated with competency evaluations as viewed through the lens of a comprehensive review of leading competency cases (See Table 4.1). These assessment techniques concentrate on those psycholegal abilities that are most relevant to a particular context (see Skeem & Golding, 1998). While each of the psycholegal abilities is "scored," this scoring is meant only to convey the relative importance of deficits in a particular area to the evaluator's integrated conclusions. The scores are not meant to be summed and are not assumed to comprise a homogeneous scale.

The other approach to competency assessment focuses on competency as a normative construct. The most highly studied instrument of this type is the MacArthur Competence Assessment Tool–Criminal Adjudication (MacCAT-CA; Hoge, Bonnie, Poythress, & Monahan, 1999; Poythress et al., 1999) which assesses the competency construct by focusing on three hypothesized lower-order constructs: understanding, reasoning, and appreciation (Bonnie, 1992).[38] It produces criterion-based scores for each lower-order construct based upon summing item scores; the scales are meant to be homogenous, and scores are referenced to a normative sample. In reality, the MacCAT-CA has an idiographic component also in that scaled scores are interpreted in light of the evaluator's integrated judgment, which includes case-specific facts and the defendant's clinical presentation.

A more detailed review of each of these approaches follows, but it is important to note that the extent to which either of these contemporary approaches better captures the open-textured nature of competency is an open empirical question. The question remains open because, with the

Table 4.1 Adjudicative competency domains and subdomains[37]

1. Capacity to comprehend and appreciate the charges or allegations
   a. Factual knowledge of the charges (ability to report charge label)
   b. Understanding of the behaviors to which the charges refer
   c. Comprehension of the police version of events
2. Capacity to disclose to counsel pertinent facts, events, and states of mind
   a. Ability to provide a reasonable account of one's behavior around the time of the alleged offense
   b. Ability to provide information about one's state of mind around the time of the alleged offense
   c. Ability to provide an account of the behavior of relevant others around the time of the alleged offense
   d. Ability to provide an account of police behavior
   e. Comprehension of the Miranda warning
   f. Confession behavior (influence of mental disorder, suggestibility, and so forth on confession)
3. Capacity to comprehend and appreciate the range and nature of potential penalties that may be imposed in the proceedings
   a. Knowledge of penalties that could be imposed (e.g., knowledge of the relevant sentence label associated with the charge, such as "five to life")
   b. Comprehension of the seriousness of charges and potential sentences
4. Basic knowledge of legal strategies and options
   a. Understanding of the meaning of alternative pleas (e.g., guilty and mentally ill)
   b. Knowledge of the plea-bargaining process
5. Capacity to engage in reasoned choice of legal strategies and options
   a. Capacity to comprehend legal advice
   b. Capacity to participate in planning a defense strategy
   c. Plausible appraisal of likely outcome (e.g., likely disposition for one's own case)
   d. Comprehension of the implications of a guilty plea or plea bargain (i.e., the rights waived on entering a plea of guilty)
   e. Comprehension of the implications of proceeding pro se (e.g., the rights waived and the ramifications of waiver)
   f. Capacity to make a reasoned choice about defense options (e.g., trial strategy, guilty plea, proceeding pro se, pleading insanity) without distortion attributable to mental illness (an ability to rationally apply knowledge to one's own case)
6. Capacity to understand the adversary nature of the proceedings
   a. Understanding of the roles of courtroom personnel (i.e., judge, jury, prosecutor)
   b. Understanding of courtroom procedure (the basic sequence of trial events)
7. Capacity to manifest appropriate courtroom behavior
   a. Appreciation of appropriate courtroom behavior
   b. Capacity to manage one's emotions and behavior in the courtroom
8. Capacity to participate in trial
   a. Capacity to track events as they unfold (not attributable to the effects of medication)
   b. Capacity to challenge witnesses (i.e., recognize distortions in witness testimony)
9. Capacity to testify relevantly
10. Relationship with counsel
    a. Recognition that counsel is an ally
    b. Appreciation of the attorney-client privilege
    c. Confidence in and trust in one's counsel
    d. Confidence in attorneys in general
    e. Particular relationship variables that may interfere with the specific attorney-client relationship (i.e., attorney skill in working with the client; problematic socioeconomic or demographic differences between counsel and client)
11. Medication issues
    a. Capacity to track proceedings given sedation level on current medication and to communicate with counsel
    b. Potentially detrimental effects of medication on the defendant's courtroom demeanor
    c. Likelihood of treatment response; treatment response history; therapeutic alliance
    d. Bases for treatment refusal

exception of Golding, Roesch, and Schreiber (1984), who compared an earlier version of the IFI with the Competency Assessment Interview (CAI; McGarry et al., 1973), and Zapf and Roesch (2001) who compared the FIT-R and the MacCAT-CA, no study has examined the comparative validity and utility of commonly used assessment strategies. The implications of this lack of comparative validity research are discussed subsequently.

Conceptualizing and Performing a Competency Evaluation

Selecting an Assessment Strategy

Many excellent resources exist for the practitioner interested in understanding different assessment models for a competency evaluation (Grisso, 2003; Roesch et al., 1999; Skeem et al., 2004; Zapf & Viljoen, 2003; Zapf & Roesch, 2009). In reality, no one model or device suffices, so in supervision, I encourage professionals to develop their own professional identity by crafting a methodology that reflects both professional practice standards and their own views. Trying out the models of others is merely a starting place. What matters most is that the practitioner can present to the court a systematic procedure, part of which is formulated based on known reliable and valid methods.[39] A competency assessment involves both an assessment as to current psychopathological symptoms or cognitive deficits and an assessment of the linkage, if any, between these and the psycholegal abilities that constitute competency (Skeem & Golding, 1998). Competency examiners, unlike clinical mental health professionals, need to be trained in both assessment domains. While a traditional comprehensive evaluation of a defendant's psychopathology and cognitive deficits, involving psychological tests,[40] diagnostic interviews and the like, would be desirable in a competency evaluation context, the pragmatic reality of most community-based evaluations is that a truncated version of such a clinical evaluation is often necessary.[41] For this reason, many competency examiners utilize prior mental health records (which almost always exist in a meaningful referral) and various screening strategies to concentrate their efforts in the "clinical phase" of a competency evaluation. Examination of prior mental health records in the preinterview stage helps set up likely areas of inquiry, screening, and subsequent focused evaluation. Little attention has been paid to this problem in the forensic assessment literature, and a review of screening strategies[42] in a competency context is needed (DeClue, 2003). Informative reviews of these and other instruments may be found in First (2003) and Rogers (2003). Much has been written about the uniqueness of forensic examiner training. An essential component of this uniqueness is the need to utilize specialized forensic assessment "tools" (Grisso, 2003; Heilbrun, 2001; Skeem et al., 2004).

All existing forensic assessment instruments are "tools" in the sense that none are meant to be solely relied upon: the assessment of competency is highly contextualized, and results from one source of information are only data that need to be integrated with other data and the context in arriving at a competency judgment. For example, the MacCAT-CA (Poythress et al., 1999) is the most psychometrically sophisticated of available competency assessment devices, but its authors specifically state that it is not meant as a "test" for competency and its nomothetic results must be integrated with facts from the case context and the individual's specific psycholegal abilities.

Among the principal forensic tools that are most commonly recommended by forensic professionals in competency examination are the CAI, the IFI-R[43] (Golding, 1993), the MacCAT-CA (Poythress et al., 1999), the FIT-R (Roesch, Zapf, & Eaves, 2006), ECST-R (Rogers et al., 2003; Rogers, Tillbrook, & Sewell, 2004). Comprehensive reviews of the strengths and weaknesses of these tools may be found in Grisso (2003), Skeem et al. (2004), Zapf and Viljoen (2003), and Zapf and Roesch (2005). Some brief comment about these instruments and their comparison is necessary.

The CAI, the IFI-R and the FIT-R are fundamentally semi-structured interviews designed to help examiners explore the domain of psycholegal abilities associated with competency. The

IFI-R is a revision of the original IFI (which, in part, was a revision of the CAI). The CAI examined 13 psycholegal abilities that McGarry and his colleagues identified from a review of the forensic literature and existing case law. It was a groundbreaking development in forensic tools for competency evaluations and is still widely used. The original IFI was developed because the CAI did not completely span the construct of competency as it was currently. IFI-R represents a subsequent update, revised to include a more extensive linkage analysis (Skeem and Golding, 1998; Skeem et al., 1998) and other psycholegal abilities associated with more modern competency cases such as *Riggins*, *Sell*, and *Godinez*. Thus, in addition to the traditional areas of psycholegal abilities, such as understanding the role of court personnel and court processes, the IFI-R adds examination of the iatrogenic effects of medication,[44] decisional competency with respect to rational choice of legal strategy, and competency to plead guilty or pro se. The 34 specific psycholegal abilities, organized into 11 more global domains that constitute the IFI-R are depicted in Table 4.1.

For each psycholegal ability, the IFI-R guides examiners through suggested inquiries meant to explore the linkage, if any, between psychopathological symptoms or cognitive deficits and impairment in each domain.[45] The IFI-R approach is very similar to the structured clinical judgment paradigm[46] advocated by many in the debate about approaches to risk assessment (actuarial versus structured clinical judgment methods). Each domain can be "scored" as to degree of impairment, but the scores are specifically *not designed to be summed into a "competency score."*

Like the IFI-R, the FIT-R (Roesch et al., 2006) was developed out of the logic used in the original IFI. Roesch and his colleagues first adapted the IFI to Canadian law (producing the FIT), and then extended the discussion of Canadian case law to include relevant U.S. cases. The FIT-R and the IFI-R are thus highly similar approaches (with subtle differences), although Roesch and his colleagues have been quite productive in producing research on the psychometrics of the FIT-R and using it in studies of juveniles, while the development of the IFI-R proceeded by further articulation of the competency domain. Nevertheless as discussed subsequently, it is interesting that only the IFI and the FIT-R have been used in comparative validity research (versus the CAI and the MacCAT respectively), and much of the research that applies to the one, logically applies to the other.

The MacCAT-CA was developed based upon Bonnie's (1992) conceptualization of competency as involving three key domains: understanding, reasoning, and appreciation. The first two domains are assessed via 16 items that reference a short vignette describing a fight and subsequent criminal charges. The understanding items reflect understanding of core aspects of the legal system, and examiners are permitted to inform defendants about misunderstood details and then assess understanding again.[47] Reasoning is assessed by probing if the defendant can identify the relevancy of information that is presented to him or her about the hypothetical case. The remaining appreciation items use the context of the defendant's case to inquire principally into psychopathological or delusional states that would lessen the defendant's appreciation of the specific case and case facts. Norms based upon a national sample of jailed individuals for whom no competency issues had been raised and a group of individuals adjudicated as incompetent are available. The first two domains, understanding and reasoning, make sense to look at nomothetically, since they are based upon a standardized vignette. The appreciation norms, based on judgments of appreciative capacity in the defendant's specific context, are really nothing more than judgments about that defendant's abilities, similar to the structure of the IFI-R, the FIT-R, or the CAI. Despite the MacCAT-CA's normative structure, its authors caution against using the three scale scores to determine competency. They stress that it is a "tool" to be integrated with clinical data and contextualized judgment.

Rogers et al. (2003) have recently introduced the ECST-R, which is a "hybrid"[48] interview protocol designed to measure the prongs of the *Dusky* standard. It groups items into three global domains: Consult With Counsel (CWC), Factual Understanding of Court Proceedings (FAC), and Rational Understanding of Courtroom Proceedings (RAC). Each item is scored by the examiner based upon standardized questions. The ECST-R also contains a scale, termed *Atypical Presentation*, based upon a structured protocol and designed to detect malingering in the competency context. Rogers and his colleagues have presented encouraging data on the factor structure of the ECST-R, the internal consistency of the scale scores, and the inter-rater reliability (Rogers et al., 2003), and on the ability of the Atypical Presentation Scale to detect feigned incompetency (Rogers, Jackson, Sewell, & Harrison, 2004). The ECST-R, like the MacCAT-CA, is a normative instrument though it is rather different in its approach to the development and scoring of competency domain items. The differences are reflected in empirical data presented by Rogers, Tillbrook, and Sewell (2004) who report that scales on the ECST-R and the MacCAT-CA have only modest convergent validity ranging from 0.32 to 0.55. The ECST-R has a great deal of appeal for examiners working in strict *Dusky* jurisdictions, but is based upon a strong normative assumption that is not widely held in the field. Scores within each domain are based upon summing items[49] within the domain and converting the total to a T-score that is then interpreted in a standard fashion. While examiners are permitted to integrate these scores with contextualized data, they are explicitly encouraged to rely upon the T-scores because such interpretations will then be accompanied by known error rates. This is a strong normative assumption that runs contrary to what appears to be the mainstream consensus that competency is a multifaceted construct that needs to be assessed in a contextualized fashion. Moreover, there is widespread agreement that severe impairment in only one area, despite no impairment in a broad range of areas, may be grounds for a finding of incompetency.

Comparative Validity and the Problem of "Gray Area" Cases

Unfortunately, little research on the comparative validity of various competency assessment approaches is available to guide forensic examiners in their selection of assessment tools. In addition, the existing validational studies mostly use a artificial contrasted groups design that arguably inflates the discriminant validities (see Zapf, Skeem, & Golding, 2005). For example, the MacCAT-CA validational sample was a "weak comparison" because it compared individuals for whom there were no competency issues raised with a group who were adjudicated incompetent. The ECST-R was validated by comparing judged "genuinely" incompetent defendants with judged feigning or simulated feigning defendants. Logically, these are weak tests of the instruments' construct validity and their ability to distinguish between groups adjudicated competent and incompetent in the context of all individuals having been subjected to original bona fide doubt as to their competency.

An additional difficulty with existing validational studies not using a contrasted groups design is that they use an unselected *Pate* referral stream. It is well known that approximately 70%–80% of all individuals referred for competency evaluations are found competent (Roesch & Golding, 1980; Roesch et al., 1999) and that the majority of competency evaluations are relatively simple determinations (Melton, Petrila, Poythress, & Slobogin, 2007; Roesch et al., 1999). Hence, the subject pool contains a relatively high proportion of clear-cut cases of clearly competent (CC) defendants. In addition, the referral stream also contains a small number of acutely psychotic, untreated, highly disorganized, and most likely clearly incompetent individuals (CI). Thus, statistically, most validational studies are weak tests and almost any instrument with some degree of criterion validity is going to look like it is highly accurate.[50] Thus, a comparative validity study among instruments in this referral stream would show at least moderate convergence by chance. In fact, even inappropriate forensic assessment approaches will look reasonably good. For example, a simple screen for absence of psychotic symptoms or presence of gross thought disorganization would be reasonably accurate in predicting competency status. A more meaningful validational study or a comparison of competency assessment instruments would be in a winnowed pool, where clear-cut competent and incompetent cases have been ideally removed, but in reality, reduced, in proportion. Thus, future validational studies of whatever type should concentrate on examining their psychometric characteristics with the "tough sample."

Reliability of Competency Assessments

Interexaminer reliability with respect to competency assessments is a function of a number of variables, the most important of which is whether or not a systematic approach to data collection and interpretation is employed by trained evaluators (Large, Nielssen, & Elliot, 2009; Skeem & Golding, 1998; Skeem et al., 1998). Thus, whether or not one adopts an idiographic or a nomothetic approach (as discussed earlier), what is critical is that the evaluator be well trained, the psycholegal context of the evaluation be well understood, and data be collected and evaluated in as neutral a fashion as possible. When allegiance issues are prominent, as they often are in politicized high-profile cases,[51] all bets on interexaminer agreement are off. In academic studies, however, interevaluator rates of agreement tend to be moderately high if they are similarly trained, vetted, and use systematic assessment techniques (Golding, Roesch, & Schreiber, 1984; Rogers & Johannson-Love, 2009). In field or applied settings, disagreements between evaluators, at the level of overall competency judgment, appear to be in the range of 20%–30% (Gowensmith, Murrie, & Boccaccini, 2012), although considerably lower at the level of agreement on specific deficits that justify the overall conclusion (Skeem et al., 1998).

Conducting a Competency Assessment

The comments and observations that follow build upon the *Interdisciplinary Fitness Interview-Revised* manual and reference the domain of psycholegal abilities referenced in Table 4.1. A competency evaluation can be thought of as occurring in a series of stages, loosely based upon Sullivan's (1953) conceptualization of a clinical interview.

Preinterview Stage

What one does before a competency evaluation is as critical as the evaluation itself. Regrettably, most jurisdictions' competency statutes do not require or facilitate the routine provision of critical materials to the evaluator, and so this must be done on one's own.[52] This stage essentially involves developing an individualized road map of "*this* defendant, facing *these charges, in light of existing* evidence, anticipating the substantial effort of a *particular* attorney with a relationship of known characteristics" (Golding & Roesch, 1988, p. 79).

"This defendant" means knowing the defendant's mental health, and criminal/forensic history, in sufficient detail to perform a meaningful evaluation. Many presumptively incompetent psychotic defendants will not be able to provide this information during an interview, and other defendants may be either unreliable historians or will deliberately shade their histories. While complete mental health histories will rarely be available at the pretrial competency evaluation phase of an adjudication, a minimum is a discharge (or other psychopathology) summary, treatment history, and social history from the most recent mental health contact, if such exists. If the individual does have a mental health history, especially in a nonforensic context, then one can perform a targeted evaluation of core symptoms and problematic patterns. Since a competency evaluation must include an assessment of malingering, or other problematic response styles, this is a minimally sufficient database concerning the longitudinal development of psychopathology to compare what this defendant claims with what is likely given his or her known history. Mental health and treatment history also provides a basis for judging the likelihood of competency restoration.

In respect of criminal history, a minimum is either a state or federal summary of prior charges and dispositions. With respect to malingering, an individual with a history of criminal justice contacts ought to present with few difficulties on basic competency abilities, though he or she may have a jaundiced view of the system. In addition, knowledge of an individual's criminal history will facilitate smoother segues during the detailed inquiry and linkage analysis stage by asking the defendant to compare his or her current situation to a prior situation.

Knowledge of a defendant's forensic history is also critical, providing invaluable information about malingering, prior symptom-impairment links, response to treatment, and prior problems in forming a therapeutic alliance. While a complete forensic history is desirable, a minimum would be the most recent forensic evaluation. These can be obtained from the moving party either directly or through the mechanism of a court-ordered disclosure.

"These charges," "existing evidence," and "substantial effort of a particular attorney" translate into a series of preevaluation inquiries. One must obtain the charging document and a summary of the state's evidence so that an informed evaluation can be made of the defendant's understanding of the charges. Consultation with the moving party (to clarify case conceptualization, the range of trial strategies, and what problems they have encountered in trying to represent this defendant) is necessary to evaluate the "rationality" of the defendant's reasoning about trial strategy in light of existing evidence.

Inception Stage

While it is important to attempt to establish rapport with a defendant, a forensic interview differs from a clinical interview in many respects (Greenberg & Shuman, 1997) and establishing rapport may be difficult because the "client" is the court that has ordered the evaluation, sometimes over the objections of the defendant. Defense attorneys have sometimes raised the competency issue against the wishes of the defendant, and at other times, the defense attorney may have warned the defendant that you are an agent of the prosecution. For whatever reason, it is not uncommon for the defendant to adopt a resistant or hostile stance towards the evaluator. In such situations, it is important to strive to maintain countertransferential neutrality and to communicate to the defendant respect for, but disagreement with, his or her perceptions that the relationship is adversarial in nature.

While it is not necessary to obtain the consent of the defendant in the context of a court-ordered evaluation, it is professionally required that one *attempt* to obtain informed assent (see American Psychological Association, 2013) and to describe the limits of privilege in the form of a "forensic warning."[53] This warning has a long legal history and is based upon a defendant's Fifth Amendment right to avoid self-incrimination (*Estelle v. Smith*, 1981). A detailed inquiry often results in various statements by the defendant that are tantamount to a confession or contradict subsequent trial testimony. While the prosecution may not introduce information obtained during a court ordered competency evaluation at either the trial or guilty phase, there is a critically important exception to this, often styled as a waiver when the defendant is deemed to have placed his or her mental state into evidence. Thus, when a mental state plea is entered, or when psychological issues are raised at the sentencing phase of a trial, *the privilege associated with all prior mental health* evaluations may be deemed waived.

Explaining the rather complex nature of this legal waiver and limits of privilege is difficult to do with competent adults, and becomes oxymoronic with individuals who are currently psychotic, manic, or have even moderate developmental disabilities. The process of attempting to obtain assent and understanding with these individuals is, in and of itself, an extremely valuable assessment window into their underlying competencies. I encourage the use of a "process approach" (Poythress, 2002) as opposed to fixed warning language or a prepared statement to be signed. A process approach involves repeated cycles of explanation of the privilege and its limits, in both abstract and concrete ways, assessing the defendant's understanding, providing further clarifying information, eliciting and responding to questions, and reassessing understanding. This approach is especially important in interviewing defendants facing severe penalties. For example, with capital murder defendants, I use the opportunity to explain how less forthcoming or exaggerated reports can backfire in the context of waiver and competency interviews. Thus, after the competency evaluation and the guilt phase of a trial, any attempts to introduce mitigating psychological evidence, such as physical and sexual abuse as a child, will blow up in the defendant's face if he or she engages in a somewhat natural tendency to exaggerate the nature of his or her own childhood abuse during a competency evaluation. When later contradicted by evidence at the penalty phase, the trier of fact is left with the impression that the defendant has a general habit of untruthfulness, which may undercut other claims.

The inception phase also offers an opportunity for informal assessment of a number of other important issues. I routinely play down my knowledge of the defendant and his or her history in order to elicit free narratives. Such free narratives, as opposed to responding to direct questions or option-posing questions, allow for an assessment of the defendant's linguistic abilities, memorial capacities, interpersonal style, and possible deceptive strategies.

The Reconnaissance Phase

This phase obtains data critical to the subsequent linkage analysis that is the heart of a competency evaluation. Having foreknowledge of a defendant's mental health history allows for a more targeted evaluation of relevant psychopathology. While it is a matter of chosen style, I prefer to mix psychopathological and psycholegal reconnaissance. The goal is to obtain an overall picture of the defendant's psychological and psychopathological strengths and weaknesses, as well as his or her psycholegal abilities, in order to determine which areas are in need of the detailed inquiry that follows in the next phase. Areas of psychopathological difficulties and their links to psycholegal abilities are successively probed in context. An illustrative sequence might be as follows:

E: "Tell me everything you can about what happened prior to your arrest."
D: [Short narrative that includes, "Before I went over to her house, I smoked part of a joint."]
E: [Loop into history and extent of all substance abuse; segue to relationship to criminal/forensic history.]
E: "Have you ever done anything that got you into legal trouble while you were high?"
D: [Relates three driving under the influence charges; interviewer segues to understanding certain aspects of legal system.]
E: "What was the outcome of those charges?"
D: [Relates one charge dropped, one resulted in fine and some jail time, last one put on probation with conditions by mental health court.]

At this point, the examiner would choose a segue to one of several relevant lines of inquiry. For example, psychopathological history, treatment and outcome history, psycholegal abilities such as understanding available pleas, possible relevance of intoxication to the alleged charge and so forth. After looping through these, the examiner would return to the main theme.

E: "OK, I understand a lot more now about how drugs have affected your life. Let's get back to the day of the incident. Tell me more about what you did before you went over to her house."

If, in describing his prior arrest and plea bargain to have charges stayed and placed under the supervision of mental health court, it was clear that the defendant understood the basic roles of court personnel, it might prove unnecessary to probe this part of the domain of psycholegal abilities further, except for a brief follow up to check for contextual differences: "Do you think there is anything different about the role of the judge, prosecutor, or your defense attorney in this case?"

Thus, rather than adopting a fixed structured interview style that examines each area sequentially, I believe that more "connected" interviews can be achieved by knowing the domains of questions well enough to flexibly flow from one topic to another, making sure that ultimately all psycholegal areas depicted in Table 4.1 have been probed.[54] At the end of the reconnaissance stage, the psycholegal abilities (potentially linked to psychopathological/cognitive symptoms) that are in play should be quite clear to the examiner and are probed in depth in the next phase.

The Detailed Inquiry Stage

Little research exists on the important topic of why defendants are evaluated or adjudicated as incompetent. Skeem et al. (1998) found that, while examiners show relatively high overall rates of agreement as to final judgments of incompetency, they were wildly discrepant in their reasons for finding an individual incompetent. I believe this is so because examiners often fail to probe the clear "linking logic" that connects symptoms and psycholegal abilities. Skeem et al. (1998) and Skeem and Golding (1998) forcefully demonstrated the general lack of "linking logic" in a random sample of competency evaluations. Thus, the most critical phase of a competency evaluation, the detailed inquiry, focuses on developing that linking logic. The issue of linkage basically comes down to providing the trier of fact with the logic that connects and substantiates the psychopathological data with the psycholegal conclusion about impairment in a relevant psycholegal ability.

For example, suppose the defendant is a paranoid schizophrenic whose symptoms are partially controlled by antipsychotic medication. A conclusion that he is incompetent on account of his being psychotic is completely without any linking logic. A conclusion that he is incompetent because he (genuinely) has a delusion that there is a government conspiracy against him, and the prosecutor, as a government agent, is part of that conspiracy is closer, but still lacks linking logic. A conclusion that he is incompetent because, on account of his delusion that the prosecutor is conspiring against him, he believes that the plea bargain[55] offered, which he "understands," must be rejected because the prosecutor cannot be trusted, even though the offer is in writing, is closer still. A conclusion that he is incompetent because, in addition to the previous, he believes that attempts by his defense counsel to explain the "pros and cons" of accepting the plea bargain prove that the defense counsel is also part of the conspiracy, and that therefore he intends to represent himself and call the head of the CIA as a witness pretty much hits the proverbial nail on the head.

The point of the detailed inquiry is to examine each of the identified potentially problematic psycholegal abilities in terms of how they relate to the individual's psychopathology and/or cognitive impairment. Implicit in the linkage analysis is a consideration of whether or not the observed deficit is more closely linked with other causes than the defendant's psychopathology. That is, the examiner must consider plausible rival hypotheses (Skeem & Golding, 1998).

Assessment of Malingering and Other Problematic Response Styles

The concept of malingering, deception, and other problematic presentation styles covers a wide territory ranging from minimization of pathology, through exaggerated symptoms or distress, to feigned pathology (see Rogers, 2012, for a detailed review). Clinical psychologists are accustomed to assessing this psychometrically with validity scales from the Minnesota Multiphasic Personality Inventory–2 (MMPI-2) or the Personality Assessment Inventory (PAI; see, for example, Arbisi & Ben-Porath, 1998; Bagby, Nicholson, Bacchiochi, Ryder, & Bury, 2002; Berry, Baer, Rinaldo, & Wetter, 2002; Edens, Cruise, & Buffington-Vollum, 2001). Given the desirability of examining converging information sources,[56] using the psychometrically sound validity indices from these instruments makes sense, when they are available or it is feasible to administer these instruments.[57] This is routinely done in inpatient forensic evaluation contexts, but often not feasible in outpatient evaluations. Regardless, in order to obtain converging information, it is necessary to assess problematic response styles from a clinical perspective (for interview strategies for malingered psychosis, see Resnick & Knoll, 2012; and, as especially applied to competency evaluations, Soliman & Resnick, 2010) and to consider convergence of these results with that of specialized forensic assessment instruments designed to assess response styles. Such instruments include those for examining problematic response styles associated with reports of psychopathological symptoms (such as Structured Interview of Reported Symptoms, or SIRS; Rogers, Bagby, & Dickens, 1992), feigned memory difficulties (such as the Test of Malingered Memory, or TOMM; Tombaugh, 1997), inadequate effort or attempts to feign inability on cognitive[58] or neuropsychological tasks (such as the Validity Indicator Profile, or VIP; Frederick, 1997), or feigned incompetency with respect to a factual understanding of court proceedings (such as the Inventory of Legal Knowledge, or ILK; Musick & Otto, 2010).

The SIRS[59] systematically assesses feigning of symptoms using a variety of interview detection strategies such as rare symptoms and improbable symptom combinations to identify various deceptive strategies. It takes between 30 minutes and an hour to administer, and is considered by most forensic psychologists to be the "gold standard" (Lalley, 2003) for the assessment of problematic symptom claims. The same logic that produced the SIRS has also been used by Rogers to develop the Atypical Presentation Scale of the ECST-R (discussed previously). Another available instrument, the Miller Forensic Assessment of Symptoms (M-FAST, Miller, 2001) is based upon the SIRS logic, though it is shorter and designed as a screening instrument. Early validity and reliability data appear promising (Jackson, Rogers, & Sewell, 2005; Miller, 2004; Vitacco, Rogers, Gabel, & Munizza, 2007; Zapf & Galloway, 2002).

TOMM (Tombaugh, 1997) has become a common means for assessing feigning with respect to memorial capacity and it appears to have decent psychometric properties.[60] Similarly, the VIP is widely used for the assessment of inadequate effort and attempts to distort one's actual cognitive abilities, especially in forensic contexts.

More recently, Musick and Otto (2010) have introduced the ILK, an instrument modeled after the logic of the VIP,[61] but specific to attempts to feign ignorance of basic and factual parameters of court processes in the context of competency evaluations. Preliminary and cross-validational data are promising and it is likely this instrument will become a standard in cases of suspect response styles in competency evaluations (Guenther & Otto, 2010; Otto, Musick, & Sherrod, 2011).

It is unfortunate that no studies exist on the detection of malingering in forensic contexts with sophisticated defendants. That is, while research suggests that many malingering cases can be reliably detected by the sorts of instruments discussed earlier (Rogers et al., 2004), the populations studied have been based on either simulation designs or contrasted groups involving "likely malingerers."[62] The problem with this research is that the items on the ILK, SIRS, or the Atypical Presentation Scale are rather obvious to sophisticated malingerers,[63] and unsophisticated malingering is much easier to detect, regardless of the method. Additionally, sophisticated and motivated defendants can, and do, research detection strategies and assessment instruments on the Internet or otherwise obtain coaching on avoiding detection from attorneys or fellow inmates (see Suhr & Gunstad, 2007, for a history of coaching issues).

Forensic evaluators should also be aware that these malingering detection instruments may be considerably less valid in certain subpopulations, particularly those who are highly suggestible, of lower intelligence, or are severely psychotic. Hurley and Deal (2006) have shown disturbingly high false positive rates in assessing malingering with either the SIRS or the TOMM[64] (Tombaugh, 1997) in mentally retarded nondefendants, even when instructed to perform optimally. This finding of overprediction of feigning symptoms with the SIRS in intellectually disabled populations has been confirmed with both the original SIRS and its updated scoring algorithm, SIRS-2 (Weiss, Rosenfeld, & Farkas, 2011).

Regardless of the approach taken, evaluation of malingering is necessary in all competency evaluations. The examiner should seek converging sources of data from traditional and forensic assessment devices,[65] and integrate that information with clinical observation. In addition to the methods described earlier, detailed observation of individuals in inpatient settings and jails, when possible, provides invaluable information. Finally, a modicum of common sense is helpful. If one knows the individual's criminal justice and mental health history in detail, claimed impairments can be evaluated in a more meaningful context.

Assessment From a Multisource Perspective

Heilbrun (2001) and Skeem et al. (2004) have appropriately stressed the importance of integrating third-party information into a competency evaluation. Police reports are important and should be compared with the defendant's ability to recall critical aspects of the alleged crime and surrounding behavior. Claims of amnesia are common and should be rigorously pursued from a multisource perspective, not relying upon the defendant's claim.[66] Police reports also help to frame the critical evidence against the defendant and hence form the basis for inquiry into the defendant's ability to engage in rational choice of defense strategy. They also allow an investigation into the defendant's ability to provide relevant information to counsel (see Table 4.1). Information should also be obtained from defense counsel concerning contextual aspects of the case (i.e., what is likely to be required of the defendant), the nature of counsel's interpersonal interactions with the defendant, and the nature of counsel's interactions with the defendant that led to a *Pate* doubt. Criminal history records provide a glimpse into the defendant's experience with the criminal justice system and the defendant's past psycholegal abilities. Mental health records provide both an opportunity to target likely realms of psychopathology, as well as important information relevant to the assessment of malingering.

A report that stresses multisource data and carefully links that data to conclusions is the goal. Examiners should also be aware that use of third-party or collateral information is potentially problematic at the guilt phase of a trial, since an argument can be made that reliance upon such data violates a defendant's right to confront and cross-examine witnesses against him (see *People v. Goldstein*, 2005 for an insightful discussion of this issue). It is for this reason that the *Specialty Guidelines for Forensic Psychology* (American Psychological Association, 2013) stress the importance of carefully documenting and attempting to corroborate such collateral data that form a critical aspect of one's opinion.[67]

Termination of the Examination

A number of defendants directly ask about the examiner's opinions at the end of an interview. Opinions about how to handle this vary widely. If the examiner has a fairly clear idea as to what will be communicated to the court and defense and prosecution counsel, I believe it is permissible to communicate the essence of one's opinion (obviously, in an appropriately tentative fashion). If one has not yet formed an opinion, this too can be communicated. I routinely ask defendants at this stage if there are any questions they have of me. Clearly one cannot respond to questions outside of one's knowledge or competence ("Do you think I'll end up serving time?"), but legitimate questions can be answered ("If the judge finds me incompetent, what is likely to happen?"). Treating the defendant with dignity in this manner helps to preserve the possibility of reasonable rapport with future examiners. Both Section 9.10 of the *Ethical Principles of Psychologists and Code of Conduct* (American Psychological Association, 2002) and Section 10.05 of *Specialty Guidelines for Forensic Psychology* (American Psychological Association, 2013) require such feedback (unless prohibited by law of the jurisdiction or institution).

A thorny issue that sometimes emerges at the end of an interview has to do with the individual who has communicated reasonable grounds for believing he or someone else is at risk or who appears to be either not treated or inappropriately treated. While the examiner is not in a clinical relationship with the defendant as client, I believe that professional standards of practice would require some reasonable action on the part of the forensic examiner. The closest any ethics code comes to addressing this issue in a forensic context is Section 4.03 of SGFP. Essentially, one should inform the party who has retained the examiner's services (e.g., attorney, legal representative, court) of one's concerns and the basis for them. Depending upon the jurisdiction, reasonable belief that there is a risk of imminent harm to another may require other actions as well.

Case analysis

Because it illustrates a number of the basic points of this chapter, I have chosen the case of Brian David Mitchell, who kidnapped and raped Elizabeth Smart. All of the details in this section, including the data sources relied upon, methodologies, and the logic and conclusions of all three state examiners are in the public domain as part of Judge Atherton's opinion, available on the Internet (Atherton, 2005). All forensic reports in this case are sealed. No aspect of those reports, not contained in Judge Atherton's opinion, nor any other detail of the case, even those testified to in open court, are included in this section.[68]

Essential Case Facts

Mr. Mitchell broke into the Smarts' home, kidnapped Elizabeth, took her as his plural wife, sexually assaulted her, and took her across state lines. He and his then-current wife (Wanda Barzee) were arrested when they returned to Salt Lake City with Elizabeth a little less than a year later. Mr. Mitchell was referred for a competency evaluation, on account of his seemingly bizarre beliefs and unwillingness to discuss critical case and mental state issues with counsel. Mr. Mitchell refused to talk with the court-appointed examiners despite several attempts to do so. After we each evaluated Mr. Mitchell using different methodologies, I opined that he was incompetent and Dr. Noel Gardner opined the opposite. Prior to a hearing, defense counsel privately retained Dr. Jennifer Skeem, and at that time Mr. Mitchell was willing to speak with her. She ultimately opined that despite serious concerns, she considered him "situationally competent" to proceed in a very specific context (pursuing a plea bargain) and needing to be reevaluated if any significant change in context occurred. Subsequently, Mr. Mitchell had a revelation that Satan was trying to trick him into accepting the plea bargain. Dr. Skeem notified counsel that she now doubted his competence even on the original narrowed grounds, and counsel moved for another reevaluation of Mr. Mitchell under *Pate* (deterioration of mental condition). He was reevaluated by all three examiners, though he now refused to speak with Dr. Skeem. Dr. Skeem and I ultimately opined that he was delusional and incompetent, and Dr. Gardner opined that he was still competent, although he had a severe narcissistic personality disorder.

Refusal of Interview

May a forensic examiner ethically opine on a psycholegal issue if the defendant refuses an interview? Yes, but only under special circumstances: (a) a sincere attempt to obtain interview data must take place; (b) the opinion must be appropriately conditioned as to limits of reliability and validity; and (c) a database sufficient to support the conditioned opinion must exist. This situation is not unusual in competency and insanity evaluation contexts with delusional defendants, those that lack insight into their psychosis (agnosognosia), or certain individuals with extreme political or religious beliefs. In this case, I agreed to attempt the evaluation, and after interviewing a variety of family members and individuals who knew Mr. Mitchell over the years, reading a number of his writings (both before and after arrest), watching a detailed interview of Ms. Smart (who was a remarkable historian of Mr. Mitchell's conversations with her and events) and FBI interviews of Mitchell immediately after his arrest, reading Ms. Smart's diary, and reviewing prior mental health and social records (a complete list of all examiners' sources is in the Court's opinion), I decided that I could satisfy Utah's burden of proof (preponderance of the evidence) in conjunction with professional standards.

Framing the Case-Specific Competency Issues

Mr. Mitchell's writings as well as videotapes and interactions with counsel left no doubt that he was quite intelligent and theoretically had no difficulties with various foundational psycholegal abilities. For example, he clearly knew, in one sense, the role of the judge, prosecutor, and defense counsel. However, in a more meaningful sense, as applied to him, there was a question of his competency in that regard because he believed that Satan especially worked through "good people" and that he had to be especially vigilant for "signs" that these people were not acting on behalf of Satan. Thus, he came to question the motives of the prosecutor (and his defense counsel, and ultimately Dr. Skeem) because he saw signs that this was the work of Satan who was tempting him to accept the plea bargain instead of following God's revelation that he was the "Davidic King" (the messiah) who needed to be martyred in order to bring on the battle between himself and the Antichrist. Similarly, he "knew" that Judge Atherton could sentence him essentially to a life term if he was found guilty, but he believed that no defense was permissible, since "he must endure sacrifice for the salvation of the righteous and must suffer a symbolic martyrdom by passively submitting to being convicted and incarcerated" (Atherton, 2005, p. 21). In addition, Mr. Mitchell claimed that, as with Peter and Paul in biblical times, he would be released within a specified time interval. Obviously, considerable doubt existed as to decisional competencies (allowing himself to be defended, making rational choice of defense strategies and the like). It was clear to all that the competency issue essentially rested on one issue: Was his belief system delusional or was it merely an extreme form of religious belief?[69] If the former, then many domains of his psycholegal abilities might be compromised, and if the latter, then his "choices" were unusual or extreme, but the result of extreme narcissism, not mental disorder.

Distinguishing Delusion From Extreme Belief and Linkage to Competency

I had confronted this issue in a prior case and, in conjunction with Dr. Skeem (who was then a graduate student), worked on a logic to address this issue. An early version of this was published as part of a forensic assessment chapter (Golding et al., 1999). Since then, additional empirical and clinical data have become available to guide decision making. Nevertheless, the issue remained such that it was important to stress to the Court that "differentiating [extreme religious belief, overvalued ideas, and delusionality] is fraught with difficulty and that no one can claim the ability to do so with great certainty or reliability" (Atherton, 2005, p. 28). This case therefore illustrates the core point of this chapter that it is the linkage between data and conclusion, and the logic of that linkage, that is central to a forensic evaluation. The essence of the (publically available) data and the linkage analysis was as follows.

Some of Mr. Mitchell's religious beliefs (personal revelation) are mainstream beliefs within the Church of Jesus Christ of Latter Day Saints (LDS); others, such as the need to reestablish plural marriage, have been abandoned by the LDS Church and are considered apostate, although held by a significant minority of "fundamentalists"; others, such as a need to be martyred to bring about the final battle with the Antichrist, or that the Antichrist will be financed by the World Bank, are extreme and rare, but not totally unique; finally, some, such as that he is the "Davidic King" or that he must capture (when indicated by God through certain "signs") particular young women to become his plural wives to build his kingdom, are totally unique and shared only by him and Ms. Barzee.[70] It would be "shaky" to use the mere content of these unique beliefs (even though they pushed the limits of subcultural "normativeness" in that only he and his wife had these beliefs) as a grounds for diagnosing delusional disorder. Modern thinking, along with some research (see Pierre, 2001) suggests that content of belief is less important than the process or manner of belief, and that degree of preoccupation, deterioration in social functioning, and distress on account of the delusion are factors that help differentiate delusion from extreme beliefs. In addition, new research and clinical observations exist on the nature of the prodromal development of psychosis (see Møller & Husby, 2000; Stanton & David, 2003). Integrating these literatures illustrates both the multisource and linkage principles discussed in this chapter.

(Public) Data and Linkage Analysis

Starting in early adolescence, Mr. Mitchell began to exhibit odd "aggressive, cruel and sadistic" behavior and speech towards his siblings, felt that his mother was trying to poison him, and that fumes from autos would infect him. Around this time, multiple family members also described a change from his childhood personality, particularly withdrawing and isolating himself. When he exposed himself to an 8-year-old, a psychological evaluation was performed and he was diagnosed with a "behavior disorder of adolescence-withdrawing reaction with some paranoid tendencies" (Atherton, 2005, p. 9). Despite recommendations, there was little follow-up by Mr. Mitchell, his family, or the state. He became heavily involved with alcohol and drugs, and dropped out of high school.

As a young adult, he became heavily involved with religion and "embarked on a self-described search for God" and "sampled" Hare Krishna, various Protestant faiths, Christian Science, and Buddhism. He subsequently had a "conversion" experience, returned to the LDS Church, obtained his GED, took university courses, and was socially involved with friends and family. After a tumultuous second marriage and divorce, he met and married Ms. Barzee, became very involved with the mainstream LDS Church, and held several positions of responsibility. He was also regularly employed. He thus achieved a fairly high level of social, interpersonal, and vocational functioning for a number of years.

After a few years, "Family members recall that [he] became more preoccupied with religious ideas and describe him as self-righteous and increasingly adamant that he had a 'special role.' . . . [They] began to isolate themselves from their families. When family members would question the two about their beliefs and conduct, they would often react defensively and appeared to become increasingly paranoid." He now saw the LDS Church as apostate and himself and Ms. Barzee as "special, unique and superior because of their religious experiences and self-understanding" (Atherton, 2005, p. 13). Eventually, they came to believe that they must rid themselves of worldly belongings. They became homeless. They began to explore a number of fringe religious, political, and alternative medicine groups. "All of these groups ultimately rejected [them] because of their overbearing attitudes with respect to their religious beliefs" (p. 13).

Their beliefs and behavior became increasingly more extreme, as did their isolation and preoccupation. At this point, Mr. Mitchell now firmly believed that his thoughts and actions—indeed his will—were controlled by God, as were the actions of others towards him. That is, he now acted as he thought God was commanding him to act. Moreover, those commands not only came in the form of revelation, but also by special signs that were sent to him by means of the "meaning" of events that happened to him. In psychopathological language, he was having passivity experiences and his thinking was becoming extremely referential. For example, he "knew" that Ms. Smart was meant to be his plural wife because of what he perceived in her face and demeanor during what was, in reality, a chance meeting at an outdoor market.

Additional data supported the extent of the breakdown of his social functioning (not recognizing former friends; being avoided by other homeless persons; being rejected even by the most extreme religious and political groups). Distress was documented in a number of ways (he experienced a great deal of subjective distress on account of his experiences; his belief system was focused on members of his family, and former friends and mentors, and led to confrontations with them).

This data—in the context of what is known about delusions, the impact of psychosis on social functioning, and the prodromal development of psychosis—led me to conclude that Mr. Mitchell's thinking was delusional, not merely extreme or narcissistic.

The connection (linking logic) between this delusionality and impairments in many of the domains of psycholegal abilities depicted in Table 4.1 are expressed in Judge Atherton's final holding:

It is the court's conclusion that the preoccupation, distress, and impaired social functioning exhibited by Defendant are symptoms of a delusional disorder and are not merely the logical outcomes of choices made by someone with extreme religious beliefs who also suffers from a narcissistic personality disorder. Defendant's religious beliefs are, therefore, delusional. Because a delusional belief is one based upon incorrect inferences about external reality . . . it necessarily follows that Defendant's ability to accurately perceive and interpret external reality is impaired and, therefore, that he lacks the capacity to realistically determine what is in his own best interests. Since having the capacity to realistically determine what is in one's own best interests is nothing more or less than having the ability to make reasoned, rational choices, it follows from the court's conclusion that because Defendant's religious belief system is the basis upon which he makes decisions concerning his criminal case, he also lacks the capacity to consult with counsel with a reasonable degree of rational understanding and is, pursuant to section 77–15–1(1), incompetent to proceed to trial. . . . The court finds that Defendant has present adequate capacity to comprehend and appreciate the charges against him, the range and nature of the possible penalties that may be imposed, and the adversary nature of the proceedings against him. See Utah Code Ann. § 77–15–5(4)(a)(i), (iii), and (v). The court further finds that Defendant has an impaired capacity to disclose to counsel pertinent facts, events, and states of mind, engage in reasoned choice of legal strategies and options, manifest appropriate courtroom behavior, and testify relevantly, if applicable. Utah Code Ann. § 77–15–5(4)(a)(ii), (iv), (vi), and (vii). The court further finds that Defendant's mental disorder substantially interferes with his relationship with counsel and, therefore, that his mental disorder has resulted in "his inability to consult with his counsel and to participate in the proceedings against him with a reasonable degree of rational understanding." Utah Code Ann. § 77–15–2(2). Therefore, the court concludes that Defendant is incompetent to proceed to trial. (pp. 58–59)

Notes

1 No attempt is made to cover the increasingly important area of competency assessments of juveniles. For reviews of this emerging area, see Grisso et al., 2003; Grisso (2005; 1998); Kruh & Grisso, 2008; Viljoen, Vincent, & Roesch, 2006.

2 In early jurisprudence, there were many rational reasons for refusing to enter a plea. For example, this acknowledged the jurisdiction of the court.

3 Youtsey's conviction was reversed and remanded based upon his epilepsy at trial, which was found to have interfered with his ability to assist counsel.

4 Indeed, the authors of the MacCAT go to great lengths to stress that it is a "tool" to be used in conjunction with other assessment procedures.

5 See Everington & Dunn (1995) as a starting place for the assessment of competency in mentally retarded defendants. This is a specialty assessment issue beyond the scope of this chapter.

6 In addition to diagnostic category relationships, Jacobs, Ryba, & Zapf (2008) have shown strong relationships between various psychotic symptoms, as measured by rating scales, and factors of the MacArthur Competence Assessment Tool-Criminal Adjudication (MacCAT-CA). Notwithstanding such relationships, the asymmetry still exists. Thus, presence of psychotic symptoms does not *equate to* incompetency.

7   Indeed, the word *psycholegal* stands for that linkage between relevant psychological and legal characteristics.

8   The issue on appeal was that the lower courts had found Dusky competent to be tried for kidnapping, based upon his factual understanding; no further inquiry was made, despite a psychiatric report that included references to disorganized thinking, psychosis, and schizophrenia.

9   Searching for case law that cites to *Dusky* within the jurisdiction, as well as case law that cites to the jurisdiction's competency statute.

10 In *Godinez v. Moran* (1993), the Supreme Court held that *Dusky* was the standard by which the various competency contexts (i.e., competency to plead guilty, to waive counsel, to stand trial with the assistance of counsel) were judged, although "States are free to adopt competency standards that are more elaborate than the Dusky formulation."

11 Professional standards of practice require examiners to maintain current knowledge within their areas of practice. Information on developments in competency law, methods, and procedures can easily be tracked in this Internet age. Electronic alerts to new federal and state cases (liibulletin at www.law.cornell.edu/bulletin; FindLaw at www.findlaw.com), articles in leading forensic journals (*Behavioral Science and the Law*; *International Journal of Forensic Mental Health*; *Journal of the American Academy of Psychiatry and the Law*; *Law and Human Behavior; Psychology, Public Policy and Law*); and discussion amongst forensic professionals (PSYLAW-L@LISTSERV.UNL.EDU) are easy to set and maintain.

12 In an analysis of competency reports, Skeem and Golding (1998) found that examiners rarely assessed decisional competencies, even when the issue was "in play."

13 Some courts have also addressed this problem in *Godinez* by distinguishing between the mental competency required to waive right to counsel and whether the waiver was "knowing and intelligent." See *Brooks v. McCaughtry* (2004) and Burrows & Herbert (2005).

14 See *Miles v. Stainer* (1997), which concerns an individual who was evaluated while compliant with medications, subsequently went off medications, became more psychotic, and wanted to plead guilty. Also see *Maxwell v. Roe* (2004), in which a clear series of events indicated a change in psychopathology between evaluation and trial.

15 This is particularly true for decisional (e.g., ability to make a reasoned choice) as opposed to foundational competencies (e.g., knowledge of the roles of court personnel), which are less likely to change. Decisional competencies are more likely to fluctuate as a function of context. See Skeem and Golding (1998) for an extended discussion of this issue.

16 As addressed later, this situation is far more common than usually realized. The psychopharmaceutical industry's mantra notwithstanding, modern research confirms that even those who do respond to antipsychotic medications often have periods of increased psychotic symptomatology, *independent* of medication compliance.

17 The issue may be inappropriately raised by counsel who believes that *any* indication of mental disorder requires a competency inquiry, as a legal tactic to obtain a psychological evaluation, to delay trial, or sometimes by the prosecution as a means of discovery or to obtain rebuttal evidence for the sentencing phase of a trial (see *Estelle v. Smith*, 1981; Roesch & Golding, 1987).

18 See, for example, Utah Annotated Code §77–15–5(1).

19 An unstudied empirical question is the extent to which such dramatic fluctuations are "normal," even in individuals considered to be "stable" on their current treatment regime.

20 A good example is *Michael v. Horn* (2006).

21 The disparities range from a 90-day limit to life.

22 A notable exception is Utah (§77–15–1 *et seq.*) which has a detailed implementation of *Jackson* tied to the underlying severity of the charge.

23 Morris and Parker (2009a) report that the Indiana Supreme Court has recently ruled that "holding criminal charges over the head of a permanently incompetent defendant, when her pretrial confinement extended beyond the maximum period of any sentence. . . violated . . . the Due Process Clause" (p. 380).

24 Morris and Parker (2009b) report findings similar to Mossman's with respect to dementia and advanced age. See also Colwell & Gianesini (2011).

25 See also Bertman et al. (2003); Scott (2003). An early controlled study by Siegel & Elwork (1990) showing superiority of psychosocial treatment is an exception.

26 Rates of competency restoration for mentally retarded defendants appear to be distinctly lower.

27 "The forcible injection of medication into a nonconsenting person's body represents a substantial interference with that person's liberty" (*Harper* at 229).

28 See Utah Code section 77–15–5(4)(c), which instructs examiners to evaluate and opine about "(i) whether the medication is necessary to maintain the defendant's competency; and (ii) the effect of the medication, if any, on the defendant's demeanor and affect and ability to participate in the proceedings."

29   Ironically, Sell ended up pleading no contest to the charges, was given credit for "time served," and is now on probation.

30   This is a generalized statement across types of medications and disorders. A comprehensive review is beyond the scope of this chapter. To pursue this complex issue see Davis, Chen, & Glick (2003), Geddes et al. (2004; 2000), Heres et al. (2006), and Whitaker (2002).

31   This is the NIMH sponsored Clinical Antipsychotic Trials of Intervention Effectiveness (CATIE) study. Stroup, Lieberman, McEvoy et al. (2006) and McEvoy, Lieberman, Stroup et al. (2006) report similar results in various follow-up studies that involve switching to other medications amongst "discontinued" groups in the original CATIE study.

32   Lieberman and his colleagues argue that such a measure is justified because it integrates both patient and clinician judgment as to effectiveness. Thus, discontinuation can occur due to ineffectiveness, side effects, or subjective dysphoria. This type of outcome criteria would make less sense in the forced medication context (they wouldn't be allowed to stop), but there are no studies of comparative medication effectiveness with forced or mandated treatment, but, as described below, the response rate is logically lower.

33   The *Riggins* Court stressed the importance of such testimony but questioned whether testimony is sufficient to overcome the prejudice (see also *Lawrence v. Georgia*, 1995).

34   See, for example, *United States v. Gomes* (2004), which included expert testimony, unchallenged, that there was a 70% likelihood of medication effectiveness.

35   See *United States v. Evans* (2006); *United States v. Lindauer* (2006), which critique puff testimony not based upon the results of controlled outcome trials, the use of formulaic conclusory *Sell* testimony, and "bland assurances" with "utter lack of substantiation."

36   See discussion of "gray-area" cases later in this chapter.

37   Adapted from Skeem, Golding, & Emke-Francis (2004).

38   With some modifications, confirmatory factor analysis of both the original normative sample and subsequent samples has found strong support for the three-factor structure of MacCAT-CA (Zapf, Skeem & Golding, 2005; Jacobs, Ryba & Zapf, 2008).

39   It is important that a competency evaluation procedure be *built upon an empirical infrastructure*. Nevertheless, as discussed, existing *validity* data for standardized forensic instruments are quite limited, and structured judgment is involved in the application of all competency assessment approaches. Even if one adopts, say, the MacCAT-CA (which has the most extensive data of any currently used instrument) as the basis of one's evaluation, in the end, it is merely a "tool," embedded in the wider context of clinical judgment and other aspects of the competency evaluation procedure. Thus, the reliability and validity of the MacCAT-CA, as used in the real world, has not been studied.

40   See Rogers (2003) for a review of tests in a forensic context.

41   Several factors are in play. Access to defendants in the kind of clinical setting conducive to adequate testing and interviews is often restricted or difficult to arrange. Furthermore, in most jurisdictions, funding of examinations places a practical limit on the number of hours an examiner can spend on a typical competency referral.

42   Some have advocated using instruments like the FIT-R (or close equivalents, such as the IFI-R) as screening tools (Roesch et al. 1999), focusing only on the detection of psycholegal deficits, leaving a full determination of possible linkage to a second stage of examination (see DeClue, 2003). In practice, this is a workable strategy, by quickly reviewing essential psycholegal abilities likely to be involved. This is the same as the reconnaissance stage discussed later.

43   Roesch, Zapf, and Eaves (2006) have made available the Fitness Interview Test-Revised (FIT-R). It is similar to the IFI (from which it was derived) but was constructed to mirror Canadian competency law, but it could be adapted to any *Dusky* jurisdiction. It differs from the IFI in being more highly structured. The IFI-R and the FIT-R are compared in Zapf & Viljoen (2003).

44   Note that the psycholegal abilities organized in Table 4.1 now also include the issues raised by *Sell*.

45   Copies of the IFI-R and its manual are available without charge at Stephen Golding's Web site, http://home.comcast.net/~slgolding.

46   With few exceptions, even strict actuarial approaches involve clinical judgment in the scoring of variables (such as psychopathy). The modern trend is to speak of structured clinical judgment. See Litwack (2001) and Westen & Weinberger (2004) for an introduction to the literature.

47   This is a valuable point for forensic examiners to consider. Either out of ignorance or cross-cultural context, a defendant may not, for example, understand the role of the judge in the U.S. system. Ignorance is not a psycholegal deficit.

48   This is the authors' description.

49   This appears to be psychometrically justified in that Rogers et al. (2003) report high internal consistency coefficients for these scales.

50   Given the base rates consistently reported in the literature, CC+CI may account for 80% of the typical referral stream.

51 A real-world example, in the case of Brian David Mitchell (discussed subsequently), is illustrative. At the state level, well-trained evaluators disagreed in a principled way about a complicated set of data and the state court ended up opining that he was incompetent. Years later, a federal prosecutor, dissatisfied with the outcome, privately retained an expert and simultaneously sent Mitchell for a reevaluation at the Bureau of Prisons by nationally recognized experts. Those experts also opined that Mitchell was incompetent. The prosecutor fired up his privately retained expert, paid that expert in excess of $750,000, and ultimately secured a federal court finding that Mitchell was competent, psychopathic, and had successfully fooled all of the prior experts.

52 Many evaluators do not engage in this preinterview stage. If suitably crossed during their testimony, they are left with the weak reply, "Well, that information was not provided to me."

53 Many jurisdictions also specify that such a warning is required. Shuman's *Psychiatric and Psychological Evidence* (2005) is an invaluable resource for tracking evidentiary issues relevant to forensic psychology.

54 In addition to the IFI-R manual, an interview "template" is also available at Stephen Golding's Web site, http://home.comcast.net/~slgolding.

55 This assumes, of course, that accepting the offered plea bargain, in light of existing evidence and chances of prevailing at trial, is a "rational choice."

56 While a detailed discussion is beyond the scope of this chapter, experts are not allowed to opine on the specific credibility of a witness or defendant (e.g. "When X claimed Y, my assessment is that he was not telling the truth"). However, assessment of malingering or minimization is the cornerstone of a forensic evaluation and a variety of testimonial approaches can be taken. For example, the "specific credibility prohibition" is not triggered if the testimony is of the form, "In reaching my conclusion that X is not psychotic, I relied in part on converging evidence from the validity scales of the MMPI-2, the PAI and clinical observation that the defendant had a response style that tended to exaggerate his level of psychopathology." Granted, this is wordsmithing, but there are important distinctions between the two testimonial forms.

57 Little research on the convergent validity of malingering assessments with different methods exists. What does exist suggests great caution given that different methods often yield dramatically different results (Farkas et al., 2006).

58 Indeed, while a *history* of mental retardation would be hard to malinger, Everington, one of the authors of the CAST-MR, has recently shown that this instrument can also be faked (Everington et al., 2007).

59 A newer version of the SIRS is available, but various highly technical issues, beyond the scope of this chapter surround its use, but not the use of the original version. See Green, Rosenfeld, and Belfi (2012) for a discussion of these issues.

60 Anyone conducting forensic evaluations needs to become sophisticated with respect to issues of diagnostic efficiency, base rates, false positive errors, and false negative errors. A discussion of these advance psychometric considerations is beyond the scope of this chapter, but the reader is encouraged to pursue the topic with Frederick & Bowden (2009) which conveniently uses forensic malingering assessment instruments as examples.

61 Both utilize the mathematical properties of forced choice responding to identify individuals whose "accuracy" is significantly lower than that expected by chance.

62 Usually based upon either clinical judgment or scores on the SIRS.

63 Incorrect answers to the more difficult items on the VIP are far from obvious.

64 TOMM is a commonly used screening for malingering in neuropsychological assessments.

65 A useful and continuously updated resource for tracking detection of malingering research may be found at Kenneth Pope's Malingering Research Update Web page, www.kspope.com/assess/malinger.php.

66 Many defendants and some attorneys erroneously believe that amnesia is a solid ground for finding a defendant incompetent. A full discussion of relevant case law (*Wilson v. United States*, 1968, is a must read case) may be found in Roesch et al. (1999).

67 Sections 9.02 and 11.03 contain excellent guidance in this regard.

68 Despite the state finding of incompetency, the Mitchell case was relitigated on federal charges. He was found competent and convicted. A detailed analysis of the differences in the forensic testimony involved is beyond the scope of this chapter. See Note 51.

69 The essence of the government's case, in the relitigation at the federal level, was that neither was true. Rather, the government's expert asserted that Mitchell was psychopathic and insincere, and that he was merely pretending to religious conviction to fool examiners and stymie court proceedings. See Note 51.

70 One of the forensic examiners of Barzee diagnosed her as folie à deux.

References

Amador, X. F., Strauss D. H., Yale, S. A., Flaum, M. M., Endicott, J., & Gorman, J. M. (1993). Assessment of insight in psychosis. *American Journal of Psychiatry, 150*, 873–879.

American Psychological Association (2002). Ethical principles of psychologists and code of conduct. Retrieved from www.apa.org/ethics/code/index.aspx.

American Psychological Association (2013). Specialty guidelines for forensic psychology. *American Psychologist, 68*, 7–19. doi: 10.1037/a0029889

Appelbaum, P. (1994). *Almost a revolution: Mental health law and the limits of change.* New York: Oxford.

Arbisi, P. A., & Ben-Porath, Y. S. (1998). The ability of Minnesota Multiphasic Personality Inventory–2 validity scales to detect fake-bad responses in psychiatric inpatients. *Psychological Assessment, 10*, 221–228. doi: 10.1037/1040–3590.10.3.221

Atherton, J. (2005). State v. Mitchell. Findings and conclusions re: Defendant's competency to proceed to trial. Available at http://home.comcast.net/~slgolding/publications.htm.

Bagby, R. M., Nicholson, R. A., Bacchioci, J. R., Ryder, A. G., & Bury, A. S. (2002). The predictive capacity of the MMPI-2 and PAI validity scales and indexes to detect coached and uncoached feigning. *Journal of Personality Assessment, 78*, 69–86. doi: 10.1207/S15327752JPA7801_05

Berry, D., Baer, R., Rinaldo, J., & Wetter, M. (2002). Assessment of malingering. In James N. Butcher (Ed.), *Clinical personality assessment: Practical approaches* (pp. 268–302). New York: Oxford University Press.

Bertman, L. J., Thompson, J. W. J., Waters, W. F., Estupinan-Kane, L., Martin, J. A., & Russell, L. (2003). Effect of an individualized treatment protocol on restoration of competency in pretrial forensic inpatients. *Journal of the American Academy of Psychiatry and the Law, 31*, 27–35.

Bonnie, R. J. (1992). The competence of criminal defendants: A theoretical reformulation. *Behavioral Sciences and the Law, 10*, 291–316. doi: 10.1002/bsl.2370100303

Brooks v. McCaughtry, 380 F. 3D 1009 (7th Cir. Wis. 2004).

Burrows, M., & Herbert, P. (2005). Competence to stand trial: Competence to stand trial does not conclusively equate to competence to waive trial counsel. *Journal of the American Academy of Psychiatry and the Law, 33*, 557–558.

Cochrane, R., Herbel, B., Reardon, M., & Lloyd, K. (2013). The *Sell* effect: Involuntary medication treatment is a "clear and convincing" success. *Law and Human Behavior, 37*, 107–116.

Colwell, L., & Gianesini, J. (2011). Demographic, criminogenic, and psychiatric factors that predict competency restoration. *Journal of the American Academy of Psychiatry and the Law, 39*, 297–306.

Cronbach, L. J., & Meehl, P. E. (1955). Construct validity in psychological tests. *Psychological Bulletin, 52*, 281–302. doi: 10.1037/h0040957

Davis, J., Chen, N., & Glick, I. (2003). A meta-analysis of the efficacy of second-generation antipsychotics. *Archives of General Psychiatry, 60*, 553–564. doi: 10.1001/archpsyc.60.6.553

Day, J., Bentall, R., Roberts, C., Randall, F., Rogers, A., Cattell, R.M.N., . . . & Power, C. (2005). Attitudes toward antipsychotic medication. *Archives of General Psychiatry, 62*, 717–724. doi: 10.1001/archpsyc.62.7.717

DeClue, G. (2003). Toward a two-stage model for assessing adjudicative competence. *The Journal of Psychiatry and Law, 31*, 305–317.

Drope v. Missouri, 420 U.S. 162 (1975).

Dusky v. United States, 362 U.S. 402 (1960).

Edens, J., Cruise, K. & Buffington-Vollum, J. (2001). Forensic and correctional applications of the Personality Assessment Inventory. *Behavioral Sciences and the Law, 19*, 519–543.

Eisenberg, T., Garvey, S., & Wells, M. (1998). But was he sorry? The role of remorse in capital sentencing. *Cornell Law Review, 83*, 1599–1637.

Estelle v. Smith, 451 U.S. 454 (1981).

Everington, C., & Dunn, C. (1995). A second validation study of the Competence Assessment for Standing Trial for Defendants with Mental Retardation (CAST-MR). *Criminal Justice and Behavior, 22*, 44–59. doi: 10.1177/0093854895022001004

Everington, C., Notario-Smull, H., & Horton, M. (2007). Can defendants with mental retardation successfully fake their performance on a test of competence to stand trial? *Behavioral Sciences and the Law, 25*, 545–560. doi: 10.1002/bsl.735

Farkas, M., Rosenfeld, B., Robbins, R., & van Gorp, W. (2006). Do tests of malingering concur? Concordance among malingering measures. *Behavioral Sciences and the Law*, *24*, 659–671.

Fogel, M., Schiffman, W., Mumley, D., Tillbrook, C., & Grisso, T. (2013). Ten year research update (2001–2010): Evaluations for competence to stand trial (adjudicative competence). *Behavioral Sciences and the Law*, *31*, 165–191. doi: 10.1002/bsl.2051

Frederick, R. (1997). *Professional manual for the Validity Indicator Profile*. Minneapolis, MN: NCS Pearson.

Frederick, R., & Bowden, S. (2009). The test validation summary. *Assessment*, *16*, 215–236. doi: 10.1177/1073191108325005

Frith's Case, 22 Howes' State Trials 307, 318 (1790).

Gaudiano, B., & Miller, I. (2006). Patients' expectancies, the alliance in pharmacotherapy, and treatment outcomes in bipolar disorder. *Journal of Consulting and Clinical Psychology, 74*, 671–676.

Geddes, J., Burgess, S., Hawton, K., Jamison, K., & Goodwin, G. (2004). Long-term lithium therapy for bipolar disorder: Systematic review and meta-analysis of randomized controlled trials. *American Journal of Psychiatry, 161*, 217–222. doi: 10.1176/appi.ajp.161.2.217

Geddes, J., Freemantle, N., Harrison, P., & Bebbington, P. (2000). Atypical antipsychotics in the treatment of schizophrenia: A systematic overview and meta-regression analysis. *British Medical Journal, 321*, 1371–1376.

Godinez v. Moran, 509 U.S. 389 (1993).

Golding, S. L. (1992). Studies of incompetent defendants: Research and social policy implications. *Forensic Reports*, *5*, 77–83.

Golding, S. L. (1993). Interdisciplinary Fitness Interview-Revised: A training manual. Unpublished monograph from State of Utah Division of Mental Health. Retrieved from http://home.comcast.net/~slgolding/publications/ifir_manual.htm.

Golding, S. L., & Roesch, R. (1988). Competency for adjudication: An international analysis. In D. Weisstub (Ed.), *Law and mental health, Vol. 4: International perspectives* (pp. 73–109). New York: Pergamon Press.

Golding, S. L., Roesch, R., & Schreiber, J. (1984). Assessment and conceptualization of competency to stand trial: Preliminary data on the Interdisciplinary Fitness Interview. *Law and Human Behavior, 8*, 321–334.

Golding, S. L., Skeem, J. L., Roesch, R., & Zapf, P. A. (1999). The assessment of criminal responsibility: Current controversies. In A. K. Hess & I. B. Weiner (Eds.), *The handbook of forensic psychology* (2nd ed., pp. 327–249). New York: Wiley.

Gowensmith, W., Murrie, D., & Boccaccini, M. (2012). Field reliability of competence to stand trial opinions: How often do evaluators agree, and what do judges decide when evaluators disagree? *Law and Human Behavior, 36*, 130–139. doi: 10.1037/h0093958

Green, D., Rosenfeld, B., & Belfi, B. (2012). New and improved? A comparison of the original and revised versions of the Structured Interview of Reported Symptoms. *Assessment, 20*, 210–218. doi: 10.1177/1073191112464389

Greenberg, S. A., & Shuman, D. W. (1997). Irreconcilable conflict between therapeutic and forensic roles. *Professional Psychology: Research and Practice, 28*, 50–57. doi: 10.1037/0735–7028.28.1.50

Greer, A., O' Regan, M., & Traverso, A. (1996). Therapeutic jurisprudence and patients' perceptions of procedural due process of civil commitment hearings. In D. Wexler & B. Winick (Eds.), *Law in a therapeutic key: Developments in therapeutic jurisprudence* (pp. 923–933). Durham, NC: Carolina Academic Press.

Grisso, T. (1988). *Competency to stand trial evaluations*. Sarasota, FL: Professional Resource Exchange.

Grisso, T. (1998). *Forensic evaluation of juveniles*. Sarasota, FL: Professional Resource Press.

Grisso, T. (Ed.). (2003). *Evaluating competencies: Forensic assessments and instruments* (2nd ed.) New York: Kluwer.

Grisso, T. (2005). *Evaluating juveniles' adjudicative competence*. Sarasota, FL: Professional Resource Press.

Grisso, T., & Appelbaum, P. S. (1998a). *Assessing competence to consent to treatment: A guide for physicians and other health professionals*. London, Oxford University Press.

Grisso, T., & Appelbaum, P. S. (1998b). *MacArthur Competence Assessment Tool for Treatment (MacCAT-T)*. Sarasota, FL: Professional Resource Press.

Grisso, T., Appelbaum, P., Mulvey, E. & Fletcher, K. (1995). The MacArthur treatment competence study II: Measures of abilities related to competence to consent to treatment. *Law and Human Behavior, 19*, 127–148. doi: 10.1007/BF01499322

Grisso, T., Steinberg, L., Woolard, J., Cauffman, E., Scott, E., Graham, S., & Schwartz, R. (2003). Juveniles' competence to stand trial: A comparison of adolescents' and adults capacities as trial defendants. *Law and Human Behavior, 27*, 333–363.

Guenther, C., & Otto, R. (2010). Identifying persons feigning limitations in their competence to proceed in the legal process. *Behavioral Sciences and the Law, 28*, 603–613. doi: 10.1002/bsl.956

Heilbrun, K. (2001). *Principles of forensic mental health assessment*. New York: Kluwer.

Heilbrun, K., & Kramer, G. (2005). Involuntary medication, trial competence, and clinical dilemmas: Implications of Sell v. United States for psychological practice. *Professional Psychology: Research and Practice, 36*, 459–466. doi: 10.1037/0735–7028.36.5.459

Heres, S., Davis, J., Maino, K., Jetzinger, E., Kissling, W., & Leucht, S. (2006). Exploratory analysis of head-to-head comparison studies of second-generation antipsychotics. *American Journal of Psychiatry, 163*, 185–194. doi: 10.1176/appi.ajp.163.2.185

Hoge, S. K., Bonnie, R. J., Poythress, N., & Monahan, J. (1999). *The MacArthur Competence Assessment Tool—Criminal Adjudication*. Odessa, FL: Psychological Assessment Resources.

Hurley, K., & Deal, W. (2006). Assessment instruments measuring malingering used with individuals who have mental retardation: Potential problems and issues. *Mental Retardation, 44*, 112–119. doi: 10.1352/0047–6765(2006)44[112:AIMMUW]2.0.CO;2

Indiana v. Edwards, 554 U.S. 164 (2008).

Jackson v. Indiana, 402 U.S. 715 (1972).

Jackson, R., Rogers, R., & Sewell, K. (2005). Forensic applications of the Miller Forensic Assessment of Symptoms (M-FAST): Screening for feigned disorders in competency to stand trial evaluations. *Law and Human Behavior, 29*, 199–210. doi: 10.1007/s10979–005–2193–5

Jacobs, M., Ryba, N., & Zapf, P. (2008). Competence-related abilities and psychiatric symptoms: An analysis of the underlying structure and correlates of the MacCAT-CA and the BPRS. *Law and Human Behavior, 32*, 64–77. doi: 10.1007/s10979–007–9086–8

Jørgensen, A., Hilden, J., & Gøtzsche, P. (2006). Cochrane reviews compared with industry supported meta-analyses and other meta-analyses of the same drugs: Systematic review. *British Medical Journal, 333*, 782–785. doi:10.1136/bmj.38973.444699.0B.

Kruh, I., & Grisso, T. (2008). *Evaluation of juveniles' competence to stand trial*. New York: Oxford University Press.

Krupnick, J. L., Sotsky, S., Simmens, S., Moyer, J., Elkin, I, Watkins, J., & Pikonis, P. A. (1996). The role of the therapeutic alliance in psychotherapy and pharmacotherapy outcome: Findings in the NIMH treatment of depression collaborative research program. *Journal of Consulting and Clinical Psychology, 64*, 532–539. doi: 10.1037/0022–006X.64.3.532

Ladds, B., & Convit, A. (1994). Involuntary medication of patients who are incompetent to stand trial: A review of empirical studies. *Journal of the American Academy of Psychiatry and the Law, 22*, 519–532. doi: 10.1080/00048670902817745

Lally, S. J. (2003). What tests are acceptable for use in forensic evaluations? A survey of experts. *Professional Psychology: Research and Practice, 34*, 491–498.

Large, M., Nielssen, O., & Elliot, G. (2009). Reliability of psychiatric evidence in serious criminal matters: Fitness to stand trial and the defence of mental illness. *Australian and New Zealand Journal of Psychiatry, 43*, 446–452.

Lawrence v. Georgia, 454 S.E.2d 446 (Ga. 1995).

Lidz, C., Hoge, S., Gardner, W., Bennett, N., Monahan, J., Mulvey, E., & Roth, L. (1995). Perceived coercion in mental hospital admission: Pressure and process. *Archives of General Psychiatry, 52*, 1034–1039. doi: 10.1001/archpsyc.1995.03950240052010

Lieberman, J., Stroup, T., McEvoy, J., Swartz, M. S., Rosenheck, R. A., Perkins, D. O., Keefe, R., Davis, S. M., . . . & Hsiao, J. K. (2005). Effectiveness of antipsychotic drugs in patients with chronic schizophrenia. *New England Journal of Medicine, 353*, 1209–1223. doi: 10.1056/NEJMoa051688

Litwack, T. R. (2001). Actuarial versus clinical assessments of dangerousness. *Psychology, Public Policy, and Law, 7*, 409–443. doi: 10.1037/1076–8971.7.2.409

Litwack, T. R. (2003). The competency of criminal defendants to refuse, for delusional reasons, a viable insanity defense recommended by counsel. *Behavioral Sciences and the Law, 21*, 135–156. doi: 10.1002/bsl.527

Marcus, D., Poythress, N., Edens, J., & Lilienfeld, S. (2010). Adjudicative competence: Evidence that impairment in "rational understanding" is taxonic. *Psychological Assessment, 22*, 716–722. doi: 10.1037/a0020131

Maxwell v. Roe, 113 Fed. Appx. 213 (9th Cir. 2004), cert. denied, 125 S. Ct. 2513 (2005).

McEvoy, J.P., Apperson, L.J., Appelbaum, P.S. et al. (1989) Insight in schizophrenia. Its relationship to acute psychopathology. *Journal of Nervous and Mental Disease, 177,* 43–47. doi: 10.1097/00005053–198901000–00007

McEvoy, J., Lieberman, J., Stroup, T., Davis, S., Meltzer, H., Rosencheck, R., . . . & Hsiao, J. (2006). Effectiveness of Clozapine versus Olanzapine, Quetiapine, and Risperidone in patients with chronic schizophrenia who did not respond to prior atypical antipsychotic treatment. *American Journal of Psychiatry, 163,* 600–610. doi: 10.1176/appi.ajp.163.4.600

McGarry, A., Lelos, D., & Lipsitt, P. (1973). *Competency to stand trial and mental illness (DHEW publication number HSM-73–9105).* Washington, D.C: National Institute of Mental Health.

Melton, G., Petrila, J., Poythress, N., & Slobogin, C. (2007). *Psychological evaluations for the courts: A handbook for mental health professionals and lawyers* (3rd ed.). New York: Guilford Press.

Michael v. Horn, No. 04–9002 (Third Cir. 2006).

Miles v. Stainer, 108 F. 3d 1109 (Ninth Cir. 1997).

Miller, H. (2001). *Miller-Forensic Assessment of Symptoms Test.* Odessa, FL.: Psychological Assessment Resources.

Miller, H. (2004). Examining the use of the M-FAST with criminal defendants incompetent to stand trial. *International Journal of Offender Therapy and Comparative Criminology, 48,* 268–280. doi: 10.1177/0306624X03259167

Møller, P., & Husby, R. (2000). The initial prodrome in schizophrenia: Searching for naturalistic core dimensions of experience and behavior. *Schizophrenia Bulletin, 26,* 217–232. doi: 10.1093/oxfordjournals.schbul.a033442

Morris, D., & DeYoung, N. (2012). Psycho-legal abilities and restoration of competence to stand trial. *Behavioral Sciences and the Law, 30,* 710–728. doi: 10.1002/bsl.2040

Morris, G. & Meloy, J. (1993). The uncivil commitment of the permanently incompetent criminal defendant. *University of California Davis Law Review, 27,*1-96.

Morris, D., & Parker, G. (2009a). *Indiana v. Davis*: Revisiting due process right of permanently incompetent defendants. *Journal of the American Academy of Psychiatry and the Law, 37,* 380–385.

Morris, D. & Parker, G. (2009b). Effects of advanced age and dementia on restoration of competence to stand trial. *International Journal of Law and Psychiatry, 32,* 156–160. doi: 10.1016/j.ijlp.2009.02.009

Mossman, D. (2007). Predicting restorability of incompetent criminal defendants. *Journal of the American Academy of Psychiatry and the Law, 35,* 34–43.

Mossman, D., Noffsinger, S., Ash, P., Frierson, R., Gerbasi, J., Hackett, M., . . . & Zonana, H. (2007). AAPL practice guidelines for the forensic psychiatric evaluation of competence to stand trial. *Journal of the Academy of Psychiatry and the Law, 35, Supplement,.* S3-S72

Musick, J., & Otto, R. (2010). *Inventory of Legal Knowledge.* Lutz, FL: Psychological Assessment Resources.

Otto, R., Musick, J., & Sherrod, C. (2011). Convergent validity of a screening measure designed to identify defendants feigning knowledge deficits related to competence to stand trial. *Assessment, 18,* 60–62. doi: 10.1177/1073191110377162

Pate v. Robinson,383 U.S. 375 (1966).

People v. Goldstein, 843 N.E. 2d 727 (Court of Appeals, New York 2005).

Pierre, J. (2001). Faith or delusion? At the crossroads of religion and psychosis. *Journal of Psychiatric Practice, 7,* 163–172. doi: 10.1097/00131746–200105000–00004

Pinals, D. (2005). Where two roads meet: Restoration of competence to stand trial from a clinical perspective. *New England Journal of Civil and Criminal Confinement, 31,* 81–108.

Pirelli, G., Gottdiener, W., & Zapf, P.A. (2011). A meta-analytic review of competency to stand trial research. *Psychology, Public Policy and Law, 17,* 1–53. doi: 10.1037/a0021713

Poythress, N. (2002). Obtaining informed consent for research: A model for use with participants who are mentally ill. *Journal of Law, Medicine and Ethics, 30,* 1-8

Poythress, N., Bonnie, R., Monahan, J., Otto, R., & Hoge, S. (2002). *Adjudicative competence: The MacArthur studies.* New York: Kluwer Academic Publishers.

Poythress, N., Nicholson, R., Otto, R.K., Edens, J.F., Bonnie, R.J., Monahan, J., & Hoge, S.K. (1999). *The MacArthur Competence Assessment Tool—Criminal Adjudication: Professional manual.* Odessa, FL: Psychological Assessment Resources.

Resnick, P., & Knoll, J. (2012). Malingered psychosis. In R. Rogers (Ed.) *Clinical assessment of malingering and deception* (3rd ed., pp. 51–68). New York: Guilford.

Riggins v. Nevada, 504 US 167 (1992).

Roesch, R., & Golding, S. L. (1979). Treatment and disposition of defendants found incompetent to stand trial: A review and a proposal. *International Journal of Law and Psychiatry, 2*, 349–370. doi: 10.1016/0160–2527(79)90012–8

Roesch, R., & Golding, S. L. (1980). *Competency to stand trial*. Champaign, IL: University of Illinois Press.

Roesch, R., & Golding, S. L. (1987). Defining and assessing competency to stand trial. In I. B. Weiner & A. K. Hess (Eds.), *Handbook of forensic psychology* (pp. 378–394). Oxford, England: Wiley.

Roesch, R., Ogloff, J., & Golding, S. L. (1993). Competency to stand trial: Legal and clinical issues. *Journal of Applied and Preventive Psychology, 2*, 43–51. doi: 10.1016/S0962–1849(05)80160-X

Roesch, R., Zapf, P. A., & Eaves, D. (2006). *The Fitness Interview Test-Revised: A structured interview test for assessing competency to stand trial*. Sarasota, FL: Professional Research Press.

Roesch, R., Zapf, P. A., Golding, S. L., & Skeem, J. L. (1999). Defining and assessing competency to stand trial. In I. B. Weiner & A. K. Hess (Eds.), *Handbook of forensic psychology* (2nd ed.; pp. 327–349). NY: Wiley.

Rogers, R. (2003). Forensic use and abuse of psychological tests: Multiscale inventories. *Journal of Psychiatric Practice, 9*, 316–320. doi: 10.1097/00131746–200307000–00008

Rogers, R. (Ed.). (2012). *Clinical assessment of malingering and deception* (3rd ed.). New York: Guilford.

Rogers, R., Bagby, R., & Dickens, S. (1992). *Structured Interview of Reported Symptoms (SIRS) and professional manual*. Odessa, FL.: Psychological Assessment Resources.

Rogers, R., Jackson, R., Sewell, K., & Harrison, K. (2004). An examination of the ECST-R as a screen for feigned incompetence to stand trial. *Psychological Assessment, 16*, 139–145. doi: 10.1037/1040–3590.16.2.139

Rogers, R., Jackson, R., Sewell, K., Tillbrook, C., & Martin, M. (2003). Assessing dimensions of competency to stand trial: Construct validation of the ECST-R. *Assessment, 101*, 344–351. doi: 10.1177/1073191103259007

Rogers, R., & Johannson-Love, J. (2009). Evaluating competency to stand trial with evidence-based practice. *Journal of the Academy of Psychiatry and the Law, 37*, 450–460.

Rogers, R., Tillbrook, C. B., & Sewell, K. (2004). *Evaluation of Competency to Stand Trial-Revised (ECST-R): Professional manual*. Lutz, FL: Psychological Assessment Resources.

Scott, C. L. (2003). Commentary: A road map for research in restoration of competency to stand trial. *Journal of the American Academy of Psychiatry and the Law, 31*, 36–43.

Sell v. United States, 539 U.S. 166 (2003).

Siegel, A. M., & Elwork, A. (1990). Treating incompetence to stand trial. *Law and Human Behavior, 14*, 57–65. doi: 10.1007/BF01055789

Skeem, J., & Golding, S. L. (1998). Community examiners' evaluations of competence to stand trial: Common problems and suggestions for improvement. *Professional Psychology: Research and Practice, 29*, 357–367. doi: 10.1037/0735–7028.29.4.357

Skeem, J. L., Golding, S. L., Cohn, N. B., & Berge, G. (1998). Logic and reliability of evaluations of competence to stand trial. *Law and Human Behavior, 22*, 519–547. doi: 10.1023/A:1025787429972

Skeem, J., Golding, S. L., & Emke-Francis, P. (2004), Assessing adjudicative competency: Using legal and empirical principles to inform practice. In W. T. Donohue & E. R. Levensky (Eds.), *Forensic psychology: A handbook for mental health and legal professionals* (pp. 175–211). New York: Academic Press

Soliman, S., & Resnick, P. (2010). Feigning in adjudicative competence evaluations. *Behavioral Sciences and the Law, 28*, 614–629. doi: 10.1002/bsl.950

Stanton, B., & David, A. (2003). First person accounts of delusions. *Psychiatric Bulletin, 24*, 333–336. doi: 10.1192/pb.24.9.333

Stroup, T., Lieberman, J., McEvoy, J., Swartz, M. et al. (2006). Effectiveness of Olanzapine, Quetiapine, Risperidone, and Ziprasidone in patients with chronic schizophrenia following discontinuation of a previous atypical antipsychotic. *American Journal of Psychiatry, 163*, 611–622. doi: 10.1176/appi.ajp.163.4.611

Suhr, J., & Gunstad, J. (2007). Coaching and malingering: A review. In G. Larrabee (Ed.), *Assessment of malingered neuropsychological deficits* (pp. 287–311). New York: Oxford University Press.

Sullivan, H. S. (1953). *The psychiatric interview*. New York: Norton.

Tandon, R. (2006). Comparing antipsychotic efficacy. *American Journal of Psychiatry, 163,* 1645. doi: 10.1176/appi.ajp.163.9.1645

Tombaugh, T. N. (1997). The Test of Memory Malingering (TOMM): Normative data from cognitively intact and cognitively impaired individuals. *Psychological Assessment, 9,* 260–268. doi: 10.1037/1040-3590.9.3.260

United States v. Bradshaw 690 F. 2d 704, 712 (9th Cir. 1982).

United States v. Evans 427 F. Supp. 2d 696 (W.D. Vir. 2006).

United States v. Gomes 387 F.3d 157 (2d Cir. 2004).

United States v. Lindauer 2006 U.S. Lexis 62872 (So. Dist. NY, 9/6/2006).

Viljoen, J., & Roesch, R. (2003). Diagnosis, current symptomatology and ability to stand trial. *Journal of Forensic Psychology Practice, 3,* 23–37. doi: 10.1300/J158v03n04_02

Viljoen, J. L., Vincent, G. M., & Roesch, R. (2006). Assessing adolescent defendants' adjudicative competence: Inter-rater reliability and factor structure of the Fitness Interview Test-Revised. *Criminal Justice and Behavior, 33,* 467–487. doi: 10.1177/0093854806287317

Vitacco, M., Rogers, R., Gabel, J., & Munizza, J. (2007). An evaluation of malingering screens with competency to stand trial patients: A known-groups comparison. *Law and Human Behavior, 31,* 249–260. doi: 10.1007/s10979-006-9062-8

Washington v. Harper, HYPERLINK "https://en.wikipedia.org/wiki/United_States_Reports" \o "United States Reports" 494 U.S. 210 (1990)

Weiss, R., Rosenfeld, B., & Farkas, M. (2011). The utility of the Structured Interview of Reported Symptoms in a sample of individuals with intellectual disabilities. *Assessment, 18,* 284–290. doi: 10.1177/1073191111408230

Westen, D., & Weinberger, J. (2004). When clinical description becomes statistical prediction. *American Psychologist, 59,* 595–613. doi: 10.1177/1073191111408230

Whitaker, R. (2002). *Mad in America: Bad science, bad medicine, and the enduring mistreatment of the mentally ill.* Cambridge, MA: Perseus.

Wilson v. United States, 391 F. 2d. 460 (1968).

Youtsey v. United States, 97 F. 937 (6th Cir. 1899).

Zapf, P. A., & Galloway, M. (2002). Test review: Miller Forensic Assessment of Symptoms Test (M-FAST). *American Psychology-Law Society Newsletter,* 16–17; 23.

Zapf, P. A., & Roesch, R. (2001). A comparison of the MacCAT-CA and the FIT for making determinations of competency to stand trial. *International Journal of Law and Psychiatry, 24,* 81–92. doi: 10.1016/S0160-2527(00)00073-X

Zapf, P. A., & Roesch, R. (2005). An investigation of the construct of competence: A comparison of the FIT, the MacCAT-CA, and the MacCAT-T. *Law and Human Behavior, 29,* 229-252.

Zapf, P. A., & Roesch, R. (2009). *Best practices in forensic mental health assessments: Evaluation of competence to stand trial.* New York: Oxford University Press.

Zapf, P. A., & Roesch, R. (2011). Future directions in the restoration of competency to stand trial. *Current Directions in Psychological Science, 20,* 43–47. doi: 10.1177/0963721410396798

Zapf, P. A., Roesch, R., & Pirelli, G. (2014). Assessing competency to stand trial. In I. B. Weiner & R. K. Otto (Eds.), *The handbook of forensic psychology* (4th ed., pp. 281–314). Hoboken, NJ: Wiley.

Zapf, P. A., Skeem, J. & Golding, S. L. (2005). Factor structure and validity of the MacArthur Competence Assessment Tool-Adjudication. *Psychological Assessment, 17,* 433–445. doi: 10.1037/1040-3590.17.4.433

Zapf, P. A., & Viljoen, J. L. (2003). Issues and considerations regarding the use of assessment instruments in the evaluation of competency to stand trial. *Behavioral Sciences and the Law, 21,* 351–367. doi: 10.1002/bsl.535

5 An Introduction to Insanity Evaluations

Richard Rogers

Insanity evaluations often evoke images of bizarre crimes with courtroom battles championed by partisan experts. Missing from these dramatized accounts is any serious consideration of the empirical knowledge and standardized measures underlying these complex evaluations. This chapter introduces the relevant legal concepts, psychological constructs, and specialized methods used in forensic evaluations of criminal responsibility. It subscribes to the *legal-empirical-forensic* paradigm propounded by Rogers and Shuman (2005). Briefly, legal formulations of insanity provide a general framework. Forensic psychologists and psychiatrists must operationalize and test empirically specialized methods for assessing the components of insanity. These empirically tested methods are subjected to judicial scrutiny regarding their admissibility in light of *Daubert* (*Daubert v. Merrell Dow Pharmaceuticals, Inc.*, 1993) and subsequent U.S. Supreme Court cases (*General Electric Company v. Joiner*, 1997; *Kumho Tire Company v. Carmichael*, 1999).

As titled, this chapter is an *introduction* to insanity evaluations. It provides a helpful overview of legal issues and clinical methods. In complementing more scholarly works, it presents a step-by-step approach to insanity assessments and discusses practical issues related to expert opinion and testimony. Forensic practitioners intending to carry out insanity evaluations must be solidly grounded in the relevant case law, legal formulations, and specialized methods. Essential texts on forensic assessments include Rogers and Shuman (2005) on criminal forensic evaluations and Otto (2013) on criminal and civil issues. For focused coverage of insanity evaluations, two books are recommended for forensic psychologists: (a) Packer's (2009) *Evaluation of Criminal Responsibility*, which provides a concise overview of relevant issues; and (b) Rogers and Shuman's (2000a) *Conducting Insanity Evaluations*, which offers extensive coverage of forensic measures and methods. In addition, forensic practitioners must become conversant with the relevant case law that is specific to their jurisdictions.

This introductory chapter does not address other issues of criminal responsibility that are sometimes addressed in U.S. jurisdictions. Examples include the mens rea defense and automatism (see Goldstein, Morse, & Packer, 2012). In addition, psychological context evidence is occasionally introduced as an affirmative defense to domestic violence in cases of battered woman syndrome. Rogers and Shuman (2005) provide an extensive treatment for these additional issues related to criminal responsibility.

Overview of Insanity Standards

The foundation of American jurisprudence on the insanity defense is based largely on the acquittal of Daniel M'Naghten in 1843 and the ensuing legal formulation that carries his name. Apparently based on delusional beliefs, M'Naghten intended to assassinate Robert Peel, the British prime minister, but mistakenly killed his personal secretary instead. In the public outrage following M'Naghten's acquittal, a special commission of 15 judges from common law courts was convened by Queen Victoria. The resulting *M'Naghten* standard relied heavily on rational abilities. It held that insanity required the defendant to be "laboring under such a defect of reason, from disease of mind as not to know the nature and quality of the act he was doing; or if he did know it, that he did not know he was doing what was wrong" (M'Naghten's Case, 1843). As observed by Rogers and Shuman (2005), this standard, relying on a "defect of reason," is composed of two cognitive prongs: (a) knowledge of "the nature and quality of the act," and (b) its legal or moral wrongfulness.

The *M'Naghten* standard was quickly imported to the United States and became the prevailing test of insanity. In some jurisdictions, its critics saw *M'Naghten* as unduly narrow in its formulation. As a result, several American insanity cases contemporaneous with *M'Naghten* (e.g., *Commonwealth v. Mosler*, 1846; cited by Keilitz & Fulton, 1983) attempted to broaden the standard by the inclusion of *irresistible impulse*. The addition of irresistible impulse was aimed at addressing the volitional prong, specifically the incapacity to control one's criminal conduct. A recent survey (Packer, 2009) found that 25 states used *M'Naghten*, with several states applying some variant of the irresistible impulse prong. Importantly, these standards vary in significant ways; for example, some states omit the nature and quality prong.

The *Durham* standard (*Durham v. United States*, 1954) was a dramatic, though brief, departure from prevailing insanity standards. Under the leadership of Judge Bazelon, the District of Columbia adopted the *product rule* that stated, "an accused is not criminally responsible if his unlawful act was a product of a mental disease or mental defect" (pp. 874–875). While tried by several jurisdictions, this experiment was deemed a failure and subsequently discarded as an insanity test with the sole exception of New Hampshire (Giorgi-Guarnieri et al., 2002).

The American Law Institute standard (ALI, 1962) represented a decade of careful study underwritten by the Rockefeller Foundation (see Rogers & Shuman, 2000a). It embraced both the cognitive and the volitional prongs, "A person is not responsible for criminal conduct, if at the time of such conduct as the result of a mental disease or defect, he lacks substantial capacity either to appreciate the criminality (wrongfulness) of his conduct or to conform his conduct to the requirements of law." The ALI standard also attempted to eliminate the possibility that psychopaths could be seen as being unable to conform their conduct; thus, it excluded any "abnormality manifested only by repeated criminal or otherwise antisocial conduct."

In the aftermath of Hinckley's highly unpopular acquittal for the attempted assassination of President Reagan, Congress passed the Insanity Defense Reform Act (IDRA, 1984). In an effort to be more restrictive, the IDRA standard held, "as a result of a severe mental disease or defect, he was unable to appreciate the nature and quality or wrongfulness of his act" (p. 201). The IDRA reverted to cognitive constructs found in *M'Naghten* and eliminated the volitional prong. Despite its fanfare, the IDRA applies to only the small percentage of insanity cases that are raised in federal jurisdictions.

Basic Components of Insanity Standards

This section provides a distilled review of the basic components common to insanity standards (see Table 5.1). Because the case law in each jurisdiction may further refine these components, a careful examination of the relevant appellate cases is required.

1   *Mental disease or defect.* The necessary precondition for all insanity standards is that the defendants suffer from a serious mental condition that significantly impairs their psychological functioning. In general, the courts have been reluctant to exclude categorically any specific disorders from consideration. While insanity acquittals are most commonly based on psychotic disorders, a significant number have mood or personality disorders as their primary diagnosis (Rogers & Shuman, 2000a).

Table 5.1 Conceptual model of insanity standards

Insanity Standard	Cognitive Prongs		Volitional Prongs		Product
	Nature and Quality	Wrongfulness	Irresistible	Conform Conduct	
M'Naghten	✓	✓			
M'Naghten/Irresistible Impulse	✓	✓	✓		
Durham					✓
ALI		✓		✓	
IDRA	✓	✓			

Note: ALI = American Law Institute; IDRA = Insanity Defense Reform Act. Please note that this table provides only a general overview and insanity standards have many minor variations (see Giorgi-Guarnieri et al., 2002). For instance, some *M'Naghten* jurisdictions omit the nature and quality prong.

2   *Nature and quality.* These closely related constructs address the defendants' awareness of their actions and their consequences; the absence of either component is sufficient to meet this prong. *Nature* typically refers to the physical actions per se. In contrast, *quality* generally refers to the likely or actual consequences of such conduct. As an example of this distinction, a female defendant with an intellectual disability knew she placed her baby into hot water (i.e., the "nature" of her actions) as a punishment for crying, but she was clearly unaware that it would cause third-degree burns (i.e., the "quality" of her actions). The nature-and-quality prong is very restrictive and applies to only the most impaired defendants.

3   *Wrongfulness.* Wrongfulness is the pivotal cognitive issue for most insanity standards. All jurisdictions with this component address legal wrongfulness, and the majority also include moral wrongfulness. For legal wrongfulness, the most common example is delusional self-defense; defendants believe that they are in imminent danger and attempt to protect themselves. Other cases may include delusionally based actions involving (a) the defense of others, (b) officially sanctioned duties, and (c) misconstrued exigencies (see Rogers & Shuman, 2005). For moral wrongfulness, Yakush and Wolbransky (2013) provide an excellent description: "the illicit behavior is sourced in mental illness (e.g., delusional ideation) and the defendant honestly believed the act was morally justified" (p. 360).

4   *Irresistible impulse.* This prong addresses an inability to refrain from the behavior. The loss of power to choose is typically the result of an overriding internal imperative, which cannot be stopped and lacks the capacity for delay (Rogers & Shuman, 2000a).

5   *Conformity of conduct.* This prong focuses on the capacity to choose between criminal and noncriminal behavior (see Knoll & Resnick, 2008). It addresses the defendant's volitional abilities to choose prosocial actions based on perceived options and decision-making abilities (Rogers & Shuman, 2000a) and refrain from criminal conduct (Donohue, Arya, Fitch, & Hammen, 2008). As observed by Packer (2009), total impairment is not required; instead, "the defendant must lack '*substantial* capacity'" (p. 12, *emphasis in the original*).

Nature of Insanity Evaluations

Retrospective Assessments

Insanity evaluations place singular demands on forensic practitioners in applying imprecise legal standards to the retrospective assessment of psychological functioning for a specific time period. The retrospective nature of these evaluations deserves special consideration.

Intervals between the criminal offenses and subsequent evaluations typically range from months to years.

Rogers (2002) provided a useful typology regarding types of retrospective assessment. First, an *ongoing episode* extends from the time in question (e.g., time of crime) to the current time. Second, a *prior episode* is limited to a past period (e.g., remission or significant amelioration of symptoms since the time of the crime). Third and finally, a *prior occurrence* refers to past symptoms of very limited duration (e.g., intoxication or other altered state at the time of the crime).

Insanity evaluations with ongoing episodes are comparatively straightforward to conduct. Clinical data are readily available from the defendant's reporting, collateral accounts, and detailed observations. The nexus between symptoms and impairment can often be established. In direct contrast, prior episodes must focus entirely on the reconstruction of the defendant's functioning at the time of the offense. The reliability of the defendant and the availability of witnesses and other collateral sources (e.g., mental health records) are critical to these insanity evaluations. Because voluntary intoxication is generally excluded as the basis for insanity, prior occurrences of very brief duration are rarely determinative of conclusions regarding criminal responsibility. Nonetheless, their role must be evaluated in ascertaining their likely effects on the defendant's cognitive and volitional capacities. Given problems with blackouts and impaired memory, use of collateral sources is often vital.

Forensic psychologists and psychiatrists are sometimes criticized for rendering expert opinions that extend beyond the current time. An important distinction should be drawn between prospective and retrospective forensic assessments. With prospective assessments, forensic practitioners *attempt to predict* low base-rate behavior for an extended period, often years, into the future. Use of general risk factors coupled with cross-situational predictions of low base-rate behaviors poses considerable dangers of overpredictions with unacceptably high false positives (Rogers, 2000). In stark contrast, retrospective assessments of insanity use a comparative analysis to *explain* the most likely motivations for criminal conduct. For insanity evaluations, particular criminal acts (e.g., murder) often have very low base rates, even in offender populations. Because the infrequent act has already occurred, however, retrospective evaluations of insanity are not vulnerable to false-positive predictions. Therefore, insanity evaluations pose very different challenges from prospective evaluations in their retrospective reconstruction of the defendant's functioning at the time of the offense.

In the context of insanity evaluations, Gutheil (2002) conceptualized hindsight analysis as a longitudinal examination that "takes into account the defendant's entire life" (p. 80). Similarly, Packer (2009) advocated a very broad perspective that includes (a) family and developmental history; (b) social, education, and employment history; (c) medical and religious history; (d) mental health and substance abuse history; and (e) criminal history. Rather than an exhaustively broad and detailed history, Rogers and Shuman (2000a) emphasized a selective review of clinical and legal issues followed by an intensive examination of the defendant's functioning during a narrowly defined period, namely the time of the offense. It is critically important to be focused on relevant patterns including the antecedent conditions, the defendant's functioning at the time of the offense, and his or her subsequent actions. Regarding mental health history, a broadened framework may help in understanding the defendant's other episodes and the effects of particular symptoms (e.g., command hallucinations) on his or her behavior.

Comparative Analysis

The overriding goal of insanity evaluations is a comprehensive reconstruction of the defendant's functioning at the time of the offense. Rogers and Shuman (2000a) provide an extensive analysis of the defendant's conduct within the context of insanity standards. This section highlights decision models and their use in the assessment of criminal responsibility.

Traditional evaluations typically employ a hypothesis-testing model as the structure of the assessment and its conclusions. With this model, forensic practitioners formulate a likely hypothesis for explaining the criminal conduct. Clinical data are collected to test this hypothesis. Despite its rich tradition, this approach is vulnerable to both confirmatory and anchoring biases (Borum, Otto, & Golding, 1993). The initial formulation of a hypothesis shapes the ensuing evaluation. Data supportive of the hypothesis tend to be overvalued, whereas data supporting alternative theories are deemphasized. As a case example, bizarre acts (e.g., the removal of human hearts with separate knives to avoid contamination) may lead to strongly held hypotheses regarding the insanity of the defendant. One solution recommended by Borum et al. (1993) is the deliberate development of alternative hypotheses.[1] This approach was vigorously endorsed by the Committee on Ethical Guidelines for Forensic Psychologists (1991, p. 661): Professional integrity is maintained by "actively seeking information that will differentially test plausible rival hypotheses." This core requirement was subsequently affirmed in the most recent forensic guidelines (Specialty Guidelines for Forensic Psychology, 2013). Consistent with these specialty guidelines, I recommend either the use of competing hypothesis, or preferably the linear best-fit model described later.

Rogers and Shuman (2000a) proposed that forensic practitioners utilize a linear best-fit model in determinations of criminal responsibility. According to this model, forensic experts systematically collect clinical data using standardized measures, where possible. Once collected, clinical judgments would be rendered about the "best fit" of the data in relation to the appropriate insanity standard. How does this approach differ from the development of alternative hypotheses?

- *Broader scope.* The linear best-fit model requires a comprehensive assessment of diagnostically relevant data. In applying standardized measures, Axis I and Axis II structured interviews[2] may be used to systematically evaluate diagnoses and salient symptoms. In contrast, alternative hypotheses may be focused in their assessments. For example, the diagnostic consideration might be between voluntary intoxication and substance-induced psychotic disorders.
- *Debiasing clinical judgment.* The linear best-fit model delays the judgment process until critical data are collected from the defendant and other relevant sources. In contrast, the alternative hypothesis involves the relative weighing of evidence throughout the assessment process. This weighing process is vulnerable to biases in clinical decision-making.

In summary, the hypothesis-testing model is susceptible to critical errors in clinical judgment (see Rogers & Shuman, 2000a). Forensic practitioners should choose between an alternative hypothesis paradigm and the linear best-fit model. In selecting the former, the alternative hypotheses should be explicitly formulated at the onset of the evaluation and include multiple perspectives. For the linear best-fit model, standardized measures should be applied to ensure a comprehensive assessment of data relevant to diagnosis and impairment.

Diagnoses and Insanity

Diagnoses, per se, have only limited relevance to determinations of criminal responsibility. Instead, diagnoses provide a useful framework for assessing salient symptoms and associated features from both longitudinal (i.e., episodes prior to the current arrest) and cross-sectional (i.e., functioning at the time of the alleged crime) perspectives. It is critically important to assess impaired functioning that arises from particular symptoms or a constellation of symptoms. Forensic practitioners must evaluate both the *level* and *type* of impairment. For example, paranoid delusions may differ substantially in their level of impairment. ranging from minimal influence to pervasive interference with day-to-day activities. Especially relevant to insanity evaluations is the type of impairment. With the example of paranoid delusions, the wrongfulness of the defendant's criminal conduct may cover a full spectrum from being unaffected (i.e., fully aware of culpability) to grossly impaired (e.g., delusionally based actions to "prevent" imminent harm).

Diagnoses in forensic evaluations are categorized into three major groups based on their methodology (Rogers & Shuman, 2005). Forensic practitioners need to decide whether to employ *unstandardized, standardized,* or *extrapolated* diagnostic methods. Unstandardized diagnoses typically rely on free-flowing clinical interviews that are characterized by flexibility in interviewing style and concomitant recording of salient findings. For diagnosis, per se, this flexibility is also its greatest detriment. Such diagnoses (see Rogers, 2001) can be limited by variability in (a) the scope of the clinical interview, (b) variability in the format and sequencing of clinical inquiries, and (c) the idiosyncratic recording of symptomatology. Rogers and Shuman (2005) summarized the accuracy of unstandardized diagnoses for major depression and schizophrenia when evaluated by mental health professionals:

- *Missed diagnoses.* Estimates for when diagnoses are overlooked range from 50% to 62% for major depression and 18% to 31% for schizophrenia.
- *Misdiagnoses.* Estimates for when diagnoses are wrongly applied range from 22% to 28% for major depression and 30% to 47% for schizophrenia.

Forensic practitioners should avoid any major reliance on unstandardized diagnoses, given their vulnerability to both missed diagnoses and misdiagnoses.

Standardized interviews provide systematic methods for assessing diagnoses. They provide a uniform structure for clinical inquiries and their correspondent ratings (Rogers, 2003). Of particular relevance to forensic consultations, practitioners can demonstrate to the court their systematic methods of assessment and their diagnostic reliability. For some standardized interviews, reliability extends beyond diagnoses and can demonstrate the consistent measurement of salient symptoms across clinicians (interrater reliability) and time (test-retest reliability).

Extrapolated diagnoses utilize scales and indexes derived from psychometric measures. These measures do not yield DSM-IV or DSM-5 diagnoses. Simply put, their clinical correlates lack the necessary precision for establishing specific diagnoses. Attempts at extrapolated diagnoses from the Minnesota Multiphasic Personality Inventory–2 (MMPI-2) and Millon Clinical Multiaxial Inventory–III scales yield unacceptably high false-positive rates that can easily exceed 50%. Likewise, indexes on the Rorschach cannot be linked to particular diagnoses. As observed by Weiner (1998), low scores on the Schizophrenia Index (SCZI) have no diagnostic significance, whereas high scores may signify a range of psychotic (e.g., schizophrenia, schizophreniform, or delusional disorder) and personality (e.g., paranoid or schizotypal personality disorder) diagnoses.[3]

One Model of Insanity Evaluations

A primary objective of this book is to present practical guidelines for conducting forensic evaluations. In that light, this section provides one model for performing insanity evaluations. Alternative approaches are readily available that address forensic evaluations in general (Heilbrun, 2001) or assessments of criminal responsibility (Packer, 2009).

Reconstruction of the Defendant's Functioning

A critically important task for forensic practitioners is the reconstruction of the defendant's thoughts, feelings, and actions at the time of the offense. Given the vulnerability of memory to external influences, a primary objective is to minimize clinician-based influences on the defendant's recall. Therefore, I recommend eliciting the defendant's account at the time of the offense in an unhurried manner. When needed the defendant can be prompted with simple, open-ended questions. The goal is to obtain the most comprehensive narrative account while minimizing memory contamination via leading questions.

How do we operationalize the "time of the offense," a critical component to insanity determinations? It is stringently defined as the period between which the criminal conduct was initiated and completed. In most instances, this period is only a matter of minutes. To better understand the "time of the offense," it is useful to consider several time perspectives:

- *Day of the offense*. An exhaustive account of this day is very helpful. In my insanity evaluations, I typically begin at the first event of the day (e.g., awakening) and attempt to catalogue each event of the day. The goal is to capture all the defendant's perceptions, thoughts, feelings, and actions.
- *Days preceding the offense*. A detailed account is sought for the several days leading up to the criminal conduct. The idea is to collect the salient thoughts, emotions, and actions. Especially important are any changes in the defendant and his or her environment. These changes may be critical in explaining the timing of the offense. Forensic practitioners must be able to address specific timing of the criminal conduct with reference to insanity, "Why then?"

Establishing good rapport is an essential requirement before proceeding with the defendant's account of the time of the offense. In beginning the interview process, it is often useful to collect background or other material that is not especially intrusive. Forensic practitioners must understand the defendants' experiences of insanity evaluations. Defendants are often asked to disclose highly personal, disturbing information, which can markedly affect their lives for the foreseeable future. Perspective taking is important for forensic practitioners in considering what is at stake for defendants being asked to provide a narrative account of their criminal actions. My own viewpoint is to approach defendants considerately and provide them with "an opportunity to disclose." I take issue with an alternative approach, specifically that forensic practitioners have "a right to know." I believe that demands, however subtle, negatively affect the professional relationship and may result in less than optimal data.

Defendants vary considerably in their level of psychological functioning and their willingness to describe the time of the offense. In some cases, they provide relatively spontaneous accounts that require very little direction. It is useful to not interrupt this process, but take detailed notes including any verbatim quotes of what the defendant and others said at the time of the offense. In some instances, a particular defendant can be encouraged to provide more detail with a comment such as, "We have plenty of time, please tell me everything."

Some defendants launch into a narrative account, but their delivery has a rehearsed quality to it. Any facile conclusions that a particular defendant has "prepared" his or her account are premature. In many instances, the defendant has been asked repeatedly about the offense and may have described his or her actions on more than a dozen occasions. Such extensive repetition can easily produce a rehearsed quality. One option is to interrupt any nonspontaneous description by slowing the process and asking questions about the experience that are often omitted from these descriptions. As an illustration, the forensic clinician could say, "Take a moment to focus on your feelings . . . What were you feeling when __ occurred?"

Many defendants need structure to their descriptions for the time of the offense. Even when spontaneous accounts are provided, open-ended inquiries are frequently necessary. Structure can be provided by simple open-ended questions such as these.

1. "What were you aware of?"
2. "What was happening?"
3. "What thoughts do you remember?"
4. "What were you feeling?"
5. "What caught your attention?"

Despite this focus on detail, defendants will frequently overlook short periods of time during the day of the offense. Therefore, my preference is to link questions to both time and chronology in order to preserve a detailed and sequential account. The following inquiries assume a relatively intact defendant; the gist of the defendant's responses is provided in brackets:

1. "When did you awake?" [7 a.m.]
2. "What happened next?" [breakfast]
3. "Before we get there, let's go moment by moment. Did you stay in bed for a bit or get right up?" [provides more details]
4. "So you got dressed and went downstairs. How long did this take?" [five minutes]
5. "Five minutes—so it's just after 7 in the morning. What were you thinking about as you went downstairs?"

The goal is to exhaust the defendant's memories regarding the day of the offense. Often, they will begin to look less certain or offer speculative remarks ("I guess"). It is important to clarify that the forensic clinician is interested in only what is actually remembered.

An alternative method in obtaining the defendant's narrative account is to ask him or her to reexperience certain components of that day. This reexperiencing typically involves a brief period of focusing (e.g., "Go back to __; picture what is going on."). The forensic clinician asks the defendant to relate what was happening as if it was occurring at the present time. The defendant might be directed: "Close your eyes and stay with the experience. Tell me what is happening." It also helps to have the defendant present this recall in the first-person present-tense. I recently used a variation of reexperiencing with a male defendant, who frequently gave tangential tirades. I asked him to imagine a video camera that captured everything at the time of the offense. He was able to give a detailed and coherent account of what the video camera would record, including actions and utterances. (Corroboration by witnesses or physical evidence is very beneficial.)

An additional alternative is attaining the defendant's narrative description in a "reverse chronology." This approach can easily disrupt descriptions that appear rehearsed. Inquiries can take the following form, "What happened just before that?" With repeated inquiries, the forensic clinician can ascertain a sequence of events with their concomitant emotions and thoughts. I recently used the "reverse chronology" with an insanity case in which a male defendant was claiming amnesia for several days following the crime. By focusing on a later "memory" and going backwards step by step, he "recovered" more than a day of his purported memory loss.

Data Sources in Reconstructing the Defendant's Functioning

The defendant is often the only available witness for the time of the offense. Even when witnesses are available, the defendant is typically the only source of information regarding internal events, including psychotic experiences. Therefore, a careful appraisal of the defendant's account involving different assessment methods is strongly advised. My own preference is the use of multiple narrative accounts for the assessment of credibility. As described in the last section, the first account involves minimal intrusions. This approach may be repeated, although it is often more focused on key components of the defendant's account. It should be noted that some inconsistencies are inevitable, given the reconstructive nature of memory recall.

Specific probes are very useful in supplementing the defendant's narrative accounts. The tenor of these probes is critical to rapport. When the probes are expressed as a need for clarification or a point of confusion, defendants are often receptive and provide additional information. When the process is presented as interrogation, defendants may respond negatively.

Collateral sources of data on the defendant's functioning at the time of the offense can be valuable in confirming or disconfirming the defendant's account. For example, a defendant with a schizophrenic disorder may engage in behaviors consistent with that diagnosis. In one instance, the defendant with paranoid delusions had sealed his window with plastic and duct tape to avoid poisonous gases. In most instances, the clinical evidence is less obvious. For instance, a paranoid defendant may become gradually more withdrawn and suspicious of others.

Defendants with prominent psychotic symptoms often do not share their bizarre perceptions or delusional thinking. In some instances, their contact with others is minimal. In other cases, they are guarded about what is shared either because of their general distrust of others or specific beliefs about individuals in their immediate environment. Therefore, a lack of corroborative data requires further investigation in light of the defendant's psychotic symptoms and characteristic responses in relationship to these symptoms.

In summary, three interview-based modalities are proposed for the reconstruction of the defendant's functioning at the time of the offense: (a) narrative accounts, (b) focused probes, and (c) collateral interviews. Equally important is the use of structured interviews for the purposes of standardizing the reported symptoms and their severity. For this purpose, the Schedule for Affective Disorders and Schizophrenia (SADS; Spitzer & Endicott, 1978) is strongly recommended.

The SADS is a semi-structured diagnostic interview that goes beyond DSM-5 inclusion criteria to assess clinical characteristics and associated features of psychotic and mood disorders. It also provides selective coverage of anxiety disorders, substance abuse, and other disorders. SADS Part I addresses the current episode from two time perspectives: the worst period and the current time (i.e., the last week). Interrater reliability is outstanding for both time perspectives and even good for the assessment of past episodes via the SADS Part II (see Rogers, 2001; Rogers, Jackson, & Cashel, 2003).

The SADS, with minor modifications, has been used successfully with insanity evaluations. Rogers and Shuman (2000a) recommended a modification of the SADS Part I so that the first time perspective (i.e., the "worst period") is used for the time of the offense. The second time perspective remains the same (i.e., the "current time"). This modification allows the forensic expert to focus specifically on the time of the offense and compare symptoms and impairment with the present time. Early research reported by Rogers and Shuman (2000a) provided solid evidence of discriminant validity for defendants clinically evaluated as sane and insane.

Forensic practitioners are more likely to be trained in the administration of the Structured Clinical Interview for DSM-IV Disorders (SCID; First, Spitzer, Williams, & Gibbon, 1997) than the SADS. Arguments for the use of the SCID in insanity evaluations include its (a) broad diagnostic coverage; (b) direct correspondence with DSM-IV criteria, which are similar to DSM-5; (c) convenient format; and (d) general popularity among mental-health professions. The first two points are valid. However, my recommendation of the SADS is based on the following four reasons:

1. *Symptom severity.* The determination of insanity relies on the severity of key symptoms rather than their mere presence. The SADS provides anchored ratings for determining the severity of symptoms. The majority of symptoms are categorized as either nonsignificant (i.e., "not at all," or "slight") or gradations of clinical significance ("mild," "moderate," "severe," or "extreme"). These gradations are based on the intensity (e.g., frequency and duration) and effect (e.g., distress and impairment) of the symptoms. Therefore, SADS ratings provide meaningful data regarding symptom severity.

2. *Symptom reliability.* Because insanity determinations often focus on individual symptoms and their severity, the SADS is very useful because of its established symptom reliability for key psychotic and mood symptoms.

3. *Retrospective assessments.* The SADS was validated for use with multiple time periods, including the worst period in an ongoing episode and past episodes. The validation is critical to retrospective evaluations of insanity.

4. *Detection strategies for likely feigning.* Rogers (2008) presented SADS data for when feigned mental disorders should be considered; these data are based on empirically validated detection strategies.

The centerpiece of insanity evaluations is the systematic use of interview methods for the establishment of retrospective diagnoses, prominent symptoms, and psychological impairment. Regarding diagnoses, the standard of practice should be standardized diagnoses using structured interviews, such as the SADS or the SCID. For the defendant's functioning at the time of the offense, interview methods encompass (a) interview-guided narrative accounts, (b) focused interviews with detailed probes, (c) collateral interviews, and (d) the SADS or SCID for standardizing the evaluation of symptoms associated with major mental disorders.

Psychological Testing and Insanity

Traditional tests often provide helpful clinical data focused on the defendant's current functioning. Except for intellectual disability, testing typically yields extrapolated diagnoses that should not be used in forensic assessments. Within the domain of mental disorders, most tests provide clinical correlates that are associated with impaired functioning. The limitation of clinical correlates is that they often represent general distress rather than specific psychopathology. Recent work on the MMPI-2–Restructured Format (MMPI-2-RF) scales is an explicit acknowledgement of how general distress can militate against discriminant validity (Ben-Porath, 2012). Unfortunately, most of the test data for the MMPI-2-RF still involves convergent validity in the form of correlates. As such, the MMPI-2-RF cannot be used to identify specific DSM symptoms or disorders.

Rogers and Shuman (2000a) provide extensive coverage of psychological tests and their relevance to the assessment of criminal responsibility. Interestingly, very few studies since 2000 have addressed the effectiveness of psychological measures for insanity evaluations. Subsequent paragraphs will focus on the MMPI-2 as the most commonly used test in insanity evaluations (Borum & Grisso, 1995). The MMPI-2-RF is not covered because PsychInfo searches have failed to uncover any peer-reviewed research on the MMPI-2-RF and assessments of criminal responsibility.

Forensic practitioners are likely to be surprised by the dearth of empirical research that examines the validity of the MMPI-2 in criminal-forensic assessments, such as insanity evaluations. Only a few investigations have evaluated differences in MMPI-2 profiles between sane and insane defendants, and these have yielded discrepant results. For example, Rogers and McKee (1995) in a descriptive study of the MMPI-2 found elevations for defendants clinically evaluated as *insane* on the *M'Naghten* insanity standards (Ms: 6 = 77, 8 = 77, 1 = 69, and 2 = 67) and ALI[4] (Ms: 8 = 82, 6 = 75, 2 = 71, 4 = 70, 7 = 70). Unexpectedly, *higher* elevations were found for pretrial defendants with Axis I disorders, who were evaluated as *sane* (Ms: 8 = 89, 6 = 86, 7 = 82, 2 = 78, 1 = 74, 4 = 72, 3 = 70). Expert conclusions by multidisciplinary teams, while not completely independent of the MMPI-2 data, yielded very few differences (i.e., scales 4 and 7 were lower for the insane groups). Clearly, these data do not suggest that higher MMPI-2 elevations can be used to identify insane defendants.

Moskowitz, Lewis, Ito, and Ehrmentraut (1999) examined the MMPI-2 profiles for a small sample of defendants found not-guilty-by-reason-of-insanity (NGRI). An advantage of this approach is that all the defendants were legally determined to be insane. However, its main drawback was the elapsed time: on average, these defendants had been hospitalized, postacquittal, for more than five years. Using averages, the complete lack of elevations on clinical scales could easily be attributable to their extensive postacquittal treatment. A large archival study of NGRI patients by Hays (1999) yielded similar results with unelevated MMPI-2 profiles that were supplemented by unremarkable Rorschach data.[5] No U.S. studies of the MMPI-2 and insanity were found for the last decade; however, recent insanity research from the Netherlands found minimal differences between their criterion groups (Barendregt, Muller, Nijman, & De Beurs, 2008).

In summary, MMPI-2 profiles do not distinguish between sane and insane defendants. Clinical elevations, per se, do not translate into greater impairment of legally relevant abilities. Instead, tests such as the MMPI-2 may provide useful data about clinical correlates and response styles (see the next section).

Response Styles and Insanity

A cornerstone of insanity evaluations is the systematic appraisal of response styles, especially the evaluation of malingering. The assessment of malingering must extend beyond the current time to the time of the offense. This extension is relatively straightforward for an *ongoing* episode that evidences relatively little change across the intervening months. When the offense in question apparently occurred in a *prior* episode, malingering becomes challenging to assess. For instance, a female defendant may accurately report her current symptoms but fabricate her symptoms and concomitant impairment for the time of the offense.

The systematic assessment of malingering relies predominantly on empirically validated detection strategies (Rogers, 2008; Rogers & Bender, 2013). These strategies emphasize the accuracy of individual classifications, rather than merely relying on group differences. For example, the *rare-symptoms* strategy uses a constellation of symptoms that are infrequently observed among genuine patients. Detection strategies are specific to both the type of dissimulation (e.g., malingering or defensiveness) and the domain (mental disorders, cognitive impairment, or medical complaints). For example, different strategies are used to evaluate feigned schizophrenia versus feigned intellectual disabilities. Forensic practitioners must be well versed in detection strategies for malingering:

1. What are the specific detection strategies found in commonly used validity indicators on psychological tests and specialized measures?
2. Which detection strategies are the most accurate for feigned mental disorders versus feigned cognitive impairment?

This section focuses on feigned mental disorders only, a common form of malingering in insanity evaluations. For issues of feigned amnesia or intellectual disability, professional resources are readily available (Boone, 2007; Rogers, 2008). Three measures of feigned psychopathology are commonly used in forensic practice: the MMPI-2, the PAI, and the SIRS/SIRS-2 (Lally, 2003). Each measure is briefly summarized with attention to its detection strategies.

MMPI-2

The MMPI-2 (Butcher et al., 2001) is used extensively to assess response styles that include malingering, defensiveness, and random responding. Rogers, Sewell, Martin, and Vitacco (2003) conducted a meta-analysis of the MMPI-2 and malingering that included 65 feigning studies that were supplemented by 12 diagnostic investigations. The key findings are summarized:

- The *F* scale is commonly elevated among genuine examinees from certain diagnostic groups, such as posttraumatic stress disorder ($M = 86.31$), schizophrenia ($M = 80.10$), and depression ($M = 71.28$). Given the large standard deviations (i.e., greater than 20 points), extreme *F* elevations (> 100T) can easily occur in genuine patients with these disorders.
- The *Fp* scale appears superior to *F* and *Fb* because of its conceptualization (i.e., a true rare-symptom strategy) and discriminability. With respect to the latter, the cut score of *Fp* > 9 for feigning produces very few false positives and can be used across a range of serious mental disorders.
- The *Ds* scale, capitalizing on the erroneous-stereotype strategy, also appears to be generally effective with comparatively few false positives.

Forensic experts should carefully review MMPI-2 conclusions by other practitioners to ensure that standard procedures were employed. For example, some defendants will respond inconsistently to MMPI-2 items. An egregious error is the interpretation of an *inconsistent* profile, often producing extreme elevations on validity scales, as a *feigned* profile. Consider for a moment that a truly random profile is likely to have a raw *F* score of 30 (i.e., 50% endorsement of 60 items). As a flagrant example of substandard practice, one insanity defendant's MMPI-2 profile was interpreted as feigned, despite a marked elevation on *Variable Response Inconsistency* (i.e., indicating an inconsistent profile) and exceedingly brief administration time (i.e., less than 10 minutes). As an important warning, computerized MMPI-2 interpretations of feigning often include inaccuracies and should not be used. As a further caution, clinicians are often tempted to use audio-recorded MMPI-2 administrations for defendants with limited reading comprehension. Audio-recorded administrations have limited validity for clinical profiles and no research whatsoever on feigning or other response styles. Any conclusions about malingering based on audio-recorded administrations are completely unsubstantiated.

PAI

The PAI (Morey, 2007) is used extensively in forensic cases because of its excellent psychometrics and easy reading level (4th grade), which is essential to many forensic assessments. Key findings for the PAI and feigning are summarized:

- Low scores on the PAI Negative Impression (NIM) scale appear useful in screening out patients for whom malingering is unlikely (Rogers, Sewell, Cruise, Wang, & Ustad, 1998; Rogers, Gillard, Wooley, & Ross, 2012).
- Extreme scores on NIM ($\geq$ 110T) or the Malingering Index (MAL $\geq$ 5) rarely occur but are indicative of feigning (Rogers et al., 1998, 2012).
- Data are mixed on the usefulness of the Rogers Discriminant Function (RDF; Rogers, Sewell, Morey, & Ustad, 1996). The RDF uses a sophisticated detection strategy, specifically *spurious patterns of psychopathology* (Rogers, 2008). However, it does not appear to function effectively in forensic assessments (Rogers & Bender, 2013) and should be avoided in insanity evaluations.
- The Negative Distortion Scale (NDS; Mogge, Lepage, Bell, & Ragatz, 2010) is a recently validated scale that appears to be highly effective (see Rogers, Gillard, Wooley, & Kelsey, 2013).

SIRS-2

The SIRS-2 (Rogers, Sewell, & Gillard, 2010) is an extensively validated measure for the assessment of feigned mental disorders via detection strategies. Its eight detection strategies are highly effective; they are composed of two domains: spurious and plausible presentations (Rogers, Jackson, Sewell, & Salekin, 2005). Key findings of the SIRS-2 are summarized:

- Its interview-based format produces highly reliable results and can be applied across a broad range of forensic populations.
- Its decision model is highly effective for identifying likely feigning and likely genuine examinees.

Pilot research (Goodness & Rogers, 1999) suggested that the original SIRS was potentially effective for retrospective evaluations of defendants for the time of the offense. However, more extensive research is needed before the SIRS-2 is used retrospectively for feigning assessments of *prior* episodes.

Determinations of Wrongfulness

This model of insanity evaluations includes sections that examine (a) the reconstruction of the defendant's functioning with (b) the integration of data sources and (c) the assessment of diagnostic issues and (d) response styles. A capstone issue for most insanity evaluations is the accurate determination of wrongfulness. As previously discussed, each forensic clinician is obliged to review general references and relevant case law. This section, adapted from Rogers and Shuman (2000a) distills key issues for the forensic determination of wrongfulness.

The first step in the evaluation of wrongfulness is an examination of the defendant's objectives in engaging in the criminal acts. Two related issues are as follows: What did the defendant hope to accomplish? From his or her perspective, what was accomplished? In the majority of insanity referrals, the defendant's objectives include a clear recognition of wrongfulness. In the remaining cases, the forensic practitioner must evaluate closely the defendant's awareness of wrongfulness and its role in conducting the acts in question. The crux of the determination can be stated simply: If the defendant's beliefs and perceptions were accurate, would they justify his or her actions?

Perceived Threats

The most common reason why a defendant does not appreciate the wrongfulness of his or her actions is because of grossly misperceived threats. Often based on delusions and markedly distorted perceptions, the defendant acts to save him- or herself, or others, from grave danger, torture, and even death.[6] The following issues must be considered:

1. What does the defendant believe would happen if he or she did not "intervene?"
2. Assuming these beliefs are chronic (e.g., delusions), why were the "interventions" initiated at this point?
3. Did the intervention achieve another goal, such as revenge?
4. What alternatives to the criminal acts were considered and why were they rejected?
5. Were the effects of severe psychopathology observed in multiple aspects of the defendant's functioning? Alternatively, were they limited to criminal conduct only?

Perceived Responsibilities

Defendants may perceive themselves as having an official capacity that requires the criminal behavior. In particular, defendants may believe they have the legal or moral authority to carry out these actions. Occasionally, defendants will see misconstrued exigencies that necessitate their intervention. For example, a female defendant may believe that her children are in imminent danger of losing their souls to an evil force. If her delusional beliefs were true, her actions could be morally justifiable. The following issues should be considered:

1. What verbalizations and behaviors have been observed that would be consistent with the defendant's misperceived responsibilities?
2. How did the defendant conclude that he or she must engage in this conduct at this time? Were communications involved?
3. If command hallucinations were present, how did the defendant decide to act on their orders at that particular time? What were the perceived consequences of not complying with these commands?

In evaluating the wrongfulness prong, forensic practitioners attempt to establish credible patterns of perceptions, thoughts, and actions. For insane defendants diagnosed with schizophrenia, a common pattern is a gradual increase of psychotic symptoms and behavior responses to these symptoms. Efforts to control the psychotic thinking become increasingly less effective. Likewise, general deterioration in day-to-day functioning is observed. For other diagnoses, similar patterns (i.e., intensification of symptoms and deterioration of functioning) are often observed. In cases of severe depression, a mother may grossly misperceive her children to be suffering unspeakably and believe that she has the moral duty to end such suffering. While deserving full investigation, it is quite possible for such a defendant to appreciate both legal and, where applicable, moral wrongfulness. Regarding the latter, relevant issues include (a) communications and beliefs about a deity's role in the demise of her children, and (b) her interpretations of and compliance with religious beliefs.

Forensic Decision Making

Rogers and Shuman (2000a) utilized a clinical database from 411 insanity cases. Its tables and accompanying text provide forensic practitioners with useful reference points for rendering insanity opinions. In addition, some forensic practitioners may wish to apply the Rogers Criminal Responsibility Assessment Scales (R-CRAS; Rogers, 1984) as a general guide to their forensic decision making. Its decision model, validated primarily on the ALI standard, operationalizes key components of criminal responsibility. The test-retest reliability (average interval of 2.7 weeks) of the ALI model is very good (M κ = .81), especially considering the retrospective nature of this assessment process. An extensive reanalysis of R-CRAS data (Rogers & Sewell, 1999) presented strong evidence of its construct validity. Without a structured format, as provided by the R-CRAS, the level of agreement is often limited for insanity evaluations (Gowensmith, Murrie, & Boccaccini, 2013).

The R-CRAS has received strong criticisms (e.g., Melton, Petrila, Poythress, & Slobogin, 1997, 2008), partially due to its endorsement of conclusory opinions. Forensic practitioners should weigh the validity data and criticisms for themselves[7] (see Rogers & Shuman, 2005). More recent reviews have taken a more measured approach (Ferguson & Ogloff, 2011; Goldstein et al., 2012; Sadoff & Dattilio, 2011). Using the R-CRAS as a template, Packer (2009) concluded that "the R-CRAS would be an aid to guide an evaluator regarding which issues to address and a framework for integrating the data into an analysis of the legal criteria" (p. 75).

Case Illustration[8]

The information included in this case illustration is technically a matter of public record; nonetheless, the identity of the defendant has been masked to avoid unnecessary intrusions on her privacy. Ms. Chavez is a 22-year-old unmarried Hispanic American woman, who was previously employed by a domestic cleaning service. Her employment was terminated after she complained vehemently about spider bites on her head and limbs. Her employers brought her to the hospital following her attempt to "burst" and "burn" the poisonous sacs she believed were deposited by the spiders. Diagnosed with a schizophrenic disorder, she was released from the hospital with antipsychotic medication. She reported that her general practitioner became increasingly concerned about her deteriorated state and had taken a personal interest in her case, including an invitation to Thanksgiving dinner.

My evaluation was conducted on three days across a period of two months. In addition to clinical interviews, I used the SADS retrospectively on two separate occasions to assess the presence and severity of her Axis I disorders at the time of the offense. The SIRS-2 and PAI were also administered. The record review included police investigative reports, prior medical and psychiatric records, and extensive documentation for the last 10 months of her behavior at the county jail.

The SIRS-2, PAI, and clinical interviews were used to evaluate Ms. Chavez for feigned mental disorders. Her PAI validity indicators were unremarkable, except for some modest evidence that she might be underreporting her psychopathology. On the SIRS-2, the decision model indicated a high likelihood of genuine (i.e., "non-feigned") responding. On the SADS and clinical interviews, a tendency to "forget" obvious details was observed. Because these denials of memory did not involve the time of the alleged offense, they were considered peripheral to the insanity evaluation.

Ms. Chavez was charged with murder and aggravated arson in causing the death of her mother. In the preceding months, she was unable to work and became increasingly preoccupied with venomous spiders and poisoned ear drops. She also became concerned that her apartment was under surveillance because her mother seemed to know too much about her activities. Ms. Chavez was convinced that several family members had conspired to cheat her out of her inheritance. Several acquaintances had persuaded her that she needed hospitalization. On the very same day that she was released from the hospital to return to her apartment, her ears became inflamed and her mother also called. These coincidental events "proved" to her that she was under surveillance by her mother, who she believed served as the ringleader in a conspiracy against her. She drove to her mother's house. Not accepting her mother's continued denials, she repeatedly stabbed her and dragged her to the bathtub. She set the house on fire and left immediately for California.

In conducting an insanity evaluation with Ms. Chavez, the onset and course of her schizophrenic disorder was well established. The SADS interview data were used to establish the paranoid delusions, disorganized thinking, and negative symptoms (e.g., diminished emotional expression). The SADS was also used to integrate data from other sources including collateral interviews and review of hospital records. Despite consistent diagnostic data, the reported involvement of her general practitioner (even after she lost her health benefits) seemed highly unusual. After several attempts, her former physician was finally contacted; unexpectedly, her doctor confirmed having informal contacts with the defendant and inviting her to Thanksgiving dinner.

In applying the *M'Naghten* standard, Ms. Chavez clearly met the "nature and quality" prong. She understood that stabbing her mother would cause serious injury and likely her death. She apparently gave her mother multiple chances to "come clean" before fatally stabbing her in the chest. Her actions in killing her mother were clearly motivated by her paranoid delusions. In this respect, she would have clearly met the New Hampshire "product rule." In evaluating the *M'Naghten* standard, however, was she motivated by delusional beliefs in self-defense? Clearly, Ms. Chavez was convinced that she was being tormented and that poison-based inflammation could lead to scarring and permanent hearing loss. However, no clinical data suggested that she believed her life was in imminent danger. Moreover, she was able to "escape" this tormenting at least when she was hospitalized and likely when not residing in her apartment. Interestingly, her ideas about family members conspiring to defraud her may have had a factual basis.

Other facets of wrongfulness included conduct required by official duties and misconstrued exigencies. Ms. Chavez has never seen herself as operating in an official capacity; she does not identify with the government and is generally suspicious of its motives. Moreover, she does not actively practice any religion or hold any unusual spiritual beliefs. Could her actions be seen as a misconstrued exigency? I do not believe so. She had experienced similar symptoms for several months. I was unable to find any misperceived catastrophe that motivated her actions.

Wrongfulness needs to be evaluated for each offense. Beyond the homicide, what were the reasons for the aggravated arson? Based on extensive interviewing, two motivations emerged for the arson: (a) purifies witchcraft and (b) eliminates fingerprints. Regarding the former, she suspected that her mother had practiced witchcraft because of her knowledge of poisons and spiders. Regarding the latter, Ms. Chavez was clearly aware that her actions were criminal, and she acknowledged that she was attempting to destroy evidence.

In summary, the case of Ms. Chavez illustrates the integration of clinical data and the subsequent analysis of insanity components. In conducting insanity evaluations, multiple data sources are essential for the corroboration of retrospective functioning. Although the defendant's account of the physician's involvement appeared implausible, it was important to confirm or disconfirm this account. In the analysis of insanity components, forensic practitioners may be tempted to equate psychotic motivations with insanity. The case of Ms. Chavez provides a useful example regarding how each facet (self-defense, defense of others, official duties, and misconstrued exigencies) of wrongfulness should be systematically evaluated for each criminal offense.

Conclusions

Insanity evaluations represent the most challenging forensic assessments within the criminal domain. Beginning forensic practitioners should seek close and competent supervision in evaluating retrospectively the defendant's diagnosis and impairment at the time of the offense. By using a linear best-fit model and standardized diagnoses, biases and misdiagnoses can be minimized. The credibility of the defendant's account must be considered from multiple measures (e.g., SIRS-2 and PAI) and collateral sources. In addition, formal response styles (e.g., malingering) should be systematically assessed. The fundamental standard for insanity evaluations is comprehensive assessment of diagnosis, symptoms, and associated features, using the best validated measures. The insanity report should address these issues in a balanced manner, bringing together sources of data from psychological measures and collateral sources.[9]

Forensic decision making is an essential component of insanity evaluations, with some forensic practitioners possibly utilizing the R-CRAS as a template (Packer, 2009). It is critically important that forensic practitioners have expert knowledge of both the legal standard (both statutes and relevant case law) and its clinical operationalization (see Rogers & Shuman, 2005). For each component of insanity, a critical analysis of the clinical data is needed within a *legal-empirical-forensic* paradigm.

Notes

1   The generation of multiple hypotheses appears to be endorsed by Goldstein et al. (2012), although it is not entirely clear that they are formally recommending the use of competing hypotheses as a standard component for insanity evaluations.
2   Although DSM-5 has eliminated the multiaxial classification, these structured interviews are commonly referred to by Axis I (major mental disorders) and Axis II (personality disorders).
3   Acklin (2008) argued that the Perceptual Thinking Index (PTI) is more accurate than the SCZI and can be used in forensic cases. However, this accuracy typically still involves a broad spectrum (e.g., psychotic disorders) rather than a specific diagnosis (see Dao & Prevatt, 2006).
4   South Carolina uses the language of the ALI standard for its guilty-but-mentally ill (GBMI) verdict.
5   In general, the scores are slightly lower than found in Exner's normative data for *nonpatient* adults.
6   Occasionally, the protection of others becomes complicated, such as the case of an ex-wife believing that her former spouse was driving their daughter to suicide.
7   Melton et al.'s analysis appears to lack objectivity; they tout their own structured format with its minimal validation while severely criticizing the R-CRAS' extensive validation (see Rogers & Shuman, 2000b).
8   Tests in this case illustration were updated for educational purposes (e.g., the SIRS-2 instead of the SIRS).
9   Fuger, Acklin, Nguyen, Ignacio, and Gowensmith (2014) provides a useful structure for evaluating the completeness of insanity reports.

References

Acklin, M. W. (2008). The Rorschach test and forensic psychological evaluation: Psychosis and the insanity defense. In C. B. Gacono & F. Evans (Eds.), *The handbook of forensic Rorschach assessment* (pp. 157–174). New York: Routledge.

American Law Institute. (1962). *Model penal code, proposed official draft*. Philadelphia: Author.

Barendregt, M., Muller, E., Nijman, H., & De Beurs, E. (2008). Factors associated with experts' opinions regarding criminal responsibility in the Netherlands. *Behavioral Sciences & the Law, 26*, 619–631. doi:10.1002/bsl.837

Ben-Porath, Y. S. (2012). *Interpreting the MMPI-2-RF*. Minneapolis: University of Minnesota Press.

Boone, K. B. (2007). *Assessment of feigned cognitive impairment*. New York: Guilford.

Borum, R., & Grisso, T. (1995). Psychological test use in criminal forensic evaluations. *Professional Psychology: Research and Practice, 26*, 465–473. doi:10.1037/0735–7028.26.5.465

Borum, R., Otto, R., & Golding, S. L. (1993). Improving clinical judgment and decision making in forensic evaluations. *Journal of Psychiatry and Law, 21*, 35–76.

Butcher, J. N., Graham, J. R., Ben-Porath, Y. S., Tellegen, A. M., Dahlstrom, W. G., & Kaemmer, B. (2001). *MMPI-2: Manual for administration and scoring* (rev. ed.). Minneapolis: University of Minnesota Press.

Committee on Ethical Guidelines for Forensic Psychologists. (1991). Specialty guidelines for forensic psychologists. *Law and Human Behavior, 15*, 655–665. doi:10.1007/BF01065858

Dao, T. K., & Prevatt, F. (2006). A psychometric evaluation of the Rorschach Comprehensive System's Perceptual Thinking Index. *Journal of Personality Assessment, 86*, 180–189. doi:10.1207/s15327752jpa8602_07

Daubert v. Merrell Dow Pharmaceutical, Inc., 509 U.S. 579 (1993).

Donohue, A., Arya, V., Fitch, L., & Hammen, D. (2008). Legal insanity: Assessment of the inability to refrain. *Psychiatry, 5*, 58–66.

Durham v. United States, 214 F.2d 862 (D.C. Cir. 1954).

Ferguson, M., & Ogloff, J. P. (2011). Criminal responsibility evaluations: Role of psychologists in assessment. *Psychiatry, Psychology and Law, 18*, 79–94. doi:10.1080/13218719.2010.482952

First, M. B., Spitzer, R. L., Williams, J. B. W., & Gibbon, M. (1997). *Structured Clinical Interview of DSM-5 Disorders (SCID)*. Washington, DC: American Psychiatric Association.

Fuger, K. D., Acklin, M. W., Nguyen, A. H., Ignacio, L. A., & Gowensmith, W. (2014). Quality of criminal responsibility reports submitted to the Hawaii judiciary. *International Journal of Law and Psychiatry, 37*, 272–280. doi:10.1016/j.ijlp.2013.11.020

Giorgi-Guarnieri, D., Janofsky, J., Keram, E., Lawsky, S., Merideth, P., Mossman, D., & . . . Zonona, H. (2002). AAPL practice guidelines for forensic psychiatric evaluation of defendants raising the insanity defense. *Journal of the American Academy of Psychiatry and the Law, 30*, S3-S40.

General Electric Co. v. Joiner, 522 U.S. 136 (1997).

Goldstein, A. M., Morse, S. J., & Packer, I. K. (2012). Evaluation of criminal responsibility. In R. K. Otto and I. B. Weiner (Eds.), *Handbook of psychology, Vol. 11: Forensic psychology* (2nd ed.) (pp. 440–472). Hoboken, NJ: Wiley.

Goodness, K. R., & Rogers, R. (1999, August). *Retrospective malingering detection: The validation of the R-SIRS and CT-SIRS*. Paper presented at the American Psychological Association annual convention, Boston.

Gowensmith, W., Murrie, D. C., & Boccaccini, M. T. (2013). How reliable are forensic evaluations of legal sanity? *Law and Human Behavior, 37*, 98–106. doi:10.1037/lhb0000001

Gutheil, T. G. (2002). Assessment of mental state at the time of the criminal offense: The forensic examination. In R. I. Simon & D. W. Shuman (Eds.), *Predicting the past: The retrospective assessment of mental states in civil and criminal litigation* (pp. 73–99). Washington, DC: American Psychiatric Press.

Hays, R. M. (1999). *A comparison of persons found not guilty by reason of insanity and mentally disordered offenders in outpatient treatment using Rorschach and MMPI-2 data*. Unpublished doctoral dissertation. Pacific Graduate School of Psychology, Palo Alto.

Heilbrun, K. S. (2001). *Principles of forensic mental health assessment*. New York: Kluwer.

Insanity Defense Reform Act of 1984, Pub. L. No. 98–473, secs. 401, 402, 20 (1984).

Keilitz, I., & Fulton, J. P. (1983). *The insanity defense and its alternatives: A guide to policy makers*. Williamsburg, VA: National Center for State Courts.

Knoll, J., & Resnick, P. J. (2008). Insanity defense evaluations: Toward a model for evidence-based practice. *Brief Treatment and Crisis Intervention, 8*, 92–110. doi:10.1093/brief-treatment/mhm024

Kumho Tire Co., Ltd. v. Carmichael, 526 U.S. 137 (1999).

Lally, S. J. (2003). What tests are acceptable for use in forensic evaluations? A survey of experts. *Professional psychology: Research and Practice, 34*, 491–498. doi:10.1037/0735–7028.34.5.491

Melton, G. B., Petrila, J., Poythress, N. G., & Slobogin C. (1997). *Psychological evaluations for the courts* (2nd ed.). New York: Guilford.

Melton, G. B., Petrila, J., Poythress, N. G., & Slobogin C. (2008). *Psychological evaluations for the courts* (3rd ed.). New York: Guilford.

M'Naghten's Case 1843 10 C & F 200.

Mogge, N. L., Lepage, J. S., Bell, T., & Ragatz, L. (2010). The negative distortion scale: A new PAI validity scale. *Journal of Forensic Psychiatry & Psychology, 21*, 77–90. doi:10.1080/14789940903174253

Morey, L. C. (2007). *Personality Assessment Inventory: Professional manual* (2nd ed.). Lutz: Psychological Assessment Resources.

Moskowitz, J. L., Lewis, R. J., Ito, M. S., & Ehrmentraut, J. (1999). MMPI-2 profiles of NGRI and civil patients. *Journal of Clinical Psychology, 55*, 659–668. doi:10.1002/(SICI)1097–4679(199905)55:5<659::AID-JCLP12>3.0.CO;2–6

Packer, I. K. (2009). *Evaluation of criminal responsibility*. New York: Oxford University Press.

Otto, R. K. (Ed.) (2013). *Comprehensive handbook of psychology: Forensic psychology*. New York: Wiley.

Rogers, R. (1984). *Rogers criminal responsibility assessment scales (R-CRAS) and test manual*. Lutz, FL: Psychological Assessment Resources.

Rogers, R. (2000). The uncritical acceptance of risk assessment in forensic practice. *Law and Human Behavior, 24*, 595–605. doi:10.1023/A:1005575113507

Rogers, R. (2001). *Handbook of diagnostic and structured interviewing*. New York: Guilford.

Rogers, R. (2002). Validating retrospective assessments: An overview of research models. In R. I. Simon & D. W. Shuman (Eds.), *Predicting the past: The retrospective assessment of mental states in civil and criminal litigation* (pp. 287–306). Washington, DC: American Psychiatric Press.

Rogers, R. (2003). Standardizing DSM-IV diagnoses: The clinical applications of structured interviews. *Journal of Personality Assessment, 81*, 220–225. doi:10.1207/S15327752JPA8103_04

Rogers, R. (Ed.) (2008). *Clinical assessment of malingering and deception* (3rd ed.). New York: Guilford.

Rogers, R., & Bender, S. D. (2013). Evaluation of malingering and related response styles. In R. K. Otto (Ed.), *Comprehensive handbook of psychology, Vol. 11: Forensic psychology* (2nd ed., pp. 517–539). New York: Wiley.

Rogers, R., Gillard, N. D., Wooley, C. N., & Kelsey, K. (2013). Cross-validation of the PAI Negative Distortion Scale for feigned mental disorders: A research report. *Assessment, 20*, 36–42. doi: 10.1177/1073191112451493

Rogers, R., Gillard, N. D., Wooley, C. N., & Ross, C. A. (2012). The detection of feigned disabilities: The effectiveness of the PAI in a traumatized inpatient sample. *Assessment, 19*, 77–88. doi: 10.1177/1073191111422031

Rogers, R., Jackson, R. L., & Cashel, M. L. (2003). SADS: Comprehensive assessment of mood and psychotic disorders. In M. Hersen, M. J. Hilsenroth, & D. J. Segal (Eds.), *The handbook of psychological assessment, Vol. 2: Personality assessment* (pp. 144–152). New York: Wiley.

Rogers, R., Jackson, R. L., Sewell, K. W., & Salekin, K. L. (2005). Detection strategies for malingering: A confirmatory factor analysis of the SIRS. *Criminal Justice and Behavior, 32*, 511–525. doi:10.1177/0093854805278412

Rogers, R., & McKee, G. R. (1995). Use of the MMPI-2 in the assessment of criminal responsibility. In Y. S. Ben-Porath, J. R. Graham, G.C.N. Hall, R. D. Hirschman, & M. S. Zaragoza (Eds.), *Forensic applications of the MMPI-2* (pp.103–126). Newbury Park, CA: Sage.

Rogers, R., & Sewell, K. W. (1999). The R-CRAS and insanity evaluations: A re-examination of construct validity. *Behavioral Sciences and the Law, 17*, 181–194. doi:10.1002/(SICI)1099–0798(199904/06)17:2<181::AID-BSL338>3.0.CO;2–4

Rogers, R., Sewell, K. W., Cruise, K. R., Wang, E. W., & Ustad, K. L. (1998). The PAI and feigning: A cautionary note on its use in forensic-correctional settings. *Assessment, 5*, 399–405. doi:10.1177/107319119800500409

Rogers, R., Sewell, K. W., & Gillard, N. D. (2010). *Structured Interview of Reported Symptoms-2 (SIRS-2) and professional manual*. Lutz, FL: Psychological Assessment Resources.

Rogers, R., Sewell, K. W., Martin, M. A., & Vitacco, M. J. (2003). Detection of feigned mental disorders: A meta-analysis of the MMPI-2 and malingering. *Assessment, 10*, 160–177. doi:10.1177/1073191103010002007

Rogers, R., Sewell, K. W., Morey, L. C., & Ustad, K. L. (1996). Detection of feigned mental disorders on the Personality Assessment Inventory: A discriminant analysis. *Journal of Personality Assessment, 67,* 629–640. doi:10.1207/s15327752jpa6703_15

Rogers, R., & Shuman, D. W. (2000a). *Conducting insanity evaluations* (2nd ed.). New York: Guilford.

Rogers, R., & Shuman, D. W. (2000b). The "Mental Status at the Time of the Offense" measure: Its validation and admissibility under *Daubert. Journal of the American Academy of Psychiatry and Law, 28,* 23–28.

Rogers, R., & Shuman, D. W. (2005). *Fundamentals of forensic practice: Mental health and criminal law.* New York: Springer.

Sadoff, R. L., & Dattilio, F. M. (2011). Criminal responsibility. In E. Y. Drogin, F. M. Dattilio, R. L. Sadoff, T. G. Gutheil (Eds.), *Handbook of forensic assessment: Psychological and psychiatric perspectives* (pp. 121–144). Hoboken, NJ: Wiley. doi:10.1002/9781118093399.ch6

Specialty guidelines for forensic psychology. (2013). *American Psychologist, 68,* 7–19. doi:10.1037/a0029889

Spitzer, R. L., & Endicott, J. (1978). *Schedule of Affective Disorders and Schizophrenia* (3rd ed.). New York: Biometrics Research.

Weiner, I. B. (1998). Rorschach differentiation of schizophrenia and affective disorder. In G. P. Koocher, J. C., Norcross, & S. S. Hill, III (Eds.), *Psychologist's desk reference* (pp. 151–154). New York: Oxford University Press.

Yakush, B. A., & Wolbransky, M. (2013). Insanity and the definition of wrongfulness in California. *Journal of Forensic Psychology Practice, 13,* 355–372. doi:10.1080/15228932.2013.820992

6 The Clinical Assessment of Psychopathy

Michael J. Vitacco, Craig S. Neumann,
Lori T. Welch, and Peter Buckley

Psychopathy continues to be one of the most researched and discussed constructs in the fields of clinical psychology, forensic psychology, and psychiatry. Although psychopathy has different definitions depending on the article or chapter that one reads, we consider it most fittingly defined as a "constellation of affective, interpersonal, and behavioral characteristics, including egocentricity; impulsivity; irresponsibility; shallow emotions; lack of empathy, guilt, or remorse; lying; manipulativeness; and the persistent violation of social norms and expectations" (Hare, 1996, p. 25). Its rich history in the field of clinical and forensic psychopathy and psychiatry was codified in Cleckley's 1941 seminal book, *The Mask of Sanity*. Psychopathy is important in clinical and forensic work given its associations to aggression, violence, and recidivism. The prototypical psychopath has been described by Hart and Hare (1997) as "grandiose, arrogant, callous, superficial, and manipulative" (p. 22) as well as "short-tempered, unable to form strong emotional bonds with others, and lacking in empathy, guilt, or remorse" (p. 23). Psychopathy, in addition to its value in risk assessment, has demonstrated utility in a variety of settings including business settings and frequently researched even in college students. In business settings, psychopathy has been linked to unethical behavior and problematic work issues (Babiak & Hare, 2006; Babiak, Neumann, & Hare, 2010). In academic settings, psychopathy continues to be one of the most widely researched forensic constructs.

Since the original chapter published by Vitacco and Neumann (2008), there have been advances in how psychopathy is viewed as a result of research using brain imaging (Yang, Raine, & Colletti, 2010), measuring biomarkers (Shirtcliff et al., 2009), and studies aimed at expanding the focus to children and adolescents (Frick & White, 2008; Vitacco, Salekin, & Rogers, 2010). Psychopathy has continued to be used in court as a risk marker for subsequent violence; unfortunately, it has also gained some traction in insanity cases, as some have argued that psychopathy can be employed to buttress claims of nonresponsibility. Moreover, the Society for the Scientific Study of Psychopathy has eclipsed its 10-year anniversary and is now firmly ensconced as the premier organization for the dissemination of psychopathy research. There appears little doubt that psychopathy will continue to see significant clinical and research attention in the foreseeable future.

While the primary focus of this chapter is on practical issues concerning how psychopathy is used and misused in court proceedings, initially, we will review psychometric properties of the Psychopathy Checklist–Revised (PCL-R; Hare, 2003), and then describe its utility in court proceedings. We will emphasize two areas of the law: risk assessment and the insanity defense. In addition, we will discuss research looking at how views of psychopathy have been altered through the use of brain scans in legal cases, often inappropriately. We also devote attention to treatment of individuals with psychopathy. An emerging development in the area of psychopathy is a change in attitude indicating that, although individuals with psychopathy are difficult to treat, they are not untreatable. Such an attitude change is reflective in the volume of research studies devoted to the treatment of psychopathy and the application of established, empirically based treatment methodologies to the disorder. Finally, we touch on emerging data dealing with psychopathic traits in the corporate world. In the wake of Wall Street scandals, Ponzi schemes, and bank failings that cost U.S. citizens billions of dollars, the application of psychopathy to business settings appears especially timely and relevant.

Psychopathy and Risk Assessment

Psychopathy and Risk Assessment With Adolescents

Although evaluating psychopathy is controversial in adolescents, it continues to be employed to assess violence risk, and has evidenced moderate predictive power in the prediction of violence. Clinical assessment for potential risk of violence continues to be a primary reason that clinicians use Psychopathy Checklist instruments. In a recent study, Viljoen, McLachlan, and Vincent (2010) surveyed 199 forensic clinicians who conduct risk assessments with adults and adolescents. Their findings indicated that clinicians frequently used PCL measures in their risk assessments to address appropriate forensic questions (also see Lally, 2003). Forth and Book (2010) stated: "Research clearly demonstrates that psychopathic traits in children predict later antisocial behavior and aggression. Nevertheless, several aspects of this relationship require clarification" (p. 274). Although there are multiple instruments developed to assess psychopathic traits in youth, the Psychopathy Checklist: Youth Version (PCL:YV; Forth, Kosson, & Hare, 2003) remains the most researched and validated tool.

Several studies have specifically addressed the utility of the PCL:YV to predict violent and aggressive behavior. A meta-analysis by Edens, Campbell, and Weir (2007) sheds the most light on the relationship between psychopathy and violence risk. This analysis included 21 nonoverlapping studies and evaluated the relationship between Psychopathy Checklist measures and violent and nonviolent recidivism. Using a weighted r, the researchers reported significant correlations for both violent ($r_w = 0.25$) and general ($r_w = 0.24$) recidivism for PCL total score. Notably, and expectedly, PCL scores were not predictive of general or violent recidivism for female offenders. In addition, sexual recidivism ($r_w = 0.07$) was not significantly predicted by PCL scores. Even in a study where psychopathy predicted sexual offenses in juveniles, the authors cautioned against reading too much into the results, given the severity of the sample (Caldwell, Ziemke, & Vitacco, 2008).

Corrado, Vincent, Hart, and Cohen (2004) used the PCL:YV with 182 male adolescent offenders and followed them for almost 15 months. In this study, the PCL:YV was predictive of violent and nonviolent offenses. Likewise, Vincent, Odgers, McCormick, and Corrado (2008) found the PCL:YV predicted recidivism with adolescent males over a three-year follow-up, but not with adolescent females over the same follow-up period. An interesting finding is psychopathy possesses incremental validity over other disruptive behavior disorders, such as conduct disorder, in predicting violent behavior (Salekin, Leistico, Neumann, DiCicco, & Duros, 2004). Salekin (2008) also reported the PCL:YV and a self-report instrument of psychopathy demonstrated incremental validity for predicting aggression over 14 variables with empirical links to antisocial behavior. These studies provide evidence for the power of psychopathy as a predictor of risk in youth. One important caveat to the predictive power of psychopathy in youth is it should only be employed for relatively short-term predictions of risk, given the rapid changes occurring in adolescence. Relying on psychopathy measurements to make risk predictions for any time frame beyond six months is unwise, as there appears to be a precipitous drop in predictive power beyond that point. And, based on the research findings, the PCL:YV does not effectively predict violence or recidivism in females (Verona & Vitale, 2006). Future research needs to continue examining this relationship; however, extant data is not supportive of its use for risk assessment with adolescent females.

Callous traits are intertwined with psychopathy, especially as they are predictive of violence and associated with risk (Frick & White, 2008). Children and adolescents with high levels of callous traits show a distinct pattern of offending, including engaging in a greater amount of violence, having an earlier onset for offending behaviors, and engaging in more police contacts (Christian, Frick, Hill, Tyler, & Frazer, 1997). In fact, individuals with callous traits have a unique course that appears somewhat unrelated to environment and parenting. The distinct etiology and pathogenesis of these traits underscore the need for distinct interventions focused on youth psychopathy, especially the interpersonal and affective characteristics. Given the behavioral correlates of psychopathic traits in youth, it is important to consider how these traits influence clinical decisions, especially as they relate to transfer to adult court.

Transfer of a juvenile to adult court is a concept that is intermingled with violence risk assessment; however, risk assessment makes up only one area of an otherwise complicated and generally contentious process. Often the court wants to know the trajectory of an adolescent who committed a serious offense. However, as noted earlier, psychopathy risk assessments in adolescents are generally valid for around six months only, due to maturation and development. Transfer evaluations for moving a juvenile to adult court often look at three constructs: (a) risk for dangerousness, (b) sophistication-maturity, and (c) amenability to treatment (see Salekin & Grimes, 2008). Based on these criteria, psychopathy is frequently misused in transfer evaluations as it would be inappropriate to conclude any adolescent high on psychopathy measures should be transferred to adult court (see Salekin, Grimes, & Adams, Chapter 13 in this volume, for a review).

Psychopathy and Risk Assessment With Adults

There have been multiple meta-analyses focusing on the associations between psychopathy and aggressive and violent behavior. Two early meta-analyses reported very strong findings for the PCL. For instance, Salekin, Rogers, and Sewell (1996) completed a meta-analysis on 18 studies and found strong relations between the PCL-R and subsequent violence. They stated, "Despite its limitations, the PCL-R appears to be unparalleled as a measure for making risk assessments with white males" (p. 211). Hemphill, Hare, and Wong (1998) found the recidivism rate of inmates meeting the criteria for psychopathy to be three times higher than inmates who did not meet the criteria for psychopathy. These early meta-analyses highlighted the strength of the PCL-R in predicting violence risk; however, they were relatively limited in scope and number of studies.

By far, the most complete and comprehensive analysis to date was completed by Leistico, Salekin, DeCoster, and Rogers (2008). This analysis included 95 nonoverlapping studies with a total of 15,826 subjects, and it found strong relationships between psychopathy scores and various forms of violent behavior. Using the traditional two-factor PCL-R model along with the total score, the authors found 94 effects for total score, 54 for PCL Factor 1 (F1), and 53 for PCL Factor 2 (F2) in reporting on four types of outcomes: recidivism, institutional infractions, nonviolent offenses, and violent offenses. Cohen's ds for PCL total ranged from 0.59 (nonviolent offenses) to 0.47 (violent offenses), for F1 ranged from 0.41 (institutional infractions) to 0.37 (recidivism and nonviolent offenses), and for F2 ranged from 0.64 (recidivism) to 0.51 (institutional infractions). Notably, effect sizes for Caucasian participants were larger compared to non-Caucasians. The researchers, while espousing the strength and utility of the PCL in violence risk assessments, also encouraged researchers and clinicians to take a broader view of psychopathy and consider additional factors that underlie violent and aggressive behavior.

Although the PCL instruments have demonstrated some predictive utility across ethnic groups (Sullivan, Abramowitz, Lopez, & Kosson, 2006), it is important to note evidence from the Leistico et al. (2008) meta-analysis suggests the PCL-R demonstrated depreciation of effect sizes when used with ethnic minorities. More recently, Walsh (2013) conducted a study with 424 adult male inmates with a special look toward how ethnicity may affect the predictive power of the PCL-R in anticipating violence risk. Regarding his findings, Walsh stated, "Specifically, psychopathy was more strongly predictive among EA [European American] relative to AA [African American] men and was not predictive among LA [Latino American] men" (p. 306). As noted by Jackson, Neumann, and Vitacco (2007) the structure of the Psychopathy Checklist–Screening Version (PCL:SV) is consistent across Blacks and Whites. PCL-R instruments and their progeny have attenuated effect sizes and cross-ethnic variability that warrant consideration, if using the PCL-R with African Americans and Latino Americans. Researchers and clinicians should consider these findings when reporting their results, and consider how the ethnic make-up of the sample increased or decreased the predictive power of their findings. For example, clinicians must be mindful that a high score on a psychopathy measure for a minority does not hold the same predictive power as the same score would in an European American male. It is our concern that these implications are frequently glossed over and the relevance of psychopathy to a specific individual is not taken into account.

Psychopathy in the Courtroom

Psychopathy and the Legal Proceedings

Two early reviews (DeMatteo & Edens, 2006; Walsh & Walsh, 2006) considered how the PCL-R was used in court proceedings to aid in decision-making processes. As expected, and consistent with the literature, courts have relied on assessment of psychopathy to assist with making decisions regarding violence risk and dangerousness. Walsh and Walsh (2006) identified five areas where the PCL-R has been admitted to assist the trier of fact. These areas include sexual predator evaluations, parole hearings, capital cases, guilt determination, and a category defined as "other." A review by DeMatteo and Edens (2006) indicated "the courts are admitting evidence of the PCL-R with increasing regularity to address a variety of pretrial, trial-related, and dispositional issues in criminal and civil cases" (p. 214). As part of this increased reliance in civil and criminal cases, there have been clear cases of the PCL-R and its progeny being misused in court.

In examining cases identified by these reviews, several types of cases came to light. For example, the "other" category included civil commitment, transfer to adult court, sentencing, and competency to stand trial. The competency to stand trial case is especially noteworthy, given the absence of any empirically based evidence to use any instrument measuring psychopathy to decide adjudicative competence. In a competency case, two psychologists determined the defendant scored in the psychopathic range on the PCL-R, and thus concluded he was using his interpersonal skills to malinger and manipulate the court system. While psychopathy is associated with a glib and superficial interpersonal style, the construct of psychopathy should not be confused with malingering. Marion et al. (2013) reported on two studies that demonstrate that psychopathy should not be confused with either malingering or even the ability to successfully malinger—one study comprising students simulating mental illness, and the other study focusing on pretrial forensic patients. Results indicated individuals with higher psychopathic traits were no better at feigning mental illness than those with lower levels of these traits. Likewise, Kucharski, Duncan, Egan, and Falkenbach (2006) reported in their study of criminal defendants "that psychopathy is not a clinically useful indicator of malingering" (p. 633). In a sample of 55 prison inmates, Poythress, Edens, and Watkins (2001) reported small (0.14) to mild negative (-0.14) correlations between scales on the Psychopathic Personality Inventory and malingering instruments. Again, the results of this study failed to support the notion that individuals with higher psychopathy were more likely to malinger or more skilled at avoiding being detected at malingering.

Psychopathy in the Courtroom: Controversial Uses and Misuses

This section explores two issues where psychopathy has been applied to psycholegal situations with significant controversy: capital sentencing and addressing risk of sexual violence. Both of these have garnered considerable attention in the literature, likely a direct result of their controversial and often contentious nature. In both cases, a substantial divide exists in what many psychologists believe the assessment and identification of psychopathy can offer and what the law requires. In addition, we will look at other questionable uses of psychopathy, including attempting to apply psychopathy as an indicator of guilt or innocence.

Research has consistently identified problems linking the presence of psychopathy with violent behavior in inmates who are on death row. Cunningham (2006; see also Cunningham, Chapter 9 in this volume) effectively argued several factors related to dangerousness (in prison and beyond) have become outdated due to changes in sentencing laws (e.g., truth in sentencing). These changes have substantially decreased the likelihood an individual convicted of a homicide will get out early, thus decreasing the likelihood of community-based violent recidivism. In addition, violent behavior within maximum-security prisons, due to the presence of external controls, is generally minimal.

However, the law often considers dangerousness from a different perspective. In *Jurek v. Texas* (1976), the U.S. Supreme Court opined that juries in capital cases can recommend the death penalty based on future dangerousness. Unfortunately, the law has typically not assisted clinicians in this task by failing to definitively define dangerousness. In case they did, it would appear psychopathy would be a useful indicator of dangerousness. In *Burns v. Commonwealth* (2001), the Virginia Supreme Court rejected the notion that future dangerousness dealt with institutional aggression only. The court held that "determination of future dangerousness revolves around the individual defendant and a specific crime." The Virginia Supreme Court added that behavior in prison is not relevant to the determination of future dangerousness and was properly excluded by the trial court. As such, from a legal perspective, psychopathy may offer probative value to capital punishment decisions, even in light of empirical data indicating very low base rates of violence within maximum-security settings.

Another area of contention revolves around laws designed to civilly commit sex offenders. Seventeen states and the federal government have enacted laws that allow for the civil commitment of sex offenders for further treatment after they have served their initial prison sentences. Although these laws are remarkably costly and their constitutionality has been closely scrutinized, to date these laws have withstood legal challenges and continue to be implemented. For individuals who are typically referred to as sexually violent predators or persons (SVP) or sexually dangerous persons, psychopathy has become a central point of argument in many commitment hearings (Walsh & Walsh, 2006). One of the primary problems identified by researchers who study SVP evaluations is adversarial allegiance. Adversarial allegiance is a phenomenon whereby clinicians appear to have a bias toward the side that retains them. As such, the results of psychopathy measures often significantly different between defense and prosecution experts (Murrie, Boccaccini, Johnson, & Janke, 2008; Murrie et al., 2009). In a case law survey of the PCL-R in sex offender evaluations, DeMatteo et al. (2014) questioned the efficacy of the PCL-R in SVP proceedings, given the problems with its use. Saleh, Malin, Grudzinskas, and Vitacco (2010) advised caution when using psychopathy in sex offender evaluations, primarily due to the extraordinary weight afforded to the construct and its lack of consistent association with sexual reoffending.

Despite the issue with partisan allegiance, the issue does not appear to be the PCL-R itself; rather, it is the inappropriate use and scoring of the PCL-R in adversarial evaluations, like those done in cases of SVP. A large number of research studies have demonstrated reliable and valid scoring of the PCL-R and its progeny. Harris, Rice, and Cormier (2013) examined scores for 58 offenders where the scoring was completed by highly trained researchers or students under supervision from trained researchers, and found both acceptable reliability and validity. As shown by multiple studies where appropriate scoring protocols were employed, the PCL-R is a reliable and valid measure. Given that, the question turns to whether the PCL-R improves decision making regarding who is most likely to sexually offend. Although the literature is questionable on the use of the PCL-R in predicting offenses against children, it appears to have predictive power for sexual sadism (Mokros, Osterheider, Hucker, & Nitschke, 2011). There is also the description of "sexual psychopath" (Porter, Campbell, Woodworth, & Birt, 2002). These individuals frequently resort to violence to commit sexual offenses, appear less restrictive in victim typology, and often manifest a higher level of deviant responding to phallometric testing (Bradford, Greenberg, Larose, & Curry, 1998). There will be continued controversy surrounding the use of the PCL-R in SVP cases. However, evaluators who score the PCL-R must be properly trained and experienced. Moreover, they must be prepared to defend their training, credentials, and scoring during voir dire and cross-examination. It appears that, too frequently, clinicians are able to make unsubstantiated statements regarding psychopathy, and often those statements are not appropriately challenged (Vincent & Hart, 2012).

In other highly questionable uses, the PCL-R has been used as an indicator of guilt and innocence. In a Wisconsin case, the defense attempted to introduce the PCL-R to indicate the defendant was not the perpetrator of a sexual offense. This evidence was not allowed due to a lack of probative value. This appears to be the correct decision, as no data exists indicating the PCL-R is related to innocence or guilt of a particular defendant. Even in individuals Meloy (2002) referred to as "polymorphously perverse," describing maladaptive sexual interpersonal relationships, psychopathy would not be considered dispositive of a judicial outcome. In fact, relying on psychopathy as a means to make these determinations is blatantly unethical, as it goes well beyond the scope, purpose, and design of the instrument. In other words, the PCL-R should not be considered as a lie detector that can separate the "wheat from the chaff" with regards to innocence and guilt.

Psychopathy and the Insanity Defense

In addition to the aforementioned descriptions, psychopathy has been increasingly considered in insanity cases. This section will present two court cases where insanity arguments on the basis of psychopathy were advanced and ultimately rejected. In the latter part of this section, we will discuss arguments for and against the inclusion of psychopathy as a legal excuse for criminal behavior. Vitacco, Lishner, and Neumann (2012) discussed the case of Stephen Stanko. The case of Mr. Stanko provides an illustrative example of how psychopathy has been employed in insanity cases. Mr. Stanko killed two people and raped a teenage girl in South Carolina a year after serving 8.5 years of a 10-year prison sentence for charges of kidnapping and battery. Dr. Thomas Sachy, a forensic psychologist, testified that Mr. Stanko was a psychopath and stated: "People with damage to the frontal lobe are prone to fits of anger or violence. We know damage to this part of the brain takes the emergency brakes off" (see Jones, 2007, p. 91). Dr. Sachy subsequently opined that Mr. Stanko was not criminally responsible for the murders and rape (i.e., was insane). His findings, in his opinion, were supported by results from a Positron Emission Topography scan showing poorly developed frontal lobes. Mr. Stanko was convicted of first-degree murder and sentenced to death in the state of South Carolina. The use of psychopathy to support an insanity plea was rejected in this case.

A similar strategy was sought by attorneys in their defense of Brian Duggan. Mr. Duggan was already serving life sentences for two rapes and murders in the state of Illinois, when additional evidence linked him to an earlier murder of a 10-year-old girl. The defense argued that Dugan was born with psychopathy, and that because individuals with psychopathy have significant impairments in behavioral control, psychopathy should act as a mitigating factor in sentencing. Dr. Kent Kiehl, a neuroscientist, testified that Mr. Duggan scored 38.5 out of 40 on the PCL-R.

He also asserted that the results of a functional Magnetic Resonance Imaging study of Mr. Duggan were consistent with psychopathy. Dr. Kiehl testified to his findings in open court. Similar to the Stanko case, the jury ultimately rejected Kiel's argument and sentenced Mr. Duggan to death. Cases like the two aforementioned cases highlight the manner in which psychopathy has invaded the courtroom in death penalty cases.

There has been a small group of scholars who have argued for psychopathy to warrant consideration in criminal responsibility cases. Unfortunately, the moral deficits observed in individuals with psychopathy have been extrapolated to mean that they are unable to appreciate the wrongfulness of their criminal behavior, a key component of insanity defenses in the United States (American Law Institute, 1962, Section 401). For example, Morse (2008) argued that some individuals with high levels of psychopathy lack the moral rationality to be considered responsible for their criminal behavior. A similar argument was advanced by Glenn, Raine, and Laufer (2011) who posited that brain anomalies in areas implicated in moral decision making mitigate criminal responsibility in individuals with psychopathy. The proposition rests on the idea that high psychopathy individuals are not responsible for their brain deficits and, by extension, their so-called inability to appreciate their criminal behavior. Yet, this notion on the lack of responsibility in psychopathic offenders is contrary to empirical evidence regarding how psychopathic individuals generally conduct themselves.

In looking at how psychopathy is related to legal responsibility, Erickson and Vitacco (2012) point out several inconsistencies between the construct of psychopathy and a finding of insanity. It is clear that psychopaths lack in moral judgment and empathy. In fact, these are deficits considered core components of psychopathy (Hare, 2003). Despite these deficits in empathy and moral development, there has not been a consistent finding that individuals with high psychopathy scores lack rationality in the commission of crimes. In other words, their illegal actions are not related to irresistible impulses and individuals with psychopathy do not lack appreciation of right and wrong. Instead, they understand the difference between right and wrong, but choose to disregard it. Additionally, it is hard to ignore the instrumental violence (both planned and goal-directed) associated with psychopathy. In a study evaluating convicted murderers, Porter, Woodworth, Earle, Drugge, and Boer (2003) reported that the murders committed by psychopaths contained more "gratuitous and sadistic violence than nonpsychopathic offenders" (p. 459).

Postoffense behavior of psychopathic offenders is also noteworthy, although there have not been a lot of studies focusing on this specific legal aspect. Extant research finds individuals with greater levels of psychopathy underestimate their own level of instrumental violence in offenses and tend to omit important details when providing an account of their offense (Porter & Woodworth, 2007). A study with 546 Finnish offenders charged with murder revealed interesting results concerning offense and postoffense behavior (Häkkänen-Nyholm & Hare, 2009). Having a higher PCL-R score was related to having multiple victims, being under the influence of drugs, and killing someone who was not a family member. What is notable is that higher PCL-R scores were related to a number of postoffense behaviors, including denying the charges, leaving the scene, and being able to successfully plea to a lesser charge of manslaughter or involuntary manslaughter instead of murder. The ability of higher psychopathy individuals to have their charges reduced is especially noteworthy and speaks to the "manipulative and deceptive features that define the disorder" (Häkkänen-Nyholm & Hare, 2009, p. 770). The findings indicate that individuals with higher levels of psychopathy are better at self-presentation, even after being arrested for a significant criminal offense. In a study with similar findings, Porter, ten Brinke, and Wilson (2009) discovered high-psychopathy offenders in Canada were over two times more likely to convince boards to grant them conditional release after serving part of their prison sentence. The apparent ability to deceive remains intact, even after what most would consider emotionally charged, anxiety provoking situations.

When taken together, the results speak to not including psychopathy as a condition that would warrant a finding of nonresponsibility of criminal behavior. To the contrary, most jurisdictions view psychopathy as increasing risk, not decreasing responsibility. In closing this section, there appears to be little doubt that individuals with psychopathy have the necessary mens rea to be held accountable for their criminal behavior. As such, individuals with psychopathy (and no comorbid mental disorder) do not meet the criteria that are associated with a successful insanity defense.

Treatment of Psychopathy

In 2008, Wong and Hare published a treatment manual for individuals with psychopathy. This was one of the first publications specifically devoted to how a treatment program for psychopathy might be implemented. From a more global perspective, it signaled a major change in philosophy and provided hope that psychopaths could indeed be successfully treated. From a primarily cognitive behavioral perspective, this manual outlined specific treatment targets and strategies for assisting the psychopathic individual to make the necessary changes to reduce recidivism. This section will highlight recent studies focusing the treatment of adolescents and adults with psychopathic traits, and conclude with recommendations geared toward the successful treatment of these individuals. Notably, most of the research conducted on the treatment of psychopathy has focused on juvenile offenders.

In considering treatment approaches for psychopathy, many approaches have been applied. There has been a gradual, yet significant, shift from viewing these young people as untreatable "super predators" to recognizing the impact significant interventions can have on improving functioning. Salekin (2002) completed a meta-analysis that included 42 treatment studies of antisocial behavior and psychopathy and found clear improvements with a wide variety of treatments. With adolescents, groundbreaking work in treatment is occurring at the Mendota Juvenile Treatment Center (MJTC) in Madison, Wisconsin. In addition to being featured in multiple publications as a "gold standard" for the treatment of antisocial youth, the program was recently featured on *Nova*, a PBS series. This particular program was titled "The Mind of a Rampage Killer" and featured ways to reduce extreme violence, with an emphasis on youth violence and school shootings.

Data from MJTC support its mission of treating extremely violent and aggressive youth. For example, Caldwell (2011) found that males with high levels of psychopathic traits treated at MJTC had significantly fewer problems in the community when followed for an average of 54 months. Interestingly, there was a treatment by facet interaction, where the Interpersonal facet of psychopathy predicted initial poorer institutional adjustment, but also indicated greater improvement with treatment. The most notable finding was that treatment reduced institutional and community violence. This follows an earlier paper by Caldwell, Skeem, Salekin, and Van Rybroek (2006) where 141 juvenile offenders were followed for an average of two years postrelease. Adolescents who received intensive treatment had significantly lower levels of recidivism and violence. Similar results for intensive treatment were found for improved institutional behavior and treatment compliance (Caldwell, McCormick, Wolfe, & Umstead, 2012). Although the costs associated with intensive treatment are higher up front, there are clear long-term financial benefits that accompany significantly reduced recidivism. Caldwell, Vitacco, and Van Rybroek (2006) reported, "In this study, the initial per diem bed cost of the MJTC program, although substantial, was offset by the treatment effectiveness of the program, and generated an annual return on the marginal investment in treatment in excess of 130 percent per year over the 4.5 years of the study" (p. 164).

Despite the success generated by the MJTC program, there have not been large-scale controlled studies demonstrating consistent effectiveness of treatment for individuals with high psychopathy. In fact, beyond juvenile offenders, the literature for effective treatment with adult offenders is mixed, at best. There has been some thought given to applying Dialectical Behavior Therapy to individuals with psychopathic traits (Galietta & Rosenfeld, 2012) with a goal of improving their ability to regulate negative emotions (Casey, Rogers, Burns, & Yiend, 2013). Wilson and Tamatea (2013) challenged the widespread pessimism associated with the untreatability of psychopathy, but provided no data to rebut negative treatment assertions. Using data from the MacArthur Study of Mental Disorder and Violence, Skeem, Monahan, and Mulvey (2002) found that more treatment sessions led to better outcomes. Notably, most individuals in their study had relatively modest levels of psychopathy and were not considered extremely high risk. However, individuals with high Affective scores may be more resistant to participate in treatment. This was recently shown in sex offenders (Olver & Wong, 2011; Roche, Shoss, Pincus, & Ménard, 2011). In addition, sex offenders with high levels of psychopathy who drop out of treatment tend to recidivate faster than similar offenders who finish treatment (Langton, Barbaree, & Peacock, 2006).

In reviewing extant research, several things become apparent. As noted by Reidy, Kearns, and DeGue (2013) methodologically sound studies need to be conducted in order to consider issues related to the treatment of psychopathic offenders. This chapter does not take a pessimistic view of the treatment of individuals with high psychopathy; however, current data does not support the notion of effective treatment with adults with high levels of psychopathic traits. If there is reason to be hopeful, it lies with the idea that intensive intervention can be effective with adolescents, including the most severe cases. For adults, the data are mixed, with some evidence that treatment can be beneficial in reducing future violence (Wong, Gordon, Gu, Lewis, & Olver, 2012). From a policy perspective, it is necessary to underscore that treatments that are effective in reducing recidivism and violence ultimately save money, both in terms of incarcerations, but also the associated costs of violent crime. Treatment needs to be intense, with an appropriate number of sessions; it needs to focus on measurable behavioral characteristics, like violence reduction; and it needs to consider how the presence of Affective and Interpersonal traits may negatively impact treatment.

Psychopathic Individuals and Business

A recent focus of psychopathy research is how psychopathy presents in corporate settings. The "successful psychopath" has always drawn some interest from researchers, but it has recently garnered a dramatic increase in attention. This increased attention has uncovered a pattern of behavior exhibited by psychopathic bosses and employees that warrants discussion and hopefully will cultivate additional research.

How does psychopathy manifest at work? There appears to be multiple answers to that question that provide essential insights into the psychopathic personality. For instance, psychopathy was associated with bullying behavior in a large sample of white-collar workers in Australia. Not surprisingly, perceived unfairness accompanies the bullying behavior exhibited by psychopaths in the workplace (Boddy, 2011). In a sample of individuals from Britain, Boddy (2013) discovered that the presence of psychopathic individuals in the workplace led to counterproductive work and decreased employee feelings of well-being. Babiak, Neumann, and Hare (2010) found that psychopathy was associated with higher rankings of charisma and strategic thinking, but negatively related to work productivity and performance reviews. In other words, as the article title implied, such individuals were good at talking and "looking the part," but less skilled at actual work performance

Based on knowledge of corporate psychopathy, it has been argued that human resource managers should implement strategies to identify and avoid hiring these individuals (Marshall, Ashleigh, Baden, Ojiako, & Guidi, 2014). To that end, there is an instrument referred to as the B-Scan 360, which has demonstrated initial promise at identifying the corporate psychopath (Mathieu, Hare, Jones, Babiak, & Neumann, 2013). However, the authors cautioned that the results were preliminary and the instrument was not yet suitable for widespread use. Likewise, the Psychopathic Personality Inventory (Lilienfeld & Windows, 2005) demonstrated applicability in identifying subclinical psychopathy in a sample of Masters of Business students (Heinze, Allen, Magai, & Ritzier, 2010). It appears the development of a validated instrument would serve a purpose, as business schools may attract a greater number of individuals with higher levels of psychopathic traits (Wilson & McCarthy, 2011). Despite the promise of corporate psychopathy, Smith and Lilienfeld (2013) rightly cautioned against widespread adaptation of the concept of corporate psychopathy due to a lack of systematic research. They recommended research focused on assessing essential correlates and behaviors of psychopathic behavior in the workplace.

The Future of Psychopathy in Court Proceedings: Recommendations for Use

There has been continued growth in clinical and research applications of psychopathy over the previous decade. There is no reason to believe that the clinical use of psychopathy and its great research base will diminish. Yet, despite all this, there remains a need for great caution as the construct, likely as a result of its growing popularity, has been subjected to significant abuses. We conclude this chapter with a circumscribed list of future directions and cautions concerning psychopathy. These cautions will focus on both how the construct can be misused by individual practitioners, but also how the use of the construct should be carefully monitored by the field of forensic mental health to avoid more systematic abuses. To that end, we provide the following recommendations and cautions.

1. Psychopathy, as measured by the PCL-R, is a valid marker of risk and violent behavior in both adolescents and adults, particularly males. Yet, there is decreased predictive power with ethnic minorities. These findings warrant continued study and consideration when completing risk assessments.
2. Multiple numbers of self-report instruments have been developed to evaluate psychopathy. Many of these instruments have provided strong empirical results in controlled research studies. However, none of the self-report instruments have yet met the exacting standards required by the court for admission in legal proceedings focusing on violence risk. Substantially more research is required before courts should consider allowing psychopathy self-report instruments as evidence in legal proceedings.
3. The PCL-R has demonstrated consistent and valid findings in multiple research studies. Yet, in adversarial proceedings, it is frequently misused with egregious scoring errors. Clinicians employing the PCL-R should be subject to rigorous cross-examination to ferret out their methodology. Likewise, if possible, courts in search of justice would benefit from appointing independent experts to score psychopathy instruments to reduce the potential for bias.
4. Psychopathy has been misapplied to cases of competency to stand trial, insanity defense, and even the ultimate question of guilt. There is no valid empirical basis for the use of psychopathy in any of these forensic areas. Clinicians should rely only on established scientifically based rationales when applying the construct of psychopathy. Clinicians must be more mindful and aware of appropriate uses of the PCL-R. If they are not, their methodologies should not pass the bar set by either the Daubert or Frye standards (see Boccaccini, Kwartner, & Harris, Chapter 21 in this volume, for a discussion of these standards).
5. Uses of the PCL-R in capital punishment and SVP cases will remain controversial. Clinicians, knowing the ultimate consequences of the outcomes of these cases, must use the PCL-R (or any psychopathy instrument) with extreme caution and ensure their results are not misinterpreted. Although this sounds fundamental, a review of court cases involving the PCL-R makes it abundantly clear that appropriate scoring procedures are often not followed.
6. Psychopaths are difficult to treat, but evidence of untreatability is slowly waning. In fact, the myths have been strongly dispelled regarding young offenders with high levels of

psychopathic traits. Large-scale controlled studies are needed in which empirically based principles can be implemented and cross-tested across populations.

7. As noted throughout this chapter, psychopathy has continued to evidence tremendous growth in clinical and research areas. Yet, there remains much to do to continue to gain necessary understanding of this construct related to applied settings in law and in corporations. This chapter attempted to synthesize new information, yet many salient questions remain. Investigators are encouraged to engage in programmatic research to begin to confront unanswered questions concerning how psychopaths present in the boardroom.

8. Ethical clinicians are encouraged to remain up-to-date on scoring and continued education training. They should not base their scoring of the PCL-R to favor the side that hired them, even at the expense of upsetting those who contracted their professional services.

Case Example

Mr. Jones, a pseudonym, is a 34-year-old European-American male who was reared in an intact family. The youngest of three boys, Mr. Jones began engaging in criminal activity in early life. His first police contact occurred at 11 years of age for stealing from local stores. He also had police contact for fighting with other children. His behavior grew increasingly more violent. Notably, Mr. Jones was the only child in the family engaging in antisocial behavior. At the age of 14, Mr. Jones joined a street gang where he ran drugs and strong-armed for money and status. These behaviors resulted in two one-year stints in juvenile correctional facilities. At those facilities, Mr. Jones did not accrue serious disciplinary infractions. Instead, records indicate that he was implicated in gambling, running contraband, and initiating fights. However, he always managed to avoid formal charges.

After turning 18, Mr. Jones moved higher within the gang and assumed a leadership role. His criminal activity escalated along with his increased role in the gang. As in the juvenile facility, Mr. Jones avoided the most serious charges although he was under investigation for drive-by shootings and one murder. However, he was arrested for and convicted on two counts of battery and one count of strong-armed robbery. Once inside prison, Mr. Jones immediately began "working" the guards and trying to assume a position of power within the prison. He succeeded by relying on his gang ties. When he was two years into his five-year sentence an unannounced room search uncovered drugs, a cell phone, and homemade weapons (i.e., "shanks"). He was immediately transferred to a maximum-security facility and placed in the Special Housing Unit (SHU), where his access to visitors was restricted. He was released three years later.

Shortly after his release, Mr. Jones became enmeshed with gang life and reentered the lifestyle. Only six months after his release, he severely beat a woman who rebuffed his advances. However, relying on his gang ties, he fled the jurisdiction and went into hiding, vowing not to serve any time. Two months later he was a passenger in a car pulled over by the police for a traffic stop. A routine identification check revealed that Mr. Jones had an outstanding warrant. He was arrested and extradited to his home jurisdiction to face charges on battery and habitual criminality. Overall, he faced a 15-year prison sentence.

Once in the county jail, Mr. Jones' behavior became increasingly bizarre. He was observed "twirling" in his cell and responding loudly to internal stimuli. When questioned by the jail staff, Mr. Jones endorsed psychotic symptoms and was prescribed antipsychotic medications to alleviate his reported symptoms. During preliminary hearings, the judge ordered a competency-to-stand-trial evaluation and an insanity evaluation (to assess if he was responsible at the time of the crime). The psychologist opined that Mr. Jones was able to stand trial, but due to a psychotic disorder, was not responsible for severely beating the young lady. He was found not guilty by reason of mental disease or defect and admitted to a forensic mental health facility.

Inside the mental health facility, Mr. Jones began bragging about how he manipulated the system; he discussed in detail his elaborate ruse and how he "played" the dumb doctors and attempted to teach genuine patients how to manipulate the system. He was overly solicitous with staff and attempted to gain favorable treatment. He frequently encouraged staff to break the rules and smuggle him contraband. Moreover, he was highly litigious; he took fastidious notes and threatened to sue when staff denied his requests. When this strategy did not succeed, Mr. Jones began to cry when he felt mistreated. However, staff noted that neither the tears nor the underlying emotion appeared genuine. In addition, Mr. Jones vandalized the facility by breaking equipment in common areas used by all patients on the living unit.

During his stay, Mr. Jones was administered the PCL-R as part of a risk assessment. Mr. Jones scored 36 out of 40 on the PCL-R. The examiner noted the absence of any real emotion and that he lacked the ability to empathize with any of his victims or peers. Beyond his antisociality, Mr. Jones was glib, superficial, and tried to impress the examiner with his knowledge of psychology. In many ways, Mr. Jones presents as the prototypical psychopath with glibness and superficiality, impulsive lifestyle, and the willingness to engage in coercive antisocial behavior.

Summary

With continued advancements in the assessment of psychopathy in the next decade, there will likely continue to be contention in how psychopathy is used and misused, especially in adversarial proceedings. Despite this contention, it also appears clear the field of psychopathy will continue to undergo exciting developments over the next several years. Researchers will continue to focus on the utility of psychopathy measurement in the lab and in real-world settings. We hope this chapter was useful to both clinicians and researchers interested in psychopathy.

References

American Law Institute. (1962). *Model Penal Code: Proposed official draft*. Philadelphia: Author.

Babiak, P., & Hare, R. D. (2006). *Snakes in suits: When psychopaths go to work*. New York: Regan Books/Harper Collins.

Babiak, P., Neumann, C. S., & Hare, R. D. (2010). Corporate psychopathy: Talking the walk. *Behavioral Sciences & the Law, 28*, 174–193. doi: 10.1002/bsl.925

Boddy, C. R. (2011). Corporate psychopaths, bullying and unfair supervision in the workplace. *Journal of Business Ethics, 100*, 367–379. doi: 10.1007/s10551–010–0689–5

Boddy, C. R. (2013). Corporate psychopaths, conflict, employee affective well-being and counterproductive work behaviour. *Journal of Business Ethics*, 107–121. doi: 10.1007/s10551–013–1688–0

Burns v. Commonwealth, 541. E.2d 872, 878 (2001).

Caldwell, M. F. (2011). Treatment-related changes in behavioral outcomes of psychopathy facets in adolescent offenders. *Law and Human Behavior, 35*, 275–287. doi: 10.1007/s10979–010–9239-z

Caldwell, M. F., McCormick, D., Wolfe, J., & Umstead, D. (2012). Treatment-related changes in psychopathy features and behavior in adolescent offenders. *Criminal Justice and Behavior, 39*, 144–155. doi: 10.1177/0093854811429542

Caldwell, M. F., Skeem, J., Salekin, R., & Van Rybroek, G. (2006). Treatment response of adolescent offenders with psychopathy features: A 2-year follow-up. *Criminal Justice and Behavior, 33*, 571–596. doi: 10.1177/0093854806288176

Caldwell, M. F., Vitacco, M., & Van Rybroek, G. (2006). Are violent delinquents worth treating? A cost-benefit analysis. *Journal of Research in Crime and Delinquency, 43*, 148–168. doi: 10.1177/002242780 5280053

Caldwell, M. F., Ziemke, M. H., & Vitacco, M. J. (2008). An examination of the Sex Offender Registration and Notification Act as applied to juveniles: Evaluating the ability to predict sexual recidivism. *Psychology, Public Policy, and Law, 14*, 89–114. doi: 10.1037/a0013241

Casey, H., Rogers, R. D., Burns, T., & Yiend, J. (2013). Emotion regulation in psychopathy. *Biological Psychology, 92*, 541–548. doi: 10.1016/j.biopsycho.2012.06.011

Christian, R. E., Frick, P. J., Hill, N. L., Tyler, L., & Frazer, D. R. (1997). Psychopathy and conduct problems in children: II. Implications for subtyping children with conduct problems. *Journal of the American Academy of Child & Adolescent Psychiatry, 36*, 233–241. doi: 10.1097/00004583-199702000-00014

Cleckley, H. (1941). *The mask of sanity*. St. Louis, MO: Mosby.

Corrado, R., Vincent, G., Hart, S., & Cohen, I. (2004). Predictive validity of the Psychopathy Checklist: Youth Version for general and violent recidivism. *Behavioral Sciences & the Law, 22*, 5–22. doi: 10.1002/bsl.574

Cunningham, M. D. (2006). Dangerousness and death: A nexus in search of science and reason. *American Psychologist, 61*, 828–839. doi: 10.1037/0003–066X.61.8.828

DeMatteo, D., & Edens, J. (2006). The role and relevance of the Psychopathy Checklist–Revised in court: A case law survey of U.S. Courts (1991–2004). *Psychology, Public Policy, and Law, 12*, 214–241. doi: 10.1037/1076–8971.12.2.214

DeMatteo, D., Edens, J. F., Galloway, M., Cox, J., Smith, S., & Formon, D. (2014). The role and reliability of the Psychopathy Checklist–Revised in U.S. sexually violent predator evaluations: A case law survey. *Law and Human Behavior, 38*, 248–255. doi: 10.1037/lhb0000059

Edens, J. F., Campbell, J. S., & Weir, J. M. (2007). Youth psychopathy and criminal recidivism: A meta-analysis of the psychopathy checklist measures. *Law and Human Behavior, 31*, 53–75. doi: 10.1007/s10979–006–9019-y

Erickson, S. K., & Vitacco, M. J. (2012). Predators and punishment. *Psychology, Public Policy, and Law, 18*, 1-17. doi:10.1037/a0024607

Firestone, P., Bradford, J. M., Greenberg, D. M., Larose, M. R., & Curry, S. (1998). Homicidal and nonhomicidal child molesters: Psychological, phallometric, and criminal features. *Sexual Abuse: Journal of Research and Treatment, 10*, 305–323. doi: 10.1023/A:1022146105664

Forth, A. E., & Book, A. S. (2010). Psychopathic traits in children and adolescents: The relationship with antisocial behaviors and aggression. In R. T. Salekin & D. R. Lynam (Eds.), *Handbook of child and adolescent psychopathy* (pp. 251–283). New York: Guilford Press.

Forth, A., Kosson, D. S., & Hare, R. D. (2003). *Manual for the Psychopathy Checklist-Youth Version*. Toronto, ON: Multi-Health Systems.

Frick, P. J., & White, S. F. (2008). Research review: The importance of callous-unemotional traits for developmental models of aggressive and antisocial behavior. *Journal of Child Psychology and Psychiatry, 49*, 359–375. doi: 10.1111/j.1469–7610.2007.01862.x

Galietta, M., & Rosenfeld, B. (2012). Adapting Dialectical Behavior Therapy (DBT) for the treatment of psychopathy. *The International Journal of Forensic Mental Health, 11*, 325–335. doi: 10.1080/14999013.2012.746762

Glenn, A. L., Raine, A., & Laufer, W. S. (2011). Is it wrong to criminalize and punish psychopaths? *Emotion Review, 3*, 302-304. doi:10.1177/1754073911402372

Häkkänen-Nyholm, H., & Hare, R. (2009). Psychopathy, homicide, and the courts: Working the system. *Criminal Justice and Behavior, 36*, 761–777. doi: 10.1177/0093854809336946

Hare, R. D. (1996). Psychopathy: A clinical construct whose time has come. *Criminal Justice and Behavior, 23*, 25–54. doi: 10.1177/0093854896023001004

Hare, R. D. (2003). *Manual for the Psychopathy Checklist-Revised* (2nd ed.). Toronto: Multi-Health Systems.

Harris, G. T., Rice, M. E., & Cormier, C. A. (2013). Research and clinical scoring of the Psychopathy Checklist can show good agreement. *Criminal Justice and Behavior, 40*, 1349–1362. doi: 10.1177/0093854813492959

Hart, S., & Hare, R. (1997). Psychopathy: Assessment and association with criminal conduct. In D. Stoff, J. Breiling, & J. Maser (Eds.), *Handbook of antisocial behavior* (pp. 22–35). Hoboken, NJ: Wiley.

Heinze, P., Allen, R., Magai, C., & Ritzier, B. (2010). Let's get down to business: A validation study of the Psychopathic Personality Inventory among a sample of MBA students. *Journal of Personality Disorders, 24*, 487–498. doi: 10.1521/pedi.2010.24.4.487

Hemphill, J., Hare, R., & Wong, S. (1998). Psychopathy and recidivism: A review. *Legal and Criminological Psychology, 3*, 139–170. doi: 10.1111/j.2044–8333.1998.tb00355.x

Jackson, R., Neumann, C., & Vitacco, M. J. (2007). Impulsivity, anger, and psychopathy: The moderating effect of ethnicity. *Journal of Personality Disorders, 21*, 289–304. doi: 10.1521/pedi.2007.21.3.289

Jones, M. R. (2007). *Palmetto predators: Monsters among us*. Mount Pleasant, SC: History Press.

Jurek v. Texas 428 U.S. 262 (1976).

Kucharski, L., Duncan, S., Egan, S. S., & Falkenbach, D. M. (2006). Psychopathy and malingering of psychiatric disorder in criminal defendants. *Behavioral Sciences & the Law, 24*, 633–644. doi: 10.1002/bsl.661

Lally, S. (2003). What tests are acceptable for use in forensic evaluations? A survey of experts. *Professional Psychology: Research and Practice, 34*, 491–498. doi: 10.1037/0735–7028.34.5.491

Langton, C. M., Barbaree, H. E., Harkins, L., & Peacock, E. J. (2006). Sex offenders' response to treatment and its association with recidivism as a function of psychopathy. *Sexual Abuse: Journal of Research and Treatment*, *18*, 99–120. doi: 10.1007/s11194–006–9004–5

Leistico, A., Salekin, R., DeCoster, J., & Rogers, R. (2008). A large-scale meta-analysis relating the Hare measures of psychopathy to antisocial conduct. *Law and Human Behavior*, *32*(1), 28–45. doi: 10.1007/s10979–007–9096–6

Lilienfeld, S. O., & Windows, M. (2005). *Manual for the Psychopathy Personality Inventory-Revised*. Florida: Psychological Assessment Resources.

Marion, B. E., Sellbom, M., Salekin, R. T., Toomey, J. A., Kucharski, L., & Duncan, S. (2013). An examination of the association between psychopathy and dissimulation using the MMPI-2-RF validity scales. *Law and Human Behavior*, *37*, 219–230. doi: 10.1037/lhb0000008

Marshall, A. J., Ashleigh, M. J., Baden, D., Ojiako, U., & Guidi, M. D. (2014). Corporate psychopathy: Can 'search and destroy' and 'hearts and minds' military metaphors inspire HRM solutions? *Journal of Business Ethics*, published online, March 5, 2014. doi: 10.1007/s10551–014–2117–8

Mathieu, C., Hare, R. D., Jones, D. N., Babiak, P., & Neumann, C. S. (2013). Factor structure of the B-Scan 360: A measure of corporate psychopathy. *Psychological Assessment*, *25*, 288–293. doi: 10.1037/a0029262

Meloy, J. (2002). The 'polymorphously perverse' psychopath: Understanding a strong empirical relationship. *Bulletin of the Menninger Clinic*, *66*, 273–289. doi: 10.1521/bumc.66.3.273.23368

Mokros, A., Osterheider, M., Hucker, S. J., & Nitschke, J. (2011). Psychopathy and sexual sadism. *Law and Human Behavior*, *35*, 188–199. doi: 10.1007/s10979–010–9221–9

Morse, S. J. (2008). Psychopathy and criminal responsibility. *Neuroethics*, *1*, 205-212. doi:10.1007/s12152-008-9021-9

Murrie, D. C., Boccaccini, M. T., Johnson, J. T., & Janke, C. (2008). Does interrater (dis)agreement on Psychopathy Checklist scores in sexually violent predator trials suggest partisan allegiance in forensic evaluations? *Law and Human Behavior*, *32*, 352–362. doi: 10.1007/s10979–007–9097–5

Murrie, D. C., Boccaccini, M. T., Turner, D. B., Meeks, M., Woods, C., & Tussey, C. (2009). Rater (dis) agreement on risk assessment measures in sexually violent predator proceedings: Evidence of adversarial allegiance in forensic evaluation? *Psychology, Public Policy, and Law*, *15*, 19–53. doi: 10.1037/a0014897

Olver, M. E., & Wong, S. (2011). Predictors of sex offender treatment dropout: Psychopathy, sex offender risk, and responsivity implications. *Psychology, Crime & Law*, *17*, 457–471. doi: 10.1080/10683160903318876

Porter, S., Campbell, M., Woodworth, M., & Birt, A. R. (2002). A new psychological conceptualization of the sexual psychopath. In S. P. Shohov & S. P. Shohov (Eds.), *Advances in psychology research, Vol. 15* (pp. 51–65). Hauppauge, NY: Nova Science.

Porter, S., ten Brinke, L., & Wilson, K. (2009). Crime profiles and conditional release performance of psychopathic and non-psychopathic sexual offenders. *Legal and Criminological Psychology*, *14*, 109–118. doi: 10.1348/135532508X284310

Porter, S., & Woodworth, M. (2007). "I'm sorry I did it . . . but he started it": A comparison of the official and self-reported homicide descriptions of psychopaths and non-psychopaths. *Law and Human Behavior*, *31*, 91–107. doi: 10.1007/s10979–006–9033–0

Porter, S., Woodworth, M., Earle, J., Drugge, J., & Boer, D. (2003). Characteristics of sexual homicides committed by psychopathic and nonpsychopathic offenders. *Law And Human Behavior*, *27*(5), 459-470. doi:10.1023/A:1025461421791

Poythress, N. G., Edens, J. F., & Watkins, M. (2001). The relationship between psychopathic personality features and malingering symptoms of major mental illness. *Law and Human Behavior*, *25*, 567–582. doi: 10.1023/A:1012702223004

Reidy, D. E., Kearns, M. C., & DeGue, S. (2013). Reducing psychopathic violence: A review of the treatment literature. *Aggression and Violent Behavior*, *18*, 527–538. doi: 10.1016/j.avb.2013.07.008

Roche, M. J., Shoss, N. E., Pincus, A. L., & Ménard, K. S. (2011). Psychopathy moderates the relationship between time in treatment and levels of empathy in incarcerated male sexual offenders. *Sexual Abuse: Journal of Research and Treatment*, *23*, 171–192. doi: 10.1177/1079063211403161

Saleh, F. M., Malin, H., Grudzinskas, A. R., & Vitacco, M. J. (2010). Paraphilias with co-morbid psychopathy: The clinical and legal significance to sex offender assessments. *Behavioral Sciences & the Law*, *28*, 211–223. doi: 10.1002/bsl.933

Salekin, R. (2002). Psychopathy and therapeutic pessimism: Clinical lore or clinical reality? *Clinical Psychology Review*, *22*, 79–112. doi: 10.1016/S0272–7358(01)00083–6

Salekin, R. (2008). Psychopathy and recidivism from mid-adolescence to young adulthood: Cumulating legal problems and limiting life opportunities. *Journal of Abnormal Psychology, 117*, 386–395. doi: 10.1037/0021–843X.117.2.386

Salekin, R. J., & Grimes, R. D. (2008). Clinical forensic evaluations for juvenile transfer to adult criminal court. In R. Jackson (Ed.), *Learning forensic assessment* (pp. 313–346). New York: Routledge.

Salekin, R., Leistico, A., Neumann, C., DiCicco, T., & Duros, R. (2004). Psychopathy and comorbidity in a young offender sample: Taking a closer look at psychopathy's potential importance over disruptive behavior disorders. *Journal of Abnormal Psychology, 113*, 416–427. doi: 10.1037/0021–843X.113.3.416

Salekin, R., Rogers, R., & Sewell, K. (1996). A review and meta-analysis of the Psychopathy Checklist and Psychopathy Checklist–Revised: Predictive validity of dangerousness. *Clinical Psychology: Science and Practice, 3*, 203–215. doi: 10.1111/j.1468–2850.1996.tb00071.x

Shirtcliff, E. A., Vitacco, M. J., Graf, A. R., Gostisha, A. J., Merz, J. L., & Zahn-Waxler, C. (2009). Neurobiology of empathy and callousness: Implications for the development of antisocial behavior. *Behavioral Sciences & the Law, 27*, 137–171. doi: 10.1002/bsl.862

Skeem, J. L., Monahan, J., & Mulvey, E. P. (2002). Psychopathy, treatment involvement, and subsequent violence among civil psychiatric patients. *Law and Human Behavior, 26*, 577–603. doi: 10.1023/A:1020993916404

Smith, S., & Lilienfeld, S. O. (2013). Psychopathy in the workplace: The knowns and unknowns. *Aggression and Violent Behavior, 18*, 204–218. doi: 10.1016/j.avb.2012.11.007

Sullivan, E. A., Abramowitz, C. S., Lopez, M., & Kosson, D. S. (2006). Reliability and construct validity of the Psychopathy Checklist–Revised for Latino, European American, and African American male inmates. *Psychological Assessment, 18*, 382–392. doi: 10.1037/1040–3590.18.4.382

Verona, E., & Vitale, J. (2006). Psychopathy in women: Assessment, manifestations, and etiology. In C. J. Patrick (Ed.), *Handbook of psychopathy* (pp. 415–436). New York: Guilford Press.

Viljoen, J. L., McLachlan, K., & Vincent, G. M. (2010). Assessing violence risk and psychopathy in juvenile and adult offenders: A survey of clinical practices. *Assessment, 17*, 377–395. doi: 10.1177/1073191109359587

Vincent, G. M., & Hart, S. D. (2012). Legal uses and assessment of psychopathy. In D. Faust (Ed.), *Coping with psychiatric and psychological testimony: Based on the original work by Jay Ziskin* (6th ed., pp. 563–586). New York, NY: Oxford University Press.

Vincent, G. M., Odgers, C. L., McCormick, A. V., & Corrado, R. R. (2008). The PCL:YV and recidivism in male and female juveniles: A follow-up into young adulthood. *International Journal of Law and Psychiatry, 31*, 287–296. doi: 10.1016/j.ijlp.2008.04.012

Vitacco, M. J., Lishner, D., & Neumann, C. S. (2012). Psychopathy assessment. In H. Hakkanen-Nyholm & J. Nyholm (Eds.), *Psychopathy and the law: A practitioner's guide* (pp. 19–38). West Sussex, UK: Wiley.

Vitacco, M. J., & Neumann, C. S. (2008). The clinical assessment of psychopathy. In R. Jackson (Ed.), *Learning forensic assessment* (pp. 129-152). New York, NY: Routledge/Taylor & Francis Group.

Vitacco, M. J., Salekin, R. T., & Rogers, R. (2010). Forensic issues for child and adolescent psychopathy. In R. T. Salekin & D. R. Lynam (Eds.), *Handbook of child and adolescent psychopathy* (pp. 374–397). New York: Guilford Press.

Walsh, Z. (2013). Psychopathy and criminal violence: The moderating effect of ethnicity. *Law and Human Behavior, 37*, 303–311. doi: 10.1037/lhb0000017

Walsh, Z., & Walsh, T. (2006). The evidentiary introduction of Psychopathy Checklist–Revised assessed psychopathy in U.S. courts: Extent and appropriateness. *Law and Human Behavior, 38*, 493–507. doi: 10.1007/s10979–006–9042-z

Wilson, M., & McCarthy, K. (2011). Greed is good? Student disciplinary choice and self-reported psychopathy. *Personality and Individual Differences, 51*, 873–876. doi: 10.1016/j.paid.2011.07.028

Wilson, N. J., & Tamatea, A. (2013). Challenging the "urban myth" of psychopathy untreatability: The High-Risk Personality Programme. *Psychology, Crime & Law, 19*, 493–510. doi: 10.1080/1068316X.2013.758994

Wong, S. P., Gordon, A., Gu, D., Lewis, K., & Olver, M. E. (2012). The effectiveness of violence reduction treatment for psychopathic offenders: Empirical evidence and a treatment model. *International Journal of Forensic Mental Health, 11*, 336–349. doi: 10.1080/14999013.2012.746760

7   Violence Risk Assessment

Michelle R. Guyton and Rebecca L. Jackson

The criminal justice system has long recognized the value in being able to estimate the likelihood that someone may be violent or engage in criminal behavior. Prosecutors, judges, parole boards, and other legal bodies have a vested interest in determining whether offenders are likely to cause harm in the community and they look to mental health professionals to aid in these determinations. Several decades ago, mental health professionals were reluctant evaluators of risk, relying on little more than clinical intuition about whether a patient might be dangerous. Early studies showed that these idiosyncratic judgments of risk were not indicative of actual risk and spurred some to suggest that flipping a coin would result in the same accuracy in identifying individuals at risk for violence (Ennis & Litwack, 1974).

However, the technology of predicting violence has surged in the last 30 years, and several measures exist for assessing both general and specific types of violence. Most assessment devices now measure certain static, historical indicators that are empirically linked to violence and recidivism. Other tools also measure more dynamic, or changeable, variables that are also linked to violence. Yet the science of violence prediction remains far from perfect. Debates continue regarding how risk decisions should be made, the role of clinical judgment in risk decisions, and the use of group actuarial data applied to individual assessments of risk.

As the use and study of risk assessment methods became more prevalent, Heilbrun (1997) suggested that psychologists must first understand the question being asked. First, risk assessment may be used for *risk prediction* purposes, to answer a question such as "What is the likelihood that Mr. X will commit a violent crime if he is released on parole?" However, risk assessment may also be understood as *risk management*, where the question might be "What are Mr. X's risk factors for violence, and how can his treatment team reduce these?" With risk prediction, there is an emphasis on empirically identifying the variables, often of a static nature, that are the most highly linked to recidivism. Risk management is more likely to focus on dynamic, or changeable, variables that can be assessed repeatedly during a follow-up period. This strategy allows mental health professionals among others to intervene and reduce risk. It is vital that mental health professionals identify the risk question posed to them, because questions of prediction and management entail different assessment and communication strategies. However, these two risk referral questions are not orthogonal; often legal decision makers are asking for assistance in how to protect communities. Both risk prediction and management can aid these kinds of decisions. Many would agree that "the eventual aim of risk assessment is not to generate a label or a number for an individual but to manage and treat the person in a way that will minimize violence risk and other risk" (Snowden, Gray, Taylor, & Fitzgerald, 2009, p. 1525).

The purpose of this chapter is to review the evolution of risk assessment and the state-of-the-art measures currently available. Only the most validated measures are presented here while newer tools that have yet to be thoroughly studied are omitted. This chapter focuses mainly on risk judgments of criminal recidivism and violent behavior, with a lesser emphasis on risk for sexual recidivism. While important, judging risk for workplace violence, domestic violence, and with child and adolescent populations is beyond the scope of this chapter. In addition, we will review the nature of risk tools that utilize various assessment strategies, such as actuarial and structured professional judgment tools and what current research suggests regarding the utility of these methods. We will also consider the limitations of risk assessment technology and how the extant research guides our clinical assessments of violence. We will briefly consider how clinicians use risk assessment tools and various strategies for communicating risk level. Finally, we will end with a vignette demonstrating the complexity of determining violence risk.

History of Violence Prediction

Mental health professionals have been called upon for decades to provide opinions about a person's risk of harm to themselves or others. Such assessments are routinely used in hospitals and other settings to determine whether a person is at imminent risk for harm and requires detention and treatment to avoid harm (see Strachan, Chapter 19 in this volume). These forms of risk assessment are often brief, with quick decision making; however, clinicians have also been asked to estimate risk level over longer periods, such as when an individual is preparing to leave the hospital or prison. Just a few decades ago, clinicians relied on their own idiosyncratic ideas to forecast risk. These judgments were unstructured and unreliable, encouraging Harris and Hanson (2010) to liken clinicians to "fortune tellers."

The U.S. Supreme Court's 1966 decision in *Baxstrom v. Herold* provided a rare opportunity to empirically investigate mental health professionals' ability to accurately predict future violence using unstructured professional judgment. Briefly, Baxstrom, a prisoner in New York's correctional system, was diagnosed as mentally disordered and transferred to a hospital for the criminally insane shortly before the expiration of his prison term. Despite New York's commitment law requiring a judicial finding of dangerousness, Baxstrom was detained at the hospital past the expiration of his original prison sentence without a hearing to determine his present dangerousness. Consequently, Baxstrom argued his right to equal protection had been violated. The Court agreed, finding that Baxstrom's rights had been violated by committing him without benefit of current finding of dangerousness as was required under New York law for all other civil commitments. As a result of this case, 967 offenders being held in hospitals without judicial determinations of dangerousness were released to lower-security civil hospitals throughout New York State. This decision presented the unique opportunity to assess the accuracy of clinicians' predictions of dangerousness, as all offenders had been deemed too dangerous to be released from maximum security hospitals. Raising doubts about clinicians' expertise, these offenders had low rates of reoffending. Overall, only about 20% of the patients were subsequently violent according to hospital and police reports. In stark contrast to predictions of dangerousness, many patients did surprisingly well. For example, 176 patients (18%) were discharged to the community within one year of transfer, and only seven (less than 1%) were subsequently returned to secure hospitals. Over a 4.5 year period, more than half of the patients were discharged to the community and fewer than 3% returned to secure hospitals (Monahan & Steadman, 2001; Steadman & Cocozza, 1974).

Proving the Baxstrom cohort was not unique, Thornberry and Jacoby (1979) published a parallel study of 586 patients released from Pennsylvania's Fairview Institution (*Dixon v. Pennsylvania*, 1971). The three-year general recidivism rate was 23.7%. Only 14% of the total sample were rearrested or returned for a violent offense during the four-year follow-up period. Both the Baxstrom and Dixon studies served to highlight two very important findings: (a) the base rate of violence among presumably "dangerous" mentally disordered offenders was relatively low, and (b) clinicians greatly overestimated the likelihood of future violence.

Early research (Goldberg, 1968; Oskamp, 1965; Quinsey & Ambtman, 1979; Steadman & Cocozza, 1974; Thornberry & Jacoby, 1979) on predictive accuracy suggested that clinicians had no special abilities to predict violent behavior. In particular, these studies suggested that training, experience, and confidence of clinicians had very little effect on their accuracy. For example, Quinsey and Ambtman (1979) demonstrated that experienced psychiatrists' predictions of violence were no better than laypersons' (i.e., schoolteachers) judgments on the same patients. Goldberg's (1968) review of the prediction literature cited several studies echoing this result: the amount of professional training and experience does not relate to predictive accuracy. In addition, he noted that the addition of information was not related to the accuracy of participants' resulting inferences. While not specific to predictions of dangerousness, Oskamp (1965) reported that the confidence of decision makers increases with the amount of information available; however, the accuracy of those predictions does not improve.

The combined influence of these findings led many mental health professionals to conclude that accurate predictions of dangerousness simply cannot be accomplished. The American Psychiatric Association (1974) declared in its task force report, *Clinical Aspects of the Violent Individual*, "Psychiatric expertise in the prediction of dangerousness is not established and clinicians should avoid conclusory judgments in this regard" (p. 30).

Monahan's (1981) *The Clinical Prediction of Violent Behavior* discredited the tradition of clinical predictions of dangerousness. This monograph articulated the many inaccuracies of clinical predictions of violent behavior and concluded that "psychiatrists and psychologists are accurate in no more than one out of three predictions of violent behavior" (p. 47). This work had such a profound influence on attitudes towards predictions of violence that Otto (2001) ironically referred to it as "too good a book" on the fallibility of clinical judgment, noting that it essentially eliminated research interest in the topic for many years. Pessimism about dangerousness predictions deterred researchers from the topic. Practically speaking, prediction research was nonexistent in the 1980s.

Paradoxically, this same period saw U.S. courts deciding on many cases that directly expanded the clinician's role in assessing dangerous behavior. For example, the Supreme Court's decision in *Barefoot v. Estelle* (1983) served to make clinical predictions of dangerousness virtually unavoidable. In *Barefoot*, the petitioner objected to the use of psychiatrists' testimony regarding his risk for future dangerousness based on the assertion that psychiatrists were not competent to predict future violence. In conjunction with this case, the American Psychiatric Association (APA) submitted an amicus brief[1] detailing their view of expert psychological testimony regarding dangerousness. In its brief, the APA cited available research, including Monahan's (1981) analysis, and concluded that psychiatrists have no expertise in predicting future violence, asserting that laypersons could do as well as "experts." The brief informed the Court that psychiatrists were wrong more often than they were right and had a tendency to overpredict violence (Monahan, 1981; Steadman & Cocozza, 1974; Thornberry & Jacoby, 1979).

The Court's response to the brief and its resultant opinion were remarkable. Essentially, the Court ignored the APA's brief, stating that "we are [not] convinced that the view of the APA should be converted into a constitutional rule barring an entire category of expert testimony" (*Barefoot v. Estelle*, 1983, p. 3387) and that it was "not persuaded that such testimony is almost entirely unreliable" (p. 3398). Despite the "experts" themselves providing evidence of their inability to predict accurately, the Court found that "neither petitioner nor the Association suggests that psychiatrists are always wrong with respect to future dangerousness, only most of the time" (p. 3398). Bolstering their argument, the Court also relied on an earlier decision (*Addington v. Texas*, 1979) which reinforced the mental health professional's role in legal proceedings. *Addington*, in referring to commitment hearings, stated, "whether the individual is mentally ill and dangerous to either himself or others . . . turns on the meaning of the facts *which must be interpreted by expert psychiatrists and psychologists*" (*Addington v. Texas*, 1979, p. 1811; emphasis added). Ironically, the prediction of dangerous and violent behavior was becoming an integral and possibly unavoidable part of psychologists' and psychiatrists' duties, leaving mental health professionals ill-suited to perform the task demanded of them (Monahan et al., 2001).

The legal system has continued to evidence greater confidence than many mental health professionals in the accuracy of clinical predictions. The American Bar Association's (1998) position on psychologists' role in risk assessments is highlighted in its *National Benchbook on Psychiatric and Psychological Evidence and Testimony*, which states that "it [clinical evaluation] is the best information available. The alternative is to deprive fact finders, judges and jurors of the guidance and understanding that psychiatrists and psychologists can provide" (p. 49). Further, Monahan et al. (2001) asserted that the general expectation is that mental health professionals can distinguish with a reasonable degree of accuracy between dangerous and nondangerous persons with mental disorders (see also Monahan, 2000; Mossman, 2000). Clearly, mental health professionals have been drafted into the field of violence risk assessment, some more readily than others.

Legal trends continue to support the use of experts in forecasting violence risk despite any reluctance they exhibit. The APA submitted another amicus brief to the U.S. Supreme Court in the case of *U.S. v. Fields* (2007). In this case, Fields was convicted of seven felonies including escape from jail, firearm possession, and murder of his former girlfriend. Fields was sentenced to death due in part to the testimony of a psychiatrist who found him to be dangerous based on a review of the legal records and a discussion with the prosecutor about the case. He did not evaluate Fields or use any tools in formulating his risk opinion, and he denied knowledge of standard procedures for assessing risk. The APA brief documents the lengthy history of research on violence risk assessment and reviews evidence-based methods such as actuarial tools for violence risk prediction. The APA requested the court to apply *Daubert* standards[2] to the admission of psychiatric testimony regarding risk assessment. The Court acknowledged the APA brief but declined to require application of *Daubert* criteria to testimony about risk. The Court suggested that the issues raised by Fields and the APA brief were addressed in *Barefoot* and did not need to be addressed again. In a similar case in 2010, *Coble v. Texas*, the Court declined to hear the case. The outcomes of these cases suggest that the Court is reluctant to reopen the admissibility of risk assessment testimony or even comment on how such assessments are conducted.

The professionals who either choose or are mandated to perform risk assessments are expected to have the requisite knowledge and expertise (Monahan et al., 2001), despite their lack of formal training in risk assessment methods. As a result of this expectation, the question has shifted from (a) "Should mental health professionals be making violence predictions?" to (b) "How do mental health professionals improve their predictions of violence?" (see Grisso & Appelbaum, 1992).

When mental health professionals are involved with clients who have the potential for violence, clinicians may be concerned about the need to report such information given *Tarasoff*-directed legislation in most states.[3] In most instances of violence risk assessment as discussed in this chapter, however, the *Tarasoff* ruling does not apply. This legal standard requires that clinicians have a duty to report information to legal authorities and potential victims when a client is at imminent risk of violence. Most typically, violence risk assessments are evaluations of long-term violence risk potential. Rarely in this context are individuals evaluated for the probability of imminent harm. In addition, legally mandated evaluations of violence risk typically include little to no expectation of confidentiality. Finally, many violence risk assessments are requested by and submitted to legal bodies such as courts, state hospitals, and parole boards. Should an issue of imminent harm arise, these agencies have the ability to proceed to reduce the likelihood of harm. Interested readers are referred to Borum and Reddy (2001) for an excellent example of assessing violence risk for imminent harm in a clinical context.

Clinical Constructs of Dangerousness and Risk Assessment

Lessard v. Schmidt (1976) established the threshold for commitment when articulating that individuals must be dangerous to themselves or others in order to be eligible for commitment. The "dangerousness" standard for civil commitment presented many difficulties for forensic psychologists. The apparent purpose of this standard is to ensure that only the most dangerous individuals are deprived of their civil liberties and freedom. Steadman (2000) argued that this requirement increased the difficulty of the psychologist's task rather than clarifying it because the term *dangerous* does not have a clinically meaningful definition. Instead, he argued, the clinical parallel to the legal concept of dangerousness is *risk of future harm*. The difference between dangerous and risk of future harm can be construed as a categorical versus dimensional judgment. Determinations of dangerousness imply a binary (yes or no) outcome. In contrast, risk is inherently a probabilistic judgment that takes into considerations notions such as individual differences, contextual elements, severity of harm, imminence of harm, and so forth. Employing the term *risk assessment* reflects the belief that the psychologist's task is one of judging probabilities, not arriving at a dichotomous decision.

From one perspective, the distinction between binary predictions of dangerousness and probabilities of future violence is useful. Construing violence as a future probability allows us to focus on those variables that increase or decrease risk. It allows us to be flexible in our assessments and tailor treatment to those variables likely to decrease risk. From another perspective, this distinction is likely to be spurious in certain contexts. Regardless of the probabilistic nature of judgments, the resulting outcome remains categorical. In the case of civil commitment, most decisions are comprised of yes/no decisions about involuntary hospitalization.

The fact remains that legal decisions (i. e., commit or not to commit) and psycholegal constructs (i. e., gradations of risk) appear at odds. Hart (1998; see also Steadman, 2000) argued for the replacement of *dangerousness* with *risk assessment* by pointing out that dangerousness implies a stable attribute about an individual. He contended that research does not support a single, global trait that operates across all individuals and situations to produce violent behavior. Instead, he defined risk assessment as "the process of evaluating individuals to (1) characterize the likelihood they will commit acts of violence and (2) develop interventions to manage or reduce that likelihood" (p. 122). Further, he argued against the term *predicting violence* on similar grounds. Predicting violence implies that the clinician is a detached observer who makes predictions and subsequently takes no action based on the prediction. In stark contrast, the express purpose for making those predictions, according to Hart, is to facilitate management of the risk. This, some would argue, is what clinicians do best anyway (Kroner, 2005). In this manner, clinicians are active participants in the evaluation process and therefore, the term *risk assessment* most accurately captures current practice.

The term *risk assessment* will be employed throughout this review because it is the most comprehensive term used to describe psychologists' activities. As noted earlier, the first prong of this term relates to characterizing an individual's likelihood of future violence. In other words, risk assessment subsumes both predictions of dangerousness and predictions of violence. Likewise, a clinician's responsibility may involve estimates of risk that change over time, situations, and legal contexts. The use of the term *risk assessment* also addresses important situational variables.

Finally, Douglas and Skeem (2005) argued that the field should shift from a focus on long-term dangerousness predictions to including examination of dynamic risk variables. For example, many risk assessments focus on *risk status*, which indicates the level of risk posed by an individual compared to others (Gardner, Lidz, Mulvey, & Shaw, 1996). However, this provides little assistance in determining how and when a high-risk person is likely to reoffend. This latter idea is conceptualized as *risk state*, and is a more dynamic concept that can be influenced by a wide variety of changeable factors (Skeem & Mulvey, 2002). Whether to focus on long-term risk or more imminent risk is largely determined by the referral question. Instruments used to assess both long-term as well as shorter-term risk levels are presented.

Reviving Risk Assessment Research

Due to the clinical concerns with unstructured clinical judgment in forecasting risk and the advent of greater empirical examination of risk factors for violence, there has been an evolution in risk assessment technology. Grisso and Appelbaum (1992) advocated a paradigm shift in the way psychologists viewed the risk assessment process. Instead of arguing the merits of psychologists' involvement, they encouraged programmatic research aimed at increasing the validity of the assessments. Since then, there has been an explosion of risk tool development. These tools vary in their methodology and emphasis on clinical input. Skeem and Monahan (2011) suggest that risk assessment tools lie upon a "continuum of rule-based structure." At one end are unstructured clinical approaches and at the other end completely structured approaches that are mechanical in nature. Between these two poles, a few different approaches exist that vary in the amount of structure applied to identify, measure, and combine risk factors into an estimate of future violence risk. Completely unstructured professional judgment allows the clinician to identify and measure the salient risk factors, and combine them to produce a risk estimate. As we have reviewed, this process is less than reliable or accurate. Newer approaches have sought to link this process to known correlates of violence; they vary in the amount that a clinician is allowed to integrate the information and determine the person's relative risk based on this summary of data. At the far end of the structured continuum are actuarial approaches that identify specific risk factors, and give specific methods for measuring the items and combining them to produce a final risk estimate. This approach is fairly mechanistic and allows very little clinical judgment (Quinsey, Harris, Rice, & Cormier, 2006). This model articulates the position that clinicians can be inaccurate and prone to error when making decisions, and therefore should be eliminated from the equation. In between these two poles, other measures allow varying amounts of clinical decision making to structure how risk factors are combined or what kind of risk judgment should be made from the evidence at hand. We will spend some time reviewing these different methodologies, how they work, and what evidence supports their use. Monahan and others have further suggested greater specificity is needed in defining violence (Monahan, 1981; Mulvey, Shaw, & Lidz, 1994). Researchers, they argued, should specifically classify what behaviors are considered violent rather than assuming everyone agrees on the definition of violent behaviors. For example, some studies employ definitions of violence that include verbal threats and aggression whereas other studies focus only on physical aspects of aggression where contact is made between perpetrator and victim. As prevalence rates of verbal and physical aggression differ, studies must employ specific definitions of violence so that their relevance to legal statutes and questions can be determined. Also, the time frame for violence risk should be clearly identified because different elements of risk are involved in immediate versus long-term risk (Douglas & Skeem, 2005).

Methodological advances have also been partially responsible for the revitalization of risk assessment research. Several researchers (Monahan, 1981; Mossman, 1994; Rice & Harris, 1995; Douglas, Ogloff, Nicholls, & Grant, 1999) have noted problems with the traditional utility estimates of prediction accuracy, such as positive predictive power, negative predictive power, sensitivity, and specificity. These indices are influenced by base rates of behavior and clinicians' preferred errors, i.e., whether they are more or less conservative in predicting violence. Douglas et al. (1999) noted that traditional 2×2 contingency tables perform maximally at base rates of the criterion at 50%. In most research of violent recidivism, base rates are often far less than 50%. When the base rates deviate from 50%, this introduces greater likelihood for error in making judgments. To counteract this sensitivity to base rates, Mossman (1994; see also Douglas et al., 1999; Rice & Harris, 1995; Swets, 1996) advocated for the adoption of Receiver (or Relative; Quinsey et al., 2006) Operating Characteristic (ROC) analysis for risk prediction research, noting that it is less influenced by base rates than traditional indices. Since Mossman's (1994) review and reanalysis of risk prediction research using ROC analysis, it has become the accuracy index of choice among violence researchers.

The ROC represents a ratio of false positives to accurate identifications by plotting false alarms on the *x*-axis and hit rate on the *y*-axis. ROCs produce a statistical index called the *Area Under the Curve* (AUC). AUCs can range from 0 (perfectly wrong predictions) to 1.0 (perfect accuracy). AUCs of .5 indicate accuracy at chance levels (see Figure 7.1). Significance testing is often

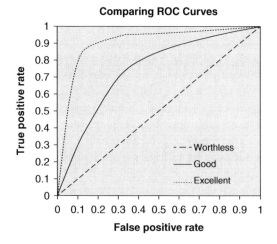

Figure 7.1 Comparing ROC curves
Source: The Area Under an ROC Curve, http://gim.unmc.edu/dxtests/ROC3.htm (Tape, n.d.)

employed to determine if the difference between the obtained AUC and chance (AUC = .50) is significantly different. The AUC value can be defined as the probability that a randomly chosen, actually violent person, will score higher on the measure than a randomly chosen nonviolent person (Douglas et al., 1999; Mossman, 1994; Rice & Harris, 1995). In terms of unaided clinical decision making, the value of AUC equals the likelihood that a clinician would rate a randomly selected violent person as more likely to be violent than a randomly selected nonviolent person. Douglas et al. (1999) reported that AUCs of .70 and above are considered large. It is noted that even when an AUC is considered large, it is far from perfect.

Importantly, both utility estimates and ROC analyses are limited in their applicability to individual decisions. As outlined previously, utility estimates are vulnerable to fluctuations in base rate. ROC analysis partially controls for this phenomenon and instead yields an "overall" AUC. Individual cut points are absent, eliminating the ability to examine a clinician's or a test's performance at different cut scores. In other words, Positive Predictive Power (PPP) and Negative Predictive Power (NPP) are not discerned from ROC analysis. In making decisions regarding future violence, and reporting the associated error rates of these predictions, PPP and NPP are perhaps of paramount importance. Further, estimates of risk yielded from ROC analyses refer to groups of individuals, not individuals per se. For example, when interpreting a score on an actuarial instrument that equates with a, for example, 61% recidivism rate, the appropriate interpretation is "of individuals who scored similarly on this instrument, 61% were known to commit another violent act." Note that this interpretation is not equivalent to testifying that the individual you examined has a 61% chance of violent recidivism. Indeed, estimates derived from ROC analysis remain limited in their application to individual cases.

The following sections review the voluminous research in actuarial and clinical predictions of violence. Actuarial scales are discussed first, followed by consideration of structured professional judgment. In most cases, ROC analyses were utilized and AUCs reported. When appropriate, this review also reports traditional analyses of predictive accuracy such as correlations and 2 × 2 contingency tables.

Actuarial Instruments

As an early and vocal advocate of statistical methods of predictions, Meehl (1954/1996) argued for the superiority of actuarial over clinical predictions of psychological and behavioral phenomena. Garb and Boyle (2003) demonstrated that unstructured clinical judgment is notably prone to error across all contexts of psychologists' decision making. Monahan (1981) applied this idea specifically to predictions of violent behavior, demonstrating that clinical predictions of future violence were wrong more often than not. His 1981 monograph influenced many professionals and researchers, who began to investigate the feasibility of actuarial (i.e., statistical) predictions of violence. Early attempts by Quinsey, Pruesse, and Fernley (1975; also Pruesse & Quinsey, 1977) to apply actuarial techniques to clinical predictions of violence found mixed results. In a sample of 60 involuntary psychiatric patients who were discharged to the community, 18 (30.0%) were rearrested during a 39-month period. Quinsey and colleagues constructed a scale in which one point was assigned for each of the variables that discriminated between successes and failure. The variables included: (a) diagnosis of a personality disorder, (b) age < 31 at discharge, (c) < 5 years spent in psychiatric hospitals, (d) admission offense not against persons, and (e) separation from a parent before age 16. This scale classified the patients with 78% accuracy. In an attempt to cross-validate this actuarial scale, Pruesse and Quinsey (1977) followed up 206 patients released from a maximum-security hospital. Accuracy of prediction dropped from 78% to 65%. Such "shrinkage" of results is not uncommon when cross-validating a measure on a new sample (Silver, Smith, & Banks, 2000).

Harris, Rice, Quinsey, and colleagues have been instrumental in the development of statistical techniques aimed at the prediction of violent behavior. As the actuarial method's most vocal proponents (Quinsey et al., 2006), they have developed the most popular actuarial instrument used to predict violent behavior, the Violence Risk Appraisal Guide (VRAG; Harris, Rice, & Quinsey, 1993).

It is worth mentioning here that items are chosen for inclusion in actuarial risk assessment schemes based on their empirical relationship with the outcome of interest (i.e., violence). Items included are not assumed to "cause" violence or serve an explanatory function, instead they are merely statistically associated with violence. It is quite possible, then, that the identified risk factors for violence are proxy variables for other more important, but as of yet unidentified, risk factors.

Violence Risk Appraisal Guide (VRAG)

Construction of the VRAG

The purpose of the VRAG is to predict long-term violence risk among individuals with prior violent episodes. The VRAG was constructed based on samples of mentally disordered offenders who had been previously followed by the researchers (Harris et al., 1993). The combined validation sample consisted of 685 men, of whom 618 had an opportunity to recidivate. The sample was derived from previous studies of Oak Ridge psychiatric patients (Rice, Harris, Lang, & Bell, 1990; Rice, Harris, & Cormier, 1992) and included violent and sexually violent offenders. Offenders in the Rice et al. (1990) study consisted of insanity acquittees and matched comparisons who had spent at least one day in Oak Ridge between the years 1975 and 1981. The offenders in the Rice et al. (1992) study included patients who spent at least two years in the therapeutic community program during the period between 1968 and 1978. While acknowledging that the construction sample consisted of men who were psychiatric patients, the authors assured "that the instrument would work as well with mentally disordered offenders as with offenders free of serious mental disorder" (Quinsey, Harris, Rice, & Cormier, 1998, p. 145).

For the purposes of scale development, the authors defined the outcome variable as any new criminal charge for a violent offense or incident that could have resulted in a criminal charge if committed in the community. Violent offenses that were included ranged in severity from assault to homicide. Institutional files and other official records were examined for incidents of violent behavior that did or would have resulted in criminal charges if committed in the community. The occurrence of violent offenses was then dichotomized for purposes of VRAG validation; the resultant outcome variable was at least one violent offense. The authors collected approximately 50 predictor variables on each of the individuals. The variables were selected on the basis of their empirical relationship to violence or the authors' curiosity about their relationship. These variables included sociodemographic variables, childhood and adult adjustment variables, characteristics of the index offense, and psychological assessment variables, including IQ. Using discriminant function analysis, 12 variables were chosen based on their independent contribution to predicting violence (Harris et al., 1993). Each item is scored according to a weighting procedure based on how different the individual is from the base rate for that item in the validation sample. Therefore, each item has its own range of scores, with total scores ranging from −26 to +38. Scores are then used to categorize individuals into "bins," where each bin is associated with a particular risk for violent recidivism.

Validation of the VRAG

Harris et al. (1993) reported a correlation between total VRAG scores and violent recidivism of .44 ($p < .01$). The AUC in the construction sample was .76, indicating that randomly drawing a violent and a nonviolent patient will result in the violent patient achieving the higher VRAG score 76% of the time. Harris et al. reported no optimal cut score in applying the VRAG, but instead assigned probabilities of risk to each VRAG category. Quinsey et al. (1998) also investigated whether individuals scoring in the highest category were also those individuals likely to commit the most violent offenses. The seriousness of each offender's act was weakly related to VRAG score ($r = .18$, $p < .01$). In cross-validating the VRAG with a sample of sex offenders, Rice and Harris (1997) utilized a sample of 159 sex offenders who were not part of the initial construction sample. Follow-up data included incidents of violence as well as sexual violence. With sex offenders, the VRAG predicted general violence as well as it did in the construction sample. Total scores on the VRAG correlated .47 (compared with .44 in the construction sample) with violent recidivism. The relationship between VRAG scores and sexual recidivism was weak ($r = .20$). The use of total scores does not allow for inspection of the VRAG's performance at various cut points.

In their updated treatise on the VRAG, Quinsey et al. (2006) documented the ability of their measure to judge risk among mentally disordered offenders, fire setters, and sex offenders released from Oak Ridge. A multitude of researchers have studied the VRAG alone (Harris, Rice, & Camilleri, 2004; Hilton & Simmons, 2001; Hilton, Harris, & Rice, 2001; Loza, Villaneuve, & Loza-Fanous, 2002) or in comparison with other risk assessment devices (Barbaree, Seto, Langton, & Peacock, 2001; Glover, Nicholson, Hemmati, Bernfeld, & Quinsey, 2002) in both forensic psychiatric and criminal populations. Kroner and Mills (2001), for example, compared the predictive abilities of the VRAG and four other measures in predicting both institutional misconduct and recidivism in a sample of male violent, nonsexual, offenders. The other four measures included were the Historical/Clinical/Risk–20 (HCR-20, extensively reviewed later in this chapter), the Psychopathy Checklist–Revised (PCL-R; Hare, 2003; see review by Vitacco, Neumann, Welch, & Buckley, Chapter 6 in this volume), the Level of Service Inventory–Revised (LSI-R; Andrews & Bonta, 2003), and the Lifestyle Criminality Screening Form (Walters, White, & Denney, 1991). Overall, there were no differences between any of the measures in ability to predict infractions and recidivism. There was a nonsignificant trend towards greater accuracy for the VRAG in classifying minor disciplinary infractions and nonviolent recidivism.

In a study of four separate Canadian forensic samples, Harris et al. (2003) compared the VRAG to three other risk assessment measures commonly used with sex offenders: the Sex Offender Risk Appraisal Guide (SORAG; Quinsey et al., 1998; reviewed briefly later in this chapter), the Rapid Risk Assessment for Sex Offender Recidivism (RRASOR; Hanson, 1997), and the Static-99 (Hanson & Thornton, 1999). The general trend showed that the VRAG and

SORAG outperformed the other two measures. Across all samples, the AUC for the VRAG in prediction of violent recidivism was .73, and for sexual recidivism was .65.

While the VRAG has demonstrated utility with a variety of groups, it works less well with populations that differ from the original validation samples. For example, several studies have shown that the VRAG is less useful when predicting violence among women. For example, Hastings, Krishnan, Tangney, and Stuewig (2011) scored the VRAG with a group of male and female jail inmates. Among males, the VRAG significantly predicted both institutional misconduct and recidivism in the first year after release. However, the VRAG was not significantly predictive of either outcome for female inmates. The VRAG did show an ability to predict recidivism in a group of female jail inmates who were followed over an average of eight years (Eisenbarth, Osterheider, Nedopil, & Stadtland, 2012). The VRAG has also shown reduced utility in predicting institutional misconduct (Endrass, Rossegger, Frischknecht, Noll, & Urbaniok, 2008; Garrett, 2012; Hastings et al., 2011).

Recently, the VRAG authors reevaluated the predictive abilities of this instrument using updated recidivism data for study subjects in three earlier VRAG follow-up studies (Rice, Harris, & Lang, 2013). Rice et al. expanded the variety of outcome variables assessed as well as significantly increased the length of the follow-up period. One VRAG item demonstrated inadequate predictive value (any female victim) and another was shown to be less applicable for sexual offense (victim injury). In addition, the authors sought to reduce the complexity of scoring the VRAG by removing the two items that required diagnostic decision making. The rationale for this was that these items required information that may not be easily accessible in legal and institutional files. Additionally, given the lengthy process of administering the PCL-R, this VRAG item was reformulated into an Antisociality item that reflects the more deviant lifestyle aspects captured in Facet 4 of the PCL-R. These items are more easily rated than the personality-based aspects of the measure. The authors suggest that the revised measure, the VRAG-R, is more time- and cost-effective in that it can be used by nonclinicians in legal settings without sacrificing its predictive utility. Until additional research has been completed validating this measure, clinicians should utilize this measure with caution.

SORAG

The SORAG (Quinsey et al., 1998), an extension of the VRAG, was developed to estimate the risk of violence among individuals who have committed sex offenses in their past. The SORAG incorporates 10 identical items from the VRAG and adds four items specific to sex offending. Given the large overlap with the VRAG, the two are highly correlated (Barbaree et al., 2001). The SORAG has demonstrated high accuracy in predicting violent recidivism and a slightly smaller yet still respectable ability to predict sexual recidivism (Barbaree et al., 2001; Harris, Rice, Quinsey, Lalumière, Boer, & Lang, 2003).

Summary and Critique of Actuarial Research

This brief review highlights the advances in actuarial predictions of violence. Actuarial methods have been shown to have better-than-chance predictive accuracy for any type of recidivistic behavior. When a clinician is asked to estimate the likelihood that a particular individual will commit any type of offense at some point in the future, actuarial methods such as the VRAG are likely to be helpful. Quinsey et al. (1998) concluded that the "VRAG performed exactly as one would have wished" (p. 150). Depending upon your view, this conclusion could be considered a marked overstatement. High scores suggest an increased probability of violence; they do not indicate certainty and they do not address the level of violence potential. Predicted violence can range from assault without bodily contact to murder. It is unknown how helpful VRAG predictions are to the clinician faced with making decisions regarding commitment to or release from a secure hospital. Litwack (2001) cogently argued this point in declaring that even a 100% chance of committing a simple assault does not necessarily justify secure commitment. Hart (2003) underscores these arguments and describes another concern: potential bias by varying definitions of the criterion behavior. In discussing how various actuarial tools are used to predict violence potential, he notes that the definition of violence used in the measure may not be the same level of violence that clinicians and legal bodies are interested in preventing. For example, noncontact sexual offenses (i.e., voyeurism, exhibitionism, etc.) may be excluded from statutory definitions of sexual violence but included as part of the predicted sexual violence. This imprecision introduces additional error into the prediction scheme.

Another concern regarding the widespread usage of actuarial risk assessments is the extent to which error rates reported for the aggregate data are transferable to individual prediction. Berlin and colleagues noted that all individuals considered high risk are not all equally likely to engage in violence (Berlin, Galbreath, Geary, & McGlone, 2003). For example, if the high-risk group has a 60% chance of recidivating, one individual's true risk might be 80% while another individual's true risk is 40%. Actuarial devices do not allow the clinician to distinguish between the two, thus contributing to the error inherent in any prediction. Berlin et al. (2003) further argued that the confidence intervals applied to aggregate data are not generalizable to individual cases: "actuarials can potentially be very misleading if one incorrectly attributes the overall risk of a previously screened group to a specific individual in it" (p. 381).

An additional consideration with the VRAG and all actuarial instruments is their sole focus on violence prediction, with no consideration of treatment or management. Actuarial tools define *risk status*, which compares individuals against others in terms of potential violence risk (Douglas & Skeem, 2005). Risk status describes the individual's long-term, nonchanging risk level and is often of great value to legal decision-making bodies. However, clinicians involved in the daily management of these individuals are more interested in determining *risk state*, which includes all factors that both contribute to and reduce violence potential. These authors argue that the violence risk a person poses is not static and inflexible, but varies as a function of his or her current levels of particular risk factors. This suggests an increased attention to dynamic, or changeable, risk factors with the assumption that targeting dynamic risk factors for change may reduce an individual's violence risk. Actuarials typically rely on static risk factors that, by definition, do not change. The exclusive use of static variables is inconsistent with comprehensive risk management. While problematic in certain contexts, their narrow focus is not necessarily a limitation when the sole purpose of the risk assessment is to determine likelihood of future violence over a long period of time, or when used in conjunction with other data as part of a larger evaluation of violence risk and management.

Supporters of the actuarial approach to risk assessment vary in their enthusiasm. Webster, Harris, Rice, Cormier, and Quinsey (1994) advocated that actuarial techniques be used as the principal, but not exclusive, method of rendering clinical decisions. They recommended that clinicians may want to adjust actuarial estimates of risk within a narrow range when there are compelling circumstances to do so. These authors have recently modified their recommendation and currently are advocating for the exclusive use of actuarial methods. They justify this position by stating that "actuarial methods are too good and clinical judgment too poor to risk contaminating the former with the latter" (Quinsey, et al., 1998, p. 171). In their more recent text, Quinsey et al. (2006) review the literature on purely clinical predictions of dangerousness and provide a less harsh conclusion: "there is still no evidence of expertise in unaided clinical judgment" (p. 66). In contrast, Hanson (2000; see also Hanson & Harris, 2000; Walters, 2006) argued for a more balanced approach, suggesting that evaluators use both clinical data (e.g., dynamic variables) and actuarial findings.

In response to many of the criticisms of actuarial models, Steadman et al. (2000) created the Iterative Classification Tree (ICT) model. Although actuarial in nature, the ICT addresses many of the shortcomings commonly associated with the use of actuarial methods.

ICT Model

Construction of the ICT

Steadman et al. (2000) note that despite actuarial tools demonstrating better accuracy than unstructured clinical judgment, they have not been readily accepted by practicing clinicians. They argue that the singular algorithm used by most actuarial scales (typically summing scores for a variety of risk factors) does not take into account the complexity of how risk factors are combined. In addition, clinicians may not see the statistical accuracy of actuarial tools as being that beneficial. To combat these issues, these authors developed a complex actuarial tool that sought to classify individuals as low or high risk by each person's specific combination of risk factors.

This new approach was derived from data gathered for the MacArthur violence risk assessment study, a large multisite study that was well-designed to prospectively measure community violence among released civil psychiatric patients (Monahan et al., 2001). For the purposes of the ICT development, the patients were followed in the community for 20 weeks via self- and collateral-report, and official arrest data, to determine whether violence had occurred (Steadman et al., 2000). From the data, 134 possible risk factors were each examined for their relationship to the outcome variable. The most highly significant was selected and participants were partitioned into two groups based on whether they possessed that risk variable or not. Each of these two groups was further partitioned by additional risk factors, thus creating smaller subgroups of individuals who possessed similar risk factors for violence and importantly also shared similar levels of violence. This process becomes iterative when individuals left unclassified as low- or high-risk were repooled and sent through the classification tree repeatedly until no new individuals are classified. The authors report that 76.6% of all participants were classified as either low- or high-risk for violence and the AUC was an impressive .82.

Research and Use of the ICT

At present, only a few studies exist that use the ICT methodology to judge risk for violence. Seeking to generalize the results to another population, Silver et al. (2000) examined the ICT model compared to logistic regression analyses of the same risk factors in a retrospective file-based review of released offenders. The sample was split to both generate the ICT model for these offenders ($n = 5,856$) and another sample was used to cross-validate the measure ($n = 5,858$). Results supported those of Steadman et al. (2000) by suggesting that the ICT approach was highly useful in classifying individuals into low- or high-risk groups, but was not linked to increased accuracy over logistic regression models of prediction. More recently, Monahan et al. (2005a; Monahan et al., 2005b) used the ICT with 700 civil psychiatric patients from three hospitals to predict community violence in the 20 weeks postdischarge. Results of the ICT showed that 76% of patients were accurately classified as low- or high-risk, with an AUC of .70.

Classification of Violence Risk (COVR)

Utilizing the MacArthur data as its basis, Monahan and colleagues developed the COVR to aid clinicians in making determinations of risk (Monahan et al., 2005; Monahan et al., 2005b). The instrument is administered via a software program the clinician uses while interviewing the examinee. The COVR was developed with civil psychiatric patients and may not be appropriate for other groups (i.e., violent offenders leaving prison). Additionally, the time frame of the risk estimation is one year rather than the lengthier time frames offered by some actuarial measures. The COVR poses a series of questions to the clinician that require dichotomous responses. Based on each of these responses, additional questions are selected until the individual's risk status is identified. The risk summary generated by the computer includes both a probabilistic estimate of risk as well as a proposed risk category. The risk indicators that contributed to the risk profile can also be viewed. Because many of the risk indicators are clinical in nature (such as substance use, active symptoms, and violent fantasies) this can aid clinicians in identifying targets for treatment.

Although the COVR is based on solid research and has good psychometric properties with the validation sample, it is a new instrument. There are very few studies to date that examine its utility. In one study, the COVR and VRAG were used to assess for institutional aggression among 52 forensic psychiatric hospital patients in the United Kingdom (Snowden et al., 2009). The base rate of verbal aggression was high, with every patient having at least one act of verbal aggression during the study period, whereas fewer patients demonstrated physical violence or property destruction. Both the COVR and VRAG were predictive of verbal and physical aggression during the next six months of hospitalization. The VRAG was a significant predictor of aggression towards property whereas the COVR was not. A similar study in the United States found that the COVR was strongly related to physical aggression by forensic inpatients (AUC = .725) and was comparable to other measures such as the VRAG, PCL-R, and HCR-20 (McDermott, Dualan, & Scott, 2011). McCusker (2007) voiced concern that the positive predictive power of the COVR was less than expected in the validation sample and worried that "high risk" related to only a 49% risk for violence. Given that so few studies have yet been completed with the COVR and that these studies have been primarily focused on inpatient aggression, cautious use of the tool is advised.

Structured Professional Judgment

The term *clinical judgment* in the risk assessment literature refers most often to *unstructured* clinical judgment. In reviewing the process of clinical predictions of risk, it becomes apparent that this lack of structure hinders the accuracy of judgments. Numerous authors (Monahan, 1981; see also Hart, 1998; Monahan & Steadman, 1994; Webster, Harris, Rice, Cormier, & Quinsey, 1994) have criticized the use of the unstructured clinical judgment approach to risk assessment (see Mossman, 2000 for a less dismal view of the unstructured clinical approach). More recently, structured methods of risk assessment have been proposed to overcome the difficulties encountered with unstructured methods. Hart (1998) argued for the adoption of structured (i.e., guided) professional judgment for risk assessment. More specifically, structured professional judgment (SPJ) involves a clinician reviewing all relevant data sources for the presence of specified static and dynamic risk factors, then making a structured final risk judgment (Douglas, Ogloff, & Hart, 2003). Douglas and Reeves (2010) noted "the SPJ approach attempts to retain the strengths associated with both clinical and actuarial approaches to decision making while limiting their weaknesses" (p. 148).

Structured approaches to risk assessment improve over unstructured approaches by standardizing how (a) evaluations are conducted and (b) variables are weighted. SPJ approaches are similar to actuarials in that they assess empirically informed risk factors and incorporate them into a model for decision making. However, SPJ approaches differ from actuarial methods in several important ways. Unlike actuarial approaches, the flexibility of clinical approaches allows for decisions to be rendered considering the "totality of the circumstances," not simply a set of static variables. The flexibility of structured approaches allows professionals, in certain circumstances, to decide that the test results are not meaningful in a given case and should be ignored. As Hart (1998) pointedly asks, "Does it matter at all what an offender's total score is on the VRAG, and how many risk factors are present or whether he scores above a specific cut-off, if he also expresses genuine homicidal intent?" (p. 126).

Advances in Structured Clinical Judgment

Structured clinical approaches to risk assessment have two main objectives. First, structured approaches strive to provide consistency. Second, they balance consistency with flexibility. The importance of these considerations led to the development of structured clinical guides to risk assessment. Currently, the HCR-20 (Webster, Douglas, Eaves, & Hart, 1997), LSI-R (Andrews & Bonta, 2003), and Sexual Violence Risk–20 (SVR-20; Boer, Hart, Kropp, & Webster, 1997) comprise the most developed and validated guides available for clinicians to aid risk assessments. Each of these measures is described in this section. Finally, no discussion of risk assessment is complete without mention of psychopathy. Although extensively covered elsewhere in this textbook (see Vitacco et al., Chapter 6 in this volume), our review will cover its relevance to judging risk. Other assessment devices are being developed but are too novel to have data to support their utility. These are also briefly mentioned.

In addition to recognizing dynamic risk factors related to violence risk, mental health professionals are slowly realizing the importance of assessing dynamic protective factors. A protective factor is a variable that if present, reduces the individual's risk level. Thus it is important to identify variables that increase risk as well as variables that reduce risk potential. The field has lagged behind in this area, and protective factors remain less well-examined than risk factors (Rogers, 2000). Schumaker and colleagues have expanded the concept of evaluation of risk and protective variables in spousal assault cases (Schumacher, Feldbau-Kohn, Slep, & Heyman, 2001). When mental health professionals are asked to provide an evaluation that contributes to risk management, consideration of protective factors (such as social support) is vital.

HCR-20

The HCR-20 identifies 20 variables that are organized into three scales: *H*istorical, *C*linical, and *R*isk Management. The original version was published in 1995, the second version in 1997, and the third version recently in 2013. The HCR-20 manual (Douglas, Hart, Webster, & Belfrage, 2013) provides definitions and scoring guidelines for each of the variables. With each version of the measure, the scoring criteria have become more explicit, with subitems and additional clarification based on both empirical analysis as well as feedback from users. The Historical scale includes 10 mostly stable, static risk variables. The Clinical scale comprises items related to current mental status. The Risk Management scale assesses future environmental factors, such as exposure to destabilizers in the environment and stress. Each of these 20 items is rated on whether it is absent, partially present, or definitely present for the individual being assessed. Evaluators are asked to judge the relevance of each of the risk factors for this particular person. The assessment of relevance allows the clinician to determine the functional relevance of that risk factor to this person's risk formulation. The emphasis on relevance of the risk factors is an effort to move between group-level and individual-level data and make the assessment as relevant as possible to this individual and his or her environment. The clinician is then asked to consider possible risk scenarios and make a general formulation of why this person might be violent. As a final step, the clinician gives categorical ratings for serious physical harm, imminent violence, and the level of risk management that needs to be employed. The HCR-20, like other SPJ tools, encourages a case formulation approach to "identify risk factors, conceptualizing their causal roles, speculating about future violence, and developing case management plans" (Hart & Logan, 2011, p. 95).

Monahan (1981) identified four common "blind spots" in the clinical prediction of violent behavior, namely, (a) the lack of specificity in defining a criterion, (b) a reliance on illusory correlations, (c) a failure to incorporate situational or environmental information; and (d) the neglect of base rates. As described earlier, the HCR-20 addresses three of Monahan's chief concerns: First, it specifically defines the items and provides scoring criteria. Second, it uses clinical and risk variables that are empirically related to violence. Third, its ratings take into consideration situational and environmental variables. In summary, the HCR-20 has a sound conceptual basis that addresses these relevant domains.

As with the VRAG, numerous studies suggest the HCR-20 performs well in predicting violence among civil and forensic psychiatric patients as well as offender groups (Chu, Thomas, Ogloff, & Daffern, 2013; Douglas et al., 2003; Grann, Belfrage, & Tengstrom; 2000; Vojt, Thomson, & Marshall, 2013). Given the recency of the third version, there are only a handful of studies examining its utility. Strub, Douglas, and Nicholls (2014) used both versions 2 and 3 of the HCR-20 with a mixed sample of offenders and civil psychiatric patients who were nearing release to the community. Participants were initially evaluated in the hospital, prison, or community and then followed approximately every four weeks. Each of the three subscales, total scales, and summary risk ratings correlated strongly between the two versions; correlations ranged from .76 to .98. Strub et al. examined the ability of Version 3 to predict violence at both four to six weeks as well as at six to eight months. The AUC for the HCR-20v3 summary scale for presence of violence at four to six weeks was .78 and at six to eight months was .77. The summary risk rating scores added incremental validity to the prediction schemes over and above the summed scales.

Several researchers have compared the HCR-20 to other risk assessment approaches. Nicholls, Ogloff, and Douglas (2004) retrospectively coded the HCR-20, Psychopathy Checklist–Screening Version (PCL:SV; Hart, Cox, & Hare, 1995), and the Violence Screening Checklist (VSC; McNiel & Binder, 1994) in a sample of male and female involuntary civil psychiatric patients. These patients were assessed for both inpatient and community violence via extensive records review. In regards to inpatient violence, AUC curves were nonsignificant for any of the three measures for any violence or physical violence. However, AUCs for any violence perpetrated by female patients were significant for the Historical (AUC = .69) and Clinical (AUC = .70) scales separately and combined (AUC = .74) and the PCL-R (AUC = .72). For physical violence, the Clinical scale (AUC = .62) and the PCL:SV (AUC = .63) were significant. The VSC performed only slightly better than chance. In the analyses of community violence, the Historical and Risk Management scales, the total HCR-20 score, and the PCL:SV showed significant prediction beyond chance for both men and women across most definitions of violence. The VSC showed AUCs at or below chance (although this is not surprising given its design to predict in-hospital violence).

In another comparison study, Douglas, Yeomans, and Boer (2005) compared the HCR-20, VRAG, PCL-R, PCL:SV, and another actuarial guide called the Violent Offender Risk Assessment Scale (VORAS). Participants were Canadian prisoners released into the community and were randomly selected from two groups: those who recidivated violently and those who did not. Conclusions from the multiple analyses run in this study suggest that the HCR-20 and VRAG tools were useful in judging which offenders would violently recidivate. The PCL-R and VORAS, while significantly correlated and at times predictive, were less sound. The results of this study along with those of Nicholls, Ogloff, and Douglas (2004) suggest that the HCR-20, an SPJ tool, is comparable to the "gold standard" actuarial methods.

In summary, the findings suggest that the HCR-20 has demonstrated predictive and postdictive accuracy that parallels that found with actuarial schemes, such as the VRAG and the Static-99, and does so in both correctional and civil samples. Demonstrating its generalizability to civil settings may provide extra support for the HCR-20. The VRAG, SORAG, and the Static-99 were developed on and validated with criminal samples. Therefore, a benefit of the HCR-20 may be its ability to predict violence in criminal and noncriminal settings. Preliminary research suggests strengths of the HCR-20 include reliability and generalizability.

The Sexual Violence Risk-20

The Sexual Violence Risk–20 (SVR-20; Boer et al., 1997), similar to the HCR-20 in construction, was developed specifically for use with sex offenders. In constructing the SVR-20, the authors attempted to identify risk factors that are empirically related to future sexual violence, and are clinically useful, yet parsimonious. The items chosen for inclusion were derived through a review of the literature on sex offenders. Special attention was given to factors that discriminate between sexual and nonsexual offenders and on those associated with recidivistic violence or sexual violence in sex offenders.

The SVR-20 has been the subject of little empirical investigation. Dutch researchers compared the SVR-20 to the Static-99 in predicting sexual recidivism among sex offenders released from a psychiatric inpatient facility (de Vogel, de Ruiter, van Beek, & Mead, 2004). While both measures showed significantly better prediction over chance, the SVR-20 risk judgment correctly identified more sexual recidivists (AUC = .83) than the Static-99 risk category (AUC = .66). MacPherson (2003) reported that individual items from SVR-20 Psychosocial Adjustment and Sexual Offenses subsections significantly differentiated noncontact sexual recidivists from contact recidivists. More recently, Smid, Kamphuis, Wever, and Van Beek (2014) compared the performance of several sex offender risk assessment instruments and determined that two versions of an actuarial instrument, the Static-99R and Static-2002R, outperformed the SVR-20 across outcome measures.

Summary and Critique of SPJ

The authors of the HCR-20 and the SVR-20 avoid offering a decision-making algorithm with associated cut scores and categories of risk. Instead, they invite clinicians to use these items as guidelines to help them assess probabilities of risk and make recommendations regarding treatment and management of offenders. They provide no guidelines to achieve this. The absence of cut scores increases the clinician's flexibility by allowing consideration of other important information in decisions regarding risk. An inherent limitation to this approach is that clinicians are left without empirically supported guidance at the most crucial step of the assessment process: making an ultimate determination.

Despite this vagueness, SPJ instruments are becoming widely validated through empirical research as useful tools in assessing and judging risk. Not only are the scale and total scores related to risk level, clinicians who use these scores to make a final judgment regarding risk demonstrate similar if not improved abilities to judge future violence. Some researchers (see Dvoskin & Heilbrun, 2001) suggest that actuarial and SPJ methods are not polar opposites but can in fact be used together. Actuarial tools can provide empirically supported knowledge about an offender's long-range risk of criminal behavior, which can be used in conjunction with SPJ methods to determine which dynamic risk factors are present, which can then become targets for intervention.

Three additional measures deserve brief mention here for their utility in assessing and/or managing risk: The Level of Service inventories (Andrews Bonta, & Wormith, 2004), the PCL-R (Hare, 2003), and the Short-Term Assessment of Risk and Treatability (START; Webster, Martin, Brink, Nichols, & Middleton, 2004). The Level of Service/Case Management Inventory (LS/CMI) was designed to measure and manage risk in the community, while the PCL-R is a measure of personality. The START was designed to predict violence as well as several other negative outcomes among individuals with mental health diagnoses. Each is briefly described in the next section.

The Level of Service Inventories

The LS/CMI (Andrews, Bonta, & Wormith, 2004) is based on the risk-need-responsivity (RNR) model espoused by Andrews, Bonta, and Hoge (1990) to assess risk factors, identify appropriate targets for intervention, and apply services that maximize the likelihood of success. This tool is based on its predecessor, the LSI-R (Andrews & Bonta, 1995) which contains 54 items grouped rationally, not empirically, onto 10 scales. It contains historical items and dynamic risk factors related to both antisocial cognitions and social relationships. Each of these items is rated as present or absent and generate both scale and total scores. The LS/CMI builds upon this earlier version by providing a plan for service delivery and ways of monitoring the case from beginning to end. It contains an additional nine sections to assess additional risk/need factors as well as development and monitoring of the case management plan. In response to feedback that the LS/CMI was too overwhelming for users, a new measure was introduced that is an intermediary between the LSI-R and LS/CMI. This newer tool, the Level of Service/Risk Need Responsivity (LS/RNR) contains only six sections

Initially developed with offenders serving short (less than two years) sentences to guide decisions regarding parole supervision, it has demonstrated validity in predicting both general and violent recidivism (Bonta & Motiuk, 1992; Kroner & Mills, 2001). In their meta-analysis of the PCL-R and LSI-R in predicting recidivism, Gendreau, Goggin, and Smith (2002) found that the LSI-R slightly outperformed the PCL-R in predicting both general and violent recidivism. In their meta-analysis of several risk tools in predicting institutional misconduct and violent recidivism, the LSI-R showed similar predictive validity to the other tools used (i.e., VRAG, HCR-20, PCL-R) with an unadjusted mean effect size of .25 (CI = .21 to .28). The focus of the LSI-R on risks and needs makes it directly applicable to management of risk (Nussbaum, 2006). Clinicians can use the scores on the differing subscales to pinpoint which areas should be of highest priority in terms of treatment and supervision of offenders or patients in the community. Case managers can then develop a specific risk management plan that identifies the specific criminogenic needs and how to address them as well as identifying and responding to any responsivity issues.

PCL-R, Second Edition (Hare, 2003)

One final measure that will be briefly discussed is the PCL-R. This highly regarded (Salekin, Rogers, & Sewell, 1996) tool measures Hare's (1991, 2003) conceptualization of psychopathy as a personality style that involves the remorseless use of others and subsequent irresponsible and antisocial behaviors. Although not originally designed as a risk assessment instrument, this measure has demonstrated utility in predicting future criminal and violent behavior (Hare, 2003). Twenty items are scored by a clinician on a 0–2 scale after ideally conducting an extensive file review, clinical interview, and sometimes collateral interviews. The instrument contains two higher-order factors, the first of which characterizes interpersonal and affective traits, and the second that measures antisocial and impulsive lifestyle. Three- and four-factor solutions have also been proposed. The three-factor solution (Cooke & Michie, 2001) separates the interpersonal and affective items into separate factors, and truncates the behavioral factor to include only impulsive and irresponsible lifestyle items. Hare (2003) similarly disaggregates both higher-order factors into two facets each, such that Factor 1 contains the Interpersonal and Affective facets while Factor 2 contains the Impulsivity and Antisocial Lifestyle facets (see Vitacco et al., Chapter 6 in this volume, for a more comprehensive review).

The PCL-R was designed as a research tool, but with its sound psychometric properties and relative ability to distinguish between psychopaths and nonpsychopaths, it has been increasingly used in jails, prisons, and forensic psychiatric units for a variety of purposes (Serin, 1992). The criminal justice system has become increasingly interested in the use of the instrument for predicting violence and recidivism after release, and a number of studies support the use of the PCL-R in identifying offenders at high risk for violence and recidivism (Hemphill & Hare, 1995; Serin, 1996). Salekin, Rogers, and Sewell (1996) conducted a meta-analysis of studies where the PCL-R was used to predict recidivism and dangerousness. The average effect size for predicting violence (institutional or recidivistic) was .79, for general recidivism was .55, and for sexual sadism or deviant sexual arousal was .61. The relationship between PCL-R scores and violence led these authors to conclude that "The PCL-R appears to be unparalleled as a measure for making risk assessments with white male inmates" (p. 211).

The START[4]

The START is a recently developed tool using a SPJ approach to determine the risk posed by psychiatric patients for a host of negative outcomes such as violence towards others, suicide risk, self-harm, self-neglect, substance use, unauthorized leave (absconding), and victimization. The START items are dynamic and thus changeable across time, lending itself to repeated assessments to track a patient's risk status. Similar to other approaches, it has 20 items that are scored on a three-point scale from present to absent. Clinicians are advocated to work in teams to assess the patient, identify specific risks and strengths, and develop an overall risk formulation from which a risk estimate is made.

Two studies in particular have demonstrated the utility of the START to predict institutional violence and adverse events (Gray et al., 2011; Nonstad et al., 2010). In both of these studies with psychiatric inpatients, START scales were predictive of violence as well as some of the other outcome variables. However, research has not yet emerged about the utility of the START in assessing community outcomes.

Selection and Utility of Risk Tools

In 2005, Kroner, Mills, and Reddon published a cleverly designed commentary on the lack of difference among the various risk assessment tools. These authors administered the VRAG, LSI-R, PCL-R, and a lesser-known tool, the General Statistical Information on Recidivism (GSIR) to 206 offenders who were nearing release from prison. They were followed for an average of 3.5 years in the community and assessed for parole violations and new criminal conviction. In addition to assessing the predictive validity of these four tools, the authors created four new tools. The authors wrote each item from each of the four measures (totaling 101 items) and put it into a coffee can. They then randomly selected 13 items from the coffee can four different times, creating four new risk measures based on elements of the four existing risk tools. Kroner et al. then examined the ability of the "Coffee Can measures" to predict the parole violations and new convictions. Amazingly, the original risk tools were no better at predicting outcomes than the randomly generated measures. Factor analysis of these 101 items with a larger sample of 1,416 subjects showed a four-factor solution: criminal history, persistent antisocial lifestyle, psychopathic personality, and drug/mental health. Kroner et al. offer two conclusions: First, our most typically used measures of violence risk are simply measuring criminal risk, nothing more. Second, no one risk tool is more sophisticated than any other nor better than a random selection of risk items. The authors advocate for development of theory regarding risk. They suggest that rather than simply using a selection of empirically derived risk factors, researchers develop theory about the etiology, expression, and management of risk.

In a large meta-analysis of the predictive utility of several violence risk schemes, Yang, Wong, and Coid (2010) compared nine commonly used risk tools, including the VRAG, HCR-20, and LSI-R. These authors determined that overall AUC values for the different instruments were fairly similar to one another (AUCs ranged from .65 to .71) and no instrument outperformed any other. Yang et al. concluded that these measures were essentially "interchangeable" with one another if the only function was to predict violence, rather than managing it. Additionally, they warned that these tools should not be the sole bases for legal decision making, such as preventative detention, due to only moderate predictive utility. Coid et al. (2011) determined that only few items of the major risk tools (PCL-R, VRAG, and HCR-20) are individually predictive of violent outcomes. The items that were predictive are indices of general criminality; many of the other items appeared less relevant. The authors argued that this produces a "glass-ceiling effect" in which no instrument appears to improve beyond the moderate predictive utility it exhibits. In other words, the predictive power of these tools lies primarily in their ability to measure general criminality, which they all do to a certain degree. Nothing else has demonstrated utility in improving these predictions.

In addition to the only moderate predictive utility noted in the studies discussed, risk assessment tools function better to identify individuals at low risk rather than high risk. In a meta-analysis of violence and recidivism prediction tools with 24,827 subjects across 13 countries, Fazel, Singh, Doll, and Grann (2012) produced a number of important findings. First, measures predicting violence performed better than measures predicting general recidivism or sexual violence. They echoed Yang et al.'s findings that all the major violence risk measures performed similarly. Of most significance, these authors reported on the positive and negative predictive values of the risk tools. Positive predictive value refers to the number of individuals identified as at risk to reoffend who actually do reoffend, whereas negative predictive value refers to the number of individuals identified as not at risk to reoffend who do not go on to reoffend. Here, Fazel et al. determined that of the people determined to be a high risk for reoffense, only 41% went on to do so. Conversely, of the people determined to be a low risk to reoffend, 91% did not reoffend. This set of statistics shows that the risk tools are quite good at identifying individuals at low risk to reoffend but less able to identify people who do reoffend. The authors contend that two people would need to be detained to prevent one person from reoffending and suggest that these tools are effective in describing a person's level of risk but not at accurately predicting which of those people will become violent or reoffend. They suggest that risk tools can be used with some confidence to identify and screen out individuals at low risk. However, they contend that risk tool estimates should not be used as the sole basis for determining the legal decisions for individuals classified as high risk, due to a relatively poor ability to discern which high-risk individual will go on to demonstrate later violence or recidivism.

In their brief review of the state of the field, Skeem and Monahan (2011) identify similar suggestions for the future direction of violence risk assessment. They noted that as violence prediction is approaching a ceiling effect in predictive utility, we should focus our efforts on a goal ripe for development: risk reduction. There are far fewer studies examining the effects of violence risk reduction strategies. Although more complicated to design and carry out, this is an important area of research that needs more effort. Given that harm prevention and reduction are typically the primary goals of violence risk assessments, more evidence is needed to determine how we can avoid or reduce possible harm.

Applying Risk Assessment Techniques to Clinical Practice

Forensic clinicians have been legitimized in their risk assessment practice by the courts (see e.g., Janus, 2000; Monahan et al., 2001). Despite the fact that research has shown that no risk assessment method is highly accurate, courts have continued to place this responsibility on clinicians, arguing that there is nothing "inherently unattainable about a prediction of future criminal conduct" (*Schall v. Martin*, 1984, p. 2417). One possible conclusion is that in the absence of a proven method, selection of a risk assessment method may depend on the clinician's personal preferences. Another possible conclusion maintains that no method has demonstrated superiority because all studies of accuracy have obscured the prediction task by asking clinicians to make overarching predictions regarding risk that are independent of situation and context (see e.g., Heilbrun, 1997; Mulvey & Lidz, 1998; Skeem, Mulvey, & Lidz, 2000).

Contextualized Risk Assessment

Twenty years ago, Monahan (1981) stated that what was needed for moral, legal, and empirical "progress in the area of prediction is a dramatic increase in the degree to which mental health professionals articulate what it is they are predicting and how they went about predicting it" (p. 17). Despite this plea, prediction research has continued to focus on the accuracy of clinicians' judgments and not on the process of decision making itself.

Most research in the area of violence prediction has been grounded in the cue-utilization model of human judgment. Grisso (1991) explained that this model frames the task of predicting dangerousness as a "clinical exercise" in applying a context-free algorithm for combining risk factors. This context-free model of risk assessment does not parallel real-life decision making in many situations. Clinicians are likely to be asked "Under what conditions is this person likely to be violent?" Importantly, the legally relevant question is: "Is this person's risk of future violence severe enough to warrant detaining him or her involuntarily?" This kind of conditional risk assessment more closely resembles the type of questions and issues that clinicians actually face.

It is naïve to suggest that (a) predictions of violence occur in a context-free framework, and (b) such predictions are accurate regardless of environmental or situational events. Similarly, Skeem, Mulvey, and Lidz (2000) criticized the cue-utilization model because it assumes that behavior is largely independent of context. As they noted, "a substantial body of research on mental health professionals' (MHPs') predictive accuracy appears to be based on a model of clinical decision making that inadequately represents the actual nature and goals of MHPs risk assessments" (p. 609).

Contextual variables that have the potential to influence the likelihood of risk include (a) situational or environmental variables and (b) legal decision-making context. Situational or environmental variables include a myriad of issues, such as inpatient or community violence, substance use, domestic disputes, and medication compliance. Legally relevant contextual variables are often intertwined with situational variables. Examples include legal determinations, such as release from a maximum security hospital or certification as a sexually violent predator.

Situational/Environmental Context

Past empirical evidence has suggested that clinicians tend to overpredict violence in their patients (Lidz, Mulvey, & Gardner, 1993; McNiel & Binder, 1991; Monahan, 1981; Steadman & Cocozza, 1974). Skeem et al. (2000) proposed that the dichotomous nature of their decisions (dangerous/not dangerous) may hide the more subtle context-specific decisions being rendered. For instance, a clinician may have predicted that a male patient will be violent toward his mother due to his alcohol intake, noncompliance with medication, and residence with his mother. However, if the patient subsequently complies with his medication and abstains from alcohol, his risk of violence is presumably lower. These contextual factors are often not made explicit when factored into binary decisions. As observed in this example, the clinician appears to have overpredicted violence because the salient situational variables are not explicated.

A fundamental problem with the notion of actuarial risk assessment techniques is that they do not take into account these contextual variables. Their use may be incompatible with the flexibility needed to incorporate environmental and situational variables into a prediction. In contrast, their use may maximize predictive ability in certain contexts. More research is needed into the contextual variables that influence decision making and the process clinicians use in formulating their judgments.

Legal Decision-Making Context

Environmental/situational contexts are important for clinicians to consider in making responsible risk assessments. Heilbrun's (1997) review of risk prediction and risk management models illustrates the importance of legal context in the decision-making process. For example, on one hand, actuarial techniques may have the most utility when binary decisions are needed, such as to commit an individual under a sex offender civil commitment act. On the other, clinically guided risk assessment may be more useful during decisions regarding graduated release. This conceptualization of prediction versus management models provides a framework for shifting the way we think about risk assessment and the decisions resulting from that process. Given this importance on clearly delineating the decision-making process and incorporating contextual variables into a management plan, we turn now to discussion of how mental health professionals can articulate risk assessment information to aid both legal and clinical decision makers.

Communicating Risk

As researchers have begun to develop more advanced ways of identifying individuals at risk for violence, clinicians have begun to use these methods to help courts and other legal and clinical bodies make decisions regarding offenders and patients. But determining what pieces of data are more useful and relevant to decision makers and how to present that information in a manner that eases understanding is no easy task. This section briefly reviews the literature on communicating violence risk and ends with suggestions for improving clarity in these communications.

In a seminal paper, Monahan and Steadman (1996) examined lessons learned about risk communication from the field of meteorology. They suggest that probabilistic statements about risk have been advanced by both meteorology and psychology in risk communication, and that these can frequently be understood by the intended audience. However, categorical statements of risk (such as naming an individual as high, moderate, or low risk for violence) may also be useful from a risk management perspective. Finally combining both categorical and probabilistic language in the same message conveying risk potential may provide multiple pathways to understanding critical information (see also Webster, Harris, Rice, Cormier, & Quinsey, 1994). For example, clinicians may note that a patient poses a "high risk" for violence due to the specified risk factors and then list ways in which to manage that risk.

In two separate surveys, Heilbrun and colleagues administered surveys to mental health professionals to determine their preference for communicating risk via reports or testimony (Heilbrun, O'Neill, Stevens, Strohman, Bowman, & Lo, 2004; Heilbrun, O'Neill, Strohman, Bowman, & Philipson, 2000). Results from both surveys were similar in that mental health professionals prefer styles of communication that included listing the identified risk factors along with suggestions for how to intervene regarding the violence potential. Participants were more likely to value this type of communication style when the risk for violence was high, perhaps because they are aware that a statement about increased risk may be viewed as prejudicial and requires more explanation.

Synthesizing information from all domains of violence risk assessment literature, Litwack, Zapf, Groscup, and Hart (2006) offer the following four guidelines for conducting an evaluation that taps both violence risk prediction and management (these authors also offer excellent and more detailed suggestions for conducting comprehensive risk assessments to which the reader is referred). These authors advocate for a clinically structured approach that may involve actuarial devices for risk prediction, but emphasizes gathering extensive clinical information regarding contextual risk factors and providing guidance with respect to risk management. First, clinicians should collect a comprehensive history of the patient's violence. This can be a tedious process during which clinicians should gather data from multiple sources, especially when concerned about the patient's response style. Second, these authors suggest that clinicians are aware of their own perceptions about violence and how these affect their judgments regarding risk potential. Some clinicians may not want to view a patient as dangerous, while in other situations they may consider any history of violence as indicative of current risk. This again emphasizes the point that it is important to gather a lot of information from multiple sources, including the patient. Direct questioning and indirect methods of assessing violent intentions, relationships with others, and insight into violence-related problems are useful. Third, clinicians are encouraged to evaluate the patient's future situation and which risk factors may be present in the environment. It would also be useful to discover how the patient has reacted to this type of environment before, and what factors either increased or decreased risk for violence. These risk factors can then become targeted for intervention. Fourth, as all psychologists learn in ethics courses, consultation is vital (see Connell, Chapter 3 in this volume). Obtaining another opinion from a clinician seasoned at violence risk assessment is often crucial when confronted with complex cases.

Reporting the results of a violence risk assessment is similar in most respects to other types of forensic communication. Evaluators should have a cogent grasp of the relevant legal standards in their jurisdiction, decide which types of information should be collected, and then carefully and at times painstakingly gather the needed data (Weiner, 2006). Weiner further suggests that once these have occurred, "what remains is for consultants to express their impressions and conclusions in a clear, relevant, informative, and defensible manner" (p. 645). Consultation of the *Specialty Guidelines for Forensic Psychology* (American Psychological Association, 2013) and with knowledgeable peers can aid this process.

Clinical Example

John Smith is a 34-year-old Caucasian male who was sentenced to seven years in prison for convictions on armed robbery and drug possession. After serving five years of his sentence, Mr. Smith is being considered for parole. The parole board has asked a forensic psychologist for an evaluation of Mr. Smith's violence potential in the community. The evaluation will aid the board in determining whether Mr. Smith will be released, and if he is, the level of community supervision required, along with what specifications might be added to his parole agreement (i.e., treatment, living situation). The forensic psychologist conducts a records review and general clinical interview with Mr. Smith, then compiles the following information.

Legal History

Mr. Smith was first arrested at the age of 16 on charges of disorderly conduct and public intoxication. He received a few more nuisance charges as a teenager but served no more than one night in juvenile detention. As an adult, Mr. Smith continued to garner more arrests related to his substance use and resulting out-of-control behavior. He served multiple jail sentences for drug possession, theft, disorderly conduct, and driving under the influence. In addition, he has two convictions for simple assault, both times when he complied with his drug dealer's requests to beat up people as payment for his drug consumption. At the age of 25, he served a three-year prison sentence for robbery and theft after attempting to rob a pharmacy. Mr. Smith was on parole for six months when he was charged with the index offense. Again, he robbed a pharmacy. When he was apprehended hours later, he was found in possession of methamphetamine.

Mr. Smith has been supervised in the community under probation and parole agreements in the past. However, his parole officers noted that he frequently does not keep his appointments, has had several positive urinalysis results for marijuana and methamphetamine, and appeared unmotivated to find stable employment. His probation officer revoked his status on two occasions, for which he served jail time. He had kept only one of three appointments during his six-month parole and had not shown up for two separate drug testing appointments.

Prison records denote that Mr. Smith has had some difficulties adjusting to prison life in the beginning of both sentences. He engaged in disruptive behavior with officers and had a couple of minor fights during the first few months. However, his behavior appeared to stabilize as he received no further disciplinary reports and was able to maintain employment in the kitchen during both sentences.

Violence History

Official records denote two arrests for simple assault, both of which resulted in minor bodily injury for the victim. During both robbery attempts, Mr. Smith used an unloaded pistol to ensure compliance with his demands. During the clinical interview, he admitted to some other instances of violence for which he has no legal charges. He admitted that he sometimes "got physical" with his long-term girlfriend when they would have arguments. He expressed genuine remorse and stated that he was usually intoxicated when this would occur. He also acknowledged a couple of fist fights at parties, which he also attributed to being "totally high."

Clinical History

Mr. Smith has no history of mental health symptoms or treatment in the community. Upon intake evaluation in the prison, he was diagnosed with an adjustment disorder and multiple substance use disorders. He entered into substance abuse treatment during his first prison sentence and was removed for noncompliance after two months. During his second sentence, Mr. Smith completed the program, although it took him five months longer than the nine months allotted. Treatment records indicate that he was frequently not forthcoming regarding the extent of his substance use and had little insight into how his substance use negatively impacted his life.

Devising the Violence Risk Assessment Protocol

First, we consider the referral question: the parole board wants to know Mr. Smith's risk of violence for the duration of his community supervision. This implies a two-prong approach that incorporates both actuarial and clinical tools. We can use actuarial tools to forecast the probability of violence and recidivism; the VRAG would provide an excellent resource. Given the lack of sexual violence in his record, specific assessment of sexual violence risk is unwarranted at this time. However, violence risk potential is also affected by a number of salient dynamic risk factors that are important to assess. Structured methods such as the PCL-R and HCR-20, along with identifying details of the antecedents and outcomes of violent behavior, will allow examination of these. Once all of this information is assembled, we can use the various data points to make a final conclusion regarding the potential risk Mr. Smith poses to his community. In addition to gathering information to score these various assessment tools, it is vital to assess Mr. Smith's response style via interview and through record review. Because he was noted in treatment notes to be guarded and hesitant to share sensitive information, he may be even less forthcoming with us due to the nature of the evaluation. Mr. Smith's ability to provide information similar to that in his records will cue us to determine the weight that is accorded to his verbal statements.

The preceding protocol may be more comprehensive than all cases require and some might suggest this is redundant (Seto, 2005). However, each instrument measures a different set of risk variables that speak to risk on multiple levels. Providing only a VRAG score and probability estimate of violence fulfills the nature of the referral question but leaves the parole board with little guidance to structure the supervision plan. Additionally, Mr. Smith would be considered a moderate to high risk for future violence based only on his VRAG score, and the Fazel et al. (2012) study would indicate we need further assessment to provide as much relevant risk information to the parole board.

Communicating Violence Risk Potential to the Parole Board

Results from the PCL-R suggest that Mr. Smith is approximately at the 50th percentile in his level of psychopathy. In other words, Mr. Smith scored higher than approximately 50% of prison inmates. His elevations on this scale are primarily the result of having a lengthy history of irresponsible and impulsive behaviors, with few interpersonal and emotional characteristics noted. Mr. Smith's score on the VRAG was in the sixth highest of nine categories of risk. Research suggests that 44% of people with scores similar to Mr. Smith recidivated within seven years while 58% did so within ten years. Another risk measure, the HCR-20, measures risk factors present in Mr. Smith's history and those he is likely to face upon release. Mr. Smith has a number of historical risk factors, which include substance use, a chaotic relationship style, and employment problems. Clinical risk factors noted are impulsivity and a lack of insight, as well as some prior unresponsiveness to treatment. Mr. Smith may be at increased risk given that his release plans include exposure to destabilizing influences like drugs and negative friends, lack of personal support, and stress. Mr. Smith appeared genuine in his efforts to lead a stable, substance-free, and law-abiding lifestyle, but showed poor insight by describing himself as impervious to environmental influences such as stress or friends using drugs.

Mr. Smith's risk of committing a violent or serious criminal act depends upon his varying level of risk factors such as substance use, acting impulsively, and an established history of breaking the law and committing violent acts while under the influence of alcohol and methamphetamine. From a static risk state framework, Mr. Smith presents a moderate to high risk of recidivism in the next several years. However, a careful and intensive supervision plan may be able to monitor and reduce the dynamic aspects of his risk. In other words, no risk plan can reduce his history of criminal involvement, but it can address the dynamic risk factors of substance use and prosocial support. We recommend that he be frequently monitored through random urinalysis and participation in a community-based substance abuse treatment program. Additionally, we recommend structuring his time with treatment, work, and other prosocial activities. Efforts should be made to increase his prosocial contacts and finding housing that supports sober living. Another potential intervention would be some type of psychoeducational class or group treatment that addresses problem-solving abilities and other coping skills. These types of supervision and treatment strategies are likely to limit Mr. Smith's exposure to destabilizing influences and allow the parole board to monitor his substance use more carefully. While this in no way guarantees a reduced risk for violence and recidivism, the plan targets the key risk factors Mr. Smith presents in an attempt to reduce them. Any protective factors, such as positive interpersonal relationships and stable employment, may also increase Mr. Smith's likelihood of successful community transition.

From an ethical perspective, we should notify the parole board of the limitations of our risk estimate given the current state of research in the field. As reviewed earlier, legal decision makers rely heavily upon the opinions of mental health professionals regarding future risk and likely do not understand the limitations of our technology. In providing our risk assessment and management plan for Mr. Smith, we should also inform them, in language easily understood by non–mental health professionals, that maybe only half of the individuals identified as "high risk" go on to reoffend and it is not within our expertise to determine in which half Mr. Smith falls.

Summary

This purpose of this chapter has been to present a general overview of the field of risk assessment, explore some of the assessment tools currently used in clinical practice and research, and contemplate how to incorporate violence risk assessment into good forensic practice. The nature of a chapter limits the depth to which these topics are explored, and the interested reader is referred to the references listed throughout. The history of violence risk assessment is long and storied, yet provides a guiding framework to understand how researchers and clinicians have developed the various assessment strategies. It is interesting to note that using clinical judgment to judge risk potential was once considered less optimal than flipping a coin, but it has enjoyed a recent resurgence. This appears to be due to a number of factors, which include the identification of numerous dynamic variables related to risk, the requirement of clinical skill to assess these factors, and a need for flexibility in integrating the various risk factors for violence. The research literature continues to grow in this area but there still exists a great skepticism regarding clinicians' abilities to step away from cognitive biases and objectively evaluate risk. Importantly, lead researchers in the field are calling for a renewed focus on risk reduction rather than the "horse race" studies of predictive utility exhibited by various risk assessment tools. In that most of the assessment tools have tied the race and no one tool has emerged as superior to the others, we must turn to other domains that require more investigation. What kind of programs, intervention strategies, and management styles work to effectively reduce violence in the community? While some studies of this exist, they are primarily in the domain of criminal justice professionals and not readily consumed by mental health professionals. This latter group needs to understand effective risk management strategies and to whom to apply the different methods of risk reduction.

In our opinion, risk prevention and reduction is the ultimate goal of risk assessment and we hope that research

Notes

1 Amicus briefs are reports submitted to the court by experts that are intended to provide triers of fact with more information with which to make a decision. The term derives from *amicus curiae*, Latin for "friend of the court."
2 *Daubert v. Merrill Dow Pharmaceuticals* (1993) developed a federal standard for the admission of expert testimony in court.
3 The *Tarasoff v. The Regents of the University of California* (1976) decision widely affected clinical practice by charging mental health professionals who gain knowledge of imminent threat to others with a duty to protect by breaking confidentiality and warning others.
4 Webster, Martin, Brink, Nicholls, & Middleton, 2004.

References

Addington v. Texas, 441 U.S. 418 (1979).

American Bar Association. (1998). *National benchbook on psychiatric and psychological evidence and testimony*. Washington, DC: Author.

American Psychiatric Association. (1974). *Clinical aspects of the violent individual*. Washington, DC: Author.

American Psychological Association. (2013). Specialty guidelines for forensic psychology. *American Psychologist, 68*, 7–19. doi: 10.1037/a0029889

Andrews, D. A., & Bonta, J. (1995) *Level of Service Inventory–Revised (LSI-R)*. Toronto, ON: Multi-Health Systems.

Andrews, D. A., Bonta, J., & Hoge, R. D. (1990). Classification for effective rehabilitation: Rediscovering psychology. *Criminal Justice and Behavior, 17*, 19-52.

Andrews, D. A., Bonta, J., & Wormith, S. (2004). *Manual for the level of service/Case Management Inventory IS/CMI*. Toronto, ON: Multi-Health Systems.

Barbaree, H. E., Seto, M. C., Langton, C. M., & Peacock, E. J. (2001). Evaluating the predictive accuracy of six risk assessment instruments for adult sex offenders. *Criminal Justice and Behavior, 28*, 490–521. doi: 10.1177/009385480102800406

Barefoot v. Estelle, 463 U.S. 880 (1983).

Baxstrom v. Herold, 383 U.S. 107 (1966).

Berlin, F. S., Galbreath, N. W., Geary, B., & McGlone, G. (2003). The use of actuarials at civil commitment hearings to predict the likelihood of future sexual violence. *Sexual Abuse: A Journal of Research and Treatment, 15*(4), 377–382.

Boer, D. P., Hart, S. D., Kropp, P. R., & Webster, C. D. (1997). *Manual for the Sexual Violence Risk–20: Professional guidelines for assessing risk of sexual violence*. Vancouver, BC: The British Columbia Institute Against Family Violence.

Bonta, J., & Motiuk, L. L. (1992). Inmate classification. *Journal of Criminal Justice, 20*, 343–353. doi: 10.1016/0047–2352(92)90018–5

Borum, R., & Reddy, M. (2001). Assessing violence risk in Tarasoff situations: A fact-based model of inquiry. *Behavioral Sciences and the Law, 19*, 375–385. doi: 10.1002/bsi.447

Chu, C. M., Thomas, S.D.M., Ogloff, J.R.P., & Daffern, M. (2013). The short- to medium-term predictive accuracy of static and dynamic risk assessment measures in a secure forensic hospital. *Assessment, 20*(2), 230–241. doi: 10.1177/1073191111418298

Coble v Texas, 1982 WL (2010). Amicus brief filed by the American Psychological Association. Retrieved from www.apa.org/about/offices/ogc/amicus/coble.aspx on June 24, 2014.

Coid, J. W., Yang, M., Ullrich, S., Zhang, T. Sizmur, S., Farrington, D., & Rogers, R. (2011). Most items in structured risk assessments do not predict violence. *The Journal of Forensic Psychiatry and Psychology, 22*(1), 3–21. doi: 10.1080/14789949.2010.495990

Cooke, D. J., & Michie, C. (2001). Refining the construct of psychopathy: Towards a hierarchical model. *Psychological Assessment, 13*, 171–188. doi: 10.1037/1040-3590.13.2.171

Daubert v Merrill Dow Pharmaceuticals, 509 U.S. 579 (1993).

de Vogel, V., de Ruiter, C., van Beek, D., & Mead, G. (2004). Predictive validity of the SVR-20 and Static-99 in a Dutch sample of treated sex offenders. *Law and Human Behavior, 28*, 235–251. doi: 10.1023/B:LAHU.0000029137.41974.eb

Dixon v. Pennsylvania, 325 F. Supp. 966 (1971).

Douglas, K. S., Hart, S. D., Webster, C. D., & Belfrage, H. (2013). *HCR-20v3 Assessing Risk for Violence User Guide.* Vancouver, BC: Mental Health, Law, and Policy Institute.

Douglas, K. S., Ogloff, J.R.P., & Hart, S. D. (2003). Evaluation of a model of violence risk assessment among forensic psychiatric patients. *Psychiatric Services, 54*(10), 1372–1379. doi: 10.1176/aapi.ps.54.10.1372

Douglas, K. S., Ogloff, J.R.P., Nicholls, T. L., & Grant, I. (1999). Assessing risk for violence among psychiatric patients: The HCR-20 violence risk assessment scheme and the Psychopathy Checklist: Screening Version. *Journal of Consulting and Clinical Psychology, 67*, 917–930. doi: 10.1037/0022-006x.67.6.917

Douglas, K. S., & Reeves, K. A. (2010). Historical-Clinical-Risk Management-20 (HCR-2). Violence risk assessment scheme. In R. K. Otto & K. S. Douglas (Eds.), *Handbook of violence risk assessment* (pp. 147–186). New York, NY: Routledge.

Douglas, K. S., & Skeem, J.L. (2005). Violence risk assessment: Getting specific about being dynamic. *Psychology, Public Policy, and Law, 11*(3), 347–383. doi: 10.1037/1076-8971.11.3.347

Douglas, K. S., Yeomans, M., & Boer, D. P. (2005). Comparative validity analysis of multiple measures of violence risk in a sample of criminal offenders. *Criminal Justice and Behavior, 32*(5), 479–510. doi: 10.1177/0093854805278411

Dvoskin, J. A., & Heilbrun, K. (2001). Risk assessment and release decision-making: Toward resolving the great debate. *Journal of the American Academy of Psychiatry and Law, 29*, 6–10.

Eisenbarth, H., Osterheider, M., Nedopil, N., & Stadtland, C. (2012). Recidivism in female offenders: PCL-R lifestyle factors and VRAG show predictive validity in a German sample. *Behavioral Sciences and the Law, 30*(5), 575–584. doi: 10.1002/bsi.2013

Endrass, J., Rossegger, A., Frischknecht, A., Noll, T., & Urbaniok, F. (2008). Using the violence risk appraisal guide (VRAG) to predict in-prison aggressive behavior in a Swiss offender population. *International Journal of Offender Therapy and Comparative Criminology, 52*(1), 81–89. doi: 10.1177/0306624x07301643

Ennis, B. J., & Litwack, T. R. (1974). Psychiatry and the presumption of expertise: Flipping coins in the courtroom. *California Law Review, 62*, 693–752. doi: 10.2307/3479746

Fazel, S., Singh, J. P., Doll, H., & Grann, M. (2012). Use of risk assessment instruments to predict violence and antisocial behaviour in 73 samples involving 24 827 people: Systematic review and meta-analysis. *British Medical Journal, 345*, e4692. doi: 10.1136/bmj.e.4692

Garb, H. N., & Boyle, P. A. (2003). Understanding why some clinicians use pseudoscientific methods: Findings from research on clinical judgment. In S. O. Lilienfeld, S. J. Lynn, & J. M. Lohr (Eds.), *Science and pseudoscience in clinical psychology* (pp. 17–38). New York: Guilford Press.

Gardner, W., Lidz, C. W., Mulvey, E. P., & Shaw, E. C. (1996). A comparison of actuarial methods for identifying repetitively violent patients with mental illnesses. *Law and Human Behavior, 20*(1), 35–48. doi: 10.1007/BF01499131

Garrett, M. W. (2012). Using the VRAG to predict institutional misconduct in male versus female inmates. Unpublished master's thesis. Pacific University.

Gendreau, P., Goggin, C., & Smith, P. (2002). Is the PCL-R really the "unparalleled" measure of offender risk? A lesson in knowledge cumulation. *Criminal Justice and Behavior, 29*(4), 397–426. doi: 10.1177/0093854802029004004

Glover, A.J.J., Nicholson, D. E., Hemmati, T., Bernfeld, G. A., & Quinsey, V. L. (2002). A comparison of predictors of general and violent recidivism among high-risk federal offenders. *Criminal Justice and Behavior, 29*, 235–249. doi: 10.1177/0093854802029003001

Goldberg, L. R. (1968). Simple models or simple processes? Some research on clinical judgments. *American Psychologist, 23*, 483–496. doi: 10.1037/h0026206

Grann, M., Belfrage, H., & Tengstrom, A. (2000). Actuarial assessment of risk for violence: Predictive validity of the VRAG and the Historical part of the HCR-20. *Criminal Justice and Behavior, 27*, 97–114. doi: 10.1177/009385480027001006

Gray, N. S., Benson, R., Craig, R., Davies, H., Fitzgerald, S., Huckle, P., . . . Snowden, R. J. (2011). The short-term assessment of risk and treatability (START): A prospective study of inpatient behavior. *International Journal of Forensic Mental Health, 10*(4), 305–313. doi: 10.1080/1499013.2011. 631692

Grisso, T. (1991). Clinical assessments for legal decision making: Research recommendations. In S. A. Shah & B. J. Sales (Eds.), *Law and mental health: Major developments and research needs* (pp. 49–81). Washington, DC: National Institute of Mental Health.

Grisso, T. & Appelbaum, P. S. (1992). Is it unethical to offer predictions of future violence? *Law and Human Behavior, 16*, 621–633. doi: 10.1007/BF01884019

Hanson, R. K. (1997). *The development of a brief actuarial risk scale for sexual offense recidivism* (User Report 1997–04). Ottawa, ON: Solicitor General of Canada.

Hanson, R. K. (2000). *Risk assessment*. Prepared for the Association for the Treatment of Sexual Abusers. Retrieved from www.atsa.com on October 4, 2014.

Hanson, R. K. & Harris, A. J. R. (2000). Where should we intervene? Dynamic predictors of sexual assault recidivism. *Criminal Justice and Behavior, 27*, 6–35. doi: 10.1177/0093855480027001002

Hanson, R. K., & Thornton, D. (1999). *Static-99: Improving actuarial risk assessments for sex offenders*. Solicitor General of Canada. Retrieved from www.publicsafety.gc.ca on June 22, 2015.

Hare, R. D. (1991). *The Revised Psychopathy Checklist*. Toronto: Multi-Health Systems.

Hare, R. D. (2003). *Hare PCL-R* (2nd ed.). Toronto: Multi-Health Systems.

Harris, A. J. R., & Hanson, R. K. (2010). Clinical, actuarial, and dynamic risk assessment of sexual offenders: Why do things keep changing? *Journal of Sexual Aggression, 16*(3), 296–310. doi: 10.1080/ 13552600.2010494772

Harris, G. T., Rice, M. E., & Camilleri, J. A. (2004). Applying a forensic actuarial assessment (the Violence Risk Appraisal Guide) to nonforensic patients. *Journal of Interpersonal Violence, 19*, 1063–1074. doi: 10.1177/0886260504268004

Harris, G. T., Rice, M. E., & Quinsey, V. L. (1993). Violent recidivism of mentally disordered offenders: The development of a statistical prediction instrument. *Criminal Justice and Behavior, 20*, 315–335. doi: 10.1177/0093854893020004001

Harris, G. T., Rice, M. E., Quinsey, V. L., Lalumière, M. L., Boer, D., & Lang, C. (2003). A multi-site comparison of actuarial risk instruments for sex offenders. *Psychological Assessment, 15*, 413–425. doi: 10.1037/1040–3590.15.3.413

Hart, S. D. (1998). The role of psychopathy in assessing risk for violence: Conceptual and methodological issues. *Legal and Criminological Psychology, 3*, 121–137. doi: 10.1111/j.2044–8333.1998.tb00354.x

Hart, S. D. (2003). Actuarial risk assessment: Commentary on Berlin et al. *Sexual Abuse: A Journal of Research and Treatment, 15*(4), 383–388.

Hart, S. D., Cox, D. N., & Hare, R. D. (1995). *Manual for the Hare Psychopathy Checklist: Screening Version (PCL:SV)*. Toronto. ON: Multi-Health Systems.

Hart, S. D., & Logan, C. (2011). Formulation of violence risk using evidence-based assessments: The structured professional judgment approach. In P. Sturmey & M. McMurran (Eds.), *Forensic case formulation* (pp. 83–106). Oxford, England: Wiley-Blackwell. doi: 10.1002/9781119977018.ch4

Hastings, M. E., Krishnan, S., Tangney, J. P., & Stuewig, J. (2011). Predictive and incremental validity of the violence risk appraisal guide scores with male and female jail inmates. *Psychological Assessment, 23*(1), 174–183. doi: 10.1037/a0021290

Heilbrun, K. (1997). Prediction versus management models relevant to risk assessment: The importance of legal decision-making context. *Law and Human Behavior, 21*, 347–359. doi: 10.1023/A:1024851017947

Heilbrun, K., O'Neill, M. L., Stevens, T. N., Strohman, L. K., Bowman, Q. & Lo, Y. (2004). Assessing normative approaches to communicating violence risk: A national survey of psychologists. *Behavioral Sciences and the Law, 22*, 187–196. doi: 10.1002/bsi.570

Heilbrun, K., O'Neill, M. L., Strohman, L. K., Bowman, Q., & Philipson, J. (2000). Expert approaches to communicating violence risk. *Law and Human Behavior, 24*, 137–148. doi: 10.1023/A:1005435005404

Hemphill, J. F., & Hare, R. D. (1995). Psychopathy Checklist factor scores and recidivism. *Issues in Criminological and Legal Psychology, 24*, 68–73.

Hilton, N. Z., Harris, G. T., & Rice, M. E. (2001). Predicting violence by serious wife assaulters. *Journal of Interpersonal Violence, 16*, 408–423. doi: 10.1177/088626001016005002

Hilton, N. Z., & Simmons, J. L. (2001). Actuarial and clinical risk assessment in decisions to release mentally disordered offenders from maximum security. *Law and Human Behavior, 25*, 393–408. doi: 10.1023/A:1010607719239

Janus, E. S. (2000). Sexual predator commitment laws: Lessons for law and the behavioral sciences. *Behavioral Sciences and the Law, 18*, 5–21. doi: 10.1002/(SICI)1099–0798(200001/02)18:1<5 :AID-BSL374>3.0.CO;2-C

Kroner, D. G. (2005). Issues in violence risk assessment: Lesson learned and future directions. *Journal of Interpersonal Violence, 20*(2), 231–235. doi: 10.1177/0886260504267743

Kroner, D. G., & Mills, J. F. (2001). The accuracy of five risk appraisal instruments in predicting institutional misconduct and new convictions. *Criminal Justice & Behavior, 28*(4), 471–489. doi: 10.1177/009385480102800405

Kroner, D. G., Mills, J. F., & Reddon, J. R. (2005). A coffee can, factor analysis, and *prediction* of antisocial behavior: The structure of criminal risk. *International Journal of Law and Psychiatry, 28*, 360–374. doi: 10.1016/j.ijip.2004.01.011

Lessard v. Schmidt, 413 F. Supp. 1318 (E.D. Wis. 1976).

Lidz, C. W., Mulvey, E. P., & Gardner, W. (1993). The accuracy of predictions of violence to others. *Journal of the American Medical Association, 269*, 1007–1011. doi: 10.1001/jama.1993.03500080055032

Litwack, T. R. (2001). Actuarial versus clinical assessments of dangerousness. *Psychology, Public Policy, and Law, 7*, 409–443. doi: 10.1037/1076–8971.7.2.409

Litwack, T. R., Zapf, P. A., Groscup, J. L., & Hart, S. D. (2006). Violence risk assessment: Research, legal, and clinical considerations. In I. B. Weiner & A. K. Hess, (Eds.), *The handbook of forensic psychology* (3rd ed., pp. 487–533). Hoboken, NJ: Wiley.

Loza, W., Villeneuve, D. B., & Loza-Fanous, A. (2002). Predictive validity of the Violence Risk Appraisal Guide: A tool for assessing violent offenders' recidivism. *International Journal of Law and Psychiatry, 25*, 85–92. doi: 10.1016/S0160–2527(01)00092–9

McNiel, D. E., & Binder, R. L. (1991). Clinical assessment of the risk of violence among psychiatric inpatients. *American Journal of Psychiatry, 148*, 1317–1321.

McNiel, D. E., & Binder, R. L. (1994). Screening for risk of inpatient violence: Validation of an actuarial tool. *Law and Human Behavior, 18*, 579–586. doi: 10.1007/BF01499176

MacPherson, G. (2003). Predicting escalation in sexually violent recidivism: Use of the SVR-20 and the PCL:SV to predict outcome with noncontact recidivists and contact recidivists. *Journal of Forensic Psychiatry and Psychology, 14*, 615–627. doi: 10.1080/14789940310001615470

McCusker, P. L. (2007). Issues regarding the clinical use of the Classification of Violence Risk (COVR) assessment instrument. *International Journal of Offender Therapy and Comparative Criminology, 51*(6), 676–685. doi: 10.1177/0306624X07299227

McDermott, B. E., Dualan, I. V., Scott, C. L. (2011). The predictive ability of the classification of violence risk (COVR) in a forensic psychiatric hospital. *Psychiatric Services, 62*(4), 430–433.

Meehl, P. E. (1954/1996). *Clinical versus statistical prediction: A theoretical analysis and a review of the evidence*. Northvale, NJ: Jason Aronson.

Monahan, J. (1981). *The clinical prediction of violent behavior*. Washington, DC: National Institute of Mental Health.

Monahan, J. (2000). Violence risk assessment: Scientific validity and evidentiary admissibility. *Washington and Lee Law Review, 57*, 901–918.

Monahan, J. & Steadman, H. J. (1994). *Violence and mental disorder: Developments in risk assessment*. Chicago, IL: University of Chicago Press.

Monahan, J. & Steadman, H. J. (1996). Violent storms and violent people: How meteorology can inform risk communication in mental health law. *American Psychologist, 51*, 931–938. doi: 10.1037/0003–066X.51.9.931

Monahan, J., & Steadman, H. J. (2001). Violence risk assessment: A quarter century of research. In L. E. Frost & R. J. Bonnie (Eds.), *The evolution of mental health law* (pp. 195–211). Washington, DC: American Psychological Association. doi: 10.1037/10414–010

Monahan, J., Steadman, H. J., Appelbaum, P. S., Grisso, T., Mulvey, E. P., Roth, L. H., . . . Silver, E. (2005a). *Classification of violence risk*. Lutz, FL: Psychological Assessment Resources.

Monahan, J., Steadman, H. J., Robbins, P. C., Appelbaum, P., Banks, S., Grisso, T. . . . Silver, E. (2005b). An actuarial model of violence risk assessment for persons with mental disorders. *Psychiatric Services, 56*, 810–815. doi: 10.1176/appi.ps.56.7.810

Monahan, J., Steadman, H. J., Silver, E., Appelbaum P. S., Robbins, P. C., Mulvey, E. P., . . . Banks, S. (2001). *Rethinking risk assessment: The MacArthur study of mental disorder and violence*. New York: Oxford University Press.

Mossman, D. (1994). Assessing predictions of violence: Being accurate about accuracy. *Journal of Consulting and Clinical Psychology, 62*, 783–792. doi: 10.1037/0022–006X.62.4.783

Mossman, D. (2000). Commentary: Assessing the risk of violence—are accurate predictions useful? *Journal of the American Academy of Psychiatry and Law, 28*, 272–281.

Mulvey, E. P. & Lidz, C. W. (1998). Clinical prediction of violence as a conditional judgment. *Social Psychiatry and Psychiatric Epidemiology, 33*, S107-S113. doi: 10.1007/s001270050218

Mulvey, E. P., Shaw, E. & Lidz, C. W. (1994). Why use multiple resources in research on patient violence in the community? *Criminal Behaviour and Mental Health, 4*(4), 253–258.

Nicholls, T. L., Ogloff, J. R. P., & Douglas, K. S. (2004). Assessing risk for violence among male and female civil psychiatric patients: The HCR-20, PCL:SV, and VSC. *Behavioral Sciences and the Law, 22*, 127–158. doi: 10.1002/bsl.579

Nonstad, K., Nesset, M. B., Kroppan, E., Pedersen, T. W., Nottestad, J. A., Almvik, R., & Palmstierna, T. (2010). Predictive validity and other psychometric properties of the short-term assessment of risk and treatability (START) in a Norwegian high secure hospital. *International Journal of Forensic Mental Health, 9*(4), 294–299. doi: 10.1080/1499013.2010.534958

Nussbaum, D. (2006). Recommending probation and parole. In I. B. Weiner, & A. K. Hess, (Eds.), *The handbook of forensic psychology* (3rd ed., pp. 426–483). Hoboken, NJ: Wiley.

Oskamp, S. (1965). Overconfidence in case study judgments. *Journal of Consulting Psychology, 29*, 261–265. doi: 10.1037/h0022125

Otto, R. K. (August, 2001). *Setting specific effects on test results in forensic cases*. Presented at the American Psychological Association Annual Convention, San Francisco, CA.

Pruesse, M. G., & Quinsey, V. L. (1977). The dangerousness of patients released from maximum security: A replication. *Journal of Psychiatry and Law, 5*, 293–299.

Quinsey, V. L., & Ambtman, R. (1979). Variables affecting psychiatrists' and teachers' assessments of the dangerousness of mentally ill offenders. *Journal of Consulting and Clinical Psychology, 47*, 353–362. doi: 10.1037/0022–006X.47.2.353

Quinsey, V. L., Harris, G. T., Rice, M. E., & Cormier, C. A. (1998). *Violent offenders: Appraising and managing risk*. Washington, DC: American Psychological Association. doi: 10.1037/10304–000

Quinsey, V. L., Harris, G. T., Rice, M. E., & Cormier, C. A. (2006). *Violent offenders: Appraising and managing risk* (2nd ed.). Washington DC: American Psychological Association.

Quinsey, V. L., Pruesse, M., & Fernley, R. (1975). Oak Ridge patients: Prerelease characteristics and postrelease adjustment. *Journal of Psychiatry and Law, 3*, 63–77.

Rice, M. E., & Harris, G. T. (1995). Violent recidivism: Assessing predictive validity. *Journal of Consulting and Clinical Psychology, 63*, 737–748. doi: 10.1037/0022–006X.63.5.737

Rice, M. E., & Harris, G. T. (1997). Cross-validation and extension of the violence risk appraisal guide for child molesters and rapists. *Law and Human Behavior, 21*, 231–241. doi: 10.1023/A:1024882430242

Rice, M. E., Harris, G. T., & Cormier, C. (1992). Evaluation of a maximum security therapeutic community for psychopaths and other mentally disordered offenders. *Law and Human Behavior, 16*, 399–412. doi: 10.1007/BF02352266

Rice, M. E., Harris, G. T., & Lang, C. (2013). Validation of and revision to the VRAG and SORAG: The Violence Risk Appraisal Guide-Revised (VRAG-R). *Psychological Assessment, 25*(3), 951–965. doi: 10.1037/a0032878

Rice, M. E., Harris, G. T., Lang, C., & Bell, V. (1990). Recidivism among male insanity acquittees. *The Journal of Psychiatry and Law, 18*, 379–403.

Rogers, R. (2000). The uncritical acceptance of risk assessment in forensic practice. *Law and Human Behavior, 24*, 595–605. doi: 10.1023/A:1005575113507

Salekin, R. T., Rogers, R., & Sewell, K. W. (1996). A review and meta-analysis of the psychopathy checklist and psychopathy checklist-revised: Predictive validity of dangerousness. *Clinical Psychology: Science and Practice, 3*, 203–215. doi: 10.111/j.1468–2850.1996.tb00071.x

Schall v. Martin, 467 U.S. 253, 264 (1984).

Schumacher, J. A., Feldbau-Kohn, S., Slep, A.M.S., & Heyman, R. E. (2001). Risk factors for male-to-female partner abuse. *Aggressive and Violent Behavior, 6*, 281–352. doi: 10.1016/S1359–1789(00)00027–6

Serin, R. C. (1992). The clinical application of the Psychopathy Checklist–Revised (PCL-R) in a prison population. *Journal of Clinical Psychology, 48*, 637–642. doi: 10.1002/1097–4679(199209)48:5<637:: AID-JCLP2270480510>3.0.CO;2-V

Serin, R. C. (1996). Violent recidivism in criminal psychopaths. *Law and Human Behavior, 20*, 207–217. doi: 10.1007/BF01499355

Seto, M. C. (2005). Is more better? Combining actuarial risk scales to predict recidivism among adult sex offenders. *Psychological Assessment, 17*, 156–167. doi: 10.1037/1040–3590.17.2.156

Silver, E., Smith, W., & Banks, S. (2000). Constructing actuarial devices for predicting recidivism: A comparison of methods. *Criminal Justice and Behavior, 27*, 733–764. doi: 10.1177/0093854800027006004

Skeem, J. L., & Monahan, J. (2011). Current directions in violence risk assessment. *Current Directions in Psychological Science, 20*(1), 38–42. doi: 10.1177/0963721410397271

Skeem, J., & Mulvey, E. (2002). Monitoring the violence potential of mentally disordered offenders being treated in the community. In A. Buchanan (Ed.), *Care of the mentally disordered offender in the community* (pp. 111–142). New York, NY: Oxford University Press.

Skeem, J. L., Mulvey, E. P., & Lidz, C. W. (2000). Building mental health professionals' decisional models into tests of predictive validity: The accuracy of contextualized predictions of violence. *Law and Human Behavior, 24*, 607–628. doi: 10.1023/A:1005513818748

Smid, W. J., Kamphuis, J. H., Wever, E. C., & Van Beek, D. J. (2014). A comparison of the predictive properties of nine sex offender risk assessment instruments. *Psychological Assessment, 26*, 691–703. doi: 10.1037/a0036616

Snowden, R. J., Gray, N. S., Taylor, J., & Fitzgerald, S. (2009). Assessing risk of future violence among forensic psychiatric inpatients with the Classification of Violence Risk (COVR). *Psychiatric Services, 60*(11), 1522–1526. doi: 10.1176/aapi.ps.60.11.1522

Steadman, H. J. (2000). From dangerousness to risk assessment of community violence: Taking stock at the turn of the century. *Journal of the American Academy of Psychiatry and Law, 28*, 265–271.

Steadman, H. J., & Cocozza, J. (1974). *Careers of the criminally insane*. Lexington, MA: Lexington Books.

Steadman, H. J., Silver, E., Monahan, J., Appelbaum, P. S., Clark Robbins, P., Mulvey, E. P. . . . Banks, S. (2000). A classification tree approach to the development of actuarial violence risk assessment tools. *Law and Human Behavior, 24*, 83–100. doi: 10.1023/A:1005478820425

Strub, D. S., Douglas, K. S., & Nicholls, T. L. (2014). The validity of version 3 of the HCR-20 violence risk assessment scheme among offenders and civil psychiatric patients. *International Journal of Forensic Mental Health, 13*(2), 148–159. doi: 10.1080/14999013.2014.911785

Swets, J. A. (1996). *Signal detection theory and ROC analysis in psychology and diagnostics*. Mahwah, NJ: Lawrence Erlbaum Associates.

Tape, T. (n.d.). The area under an ROC Curve. Interpreting diagnostic tests. Retrieved from http://gim. unmc.edu/dxtests/ROC3.htm.

Thornberry, T., & Jacoby, J. (1979). *The criminally insane: A community follow-up of mentally ill offenders*. Chicago: University of Chicago Press.

United States v. Fields, 483 F 3d 313 (2007).

Vojt, G., Thompson, L.D.G., & Marshall, L. A. (2013). The predictive validity of the HCR-20 following clinical implementation: Does it work in practice? *The Journal of Forensic Psychiatry and Psychology, 24*(3), 371–385. doi: 10.1080/14789949.2013.800894

Walters, G. D. (2006). Risk-appraisal versus self-report in the prediction of criminal justice outcomes: A meta-analysis. *Criminal Justice and Behavior, 33*, 279–304. doi: 10.1177/0093854805284409

Walters, G. D., White, T. W. & Denney, D. (1991). The lifestyle criminality screening form: Preliminary data. *Criminal Justice and Behavior, 18*, 406–418. doi: 10.1177/0093854891018004003

Webster, C. D., Douglas, K. S., Eaves, D., & Hart, S. D. (1997). *HCR-20: Assessing risk for violence (Version 2)*. Burnaby, BC: Mental Health, Law, and Policy Institute, Simon Fraser University.

Webster, C. D., Harris, G. T., Rice, M. E., Cormier, C., & Quinsey, V. L. (1994). *The violence prediction scheme: Assessing dangerousness in high-risk men.* Toronto, Canada: University of Toronto, Centre of Criminology.

Webster, C. D., Martin, M. L., Brink, J., Nicholls, T. L., & Middleton, C. (2004). *Short-term Assessment of Risk and Treatability (START).* Port Coquitlam, BC: St. Joseph's Healthcare Hamilton, Ontario, and Forensic Psychiatric Services Commission.

Weiner, I. B. (2006). Writing forensic reports. In I. B. Weiner & A. K. Hess, (Eds.), *The handbook of forensic psychology* (3rd ed., pp. 631–651). Hoboken, NJ: Wiley.

Yang, M., Wong, S. C., & Coid, J. (2010). The efficacy of violence prediction: A meta-analytic *comparison* of nine risk assessment tools. *Psychological Bulletin, 135*(5), 740–767. doi: 10.1037/a0020473

8 Evaluations for Sexual Offender Civil Commitment

Amy Phenix and Rebecca L. Jackson

The nation's first civil commitment law for sex offenders was enacted in Washington state following a series of tragic events in the 1980s and the perceived failure of the legal system to prevent them.

Gene Raymond Kane was on work release from the prison where he had been serving a sentence for sexually assaulting two women. During this time, he kidnapped and murdered a young Seattle woman. The state's "sexual psychopathy" treatment program, operated by a state psychiatric hospital, had deemed him "too dangerous to handle."

Earl Shriner was released from a Washington prison after serving 10 years for kidnapping and assaulting two teenage girls. In addition to this charge, Shriner had a history of sexual violence. Despite information suggesting he would harm children after his release, the state was unable to commit him through traditional civil commitment statutes because there was no "recent overt act" or imminent dangerousness. Two years after his release from prison, Shriner raped and mutilated a 7-year-old boy.

In response to these crimes, the then-governor, Gardner, appointed a task force on Community Protection and charged it with the duty of making recommendations to change the existing laws pertaining to sex offenders. During this period of time, Wesley Allen Dodd, a confessed killer of young boys, was apprehended trying to abduct a 6-year-old boy. The need to alter current laws, with an eye both toward harsher penalties for sex offenses as well as their prevention, met with great public support. The task force's findings and recommendations were included in a comprehensive bill addressing sex offenses. Included in this bill were the state's sex offender registry and community notification program as well as the civil commitment law for "sexually violent predators." Washington State's Community Protection Act was passed in 1990.

Heinous crimes, especially ones that in hindsight "should" or "could" have been prevented, often trigger action in attempts to prevent future tragedies. Many jurisdictions have instituted laws to prevent sex crimes. Florida, for example, requires released sex offenders to wear GPS tracking devices so that their movements can be monitored. Many states have passed laws restricting where sex offenders may live. In 1996 the then-president, Bill Clinton, required all states to establish and maintain a sex offender registry. Legislating mandatory sentences of increased length for sex offenders became routine for state legislatures in the 1990s, and many adopted severe penalties for second strike offenders with the goal of incapacitating these offenders for longer periods of time. Many of these legislative initiatives, however, leave a significant number of potentially dangerous offenders free in communities as a result of plea bargains or expiration of prison sentences. Many legislatures found civil commitment an attractive solution to the gaps and loopholes they saw in their extended criminal penalties.

Civil commitment laws for sexual offenders, also known as sexually violent predator/person (SVP) or sexually dangerous person (SDP) statutes, allow for the involuntary civil commitment of sex offenders following the expiration of their prison terms. All 50 states have sex offender registries, but only 21 jurisdictions have taken the additional step of creating civil commitment laws especially designed for sex offenders. Following the enactment of Washington's law in 1990, 20 other jurisdictions have established similar laws (Arizona, California, Florida, Iowa, Illinois, Kansas, Massachusetts, Minnesota, Missouri, Nebraska, New Hampshire, New Jersey, New York, North Dakota, Pennsylvania [juveniles aging out of juvenile system only], South Carolina, Texas, Virginia, Wisconsin, and the U.S. government).

This chapter aims to introduce readers to the SVP laws and present recommendations for conducting empirically supported evaluations. The practice of civilly committing sex offenders remains controversial despite the presence of these laws now for more than 20 years. Although this chapter will touch upon some of the challenges unique to SVP evaluations, for comprehensive and detailed reviews of the clinical, legal, and ethical controversies, the reader is referred to several reviews provided by Doren (2002); Jackson and Covell (2013); Murrie, Boccaccini, and Turner (2010); Schlank (2014); Vlahakis (2010); and Winick and La Fond (2003).

The notion of civilly committing sex offenders is not entirely new. Sexual psychopath laws were initially enacted in the 1930s and 1940s to allow for the prolonged commitment of sexually violent individuals for the purposes of treatment. The early sexual psychopath laws were enacted to help society deal with sexual offenders who were "too sick to deserve punishment" (Janus, 2000). In these laws, treatment replaced punishment. In contrast, the "second generation" of commitment laws was enacted as a public safety measure in extending the incapacitation of offenders who had already served their criminal sentences. In this new model, treatment followed punishment.

Initially challenges to the SVP laws focused on whether it was truly civil commitment for the purpose of treatment or whether it was simply additional punishment after the offender had already served his[1] sentence. SVP/SDP laws were found to be constitutional pursuant to the *Kansas v. Hendricks* (1997) decision. In *Hendricks*, the Court upheld the state's police power rights and legitimized the constitutionality of SVP commitment laws. Briefly, Hendricks was a convicted child molester serving a sentence in a Kansas state penal institution. Shortly before his release in 1994, the state petitioned to have Hendricks civilly committed under a newly enacted sexually violent predator law (see Kan. Stat. Ann. 59–29[a], 1994). Hendricks argued against the constitutionality of this law and was eventually denied relief by the U.S. Supreme Court. The Kansas statute allows for the commitment of "any person who has been convicted of or charged with a sexually violent offense and who suffers from a mental abnormality which predisposes the person to commit sexually violent offenses in a degree constituting such person a menace to the health and safety of others" (Kan. Stat. Ann. 59–29[a], 1994).

Although state-to-state variation exists in the exact language of these laws, and who qualifies, each shares four common elements or prongs: (1) a past act of sexually harmful conduct; (2) a current mental disorder or abnormality; (3) a finding of risk of future sexually harmful conduct; and (4) some relationship between the mental abnormality and the likelihood of sexual violence. Table 8.1 summarizes the language used in each of the statutes, allowing for easy comparison across statutes. As always, clinicians should become familiar with current statutes, definition of legal terms in the law, and case law in the jurisdiction in which they practice. For the purposes of this chapter, we will focus on those issues that are common to most, if not all, of the statutes and provide a wide framework for understanding. Some fine-tuning will be required depending upon the particular jurisdiction.

In the first section, each of the four elements of the qualifying criteria will be reviewed, highlighting some of the more common issues faced by evaluators. In the second section, methodologies for the evaluation itself are outlined and recommendations for empirically based evaluations are presented.

Table 8.1 Civil commitment of sexual offenders: Statute details by state

State	Nomenclature	Eligibility	Standard of Dangerousness	Qualifying Disorders
Arizona	Sexually violent person	Convicted, found guilty but insane, or incompetent to stand trial for a sexually violent offense	Likely to engage in acts of sexual violence	Mental disorder: a paraphilia, personality disorder or conduct disorder or any combination of paraphilia, personality disorder and conduct disorder
California	Sexually violent predator	Convicted of a sexually violent offense against one or more victims	Likely to engage in sexually violent criminal behavior	Mental disorder: congenital or acquired condition affecting the emotional or volitional capacity that predisposes the person to the commission of criminal sexual acts in a degree constituting the person a menace to the health and safety of others
Florida	Sexually violent predator	Convicted, adjudicated delinquent, or found not guilty by reason of insanity for a sexually violent offense	Likely to engage in acts of sexual violence	Mental abnormality or personality disorder; mental abnormality: a mental condition affecting a person's emotional or volitional capacity
Illinois	Sexually violent person	Convicted, adjudicated delinquent, or found not guilty of or not responsible for a sexually violent offense by reason of insanity, mental disease, or mental defect	Substantial probability that the person will engage in acts of sexual violence	Mental disorder: congenital or acquired condition affecting the emotional or volitional capacity that predisposes a person to engage in acts of sexual violence
Iowa	Sexually violent predator	Convicted, found not guilty by reason of insanity, or found incompetent to stand trial for a sexually violent offense	Likely (defined as more likely than not) to engage in predatory acts constituting sexually violent offenses	Mental abnormality: a congenital or acquired condition affecting the emotional or volitional capacity predisposing that person to commit sexually violent offenses
Kansas	Sexually violent predator	Convicted, found incompetent to stand trial, or found not guilty by reason of insanity for a sexually violent offense	Likely to engage in repeat acts of sexual violence	Mental abnormality or personality disorder; mental abnormality: a congenital or acquired condition affecting the emotional or volitional capacity which predisposes the person to commit sexually violent offenses in a degree constituting such person a menace to the health and safety of others
Massachusetts	Sexually dangerous person	Convicted, adjudicated delinquent, or found incompetent to stand trial for a sexual offense or previously adjudicated as such by a court and whose misconduct in sexual matters indicates a general lack of power to control his sexual impulses	Likely to engage in sexual offenses if not confined to a secure facility	Mental abnormality or personality disorder; mental abnormality: a congenital or acquired condition that affects the emotional or volitional capacity of the person that predisposes that person to commit sexually violent offenses

Minnesota	Sexually dangerous persons (SDP)/sexual psychopathic personality (SPP)	Engaged in a course of harmful sexual conduct that creates a substantial likelihood of serious physical or emotional harm to victims (SDP) or the person has evidenced, by a habitual course of misconduct in sexual matters, an utter lack of power to control the person's sexual impulses and, as a result, is dangerous to other persons (SPP)	Likely to engage in acts of harmful sexual conduct (SDP) is dangerous to other persons (SPP)	Sexual, personality, or other mental disorder or dysfunction (SDP)/emotional instability, or impulsiveness of behavior, or lack of customary standards of good judgment, or failure to appreciate the consequences of personal acts, or a combination of any of these considerations, which render the person irresponsible for personal conduct with respect to sexual matters (SPP)
Missouri	Sexually violent predator	Pled guilty, found guilty, or found not guilty by reason of mental disease of a sexually violent offense or has been committed as a sexual psychopath	More likely than not to engage in predatory acts of sexual violence if not confined in a secure facility	Mental abnormality: congenital or acquired condition affecting the emotional or volitional capacity that predisposes the person to commit sexually violent offenses
Nebraska	Dangerous sex offender	Sex offenders who have completed their sentences but continue to pose a threat of harm to others	Neither voluntary hospitalization nor other treatment alternatives less restrictive of the subject's liberty than inpatient or outpatient treatment ordered by the mental health board are available or would suffice to prevent the harm	Mental illness or personality disorder
New Hampshire	Sexually violent predator	Adjudicated guilty, adjudicated not guilty by reason of insanity, or found incompetent to stand trial for a sexually violent offense	Likely to engage in sexual violence (the person's propensity to commit acts of sexual violence is of such a degree that the person has serious difficulty in controlling his behavior as to pose a potentially serious likelihood of danger to others)	Mental abnormality; mental abnormality: a mental condition affecting a person's emotional or volitional capacity which predisposes the person to commit sexually violent offenses

(Continued)

Table 8.1 Continued

State	Nomenclature	Eligibility	Standard of Dangerousness	Qualifying Disorders
New Jersey	Sexually violent predator	Convicted, adjudicated delinquent, or found not guilty by reason of insanity for commission of a sexually violent offense, or found incompetent to stand trial for commission of a sexually violent offense	Likely to engage in acts of sexual violence (further defined in case law as "highly likely")	Mental abnormality or personality disorder; mental abnormality: a mental condition that affects a person's emotional, cognitive or volitional capacity in a manner that predisposes that person to commit acts of sexual violence
New York	Sexually violent predator	Convicted and is serving a sentence for a felony sex offense, including a "specified felony" such as murder, burglary, or kidnapping determined to be sexually motivated	Likely to reoffend if not confined to a secure facility	Mental abnormality that results in a serious difficulty controlling illegal sexual behavior
North Dakota	Sexually dangerous individual	Shown to have engaged in sexually predatory conduct	Likely to engage in further acts of sexually predatory conduct that constitute a danger to the physical or mental health or safety of others	A congenital or acquired condition that is manifested by a sexual disorder, personality disorder, or other mental disorder or dysfunction
Pennsylvania	Sexually violent person	Sexually violent delinquent child: found delinquent for an act of sexual violence and remaining in the institution or facility upon attaining 20 years of age ("aging out" juveniles)	Likely to engage in an act of sexual violence	Mental abnormality or personality disorder: congenital or acquired condition of a person affecting the person's emotional or volitional capacity
South Carolina	Sexually violent predator	Convicted of, found incompetent to stand trial, found not guilty by reason of insanity, or guilty but mentally ill of sexually violent offense	Likely to engage in acts of sexual violence if not confined in a secure facility	Mental abnormality or personality disorder; mental abnormality: mental condition affecting a person's emotional or volitional capacity
Texas (outpatient commitment only)	Sexually violent predator	Repeat sexually violent offender	Likely to engage in a predatory act of sexual violence	Behavioral abnormality: a congenital or acquired condition that affects a person's emotional or volitional capacity
U.S. government	Sexually dangerous person	Engaged or attempted to engage in sexually violent conduct or child molestation	Serious difficulty in refraining from sexually violent conduct or child molestation	Serious mental illness, abnormality, or disorder

State	Term			
Virginia	Sexually violent predator	Convicted of a sexually violent offense, or unrestorably incompetent to stand trial	Likely to engage in sexually violent acts	Mental abnormality or personality disorder: emotional or volitional capacity that renders the person so likely to commit sexually violent offenses that he constitutes a menace to the health and safety of others. Because of mental abnormality or personality disorder, finds it difficult to control his predatory behavior.
Washington	Sexually violent predator	Convicted of or charged with a crime of sexual violence	Likely (defined as more probably than not) to engage in predatory acts of sexual violence	Mental abnormality and/or personality disorder: a congenital or acquired condition affecting the emotional or volitional capacity which predisposes the person to commit criminal sexual acts
Wisconsin	Sexually violent person	Convicted of, or adjudicated delinquent for, a sexually violent offense, not guilty of or not responsible for a sexually violent offense by reason of insanity or mental disease, defect, or illness	More likely than not that the person will engage in acts of sexual violence	Mental disorder: a congenital or acquired condition affecting the emotional or volitional capacity that predisposes a person to engage in acts of sexual violence

Components of SVP Statutes

A Past Act of Sexually Harmful Conduct

Each state statute (see Table 8.1) is specific to sexual offending, but states differ on the exact requirements for eligibility. Of the four prongs, this is the least likely to be an issue for the evaluator because qualifying sex offenses are generally statutorily defined in each jurisdiction with SVP/SDP laws. Most states have a screening process that identifies qualifying offenses, and those cases are identified for further review or evaluation. In other words, the evaluation is triggered by the determination that an offender has met at least this statutory requirement. In some states the offense is deemed qualifying by the prosecuting attorneys. Less often, for example in California, the evaluators in their evaluations are tasked with determining what offenses qualify according to the Sexually Violent Predator Act.

As Table 8.1 demonstrates, variations exist in terms of (1) language, e.g., sexual offense, sexually violent offense; (2) number of victims; and (3) adjudication of past sex crimes, e.g., charged vs. convicted, incompetent to stand trial, not guilty by reason of insanity.

Perhaps most important to the evaluator, states also differ on the types of sexual behavior covered under the law. As an evaluator, you will want to be familiar with the types of sexual conduct that qualify an individual for commitment. For example, exhibitionism is a qualifying behavior only in some states. Other states (e.g., Washington) exclude incest offenders from civil commitment.

A Current Mental Disorder or Abnormality

Almost all jurisdictions define mental abnormalities or disorders as congenital or acquired conditions that affect a person's emotional, cognitive, or volitional capacity that predisposes the person to commit sexually violent offenses (Miller, Amenta, & Conroy, 2005). As you can see, this definition is sufficiently broad that the evaluator has discretion in determining qualifying diagnoses. In addition, this definition of mental abnormality is different than the definition of mental disorder found in the *Diagnostic and Statistical Manual of Mental Disorders*, fifth edition (DSM-5) that equates a mental disorder with "distress and impairment in social, occupational or other important activities." (American Psychiatric Association, 2013). Beyond this definition of mental abnormality, some states also explicitly allow personality disorders (e.g., Florida, Washington) or sexual disorders (e.g., Arizona, Minnesota, North Dakota). In such cases, the connection to psychological disorders within the DSM-5 is more apparent. The much more vague "mental disorder," "mental abnormality," and "behavioral abnormality" provide evaluators with less guidance in conducting the diagnostic prong of an SVP/SDP evaluation. The definition of "mental abnormality" in the SVP law includes the "predisposition" to commit sexual violence. Because every diagnosis in the DSM-5 would not predispose an individual to commit sexual violence, diagnoses in SVP cases are most frequently paraphilic disorders, which are the most directly related to sexual offending. Other common diagnoses in SVP evaluations include substance abuse disorders and personality disorders.

Although no disorders are explicitly excluded from consideration as a mental abnormality, some disorders are much more likely to be present than others. Certain disorders lend themselves more readily to SVP cases. The most obvious qualifying disorders are the paraphilic disorders. Indeed, Becker, Stinson, Tromp, and Messer (2003) reported that the most common disorders among a sample of civilly committed sex offenders are paraphilic disorders. Research in the state of Washington replicates the trend, with the most common disorder being pedophilia, followed closely by antisocial personality disorder and substance abuse disorders (Jackson & Richards, 2007).

The paraphilias are the most likely disorders to qualify for "disorders" or "abnormalities" for the purposes of civil commitment. Within the paraphilias, pedophilia and other specified paraphilic disorders involving sexual arousal to forced sex with adults are the most common diagnoses. Although not an official diagnosis in the DSM-5, paraphilias involving sexual arousal to forced sex is commonly used by clinicians in SVP/SDP cases. It is used to describe an individual who has demonstrated a preference for, or has repeatedly engaged in, nonconsensual sex such as a serial rapist, who is aroused by the forced aspects of the sexual activity. Paraphilias indicated by noncontact sex offenses (such as exhibitionism, voyeurism) are rare as primary disorders (and would be disallowed in some states as qualifying disorders), but are often comorbidly present (Becker et al., 2003).

Psychotic disorders are most often present in individuals referred for more traditional civil commitment such as those who are found incompetent to stand trial, not criminally responsible, or subject to civil commitment due to imminent threat of harm to self or others. In contrast, psychotic disorders are rarely seen among civilly committed sex offenders (Becker et al., 2003; Vess, Murphy, & Arkowitz, 2004; Zander, 2005).

Psychopathy

Only one state, Texas, (Bailey, 2002) specifically mentions psychopathy in the statute and requires an assessment of psychopathy as part of a precommitment evaluation. High levels of psychopathy, however, are quite common among civilly committed sex offenders, primarily rapists (Vess et al., 2004). As reviewed in Vitacco, Neumann, Welch, and Buckley (Chapter 6 in this volume), psychopaths are more violent, criminally versatile, callous, and impulsive than their nonpsychopathic counterparts. In addition, psychopaths demonstrate less empathy and remorse than do others. There is convincing data that shows that high psychopathy and high psychopathy coupled with sexual deviance are both risk factors for sexual reoffense (Hanson & Morton-Bourgon, 2005; Hildebrand, de Ruiter, & de Vogel, 2004; Looman, Morphett, & Abracen, 2012; Rice & Harris, 1997). Hanson and Morton-Bourgon (2005) in a meta-analysis updating Hanson and Bussiere's classic 1998 study that identified the primary risk factors for sexual reoffense found that psychopathy was a "promising risk factor" in predicting sexual reoffense ($d = .29$). Although the single sample studies on assessing the interaction between psychopathy and sexual deviance have had mixed results (Hildebrand et al., 2004; Looman et al., 2012; Rice & Harris, 1997) a recent meta-analysis has shown greater risk of sexual reoffense with the presence of psychopathy and sexual deviance (Hawes, Boccaccini, & Murrie, 2012). Assessing psychopathy can inform a state-of-the-art risk assessment.

Related to, but not synonymous with, psychopathy is antisocial personality disorder (ASPD). Among the DSM-5 personality disorders, antisocial personality disorder is the most common in civilly committed sex offenders (Becker et al., 2003) as it is for offenders in prison (Hare, 1983). Sreenivasan, Weinberger, and Garrick (2003) noted that no statutes explicitly exclude ASPD as a qualifying diagnosis, ergo, it is possible that an individual will qualify based on this alone. While it is true that SVP/SDP laws allow for a diagnosis of ASPD to qualify alone as a mental abnormality for civil commitment, it is a matter of clinical debate in the literature. Vognsen and Phenix (2004) argue cogently that ASPD on its own is insufficient to warrant civil commitment, but that a diagnosis of paraphilia must also be present. The central argument here is that a qualifying disorder must predispose the offender to commit acts of sexual violence. The DSM-5 definition of ASPD does not include any criteria regarding sexual acts. Individuals with ASPD are clearly predisposed toward criminal acts, but not necessarily sexual acts specifically. In other words, it fails to adequately distinguish the SVP from the "dangerous, but typical recidivist" as outlined in *Hendricks* (1997).

Serious Difficulty With Volition

A crucial component of a legal mental disorder is that it "predisposes the individual to commit acts of sexual violence" (Schopp, 1998; Schopp & Sturgis, 1995). What is legally significant in establishing this link is that it also establishes a "serious difficulty" in volitional control. The challenge for the evaluator is to assess if the offender being evaluated by reason of his mental disorder also suffers from serious difficulty in volitional control as outlined in *Kansas v. Crane* (2002). In other words, how much volitional impairment is necessary under the law and how can we measure volitional impairment?

All SVP statutes require a nexus between the clinical condition (e.g., mental disorder or abnormality; personality disorder; sexual disorder) and ability to control behavior within a *legal* definition. Legal scholars (e.g., Janus, 1998; Schopp, 1998) have articulated the distinction between *legal* and *clinical* mental disorders. Legally, a disorder requires an impairment in volitional control (*Kansas v. Crane*, 2002; Schopp, 1998). The simple presence of a clinical disorder and lack of control is not sufficient; the key element is that the disorder *causes* the lack of control. The issue of degree of impairment was addressed in *Kansas v. Crane*. Michael Crane, a convicted sex offender, argued that *Hendricks* required a complete lack of control of sexual impulses and behavior. He argued that, since he retained some control, he was ineligible for civil commitment. The U.S. Supreme Court disagreed and found that "serious," but not complete volitional impairment was required for commitment.

Hendricks (1997) and *Crane* (2002) provided guidelines for the required impairment in volitionality. However, the Court purposefully avoided operationalizing the construct by suggesting that "safeguards of human liberty in the area of mental illness and the law are not always best enforced through precise bright-line rules" (*Crane*, 2002, p. 868). *Crane* clarified that the statutes do not require a total lack of control, only a "serious difficulty" in controlling behavior (p. 868). In the absence of bright-line criteria, clinicians are faced with the challenging task of defining volitionality for themselves. The clinician must differentiate the definition of "serious difficulty," distinguishing it from "some" difficulty or "moderate" difficulty. What is clear from the statutes, coupled with the findings in *Hendricks* (1997) and *Crane* (2002) is that a mental disorder and high risk are not enough. The link between the two is the crux of the civil commitment. Without this link, the offender is more suitable for criminal punishment rather than civil commitment.

Practical guidance is provided in understanding the various components that indicate serious difficulty according to the Federal Code (Federal Code § 549.95). In Federal Adam Walsh cases, which are similar to state SVP/SDP cases, the evaluator is asked to determine "serious difficulty in refraining from sexually violent conduct or child molestation if released."

The code advises "In determining whether a person will have serious difficulty in refraining from sexually violent conduct or child molestation if released, Bureau mental health professionals are advised to consider the following, but are not limited to the following evidence:

(a) of the person's repeated contact, or attempted contact, with one or more victims of sexually violent conduct or child molestation;

(b) of the person's denial of or inability to appreciate the wrongfulness, harmfulness, or likely consequences of engaging or attempting to engage in sexually violent conduct or child molestation;

(c) established through interviewing and testing of the person or through other risk assessment tools that are relied upon by mental health professionals;

(d) established by forensic indicators of inability to control conduct, such as:
   (1) offending while under supervision;
   (2) engaging in offense(s) when likely to get caught;
   (3) statement(s) of intent to reoffend; or
   (4) admission of inability to control behavior; or

(e) indicating successful completion of, or failure to successfully complete, a sex offender treatment program."

Providing Diagnoses in SVP Evaluations

To qualify as a SVP/SDP the individual's mental disorder or abnormality must be associated with serious difficulty with volition and lead to criminal sexual acts. Evaluators conducting these evaluations would benefit from evaluating this issue using a two-prong process. First, the evaluator should establish if the offender has a mental disorder using the DSM-5. Second, the evaluator makes a determination whether the offender has sufficient control or not to prevent sexual reoffense. The evaluator is reminded that the DSM-5 provides a cautionary note that "When used appropriately, diagnoses and diagnostic information can assist legal decision makers in their determinations" (American Psychiatric Association, 2013, p. 25). The evaluator is cautioned, however, that there is an imperfect fit between clinical diagnoses and diagnoses defined in mental health law. For every given diagnosis, it does not "imply that an individual with such a condition meets legal criteria for the presence of a mental disorder or a specified legal standard" (p. 25). Further, it is noted that "impairments, abilities, and disabilities vary widely within each diagnostic category that assignment of a particular diagnosis does not imply a specific level of impairment or disability" (p. 25), nor does a clinical diagnosis carry any necessary implications regarding the degree of control over behaviors that are typical of the disorder.

Risk Assessment in Civil Commitment Evaluations

As discussed in "Violence Risk Assessment" (Guyton & Jackson, Chapter 7 in this volume), the practice of violence risk prediction and sex offender risk prediction in psychology and psychiatry has evolved tremendously since early condemnations of its accuracy (e.g., Harris & Hanson, 2010; Monahan, 1981). Because the purpose of civil commitment laws is to prevent high-risk individuals from committing further sexually violent offenses, rather than punishing them for violence already committed, the ability to estimate future risk is integral to SVP evaluations.

The question now is not whether risk assessments should be completed for sex offenders, but what methodology should be used. To examine this question Hanson and Morton-Bourgon (2009) meta-analytically examined 118 prediction studies to determine the predictive accuracy of the method of prediction. For all outcomes the actuarial method of predicting sexual reoffense was superior ($d = .67$). Unstructured professional judgment was significantly less accurate than actuarial methods ($d = .42$). The accuracy of structured professional judgment was intermediate between the accuracy found for actuarial measures and for unstructured professional judgment.

Actuarial predictors of future risk are the most commonly used and empirically supported methods employed for estimation of risk (Hanson & Morton-Bourgon, 2009). Further, the Association for the Treatment of Sexual Abusers (ATSA, 2001) recommends their use in all SVP evaluations. Secondary to this research, it is mandatory practice today to use one or more actuarial instruments to measure static, or historical, risk factors. Static risk factors rarely change (although they can increase with new offending) and they can provide a baseline of risk for a sexual offender. Examples of static risk factors include number of prior sex offenses, total criminal offenses, and gender of the victim.

More recent research has identified the dynamic or changeable risk factors for sexual reoffense that are generally the targets of treatment (Mann, Hanson, & Thornton, 2010). These dynamic risk factors, also called *long-term vulnerabilities* or *psychological risk factors*, have been incorporated into structured instruments to assess relevant risk factors (e.g., Fernandez, Harris, Hanson, & Sparks, 2012; Helmus, Hanson, Thornton, Babchishin, & Harris, 2012a; McGrath, Lasher, & Cumming, 2012). Contemporary risk assessments should contain an assessment of both one or more actuarial instruments and a review of relevant dynamic risk factors.

Risk Assessment in SVP Evaluations

Estimating risk within the context of SVP evaluation encompasses three distinct considerations: First, the risk must be of a statutorily defined likelihood. Second, the risk must be of sexual violence specifically, not general violence. Third, as noted earlier, the type of violence must be included in the statute.

Concerning the first consideration, states vary regarding the standard of dangerousness needed to meet statutory criteria. Many states require that an individual be "likely" to commit future acts of sexual violence. Others use the more stringent "more likely than not" (see Table 8.1). The more likely than not criteria seems reasonably analogous to a greater than 50% chance. However, no such "logical" definition of likely exists. In fact, in California the *Ghilotti* decision termed "likely" as a "reasonable and well-founded risk" (*People v. Superior Court [Ghilotti]*, 2002). When familiarizing yourself with your state's law, be sure to read it in its entirety. Definitions often appear embedded in the statute that clarify the language put forth in the statute proper. For example, Washington's law requires that the offender be "likely" to commit predatory acts if not confined in a secure facility. "Likely" is further defined in the statute as meaning "more likely than not." The evaluator will also need to be cognizant of the relevant case law that may further clarify the meaning of these probability descriptors within a given jurisdiction.

Regarding the second consideration, the type of violence must be sexual in nature. Beyond being at risk for committing sexual violence, the offender must be at risk of committing the type of violence the state has established as relevant. A finding, even that the individual is 100% likely to commit some sort of violence (even if that were possible) is not sufficient. The risk must be specific to sexual violence. Actuarial measures that have been developed for risk assessment purposes differ on the type of violence they predict. As will be discussed in the second half of this chapter, a few well-validated instruments exist for aiding in sexual violence prediction.

The use of actuarials requires the ability to accurately interpret the instruments and communicate their results. As discussed more fully in "Violence Risk Assessment" (Guyton & Jackson, Chapter 7 in this volume) estimates of risk derived from actuarial measures must be interpreted and communicated with care. For example, actuarial instruments offer measures of relative risk such as low, medium, and high. No clinical or legal criteria have been established to translate the results into legally meaningful estimates. The evaluator must still render a judgment whether an individual who is medium-high on a risk assessment instrument meets the state's "likely" or "more likely than not" risk criterion. Even when associated percentages are included (e.g., 30% of offenders in this risk category reoffended over the 10-year follow-up), evaluators must judge associated "likelihood" as defined in the statute in consideration of all means of assessment and case factors. Further, the sexual reoffense risk assessment task is over the offender's lifetime, not only the five- or 10-year follow-up captured by the instruments.

Evaluation

SVP/SDP statutes require that the individual undergo an evaluation. In most of these proceedings the respondent is evaluated by one or more state evaluators and one or more evaluators representing the respondent. The nature of these evaluations is not well articulated but each calls for a determination that the individual (respondent) is at increased risk for committing sexual violence, and that this risk is connected to a mental disorder, abnormality, or personality disorder. While these statutes provide for the final determination to be made by the court, the role of the mental health professional is integral. These legal determinations are informed by mental health professionals' findings.

Few professional standards exist to guide SVP evaluations. ATSA has published a statement regarding SVPs, only a small portion of which directly pertains to the evaluation process (see section on risk for future violence). The American Psychiatric Association has publicly denounced the practice of civil commitment for sex offenders and, therefore, provides no guidance for psychiatrists engaged in their evaluation (Zanona, Bonnie, & Hoge, 2001). The American Psychological Association has taken no public stance on the laws. In the absence of more specific guidelines, its *Specialty Guidelines for Forensic Psychology* (American Psychological Association, 2013) remain applicable.

Preparing for the Assessment

SVP evaluations have been conceptualized as a series of interrelated questions (Rogers & Jackson, 2005). Each question roughly corresponds to one of the four prongs of the laws: (1) a past act of sexually harmful conduct; (2) a current mental disorder or abnormality; (3) some relationship between the mental abnormality and the likelihood of sexual violence; and (4) a finding of risk of future sexually harmful conduct. It is often helpful to organize your final report around these sections, fully answering one question before addressing the next.

The Evaluation Context and Approach

Clinicians face a formidable task when they agree to conduct an assessment and offer testimony in a SVP evaluation. Similar to other referral questions, such as competency to stand trial and criminal responsibility, the expert is expected to understand the legal standard and apply it appropriately in his psychological evaluation and eventual testimony. The *Specialty Guidelines for Forensic Psychologists* (American Psychological Association, 2013) clearly states that clinicians must provide "information that is most relevant to the psycholegal issue" (p. 15); This requires the evaluator to be well versed in law—and not only the law in the state where you conduct evaluations, but also the appellate law that forms the basis for interpreting the law over time.

A common first step in forensic assessment is to gather relevant records and potential collateral sources. The universe of relevant information is often quite large as the evaluator will want to review information regarding the respondent's childhood, family, sexual, and criminal histories as well as psychological, treatment, and incarceration histories. These records will provide important data for both diagnostic and risk assessment purposes. In some cases, they will be the only information available to the evaluator, such as in the absence of a clinical interview. In other cases, they will be used to confirm or refute a respondent's account given in the interview. The evaluator may also have past trial transcripts and depositions for past proceedings, particularly when the individual is subject to annual evaluations or conditional or unconditional release trials from SVP/SDP facilities. Much more than is true for other psycholegal assessments, SVP evaluations are very comprehensive and in some cases may involve the review of thousands of pages of discovery. All details of the individual's history and lifestyle are potentially relevant.

One caution deserves mention here: reviewing such a large number of documents virtually guarantees that the examiner will review information that he or she finds appalling or, alternatively, information that makes him overly sympathetic to the respondent. Esses and Webster (1988), Lynett and Rogers (2000), and Jackson, Rogers, and Shuman (2004) have all demonstrated the biasing effect that emotionally provocative information has on forensic decision making. One suggestion for combating this potential bias is to score the actuarial instrument(s) you will use during this initial portion of the evaluation. Jackson et al. (2004) demonstrated that "anchoring" assessments with actuarial information may protect the examiner against the biasing effects of emotionally powerful information. This is likely also true of reviewing dynamic or psychological risk factors in a structured fashion so the evaluator does not over- or underweight a particular risk factor.

Clinical Interview

The *Specialty Guidelines for Forensic Psychology* (American Psychological Association, 2013) state that, "Forensic practitioners recognize their obligations to only provide written or oral evidence about the psychological characteristics of particular individuals when they have sufficient information or data to form an adequate foundation for those opinions or to substantiate their findings" (p. 15). At times, the respondent will decline to participate in the interview. Absent the opportunity to interview, evaluations can be completed on record review alone but forensic psychologists "strive to make clear the impact of such limitations on the reliability and validity of their professional products, opinions, or testimony" (p. 15).

Respondents may or may not participate in an interview for a variety of reasons; no particular meaning should be interpreted from their participation or refusal. Benefits of conducting an interview include providing the respondent an opportunity to confirm or refute information garnered from his records; conducting a structured or semi-structured interview for diagnostic or risk assessment purposes, including the Psychopathy Checklist–Revised (PCL-R; Hare, 2003); and gathering information from the respondent regarding current thoughts, feelings, fantasies, and behavior relevant to the referral questions.

A challenge in all forensic assessment is gauging the value of an examinee's self-report. Research suggests that sex offenders are unreliable in their self-reports (Langevin, 1988; Rogers & Dickey, 1991; Sewell & Salekin, 1997). Most notably, sex offenders are characterized by their denial, minimization, or externalization of blame (Kennedy & Grubin, 1992; Langevin, 1988). Kennedy and Grubin (1992) identified a number of different denial patterns common among sex offenders. Importantly, two of the four patterns identified were characterized by externalization of responsibility. These offenders acknowledged the offense, but attributed the cause of their behavior to an external force out of their immediate control (see also Sewell & Salekin, 1997). These studies are directly relevant to SVP evaluations in that behavioral control is a central referral question.

A Past Act of Sexually Harmful Conduct

As discussed previously, this requirement is statutorily defined. As an evaluator, you will typically not need to make a determination regarding whether this requirement has been met. Instead, the following discussion will focus only on the additional three components of the statutes. However, a thorough narrative of the facts of the sexual offenses is useful to highlight the offender's modus operandi, sexually deviant arousal pattern, victim type, and level of violence. This information is helpful diagnostically and in conducting a risk assessment.

Current Mental Disorder or Abnormality

The first question is: Does the respondent suffer from a mental disorder or abnormality (as defined by the relevant statute)? Record review is often helpful in this regard to gather a history of psychiatric diagnosis and treatment, and criminal behavior that will be useful in assessing the possibility of antisocial personality disorder and the paraphilias.

Provided the respondent agrees to a clinical interview, most mental disorders can be assessed reliably through the use of structured and semi-structured interviews for mental disorders (see Rogers, 2001 for a comprehensive discussion of diagnostic and structured interviews). The PCL-R should also be administered to assess the various personality traits and behavior associated with this disorder. Additionally high scores on the PCL-R are associated with increased risk of violent and sexual offending (Murrie et al., 2010). Although the PCL-R can be scored without the benefit of an interview, the recommended method of administration includes a clinical interview.

Perhaps of paramount importance for SVP evaluations is a comprehensive assessment of the paraphilias. Few standardized approaches exist for assessing the various sexual disorders (Miller et al., 2005). Several diagnostic issues make the systematic evaluation of paraphilias imperative. First, research suggests that during the use of unstructured interviews, clinicians will often cease their diagnostic inquiry prematurely (Rogers, 2001). Yet, research in Washington state suggests that the typical SVP has more than one paraphilia (Jackson & Richards, 2007). Important diagnostic data will be missed if diagnostic inquiries are prematurely terminated. Second, clinicians tend to overrely on unique or sensational data (Borum, Otto, & Golding, 1993). A particularly heinous sexual offense may bias the clinician in favor of a related diagnosis, or alternatively, overshadow less heinous yet still meaningful data. The related issues of confirmatory and hindsight bias (Borum et al., 1993) reinforce the need for comprehensive and structured assessments. Evaluators are encouraged to conduct a systematic evaluation of all the paraphilias.

Determining Risk of Sexually Violent Conduct—Actuarial Instruments

The use of actuarial estimates of risk has been established as the *standard of practice* for SVP evaluations (Association for the Treatment of Sexual Abusers, 2001). Furthermore, state statutes may require the use of actuarial measures as well. For example, Virginia's code requires the use of the Static-99 or a "comparable, scientifically valid instrument." The most common actuarial instruments used in civil commitment evaluations are outlined in this section. Information provided here was current as of the writing of this chapter. However, sex offender recidivism and risk assessment is an active area of research, with several new articles being published each year. Students and practitioners are encouraged to attend conferences and stay current with the literature to ensure most up to date information and practice. As of this writing, the most commonly used and best validated actuarial measures for assessing sexual recidivism risk are the Static-99, Static-99 Revised (Static-99R), Static-2002R, and the Violence Risk Appraisal Guide (VRAG; Hanson, Helmus, & Thornton, 2010; Hanson & Thornton, 2000; Rice, Harris, & Lang, 2013)

Static-99

The original Static-99 was developed by Karl Hanson and David Thornton (2000) to assess risk of sexual and violent recidivism with sexual offenders. The Static-99 is the combination of static, historical risk factors that were initially included in two earlier tools, the Rapid Risk Assessment for Sex Offender Recidivism (RRASOR) and the Structured Anchored Clinical Judgment (SACJ-Min; Grubin, 1998; Hanson & Bussiere, 1998; Hanson & Thornton, 2000).

The 10-item Static-99 includes the following variables: number of prior sexual offenses, four or more prior sentencing occasions, any conviction for a noncontact sexual offense, any nonsexual violent conviction in conjunction with the index sexual offense, any prior conviction for a nonsexual violent offense, any male victim, any unrelated victim in a sexual offense, any stranger victim in a sexual offense, young age at release (under 25), and never lived with an intimate partner for at least two years. The Static-99 differs from the Static-99R only on Item 1, the age item, which now has four categories of age versus two in Static-99.

The scoring of Static-99 (along with the Static-99R and the Static-2002R—both discussed later in this chapter) is contained in a comprehensive coding manual available on the Static-99 Clearinghouse (www.static99.org), a Web site dedicated to providing resources for the instrument including training, research, and other documents related to the use of various Static tools. The Web site also allows for submitting questions on the scoring of Static-99 and receiving responses from the Web site manager.

The Static-99 measures the risk of sexual or violent reconviction among males who have sexually offended. Because many offenses go undetected, particularly sexual offenses, the resulting risk estimates should be considered an underestimate of the true risk of recidivism (Bonta & Hanson, 1994).

Static-99 Development Sample and Results

The assumptions leading to the construction of the Static-99 were assessed in the Static-99 development sample, which consisted of four subsamples: three from Canada and one from England. Because the recidivism rates for all four samples were so similar, Hanson and Thornton (2000) combined them into a single sample ($n = 1{,}208$) for further analyses. Area Under the Curve (AUC) was used to test the predictive accuracy of each of the tools. The Static-99 (AUC = .71), RRASOR (AUC = .69), and SACJ-Min (AUC = .67) each predicted sexual recidivism at significantly better than chance levels. Generally, these levels of accuracy would be considered to be in the moderate to large range. Additional analyses demonstrated that the predictive accuracy of the Static-99 was greater than either the RRASOR ($Z = 2.38$, $p < .05$) or the SACJ-Min ($Z = 2.84$, $p < .01$).

Static-99 Reliability

Reliability studies have typically shown excellent levels of reliability for Static-99 scores in both research and applied settings (Hanson & Morton-Bourgon, 2009; Helmus, 2009), in community supervision and treatment settings (Hanson, Harris, Scott, & Helmus, 2007; Storey, Watt, Jackson, & Hart, 2012), and in the field (Boccaccini, Murrie, Mercado, & Quesada, 2012).

This is also true for interrater reliability studies that have been conducted in the field for SVP evaluators. An early unpublished study by Hanson (2001) examined 55 cases from SVP evaluations in California and found an interclass correlation coefficient (ICC) of .87. Levenson (2004) conducted a larger field reliability study in Florida and also found strong rater agreement in Static-99 total scores for 281 offenders evaluated for SVP commitment in Florida (ICC = .85).

Murrie et al. (2009) examined interrater agreement for Texas SVP evaluators with a relatively smaller sample. Reliability of Static-99 scores was high when comparing scores of experts on the same side of a case (ICC = .84 for petitioners' experts and ICC = .95 for respondents' experts). However, when comparing scores of petitioners' experts with respondents' experts, the ICCs dropped into the .60 range, suggesting the possibility of adversarial allegiance effects.

Cross-Validations of Static-99

The Static-99 has been validated on large and diverse samples from all over the world. Although readers are recommended to use Static-99R, these validations are reported because they are relevant to the validity of Static-99R since only one item was changed in the revision. There were 63 validations on Static-99 in Hanson and Morton-Bourgon's (2009) meta-analysis, substantially more than any other actuarial instrument that measures risk for sexual recidivism, and a number that continues to grow. Approximately 20,000 sexual offenders have been sampled in these studies. As noted by Hanson and Morton-Bourgon, the weighted average AUC across those studies was .67 (95% CI of .62 – .72) and the median AUC was .74.

AUC values indicating moderate to strong predictive accuracy for sexual recidivism with the Static-99 have been very robust across nations, settings, and populations. Overall, the Static-99 shows moderate to strong predictive accuracy in Canada, the United States, the United Kingdom, Europe, Australia, and New Zealand, with the largest effect sizes in the United Kingdom, Australia, New Zealand, and California (Hanson, Lunetta, Phenix, Neely, & Epperson, 2014; Helmus, Hanson, & Morton-Bourgon, 2011).

Similarly, the Static-99 has shown moderate to large effect sizes for sexual offenders released from prison (Beggs & Grace, 2010; Brown, 2003; Craig, Beech, & Browne, 2006; Epperson, 2003; Friendship, Mann, & Beech, 2003; Hanson et al., 2014; Hood, Shute, Feilzer, & Wilcox, 2002;

Langstrom, 2004; McGrath, Hoke, Livingston, & Cumming, 2001; Skelton, Riley, Wales, & Vess, 2006; Ternowski, 2004; Thornton, 2002) and for sexual offenders in community samples (Beech, Friendship, Erikson, & Hanson, 2002; Craissati, Webb, & Keen, 2005; Endrass, Urbaniok, Held, Vetter, & Rossegger, 2009; Epperson, 2003; Hanson et al., 2007; Stalans, Seng, & Yarnold, 2002).

Moderate predictive accuracy has been demonstrated for sexual offenders in forensic hospitals (Bengston & Langstrom, 2007; de Vogel, de Ruiter, van Beek, & Mead, 2004; Ducro & Pham, 2006; Harris, Rice, Quinsey, Lalumiere, Boer, & Lang, 2003; Nunes, Wexler, Firestone, & Bradford, 2003). Varying levels of predictive accuracy, from small to large, have been documented in validations with more specialized groups of sexual offenders, such as developmentally delayed sexual offenders (Hanson, Sheahan, & VanZuylen, 2013; Tough, 2001), juvenile offenders (Beech, 2005; Poole, Liedecke, & Marbibi, 2000; Ralston & Epperson, 2013), subtypes of sexual offenders (rape, child molest) (Bartosh, Garby, Lewis, & Gray, 2003; Brouillette-Alarie & Proulx, 2013; Ducro & Pham, 2006), treated offenders (Allan, Grace, Rutherford, & Hudson, 2007; Friendship, Mann, & Beech 2003; McGrath et al., 2012; Seager, Jellicoe, & Dhaliwal, 2004; Thornton, 2002), and offenders who committed sexually motivated homicides (Hill, Habermann, Klusmann, Berner, & Briken, 2008).

A recent meta-analysis involving 43 studies and 31,426 sexual offenders from 11 countries examined the predictive accuracy of 15 risk assessment tools for sexual offenders. The total sample for analyses of the Static-99 was comprised of 20,727 sexual offenders from 30 studies. All of the reviewed tools produced at least a moderate effect size in predicting sexual reoffense, including Static-99 (AUC = .69; Tully, Chou, & Browne, 2013).

There are mixed results of replications of Static-99 in the field versus research settings. An actuarial instrument may work well in a research setting, where there is quality control over fidelity to scoring rules, but not in an applied context where there is more opportunity for "coder drift." The field validity of Static-99 was tested for 1,928 sexual offenders screened for possible civil commitment as SVPs in Texas. Sexual offenders in this study were either subject to discharge, mandatory supervision, or civil commitment (outpatient intensive supervision in Texas). The results demonstrated modest predictive accuracy (AUC = .55 for SVPs and AUC = .57 for sex offenders who were not determined to be SVPs; Boccaccini, Murrie, Caperton, & Hawes, 2009). Potential problems with this study included a very low sexual recidivism base rate, relatively short follow-up time, lower interrater reliability, and the level of supervision received by higher scoring sexual offenders, with each of these contributing to decreased variance in the outcome measure. This was likely most true for higher scoring offenders given the increased supervision that they received.

In contrast, very positive results emerged in a recent field study in California (Hanson et al., 2014). This study examined the predictive accuracy of Static-99 and Static-99R in a prospective study of 475 randomly selected adult males released in 2006 and 2007 and followed for five years. The California study revealed strong predictive accuracy for Static-99 (AUC = .82). This study demonstrated that the higher levels of predictive accuracy obtained in research settings can also be achieved in the field. While the reasons for the relatively higher AUCs are not fully understood, it is likely that California's comprehensive and structured training program for scoring Static-99R for probation and parole officers in California was a contributing factor. This program requires certification and recertification of scorers every two years, resulting in scoring that demonstrated very broad-based reliability *and* consistency with scoring rules.

Although the majority of Static-99 validation studies were conducted with retrospective samples, the study just described used a prospective design. In addition to the study just described, there have been other prospective validation studies. The Dynamic Supervision Project (Hanson et al., 2007) followed more than 997 Canadian probationers for three years, and the Static-99 showed high predictive accuracy (AUC = .74) in this large contemporary sample (Hanson et al., 2007). An Austrian prospective study was conducted on 1,142 sexual offenders released from

Austrian prisons and yielded statistically significant indices of predictive accuracy for the total sample (AUC = .73) and separately for child abusers (AUC = .77) and rapists (AUC = .69; Eher, Schilling, Haubner-MacLean, Jann, & Rettenberger, 2012).

Static-99R

The Static-99R was released for clinical use in 2009 (Hanson, Phenix, & Helmus, 2009; Helmus, Thornton, Hanson, & Babchishin, 2012b). The reasons for revising Static-99 were twofold. First, it was discovered that Static-99 did not adequately account for reductions in recidivism with advancing age at release (Hanson, 2002; Helmus et al., 2012b). Second, more contemporary samples showed substantial reductions in sexual recidivism base rates relative to those in the Static-99 development samples. The Static-99R development team has recommended the Static-99R replace the use of Static-99.

Static-99R Development and Validation Samples

The Static-99R (Helmus et al., 2012b) was developed and validated with 23 samples, which were drawn from eight different countries. Eleven samples were from Canada, six were from the United States, two were from the United Kingdom, and one each was drawn from Austria, Denmark, Germany, Sweden, and New Zealand. A total of 8,390 sexual offenders were included in the 23 samples.

For analyses to recode age at release, the sample was divided into construction and validation subsamples. All offenders with a follow-up period of less than 10 years were included in the construction sample ($n = 5,714$) and all offenders with a longer follow-up period were included in the validation sample ($n = 2,392$). The entire sample was used to renorm the Static-99R and to address the issue of variability of sexual recidivism base rates across the samples. More details on the samples are available in Helmus et al. (2012b).

Age at Release Item

In Static-99, age at release (following the last sexual offense) was classified and scored using two categories: under age 25 (1 risk point) or age 25 and older (0 risk points). Additional analyses indicated age was not fully accounted for in Static-99, and the age item was revised to include four age categories with decreasing risk points for increased age as follows: 18 to 34.9 (1 point), 35 to 39.9 (0 points), 40 to 59.9 (−1 point), and 60 and older (−3 points; Helmus et al., 2012b). This new scoring reflects increased risk for younger offenders and decreased risk with advancing age. All other Static-99R scoring is identical to that of the Static-99.

Validity of the Static-99R

Relative Risk

The *Static-99R and Static-2002R Evaluator Workbook* (Phenix, Helmus, & Hanson, 2015) contains scoring guidelines for measures of relative risk such as percentiles and relative risk ratios. While these measures are useful for developing policy and procedures in the management of sexual offenders, they may be less informative in SVP/SDP evaluations that require an estimate of how likely the offender is to go on to sexually reoffend.

Absolute Risk

Sexual recidivism rates of more contemporary samples in Static-99R were approximately 60% of the rate observed in the original Static-99 samples, with the greatest reductions occurring at higher scores (4 and higher; Helmus, 2009). These findings highlighted the need for updated norms for absolute risk estimates (predicted probabilities of sexual recidivism) associated with each score and/or risk category.

An additional finding in the new data was that sexual recidivism base rates varied significantly across samples, which contrasted with the homogeneity of sexual recidivism base rates in the original Static-99 development samples. Helmus (2009) examined a number of variables that might moderate the observed variability; of these potential moderator variables, only sample type warranted further consideration.

This finding, and further analyses in 2009, led to the adoption of new contemporary norms for four separate groups based on level of preselection: routine correctional samples, preselected for treatment samples, preselected for high risk/high needs samples, and other nonroutine correctional samples. In 2015 new norms were again released that included three new routine samples and the removal of the Thornton and Knight (2013) sample from the *High Risk/High Needs Norms*. The *Routine Norms* are based on correctional samples comprised of sexual offenders selected in relatively random and unselected ways. This group has the lowest recidivism rates for each cutoff score.

The *High Risk/High Needs Norms* are based on sexual offenders selected (on the basis of perceived risk) for relatively "rare or infrequent measures or interventions or sanctions, such as psychiatric commitments and being held past their release date" (Hanson et al., 2009; Phenix, Helmus, & Hanson, 2012). More detailed descriptions of the defining characteristics of each normative group, as well as a listing of the risk estimates for each group, are provided in the *Evaluator Workbook* (Phenix et al., 2015).

Increasingly, research evidence confirms that that the variability in sexual recidivism base rates in the Static-99R samples is due to differences in the presence of unmeasured risk factors external to Static-99R (Hanson & Thornton, 2012). These external risk factors are often referred to as psychological needs or dynamic risk factors. Many such enduring psychological/ dynamic needs or long-term vulnerabilities were identified meta-analytically by Mann et al. (2010) and are discussed later in this chapter.

Looman and Abracen (2012) examined 348 high-risk sexual offenders who were divided into two groups based on the level of preselection (detained and not detained past release date). Offenders in the detained (preselected) group evidenced greater levels of hostility, cognitive distortions supportive of offending, sexual obsessions, and sexually deviant behaviors. They also showed less assertiveness and greater psychiatric histories. These results supported the findings by Hanson and Thornton (2012) that preselection is associated with greater levels of dynamic needs.

Importantly, these dynamic needs add incremental validity to Static-99R (Hanson & Thornton, 2012). Offenders with low to moderate dynamic needs are most similar to offenders in the *Routine Norms*, and offenders with high dynamic needs are most similar to offenders in the *High Risk/High Needs Norms* Similarly, sexual offenders with identical scores on the Static-99R have different rates of sexual recidivism based on the density of psychological/dynamic needs, with higher needs sexual offenders exhibiting higher rates of sexual recidivism than lower needs sexual offenders with the same score (Hanson & Thornton, 2012; Thornton & Knight, 2013).

Concurrent with research documenting the additional explanatory power of psychological/ dynamic needs external to the Static-99, empirically derived and validated tools measuring the density of such needs emerged. Examples of such tools include the Stable-2007 (Fernandez, et al., 2012; Helmus et al., 2012a; Hanson et al., 2007), Structured Risk Assessment–Forensic Version (SRA-FV; Thornton & Knight, 2013) and the Violence Risk Scale–Sex Offender Version (VRS-SO; Olver, Wong, Nicholaichuk, & Gordon, 2007). These tools provide methods for reliably quantifying the density of psychological/dynamic needs and informing the selection of an appropriate Static-99R norm group. For example, the SRA-FV manual contains a Level of Need Inventory (LONI) that gives specific cutoff scores to select the appropriate Static-99R norm group (for details on obtaining the SRA-FV manual, see Thornton & Knight, 2013). Similarly, the Stable-2007 provides recidivism rates depending on the score on Static-99R and Stable-2007 combined.

Reliability of the Static-99R

Given that the scoring for the Static-99R differs from the Static-99 on only one of 10 items, it can draw from the vast research confirming the ability to reliably score the Static-99. Still, it is technically a different tool, so it was important to independently document the reliability of scores using the Static-99R. McGrath et al. (2012) reported very high reliability for the Static-99R (ICC = .89).

Noting the importance of assessing reliability of scores produced by field-workers, Hanson et al. (2014) assessed the reliability of Static-99R scores from 55 corrections and probation officers in California scoring a common set of 14 cases. Overall rater reliability was acceptable (ICC = .78). There was a substantial difference in the reliability of scores from experienced scorers (ICC = .85) and less experienced scorers (ICC = .71), pointing to the importance of recent practice. Experienced scorers were those who had scored 26 or more sexual offenders on the Static-99R in the previous 12 months.

Cross-Validations of the Static-99R

Validity of the Static-99R was well established through the use of separate construction and validation samples. As noted earlier, the AUC of .72 in the validation sample ($n = 2,392$) was statistically significant and nominally higher than that for the Static-99 (AUC = .71; Helmus et al., 2012b). Because the Static-99 and Static-99R are identical except for the age item, Static-99 cross-validations can be informative about the predictive accuracy for both Static-99 and Static-99R.

In a separate cross-validation of the Static-99R in California, Hanson et al. (2014) reported high relative risk validity (discrimination) and good absolute risk validity (calibration). This was a prospective field study of 475 randomly selected adult males released from California prisons in 2006–2007 and followed for five years. The resulting AUC = .817 (95% CI .716 – .919) demonstrated strong relative predictive accuracy.

Hanson et al. (2014) also looked at the predictive accuracy of the Static-99R for five-year sexual recidivism separately for Black (AUC = .765), Hispanic (AUC = .734), and White (AUC = .850) sexual offenders. The levels of predictive accuracy were statistically significant ($p < .05$) for Blacks and Whites, but not for Hispanics. That latter nonsignificant finding resulted from a very wide 95% confidence interval, which was at least in part due to the small sample size of Hispanic sexual recidivists ($n = 5$). Logistic regression equations for Black, Hispanic, and White sexual offenders revealed no significant differences in the adjusted base rate (predicted value for a Static-99R score of 2) or in the rate of change in relative risk for a one-unit increase in Static-99R score. In other words, discrimination and calibration were not different based on ethnicity.

Performance of the Static-99R with Black, Latino, and White sexual offenders was also examined in the large Texas study described earlier (Varela, Boccaccini, Murrie, Caperton, & Gonzalez, 2013). The Static-99R did not perform well overall in this study, but its sexual recidivism predictive accuracy for relative risk was roughly equivalent with Blacks (AUC = .65), Latinos (AUC = .57), and Whites (AUC = .59). Only the AUC for Blacks was statistically significant.

In a sample of 319 Canadian Aboriginals and 1,269 Canadian non-Aboriginals across five independent samples, Babchishin, Blais, and Helmus (2012) found similar, statistically significant levels of predictive accuracy for the Static-99R with both groups, AUC = .698 and AUC = .726 respectively. Predictive accuracy at the item level was also similar for the two groups of sexual offenders. In contrast, with a smaller sample of Australian Aboriginals ($n = 67$) and non-Aboriginals (n = 399) with a relatively short follow-up period (M = 29 months), Smallbone and Rallings (2013) reported statistically significant sexual recidivism predictive accuracy for the Static-99R with Australian non-Aboriginal sexual offenders (AUC = .79) but not for Australian Aboriginal sexual offenders (AUC = .61).

As with the Static-99, a clear pattern based on race/ethnicity does not emerge. This variability of results should be a consideration in applied risk assessments with sexual offenders identified as a racial/ethnic minority.

Static-2002 and Static-2002R

Development and Initial Validation

STATIC-2002

The Static-2002 was developed by Hanson and Thornton (2003) with the intent of creating a risk assessment tool with improved reliability and predictive accuracy, as well as increased conceptual clarity and coherence. Like Static-99, the Static-2002 was designed to be a brief actuarial measure of relative and absolute risk for sexual recidivism that could be scored from commonly available information in correctional files.

Potential items were identified through a review of existing research literature at the time, as well as a review of items in some other validated actuarial tools. Items were selected, weighted, and combined in some cases based on meta-analyses of 10 samples, including three of the four samples to develop the Static-99 (Institut Philippe Pinel, Millbrook, and Her Majesty's Prison Service in the United Kingdom; Hanson & Thornton, 2003). Two federal Canadian samples were also utilized. Other Canadian samples were from Edmonton, British Columbia, and Manitoba. Two samples were included from the United States: one from California and one from Washington state. In all, 4,596 sexual offenders were included in the development sample with an average follow-up period of seven years.

The Static-2002 resulted in inclusion of 14 items, which were organized into five meaningful subscales of risk: age, persistence of sexual offending, deviant sexual interests, relationship to victims, and general criminality. Age at release consisted of a single item and the other four categories consisted of two to five items. Organization of the 14 items into five subcategories was intended to provide greater conceptual clarity and potentially enable treatment providers to identify specific areas of risk to better develop treatment plans and interventions. The range of total scores is 0–14. Indices of relative risk including percentiles and relative risk ratios are available in the first version of the *Evaluator Workbook* (Phenix et al., 2012).

To estimate the predictive accuracy, Hanson and Thornton (2003) compared the performance of the Static-2002 to the Static-99 and the RRASOR using eight of the 10 samples. The performance of the three tools in predicting sexual recidivism across the eight samples was comparable, as reflected in unweighted average AUCs of .678 for the RRASOR, .688 for the Static-99, and .716 for the Static-2002. There was also little difference in the performance of the three tools separately for child molesters (respective AUCs of .671, .700, .687) and rapists (respective AUCs of .693, .671, .734). One advantage of the Static-2002 is that it had less variability across samples. Although absolute risk estimates were generated for the Static-2002, they are not reported here because they have been deemed outdated by the developers and replaced with new absolute risk estimates in conjunction with the development of the Static-2002R.

STATIC-2002R

The Static-2002 Revised (Static-2002R) is a revision from the prior Static-2002. Static-2002R was developed for the same reasons as the Static-99R, to better reflect decreasing risk with advancing age and to adjust for decreasing base rates of sexual recidivism and variability in those base rates in generating absolute risk estimates. The analyses and results were parallel to those described earlier for the Static-99R and both sets of analyses are provided by Helmus et al. (2012a, b), so only the differences between the Static-99R and Static-2002R analyses and results are described here.

One important difference is that there were only seven Static-2002 samples ($n = 2,609$) available. Analyses to determine the need for new scoring of the age at release item utilized the samples from these studies. The Static-2002R age at release item is scored: 2 for age 18–34.9, 1 for age 35–39.9, 0 for age 40–59.9, and −2 for age 60 and older. For both Static-99R and Static-2002R, age is fully accounted for within the instrument.

With these seven samples, the relative predictive validity for five-year sexual recidivism was nominally higher on Static-2002R (AUC = .713) than the Static-2002 (AUC = .709). As with other actuarial tools, relative risk can be reported as nominal risk categories, percentiles, or relative risk ratios. Static-2002R nominal risk categories, percentiles, and relative risk ratios are available at the Static-99 Clearinghouse Web site.

These norm groups, first presented by Hanson et al. (2009), reflect level of preselection, similar to the Static-99R norm groups. There were originally three sets of norms available for Static-2002R: they were identical to Static-99R, except Static-2002R did not have *Preselected for Treatment Norms* due to lack of sufficient samples. Currently the Static-2002R has the same two norm groups as Static-99R, *Routine Norms* (based on routine and representative correctional samples) and *High Risk/High Needs Norms* (based on samples of sexual offenders selected based on perceived risk for significant but relatively infrequent interventions or sanctions, such as psychiatric commitments and being held past their release date). The two sets of norms for absolute risk are provided on the Static-99 Clearinghouse Web site.

Reliability

Five studies reporting interrater reliability for the Static-2002 scores were identified, and all reported high indices of reliability (Bengston, 2008; Haag, 2005; Knight & Thornton, 2007; Langton et al., 2007). Published reports of reliability for the Static-2002R could not be found. However, the latter tool differs from the Static-2002 only in the scoring of one item. Given that there were no meaningful differences in the reliability achieved with the Static-99R versus the Static-99, one would not expect reliability with the Static-2002R to differ from that of the Static-2002. This should be confirmed through appropriate lab and field assessments.

Cross-Validations

Hanson, Helmus, and Thornton (2010) reviewed and performed meta-analyses on samples from eight studies ($n = 3,034$), published and unpublished, to assess the predictive accuracy of the Static-2002 on independent samples in comparison to the Static-99. Across the eight studies, the AUCs for sexual recidivism ranged from .64 to .79, and all 95% CIs excluded .50, reflecting statistically significant predictive accuracy in each of the studies. A similar pattern was evident for violent recidivism (AUCs ranged from .64 to .77 and all were statistically significant).

Across all eight studies, the weighted average predictive accuracy for sexual recidivism was slightly higher for the Static-2002 (AUC = .685) and the Static-99 (AUC = .665). Predictive accuracy for violent recidivism exhibited a similar pattern, with the Static-2002 (AUC = .702) being slightly higher than the Static-99 (AUC = .662). The differences between the two instruments were statistically significant in both cases, with the predictive accuracy of the Static-2002 superior to that of the Static-99. Although there was significant variability in AUCs across studies, the difference between the Static-2002 and the Static-99 was stable.

Babchishin, Hanson, and Helmus (2012) compared the predictive accuracy of the Rapid Risk Assessment for Sex Offender Recidivism (RRASOR), Static-99R, and Static-2002R for 7,491 offenders (20 samples from the Static-99R renorming project) primarily from Canada and the United States, but also offenders from Austria, Denmark, Germany, New Zealand, Sweden, and the United Kingdom. Total scores of Static-2002R (AUC = .686) predicted sexual recidivism. This level of predictive accuracy was similar to that for the Static-99R (AUC = .684).

Another recent meta-analysis (Tully, Chou, & Browne, 2013) of 43 studies and 31,426 sexual offenders from 11 countries examined the predictive accuracy of 15 risk assessment tools for sexual offenders (the number of studies and sexual offenders varied for each instrument). All of the reviewed tools produced at least a moderate effect size in predicting sexual reoffense, including the Static-2002 (AUC = .70). The Static-99 performed similarly (AUC = .69).

Babchishin, Blais, & Helmus (2012) examined the predictive accuracy of the Static-2002 and the Static-2002R with three samples of Canadian Aboriginals (*n* = 209) and non-Aboriginals (*n* = 955). Predictive accuracy for sexual recidivism was statistically significant in the total sample for the Static-2002 (AUC = .740) and the Static-2002R (AUC = .733) and in the non-Aboriginal sample for the Static-2002 (AUC = .763) and the Static-2002R (AUC = .759). In contrast to the Static-99 and Static-99R, there was a substantial drop in predictive accuracy in the Aboriginal sample for both the Static-2002 (AUC = .617) and the Static-2002R (AUC = .608), though the accuracy for the Static-2002 remained statistically significant.

VRAG

One of the first actuarial instruments measuring violence, the VRAG was developed by clinical researchers at the Mental Health Centre in Penetanguishene, Ontario, Canada. Both the VRAG and Sex Offender Risk Appraisal Guide (SORAG, to be discussed later) were developed on samples of forensic patients and convicted offenders; they predict any new criminal charge for a violent offense. Although the VRAG is not used for evaluating sexual offenders, related instruments developed by the same authors (the SORAG and VRAG-Revised discussed in this chapter) are actuarial instruments designed to evaluate sexual offenders. An understanding of the development, validation, and use of the VRAG is useful to understand the development and use of the SORAG.

Development of the VRAG

The VRAG items were selected from 50 potential predictor variables using multiple regression that identified variables with independent and incremental contributions to predicting violent recidivism. Potential items without a bivariate relationship with violent recidivism were not considered further. The Nuffield (1982) method where weights are computed actuarially using the item's base rate relationship with the outcome variable (recidivism) was used to weigh the individual factors. Scores on the VRAG ranged from –26 to +38. Nine risk groups were formed by dividing the range of scores (63 points) into nine equal-sized categories of reoffense probabilities for each cutoff score based on seven- and ten-year follow-ups. Percentiles are also reported for each of the nine categories. The construction sample showed large predictive accuracy (AUC = .76).

Interrater reliability of the VRAG using independent coding by two trained raters for each of the 12 VRAG variables with 20 randomly selected offenders revealed a correlation coefficient of .90 (Harris, Rice, & Quinsey, 1993).

The VRAG has a total of 12 items that are scored from the offender's psychosocial history. The items on VRAG include the following: lived with both biological parents to age 16; elementary school maladjustment; history of alcohol problems; marital status; criminal history score for convictions and charges for nonviolent offenses prior to the index offense; failure on prior conditional release, age at index offense; victim injury; any female victim; meets DSM-III criteria for any personality disorder; meets DSM-III criteria for schizophrenia; PCL-R score.

An extensive manual is available for VRAG that includes scoring instructions, norms, frequently asked questions, instructions to compile psychosocial histories, practice material, and recommended report formats (Quinsey, Harris, Rice, & Cormier, 2006: Harris, Rice, Quinsey, & Cormier, 2015).

VRAG Cross-Validations

The accuracy of the VRAG in predicting violent recidivism and sexually violent recidivism has been tested. It demonstrated moderate to high predictive accuracy (AUC = .60 to .85) in more than 70 different samples of serious offenders with an average predictive accuracy of .72. Cross-validations of VRAG have been conducted for forensic psychiatric patients, convicted offenders, and sex offenders with intellectual disabilities (see Harris et al., 2015 for a comprehensive review) The VRAG has also been cross-validated on samples of female sex offenders (Eisenbarth, Osterheider, Nedopil, & Stadtland, 2012), jail inmates (Hastings, Krishnan, Tangney, & Stuewig, 2011), and ethnic minorities (Snowden, Gray, & Taylor, 2010).

SORAG

Because the violent recidivism rates were higher than expected for sex offenses based on the VRAG, the authors of the VRAG developed different norms to improve predictions for men institutionalized for sex offenses against minors and women. The SORAG, an actuarial instrument that is the outgrowth of the VRAG, was designed to be used to measure violent, including sexual, recidivism for sex offenders (Quinsey et al., 2006).

Development of the SORAG

The SORAG was developed on 288 sex offenders, 129 of whom were in the developmental sample for the VRAG (Rice & Harris, 1997). The variables were chosen using stepwise multivariate methods with the goal to predict at least one reconviction for a violent or sexual offense. The SORAG's interrater reliability was equivalent to that of the VRAG (ICC = .90). Similarly high reliability coefficients have been reported in replication studies (Rice & Harris, in press).

As with the VRAG, SORAG scores are associated with one of nine categories, each with a measured rate of violent recidivism in seven years, increasingly linearly from 7% to 100%. There are norms for both five and 12 years of offense opportunity; percentiles are also reported. The predictive accuracy in the construction sample was in the high range at .77 (Rice, Harris, & Lang, 2013).

The SORAG includes 10 of the VRAG items noted earlier (victim injury and any female victim were dropped), but it also has four additional items unique to sex offenders added to those of the VRAG, including criminal history score for convictions and charges for violent offenses prior to the index offense, prior convictions for offenses known to be sexual, history of offenses against girls under the age of 14 only, and deviant phallometric preferences. Like the VRAG, the items were weighted using the Nuffield method (1982). The range of scores for the SORAG is −26 to +42.

An extensive manual is available for the SORAG that includes scoring instructions, updated norms, frequently asked questions, instructions to compile psychosocial histories, practice material, and recommended report formats (Harris et al., 2015).

Cross-Validations of the SORAG

For the SORAG there have been 10 cross-validations on male offenders, resulting in an average AUC of .74. It has shown moderate to high predictive accuracy on offenders in prisons and forensic settings. Harris et al. (2015) examined new follow-up data on 750 sex offenders included in one or more of their previous follow-up studies (Harris et al., 1993, 2003; Rice & Harris, 1995, 1997). New follow-up data were gathered, where possible, up to 2007, resulting in an average follow-up time of more than 20 years. The AUC for the prediction of violent recidivism over the entire follow-up using the SORAG was .73.

VRAG–Revised (VRAG-R)

The Violence Risk Appraisal Guide–Revised (VRAG-R) is the third and newest instrument developed by researchers at Waypoint Centre (formerly called the Mental Health Centre in Penetanguishene, Ontario, Canada; Rice, Harris, & Lang, 2013). Like the VRAG and the SORAG, the new VRAG-R is an actuarial measure of violent (including sexual) recidivism. The new instrument was developed with the goal of including updated and simpler scoring of items and having one actuarial instrument for violent offenders and sex offenders. Although the VRAG and SORAG are well-validated tools, the developers hope that the VRAG-R will eventually replace the other two tools.

The total sample for the VRAG-R was comprised of 1,261 subjects who were coded for earlier studies, including the construction samples for VRAG and SORAG. The average follow-up for the sample was 20 years, but spanned over 40 years for a smaller sample.

The construction sample included 961 sex offenders and the validation sample consisted of 300 subjects. The validation also was subject to 1,000 bootstrap samples. Items were weighted using the Nuffield system (1982). The sample was divided into nine approximately equal-sized bins used to obtain probabilities of violent or sexual reoffense for five years and 12 years. Possible scores range from –34 to +46. The ICC for the VRAG-R was .99. The predictive accuracy of the VRAG-R for the prediction of dichotomous violent recidivism on the entire sample of 1,261 offenders over the mean 20-year follow-up was .76.

The items on the new VRAG-R include: lived with both biological parents to age 16, elementary school maladjustment (up to and including Grade 8), history of alcohol and drug problems, marital status at time of the index offense, Cormier-Lang score for nonviolent convictions and charges prior to index, failure on conditional release, age at index offense (at most recent birthday), Cormier-Lang score for violent convictions and charges prior to index, number of prior admissions (of one day or more) to correctional institutions, conduct disorder indicators (before age 15), sex offending, and antisociality.

An extensive manual is available for VRAG-R that includes scoring instructions, norms, frequently asked questions, instructions to compile psychosocial histories, practice material, and recommended report formats (Harris et al., 2015). The VRAG-R is able to predict time to first violent recidivism offense, severity of all violent recidivism offenses, and a composite score reflecting both speed and severity of violent recidivism.

The Use of Multiple Actuarial Instruments

Evaluators in the field are tasked with determining which actuarial instruments they will use to evaluate a sexual offender's risk to sexually reoffend in SVP/SDP evaluations. Evaluators should consider aspects of the development of the instrument, predictive accuracy, reliability, and replications of the instrument, among other things, in choosing an actuarial instrument. Incremental validity of risk instruments is a key to deciding what combination of instruments to use. Incremental validity is the extent to which new information improves the accuracy of a prediction above and beyond that of the previous instrument(s) used.

Seto (2005) examined the incremental validity of several routinely used scales (i.e., RRASOR, Static-99, SORAG, and VRAG) and found the scales did not add incrementally to each other in the prediction of sexual recidivism. Evaluators were advised to choose the "best" instrument, which was identified as the RRASOR in his sample. However, this study was limited by a small sample size, and subsequent studies did not support the RRASOR as having superior predictive accuracy relative to other instruments. However, as a result of this study, many evaluators followed Seto's advice and have continued to use only one scale.

The use of multiple actuarial instruments was revisited more recently by Babchishin, Hanson, and Helmus (2012). This study examined potential incremental validity of the RRASOR, Static-99R, and Static-2002R in a large cohort of 7,491 sex offenders from 20 samples in the Static-99 renorming project. Contrary to Seto's (2005) prior findings, all three scales provided incremental validity to the prediction of sexual recidivism. This is despite the similarity in items on the scales. This robust finding confirmed clear potential improvements by considering multiple scales. Even though the Static-99R and Static-2002R are highly correlated scales, the incremental validity of each indicates that there is better coverage of relevant static risk factors by using both. This finding may generalize to other scales when samples are large enough to have sufficient statistical power.

Decision rules for combining static, actuarial risk instruments for sexual offenders in the overall evaluation of risk were examined by Lehmann et al. (2013). In this study, the RRASOR, Static-99R, and Static-2002R all predicted sexual recidivism (AUCs of .69 to .71) and provided incremental validity to each other. In regard to using multiple risk instruments, the authors examined whether choosing the highest, the lowest, or averaging absolute risk estimates (probabilities) optimized accuracy. Their findings supported averaging the probabilities obtained on Static-99R and Static-2002R for the follow-up period of interest (five or 10 years).

McGrath et al. (2012) developed the Sex Offender Treatment Intervention and Progress Scale (SOTIPS), a new rating scale to assess dynamic risk among adult male sex offenders. SOTIPS predicted sexual, violent, and any criminal recidivism, as well as returns to prison, across time. However, combined SOTIPS and Static-99R scores predicted all recidivism types better than either instrument alone. These results bolster previous sexual offender studies documenting the incremental validity of layering assessments of dynamic risk factors onto assessments of static risk factors (Beggs & Grace, 2010; Hanson et al., 2007; Knight & Thornton, 2007; Olver et al., 2007; Thornton & Knight, 2013). These findings collectively indicate that a comprehensive risk assessment should include multiple actuarial instruments, including measures of both static and dynamic risk factors. As discussed earlier, this practice can also make the selection of Static-99R and Static-2002R norms more empirically based.

Choosing an Actuarial Instrument to Use

In light of recent research on the use of multiple instruments, it is not necessary to choose between them, unless time or resources limit options to one or the other, because risk estimates may be more accurate if they are averaged across the two tools.

Regardless of which tool(s) is used, a number of best practices have emerged from the evolving work on developing actuarial instruments. The first is that relative risk should always be reported: relative risk has been far more stable over time, as reflected in various temporal cohorts in samples. Relative risk should be presented in multiples ways, including nominal relative risk categories, percentiles, and relative risk ratios when available.

For SVP/SDP evaluations absolute risk estimates are needed. They should be based on contemporary local norms, if available, and/or the appropriate contemporary norm group estimates provided by the authors. Historically, for Static-99R and Static-2002R some degree of clinical judgment was required in determining which norm group is most appropriate for an individual offender based on the degree of preselection for treatment and/or *High Risk/High Needs* interventions. More recent research has begun to provide cutoffs on measures of dynamic risk factors/needs (e.g., SRA-FV, Stable-2007, VRS-SO) to inform the selection of norm group. Research on the three actuarial instruments discussed in this chapter is ongoing, so normative information and recommendations may change. Thus, people using the Static tools should periodically check the Static-99 Clearinghouse Web site to ensure that current normative information and language is being used and that they are using the most appropriate methods for selecting absolute risk norm groups.

Psychologically Meaningful Risk Factors

While the static risk factors have long been established, the changeable risk factors that predict sexual reoffense have been subject to more recent research (Mann et al., 2010). Psychologically meaningful risk factors, also called *dynamic risk factors* and *long-term vulnerabilities*, are the targets of treatment because when they are lowered, risk is decreased. These risk factors can be conceptualized as individual propensities, which may or may not manifest during any time in the individual's life. Assessment of these risk factors is an integral part of a contemporary risk assessment. Although there are many single sample studies identifying potentially changeable risk factors, the Mann et al. (2010) meta-analysis categorized potential risk factors according to the strength of the evidence for their relationship with offending.

Risk factors with sufficient research support to be included in current risk assessments and their effect sizes are listed in Table 8.2, which provides a summary of data available in Mann et al. (2010).

Like static risk factors for sexual reoffense, many of the psychologically meaningful risk factors have low to moderate effect sizes, so evaluating them collectively will increase predictive

Table 8.2 Risk factors and their effect sizes

Risk Factor	Effect Size (d score)
Sexual preoccupation	.39
Any deviant sexual interest	.31
Sexual preference for children (PPG)	.32
Sexualized violence	.18
Multiple paraphilias	.21
Offense-supported attitudes	.22
Emotional congruence with children	.43
Lack of emotionally intimate relationships with adults	
Never married	.32
Conflicts in intimate relationships	.36
Lifestyle impulsivity/General self-regulation problems	.37
Impulsivity, recklessness	.25
Employment instability	.22
Poor cognitive problem solving	.22
Resistance to rules and supervision	
Childhood behavior problems	.30
Noncompliance with supervision	.62
Violation of conditional release	.50
Grievance/hostility	.20
Negative social influences	.26

accuracy. As a result three validated instruments have been developed to assess psychologically meaningful risk factors in a structured and thorough way.

Stable-2007

The Stable-2007 measures sex offender risk factors that are changeable over time. It can be used to formulate case management and identify treatment/supervision targets. This instrument can also inform treatment providers and supervision officers when offenders are becoming more or less dangerous over time. Because the Stable-2007 was developed and validated on a community sample it is very appropriate for offenders on community supervision. It is more difficult to score on offenders who have been in prison for lengthy periods of time, such as offenders subject to SVP/SDP proceedings.

The Stable-2007 is an outgrowth of the Dynamic Predictors Project (Hanson & Harris, 1998) which provided a retrospective file review study and interview with probation, police, and parole officers supervising sexual offenders in the community. The Dynamic Predictors Project identified a list of the most likely dynamic risk factors, and that list was used to create the Stable-2007's predecessors: the SONAR (Hanson & Harris, 2000), the Stable-2000, and the Acute-2000 (Hanson & Harris, 2004). The Dynamic Supervision Project was launched to develop an instrument on prospective data. The Dynamic Supervision Project followed approximately 1,000 sexual offenders for an average of 43 months. Community supervision officers and law enforcement were trained in risk assessment instruments (Static-99, Stable-2000, Acute-2000) and followed offenders on their caseload until the offenders recidivated or the study period ended. The officers were instructed to score the Static-99 once at the beginning of the project and the Stable-2000 every six months, and the Acute-2000 every supervision visit. Data was collected across Canada and in the U.S. states of Iowa and Alaska (Hanson et al., 2007). These data informed the revision from Stable-2000 to Stable-2007.

Stable-2007 contains five categories of risk factors and three of the items have multiple factors. The items on Stable-2007 include: significant social influences; intimacy deficits (capacity for relationship stability; emotional identification with children; hostility toward women; general social rejection and/or loneliness; lack of concern for others); sexual self-regulation (sex drive/preoccupation; sex as coping; deviant sexual interests); general self-regulation (impulsive acts; poor cognitive problem solving; negative emotionality/hostility); and cooperation with supervision.

The interrater reliability was measured for the Stable-2007 in a maximum security penitentiary (Fernandez, 2008) and resulted in an ICC of .92 for the total score on Stable-2007. The Stable-2007 was cross-validated by Eher et al. (2012), who found that Stable-2007 was significantly related to sexual recidivism, violent recidivism, and general reoffense (AUC of .67 to .71). In a small sample of 261 rapists and child molesters, Stable-2007 did not add incrementally above Static-99. In a subsequent validation by Eher et al. (2013) with an increased sample ($n = 370$) incremental validity was found for Stable-2007.

SRA-FV

The SRA-FV was developed by David Thornton on a sample from the Massachusetts Treatment Center. This instrument has been available for use since 2010 (Thornton & Knight, 2013). Since it was developed and validated on incarcerated offenders from the former sexual psychopath program in Massachusetts, the SRA-FV is particularly suited for SVP/SDP evaluations in adversarial conditions. It is based on previous research using the Structured Risk Assessment (SRA) framework (Thornton, 2002). According to Thornton's SRA, long-term risk factors can be divided into static risk indicators and enduring psychological risk factors that he refers to as *needs or long-term vulnerabilities*. According to the SRA model, these long-term vulnerabilities can be organized into four domains: sexual interests, distorted attitudes, relational style, and self-management.

The SRA-FV contains three of the four domains identified in the SRA framework. It has items measuring sexual interests, relational style, and self-management. Distorted attitudes were omitted because it is difficult to measure them in adversarial circumstances. Most of the items used in SRA-FV were selected and their scoring rules written on the basis of previous research. Facets 2, 3, and 4 of the PCL-R were used to represent the SRA factors of Callousness, Lifestyle Impulsiveness, and Resistance to Rules and Supervision. When an interview is not conducted or a PCL-R is not scored as part of the evaluation process, an alternative version of the SRA-FV may be utilized (SRA-FV Light).

Item scoring rules were written so that self-report could be taken into account when this was available, but also the factors could be coded on the basis of the kind of behavioral history information that was commonly available to the evaluators in the archival files.

All offenders in the construction and cross-validation samples were sexual offenders who had been evaluated between 1959 and 1984 at the Massachusetts Treatment Center for Sexually Dangerous Persons in Bridgewater, Massachusetts and were released from the Center in or before 1984. The instrument was developed on 93 to 96 offenders and cross-validated on 365 to 444 offenders with five or more years follow-up. The validation produced an AUC for a five-year follow-up of .72 and that was unchanged for a 10-year follow-up. Additionally substantial and highly statistically significant incremental validity was exhibited at five and 10 years.

The SRA-FV has a comprehensive coding manual that provides directions to score each item 0 (absent), 1 (some presence), and 2 (fully present). Additionally, the total score on SRA-FV can be used to pick the appropriate norms for Static-99R, which is another advantage for SVP/SDP evaluations.

VRS-SO

The VRS-SO (Olver, Wong, Nicholaichuk, & Gordon, 2007) is a rating scale designed to assess risk and predict sexual recidivism, to measure and link treatment changes to sexual recidivism, and to inform the delivery of sexual offender treatment. The VRS-SO assesses and measures change in treatment by using a modified application of the transtheoretical model of change (TTM). The TTM presumes that individuals in sex offender treatment progress through a series of stages known as precontemplation, contemplation, preparation, action, and maintenance; these stages are measured by the VRS-SO.

The VRS-SO was developed on 321 male federal Canadian offenders who had participated in a high-intensity sex offender treatment program at a maximum-security forensic mental health facility in Canada between 1983 and 1997. The VRS-SO is modeled closely after the Violence Risk Scale (Wong & Gordon, 2006) that is designed to assess nonsexual violence risk and needs. The VRS-SO is a 24-item scale comprising seven static and 17 dynamic items. The items are rated on a Likert-type scale with scores ranging from 0 to 3. Evaluators rate the scale on the basis of a file review and semi-structured interview.

The static and dynamic items were developed differently. The static items were developed with statistical-actuarial procedures on close to one randomly selected half of the sample ($n = 152$) and cross-validated on the remaining portion of the sample ($n = 169$). A collection of 24 static variables identified from the literature was initially coded and correlated with sexual recidivism. Items with the strongest univariate relationships to outcome were retained and rescaled to a four-point scoring format. The static items can be summed to derive a total risk score. The dynamic items were developed through a review of sex offender prediction and treatment literature.

A comprehensive scoring manual is available. As with all of the static and dynamic instruments the evaluator is advised to participate in formal training before using the instruments. The different dynamic items are potentially changeable by varying degrees. Change on the dynamic items is assessed and quantified through the assessment of a modified TTM. Each of the five stages of change has been operationalized for each of the 17 dynamic items. The advancement in the stages of change (e.g., from contemplation at pretreatment to action at posttreatment) shows the extent to which the offender has improved by developing positive coping skills and abilities that are stable and consistent with respect to each dynamic factor. Baseline ratings and ratings as the offender progresses through treatment give an assessment of positive treatment progress.

A factor analysis of the dynamic items of VRS-SO revealed three factors, labeled *Sexual Deviance, Criminality*, and *Treatment Responsivity*. Interrater reliability for VRS-SO for the dynamic items was assessed on 35 randomly selected cases and produced an ICC of .74 for pretreatment dynamic items and .79 for posttreatment dynamic items. The sample was followed up for 20 years. Predictive accuracy of the VRS-SO static factors was .74; for pretreatment dynamic factors was .66; and for dynamic posttreatment items was .67. The extent to which the dynamic items made unique contributions to the prediction of sexual recidivism after Static-99 and the static items of the VRS-SO were controlled for was examined through Cox regression survival analysis. Significant independent contributions were made by the VRS-SO static item total and dynamic item total. Independent contributions were also observed when these analyses were repeated for Static-99 and the dynamic items, indicating the total dynamic score made significant incremental contributions to predicting sexual recidivism over and above that of the Static-99.

The VRS-SO has been subject to one independent cross-validation by Beggs and Grace (2010) on a sample of 218 child molesters who received treatment at a prison-based program in New Zealand. The VRS-SO showed good interrater reliability for 23 cases and two raters for pretreatment scores (ICC = .90) and for posttreatment items (ICC = .92). It also showed concurrent validity and high predictive accuracy for the static and dynamic risk factors both pre- and posttreatment (AUCs = .70 to .81). The dynamic scale made significant incremental contributions after controlling for static risk.

Measures of relative risk (Low, Moderate-Low, Moderate-High, and High) are available for VRS-SO and absolute probabilities of sexual reoffense for the four risk groups are available for three, five, and 10 years.

Contemporary Risk Assessment Protocol for SVP/SDP Evaluations

Contemporary risk assessment for SVP/SDP evaluations should include the use of multiple validated actuarial instruments and validated dynamic risk assessment instruments as outlined in this chapter. Evaluators need to avail themselves of formal training prior to use of these instruments to ensure the reliability and validity of scores. Because these instruments do not contain all relevant risk factors and contextual factors, additional empirically related factors may be considered. Such additional variables are often referred to as *special considerations*.

Most frequently, additional risk factors considered are those that are compelling but occur with sufficient infrequency that it is not possible to include them on an actuarial risk assessment tool. For example, offenders being assessed for SVP/SDP proceedings are often aging offenders with many prior sexual offenses. As offenders age, they may become sufficiently infirm that the evaluator should consider changes in health and mobility as it relates to decreasing risk to sexually reoffend. Less often, in part because of the adversarial nature of SVP/SDP proceedings, offenders will self-report intent to reoffend, but when they occur such statements should factor into a risk assessment. Though not measured in actuarial instruments, such risk factors can provide compelling data in a risk assessment. The additional contextual factors most frequently considered are variables such as treatment completion, length of supervision, and intensity of supervision.

Evaluators are cautioned not to "double dip" by using a risk factor included in a tool as a special consideration. For example, if using Static-99R, offending against a male victim should not be considered as a special consideration because the instrument fully accounts for this risk factor. In addition, factors that are not empirically associated with sexual recidivism also should not be used as special considerations. Finally, evaluators should strive to remain current on the research that supports instruments they use and on new, evolving research that furthers the field of risk assessment with sexual offenders.

Case Study

Mr. M. is a 42-year-old male nearing the end of a prison term. His current (index) offense is for two counts of child sexual abuse. The victim was a 9-year-old boy he met at a video arcade. According to police reports, he approached the child and offered to pay for video gaming if the child would go into the bathroom with him. Once in the restroom, Mr. M. pulled down the boy's pants and performed oral sex on him and also forced the child to masturbate his penis. The child exited the bathroom and told his father, who reported it to the police. Mr. M. was sentenced to 10 years in prison. He is now being referred to possible civil commitment under the state's Sexually Violent Predator statute. Mr. M. was reported to frequent the video gaming establishment and play videos with younger males. He told his probation officer that he feels more comfortable with younger kids.

A record review reveals that Mr. M. is the youngest of three children who were raised by a single mother. The presentencing report indicated that Mr. M.'s biological father left the family during his mother's pregnancy. Mr. M. has reportedly had no contact with his biological father. Mr. M.'s mother was noted to have a series of boyfriends, some of whom lived with the family. Mr. M. reported to a probation officer that one of the boyfriends sexually abused him between the ages of 5 to 7. Despite this Mr. M. stated in the interview that he loved his mother and they are very close. They sometimes talk daily when his mother can afford it. He was also frequently cared for by his aunt and they still have a close relationship.

When Mr. M. was 18, he was arrested and convicted of public exposure in a public park. Several boys between the ages of 6 and 9 reported seeing Mr. M. in the bushes masturbating while they were playing on the playground and they reported it to their parents. Mr. M. was sentenced to a term of five years' probation. Mr. M. violated his probation after only one year when his probation officer arrived at his house to find an 8-year-old boy at his home. The boy reported to the probation officer that Mr. M. gave him candy and video games in exchange for allowing Mr. M. to fondle his penis. Although his probation was violated, no new criminal charges were brought against him. The boy's mother would not allow him to testify against Mr. M.

During his current term of incarceration, Mr. M. received two institutional rule violations, one for being out of bounds and one for engaging in sex with another inmate in the shower. Mr. M. was employed in the institution's kitchen and also participated in a cabinetry-making vocational program. Mr. M. was offered sex offender treatment, but declined to participate. He told his case worker he did not want to transfer to the prison in which the treatment program was operated because it would be too far for his mother to visit. He also did not think he had a problem that would lead to molesting again.

Mr. M. has never been married. He reported to the evaluator that he has dated both men and women. He had short-term sexual relationships with both men and women, sometimes very frequently, but reported he had never been "in love" with anyone. He said most of his sexual experiences were one-night stands. He has one pen pal, a volunteer from a religious group who conducts services in the institution. Otherwise, he appears to be a loner with few close friends. In the interview he said he prefers to spend time alone as he is uncomfortable around others, who have at times rejected him.

In the clinical interview Mr. M. denied experiencing sexual arousal to children or ever having sexual fantasies of children. He said his child molest offense was just "experimenting." He also thought it might have occurred because of job stress. His boss threatened to fire him if he could not improve his job performance. When he exposed himself to boys in the park he said he was struggling to take a few college courses but was failing. He denied the use of child pornography but admitted he is "addicted" to the use of adult heterosexual pornography. He admitted to masturbating daily and sometimes more often. He said he has tried to stop using pornography but he has been unsuccessful.

Risk Assessment for Mr. M.

Static-99R

Item	Risk Factor	Value	Score
1	Age at release? (Score range is −3 to 1)	42	−1
2	Ever lived with (no two year relationship)?	No	1
3	Index non-sexual violence, any conviction?	No	0
4	Prior non-sexual violence, any convictions?	No	0
5	Prior sex offenses? (Score range is 0–3)	1 conv. and 1 conditional release viol.	1
6	Prior sentencing dates (excluding index)?	2	0
7	Convictions for noncontact sex offenses?	Yes	1
8	Any unrelated victims?	Yes	1
9	Any stranger victims?	Yes	1
10	Any male victims?	Yes	1
	TOTAL SCORE =		**5**
	RISK CATEGORY = Moderate		**High**

Static-2002R

	Category	Sub-Score*	Possible Range	
I.	Age (1 item)	0	−2	2
II.	Persistence of sexual offending (3 items)	1	0	3
III.	Deviant sexual interests (3 items)	3	0	3
IV.	Relationship to victim (2 items)	2	0	2
V.	General criminality (5 items)	2	0	3
	TOTAL SCORE =	**8**	**−2**	**13**

SRA-FV-Light

Because the PCL-R is unavailable the SRA-FV-Light was utilized in the evaluation.

Domain		Factor Scores		Domain Scores
Sexual Interests Domain SID				
Sexual Preference for Children SID1		2		
Sexualized Violence SID2		0		
Sexual Preoccupation SID3				
Rule-based	2			
Concept-based	2			
Rule + Concept =	4			
	÷ 2 =	2		
Sexual Interests Domain Total Score		4	÷ 3 =	1.33
Relational Style Domain RSD				
LEIRA—RSD1	2			
Emotional Congruence with Children RSD2	2			
Grievance Thinking RSD4				

Domain	Factor Scores		Domain Scores
Internal grievance thinking	0		
Poorly managed anger	0		
IGT + PMA =	0		
	÷ 2 =	0	
Relational Interests Domain TOTAL Score	4	÷ 3 =	**1.33**
Self-Management Domain SMD			
Dysfunctional Coping SMD3	2		
Self-Management Domain TOTAL Score	2	÷ 2 =	**1**
* minus omitted (X) items **Total Need Score (0–6) =**			**3.67**

Discussion of the SRA-FV

Sexual Interests

- Sexual Preference for Children: This item refers to an intense interest in or preference for sexual activity with children. Mr. M. has more than three male child victims of exposure and child molest over a period greater than six months which earns a score of 2.
- Sexualized Violence: Individuals who have an intense interest or preference for sexual activity involving sex upon an unwilling recipient have aspects of this factor. The coercive element must be the source of the sexual arousal and not a means to overcome resistance. This factor is not present for Mr. M.
- Sexual Preoccupation: This factor is divided into two categories, rule based and concept based. Rule-based sexual preoccupation refers to an intense interest in sex; much of the individual's behavior is sexually motivated. Concept-based sexual preoccupation refers to hypersexuality that exceeds what would be normative for an adult. Mr. M has reported masturbating once a day or more frequently at times. He said he was addicted to adult pornography. He admitted to frequent one-night stands and repetitive casual sex.

Relational Style

- LEIRA: This acronym stands for Lack of Emotional Intimate Relationships with Adults. Individuals who have few long-term intimate relationships or engage in relationships that are dysfunctional have elements of this factor. Mr. M. has never had a sustained intimate relationship.
- Emotional Congruence With Children: Individuals who relate to children easier than adults or prefer the company and companionship with children to that of adults have elements of this factor. Mr. M. reported in the clinical interview that he frequented places where younger males would "hang out" because he was most comfortable with younger males.
- Grievance Thinking: This factor is divided into two separate items. Internal grievance thinking refers to an individual who easily feels wronged, suspicious, ruminates angrily, and tends to not see or accept others' points of view. Poorly managed anger refers to a persistent pattern of verbal aggression, angry outbursts, threatening and intimidating behavior, or physical assaults of a nonsexual variety. Neither grievance thinking nor poorly managed anger is present for Mr. M.

Self-Management

- Dysfunctional Coping: This factor is defined when an individual reacts to stress or problems in an impulsive/reckless way or there is an absence of effective systematic problem-solving skills or problem-solving abilities. Mr. M. has committed two sexual offenses and he has declined to participate in sex offender treatment. He does not think he has "a problem" with sexual offending. He has poor problem identification and problem solving skills.

Mr. M scored a 3.67 on the SRA-FV-Light Need Assessment. Groups of offenders with this level of need are expected to have a recidivism rate above that indicated by the Static-99R High Risk/Need Norms.

Stable-2007

Scoring Item	Notes	Total
Significant Social Influences	Mr. M. has few friends and his only community supports when he is released are his mother, aunt, and his probation officer. He has no negative influences.	0
Capacity for Relationship Stability	Mr. M. has never lived in a two- year relationship or had any sustained intimate relationships.	2
Emotional ID with Children	Mr. M. reported he is most comfortable with children and he frequents places where children are drawn.	2
Hostility Toward Women	This factor is not present for Mr. M.	0
General Social Rejection	Mr. M. reported he has few friends and that he is uncomfortable around other adults. It appears he does not feel lonely but prefers to be alone.	1
Lack of Concern for Others	Mr. M. is not callous or indifferent towards others. He has a close relationship with his mother and a maternal aunt with whom he described a loving relationship.	0
Impulsive	Mr. M described himself as impulsive at times primarily in his sex life. He is prone to have one-night stands without thinking about risky sexual behavior. He reported he has impulsively quit jobs without having one lined up, fearing he is not doing a good job	1
Poor Problem-Solving Skills	Mr. M. has committed three sexual offenses and he has declined to participate in sex offender treatment. He does not think he has "a problem" with sexual offending. He has poor problem identification and problem-solving skills.	2
Negative Emotionality	Mr. M described his mood as "fine" most of the time. He denied feeling down except occasionally when he misses his mother. He does not blame his victims for telling their parents and he thought his sentence was fair.	0
Sex Drive/Sex Preoccupation	Mr. M. has reported masturbating once a day or more frequently at times. He said he was addicted to adult pornography. He admitted to frequent one night stands and repetitive casual sex.	2
Sex as Coping	Mr. M. reported in the clinical interview that he frequented places where younger males would "hang out" because he was most comfortable with younger males.	2
Deviant Sexual Preference	Mr. M. has three to seven male victims. He has two or more deviant victims and multiple incidents of deviant activity. It is strongly indicated that he has a deviant sexual interest in prepubescent boys.	2
Cooperation with Supervision	Mr. M. has two prison rules violations, with only one of them serious. Mr. M. violated the terms of his probation by committing another sexual offense. However, staff in prison have described him as a good worker and compliant with their instructions.	1
Total Score		**14**

Based upon the information provided, it appears that Mr. M. suffers from pedophilic disorder, sexually attracted to males, nonexclusive type. In regard to the actuarial instruments, his score on Static-99R (5) is in the Moderate-High range. His score on Static-2002R (8) is similarly in the Moderate-High range of risk. His risk is also high on the dynamic risk instruments used. His score on the Stable-2007 is in the High Range. Mr. M.'s score on the SRA-FV-Light was 3.67, which is in the Very High Range. His overall risk is in the High Range.

In terms of absolute risk level, both the Routine Risk estimates and High Risk/High Needs estimates will be reported. Offenders from routine correctional samples with the same score as Mr. M. have been found to sexually reoffend at a rate of 11.4% percent in five years. Offenders in the High Risk/High Needs samples have been found to sexually reoffend at a rate of 25.2% over five years and 35.5% over 10 years.

Although we are not suggesting whether or not Mr. M. should be recommended for commitment, evaluators would consider if Mr. M. had a mental abnormality and if he met the statutory standard of likeliness to reoffend in their jurisdiction.

Summary

This chapter has provided an introduction to civil commitment laws for sex offenders and provided an overview of the assessment process. We focused on the initial precommitment evaluations because they present the majority of the assessment challenges the evaluator is likely to face. Precommitment evaluations are not the sole issue within civil commitment laws. Periodic reviews of SVPs are often written into the statutes, requiring an evaluation of treatment progress and conclusions regarding whether the respondent continues to meet commitment criteria. Although the psycholegal standard remains the same, the evaluator must assess any treatment gains achieved, such as improvements in self-regulation or a reduction in sexually deviant interests. In addition, nontreatment issues may also alter an individual's risk to reoffend, such as increasing age or failing health. The issues involved in periodic reviews are not trivial, yet space limits our ability to adequately cover them in this chapter. Individuals involved in SVP treatment programs or in conducting civil commitments for sex offenders should familiarize themselves with these issues.

Note

1   The vast majority of civilly committed sexual offenders are male. The use of the male pronoun will be utilized throughout the remainder of this chapter.

References

Allan, M., Grace, R. C., Rutherford, B., & Hudson, S. M. (2007). Psychometric assessment of dynamic risk factors for child molesters. *Sex Abuse, 19*, 347–367. doi:10.1177/107906320701900402

American Psychiatric Association. (2013). *Diagnostic and statistical manual of mental disorders* (5th ed.). Washington, DC: Author.

American Psychological Association. (2013). Specialty guidelines for forensic psychology. *American Psychologist, 68*, 7–19. doi:10.1037/a0029889

Association for the Treatment of Sexual Abusers. (2001). *Practice standards and guidelines for members of the association for the treatment of sexual abusers*. ATSA Professional Issues Committee. Beaverton, OR: Author.

Babchishin, K. M., Blais, J., & Helmus, L. (2012). Do static risk factors predict differently for Aboriginal sex offenders? A multi-site comparison using the original and revised Static-99 and Static-2002 Scales. *Canadian Journal of Criminology and Criminal Justice, 54*, 1–43. doi:10.3138/cjccj.2010.E.40

Babchishin, K. M., Hanson, R. K., & Helmus, L. (2012). Even highly correlated measures can add incrementally to predicting recidivism among sex offenders. *Assessment, 19*, 442–461. doi:10.1177/1073191112458312

Bailey, R. K. (2002). The civil commitment of sexually violent predators: A unique Texas approach. *Journal of the American Academy of Psychiatry and Law, 30*, 525–532.

Bartosh, D. L. Garby, T., Lewis, D., & Gray, S. (2003). Differences in the predictive validity of actuarial risk assessments in relation to sex offender type. *International Journal of Offender Therapy and Comparative Criminology, 47*, 422–438. doi:10.1177/0306624X03253850

Becker, J. V., Stinson, J., Tromp, S., & Messer, G. (2003). Characteristics of individuals petitioned for civil commitment. *International Journal of Offender Therapy and Comparative Criminology, 47*, 185–195. doi:10.1177/0306624X03251114

Beech, A. R. (2005, November). *An evaluation of the effectiveness of Static-99 with juveniles.* Presentation at the 24th Annual Research and Treatment Conference of the Association for the Treatment of Sexual Abusers, Salt Lake City, UT.

Beech, A. R., Friendship, C., Erikson, M., & Hanson, R. K. (2002) The relationship between static and dynamic risk factors and reconviction in a sample of UK child abusers. *Sexual Abuse: A Journal of Research and Treatment, 14*, 155–167. doi:10.177/107906320201400206

Beggs, S. M., & Grace, R. C. (2010). Assessment of dynamic risk factors: An independent validation study of the Violence Risk Scales: Sexual Offender Version. *Sexual Abuse: A Journal of Research and Treatment, 22*, 234–251.

Bengston, S. (2008). Is newer better? A cross-validation of the Static-2002 and the Risk Matrix 2000 in a Danish sample of sexual offenders. *Psychology, Crime & Law, 14*, 85–106. doi:10.1080/10683160701483104

Bengston, S., & Langstrom, N. (2007). Unguided clinical and actuarial assessment of reoffending risk: A direct comparison with sex offenders in Denmark. *Sexual Abuse: A Journal of Research and Treatment, 19*, 135–153. doi:10.1177/10790632701900205

Boccaccini, M. T., Murrie, D.C., Caperton, J. D., & Hawes, S. W. (2009). Field validity of the STATIC-99 and MnSOST-R among sex offenders evaluated for civil commitment as sexually violent predators. *Psychology, Public Policy, and Law, 15*, 278–314. doi:10.1037/a0017232

Boccaccini, M. T., Murrie, D.C., Mercado, C., & Quesada, S. (2012). Implications of Static-99 field reliability findings for score use and reporting. *Criminal Justice and Behavior, 39*, 42–58. doi:10.1177/0093854811427131

Bonta, J., & Hanson, R. K. (1994). *Gauging the risk for violence: Measurement, impact and strategies for change.* (User Report No. 1994–09). Ottawa, ON: Department of the Solicitor General of Canada.

Borum, R., Otto, R., & Golding, S. (1993). Improving clinical judgment and decision making in forensic evaluation. *Journal of Psychiatry and Law, 21*, 35–76.

Brouillette-Alarie, S., & Proulx, J. (2013). Predictive validity of the Static-99R and its dimensions. *Journal of Sexual Aggression, 19*, 311–328. doi:10.1080/13552600.2012.747630

Brown, J. A., (2003). *A comparison of actuarial methods of predicting sexual dangerousness.* Dissertations Abstracts International, 55 (02), 1068B. (UMI No. 3120894).

Community Protection Act, Rev. Code of WA § 71.09 (1990).

Craig, L. A., Beech, A. R., & Browne, K. D. (2006). Evaluating the predictive accuracy of sex offender risk assessment measures on UK samples: A cross-validation of the Risk Matrix 2000 Scales. *Sexual Offender Treatment, 1*, 1–17.

Craissati, J., Webb, L., & Keen, S. (2005). *Personality disordered sex offenders.* Unpublished report. London, UK: Bracton Centre (Oxleas NHS Trust), London Probation Area and Home Office.

de Vogel, V., de Ruiter, C., van Beek, D., & Mead. G. (2004). Predictive validity of the SVR-20 and Static-99 in a Dutch sample of treated sex offenders. *Law and Human Behavior, 28*, 235–251. doi:10.1023/B:LAHU.0000029137.41974.eb

Doren, D. M. (2002). *Evaluating sex offenders: A manual for civil commitment and beyond.* Thousand Oaks, CA: Sage.

Ducro, C., & Pham, T. (2006). Evaluation of the SORAG and the Static-99 on Belgian sex offenders committed to a forensic facility. *Sexual Abuse: A Journal of Research and Treatment, 18*, 15–26. doi:10.1007/x11194–006–9003–6

Eher, R., Matthes, A., Schilling, F., Haubner-MacLean, T., & Tettenberger, M. (2012). Dynamic risk assessment in sexual offenders using Stable-2000 and the Stable-2007: An investigation of predictive and incremental validity. *Sexual Abuse: A Journal of Research and Treatment, 24*, 5–28. doi:10.1177/1079063211403164

Eher, R., Rettenberger, M., Gaunersdorfer, K., Haubner-MacLean, T., Matthes, A., Schilling, F., & Mokros, A. (2013). Über die Treffsicherheit standardisierter Risikoeinschätzungsverfahren bei aus der Maßregel entlassenen Sexualstraftätern [About the accuracy of standardized risk assessment procedures for the evaluation of discharged sex offenders]. *Forensische Psychiatrie, Psychologie, Kriminologie, 7*, 264–272. doi:10.1007/s11757–013–0212–9

Eisenbarth, H., Osterheider, M., Nedopil, N., & Stadtland, C. (2012). Recidivism in female offenders: PCL-R lifestyle factor and VRAG show predictive validity in a German sample. *Behavioral Sciences and the Law, 30*, 575–584. doi:10.1002/bsl.2013

Endrass, J., Urbaniok, F., Held, L., Vetter, S., & Rossegger, A. (2009). Accuracy of the Static-99 in predicting recidivism in Switzerland. *International Journal of Offender Therapy and Comparative Criminology, 53*, 482–490. doi:10.1177/0306624X07312952

Epperson, D. L. (2003). *Validation of the MnSOST-R, Static-99, and RRAZOR with North Dakota Prison and Probation Samples*. Technical Assistance Report.

Esses, V. M., & Webster, C.D. (1988). Physical attractiveness, dangerousness, and the Canadian Criminal Code. *Journal of Applied Social Psychology, 18*, 1017–1031. doi:10.1111/j.1559–1816.1988.tb01190.x

Federal Code 28 C.F.R. § 549.95

Fernandez, Y. (2008). *An examination of the interrater reliability of the STATIC-99 and Stable-2007*. Poster presentation at the 27th Annual Research and Treatment Conference of the Association for the Treatment of Sexual Abusers, Atlanta, GA.

Fernandez, Y., Harris, A.J.R., Hanson, R. K., & Sparks, J. (2012). *Stable-2007 coding manual—revised 2012*. Unpublished report. Ottawa, ON: Public Safety Canada.

Friendship, C., Mann, R. E., & Beech, A. R. (2003). Evaluation of a national prison-based treatment program for sexual offenders in England and Wales. *Journal of Interpersonal Violence, 18*, 744–759. doi:10.1177/0886260503253236

Grubin, D. (1998). *Sex offending against children: Understanding the risk*. Police Research Series Paper 99. London: Home Office.

Haag, A. M. (2005). *Do psychological interventions impact on actuarial measures: An analysis of the predictive validity of the Static-99 and Static-2002 on a re-conviction measure of sexual recidivism*. Unpublished doctoral dissertation. Department of Applied Psychology, University of Calgary, Calgary, Alberta.

Hanson, R. K. (2001). *A report on the reliability of the Static-99 as used by California Department of Mental Health Sex Offender Commitment Program*. Unpublished report.

Hanson, R. K. (2002). Introduction to the special section on dynamic risk assessment with sex offenders. *Sexual Abuse: A Journal of Research and Treatment, 14*, 99–101.

Hanson, R. K., & Bussiere, M. T. (1998). Predicting relapse: A meta-analysis of sexual offender recidivism studies. *Journal of Consulting and Clinical Psychology, 66*, 348–362. doi:10.1037/0022–006X.66.2.348

Hanson. R. K., & Harris. A. (1998). *Dynamic predictors of sexual recidivism*. Corrections Research Ottawa: Department of the Solicitor General Canada.

Hanson, R. K., & Harris, A.J.R. (2000). *The Sex Offender Need Assessment Rating (SONAR): A method for measuring change in risk levels*. User Report No. 2000–1. Department of the Solicitor General of Canada, Ottawa, Canada.

Hanson, R. K., & Harris, A.J.R. (2004). Stable-2000/Acute-2000: Scoring manuals for the Dynamic Supervision Project. Unpublished scoring manuals. Corrections Research, Public Safety Canada, Ottawa, Ontario, Canada.

Hanson, R. K., Harris, A.J.R., Scott, T., & Helmus, L. (2007). *Assessing the risk of sexual offenders on community supervision: The Dynamic Supervision Project*. Ottawa, ON: Department of the Solicitor General of Canada.

Hanson, R. K., Helmus, L., & Thornton, D. (2010). Predicting recidivism among sexual offenders: A multi-site study of STATIC-2002. *Law and Human Behavior, 34*, 198–211. doi:10.1007/s10979–009–9180–1

Hanson, R. K., Lunetta, A., Phenix, A., Neeley, J., & Epperson, D. (2014). The field validity of Static-99/R sex offender risk assessment tool in California. *Journal of Threat Assessment and Management, 1*, 102–117. doi:10.1037/tam0000014

Hanson, R. K., & Morton-Bourgon, K. E. (2005). The characteristics of persistent sexual offenders: A meta-analysis of recidivism studies. *Journal of Consulting and Clinical Psychology, 73*, 1154–1163. doi:10.1037/0022–006X.73.6.1154

Hanson, R. K., & Morton-Bourgon, K. E. (2009). The accuracy of recidivism risk assessments for sexual offenders: A meta-analysis of 118 prediction studies. *Psychological Assessment, 21*, 1–21. doi:10.1037/a0014421

Hanson, R. K., Phenix, A., & Helmus, L. (2009, September). *Static-99 and Static-2002: How to interpret and report scores in light of recent research.* Workshop presented at the ATSA 28th Annual Research and Treatment Conference, Dallas, TX.

Hanson, R. K., Sheahan, C. L., VanZuylen, H. (2013). STATIC-99 and RRASOR predict recidivism among developmentally delayed sexual offenders: A cumulative meta-analysis. *Sexual Offender Treatment, 8*, 1–14.

Hanson, R K., & Thornton, D. (2000). Improving risk assessments for sex offenders: A comparison of three actuarial scales. *Law and Human Behavior, 24*, 119–136. doi:10.1023/A:1005482921333

Hanson, R. K. & Thornton, D. (2003). *Notes on the development of Static-2002.* User Report 2003–01. Ottawa: Department of the Solicitor General of Canada.

Hanson, R. K., & Thornton, D. (2012, October). *Preselection effects can explain group differences in sexual recidivism base rates in Static-99R validation studies.* Paper presented at the 31st Annual Research and Treatment Conference of the Association for the Treatment of Sexual Abusers, Denver, CO.

Hare, R. D. (1983). Diagnosis of antisocial personality disorder in two prison populations. *The American Journal of Psychiatry, 140*, 887–890. doi:10.1176/ajp.140.7.887

Hare, R. D. (2003). *Manual for the Revised Psychopathy Checklist* (2nd ed.). Toronto, ON: Multi-Health Systems.

Harris, A. J. R., & Hanson, R. K. (2010). Clinical, actuarial and dynamic risk assessment of sexual offenders: Why do things keep changing? *Journal of Sexual Aggression, 16*, 296–310. doi:10.1080/13552600.2010494772

Harris, G. T., Rice, M. E., Quinsey, V. L. (1993). Violent recidivism of mentally disordered offenders: The development of a statistical prediction instrument. *Criminal Justice and Behavior, 20*, 315–335. doi:10.1177/0093854893020004001

Harris, G. T., Rice, M. E., Quinsey, V. L., & Cormier, C.A. (2015). *Violent offenders: Appraising and managing risk* (3rd ed.). Washington, DC: American Psychological Association.

Harris, G. T., Rice, M. E., Quinsey, V. L., Lalumiere, M. L., Boer, D., & Lang, C. (2003). A multi-site comparison of actuarial risk instruments for sex offenders. *Psychological Assessment: A Journal of Consulting and Clinical Psychology, 15*, 413–425. doi:10.1037/1040–3590.15.3.413

Hastings, M. E., Krishnan, S., Tangney, J. O., & Stuewig, J. (2011). Predictive and incremental validity of the Violence Risk Appraisal Guide scores with male and female jail inmates. *Psychological Assessment, 23*, 174–183. doi:10.1037/a0021290

Hawes, S. W., Boccaccini, M. T., & Murrie, D.C. (2012). Psychopathy and the combination of psychopathy and sexual deviance as predictors of sexual recidivism: Meta-analytic findings using the Psychopathy Checklist-Revised. *Psychological Assessment, 25*, 233–242. doi:10.1037/a0030391

Helmus, L. (2009). *Renorming STATIC-99 recidivism estimates: Exploring base rate variability across sex offender samples.* Unpublished master's thesis. Carleton University, Ottawa.

Helmus, L., Hanson, R. K., & Morton-Bourgon, K. E. (2011). International comparisons of the validity of actuarial risk tools for sexual offenders, with a focus on Static-99. In D. P. Boer, R. Eher, L. A. Craig, M. H. Miner, & F. Pfäfflin (Eds.), *International perspectives on the assessment and treatment of sexual offenders: Theory, practice, and research* (pp. 57–83). West Sussex, UK: Wiley-Blackwell.

Helmus, L., Hanson, R. K., Thornton, D., Babchishin, K. M., & Harris, A. J. R. (2012a). Absolute recidivism rates predicted by Static-99R and Static-2002R sex offender risk assessment tools vary across samples: A meta-analysis. *Criminal Justice & Behavior, 39*, 1148–1171. doi:10.1177/0093854812443648

Helmus, L., Thornton, D., Hanson, R. K., & Babchishin, K. M. (2012b). Improving the predictive accuracy of Static-99 and Static-2002 with older sex offenders: Revised age weights. *Sexual Abuse: A Journal of Research and Treatment, 24*, 64–101. doi:10.1177/1079063211409951

Hildebrand, M., de Ruiter, C., & de Vogel, V. (2004) Psychopathy and sexual deviance in treated rapists: Association with sexual and nonsexual recidivism. *Sexual Abuse: A Journal of Research and Treatment, 16*, 1–24. doi:10.1177/107906320401600101

Hill, A., Habermann, N., Klusmann, D., Berner, W., & Briken, P. (2008). Criminal recidivism in sexual homicide perpetrators. *International Journal of Offender Therapy and Comparative Criminology, 52,* 4–20 doi:10.1177/0306624X07307450

Hood, R., Shute, S., Feilzer, M., & Wilcox, A. (2002). Sex offenders emerging from long-term imprisonment: A study of their long-term reconviction rates and of parole board members' judgments of their risk. *British Journal of Criminology, 42,* 371–394. doi:10.1093/bjc/42.2.371

Jackson, R. L., & Covell, C. N. (2013). Sex offender civil commitment: Legal and ethical issues. In K. Harrison & B. Rainey (Eds.), *The Wiley-Blackwell handbook of legal and ethical aspects of sex offender treatment and management* (pp. 406–423). West Sussex, UK: Wiley Blackwell. doi:10.1002/9781118314876. ch24

Jackson, R. L., & Richards, H. J. (2007). Diagnostic and risk profiles among civilly committed sex offenders in Washington state. *International Journal of Offender Therapy and Comparative Criminology, 51,* 313–323. doi:10.1177/0306624X06292874

Jackson, R. L., Rogers, R., & Shuman, D. W. (2004). The adequacy and accuracy of sexually violent predator evaluations: Contextualized risk assessment in clinical practice. *International Journal of Forensic Mental Health, 3,* 115–129. doi:10.1080/14999013.2004.10471201

Janus, E. S. (1998). *Hendricks* and the moral terrain of police power civil commitment. *Psychology, Public Policy, and Law, 4,* 297–322. doi:10.1037/1076–8971.4.1–2.297

Janus, E. S. (2000). Sexual predator commitment laws: Lessons for law and the behavioral sciences. *Behavioral Sciences and the Law, 18,* 5–21. doi:10.1002/(SICI)1099–0798(200001/02)18:1

Kansas Stat. Ann. 59–29 (a); SB 671 (1994).

Kansas v. Crane, 534 U.S. 407 (2002).

Kansas v. Hendricks, 521 U.S. 346 (1997).

Kennedy, H. G., & Grubin, D. H. (1992). Patterns of denial in sex offenders. *Psychological Medicine, 22,* 191–196. doi:10.1017/S0033291700032840

Knight, R. A., & Thornton, D. (2007). *Evaluating and improving risk assessment schemes for sexual recidivism: A long-term follow-up of convicted sexual offenders.* Unpublished report to the U.S. Department of Justice.

Langevin, R. (1988). Defensiveness in sex offenders. In R. Rogers (Ed.), *Clinical assessment of malingering and deception* (pp. 269–290). New York: Guilford Press.

Langstrom, N. (2004). Accuracy of actuarial procedures for assessment of sexual offender recidivism risk may vary across ethnicity. *Sexual Abuse: A Journal of Research and Treatment, 16,* 107–120.

Langton, C. M., Barbaree, H. E., Seto, M.C., Peacock, E. J., Harkins, L., & Hansen, K. T. (2007). Actuarial assessment of risk for reoffense among adult sex offenders. *Criminal Justice and Behavior, 34,* 37–59. doi:10.1177/0093854806291157

Lehmann, R.J.B., Hanson, R. K., Babchishin, K. M., Gallasch-Nemitz, F., Biedermann, J., & Dahle, K. P. (2013). Interpreting multiple risk scales for sex offenders: Evidence for averaging. *Psychological Assessment, 25,* 1019–1024. doi:10.1037/a0033098

Levenson, J. S. (2004). Reliability of sexually violent predator civil commitment criteria in Florida. *Law and Human Behavior, 28,* 357–368. doi:10.1023/B:LAHU.0000039330.22347.ad

Looman, J., & Abracen, J. (2012). The Static-99: Are there really differences between the treatment need and high risk normative groups? *International Journal of Offender Therapy and Comparative Criminology, 57,* 888–907. doi:10.1177/0306624X12443657

Looman, J., Morphett, N.A.C., & Abracen, J. (2012). Does consideration of psychopathy and sexual deviance add to the predictive validity of the Static-99R? *International Journal of Offender Therapy and Comparative Criminology, 57,* 939–965. doi:10.1177/0306624X12444839

Lynett, E., & Rogers, R. (2000). Emotions overriding forensic opinions? The potentially biasing effects of victim statements. *The Journal of Psychiatry and Law, 28,* 457.

Mann, R. E., Hanson, R. K., & Thornton, D. (2010). Assessing risk for sexual recidivism: Some proposals on the nature of psychologically meaningful risk factors. *Sexual Abuse: A Journal of Research and Treatment, 22,* 191–217. doi:10.1177/1079063210366039

McGrath, R. J., Hoke, S. E., Livingston, J. A., & Cumming, G. F. (2001, November). *The Vermont Assessment of Sex-Offender Risk (VASOR): An initial reliability and validity study.* Presentation at the 20th Annual Research and Treatment Conference of the Association for the Treatment of Sexual Abusers, San Antonio, TX.

McGrath, R. J., Lasher, M. P., & Cumming, G. F. (2012). The Sex Offender Treatment Intervention and Progress Scale (SOTIPS): Psychometric properties and incremental predictive validity with Static-99R. *Sexual Abuse: A Journal of Research and Treatment 24*, 431–458. doi:10.1177/1079063211432475

Miller, H. A., Amenta, A. E., Conroy, M. A. (2005). Sexually violent predator evaluations: Empirical evidence, strategies for professionals, and research directions. *Law and Human Behavior, 29*, 29–54. doi:10.1007/s10979–005–1398-y

Monahan, J. (1981). *The clinical prediction of violent behavior*. Washington, DC: National Institute of Mental Health.

Murrie, D.C., Boccaccini, M. T., & Turner, D. T. (2010). Ethical challenges in sex-offender civil commitment evaluations: Applying imperfect science in adversarial settings. In A. Schlank (Ed.), *The sexual predator: Vol. 4* (pp. 8–1–8–35). Kingston, NJ: Civic Research Institute.

Murrie, D. C., Boccaccini, M. T., Turner, D. B., Meeks, M., Woods, C., & Tussey, C. (2009). Rater (dis) agreement on risk assessment measures in sexually violent predator proceedings. *Psychology, Public Policy and Law, 15*, 19–53. doi:10.1037/a0014897

Nuffield, J. (1982). *Parole decision-making in Canada: Research towards decision guidelines*. Ottawa. ON: Solicitor General of Canada.

Nunes, K. L., Wexler, A., Firestone, P., & Bradford, J. M. (2003). *Incarceration and recidivism in a sample of sexual offenders*. Paper presented at the annual Research and Treatment Conference of the Association for the Treatment of Sexual Abusers, St. Louis, MO.

Olver, M. E., Wong, S. C. P., Nicholaichuk, T., & Gordon, A. (2007). The validity and reliability of the Violence Risk Scale—Sexual Offender Version: Assessing sex offender risk and evaluating therapeutic change. *Psychological Assessment, 19*, 318–329. doi:10.1037/1040–3590.19.3.318

People v. Superior Court (Ghilotti), 27 Cal 4th 888 (2002).

Phenix, A., Helmus, H. M., & Hanson, R. K. (2012). *Static-99R and Static-2002R Evaluator Workbook*. Retrieved from www.static99.org.

Phenix, A., Helmus, H. M., & Hanson, R. K. (2015) *Static-99R and Static-2002R Evaluator Workbook*. Retrieved from www.static99.org.

Poole, D., Liedecke, D., & Marbibi, M. (2000). *Risk assessment and recidivism in juvenile sexual offenders: A validation study of Static-99*. Austin: Texas Youth Commission.

Quinsey, V. L., Harris, G. T., Rice M. E., & Cormier, C. A. (2006). Violence Risk Appraisal Guide (VRAG). In V. L. Quinsey, G. T. Harris, M. E. Rice, & C. A. Cormier (Eds.), *Violent offenders: Appraising and managing risk* (2nd ed.). *The law and public policy*. Washington, DC: American Psychological Association.

Ralston, C. A., & Epperson, D. L. (2013). Predictive validity of adult risk assessment tools with juveniles who offended sexually. *Psychological Assessment, 3*, 905–916. doi:10.1037/a0032683

Rice, M. E., & Harris, G. T. (1997). Cross-validation and extension of the violence risk appraisal guide for child molesters and rapists. *Law and Human Behavior, 21*, 231–241. doi:10.1023/A:1024882430242

Rice, M. E., & Harris, G. T. (in press). The Sex Offender Risk Appraisal Guide. In A. Phenix & H. Hoberman (Eds.), *Sexual offenders: Diagnosis, risk assessment, and management*. New York: Springer.

Rice, M. E., Harris, G. T., & Lang, C. (2013). Validation of and revision to the VRAG and SORAG: The Violence Risk Appraisal Guide–Revised (VRAG-R). *Psychological Assessment, 25*, 951–965. doi:10.1037/a0032878

Rogers, R. (2001). *Handbook of diagnostic and structured interviewing*. New York: The Guilford Press.

Rogers, R., & Dickey, R. (1991). Denial and minimization among sex offenders: A review of competing models of deception. *Annals of Sex Research, 4*, 49–63.

Rogers, R., & Jackson, R. L. (2005). Sexually violent predators: The risky enterprise of risk assessment. *Journal of the American Academy of Psychiatry and the Law, 33*, 523–528.

Schlank, A. (2014). Update on legal issues involving sexually violent predators. In A. Schlank (Ed.), *The sexual predator: Vol. 5* (pp. 2–1–2–10). Kingston, NJ: Civic Research Institute.

Schopp, R. F. (1998). Civil commitment and sexual predators: Competence and condemnation. *Psychology, Public Policy, and Law, 4*, 323–376. doi:10.1037/1076–8971.4.1–2.323

Schopp, R. F., & Sturgis, B. J. (1995). Sexual predators and legal mental illness for civil commitment. *Behavioral Sciences & the Law, 13*, 437–458. doi:10.1002/bsl.2370130402

Seager, J. A., Jellicoe, D., & Dhaliwal, G. K. (2004). Refusers, dropouts, and completers: Measuring sex offender treatment efficacy. *International Journal of Offender Therapy and Comparative Criminology, 48*, 600–612. doi:10.1177/0306624X04263885

Seto, M. C. (2005). Is more better? Combining actuarial risk scales to predict recidivism among adult sex offenders. *Psychological Assessment, 17*, 156–167. doi:10.1037/1040–3590.17.2.156

Sewell, K. W., & Salekin, R. T. (1997). Understanding and detecting dissimulation in sex offenders. In R. Rogers (Ed.), *Clinical assessment of malingering and deception* (2nd ed., pp. 328–350). New York: Guilford Press.

Skelton, A., Riley, D., Wales, D., & Vess, J. (2006). Assessing risk for sexual offenders in New Zealand: Developing and validation of a computer-scored risk measure. *Journal of Sexual Aggression, 12*, 277–286. doi:10.1080/13552600601100326

Smallbone S., & Rallings M. (2013). Short-term predictive validity of the Static-99 and Static-99-R for indigenous and nonindigenous Australian sexual offenders. *Sexual Abuse: A Journal of Research and Treatment, 3*, 302–316. doi:10.1177/1079063212472937

Snowden, R. J., Gray, N. S., & Taylor, J. (2010). Risk assessment for future violence in individuals from an ethnic minority group. *International Journal of Forensic Mental Health, 9*, 118–123. doi:10.1080/14999013.2010.501845

Sreenivasan, S., Weinberger, L. E., & Garrick, T. (2003). Expert testimony in sexually violent predator commitments: Conceptualizing legal standards of mental disorder and likely to reoffend. *Journal of the American Academy of Psychiatry & Law, 31*, 471–485.

Stalans, L. J., Seng, M., & Yarnold, P. R., (2002). *Long-term impact evaluation of sex offender probation programs in DuPage, Lake, and Winnebago Counties.* Illinois Criminal Justice Information Authority. Retrieved from www.icjia.state.il.us/public/pdf/ResearchReports/Long-termDuPageWinnebago.pdf.

Storey, J. E., Watt, K. A., Jackson, K. J., & Hart, S. D. (2012). Utilization and implications of the Static-99 in practice. *Sexual Abuse: A Journal of Research and Treatment, 24*, 289–302. doi:10.1177/1079063211423943

Ternowski, D. R. (2004). *Sex offender treatment: An evaluation of the Stave Lake Correctional Centre Program.* Unpublished doctoral dissertation. Simon Fraser University, Burnaby, BC.

Thornton, D. (2002). Constructing and testing a framework for dynamic risk assessment. *Sexual Abuse: A Journal of Research and Treatment, 14*, 137–151. doi:10.1077/107906320201400205

Thornton, D., & Knight, R. A. (2013). Construction and validation of the SRA-FV. *Sexual Abuse: A Journal of Research and Treatment.* Published online December 30, 2013. doi:10.1177/1079063213511120

Tough, S. E. (2001). *Validation of two standardized risk assessments (RRASOR, 1997; Static-99, 1999) on a sample of adult males who are developmentally disabled with significant cognitive deficits.* Unpublished master's thesis, University of Toronto, Toronto, ON.

Tully, R. J., Chou, S., & Browne, K. D. (2013). A systematic review on the effectiveness of sex offender risk assessment tools in predicting sexual recidivism of adult male sex offenders. *Clinical Psychology Review, 33*, 287–316. doi:10.1016/j.cpr.2012.12.002

Varela, J. G., Boccaccini, M. T., Murrie, D.C., Caperton, J. D., & Gonzalez, E. (2013). Do the Static-99 and Static-99R perform similarly for Black, White, and Latino sex offenders? *International Journal of Forensic Mental Health, 12*, 231–243. doi:10.1080/14999013.2013.846950

Vess, J., Murphy, C., & Arkowitz, S. (2004). Clinical and demographic differences between sexually violent predators and other commitment types in a state forensic hospital, *Journal of Forensic Psychiatry and Psychology, 15*, 669–68. doi:10.1080/14789940410001731795

Vlahakis, J. C. (2010). Legal issues involving sexually violent persons. In A. Schlank (Ed.), *The sexual predator: Vol 4.* (pp. 2–2–2–30). Kingston, NJ: Civil Research Institute.

Vognsen, J., & Phenix, A. (2004). Antisocial personality disorder is not enough: A reply to Sreenivasan, Weinberger, and Garrick. *Journal of the American Academy of Psychiatry and Law, 32*, 440–442.

Winick, B. J., & La Fond, J. Q. (Eds.) (2003). *Protecting society from sexually dangerous offenders: Law, justice, and therapy.* Washington, DC: American Psychological Association. doi:10.1037/10492–000

Wong, S. C. P., & Gordon A. E. (2006). The validity and reliability of the Violence Risk Scale: A treatment-friendly violence risk assessment tool. *Psychology, Public Policy, and Law, 12*, 279–309. doi:10.1037/1076–8971.12.3.279

Zander, T. K. (2005). Civil commitment without psychosis: The law's reliance on the weakest links in psychodiagnosis. *Journal of Sexual Offender Civil Commitment: Science and the Law, 1*, 17–82.

Zonana, H., Bonnie, R. J., & Hoge, S. K. (2001). In the wake of Hendricks: The treatment and restraint of sexually dangerous offenders viewed from the perspective of American psychiatry. In B. J. Winick & J. Q. La Fond (Eds.), *Protecting society from sexually dangerous offenders: Law, justice, and therapy* (pp. 131–145). Washington, DC: American Psychological Association.

9 Forensic Psychology Evaluations at Capital Sentencing[1]

Mark D. Cunningham

The U.S. Supreme Court in *Satterwhite v. Texas* (1988) described psychiatric testimony at capital sentencing as "a life or death matter" (at 1802). This characterization aptly captures the unparalleled gravity and implications of evaluations by mental health experts in these ultimate determinations. The demands for competence and professionalism from psychologists practicing in this arena are correspondingly high. The foundation for such competence and professionalism requires a clear understanding of the psycholegal issues involved in these determinations. It also calls for a sophisticated awareness of the implications and repercussions of the evaluation procedures and parameters. Finally, as in any arena of forensic practice, competence and professionalism rest on the empirical data that inform the conclusions and applications of the evaluation (for an extended discussion of parameters and standards for mental health evaluations at capital sentencing see American Bar Association, 2008; Cunningham, 2006b, 2010; Cunningham & Goldstein, 2013; DeMatteo, Murrie, Anumba, & Keesler, 2011).

The Modern Death Penalty Era

The modern era of the death penalty in the United States began and has evolved through a series of U.S. Supreme Court decisions. These decisions in turn have shaped state and federal statutes. This began with *Furman v. Georgia*, a 1972 landmark decision by a divided U.S. Supreme Court declaring that the death penalty was unconstitutional. This was not a determination that the death penalty per se was unconstitutional, rather the existing death penalty was unconstitutional in its procedures and application. State legislatures throughout the country responded by redrafting their death penalty statutes, attempting to address the concerns of the Court that the death penalty had been applied in an unreliable, capricious, arbitrary, or prejudicial fashion. The various revised capital statutes were initially tested and modified by the Court in *Woodson v. North Carolina* (1976), *Gregg v. Georgia* (1976), *Jurek v. Texas* (1976), and *Lockett v. Ohio* (1978). Capital litigation procedures emerging from these and subsequent U.S. Supreme Court decisions broadly reflect three primary themes, discussed in this section.

Restricted Class of Death—Eligible Offenses

Armed robbery and rape are no longer death-penalty eligible offenses as they were in many jurisdictions pre-*Furman*. Though some jurisdictions considered legislation making repeat child molestation a capital offense, this did not pass constitutional muster (*Kennedy v. Louisiana*, 2008, see also *Coker v. Georgia*, 1977). Capital murder in the modern era is restricted to particular circumstances, such as murder in the course of a felony, accompanied by specified aggravating factors, or involving a particular class of victims such as police officers or children.

Individualized Capital Sentencing

Death is never a mandatory penalty, regardless of the offense. Rather, the jury is tasked with making an *individualized* determination of death-worthiness. This individualized consideration requires a bifurcated (two-stage) or trifurcated (three-stage) trial process involving a guilt phase, an eligibility phase, and a sentencing phase where the jury separately deliberates guilt and punishment. An individualized determination of punishment in a capital case, however, is not simply a matter of trial structure. It also requires the weighing of mitigating as well as aggravating factors. Violence risk assessment perspectives are a part of this individualized consideration in some jurisdictions.

Heightened Standards of Reliability

Reliability in capital cases is enhanced by several post-*Furman* mechanisms. Two attorneys are appointed to defend a capitally charged defendant. In many jurisdictions one or both of these attorneys must have experience or training in capital cases. Death verdicts also come under increased scrutiny and multiple stages of appellate review. Appellate review occurs in two stages: direct appeal, and postconviction proceedings. In state capital cases, each of these appellate stages is examined at a state and federal level. Legal errors that may have occurred at trial as a result of various rulings of the trial court in response to pretrial motions, jury selection, or objections during the trial itself are reviewed on direct appeal. The second stages of appellate review are called *postconviction* proceedings at a state level and *habeas* proceedings at a federal level. These proceedings investigate issues that may not be apparent from the trial record alone. Most often postconviction claims assert that the defense attorneys provided inadequate representation, referred to as *ineffective assistance of counsel* (see American Bar Association, 2003, 2008; *Strickland v. Washington*, 1984). For example, the defense may have failed to conduct an adequate mitigation investigation of the defendant's development and limitations (see *Wiggins v. Smith*, 2003; *Rompilla v. Beard*, 2005). On occasion, these claims may also assert prosecutorial misconduct (e.g., withholding evidence, knowingly eliciting perjury), juror misconduct (e.g., conducted an independent investigation), and other miscarriages of justice.

As will become apparent in the sections that follow, psychological evaluations at capital sentencing are an extension of these themes of narrowing of the class of offenders eligible for the death penalty, individualized consideration, and heightened reliability.

Conceptual Issues at Capital Sentencing

The psycholegal issues that are the focus of psychological evaluations in capital sentencing at a trial level can be broadly divided into two factors: mitigation and violence risk assessment (Cunningham, 2010; Cunningham & Goldstein).

Mitigation

The U.S. Supreme Court in *Lockett v. Ohio* (1978) described mitigation at capital sentencing as including: "any aspect of a defendant's character or record, or any of the circumstances of the offense that the defendant proffered as a basis for a sentence less than death." What may be considered as mitigating, then, is extraordinarily broad and multifaceted. Though mitigation is a multifaceted consideration, a central component is the concept of moral culpability. Moral culpability involves what the Supreme Court in *Woodson v. North Carolina* (1976) characterized as "the diverse frailties of humankind" (at 304; see also *Burger v. Kemp*, 1987). The concept of moral culpability acknowledges an elementary psychological reality: we do not all arrive at our choices out of equivalent raw material (see *Eddings v. Oklahoma*, 1982; *Penry v. Lynaugh*, 1989). It follows that the degree of "blameworthiness" of an individual for criminal or even murderous conduct may vary depending on what factors and experiences shaped, influenced, or compromised that choice. More specifically, the nature and quality of understanding, perception, impulse control, judgment, and values that underlie choice—even choice that results in heinous violence—are influenced by developmental, cognitive, neuropsychological, relationship, cultural, community, and situational factors (Haney, 1995). Haney (1997), as well as others (Hawkins et al., 2000; Monahan, 1981, 1996; Shah, 1978; U.S. Department of Justice, 1995) have identified this "interactional" convergence of nature, situation, context, and structure as the primary explanation for criminal violence (Cunningham, 2010).

The relationship of developmental damage and other impairing factors to the exercise of choice, and subsequently to moral culpability, is illustrated in the graphic models depicted in Figures 9.1 and 9.2. As the damaging and impairing factors (e.g. neglect, abuse, psychological disorder, neuropsychological deficits, substance dependency/intoxication, etc.) increase, choice is exercised on an increasing slope, and moral culpability is correspondingly reduced.

The greater the damaging or impairing factors, the steeper the angle or slope on which the choices are made, and the lower is the level of moral culpability. This is the rationale of *Atkins v. Virginia* (2002)—i.e., mental retardation represents such a significant impairment that the afflicted defendant simply cannot possess the requisite level of moral culpability to be eligible for the death penalty. A related moral culpability rationale, this time implicating developmental immaturity, underlies *Roper v. Simmons* (2005), the U.S. Supreme Court decision barring the execution of offenders who were less than 18 years old at the time of the capital offense. Of course, an analysis of moral culpability is not limited to mental retardation or adolescence. Rather, formative or limiting impacts from any source of developmental damage or impairment are relevant in the weighing of moral culpability.

Though equally *criminally responsible*, capital defendants may vary markedly in their *moral culpability* and, ultimately, in their blameworthiness. Accordingly, it is critically important for psychologists undertaking a capital sentencing evaluation to differentiate between these distinct psycholegal issues. Criminal responsibility (i.e., sanity, guilt-phase issue) and moral culpability (i.e., blameworthiness, sentencing-phase issue), and their associated corollary queries are

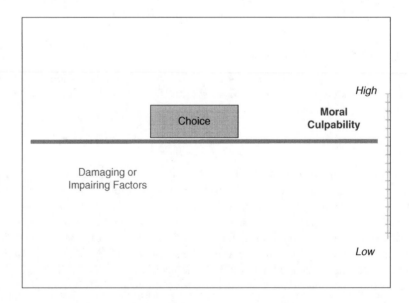

Figure 9.1 Few damaging and impairing factors.

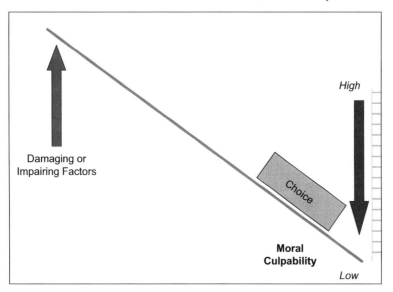

Figure 9.2 Extensive damaging and impairing factors.

Table 9.1 Criminal responsibility and moral culpability

Criminal Responsibility	Moral Culpability
Guilt phase	**Sentencing phase**
Sanity	Punishment
Dichotomous	Continuum
Queries:	*Queries*:
Could he or she control himself?	What diminished his or her control?
Did he or she have a choice?	What shaped the choice?
Did he or she know right from wrong?	What shaped his or her morality and value system?

contrasted in Table 9.1. That a capital defendant is criminally responsible is a settled issue when a guilty verdict is returned. On the basis of this criminal responsibility, the defendant will receive a sentence of either life in prison or the death penalty. In determining which of these most severe sanctions will be imposed, the questions of criminal responsibility are of no value to the jury in individualizing the punishment (i.e., it has already answered "yes" with a guilty verdict). Stated differently, in the absence of choice, wrongful awareness, or the ability to exert self-control, the defendant would have lacked some necessary element of the offense or been not guilty by reason of insanity.

Accordingly, if a weighing of mitigation is in terms of whether the capital defendant had a choice or possessed wrongful awareness, the presentation of the defendant's circumstances, character, and background would be without individualizing or particularizing value in the application of the death penalty. A moral culpability analysis at capital sentencing, then, is not a dichotomous determination of whether the defendant had a choice or wrongful awareness. Rather, it is an appraisal of the extent to which the background and circumstances of the defendant influenced, predisposed, or diminished the defendant's moral sensibilities and that exercise of volition or free will. Stated more plainly, how steep was the angle from which the choices were made?

Admittedly, a perspective that interacting, adverse bio-psycho-social factors were integral to the defendant's criminal trajectory and capital conduct is more congruent with the defense theory at sentencing. The view advanced by the prosecution, by contrast, typically emphasizes the operation of willful choice, asserting that "a defendant's crime stems entirely from his evil makeup and that he therefore deserves to be judged and punished exclusively on the basis of his presumably free, morally blameworthy choices" (Haney, 1997, p. 1459). For this reason, the role of a mental health professional retained by the State at capital sentencing is more often to provide second opinions regarding the assessment findings and the scholarly applications of the defense-retained experts.

Violence Risk Assessment

A second psycholegal issue at capital sentencing in many jurisdictions examines the likelihood of future violent acts by the defendant, sometimes referred to as "future dangerousness" (see Krauss, McCabe, & McFadden, 2009). Depending on the jurisdiction, this question may be inadmissible unless introduced by the defense (e.g., California). In two jurisdictions (i.e., Oregon, Texas), this question is a mandatory "special issue" in all capital determinations. In many other jurisdictions consideration of future violence is available as either a statutory or nonstatutory aggravating factor. "Positive prisoner evidence" or "*Skipper* evidence" (i.e., factors pointing to a positive adjustment to a life term in prison) can also be introduced as a mitigating factor (*Skipper v. South Carolina*, 1986).

The consideration of future violent conduct as a special issue or aggravating factor was introduced as part of the capital sentencing scheme by the Texas legislature in 1973 (see Cunningham, 2006a), and affirmed by the U.S. Supreme Court in *Jurek v. Texas* (1976) and *Barefoot v. Estelle* (1983). This special issue at capital sentencing states: "whether there is a probability that the defendant would commit criminal acts of violence that would constitute a continuing threat to society" (see Texas Code of Criminal Procedure, Article 37.071 §2(b)1).

Problematically, appellate courts (e.g., *James v. Collins*, 1993) have declined to provide operational definitions of "probability," "acts of violence," "continuing threat," or "society." This necessarily invites ambiguity and controversy in the application of these terms. Inferential guidance, though, can be derived from recognition that this and other capital sentencing considerations drafted in the aftermath of *Furman* exist to "individualize" the application of the death penalty. If "probability" is construed to mean "any possibility," then the question would always be answered in the affirmative and the issue would serve no individualizing or narrowing function. Something more than "any possibility," then, must be contemplated by the special issue.

The rationale of an *individualized* determination of death-worthiness also informs an understanding of the severity and context of the future violent acts that are contemplated by "criminal acts of violence that constitute a continuing threat to society." Because the shoving of another inmate, occasional belligerence with staff, and even a mutual fistfight are routine if not ubiquitous acts among prison inmates, these behaviors are of little value in individualizing or narrowing the application of the death penalty. Additionally, reasonable proportionality would require that "threat to society" be limited to acts of sufficient severity that a sanction of death is a reasonable preventative intervention (Cunningham, Sorensen, Vigen, & Woods, 2011), i.e., the "intervention" should be proportional to the harm it is intended to prevent (Slobogin, 2009).

Extending this line of analysis, no individualizing function is achieved if society is construed to mean the free community as opposed to prison. Under what circumstances is a capital offender not a substantial risk of violence if at large at the time of sentencing? Despite the appeal of this logic and the availability of life-without-parole sentencing in every U.S. jurisdiction with the death penalty, courts are divided on whether risk assessment determinations by capital juries are limited to a prison context. State appellate courts in both Texas (*Coble v. Texas*, 2010) and Virginia (*Porter v. Commonwealth*, 2008) have opined that "society" is not restricted to prison,

Table 9.2 Future dangerousness versus violence risk assessment

Future Dangerousness	Violence Risk Assessment
• Violence potential	• Probability of violent act
• Personal attribute	• Time and context dependent
• Dichotomous decision	• Continuous variable
• All violent felons are dangerous	• Varying probability
• No particularizing function	• Particularized by risk (probability)
• Unresponsive to preventive efforts	• Altered by preventive action

even when the alternative to the death penalty is life without parole. Federal district courts, by contrast, have restricted the "society" under consideration to prison.

A caution regarding terminology is also in order. The term *future dangerousness* is utilized with unfortunate regularity at capital sentencing as shorthand for *probability of criminal acts of violence that would constitute a continuing threat to society*. This shorthand may variously be framed in terms of whether the defendant is "dangerous," or will be "a danger" in the future. Whatever its convenience, reframing the operational definition in this manner has significant potential to alter and confuse the issue. To illustrate, "future dangerousness" and "risk of violent acts" are contrasted in Table 9.2.

Most problematically, when construed as "dangerousness" the issue loses any individualizing value. All violent felons, including all capital offenders, are dangerous. Their dangerousness is a significant rationale for their long-term confinement in a highly secure correctional facility. Probability of acts, by contrast, can be specified and will vary from defendant to defendant—thus preserving an individualizing function for this consideration.

Targets and Issues for Informed Consent

Informed consent is a fundamental ethical consideration in the provision of both clinical and forensic services (American Psychological Association, 2002, 2013). Informed consent occurs when "the recipient or target of services has sufficient information regarding the pending procedures, including the associated potential benefits and hazards, to exercise a meaningful or illuminated choice regarding whether to participate" (Cunningham, 2006b, p. 452). Because the necessity and extent of informed consent disclosures increase with the potential severity of adverse repercussions, evaluations by psychologists in death penalty cases call for particular attention to informed consent. Basic informed consent information is, of course, conveyed directly to the defendant or third parties at the outset of any interview. Regardless of whether retained by the defense or the prosecution, this disclosure should include a clear statement of who has retained the psychologist, the purpose and parameters of the evaluation, the pending procedures and potential applications, and any limitations to confidentiality.

Discussion of these factors, however, is more akin to a warning than a fully illuminated disclosure. The consent of the defendant may also be illusory, particularly in evaluations by prosecution-retained psychologists (Cunningham, 2006b). To explain, the defendant in most instances cannot decline the evaluation by a state-retained mental health expert without sanctions by the court that may include barring the defense from calling mental health experts and/or asserting some mitigating factors at sentencing.

Though warnings to the capital defendant are essential, Cunningham (2006b) asserted that defense counsel is the *primary* target of informed consent disclosures, who then acts as both a conduit in conveying this information to the defendant and an advisor in making strategic use of it. Defense counsel is the point of contact before the retention is secured and has greater appreciation of the complex issues surrounding mental health evaluations in capital litigation, as well as how the evaluation and its parameters will impact trial strategy and the constitutional rights of the defendant.

Cunningham (2006b) asserted that a prosecution-retained psychologist also has informed consent obligations to defense counsel that extend beyond "warning" disclosures to the defendant or third parties who are interviewed. These proposed obligations include providing meaningful notice, as well as information regarding the limitations and potential applications of the proposed evaluation procedures (see Cunningham, 2006b, for proposed timing and elements of this notice).

Informed consent by defense-retained psychologists involves a broad range of considerations. These include the expertise and experience of the psychologist, the referral question and focus of the evaluation, the role the psychologist will occupy, and various parameters of the evaluation. Informed consent does not dictate the election of the psychologist in these matters; only that defense counsel is informed of the rationale, options, and repercussions in advance of the retention. The sections that follow are intended to illuminate these considerations for the psychologist and subsequently for informed consent discussions.

Roles for Psychologists at Capital Sentencing

Advocacy and Bias

Psychologists may occupy one of two roles when retained in a capital or other forensic case: consultant or testifying expert. As a consultant in capital or other forensic cases, the psychologist is unabashedly aligned with one party in the litigation and advocates for that party's desired *outcome*. Consultant activities include jury selection, focus groups, shadow juries, preparation of opening and closing statements, preparation of witnesses, and development of trial strategy. A testifying expert, by contrast, is an advocate for the *data* and associated expert opinion rather than the outcome. A testifying psychologist, whether retained by the defense or the State, only has an investment in the skill, objectivity, and professionalism of the evaluation, and in providing informed choice regarding the options for this evaluation. Involvement of a testifying expert in consultant activities would represent a dual role, and is obviously inconsistent with the neutrality and objectivity required in expert testimony. Accordingly, the role desired from the psychologist should be clarified at the outset.

Maintaining clear role boundaries and professional neutrality is particularly challenging for testifying experts in capital cases. The complexity of capital litigation requires the involvement of multiple attorneys, investigators, and experts who must interact and coordinate their activities during the extended course of the case. This results in subtle pressures to align with the perspectives and goals of the defense or prosecution team (Cunningham & Goldstein, 2013). Capital cases are also characterized by intense advocacy by both the prosecution and the defense, and the expert must guard against compromising assessment methods and opinions in the service of this intense advocacy.

Bundled Evaluations

Psychologists are sometimes asked to simultaneously or sequentially evaluate sentencing considerations *and* other issues in a given capital case. At times this involves a specific request to expand the evaluation to include competency to stand trial or mental state at time of offense. In other instances multiple evaluations are embedded in an unfocused referral to "go see this defendant and tell me what you think." Such bundled evaluations of sentencing and other psycholegal issues are typically ill advised for a number of reasons:

1. A less comprehensive sentencing evaluation may result from defusing the focus of the assessment.

2. Constitutional protections may be forfeited. But for the participation of the same expert for competency and sentencing issues, the findings of the competency to stand trial evaluation might not be admissible for any other purpose.

3. Evaluation of mental state at time of offense necessarily requires inquiry regarding the time period of the offense. Such an inquiry, however, would be discretionary if the evaluation focused on sentencing issues of formative developmental factors. Any denials of guilt by the defendant in the course of such a mental state inquiry are likely to be asserted by the State at sentencing as evidence of lack of remorse.

4. The sentencing jury is at risk of confusing competency, sanity, and moral culpability issues—inappropriately forming a nexus between the former two and the latter.

5. If the jury does not find the criminal responsibility (i.e., insanity related) testimony of the expert to be credible in the guilt phase, acceptance of the expert's findings at the sentencing phase may be compromised. Further, the jury may fatigue to the repeated testimony of the same expert.

Testifying Roles

The testimony of a psychologist at capital sentencing may involve any of three overlapping roles: teaching witness, evaluation without direct assessment contact with the defendant, and evaluation with direct assessment contact with the defendant (see Cunningham, 2006b, 2010).

As a *teaching witness*, the psychologist describes research findings that illuminate a factor being considered at sentencing. For example, a teaching witness might describe risk and protective factors for delinquency and violence, or the effects of disrupted attachment, childhood maltreatment, etc. Alternatively, a teaching witness might outline violence risk assessment methodology and detail relevant rates and correlates of inmate violence. This testimony would assist the jury in applying relevant risk factors in light of the group statistical data on various forms of prison violence.

In *evaluation without direct assessment contact*, the psychologist reviews records and interviews third parties, but does not interview or perform testing on the defendant. This procedure is typically the result of the unwillingness of the defense to allow the defendant to be interviewed by State-retained mental health experts, which would be triggered in some jurisdictions if the defendant were interviewed by a testifying defense-retained psychologist. The findings of an evaluation without interview are offered more tentatively, and usually focus on historical factors rather than diagnosis or personality descriptions.

Whether opinions can be reliably and ethically offered in the absence of direct evaluative contact with the defendant will vary depending on the nature of the issue under consideration and the adequacy of data from other sources (see Cunningham, 2006b). Mitigation at capital sentencing often focuses on historical adverse developmental factors. The defendant is neither the sole nor the most reliable source of historical information regarding important developmental events and formative influences in his or her own life. Records, as well as information obtained from family, community members, and other third parties, represent important alternative and potentially preferable sources of developmental information.

The nexus drawn by the mental health expert between particular adverse factors and criminally violent outcomes in adolescence or adulthood relies on research studies examining the impact of these risk factors, not on the insight of the defendant. Similarly, the most important types of data in a capital violence risk assessment involve the defendant's pattern of behavior when incarcerated, various demographic and historical factors, and the base rates of institutional violence in various inmate groups (Cunningham, 2010; Cunningham & Reidy, 1998b; Cunningham et al., 2011), none of which is fundamentally reliant on interview or testing of the capital defendant.

Even recognizing these limitations of direct evaluation of the defendant and alternative sources of information, *evaluation with direct assessment contact* is the preferable basis for testimony and provides the most comprehensive investigation and foundation for expert opinions. This role would be essential in quantifying current intellectual or neuropsychological capabilities. It may also be the only vehicle for obtaining historical information that is known only to the defendant (e.g., sexual abuse, substance abuse, observed community violence, corruptive influences, etc.). As will be discussed in the sections that follow, however, interview of the defendant is only one component of a far more widely ranging capital sentencing evaluation.

Procedures and Parameters of Evaluation

Parameters of the Interview of the Defendant

An essential issue to resolve with defense counsel prior to interview of the defendant is whether inquiry is permitted regarding the capital offense and/or any unadjudicated conduct. Such a consideration is complex (see Cunningham, 2006b; 2010). Interviewing the defendant about the capital offense could help establish whether his or her capacities at that time were undermined by a major Axis I disorder. The defendant's accounts of the instant offense and/or prior unadjudicated offense(s), however, do not typically inform a mitigation analysis of damaging developmental trajectory (i.e., how the defendant came to be damaged), nor do these accounts contribute to a violence risk assessment. Further, if the defense-retained expert elicits such a history the state-retained expert will likely be allowed to also inquire regarding these matters, depriving the defendant of important Fifth Amendment protections. Finally, there is the potential that the account of the defendant will be inconsistent with defense assertions of innocence at the guilt phase, or the jury's finding of guilt. The benefits, limitations, and implications of the defendant's self-incriminating statements should be disclosed to defense counsel prior to interviewing the defendant.

The Role of Personality Testing

Personality testing adds to the descriptive richness and depth of a psychological assessment, and it may be relevant to mitigation assertions of a major Axis I disorder. Personality testing in capital sentencing evaluations, however, also has important limitations and adverse implications that can render its use inadvisable (Cunningham, 2010). To summarize these, personality testing has not been standardized on a population facing capital murder charges, and testing profile patterns including Minnesota Multiphasic Personality Inventory (MMPI) (Megargee 1984) profile classifications (i.e., typology of MMPI code types among prison inmates) routinely change over time. Personality assessment does little to illuminate the damaging developmental trajectory that is fundamental to mitigation. Personality assessment is likely to implicate the presence of a personality disorder and associated descriptions of maladaptive traits—an unsurprising finding in an individual who is assumed for purposes of the assessment to have been so damaged as to perpetrate a capital murder. Finally, because personality testing does not reliably differentiate those inmates who commit acts of serious violence in prison from those who do not, it is of negligible value in violence risk assessments for this institutional context (see Edens, Buffington-Vollum, Keilen, Roskamp, & Anthony, 2005).

Additional Preconsultation Issues

Other essential informed consent discussion topics include fee estimates, how the interviews will be memorialized, whether a report will be prepared, any personal advocacy positions regarding the death penalty, and any complaints or judgments that might affect the attorney's decision to retain the expert.

Evaluation of Mitigation and Moral Culpability

Comprehensive Investigation

The range of factors that impact developmental trajectory and adult functioning are extraordinarily broad. Accordingly, a mental health expert addressing mitigation and moral culpability at capital sentencing faces the daunting task of identifying any factors that might adversely impact physical, neuropsychological, psychoeducational, personality, social/interpersonal, moral, and vocational development and capability (Cunningham, 2010; Cunningham & Reidy, 2001; DeMatteo et al., 2011). The comprehensiveness of this assessment task is well beyond any other forensic mental health consultation and requires evaluation procedures of unique thoroughness. This is not an investigation that rests entirely or even primarily on the defense-retained psychologist.

In addition to two defense attorneys, capital defense teams typically include a social worker or "mitigation specialist" who initiates an investigation of the defendant's individual and family history well prior to a psychologist being retained. This mitigation specialist performs a comprehensive records search regarding the defendant and the defendant's family, including medical, educational, social services, mental health, juvenile, military, employment, criminal, and offense records. These records are ultimately made available to the psychologist. The mitigation investigator also locates and interviews a large number of family members and other third parties who are familiar with the defendant, his or her family history, or his or her social context. Summaries of each of these interviews are prepared. The mitigation investigator then integrates the information obtained from these records and interview summaries into a detailed chronology or time line of the defendant's generational family history. The mitigation specialist routinely invests hundreds of hours in this comprehensive investigation of a capital defendant's life. Depending on the discovery rules and trial strategy of the defense, the interview summaries and chronologies are provided to the psychologist.

The evaluation activities, inquiries, and time investment of the psychologist will vary markedly depending on the focus of the referral. For example, a psychologist may be asked to evaluate a particular developmental factor (e.g., disrupted attachment, sexual abuse, substance dependence) or deficiency (e.g., intellectual functioning, neuropsychological deficits). Alternatively, the psychologist may be involved in investigating the presence and implications of all of the adverse developmental, family, and community factors in a defendant's background. Table 9.3

Table 9.3 Potential adverse developmental factors

Neurological and Hereditary Factors	*Family Factors*
• Chromosomal abnormalities	• Multigenerational family distress
• Prenatal alcohol or drug exposure	• Parental substance dependence
• Perinatal complications	• Parental psychological disorder
• Intellectual disability or deficient intelligence	• Parental criminality
• Closed head injuries	• Mother a teen at outset of child rearing
• Toxin exposures	• Father absence
• Inhalant and other substance abuse	• Disrupted primary attachment
• Attention deficit hyperactivity disorder	• Abject poverty
• Learning disabilities	• Physical and emotional abuse and neglect
• Chronic trauma exposure	• Observed domestic violence
• Type II alcoholism	• Sexually traumatic exposures
• Substance dependency and intoxication effects	• Corruptive socialization
• Youthfulness	• Large family size
• Genetic predisposition to substance dependence	• Insufficient supervision and guidance
• Genetic predisposition to psychological disorders	

provides a sample of such factors. As this admittedly incomplete listing reflects, the spectrum of possible factors can be daunting. It is not uncommon for 15 or more adverse developmental factors to be present in a given capital defendant's history. As this listing reflects, the primary emphasis of a mitigation evaluation is developmental and explanatory, rather than simply diagnostic and personality descriptive.

Review of Records

Depending on the extent of the issues involved in the referral, the psychologist will review a varying volume of records. If tasked with considering all psychological and adverse developmental factors, the psychologist may ultimately review all records retrieved regarding the defendant, his or her family, and his or her community setting.

Interview of the Defendant

In a role of a testifying expert with direct assessment of the defendant, the psychologist will spend 8–20 hours obtaining a comprehensive and detailed bio-psycho-social multigenerational history from the capital defendant. Such extended interviewing is required to secure candid anecdotal description of specific events, particularly of trauma and victimization. Extended interviews also help build trust and rapport, and counter the tendency of most capital defendants to minimize or deny dysfunctional family processes and traumatic experience (Connell, 2003; Cunningham, 2010; Cunningham & Reidy, 2001; Dekleva, 2001).

Interview of Third Parties

Family members and other third parties are often better historians than the defendant and represent more credible sources as well. Typically, the psychologist will conduct numerous in-person or telephone interviews with these third parties. Contrary to expectations that family members would fabricate generational and childhood pathology in an effort to save their loved one, the relatives of capital defendants routinely minimize dysfunctional aspects of their family history so as to place themselves and their family in the best possible light. Obtaining an accurate and candid history of the defendant and extended family can be facilitated by orienting family members to the purpose of the evaluation, employing patiently probing interviews, and sampling from a wide range of family members. The psychologist should maintain detailed notes of these interviews, and have these available at the time of testimony.

Referrals for Specialized Assessment

Complete neuropsychological assessment is indicated in most capital sentencing workups. Not uncommonly, referrals for neurological evaluation, EEG, and neuroimaging are made as well. These referrals are driven by the routine presence of neurological insults and indicators of neuropsychological dysfunction in the histories of capital offenders (Cunningham, 2012; Cunningham & Vigen, 1999, 2002), as well as a disproportionate incidence of such histories among violent offenders (see Fabian, 2010). Often other factors are identified that require referral for more specialized consultation. These may include toxicology, endocrinology, intellectual disability, psychopharmacology, learning disabilities, addiction medicine, and other specialized fields of expertise (Cunningham, 2010; Cunningham & Goldstein, 2013).

Nexus With Developmental Trajectory and Outcome

The identification of impairments and adverse developmental factors is only a critical *first* step in a capital sentencing evaluation. Without knowledge of research findings on the impact such factors have on developmental trajectory and criminality, members of the jury have no mechanism to give informed weight to the mitigating factors they hear. Accordingly, a second and equally important aspect of a psychological evaluation at capital sentencing involves detailing the influence of such impairments and adverse factors on developmental trajectory—particularly as these may have been demonstrated to have a nexus with criminal violence in late adolescence or adulthood. A literature review regarding the life trajectory impact of commonly encountered developmental factors in capital cases is well beyond the scope of this chapter. Any review would be incomplete, though, without reference to research studies and summaries sponsored by the U.S. Department of Justice that identify risk and protective factors for chronic delinquency and serious violence in the community (e.g., Chaiken, 2000; Hawkins et al., 2000; Kelley, Thornberry, & Smith, 1997; Thornberry, 1994; Thornberry, Smith, Rivera, Huizinga, & Stouthamer-Loeber, 1999; U.S. Department of Justice, 1995; Wasserman et al., 2003; Widom, 2000). To illustrate, Table 9.4 details developmental risk factors for delinquency and criminal violence in the community as reported by Hawkins et al. (2000). This and other relevant papers can be accessed through the Web site for the Office of Juvenile Justice and Delinquency Prevention, U.S. Department of Justice (www.ojjdp.gov/publications/PubResults.asp).

These studies are consistent with a well-established developmental perspective that adult outcome is a function of the cumulative saturation of risk factors, as well as the interaction and balance of predisposing, risk, and protective factors in childhood. In other words, as predisposing and risk factors increase and protective factors decrease, there is an increasing probability of adult maladjustment, substance abuse, psychological disorders (including personality disorders), delinquency, criminality, and criminal violence.

In considering this nexus between damaging developmental factors and adverse outcomes in adulthood, it is important to note that everyone need not totally succumb to adverse developmental exposures in order for a toxic effect to be implicated. Correspondingly, all similarly situated persons need not commit acts of criminal violence or suffer adverse life outcomes in order to demonstrate a relationship between background and outcome. The analysis of risk, vulnerabilities, and protective factors in the etiology of criminal violence and other adverse life outcomes is quite similar to explanations of why some individuals contract cancer and others do not (i.e., toxin exposure, predisposing factors, and protective factors; see National Cancer Institute, 2006). Thus a history of adverse developmental experiences does not invariably result in a criminally

Table 9.4 U.S. Department of Justice Model: Predictors of Youth Violence

Individual Psychological Factors

- Internalizing disorders
- Hyperactivity, concentration problems, restlessness, and risk taking
- Aggressiveness
- Early initiation of violent behavior
- Involvement in other forms of antisocial behavior
- Beliefs and attitudes favorable to deviant or antisocial behavior

Family Factors

- Parental criminality
- Child maltreatment
- Poor family management practices
- Low levels of parental involvement
- Poor family bonding and family conflict
- Parental attitudes favorable to substance use and violence
- Parent–child separation

School Factors

- Academic failure
- Low bonding to school
- Truancy and dropping out of school
- Frequent school transitions
- High delinquency rate schools

Peer-Related Factors

- Delinquent siblings
- Delinquent peers
- Gang membership

Community and Neighborhood Factors

- Poverty
- Community disorganization
- Availability of drugs and firearms
- Neighborhood adults involved in crime
- Exposure to violence and racial prejudice

Source: From Hawkins et al. (2000).

violent or markedly impaired adult outcome—only a much increased likelihood of it. These general perspectives regarding risk and protective factors, as well as recurrent problematic outcomes in the defendant's extended family, are often critical to rebutting the very predictable argument of the State that "many people have tough childhoods" or that the developmental history of the defendant is only an "abuse excuse."

Violence Risk Assessment at Capital Sentencing

Reliable assessments of the "probability of future criminal acts of violence" require knowledge of a highly specialized and often counterintuitive literature and associated correctional group statistical data (e.g., Cunningham, 2010; Cunningham, Sorensen, & Reidy, 2009; Cunningham et al., 2011; Edens et al., 2005; Otto & Douglas, 2010; Reidy, Sorensen, & Cunningham, 2013). A number of essential conceptualizations and conclusions emerge from this research.

Prison Is Typically the Only Relevant Context for Expert Assessment

Capital inmates sentenced to life-without-parole will *never* be in the open community again. Though juries may utilize a broader perspective, prison would appear to be the only relevant context for a violence risk assessment by mental health experts at capital sentencing (Cunningham, 2010).

Prison Violence Is Not Reliably Predicted from Community Violence

A well-known predictive maxim is that the best predictor of future behavior is past behavior. This is known as a *past pattern* or *anamnestic* approach. The reliability of an anamnestic approach rests on sufficient behavior to form a pattern and adequate similarity in the context of prediction (see Morris & Miller, 1985). It is not surprising then that the marked differences between the community and prison (see Cunningham et al., 2009; Cunningham et al., 2011; Reidy, Sorensen, & Cunningham, 2012, 2013; Sorensen & Cunningham, 2010) result in violent behavior in the former being a poor predictor of violent behavior in the latter. Simply stated, for most inmates there is not a continuing trajectory of serious violence that crosses the community to prison boundary.

To demonstrate, at the end of August 2013, 55.7% of the inmates in the Texas Department of Criminal Justice (TDCJ) were serving sentences for violent offense convictions and 37% had served a prior sentence in the Texas prison system (Texas Department of Criminal Justice, 2014b). Despite this concentration of individuals whose community conduct had been recurrently criminal and violent, the rate of serious violence in TDCJ in 2013 was quite low. The rate of inmate-on-inmate homicide in TDCJ was only 2.6 per 100,000 inmates in 2013 (Texas Department of Criminal Justice, 2014a), about one-third the 7.8 per 100,000 rate of homicide among males in the open community of the United States in 2011 (see Smith & Cooper, 2013). Similarly, Mumola and Noonan (2008) reported stable rates of inmate-on-inmate homicide of about 4 per 100,000 inmates nationwide 2001–2006. This ratio, however, does not fully reflect the infrequency of prison homicide as compared to community rates. Mumola (2005) reported that when standardized to match the demographics of the state prison population, the resident (i.e., nonincarcerated) population of the United States in 2002 had a homicide rate that was nearly nine times higher (i.e., 35 per 100,000 community members) than that occurring in U.S. prisons. Also quite low in TDCJ in 2013 were annual rates of serious assault (i.e., resulting in more than first-aid injury) of a staff member (0.00062) or another inmate (0.0077).

A conviction for murder is also not predictive for prison violence. Sorensen and Cunningham (2010), utilizing a retrospective comparative review of the prison disciplinary records of 51,527 inmates, including 9,586 who had been convicted of some degree of homicide, found that convicted murderers did not account for a disproportionate share of prison violence, however defined.

Capital Offenders Are Neither Inevitably nor Disproportionately Violent in Prison

A number of studies have examined rates of assaultive misconduct in the general prison population by capital inmates who were either sentenced to life terms at their trials or obtained relief from their death sentences (for a review of pre-2000 data, see Cunningham & Reidy, 1998b). These data, reflected in Table 9.5, demonstrate that the majority of capital offenders do not engage in serious prison violence (see also Reidy et al., 2013) and comparatively are not a disproportionate source of this misconduct. Recent large-scale comparisons found that homicide offenders were also not a disproportionate source of assaultive misconduct in prison (Reidy, Sorensen, & Cunningham, 2012; Sorensen & Cunningham, 2010).

Table 9.5 Assaultive rule violations of murderers, capital murderers, and comparison inmates

Study	Sample	Study Interval	Rate of Assaults	
			Capital Inmates	Comparison Inmates
Convicted murderers in the general prison population				
Sorensen & Cunningham, 2010	51,527 system-wide, Florida	2003 (12 months)		0.034 annual
	5,010 1st degree murderers			0.032 annual
	3,256 2nd degree murderers			0.038 annual
	1,320 lesser homicide			0.021 annual
	837 any homicide	(2002 admission)		0.042 annual
	13,251 no homicide	(2002 admission)		0.037 annual
	450 any homicide	(2002 admission, close custody)		0.044 annual
	3,663 no homicide	(2002 admission, close custody)		0.082 annual
Sorensen & Cunningham, 2007	1,659 murderers, Texas	2001–2003 (initial)		
		$M = 20$ months		
	223 lesser homicide			0.045 cum. preval.
	1,108 murder			0.070 cumulative prevalence
	328 capital murder (life)		0.162 cumulative prevalence	
Sorensen & Pilgrim, 2000	6,390 murderers, Texas	1990–1999 (initial)		0.024 annual
		$M = 4.5$ years		0.084 cumulative prevalence (serious assault)
Life-without-parole inmates				
Cunningham, Reidy, & Sorensen, 2005	149 MS-DS, Missouri	1991–2002 ($M = 6.7$ yrs)	0.076 annual	
	1,054 LWOP	($M = 4.3$ yrs)		0.096 annual
	2,199 parole eligible	($M = 1.5$ yrs)		0.425 annual

(Continued)

Table 9.5 Continued

Study	Sample	Study Interval		Rate of Assaults
Cunningham & Sorensen, 2006	9,044 long-term inmates in close custody, Florida	1998–2003 (initial)		
	1,897 LWOP	*M* = 3.4 years		0.074 cumulative prevalence
	1,985 30+ year sentence	*M* = 3.4 years		0.061 cumulative prevalence
	1,726 20–29 year sentence	*M* = 3.2 years		0.072 cumulative prevalence
	1,469 15–19 year sentence	*M* = 3.3 years		0.097 cumulative prevalence
	1,967 10–14 year sentence	*M* = 3.2 years		0.117 cumulative prevalence
Sorensen & Wrinkle, 1996	648 murderers, Missouri	1977–92		0.218 cumulative prevalence
	93 death row	*M* = 6.62 years	0.237 cumulative prevalence	
	323 LWOP	*M* = 6.66 years	0.176 cumulative prevalence	
	232 LWP (2nd degree)	*M* = 7.13 years		0.224 cumulative prevalence
Capital murderers sentenced to life terms				
Cunningham & Sorensen, 2007	136 capital murderers, Texas	2001–2004 (initial)	0.094 annual	
		M = 2.37 years	0.14 cumulative prevalence	
Cunningham, Reidy, & Sorensen, 2008	145 capital murderers, BOP	1991–2005 (*M* = 6.17 yrs)	0.01676 annual	
			0.09 cumulative prevalence	
	18,561 high security, BOP	2001–2005		0.01165 annual
Cunningham, Sorensen, Vigen, & Woods, 2011	111 DR, Texas	1974–2008 (*M* = 9.9 yrs)	0.036 cumulative prevalence	
	111 FDR, Texas	1989–2008 (*M* = 8.4 yrs)	0.045 cumulative prevalence	
	1,757 LWP, Texas	2008	0.014 prevalence (serious assault)	
Marquart, Ekland-Olson, & Sorensen, 1989	90 FDR, Texas	1974–1988 (*M* = 6.3 yrs)	0.016 annual	
	107 CLS murderers, Texas	1974–1988 (*M* = 7.2 yrs)		0.026 annual
	38,246 system-wide, Texas	1986		0.12 annual

Study	Sample	Study Interval	Rate of Assaults
	1,712 high security, Texas	1986	0.20 annual
Sorensen & Wrinkle, 1996	*See same study above*		
Former death-sentenced murderers			
Akman, 1966	69 FDR, Canada	1964–1965 (2 yrs)	0 cumulative prevalence
	7,447 System-wide, Canada	1964–1965 (2 yrs)	0.007 annual
Bedau, 1964	55 FDR, New Jersey	1907–1960 (53 yrs)	0 cumulative prevalence (serious assault)
Cunningham et al, 2011	*See same study above*		
Edens et al., 2005	*See same study below*		
			(serious assault)
Marquart, Ekland-Olson, & Sorensen, 1989	*See same study above*		
Marquart, Ekland-Olson, & Sorensen, 1994	47 FDR, Texas	1973–1988 (M = 10 yrs)	0.07 cumulative prevalence
			(serious assault)
	156 LS, Texas	1973–1988 (M = 11 yrs)	0.10 cumulative prevalence (serious assault)
	(128 murderers/28 rapists)		
Marquart & Sorensen, 1989	533 FDR, nationwide	1973–1988	0.031 cumulative prevalence
	(453 murderers, 80 rapists)		
Reidy, Cunningham, & Sorensen, 2001	39 DR/FDR, Indiana	1972–1999	0.038 annual
		On DR (M = 6.7 years)	0.054 annual
		Post-DR (M = 9.3 years)	0.028 annual
			(serious assault)
Sorensen & Cunningham, 2009	80 FDR, Arizona	1975–2005 (M = 13.1 yrs)	0.163 cumulative prevalence (serious assault)
Wagner, 1988	100 FDR, Texas	1924–72 (M = 12 yrs)	0.20 cumulative prevalence
Death row inmates			
Cunningham, Sorensen, & Reidy, 2009	35 DR, BOP	1993–2006	0.0 cumulative prevalence
			(serious assault)

(*Continued*)

Table 9.5 Continued

Study	Sample	Study Interval	Rate of Assaults
Cunningham et al., 2011	*See same study above*		
Edens et al., 2005	155 DR, expert predicted, Texas		
	5 DR executed	*M* = 12 years	0.046 cumulative prevalence
	42 DR, Texas	*M* = 8 years	0.071 cumulative prevalence
	48 DR/FDR	*M* = 22 years	0.042 cumulative prevalence (serious assault)
Marquart et al., 1994	421 DR, Texas	1974–1988	0.107 cumulative prevalence
Reidy, Cunningham, & Sorensen, 2001	*See same study above*		
Aggravated murder inmates			
Reidy, Sorensen, & Cunningham, 2013	115 agg. murderers, Oregon (65 LS, 50 DR)	1985–2008 *M* = 15.3 years	0.183 cumulative prevalence (outpt. min. injury) 0.061 cumulative prevalence (outpt. moderate injury) 0.009 cumulative prevalence (inpt. serious injury)
Mainstreamed death-sentenced inmates			
Cunningham, Reidy, & Sorensen, 2005	*See same study above*		

Abbreviations used in this table: Agg. = aggravated; BOP = federal Bureau of Prisons; CLS = capital life sentence; DR = death row; FDR = former death row; LS = life sentence; LWOP = life without paroled; LWP = life with parole eligibility; MS-DS = mainstreamed death-sentenced

Antisocial Personality Disorder Is Not Reliably Predictive of Prison Violence

Despite its notorious frequency of appearance in violence risk assessments at capital sentencing (Cunningham & Reidy, 1998a, 1999; Edens et al., 2005), there is no research demonstrating that antisocial personality disorder (ASPD) or its progeny (e.g., sociopathy, psychopathy) are reliably predictive of serious violence in U.S. prisons (Edens et al., 2001, 2005; see also Vitacco, Neumann, Welch, & Buckley, Chapter 6 in this volume). The poor predictive performance of such personality pathology is not surprising given the intersection of the high prevalence rate of ASPD among prison inmates and the low rate of serious violence in prison. Aggregating various studies, it is estimated that 75% of inmates in U.S. prisons meet diagnostic criteria for ASPD (see Cunningham & Reidy, 1998a, 2002; Meloy, 1988; Widiger & Corbitt, 1995). Any characteristic that is present in the majority of subjects in a targeted population will fail to predict a low base-rate (i.e., highly infrequent) behavior. ASPD is normative among a prison population and, accordingly, does not denote a particularly malignant or violence-prone inmate. Similarly, histories associated with the etiology or expression of this personality disorder (e.g., childhood maltreatment or misconduct, impulsivity, lack of remorse, irresponsibility, dishonesty, substance dependence, etc.) are so frequent among a prison population that these features also fail to predict serious violence in a prison context (see Cunningham, 2012; Cunningham & Vigen, 2002).

Psychopathy (see the Psychopathy Checklist–Revised [Hare, 2003]), though representing an extreme end of the ASPD continuum and present in a much smaller proportion (25%) of inmates, has fared no better as a predictive construct for serious violence in U.S. prisons (see Cunningham & Reidy, 1998a, 2002; Edens et al., 2005; Edens, Petrila, & Buffington-Vollum, 2001).

Prison Violence Usually Represents an Interaction of Factors

The proclivities of an inmate are only one factor, and potentially not the primary factor, influencing the occurrence of serious violence in prison. Rather, violent acts in most contexts represent the pathological intersection of person-interaction-context (Monahan, 1981, 1996; Shah, 1978). Consistent with this early risk assessment formulation, a triad of factors has increasingly been recognized as contributing to prison violence (see Cunningham, Sorensen, & Reidy, 2005). These include importation factors (i.e., variables that the inmate brings with him into prison), deprivation factors (i.e., hardships associated with confinement), and situational factors (Jiang & Fisher-Giorlando, 2002). Consistent with this view, Gendreau, Goggin, and Law (1997), in a meta-analysis of studies of prison misconduct, found that "institutional factors produced larger correlations with the criterion than did any other predictor domain" (p. 425).

Not surprising in light of the described conceptualizations, there are no personality test profiles or risk assessment instrument scores that currently reliably predict serious violence in U.S. prisons (for reviews see Cunningham & Reidy, 1998a, 1998b, 2002; Cunningham et al., 2005; Edens et al., 2005).

Though simplistically attractive at capital sentencing, a single-dimensional view that prison aggression is solely a function of the individual is not supported by correctional data. Because of the low base rate of serious violence in prison and the interacting contribution of factors that result in this violence, it is doubtful a model can be developed from preconfinement factors that will result in a "more-likely-than-not" probability of serious violence in prison.

Varying Levels of Improbability

A finding that offenders similar to the defendant present a low and not disproportionate risk of serious violence in prison will be reached with high reliability in most capital cases through the application of base rate and actuarially derived data. The specified improbability will vary in relation to the severity of violence being forecasted. Further, even that low probability can be reduced by the application of correctional interventions including more secure confinement.

To illustrate, Cunningham and Sorensen (2010) reported on 73 defense-sponsored capital risk assessments for prison (1995–2007) by the first author. In all cases, the first author had utilized base rates in forecasting that there was only a low likelihood of the defendant committing serious violence while confined for life in prison. These offenders had averaged 4.4 years in prison at the time of follow up. The prevalence of assaultive misconduct was inversely related to severity: 12.3% for assaultive misconduct and 1.4% for attempted serious assault. No assaults had occurred resulting in serious injury. If treated as dichotomous "predictions" of improbability of serious violence, these assessments reflected an accuracy rate exceeding 98%.

By contrast, assertions at capital sentencing of high and disproportionate risk of violence in prison are, in most instances, highly inaccurate. Illustrating this unreliability, Edens et al. (2005) reported on the predictive accuracy of mental health experts whose testimony had asserted "future dangerousness" in 155 capital sentencing cases in Texas. If the assertions of future dangerousness were intended to reflect a serious assault, the expert prediction was wrong 95% of the time. If the expert assertions of dangerousness were intended to reflect a probability of a homicide in prison, the predictions were wrong in every instance. The extraordinarily high error rates in these predictions of violence reflected the adoption of illusory correlations (i.e., factors erroneously believed to be associated with prison violence) and a neglect of base rate data.

Prosecutors and capital jurors fare no better when asserting that serious violence *will* occur. Cunningham, Reidy, and Sorensen (2008) examined 145 cases where future dangerousness was alleged by the government as a nonstatutory aggravating factor in federal death penalty prosecutions, but the defendant was sentenced by plea bargain or to life-without-release. Averaging 6.6 years postadmission to federal prison, only 0.09 of the violence-predicted offenders engaged in a serious assault and only 0.007 perpetrated an assault resulting in a hospital admission for non–life threatening injury. Thus, at the time of the study, predictive error rates were 91% and 99.3% depending on the definition of "criminal acts of violence that would constitute a continuing threat to society."

A number of studies have examined the abilities of capital juries to predict future prison violence (see Reidy et al., 2013). These studies demonstrate that capital jurors are wrong 90% of the time in predicting serious assaults and virtually always wrong in anticipating life-threatening assaults. Even more disturbing, these juries show no improvement over random guesses. Whether finding that the capital defendant is likely or unlikely to commit serious violence in prison, the performance of these juries simply reflects the underlying base rates. This finding has grave public policy implications (see also Krauss et al., 2009; Shapiro, 2009). As Reidy et al. (2013) conclude: "no authentic 'individualization' is occurring regarding the only setting where the offender could exhibit violence. Such arbitrary guesses are the antithesis of a reasoned, individualized death penalty determination" (p. 303).

How can assertions of low likelihood be sound, while conclusions of high likelihood are not? The answer, of course, is base rates (i.e., group data). Only a minority of capital offenders engage in serious violence in prison. There is currently no mechanism for reliably identifying from preconfinement variables a subgroup that are more likely than not to perpetrate such violence in prison. This reality results in varying levels of improbability (see Cunningham, 2010; Cunningham & Sorensen, 2010).

Risk Assessment Includes Consideration of Risk Management

Violence risk assessment also includes consideration of what risk management procedures could be applied to reduce any risk (see Cunningham & Reidy, 2002; Heilbrun 1997; Heilbrun, O'Neil, Strohman, Bowman, & Philipson, 2000; Otto & Douglas, 2010). These may include mental health treatment, preventive and rehabilitation programming, classification, or more secure confinement options. Regarding this latter intervention, super-maximum confinement is an available option in almost all correctional jurisdictions in the United States. At this security level an inmate is typically single-celled, confined to the cell 23 hours a day, handcuffed when removed from the cell, and has no physical contact with other inmates. Any opportunity to exhibit serious violence when maintained at this security level is markedly reduced.

Practical Applications

The following steps for making a violence risk assessment at capital sentencing are suggested (see Cunningham, 2006c):

1. Retrieve and review correctional and empirical group statistical/actuarial modeling data. Review capital violence risk assessment literature.
2. Review the defendant's jail and prison records. Identify any pattern of serious violence in jail or prison. (Note: Mutual fist fights are not considered serious violence.) Seek rates of inmate weapons infractions and assaults in the relevant facilities for comparison.
3. If the defendant is interviewed, seek information regarding past and current celling and custody, involvement in inmate work or educational programming, any disciplinary infractions and the defendant's explanation of these, family contact and visitation, mental health consultations and medication support, community employment history, educational attainment, and past response to structured settings.
4. Interview correctional staff and other third parties regarding the defendant's adjustment to incarceration.
5. Examine relevant group rates (i.e., base rates) and establish anchor points of risk corresponding to the severity of various predicted acts.
6. Modestly adjust the group rates in light of individual factors that are sufficiently infrequent to deviate from the respective group.
7. Consider interpersonal-situational-contextual components as well as personal disposition factors in individualizing group data.
8. If the risk estimate is a substantial departure from the base rate, consider whether the underlying observations and data are sufficiently reliable and empirically validated to justify this departure (see Cunningham et al., 2009, 2011; Reidy et al., 2013).
9. Consider what risk management interventions might be brought to bear, and the impact of these on the risk estimate.
10. Identify how the risk estimate is likely to change as the defendant ages during a capital life term.
11. Scrutinize the risk assessment for common errors (see Cunningham & Reidy, 1999).

Evaluations for Intellectual Disability (Atkins) Proceedings

Psychologists may be retained to provide evaluation services many years after a defendant has been sentenced to death. This may occur if a capital defendant was sentenced to death prior to *Atkins v. Virginia* (2002), or if evidence emerges that a death-sentenced inmate may be a person with intellectual disability (formerly *mental retardation*). The standards and procedures for making these determinations remain dynamic and evolving in the scholarly literature (see Macvaugh & Cunningham, 2009), statutes, and case law (e.g., *Hall v. Florida*, 2014). Regardless, from an assessment standpoint, a number of activities, factors, and conceptualizations appear relevant (see Macvaugh & Cunningham, 2009 for a fuller discussion):

1. Attempt to retrieve all prior intellectual assessments performed on the defendant. To the extent that test protocols or subtest scores are available, recheck scoring, addition, and related IQ tables for errors.

2. Interpretation of IQ scores in not a clerical enterprise. Rather, IQ score interpretation requires integration of psychometric research, norm obsolescence, and reliability considerations. Postpublication research on various intellectual assessment instruments may demonstrate validity issues, either broadly or in particular IQ score ranges. Thus, the test manual should not be considered the last word on psychometric features of the test. Second, by definition, IQ scores reflect relative position in the population. Accordingly, interpretation of prior and current test scores should include correction for the "Flynn effect" (Cunningham & Tassé, 2010; Flynn, 2006; Kaufman, 2010; Schalock et al., 2007; American Psychiatric Association, 2013; but see Hagan, Drogin, & Guilmette, 2008). The Flynn effect is a well-established finding that IQ scores are inflating (becoming increasing overestimates) by approximately 0.3 points per year from the date of test standardization to the date of test administration. The Flynn effect is more pronounced for performance (i.e., nonverbal or fluid) intelligence. Qualifying IQ scores for a diagnosis of intellectual disability should also acknowledge the standard error of measurement (American Psychiatric Association, 2013; Schalock et al., 2007). The factors outlined here point to the hazards of simplistic "bright line" applications of IQ scores in making diagnoses of intellectual disability, particularly in a capital context where the stakes are so grave.

3. Current test administration should reflect the most recently standardized version of an individually administered, multiple-subtest instrument that is appropriate for the defendant's language and national origin. The instrument(s) selected should be administered in its entirety. Carefully recheck all scoring and calculations.

4. Procedures should be employed to evaluate the defendant's test effort. In interpreting effort-testing scores, seek normative data for persons with deficient and borderline IQ scores. Avoid broad personality assessment measures in effort evaluation as these have not been standardized on persons of deficient intelligence.

5. Assessments of adaptive functioning are complex as these are community based and thus are likely to be retrospective in a capital context. When many years have transpired since the defendant was in the community, use of standardized adaptive behavior instruments is problematic as these instruments were normed utilizing *contemporaneous* observations of activities in the *community*. Seek prior educational, mental health, employment, and other descriptive records that illuminate adaptive functioning. Historical observations regarding the defendant should be sought from numerous third parties.

6. When a significant interval of years has transpired between the capital offense and the current assessment, the evaluation will need to consider whether the issue is *current* functioning or functioning *at the time of the offense*. This differential and its moral culpability implications may not be addressed by statute or case law.

Evaluations for Postconviction and Federal Habeas Proceedings

Potentially years after the capital sentencing trial, a psychologist may be retained to evaluate what could have been presented by the defense in mitigation or in violence risk assessment for prison had an adequate investigation and psychological assessment occurred. This is associated with a postconviction or federal habeas claim that counsel did not provide a reasonable sentencing defense. This claim is termed *ineffective assistance of counsel*. These psychological evaluations may be as extensive as would be performed at trial, or may be limited to summarizing and describing the implications of history uncovered in posttrial investigations. Typically, a detailed affidavit is prepared. This may be followed by testimony at an evidentiary hearing where a determination is made of whether failures of trial counsel were so grave that the defendant was deprived of a fair trial and is entitled to a new sentencing phase.

Case Study

Julian Johnson was arrested at age 24 for the capital murder of two rival drug dealers in an inner-city urban area. A forensic psychologist was contacted to provide capital sentencing evaluation services after Julian had been in custody for nine months. Julian's capital trial was scheduled for the following year. Prior to confirming the retention, the psychologist and defense counsel engaged in an extended discussion regarding the areas of expertise of the psychologist and the alternatives for the focus, parameters, and methods of the evaluation. From this informed consent discussion it was agreed that the psychologist would evaluate the presence and implications of any adverse developmental factors. Julian would be interviewed, but not regarding the capital offense or any prior unadjudicated conduct.

An extensive investigation entailing several hundred hours had already been accomplished by a social worker who was serving as a mitigation specialist. The social worker provided the psychologist with voluminous records that had been retrieved regarding Julian, as well as summaries from interviews of 28 family members and other third parties, and a lengthy chronology that integrated the interview and records data regarding critical events. After reviewing these materials, the psychologist interviewed Julian in the county jail, obtaining a highly detailed generational history from him that was meticulously documented with notes. These interviews on two successive days totaled 12 hours. Individual follow-up interviews, either in person or by phone, were conducted with all of the parties interviewed by the mitigation investigator. In the sections that follow, Mr. Johnson will be referred to as "Julian," as this convention better reflects his developmental status at the time of many of the described events.

The history that emerged revealed Julian was the product of paternal and maternal family systems characterized by generational dysfunction, including systemic poverty, teen pregnancies, parental neglect and abandonment, child abuse and domestic violence, criminality, personality disorders, and substance dependence. Not surprising in this family system, Julian's mother, Rachelle, was unmarried and in her mid-teens when she gave birth to him. She had had a pattern of drinking heavily on weekends prior to becoming aware of her pregnancy with Julian at 11 weeks. Julian's biological father was sentenced to prison for armed robbery during the pregnancy and was not paroled until Julian was age 14.

Until age 9, Julian resided in the public housing project apartment of his maternal grandmother, sharing this residence with various combinations of up to 18 aunts, uncles, cousins, siblings, and paramours. His care was shared by the household adults and older cousins. Rachelle had periods of crack cocaine dependence and was an intermittent presence in the home. Julian's grandmother died when he was age 9, and he then resided with his mother and a series of her abusive and domestically violently alcoholic or drug-dependent boyfriends.

Julian was hyperactive, impulsive, and inattentive throughout childhood. After being retained in both first and second grades, he was identified as learning disabled and received special education assistance. His academic achievement was never at grade level and he dropped out of school at age 15. Julian sustained three head injuries in childhood that were accompanied by loss of consciousness for 3–5 minutes. In light of this history, the psychologist recommended to the attorney that Julian be referred for neuropsychological assessment, and this evaluation subsequently demonstrated mild impairment in functions associated with the frontal lobes.

Julian began to drink from unattended cans of beer or mixed drinks at family parties in middle childhood. By his middle teens he was drinking a pint of Remy Martin and smoking three–four blunts daily. There was frequent gunfire in the projects and he saw victims being loaded into ambulances on a number of occasions. Julian could name 17 teen and young adult males he had been acquainted with while growing up who had been shot to death, and a far larger number who had prison histories. Julian began to deal drugs at age 12, initially being fronted small amounts for street sales and eventually progressing to trafficking in weight.

The psychologist performed literature reviews regarding the implications of the identified adverse developmental factors, and particularly the nexus of these factors with delinquency, criminality, and violence. This included retrieval and review of a number of studies published by the U.S. Department of Justice. Extended telephone conferences were held with defense counsel. When notified that a report was desired for discovery, the psychologist prepared a several-page report summarizing the evaluation and his findings. Digital demonstrative (i.e., Microsoft PowerPoint) exhibits were prepared by the psychologist to illustrate key aspects of the anticipated testimony and these were also provided by defense counsel to the prosecution in discovery. Because of the number and breadth of damaging developmental factors in Julian's background, the testimony of the psychologist at capital sentencing lasted a full day.

Final Thoughts

Psychological evaluations for capital sentencing have literal life and death implications, and call for corresponding standards of thoroughness and scholarship. Complex repercussions may ensue from evaluation access and parameters that require special attention to informed consent. This chapter is intended to provide an overview and outline of key concepts and resources that can facilitate self-study and reflection. It is not intended to provide adequate preparation to provide these evaluations. Mental health professionals who desire to perform these evaluations are encouraged to familiarize themselves with current developmental and capital violence risk assessment literature, as well as seek specialized continuing education training. Workshops addressing the role of forensic psychologists in death penalty sentencing evaluations are offered under the auspices of the American Academy of Forensic Psychology. Seminars regarding death penalty litigation are also offered by the National Legal Aid and Defender Association, National Association of Criminal Defense Lawyers, California Attorneys for Criminal Justice, and other organizations.

Note

1 Portions of this chapter have been adapted with permission from other publications of the author including: Cunningham (2010, 2006b); Cunningham and Goldstein (2013) and Cunningham and Reidy (1998b, 2001).

References

Akman, D. D. (1966). Homicides and assaults in Canadian penitentiaries. *Canadian Journal of Corrections, 8*, 284–299.

American Bar Association. (2003). *ABA guidelines for the appointment and performance of counsel in death penalty cases*. Chicago: Author.

American Bar Association. (2008). Supplementary guidelines for the mitigation function of defense teams in death penalty cases. *Hofstra Law Review, 36*, 677–692. Retrieved from www.americanbar.org/content/dam/aba/uncategorized/Death_Penalty_Representation/Standards/National/2008_July_CC1_Guidelines.authcheckdam.pdf

American Psychiatric Association. (2013). *Diagnostic and statistical manual of mental disorders, Fifth Edition* (DSM-5). Washington DC: Author.

American Psychological Association. (2002). Ethical principles and code of conduct. *American Psychologist, 57*, 1060–1073.

American Psychological Association. (2013). Specialty guidelines for forensic psychology. *American Psychologist, 68*, 7–19.

Atkins v. Virginia, 536 U.S. 304 (2002).

Barefoot v. Estelle, 463 U.S. 880 (1983).

Bedau, H. A. (1964). Death sentences in New Jersey, 1907–1960. *Rutgers Law Review, 19*, 1–64.

Burger v. Kemp, 483 U.S. 776 (1987).

Coble v. Texas, 330 S.W.3d. 253 (Tex. Crim. App. 2010).

Coker v. Georgia, 433 U.S. 584 (1977).

Chaiken, M. R. (2000, March). Violent neighborhoods, violent kids. (Juvenile Justice Bulletin NCJ 178248). Washington, DC: U.S. Department of Justice, Office of Juvenile Justice and Delinquency Prevention. Retrieved from www.ncjrs.gov/pdffiles1/ojjdp/178248.pdf.

Connell, M. A. (2003). A psychobiographical approach to the evaluation for sentence mitigation. *Psychiatry and the Law, 31*, 319–354.

Cunningham, M. D. (2006a). Dangerousness and death: A nexus in search of science and reason. *American Psychologist, 61*, 828–839. doi:10.1037/0003–066X.61.8.827

Cunningham, M. D. (2006b). Informed consent in capital sentencing evaluations: Targets and content. *Professional Psychology: Research and Practice, 37*, 452–459. doi:10.1037/0735–7028.37.5.452

Cunningham, M. D. (2006c). Special issues in capital sentencing. In M. A. Conroy, P.M. Lyons, Jr., & P. P. Kwartner (Eds.), *Forensic Mental Health Services in Texas* [Special Issue]. *Applied Psychology in Criminal Justice, 2* (3).

Cunningham, M. D. (2010). *Evaluation for capital sentencing.* New York: Oxford University Press.

Cunningham, M. D. (2012). Death-sentenced inmates. In L. Gideon (Ed.), *Special needs offenders in correctional institutions.* Thousand Oaks, CA: Sage.

Cunningham, M. D., & Goldstein, A. M. (2013). Sentencing determinations in death penalty cases. In R. Otto (Ed.), *Forensic psychology, Vol. 11.* In I. Weiner (Ed.), *Handbook of psychology* (2nd ed., pp. 473–514). New York: Wiley.

Cunningham, M. D., & Reidy, T. J. (1998a). Antisocial personality disorder and psychopathy: Diagnostic dilemmas in classifying patterns of antisocial behavior in sentencing evaluations. *Behavioral Sciences & the Law, 16*, 333–351.

Cunningham, M. D., & Reidy, T. J. (1998b). Integrating base rate data in violence risk assessments at capital sentencing. *Behavioral Sciences & the Law, 16*, 71–95.

Cunningham, M. D., & Reidy, T. J. (1999). Don't confuse me with the facts: Common errors in violence risk assessment at capital sentencing. *Criminal Justice and Behavior, 26*, 20–43. doi:10.1177/0093854899026001002

Cunningham, M. D., & Reidy, T. J. (2001). A matter of life or death: Special considerations and heightened practice standards in capital sentencing evaluations. *Behavioral Sciences & the Law, 19*, 473–490. doi:10.1002/bsl.460

Cunningham, M. D. & Reidy, T. J. (2002). Violence risk assessment at federal capital sentencing: Individualization, generalization, relevance, and scientific standards. *Criminal Justice and Behavior, 29*, 512–537. doi:10.1177/009385402236731

Cunningham, M. D., Reidy, T. J., & Sorensen, J. R. (2005). Is death row obsolete? A decade of mainstreaming death-sentenced inmates in Missouri. *Behavioral Sciences & the Law, 23*, 307–320. doi:10.1002/bsl.608

Cunningham, M. D., Reidy, T. J., & Sorensen, J. R. (2008). Assertions of "future dangerousness" at federal capital sentencing: Rates and correlates of subsequent prison misconduct and violence. *Law and Human Behavior, 32* (1), 46-63. doi:10.1007/s10979-007-9107-7

Cunningham, M. D., & Sorensen, J. R. (2006). Nothing to lose? A comparative examination of prison misconduct rates among life-without-parole and other long-term high security inmates. *Criminal Justice and Behavior, 33*, 683–705. doi:10.1177/0093854806288273

Cunningham, M. D., & Sorensen, J. R. (2007). Capital offenders in Texas prisons: Rates, correlates, and an actuarial analysis of violent misconduct, *Law and Human Behavior, 31, 553–571.* doi:10.1007/s10979–006–9079-z

Cunningham, M. D., & Sorensen, J. R. (2010). Improbable predictions at capital sentencing: Contrasting prison violence outcomes. *Journal of the American Academy of Psychiatry and the Law, 38*, 61–72.

Cunningham, M. D., Sorensen, J. R., & Reidy, T. J. (2005). An actuarial model for assessment of prison violence risk among maximum security inmates. *Assessment, 12*, 40-49. doi:10.1177/1073191104272815

Cunningham, M. D., Sorensen, J. R., & Reidy, T. J. (2009). Capital jury decision-making: The limitations of predictions of future violence. *Psychology, Public Policy, and Law, 15*, 223–256. doi:10.1037/a0017296

Cunningham, M. D., Sorensen, J. R., Vigen, M. P., & Woods, S. O. (2011). Correlates and actuarial models of assaultive prison misconduct among violence-predicted capital offenders. *Criminal Justice and Behavior, 38,* 5–25. doi:10.1177/0093854810384 830

Cunningham, M. D., & Tassé, M. (2010). Looking to science rather than convention in adjusting IQ scores when death is at issue. *Professional Psychology: Research and Practice, 41,* 413–419. doi:10.1037/a0020226

Cunningham, M. D., & Vigen, M. P. (1999). Without appointed counsel in capital postconviction proceedings: The self-representation competency of Mississippi death row inmates. *Criminal Justice and Behavior, 26,* 293–321. doi:10.1177/0093854899026003002

Cunningham, M. D., & Vigen, M. P. (2002). Death row inmate characteristics, adjustment, and confinement: A critical review of the literature. *Behavioral Sciences & the Law, 20,* 191–210. doi:10.1002/bsl.473

Dekleva, K. B. (2001). Psychiatric expertise in the sentencing phase of capital murder cases. *Journal of the American Academy of Psychiatry and the Law, 29,* 58–67.

DeMatteo, D., Murrie, D. C., Anumba, N. M., & Keesler, M. E. (2011). *Forensic mental health assessments in death penalty cases.* New York: Oxford University Press. doi:10.1093/acprof:oso/9780195385809.001.0001

Eddings v. Oklahoma, 455 U.S. 104 (1982).

Edens, J. F., Buffington-Vollum, J. K., Keilen, A., Roskamp, P., & Anthony, C. (2005). Predictions of future dangerousness in capital murder trials: Is it time to "disinvent the wheel"? *Law and Human Behavior, 29,* 55–86. doi:10.1007/s10979–005–1399-x

Edens, J. F., Petrila, J., & Buffington-Vollum, J. K. (2001). Psychopathy and the death penalty: Can the Psychopathy Checklist–Revised identify offenders who represent "a continuing threat to society"? *Journal of Psychiatry and Law, 29,* 433–481.

Fabian, J. M. (2010). Neuropsychological and neuropsychological correlates in violent and homicidal offenders: A legal and neuroscience perspective. *Aggression and Violent Behavior, 15,* 209–223. doi:10.1016/j.avb.2009.12.004

Flynn, J. R. (2006). Tethering the elephant: Capital cases, IQ, and the Flynn Effect. *Psychology, Public Policy, and Law, 12,* 170–189. doi:10.1037/1076–8971.12.2.170

Furman v. Georgia, 404 US 238 (1972).

Gendreau, P., Goggin, C. E., & Law, M. A. (1997). Predicting prison misconducts. *Criminal Justice and Behavior, 24,* 414–431. doi:10.1177/0093854897024004002

Gregg v. Georgia, 428 U.S. 153 (1976).

Hagan, L. D., Drogin, E. Y., & Guilmette, T. J. (2008). Adjusting IQ scores for the Flynn Effect: Consistent with the standard of practice? *Professional Psychology: Research and Practice, 39,* 619–625. doi:110.1037/a0012693

Hall v. Florida, 134 S. Ct. 1986 (2014).

Haney, C. (1995). Symposium: The social context of capital murder: Social histories and the logic of mitigation. *Santa Clara Law Review, 35,* 547–609.

Haney, C. (1997). Violence and capital law. *Stanford Law Review, 49,* 1447–1486.

Hare, R. (2003). *The Hare Psychopathy Checklist–Revised.* Toronto, ON: Multi-Health Systems.

Hawkins, J. D., Herrenkohl, T. I., Farrington, D. P., Brewer, D., Catalano, R. F., Harachi, T. W., & Cothern, L. (2000, April). Predictors of youth violence. (Juvenile Justice Bulletin NCJ 1790650). Washington, DC: U.S. Department of Justice, Office of Juvenile Justice and Delinquency Prevention. Retrieved from www.ncjrs.gov/pdffiles1/ojjdp/179065.pdf.

Heilbrun, K. (1997). Prediction versus management models relevant to risk assessment: The importance of legal decision-making context. *Law and Human Behavior, 21,* 347–359. doi:10.1023/A:1024851017947

Heilbrun, K., O'Neil, M. L., Strohman, L. K., Bowman, Q., & Philipson, J. (2000). Expert approaches to communicating violence risk. *Law and Human Behavior, 24,* 137–148. doi:10.1023/A:1005435005404

James v. Collins, 987 F2d 1116 (5th Cir. 1993).

Jiang, S. & Fisher-Giorlando, M. (2002). Inmate misconduct: A test of the deprivation, importation, and situational models. *The Prison Journal, 82,* 335–358. doi:10.1177/003288550208200303

Jurek v. Texas, 428 U.S. 153 (1976).

Kaufman, A. S. (2010). Looking through Flynn's rose-colored scientific spectacles. *Journal of Psychoeducational Assessment, 28*(5), 494–505. doi:10.1177/0734282910373573

Kelley, B. T., Thornberry, T. P., & Smith, C. A. (1997, August). In the wake of childhood maltreatment. (Juvenile Justice Bulletin NCJ 165257). Washington, DC: U.S. Department of Justice, Office of Juvenile Justice and Delinquency Prevention. Retrieved from www.ncjrs.gov/pdffiles1/165257.pdf.

Kennedy v. Louisiana, 554 U.S. 407 (2008).

Krauss, D. A., McCabe, J. G., & McFadden, S. (2009). Limited expertise and experts: Problems with the continued use of future dangerousness in capital sentencing. In R. F. Schopp, R. L. Weiner, B. H. Bornstein, & S. L. Willborn (Eds.), *Mental disorder and criminal law: Responsibility, punishment, and competence* (pp. 135–157). New York: Springer. doi:10.1007/978–0–387–84845–7_6

Lockett v. Ohio, 438 U.S. 604 (1978).

Macvaugh, G., & Cunningham, M. D. (2009). *Atkins v. Virginia*: Implications and recommendations for forensic practice. *Journal of Psychiatry and Law, 37*, 131–187.

Marquart, J. W., Ekland-Olson, S., & Sorensen, J. R. (1989). Gazing into the crystal ball: Can jurors accurately predict dangerousness in capital cases? *Law & Society Review, 23*, 449–468. doi:10.2307/3053829

Marquart, J. W, Ekland-Olson, S., Sorensen, J. R. (1994). *The rope, the chair, and the needle: Capital punishment in Texas, 1923–1990*. Austin: University of Texas Press.

Marquart, J. W., & Sorensen, J. R. (1989). A national study of the Furman-commuted inmates: Assessing the threat to society from capital offenders. *Loyola of Los Angeles Law Review, 23*, 5–28.

Megargee, E. I. (1984). Derivation, validation, and application of an MMPI-based system for classifying criminal offenders. *Medicine and Law, 3*, 109–118.

Meloy, J. R. (1988). *Psychopathic mind: Origin, dynamics, and treatment*. Northvale, NJ: Jason Aronson. doi:10.1093/mind/XCVII.388.632

Monahan, J. (1981). *Predicting violent behavior: An assessment of clinical techniques*. Beverly Hills, CA: Sage.

Monahan, J. (1996). Violence prediction: The past twenty years. *Criminal Justice and Behavior, 23*, 107–120. doi:110.1177/0093854896023001008

Morris, N., & Miller, M. (1985). Predictions of dangerousness. In M. Tonry & N. Morris (Eds.), *Crime and justice: An annual review of research* (Vol. 6., pp. 1–50). Chicago: University of Chicago Press.

Mumola, C. J. (2005). Suicide and homicide in state prisons and local jails (NCJ 210036). Washington, DC: U.S. Department of Justice, Office of Justice Programs, Bureau of Justice Statistics. Retrieved from www.bjs.gov/content/pub/pdf/shsplj.pdf.

Mumola, C. J., & Noonan, M. E. (2008). Deaths in custody reporting program. U.S. Department of Justice, Office of Justice Programs, Bureau of Justice Statistics. Retrieved from www.bjs.gov/content/dcrp/dcst.pdf

National Cancer Institute (2006). Tobacco control research: Cancer control and population science. U.S. National Institutes of Health. Retrieved from http://cancercontrol.cancer.gov/tcrb/monographs/

Otto, R. K., & Douglas, K. (Eds.). (2010). *Handbook of violent risk assessment*. New York: Routledge.

Penry v. Lynaugh, 492 U.S. 302 (1989).

Porter v. Commonwealth, 661 S.E.2d. 415 (2008).

Reidy, T., Cunningham, M. D. & Sorensen, J. (2001). From death to life: Prison behavior of former death row inmates in Indiana. *Criminal Justice and Behavior, 28*, 62–82. doi:10.1177/0093854801028001003

Reidy, T. J., Sorensen, J. R., & Cunningham, M. D. (2012). Community violence to prison assault: A test of the behavior continuity hypothesis. *Law and Human Behavior, 36*(4), 356–363. doi:10:1037/h0093934

Reidy, T. J., Sorensen, J. R., & Cunningham, M. D. (2013). Probability of criminal acts of violence: A test of jury predictive accuracy. *Behavioral Sciences and the Law, 31*, 286–305. doi:10.1002/bsl.2064

Rompilla v. Beard, 545 U.S. 374 (2005).

Roper v. Simmons, 543 U.S. 551 (2005).

Satterwhite v. Texas, 486 U.S. 249 (1988).

Schalock, R. L., Buntinx, W.H.E., Borthwick-Duffy, S., Luckasson, R., Snell, M. E., Tassé, M. J., & Wehmeyer, M. L. (2007). *User's guide: Mental retardation: definition, classification, and systems of supports, 10th ed.: Applications for clinicians, educators, disability program managers, and policy makers*. Washington, DC: American Association on Intellectual and Developmental Disabilities.

Shah, S. (1978). Dangerousness: A paradigm for exploring some issues in law and psychology. *American Psychologist, 33*, 224–238. doi:10.1037/0003–066X.33.3.224

Shapiro, M. (2009). An overdose of dangerousness: How "future dangerousness" catches the least culpable capital defendants and undermines the rationale for the executions it supports. *American Journal of Criminal Law, 35*, 101–156.

Skipper v. South Carolina, 476 U.S. 1 (1986).

Slobogin, C. (2009). Capital punishment and dangerousness. In R. F. Schopp, R. L. Wiener, B. H. Bornstein, & S. L. Willborn (Eds.), *Mental disorder and criminal law: Responsibility, punishment, and competence* (pp. 119–134). New York: Springer. doi:10.1007/978–0–387–84845–7_5

Smith, E.L., & Cooper, A. (2013, December). Homicides in the U.S. known to law enforcement, 2011 (NCJ243035). Washington, DC: U.S. Department of Justice, Office of Justice Programs, Bureau of Justice Statistics.

Sorensen, J.R., & Cunningham, M.D. (2007). Operationalizing risk: The influence of measurement choice on the prevalence and correlates of violence among incarcerated murderers, *Journal of Criminal Justice, 35*, 546–555. doi:10.1016/j.jcrimjus.2007.07.007

Sorensen, J. R., & Cunningham, M. D. (2009). Once a killer always a killer? Prison misconduct of former death-sentenced inmates in Arizona. *Journal of Psychiatry and Law, 37* (2-3), 237–267.

Sorensen, J.R., & Cunningham, M.D. (2010). Conviction offense and prison violence: A comparative study of murderers and other offenders, *Crime & Delinquency, 56*, 103–125. doi:10.1177/0011128707307175

Sorensen, J.R., & Pilgrim, R.L. (2000). An actuarial risk assessment of violence posed by capital murder defendants. *Journal of Criminal Law & Criminology, 90*, 1251–1270. doi:10.2307/1144202

Sorensen, J.R., & Wrinkle, R.D. (1996). No hope for parole: Disciplinary infractions among death-sentenced and life-without-parole inmates. *Criminal Justice and Behavior, 23*, 542–552. doi:10.1177/0093854896023004002

Strickland v. Washington, 466 U.S. 668 (1984).

Texas Code of Criminal Procedure. Article 37.071 (b), Supp. (1975–1976).

Texas Department of Criminal Justice. (2014a, September). Emergency Action Center select statistics: August 2014. Executive Services Department. Huntsville, TX: Author.

Texas Department of Criminal Justice (2014b). Statistical Report: Fiscal Year 2013. Huntsville, TX: Author.

Thornberry, T. P. (1994, December). Violent families and youth violence. Fact sheet #21. National Criminal Justice Resources and Statistics. U.S. Department of Justice, Office of Juvenile Justice and Delinquency Prevention. Washington, DC: U.S. Department of Justice.

Thornberry, T.P., Smith, C.A., Rivera, C., Huizinga, D., & Stouthamer-Loeber, M. (1999, September). Family disruption and delinquency. (Juvenile Justice Bulletin, NCJ 178285). Washington, DC: U.S. Department of Justice, Office of Juvenile Justice, and Delinquency Prevention. Retrieved from www.ncjrs.gov/pdffiles1/ojjdp/178285.pdf.

U.S. Department of Justice (1995, May. Guide for implementing the comprehensive strategy for serious, violent, and chronic juvenile offenders. (NCJ 153681). U.S. Department of Justice, Office of Justice Programs, Office of Juvenile Justice and Delinquency Prevention. Washington, DC: U.S. Office of Juvenile Justice and Delinquency Prevention. Retrieved from www.ncjrs.gov/pdffiles/guide.pdf.

Wagner, A. (1988). *A commutation study of ex-capital offenders in Texas, 1924–1971.* Unpublished dissertation. Sam Houston State University, Huntsville, TX.

Wasserman, G.A., Keenan, K., Tremblay, R.E., Coie, J.D., Herrenkohl, T.I., Loeber, R., & Petechuk, D. (April, 2003). Risk and protective factors of child delinquency. (Child Delinquency Bulletin Series NCJ 193409). Washington, DC: U.S. Department of Justice.

Widiger, T. A., & Corbitt, E. (1995). Antisocial personality disorder. In W.J. Livesley (Ed.), *The DSM IV personality disorders* (pp.103–134). New York: Guilford Press.

Widom, C.S. (January, 2000). Childhood victimization: Early adversity, later psychopathology. *National Institute of Justice Journal.*

Wiggins v. Smith, 539 U.S. 510, 530 (2003).

Woodson v. North Carolina, 438 US 304 (1976).

10 Competency for Execution

Patricia A. Zapf

Competency for Execution (CFE)—the "last competency" temporally in a series of opportunities throughout the criminal adjudication process to raise the question of competency for a criminal defendant (see Brodsky, Zapf, & Boccaccini, 2001)—can be raised for any criminal defendant who has been sentenced to death and who appears to be or to have become severely mentally ill while awaiting execution. More than any other area within the field of forensic assessment, CFE has been fraught with controversy and debate regarding whether, and to what extent, psychologists (or psychiatrists and other mental health professionals) should become involved in this type of evaluation. Indeed, the personal outcome for the defendant who serves as the evaluee in this type of evaluation weighs heavily in this debate. The point of this chapter is not to deal with the controversy regarding whether psychologists should become involved, but rather, to delineate appropriate assessment techniques and considerations for those psychologists who choose to become involved in this type of assessment. Given that the focus of this chapter is on assessment, the issue of restoration of competency to be executed will not be discussed. Those readers who are interested in reading more about the controversy regarding participation in this type of evaluation are referred to Appelbaum (1986), Bonnie (1990), Brodsky (1990), Shapiro (2005), and Lichtenstein (2013) for ethical discussions, to Brodsky, Zapf, and Boccaccini (2001, 2005) for an overview of the legal, ethical, and professional issues regarding participation, and to Neal (2010) for a framework to guide decisions regarding whether to become involved in the evaluation of CFE. Those readers who are interested in the controversy regarding participation in competency restoration efforts are referred to Hensl (2005), Mossman (1995), and Weinstock, Leong, and Silva (2010).

This chapter will begin with a review of legal decisions pertaining to the assessment of CFE. A description of the research and commentary with respect to the assessment of CFE will follow and, finally, the assessment of CFE, including a description of the forensic assessment instruments that have been developed for use in this type of evaluation, will be presented.

Legal Review of CFE

The mentally incompetent have been excluded from execution since medieval times (Broderick, 1979; Ward, 1986). English common law and early U.S. law excluded the mentally incompetent from executions based on religious, humane, and societal reasons. Several additional reasons for exclusion are currently recognized in U.S. law, including issues focusing on retribution, the ability to provide information for the appeals process, and the ability to "psychologically" prepare for death (Brodsky, Zapf, & Boccaccini, 1999; Heilbrun, 1987). The U.S. Supreme Court has reviewed several cases in which inmates have alleged mental incompetence at the time of their scheduled executions—earlier cases focused primarily on issues of procedure and due process whereas the constitutionality of executing the insane was not addressed by the Supreme Court until 1986 in *Ford v. Wainwright*.

The first CFE case heard was in 1897 wherein the U.S. Supreme Court granted certiorari to establish whether a defendant had a due process right for a jury to determine his competency to be executed (*Nobles v. Georgia*, 1897) In *Nobles*, the Supreme Court held that the condemned defendant did not have a guaranteed right to a jury trial on the question of CFE and that it was the responsibility of each state to resolve the question of CFE.

Fifty-one years later, in 1948, the Supreme Court was asked to consider the constitutionality of executing the insane (*Phyle v. Duffy*, 1948). The Supreme Court in *Phyle* granted certiorari to determine whether the due process clause of the Fourteenth Amendment forbade the execution of the insane and whether a person could be executed upon an unreviewable ex parte determination of sanity. The Court later refused to address the first question, stating that it lacked jurisdiction to hear the petition; however, the *Phyle* Court did address the second question and ruled that a state could not constitutionally allow a single individual to make an ex parte determination of sanity without judicial supervision or review (Pastroff, 1986).

In 1950, the U.S. Supreme Court upheld the state of Georgia's procedures for the disposition of condemned inmates' insanity claims (*Solesbee v. Balkcom*, 1950). At that time, Georgia's governor was responsible for deciding whether to hospitalize a condemned inmate who claimed insanity. The governor possessed the legal authority to call upon experts to assist him with this decision. The *Solesbee* Court ruled that the petitioner failed to establish that the governor refused to consider the information submitted to him by the petitioner when rendering his decision. Justice Frankfurter dissented in this case and addressed the constitutionality of executing the insane arguing that the Constitution prohibits the execution of the insane and pointing out that no individual state permitted the execution of insane persons. He concluded that insane inmates are protected from being executed by the Fourteenth Amendment.

Eight years later, a death row inmate challenged a California procedure permitting only a prison warden to take the first step in instituting court proceedings for the determination of CFE (*Caritativo v. Cal.*, 1958). The U.S. Supreme Court, in *Caritativo*, upheld the lower court's approval of this procedure. Again, Justice Frankfurter dissented and strongly criticized the California procedure as violating the inmate's right to due process.

In the time between *Caritativo* and *Ford v. Wainwright*, the Supreme Court ruled that capital punishment was both cruel and unusual and violated both the Eighth and Fourteenth Amendments (*Furman v. Ga.*, 1972). The Court also ruled that those states with the death penalty must "refine" their statutes relevant to capital punishment; however, the *Furman* ruling was vague and temporary. Five Supreme Court justices agreed that the death penalty violated the two amendments, but each justice had unique opinions as to the reason for this violation. Further, the Court did not specify what the ruling forbade and what it permitted. As a result, the death penalty was not abolished outright and by 1986 capital punishment had been reinstated in many states.

When the U.S. Supreme Court decided *Ford v. Wainwright* in 1986, 37 states had authorized capital punishment and had laws relating to CFE; 23 states had statutory provisions that prohibited the execution of the mentally incompetent, and most granted the authority to stay the execution to prison wardens or to governors (Miller, 1988); four states (Colorado, Kentucky, New Jersey, and Texas) relied on individual case law; and six states required the immediate transfer of mentally incompetent inmates to a secure mental hospital for treatment. Moreover, these states, as well as others, required inmates be treated in order to restore competence and then returned for execution.

Wide variation between states existed with respect to procedures for determining legal competency, including: (1) who is qualified to raise the question of an inmate's CFE, (2) what specific procedures apply once the question is raised, (3) who examines the inmate and how thoroughly, (4) what standards or tests of competence are to be used in the evaluation procedure, (5) who makes the final determination regarding competency, and (6) what procedures are followed for the restoration of competency (see Ward, 1986).

Immediately following *Ford*, Heilbrun (1987) offered a comprehensive examination of the standards used by the various states. He reported that out of the 23 states with statutory provisions, two relied on the "understand" element, which requires that the inmate be aware of the fact that he or she was convicted and is being punished by execution; six states relied on the "understand and assist" element, which requires that the inmate be able to effectively assist his or her attorney in the preparation of a defense that may ultimately render him or her innocent; and 16 other states used brief and vague definitions of competency to be executed and simply asserted that any inmate who is "mentally ill" cannot be executed.

In 1986, the U.S. Supreme Court had the opportunity to provide specific guidelines both for raising and evaluating a claim of CFE. In *Ford v. Wainwright*, the Court ruled that the Constitution's Eighth Amendment prohibited "cruel and unusual punishment" and therefore prohibited the execution of an "insane" person. The Court reasoned: (1) execution of the insane would offend humanity, (2) executing the insane would not serve to set an example and would not reaffirm the deterrence value believed to exist with capital punishment, (3) any individual who is believed to be insane is also believed unable to prepare "spiritually" for death, (4) madness itself is punishment and, therefore, negates the punishment value of execution, and (5) no retributive value is believed to be served by executing the mentally incompetent.

The Court also ruled that when questions of CFE were raised, due process entitled a defendant to an evidentiary hearing. Further, the Court stated that this evidentiary hearing is required only when defendants make a "high threshold showing" that their competency to be executed is in question. The justices, however, did not define the precise nature of the "high threshold." Moreover, when such a threshold was met, a majority of justices could not agree on the specific fact-finding procedures: four justices required full "panoply" of trial-type procedures; three justices argued that a more relaxed hearing was acceptable if due process was ensured; and two justices argued that the most minimal "pro forma" procedures were acceptable.

In addition to being divided on fact-finding procedures, the U.S. Supreme Court also failed to specify a proper legal test of incompetence in the execution context. Melton, Petrila, Poythress, and Slobogin (2007) noted that the Court failed to provide a legal standard or specific guidelines for evaluating this type of competency because the very issue was never raised. Only Justice Powell, in his concurring opinion to *Ford v. Wainwright* (1986), addressed the issue of the legal test for CFE, stating that the Eighth Amendment "forbids the execution only of those who are unaware of the punishment they are about to suffer and why they are to suffer it" (p. 2608). Further, he concluded that the proper test of competency should be whether defendants can comprehend the nature, pendency, and purpose of their execution. Justice Powell argued that the retributive goal of criminal law is satisfied only when defendants are aware of the connection between their crime and the punishment, and defendants can prepare for death only if they are aware that it is pending shortly. Further, Justice Powell asserted that the states were free to adopt "a more expansive view of sanity" that included the "requirement that the defendant be able to assist in his own defense" (p. 2608).

Despite the charge given to individual states to develop procedures to ensure that the insane would not be executed, many states provide no specific guidelines for evaluating CFE and those guidelines that do exist vary widely. The *Ford v. Wainwright* decision established that it was unconstitutional to execute the insane, setting the stage for psychological evaluations of death row inmates whose mental status for execution is questionable. However, the *Ford* Court left open two critical issues. First, the Court did not specify the necessary fact-finding procedures to enforce the *Ford* decision. Second, the Court failed to specify the proper legal test to be implemented in cases of CFE (see ex parte *Jordan*, 1988). Since the *Ford* decision, only a handful of cases addressing CFE have been decided, each attempting to define more clearly the facts set forth in *Ford v. Wainwright*. Three state rulings that followed directly after *Ford* are representative of the ways in which *Ford* raised more questions than it answered.

In 1987, a divided Florida Supreme Court dissolved a stay of execution and upheld the trial court's determination that the defendant understood the reasons he was given the death penalty. In *Martin v. Florida* (1987), the defendant argued that the trial court did not distinguish between a "rational and factual" understanding of why the death penalty was to be carried out (p. 189). The Florida Supreme Court asserted that rational versus factual understanding pertained to competency to stand trial, not CFE. The Florida Supreme Court further concluded that Martin's belief that his conviction resulted from a satanic conspiracy did not negate his rational understanding of why he was being executed.

In 1988, the Court of Criminal Appeals of Texas was faced with the issue of CFE (Ex parte *Jordan*). After the trial, the defendant, Jordan, was found incompetent to face execution under the criterion set forth in *Ford v. Wainright*. The trial court, noting the lack of any Texas statutes specifying the procedures to be followed in raising and determining a defendant's CFE, then created its own procedure requiring that a psychiatric examination of the defendant be conducted every 90 days. The defendant subsequently petitioned for a writ of habeas corpus asking the appeals court to set aside his execution and order his transfer to a state hospital for treatment. The appellate court argued that a defendant judged incompetent for execution was not legally entitled to have his execution set aside, but was only entitled a stay of execution pending regained competency. Further, the court denied Jordan's request for transfer to state hospital for treatment, stating that the *Ford* statute only prohibits execution of the insane and does not mandate treatment. The court also noted the Texas statute prohibits any transfers of inmates on death row and Jordan's request for transfer would be in direct violation of statutory language and intent.

In 1990, the Washington Supreme Court argued that adoption of a broader "ability to assist" test, as allowed by *Ford*, and any other definition of CFE in the state of Washington "must be based on the common law or the Washington State Constitution" (*Washington. v. Harris*, 1990, p. 65). The standard for CFE in the state of Washington was set forth in *Washington v. Rice* (1988). According to *Rice*, a defendant is incompetent for execution if unable to understand that he or she has been sentenced to death and/or is unable to communicate rationally with counsel.

In *Harris*, the Washington Supreme Court defined the criterion of "able to assist" to mean that the defendant is not required to be able to think of new issues for counsel to raise or to recall events surrounding the crime, but rather, the defendant must understand that he or she has "been sentenced to death for murder and be able to communicate rationally with counsel" (1990, p. 65). Relying on cases involving competency to stand trial, the Court held that a defendant is competent to be executed if he or she is, "capable of properly appreciating his [or her] peril and of rationally assisting in his [or her] own defense" (p. 65). The Court also stated that the standard of ability to assist, "applies equally in the context of a person's insanity at the time of punishment as it does at the time of trial" (p. 65). Finally, the Washington Supreme Court argued that the appropriate parties were responsible for informing the court of any change in the defendant's condition that would result in the dissolution of the stay of execution.

The American Bar Association (ABA) has also expressed interest in the issue of CFE and has adopted its own specific standard as presented in the *ABA Criminal Justice Mental Health Standards* (ABA, 1989), consisting of two parts. The first part states:

> Convicts who have been sentenced to death should not be executed if they are currently mentally incompetent. If it is determined that a condemned convict is currently mentally incompetent, execution should be stayed. (p. 290)

This part of the ABA standard reflects both the constitutional and common-law prohibition against executing any defendant currently judged to be incompetent. According to the commentary presented in the *ABA Criminal Justice Mental Health Standards*, the reason for this part of the standard is to preserve both the sanctity and integrity of the criminal justice system. The ABA stated:

> The integrity of the criminal justice system is eroded by the execution of a defendant who is incapable of understanding the penalty that is about to be imposed or who is unable to communicate exculpatory or mitigating information that might affect the decision regarding capital punishment. (p. 291)

Indeed, this part of the ABA's standard reveals its zealous concern for preserving the integrity of the criminal justice system rather than providing sympathy for the sentenced convict.

The ABA also provides a legal test to determine CFE. This legal test is defined in the second part of the standard:

> A convict is incompetent to be executed if, as a result of mental illness or mental retardation, the convict cannot understand the nature of the pending proceedings, what he or she was tried for, the reasons for the punishment, or the nature of the punishment. A convict is also incompetent if, as a result of mental illness or mental retardation, the convict lacks sufficient capacity to recognize or understand any fact which might exist which would make the punishment unjust or unlawful, or lacks the ability to convey such information to the court. (p. 290)

The ABA's standard of CFE follows directly from the U.S. Supreme Court's decision in *Ford* and from several state statutes; however, the standard differs in that it employs the term "incompetent" rather than the terms "insane" or "insanity" used in earlier case laws and statutes. These latter terms were rejected primarily because of their customary use in the context of criminal responsibility. Specifically, the ABA believed that the terms might result in the erroneous conclusion that the appropriate inquiry for competence to be executed is identical to that involved in determining criminal responsibility.

Zapf (2002; Zapf, Boccaccini, & Brodsky, 2003) commented on the relatively *low* standard of competence for execution as set out by the *Ford* decision and the necessity for evaluators to perform comprehensive assessments of *all* relevant aspects of competency—including those that go above and beyond the standard set out in *Ford* (such as some of the issues raised in the ABA's standard). The argument is that competence-related abilities such as rational understanding and appreciation (in addition to factual understanding) need to be addressed in the evaluation and discussed in the report to court so as not to interpret the *Ford* criteria for the court, but rather to describe all relevant aspects of competency to both educate the courts and to allow the courts to make an informed decision in each case.

Clarification of the (low) standard set out in *Ford* was part of the reason the U.S. Supreme Court granted certiorari in the 2007 case of *Panetti v. Quarterman* (in addition to procedural clarifications not relevant to the discussion here). On June 28, 2007, the Supreme Court decided, in *Panetti*, that the Fifth Circuit used an improperly restrictive test when it did not consider Panetti's rational understanding (and only focused on his factual understanding) in determining his competence for execution. The Court's decision in *Panetti* broadened the legal standard for CFE and changed the landscape for evaluation of CFE. Rather than ignore the inmate's rational understanding abilities and focus solely on factual understanding abilities, the Supreme Court decided that these must be taken into consideration in making a determination of an inmate's competence for execution. Although the Supreme Court rejected the Fifth Circuit's standard, it did not attempt to specify a standard for competency determinations; instead, it remanded the case back to the Federal District Court to make the initial attempt at setting this standard. The subsequent decision of the district court included a clear reference to both factual and rational understanding as well as the retributive connection between the crime and the punishment. This ruling represents the first time that both factual *and* rational understanding have been (formally) taken into consideration in determining an inmate's CFE.

Zapf (2009) reviewed the *Ford* and *Panetti* decisions in detail and in light of the *Dusky* (1960) and *Godinez* (1993) decisions regarding trial competence, and cautioned evaluators about limiting their evaluations to only the understanding prong while ignoring the ability to assist:

> The necessity of evaluating the broadest standard or test for CFE arises from the fact that, as mental health professionals, we cannot assume that we know how a particular court will interpret a particular standard. This is especially true with respect to CFE, where the courts continue to delineate the standard. If the evaluators in *Panetti* had stuck to a literal interpretation of the *Ford* standard (as had been done for over 20 years), the issue of rational understanding (appreciation) may never have arisen. Thus, caution is warranted to ensure that we do not interpret the standard for the court. Rather, full evaluation and delineation of all competence-related abilities—including the inmate's factual understanding, rational understanding (appreciation), and ability to assist counsel (including rational decision-making)—ensures that the legal decision maker is presented with the full panoply of potentially relevant information to consider in making the ultimate decision regarding an inmate's CFE. (p. 298)

Thus, evaluators are encouraged to complete full and detailed evaluations of CFE that take into consideration all relevant competence-related abilities. The reader is referred to Zapf (2009) for a detailed discussion as well as specific recommendations regarding guidelines for evaluators. The reader is also referred to Saks (2009), who extends the analysis in *Panetti* to include patently false beliefs about other relevant aspects of CFE.

Research and Commentary on CFE

There has been a dearth of empirical research conducted on competency to be executed. Part of the explanation may be the fact that only a handful of individuals have made successful claims of incompetency to be executed. In addition, this particular type of competency tends to evoke strong emotion in individuals, which in turn, may impact upon the motivation of involved professionals to conduct research in this area. The limited amount of empirical research that has been conducted has been confined to surveys, usually of legal professionals (e.g., Miller, 1988). No studies thus far have examined the issue of competency to be executed in a sample of offenders sentenced to death.

Four studies have investigated the attitudes of mental health professionals on issues of CFE. In 1982, a time when many states were reinstituting the death penalty and thus guidelines for capital participation were being put forward by the American Psychological Association (APA) as well as independent authors, White (1982) surveyed the attitudes of a sample of 72 psychologists in attendance at the conference of the Ohio Psychological Association to determine their level of agreement with the various proposed participation guidelines. The vast majority (90%) of the respondents reported having forensic experience and 57% reported testifying in court at least once. White (1982) found that most participants (72%) supported the participation of psychologists in capital cases when proper guidelines were implemented; 4% believed that no restrictions should be implemented and 18% were against participation completely.

Deitchman, Kennedy, and Beckham (1991) examined whether attitudes towards the death penalty and attributions of criminal responsibility predicted willingness to participate in competency evaluations in a sample of 222 psychologists and psychiatrists who responded to a mailed questionnaire. Deitchman and colleagues found that forensic examiners who expressed a willingness to participate in CFE evaluations, compared to those who were unwilling, were significantly more likely to be in favor of capital punishment and significantly less likely to view participation as a violation of professional ethics. In addition, Deitchman and colleagues found a significant association between actual and predicted classifications of willingness using a combination of attitude and attribution characteristics.

Leong, Silva, Weinstock, and Ganzini (2000) surveyed 290 board-certified forensic psychiatrists regarding their views on capital punishment and physician-assisted suicide. Leong and colleagues found no significant effects for any demographic variables—including age, importance of religion, and region of practice—on views towards capital punishment or participation in capital cases. They found age to be the only variable related to participation in competency restoration, with older participants being more likely to support such participation.

Pirelli and Zapf (2008) surveyed 231 forensic psychologists regarding their attitudes and practices with respect to capital participation. These researchers found that opposition to participation in six types of capital evaluations was predicted by religiosity, views on the death penalty, personal values, and self-reported adequacy of experience/training specific to participation in capital cases. In addition, while most forensic psychologists were not opposed to participation in all other types of criminal forensic evaluations in the capital context, only 46% indicated a willingness to participate in CFE evaluations.

Current Practices in the Evaluation of CFE

To evaluate current practices in the evaluation of CFE and identify assessment issues considered important by professionals who conduct this type of evaluation, Zapf et al. (2003) interviewed seven mental health professionals who had been involved in evaluating competency to be executed. The practicing professionals were asked about their past experiences with specific cases in an attempt to determine how they conceptualized the nature of this type of competency and the pertinent issues involved in conducting this type of evaluation.

All seven of the mental health professionals interviewed held a PhD degree; one also held a JD and one held a MSEd degree in addition to the PhD. Two individuals had conducted (or were actively involved in) CFE evaluations during the current year (in Arkansas and Tennessee), three others had conducted their last evaluation of this type in the 1990s (in Alabama, Missouri, and Texas), and two of the professionals last conducted a CFE evaluation in 1989 (in Utah and Arkansas).

When asked about current practices in the evaluation of CFE, the professionals identified a number of components that they believed make up the structure of a thorough CFE evaluation. Identified components included reviewing case materials, prison records, medical records, trial transcripts, and psychiatric records (including those during and prior to the offender's incarceration on death row); examining statutes or relevant court decisions to determine the applicable criteria for a given jurisdiction; consulting with the retaining attorney; interviewing and conducting psychological or other relevant testing with the offender; interviewing family members of the offender; interviewing prison officials, correctional officers, and other offenders who have had contact with the offender; and observing the offender in his cell on death row.

The evaluators reported using a number of different psychological tests during CFE evaluations including: the Minnesota Multiphasic Personality Inventory (MMPI or MMPI-2), Millon Clinical Multiaxial Inventory (MCMI or MCMI-II), Personality Assessment Inventory (PAI), Schedule for Affective Disorders and Schizophrenia (SADS), or Present State Examination (PSE) to assess psychopathology and test-taking style; the Structured Interview of Reported Symptoms (SIRS), Validity Indicator Profile (VIP), or Rey 15 to assess malingering (when indicated); the Wechsler Adult Intelligence Scale–Revised (WAIS-R)[1], Shipley Institute of Living Scale, Test of Nonverbal Intelligence (TONI), or Kaufman Functional Academic Skills Test (KFAST) to assess intellectual functioning or to diagnose mental retardation; the Peabody Picture Vocabulary Test–Revised (PPVT-R) to assess language functioning; the Beery-Buktenica Developmental Test of Visual Motor Integration (BEERY) or Boston Naming Test (BNT) to assess dementia;

the Psychopathy Checklist–Revised (PCL-R) to assess psychopathy (when indicated); the Interdisciplinary Fitness Interview (IFI) to assess reasoning ability; and the Halstead-Reitan to assess neuropsychological functioning (when indicated). There was some disagreement about whether or not to use projective techniques for this type of evaluation, with one professional indicating that he would use the Rorschach "when indicated," and another stating that he would "never" use the Rorschach or any other projective technique for this type of evaluation. None of the other CFE evaluators mentioned projective techniques.

In response to inquiries about the assessment of the specific criteria for incompetency, all of the evaluators indicated that they asked the offenders specifically about each of the relevant criteria (for their respective jurisdictions). All of the evaluators reported that they focused specifically on the offender's understanding of death and the reasons for it. Three of the evaluators indicated that they made an attempt to assess the offenders' reasoning abilities, in addition to simple factual understanding, with respect to death.

When asked about the most challenging aspects of the evaluation of an offender's CFE, three global issues were identified: (1) the nature of the inquiry itself and the gravity of the consequences, (2) the difficulty the evaluator may experience in trying to remain objective, and (3) the evaluator's own personal difficulties with the death penalty.

With regard to the gravity issue, the CFE evaluators reported feeling that the magnitude and the immediacy of the consequences for the offender had an impact upon their evaluation in terms of the amount of time and energy they put into ensuring that they conducted a thorough and comprehensive evaluation. With regard to objectivity, one professional, speaking candidly, indicated that he found it difficult to maintain objectivity for three reasons: (1) you become sharply aware of your own personal beliefs about the death penalty, (2) you get to know the offender and may not see anything to prevent the offender from being executed, and (3) it is difficult to resist the pull to affiliate with the attorneys who retained you as the case is always presented to you from their point of view. Finally, with regard to the personal difficulties, several CFE evaluators reported feeling that this type of evaluation can be emotionally difficult for the evaluator because the task forces the evaluator to deal with his or her own feelings and beliefs about capital punishment. When asked if they would consider conducting another CFE evaluation in the future, six of the seven evaluators indicated that they would. Each of these evaluators felt that they were prepared to do these evaluations with what they perceived as the necessary amount of comprehensiveness and scrutiny. In addition, they felt that they would be leaving this task to someone who might not do as thorough a job if they declined. The one evaluator who indicated that he would not conduct another CFE evaluation stated that he has had a change of heart with respect to capital punishment and no longer considers the death penalty to be an acceptable form of punishment. This evaluator believes that individuals who conduct this type of evaluation have to be in favor of the death penalty. The other evaluators were not polled about their opinions on this matter.

Specific problems that were encountered by these professionals in conducting CFE evaluations included difficulty in accessing medical records from other facilities, difficulty in finding a proper setting for this type of evaluation, difficulty in gaining access to the offender at times (i.e., are required to interview behind glass at some facilities), difficulty in establishing or maintaining rapport with embittered offenders or those who refused to cooperate, and insufficient allocation of resources by the court (i.e., in terms of time required to obtain all the relevant records as well as compensation).

When asked to give their opinions about their respective jurisdiction's criteria for CFE, most of the evaluators indicated that they believed the criteria to be very minimal standards that were patterned after *Ford*, which has a very low threshold for competence. Several evaluators felt that the courts interpret the *Ford* criteria as *factual* understanding, whereas they believe that the courts should consider the higher standard of *rational* understanding when making CFE determinations (this research was conducted prior to the *Panetti* decision). Similarly, when asked about the most difficult aspect of the CFE criteria to assess, a number of evaluators indicated that it was difficult to distinguish between a factual and rational understanding of death. One evaluator stated that this was especially the case given that there is no "gold standard" for understanding death. When asked how they might change the CFE criteria if they could, a number of CFE evaluators stated that they would further define the required level of understanding.

Current Practices in Texas

Boccaccini and colleagues (Young, Boccaccini, Lawson, & Conroy, 2008) interviewed 16 mental health professionals (eight psychologists and eight psychiatrists) who conduct CFE evaluations in Texas about their practices and opinions regarding the standard for CFE. Approximately one-third of their sample ($n = 5$) reported that they had conducted one CFE evaluation, two-thirds ($n = 10$) had conducted between two and five CFE evaluations, and the remaining evaluator had conducted eight CFE evaluations.

When asked about essential assessment procedures, all 16 evaluators indicated that an interview was essential; 14 noted that reviewing collateral records and reports was essential; and six indicated that interviewing others was essential. With respect to psychological testing, four of the eight psychologists indicated that psychological tests were an essential component of the CFE evaluation. The tests that the evaluators indicated they used were intelligence tests (i.e., WAIS-III) and personality inventories (i.e., MMPI-2, MCMI-III, PAI).

Evaluators were asked whether they believed that the Texas standard for CFE consisted of factual understanding only or whether it also encompassed rational understanding (this research was conducted prior to the Court's decision in *Panetti*). The vast majority (14 of 16 evaluators) believed that rational understanding *should* be required for competence but only five evaluators indicated that the Texas standard required an assessment of rational understanding; seven evaluators indicated that the Texas standard required only factual understanding; and two evaluators reported that the Texas statute did not specify the level of understanding or did not know which type of understanding was required.

When asked about how to assess an inmate's rational understanding of death, all 16 evaluators indicated that they would assess this using an interview but only 12 reported that they would ask questions about death. Specifically, with respect to the assessment of an inmate's understanding of death, evaluators reported using the interview to assess the inmate's understanding of the finality of death ($n = 4$), beliefs about what happens to people when they die ($n = 3$), whether the inmate had made any preparations for death ($n = 2$), and religious or spiritual beliefs related to dying ($n = 1$).

Finally, when asked about whether they also assess an inmate's ability to consult with an attorney as part of a CFE evaluation, 12 evaluators reported that they do assess ability to assist, two reported that they do *not* assess ability to assist, and two indicated that it depends on the specifics of the case. Most evaluators ($n = 11$) reported that it was important to assess ability to assist even when it was not required by statute.

Commentary on CFE

There has been more commentary on the assessment of competency to be executed than there has been research. Heilbrun (1987) discussed the implications of the *Ford* decision for the assessment of competency to be executed and made five practical suggestions. First, with regard to the mental health professionals who are selected to evaluate an inmate's competency to be executed, Heilbrun argues that these evaluators need to have demonstrated skill in general clinical as well as clinical-legal areas. In addition, he makes the case that these professionals need to be chosen in a manner that eliminates the possibility of any systematic bias operating in the evaluation. For example, systematically eliminating (or including) only those evaluators that favor the death penalty from the potential pool of professionals who will conduct these evaluations may serve to introduce bias into the process that may not have otherwise existed. Second, Heilbrun contends that evaluators must (and, in fact, are ethically obliged to) inform any individual of the nature and purpose of a forensic evaluation before beginning. This is especially true in the case of competency to be executed. Evaluators should attempt to ensure that the inmate understands this notification of purpose (e.g., present the information using easily understood language; ask questions to attempt to determine the inmate's understanding of the information). Third, Heilbrun emphasizes the importance of a comprehensive evaluation: that is, including an assessment of intellectual functioning, personality characteristics, and motivation in addition to symptoms of psychopathology; having more than one contact with the inmate whose competence is being evaluated; an assessment of the possibility of malingering; and the use of collateral or third-party information. Fourth, the evaluator needs to take into consideration circumstances of the evaluation, which include the people who are present in the daily life of the inmate as well as the physical environment. Finally, Heilbrun underscores the importance of comprehensive documentation, usually in the form of a written report, to assist the decision maker and to allow others access to the procedures and reasoning processes used by the evaluator.

Heilbrun and McClaren (1988) discussed the assessment of CFE in terms of both preadjudication (before a formal legal judgment about an inmate's CFE has been made) as well as postadjudication (after an inmate has been legally deemed incompetent for execution). Given that only a handful of individuals have ever been found to be incompetent for execution (and would therefore require postadjudicative assessment of this type of competency), preadjudicative assessment of CFE is certainly the more prevalent type of assessment. Of course, the reader must keep in mind that assessments of CFE are much less common than assessments of almost any other type of competency.

With regard to the preadjudicative assessment of CFE, Heilbrun and McClaren (1988) outlined a number of "minimum requirements for performing an excellent evaluation" and suggested that evaluators make their participation contingent upon having these minimum requirements met (p. 208). In addition, Heilbrun and McClaren argue strongly for the formal assessment of intellectual functioning, motivation, and psychopathology using well-validated and standardized assessment instruments.

With respect to the legal criteria that need to be assessed, evaluators should be aware of the particular legal criteria that define the standard for competency within the relevant jurisdiction. If the criteria for CFE within a particular jurisdiction are not specified, Heilbrun and his colleagues (Heilbrun, 1987; Heilbrun & McClaren, 1988) advise that evaluators should consider the standard in its broadest form and then leave it up to the court to determine what is applicable and what is not. As previously mentioned, Zapf and colleagues (Zapf, 2002; Zapf et al., 2003) argued that, regardless of the specific criteria set out in a particular jurisdiction, a comprehensive evaluation of all relevant aspects of CFE be conducted and delineated in the report to court.

With regard to the postadjudicative assessment of competency to be executed, Heilbrun and McClaren (1988) maintain that evaluators who are involved in the assessment of CFE at this stage should be independent of those who are responsible for treating the inmate for the purposes of restoring competence.

Mathias (1988) also observed the importance of taking the physical and social environment of the inmate into account when evaluating an individual's mental state on death row. He indicated that there are many variables that operate in the environment of death row that may affect an inmate's psychological functioning and presentation and that may impact upon a mental health evaluation in a variety of different ways. The nature of a maximum-security setting can have a great impact upon an inmate's mental health and may affect competency status. Mathias argued that evaluators of an individual's competency need to consider these variables when conducting evaluations of competency to be executed.

Small and Otto (1991) explored the legal context and the clinical aspects of evaluations of competency to be executed. These authors encouraged the use of evaluation techniques that focus on the functional capacity of the inmate. Differing slightly from Heilbrun and his colleagues (Heilbrun, 1987; Heilbrun & McClaren, 1988) with respect to the use of traditional psychological testing, Small and Otto stated, "evaluations that emphasize traditional psychological testing and assessment are unlikely to assist the decision maker in assessing functional abilities" (1991, p. 152; see also Melton, Petrila, Poythress, & Slobogin, 2007). Consistent with this argument is the fact that the education level and/or mental state of many offenders on death row may be problematic in terms of rendering many traditional psychological tests invalid. Small and Otto did, however, concede that psychological testing may assist in identifying the core mental disorder, making treatment recommendations, or detecting the possibility of malingering.

Brodsky, Zapf, and Boccaccini (2001) reviewed the legal, ethical, and professional ambiguities regarding the assessment of CFE and gave the following ten recommendations for practice (pp. 21–23).

1. *The temperament issue*. Not for the timid or faint of heart. The preceding review has marked a number of dimensions on which CFE evaluators may expect personal or professional controversies and uncertainties. Because assessments are part of contentious, politicized, and life or death proceedings, participation requires a clear vision of the tasks and an internal locus of motivation and control.

2. *The impact issue*. CFEs are low demand, high impact evaluations. Relatively few are conducted. Indeed, CFEs probably represent the lowest incidence of any competency assessments. The opinions and reports will be publicized, debated, and often quickly linked into other issues quite apart from the legal-psychological issues.

3. *Objectivity*. A profound commitment to objectivity and detachment is needed in CFE assessments. Although all forensic work calls for objectivity, the deeply held opinions about the death penalty and ukases against professionals engaging in any activity relating to capital punishment means that evaluators must be able to define and maintain a scrupulously objective posture.

4. *Specific legal foundations*. Knowledge of applicable statutory and case law is essential. Such law is not routinely taught or communicated in day-to-day forensic practice, and evaluators may have to seek it out.

5. *Ford*. Extrapolation of *Ford v. Wainwright* to psychological constructs is neither simple nor obvious. It draws on scholarly and legal literature and operational definition of ambiguous constructs.

6. *Structure*. Use a systematic, structured approach to CFE assessments. The methodology should not be exclusively case specific but driven by *Ford* and other legal constructs.

7. *Collateral information*. Redefining of collateral information. Current history is a central issue. Other death row inmates, officers, medical staff, and psychological sources should be interviewed.

8. *Situational and contextual factors*. Being on death row, under a sentence of death, and living in this particular environment all can have an effect. These situational factors need to be assessed.

9. *Measures and instruments*. This specific forensic issue is without quantitative and qualitative measures. CFE assessors are greatly in need of organized, useful, reliable methodology. The desirable first steps en route to standardized CFE assessment instruments are a CFE checklist for assessors and death appreciation measures.

10. *The threshold issue*. A high legal threshold exists for not being CFE, with almost all CFE findings being competency. The assessor must walk a thin line, not anticipating the ultimate decision, but at the same time providing enough psychological information to allow the fact finders to address the legal threshold.

Evaluation of CFE

Minimum standards for CFE evaluations should parallel those standards that apply to other types of forensic assessments. That is, standardized procedures that are used during the evaluation should be described to the subject of the evaluation as well as in the examiner's report, assessment measures should be specific to the referral issue(s), and the examiner should have a sound and sophisticated conceptualization of the criteria for being not competent for execution. In addition, the knowledge base of examiners should cover three domains: general legal competencies, forensic assessment methodologies, and execution-related substantive content. Finally, collateral information should be gathered. This might include (but would not be limited to) information regarding life history, psychological history and disorders, deterioration-related data, previous and current written reports, and interviews with persons who have had extensive opportunities to observe the evaluee.

Although *minimum* standards for CFE evaluations can be identified, these should not be equated with *professional* standards or guidelines for these evaluations. Professional standards or guidelines are more encompassing than minimum standards and form the basis for sound forensic practice. Whereas an evaluation that meets only the minimum standards might address the relevant issue in a perfunctory manner, an evaluation that also meets professional standards or guidelines would go above and beyond simply addressing the issue in an obligatory manner. An evaluation that meets minimum standards might be a brief, narrowly focused, concrete and surface inquiry into the psycholegal issue.[2] However, evaluations that meet professional standards should include informative and useful statements about the individual being evaluated and supply a detailed analysis of the issue to be addressed in the form of observations and statements that provide justification for the findings and opinions. An evaluation that meets professional standards should not only be useful to the court; it should ultimately be defensible in court.

What follows is a discussion of the framework and approach for evaluations of CFE that would meet professional standards. The astute reader will note that many of these recommendations have been extrapolated from various other types of competency evaluations. As Zapf, Viljoen, Whittemore, Poythress, and Roesch (2002) noted when summarizing the past and surmising about the future of competency research and practice, it is important to be familiar with all aspects of the literature on competency to stand trial since this is the most well-developed literature of all the criminal competencies. Practice and research regarding the various other types of criminal competencies, and especially competency to be executed, will benefit by extrapolating from this literature.

Knowledge Base

Before conducting a CFE evaluation, evaluators should be familiar with the relevant statutes, definitions, and criteria for CFE that exist within their jurisdiction as well as any Supreme Court decisions relevant to CFE. In addition, CFE evaluators should be familiar with the procedural aspects of competence for execution cases within their jurisdiction (i.e., knowing how, when, and by whom the issue of competence for execution may be raised; who determines that an evaluation is to occur; procedures specific to the evaluation process). A competent evaluator should be knowledgeable about these legal requirements and procedures before beginning an evaluation of CFE. As in other types of forensic evaluations, the evaluator should consult with whoever has ordered the evaluation to clarify the referral question and to ensure that all parties involved understand what is to be evaluated.

General Evaluation Procedures and Considerations

CFE evaluations should be conducted in a place with adequate space and privacy that is free from distractions. In addition, CFE evaluators should seek to meet with the offender on more than one occasion as part of an assessment of consistency, deterioration, improvement, and other changes. Finally, CFE evaluations should include a clinical-forensic interview in which the offender's psychiatric history, symptom validity, and understanding of the relevant legal criteria for CFE in the particular jurisdiction are assessed. The relevant psycholegal criteria should be assessed in a structured and replicable manner. The information gained from the interview should be considered in light of collateral information that has been collected.

It is important for the evaluator to be clear about the referral question as well as his or her role in the evaluation. It may be the case that an evaluator is the only expert retained, or he or she may be one of several and assigned to evaluate a specific aspect of functioning (e.g., mental retardation). In this instance, it would be necessary for the evaluator to be clear about the boundaries of the specific case.

Clinical-Forensic Interview

At the beginning of the forensic interview, CFE evaluators should inform the offender of the nature and purpose of the evaluation, the possible outcomes of the evaluation, for whom the evaluation is being performed, who will have access to the results of the evaluation, and the consequences of not participating in the evaluation. Any indication of a lack of understanding on the part of the offender should be noted and appropriate measures taken to determine whether or not to continue with the evaluation. During the interview, evaluators should assess the offender's understanding of the relevant information in the jurisdiction, the offender's appreciation of his or her situation, and his or her reasoning about these issues. In addition, the evaluator should inquire about the offender's previous and current psychological functioning and psychiatric history as well as any medication that the offender may be prescribed and its effect on the offender.

Assessment Measures

CFE evaluators should be aware of the psycholegal abilities required of a competent offender. In the absence of a standardized assessment instrument specifically developed to assess the psycholegal criteria for a given jurisdiction, the evaluator should operationalize the applicable psycholegal criteria. Evaluators should focus on the functional abilities of the offender, in addition to the mental state of the offender and the appropriate diagnosis of a mental disorder, and should document how any functional deficits may be causally related to mental, emotional, or intellectual deficits. If it is a requirement of the jurisdiction that the offender be able to assist his or her attorney, then a true functional assessment would include observing the interaction of the offender with his or her attorney and attempting to determine whether or not the offender is able to assist the attorney (e.g., disclose relevant information to the attorney, understand what it is that the attorney is attempting to accomplish).

Since death row offenders are disproportionately intellectually limited and academically deficient (Cunningham & Vigen, 1999, 2002), it is important for evaluators to use language that is straightforward and understandable when evaluating a particular offender. If a particular offender holds a known delusional system, it would be important for an evaluator to assess this delusional system directly with respect to the execution process, the reasons why this individual is to be executed, and what it means to be executed, as well as the offender's beliefs about the perceived role that his or her attorney plays in this process.

Finally, CFE evaluators should examine the possibility of response sets such as defensiveness, uncooperativeness, or malingering. Every effort should be made to use instruments that have established reliability and validity; after all, the motivation to malinger in this situation may be high. It may be necessary to use an instrument specifically designed to evaluate the potential for malingering or the authenticity of reported symptoms. The evaluator should use other psychological tests in the evaluation of CFE as indicated in a particular case (e.g., use neuropsychological tests if there is some question of cognitive or neuropsychological impairment).

Collateral Information

CFE evaluators should collect collateral information about the offender's previous and current functioning, as well as his or her functioning while on death row (including any specific behaviors that the offender has engaged in that might be relevant to psycholegal understanding[3]). Friends and family of the offender who can comment on previous and current functioning and characteristics should be interviewed. Correctional officers, prison physicians and psychologists, and other prisoners should be asked to comment on the behavior of the offender while in the institution. Medical records and psychiatric history both within and outside of the correctional institution should be gathered and evaluated.

Presentation of the Results of the Evaluation

CFE evaluators should carefully document the evaluation procedures as well as all other relevant information. Record keeping, note taking, and recording[4] the interview are important considerations and should be meticulous as these assessments are likely to undergo serious scrutiny. It is appropriate practice for CFE evaluators to speak to the individual who retained their services before preparing a report. Although it remains arguable whether CFE evaluators should speak to the ultimate legal issue, they should certainly present the evidence before the triers of fact in a manner that will be of assistance in reaching a decision about whether the offender is capable of a specific psycholegal ability or required capacity (e.g., include a full history, observations, and testing including descriptions or observations of the offender and perhaps extensively quoting the offender's responses).

Measures of CFE

To date, there have been less than a handful of published measures of CFE. As was the case with competency to stand trial, the first measures have taken the form of checklists or aide-mémoires for evaluators. Given that the research on CFE is in its infancy, when compared to the literature on competency to stand trial, it is expected that these checklists will be further elaborated and expanded in the future as the research and literature in this area continues to develop.

Interview Checklist for Evaluations of CFE

Zapf et al. (2003) published a checklist for evaluations of CFE. This checklist was compiled after reviewing the available literature on criminal competencies, reviewing the available case law on CFE, and conducting interviews with professionals who have been involved in conducting evaluations of CFE (the reader is referred to Zapf et al., 2003 for full details).

The checklist is divided into four sections: (1) understanding the reasons for punishment, (2) understanding the punishment, (3) appreciation and reasoning (in addition to simple factual understanding), and (4) ability to assist attorney. These four sections are representative of the legal criteria for CFE that have been set out by various states (see Acker & Lanier, 1997; Harding, 1994).

Most states model their statutes after the criteria set out in *Ford* and, therefore, consider only the prisoner's ability to understand the punishment that is being imposed and the reasons why it is being imposed. The first two sections of the checklist parallel these two *Ford* criteria. The first section targets the offender's understanding of the reasons for punishment. That is, his or her understanding of the crime and other conviction-related information. Specific topic areas include the offender's understanding of the reasons why he or she is in prison; his or her place of residence within the prison; the crime for which he or she was convicted, including an explanation of the criminal act and victim identifying information; the perceived justice of the conviction; reasons why other people are punished for the same offense; and any self-identified, unique, understandings of the offense and trial that the offender might have.

The second section targets the offender's understanding of the punishment: that is, that the punishment he or she is facing is death. Specific topic areas include the offender's understanding of the sentence, the meaning of a sentence of death, what it means for a person to be dead, specific understandings about death from execution, and the reasons for execution. Questions about death are asked from a number of different angles (i.e., meaning of death, specific understandings about death from execution) so as to facilitate a thorough evaluation of any irrational beliefs or ideas that the offender may hold regarding death.

The literature on other types of competence (i.e., competence to consent to medical treatment) indicates that there is often a relationship between the severity of the consequences (to the individual being assessed) and the stringency of the standard used to evaluate competence (e.g., see Roth, Meisel, & Lidz, 1977). Thus, given the gravity of the consequences in the particular instance of CFE, it seems appropriate and important to assess the offender's appreciation and reasoning abilities (in addition to simple factual understanding). Therefore, the third section of the checklist lists topic areas specific to the assessment of an offender's appreciation and reasoning abilities with respect to death and execution; areas that may go above and beyond the specific *Ford* criteria but that are arguably important to a comprehensive evaluation of CFE. Indeed, the *Panetti* decision, occurring more than four years after the development of this interview checklist, confirms that an inmate's rational understanding is important and relevant to the determination of CFE. Specific content areas in this section include the offender's appreciation of the personal importance of the punishment and the personal meaning of death; the offender's rationality or reasoning about the physical, mental, and personal changes that occur during and after execution; beliefs regarding invulnerability; inappropriate affect; acceptance or eagerness for execution; and beliefs against execution.

Finally, the last section of the checklist identifies issues related to the offender's ability to assist his or her attorney. This section will be especially relevant in jurisdictions that rely upon criteria that are broader in nature than those outlined in *Ford* and *Panetti*, such as the capacity to comprehend the reasons that might make the capital sentence unjust and to communicate these reasons effectively. Specific topic areas in this section include the identity of the offender's attorney and the amount of time that the attorney has been working for the offender, the offender's trust in the attorney, awareness of execution date, status of appeals, what the attorney is attempting to accomplish through the appeals, how the appeals will be processed and assessed, the actual substance of the appeals, important content that the offender may have withheld from the attorney, and any pathological reasons for not planning or discussing appeals.

The purpose of the checklist is to guide evaluators through the interview portion of a CFE evaluation. As is the case with any forensic assessment instrument, all relevant issues for a particular case may not be addressed thus evaluators need to remain mindful of this and pay special attention to additional, relevant issues that may arise. The checklist includes specific areas of inquiry for each of the topic areas; however, specific questions were deliberately not included so as to encourage evaluators to develop their own style of questioning for each of the content areas. Of course, as is the case for any type of forensic evaluation, it is important for evaluators to phrase questions in such a way so as not to lead the offender to exaggerated or malingered pathological responses.

Instrument to Evaluate an Inmate's Level of Competency

Ebert (2001) published an overview and commentary on CFE that included a table of 12 items that he called "A proposed competency to be executed instrument." The 12 items are as follows: (1) ability to identify what is about to happen, (2) ability to understand and conceptualize that the person is housed on death row, (3) ability to understand the meaning of the term and concept of punishment, (4) ability to work with attorney, (5) ability to understand the sentence of death, (6) ability to understand the reason for the punishment of death, (7) ability to conceptualize what will happen when the punishment is carried out, (8) ability to describe the role of key people involved in the punishment, (9) ability to provide recent facts that may be helpful to deal with the issue of current competency, (10) ability to voluntarily control thoughts, (11) ability to perceive reality in the present, and (12) self-serving versus self-defeating motivation. Ebert provides a six-point scale on which each item is to be rated: 0 = no capacity, 1 = some incapacity, 2 = mild incapacity, 3 = moderate incapacity, 4 = severe incapacity, and 5 = severe incapacity. No elaboration regarding how to determine the level of capacity or incapacity for each of the 12 areas is given and he provides no explanation for how a rating of a 4 or a 5 differ from each other (with both being called "severe incapacity"). In addition, Ebert does not indicate whether or how one is to use the ratings for making a determination about an individual's CFE. Evaluators who choose to use this instrument as part of their CFE evaluation should be careful to consider both factual as well as rational understanding as highlighted by *Panetti*.

CFE Research Rating Scales

The CFE Research Rating Scales (CERRS) was developed to assist mental health professionals in the evaluation of CFE (Ackerson, Brodsky, & Zapf, 2005) and is the only instrument that has been the focus of research. The CERRS was developed from a survey of judges authorized to give death penalty sentences regarding those content areas that were important for determining CFE and is comprised of four sections: (1) understanding and appreciating punishment, (2) understanding and appreciating death, (3) capacity to work with counsel, and (4) relevant clinical information.

The first section is comprised of eight items that evaluate an inmate's understanding and appreciation of punishment, including global understanding of punishment, understanding of why the inmate is being punished by the legal system, appreciation of punishment, understanding that the inmate has received the death penalty, appreciation of the death penalty, capacity to appreciate that the death penalty is impending, understanding of the crime, and appreciation of the crime. The second section is comprised of two items: understanding of death and appreciation of death. The third section consists of four items surrounding the capacity to work with counsel, including ability to converse with counsel, ability to make a rational choice about working with counsel, understanding of legal issues, and ability to provide information that would make the punishment unjust. The final section consists of three items, each corresponding to a relevant area of clinical information, including severity of mental illness, severity of deficits in cognitive abilities (including memory capacities, reasoning skills, and comprehension skills), and impairment of judgment and insight.

Each of the items in each section are to be considered by the evaluator and rated on a 5-point Likert-type scale in terms of the degree of incapacity: 1 = severe, 2 = moderately severe, 3 = moderate, 4 = mild, and 5 = none. The items are not to be summed, but rather are to be considered by the evaluator within the context of each inmate's individual case.

In addition to publishing the CERRS, Ackerson et al. (2005) also reported the results of research conducted with the CERRS. Ninety forensic-clinical psychologists were asked to make CFE judgments for nine fictional vignettes; approximately half ($n = 41$) were given the CERRS to aid in their judgments, while the other half ($n = 49$) were not. Results indicate that judgments made by the two groups differed significantly for those vignettes wherein the legal criteria were ambiguous (as opposed to clearly either meeting or not meeting legal criteria for CFE), with the group given the CERRS to aid in their judgments being more likely to be influenced by legal information presented in the vignettes. In addition, it was found that 48% of the variance in the judgments made by the group given the CERRS was accounted for by both legal criteria and diagnostic symptomatology (as compared to 37% of the variance in the group not given the CERRS to use); thus, it appears that the CERRS guided respondents to consider both legal and clinical factors when making judgments about CFE.

Response Styles

As previously mentioned and as is the case with any forensic evaluation, it is important to consider and evaluate the possibility of various response sets in the evaluation of CFE. Given that the outcome of a CFE evaluation is important, literally, to the life or death of an individual, motivation to malinger may be high. Evaluators need to evaluate, informally if not formally, the possibility that the evaluee might be malingering in every CFE evaluation.

Two types of malingering can occur in any forensic evaluation—falsely claiming or exaggerating psychiatric symptomatology or cognitive deficits. If an informal evaluation of malingering leads an evaluator to suspect that an evaluee is exaggerating his or her symptomatology (psychiatric or cognitive), a formal evaluation of malingering should be undertaken as part of the CFE evaluation. Instruments that have established reliability and validity and that were specifically designed to evaluate the potential for malingering or the authenticity of reported symptoms should be used for this purpose. With respect to the false production or exaggeration of psychiatric symptoms, forensic assessment instruments such as the SIRS (Rogers, Bagby, & Dickens, 1992), SIRS-2 (Rogers, Sewell, & Gillard, 2010), or the Miller Forensic Assessment of Symptoms Test (M-FAST; Miller, 1995) would be appropriate for use. Forensic assessment instruments such as the Test of Memory Malingering (TOMM; Tombaugh, 1996) or the VIP (Frederick, 1997) would be appropriate for the evaluation of malingered cognitive deficits.

The available research on death row offenders indicates that they are disproportionately intellectually limited and academically deficient (Cunningham & Vigen, 1999, 2002); therefore, it is important for evaluators to consider this alongside the possibility of malingering cognitive deficits. The sensitive nature of CFE evaluations, in general, coupled with the potentially devastating consequences of being *mis*labeled a malingerer should underscore just how important it is for an evaluator to be as sure as possible of the true mental state of the individual being evaluated.

Conclusions

This chapter has provided an overview of the legal issues and decisions pertaining to competency, a review of the commentary and empirical research in this area, and a discussion of the assessment of CFE. As is the case with all developing areas within forensic assessment, future work will no doubt continue to expand and elaborate upon the work that has been completed to this point. Perhaps more so than other areas in the field of forensic assessment, research on CFE is difficult and slow given the relatively small number of evaluations that are conducted each year and the difficulty in accessing this population for research purposes. Researchers and evaluators should be encouraged to continue to extrapolate the information obtained through practice and research on other types of criminal competencies to CFE. It is in this way that we will be able to continue to develop this important area of forensic assessment.

Notes

1   The reader is reminded that the majority of these evaluations were conducted a number of years ago. Therefore, some of the instruments reported, while perhaps out of date now, were not out of date at the time of the evaluations.

2   For instance, an examiner could conceivably conduct the interview portion of a CFE evaluation by asking only two questions: (1) Are you going to die? and (2) Do you know why you are going to die?

3   These might include, but not be limited to, discussions of execution content with correctional personnel or chaplains, writing letters of good-bye or issue resolution, writing a will, giving away possessions, selecting witnesses, or making preferences for a last meal.

4   Video or audio recording is useful in that the evaluator is able to review the evaluation as well as present the tape to complement his or her testimony; however, recording the evaluation is also subject to legal-strategic decisions by the attorney and, therefore, should be discussed with the retaining attorney beforehand.

References

Acker, J. R., & Lanier, C. S. (1997). Unfit to live, unfit to die: CFE under modern death penalty legislation. *Criminal Law Bulletin, 33*, 107–150.

Ackerson, K. S., Brodsky, S. L., & Zapf, P. A. (2005). Judges' and psychologists' assessments of legal and clinical factors in competence for execution. *Psychology, Public Policy, and Law, 11*, 164–193 doi: 10.1037/1076–8971.11.1.164

American Bar Association. (1989). *American Bar Association criminal justice mental health standards.* Washington, DC: Author.

Appelbaum, P. S. (1986). Competence to be executed: Another conundrum for mental health professionals. *Hospital and Community Psychiatry, 37*, 682–684.

Bonnie, R. (1990). Dilemmas in administering the death penalty: Conscientious abstention, professional ethics, and the needs of the legal system. *Law and Human Behavior, 14*, 67–90. doi: 10.1007/BF01055790

Broderick, D. J. (1979). Insanity of the condemned. *Yale Law Journal, 88*, 533-564.

Brodsky, S. L., Zapf, P. A., & Boccaccini, M. (1999). Post conviction relief: The assessment of competence for execution. *Proceedings of Psychological Expertise and Criminal Justice: An APA/ABA Conference for Psychologists and Lawyers* (vol. 2, pp. 189-201). Washington, DC: American Psychological Association.

Brodsky, S. L., Zapf, P. A., & Boccaccini, M. T. (2001). The last competency: An examination of legal, ethical, and professional ambiguities regarding evaluations of competence for execution. *Journal of Forensic Psychology Practice, 1*, 1–25. doi: 10.1300/J158v01n02_01

Brodsky, S. L., Zapf, P. A., & Boccaccini, M. T. (2005). CFE assessments: Ethical continuities and professional tasks. *Journal of Forensic Psychology Practice, 5*, 65–74. doi: 10.1300/J158v05n04_04

Caritativo v. California, 357 U.S. 549, 785 S. Ct. 1263 (1958).

Cunningham, M. D., & Vigen, M. P. (1999). Without appointed counsel in capital postconviction proceedings: The self-representation competency of Mississippi death row offenders. *Criminal Justice and Behavior, 26*, 293–321. doi: 10.1177/0093854899026003002

Cunningham, M. D., & Vigen, M. P. (2002). Death row inmate characteristics, adjustment, and confinement: A critical review of the literature. *Behavioral Sciences and the Law, 20*, 191–210. doi: 10.1002/bsl.473

Deitchman, M. A., Kennedy, W. A., & Beckham, J. C. (1991). Self-selection factors in the participation of mental health professionals in CFE evaluations. *Law & Human Behavior, 15*, 287–303. doi: 10.1007/BF01061714

Dusky v. United States, 362 U.S. 402 (1960).

Ebert, B. (2001). Competency to be executed: A proposed instrument to evaluate an inmate's level of competency in light of the Eighth Amendment prohibition against the execution of the presently insane. *Law and Psychology Review, 25*, 29–57.

Ex parte Jordan, 758 S.W.2d. 250 (Tx. Ct. App.1988).

Ford v. Wainwright, 477 U.S. 399, 106 S.Ct. 2595 (1986).

Frederick, R. (1997). *The Validity Indicator Profile: Professional Manual.* Odessa, FL: Psychological Assessment Resources.

Furman v. Georgia, 408 U.S. 238, 92 S. Ct. 2726 (1972).

Godinez v. Moran, 113 S. Ct. 2680 (1993).

Harding, R. M. (1994). "Endgame": Competency and the execution of condemned offenders—A proposal to satisfy the Eighth Amendment's prohibition against the infliction of cruel and unusual punishment. *St. Louis University Public Law Review, 14*, 105–151.

Heilbrun, K. S. (1987). The assessment of CFE: An overview. *Behavioral Sciences and the Law, 5*, 383–396. doi: 10.1002/bsl.2370050403

Heilbrun, K. S., & McClaren, H. A. (1988). Assessment of CFE? A guide for mental health professionals. *Bulletin of the American Academy of Psychiatry and the Law, 16*, 205–216.

Hensl, K. B. (2005). Restoring CFE: The paradoxical debate continues with the case of Singleton v. Norris. *Journal of Forensic Psychology Practice, 5*, 55–68. doi: 10.1300/J158v05n03_03

Leong, G. B., Silva, J. A., Weinstock, R., & Ganzini, L. (2000). Survey of forensic psychiatrists on evaluation and treatment of prisoners on death row. *Journal of the American Academy of Psychiatry & the Law, 28*, 427–432.

Lichtenstein, B. (2013). Beyond Abu Ghraib: The 2010 APA Ethics Code Standard 1.02 and CFE Evaluations. *Ethics and Behavior, 23*, 67–70. doi: 10.1080/10508422.2013.757958

Martin v. Florida, 515 So.2d. 189 (Fla. 1987).

Mathias, R. E. (1988). Assessment of CFE: Assessment and dissonance on death row: The dilemma of consultation. *Forensic Reports, 1*, 125–132.

Melton, G. B., Petrila, J., Poythress, N. G., & Slobogin, C. (2007). *Psychological evaluations for the courts: A handbook for mental health professionals and lawyers* (3rd ed.). New York: Guilford Press.

Miller, H. A. (1995). *Miller Forensic Assessment of Symptoms Test*. Odessa, FL: Psychological Assessment Resources.

Miller, R. D. (1988). Evaluation of and treatment for competency to be executed: A national survey and an analysis. *Journal of Psychiatry & Law, 16*, 67–90.

Mossman, D. (1995). Denouement of an execution competency case: Is *Perry* pyrrhic? *Bulletin of the American Academy of Psychiatry and the Law, 23*, 269–284.

Neal, T.M.S. (2010). Choosing the lesser of two evils: A framework for considering the ethics of competency-for-execution evaluations. *Journal of Forensic Psychology Practice, 10*, 145–157. doi: 10.1080/15228930903446724

Nobles v. Georgia, 168 U.S. 398, 18 S. Ct. 87 (1897).

Panetti v. Quarterman, 551 U.S. 930 (2007), 127 S. Ct. 2842 (2007).

Pastroff, S. M. (1986). Eighth amendment-the constitutional rights of the insane on death row. *The Journal of Criminal Law and Criminology, 77*, 844–866. doi: 10.2307/1143441

Phyle v. Duffy, 334 U.S. 431, 68 S. Ct. 1131 (1948).

Pirelli, G., & Zapf, P. A. (2008). An investigation of psychologists' practices and attitudes toward participation in capital evaluations. *Journal of Forensic Psychology Practice, 8*, 39–66. doi: 10.1080/15228930801947294

Rogers, R., Bagby, R. M., & Dickens, S. E. (1992). *Structured Interview of Reported Symptoms (SIRS) and professional manual*. Odessa, FL: Psychological Assessment Resources.

Rogers, R., Sewell, K. W., & Gillard, N. D. (2010). *Structured Interview of Reported Symptoms (SIRS)* (2nd Ed.), *professional manual*. Lutz, FL: Psychological Assessment Resources, Inc.

Roth, L. H., Meisel, A., & Lidz, C. W. (1977). Tests of competency to consent to treatment. *American Journal of Psychiatry, 134*, 279–284.

Saks, E. (2009). Retributive constraints on the concept of competency: The required role of "patently false beliefs" in understanding competency to be executed. *Behavioral Sciences and the Law, 27*, 1–27. doi: 10.1002/bsl.852

Shapiro, D. (2005). Ethical dilemmas in CFE evaluations. *Journal of Forensic Psychology Practice, 5*, 75–82. doi: 10.1300/J158v05n04_05

Small, M. A., & Otto, R. K. (1991). Evaluations of competency to be executed: Legal contours and implications for assessment. *Criminal Justice and Behavior, 18*, 146–158. doi: 10.1177/0093854891018002003

Solesbee v. Balkcom, 339 U.S. 9, 70 S. Ct. 457 (1950).

Tombaugh, T. N. (1996). *Test of Memory Malingering*. Toronto: Multi-Health Systems.

Ward, B. A. (1986). CFE: Problems in law and psychiatry. *Florida State University Law Review, 14*, 35–101.

Washington v. Harris, 789 P.2d. 60, 114 Wash. 2d 419 (Wash. 1990).

Washington v. Rice, 757 P.2d. 889, 110Wash. 2d 577 (Wash. 1988).

Weinstock, R., Leong, G. B., & Silva, J. A. (2010). Competence to be executed: An ethical analysis post *Panetti. Behavioral Sciences and the Law, 28*, 690–706. doi: 10.1002/bsl.951

White, C. G. (1982). Ethical guidelines for psychologist participation in death penalty proceedings: A survey. *Professional Psychology, 13*, 327–329. doi: 10.1037/h0078002

Young, B., A., Boccaccini, M. T., Lawson, K., & Conroy, M. A. (2008). Competence-for-execution evaluation practices in Texas: Findings from a semi-structured interview with experienced evaluators. *Journal of Forensic Psychology Practice, 8*, 280–292. doi: 10.1080/15228930802282022

Zapf, P. A. (2002, March). *The assessment of CFE: Going above and beyond the* Ford *criteria*. Invited participant, Mini Conference on Capital Case Litigation, Biennial Meetings of the American Psychology-Law Society, Austin, TX.

Zapf, P. A. (2009). Elucidating the contours of CFE: The implications of *Ford* and *Panetti* for the assessment of CFE. *The Journal of Psychiatry and Law*, 37, 269–307.

Zapf, P. A., Boccaccini, M. T., & Brodsky, S. L. (2003). Assessment of CFE: Professional guidelines and an evaluation checklist. *Behavioral Sciences and the Law, 21*, 103–120. doi: 10.1002/bsl.491

Zapf, P. A., Viljoen, J. L., Whittemore, K. E., Poythress, N. G., & Roesch, R. (2002). Competency: Past, present, and future. In J. R. P. Ogloff (ed.), *Taking psychology and law into the twenty-first century* (pp. 171–198). New York: Kluwer Academic/Plenum.

Part III

Juvenile Forensic Assessment

11 The Capacity of Juveniles to Understand and Waive Arrest Rights

*Ronald Roesch, Kaitlyn McLachlan, and
Jodi L. Viljoen*

The juvenile justice system in the United States was created well over a hundred years ago as an informal system that focused on the best interests of the child. As a consequence, procedural safeguards were not paramount, since the prevailing philosophy was one of rehabilitation rather than punishment. Beginning in the early part of the last century, juvenile courts "viewed children as more malleable and more amenable to rehabilitation than adults and believed that they were not solely responsible for their criminal conduct, which was thought to be due to poverty and parental neglect" (Redding, Goldstein, & Heilbrun, 2005, p. 7). This benevolent philosophy was dominant for decades but began to change in the 1960s, owing in part to legal decisions extending the rights of adults to adolescents and in part to changing attitudes that youth should be held more accountable and punished for delinquent and criminal behavior. Owen-Kostelnik, Reppucci, and Meyer (2006) noted that "the characterization of young people has shifted between *paternalistic logic* models, which portray youths as children in need of protection and thus deprive them of certain rights when being questioned, and *liberationist logic* models, which depict youths as autonomous individuals entitled to the same rights as adults when being questioned" (pp. 287–288).

The legal foundation for the major shift in juvenile justice practice perhaps began with a decision affecting adults in the criminal justice system. *Miranda v. Arizona* (1966) required states to warn suspects prior to interrogation or questioning of several rights, including their right to remain silent, that anything they say can be used against them in a court of law, the right to the presence of an attorney, and the right to free counsel if they cannot afford the cost of an attorney. These warnings were viewed as strengthening individuals' protection against incriminating themselves during police interrogation. These rights were extended to juveniles soon after the *Miranda* decision. *Kent v. United States* (1966) and *In re Gault* (1967) required courts to provide these procedural safeguards to youth. However, the seemingly straightforward downward extension of rights from the adult to juvenile courts has not been as easy to implement in practice, due largely to the differences in decision-making capacities of youth compared to adults. As Feld (2000) noted: "In reality, juveniles receive a very different form of procedural justice. Oftentimes, delinquents waive *Miranda* rights without appreciating the legal significance of confessing, and relinquish their right to counsel prior to trial and face the power of the state alone and unaided" (p. 105). Indeed, Feld (2013) observed that "the Supreme Court has decided more cases about interrogating youths than any other aspect of juvenile justice" (p. 1).

This chapter will focus on the assessment of youths' capacity to understand and waive their legal rights at the time of arrest. The intent of this chapter is to provide clinicians with an overview of how to approach an assessment of capacity to waive these rights at arrest. In order to effectively assess youths' capacities, it is necessary to understand relevant laws, research on adolescents' *Miranda* rights comprehension, and important developmental considerations. Therefore, we first discuss these issues. Following that, instruments and approaches for assessing youths' capacity to understand and waive *Miranda* rights are discussed. A case report is also presented.

The Application of *Miranda* Standards to Youth

The importance of ensuring that procedural safeguards provide adequate protection of the rights of youth is underscored by the fact that not all juveniles are kept in juvenile court. The philosophical shift to accountability and punishment has resulted in an increasing number of youth who are transferred to adult criminal court, and consequently sentenced to prison rather than juvenile facilities (Penney & Moretti, 2005). It is important to emphasize the fact that decisions about the determination of a young offender's transfer to adult court, and the imposition of severe adult penalties occur after the young person has been arrested, given the opportunity to exercise *Miranda* rights, and interrogated. The possibility thus exists that a 16-year-old could be raised to adult court and be sentenced to a lengthy prison term, including life without parole (although *Graham v. Florida*, 2010 held that a life without parole sentence could not be given automatically, as had been the case).

This transfer can occur in one of three ways (see Salekin, Grimes, and Adams, Chapter 13 in this volume). *Judicial waiver* allows a judge to transfer a youth to adult court following a hearing in which it is determined that a youth satisfies the criteria established in *Kent v. United States* (1966). These criteria focus on both the youth (e.g., treatment amenability, sophistication and maturity, prior record) as well as risk to the community. *Automatic waiver* is used in over half of the states. The waiver is automatic if a youth is charged with certain offenses, such as murder or other serious violence. Some states limit this to those aged 16 or 17, while other states do not provide any age restriction. In fact, young offenders as young as age 8 can face adult penalties for serious offences. Nevada is one of just a few states that do not specify any age limit for exclusion of certain serious offenses (see also Delaware, Mississippi, Nevada, Ohio, and Pennsylvania). In Nevada, anyone charged with murder or attempted murder is tried in adult court. Those 14 and older charged with other crimes could also be raised to adult court. In cases where this may occur, the youth's understanding, at the time of the *Miranda* warning, of the possibility of transfer to adult court should be assessed. A third option, which is available in nearly a third of the states, is *prosecutor direct file*, in which prosecutors can decide whether to try the youth in adult or juvenile court.

One other consequence of youth interrogation that should be mentioned is the possibility of false confessions. Youth, especially younger adolescents and preteens, may be especially vulnerable to making false confessions due to immaturity and poor judgment (Kassin, 2005; Lassiter, 2004). Drizen and Leo (2004) cited cases in which youths confessed on the misguided belief that they would then be released. In a study of false confessions, Goldstein, Condie, Kalbeitzer, Osman, and Geier (2003) found that adolescents aged 15 and under were more prone to false confessions (see also Redlich & Goodman, 2003). Malloy, Shulman, and Cauffman (2014) interviewed adolescent offenders and found that just over one-third of the sample claimed to have made a prior false confession or false guilty plea to legal authorities. Cleary (2014) analyzed recorded transcripts from police interrogations with young offenders and found that many provided confessions or inculpatory statements after administration of their rights, suggesting that they may not fully understand and appreciate the importance of their arrest rights at the time of waiver. As part of an evaluation of capacity to waive *Miranda* warnings, clinicians may be asked to evaluate the validity of a confession. If this is the case, Oberlander, Goldstein, and Goldstein (2003) is a helpful resource.

It should also be noted that courts typically accept waivers. Feld (2000) reported that courts will typically validate *Miranda* waivers when police follow typical procedures of advising youth of their rights and obtaining a "yes" answer in response when they are asked if they understood those rights. Feld is critical of this practice, commenting that "If most juveniles lack the cognitive capacity to understand the warning or the psychosocial ability to invoke or exercise rights, then ritualistic recitation of the *Miranda* litany hardly accomplishes those purposes [to enable youth to assert their rights and to ensure that rights were knowingly and intelligently waived]" (p. 115). He also noted that courts typically do not consider low intellectual ability, including mental retardation, as necessarily resulting in a finding of inadmissibility of confessions. We will discuss this issue later in this chapter.

Miranda Warnings in Practice

In most jurisdictions, adolescents can choose to waive their *Miranda* rights independently, without the assistance of an attorney or parent. A key assumption underlying the extension of *Miranda* rights and other procedural safeguards is that adolescents are able to make informed use of them. Adolescents' capacity to exercise and validly waive their *Miranda* rights must be based on their ability to both understand the legal right and to appreciate the consequences of decisions to waive or exercise their legal rights (Grisso, 1998a).

Grisso (1981) conceptualized appreciation of the significance of rights to comprise three main parts. First, suspects must recognize the interrogative nature of police questioning. Second, suspects must perceive the defense attorney as an advocate who will defend and advise them, and be willing to disclose confidential information to him or her (appreciation of the right to counsel). Finally, suspects must perceive the right to silence as a right that cannot be revoked, and that statements made by suspects can be used in court (appreciation of the right to silence).

The legal test applied in determining the validity of a waiver is that the waiver is "knowing, intelligent, and voluntary" (Grisso, 1981). The courts have outlined two standards for determining whether or not an adolescent has competently waived their *Miranda* rights. First, in *Fare v. Michael C.* (1979), a totality of circumstances approach was adopted, in which the validity of a waiver is decided based on a variety of factors and circumstances including for example the youth's age and education, the length of the interrogation, and understanding of the *Miranda* warning. The other decision rule is known as the *per se* standard, in which a single factor (e.g., age, mental retardation) invalidates a *Miranda* waiver regardless of other factors related to the youth and the circumstances surrounding the waiver. However, as Grisso (2003) noted: "Currently, no states have *per se* rules based on capacities or characteristics of suspects alone. For example, no statute considers all mentally retarded defendants or all children automatically incompetent to waive *Miranda* rights. Some states, however, consider juveniles incompetent to waive their rights *unassisted*. In those states, juveniles' waivers are automatically *(per se)* invalid if they have not been advised by parents or other 'friendly adults' (that is, if one of these persons was not present at the waiver)" (p. 154).

The Role of Police in Interrogations and *Miranda* Administration

There is a considerable range in the types of police questioning of juveniles, from informal talks on the street or at a youth's home to the much more formal, sometimes audio- or video-taped, interrogations in detention. A youth could confess to a crime even before a *Miranda* warning is given if the youth was not considered to be in custody, but the court could be asked to review "whether the police officers' questions were directed toward obtaining a confession and whether they subsequently took the youth into custody, endeavored to meet all procedural requirements. . . and the youth then waived the rights and repeated the confession" (Grisso, 1998b, p. 40). Further, in *J.D.B. v. North Carolina* (2011) the Court ruled that age was an objective factor, and thus police officers must evaluate the "effect of relative age" (p. 16) when determining whether a youth suspect is in custody for the purposes of *Miranda* warnings. As Grisso (1998b) notes, *Miranda* warnings are not necessary in many police encounters with youth. The warning is required only when youth are questioned in custody. This does not necessarily mean that the youth is in detention, as it could include situations on the street or in the youth's home when the youth is apprehended or arrested.

Once youth waive their arrest rights, confessions often immediately follow. Feld (2013) obtained interrogation videos and police files of 307 real interrogations of juvenile suspects. He found that the majority (86.6%) had been formally arrested prior to questioning, and more than three-quarters (78.8%) were interrogated in an interrogations room at either a police station or a juvenile detention center. However, many interrogations took place in less formal places, including the back of a police car at the place of arrest (8.1%), in the juvenile's home (6.2%), and in schools (6.2%). In Feld's (2013) study, all interrogated youth received a proper *Miranda* warning prior to interrogation, though only about a fifth (19.5%) of the files included a signed warning form. Feld found that more than half of the youth confessed within a few minutes of waiving *Miranda* and did not require any prompting by police.

Police officers play a critical role in the administration of valid *Miranda* warnings prior to interrogation and in ensuring that juvenile suspects waive their rights under appropriate conditions. However, the priority of police during a criminal investigation is to solve crimes and obtain evidence, often through interrogation and confessions, about a suspect's guilt. The majority of police trained in the interrogation of juvenile suspects learn the Reid Method (Leo, 2008). The Reid Method has been heavily criticized for explicitly training investigators to use coercive and psychologically manipulative tactics to scare or intimidate suspects, or alternatively, to gain their trust and encourage confessions (King & Snook, 2009; Leo & Drizen, 2010). Importantly, the Reid Method does not train alternative or modified approaches to interrogation that take into consideration developmental differences between youth and adult suspects (Feld, 2013, Owen-Kostelnik et al., 2006). Feld's (2013) data confirms frequent use of such techniques during the administration of *Miranda* warnings specifically. He found that

> Police sometimes framed a Miranda waiver as a prerequisite to a juvenile's opportunity to tell his side of the story. Police communicated the value of talking—"telling her story"— and telling the truth before they gave a Miranda warning. Officers characterized the warning as an administrative formality to complete before the suspect can talk. Officers sometimes referred to the warning as "paper-work" to emphasize its bureaucratic quality or as a ritual with which to comply . . . " Officers regularly referred to youths' familiarity with Miranda from television and movies. Miranda's cultural ubiquity may detract from youths' understanding, as the warning becomes background noise at an interrogation. (pp. 10–11)

The Content and Complexity of **Miranda Warnings**

The exact wording and complexity of *Miranda* warnings varies quite substantially across states (Grisso, 1998a; Helms, 2003). Each warning typically contains the four prongs already described and outlined in *Miranda*. A fifth warning prong has been added in many jurisdictions, which informs suspects that they can choose to stop questioning and consult with an attorney at any time (Goldstein et al., 2003). Additionally, some jurisdictions have included cautionary statements to juveniles regarding the possibility of having their case remanded to adult court or serving an adult sentence. While the content of the warnings may remain somewhat static, wording complexity and the format in which the warnings are administered vary considerably across jurisdictions. For example, Helms (2003) investigated the readability of adult and juvenile *Miranda* warning cards carried by police officers and waiver forms employed across most U.S. states. In his analyses, Helms (2003) determined that the Flesch-Kincaid grade reading levels of protocols obtained at the state level ranged substantially, from 4.0 in South Dakota, to 9.9 for forms used by the U.S. Bureau of Alcohol, Tobacco, and Firearms. Remarkably, of the states that employed separate warning cards or forms for juveniles, Helms found that the reading grade level of the warnings actually increased, while the ease of readability decreased, making the juvenile forms more difficult than their adult counterparts in the majority of cases. More recently, Rogers, Hazelwood, Sewell, Shuman, and Blackwood (2008) looked at 122 juvenile *Miranda* warnings from across the states and found Flesch-Kincaid reading estimates varied dramatically from Grade 2.2 to postcollege.

An example of a *Miranda* waiver form used by police in the state of Washington includes the four traditional *Miranda* warnings as well as the two additional prongs utilized in some U.S. jurisdictions:

- I have the right to remain silent and not make any statement at all.
- Any statement that I do make can and will be used against me in a court of law.
- I have the right to consult with and have an attorney present before and during questioning or the making of any statement.
- If I desire an attorney but cannot afford one, an attorney will be appointed for me at public expense prior to any questioning.
- I may exercise these rights at any time before or during questioning.
- If I am under 18 years of age I am considered a juvenile, but I do realize that this matter may be remanded to adult court for criminal prosecution, where I would be treated as an adult in all respects.

After initialing each of the above statements, the youth is asked to sign the form after reading the following:

- I understand each of these rights that I have read or had read to me. I understand that I may exercise these rights at any time before or during questioning. I do wish to waive my right to remain silent, and I do wish to waive my right to an attorney at this time.

A Flesch-Kincaid reading level analysis conducted on this warning form yielded a grade level of 9.2. This suggests that in order for an individual to be able to read the Washington *Miranda* warning, he or she would have to be able to read just slightly above a Grade 9 level. This diffi-culty level is concerning, given the fact that youths much younger than 14 years old (a typical age for Grade 9 students) may be presented with the same form, and also that even those 14 or older may have reading levels below the Grade 9 level. Clinicians should be aware of the reading level for the warning in their jurisdiction, and may wish to assess reading level of the youth if there is reason to believe that his or her reading level falls below this grade level.

Role of Parents or Significant Adult

A number of scholars have concluded that it would be appropriate for all states to require the presence of an adult before a youth could waive rights, with some arguing that a lawyer rather than a parent or other adult would be the most suitable person (see Feld, 2000). Some states require consultation with a parent or interested adult, apparently assuming that "parental pres-ence will assure the accuracy of any statements obtained, involve parents in the process at the initial stages, ensure that police fully advise and a juvenile actually understand those advisories, and relieve police of the burden of making judgments about a youth's competency" (Feld, 2000, p. 117).

Parents cannot waive the constitutional rights of their child, but they do have an influence. However, the expectation that they would help ensure understanding and protect the rights of their child may sometimes not be realized in practice. Parents may place coercive pressures on youth to talk to the police because they are upset or angry with their child. They also may advise their children to waive their right to an attorney, encourage them to cooperate, and even adopt an adversarial attitude toward their own children. In their study of youth in pretrial detention,

Viljoen, Klaver, and Roesch (2005) found 89% of youth indicated their parents wanted them to confess or tell the truth, 11% indicated that their parents wanted them to deny the offense, and none reported that their parents advised them to remain silent.

Also, parents may not fully understand or appreciate the legal situation and, indeed some parents may themselves have incapacities in terms of ability to waive *Miranda* rights (Woolard, Cleary, Harvell, & Chen, 2008). Owen-Kostelnik et al. (2006), after reviewing the developmental research, concluded that "serious consideration should be given to the *per se approach*, which advocates mandating that juveniles be afforded the protection of an advocate during questioning. Further, this advocate should be an attorney, as opposed to a parent because studies . . . have shown that parents often do little to encourage their children to assert their constitutional rights" (p. 301).

Research on Adolescents' *Miranda* Rights Comprehension

As we have discussed, trends in the juvenile justice system have emphasized the increased availability of severe punishments for young persons convicted of serious crimes. Given the potentially serious and long-term consequences that can arise in these circumstances, increased emphasis is placed on ensuring that young persons are able to understand and make informed decisions regarding their legal rights (Grisso, 1997).

Specifically, comprehension refers to a young person's simple understanding of *Miranda* rights, while appreciating the significance of a right goes beyond simple understanding and requires an individual to understand why they are important. For example, a young male may clearly understand a statement informing him that he can consult with a lawyer prior to interrogation—but without an appreciation of the role and function of a lawyer, this understanding is meaningless (Grisso, 1998a). In order for young people to benefit from these due-process extensions, they must know that they are entitled to certain rights, understand the protections these rights afford them, and understand the consequences of exercising or waiving these rights. However, research to date demonstrates that young persons, especially individuals under the age of 15, show poor comprehension of these rights generally (Abramovitch, Peterson-Badali, & Rohan, 1995; Colwell et al., 2005; Goldstein et al., 2003; Grisso et al., 2003; McLachlan, Roesch, & Douglas, 2011; Redlich, Silverman, & Steiner, 2003; Viljoen & Roesch, 2005). It is perhaps not surprising that research also shows that most juvenile suspects opt to waive their rights when being questioned by police (Grisso, 1981; Peterson-Badali, Abramovitch, Koegl, & Ruck, 1999; Viljoen et al., 2005).

Researchers to date have investigated the influence of numerous factors on juvenile rights comprehension, including age, IQ, and intellectual functioning, ethnicity, socioeconomic status, psychopathology, psychosocial maturity, and interrogative suggestibility (Abramovitch et al., 1995; Colwell et al., 2005; Frumkin, Lally, & Sexton, 2012; Goldstein et al., 2003; Grisso et al., 2003; Peterson-Badali et al., 1999; Redlich et al., 2003; McLachlan et al., 2011; McLachlan, Roesch, Viljoen, & Douglas, 2014; Rogers, Steadham, Fiduccia, Drogin, & Robinson, 2014). Studies consistently find that rights comprehension in young persons is significantly more impaired for younger adolescents compared with older adolescents and adults. Further, comprehension is most impaired among younger adolescents with lower IQ and other intellectual disabilities. The interaction between age and IQ seems to most strongly predict poor rights comprehension. Results from studies evaluating the influence of the other factors have been less clear.

One interesting line of inquiry has evaluated the role of prior police or justice system experience, following the supposition that criminally entrenched juvenile suspects who have heard and waived their rights more often may better understand and appreciate the significance of *Miranda* warnings. However, numerous studies have now found that even the most experienced juvenile offenders show no significant advantage in *Miranda* recall or comprehension when compared with defendants who have few arrests or justice system contact, and that repeated exposure to

Miranda warnings did not improve understanding or dispel misconceptions (McLachlan et al., 2011; Rogers, Rogstad, Steadham, & Drogin, 2011; Rogers, Fiduccia, Robinson, Steadham, & Drogin, 2013; Viljoen & Roesch, 2005).

Another important line of research has focused on the role of interrogative suggestibility in the context of *Miranda* comprehension and false confessions during interrogation. Gudjonsson and Clark (1986) defined *interrogative suggestibility* as "the extent to which, within a closed social interaction, people come to accept messages communicated during formal questioning, as the result of which their subsequent behavioral response is affected" (p. 4). They developed a theoretical model of interrogative suggestibility combining two distinct aspects of suggestibility relevant to police questioning: Yield and Shift. The first reflects the extent to which individuals tend to give into leading questions (Yield), and the second refers to individuals' tendency to shift responses under conditions of interpersonal pressure (Shift; Gudjonsson, 1984). Gudjonsson developed a series of clinical tools to evaluate interrogative suggestibility called the *Gudjonsson Suggestibility Scales* (GSS, Gudjonsson, 1997, described later in this chapter). Research using the GSS shows that, in general, children are more suggestible than adolescents and adults, and that suggestibility decreases steadily as age increases (Danielsdottir, Sigurgeirsdottir, Einarsdottir, & Haraldsson, 1993; Warren, Hulse-Trotter, & Tubbs, 1991). Studies evaluating the suggestibility of a wide range of adolescents, including offenders and forensic samples, show that when compared with adults, adolescents are no more likely to yield to leading questions, but are significantly more susceptible to interrogative pressure in the form of negative feedback and interpersonal pressure (Muris, Meesters, & Merckelbach, 2004; Redlich et al., 2003; Redlich & Goodman, 2003; Richardson & Kelly, 2004; Singh & Gudjonsson, 1992). Suggestibility is also negatively correlated with IQ in both adults and adolescents (McLachlan et al., 2011; Muris et al., 2004; Pollard et al., 2004; Richardson & Kelly, 1995; Singh & Gudjonsson, 1992).

Research suggesting that youthful suspects with impaired intellectual abilities are more likely to have both poor understanding and appreciation of their rights, and have higher levels of suggestibility, underscores the importance of evaluating suggestibility in the context of an assessment for the validity of a *Miranda* waiver. This is particularly critical because studies have shown that interrogative suggestibility may increase the likelihood of false confessions (Gudjonsson, 1990). For example, in a laboratory study, Redlich and Goodman (2003) found that younger and more suggestible adolescents were more likely than young adults to falsely take responsibility for crashing a computer. In particular, those who were more likely to yield to misleading questions on the GSS were also more likely to agree with an experimenter's request to (falsely) sign a confession form. It is troubling to consider the implications of this line of research. Given that young age, high suggestibility, and impaired intellectual abilities are each risk factors for poor rights comprehension, as well as false confessions (Kassin et al., 2010) this introduces the possibility of a possibly dangerous cycle. Once in police contact a young person's chances of being interrogated by police are heightened along with the opportunity to receive an arrest rights warning by police. Poor rights comprehension has been identified as an important factor that may contribute to a young person's decision to then waive those rights, which, in combination with high suggestibility, increases the chances of self-incrimination, false confession, and the possibility of prosecution (Kassin et al., 2010; Muris et al., 2004; Redlich et al., 2003; Richardson & Kelly, 1995).

Research Limitations

Although research has been helpful in identifying areas in which capacity may be impaired, it is important that clinicians keep in mind that an important limitation of the research on adolescents' capacity to waive rights is that many studies have been conducted in laboratory settings, using hypothetical scenarios and nondelinquent samples. While some studies have assessed the understanding and capacity of juvenile offenders, most research is nevertheless conducted under "ideal" conditions with a friendly examiner. This has meant that studies have failed to capture the stressful nature of police interrogations. Under stressful circumstances, juveniles' understanding, appreciation, and reasoning about interrogation rights may be poorer than these findings suggest (Grisso, 1997). For instance, experimental studies show that when stressful "interrogation" conditions are induced (e.g., students are accused of lying or cheating during an experiment) comprehension of arrest warnings goes down (Scherr & Madon, 2012, 2013).

Developmental Considerations

Adolescents are different from adults in one important way: They are at a stage in development where they are still undergoing important maturational changes, including significant physical maturation, budding sexuality, an increased awareness and sensitivity towards peers, and an increased desire for independence and identity development, to name only a few (Kazdin, 2000). These intersecting factors and developmental influences affect the way that youth make decisions, and in turn might affect how we view adolescents in conflict with the law. The U.S. Supreme Court decision in *Roper v. Simmons* (2005) is important for what it concludes about the decision making and judgment capacities of young people, and thus has implications for the manner in which our system of justice should deal with young people who are suspected of engaging in criminal activity. In *Roper*, the Court considered whether it was permissible, under the U.S. Constitution, to execute a juvenile offender (older than 15 but younger than 18) when a capital crime was committed. Christopher Simmons was 17 when he murdered a woman during an attempt to burglarize her home. Due to his age, he was automatically raised to adult court in the state of Missouri. Simmons confessed to the crime and was sentenced to death.

The Court considered briefs by a number of groups that presented evidence on the capacities of adolescents. Notable among these briefs to the court was one submitted by the American Psychological Association (APA, 2004). The APA brief reviewed the developmental research that shows that adolescents have considerably less capacity than adults in terms of judgment and decision making. Adolescence is marked by an increase in risk taking (Arnett, 1992), including engaging in criminal behavior. As Moffitt (1993) notes, this involvement in criminal activity, particularly when initiated in adolescence rather than childhood, typically does not persist into adulthood, and may reflect the fact that adolescents are immature and more heavily influenced by peers (Haynie, 2002). Adolescents are also less future oriented, and are less likely to weigh the consequences of their decisions (Cauffman & Steinberg, 2000). In other words, they often act impulsively (Halpern-Felsher & Cauffman, 2001). One compelling explanation for these differences between adolescents and adults is that cognitive capacities of adolescents are simply underdeveloped. Recent research on brain development shows that adolescent brains have not reached adult maturity, particularly in the frontal lobes, which control executive functions of the brain related to decision making. This area of the brain is typically not fully developed until the early 20s (Giedd et al., 1999; Steinberg, 2008). Younger children and adolescents are simply less likely to think strategically about their decisions (Peterson-Badali & Abramovitch, 1993). As adolescents mature, they typically become better problem solvers, are less influenced by peers, less impulsive, and more sophisticated in the way they think.

Even if a young person adequately understands the meaning of a *Miranda* warning, his or her appreciation of the consequences of the decision to either waive or exercise those rights may suffer given the relative level of maturity and development. Feld (2000) provided an example: "Inexperienced youths may waive their rights and speak to police in the short-sighted and unrealistic belief that their interrogation will end more quickly and secure their release" (p. 115). Moreover, development and maturation unfolds at varying rates from young person to young person, and it is key to remember that a great degree of variability in rights comprehension and decisional maturity may be attributed to individual differences between youths. A bright 12- or

13-year-old may have excellent understanding of *Miranda* rights while a less intellectually capable adult may struggle to comprehend the content of typical *Miranda* warnings.

Mental Health Professionals' Role in *Miranda* Comprehension Assessments

Mental health professionals may be asked to undertake an evaluation of a young person's *Miranda* comprehension and capacity to have waived the warnings. Often, such requests are made long after the time of waiver, when the validity or admissibility of a waiver and/or statement or confession has been brought into question. This type of retrospective evaluation can be challenging for a number of reasons. It can be difficult to assess an individual's capacities in the past, as replication of the circumstances under which a young person was asked to provide a waiver is impossible. Youth may have gained knowledge about arrest rights subsequent to the arrest. Parents, attorneys, and others may have informed them of what rights they had and what they should have done. They may have learned, through experience, the consequences of providing a waiver, and those consequences may have been poorly appreciated at the time of waiver. This is a retrospective evaluation, and what is relevant is what the youth knew and understood at the time of the arrest, not what they know and understand at the time of the evaluation. Evaluators need to keep this important distinction in mind as the evaluation proceeds.

As with any forensic evaluation, it is first key to clarify the nature and purpose of the evaluation. Next, it is important to inform youth about the purpose of the assessment, what information will be conveyed to the courts, and limits of confidentiality. The youth's understanding of this information should be assessed as it can provide relevant information on reasoning and understanding. Evaluators may wish to ask the youth to repeat what was said in their own words and probe when misunderstandings seem evident. Difficulties in understanding and providing informed consent may be included in the report as difficulties in this area may validate concerns about the validity of the *Miranda* waiver.

There are several sources of information that clinicians should obtain as part of a comprehensive evaluation of juvenile waiver of *Miranda* rights. First, details about the initial police contact should be gathered. How did police officers convey the *Miranda* warning to the youth? Where was the warning delivered and at what time? This information should be available in arrest reports, and there should be documentation showing that the youth was advised of his or her rights. This is often in the form of a signed waiver, in which youth initial the components of the waiver and sign indicating that the rights were understood. Ideally, an evaluator should obtain a copy of both the verbal warnings issued and any written waivers completed in order to evaluate the complexity and reading level of any waivers the young person was asked to make. If the youth has been arrested, he or she may then be interrogated by detectives. Detectives often repeat the warning to youth, and there may be either audiotape or videotape records of this waiver. Second, the youth's perspective should be obtained. Interviews with youth should focus on details of their experience with the police and with detectives, and what they understood at the time of the waiver. Information about the circumstances leading up to the waiver might also be critical, including whether the young person was well rested, stressed, emotionally aroused, as these types of factors may have had an influence on his or her state of mind and level of reasoning ability at the time warnings were administered. Third, parents or guardians should be interviewed to determine their role, if any, in the waiver. As we note elsewhere, parents may be involved and, indeed, may have encouraged their child to talk to the police. Fourth, various records should be obtained as appropriate and available from schools, mental health treatment providers, social services agencies, and criminal record. If possible, it may be useful to interview teachers. Prior testing, particularly intellectual functioning and personality assessments, should be obtained if available as they can provide an indication of the youth's functioning prior to arrest. Overall however, clinicians should be cognizant of the fact that the evaluation assesses *present* abilities and they should be cautious about making inferences about performance in the waiver situation (Grisso, 2003). Grisso (2003) also cautioned that clinicians should not testify about the ultimate legal issue before the court. He stated that,

> When circumstances allow the examiner to conclude that the individual probably understood very little about the rights at the time that they were waived, this still does not justify expert testimony regarding the validity of the waiver (i.e., testimony that the waiver was or was not made "knowingly, intelligently, and voluntarily"). Nothing about the empirical nature of the forensic assessment instruments justifies testimony by expert witnesses on questions that require moral and social judgments in the application of the legal standard. (p. 192)

Forensic Assessment Instruments

Miranda *Rights Comprehension Instruments*

In 1998, Grisso published the *Instruments for Assessing Understanding and Appreciation of* Miranda *Rights* for clinical use in assessing defendants' capacities to understand and appreciate the significance of their *Miranda* rights. These instruments have been widely adopted by forensic clinicians (Ryba, Brodsky, & Shlosberg, 2007). However, their content and normative data had not been revised since their original development more than 30 years ago. Goldstein, Zelle, and Grisso (2014) undertook a major revision of the tools, culminating in the recent publication of the Miranda *Rights Comprehension Instruments* (MRCI).

Like the original version, the MRCI includes four primary subscales: Comprehension of *Miranda* Rights–II (CMR-II, which assesses understanding of *Miranda* warnings through correctly paraphrasing their meaning); Comprehension of *Miranda* Rights-Recognition–II (CMR-R-II, which parallels the CMR-II but uses a recognition test format); Comprehension of *Miranda* Vocabulary–II (CMV-II, which examines understanding of vocabulary items in the *Miranda* warnings); and Function of Rights in Interrogation (FRI, which assesses appreciation of the meaning and function of the warnings using picture stimuli and contextualized vignettes). The revised instruments require 30 to 45 minutes to complete, an increase over the original instruments, largely owing to the addition of items across the CMR-II, CMR-R-II, and CMV-II.

Given the evolution of *Miranda* warnings across U.S. jurisdictions over time, Goldstein and her colleagues acknowledged a need for updating the original instruments. As such, the MRCI comprises key revisions to ensure the applicability of this measure to 21st-century clinical practice. First, given that the wording and language complexity of the original instruments may no longer generalize to modern-day warnings used by police forces, the authors simplified the item wording (now a Grade 7 reading level) and updated the vocabulary to better reflect an "average" *Miranda* warning. They also introduced a fifth warning prong (informing suspects they may stop questioning at any time). These updates appear well grounded in a review of the literature and analysis of approximately 50 warnings sampled from across the United States, although their discussion around their sampling procedure is somewhat limited. Scoring criteria for the new fifth warning and additional vocabulary items were developed in consultation with legal and psychological experts, and they were drafted in the same format as the original items.

Normative data comprising two samples of adolescents across the four instruments is presented in the manual. The first group consisted of 183 youth (43 girls) drawn from juvenile justice facilities in Massachusetts and Pennsylvania (ages 11 through 19), and the second, 64 youth (33 girls) attending a single mid-Atlantic college preparatory school (ages 10 through 16). While the juvenile justice sample was racially diverse, the school sample consisted primarily of Caucasian adolescents. The authors presented a variety of descriptive data characterizing the samples, including IQ and academic achievement scores, mental health symptom report data, and criminal justice system and *Miranda* experience, helping clinicians to contextualize the fit between a given examinee and the norms.

Goldstein and colleagues (Goldstein et al., 2011, 2014) have evaluated the psychometric properties of the new instruments using approaches parallel to those published with the original measures, as well as modern techniques. With respect to reliability indicators, the authors first assessed internal consistency. Scores ranged from low to moderate in value (.54 for the FRI through .75 for the CMV-II), though as was true for the original instruments, the authors caution that the short length of each scale and heterogeneity of the item content (drawn from real-world warnings) dampen these values and may not be the best indicator of stability for this type of tool. Subtotal-total and item-total scores generally fell within the moderate to high range. Based on data for 47 participants from the juvenile justice sample, test-retest reliability was moderate to high over an eight-day period, ranging from .53 (FRI) to .84 (CMV-II). Lastly, interrater reliability data for the entire juvenile justice sample across both trained and untrained raters suggested good stability, with intraclass correlation coefficients ranging from .83 (FRI, untrained rater) to .96 (CMV-II, untrained rater) and Pearson correlation coefficients of .80 (untrained raters) to .90 (trained raters) for the CMR-II.

The authors also presented strong evidence that supports the validity of the tool. The test development procedures, which included sampling of actual police warnings, suggest the measure has good content validity. No significant differences were found between scores on the old and revised instruments in a subsample of participants ($n = 16$), suggesting good criterion validity. Similarly, Cooper and Zapf (2008) administered the old and revised instruments[1] in a sample of 75 psychiatric inpatients and found no differences in performance on the instruments. Test authors reported moderate to large correlations, with both samples, between MRCI scores and measures thought to capture related constructs, including intellectual and academic functioning scores, lending evidence to the instruments' convergent validity. Similarly, strong intercorrelations between the four measures were demonstrated, ranging from .39 to .64 across both samples. Test users can also review additional psychometric data in a recent peer-reviewed publication of the MRCI (Goldstein et al., 2011).

The MRCI manual also includes a systematic law review of cases involving this tool (the original version) and extensive discussion around the legal relevance of the MCRI and assessments of capacity to waive *Miranda* more generally that clinicians may find helpful. This feature may be particularly useful in preparing clinicians for questions they may face in legal contexts as well as aiding in their conceptualization of the tool's admissibility in court.

Limitations

Grisso, and Goldstein and colleagues, provide a thoughtful discussion of the limitations of the MRCI and its predecessor. They emphasize that the MRCI cannot be used to measure totality of circumstances (e.g., other factors relevant to a capacity evaluation beyond understanding and appreciation of the *Miranda* warnings, such as fatigue or police pressure), as well as the aforementioned challenges inherent in undertaking retrospective forensic evaluations. A key challenge that arises in assessing *Miranda* rights comprehension is that the wording of the warnings differs considerably across jurisdictions (Helms, 2003; Rogers, Harrison, Shuman, Sewell, & Hazelwood, 2007). The earlier version of this tool was sometimes criticized on this basis both in academic contexts (e.g., Rogers, Jordan, & Harrison, 2004) and legal cases (e.g., *State v. Griffin*, 2005; *People v. Cole*, 2005). While it is unclear if this criticism will be allayed entirely in the updates to the tool, the authors provide sound clinical guidance and discussion regarding this issue. Specifically, they note the potential benefits of using a standardized approach (i.e., the ability to compare the youth to individuals with similar ages and IQ), and make the excellent point that the instruments are designed to assess understanding of concepts rather than simply their understanding of a simple set of words. The revised version is more likely to be representative of and consistent with the warnings used in various areas, and as such, concerns may be less likely to arise in this regard. Nevertheless, in instances in which significant discrepancies between the MRCI and local warnings arise, the authors wisely suggested a combined approach whereby clinicians would first administer the MRCI using standardized instructions, followed by a more qualitative analysis of understanding of local warnings. Future editions of the manual may offer more specific guidance on how an evaluator might undertake this challenge.

Prospective test users may also have questions about the normative data featured in the current edition of the test manual. While the juvenile justice sample appears relatively representative in terms of IQ, academic functioning, and ethnicity, it is possible that evaluators will be left with questions concerning the utility of the second community sample of youth, who had, overall, much higher intellectual scores than might be expected in general forensic practice. Some users might be interested in further clinical guidance regarding how best to use these data when interpreting scores from an average young person in relation to this sample of youth. Further normative data, including adult norms and psychometric data, will most certainly be forthcoming, and will strengthen the applicability of the instruments from a comparative perspective.

Other Assessment Issues and Measures

Intellectual and Achievement Measures

Intellectual ability and educational achievement form important elements of any assessment. Under the legal totality of circumstances test, these factors have been recognized by U.S. courts as contributing to a juvenile's overall comprehension of their *Miranda* rights at the time of waiver, and psychologists who conduct evaluations of *Miranda* rights comprehension report that they routinely evaluate intelligence and achievement (Ryba & Brodsky, 2005). As earlier described, intellectual ability strongly predicts rights comprehension, particularly in younger adolescents. Young suspects with intellectual disabilities are at particular risk for having poor rights comprehension (Everington & Fulero, 1999). Additional assessment steps should be taken if during the course of an evaluation clinicians' suspect that an examinee may have significant impairments in intellectual ability. However, in-depth assessment of intellectual and academic functioning may not be necessary in every case. For example, if an evaluator has access to the adolescent's school records and these demonstrate satisfactory, above-average academic achievement, there may be little reason to suspect that difficulties in intellectual ability may have impaired an examinee's rights comprehension.

Suggestibility

Assessors may consider evaluating a young person's suggestibility as an additional factor that could have influenced comprehension or capacity at the time of a *Miranda* waiver. Lawyers or judges often want evaluators to comment on the overall reliability of a statement or confession, and whether or not it was distorted or false in some way. It is important for clinicians to understand that the reliability of statements is a separate issue from the validity of *Miranda* rights waiver, which focuses on understanding and appreciation of *Miranda* rights. However, the GSS may provide some relevant information for evaluators during the course of such an assessment as one factor at play in the overall totality of circumstances surrounding a *Miranda* warning and waiver.

The GSS (Gudjonsson, 1997) measures interrogative suggestibility and taps into two distinct forms of suggestibility: the extent to which people yield to misleading questions, and the extent to which people shift their answers after receiving negative feedback. Two parallel forms of the GSS (GSS and GSS 2) are designed to measure "individual differences in the degree to which they may yield to suggestions by police officers" (Grisso, 2003, p. 164), and whether a person's confession may have been distorted or false (Gudjonsson, 1997). The measure is presented as an auditory memory test. After listening to a short fictional story, examinees are prompted to recall as many details from the story as they can both immediately, and again after a 50-minute delay. The second portion of the GSS asks participants 20 specific questions about the content of the story, 15 of which incorporate increasingly suggestive prompts. Regardless of an examinee's actual performance, the examiner provides negative feedback and then sternly asks the partici-pant to answer the questions again while trying to provide more accurate answers.

Five GSS subscale scores can be calculated: short and long delay recall memory scores are calculated by assigning one point for each element of the story that examinees are able to recall, ranging from 0 to 40. Two scores measuring the impact of suggestive questions (Yield 1 and Yield 2) can be calculated, and one point is assigned for each instance where examinees acknowledge the content of each of 15 suggestive questions (scores range from 0 to 15 for both subscales). One score measuring the impact of interrogative pressure (Shift) is calculated by assigning a point for each instance where the examinee provides a different response during the second round of questioning after receiving negative feedback (e.g., changing their answer from "Yes" to "No" or from "I do not remember" to "Yes"). Shift scores range from 0 to 20. A total suggestibility score is also calculated by summing the Yield 1 and Shift subscales. Clinicians can compare an examinee's performance on the GSS with normative data found in the GSS manual (Gudjonsson, 1997). The normative samples cover a wide range of demographic characteristics, and include adult and juvenile normative, correctional, custodial, and forensic populations, as well as norms for intellectually disabled adults.

Factor analysis conducted on both GSS forms clearly demonstrated that the two types of items (Yield and Shift) load on two separate factors. The GSS and GSS 2 subscales also yield good reliability, and the Yield and Shift subscales of the GSS yield acceptable reliability (Gudjonsson, 1997; Richardson & Smith, 1993).

Gudjonsson also developed the Gudjonsson Compliance Scale (GSC) as a self-report measure of compliance, and clinicians can also use this measure to complement the GSS assessment of suggestibility.

Mental Health Assessment

Mental health issues may also be a focus of an evaluation of capacity to waive *Miranda* rights. Research has consistently shown that mental health problems are especially prevalent in youth who are in conflict with the law (Penner, Roesch, & Viljoen, 2011). For example, a study by Teplin, Abram, McClelland, Dulcan, and Mericle (2002) of 1,829 youth in detention in Cook County, Illinois showed that two-thirds of the male youth and three-quarters of the female youth had one or more psychiatric disorders; about half the sample had indications of substance abuse; about 20% had a major depression; and approximately 16% of male offenders and 21% of female offenders were considered to have attention deficit hyperactivity disorder (ADHD). While psy-chotic disorders were rare, about 21% of male offenders and 31% of female offenders had an anxiety disorder. Other research has shown that conduct disorder is quite high, in some studies up to 90%, so the presence of conduct disorder is not particularly useful as an assessment focus or a guide for intervention. Finally, comorbidity is also common for young offenders, especially depression with substance abuse, ADHD, and anxiety disorders (Lexcen & Redding, 2002).

In addition, estimates suggest the prevalence of fetal alcohol spectrum disorder (FASD) is high in justice settings, with one Canadian estimate among youth in a forensic inpatient unit finding 23.3% of patients met diagnostic criteria for FASD (Fast, Conry, & Loock, 1999). FASD refers to a number of conditions stemming from prenatal exposure to alcohol that comprise a charac-teristic facial dysmorphology, growth restriction, and neurobehavioral impairments in function-ing. McLachlan and colleagues (2014) found that the majority of young offenders in their study had deficits in their understanding of Canadian arrest warnings (comparable to U.S. *Miranda* warnings). Individuals with FASD often present with deficits in intellectual ability, executive functioning, attention and impulse control, memory, adaptive functioning, and language and communication (see Mattson, Crocker, & Nguyen, 2011, for a review), as well as psychosocial immaturity, suggestibility, and a strong desire to please others (Brown, Gudjonsson, & Connor, 2011). McLachlan et al. (2014) caution that young offenders with FASD may be particularly vulnerable in the context of *Miranda* waivers and evaluators may want to query any history of prenatal exposure to alcohol or previous assessment/diagnosis for FASD in their evaluation.

It is not always immediately clear how mental health issues can affect waiver capacity. Research looking at groups and examining the influence of mental health symptoms such as depression and anxiety have failed to identify a relationship between psychopathology and *Miranda* rights comprehension per se (e.g., Viljoen & Roesch, 2005). However, given the totality of circumstances approach to a determination of the validity of rights waiver, an evaluation of an examinee's individual mental health symptoms may be important in some assessments. For example, it seems reasonable to suggest that adolescents who suffer from severe depression and suicidal ideation or attempts may not carefully evaluate and understand their legal rights or appreciate the consequences of waiving those legal rights. Viljoen and Roesch (2005) found that psychomotor agitation symptoms associated with ADHD inversely impacted scores on Grisso's (1998a) CMR and CMR-R Instruments. Suspects with ADHD or other attention-related problems may have difficulty concentrating long enough to understand and appreciate the *Miranda* waiver process, particularly if lengthy forms or explanatory protocols are in place. Given that these symptoms are common among adolescent offenders, consideration of assessing these factors should be made on a case-by-case basis.

In order to further illustrate the use of these instruments in practice, a case example is provided in the following section. For other examples of evaluations of *Miranda* rights comprehension, readers are advised to consult Heilbrun, Marczyk, and DeMatteo (2002) and Goldstein and Goldstein (2010).

Case Example

The following case example is based on a consultation by one of the chapter authors. Names and identifying information have been changed.

Daniel is a 13-year-old male of mixed race (African American/Caucasian) who was referred by his defense attorney for an assessment of his competency to waive his *Miranda* rights.[2] He appears small for his age. At the time of the evaluation, he was in detention at the Youth Services Center awaiting adjudication on charges of Rape in the Third Degree and Incest in the First Degree. At the time of his arrest, Daniel was a student in Grade 8 in special education.

The following tests were administered: Woodcock-Johnson III (WJ III), the MRCI, and the GCS. I also reviewed the following documents: Police Department Incident Report, Superior Court for County Juvenile Department Notice and Summons-Dependency, Department of Social and Health Services reports, court documents, police records, Child Protective Services (CPS) reports, and school records.

Daniel was living with both parents and his brother at the time of his arrest. Daniel's family has a history of economic difficulties. His parents have been unemployed for extended periods, were homeless for a time, and have lived in motels supported by state funds. CPS reports note a history of possible sexual abuse by a female babysitter. Daniel's mother was reported to have been sexually abused as a child. Several incidents of domestic violence involving Daniel's parents have been reported, as well as prior reports of Daniel's sexual abuse of his brother Mark, dating back to 2004. Daniel also has a history of seizures.

Daniel was arrested on January 10, 2012. Police officers responded to a call from a CPS social worker who had been notified by Daniel's brother Mark's school that Mark had reported that he had been sexually assaulted by Daniel. Officer B went to Daniel's home and first interviewed

Mark, who informed him that "his brother had sex with him and had inserted his penis into his body." The officer subsequently interviewed Daniel and asked him if "he had penetrated his brother with his penis." Daniel responded "yes." Based on these interviews, Officer B took Daniel into custody for investigation of Rape I. Daniel was not read his *Miranda* rights until he was at the East Precinct. Daniel was asked if he understood his rights and he responded, "Yes, I do." He was then asked to again relate the incident involving his brother.

Daniel commented in my interview with him that the police started asking him questions when he was first contacted and did not inform him that he did not have to talk to them. He also commented that he was scared because he had never been arrested before and had no prior contact with police.

Assessment

The assessment focused on two areas: cognitive functioning and capacity to waive *Miranda* rights.[3]

Cognitive Functioning

The WJ III is a comprehensive measure of cognitive functioning that research has indicated is accurate and reliable. Daniel was cooperative with testing, and appeared at ease and comfortable. However, he was fidgety and restless, and often distracted. To compensate for this, he was given an opportunity to take numerous short breaks. Although he attempted difficult tasks, he tended to give up easily, and was frequently impulsive and careless in responding.

On the WJ III, Daniel achieved a General Intellectual Ability score in the Very Low range (54). This suggests that Daniel's cognitive functioning is comparable to that of an average individual aged 7 years and 1 month. The WJ III provides three cognitive performance clusters in addition to the overall General Intelligence Ability score. On Thinking Ability (a measure of intentional cognitive processing), Daniel's score fell in the Borderline range (72). Daniel's performance on Verbal Ability fell in the in the Low range (68). His score on Cognitive Efficiency (a measure of automatic cognitive processing) was significantly lower (54).

The results of the WJ III are largely consistent with prior testing. At age 9, he was administered the Wechsler Intelligence Test for Children–III and obtained a full scale score of 73, which placed him in the Borderline range of functioning. His scores on achievement tests in the past have indicated significant delays in academic skills, including reading, writing, and math. Language comprehension deficits have also been documented.

Assessing Understanding and Appreciation of Miranda Rights

Daniel's behavior at arrest, when he was read his *Miranda* rights, and the subsequent interview by police, was assessed with several instruments. The MRCI was developed for clinical use in assessing defendants' capacities to understand and appreciate the significance of their *Miranda* rights. There are four subtests comprising this instrument. While these tests cover issues related to *Miranda* rights, they also provide an assessment of comprehension and understanding of legal issues and rights more broadly. Normative samples of juveniles drawn from both community and juvenile justice settings allow comparisons of an individual's score to other youth, including offenders.

The CMR-II assesses understanding of *Miranda* warnings through correctly paraphrasing their meaning. Daniel obtained a score of 10 of a possible 10, consistent with only 11.6% of juvenile offenders on this subtest. The CMR-R-II requires an ability to recognize the similarity between each right and three sentences related to each of these rights. Daniel obtained a score of 13 of 15, a score that was better than about 92% of juvenile offenders. The CMV-II evaluates understanding of vocabulary used in communicating *Miranda* rights. Daniel obtained a score of 10 of 12, which places him in the top one-third. The FRI uses drawings to assess perceptions of the functions of the *Miranda* warnings. Daniel obtained a score of 17 of a possible 32. His score was about two points below the mean for 13-year-olds. Daniel had difficulty in particular with the Right to Silence subtest of the FRI, in which he obtained a score of 4 of a possible 10. Overall, Daniel's scores on the CMR-II, CMR-R-II and CMV-II tests suggest that at present Daniel has an adequate understanding of the vocabulary used and the rights expressed in *Miranda* warnings—but his scores on the FRI subtests, all of which were below the mean for other juveniles, suggest that Daniel may have had difficulties understanding the nature of interrogation and his right to an attorney at the time he was questioned by police.

As part of the assessment of Daniel's understanding of his rights and his behavior during interrogation by the police, one additional instrument was used. The GCS is a self-report questionnaire that measures compliance with authority. Gudjonsson (1997) noted that, "Within the context of police interviewing and custodial confinement, of particular importance is the tendency of some individuals to comply with requests and obey instructions that they would rather not do, for instrumental gains (e.g., in order to terminate the police interview, be released from custody more quickly, escape from the stress of the situation, or to please the interviewer)" (p. 5). This instrument was administered by reading questions to Daniel, who was given a copy of questions to follow along, on which he circled his responses. Daniel's score on this instrument (12) was considerably higher than the average score of other juvenile offenders (M = 8.9, SD = 3.2). This suggests that he may be more compliant with authority figures, such as police, than other juvenile offenders.

Opinion About Competence to Waive *Miranda* Warning

Daniel's scores on the *Miranda* competency instrument raised some concerns about his competence to waive his *Miranda* rights. He had an adequate understanding of the basic vocabulary used in *Miranda* but had some confusion about his rights to remain silent and that he could have obtained an attorney prior to questioning. His level of cognitive functioning also raised concerns about his competence to understand and waive arrest rights.

Daniel was questioned about his behavior with his brother before he was read his *Miranda* warning. By that time, he had already responded to questions by the police officer, and was then asked to repeat them after he was taken into custody and was in a police station. The sequence of questioning is important to appreciate in terms of Daniel's understanding of his rights. By the time the *Miranda* warning was read to him, Daniel had already provided the arresting officer with information about the incident, and he may have felt that he should continue to respond to the same questions once the *Miranda* warning was read, since he had already provided this information to the police. His score on the compliance measure suggested that he may be more compliant with authority figures, compared to other juveniles, which may have influenced both his initial response to questions by the police officer as well as his acquiescence after receiving the *Miranda* warning at the police station.

I also showed Daniel the Explanation of Rights form he signed. He recalled signing it and said that his case worker and a male were present. He thought the male, who was actually Detective G, was his lawyer. I asked him if he understood he was giving up his right to silence and he said that he did. He believed he had to talk because Detective G told him that he had to tell him everything that happened.

It should also be noted that Daniel may be untruthful if he feels it will serve some purpose. For example, while he has been in detention, he told his mother that he had been beaten and threatened with rape. These allegations were investigated by a juvenile probation counselor, who stated that "Daniel finally admitted he had told his mother that these two things were happening because he thought she would be able to get him out of detention." He has also told several versions of the incident with his brother that differ from the original statement to the police.

Summary

Our legal system requires that in order to validly waive interrogation rights, including the rights to silence and counsel, juvenile (and adult) suspects must understand and appreciate the significance of these rights (*Miranda v. Arizona*, 1966; *In re Gault*, 1967; *Fare v. Michael C.*, 1979). The point of these laws is not to let guilty adolescents go free or get more lenient dispositions, but instead to ensure that confessions made are reliable, accurate, and obtained through fair means. As the legal system has become more punitive towards juvenile offenders, it has become more critical that youth understand and appreciate their *Miranda* rights. Research has demonstrated that adolescents, particularly young adolescents, may have higher rates of deficits in their comprehension of *Miranda* rights as a result of developmental immaturity (Goldstein et al., 2003; Viljoen & Roesch, 2005). In addition, in comparison to adults, adolescents may be more likely to yield to interrogative pressure (Richardson & Kelly, 2004), more likely to waive their interrogation rights (Viljoen et al., 2005), and more likely to falsely take responsibility for acts they did not commit (Redlich & Goodman, 2003). While courts may allow youths' parents to be present as a form of additional protection for young suspects, parents may encourage their children to waive their rights (Viljoen et al., 2005).

It is important for clinicians to take into account these developmental differences in youths' comprehension of *Miranda* rights and their ability to reason about waiver decisions. However, given individual variability in youths' capacities, clinicians cannot automatically assume that young age equates to poor comprehension. Indeed, although capacity increases with age, there is considerable variability and some 16- and 17-year-old adolescents may have less capacity than some 13- or 14-year-old adolescents.

In assessing youth's comprehension of *Miranda* rights, the MRCI may be a useful series of tools. The instruments were recently updated to modernize Grisso's original instruments, which are widely used by clinicians. During assessments, police records, accounts of the arrest, and other relevant collateral information should be carefully reviewed. In addition, depending on the characteristics of the case, clinicians should assess the youth's intelligence, achievement, suggestibility, and mental health, as well as the impact of caretaker involvement on the interrogation.

Notes

1   Cooper and Zapf (2008) employed an earlier, prepublication version of the MRCI-II that included two additional vocabulary items and minor differences on the CMR-II.
2   In order to protect client confidentiality, all identifying information regarding this case was removed and critical case details were extensively altered.
3   This assessment also included an evaluation of Daniel's competence to stand trial (adjudicative competence). This aspect of the evaluation is not covered here, however, it is discussed in "Assessing Adolescents' Adjudicative Competence" (Roesch & Viljoen, Chapter 12 in this volume).

References

Abramovitch, R., Peterson-Badali, M., & Rohan, M. (1995). Young people's understanding and assertion of their rights to silence and legal counsel. *Canadian Journal of Criminology, 37*, 1–18.

American Psychological Association. (2004). *Brief for the American Psychological Association, and the Missouri Psychological Association as amici curiae supporting respondent*. Washington, DC: Author.

Arnett, J. (1992). Reckless behavior in adolescence: A developmental perspective. *Developmental Review, 12*, 339–373. 10.1016/0273–2297(92)90013-R

Brown, N.N., Gudjonsson, G., & Connor, P. (2011). Suggestibility and fetal alcohol spectrum disorders (FASD): I'll tell you anything you want to hear. *Journal of Psychiatry and Law, 39*, 39–71.

Cauffman, E., & Steinberg, L. (2000). Immaturity of judgment in adolescence: Why adolescents may be less culpable than adults. *Behavioral Sciences & the Law, 18*, 741–760. doi: 10.1002/bsl.416

Cleary, H.M.D. (2014). Police interviewing and interrogation of juvenile suspects: A descriptive examination of actual cases. *Law and Human Behavior, 38*, 271–282. doi: 10.1037/lhb0000070

Colwell, L. H., Cruise, K. R., Guy, L. S., McCoy, W. K., Fernandez, K., & Ross, H. H. (2005). The influence of psychosocial maturity on male juvenile offenders' comprehension and understanding of the Miranda warning. *Journal of the American Academy of Psychiatry and Law, 33*, 444–454.

Cooper, V. G., & Zapf, P. A. (2008). Psychiatric patients' comprehension of Miranda rights. *Law and Human Behavior, 32*, 390–405. doi: 10.1007/s10979–007–9099–3

Danielsdottir, G., Sigurgeirdottir, S., Einarsdottir, H. R., & Haraldsson, E. (1993). Interrogative suggestibility in children and its relationship with memory and vocabulary. *Personality and Individual Differences, 14*, 499–502. doi: 10.1007/s10979–007–9099–3

Drizen, S., & Leo, R. (2004). The problem of false confessions in the post-DNA world. *North Carolina Law Review, 82*, 891–1011.

Everington, C., & Fulero, S. M. (1999). Competence to confess: Measuring understanding and suggestibility of defendants with mental retardation. *Mental Retardation, 37*, 212–220. doi: 10.1352/0047–6765(1999)037<0212:CTCMUA>2.0.CO;2

Fare v. Michael C., 442 U.S. 707 (1979).

Fast, D. K., Conry, J., & Loock, C. A. (1999). Identifying fetal alcohol syndrome among youth in the criminal justice system. *Journal of Developmental & Behavioral Pediatrics, 20*, 370–372. doi: 10.1097/00004703–199910000–00012

Feld, B. C. (2000). Juveniles' waiver of legal rights: Confessions, Miranda, and the right to counsel. In T. Grisso & R. G. Schwartz (Eds.), *Youth on trial: A developmental perspective on juvenile justice* (pp. 105–138). Chicago: University of Chicago Press.

Feld, B. C. (2013). Real interrogation: What actually happens when cops question kids. *Law & Society Review, 47*, 1–36. doi: 10.1111/lasr.12000

Frumkin, I., Lally, S. J., & Sexton, J. E. (2012). The Grisso tests for assessing understanding and appreciation of Miranda warnings with a forensic sample. *Behavioral Sciences & The Law, 30*, 673–692. doi:10.1002/bsl.2018

Giedd, J., Blumenthal, J., Jeffries, N., Castellanos, F., Liu, H., Ijdenbos, A., . . . Rapoport, J. (1999). Brain development during childhood and adolescence: A longitudinal MRI study. *Nature Neuroscience, 2*, 861–863. doi: 10.1038/13158

Goldstein, A. M., & Goldstein, N.E.S. (2010). *Evaluating capacity to waive Miranda rights*. New York: Oxford University Press.

Goldstein, N.E.S., Condie, L. O., Kalbeitzer, R., Osman, D., & Geier, J. L. (2003). Juvenile offenders' Miranda rights comprehension and self-report likelihood of offering false confessions. *Assessment, 10*, 359–369. doi: 10.1177/1073191103259535

Goldstein, N.E.S., Riggs Romaine, C., Zelle, H., Kalbeitzer, R., Mesiarik, C., & Wolbransky, M. (2011). Psychometric properties of the Miranda Rights Comprehension Instruments with a juvenile justice sample. *Assessment, 18*, 428–441. doi: 10.1177/1073191111400280

Goldstein, N.E.S., Zelle, H., & Grisso, T. (2014). *The Miranda Rights Comprehension Instruments: Manual for use with juveniles and adults*. Sarasota, FL: Professional Resource Press.

Graham v. Florida, 560 U.S. 48 (2010).

Grisso, T. (1981). *Juvenile's waiver of rights: Legal and psychological competence*. New York: Plenum. doi: 10.1007/978–1–4684–3815–4

Grisso, T. (1997). The competence of adolescents as trial defendants. *Psychology, Public Policy, and Law, 3*, 3–32. doi: 10.1037/1076–8971.3.1.3

Grisso, T. (1998a). *Instruments for assessing understanding and appreciation of* Miranda *rights*. Sarasota, FL: Professional Resources.

Grisso, T. (1998b). *Forensic evaluations of juveniles*. Sarasota, FL: Professional Resource Exchange.

Grisso, T. (2003). *Evaluating competencies: Forensic assessments and instruments*. New York: Kluwer Academic/Plenum Press.

Grisso, T., Steinberg, L., Woolard, J., Cauffman, E., Scott, E., Graham, S. . . . Schwartz, R. (2003). Juveniles' competence to stand trial: A comparison of adolescents' and adults' capacities as trial defendants. *Law and Human Behavior, 27*, 333–363. doi: 10.1023/A:1024065015717

Gudjonsson, G. H. (1984). A new scale of interrogative suggestibility. *Personality and Individual Differences, 3*, 303–314. doi: 10.1016/0191–8869(84)90069–2

Gudjonsson, G. H. (1990). The relationship of intellectual skills to suggestibility, compliance and acquiescence. *Personality and Individual Differences, 11*, 185–186. doi: 10.1016/0191–8869(90)90012-G

Gudjonsson, G.H. (1997). *Gudjonsson Suggestibility Scales*. East Sussex: Psychology Press.

Gudjonsson, G.H., & Clark, N.K. (1986). Suggestibility in police interrogation: a social psychological model. *Social Behaviour, 1*, 83–104.

Halpern-Felsher, B.L., & Cauffman, E. (2001). Costs and benefits of a decision. Decision-making competence in adolescents and adults. *Journal of Applied Developmental Psychology, 22*, 257–273. doi: 10.1016/S0193–3973(01)00083–1

Haynie, D.L. (2002). Friendship networks and delinquency: The relative nature of peer delinquency. *Journal of Quantitative Criminology, 18*, 99–134. doi: 10.1023/A:1015227414929

Heilbrun, K., Marczyk, G.R., & DeMatteo, D. (2002). *Forensic mental health assessment: A casebook*. New York: Oxford University Press.

Helms, J. (2003). Analysis of Miranda reading levels across jurisdictions: Implications for evaluating waiver competency. *Journal of Forensic Psychology Practice, 3*, 25–37. doi: 10.1300/J158v03n01_03

In re Gault, 387 U.S. 1 (1967).

J.D.B. v. North Carolina, 131 S.Ct. 2394 (2011).

Kassin, S.M. (2005). On the psychology of confessions: Does innocence put innocents at risk? *American Psychologist, 60*, 215–228. doi: 10.1037/0003–066X.60.3.215

Kassin, S.M., Drizin, S.A., Grisso, T., Gudjonsson, G.H., Leo, R.A., & Redlich, A.D. (2010). Police-induced confessions: Risk factors and recommendations. *Law and Human Behavior, 34*, 3–38. doi: 10.1007/s10979–009–9188–6

Kazdin, A.E. (2000). Adolescent development, mental disorders, and decision making of delinquent youths. In T. Grisso & R.G. Schwartz (Eds.), *Youth on trial: A developmental perspective on juvenile justice* (pp. 33–65). Chicago: University of Chicago Press.

Kent v. United States, 383 U.S. 541 (1966).

King, L., & Snook, B. (2009). Peering inside a Canadian interrogation room: An examination of the Reid model of interrogation, influence tactics, and coercive strategies. *Criminal Justice and Behavior, 36*, 676–694. doi: 10.1177/0093854809335142

Lassiter, G.D. (Ed.). (2004). *Interrogations, confessions, and entrapment, Vol. 20*. New York: Kluwer Academic/Plenum. doi: 10.1007/978–0–387–38598–3

Leo, R.A. (2008). *Police interrogation and American justice*. Cambridge, MA: Harvard University Press.

Leo, R.A., & Drizin, S.A. (2010). The three errors: Pathways to false confession and wrongful conviction. In G. Lassiter & C.A. Meissner (Eds.), *Police interrogations and false confessions: Current research, practice, and policy recommendations* (pp. 9–30). Washington, DC: American Psychological Association. doi: 10.1037/12085–001

Lexcen, F., & Redding, R. (2002). Mental health needs of juvenile offenders. *Juvenile Correctional Mental Health Report, 3*, 1–16.

Malloy, L.C., Shulman, E.P., & Cauffman, E. (2014). Interrogations, confessions, and guilty pleas among serious adolescent offenders. *Law and Human Behavior, 38*, 181–193. doi: 10.1037/lhb0000065

Mattson, S.N., Crocker, N., & Nguyen, T.T. (2011). Fetal alcohol spectrum disorders: neuropsychological and behavioral features. *Neuropsychology Review, 21*, 81–101. doi: 10.1007/s11065–011–9167–9

Miranda v. Arizona, 384 U.S. 436 (1966).

McLachlan, K., Roesch, R., & Douglas, K.S. (2011). Examining the role of interrogative suggestibility in Miranda rights comprehension in adolescents. *Law and Human Behavior, 35*, 165–177. doi: 10.1007/s10979–009–9198–4

McLachlan, K., Roesch, R., Viljoen, J.L., & Douglas, K.S. (2014). Evaluating the psycholegal abilities of young offenders with fetal alcohol spectrum disorder. *Law and Human Behavior, 38*, 10. doi: 10.1037/lhb0000037

Moffitt, T.E. (1993). Adolescence-limited and life-course-persistent antisocial behavior: A developmental taxonomy. *Psychological Review, 100*, 674–701. doi: 10.1037/0033–295X.100.4.674

Muris, P., Meesters, C., & Merckelbach, H. (2004). Correlates of the Gudjonsson Suggestibility Scale in delinquent adolescents. *Psychological Reports, 94*, 264–266. doi: 10.2466/pr0.94.1.264–266

Oberlander, L.B., Goldstein, N.E., & Goldstein, A.M. (2003). Competence to confess. In A.M. Goldstein (Ed.), *Handbook of psychology, Vol. 11: Forensic psychology* (pp. 335–357). New York: Wiley.

Owen-Kostelnik, J., Reppucci, N.D., & Meyer, J.R. (2006). Testimony and interrogation of minors: Assumptions about maturity and morality. *American Psychologist, 61*, 286–304. doi: 10.1037/0003–066X.61.4.286

Penner, E. K., Roesch, R., & Viljoen, J. L. (2011). Juvenile offenders: An international comparison of mental health assessment and treatment practices. *International Journal of Forensic Mental Health, 10,* 215–232. doi: 10.1080/14999013.2011.598427

Penney, S. R., & Moretti, M. M. (2005). The transfer of juveniles to adult court in Canada and the United States: Confused agendas and compromised assessment procedures. *International Journal of Forensic Mental Health, 4,* 19–37. doi: 10.1080/14999013.2005.10471210

People v. Cole, 807 N. Y.S.2d 166 (N. Y. App. Div. 2005).

Peterson-Badali, M., & Abramovitch, R. (1993). Grade related changes in young people's reasoning about plea decisions. *Law and Human Behavior, 17,* 537–552. doi: 10.1007/BF01045072

Peterson-Badali, M., Abramovitch, R., Koegl, C. J., & Ruck, M. D. (1999). Young people's experience of the Canadian youth justice system: Interacting with police and legal counsel. *Behavioral Sciences and the Law, 17,* 455–465. doi: 10.1002/(SICI)1099–0798(199910/12)17:4<455::AID-BSL358>3.0.CO;2-R

Pollard, R., Trowbridge, B., Slade, P. D., Streissguth, A. P., Laktonen, A., & Townes, B. D. (2004). Interrogative suggestibility in a U.S. context: Some preliminary data on normal subjects. *Personality and Individual Differences, 37,* 1101–1108. doi: 10.1016/j.paid.2003.12.004

Redding, R. E., Goldstein, N.E.S., & Heilbrun, K. (2005). Juvenile delinquency: Past and present. In K. Heilbrun, N.E.S. Goldstein, & R. E. Redding (Eds.), *Juvenile delinquency: Prevention, assessment, and intervention* (pp. 3–18). New York: Oxford University Press.

Redlich, A. D., & Goodman, S. (2003). Taking responsibility for an act not committed: The influence of age and suggestibility. *Law and Human Behavior, 27,* 141–156. doi: 10.1023/A:1022543012851

Redlich, A. D., Silverman, M., & Steiner, H. (2003). Pre-adjudicative and adjudicative competence in juveniles and young adults. *Behavioral Sciences and the Law, 21,* 393–410. doi: 10.1002/bsl.543

Richardson, G., & Kelly, T. P. (1995). The relationship between intelligence, memory and interrogative suggestibility in young offenders. *Psychology, Crime & Law, 1,* 283–290. doi: 10.1080/10683169508411965

Richardson, G., & Kelly, T. P. (2004). A study in the relationship between interrogative suggestibility, compliance and social desirability in institutionalized adolescents. *Personality and Individual Differences, 36,* 485–494. doi: 10.1016/S0191–8869(03)00263–0

Richardson, G., & Smith, P. (1993). The inter-rater reliability of the Gudjonsson Suggestibility Scale. *Personality and Individual Differences, 14,* 251–253.

Rogers, R., Fiduccia, C. E., Robinson, E. V., Steadham, J. A., & Drogin, E. Y. (2013). Investigating the effects of repeated Miranda warnings: Do they perform a curative function on common Miranda misconceptions? *Behavioral Sciences and the Law, 41,* 397–410. doi: 10.1002/bsl.2071

Rogers, R., Harrison, K. S., Shuman, D. W., Sewell, K. W., & Hazelwood, L. L. (2007). An analysis of Miranda warnings and waivers: Comprehension and coverage. *Law and Human Behavior, 31,* 177–192. doi: 10.1007/s10979–006–9054–8

Rogers, R., Hazelwood, L. L., Sewell, K. W., Shuman, D. W., & Blackwood, H. L. (2008). The comprehensibility and content of juvenile *Miranda* warnings. *Psychology, Public Policy, and Law, 14,* 63-87.

Rogers, R., Jordan, M. J., & Harrison, K. S. (2004). A critical review of published competency-to-confess measures. *Law and Human Behavior, 28,* 707–718. doi: 10.1007/s10979–004–0794-z

Rogers, R., Rogstad, J. E., Steadham, J. A., & Drogin, E. Y. (2011). In plain English: Avoiding recognized problems with Miranda miscomprehension. *Psychology, Public Policy, and Law, 17,* 264–285. doi: 10.1037/a0022508

Rogers, R., Steadham, J. A., Fiduccia, C. E., Drogin, E. Y., & Robinson, E. V. (2014). Mired in Miranda misconceptions: A study of legally involved juveniles at different levels of psychosocial maturity. *Behavioral Sciences and the Law, 32,* 104–120. doi:10.1002/bsl.2099

Roper v. Simmons, 543 U.S. 541 (2005).

Ryba, N. L., & Brodsky, S. L. (2005, March). *Competency to waive Miranda rights: Frequency and style of test usage.* Paper presented at the American Psychology-Law Society Conference, La Jolla, CA. doi: 10.1177/1073191110730284

Ryba, N. L., Brodsky, S. L. & Shlosberg, A. (2007). Evaluations of capacity to waive Miranda rights: A survey of practitioners' use of the Grisso Instruments. *Assessment, 14,* 300–309.

Scherr, K. C., & Madon, S. (2012). You have the right to understand: The deleterious effect of stress on suspects' ability to comprehend Miranda. *Law and Human Behavior, 36,* 275–282. doi: 10.1037/h0093972

Scherr, K. C., & Madon, S. (2013). "Go ahead and sign": An experimental examination of Miranda waivers and comprehension. *Law and Human Behavior, 37,* 208–218. doi: 10.1037/lhb0000026

Singh, K. K., & Gudjonsson, G. H. (1992). Interrogative suggestibility among adolescent boys and its relationship with intelligence, memory, and cognitive set. *Journal of Adolescence, 15,* 155–161. doi: 10.1016/0140–1971(92)90044–6

State v. Griffin, 869 A.2d 604 (Conn. 2005).

Steinberg, L. (2008). A social neuroscience perspective on adolescent risk-taking. *Developmental Review, 28,* 78–106. doi: 10.1016/j.dr.2007.08.002

Teplin, L. A., Abram, K. M., McClelland, G., M., Dulcan, M. K., & Mericle, A. A. (2002). Psychiatric disorders in youth in juvenile detention. *Archives of General Psychiatry, 59,* 1133–1143. doi: 10.1001/archpsyc.59.12.1133

Viljoen, J. L., Klaver, J., & Roesch, R. (2005). Legal decisions of preadolescent and adolescent defendants: Predictors of confessions, pleas, communication with attorneys, and appeals. *Law and Human Behavior, 29,* 253–257. doi: 10.1007/s10979–005–3613–2

Viljoen, J. L., & Roesch, R. (2005). Competence to waive interrogation rights and adjudicative competence in adolescent defendants: Cognitive development, attorney contact, and psychological symptoms. *Law and Human Behavior, 29,* 723–742. doi: 10.1007/s10979–005–7978–y

Warren, A., Hulse-Trotter, K., & Tubbs, E. C. (1991). Inducing resistance to suggestibility in children. *Law and Human Behavior, 15,* 273–285. doi: 10.1007/BF01061713

Woolard, J. L., Cleary, H. M., Harvell, S. A., & Chen, R. (2008). Examining adolescents' and their parents' conceptual and practical knowledge of police interrogation: A family dyad approach. *Journal of Youth and Adolescence, 37,* 685–698. /10.1007/s10964–008–9288–5

12 Assessing Adolescents' Adjudicative Competence

Ronald Roesch and Jodi L. Viljoen

It is a long-held principle within adult criminal court that individuals charged with crimes must be competent to proceed to adjudication (competent to stand trial), meaning that they must be able to adequately understand and participate in legal proceedings against them. While historically the requirement that defendants must be competent did not apply to juvenile defendants, over the past several decades courts have increasingly required that juvenile defendants must be competent to proceed to adjudication (Kruh & Grisso, 2009). This trend has led to growth in the numbers of competency evaluations requested for juveniles (Grisso & Quinlan, 2005; Redding & Frost, 2002).

This chapter describes currently available information regarding the assessment of adolescents' competency and focuses on the unique developmental considerations that may arise in evaluating adolescents' competency.[1] To start, relevant legal standards and processes are discussed, and research on adolescents' legal capacities is reviewed. Following that, the evaluation process is described.

Background on Juvenile Competence

Legal Requirements for Adolescents' Competence

Competence in Adult Criminal Court

Since as far back as the 17th century, the criminal justice system has required that adult defendants accused of crimes must be competent to proceed to adjudication (Bonnie, 1992). This requirement aims to protect the fairness and dignity of legal proceedings, the accuracy of adjudications, and defendants' decision-making autonomy.

The modern U.S. legal standard for competence to stand trial was established in 1960 in *Dusky v. United States*. According to *Dusky*, defendants must have "rational as well as factual understanding of proceedings" and "sufficient present ability to consult with his lawyer" (p. 402). Later court cases have emphasized that defendants must be able to assist his or her attorney (*Drope v. Missouri*, 1975) and adequately reason about specific legal decisions, such as how to plead and whether to assert or waive the right to counsel (*Godinez v. Moran*, 1993). Bonnie (1992) has referred to these reasoning abilities as "decisional competence," whereas he considers factual and rational understanding and the ability to communicate with counsel to be "foundational" abilities.

The Canadian legal standard for adjudicative competence (fitness to stand trial) is similar to the U.S. standard, but is narrower in scope and focuses on the "foundational" abilities of understanding and communication (Zapf & Roesch, 2001). In particular, as defined in the Criminal Code of Canada (1985, S. 2), defendants must "understand the nature and object of legal proceedings," "understand the possible consequences of legal proceedings," and be able to "communicate with counsel."

Although adjudicative competence is often raised at the same time as the insanity defense, they are separate issues. Specifically, while the insanity defense focuses on a defendant's mental state at the time of the offense, adjudicative competence focuses on a defendant's mental state and legal capacities at the time of adjudication.

The Growing Importance of Juvenile Competency

While the initial focus of the juvenile justice system was on rehabilitation, the juvenile justice system has gradually evolved to become more punishment oriented. Scott and Steinberg (2008) commented that "In less than a generation, a justice system that had viewed most young law-breakers as youngsters whose crimes were the product of immaturity was transformed into one that stands ready to hold many youths to the same standard of criminal accountability it imposes on adults" (p. 16).

During the 1960s and 1970s, there was growing disillusionment about the system's effectiveness in treating youth as well as civil liberty concerns about the lack of consistency and procedural safeguards for youth. In 1966, Justice Fortas argued that a child handled by the juvenile justice system "receives the worst of both worlds . . . he gets neither the protection afforded to adults nor the solicitous care and rejuvenative treatment postulated for children" (*Kent v. United States*, 1966, pp. 555–556).

The following year, *In re Gault* (1967) extended a number of rights that apply to adults involved in criminal proceeding to juveniles involved in delinquency proceedings. These rights included the rights of notice of charges, assistance of counsel, cross-examination of witnesses, and privilege against self-incrimination. The rights of adolescents were extended further in the case of *In re Winship* (1970), which established that findings of guilt in juvenile court must, as in adult court, be established beyond a reasonable doubt.

Although these cases did not specifically establish a requirement for juveniles to be competent, they emphasized an increasing concern regarding juveniles' rights and protections, and opened the door for juvenile competency to be considered. By the late 1980s, approximately one-third of states recognized the right of juveniles to be competent to stand trial in juvenile court (Grisso, Miller, & Sales, 1987). Nevertheless, the issue of adjudicative competence was rarely raised at that time.

During the 1990s, violent crime by juveniles was perceived to have increased (Snyder, Sickmund, & Poe-Yamagata, 1996), a perception that some scholars have considered inaccurate (Slobogin & Fondacaro, 2011). Although this trend has since abated, public alarm over juvenile violence was sufficient enough to lead to a number of dramatic changes in the juvenile justice system. These changes, which remain in place, effectively made the juvenile justice system more similar to the adult criminal justice system. Specifically, four substantive changes in the manner in which youth are charged with criminal offenses have made juvenile competence to stand trial an issue that is now more frequently considered. First, while *parens patriae* (the notion of a benevolent court system that considered rehabilitation paramount) was once the guiding philosophy of the juvenile justice system, juvenile court dispositions have become lengthier and more severe (Bonnie & Grisso, 2000; Gilles & Jackson, 2003). Second, the age at which a youth can be charged with a criminal offense has been lowered in many jurisdictions, and some states allow youth as young as 7 to be charged in juvenile court or even possibly transferred to adult court. Stahl et al. (2007) reported that over half of all juvenile cases involved youth under 15, with a 24% increase in charges against youth 12 or under. As we will discuss later in this chapter, findings of incompetence are higher for youth under 15. Third, transfer to adult court has increased substantially, which results in many adolescents being processed in adult court and receiving adult sentences, placing youth at increased risk for physical and sexual abuse in prisons (Mulvey & Schubert, 2012; Redding, Goldstein, & Heilbrun, 2005). These transfers can result from prosecutorial discretion in which a juvenile hearing determines whether the youth remains in the juvenile system or is waived to the adult criminal justice system, but many jurisdictions allow for automatic transfer so that a youth charged with a violent offense is waived to adult court without any court hearing. Even when youth remain in the juvenile justice system, juvenile offenses can be included when three-strikes laws are applied to adults (Kruh & Grisso, 2009). Fourth, it is no longer guaranteed that juvenile court hearings in some states will be held confidential or that a youth's juvenile court records will be expunged upon turning 18 years old.

These changes have made it more important that youth are able to understand and effectively participate in legal proceedings against them. Therefore, more and more jurisdictions have explicitly established a requirement that juveniles tried in juvenile court as well as criminal court must be competent (Bonnie & Grisso, 2000; Scott & Grisso, 2005; Redding & Frost, 2002; Youth Criminal Justice Act, 2002).

Standards of Juvenile Competence

Although there is growing consensus that juveniles must be competent, there is less agreement as to what legal standard of competence should apply. In general, the adult standard of competency has been applied to youth tried in adult criminal court (Redding & Frost, 2002). This means that youth tried in criminal court must be able to understand legal proceedings and consult with counsel. Presumably, youth must also have adequate decision-making capacities, as required by *Godinez v. Moran* (1993).[2]

For youth tried in juvenile court, however, legal standards remain unclear and inconsistent. The most recent statistics indicate that less than half the states have statutes that explicitly addressed juvenile competency (National Conference of State Legislatures, 2014; see also Brown, 2012). Other states have addressed the issue by ruling that adjudicative competence requirements apply to juveniles tried in juvenile court, but a number of states have not yet even addressed the issue (Redding & Frost, 2002; Scott & Grisso, 2005). Courts that have ruled that juveniles tried in juvenile court must be competent have typically held that juveniles must possess the same types of legal capacities as adults (factual and rational understanding, and communication). However, courts differ as to whether juveniles required the same *levels* of these legal capacities as adults (Redding & Frost, 2002). Specifically, some courts have ruled that lower levels of these abilities may suffice for juveniles tried in juvenile court. Slobogin and Fondacaro (2011) suggest that the standard for adjudicative competence might well be different in juvenile court:

> To meet the due process standard of adjudicative competence, the juvenile offender would still need to be able to provide and follow factual accounts well enough to be able to challenge erroneous information about the triggering act and the relevant risk factors. But more elaborate cognitive abilities may not be necessary, at least if an attorney is also present. Thus, a demonstration that the child is competent to testify . . . along with assurance that the youth's attorney knows how to deal with young, often reticent, clients, may suffice for adjudicative competence. (p. 115)

Slobogin and Fondacaro (2011) also note that decisional competence may be less important. Citing the literature on maturity and autonomy (which will be discussed later in this chapter), they suggest that given the finding that juveniles "have less autonomy than adults and thus need or are perceived to need more paternalistic oversight, then perhaps juvenile offenders should not have complete control of the decisions in their case" (pp. 115–116).

Kruh and Grisso (2009) provided an excellent discussion of whether adult criminal court standards should be applied in juvenile cases. They summarized three approaches applying different schemes for differentially applying the *Dusky* standard in juvenile court. The *adjusted bar* holds that different demands are placed on juvenile court defendants compared to adult defendants, suggesting that different abilities may be needed. For example, cases involving the possibility of waiver to adult court may require a higher level of rational understanding and decision-making abilities than cases involving juvenile court adjudications that are more limited in their consequences. The *lower bar* standard recognizes the *Dusky* abilities but proposes that a lower level of those abilities may be acceptable in juvenile court. Kruh and Grisso noted that the juvenile justice system is intended to provide services that benefit youth, which would be prevented by a finding of incompetence. Kruh and Grisso were skeptical about applying either of these standards as both raise significant threats to due-process protections. However, they saw some merit in the *flexible bar* standard, in which the level of competence required would match the level of needed protection. A lower threshold would apply in cases involving less serious offenses or sanctions, whereas a similar standard to adult court would apply in cases in which the juvenile faces sanctions similar to adult court sanctions. We believe this hybrid option has merit as it is consistent with the functional approach to assessing competence that has been advocated for competence evaluations of adults as well as juveniles (Kruh & Grisso, 2009; Zapf & Roesch, 2009).

Still another source of uncertainty regarding legal standards for juvenile competence is what constitutes an acceptable basis for a finding of incompetence. Historically, legal standards of competence have focused on mental illness and mental retardation as possible causes of legal deficits (Grisso, 2005; Criminal Code of Canada, 1985). For adolescents, legal deficits may result from mental illness, but may also stem from age-related factors such as developmental immaturity (see Viljoen, Penner, & Roesch, 2012 for a review). While some states (e.g., California, Louisiana) explicitly recognize immaturity as a basis for a finding of incompetence, most states have not yet offered a finding on this issue (Grisso, 2005). Indeed, there is considerable scholarly debate about whether immaturity should be a consideration as a factor in determining the competence of juveniles (see Sanborn, 2009, and Wingrove, 2007 for opposing views). Many juvenile court judges appear to recognize developmental immaturity and other age-related factors as a basis for findings of incompetence even without a specific legal mandate to do so (Cox, Goldstein, Dolores, Zelechoski, & Messenheimer, 2012; Viljoen & Wingrove, 2008). It is likely that many states will adopt explicit language about immaturity as various groups pressure legislators to address this issue. For example, the Models for Change initiative has presented guidelines to assist states considering developing or amending juvenile competence to stand trial statutes, recommending a multitiered system that takes both age and developmental immaturity into account (Larson & Grisso, 2012).

The Legal Process

There are a number of stages in legal proceedings involving competence (Grisso, 2003). First, a competence evaluation is requested; this step is often called *raising the issue* of competence. Following this, if the court orders an evaluation, a mental health professional typically will evaluate the defendant's competence and then the court will make a determination as to whether the defendant is incompetent. If a defendant is deemed incompetent, efforts are made to "restore" the defendant to competence, and the defendant's competence is periodically reevaluated through court hearings. In the following section, these stages in juvenile competence proceedings are examined.

Raising the Issue of Competence

When it appears that a juvenile defendant may lack the necessary legal capacities to understand and/or participate in the adjudicative process, the issue of competence must be raised by the defense attorney, judge, or prosecutor. It is unclear exactly how commonly the issue of juvenile competence is raised. However, there is evidence that the number of requests for evaluations is increasing significantly (Grisso & Quinlan, 2005; Redding & Frost, 2002).

As with adults, concerns have been expressed that the issue of juvenile competence may be inappropriately raised to delay the trial or to obtain mental health treatment when more direct means are not easily attainable (Barnum & Grisso, 1994; Grisso et al., 1987; Roesch & Golding, 1980). While obtaining treatment may be an important goal, using competency evaluations to do this may have negative effects, such as delaying the trial and leading to possible stigma for the youth.

Although overuse of competency referrals is a serious concern, an even greater concern is that juvenile defendants who are potentially incompetent are not identified (Barnum & Grisso, 1994). In order to prevent underidentification of potentially incompetent youth, Grisso et al. (1987) recommended that a juvenile defendant's competence automatically be evaluated when a youth is 12 years old or younger; has a prior diagnosis of or treatment for mental illness or mental retardation; has intellectual deficits or a learning disability; and/or appears to have deficits in memory, attention, or reality testing.

Competency Evaluation and Judicial Determination

Once the issue of competence is raised, courts generally order that an evaluation be conducted. In several U.S. jurisdictions, including Virginia and the District of Columbia, competence must be evaluated whenever a youth is transferred to adult court (Redding & Frost, 2002). However, the large majority of jurisdictions do not have such a rule.

Typically, state statutes require that juvenile competency evaluations be conducted by a licensed physician, psychiatrist, or psychologist, and some states require two separate competency evaluations. As with adult defendants, there is a preference for juvenile evaluations to be conducted on an outpatient basis unless an inpatient setting is considered necessary (Redding & Frost, 2002).

The length of time given to complete a competence evaluation varies considerably across states, ranging from 10 days to 90 days (Grisso, 1998). While short evaluation periods may help prevent unnecessary trial delays for youth, it may be challenging for evaluators to conduct comprehensive evaluations in short periods. Based on a survey of over 80 juvenile court clinics, Grisso and Quinlan (2005) found that the average time that evaluators spend on juveniles' competency evaluations ranges from 2 to 30 hours, with an average of 8 hours.

As with adult defendants, relatively few youth (14%–18%) who are referred for competence evaluations appear to be found incompetent (Cowden & McKee, 1995; McKee, 1998; McKee & Shea, 1999). However, young adolescents may be more likely than older adolescents to be found incompetent. For instance, a study from South Carolina reported that only 17% of defendants younger than 12 were judged competent to stand trial as compared to 84% of 15-year-olds (Cowden & McKee, 1995; see also Baerger, Griffin, Lyons, & Simmons, 2003). In a study in Washington state, Kruh, Sullivan, Ellis, Lexcen, and McClellan (2006) found that over half of the youth between 9 and 14 were found incompetent.

While the large majority of adults who are judged incompetent have psychotic disorders, only a small percentage of youth found incompetent have psychotic disorders (Kruh et al., 2006; McGaha, Otto, McClaren, & Petrila, 2001). On one hand, to a large extent, this is because psychotic disorders often do not develop until late adolescence or early adulthood (American Psychiatric Association, 2013). On the other, mental retardation may be fairly common among adolescent defendants according to figures from Florida (McGaha et al., 2001).

Once an evaluation of competence is complete, a judicial determination regarding competence is made. Since competency is a legal issue, a judge must make the final determination. However, research with adult defendants has indicated that courts defer to the opinions of mental health professionals in the large majority of cases (Zapf, Hubbard, Cooper, Wheeles, & Ronan, 2004). It is likely that courts also defer to clinicians in cases involving youth, although research has not yet investigated this.

Treatment and Rehearings for Youth Found Incompetent

If a defendant is deemed incompetent by the court, the court must determine whether a youth can be rendered competent through treatment. With adults, the term *restored to competence* is used because it is assumed that the defendant was previously competent but was rendered incompetent by a transient condition, most often mental illness. For adolescents, however, the notion of restoration may be misleading because an adolescent may be incompetent as a result of developmental immaturity and therefore may never yet have attained competence.

With adult defendants, the 1972 case of *Jackson v. Indiana* established that adult defendants could not be held indefinitely if they had no prospect of being restored to competence. Therefore, states set time limits (typically around 6–18 months) on the length of time adult defendants could be held as incompetent (Roesch, Ogloff, & Golding, 1993). While many states do not yet have guidelines regarding the remediation or restoration of juvenile competence, a number of states have set maximum durations on restoration services (Redding & Frost, 2002). Length of time allowed for juvenile restoration services varies considerably. Often, longer periods of time are permitted for felony charges than misdemeanor offenses, and some maximum duration time limits are quite long. For instance, in North Carolina a youth may be committed to restoration services for 10 years for a felony, or for five years for a misdemeanor (Redding & Frost, 2002).

In general, there is a preference for juvenile restoration services to occur in the community, unless there is evidence that an inpatient setting is needed (Redding & Frost, 2002). If treatment is ordered, then competence is periodically reevaluated. While the requirements for reevaluations and rehearings vary across states, Redding and Frost argue that frequent reviews may be particularly important for youth because of the "relatively malleable nature of child and adolescent mental status and the need to ensure that adjudication is not delayed any longer than necessary" (p. 391).

Little research has examined whether youth can be restored to competence and if so, which remediation approaches are most effective. Given youths' developmental immaturity and the possibility that legal deficits may stem from incomplete developmental processes, it may be difficult to remediate youth. Cooper (1997), for instance, found that although youth evidenced improved legal abilities following viewing an educational videotape, the large majority of youth still did not meet adult cut-off scores for competence. Similarly, Viljoen, Odgers, Grisso, and Tillbrook (2007) found that teaching did not erase important developmental differences in youths' and adults' legal understanding. Nevertheless, McGaha et al. (2001) found that most youth who were found incompetent in Florida were restored to competence. As that study examined only judicial determinations of competence rather than defendants' functional legal deficits, it is unclear to what extent these youths' legal capacities improved following treatment. In some cases, there may have been pressure to find the youth competent in order to proceed with adjudication even if the youths' legal capacities were questionable.

A promising community-based approach has been developed by Warren and colleagues (2009). They used an intensive case management approach, with developmentally informed interactive educational tools, and case integration and mentoring by trained counselors. The majority of youth were restored within four months, except for those with a diagnosis of mental retardation. Less than half of this group were successfully restored.

At the present time, there is considerable debate as to what is the appropriate disposition or outcome for youth considered to be unrestorable. Bonnie and Grisso (2000) suggested that if a youth is found incompetent in adult court, the case could be heard in juvenile court provided that the sanctions in juvenile court are less severe than those in adult court (see also Scott & Grisso, 2005). Other options may be to drop charges, initiate civil commitment or other mental health services, and/or initiate dependency proceedings.

Legal Capacities of Adolescents

As with adult defendants, all states presume that youth are competent, and the defense counsel bears the burden of proving otherwise (Redding & Frost, 2002). However, research has convincingly demonstrated that adolescents, especially young adolescents, have high rates of legal deficits in comparison to older adolescents and adults. In an important recent study, Grisso et al. (2003) found that one-third of youth aged 11–13 and one-fifth of youth aged 14–15 demonstrated significant impairments in understanding of legal proceedings and/or legal reasoning (see also Burnett, Noblin, & Prossor, 2004; Peterson-Badali & Abramovitch, 1992; Viljoen & Roesch, 2005). Also, young adolescents have been found to be more likely than older individuals to waive their legal rights, such as the right to silence and counsel (Viljoen, Klaver, & Roesch, 2005).

Research has revealed that age-related differences in legal capacities stem, in part, from immature cognitive development (Viljoen & Roesch, 2005; see Kruh & Grisso, 2009 for a detailed definition of developmental maturity). In addition, psychosocial development appears to influence the acquisition of the legal capacities, particularly reasoning and judgment (Steinberg & Cauffman, 1996; Scott, Reppucci, & Woolard, 1995). Specifically, research has indicated that adolescents aged 11–13 are less likely to recognize risks and long-term consequences of legal judgments than older adolescents and adults (Grisso et al., 2003). Kivisto, Moore, Fite, and Seidner (2011) analyzed data from a sample of 927 youth from the MacArthur Juvenile Adjudicative Competence Study. Age, intellectual ability, and future orientation were found to be positively associated with competence, but psychiatric symptomatology was only weakly negatively related to competence. Kivisto et al. (2011) added that the development of a future orientation partially mediated the relationship between age and competence. They concluded that "the evaluation of an adolescent's future orientation may represent a causal factor contributing to deficits in the adolescent's psycholegal abilities, thereby informing the evaluator's prognosis for competency restoration" (p. 324). The importance of future orientation was highlighted in a study of 935 individuals between 10 and 30 years old. Steinberg et al. (2009) found that younger adolescents had weaker future orientations, as they were more likely to accept immediate versus delayed rewards and reported they were less concerned about the future and did not anticipate the consequences of their decisions.

These findings suggest that clinicians who conduct competency evaluations should be especially vigilant in examining the legal capacities of young defendants, and be sensitive to the possible impact of cognitive and psychosocial development on legal capacities. Notably, however, there can be considerable variability within age categories. Therefore, clinicians should not infer incompetence on the basis of young age alone.

In addition to young age and immaturity, a number of other factors may place an adolescent at risk of legal deficits, including attention deficits and hyperactivity, impaired verbal abilities, and low intelligence (Viljoen & Roesch, 2005). Research has indicated that low intelligence may be a particularly strong risk factor among young adolescents compared to older adolescents, possibly because legal capacities are less ingrained at a young age and therefore more strongly associated with cognitive ability (Viljoen & Roesch, 2005). Severe psychopathology appears to be another important risk factor for incompetence (Cowden & McKee, 1995). However, given that many youth with severe mental disorders are found competent, severe psychopathology cannot be equated with incompetence.

While it is often assumed that youth who have been previously arrested or convicted will be knowledgeable about legal proceedings, this assumption generally has not been supported by research (Grisso, 1997; Grisso et al., 2003). Therefore, evaluators should be careful not to assume that youth with prior arrests or convictions are competent.

Evaluation

Juvenile competency evaluations differ in important ways from general clinical evaluations. Unlike general psychological evaluations, the primary goal of juvenile competency evaluations is not to provide information about a youth's diagnosis and treatment needs. Instead, the primary purpose is to collect information about the youth's legal capacities and any deficits that may affect his or her ability to function as a defendant (Kruh & Grisso, 2009).

In the following sections, the process of conducting a juvenile competency evaluation is described, including preparation for the evaluation, collecting data, and interpreting data. Following that, several competency assessment tools that may potentially be useful are examined. To demonstrate how these principles apply in practice, a case example is provided.

Readers are strongly encouraged to read Kruh and Grisso's (2009) book detailing the best practices for conducting juvenile competency evaluations. For useful examples of juvenile competency reports, readers are referred to the MacArthur Juvenile Court Training Curriculum (Rosado, 2000), Heilbrun, Marczyk, and DeMatteo (2002), and Grisso (2005).

Preparation for Evaluation

Kruh and Grisso (2009) recommend a comprehensive yet flexible evaluation model. In preparing to conduct a juvenile competency evaluation, evaluators should seek relevant records, including educational, medical, mental health, juvenile justice, and social service records (Grisso, 2005). Because these records can often take a while to obtain, they should be sought early on in the evaluation process. The youth's attorneys may be able to assist with the process of obtaining relevant records. Despite the importance of reviewing background records, research has indicated that clinicians often fail to obtain relevant records (Christy, Douglas, Otto, & Petrila, 2004).

To ensure that the evaluation provides useful and relevant information, evaluators should discuss the reason for the referral with the party initiating the referral, typically the defense attorney (Kruh & Grisso, 2009). Evaluators should speak with the defense attorney about their observations regarding the youth's legal capacities (see Grisso, 2005 for a questionnaire clinicians may use), and they should ask the defense attorney if she or he would like to be present during the evaluator's interviews with the youth.

Evaluators should also contact the youth's caretakers to notify them about the evaluation and to determine how they might be able to participate in the evaluation. While there is typically no legal obligation to involve caretakers, there are important ethical and practical reasons to do so (Grisso, 2005). In general clinical practice, it is very uncommon to evaluate juveniles without involving parents or guardians. Additionally, caretakers can provide important information about children and may be able to help evaluators to access relevant records.

Conducting the Evaluation

Juvenile competency evaluations should contain information about youths' developmental history and current developmental status, their clinical history and current clinical features, and their legal circumstances and legal capacities (Grisso, 2005). Research has indicated that clinicians often do quite well in presenting information about youths' clinical features (Christy et al., 2004). However, information on youths' legal capacities is often lacking.

In gathering information relevant to these domains, evaluators should review records and conduct interviews with youth and their caretakers. Prior to each interview, examiners should clearly explain their identity and the nature of the evaluation. In addition, examiners must explain the limits of confidentiality, particularly that statements made during the interview will not be kept confidential but rather will be given to the court.

Psychological testing may be useful. Intelligence tests, particularly the Wechsler tests, and personality tests, particularly the Minnesota Multiphasic Personality Inventory–Adolescent and Minnesota Multiphasic Personality Inventory–2, are used fairly commonly in juvenile competency evaluations (Christy et al., 2004; Ryba, Cooper, & Zapf, 2003). While competency assessment tools are used less frequently, the use of such tools is recommended (competency assessment tools are described later in the chapter). In choosing appropriate tests, the evaluator should consider the characteristics of the child—such as his or her age and clinical presentation, the availability of other data about a youth such as prior psychological testing, and practical constraints such as the amount of time available to conduct an evaluation (Grisso, 2005).

Data Interpretation and Preparation of the Report

In order to protect youths' rights against self-incrimination, clinicians should be careful to avoid including incriminating information about the youth's current charge in their reports (Grisso, 2005). As data are collected and the report is written, examiners should consider how results apply to each of the primary legal questions at issue in juvenile competency evaluations. These questions, which are described in more detail in this section, are based on the evaluation model developed by Grisso (Kruh & Grisso, 2009, p. 103):

1. *Functional question*: Does the defendant demonstrate deficits in psycholegal functioning?
2. *Causal question*: What are the clinical and/or developmental causes of any deficits?
3. *Contextual question*: How will the deficits impact the defendant in her or his jurisdiction?
4. *Conclusory question*: Does the impairment rise to a level rendering the defendant IST [incompetent to stand trial]?
5. *Remediation question*: If the defendant is IST, can the deficits be remedied? If so, how?

What Are the Defendant's Functional Legal Abilities?

Kruh and Grisso (2009) note that "The main functional question asks whether the youth is capable of knowing, understanding, believing, doing, and deciding within the role of being a defendant at the current time and as the adjudication proceeds" (p. 167). In general, legal standards for juvenile competency focus on whether the youth is able to understand and appreciate the charges, the consequences of a finding of guilt or delinquency, the role of key legal players, and the meaning of evidence and pleas. In addition, youth must typically be able to communicate adequately with their attorney, conduct themselves appropriately during legal proceedings, and reason about legal decisions such as how to plead. Therefore, information relevant to each of these areas should be described in the report, with a particular focus on any deficits as well as strengths that might serve to compensate for any deficits (Kruh & Grisso, 2009).

What Are Possible Causes of Legal Deficits?

If a youth exhibits legal deficits, it is important to delineate the possible clinical and/or developmental causes of legal deficits, such as psychopathology, cognitive impairments, impulsivity, and immaturity. As described earlier, although legal standards have traditionally focused on psychopathology and mental retardation as possible causes of legal deficits, courts appear to be increasingly recognizing immaturity as a possible basis for findings of incompetence (Grisso & Quinlan, 2005). If mental illness is a possible causal factor, the report should be specific about the defendant's symptoms and how a particular symptom may impact competency. As Kruh and Grisso (2009) comment, "the causal analysis involving childhood mental illnesses may be most useful when examiners offer the best diagnostic picture possible, but then move beyond the disorders themselves to discuss problems at the level of symptoms and functional impacts" (p. 172).

There are two primary reasons that knowledge of the causes of legal deficits is relevant (Grisso, 2003). First, knowledge about potential causes of functional legal deficits is useful in planning treatment to remediate legal deficits. Second, courts are interested in causal explanations for functional deficits in order to rule out the possibility of feigned deficits, or if legal deficits may stem from sources that could be easily remediated without psychiatric treatment, such as simply a lack of education. Despite the importance of information on causes of legal deficits, many reports lack this information (Christy et al., 2004).

In rare cases, it is possible that adolescents may feign mental illness. Research has suggested that clinicians may not be good at recognizing simulated impairments in adolescents (Faust, Hart, Guilmette, & Arkes, 1988), and measures of competence may be vulnerable to feigning (Rogers, Sewell, Grandjean, & Vitacco, 2002). However, little research exists by which to assist clinicians in evaluating malingered incompetence in youth. As a general strategy, evaluators should examine inconsistencies in performance that may be indicative of feigning. With respect to clinical presentations, evaluators should be vigilant of absurd and implausible symptoms, unusual combinations of symptoms, overendorsement of diverse symptoms, sudden onset and resolution of symptoms, inconsistent reports of symptoms, and discrepancies between self-report and clinical observations (McCann, 1998; Rogers, 1997). Clinicians may find the Structured Interview of Reported Symptoms useful in detecting malingering of psychopathology, as research has supported the use of this instrument with adolescents (Rogers, Hinds, & Sewell, 1996).

In addition to ruling out malingering, clinicians should rule out the possibility that legal deficits stem from simply a lack of education that is easily remediable (Grisso, 2003, 2005). To do so, evaluators can attempt to teach the youth information and then reassess whether his or her legal understanding improves. If there is improvement, evaluators should examine if this is retained even after several days have passed.

What Contextual Factors May Affect the Legal Abilities Required by the Defendant?

Due to differences in legal standards, the particular functional abilities that evaluators should examine may vary somewhat from jurisdiction to jurisdiction. Evaluators should, therefore, be familiar with the legal standards that are applied in their jurisdiction of practice. Legal requirements regarding the nature and degree of defendants' legal capacities are not absolute and invariant (Grisso, 2003). Instead, the specific legal abilities required by youth may depend on the particular characteristics of their case. Therefore, it is important for evaluators to examine contextual factors that may affect the nature and degree of legal capacities that may be required, such as the complexity of the trial, whether the defendant may be required to testify, the likely length of the trial, and social supports available to the defendant (Grisso, 2003).

For youth, several contextual factors are of particular importance. First, whether a juvenile is tried in adult criminal or juvenile court may affect the types and levels of legal capacities that are required (Bonnie & Grisso, 2000; Grisso, 2005), as a trial in criminal court may place greater demand on youths' capacities than trial in juvenile court. If transferred to criminal court, a youth may require an understanding of certain legal concepts that may not arise in juvenile court, such as the role of juries.

Another contextual factor that is important to consider in juvenile competency cases is caretaker involvement (Grisso, 2005). Although caretakers may facilitate youths' legal capacities at times, there may be situations in which caretakers may hinder youths' ability to effectively function as trial defendants. While young defendants alone (provided they are deemed competent) have the power to make legal decisions regarding their adjudication, caretakers may assume that they have this authority and place excessive pressure on their children to make certain decisions (Woolard, 2005). In addition, caretakers may have inadequate legal capacities themselves (Woolard, Cleary, Harvell, & Chen, 2008), and may provide children with advice that, from a legal perspective, is not necessarily optimal, such as advice to waive their rights (Grisso & Pomicter, 1978).

Does the Impairment Render the Defendant Incompetent to Stand Trial?

This is the conclusory, or ultimate, question that is of concern to the court. The specific question to be addressed is "Are the defendant's functional abilities caused by legally relevant factors and are they so limited that the defendant should be considered incompetent to proceed?" (Kruh & Grisso, 2009, p. 183). In general, conclusory opinions by evaluators are permitted within evidentiary law (Heilbrun, 2001). In Florida an opinion about a defendant's competence is even required by law (Christy et al., 2004).

Evaluators should be aware that there is considerable debate about whether evaluators should offer ultimate opinions (see Kruh & Grisso, 2009, p. 184 for a review of arguments for and against ultimate opinions). Given that legal standards for juvenile competence are currently unclear, it may be difficult for examiners to legitimately offer an ultimate conclusion as to whether a youth meets legal criteria for incompetence (see Grisso, 2005). Instead, it may be most appropriate to simply describe the youth's legal capacities in detail and allow the court to make a decision. Kruh and Grisso (2009) conclude that ultimate-issue opinions are inappropriate except in some extreme cases, and they caution that when ultimate opinions are offered, "the rationale for the opinion should be transparent, so that the court is adequately equipped to consider the merits of the examiner's opinion and reach its own independent determination" (p. 186).

What Are Possible Interventions for Legal Deficits?

In cases in which a youth demonstrates legal deficits, evaluators should consider whether an appropriate intervention exists, the specific type of intervention required, and how and where this intervention could be obtained (Grisso, 2005). Evaluators should also offer an opinion regarding the likelihood that the proposed intervention will be effective in remediating the particular legal deficits exhibited by a youth, and how long this would take. Research in Florida has indicated that a sizable proportion of juvenile competency reports do not contain this information (Christy et al., 2004).

In considering potential interventions, evaluators should consider both the particular legal deficits exhibited by a youth and the causes of the legal deficits. In many cases, such as when a youth is found incompetent due to mental retardation or developmental immaturity, evaluators may chose to recommend psycho-educational interventions, in which youth are taught relevant concepts and skills in the areas in which they demonstrate deficits. If legal deficits appear to stem from an underlying mental disorder, evaluators may recommend treatment of the disorder using empirically supported interventions.

There is limited research on competency restoration of adults (Zapf & Roesch, 2011), and even less research on juveniles found incompetent. It may be difficult to remediate legal deficits in adolescents. For instance, on one hand Viljoen et al. (2007) reported that young adolescents were less likely than older individuals to show improved understanding of basic legal concepts following brief teaching. It may be even more difficult to teach youth how to apply legal concepts to their own cases, and how to reason about legal decisions. On the other hand, Warren et al. (2009) found that 91% of youth who did not have mental illness nor mental retardation, and 84% of youth with mental illness only, were restored to competence after completing their community-based competence restoration program (rates of restoration were much lower in youth with mental retardation). As such, positive results may be attainable for some youth with specialized, intensive approaches.

Multicultural Considerations

As with all forensic evaluations, there are a number of important cultural considerations in conducting juvenile competency evaluations. Due to experiences with prejudice and discrimination, ethnic minority youth and their families may be understandably mistrustful and guarded with anyone associated with mainstream culture (Sue & Sue, 1999). As such, evaluators should work hard to establish adequate rapport. If a minority youth appears guarded or uncooperative in the context of a juvenile competency evaluation, evaluators should be sensitive to how cultural factors may contribute to this presentation.

Evaluators should strive to use psychological instruments that have been validated with ethnic minority youth. Unfortunately, at the present time, many adolescent psychological instruments lack adequate data with diverse youth. Evaluators should also be sensitive to language issues. An interpreter should be obtained if the youth or their caretakers would like to communicate in a language in which the evaluator is not fluent. If a youth has difficulty communicating with their attorney simply because English is not the primary language, he or she would not be considered incompetent by legal standards. However, in such cases, evaluators could offer recommendations in order to accommodate for language issues, and ensure that the defendant receives a fair trial.

In general, research has not found differences between the legal abilities of non-Hispanic Caucasian youth and minority youth once other relevant factors, such as IQ and socioeconomic status are controlled (Grisso et al., 2003; Viljoen & Roesch, 2005). However, some research has indicated that juvenile defendants from ethnic minority groups may have lower levels of trust in their attorneys than Caucasian defendants (Pierce & Brodsky, 2002), and are less likely to report that they would disclose important information to their attorneys (Viljoen et al., 2005). As such, this may be an especially important area to assess.

At times, youth from diverse cultural backgrounds, such as youth who have recently immigrated to the United States, may have inadequate legal abilities due simply to limited experiences with mainstream, North American legal systems. In such cases, evaluators should assess whether such youth have the capacity to easily learn this information.

Competency Assessment Instruments

Competency assessments instruments differ from standard psychological instruments in that they are designed specifically to assess defendants' functional legal abilities that are relevant to adjudication. While research has indicated that clinicians consider such instruments to be useful in juvenile competency evaluations (Ryba et al., 2003), competency assessment instruments are used in a small proportion of juvenile competency evaluations only (Christy et al., 2004). In part, this may be due to the dearth of developmentally appropriate tools for youth.

Grisso (2005), however, developed a competency assessment tool specifically for youth, the Juvenile Competency Assessment Interview (JACI). In the following section, we describe the JACI, as well as several tools that were originally developed for adults, namely the Fitness Interview Test–Revised (FIT-R; Roesch, Zapf, & Eaves, 2006), the MacArthur Competence Assessment Tool-Criminal Adjudication (MacCAT-CA; Poythress et al., 1999), and the Competence Assessment for Standing Trial for Defendants With Mental Retardation (CAST-MR; Everington & Luckasson, 1992). We chose to describe these instruments because the FIT-R was recently validated with adolescents (Viljoen et al., 2006), and the MacCAT-CA and CAST-MR appear to be used fairly frequently in juvenile competence evaluations (Ryba et al., 2003).[3]

JACI

The JACI is a structured set of questions designed to assess youths' legal capacities relevant to adjudication. At the present time, the JACI is the only existing competency assessment tool that was developed specifically for youth. As Grisso (2005) describes, the JACI is not currently a standardized instrument. It does not provide item scores or cutoffs to make determinations regarding juveniles' competency, and it has not yet been empirically investigated. Instead, the JACI functions as a guide to ensure that clinicians consider the relevant legal capacities and developmental issues in assessing juveniles' adjudicative competence.

In the introduction to the JACI, evaluators are provided with a general set of guidelines as a frame of reference for their evaluation. In particular, definitions of "Understanding,"

"Appreciation," and "Reasoning and Decision Making" are offered and clinicians are oriented to key developmental concepts, which are relevant to juvenile competency evaluations (i.e., perceived autonomy, perceptions of risk, time perspective, abstract/concrete thinking). Following this introduction, evaluators are provided with a series of questions to assess youths' adjudicative capacities. These questions are divided into four sections.

The first section focuses on the "Juvenile Court Trial and its Consequences," including the nature and seriousness of the offense, nature and purpose of the juvenile court trial, possible pleas, and guilt and punishment/penalties. The second section focuses on the "Roles of the Participants," including role of the prosecutor, juvenile defense lawyer, probation officer, and juvenile court judge. The third section focuses on "Assisting Counsel and Decision Making," including assisting the defense lawyer, and plea bargains/agreements. This section also includes an item on reasoning and decision making. For that item, youth are asked to make a choice about various legal decisions (e.g., whether to assert the right to a lawyer, or plead guilty or not guilty). They must then explain their choices. Importantly, judgments about whether a youth exhibits deficits in this area are not made on the basis of what choice they made but rather the reasons that led to their choice. The fourth section focuses on "Participating at the Juvenile Court Hearing." This section does not include specific questions to be administered but instead provides space for examiners to make observations about the youth's ability to pay attention, maintain self-control, and testify.

With the exception of items in the fourth section and the item on reasoning and decision making, items on the JACI are designed to assess not only youths' understanding of concepts but also their *appreciation* of how this information applies to their own case. In addition, the JACI contains several "Capacity Checks," whereby evaluators can teach youth who do not adequately understand a legal concept about that concept and then reassess their understanding immediately after teaching, as well as several days later.

The structure of the JACI is flexible. Evaluators can adjust item wording to take into account the varying ages, maturity levels, and cognitive abilities of youth (Grisso, 2005). In addition, evaluators do not need to administer every item on the JACI if some items appear unnecessary or inappropriate. For instance, if a youth fails to give an acceptable response for the understanding item, it may not be necessary to administer the parallel appreciation item for that concept. While the JACI does not include specific scoring criteria for items, evaluators are provided with guidelines regarding the key concepts that the youth must demonstrate.

The JACI has not undergone research on standard psychometric properties (e.g., interrater reliability, predictive validity), in part because of its flexible format. However, an implementation project, in which the JACI was adopted in a juvenile court clinic in Washington state, reported that the JACI enabled evaluators to collect more nuanced information regarding competence and led to an improvement in the quality of competence assessment reports (Lexcen, Heavin, & Redick, 2010).

The JACI holds a number of important advantages over other tools. As described, it is the only tool that was designed specifically for youth. The wording and format were carefully chosen so as to be easy to understand and developmentally appropriate. Evaluators are directed to consider key developmental constructs and issues (e.g., perceived autonomy, perceptions of risk, time perspective, abstract/concrete thinking), which otherwise might easily be overlooked. In addition, Grisso (2005) has provided a number of useful resources that may be used with the JACI, including an attorney questionnaire, a parent interview, templates for developmental and clinical interviews, and a records worksheet.

FIT-R

The FIT-R is a semi-structured clinical interview that was originally developed for adult criminal defendants. Although the FIT-R was developed in Canada, it is relevant to U.S. legal standards (Grisso, 2003) and a U.S. manual for this instrument was recently published (Roesch et al.,

2006). There are 16 items on the FIT-R, which is divided into three sections. To assess each item, evaluators are provided with a number of questions. However, evaluators may rephrase questions if an examinee appears confused by the particular wording or format of a question, and may ask additional questions to further clarify and probe a defendant's response.

The first section, "Understanding the Nature or Object of the Proceedings" ("Factual Knowledge of the Criminal Procedure")[4], examines a defendant's understanding of the arrest process, current charges, role of key participants, legal process, pleas, and court procedures. The second section, "Understanding the Possible Consequences of the Proceedings" ("Appreciation of Personal Involvement in and Importance of the Proceedings") examines a defendant's appreciation of the possible penalties, available legal defenses, and likely outcome. The third section, "Communication with Counsel" ("Ability to Participate in Defense"), examines a defendant's ability to communicate facts, relate to lawyers, plan legal strategy, engage in the defense, challenge witnesses, testify relevantly, and manage courtroom behavior.

Items are rated on a three-point scale, with higher scores indicating greater impairment. In rating sections, evaluators must make structured clinical judgments regarding the examinee's level of impairment on that factor. Once items and sections on the FIT-R are rated, evaluators come to a final conclusion as to whether the defendant is "fit," "questionable," or "unfit." This rating is not based on a cut-off score but rather requires a separate structured clinical judgment.

Research with adults has indicated that overall judgments made using the FIT-R have adequate interrater reliability (Viljoen, Roesch, & Zapf, 2002), and show high agreement with judgments made by clinicians (Zapf, Roesch, & Viljoen, 2001). Recently, Viljoen, Vincent, and Roesch (2006) investigated the interrater reliability and validity of the FIT-R with adolescents. Results indicated that the interrater reliability of sections and overall judgment of competence were good. In addition, support was found for a three-factor model that generally paralleled the sections on the FIT-R. These factors ("Understanding and Reasoning about Legal Proceedings," "Appreciation of Case-Specific Information," and "Ability to Communicate with Counsel") were united by a dominant unidimensional factor. As expected, FIT-R scores are inversely correlated with age, with young adolescents, particularly those with low IQ scores, showing greater impairment than older adolescents and adults (Viljoen & Roesch, 2005).

The FIT-R has a number of strengths regarding its use with juveniles. At the present time, it is the only instrument that has specifically been validated for use with adolescents. It uses simply worded questions that are directly relevant to a youth's own legal situation, and has a flexible format. However, as with other instruments that were originally developed for adults, the FIT-R does not specifically examine how developmental immaturity may relate to a youth's legal capacities. As such, it cannot be used as a sole indicator of juveniles' competence and must be used in conjunction with other information.

MacCAT-CA

The MacCAT-CA is a structured interview that consists of 22 items. It was developed for adult criminal defendants and is based on Bonnie's theory of legal competence, which distinguishes between competence to assist counsel and decisional competence (Bonnie, 1992). The MacCAT-CA has three sections.

The first section, "Understanding," includes eight items that examine defendants' knowledge of legal concepts, such as the role of attorneys, the definitions of specific offenses, and the consequences of conviction. To assess defendants' understanding of these concepts, defendants are read a brief vignette about two men who get into a fight in a bar while playing pool and are then asked questions about how these legal concepts apply to this scenario. For six items on this subscale, defendants may be taught information relevant to this concept if they initially demonstrate inadequate understanding of that concept. They are then immediately retested to examine if their understanding improves.

The second section of the MacCAT-CA, "Reasoning," includes eight items that also pertain to the hypothetical vignette about the bar fight. For five of these items, defendants are given two facts and are asked which of these facts would be more important to tell their attorney. For the remaining three items, defendants are given choices between possible plea options. Defendants are evaluated on their ability to adequately reason about these choices.

The third section, "Appreciation," includes six items about the defendant's own legal situation. Specifically, defendants are asked whether they are "more likely, less likely, or just as likely" as other people to be treated fairly in legal proceedings, be assisted by their attorneys, disclose information to their attorneys, plead guilty, be found guilty, and receive the same sentences as others if found guilty. Defendants' responses are scored according to whether their response appears plausible or appears influenced by symptoms of mental illness (e.g., delusions).

Items are scored on a three-point scale, with higher scores indicating better performance. Item scores for each section are then totaled, and norms may be used to classify whether a defendant shows "minimal or no impairment," "mild impairment," or "clinically significant impairment" on a section. No overall competence score is calculated.

Research with adults has indicated that the MacCAT-CA has good interrater reliability, is correlated with clinical ratings of competence, and is able to discriminate between adults found incompetent and those presumed to be competent (Otto et al., 1998). In addition, as a competence assessment tool, the MacCAT-CA has a number of unique strengths, including its strong theoretical grounding, structured scoring procedures, and inclusion of a teaching component.

One study used item response theory to test if the MacCAT-CA functions similarly in adolescents as in adults (Viljoen, Slaney, & Grisso, 2009). In general, there was little evidence of systematic age-related measurement bias. In other words, it does not appear as though the MacCAT-CA consistently underestimates youths' legal capacities. Several studies have suggested that the interrater reliability of the Appreciation subscale may be fairly low when used with adolescents (Burnett, Noblin, & Prosser, 2004; Grisso et al., 2003). Because the Appreciation subscale was designed specifically to examine the impact of mental illness on defendants' appreciation of case-specific information, it may be less appropriate for adolescents, as legal deficits in adolescents may stem from immaturity rather than mental illness (Grisso et al., 2003). In addition, some of the items on the MacCAT-CA, such as understanding the role of juries, may be less relevant to adolescents (Woolard & Harvell, 2005). (This can also be said of other instruments that were originally developed for adults.)

As more information accumulates, evaluators will be able to make better informed decisions regarding the use of the MacCAT-CA with adolescents. If the MacCAT-CA is used in clinical evaluations with youth, evaluators should seek additional information, such as regarding developmental immaturity (Grisso, 2005).

CAST-MR

The CAST-MR was developed specifically for assessing the competency of adult defendants with mental retardation. It comprises 50 items, which are organized into three sections. Section I ("Basic Legal Concepts") includes 25 multiple choice questions that assess defendants' knowledge of legal concepts and processes, such as pleas and the role of judges and attorneys. Section II ("Skills to Assist the Defense") includes 15 multiple-choice questions that assess defendants' understanding of appropriate courtroom behavior and the attorney-client relationship, such as whether they would disclose important information to their attorney. Section III ("Understanding Case Events") includes 10 open-ended questions that assess defendants' understanding of information pertaining to their specific case, including their ability to coherently describe the incident that led to their arrest and charges.

In order to familiarize defendants with the response format, examinees are administered several practice items prior to beginning each new section. Questions are read aloud to defendants, and may be reread if the defendant does not appear to adequately understand. All of the multiple choice questions include three options that are read to defendants, and defendants are instructed to listen to each of the three options prior to selecting an answer.

Correct responses to questions in Sections I and II are scored 1 point; the scoring system is objective and does not require any evaluator judgment. Items on Section III are scored on a three-point scale, which includes scores of 0, .5, or 1. Although scoring for Section III does require some evaluator judgment, detailed scoring instructions are provided in the test manual. A total score on the instrument is calculated by adding up each of the section scores.

Thus far, no research has examined the psychometric properties of the CAST-MR with youth. Studies with adult samples have reported that the interrater agreement for items on Section III is at least .80 (Section I and II do not require evaluator judgment), and internal consistency for all three sections generally appears adequate (Everington, 1990; Everington & Dunn, 1995). As evidence of validity, CAST-MR scores have been found to be significantly correlated with IQ, and have differentiated mentally retarded adult defendants who were found competent and incompetent.

The CAST-MR is perhaps the instrument used most commonly in juvenile competency evaluations (Ryba et al., 2003). On one hand, the multiple-choice format may place fewer demands on youths' expressive language abilities, and may help avoid acquiescent responding (Grisso, 2005). On the other, in order to competently stand trial, defendants may be required to employ expressive language abilities. Therefore, it may be important to understand how defendants might respond to open-ended questions that are similar to those they may be asked in actual legal proceedings (Grisso, 2003). In addition, if the CAST-MR is in fact easier than other competency assessment instruments, then the use of the CAST-MR may inadvertently and unfairly result in lower expectations and standards regarding juveniles' competency (McKee, 1998).

In order to further illustrate the use of these competency assessment instruments, a case example is provided in the following section. This example aims to demonstrate the importance of using empirically based assessment methods, obtaining information from multiple sources (including parents), and considering developmental and contextual factors that may affect youths' legal capacities (e.g., compliance with adults).

Case Example

Daniel is a 13-year-old male of mixed race (African American/Caucasian) who was referred for a competence evaluation by his defense attorney.[5] He was awaiting adjudication in juvenile court on charges of Rape in the Third Degree and Incest in the First Degree. The victim of the alleged charges was Daniel's 11-year-old brother Mark. Daniel's defense attorney reported that he raised the issue of competence because Daniel "doesn't say much and it's hard to tell if he gets what I'm telling him."

The consulting psychologist interviewed Daniel, his attorney, his parents, and his teacher, and reviewed his school, juvenile court, and mental health records. In addition, psychological tests were administered to assess Daniel's cognitive functioning, mental health, and legal capacities.

According to records, Daniel had no prior court contacts. He was living with his mother, father, and brother at the time of his arrest. His family has a history of economic difficulties, and was homeless in the past. Daniel was reported to have been sexually abused by a female babysitter when he was 6 years old, and has witnessed domestic violence between his parents. In second grade, Daniel began receiving special education services. Currently, he is in eighth grade in a special education program. Daniel's teacher noted that Daniel is frequently disruptive in the classroom and described him as "socially immature."

Daniel's parents indicated that they want Daniel to plead guilty so that he can "take responsibility for what he has done." They believe that the judge will let Daniel "come home" if he is found guilty. However, Daniel's attorney reported that this is extremely unlikely, and Daniel will probably face at least six months in a juvenile detention facility.

On the Woodcock-Johnson III, Daniel achieved a General Intellectual Ability score in the Very Low range (54). During the interview with Daniel's parents, they reported that Daniel is unable to independently make decisions and needs assistance with simple tasks, such as picking out his clothing. Daniel did not report any significant psychological symptoms, such as depression and anxiety, on the Massachusetts Youth Screening Instrument–Version 2. However, based on records and interviews with Daniel and his parents, he exhibits symptoms consistent with a diagnosis of attention deficit hyperactivity disorder.

Daniel's legal capacities relevant to adjudication were assessed with the FIT-R and the CAST-MR. On the FIT-R, Daniel generally demonstrated basic understanding of the adjudicative process and court procedure, and the role of key players, such as the judge and the defense attorney. Also, Daniel's appreciation of the seriousness of his charges and likely penalties appeared fairly realistic, and he reported a high degree of trust and confidence in his attorney.

However, based on his FIT-R performance, Daniel may have difficulty communicating relevant facts about his case to his lawyer: his accounts of case-related events were confusing and difficult to follow. Also, Daniel appears to have difficulty reasoning about legal decisions. His responses demonstrated a high degree of compliance with potential suggestions of a lawyer. For instance, when asked what he would do if "the prosecutor makes some legal errors and your lawyer wants to appeal," Daniel reported that he would go with what his lawyer says because his lawyer is "a cool guy." The FIT-R assessment also suggested potential deficits in Daniel's ability to recognize and report inaccuracies in witness testimony, testify relevantly, and manage his courtroom behavior.

On the CAST-MR, Daniel showed adequate understanding of basic legal concepts and case events. However, consistent with his performance on the FIT-R, he demonstrated deficits on a scale that measures skills to assist his defense attorney. Specifically, he obtained a significantly lower score than the average score obtained by mentally retarded adult defendants who are found incompetent to stand trial.

In the consulting psychologist's opinion, Daniel has a limited ability to communicate with his attorney and reason about legal decisions, such as plea bargains, due to his cognitive deficits and his acquiescence to adults, including his attorney and parents. If there is a formal trial, it is questionable as to whether Daniel can adequately testify and manage his courtroom behavior given his attention deficits and impulsivity. If Daniel is found incompetent to stand trial, medication may be useful in helping to mitigate his attention deficits and impulsivity. However, it is unlikely that he can be taught to communicate more effectively, reason about the consequences of various legal decisions, and function more autonomously within the time limit permitted for remediation.

Summary

A large body of research has examined adjudicative competency in adults, and a number of instruments have been developed for adults. However, in assessing adolescents, a number of unique developmental considerations arise. As such, adult approaches cannot automatically be applied to youth.

Because legal deficits in youth may stem from immaturity, evaluators must routinely consider immaturity when conducting juvenile competency evaluations. Also, evaluators must consider contextual issues that are unique to adolescents, including the impact of caretaker involvement in legal proceedings and the possibility of trial in juvenile or adult criminal court. In evaluating adolescents' competence, it is important to include parents in the evaluation process, as parents may be able to provide useful information regarding youths' developmental and clinical history, current presentation, and legal capacities.

In addition, it is essential that evaluators use instruments that are developmentally appropriate. Because youth evaluated for competency vary widely in age, from 8 to 17, it is likely that evaluators will need to adopt different approaches for youth of different ages. The JACI is the only tool that was developed specifically for assessing adjudicative competency in youth. At the present time, the JACI is a guide rather than a standardized, validated instrument. While a number of adult instruments, such as the FIT-R, MacCAT-CA, and CAST-MR, may have utility in juvenile competency evaluations, they should not be relied upon as the sole source of information about a youth's legal capacities but rather as an adjunct source of information. An important area for future research will be the development of standardized tests for assessing juveniles' competence.

The lack of research on assessing juveniles' competence makes it a challenging area of practice for clinicians. However, there have been a number of important new developments in this area, including the publication of the JACI, Grisso's (2005) book on assessing youths' adjudicative competence, Kruh and Grisso's (2009) best practices book on evaluating juvenile competence, and the growing body of research on assessing youths' legal capacities summarized in this chapter. Clinicians are advised to frequently consult the literature as the relevant research and resources continue to grow.

Notes

1   The terms *competence* and *competency* are used interchangeably in this chapter.
2   As argued by Scott, Reppucci, and Woolard (1995) and Steinberg and Cauffman (1996), reasoning and decision making may be especially relevant to juvenile competency because adolescents may make different and potentially riskier legal decisions as a result of psychosocial immaturity.
3   Due to space constraints, we were unable to discuss all of the competency assessment instruments that were developed for adults (see Grisso, 2003, and Zapf & Roesch, 2009, for information on adult competency assessment instruments).
4   The FIT sections each have two titles, which correspond with the relevant Canadian and American legal standards.
5   In order to protect client confidentiality, all identifying information regarding this case was removed and critical case details were extensively altered.

References

American Psychiatric Association. (2013). *Diagnostic and statistical manual of mental disorders* (5th ed.). Arlington, VA: American Psychiatric Publishing.

Baerger, D.R., Griffin, E.F., Lyons, J.S., & Simmons, R. (2003). Competency to stand trial in preadjudicated and petitioned juvenile defendants. *Journal of the American Academy of Psychiatry and the Law, 31*, 314–320.

Barnum, R., & Grisso, T. (1994). Competence to stand trial in juvenile court in Massachusetts: Issues of therapeutic jurisprudence. *New England Journal on Criminal and Civil Confinement, 20*, 321–344.

Bonnie, R.J. (1992). The competence of criminal defendants: A theoretical reformulation. *Behavioral Sciences and the Law, 10*, 291–316. doi: 10.1002/bsl.2370100303

Bonnie, R.J., & Grisso, T. (2000). Adjudicative competence and youthful offenders. In T. Grisso & R.G. Schwartz (Eds.), *Youth on trial: A developmental perspective on juvenile justice* (pp.73–103). Chicago: University of Chicago Press.

Brown, S.A. (2012). *Trends in juvenile justice state legislation: 2001–2011*. Denver, CO: National Conference of State Legislatures. Retrieved from www.ncsl.org/documents/cj/TrendsInJuvenileJustice.pdf.

Burnett, D.M.R., Noblin, C.D., & Prosser, V. (2004). Adjudicative competency in a juvenile population. *Criminal Justice and Behavior, 31*, 438–462. doi: 10.1177/0093854804265175

Christy, A., Douglas, K., Otto, R., & Petrila, J. (2004). Juveniles evaluated incompetent to proceed: Characteristics and quality of mental health professionals' evaluations. *Professional Psychology: Research and Practice, 35*, 380–388. doi: 10.1037/0735–7028.35.4.380

Cooper, D.K. (1997). Juveniles' understanding of trial-related information: Are they competent defendants? *Behavioral Sciences and the Law, 15*, 167–180. doi: 10.1002/(SICI)1099–0798(199721)15:2<167::AID-BSL266>3.0.CO;2-E

Cowden, V.L., & McKee, G.R. (1995). Competency to stand trial in juvenile delinquency proceedings—cognitive maturity and the attorney-client relationship. *University of Louisville Journal of Family Law, 33*, 629–660.

Cox, J. M., Goldstein, N. E. S., Dolores, J., Zelechoski, A. D., & Messenheimer, S. (2012). The impact of juveniles' ages and levels of psychosocial maturity on judges' opinions about adjudicative competence. *Law and Human Behavior, 36*, 21–27. dx.doi.org/doi: 10.1037/h0093953

Criminal Code of Canada (1985), R. S. C., C-46.

Drope v. Missouri, 420 US 162 (1975).

Dusky v. the United States, 362 U.S. 402 (1960).

Everington, C. T. (1990). The Competence Assessment for Standing Trial for Defendants with Mental Retardation (CAST-MR): A validation study. *Criminal Justice and Behavior, 17*, 147–168. doi: 10.1177/0093854890017002001

Everington, C. T., & Dunn, C. (1995). A second validation of the Competence Assessment for Standing Trial for Defendants with Mental Retardation (CAST-MR). *Criminal Justice and Behavior, 22*, 44–59. doi: 10.1177/0093854895022001004

Everington, C. & Luckasson, R, (1992). *The competence assessment for standing trial for defendants with mental retardation (CAST-MR).* Worthington, OH: IDS.

Faust, D., Hart, K. J., Guilmette, T. J., & Arkes, H. R. (1988). Neuropsychologists' capacity to detect adolescent malingerers. *Professional Psychology: Research and Practice, 19*, 508–515. doi: 10.1037/0735–7028.19.5.508

Gilles, C., & Jackson, M. (2003). Bill C-7: The new Youth Criminal Justice Act: A darker Young Offenders Act? *International Journal of Comparative and Applied Criminal Justice, 1*, 19–38. doi: 10.1080/01924036.2003.9678699

Godinez v. Moran, 113 S.Ct. 2680 (1993).

Grisso, T. (1997). The competence of adolescents as trial defendants. *Psychology, Public Policy, and Law, 3*, 3–32. doi: 10.1037/1076–8971.3.1.3

Grisso, T. (1998). *Forensic evaluations of juveniles.* Sarasota, FL: Professional Resource Exchange.

Grisso, T. (2003). *Evaluating competencies: Forensic assessments and instruments* (2nd ed.). New York: Kluwer Academic/Plenum.

Grisso, T. (2005). *Evaluating juveniles' adjudicative competence: A guide for clinical practice.* Sarasota, FL: Professional Resource Press.

Grisso, T., Miller, M. O., & Sales, B. (1987). Competency to stand trial in juvenile court. *International Journal of Law and Psychiatry, 10*, 1–20. doi: 10.1016/0160–2527(87)90009–4

Grisso, T., & Pomicter, C. (1978). Interrogation of juveniles: An empirical study of procedures, safeguards, and rights waiver. *Law and Human Behavior, 1*, 321–342. doi: 10.1007/BF01048593

Grisso, T., & Quinlan, J. (2005). *Juvenile court clinical services: A national description.* Worcester, MA: Law and Psychiatry Program, University of Massachusetts Medical School.

Grisso, T., Steinberg, L., Woolard, J., Cauffman, E., Scott, E., Graham, S., . . . Schwartz, R. (2003). Juveniles' competence to stand trial: A comparison of adolescents' and adults' capacities as trial defendants. *Law and Human Behavior, 27*, 333–363. doi: 10.1023/A:1024065015717

Heilbrun, K. (2001). *Principles of forensic mental health assessment.* New York: Kluwer Academic.

Heilbrun, K., Marczyk, G. R., & DeMatteo, D. (2002). *Forensic mental health assessment: A casebook.* New York: Oxford University Press.

In re Gault, 387 U.S. 1 (1967).

In re Winship, 397 U.S. 358 (1970).

Jackson v. Indiana, 406 US 715 (1972).

Kent v. United States, 383 U.S. 541 (1966).

Kivisto, A. J., Moore, T. M., Fite, P. A., & Seidner, B. G. (2011). Future orientation and competence to stand trial: The fragility of competence. *Journal of the American Academy of Psychiatry and the Law, 39*, 316–26.

Kruh, I., & Grisso, T. (2009). *Evaluation of juveniles' competence to stand trial.* New York: Oxford University Press.

Kruh, I. P., Sullivan, L., Ellis, M., Lexcen, F. & McClellan, J. (2006). Juvenile competence to stand trial: A historical and empirical analysis of a juvenile forensic evaluation service. *International Journal of Forensic Mental Health, 5*, 109–123. doi: 10.1080/14999013.2006.10471236

Larson, K., & Grisso, T. (2012). *Developing statutes for competence to stand trial in juvenile delinquency proceedings: A guide for lawmakers.* Chicago, IL: John D. and Catherine T. MacArthur Foundation. Retrieved from www.modelsforchange.net.

Lexcen, F., Heavin, S., & Redick, C. (2010). A clinical application of the Juvenile Adjudicative Competence Interview (JACI). *Open Access Journal of Forensic Psychology, 2,* 287–305.

McCann, J.T. (1998). *Malingering and deception in adolescents: Assessing credibility in clinical and forensic settings.* Washington, DC: American Psychology Association.

McGaha, A., Otto, R. K., McClaren, M. D., & Petrila, J. (2001). Juveniles adjudicated incompetent to proceed: A descriptive study of Florida's competence restoration program. *Journal of the American Academy of Psychiatry and the Law, 29,* 427–437.

McKee, G.R. (1998). Competency to stand trial in preadjudicatory juveniles and adults. *Journal of the American Academy of Psychiatry and the Law, 26,* 89–99.

McKee, G.R., & Shea, S.J. (1999). Competency to stand trial in family court: Characteristics of competent and incompetent juveniles. *Journal of the American Academy of Psychiatry and the Law, 27,* 65–73.

Mulvey, E., & Schubert, C. (2012). Youth in prison and beyond. In B.C. Feld & D. Bishop (Eds.), *The Oxford handbook on juvenile crime and juvenile justice* (pp. 843–867). New York: Oxford University Press.

National Conference of State Legislatures (2014). *Juvenile justice: States with juvenile competency law.* Retrieved on July 19, 2014 from www.ncsl.org/research/civil-and-criminal-justice/states-with-juvenile-competency-laws.aspx.

Otto, R. K., Poythress, N. G., Nicholson, R. A., Edens, J. F., Monahan, J., Bonnie, R. J., Hoge, S. K., & Eisenberg, M. (1998). Psychometric properties of the MacArthur Competence Assessment Tool–Criminal Adjudication (MacCAT-CA). *Psychological Assessment, 10,* 435–443. doi: 10.1037/1040–3590.doi: 10.4.435

Peterson-Badali, M., & Abramovitch, R. (1992). Children's knowledge of the legal system: Are they competent to instruct legal counsel? *Canadian Journal of Criminology, 34,* 139–160.

Pierce, C.S., & Brodsky, S.L. (2002). Trust and understanding in the attorney-juvenile relationship. *Behavioral Sciences and the Law, 20,* 89–107. doi: 10.1002/bsl.478

Poythress, N., Nicholson, R., Otto, R. K., Edens, J. F., Bonnie, R. J., Monahan, J., & Hoge, S. K. (1999). *The MacArthur Competence Assessment Tool–Criminal Adjudication: Professional manual.* Odessa, FL: Psychological Assessment Resources.

Redding, R. E., & Frost, L. (2002). Adjudicative competence in the modern juvenile court. *Virginia Journal of Social Policy and the Law, 9,* 353–410.

Redding, R.E., Goldstein, N.E.S., & Heilbrun, K. (2005). Juvenile delinquency: Past and present. In K. Heilbrun, N.E.S. Goldstein, & R. E. Redding, (Eds.), *Juvenile delinquency: Prevention, assessment, and intervention* (pp. 3–18). New York: Oxford University Press.

Roesch, R., & Golding, S.L. (1980). *Competency to stand trial.* Urbana: University of Illinois Press.

Roesch, R., Ogloff, J.R.P., & Golding, S.L. (1993). Competency to stand trial: Legal and clinical issues. *Applied and Preventive Psychology, 2,* 43–51. doi: 10.1016/S0962–1849(05)80160-X

Roesch, R., Zapf, P.A., & Eaves, D. (2006). *Fitness Interview Test–Revised: A structured interview for assessing competency to stand trial.* Sarasota, FL: Professional Resource Press.

Rogers, R. (1997). *Clinical assessment of malingering and deception* (2nd ed.). New York: Guilford.

Rogers, R., Hinds, J.D., Sewell, K.W. (1996). Feigning psychopathology among adolescent offenders: Validation of the SIRS, MMPI-A, and SIMS. *Journal of Personality Assessment, 67,* 244–257. doi: 10.1207/s15327752jpa6702_2

Rogers, R., Sewell, K. W., Grandjean, N. R., & Vitacco, M. (2002). The detection of feigned mental disorders on specific competency measures. *Psychological Assessment, 14,* 177–183. doi: 10.1037/1040–3590.14.2.177

Rosado, R. (2000). *Understanding adolescents: A juvenile court training curriculum.* Washington, DC: American Bar Association Juvenile Justice Center.

Ryba, N.L., Cooper, V.G., & Zapf, P.A. (2003). Juvenile competence to stand trial evaluations: A survey of current practices and test usage among psychologists. *Professional Psychology: Research and Practice, 34,* 499–507. doi: 10.1037/0735–7028.34.5.499

Sanborn, J.B. (2009). Juveniles' competency to stand trial: Wading through the rhetoric and the evidence. *Journal of Criminal Law & Criminology, 99,* 135–213.

Scott, E.S., & Grisso, T. (2005). Developmental incompetence, due process, and juvenile justice policy. *North Carolina Law Review, 83,* 101–147.

Scott, E. S., Reppucci, N. D., & Woolard, J. L. (1995). Evaluating adolescent decision-making in legal contexts. *Law and Human Behavior, 19,* 221–244. doi: 10.1007/BF01501658

Scott, E., & Steinberg, L. (2008). Adolescent development and the regulation of youth crime. *The Future of Children, 18,* 13–33.

Slobogin, C., & Fondacaro, M. R. (2011). *Juveniles at risk: A plea for preventive justice.* New York: Oxford University Press.

Stahl, A. L., Puzzanchera, C., Livsey, S., Sladky, A., Finnegan, T. A, Tiernney, N., & Snyder, H. N. (2007). *Juvenile court statistics 2003–2004.* Pittsburgh, PA: National Center for Juvenile Justice.

Steinberg, L., & Cauffman, E. (1996). Maturity of judgment in adolescence: Psychosocial factors in adolescent decision making. *Law and Human Behavior, 20,* 249–272.

Steinberg, L., Graham, S., O'Brien, L, Woolard, J. L., Cauffman, E., & Banich, M. (2009). Age differences in future orientation and delay discounting. *Child Development, 80,* 28–43. doi: 10.1007/BF01499023

Sue, D. W., & Sue, D. (1999). *Counseling the culturally different: Theory and practice* (3rd ed.). Hoboken, NJ: Wiley.

Snyder, H. N., Sickmund, M., & Poe-Yamagata, E. (1996). *Juvenile offenders and victims: 1996 update on violence.* Washington, DC: U.S. Department of Justice, Office of Justice Programs, Office of Juvenile Justice and Delinquency Prevention.

Viljoen, J. L., Klaver, J., & Roesch, R. (2005). Legal decisions made by preadolescent and adolescent defendants: Predictors of confessions, pleas, appeals, and communication with attorneys. *Law and Human Behavior, 29,* 253–277. doi: 10.1007/s10979–005–3613–2

Viljoen, J. L., Odgers, C., Grisso, T., & Tillbrook, C. (2007). Teaching adolescents and adults about legal proceedings: A comparison of pre- and post-teaching scores on the MacCAT-CA. *Law and Human Behavior, 31,* 419–432. doi: 10.1007/s10979–006–9069–1

Viljoen, J. L., Penner, E., & Roesch, R. (2012). Competence and criminal responsibility in adolescent defendants: The role of mental illness and adolescent development. In B. C. Feld & D. Bishop (Eds.), *The Oxford handbook on juvenile crime and juvenile justice* (pp. 526–548). New York: Oxford University Press.

Viljoen, J. L., & Roesch, R. (2005). Competence to waive interrogation rights and adjudicative competence in adolescent defendants: Cognitive development, attorney contact, and psychological symptoms. *Law and Human Behavior, 29,* 723–742. doi: 10.1007/s10979–005–7978-y

Viljoen, J. L., Roesch, R., & Zapf, P. A. (2002). Interrater reliability of the Fitness Interview Test across four professional groups. *Canadian Journal of Psychiatry, 47,* 945–952.

Viljoen, J. L., Slaney, K. L., & Grisso, T. (2009). The use of the MacCAT-CA with adolescents: An item response theory investigation of age-related measurement bias. *Law And Human Behavior, 33*(4), 283–297. doi: 10.1007/s10979–008–9154–8

Viljoen, J. L., Vincent, G. M., & Roesch, R. (2006). Assessing child and adolescent defendants' adjudicative competency: Interrater reliability and factor structure of the Fitness Interview Test. *Criminal Justice and Behavior, 33,* 467–487. doi: 10.1177/0093854806287317

Viljoen, J. L., & Wingrove, T. (2008). Adjudicative competence in adolescent defendants: Judges' and defense attorneys' views of legal standards for adolescents in juvenile and criminal court. *Psychology, Public Policy, and Law, 13,* 204–229. doi: 10.1037/1076–8971.13.3.204

Warren, J. I., DuVal, J., Komarovskaya, I., Chauhan, P., Buffington-Vollum, J., & Ryan, E. (2009). Developing a forensic service delivery system for juveniles adjudicated incompetent to stand trial. *International Journal of Forensic Mental Health, 8,* 245–262. doi: 10.1080/14999011003635670

Wingrove, T. A. (2007). Is immaturity a legitimate source of incompetence to avoid standing trial in juvenile court? *Nebraska Law Review, 86,* 488–514.

Woolard, J. (2005, March). *Parental involvement and juvenile participation: Comparing parents' and youths' decision-making about the juvenile justice process.* Paper presented at the Annual Meeting of the American Psychology-Law Society, La Jolla, California.

Woolard, J. L., Cleary, H., Harvell, S., & Chen, R. (2008). Examining adolescents' and their parents' conceptual and practical knowledge of police interrogation: A family dyad approach. *Journal of Youth and Adolescence, 37,*685–698. doi: 10.1007/s10964–008–9288–5

Woolard, J. L., & Harvell, S. (2005). MacArthur Competence Assessment Tool–Criminal Adjudication. In T. Grisso, G. Vincent, & D. Seagrave (Eds.), *Mental health screening and assessment in juvenile justice* (pp. 283–294). New York: Guildford Press.

Youth Criminal Justice Act, S.C. 2002, c. 1.

Zapf, P. A., Hubbard, K. L., Cooper, V. G., Wheeles, M. C., & Ronan, K. A. (2004). Have the courts abdicated their responsibility for determination of competency to stand trial to clinicians? *Journal of Forensic Psychology Practice, 4*, 27–44. doi: 10.1300/J158v04n01_02

Zapf, P. A., & Roesch, R. (2001). A comparison of the MacCAT-CA and the FIT for making determinations of competency to stand trial. *International Journal of Law and Psychiatry, 24*, 81–92. doi: 10.1016/S0160–2527(00)00073-X

Zapf, P. A., & Roesch, R. (2009). *Best practices in forensic mental health assessment: Evaluation of competence to stand trial.* New York: Oxford University Press.

Zapf, P. A., & Roesch, R. (2011). Future directions in the restoration of competence to stand trial. *Current Directions in Psychological Science, 2, 20*, 43–47. doi: 10.1177/0963721410396798

Zapf, P. A., Roesch, R., & Viljoen, J. L. (2001). The utility of the Fitness Interview Test for assessing fitness to stand trial. *Canadian Journal of Psychiatry, 46*, 426–432.

13 Clinical Forensic Evaluations for Juvenile Transfer to Adult Criminal Court

Randall T. Salekin, Ross D. Grimes,
and Elizabeth W. Adams

The past two decades evidenced marked advances in theoretical and scientific work on the topic of juvenile transfer to adult criminal courts. Melton, Petrila, Poythress, and Slobogin (1987, 1997) produced one of the first chapters discussing juvenile transfer evaluations and provided initial information on how psychologists might address the amenability to treatment question. Subsequently, Ewing (1990) wrote one of the first journal articles on juvenile transfer evaluations and discussed specific ways in which psychologists could address the questions of dangerousness, sophistication-maturity, and amenability—constructs widely accepted to be relevant in the transfer decision (and disposition in general). Ewing noted that psychologists, because of their clinical training might be in a particularly good position to address questions of developmental maturity. Later, Kruh and Brodsky (1997) wrote an article on transfer to adult courts and outlined ways in which youth might be assessed on the constructs of dangerousness, developmental maturity, and amenability to treatment. At the time, Kruh and Brodsky argued that clinicians might be in a better position to address questions of developmental maturity, but also provided suggestions for ways in which amenability and dangerousness could be evaluated. Their paper also pointed to future research that was needed if transfer evaluations were to be conducted in a sound manner. That same year, Witt and Dyer (1997) provided information for how clinicians might conduct scientifically grounded waiver-of-jurisdiction evaluations. Grisso (1998, 2000, 2013) also provided information on how to conduct forensic evaluation of youth facing transfer and provided a specific structure for the evaluation. His work suggested that clinicians should focus on family, peers, community, academic and vocational skills, and personality functioning. Salekin (e.g., Salekin, Yff, Neumann, Leistico, & Zalot, 2002) provided empirical data on the core criteria that underpin the *Kent* (1966) constructs of dangerousness, sophistication-maturity, and amenability to treatment and also highlighted in a series of articles (Salekin, 2002a, 2002b; Salekin, Rogers, & Ustad, 2001) ways in which transfer cases might be addressed.

Witt (2003) provided an illustrative case example of a transfer evaluation that highlighted how the evaluation could be conducted and interpreted. More recently, Salekin (2015), in his monograph on disposition and transfer titled *Forensic Evaluation and Treatment of Juveniles: Innovation and Best Practice* has provided details on both disposition and transfer evaluations by compiling research on the three key constructs of risk, developmental maturity, and amenability, and by providing detailed information on how to collect and interpret information for the evaluation. Information is offered pertaining to the specific tests to use, such as structured interviews, and information is also provided on how to write reports and offer expert testimony. The Salekin (2015) book offers best practice information regarding the forensic evaluation and treatment of juveniles.

At present, there is little knowledge about the training of the mental health professionals who perform these evaluations (Grisso, 2013; Salekin, 2015). Given what we know about traditional models for training in psychology, it is possible that clinicians currently conducting these evaluations have the necessary education in some areas of relevance (e.g., forensic psychology primarily with adult samples) but perhaps not in other areas of relevance (e.g., child clinical and developmental psychology). Thus, clinicians conducting waiver evaluations may be only partially prepared for the task, have a smaller literature base from which to work, and have no formal set of experts to whom they can easily turn to obtain guidance. Moreover, a concern in the past has been that the constructs forensic clinicians are evaluating have often been ill-defined or not well understood (see Salekin, Yff et al., 2002). Given the large volume of waiver evaluations in most courts and the importance of psychological information to these decisions, the dearth of information in the literature about any aspect of evaluation in waiver-of-jurisdiction cases is concerning and signals the need for further research and theory on transfer evaluations. Fortunately, as can be seen earlier, research and relevant monographs are emerging on this topic as are training opportunities (see Salekin, 2015).

The purpose of the current chapter is to offer clinicians a starting point for conducting evaluations of youth who are facing transfer to adult criminal courts. In order to help with this process, the current chapter first discusses the rationale for removing some youth from the juvenile justice system. Next, this chapter discusses the mechanisms for transfer of juveniles to adult court. This section provides an overview of the various ways in which youth can be transferred to adult court (or sent back to juvenile courts from adult court). Then, the chapter looks at the three main standards used to guide judicial decision making in transfer cases and how those standards vary across jurisdictions. Under the broader umbrella of these "standards," are the more specific criteria for transfer. The chapter also provides a brief overview of these criteria, which generally are derived from the factors delineated in *Kent v. U.S.* (1966). The chapter suggests that the *Kent* criteria are key to the psychological evaluation and can be reduced to three primary psycholegal factors: (a) risk for dangerousness, (b) sophistication-maturity, and (c) treatment amenability. Next, in order to provide information on how such evaluations can be grounded in theory and science, the chapter discusses the most recent literature on risk for dangerousness, sophistication-maturity, and amenability to treatment.

In addition to these purposes, the current chapter offers suggestions regarding psychological measures that might be used to help with the evaluation as well as offering a model for how mental health professionals can conceptualize and assess youth in order to present this information to the courts. The perspective of proper transfer evaluations put forth in this chapter is based on the available research and theory on the topic. However, much of the hope in developing scholarly research chapters on such a topic is to also stimulate further empirical inquiry to refine the evaluation process and to further policy changes. The last section of the chapter offers concluding observations about the role and value of forensic evaluations of youth facing transfer, including the potential for clinical evaluations to influence the legal definition and application of waiver laws to maximize the healthy development and well-being of young people. Finally, we provide a brief illustrative case example based on our model.

Historical Purposes for Waiver of Jurisdiction

Traditionally, the rationale and juvenile court's interest in upward waiver has been fourfold. First, the juvenile justice system was initiated, in part, to reform and rehabilitate delinquent individuals. One historical purpose of upward waiver was to avoid the inclusion of young people whose "ingrained criminality" and potential dangerousness might detract from the rehabilitative aim of programs that were intended to benefit children and adolescents in juvenile settings. Therefore, the waiver mechanism has been used to remove certain youth from a system intended to treat young people they believed were displaying conduct problems, perhaps for developmental reasons, but were also viewed as amenable to the juvenile justice system's intervention.

Second, and relatedly, the juvenile justice system has the corresponding aim of protecting the public. In most states, the juvenile justice system is required to release youth in their custody when they reach a certain age (typically 17 or 18 years). However, if it is believed that a juvenile is unlikely to be rehabilitated prior to that time, the legal system allows juvenile court judges to waive jurisdiction. This alleviates any potential threat the youth might pose to public safety at the time of mandatory release or in terms of escape from juvenile facilities, which are occasionally viewed as less able to contain dangerous young individuals than are adult facilities.

Third, and related to the previous two points, in cases in which there is a slim chance for rehabilitation, it has been argued that the state has an interest in avoiding the use of rehabilitation resources that are in short supply. As Grisso notes (2000), although the state has an obligation to initiate and develop services for youths whose needs exceed the juvenile system's current capacities, historically, upward waiver has been accepted as a legal mechanism for avoiding the use of existing resources when the availability of the typically effective treatments would be unlikely to result in rehabilitation (see also Mulvey, 1984).

Fourth, until waiver and transfer laws were enacted, it was legally presumed that all juveniles below a certain age (typically 18 years) were not sufficiently mature to be held criminally responsible for their antisocial acts (Bechtold & Cauffman, 2014; Ewing, 1990). Young people below this age were automatically treated as juveniles under the principle of *parens patriae*. This guiding principle remains as a rebuttable presumption based, at least in part, on the juvenile's level of maturity. Thus, juveniles may be transferred if they are viewed as mature participants in the crime. Although it is unlikely that a juvenile court judge would ever take this factor of maturity into consideration, in isolation, it is possible that a judge may consider the concept of developmental maturity in conjunction with risk for future offending and amenability to treatment (see Brannen et al., 2006). The next section of this chapter discusses the various mechanisms for transfer.

Mechanisms for Transfer: Routes to and From Juvenile Courts

Juvenile courts, since their inception, have always had an option of waiving their jurisdiction over some young individuals, allowing their charges to be filed in criminal court. There are different mechanisms by which the justice system achieves transfer. Transfer mechanisms can be grouped into three categories: judicial (upward) waiver, statutory exclusion, and direct file. Transfer mechanisms are determined by state law, and states may use any combination of mechanisms in order to achieve their desired policy outcomes. Every state now allows for the transfer of youthful offenders to adult court (Redding & Murrie, 2010; Salekin, 2015). Judicial waiver is the most common method for transferring cases to adult criminal court. Currently, 45 states allow judicial waiver transfer for certain types of cases on the basis of juvenile court judges' decisions about the appropriateness of trying an adolescent in adult criminal court (Chen & Salekin, 2012). Under this method, juvenile court judges make a determination about whether the juvenile should be tried in juvenile or adult court. Juvenile court judges may consider a range of factors in making this decision, including psychological evaluations that address the psychological makeup of the youth as they pertain to *Kent* criteria.

National trends in juvenile law in the mid-1980s and early 1990s introduced two other mechanisms by which youths may be transferred to criminal court for trial: (a) statutory exclusion and (b) prosecutorial direct file. At present, 29 states provide a statutory exclusion. In these states, certain age and criminal offense types (serious offenses such as murder and assault) are by design outside the jurisdiction of the juvenile court (Chen & Salekin, 2012). As such, the charge is filed directly in criminal court without any formal evaluation of the young person's characteristics or input from juvenile court judges. Under this system, the age of the offender and the type of offense may automatically move the case to go to adult court. For example, a state may legislate that any offender aged 14 and up accused of homicide will be tried in adult court. States may codify any combination of ages and offense categories to be transferred, taking the discretion of the juvenile court judges out of the decision-making process (Penney & Moretti, 2005; Snyder & Sickmund, 2006).

The second transfer mechanism adopted in 15 states in the late 1980s and early 1990s is called *prosecutorial direct file* (Salekin, 2015). This mechanism allows prosecutors to file charges against youths in either juvenile or criminal court for certain types of offenses. With this mechanism, prosecutors have the discretion to file the case in juvenile or adult court. This method may also be limited to certain offenses or ages. Similar to statutory exclusion, there is no psychological evaluation of the youth or hearing at the juvenile level prior to the prosecutor's filing of the case directly in adult criminal court. With all the mentioned transfer mechanisms, the age at which a juvenile may be transferred varies between states and between transfer mechanisms.

The majority of states allow transfer for youths aged 14 and over; however, a number of states also allow transfer of youths between 10 and 13 years of age, depending on the type of offense or method of transfer. Thus, the minimum offender age range for transfer by judicial waiver, statutory exclusion, and prosecutorial discretion varies across the 50 states from 10 to 17 years of age. Recent estimates of the percentage of juveniles transferred to adult court under each type of transfer indicate that although newer routes have been introduced, judicial transfer from juvenile courts remains a relatively common mechanism for transfer (Griffin, Torbet, & Szymanski, 1998; Puzzanchera, 2003; Snyder & Sickmund, 2006) and waiver rates differ based on the types of crimes committed and what is occurring in various communities with respect to the level of juvenile violence. Figure 13.1 shows the high rate of violence in the mid-1980s and early 1990s that resulted in a high rate of transfer to adult courts. Interestingly, the use of transfer mechanisms also declined as the rate of youth violence declined (Snyder & Sickmund, 2006), and in 2010, 55% fewer cases were waived in comparison to the 1990s (Office of Juvenile Justice and Delinquency Prevention, 2014). The Office of Juvenile Justice and Delinquency Prevention (OJJDP) suggests that the decline in waiver cases may be due to new and expanded waiver laws allowing cases previously subject to waiver proceedings to bypass the juvenile court filing directly to criminal court.

Protective mechanisms are also in place if decision errors occur in the transfer process. That is, even in situations in which automatic transfer or prosecutorial direct file occur, psychological evaluations of young people are sometimes requested by criminal court judges to determine whether young individuals should remain in adult court or be returned to juvenile court (Fagan & Zimring, 2000; Grisso, 1998, 2013; Salekin, 2015). Specifically, judges have the opportunity to reverse transfer (decertify) youth. It is interesting that in some states where judicial transfer

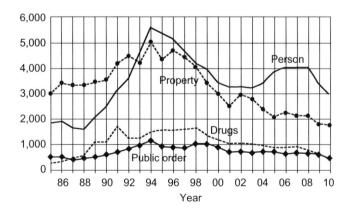

Figure 13.1 Cases judicially waived to criminal court
Source: OJJDP National Report. (2014). *Delinquency cases waived to criminal court, 2011.* Washington, DC: Author.

(upward waiver) is used, reverse transfer is an option (Griffin et al., 1998; Snyder & Sickmund, 2006). The reverse transfer process, available in 25 states, serves as a safety net for those youths who are inappropriately transferred to adult courts (e.g., they are immature or incompetent to stand trial); however, this mechanism typically requires that someone notice the developmental immaturity and/or the potential amenability of the youth and plan a pretrial hearing in criminal court, which then allows the criminal court judge to transfer jurisdiction back to juvenile court (Griffin et al., 1998; Grisso, 1998, 2013; Salekin, 2002a, 2002b; Snyder & Sickmund, 2006; Salekin, in press). There are six states in which a criminal court judge can oppose a juvenile court judge's ruling, returning the youth to juvenile court (Salekin, in press).

There is also the potential for blended sentencing wherein the trial occurs in one setting, but sentencing occurs in a different setting or combination of settings. Such a system can result in the imposition of both juvenile and criminal sanctions for the same offense (Salekin et al., 2013; Woolard, Odgers, Lanza-Kaduce, & Daglis, 2005). Blended sentencing and other transfer mechanisms are attempts to balance the need for protecting society against the recognition that children and adolescents may possess diminished capacity compared to adults and therefore deserve a judicial process that takes such factors into account. Given the different routes in which children and adolescents can find themselves in adult court, clinicians conducting transfer evaluations should be aware of the specific mechanisms and laws governing transfer for the state in which they are conducting their evaluations. Similar types of information may be considered in the upward transfer and decertification hearings; however, it is important for the child and adolescent forensic examiners to have knowledge of the mechanisms in play and the specific "standard" applied for the state in which they are conducting the evaluation. We elaborate on this latter point in the following section.

Legal Standards for Transfer to Adult Court

With each of the mechanisms for transfer, the judge typically applies a "standard" to determine whether or not the youth should be tried in adult court (Grisso, 2013). The purpose of any forensic clinical evaluation is to provide information to a decision maker that is relevant for a legal decision. This requires that the clinical forensic examiner be aware of the legal standard the legal decision maker will apply to reach his or her decision; this then allows the clinician to use the specific standard to help guide the evaluation process (Grisso, 1986, 2000; Melton et al., 1997). These standards can be found in the state statutes for transfer. Laws governing waiver require hearings to address whether evidence supports the statutory criteria for transfer. Some states have two to three levels of legal standards for waiver of jurisdiction. The first is a set of threshold conditions that are to be met before proceeding further (e.g., age, charged with a certain offense, a special history of prior offenses). If threshold measures are met, then courts in most states can proceed to the point of applying one of typically three standards referred to as "public safety" (or "danger to others"), "amenability to rehabilitation," and "the best interest of the child/community." More frequently, the state statutes simply explicitly list the condensed *Kent* criteria of risk for dangerous behavior, developmental maturity, and amenability in their statutes.

Many of these standards have similar meaning. Specifically, they are attempting to balance the development of the youth against the protection of society. The "danger to others" standard requires that youths cannot be waived to criminal court unless they present a serious risk of harm to others. The same standard would generally be applied in reverse waiver (requiring that the youth not present a serious risk of harm if the waiver were approved). This standard typically occurs in a brief phrase at the beginning of a statute that identifies it, such as "protection to the community," "danger to public," or "public safety" (Grisso, 2000; Grisso, Tomkins, & Casey, 1988). The "amenability to rehabilitation" standard allows the court to waive jurisdiction and remand the youth for criminal court trial only if the youth is found to be not amenable to rehabilitation with the resources available to the juvenile court (e.g., *Kent v. U.S.*, 1966) and/or "is not a

Table 13.1 Legal standards for transfer and the percentage of states using each standard

Method	Percentage of States
Public Safety	16%
Interests of Juvenile	18%
Balance of Public Safety and Interests of Juvenile	34%
List of criteria to consider (*Kent* criteria)	18%

Note: percentages do not equal 100 because some states do not allow judicial waiver, and some do not clearly define how the decision should be made.

fit and proper subject" for juvenile custody (Grisso, 2000; Grisso et al., 1988). The "best interest of the child/community" standard requires that the juvenile court judge consider issues such as dangerousness and amenability, and attempt to provide the best placement for the youth. Finally, as mentioned, it appears that increasingly states do not list a broader standard but rather list *Kent-like* criteria. All three standards and/or the listing of *Kent* criteria exist because of a concern for risk of harm to the public. Judgments about one standard (dangerousness) are often related to judgments about another (amenability) and all appear to draw on *Kent* criteria. Table 13.1 lists the four different systems and the percentage of states that use each.

Criteria Underpinning the Standards: The *Kent* Criteria

Under each standard within state statutes exist a set of criteria that judges consider in order to address the broader legal standard. Many of these factors listed in state statutes mimic *Kent* criteria. Specifically, in *Kent v. U.S.* (1966), the U.S. Supreme Court recommended eight factors, and most states have etched some permutation of these factors into their statutes or case law. The *Kent* criteria can be separated into straightforward legal criteria and others that are psychological or psycholegal in content. For example, some *Kent* criteria, such as whether the case has prosecutorial merit, or the desirability of trial in criminal court because the case involved adult associates, are primarily factors that the judges can determine without psychological input. Other elements of *Kent* ask about danger to others, sophistication-maturity, and amenability to treatment; these are pertinent psychological constructs for which judges often request psychological information via reports and testimony.

Eight Kent Factors Distilled to Three Key Psychological Constructs

While the *Kent* case has been very instructive in reducing the arbitrariness of the transfer process, disparity exists regarding the number of factors that psychologists feel ought to be considered in transfer decisions. In essence, researchers and legal theorists have claimed that anywhere from one to five factors should be considered. For example, Melton et al. (1997) suggested amenability to treatment should be the primary factor considered in transfer evaluations (this was likely based on the amenability standard). Grisso et al. (1988) found dangerousness and amenability to treatment to be key, although they too were focusing primarily on legal standards. Ewing (1990), however, suggested three factors likely derived more directly from *Kent* criteria: (a) dangerousness, (b) sophistication-maturity, and (c) amenability to treatment. Kruh and Brodsky (1997) also believed that three factors were important. Heilbrun, Leheny, Thomas, and Huneycutt (1997) reviewed juvenile transfer statutes and found five pertinent factors: (a) treatment needs and amenability, (b) risk assessment for future criminality, (c) sophistication-maturity, (d) the presence of intellectual disability or mental illness, and (e) offense characteristics. Given this disparity, one might ask, how did we arrive at three concepts? We provide a rationale next.

Three factors probably best capture criteria pertinent to transfer determinations as well as offer a parsimonious model. In our opinion, considering amenability to treatment alone is under-inclusive (and this simply focuses on one standard and one *Kent* criterion). Practically, juvenile court judges will want to evaluate dangerousness and developmental maturity when weighing the protection of society against the development of the youth. Similarly, with five factors, redundancy exists. Specifically, the criterion of intellectual disability could be subsumed under the sophistication-maturity umbrella. That is, juveniles who are intellectually disabled are unlikely to be sophisticated or mature. Similarly, offense characteristics could be subsumed under the broader construct of risk for dangerous behavior. Therefore, factors from juvenile statutes and *Kent v. U.S.* (1966) directly relevant to the psychological functioning of juveniles can be distilled to (a) potential dangerousness, (b) sophistication-maturity, and (c) treatment amenability (Chen & Salekin, 2012; Salekin, in press). Juvenile court guidelines written by the National Council of Juvenile and Family Court Judges (NCJFCJ) (2005) echoed that these three concepts are necessary criteria in transfer decisions. However, it should be noted that the criteria that underlie these superordinate constructs are broad (e.g., intelligence and mental retardation would be included under the sophistication-maturity construct along with emotional stability, perspective taking, and decision-making characteristics). While we note that the eight *Kent* criteria can be distilled to three psychological concepts, not every state requires that these three factors be assessed. While dangerousness is always a criterion to consider, developmental maturity is mentioned explicitly in only about half of the states and implicitly in another 11 states. Amenability is also almost always mentioned as a criterion to consider in transfer evaluations. When deciding a transfer case, it is important to note that the court may weigh characteristics of the youth differently, allotting more weight to certain constructs (Brannen et al., 2006).

Recent U.S. Supreme Court Cases and New Ways of Processing Juveniles

Significant rulings at the federal level have reshaped the juvenile justice system again. In 2005, *Roper v. Simmons* removed the possibility of the death penalty for juveniles based in part, on the notion that juveniles' brains are not fully developed, affecting mental abilities such as self-control. This was extended in 2010 when the U.S. Supreme Court ruled that life without possibility of parole was cruel and unusual when applied to youth convicted of nonhomicide crimes (*Graham v. Florida,* 2010). In 2012, the Supreme Court further extended that principle by banning mandatory sentences of life without parole even for youths convicted for homicide (*Miller v. Alabama,* 2012*)*. Of particular note to clinicians was the role that various outside experts played in the Court's decision making process in these cases (through the submission of amicus briefs), including the American Psychological Association. In essence, these cases have reaffirmed the importance of considering both youths' specific situations and circumstances as well as the importance of examining general developmental differences between youths and adults. They also highlight the importance of forensic clinical evaluations of young people involved with the law to assist judges in their task with transfer decisions.

Conducting Evaluations of Youth Facing Transfer

Once mental health professionals know the standard being evaluated, the criteria that underlie the standard, and the psychological concepts they will evaluate, they can proceed to the next stage of the evaluation, which is to comprehensively assess the young person. On beginning the evaluation, it is important that the forensic expert allow adequate time to gather and assess the data required by this complex process. The first step should be to review all the relevant documents, including police, medical, psychiatric, social, and school reports. The areas for evaluation are extensive. A carefully constructed developmental history will be a composite of information gathered from home, school, workplace, and neighborhoods. Contacting teachers and court personnel facilitates the evaluation. A broad perspective in gathering the information is important because context may be at least as relevant as personality and behavior. The specific nature of the interviews should be clarified to the young person. It should be explained that the evaluation is not part of treatment, and the juvenile must be warned that his or her confidentiality *will not* be preserved. The expectation of a report to the court and possible court testimony about the juvenile should be made explicit. This must be thoughtfully communicated with sensitivity to the child or adolescent's comprehension of the situation.

Once these factors have been carefully considered, the transfer evaluation is likely to center on *Kent* criteria. The evaluation of juvenile offenders being considered for transfer thus entails the consideration of three broad factors: (a) risk of dangerous behavior in the community, (b) level of developmental maturity (and sophistication-maturity), and (c) amenability to treatment. Traditionally, these factors have been evaluated by clinical interview alone. Salekin (2015) provides a structure for the evaluations that includes assessment of personality (character) and psychopathology. Two other broad concepts are essential to evaluate. These include the truthfulness of the young person's report (and collateral source reporting) and, as mentioned, the young person's placement on relevant psycholegal constructs. With regard to this latter point, tools have been designed for the assessment of young offenders on pertinent constructs. For example, the Risk-Sophistication-Treatment-Inventory (RSTI; Salekin, 2004; see also Salekin, 2006 and Iselin & Salekin, 2008), Structured Assessment of Violence Risk in Youth (SAVRY; Borum, Bartel, & Forth, 2005), and the Youth Level of Service/Case Management Inventory (YLS/CMI; Hoge, 2005) are all measures that should be considered when developing a test battery for the examination of young people involved with the law. The SAVRY or YLS/CMI might be utilized for risk for violence questions. Similarly, the YLS/CMI and RSTI could be used to address questions of amenability and treatment needs. Importantly, all measures allow for the assessment of protective factors, which are linked to amenability issues. With respect to developmental maturity, only the RSTI allows for the assessment of this important juvenile psycholegal construct. Importantly, a self-report and briefer version of the RSTI is in development (the RSTI-SR).

While the aforementioned measures provide structure to the evaluation process, they do not supplant the need for extensive knowledge about adolescent development and the need to keep abreast of the current literatures on transfer, risk for violence in youth, maturity, and treatment amenability. That is, examiners should look to the body of knowledge about which they are experts—scientific, theoretical, and clinical knowledge—for the factors they will use to address the questions posed by the legal standards. Recent updates on this science are provided in Salekin (2015). Forensic clinicians should be cognizant of new developments in these areas and should be able to discuss them in the context of their evaluations. In the next sections, we discuss risk for dangerousness, sophistication-maturity, and amenability to treatment, in turn.

Risk for Dangerous Behavior: A Research Update

At the time we wrote one of our first papers on transfer to adult court (Salekin, 2002a, 2002b, 2002c), we provided a number of broad factors that could be considered in dangerousness assessments. We also reviewed the current state-of-knowledge on risk for dangerousness assessments. We mentioned that when Ewing (1990) wrote his paper on the assessment of youth being transferred to adult court, he recommended against assessments of dangerousness because empirical evidence during that era suggested that clinicians were not particularly accurate at predicting its occurrence. During that same time, Barnum (1987) concurred with this belief and suggested that clinicians were better equipped to conduct evaluations of amenability to treatment than dangerousness. In recent years, however, advances in risk assessment have demonstrated that mental health professionals are in a better position to offer information on risk of future dangerousness (Borum, 1996). We also noted that the increased accuracy for risk prediction stemmed from the manner in which the evaluations were structured. Creating more proximal time lines for prediction as well as making predictions along a continuum of probabilities improved the accuracy of dangerousness assessments (Grisso & Appelbaum, 1992; Kruh & Brodsky, 1997). Aside from reviewing the general beliefs about assessing dangerousness in youth, we provided a general framework for such evaluations, suggesting that core criteria from juvenile court and psychological perspectives would be important to consider (Salekin, Yff et al., 2002). We also suggested, as did Kruh and Brodsky (1997), that antisocial pathways and psychopathy assessments might further add to the risk for dangerousness equation. Within this section, we discuss three main sources of information from prototypical analyses research as well as antisocial pathway and psychopathy research, to provide important updates on their validity so as to best inform decisions about risk for dangerousness.

One aspect of dangerousness evaluations involves examining the prototypes for dangerousness that juvenile court judges and clinical psychologists provide. In two prototypical analyses (Salekin et al., 2001; Salekin, Yff et al., 2002), factors that clinicians and juvenile court judges found to be pertinent in the assessment of dangerousness included youth who engaged in extreme unprovoked violence, had severe antisocial personalities, lacked remorse/guilt and empathy, had violent histories, and had shown a leadership role in a crime. These factors tend to align with characteristics in the social science literature that suggest a higher likelihood for, and stability of, future offending (e.g., Loeber & Stouthamer-Loeber, 1998; Lynam, Miller, Vachon, Loeber, & Stouthamer-Loeber, 2009; Moffitt, 1993, 2003).

Over the last decade a great deal of research has begun to suggest that psychopathy may be a moderate predictor of violence and aggression in youth (Forth & Burke, 1998; Frick & Morris, 2004; Lynam & Gudonis, 2005; Salekin, 2006; Salekin & Lynam, 2010). Research suggests that personality characteristics such as those found in psychopathic individuals are important considerations in predicting both general and violent recidivism in adults (Leistico, Salekin, DeCoster, & Rogers, 2008; Salekin, Rogers, & Sewell, 1996). Regarding dangerousness and treatment amenability, evidence of psychopathic traits may be used in the future to support transfer to adult court or reverse transfer to juvenile court (Vitacco & Vincent, 2006; Vitacco & Salekin, 2013; Vitacco, Salekin, & Rogers, 2010). The use of at least a component of psychopathy may become more frequent, given the addition of the limited prosocial emotion specifier to the DSM-5 diagnosis of conduct disorder (CD) (American Psychiatric Association, 2012, 2013). Although it should be noted that CD+limited prosocial emotion (LPE) may not equate to psychopathy and there may be a need to further specify CD (see Salekin, in press). In the past two decades, research on adolescent psychopathy has grown substantially (Salekin & Lynam, 2010). From this research, psychopathy in youth is found to be predictive of later offending and of violent offending for a timeline of at least two to three years (Asscher et al., 2011; Leistico et al., 2008). However, there are limitations to our knowledge of long-term life outcomes of youth with psychopathic traits and limitations to assessment and predictive capabilities (Vitacco, Salekin, & Rogers, 2010).

While some research suggests that psychopathy is predictive of some forms of dangerousness with youth (e.g., Gretton, McBride, Hare, O'Shaughnessy, & Kumka, 2001; Salekin, Ziegler, Larrea, Anthony, & Bennett, 2003), other research has concerned the appropriateness of the construct to children and adolescents. There are some very good arguments to suggest that we do not actually know if this is psychopathy per se or something else. Although, increasingly, there is data to show that at least a portion of the youth carry their psychopathic symptoms through to adulthood, many of the children assessed do not (Andershed, 2010; Lynam et al., 2009). With respect to risk assessment, because the descriptors used in the measures tend to be predictive, they may be indicated for use in transfer evaluations—but psychologists should be clear in stating that there is no evidence that the disorder is untreatable (see Caldwell, Skeem, Salekin, & Van Rybroek, 2006; Salekin, 2002c; Salekin, Rogers, & Machin, 2001; Salekin, Tippey, & Allen, 2012). In fact, reductions in offending after treatment with these youth can be found (Salekin, 2010; Salekin, Worley, & Grimes, 2010; Salekin et al., 2012). Finally, the longitudinal studies that are emerging suggest we can predict only a few years out, although more data has been emerging on this topic (see Salekin, Debus, MacDougall, & Clark, Chapter 14 in this volume). If clinicians use proximal terms such as *psychopathy-like features,* then they need to be very active in providing relevant court personnel with accurate information regarding treatment amenability, comorbidity, and other pertinent information in their reports and testimony.

Over the last two decades, violent and antisocial pathways have been conceptualized in ways that may facilitate determinations of dangerousness (e.g., Loeber & Stouthamer-Loeber, 1998; Moffitt, 2007). Developmental pathways may assist in the determination of future dangerousness by distinguishing among different types of offenders. In 1993, Moffitt proposed two distinct pathways to antisocial behavior: (a) "adolescent-limited," and (b) "life-course persistent" delinquents. This model is particularly important because it addresses the issue of why many adolescents engage in antisocial behaviors and then later desist and live normal lives. Moffitt (2007) suggested that "life-course persistent" offenders begin committing crimes early in childhood, continue well into adulthood, and manifest characteristics that seem categorically antisocial. Severe, early, and frequent antisocial behavior is predictive of more negative outcomes (Farrington, Loeber, Stallings, & Homish, 2008; Kreuter & Muthén, 2008). In contrast, "adolescent-limited" offenders tend to commit their first offense in mid-adolescence and desist from illegal behavior as they enter adulthood. This taxonomy has been widely accepted as evidenced by its being codified in the DSM-IV and DSM-5 (American Psychiatric Association, 1994, 2013), invoked in *Child and Adolescence Violence Research* from the National Institute of Mental Health (2000) and the U.S. Surgeon General's report, *Youth Violence* (U.S. Department of Health and Human Services, 2001), and presented in abnormal psychology and criminology textbooks. In 2003, Moffitt provided a 10-year review of her developmental taxonomy; subsequently she has updated what we know about the taxonomy (Moffitt, 2007). Her work has shown that, in general, there is support for her model. However, Moffitt also pointed to the need for further research on these CD trajectories across time and the need to continue to report differences across race, gender, and age groups. For example, although the pathway research generally applies to young people, not all young people who are categorized as adolescent-limited desist from criminal behavior in later life. Also, we now know that not all early starters are antisocial throughout the life span. Providing the most recent data on these pathways, how youth fit into the pathways, and the percentage of youth that persist on a pathway, may be helpful to the court.

Previously Kruh and Brodsky (1997) suggested that other constructs may offer clinicians important information regarding dangerousness in very circumscribed areas. For instance, the Overcontrolled Hostility scale (OH; Megargee, 1966) may be useful in identifying offenders with a history of infrequent, but extremely severe, violence (Du Toit & Duckitt, 1990). The generalizability of the overcontrolled hostility construct to juvenile offenders has been suggested as a possible predictor of certain types of offenses in certain types of adolescents. Specifically, Kruh and Brodsky (1997) suggested that this scale may help to identify weapon-related violence with homicidal intent against other individuals during periods of disinhibition. Unfortunately, we have limited knowledge on the validity of the OH subtype scheme for adolescent offenders. Specifically, only a few studies (e.g., McGrory, 1991; Salekin, Ogloff, Ley, & Salekin, 2002) back this finding. Clearly, more research is needed with the OH construct before mental health professionals consider its use in transfer evaluations.

The foregoing reveals theoretical and empirical research suggesting at least three avenues psychologists may want to use to inform courts about the dangerousness of youth. First, knowledge of antisocial pathways may assist mental health professionals and the courts in predicting the likelihood of future criminal and violent behavior. Pathways may allow clinicians to classify and speak to the percentages of youth who decelerate, maintain, or escalate to serious crime and violence. Second, measures of psychopathy-like characteristics have been shown to have predictive validity with adolescent offenders and may prove moderately useful to risk assessments with juvenile offenders. Third, utilization of specific characteristics such as those found in prototypical analyses may also prove effective. In general, these characteristics overlap with factors found to be important in distinguishing developmental pathways for youth, as well as those factors from the literature on interpersonal callous traits. Combining approaches may further improve the court's ability to make appropriate decisions with respect to dangerous behavior (see Salekin, 2004; Spice, Viljoen, Gretton, & Roesch, 2010).

Although psychologists are now in a better position to incorporate dangerousness evaluations into transfer cases than in the past, a word of caution is necessary. Despite some advances in the assessment technology for child and adolescent forensic populations, the current empirical basis for juvenile risk assessment is still limited. Even when the previously mentioned factors are used in making predictions about dangerousness, it is recommended that psychologists be very clear regarding the continuing limitations of risk assessment with adolescent populations. One important consideration here is that while theory suggests that certain youth will persist in criminality well into adulthood, empirical evidence tracking juvenile recidivism rates is limited. However, psychologists could add important comparative statistical information such as the percentage of youth who continue on a certain pathway, the percentage of youth who drop off of specific pathways, and what factors account for continuation or discontinuation of a particular pathway. These data help frame the information that pertains to the judge's decision. In addition, with regard to risk assessments, we also believe that Grisso (1998) offered some important considerations for these evaluations. Specifically, Grisso (1998) suggested that clinicians make their risk estimates conditional with regard to future situational contexts. This simply means that mental health professionals should recognize that the likelihood of future violence is not merely a product of an individual's characteristics but also is dependent upon the situation and setting (conditions) in which the young individual will find him- or herself in the future (Grisso, 2000; Swanson, Borum, Swartz, & Monahan, 1996).

Developmental Maturity (Sophistication-Maturity): A Research Update

Most states either explicitly list or implicitly mention developmental maturity as a factor to consider in transfer cases. Ewing (1990) suggested that developmental maturity (and sophistication-maturity) is one construct about which forensic clinicians are especially capable of offering the courts useful information. He advised that clinicians attempt to assess both cognitive and emotional maturity. With regard to cognitive maturity, Ewing recommended that juveniles evaluated for transfer be administered intelligence (e.g., Wechsler Intelligence Scale for Children-5th edition) and achievement (e.g., Wide Range Achievement Test-4th edition) tests. Ewing argued that such measures evaluate a young person's general intellect, but also evaluate factors such as "perception, cognitive processing, attention, and judgment all of which can be reflective of a youth's sophistication-maturity. . . [and the youth's] level of criminal responsibility" (p. 8). Similarly, the rationale for using achievement testing is based on the notion that many juvenile delinquents have co-occurring learning disabilities that may negatively affect academic performance and contribute to their lack of age-appropriate maturity. Ewing (1990) recommended that a juvenile's level of emotional maturity also may be examined through interviewing and psychological testing. With respect to psychological testing techniques, he recommended that self-report measures such as the Millon Adolescent Clinical Inventory (MACI) (Millon, 1993), and projective techniques such as the Thematic Apperception Test (TAT; Murray, 1937) and the Rorschach Inkblot test, be used to provide "indications of the juvenile's internal controls, ability to organize thoughts coherently, and reality testing" (p. 9). Although projective testing has been criticized of late, there are some basics that can likely be determined from projective tests. For instance, Arden, Trzaskowski, Garfield, and Plomin (2014) found that human figure drawings predicted intelligence many years after the drawings were created. This is not to suggest that these methods be used, only to state that there are a number of factors that clinicians can use their clinical acumen for and research to begin to develop hypotheses regarding a young person's developmental maturity. Salekin (2015) provides some information on how broad strands of information can be used to help understand a young person's level of maturity.

We would add that the forensic clinicians who work with juvenile offenders are often aware of the need to extend these assessments of traditional intellect and maturity to examine the greater issue of sophistication-maturity in the legal context. Certain abilities not tapped by traditional assessment procedures may be important for clinicians to assess in order to inform the court. Occasionally, youth may have a significant degree of practical knowledge for survival outside of academic settings but score low on traditional measures of intellect and achievement. Information regarding maturity can also be assessed through clinical interviewing and gauging a young person's developmental maturity in relation to his or her moral maturity.

Converging information (Salekin et al., 2001; Salekin, Yff et al., 2002) suggests that the legal term and construct of sophistication-maturity may consist of a complex set of interrelated factors: autonomy or adult-like self-reliance, understanding of behavior norms, foresight, and the ability to engage in balanced judgment. With respect to criminal sophistication, areas such as autonomy, and cognitive and emotional abilities, may still apply but tend to be used for antisocial purposes. Thus, autonomy, in this case, appears to be one of increased levels of self-reliance and self-concept that may be antisocial in nature, with the adolescent tending to embrace a criminal lifestyle. This may be evidenced by progressively more involvement (and perhaps increasingly sophisticated involvement) in crime. Factors that lead to decisions about maturity include the extent to which youth engage in planned and premeditated crimes, their ability to give thought to the consequences in a larger frame, and their decision-making skills more generally (engage in cost benefit analysis with respect to decision making). Another way to think about this is that developmental maturity may be moderated by other factors such as criminal thinking styles or even psychopathy.

Finally, with regard to sophistication-maturity, mental health professionals should attempt to assess moral development. Whereas very young children promote self-interest by "taking care of number one," older children and adolescents move through different stages that reflect more well-reasoned perspectives on morality (Kohlberg, 1981; Sternberg, 2000). Psychologists should assess whether there is a mismatch between the youth's level of moral development, his or her cognitive development, and his or her behavior. For example, a youth may understand that physical aggression is wrong for a variety of reasons (including very high levels of moral reasoning) but may still engage in this antisocial behavior.

Assessing varying degrees of developmental maturity amongst youth will likely provide the courts with a more complete picture that will assist them in weighing concerns about the protection of society against the development of the youth. If youth are assessed as low in developmental maturity (and/or prosocial in maturity), then they may well be provided further opportunities to develop in the community while remaining under the juvenile jurisdiction. In addition, developmental maturity might also be viewed as a treatment target, and something to be built upon, in youth who are showing low levels of maturity or in those showing higher levels of maturity but who lack prosocial decision making.

Of the three constructs related to transfer, developmental maturity (and sophistication-maturity) is likely to pose the most problems for psychologists in terms of juvenile transfer evaluations. On the one hand, higher levels of maturity might produce better treatment results and allow for better decision making. Youth with high-level cognitive skills, moral knowledge, emotion regulation, and clearer identity (including at least some aspect of prosocial identity) are likely to benefit from psychological therapy (Garfield, 1994; Jordan, 2009; Salekin, 2015). For example, emotion regulation would help promote stable functioning and would facilitate youth in reaching their treatment goals. On the other hand, higher maturity might be indicative of more sophisticated criminal conduct that may (or may not) be particularly malleable or amenable to treatment. An important question is whether such youth are able to utilize their higher levels of maturity toward changing their antisocial beliefs and conduct. Although this issue is a complex one for clinicians to resolve, assessment of the amenability to treatment construct (e.g., motivation to change and protective factors) may help to elucidate whether a youth high in maturity has the capability to make positive changes in his or her life.

Next we provide a model for examining developmental maturity in adolescents that considers developmental status (e.g., age), the environment in which young individuals currently live, any potential psychopathology they may exhibit, and the context or situation in which young individuals make their decisions (see Figure 13.2). This model suggests that developmental status, which includes developmental maturity, has a two-way interaction with the environment (e.g., parenting, family socioeconomic status, and so forth) that also must be viewed through any form of psychopathology (or lack of pathology) that the young individual may have (e.g., attention deficit hyperactivity disorder, depression). Although we have not drawn arrows for the paths from decision making back to developmental status, we believe that decision making has a cumulative effect on developmental maturity. Psychopathology is included because we know that a number of juveniles have high levels of psychopathology and that some of this pathology may impact decision making and opportunities for growth in developmental maturity. In sum, the model suggests that there are a number of factors that should be considered in examining a young individual's level of developmental maturity.

Amenability to Treatment: A Research Update

Researchers (Cauffman & Steinberg, 2000; Salekin, 2002c; Steinberg & Cauffman, 1999, 2000; Zimring, 1998) have suggested that youth are more malleable than adults and are therefore more amenable to treatment. Although not well tested, there is some evidence to suggest that the earlier a disease or disorder is detected, the better the prognosis. This notion has been, in part, the basis for treating rather than punishing errant youth who may have externalizing disorders such as oppositional defiant disorder (ODD), CD, or other antisocial behavior problems. The idea of early detection and treatment would suggest that many youth who come into contact with the law

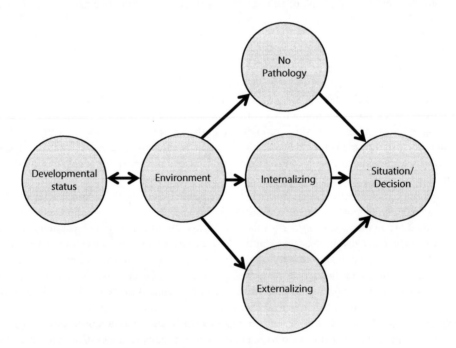

Figure 13.2 Model of developmental sophistication-maturity

can be directed toward more prosocial lifestyles. Personality research also backs this contention, with the earlier years showing less stability (more opportunity for change) in personality than later years (Roberts & DelVecchio, 2000).

An important step in the amenability to treatment construct is understanding juvenile characteristics that are predictive of positive and negative treatment outcomes. Several early studies (e.g., Adams, 1970; Carlson, Barr, & Young, 1994; Izzo & Ross, 1990) suggested that factors such as cognition, self-evaluation, expectation, an understanding and appraisal of the world, and values are important in the treatment prognosis of young individuals. Amenable young persons have also been described as being smart, verbal, anxious, insightful, aware of their difficulties, and motivated toward change. Young individuals without some of these characteristics are also likely amenable, but some standard interventions for youth may need to be altered.

When clinical psychologists (Salekin et al., 2001) and juvenile court judges (Salekin, Yff et al., 2002) were asked to rate core characteristics for treatment amenability, important elements included motivation to engage in treatment, awareness of difficulties, expectations that treatment would be beneficial, remorse/guilt, empathy, knowledge of right from wrong, anxiety about the circumstances, and a stable and supportive family environment. Many of the characteristics mentioned here have been studied in relation to treatment outcome and have been found to be positive signs for subsequent gains in psychotherapy (e.g., Carlson et al., 1994; Frank, 1959; Garfield, 1994). Three other prognostic variables that should be evaluated by forensic clinicians involved in transfer evaluations include the degree and type of psychopathology, family/support system considerations, and protective factors (e.g., prosocial role model or interests/hobbies).

Strong conclusions should not be drawn, however, between severe antisocial personality and poor treatment prognosis. Important in this regard are meta-analyses on psychopathy and treatment (Salekin, 2002c, 2010) that have shown that psychopathy, particularly in children and adolescents, may be more amenable to treatment than previously thought (see also Caldwell, Skeem, Salekin, & Van Rybroeck, 2006; Hawes & Dadds, 2005). Considerations of whether, and how ingrained, youth are in a violent criminological lifestyle coupled with considerations for whether youth have stable psychopathic-like characteristics may be more relevant in determining the severity of treatment resistance and the need for disorder specific interventions. For instance, Salekin et al. (2012) found that the mental models intervention was effective at reducing interpersonal callous traits even in a residential sample of youth who had run the course of probation, numerous detention stays, and police contact before arriving at a residential facility.

Disorders other than conduct problems—such as psychotic disorders, posttraumatic stress disorder (PTSD), and depression—may be severe and difficult to treat but they are often treated differently by the courts (Barnum, 1987; Grisso, 1998). Barnum (1987) contended that assessing signs of low risk for career criminality and treatable violence-related psychopathology (such as depression and posttraumatic stress) is necessary in such evaluations and should be reported to the judge. Mental health professionals may want to inform the court that appropriate treatment (psychopharmacological/behavioral or other) would likely reduce offenses that were previously linked to psychotic thinking, depressive conditions, or PTSD symptomatology. Thus, although clinicians may want to provide information on the chronicity, severity, and associated treatment difficulties of a disorder, they may also want to provide information to the courts about how the psychopathology is associated with antisocial conduct and outline ways in which interventions may reduce antisocial behavior. Evaluators of youth facing transfer should also look for the presence of protective factors that may cancel or attenuate the influence of known risk factors. Variables such as social competence, intelligence, positive peer relations, positive peer response to authority, and effective use of leisure time can serve as buffers in the presence of risk factors (e.g., Luthar, 1991).

Family is also a critical component related to how well children and adolescents respond to psychotherapy. Parental resistance to viewing a youth's problems, at least in part, as a symptom of family difficulties can be a negative factor for amenability to treatment. Kazdin (1985) concluded that assessment of parents' expectations of treatment for their adolescent children may be a useful predictor regarding amenability to treatment. He found that parents' expectations influenced the degree to which children complied and changed with psychotherapy. Examiners might look for other strong attachment figures the youth has who could facilitate treatment, such as family or community members.

Ewing (1990) and Mulvey and Iselin (2008) have suggested that other factors to be considered include whether (a) the dispositions available to the juvenile court are likely to rehabilitate the juvenile before that court's jurisdiction ends, and (b) the services available to the juvenile in the criminal justice system are appropriate to the youth's needs. Also, as Ewing (1990) points out, in some states there are provisions for state-funded, out-of-state treatment of serious juvenile offenders, but only if the offender is assessed as being amenable to treatment and the agency or facility providing treatment is able to accept the youth pursuant to court order. Although it is important to have current knowledge of the range of services available to juveniles in both the juvenile justice system and the criminal justice system in the jurisdiction where one is operating, Kruh and Brodsky (1997) contended that child forensic psychologists should be less concerned with this issue than the issue of whether or not amenability is possible at all. According to these authors, a finding of amenability places some pressure on the courts to provide adequate treatment to youth who are amenable to treatment. If clinicians recommend that the youth is not amenable simply because facilities are not available in the district, then this may diminish constructive attempts to process and treat youth in juvenile facilities.

Taken together, child forensic psychologists assessing treatment amenability of youth facing transfer would want to consider and assess the degree and type of psychopathology, protective factors, and family functioning as well as motivation and expectation for change, level of anxiety or concern, and remorse and empathy for the current offense and/or previous offense(s). These factors could be assessed through interviews, collateral source data, police and court records, and other relevant information as well as administration of the RSTI. The clinician will want to understand whether previous treatments were adequate or appropriate, and why such rehabilitative efforts may have failed. In view of the generally unsatisfactory state of juvenile rehabilitative efforts throughout the country, counsel for the child should always explore exactly what has been done for the child in the past (e.g., nature of the prior treatment, frequency of efforts made to work with him or her, and whether the youth was given a chance to "resocialize"). Some youth are placed on probation or in a "training" school but then are, for the most part, neglected (Grisso, 2000; Strasburger, 1989).

Three aspects of youthful behavior further complicate juvenile assessment of amenability. First, juveniles, in contrast to adults, rarely wish to appear sick no matter how advantageous this may be legally. Adolescents sometimes assume a "tough guy/girl" stance, preferring to be seen as "bad" rather than "mad." Second, some youth do not fully understand the purpose of the evaluation (see Salekin, Kubak, & Lee, 2008). Third, juveniles may be suspicious of the evaluation and not provide adequate information. Some researchers note that adolescents can be frightened by the process and may have unrealistic ideas of the examiner. For instance, youth may not believe they have to provide comprehensive information because mental health professionals, with their special expertise, can fill in the gaps. Of course, the more comprehensively that adolescents report information to the mental health professional, the better the evaluation will be. Because of the intrusiveness of the consequences into the lives of juveniles, they may be unmotivated to cooperate with evaluation. Because of this parameter, care must be exercised with the evaluation of a young individual.

Fortunately, the literature indicates that adolescents are remarkably resilient and subject to positive change through both development and treatment (Woolard, Fondacaro, & Slobogin, 2001). Youth who are motivated to change may be less likely to offend (Salekin, Lee, Schrum Dillard, & Kubak, 2010). Those who are amenable to treatment may demonstrate less violent conduct and be less likely for transfer to adult court (Spice et al., 2010). Because of the potentially severe consequences in juvenile transfer evaluations, these factors must be given substantial weight. Also, it should be noted that many of the treatment amenability factors are also dynamic and subject to change even with oppositional young individuals. Some of this might be accomplished through motivational interviewing and attempts to change the young individual's outlook.

To this point in the chapter, we have discussed the rationale for waiver, the various mechanisms for waiver, the standards that are applied by judges in determining whether a youth should be transferred, as well as the criteria that underlie each standard. We also suggested that the most parsimonious model for waiver evaluations is one that considers (a) the truthfulness of reporting; (b) the young individual's personality and type/level of psychopathology (if any); and the three psycholegal factors, namely (c) risk for dangerousness, (d) sophistication-maturity, and (e) treatment amenability. These five issues are important to the evaluation. In the next section of this chapter, we discuss how this information can be coherently evaluated and reported upon in a psychological report as well as in testimony. We suggest several psychological measures that can be used in transfer evaluations but focus the section on the RSTI, which provides a structure for evaluating risk, maturity, and amenability.

The Evaluation and Psychological Report: Putting It All Together

After a full investigation of the young person's history, records, family life, and legal consequences, the clinician's report to the court should be informative, clear, and concise. The report should contain identifying data, an introduction outlining the forensic issue (the psycholegal question being addressed), the circumstances initiating referral for evaluation, the sources of information on which the evaluation was based, a description of the offense, and background information. The background information should include developmental, social, educational, vocational, and legal information. In addition, this section should include medical history and psychiatric history. The report should also include a behavioral observation section (including mental status) and specific information pertaining to risk, developmental maturity, and amenability. These latter psycholegal factors can be subsections within the report. Finally, the report should include a summary, a diagnostic impression, and a conclusion to the forensic question. The mental health professional's greatest contribution to the court in transfer cases is the careful reporting of observable data and the conclusions derived from the data. If the data are insufficient to support an opinion, we suggest, as did Grisso (2000), that no opinion be offered.

It is difficult to address questions of dangerousness, sophistication-maturity, and treatment amenability in the absence of assessment technology designed specifically for the measurement of these constructs. The RSTI (Salekin, 2004) is one such measure as it was designed to meet the specific needs of mental health professionals who provide general dispositional rehabilitation evaluations for the juvenile courts. The RSTI addresses the three important psychological constructs mentioned earlier, namely (a) a juvenile's level of dangerousness, (b) level of sophistication-maturity, and (c) the degree to which the youth is amenable to treatment. It provides a focused assessment by producing ratings that provide a basis for nuanced descriptions of the complex prongs delineated in the *Kent* decision that inform court placement and treatment decisions. The RSTI can be used prior to disposition decisions or to assist with legal decisions regarding treatment and design of individualized treatment plans.

The RSTI comprises a semi-structured interview (90 minutes) and rating scale designed to help clinicians assess juvenile offenders (aged 9–18 years) in three important areas. The RSTI measures each of the areas mentioned earlier using three scales composed of 15 items. Items are rated on three-point scales (0 = *absence of the characteristic/ability*, 1 = *subclinical/moderate*, 2 = *presence of the characteristic/ability*), which reflect the extent to which the individual demonstrates the specific characteristic or ability. Each scale contains three subscales, referred to as *clusters*. The Risk for Dangerousness scale is comprised of the Violent and Aggressive Tendencies (R-VAT), Planned and Extensive Criminality (R-PEX), and Psychopathic Features (R-PPF) clusters. The clusters of the Developmental Maturity (and Sophistication-Maturity) scale are Autonomy (S-AUT), Cognitive Capacities (S-COG), and Emotional Maturity (S-EMO). The Sophistication-Maturity Scale is neither prosocial nor antisocial. It measures developmental maturity broadly while also allowing clinicians to then rate the extent to which the related emotional/cognitive skills are used for criminological purposes. Finally, the Treatment Amenability clusters are Psychopathology-Degree and Type (T-PAT), Responsibility and Motivation to Change (T-RES), and Consideration and Tolerance of Others (T-CAT). Table 13.2 lists the items for each RSTI scale and cluster.

Table 13.2 Items for the RSTI scales and clusters

Risk for Dangerousness Scale

R-VAT	R-PEX
Engages in unprovoked violent behavior	Severe antisocial behavior
Violence toward individuals	Premeditated crimes
Violence toward animals	Leadership role in crimes
Easily angered and physically aggressive	Frequency of past criminal acts
Generally oppositional and cruel	Age of onset of antisocial behavior
	Delinquent peer group

R-PPF	
Lacks remorse	
Lacks empathy	
Egocentric	
Manipulative	

Developmental Maturity (and Sophistication-Maturity) Scale

S-AUT	S-COG
Autonomy	Aware of wrongfulness of crimes
Internal locus of control	Understanding of behavioral norms
Development of self-concept	Able to identify alternative actions
Self-reflection	Foresight (has future time perspective)
Ability to anticipate consequences	Cost-benefit analysis in decision making

S-EMO	
Able to delay gratification	Conflict resolution
Moral development	Interpersonal skills
Self-regulation of emotion	

Treatment Amenability

T-PAT	T-RES
Degree of psychopathology	Motivated to engage in treatment
Treatability of psychopathology	Takes responsibility for actions
Aware of difficulties and problems	Open to change
Insight into cause of problems	Expects change
Limited police/court/probation involvement	Positive involvement by parents

T-CAT

Anxiety about the circumstance
Feels guilt/remorse
Considers and generally cares about others
Has protective factors
Has positive attachments

The *RST-I Interview Booklet* (Salekin, 2004) contains queries designed to obtain background, clinical, and historical information, as well as a sample of the juvenile's behavioral and psychological functioning. Items on the rating form reflect information central to the three scales. Scoring of items involves reviewing and synthesizing information from an interview; collateral sources such as school, police, detention, and previous treatment records; and consultations with parents or guardians. Proper administration and coding of the RSTI requires professional knowledge, skill, and experience with juvenile offenders. Forensic clinicians can learn how to best administer the RSTI by working with other professionals who have administered the instrument, or attending workshops on the RSTI. As reported in the manual (Salekin, 2004), the RSTI has promising psychometric properties. For instance, Zalot (2002a, 2002b) found interrater interclass correlation coefficients (ICCs) of .84, .73, and .83; Leistico (2002) found ICCs of .94, .74, and .91 on the Risk of Dangerousness, Sophistication-Maturity, and Treatment Amenability scales, respectively. Spice et al. (2010) also found good reliability estimates for the RSTI (ICCs of .68, .60, .72; Cronbach's alpha .77, .69, .87). The validity of the RSTI appears to be promising (e.g., Leisitco & Salekin, 2003; Salekin, 2004; Spice et al., 2010) and there are two shorter research versions of the measure undergoing testing. For instance, Ang, Salekin, Sellbom, and Lee (2014) found convergent validity of the RSTI self-report (RSTI-SR), demonstrating that developmental maturity was positively correlated with conscientiousness (.43), problem-focused coping (.42), and emotion-focused coping (.30). Additionally, sophistication-maturity was found negatively related to neuroticism (−.35) showing discriminant validity. In addition, an abbreviated measure of the RSTI (RSTI-Abbreviated) has been developed, and this measure is showing promising reliability and validity estimates (see Gillen et al., 2015).

Although the RSTI is one potential measure to use in such evaluations, it should not be the sole measure utilized in evaluations, and it is not a tool that directly links to legal decisions. Rather, forensic assessments should incorporate a battery of measures of standard intelligence testing, child and adolescent psychopathology, and other areas. The RSTI is useful because its scoring design allows for systematic follow-up regarding recidivism, treatment compliance, and other outcome indicators, and the scales appear to be change sensitive, indicating that following intervention risk scores go down, whereas developmental maturity and amenability can be elevated. Even though the RSTI directly taps important juvenile psycholegal constructs it should be kept in mind that the ultimate decision is left to the juvenile court judges. Also, there has been some discussion as to whether these are psychological concepts, psycholegal concepts, or legal concepts. With respect to our research, we view these concepts as psychological. However, they become legal concepts in terms of the level at which juvenile court judges deem the information pertinent to transfer. Another area where the concepts become psycholegal is how judges decide to balance the concepts along with other information when they decide upon waiver (e.g., public safety is more important than questions of amenability).

Although the RSTI has a normative sample, it intentionally does not provide, or suggest, cutoff scores that would dictate or exclude a particular disposition for a given youth. It is necessary for mental health professionals to use scores in conjunction with their clinical acumen to arrive at decisions regarding a young person's dimensional level of risk, maturity, and treatment amenability. Examiners are encouraged to consider contextual factors not only when scoring the RSTI items, but also when interpreting scale scores within the broader clinical context. For instance, as a result of their predominant environment, young individuals may lead a lifestyle that relies on risky behavior for survival. The RSTI interview allows clinicians to obtain this information, which should be brought to light in the context of evaluations and testimony.

Using Clinical Information to Address the Legal Standards and Criteria Delineated in the Statutes

Upon concluding their evaluations and arriving at opinions relevant to the questions of risk, developmental maturity, and amenability to rehabilitation, examiners should be able to clearly explain how they arrived at those opinions by showing what information from the evaluation was relevant, and what reasoning was used to move from the psychological material to the clinical opinion (Grisso, 2000; Salekin, 2015). Earlier, we suggested use of the RSTI as a coherent structure for evaluating juvenile offenders that takes into consideration theories of developmental pathways to antisocial behavior and prototypical analyses results to arrive at decisions about risk for offending. These theoretical underpinnings to the RSTI closely follow the theories of juvenile offenders developed and tested by Quay (1964) as well as the empirical work of others (DiCataldo & Grisso, 1995; Moffitt, 1993, 2003; Loeber, 1991).

The point of this chapter is to suggest that the examiner should have some model for describing the youth, whether it be for a general disposition or in more serious cases. This model should derive from a theory of child and adolescent development, personality, and delinquency. Thus, it might include classification of the young people according to a number of typologies and systems for personality description. The field provides a number of useful theories and typologies devised in extensive research specifically for delinquent youths that clinicians can draw upon (e.g., Achenbach, 1991; Jesness & Wedge, 1983, 1984; Loeber, 1991; Moffitt, 2003; Quay, 1987; Witt, 2003). However, some of the former typology theories are dated and less commonly known by juvenile court judges. Thus, a more parsimonious model such as one that examines truthfulness, personality, mental health, risk, developmental maturity, and amenability to treatment is advised (see Salekin, 2015).

Providing Context to the Evaluation

Reports should examine and characterize the extent of involvement with the law, how severe the past crimes have been, and if there exist personality characteristics (e.g., interpersonal callousness) that might contribute to a risk for further offending. With respect to developmental maturity, the reports should center on the extent to which the young person is a mature participant and how much maturity he or she exhibits, including autonomy, cognitive, and emotional maturity. Although the law might be interested in these factors for legal purposes (culpability), psychologists should shed light on how these factors might improve treatment outcome, should youth effectively use their autonomy, cognitive, and emotional skills to make substantive changes in their lives. Since a number of the factors are dynamic (e.g., autonomy, use of cognitive and emotional skills), it is quite possible that a number of these factors could be established as treatment targets.

Although the current chapter addresses the practice of assessing dangerousness, sophistication-maturity, and amenability to treatment, it does not inform clinicians of the complex issue of weighing these constructs (see Brannen et al., 2006). This task is difficult and weighting of factors will be left to judges in juvenile courts, at least with regard to the ultimate decision. Nevertheless, psychologists should provide more detail than simply a young person's level of risk for dangerous behavior, developmental maturity (and sophistication), and treatment amenability in isolation. We would suggest that if psychologists view the young person as amenable to treatment and can develop an appropriate roadmap for change that they highlight those points in their psychological reports. Psychological reports and testimony can be used to convey the ways that potential dangerousness could be managed while treatment is ongoing.

Thus, transfer evaluations should aim to not only describe the youth but also to determine and delineate what needs to change, outline what the optimal rehabilitation plan is, and what the probable outcome would be if the plan were implemented. With respect to describing what needs to change, the examiner should formulate a theory about the relation between the developmental picture of the young person and the young individual's delinquency. This theory, according to Grisso (2000), becomes the basis for identifying what aspects of the juvenile and/or family need to change in order to meet the juvenile justice system's objectives (to provide for the welfare of the youth and to promote public safety). Estimating the probable outcomes of future rehabilitative efforts requires that the examiner take into consideration factors that have been found to be related to the likelihood of change in psychotherapeutic interventions, including an individual's capacity to form attachments to caregivers, degree of anxiety or psychological discomfort (which can be used to motivate change), and the chronicity of the condition that must be modified (Grisso, 1998, 2013; Salekin, 2015). Relevant considerations may range from factors borrowed from criminology (e.g., as noted earlier, the fact that youths with certain histories tend not to persist in delinquency past the adolescent years; Moffitt, 1993; Loeber & Farrington, 1998) to knowledge derived from psychopharmacology regarding the likely response of a youth to a proposed trial on a particular medication (Grisso, 2000).

The Ultimate Opinion Regarding Transfer

Once the clinician has offered an opinion about the degree of risk that the case poses, it is the role of the judge to determine whether that level of risk is sufficient to meet the legal requirements for a conclusion that the youth is dangerous or should be waived to criminal court or alternately, the young person poses low levels of risk, and should remain in juvenile court. Thus, as mentioned, risk for dangerousness, developmental maturity, and treatment amenability are important in any juvenile evaluation, however, the concepts as they relate to transfer standards have more to do with the *degree* or *level* to which a youth possesses characteristics of a given construct and how the judge *balances* the constructs. Another example of how the decisions are legal is the amenability to rehabilitation standard, which, as stated in most states, does not ask simply whether the youth's conduct can be modified. It asks whether it can be modified within the resources and time available to the juvenile court (Mulvey & Iselin, 2008). Although the psychological concept of amenability does not typically factor in a time limit, the juvenile justice system requires this consideration. Thus, according to the legal system the amenability question is not answered merely by evaluation of the characteristics of a youth, or whether the youth is "malleable." The question also requires matching those characteristics with the options available for rehabilitation and considering whether treatment gains can be made within a specific time frame. When clinicians do not know what resources are available, their role is to describe what the youth needs and to let others in the legal system obtain from other sources (e.g., probation officers, other mental health professionals) the information needed to identify whether there are appropriate rehabilitation services to meet those needs.

Transforming the Law: How Difficult Evaluations Can Eventually Inform Policy

Assessments for waiver of jurisdiction cases serve many important purposes for policy makers and society if they are performed properly. First, these evaluations can be instrumental in identifying youths who are likely to desist in their delinquent behavior as they age out of adolescence. Second, these assessments can identify youths who are developing serious mental disorders and who need psychiatric and psychological treatment. Third, properly performed forensic clinical evaluations can contribute to the fairness of the legal process in transfer cases. As Salekin (2015) and Grisso (2013) note, if they are designed appropriately, guided by legal standards and requirements, they assure that the court does not overlook important psychological variables, and they provide a relevant structure within which the courts can think about the cases before them in relation to the legal standards and criteria underpinning the legal standard. If they are performed carefully, guided by a scientific foundation, they protect against bias and potentially faulty presumptions, enhancing the quality of justice (Brannen et al., 2006; Grisso, 2000; Penney & Moretti, 2005; Salekin, 2015).

Finally, we believe that one way to improve transfer evaluations is to further examine the dynamic risk factors and to have the evaluations conducted frequently. At present, single-point predictions are limited in what they can offer (Douglas & Skeem, 2005). This may not be particularly helpful as the young person grows. With policy change and a juvenile justice system that is transformed, the concepts of violence prevention, management, and treatment could very well be infused into contemporary thinking of juvenile evaluations and treatment. This conceptual development might underscore the necessity for identifying, measuring, and monitoring changeable risk factors in youth over time because these factors are the most promising targets for risk reduction efforts. To be maximally effective, the chief task with youth risk assessment and management contexts might be to evaluate risk factors and their variability over time, rather than assuming that single-point estimates will remain valid indefinitely (Douglas, Cox, & Webster, 1999). Developmental maturity and amenability offer two concepts that are potentially changeable and may impact youth violence and treatment potential over time, but single-point predictions do not allow for the development of these concepts (Salekin, 2015). As such, one policy change might be to more frequently adopt the blended sentence option so that youth can be monitored not only retrospectively but also prospectively over longer periods of time before making a decision about transfer.

Summary

On one hand, courts influence the clinical forensic process by providing legal guidance for clinicians. On the other hand, the ways that clinicians frame their opinions and reports for use by the legal decision maker have an effect on the way the courts structure their application of legal standards to questions of transfer. Grisso (2000) suggested that out of this two-way interaction emerges and evolves the meaning of the legal standards that guide judicial decisions about juvenile waiver in practice. What the current chapter indicates is that more than one assessment over time might better inform whether youth should be transferred to adult courts. This may mean that one important consideration for policy change might be to expand the use of blended sentencing so that clinicians and juvenile court personnel can monitor the future of adolescent risk, developmental maturity, and amenability, to determine if youth can be returned to the community for healthy development rather than be transferred to adult court where rehabilitation is less likely.

Case Study

The following presents a sample case study focusing on the issues we have discussed in the present chapter. Because of the variability in state laws regarding transfer the following discussion may be more or less relevant depending on the specific statutes governing the transfer process in any one state. We have generally used the most common aspects of state transfer laws and combined them with the aspirational goals outlined in the chapter.

Summary of Case

Michael is a 15-year-old boy who was apprehended by the police after attempting to rob a convenience store. During the robbery, which was committed with two adult accomplices, one of the clerks was injured and sustained a broken arm after being hit with a club by one of Michael's accomplices. Michael lives with his mother and has had no contact with his father since he was 5 years old. With respect to past legal history, Michael has had some prior involvement with the judicial system. Specifically, he has been charged with truancy at age 13, running away from home at age 14, and defacing property at age 15. As a result of his past legal contacts, Michael had been detained and received treatment in a detention center where he resided for 60 days. In the current case, the juvenile court prosecutor moved for the case to be heard in criminal court, in light of the seriousness of the offense, the injuries sustained by the clerk, and Michael's previous involvement with the juvenile court. Michael's attorney objected to this move, and the court convened a hearing to determine whether or not the case should be processed in adult court. The juvenile court judge also ordered a psychological evaluation to assist in the determination.

Psychological Evaluation

The measures administered by the psychologist included an intelligence test, an achievement test, a structured interview, a self-report measure, and the Psychopathy Checklist: Youth Version (PCL:YV) and RSTI. This latter measure is designed specifically to look at constructs relevant to juvenile offenders and indexes three broad domains: risk, developmental maturity (and sophistication/maturity), and treatment amenability. The psychological evaluation ordered by the court revealed that Michael has average intelligence and below average academic achievement. The interviewing and psychological testing revealed that Michael met criteria for CD. School records indicated he was retained in first grade and has been suspended from school multiple times for defiance, disrupting the classroom, and occasionally bullying peers. His school suspensions date back to early elementary school. He saw a school counselor for several sessions in third grade; however, lack of funding resulted in these sessions being discontinued, with minimal progress. After completing the interview and rating scale for the RSTI, results showed that Michael scored in the low-to-average range, indicating low-to-average risk. On the developmental maturity (sophistication/maturity) scale, Michael scored in the low-moderate offender range, suggesting some developmental maturity but also a need for growth in this area. This scale was also retrospectively scored for the time at which Michael had potentially been involved in the alleged crime. It was noted that his maturity was even lower at the time of the offense. These two time points suggest that some growth in developmental maturity had already occurred. On the treatment amenability scale, Michael scored in the middle range. Cluster scores for all of the scales were in the average to low range.

The psychologist also administered the PCL:YV, a measure of psychopathy-like features in youth. After an extensive interview and review of records, the psychologist determined that Michael scored 15 out of 40. While there is no generally accepted cutoff for diagnosing psychopathy, individuals generally must score between 25 and 30 to be considered high scorers on adult measures. During the evaluation, Michael showed features of irresponsibility and stimulation seeking; however, the psychologist determined that Michael did not display the interpersonal callousness and emotional detachment usually associated with psychopathy, that he had taken responsibility for his role in the crime, and that he was remorseful about its effect on the victim.

Finally, based on a general clinical interview with Michael, his mother, and his teachers, and the administration of a general psychopathology scale, the psychologist determined that Michael met diagnostic criteria for CD. Both his mother and teachers reported that Michael had been in trouble with the law, had engaged in some fighting, and had on occasion lied and/or refused to comply with rules. He often does not seem to understand why others are upset with him and therefore does not change his behavior to improve his relationships. His mother reported that she has never really considered nor does she have the financial or practical ability to take him to treatment or therapy sessions.

Based on the results of the interviews and clinical measures completed by Michael, his parents, and his teachers, the psychologist provided to the court a report outlining his findings in three areas: Michael's risk of future dangerousness, Michael's overall level of developmental maturity, and the likelihood that he will be amenable to the treatment facilities available to the juvenile court within the time frame of its jurisdiction. In the area of dangerousness, she concluded that with appropriate supervision, Michael was unlikely to present a significant danger; however, she noted that Michael's parents were unlikely to provide such an environment without additional support. In the area of developmental maturity and sophistication/maturity, she concluded that Michael presented himself as low to moderate with regard to developmental maturity but that he had made some gains in this regard, showing greater levels of prosocial autonomy, cognitive skills (better decision making), and emotional skills (emotion regulation). It was noted that he also engaged in some planning and forethought before acting, and that he was showing some escalation in criminal activity, but in the case being considered he was viewed as having taken much less of a leadership role in the crime. Finally, in the area of amenability to treatment, the psychologist concluded that Michael was likely amenable to treatment, but that previous attempts at short-term treatment had been ineffective and that he required relatively intensive services, particularly relating to his association with a deviant peer group and poor familial relations. She noted that Michael had expressed some willingness to undergo psychological therapy. Moreover, she determined that Michael did have genuine interest in treatment. Pursuant to generally accepted practice, the psychologist provided guidance on the key juvenile constructs pertinent to transfer.

Interpretation of Law

According to state law, the judge must balance "the interests of the juvenile" against "the welfare of the public." Probable cause for charging Michael in the robbery is assumed for purposes of the transfer hearing. The relevant statutes lists eight factors that should be considered in making a transfer determination, grouped under the three major areas of dangerousness/risk to others, sophistication/maturity, and amenability to treatment. Table 13.3 presents seven factors to be considered (note: specific factors vary slightly by state, the following are the most common ones listed), along with one-sentence summaries of the prosecution case, defense case, and any data

Table 13.3 Factors for transfer determination: An example

Threshold Criteria

Criteria: Age
Data/Evidence From Psychological Report: Michael is 15 years old. This is within the age range allowed for transfer to adult court.

Criteria Impacting Dangerousness

Criteria: Seriousness of Offense
Data/Evidence From Psychological Report: Report indicated that Michael did not intend to hurt the clerk and was not the party committing the act in the alleged offense.
Criteria: Public Safety
Data/Evidence From Psychological Report: Without effective treatment and monitoring, Michael is likely to engage in increasingly dangerous behavior.

Criteria Impacting Sophistication and Maturity

Criteria: Sophistication and Maturity of the Minor (Sophistication/Maturity)
Data/Evidence From Psychological Report: Michael has low average intelligence and emotional maturity. Michael's criminal history suggests some increasing sophistication, but it is not extensive at this point. Moreover, his increasing developmental maturity could be used to his benefit in treatment.

Criteria Impacting Treatment Amenability

Consideration: Availability, willingness, and amenability to treatment (Treatment Amenability)
Data/Evidence From Psychological Report: Michael expressed some willingness to engage in treatment, but that treatment would have to be intensive in order to be effective.

Criteria Impacting Multiple Constructs

Criteria: Culpability of Minor (Dangerousness, Sophistication/Maturity)
Data/Evidence From Psychological Report: Report indicated that Michael was not directly involved with the alleged violent act.
Criteria: Prior record of delinquency and previous contacts with social service agencies (Dangerousness, Sophistication/Maturity, Treatment Amenability)
Data/Evidence From Psychological Report: Michael is following a slight escalating trajectory of delinquency, however, the late start of his delinquency is consistent with an adolescent-limited pathway.

or evidence obtained by the psychologist that is relevant to the factor at issue. Age is considered from a threshold standpoint as to whether or not the juvenile is old enough per statute to be transferred. These factors, the most common ones listed in state statutes, are similar to the criteria originally listed in *Kent*, though some purely legal criteria are excluded. Some of these considerations may include evidence relevant to multiple constructs.

As can be seen, some of these criteria may provide information on more than one of the psychologically relevant constructs. Those involved in juvenile transfer evaluations should also be aware that legal issues such as prosecutive merit and a preference for joint versus severed trials for multiple defendants may play a role in the final decision making.

Deliberation and Outcome

In making his determination, the juvenile court judge considers the prosecution and defense cases, as well as the results of the psychological exam. After deliberation the judge finds that Michael's case should not be transferred to adult court. Specifically, he concludes that Michael currently lacks the developmental maturity and especially the sophistication and maturity of the criminal type to be equal to an adult criminal, that he was less culpable in the planning and execution of the crime, and that the treatment facilities available to the juvenile court system are sufficient for his rehabilitation prior to adulthood, that with appropriate supervision and monitoring (remedies available to the juvenile court through probation and/ or detention) he will not represent a substantial danger to the public. Although his escalating and relatively long history of offending and school behavior problems weighs in favor of transfer, this must be balanced against the fact that he has never received appropriate treatment. Given his family situation, treatment through the juvenile court system is more appropriate in this situation due to the level of monitoring and support he will have. The judge concludes that transferring Michael's case to adult court will prevent Michael from receiving the treatment and assistance he needs in order to become a productive member of society by the time he reaches adulthood. Treatment outcome monitoring is recommended with respect to risk, developmental maturity, and treatment amenability. In particular the judge requests regular updates from the therapist and probation officer assigned to Michael's case regarding his compliance with treatment, which is intended for use in determination of probation and supervision requirements.

Conclusion

The case study illustrates some of the common considerations in juvenile transfer hearings, as well as the difficult nature of balancing the competing interests of public safety and a commitment to the original ideals of the juvenile justice system of rehabilitation and treatment. As we noted earlier, mental health professionals who conduct juvenile forensic evaluations bear a responsibility to become familiar with the procedures, processes, and factors that apply in the state in which they practice. By framing the debate in terms of the increasingly well-validated psycholegal constructs of risk for dangerous behavior, developmental maturity (sophistication/maturity), and treatment amenability, we believe that psychologists can provide a valuable and critical service to the courts and to the juveniles that that the courts were created to serve. Two other important issues to assess include the truthfulness of the young person's reporting, and information on their character and psychopathology. Also, new methods for integrating and evaluating youth for disposition and transfer can be found in Salekin (2015). We believe that monitoring these psychological concepts over time will allow for better judgments regarding transfer, particularly when the cases are ambiguous. Blended sentencing and other nontraditional sentencing mechanisms may allow for new (e.g., changes in maturity and treatment) information to inform judicial and/or legal decisions about cases, which more traditional waiver mechanisms do not allow for, thereby maximizing the opportunity for healthy development in young people involved with the law.

References

Achenbach, T. (1991). The derivation of taxonomic constructs: A necessary stage in the development of developmental psychopathology. In D. Cicchetti & S. L. Toth (Eds.), *Rochester symposium on developmental psychopathology, Vol. 3: Models and integrations* (pp. 43–74). Rochester, NY: University of Rochester Press.

Adams, B. & Addie, S. (2011). *Delinquency cares waived to criminal court, 2008.* OJJDP. Fact sheet.

Adams, S. (1970). The PICO project. In N. Johnson, L. Savitz, & M. E. Wolfgang (Eds.), *The sociology of punishment and correction* (2nd ed.) (pp. 548–561). New York: Wiley.

American Psychiatric Association. (1994). *Diagnostic and statistical manual of mental disorders* (4th ed.). Washington, DC: Author.

American Psychiatric Association. (2012). Callous and unemotional specifier for conduct disorder. *DSM-5 Development: Proposed revisions. disruptive, impulse control, and conduct disorders.* Washington, DC: Author. Retrieved from www.dsm5.org/ProposedRevision/Pages/proposedrevision.aspx?rid=424#.

American Psychiatric Association. (2013). *Diagnostic and statistical manual of mental disorders* (5th ed.). Washington, DC: Author.

Andershed, H. (2010). Stability and change of psychopathic traits. What do we know? In R. T. Salekin & D. R. Lynam (Eds.), *Handbook of child and adolescent psychopathy* (pp. 233–250). New York: Guilford.

Ang, X., Salekin, R. T., Sellbom, M., & Lee, Z. (2014, March). *Assessment of sophistication-maturity with the Risk-Sophistication-Treatment Inventory Self-Report (RSTI-SR).* Poster presented at the American Psychology Law Association, New Orleans, LA.

Arden, R., Trzaskowski, M., Garfield, V., & Plomin, R. (2014). Genes influence young children's human figure drawings and their association with intelligence a decade later. *Psychological Science, 25,* 1843-1850.

Asscher, J.J., van Vugt, E.S., Stams, G.M., Dekovic̀, M. Eischelsheim, V.I., Yousfi, S. (2011). the relationship between juvenile psychopathic traits delinquency and (violent) recidivism: a meta-analysis. *Journal of Child Psychology and Psychiatry, 52,* 1134–1143. doi:10.1111/j.1469-7610.2011.024212.x

Barnum, R. (1987). Clinical evaluation of juvenile delinquents facing transfer to adult court. *Journal of the American Academy of Child and Adolescent Psychiatry, 26,* 922–925. doi:10.1097/00004583-198726060–00018

Bechtold, J., & Cauffman, E. (2014). Tried as an adult, housed as a juvenile: A tale of youth from two courts incarcerated together. *Law and Human Behavior, 38,* 126–138. doi:10.1037/lhb0000048

Borum, R. (1996). Improving the clinical practice of violence risk assessment: Technology, guidelines, and training. *American Psychologist, 51,* 945–956. doi:10.1037/0003–066X.51.9.945

Borum, R., Bartel, P., & Forth, A. (2005). Structured assessment of violence risk in youth. In T. Grisso, G. Vincent, & D. Seagrave (Eds.), *Mental health screening and assessment in juvenile justice* (pp. 311–323). New York: Guilford Press.

Brannen, D. N., Salekin, R. T., Zapf, P. A., Salekin, K. L., Kubak, F. A., & DeCoster, J. (2006). Transfer of youth to adult courts: A National study of how juvenile court judges weigh pertinent *Kent* factors. *Psychology, Public Policy, and Law, 12,* 332–355. doi:10–1037/1076–8971.12.3.332

Caldwell, M., Skeem, J. L., Salekin, R. T., & Van Rybroek, G. (2006). Treatment response of adolescent offenders with psychopathy features: A 2-year follow-up. *Criminal Justice and Behavior, 33,* 571–596. doi:10.1177/0093854806288176

Carlson, B. E., Barr, W. B., & Young K. J. (1994). Factors associated with treatment outcomes of male adolescents. *Residential Treatment for Children and Youth, 12,* 39–58. doi:10.1300/J007v12n01_03

Cauffman, E., & Steinberg, L. (2000). (Im)maturity of judgment in adolescence: Why adolescents may be less culpable than adults. *Behavioral Sciences and the Law, 18,* 741–760. doi:10.1002/bsl.416

Chen, D. R., & Salekin, R. T. (2012). Transfer to adult court: Enhancing clinical forensic evaluations and informing policy. In E. L. Grigorenko (Ed.), *Handbook of juvenile forensic psychology and psychiatry* (pp. 105–125). New York: Springer Science + Business Media. doi:10.1007/978–1–4614–0905–2_8

DiCataldo, F., & Grisso, T. (1995). A typology of juvenile offenders based on the judgments of juvenile court professionals. *Criminal Justice and Behavior, 22,* 246–262. doi:10.1177/0093854895022003004

Douglas, K., Cox, D., & Webster, C. (1999). Violence risk assessment: Science and practice. *Legal and Criminological Psychology, 4,* 149–184. doi:10.1348/135532599167824

Douglas, K., & Skeem, J. L. (2005). Violence risk assessment: Getting specific about being dynamic. *Psychology, Public Policy, And Law, 11,* 347–383. doi:10.1037/1076–8971.11.3.347

Du Toit, L., & Duckitt, J. (1990). Psychological characteristics of over- and undercontrolled violent offenders. *Journal of Psychology, 124,* 125–141. doi:10.1080/00223980.1990.1543210

Ewing, C. P. (1990). Juveniles or adults? Forensic assessment of juveniles considered for trial in criminal court. *Forensic Reports, 3,* 3–13.

Fagan, J., & Zimring, F. E. (Eds.). (2000). *The changing borders of juvenile justice: Transfer of adolescents to the criminal court.* Chicago: University of Chicago Press.

Farrington, D. P., Loeber, R., Stallings, R., & Homish, D. L. (2008). Early risk factors for young homicide offenders and victims. In M. J. Delisi & P. J. Conis (Eds.), *Violent offenders: Theory, research, public policy, and practice* (pp. 79–96). Sudbury, MA: Jones and Barlett.

Forth, A. E., & Burke, H. C. (1998). Psychopathy in adolescence: Assessment, violence, and adolescent precursors. In D. J. Cooke, A. E. Forth, & R. D. Hare (Eds.), *Psychopathy: Theory, research, and implications for society* (pp. 205–229). Dordrecht, The Netherlands: Kluwer. doi: 10.1007/978–94–011–3965–6_10

Frank, J. D. (1959). The dynamics of the psychotherapeutic relationship. *Psychiatry, 22,* 17–39.

Frick, P., & Morris, A. (2004). Temperament and developmental pathways to conduct problems. *Journal of Clinical Child and Adolescent Psychology, 33,* 54–68. doi:10.1207/515374424JCCP3301_6

Garfield, S. L. (1994). Research on client variables in psychotherapy. In S. L. Garfield & A. E. Bergin (Eds.), *Handbook of psychotherapy and behavior change* (3rd ed., pp. 190–228). New York: Wiley.

Gillen, C. T. A., MacDougall, E. A. M., Salekin, R. T., & Forth, A. E. (2015). The validity of the Risk-Sophistication-Treatment Inventory–Abbreviated (RSTI-A): Initial evidence in support of a measure designed for juvenile evaluations. *Psychology, Public Policy, and Law, 21,* 205-212. doi: 10.1037/law0000044

Graham v. Florida, 130 S. Ct. 2011 (2010).

Gretton, H. M., McBride, M., Hare, R. D., O'Shaughnessy, R., & Kumka, G. (2001). Psychopathy and recidivism in adolescent sex offenders. *Criminal Justice and Behavior, 28,* 427–449. doi:10.1177/009385480102800403

Griffin, P., Torbet, P., & Szymanski, L. (1998). *Trying juveniles as adults in criminal court: An analysis of state transfer provisions.* Washington, DC: U.S. Department of Justice Office of Juvenile Justice and Delinquency Prevention.

Grisso, T. (1986). Psychological assessment in legal contexts. In W. J. Curran, A. L. McGarry, & S. A. Shah (Eds.), *Forensic psychiatry and psychology: Perspectives and standards for interdisciplinary practice* (pp. 103–128). Philadelphia: F. A. Davis.

Grisso, T. (1998). *Forensic evaluation of juveniles.* Sarasota, FL: Professional Resource Press.

Grisso, T. (2000). Forensic clinical evaluations related to waiver of jurisdiction. In J. Fagan & F. E. Zimring (Eds.), *The changing borders of juvenile justice: Transfer of adolescents to the criminal court* (pp. 321–352). Chicago: University of Chicago Press.

Grisso, T. (2013). *Forensic evaluation of juveniles* (2nd ed.). Sarasota, FL: Professional Resource Press.

Grisso, T., & Appelbaum, P. S. (1992). *Manual for rational thinking about treatment.* Worcester, MA: Massachusetts Medical School.

Grisso, T., Tomkins, A., & Casey, P. (1988). Psychosocial concepts in juvenile law. *Law and Human Behavior, 12,* 403–437. doi:10.1007/BF01044626

Hawes, D. J., & Dadds, M. R. (2005). The treatment of conduct problems in children with callous-unemotional traits. *Journal of Consulting and Clinical Psychology, 73,* 737. doi:10.1037/0022–006X.73.4.737

Heilbrun, K., Leheny, C., Thomas, L., & Huneycutt, D. (1997). A national survey of U.S. statutes on juvenile transfer: Implications for policy and practice. *Behavioral Sciences and the Law, 15,* 125–149. doi:10.1002/(SICI)1099–0798(199721)15:2<125::AID-BSL265>3.0.CO;2-R

Hoge, R. (2005). Youth Level of Service/Case Management Inventory. In T. Grisso, G. Vincent, & D. Seagrave (Eds.), *Mental health screening and assessment in juvenile justice* (pp. 283–294). New York: Guilford Press.

Iselin, A., & Salekin, R. T. (2008). *The Risk-Sophistication Treatment Inventory-Self Report.* Unpublished test. Tuscaloosa, AL: Department of Psychology, University of Alabama.

Izzo, R. L., & Ross, R. R. (1990). Meta-analysis of rehabilitation programs for juvenile delinquents: A brief report. *Criminal Justice and Behavior, 17,* 134–142. doi:10.1177/0093854890017001008

Jesness, C., & Wedge, R. F. (1983). *Classifying offenders: The Jesness Inventory classification system.* California Department of Youth Authority, Program Research and Review Division. Sacramento, CA.

Jesness, C., & Wedge, R. F. (1984). Validity of a revised Jesness Inventory I-Level Classification with delinquents. *Journal of Consulting and Clinical Psychology, 52,* 997–1010. doi:10.1037/0022–006X.52.6.997

Jordan, M. J. (2009). *Readiness for change as a predictor of treatment effectiveness: An application of the transtheoretical model.* Dissertation. *Abstracts International, 70,* 2575.

Kazdin, A. E. (1985). *Treatment of antisocial behavior in children and adolescents.* Homewood, IL: Dorsey Press.

Kent v. U.S., 383 U.S. 541 (1966).

Kohlberg, L. (1981). *Stages and aging in moral development.* San Francisco: Harper & Row. doi:10.1093/geront/13.4.497

Kreuter, F., & Muthén, B. (2008). Analyzing criminal trajectory profiles: Bridging multilevel and group-based approaches using growth mixture modeling. *Journal of Quantitative Criminology, 24,* 1–31. doi:10.1007/s10940–007–9036–0

Kruh, I. P., & Brodsky, S. L. (1997). Clinical evaluations for transfer of juveniles to criminal court: Current practices and future research. *Behavioral Sciences and the Law, 15,* 151–165. doi:10.1002/(SICI)1099–0798(199721)15:2<151::AID-BSL267>3.0.CO;2-U

Leistico, A.M.R. (2002). *Juvenile transfer to adult court: Risk, sophistication-maturity, treatment amenability, and related constructs.* Doctoral dissertation. University of Alabama, Tuscaloosa.

Leistico, A.M.R., & Salekin, R. (2003). Testing the reliability and validity of the Risk, Sophistication-Maturity, and Treatment Amenability Instrument (RST-I): An assessment tool for juvenile offenders. *International Journal of Forensic Mental Health, 2,* 101–117. doi:10.1080/14999013.2003.10471182

Leistico, A.M.R., Salekin, R. T., DeCoster, J., & Rogers, R. (2008). A large-scale meta-analysis relating the Hare measures of psychopathy to antisocial conduct. *Law and Human Behavior, 32,* 28–45.

Loeber, R. (1991). Risk factors and the development of disruptive and antisocial behaviour in children. *Forum on Corrections Research, 3,* 22–28.

Loeber, R., & Farrington, D. (1998). Never too early, never too late: Risk factors and successful interventions for serious and violent juvenile offenders. *Studies on Crime & Crime Prevention, 7,* 7–30.

Luthar, S. S. (1991). Vulnerability and resilience: A study of high risk adolescents. *Child Development, 62,* 600–616. doi:10.2307/1131134

Lynam, D. R., & Gudonis, L. (2005). The development of psychopathy. *Annual Review of Clinical Psychology, 1,* 381–407. doi:10.1146/annurev.clinpsy.1.102803.144019

Lynam, D. R., Miller, D. J., Vachon, D., Loeber, R., & Stouthamer-Loeber, M. (2009). Psychopathy in adolescence predicts official reports of offending in adulthood. *Youth Violence and Juvenile Justice, 7,* 189–207. doi:10.1177/1541204009333797

Lyons, C. L., Adams, A. N., & Dahan, A. L. (2012). Commentary: Nuances of reverse-waiver evaluations of adolescents in adult criminal court. *Journal of the American Academy of Psychiatry and the Law, 40,* 341–347.

McGrory, J. J. (1991). *Violent young offenders: An investigation of the overcontrolled/undercontrolled personality typology.* Unpublished doctoral dissertation. University of Toronto, Ontario, Canada.

Megargee, E. I. (1966). Undercontrolled and overcontrolled personality traits in extreme antisocial aggression. *Psychological Monographs, 80,* (3, Whole No. 611). doi:10.1037/h0093894

Melton, G. B., Petrila, J., Poythress, N. G., & Slobogin, C. (1987). *Psychological evaluations for the courts.* New York: Guilford Press.

Melton, G. B., Petrila, J., Poythress, N. G., & Slobogin, C. (1997). *Psychological evaluations for the courts: A handbook for mental health professionals and lawyers* (2nd Ed.). New York: Guilford Press.

Miller v. Alabama, 132 S.Ct. 2455 (2012).

Millon, T. (1993). *Millon Adolescent Clinical Inventory manual.* Minneapolis, MN: National Computer Systems.

Moffitt, T. E. (1993). Adolescent-limited and life-course persistent antisocial behavior: A developmental taxonomy. *Psychological Review, 100,* 674–701. doi: 10.1037/0033–295X.100.4.674

Moffitt, T. E. (2003). Life-course persistent and adolescent-limited antisocial behavior: A 10-year research review and research agenda. In B. B. Lahey, T. E. Moffitt, & A. Caspi (Eds.), *Causes of conduct disorder and juvenile delinquency* (pp. 49–75). New York: Guilford Press.

Moffitt, T. E. (2007). A review of research on the taxonomy of life-course persistent versus adolescent-limited antisocial behavior. In D. J. Flannery, A. T. Vazsonyi, & I. D. Waldman (Eds.), *The Cambridge handbook of violent behavior and aggression* (pp. 49–74). New York: Cambridge University Press.

Mulvey, E. P. (1984). Judging amenability to treatment in juvenile offenders: Theory and practice. In N. D. Reppucci, L. A. Weithorn, E. P. Mulvey, & J. Monahan (Eds.), *Children, mental health, and the law* (pp. 195–210). Beverly Hills, CA: Sage.

Mulvey, E. P., & Iselin, A. R. (2008). Improving professional judgments of risk and amenability in juvenile justice. *The Future of Children, 18,* 35–57. doi:10.1353/foc.0.0012

Murray, H. A. (1937). *Thematic Apperception Test manual.* Cambridge, MA: Harvard University Press.

National Council of Juvenile and Family Court Judges. (2005). *Juvenile delinquency guidelines: Improving court practice in juvenile delinquency cases.* Washington, DC: U.S. Department of Justice, Office of Juvenile Justice and Delinquency Prevention. Retrieved from www.ncjfcj.org/images/stories/dept/ppcd/pdf/JDG/juveniledelinquency-guidelinescompressed.pdf.

National Institute of Mental Health. (2000). *Child and adolescence violence research* (NIH Publication No. 00–4706). Bethesda, MD: Author.

Office of Juvenile Justice and Delinquency Prevention. (2014). National Report. Retrieved August 14, 2014 from www.ojjdp.gov/ojstatbb/publications/StatBBAbstract.asp?BibID=265117.

Penney, S. R., & Moretti, M. M. (2005). The transfer of juveniles to adult court in Canada and the United States: Confused agendas and compromised assessment procedures. *International Journal of Forensic Mental Health, 4,* 19–37. doi:10.1080/14999013.2005.10471210

Puzzanchera, C. (2003). Delinquency cases waived to criminal court, 1990–1999. *OJJDP Fact Sheet, 4,* FS-200304.

Quay, H. (1964). Dimensions of personality in delinquent boys as inferred from the factor analysis of case history data. *Child Development, 35,* 479–484.

Quay, H. (1987). *Handbook of juvenile delinquency.* Oxford, England: Wiley.

Redding, R. E., & Murrie, D.C. (2010). Judicial decision making about forensic mental health evidence. In A. M. Goldstein (Ed.), *Forensic psychology: Emerging topics and expanding roles* (pp. 683–707). Hoboken, NJ: Wiley.

Roberts, B. W., & DelVecchio, W. F. (2000). The rank-order consistency of personality traits from childhood to old age: a quantitative review of longitudinal studies. *Psychological Bulletin, 126,* 3–25. doi:10.1037/0033-2909.126.1.3

Roper v. Simmons, 543 U.S. 551 (2005).

Salekin, R. T. (2002a). Clinical evaluation of youth considered for transfer to adult criminal court: Refining practice and directions for science. *Journal of Forensic Psychology Practice, 2,* 55–72. doi:10.1300/J158v02n02_03

Salekin, R. T. (2002b). Juvenile waiver to adult court: How can developmental and child psychology inform policy decision making. In B. Bottoms, M. B. Kovera, & B. McAuliff (Eds.), *Children and the law: Social science and U.S. law* (pp. 203–232). Cambridge, MA: Cambridge University Press. doi:10.1017/CBO9780511500114.009

Salekin, R. T. (2002c). Psychopathy and therapeutic pessimism: Clinical lore or clinical reality? *Clinical Psychology Review, 22,* 79–112. doi:10.1016/S0272-7358(01)0083-6

Salekin, R. T. (2004). *Risk-Sophistication-Treatment Inventory (RST-I).* Lutz, FL: Psychological Assessment Resources.

Salekin, R. T. (2006). Psychopathy in children and adolescents: Key issues in conceptualization and assessment. In C. J. Patrick (Ed.), *Handbook of psychopathy* (pp. 389–414). New York: Guilford Press.

Salekin, R. T. (2010). Treatment of child and adolescent psychopathy: Focusing on change. In R. T. Salekin, D. R. Lynam (Eds.), *Handbook of child and adolescent psychopathy* (pp. 343–373). New York: Guilford Press.

Salekin, R. T. (2015). *Forensic evaluation and treatment of juveniles: Innovation and best practice.* Washington, DC: American Psychological Association.

Salekin, R. T. (in press). Psychopathy in childhood: Toward better informing the DSM-5 and ICD-11 Conduct Disorder specifiers. *Personality Disorders: Theory, Research, and Treatment.*

Salekin, R. T., Barker, E. D., Ang, X., & MacDougall, E. (2012). Indexing adolescent psychopathy: Commentary on Dawson, McCuish, Hart, and Corrado. *International Journal of Forensic Mental Health, 11,* 80–86. doi:10.1080/14999013.2012.676150

Salekin, R. T., Kubak, F. A., & Lee, Z. (2008). Children and deception. In R. Rogers (Ed.), *Clinical assessment of malingering and deception* (3rd ed., pp. 343–364). New York: Guilford Press.

Salekin, R. T., Lee, Z., Schrum Dillard, C. L., & Kubak, F. A. (2010). Child psychopathy and protective factors: IQ and motivation to change. *Psychology, Public Policy, and Law, 16,* 158–167. doi:10.1037/a0019233

Salekin, R. T., & Lynam, D. R. (2010). Child and adolescent psychopathy: The road ahead. In R. T. Salekin, D. R. Lynam (Eds.), *Handbook of child and adolescent psychopathy* (pp. 401–419). New York: Guilford Press.

Salekin, K. L., Ogloff, J. R. P., Ley, R., & Salekin, R. T. (2002). The overcontrolled hostility scale: An evaluation of its applicability with an adolescent population. *Criminal Justice and Behavior, 29,* 718–733. doi:10.1177/009385402237924

Salekin, R. T., Price, K. M., Tant, K. E., Adams, E. W., Ang, X., & Rosenbaum, J. (2013). Evaluation for disposition and transfer of juvenile offenders. In R. Roesch & P. A. Zapf (Eds.), *Forensic assessments in criminal and civil law: A handbook for lawyers* (pp. 249–263). New York: Oxford University Press.

Salekin, R. T., Rogers, R., & Machin, D. (2001). Psychopathy in youth: Pursuing diagnostic clarity. *Journal of Youth and Adolescence, 30,* 173–195. doi:10.1023/A:1010393708227

Salekin, R. T., Rogers, R., & Sewell, K. W. (1996). A review and meta-analysis of the Psychopathy Checklist and Psychopathy Checklist–Revised: Predictive validity of dangerousness. *Clinical Psychology: Science and Practice, 3,* 203–215. doi:10.111/j.1468-2850.1996.tb00071.x

Salekin, R. T., Rogers, R., & Ustad, K. L. (2001). Juvenile waiver to adult criminal courts: Prototypes for dangerousness, sophistication-maturity, and amenability to treatment. *Psychology, Public Policy, and Law, 7,* 381–408. doi:10.1037/1076-8971.7.7.381

Salekin, R. T., Tippey, J., & Allen, A. (2012). Treatment of conduct problem youth with interpersonal callous traits using mental models: Measurement of risk and change. *Behavioral Sciences and the Law, 30,* 470–486. doi:10.1002/bsl.2025

Salekin, R. T., Worley, C., & Grimes, R. D. (2010). Treatment of psychopathy: A review and brief introduction to the mental model approach for psychopathy. *Behavioral Sciences and the Law, 28,* 235–266. doi:10.1002/bsl.928

Salekin, R. T., Yff, R., Neumann, C., Leistico, A., & Zalot, A. (2002). Juvenile transfer to adult courts: A look at the prototypes for dangerousness, sophistication-maturity, and amenability to treatment through a legal lens. *Psychology, Public Policy, and Law, 8,* 373–410. doi:10.1037/1076–8971.8.4.373

Salekin, R. T., Ziegler, T. A., Larrea, M. A., Anthony, V. L., & Bennett, A.D. (2003). Predicting dangerousness with two Millon Adolescent Clinical Inventory psychopathy scales: The importance of egocentric and callous traits. *Journal of Personality Assessment, 80,* 154–163. doi:10.1207/S15327752JPA8002_04

Snyder, H. N., & Sickmund, M. (2006). *Juvenile offenders and victims: 2006 national report.* Washington, DC: U.S. Department of Justice, Office of Justice Programs, Office of Juvenile Justice and Delinquency Prevention. doi:10.1037/e501002006–001

Spice, A., Viljoen, J. L., Gretton, H. M., & Roesch, R. (2010). Psychological assessment for adult sentencing of juvenile offenders: An evaluation of the RSTI and the SAVRY. *International Journal of Forensic Mental Health, 9,* 124–137. doi:10.1080/14999013.2010.501846

Steinberg, L., & Cauffman, E. (1999). A developmental perspective on serious juvenile crime: When should juveniles be treated as adults? *Federal Probation, 63,* 52–57.

Steinberg, L., & Cauffman, E. (2000). A developmental perspective on judicial boundary. In J. Fagan and F. E. Zimring (Eds.), *The changing borders of juvenile justice: Transfer of adolescents to criminal court* (pp. 379–406). Chicago: University of Chicago Press.

Sternberg, R. J. (2000). Implicit theories of intelligence as exemplar stories of success: Why intelligence test validity is in the eye of the beholder. *Psychology, Public Policy, and Law, 6,* 159–167. doi:10.1037/1076–8971.6.1.159

Strasburger, L. H. (1989). The juvenile transfer hearing and the forensic psychiatrist. In R. Rosner (Ed.), *Juvenile psychiatry and the law* (pp. 391–403). New York: Plenum Press.

Swanson, J., Borum, R., Swartz, M., & Monahan, J. (1996). Psychotic symptoms and disorders and the risk of violent behaviour in the community. *Criminal Behaviour and Mental Health, 6,* 309–329. doi:10.1002/cbm.118

U.S. Department of Health and Human Services. (2001). *Youth violence: A report of the Surgeon General.* Washington, DC: U.S. Department of Justice.

Vitacco, M. J., & Salekin, R. (2013). Adolescent psychopathy and the law. In K. A. Kiehl & W. P. Sinnott-Armstrong (Eds.), *Handbook on psychopathy and law* (pp. 78–89). Oxford University Press.

Vitacco, M. J., Salekin, R. T., & Rogers, R. (2010). Forensic issues for child and adolescent psychopathy. In R. T. Salekin & D. R. Lynam (Eds.), *Handbook of child and adolescent psychopathy* (pp. 374–400). New York: Guildford Press.

Vitacco, M. J., & Vincent, G. M. (2006). Applying adult concepts to youthful offenders: Psychopathy and its implications for risk assessment and juvenile justice. *International Journal of Forensic Mental Health Assessment, 5,* 29–38. doi:10.1080/14999013.2006.10471228

Witt, P. H. (2003). Transfer of juveniles to adult court: The case of H. H. *Psychology, Public Policy, and Law, 9,* 361–380. doi:10.1037/1076–8971.9.3–4.361

Witt, P. H., & Dyer, F. J. (1997). Juvenile transfer cases: Risk assessment and risk management. *Journal of Psychiatry and Law, 25,* 581–614.

Woolard, J. L., Fondacaro, M. R., & Slobogin, C. (2001). Informing juvenile justice policy: Directions for behavioral science research. *Law and Human Behavior, 25,* 13–24. doi:10.1023/A:1005635808317

Woolard, J. L., Odgers, C., Lanza-Kaduce, L., & Daglis, H. (2005). Juveniles within adult correctional settings: Legal pathways and developmental considerations. *International Journal of Forensic Mental Health, 4,* 1–18. doi:10.1080/14999013.2005.10471209

Zalot, A. A. (2002a). *How do dangerousness, sophistication-maturity, and amenability to treatment influence the juvenile transfer decision?* Unpublished master's thesis, University of Alabama, Tuscaloosa.

Zalot, A. A. (2002b). Taylor Hardin Secure Medical Facility Project. Unpublished raw data.

Zimring, F. E. (1998). *American youth violence.* New York: Oxford University Press.

14 Assessing Child and Adolescent Psychopathy

Randall T. Salekin, Sara A. Debus-Sherrill, Emily A. M. MacDougall, and Abby P. Clark

Adolescent psychopathy has already made its way into the field of forensic practice. Some recent cases have used expert testimony on child psychopathy to make decisions regarding trying a child as an adult. In these cases, expert witnesses typically report that the child in question is a risk to the community or is unlikely to improve with treatment within the juvenile justice system due to psychopathic personality traits. For instance, in a case reviewed by Walsh and Walsh (2006), the Psychopathy Checklist–Revised (PCL-R; Hare, 1991/2003) was used by the prosecution to support the defendant's transfer to adult court. The defendant, "John Doe #3," who was 21 at the time of trial, was charged with 10 acts committed while a minor, including armed robbery, kidnapping, murder, and distribution of cocaine, among others (*United States v. Doe #3*, 2000). The testifying psychologist concluded that John Doe's psychopathy score, although slightly below the cutoff of 30 for adults, indicated a high risk for recidivism (*United States v. Doe #3*, 2000). Although the defendant was transferred to adult court, the judge stated that it could not be concluded that John Doe #3 was in fact a psychopath (*United States v. Doe #3*, 2000). A recently published court case of a youth convicted of sexual abuse also relied on whether the defendant, who was 13 years old at the time of the evaluation, could be diagnosed with "either . . . antisocial personality disorder or . . . psychopathy" to determine the defendant's risk for reoffending (*In re Harold W., a Minor* [*The People of the State of Illinois, Petitioner-Appellee, v. Harold W., Respondent-Appellant*], 2014, para. 9). The court noted that "testing" completed by a clinical social worker indicated that the defendant did not have "either an antisocial personality disorder or any psychopathy" (*In re Harold W., a Minor* [*The People of the State of Illinois, Petitioner-Appellee, v. Harold W., Respondent-Appellant*], 2014, para. 10). Based on the evaluation, the social worker "opined that respondent was a low risk to reoffend."

Another recent court case involved an adolescent defendant charged with aggravated sexual assault. The defendant was 17 years old at the time of the crime (*The People of the State of Illinois v. Rickie T. Nichols*, 2012). This case also cited psychopathy information in making statements regarding risk for reoffending. Based on factors such as the defendant's age and "potential for psychopathy," the evaluator found that the defendant was at a moderate risk to reoffend (*The People of the State of Illinois v. Rickie T. Nichols*, 2012, para. 79).

Another more highly publicized example of the use of the psychopathy construct in legal settings came to light in the Cody Posey murder trial in February 2006. Posey was convicted of first-degree murder, second-degree murder, voluntary manslaughter, and four counts of evidence tampering for the deaths of his stepsister, stepmother, and father and the subsequent cover-up of their murders (Brown, 2006). To help determine the question of whether Posey should be sentenced as a child or an adult, Posey was administered the Psychopathy Checklist: Youth Version (PCL:YV; Forth, Kosson, & Hare, 1996/2003). The prosecution's expert witness testified that Cody Posey received a score of 19 on this assessment instrument (Grinberg, 2006). Another expert witness reportedly stated that there was a "slim to none" chance of changing psychopathic traits in people. The prosecution then used this information to say that Posey was a psychopath and that "no one knows how to treat psychopathy" (Brown, 2006).

The cases described provide the reader with several examples of the uses and potential misuses of psychopathy classifications in adolescent forensic cases. The latter example is probably best characterized as a misuse because the statements offered go beyond the purposes of the PCL:YV. The PCL:YV manual states that the measure is not intended for legal decision making (Forth et al., 1996/2003). In addition, the developers of the PCL:YV do not provide a specific cutoff score because with the current level of research, it is inappropriate to diagnose a child or adolescent with psychopathy (Forth et al., 1996/2003). Even at the adult level, the cutoff score for diagnosing someone as psychopathic in adulthood is 30 (Hare, 1991/2003), which Posey did not meet. Thus, it could be argued that in the Posey case, the term *psychopathy* is contraindicated for two primary reasons: (a) Posey's score on the PCL:YV was relatively low, and (b) the use of the term *psychopathy* even in high scorers is not recommended. In addition to the aforementioned points, general conclusions that accompany high scorers—such as poor treatment prognosis—should not be applied to low scorers, especially as there is some emerging evidence to show that psychopathy may be an alterable condition, especially with younger populations (Hawes, Price, & Dadds, 2014; Salekin, 2002; Salekin, Tippey, & Allen, 2012; Salekin, Worley, & Grimes, 2010; Skeem, Monahan, & Mulvey, 2002). These case examples highlight the emergence of child psychopathy into adolescent forensic cases and at least one of the cases underscores the potential misapplication of the psychopathy construct.

The aim of the current chapter is to provide detailed information on the psychopathy concept as it applies to children and adolescents and to discuss how it might be appropriately used in clinical or clinical forensic settings. Specifically, the purpose of the current chapter is fivefold. First, we describe psychopathy and discuss why the concept might be important to consider in child samples as well as discuss differences between psychopathy and the DSM disruptive disorders (DBDs) at a descriptive and conceptual level (American Psychiatric Association, 2013). Second, we briefly discuss the developmental appropriateness of the psychopathy construct for children and adolescents. This section of the chapter touches on some of the concerns typically raised regarding the appropriateness of the psychopathy concept to child and adolescent samples and also addresses what science can currently tell us regarding the appropriateness of the term for youth. This section also suggests that there are hints in the literature that the disorder has its roots in childhood, or earlier. Third, we examine the structural stability and validity of the psychopathy measures. This section is the most extensive section of the chapter because it is imperative that researchers and clinicians alike understand the current state of knowledge on the assessment of psychopathy if they are to apply the diagnosis in forensic settings. Each of these sections is designed to help both researchers and clinicians understand what can be said about the child psychopathy concept within the terms of scientific evidence. Fourth, if clinicians choose to use the diagnosis, we offer specific clinical recommendations for employing the psychopathy concept in forensic practice. Finally, we provide a case example that is intended to help illustrate the proper use of the concept in forensic settings.

Psychopathy in Youth and Its Differentiation From DSM-5 Disruptive Disorders

Psychopathy in children and adolescents is thought to look much like it does in adulthood (e.g., Lynam & Gudonis, 2005; Salekin & Lynam, 2010). Specifically, although there is some debate about the appropriateness of several of the items as well as some need to specify developmental considerations for each of the items (Salekin & Frick, 2005; Salekin, Rogers, & Machin, 2001; Schrum & Salekin, 2006; Vincent & Hart, 2002), psychopathy in youth is thought to be composed of interpersonal, affective, lifestyle, and perhaps antisocial characteristics, as it is in adulthood (Hare, 1991/2003; Forth et al., 1996/2003; Frick et al., 2000; Frick & Hare, 2001; Lynam, 1997; Salekin et al., 2001). Within the interpersonal characteristics, psychopathic youth are thought to be glib, superficially charming, manipulative, deceitful, and intelligent (or, at least, to not have a deficit in intelligence). Affective characteristics include lack of empathy, callousness, and a lack of remorse. Lifestyle characteristics include sensation seeking, irresponsible behavior, and an inability to plan. Antisocial characteristics include criminal versatility, criminal conduct, and moral transgressions. Because many of the characteristics described earlier are personality features, clinicians have, on one hand, been reluctant to use the term *psychopathy* given that youth may undergo character change over the formative years of their lives. On the other hand, many researchers believe that temperament and personality are in place early, and, thus stability should be evidenced early on. To the extent that these traits manifest early in the developmental trajectory, they may well be important to better understanding adolescent offenders.

Researchers and clinicians have considered the existence of psychopathy in children for over half a century (Salekin & Frick, 2005). Some important insights can be gleaned from examining this early literature. For instance, Cleckley noted the possibility of child psychopathy in the early 1940s but also delineated his concern regarding the possibility of misclassifications due to developmental factors. Karpman (1949) organized two consecutive round table discussions to examine the possibility of the existence of psychopathy in children and adolescents. Much of the theoretical exchange centered on whether psychopathy was biologically or environmentally determined and whether the syndrome was treatable—two issues that are still currently investigated today. Later, McCord and McCord (1964) examined the concept of psychopathy in children and adolescents and determined that it was rarer than that of conduct disorder (CD) but emphasized that meanness could be a distinguishing factor. Finally, Quay (1964) conducted one of the first factor analytic studies to show that symptoms of disruptive behavior in youth separated into at least two clusters, one of which he considered to resemble psychopathy. Despite this remarkable start to the study of psychopathy in youthful populations, research in the ensuing decades was sparse (Salekin & Frick, 2005; Salekin & Lynam, 2010). It was not until the early 1990s that interest in child and adolescent psychopathy was revitalized when researchers attempted to systematically measure psychopathy in child and adolescent samples (e.g., Forth, Hart, & Hare, 1990).

Research in the early 1990s (e.g., Forth et al., 1990), like the research before it (Quay, 1964, 1965, 1987), claimed that CD was a heterogeneous class. Researchers suggested that psychopathy may be an important disorder to consider in youth, because factor analytic work continued to demonstrate that the syndrome was composed of symptom compositions that extended beyond the DSM-IV, and now DSM-5, descriptor sets for the DBDs which include CD, oppositional defiant disorder (ODD), and attention deficit hyperactivity disorder (ADHD). These early factor analytic studies (e.g., Frick, O'Brien, Wootton, & McBurnett, 1994) have since been replicated with confirmatory factor analytic work (Jones, Cauffman, Miller, & Mulvey, 2006; Kosson et al., 2013; Neumann, Kosson, Forth, & Hare, 2006; Salekin, Brannen, Zalot, Leistico, & Neumann, 2006) suggesting that there are basic descriptive and factor structure differences between the DBDs and psychopathy. To elaborate on this point, CD is defined as serious violation of the rules, but does not take into consideration personality or motivational features to the same degree as psychopathy. However, the DSM-5 specifier, termed *limited prosocial emotion*, has brought CD somewhat closer to psychopathy definitions. Nonetheless, of the 15 items that constitute CD criteria, and the additional four specifier items, only four items, in total, overlap with Cleckley's definition of psychopathy and only six items in total overlap with Hare's criteria (Salekin, in press). Therefore, the specifier still falls quite short of tapping something that will resemble psychopathy. Especially absent are grandiose-manipulative and daring-impulsive traits. ODD is defined as oppositional attitudes and behaviors; although it may have some links to psychopathy, it offers very little in terms of explicit representation of psychopathic traits. ADHD is defined as either hyperactivity or attention problems (or both) but, again, ADHD does not address the interpersonal and affective features thought to compose psychopathy and may have only a very limited contribution to the daring impulsive traits of psychopathy.[1]

Beyond descriptive-level differences, there are conceptual differences between psychopathy and the DBDs of the DSM-5. Difference between conduct problems and psychopathy has a great deal to do with interpersonal, affective characteristics of psychopathy but also possibly motivational considerations (Kazdin 1997). These important conceptual differences have to some extent been reflected in research suggesting that psychopathy differs from CD and other conduct problems on important factors such as severity of offending, type of aggressive behavior exhibited (e.g., reactive versus proactive aggression), social skills (Cleckley, 1941/1976; Quay, 1964, 1986, 1987), and intellectual (Loney, Frick, Ellis, & McCoy, 1998; Salekin, Neumann, Leistico, & Zalot, 2004) and emotional functioning. These differences could help to explain some of the heterogeneity in CD.[2] Greater partitioning and augmentation of the CD construct might help to improve the predictive utility of CD, which has been a concern in the past, and better inform treatment planning for CD subtypes or specifiers (APA, 2013). Some have argued that Cleckley (1941/1976) or Hare (1991/2003) models of psychopathy might be one diagnostic approach that would allow for greater specificity for identifying a specific class of conduct problem youth and the partitioning of criteria could provide for further resolution regarding CD specifiers (Salekin, in press). In Table 14.1, we provide the defining features of ODD, CD, and Cleckley's criteria for psychopathy.

Table 14.1 Criteria for ODD, CD, and psychopathy

ODD	CD	Cleckley Psychopath
1. Often loses temper	1. Often bullies, threatens, and intimidates	1. Superficial charm and good intelligence
2. Often argues with adults	2. Often initiates physical fights	2. Absence of delusions and irrational thinking
3. Often actively defies or refuses to comply with adults' requests or rules	3. Has used a weapon that can cause serious physical harm to others	4. Unreliability
4. Often deliberately annoys people	4. Has been physically cruel to people	5. Untruthful and insincere
5. Often blames others for his or her mistakes	5. Has been physically cruel to animals	6. Lack of remorse or shame
6. Is often touchy or easily annoyed	6. Has stolen while confronting a victim	7. Inadequately motivated antisocial behavior
7. Is often angry and resentful	7. Has forced someone into sexual activity	8. Poor judgment/failure to learn from experience
8. Is often spiteful or vindictive	8. Has deliberately engaged in fire-setting with intention of causing serious damage	9. Pathological egocentricity/incapacity for love
	9. Has deliberately destroyed property	10. General poverty of affective reactions
	10. Has broken into someone else's house, building, car	11. Specific loss of insight
	11. Often lies to obtain goods or favors or to avoid obligations	13. Fantastic and uninviting behavior
	12. Has stolen items of nontrivial value w/o confronting a victim	14. Suicide rarely carried out
	13. Often stays out at night despite parental prohibitions	15. Sex life impersonal, trivial, poorly integrated

(Continued)

Table 14.1 Continued

ODD	CD	Cleckley Psychopath
	14. Has run away from home overnight at least twice while living in parental or parental surrogate home 15. Is often truant from school	16. Failure to follow a life plan
	Limited prosocial emotion specifier 1. Lack of remorse or guilt 2. Callous—lack of empathy 3. Unconcerned about performance 4. Shallow or deficient affect	

In the next section, we discuss theory and some empirical evidence from developmental psychology to suggest that the disorder may be observable very early in development. Although there is quite a large body of highly relevant developmental literature on the topic (e.g., empathy development, conscience development, and other related research areas) to suggest that psychopathy has its roots in childhood (or even earlier), there is less in the way of research that examines psychopathy throughout the life span. For these reasons, we suggest that clinicians be very cautious with their conclusions regarding psychopathy in forensic settings.

Development of Psychopathy From an Early Age: What Do We Know?

Although psychopathy has been considered as a possible diagnosis in youth for some time now, its development from an early age is not fully understood. Salekin (2006) reviewed developmental literature related to the topic of psychopathy and showed that there exists some indirect theory and evidence to suggest that the disorder may manifest itself early in the developmental process. Hints to the possible existence of psychopathy come from developmental research on related topics such as emotion, empathy development, conscience development, and temperament. We discuss briefly some of this research in order to examine whether the disorder could, theoretically, be observed early in the development of children and adolescence. We make several points based on developmental literature to support the supposition that it may be observable from an early age.

There is considerable information that could lead to important etiological information regarding the development of psychopathy. These etiological keys could very well open doors to a better understanding of the observability of psychopathy from an early age as well as fuel the development of prevention and intervention programs. The relevant developmental literature is vast and it is beyond the scope of this chapter to provide a comprehensive review. However, we highlight several important research findings to demonstrate the early observability of child psychopathy-like symptoms. First, there is considerable research to suggest that basic emotions are present from the earliest days of life (Izard, 1977; Izard & Harris, 1995; Plutchik, 1980). Thus, as Johnstone and Cooke (2004) note, the capability to assess emotion and perhaps even psychopathy related symptoms such as shallow affect, sensation seeking, and emotional responsiveness may be possible from an early age. Second, some evidence suggests that conscience development and the internalization of societal values occurs very early in the toddler years (Kochanska, 1991, 1993). Several researchers have also highlighted the importance of early social referencing, during which mothers and young children negotiate affective meanings of acts. Relatedly, Barrett and Campos (1987) proposed that social referencing endows events with social significance, including emotional marking of acts that parents consider undesirable or forbidden. In addition, research has shown that early social referencing is essential in establishing initial prohibitions against inappropriate acts (Emde, Biringen, Clyman, & Oppenheim, 1991). Research by Emde et al. (1991) and others has indicated that parental practices can either facilitate or undermine early elements of internalization of conscience, such as awareness of standards, the development of the self, early social emotions, and emerging self-regulation. Developmental psychology has also shown that by 18 months of age the cognitive prerequisites for emotions such as perspective taking and differentiation between self and other are well established, and indices of empathic responding have been recorded even in this early developmental phase, with youth showing concern and compassion for others as well as moral sensitivity to the desires and needs of others (Dunn, 1987; Eisenberg & Mussen, 1989; Hann, Aerts, & Cooper, 1987; Johnstone & Cooke, 2004; Radke-Yarrow & Zahn-Waxler, 1984; Zahn-Waxler & Radke-Yarrow, 1990; Zahn-Waxler, Radke-Yarrow, Wagner, & Chapman, 1992). Other research has shown that although lying is experimented with in adolescence, chronic lying is a rare occurrence, and chronic lying is predictive of delinquency (Stouthamer-Loeber, 1986; Loeber & Stouthamer-Loeber, 1986). Further evidence for the early development of psychopathy can be derived from the research on temperament. Temperament may act to moderate the child's perception and acceptance of the parental messages (Patterson, 1976). In particular, the temperamental dimensions of fearfulness, anxiety, and inhibitory control have been linked to the regulation of moral conduct and moral emotions (Kochanska, 1993). Thus, taken together, these findings suggest that the development of the disorder might well be observable early in childhood in part due to genetics (Larsson, Andershed, & Lichenstein, 2006; Viding, Blair, Moffitt, & Plomin, 2004) but also the manner in which the child interacts with the environment even at a very early age (see also Lykken, 1995).

While the above section provides a brief description of the developmental literature to indicate that the syndrome is observable early in childhood and adolescence, much more research is needed to (a) determine the earliest age at which psychopathic characteristics manifest themselves, (b) examine the developmental trajectories of psychopathy throughout childhood and adolescence, and (c) address the continuity between childhood psychopathy and adult psychopathy (see Kotler & McMahon, 2005, 2010). Moreover, there needs to be greater integration between research on empathy development, conscience development, and research on psychopathy, more generally. These research endeavors are likely to take some time to accomplish but such research efforts are necessary before we are able to shed light on the topic of onset and continuity. Furthermore, such research exertions are necessary before we can more firmly use the term *psychopathy* in forensic settings and be sure that it is in fact psychopathy—a disorder originally delineated by Cleckley (1941/1976), or Hare (1991/2003) to describe a condition (a) with an enduring course that is (b) responsible for moral transgressions and criminal behavior across the life span, and (c) difficult to treat.[3] For this reason, although science is pointing toward the observability of the disorder from an early age, much more data is needed that follows youth across the life span to examine the onset and potential offset of symptoms (see Klaver, 2006). Research is also needed to determine which factors maintain, amplify, and/or protect against the development of the disorder and thus offer information regarding the developmental trajectories for young people considered to be at risk for psychopathy. Without these data, we do not have adequate information on the psychopathy concept as it may manifest in children. Rather, what we have are two isolated pools of research that typically examine (a) the nomological net that surrounds child psychopathy, and (b) the nomological net that surrounds adult psychopathy. These single–time point cross-sectional investigations may provide partial support for the construct of psychopathy in children and adolescents, but they do not provide the chief information needed to allow for clinicians to firmly utilize the terms *psychopathy* or *psychopathic personality* in forensic practice. Because these data are very important to forensic evaluations, the following sections examine what we currently know about the concept of psychopathy in children and adolescents. Fortunately, a number of longitudinal studies have emerged in this area to shed some light on the continuity of psychopathy. We review this longitudinal research in the present chapter. Prior to covering the construct validity and stability research, we first briefly discuss several commonly researched child and adolescent psychopathy measures that will be referred to throughout the chapter.

Measurement of Psychopathy in Youth

At present, a variety of measures on the concept of psychopathy have been developed. We cover three of the most popular measures derived from the PCL-R: the Antisocial Process Screening Device (APSD), the PCL:YV, and the Child Psychopathy Scale (CPS). We also describe the Youth Psychopathic Traits Inventory (YPI), and two of the Millon Adolescent Clinical Inventory (MACI) content scales (Murrie & Cornell, 2002; Salekin et al., 2003) intended to assess psychopathy. We also briefly introduce a new measure that may be helpful for cross-informant reporting and is designed to be change sensitive. It should be recognized that a variety of measures exist on the concept and that research in this area is proliferating. As such, we are not able to cover all measures. For instance, there are content scales on the Minnesota Multiphasic Personality Inventory-Adolescent such as the Psychopathic Deviate scale (e.g., MMPI-A Pd scale) and the California Personality Inventory Socialization scale (CPI-So scale) that might be used to assess psychopathy in youthful populations. However, these measures are not discussed in this chapter. Additionally, measures such as the Inventory of Callous and Unemotional traits (ICU; Frick, 2004) are not reviewed because they tap only one aspect of psychopathy and therefore are less well suited for forensic practice. (Vitacco & Salekin, 2013).

APSD

The APSD is a measure intended to screen for psychopathic traits in children; it has parent, teacher, and self-report formats (Frick & Hare, 2001). Its 20 items, based on Hare's model of psychopathy, are scored on a three-point scale with the following response options: 0 = *not at all true*, 1 = *sometimes true*, 2 = *definitely true*. However, not all Hare PCL-R items were included in this measure, such as "parasitic lifestyle," "promiscuous sexual behavior," "many short marital relationships," and "revocation of conditional release." In place of these items, the APSD supplants items thought to be more developmentally appropriate (e.g., "keeps same friends," and "is concerned about school work"). The APSD has been shown to generally have relatively good psychometric properties with generally high levels of reliability and construct validity (Frick & Marsee, 2006; Salekin, 2006). However, of the three factors of psychopathy that it purports to assess, the Callous-Unemotional factor appears to fare the worst in terms of reliability and item functioning (see Dillard, Salekin, Barker, & Grimes, 2013). Because we will examine reliability and validity in more detail at a later point in this chapter, we do not cover this material in detail here.

CPS

The CPS (Lynam, 1997) is a psychopathy assessment tool with 41 items originally derived from the PCL-R, the Child Behavior Checklist (CBCL; Achenbach, 1991), and the Common-Language Q-Sort (CCQ; Caspi et al., 1992). There is a parent-report and self-report version. Using descriptions of PCL-R items previously collected from caregivers on the CBCL and the CCQ, the CPS was originally developed to map onto the PCL-R. A total of 41 items were used to parallel contemporary models of psychopathy. According to Lynam et al. (2005), a revision of the CPS was undertaken in order to (a) simplify complex items, and (b) increase the reliability and validity of several items which were not optimally operationalized in the original version. Additionally, items measuring antisocial behavior were removed and replaced with items designed to assess boredom susceptibility. Thus, the revised CPS assesses 13 of the 20 PCL-R items (glibness, untruthfulness, boredom susceptibility, manipulation, lack of guilt, poverty of affect, callousness, parasitic lifestyle, behavioral dyscontrol, lack of planning, impulsiveness, unreliability, and failure to accept responsibility). Salekin et al. (2005) rationally developed three scales for the CPS based on the Cooke and Michie (2001) model. Factor 1 (Arrogant and Deceitful Interpersonal Style, or ADI) comprises glibness, grandiosity, untruthfulness, and manipulation. Factor 2 (Deficient Affective Experience, or DAE) comprises lack of guilt, poverty of affect, callousness, and failure to accept responsibility. Factor 3 (Irresponsible and Impulsive Behavior, or IIB) comprises parasitic lifestyle, boredom susceptibility, impulsiveness, lack of planning, and unreliability.

PCL-YV

The PCL:YV is a 20-item rating scale designed for the assessment of psychopathy-like characteristics in youth (Forth et al., 1996/2003). The items are scored on the basis of information from a semi-structured interview and file review. The PCL:YV has modified item descriptions but has retained essentially the same 20 items that appear on the adult measure (PCL-R; Hare, 1991/2003). These modifications are intended to take into consideration adolescent life experiences with an increased emphasis on peer, family, and school adjustment (see Forth & Burke, 1998). For example, the PCL-R item "Many Short-Term Marital Relationships" was replaced with "Unstable Interpersonal Relationships." In addition, the PCL-R item "Superficial Charm" was replaced with "Impression Management." The PCL:YV is scored on a three-point scale with 0 indicating the characteristic is *consistently absent*, 1 indicating the characteristic is *inconsistently present*, and 2 indicating the characteristic is *consistently present*. What is unique about the rating system is that judgments require the integration of information provided by self-report, collateral sources, and direct observation of the youth's presentation. The PCL:YV is also noted to be interpretable from three- and four-factor models. The three-factor model includes the facets ADI, DAE, and IIB. The four-factor model adds Antisocial Behaviors (AB).

YPI

The YPI was developed in early 2000 and reported on in 2002 in Andershed, Kerr, Stattin, and Levander, (2002). This self-report measure has 50 items phrased in socially desirable ways, with four response options ranging from *does not apply at all* to *applies very well*. The YPI consists of 10 subscales, including: dishonest charm, grandiosity, lying, manipulation, callousness, unemotionality, remorselessness, impulsiveness, thrill-seeking, and irresponsibility. Developed for youth 12 years of age and older, the test takes approximately 15 minutes to complete. The YPI has performed rather impressively in terms of its internal reliability, test-retest reliability, and predictive validity. Specifically, the YPI is predictive of a range of deviant behaviors and institutional infractions (Campbell, Doucette, & French, 2009; Larsson et al., 2006; Skeem & Cauffman, 2003). There is now a shorter version of the scale titled the YPI-S, with 18 items. This scale is also evidencing promising psychometric properties.

Millon Adolescent Clinical Inventory—Psychopathy Scales

This personality inventory is designed for examining a broad range of psychopathology and takes approximately one hour to complete. Three studies assessing adolescent psychopathy have been conducted with this measure. The Murrie-Cornell Psychopathy Scale (MC-P; Murrie & Cornell, 2002) is a 20-item self-report measure drawn from the MACI (Millon, 1993) and exhibiting a two-factor structure. The Psychopathy Scale–16 (P-16; Salekin, Ziegler, Larrea, Anthony, & Bennett, 2003) is also drawn from the MACI items but has a three-factor structure. Approximate time to complete both measures when not embedded in the broader MACI measure is 5–10 minutes. Internal consistency reliability for the total score has been good ($\alpha = .86$). In the Murrie and Cornell (2002) study, the MC-P was superior to the APSD in terms of diagnostic efficacy, using the PCL:YV as the gold standard with an Area Under the Curve (AUC) of .76; in addition, it correlated moderately with the PCL:YV ($r = .49$). In the second study (Salekin et al., 2003), a new scale was designed that is based, in part, on Cooke and Michie's (2001) model of psychopathy, which separates the first factor into two components. However, this scale also includes antisocial items that are not part of the Cooke and Michie (2001) model for psychopathy, but do fit Hare's (1991/2003) model. Although preliminary research is promising for these scales, much more research is needed with both scales, particularly if they are to be used in forensic practice.

Interpersonal Callous Emotion–Self Report (ICE-SR; Salekin, 2014)

Recently, we developed a scale for the assessment of psychopathy that is based on the work of Cleckley (1941/1976). The measure is also designed to have cross-informant ratings, be sensitive to treatment targets, and be change sensitive. The scale has 36 items and has three primary dimensions including arrogance and deceit, cold and uncaring affect, and daring impulsive traits. Each primary scale also has subscales that might also be treatment targets. Thus far, the reliability and validity of the scale appear to be promising. The goal for future studies is to test its ability to perform across raters and to assess the various dimensions of psychopathy in conjunction with CD as well as to examine change in treatment studies. In the next section, we discuss the current state of knowledge on child and adolescent psychopathy broadly. This section of the chapter is critical to consider when applying the concept in clinical forensic settings.

Current State of Knowledge on Child and Adolescent Psychopathy

While there is some theory and empirical research for early onset of the disorder as well as research to show the ability to index child psychopathy-like characteristics, much research is needed on the concept across time. This type of research is imperative because scientists have argued that many of the elements of child and adolescent psychopathy are part of normal adolescent development (e.g., egocentricity) and as such we cannot be certain that the child psychopathy measures are actually tapping psychopathy. Some researchers have noted that adolescent psychopathy measures have been downwardly extended from adulthood with relatively few developmental considerations (see Kotler & McMahon, 2005, 2010) or that they do not involve important bottom-up considerations (see Salekin, Rogers, & Machin, 2001). We do not critically evaluate the psychopathy measures for the extent to which they incorporate important developmental considerations or bottom-up research efforts. Instead, we examine the construct validity of these psychopathy measures as they currently exist. Nonetheless, we acknowledge, as did Kotler and McMahon (2005, 2010), that further research efforts are needed to examine the developmental sensitivity of each of the measures being employed in research and practice.

The following section builds on previous reviews on the topic of child and adolescent psychopathy (Forth & Burke, 1998; Hart, Watt, & Vincent, 2002; Salekin, 2006; Salekin & Lynam, 2010; Vincent & Hart, 2002). It is critical to evaluate the structure and validity of the measures if they are to be used in forensic practice even for short-term prediction. By examining the psychometric properties of the psychopathy measures systematically and comprehensively, concerns as to whether the cardinal symptoms of psychopathy are applicable to this youthful population can be partially addressed. Also, it is important to examine what is currently known about the concept of psychopathy in youth with respect to the nomological net that surrounds the disorder. We start by examining the reliability of the construct to determine if there exists structural stability and agreement across raters. We then turn to more general construct validity data on the child and adolescent psychopathy concept.

Scale Homogeneity: Internal Consistency of Measures

If psychopathy is to be used in clinical or clinical forensic practice then it should be a reliable concept. Various types of reliability in youth psychopathy measures, including internal consistency, inter-rater reliability, and test-retest reliability are generally supportive for the construct of psychopathy in children and adolescents. Multiple measures of psychopathic features designed for younger populations have shown satisfactory internal consistency at both the factor structure level and the total score level, but the level of reliability in the scales and subscales does vary across measures. For the purpose of examining scale homogeneity, we discuss total, as well as two-, three-, and four-factor alpha coefficients (α). In order to facilitate the discussion of reliability, we briefly describe the various factor models for psychopathy. However, we cover the factor structure models in greater detail at a later point in this chapter.

Originally, a two-factor model for psychopathy was proposed (Harpur, Hare, & Hakstian, 1989). In the two-factor model, Factor 1 (F_1) was labeled *Interpersonal/Affective Traits* and Factor 2 (F_2) was labeled *Socially Deviant Lifestyle*. Cooke and Michie (2001) proposed a three-factor model for psychopathy. This model split the traditional F_1 into two factors: Interpersonal and Affective. With respect to traditional F_2, Cooke and Michie (2001) dropped the antisocial items and maintained the impulsive items. Hare (1991/2003) later reincorporated the antisocial items to develop a four-factor model that is virtually identical to the Cooke and Michie three-factor model although he added a fourth factor, Antisocial. Two- and three-factor models also generally describe the APSD factors, although the factors are titled Callous-Unemotional and Impulsivity/Conduct Problems for the two-factor model, and Narcissism, Callous-Unemotional, and Irresponsible Behavior for the three-factor model. A four-factor model of the APSD has not been proposed, partially because the APSD does not incorporate antisocial items beyond risky behavior and it has only a single antisocial item. The replicability and robustness of findings for the broad two-factor model, and refined three- and four-factor models, have been remarkable and span research groups, samples (e.g., girls, boys, forensic, community), and models for psychopathy (Hare, 1991/2003; Kosson et al., 2013; Olver & Stockdale, 2010; Patrick, 2010; Salekin & Lynam, 2010).

Considerable data exists on the scale homogeneity of psychopathy. Across 14 studies, internal consistency for the PCL:YV total score ranged from $\alpha = .72$ to $\alpha = .90$. Another study using only file information and no interview found internal consistency of $\alpha = .92$. One more recent study using incarcerated females only found internal consistency of $\alpha = .82$. For the traditional two-factor model, internal reliability estimates range from .64 to .90 for F_1 and range from .45 to .90 for F_2. In the three-factor model (Cooke & Michie, 2001), results range from $\alpha = .52$ to $\alpha = .72$ for ADI, from .56 to .69 for DAE, and from .22 to .68 for IIB. Spain, Douglas, Poythress, and Epstein (2004), utilizing the four-factor model, reported $\alpha = .53$, .54, .42, and .51 for Factors 1, 2, 3, and 4, respectively on the PCL:YV (see Table 14.2).

Across 12 studies the internal consistency (α) for the total score of the self-report version of the APSD ranged from .62 to .84. One study (Frick et al., 2003) found that $\alpha = .92$ for the teacher version of the APSD. This same study found internal reliability estimates to range from .86 to .89 for the parent version of the APSD across four time points. Other studies examining the parent version found the internal consistency to range from $\alpha = .84$ to $\alpha = .88$ (Bijttebier & Decoene, 2009; Falkenbach et al., 2003; Murrie et al., 2004), but other studies have not always found such high estimates. Like the PCL-R, initially, the developers proposed a two-factor structure with a

Table 14.2 Scale homogeneity of psychopathy scales

Psychopathy Scale	Total	F1	F2	F3	F4	N
APSD–Self Report	.766					9
Two-Factor Model		.673	.573			3
Three-Factor Model		.634	.540	.596		8
APSD-Parent	.872					2
Two-Factor Model		.720	.560			1
Three-Factor Model		.743	.805	.708		1
APSD–Teacher	.920	.820	.900	.830		1
APSD–Staff Report	.880					1
CPS–Self Report	.830					4
Two-Factor Model		.685	.695			2
Three-Factor Model		.680	.675	.760		2
CPS–Parent Report	.910	.850	.760			2
PCL:YV	.815					13
Two-Factor Model		.853	.823			3
Three-Factor Model		.610	.640	.580		3
Four-Factor Model		.530	.540	.420	.510	1
Millon P-16	.860	.620	.630	.560		1
Millon MC-P	.840	.590	.560	.510		1
YPI	.907	.883	.693	.807		3

Note. *N* is the number of studies used to compute the estimate. The following studies were used for this table: Andershed et al., 2002; Brandt, Kennedy, Patrick, & Curtin, 1997; Campbell, Porter, & Santor, 2004; Corrado, Vincent, Hart, & Cohen, 2004; Dolan & Rennie, 2006; Falkenbach, Poythress, & Heide, 2003; Forth et al., 1990; Frick, Kimonis, Dandreaux, & Farrell, 2003; Gretton, McBride, Hare, O'Shaughnessy, & Kumka, 2001; Kosson, Cyterski, Steuerwald, Neumann, & Walker-Matthews, 2002; Lee, Vincent, Hart, & Corrado, 2003; Lynam et al., 2005; Murrie, Cornell, Kaplan, McConville, & Levy-Elkon, 2004; O'Neill, Lidz, & Heilbrun, 2003; Poythress, Dembo, Wareham, & Greenbaum, 2006; Poythress, Douglas et al., 2006; Salekin, Leistico, Trobst, Schrum, & Lochman, 2005; Skeem & Cauffman, 2003; Spain et al., 2004; Vitacco, Rogers, & Neumann, 2003; Vitale et al., 2005

Callous-Unemotional traits factor and an Impulsive/Conduct Problems factor. In order to simplify, the different versions of the APSD (i.e., parent-report, self-report, teacher-report) were combined for the following internal reliability estimates. The Callous-Unemotional factor αs ranged from .39 to .73, and the Impulsive/Conduct Problems factor had αs that ranged from .57 to 84. The three-factor model describes the factors as the following: Narcissism, Callous-Unemotional traits, and Impulsivity. Studies have shown the Narcissism factor to have α ranging from .55 to .90, the Callous-Unemotional traits factor to have αs ranging from .22 to .82, and the Impulsivity factor to have αs ranging from .44 to .83. Of the subscales, the Callous-Unemotional factor has evidenced the lowest reliabilities across more than just a few studies now and appears to be the least reliable scale of the psychopathy scales.

Three studies evidenced internal reliability estimates (α) for the total score of the parent-report version of the CPS of .81, .90, and .91 (Bijttebier & Decoene, 2009; Falkenbach et al., 2003; Lynam, 1997). The child-report version of the CPS had αs ranging from .68 to .88. The CPS does not have an empirically derived factor structure, but researchers have proposed both two and three-factor models. The two-factor model is identical to that of the PCL:YV with Factor 1 representing Interpersonal/Affective traits and Factor 2 representing Socially Deviant Lifestyle. Factor 1 internal reliability estimates range from .25 to .85 and Factor 2 internal reliability estimates range from .36 to .75 for the parent-report version of the CPS. For the child-report version of the CPS, total score αs range from .77 to .88. Factor 1 internal reliability estimates range from .14 to .68 and Factor 2 internal reliability estimates range from .21 to .66 for the two-factor model. Spain et al. (2004) and Salekin et al. (2005), using the three-factor model, found much better estimates with Factor 1 (Interpersonal traits) internal reliabilities of .73 and .63, Factor 2 (Affective traits) internal reliabilities of .68 and .67, and Factor 3 (Behavioral traits) internal reliabilities of .71 and .81, respectively.

The YPI has demonstrated internal reliability, with total score αs ranging from .88 to .93 and αs ranging from .84 to .91 for Factor 1 (Grandiose-Manipulative), .57–.78 for Factor 2 (Callous-Unemotional), and .78–.82 for Factor 3 (Impulsive-Irresponsible). The MACI-based Psychopathy measures also were found to show structural stability, with the MC-P showing high αs for its two-factor model. Specifically, the αs for the P-16 scale were generally high with a total-score $\alpha = .86$ (factor scores of .62, .63, .56). Similar αs were found for the MC-P total score (.82) and egocentricity (.59), antisocial (.56), and substance abuse scales (.51) (Salekin et al., 2003). The ICE-SR has promising preliminary results and full study findings should be available soon (see Table 14.2).

Interrater Reliability

Youth psychopathy measures have also shown sufficient interrater reliability (IRR), demonstrating that two raters can achieve relative agreement in identifying and evaluating psychopathic characteristics in children and adolescents (see Table 14.3). The PCL:YV has evidenced a range of intra-class coefficients from .80 to .98 on total scores. Average weighted kappas (κ) have also ranged from .49 to .91. In a meta-analytic study by Olver and Stockdale (2010), 36 research studies from 2000 to 2010 were used to examine PCL:YV interrater reliability. The mean IRRs of the PCL:YV were .90 overall (effect size heterogeneity measured by Q showed $Q = 75.38, p < .01$), not differing between unweighted or weighted effect sizes based on sample size (unweighted $\kappa = 36$; weighted $\kappa = 31$). At the factor level, each factor has shown good interrater reliability for both the two-factor and three-factor models. For the two-factor model, F_1 intra-class correlations (ICCs) range from .75–1.0 and F_2 ICCs range from .83-.99. The three-factor model has displayed good interrater reliability with ICCs of .77, .84, and .86 for ADI, DAE, and IIB, respectively. Olver and Stockdale (2010) further reported that the two-factor model, which had relatively fewer studies ($\kappa = 11$, 9 respectively), also had excellent IRR with Factor 1 $IRR_{unweighted} = .80$ and $IRR_{weighted} = .77$ ($Q = 21.85, p < .01$) and Factor 2 $IRR_{unweighted} = .84$ and $IRR_{weighted} = .84$ ($Q = 45.49, p < .001$). Finally, this meta-analytic study also examined α of the four-factor model: Interpersonal, Affective, Lifestyle, and Antisocial. All of the factors' interrater reliability was consistent with Lifestyle having the lowest of .75 and Antisocial having the highest of .85. The effect size heterogeneity for the Interpersonal, Affective, Lifestyle, and Antisocial factors were 35.75, 50.52, 29.82, and 45.94, respectively (all significant to $p < .01$).

In addition, on the Callous-Unemotional scale of the APSD, the average correlation between parent-reported and teacher-reported traits was .38 (Kimonis, Frick, & Barry, 2004) in one study, but has been more variable in others (Kotler & McMahon, 2010). Furthermore, the correlation between informants increased when two teachers rated the child, resulting in a correlation of .54 between the two teacher-reported APSD total scores (Stevens, Charman, & Blair, 2001). Although the interrater reliability for the APSD between parent and teacher ratings is generally lower than that of the PCL:YV interrater reliabilities, there are a number of potential reasons for this. First, there could be real differences in what various individuals see in different settings (parent, teacher, child). Second, there may be a lack of knowledge with respect to teacher and parent understanding of clinical concepts such as psychopathy and thus perhaps greater variability in the scores (see Table 14.3).

The research discussed earlier on reliability shows evidence of moderate-to-strong reliability of the measurement of psychopathic features in younger populations—although, as can be seen, it does depend on the measure used. Although the aforementioned section on reliability shows that there is agreement for a number of existing youth psychopathy measures, this does not in and of itself inform researchers or clinicians that it is, in fact, psychopathy that is being measured.

Table 14.3 Interrater reliability

	R	ICC	N
APSD	.39	—	1
CPS	.37	—	1
PCL:YV	—	.88	14
MC-P	N/A	N/A	2
P-16	N/A	N/A	1
YPI	—	—	1

Note. The IRR for APSD is between parents and teachers. The IRR for the CPS is between caregiver and self-report. The IRR for the PCL:YV is based on two interviewers independently rating an individual. *N* is the number of studies used to compute the estimate. The following studies were used for this table: Brandt et al., 1997; Campbell et al., 2004; Catchpole & Gretton, 2003; Corrado et al., 2004; Dolan & Rennie, 2006; Forth et al., 1990; Gretton et al., 2001; Kosson et al., 2002; O'Neill et al., 2003; Salekin et al., 2004; Salekin et al., 2005; Skeem & Cauffman, 2003; Spain et al., 2004

Rather, what we know is that if we downwardly extend the adult psychopathy items to youth, the items tend to be moderately reliably assessed in younger populations. The next chief question is to determine whether the same nomological net that surrounds adult psychopathy also surrounds child and adolescent psychopathy. Two steps are necessary before we examine the validity of child psychopathy. First, we review the various factor structures proposed for child psychopathy as this could be important to understanding the psychopathic personality in childhood. Second, we examine the research on the temporal stability of psychopathy. Following these important sections, we turn to addressing the nomological network of child psychopathy.

Factor Structure for Psychopathy in Youth

Traditionally, psychopathy has been viewed as a two-factor concept (Harpur, Hakstian, & Hare, 1989). In the traditional two-factor model, F_1 represents interpersonal and affective characteristics and F_2 represents impulsivity and social deviancy. Cooke and Michie (2001) proposed and tested an alternate factor structure for the PCL-R. This factor structure was a hierarchical three-factor model that separated F_1 into two factors, (1) interpersonal and (2) deficient affective experience, and dropped the antisocial items from the original F_2 to result in a third factor that was represented only by (3) irresponsible and impulsive items. Hare (1991/2003) has argued that four factors underpin psychopathy and proposed a two-factor model with four facets. As mentioned, this model is virtually the same as the Cooke and Michie (2001) three-factor model but adds the fourth factor or facet containing antisocial items.

Frick et al. (1994) and Forth (1995) conducted early research on the factor structure of psychopathy in children and in adolescents, respectively. Frick and colleagues conducted an exploratory factor analysis of parent and teacher ratings of 95 clinic referred children between the ages of 6 and 13. The authors suggested that, consistent with the literature on adult psychopathy, child psychopathy yielded a parallel factor structure characterized by Impulsive/Conduct Problems and callous-unemotional features. Differences in opinion exist as to the extent to which this factor structure replicated adult factor structure data for psychopathy (see Vincent & Hart, 2002). Forth (1995) also contended the traditional two-factor model for psychopathy was replicated via exploratory factor analysis in adolescents, although the items that loaded on each factor differed from the traditional model. Brandt et al. (1997) using confirmatory factor analysis also stated that the two-factor model was a good fit for psychopathy although as noted by Cooke and Michie (2001), the Comparative Fit Index (CFI) was low at .83, below the standard of .95, or even the more liberal standard of .90. Kosson et al. (2002) tested the factor structure of the PCL:YV via confirmatory factor analysis and were unable to validate either the two- or three-factor structure conclusively among 12–16-year-old males on probation.

Salekin and colleagues (Salekin et al., 2004, Salekin et al., 2006) tested the three- and four-factor models in two separate studies. The first was a study that examined the factor structure of psychopathy in relation to intelligence (Salekin et al., 2004). The second study directly tested the factor structure of psychopathy and compared two-, three-, and four-factor models (Salekin et al., 2006). Both studies reported good fit indices for the three-factor model. The second study showed that three- and four-factor models were justifiable but that the three-factor model produced a better fit to the data and that the fourth factor had a relatively weak loading. Two other studies have furthered knowledge on the factor structure of psychopathy. Specifically, Jones, Cauffman, Miller, and Mulvey (2006) tested the factor structure for psychopathy in a large sample of adolescents. Their findings extended the results mentioned above by demonstrating a good fit for three- and four-factor models and invariance across race and gender. Neumann, Kosson, Forth, and Hare (2006) tested the rivaling models and found that two-, three-, and four-factor models fit the data. More recently, Kosson, Neumann, Forth, Salekin, Hare, Krischer, and Sevecke (2013) found that both three- and four-factor models for psychopathy were also applicable to girls.

Stability: Test-Retest Reliability of Psychopathy

Until recently, evidence for the chronicity of psychopathy has been derived almost exclusively from analyses of retrospective data from adults with antisocial personality disorders, although the plight of research in this area is changing. In her classic study, Robins (1966, 1978) traced the onset of psychopathic symptoms back to the age of 6–10 years using case file information from individuals who had been assessed at a child and guidance clinic in St. Louis two decades prior to her discovery of the files. Many of these youth were considered to have sociopathic, delinquent, and conduct-problem symptoms at the time of initial assessment. Twenty years after their original assessment, Robins embarked on a research endeavor to identify and interview this sample of individuals as adults. She reported that many of these adults continued to have primarily antisocial lifestyles over two decades later in time.

One other study has addressed the stability issue in a less direct way. Harpur and Hare (1994) compared the prevalence rates of psychopathy classifications and the mean level of psychopathy traits in six different age subgroups of adult offenders (overall age range of sample is 16–70 years). These authors found that overall rates of psychopathy declined with age, especially after the age of 45. This decline was strong for the impulsive and antisocial features of psychopathy (F_2), whereas the average level of interpersonal and affective traits (F_1) remained relatively steady across age groups. It is important to note that this was a cross-sectional study in which variations in psychopathy levels were examined across different-aged cohorts, and thus the study was not a direct test of temporal stability. Other studies have also investigated the temporal stability of psychopathy in adult samples. Schroeder et al. (1983) reported a stability coefficient of .89 over a 10-month period. Rutherford, Cacciola, Alterman, McKay, and Cook (1999) reported two-year stability estimates of .60 in methadone patients.

More recently, studies which test the temporal stability of psychopathy in young people, longitudinally, have surfaced. One of the first studies in this regard was conducted by Frick and colleagues (2003) and tested youth on the APSD over four time points, prospectively. The sample consisted of non-referred children who were in the third, fourth, six, and seventh grades at the time of the first assessment. Assessments included parent- and self-report versions of the APSD. For parent ratings of overall psychopathic traits, stability estimates using intra-class correlation coefficients ranged from .80 to .88 across two to four years, with a stability estimate of .93 across all four assessments. These coefficients suggest that parent ratings are reasonably

Table 14.4 Stability of psychopathy

Authors	Psychopathy Conceptualization/Factor	Duration	Stability
Blonigen et al. (2008)		7 years	
	Fearless / Dominance		85.0%
	Impulsive Antisociality		51.6%
Forsman, Lichtenstein, Andershed, & Larsson (2008)	Psychopathy total	3 years	
	Grandiose-manipulative		91.2%
	Callous-unemotional		91.7%
	Impulsive-irresponsible		80.9%
Frick et al. (2003)	Psychopathy total	4 years	.89
Harpur & Hare (1994)	Psychopathy total	cross-sectional	—
	Factor 1	18-50 years	stable
	Faxtor 2	18-50 years	declining
Lynam et al. (2007)	Psychopathy total	11years	.32
Pardini et al. (2003)	Interpersonal	9 year	.50
Robins (1966)	Antisocial total	20 years	50%
Rutherford, Cacciola, Alterman, McKay, & Cook (1999)	Psychopathy total	1 year	.65
Schroeder, Schroeder, & Hare (1983)	Psychopathy total	10 months	.89
Skeem & Cauffman (2003)	Psychopathy total	1 month	.74

Note. The stability estimate in Lynam, Caspi, Moffitt, Loeber, and Stouthamer-Loeber (2007) is a correlation-coefficient. Percentages represent the percentage of individuals who met criteria at time one and time two for example. In the Blonigen et al. article, the percentage represents the percentage of individuals who remained the same on the psychopathic traits, respectively, on the basis of the Reliable Change Index.

consistent across time. Stabilities for individual subscales of the APSD (narcissism [interpersonal], callous-unemotional [affective], and impulsivity) were also quite high based on parent report, ranging from .71 to .92.

Even more recently, researchers have attempted to address the stability of psychopathy. To date studies range in follow-up periods from one to 13 years and generally show moderate stability (Barker & Salekin, 2012; Barry, Barry, Deming, & Lochman, 2008; Munoz & Frick, 2007; Obradovic, Pardini, Long, & Loeber, 2007; Loeber, Pardini, Hipwell, Stouthamer-Loeber, Keenan, & Sembower, 2009; Pardini, Lochman, & Powell, 2007; Van Baarewijk, Vermeiren, Stegge, & Doreleijers, 2011). In general, however, the longer the follow-up period, the lower the stability estimate—and a number of factors appear to affect stability estimates. For example, one influence on stability is the reporter used to assess psychopathy.

In one informative study, Forsman et al. (2008) reported that the stability of psychopathy traits from 16 to 19 years ($N = 1,467$) was .43 and $r = .54$ (p < .05) for boys and girls retrospectively. In a sample of older adolescents, Blonigen, Carlson, Hicks, Krueger, and Iacono (2008) reported a stability of .60 (p < .001) from ages 17 to 24 (n = 1252). Two studies provide information on the stability of psychopathic traits from childhood to young adulthood. Burke et al. (2007) reported that both parent- and teacher-rated interpersonal traits assessed at ages 7–12 in a sample of clinic referred boys ($N = 177$) were significantly related to clinician-rated psychopathy at aged 18 and 19. Lynam, Caspi, Moffitt, Loeber, & Stouthamer-Loeber (2007) reported that self-report of psychopathic traits at age 13 ($N = 250$) was significantly associated with clinician ratings of psychopathic traits at age 24 ($r = .31$, $N = 250$). These estimates clearly suggest that psychopathy from childhood to adolescence is not unalterable, given that only 9% of the variance of age 24 scores were accounted for by the scores at age 13. Thus, although psychopathy is a risk factor for future psychopathy, the findings indicate that there is stability but also considerable change evidenced in psychopathy ratings. It should be noted, however, that children who were in the upper 10% of psychopathic traits at age 13 were 3.22 times more likely than other children to show elevations on the adult measure 11 years later. At the same time, it is also important to keep in mind that most children show a decline in psychopathic traits over time. Thus, one important question regarding the applicability of the psychopathy construct to children continues to be whether youth who are assessed as being psychopathic will actually meet cutoff scores for psychopathy at later points in time.

Construct Validity of Child and Adolescent Psychopathy: Examining the Nomological Net

While a great deal of the research has examined the reliability and structural stability of the psychopathy concept, it is important to note here that child psychopathy measures will be useful only if they make conceptual sense and offer some predictive value. That is, the measures and concepts must show a nomological net that corresponds with theoretical models. If this does not occur, then the concept either (a) is inapplicable, (b) is applicable to a lesser degree, and/or (c) requires important developmental considerations that should be charted over time (Salekin & Frick, 2005; Salekin & Lynam, 2010). The degree to which developmental differences exist requires careful consideration as the findings may have important implications for risk assessment and treatment amenability.

As mentioned earlier, as part of any nomological net, the concept must be predictive of a set of behavior(s). This is similar to any diagnostic category in that if a diagnostic entity is established, it is assumed that the category, or class, will be predictive of some set of behaviors. If the class is not predictive, then there is little value in making the diagnosis. For example, depression might be predictive of poor sleep, poor work performance, poor concentration, suicidal ideation, and even suicide. In a similar vein, child psychopathy should be predictive of negative outcomes such as, for example, poor relationship quality, antisocial conduct, impaired emotional responses to others, moral transgressions, as well as potentially underlying neurological deficits. In this section, we examine construct validity of psychopathy to determine the extent to which a meaningful nomological net surrounds the concept of child and adolescent psychopathy. Understanding the degree to which a nomological net has been established is critical to forensic assessments in that clinicians will have to know the various correlates of psychopathy and its sub-factors if they are to use the construct competently in practice. The next few sections examine psychopathy's relation to (a) general models of personality, (b) other forms of DSM psychopathology, (c) performance tasks, (d) antisocial conduct, and (e) treatment outcome. We start by discussing psychopathy and general models of personality in children and adolescents.

Psychopathy and Personality

The relations between psychopathy and personality are now fairly well charted. Hart and Hare (1994) initiated work on psychopathy and the Big 5; Lynam and Widiger (Lynam 2002a, 2002b; Widiger & Lynam, 1998) greatly expanded on this topic with adults and later children and adolescents. The Big 5 factors of personality emphasize broad domains identified as Extraversion, Agreeableness, Conscientiousness, Neuroticism, and Openness. Widiger and Lynam (1998) and their colleagues (Brinkley, Newman, Widiger, & Lynam, 2004; Lynam, Whiteside, & Jones, 1999; Miller, Lynam, Widiger, & Luekefeld, 2001; Widiger & Lynam, 1998) argued that psychopathy can be understood from the perspective of the Five-Factor Model (FFM; McCrae & Costa, 1990). This model has considerable empirical support with convergent and discriminant validity across self, peer, and spouse ratings (Costa & McCrae, 1988, 1989), good temporal stability (7–10 years; Costa, Herbst, McCrae, & Siegler, 2000; Costa & McCrae, 1994) and heritability evidence (Jang, McCrae, Angleitner, Reimann, & Livesley, 1998; Plomin & Caspi, 1999). According to theory, psychopathy should be negatively associated with Conscientiousness and Agreeableness, an association that has already been demonstrated with adults (e.g., Miller et al., 2001; Salekin, Trobst, & Krioukova, 2001). Importantly, a number of studies have now examined psychopathy and its relation to the Big 5 factors of personality in children and adolescents. These results parallel those found with adults and appear to be replicated even in preschool samples (Assary, Salekin, & Barker, in press; Lynam, 2002b; Lynam et al., 2005; Salekin, Debus, & Barker, 2010).

From these studies, there appears to be consistency across the findings for the domains of Agreeableness and Conscientiousness. Child and adolescent psychopathy, across measurements, is negatively related to Agreeableness and Conscientiousness. There is less agreement across studies for the domain of Neuroticism. Lynam (2002b) found that child psychopathy was negatively related to Neuroticism, whereas other studies found that it was positively related (see Salekin et al., 2005). Berg et al. (2013) have also found that the ICU measure (which taps a component of psychopathy) is saturated with negative affect. Similarly, Latzman, Lilienfeld, Latzman, and Clark (2013) found neuroticism was associated with psychopathy. These differences could be due to the complex relation that psychopathy has with neuroticism and the differential weighting that the various components of Neuroticism receive across studies. Aspects of Neuroticism associated with self-consciousness, anxiety, and vulnerability should be negatively related to psychopathy, whereas aspects of Neuroticism associated with angry hostility and impulsiveness/urgency should be positively related (Derefinko & Lynam, 2006). While one argument is that there is variability in the Neuroticism scale items accounting for differences across studies, an alternate explanation might be that there are developmental differences with child and adolescent samples experiencing higher levels of anxiety than their adult counterparts.

To the extent that psychopathy is personality, it has been argued that basic research on personality is relevant to the concept of psychopathy for several reasons. First, personality traits that characterize psychopathy appear to be relatively stable across adolescence and into adulthood. For example, Block (1993) provided evidence for a 10-year stability of ego-control (a specific constellation of the Big 5 factors of personality), reporting a test-retest correlation of .67 between ages 14 to 23. In a meta-analysis, Roberts and DelVecchio (2000) found moderate to large stability coefficients for each of the Big 5 factors across ages 12 to near 18. Although they do not suggest that personality is immutable across adolescence, the coefficients from the meta-analysis are similar to those found for stabilities in early to mid-adulthood. Some researchers have argued that these results suggest that the most psychopathic individuals in adolescence will be the most psychopathic in adulthood (Lynam & Gudonis, 2005).

Psychopathy and Coexisting Childhood Psychopathology

One concern regarding the applicability of the psychopathy construct to children and adolescents has been the overlap with other forms of psychopathology. Research indicates that comorbidity of mental disorder is somewhat normative in child and adolescent samples (Achenbach, 1995; Biederman, Newcorn, & Sprich, 1991; Caron & Rutter, 1991; Frick, 2002; Lahey, Loeber, Burke, Rathouz, & McBurnett, 2002). This is true for youth who are diagnosed with externalizing disorders such as ODD or CD (Lahey et al., 2002; Seagrave & Grisso, 2002). For example, disorders frequently co-occurring with CD include various forms of depression, anxiety, substance use/abuse, and attention problems (Hinshaw & Zupan, 1997). Some researchers have argued that because of the high comorbidity evident for CD and ODD, psychopathy may also show an elevated overlap with other forms of pathology when diagnosed early in life (Hart, Watt, & Vincent, 2002; Vincent & Hart, 2002; Seagrave & Grisso, 2002).

Several studies have explored the relation between child psychopathy and general psychopathology (Bauer & Kosson, 2000; Bauer, Whitman, & Kosson, 2011; Epstein, Douglas, Poythress, Spain, & Falkenbach, 2002; Kosson et al., 2002; Lynam, 1997; Myers, Burket, & Harris, 1995). Brandt et al. (1997) found significant correlations between total scores on the PCL-R and Scales

4 ($r = .17$) and 9 ($r = .23$) of the MMPI. Modest correlations were also found between the PCL-R and the aggressive and externalizing disorder subscales of the CBCL, $rs = .31$ and .23, respectively. Somewhat unexpectedly, however, the diffuse pathology scale of the CBCL, defined by overall elevations on its constituent scales, also correlated significantly with PCL-R total scores ($r = .24$). Comparable correlations were found for the immature ($r = .20$), self-destructive ($r = .20$), and unpopular ($r = .18$) subscales of the CBCL.

Epstein et al. (2002) found the PCL:YV was associated positively with alcohol dependence ($r = .29$) and substance dependence ($r = .51$), but not with anxiety ($r = .07$) or depression ($r = .04$) in a sample of 60 adolescent offenders. However, overall APSD scores showed significant positive relations with anxiety ($r = .28$) and ADHD ($r = .23$). In a study that focused on female offenders, Bauer and Kosson (2000) examined 80 adolescent girls detained at the Illinois Youth Center, and reported that psychopathy as indexed by the PCL:YV was significantly and positively associated with a number of psychiatric diagnoses, even after removing CD from the analyses. Rates of comorbidity that psychopathy (PCL:YV > 30) showed with other diagnoses in this sample were generally very high: alcohol dependence (61%), drug dependence (72%), ADHD (71%), dysthymia (22%), depression (52%), and PTSD (19%).

Myers et al. (1995) examined relations among psychopathy as measured by the PCL-R, Axis I and II psychopathology, and delinquent behaviors in 30 psychiatrically hospitalized male and female adolescents. These authors found significant relations among psychopathy, CD, delinquent behavior, substance abuse, and narcissistic personality disorder. The authors noted that many participants in this sample had multiple personality problems and, aside from age requirements, would have met criteria for many of the personality disorders (i.e., approximately one-third of the sample had met criteria for four or more personality disorders). However, this high comorbidity may be in part reflective of the setting (i.e., psychiatric hospital).

Salekin, Neumann, Leistico, DiCicco, and Duros (2004) examined the construct of psychopathy in 130 adolescent offenders utilizing three psychopathy measures (APSD, PCL:YV, and a modified version of the Self Report of Psychopathy–II [SRP-II]) and a wide range of DSM-IV Axis I diagnoses and psychosocial problems (indexed by the Adolescent Psychopathology Scale; Reynolds, 1998). Pearson product-moment correlations indicated that psychopathy evidenced less comorbidity than did ODD or CD. This evidence for the discriminant validity of the psychopathy construct in youth suggests that it could offer a refinement over existing DSM-IV disruptive behavior disorders in terms of differentiation from other conditions (see also Lahey et al., 2002). However, it is important to note that comorbidity was not absent for the diagnosis of psychopathy in comparison with CD; it merely evidenced lower rates of comorbidity with other conditions than the DSM-IV disruptive behavior disorders. Furthermore, anxiety and depression were evident at higher rates among psychopathic youth than expected based on theory (Cleckley, 1941/1976).

Psychopathy, Performance Tasks, and Biological Deficits

The adult literature has attempted to link psychopathy to theoretical biological or cognitive deficits. In recent years, these models have been extended to child and adolescent populations (Lynam & Gudonis, 2005). A review of the existing literature has suggested primary deficits in at least two areas: (a) behavioral inhibition or impulsivity, and (b) emotional processing. The following summary is focused primarily on the deficit and its operational definition, with little emphasis on models or theories upon which they are based.

Several studies have examined the relation between child and adolescent psychopathy and measures of behavioral inhibition or impulsivity. This particular deficit has received some support among adult psychopaths. For example, two studies have used adaptations of a card-playing task developed originally to measure response modulation in adult psychopaths (Newman, Patterson, & Kosson, 1987). This task contains 100 cards, and its rate of reward per 10 trials drops from 100% to 10%. Participants must make a decision whether to play another card or whether to quit the task. Previous research has shown that adult psychopaths play more cards than do adult nonpsychopaths. Similar results have been obtained among children (Fisher & Blair, 1998) although in a very small sample of participants ($n = 39$). Specifically, Fisher and Blair found positive correlations between the number of cards played and total scores on the APSD and scores on the impulsive/conduct problems subscale. In a mixed-gender sample ($n = 132$), O'Brien and Frick (1996) found that nonanxious psychopathic children played the greatest number of cards. Originally, Lynam (1997) reported that scores on the CPS were not correlated with the number of cards played, but a reanalysis of those data showed a positive correlation among White participants (Lynam & Gudonis, 2005).

Two additional studies have examined in juveniles different behavioral tasks designed to assess a reward-dominant response style. Blair, Colledge, and Mitchell (2001) used the Iowa Gambling Task, which consists of four decks of cards that differ from one another in terms of the rewards and punishments accompanying each deck. Two decks are associated with net rewards, whereas two are associated with net losses; individuals are expected to learn to play from the decks associated with the net rewards. Blair et al. (2001) found that boys with psychopathic tendencies assessed with the APSD made more selections from the disadvantageous decks across time, paralleling findings in adult psychopaths (Mitchell, Colledge, Leonard, & Blair, 2002). However, these findings were based on a relatively small sample of 51 juvenile boys. Lynam (1998) reported that boys scoring high on the CPS were more likely to choose a smaller, but immediately available, monetary reward over a larger delayed reward.

A second set of deficits found within the child literature is deficits in nonverbal emotional processing. This follows directly from adult literature that suggests psychopathic deficits in this domain are due to dysfunction found within neurophysiological systems modulating fear behavior and systems mediating empathy (Blair 1995, 1999; Lynam & Gudonis, 2005). Blair and Coles (2000) examined expression recognition further using faces composed of six different emotional facial expressions (happiness, surprise, fear, sadness, disgust, and anger). Results indicated a significant inverse relation between APSD F_1 and the ability to recognize sadness and fearfulness, and a significant inverse correlation between F_2 and the ability to recognize fear. Similarly, children with psychopathic tendencies demonstrated deficiencies in noticing sad vocal tones (Stevens et al., 2001) and a sensitivity to sad and fearful emotional expressions (Blair et al., 2001). These findings mirror the selective recognition results found in adults.

A final deficit noted in research on psychopathy is a discrepancy between psychopathic individuals' verbal descriptions of themselves and their behavior (Hare, 1993). Raine et al. (1990) investigated this hypothesis with a group of male adolescent offenders using a cluster analysis technique for diagnosing psychopathy. Utilizing a verbal dichotic listening task composed of consonant vowel pairs, the authors found adolescent psychopathic individuals had differential hemispheric functioning which supported previous work by Hare and McPherson (1984) that suggests psychopathic individuals have reduced brain lateralization for verbal material. Loney, Frick, Clements, Ellis, and Kerlin (2003) examined the performance of 65 adolescent males on an emotional-lexical decision task originally used by Williamson, Harpur, and Hare (1991) in adult psychopaths. This task requires participants to identify a string of letters as either a word or nonword. The words are equally divided among three emotional valences: positive, negative, and neutral. Differences between speed of recognition for emotional and neutral words provided indices of facilitation for emotional words. Loney et al. (2003) found few relations between adolescent psychopathy and facilitation to either positive or negative words. One noteworthy finding was a significant, negative relation between scores on the callous-unemotional subscale of the APSD and facilitation for negative words only after parsing out the impulsive conduct problems subscale of the APSD. Frick et al. (2003) in a sample of 85 nonreferred children did find a negative relation between callous-unemotional traits and facilitation to negative words, but this relation held only among children in the third and fourth grades and not among children from the fifth and sixth grades. These results do not map onto results from the original study conducted in adults by Williamson et al. (1991), which showed psychopaths showed less facilitation to both positive and negative words than did nonpsychopaths. These findings are consistent with more recent studies, which have found this relation to be less than robust (see Lorenz & Newman, 2002a; 2002b) and potentially dependent upon race and handedness, amongst other factors.

More recently, psychopathy in youth has been explored using performance tasks with fMRI and EEG data. In a study by Marsh et al. (2013), there was a significant negative correlation between the level of empathic pain responses in the amygdala and rostral anterior cingulate cortex and a juvenile's psychopathy scores on the PCL:YV. Moreover, Marsh et al. found that reduced empathic pain response levels in these brain areas could predict symptom severity on the PCL:YV. Psychopathic traits were also negatively associated with right amygdala activity during a judgment of fear task (Marsh & Cardinale, 2014). Furthermore, psychopathy was positively associated with increased activity in the middle frontal gyrus during the same task. In an extension of the adult literature, White et al. (2013) found that a large cavum septum pellucidum was associated with a DBD diagnosis, proactive aggression, and psychopathic traits in youth.

Aside from imaging studies, several studies have been conducted using EEG to measure brainwave activity. Patrick, Durbin, and Moser (2012), highlighted what is known about P300 (a component of ERP) and psychopathy, stating that adolescents at risk for or with impulse control and externalizing behaviors have exhibited lower P300 amplitudes than control groups. Gao, Raine, Venables, Dawson, & Mednick (2010) conducted a longitudinal study in which P300 amplitude was measured during a continuous performance task at ages 11 and 23 and found that lowered P300 amplitude at age 11 was significantly associated with antisocial behavior at age 11 and age 23. Overall, these fMRI and EEG studies have begun to examine the biological and cognitive development of psychopathy in adolescents. These studies are extremely important in understanding the genetic predisposition and brain functioning abnormalities associated with risk of developing psychopathy. This area continues to be studied and further research is promising.

Psychopathy and Antisocial Conduct

In general, the research thus far has shown that child and adolescent psychopathy is predictive of delinquency and later recidivism as it is in adulthood (Leistico, Salekin, DeCoster, & Rogers, 2008; Salekin, Rogers, & Sewell, 1996). Moreover, psychopathy appears to be related to institutional misconduct when psychopathic individuals are captive (Guy, Edens, Anthony, & Douglas, 2005). Psychopathy scores on the PCL:YV have been found to be associated with a younger age of first conviction, first drug use, and onset of school misconduct (Corrado et al., 2004). Furthermore, a number of researchers have found psychopathy scores to be associated with the number of prior convictions and previous violence (Campbell, Porter, & Santor, 2004; Dolan & Rennie, 2006; Salekin, Neumann, Leistico, DiCicco, & Duros, 2004; Vincent, Vitacco, Grisso, & Corrado, 2003) and specifically prior violent criminal behavior (Dolan & Rennie, 2006; Leistico et al., 2008; Murrie et al., 2004; Salekin et al., 2004, Vincent et al., 2003). In addition, Kimonis et al., (2004) showed that children rated high on conduct problems and callous-unemotional traits by their parents and teachers were more likely to associate with a deviant peer group across a four-year time period. Kostos and Kimonis (2014) have found that grandiose and manipulative traits are related to bullying behavior. Most recently, Asscher and colleagues (2011) provided additional information on psychopathy and recidivism and noted that the PCL:YV was the best predictor of recidivism over other child measures although each have some predictive ability.

Psychopathy and Treatment

Salekin and colleagues (2002, 2010) examined the psychopathy-treatment literature and concluded that there was little-to-no evidence to demonstrate that psychopathy was an untreatable disorder. In fact, some of the research indicated that psychopathy was a treatable condition and that youth might be the most likely to benefit from treatment. Skeem et al. (2002) generated similar conclusions after conducting a study with civil psychiatric patients. Caldwell, Skeem, Salekin, and Van Rybroeck (2006) found that treatment of psychopathy reduced antisocial conduct in young offenders. Despite some limitations regarding the treatment literature thus far (Harris & Rice, 2006; Salekin, 2002; Wong & Hare, 2005), reviews of the literature on psychopathy and treatment result in a very similar conclusion —specifically, that there are not yet sufficient well controlled treatment studies and thus no evidence that psychopathy is an untreatable disorder. Subsequent reviews have shown that there have been successful attempts to treat psychopathy in open trial and other research designs. For instance, Salekin, Tippey, and Allen (2012) in an operational study showed that psychopathy could be reduced even in deep-end offenders who are living in residential facilities. This study showed that there was a reduction in psychopathic traits across the intervention as well as improved behavior on the campus. On balance, the findings thus far indicate that psychopathy may very well be a treatable disorder.

Conclusions

In the current chapter, we sought to answer several questions on the development and utility of child and adolescent psychopathy. First, we were interested in examining how psychopathy differs from DSM-5 DBDs. Second, we were interested in whether there was theoretical evidence to suggest that the disorder could start early in development. Third, we were interested in the homogeneity and temporal stability of the construct. Finally, we were interested in examining the nomological net that surrounds child and adolescent psychopathy. We reviewed a number of recent studies that suggest psychopathy in children and adolescents looks roughly similar to psychopathy in adults. Similar characteristics are present in these individuals at developmental time points. Additionally, child and adolescent psychopathy predicts antisocial conduct like that of adult psychopathy. Like their adult counterparts, child and adolescent psychopaths tend to be more stable in their offending. They are prone to externalizing disorders but also exhibit some internalizing disorders. Child and adolescent psychopathy is characterized by low levels of agreeableness and conscientiousness. Psychopathic youth may show processing deficits that are somewhat similar to those found in adults. There are likely developmental differences as well; more research is needed on this topic.

This leads us to conclude that although the construct of psychopathy in youth is garnering additional research support, its use should be limited in court settings (Vitacco & Salekin, 2013; Vitacco, Salekin, & Rogers, 2010). More research is needed, not only on symptomatology and assessment instruments, but also on the efficacy of interventions for this new, younger version of psychopathy. It is also possible that the term *psychopathy* may have become too stigmatizing to use with children when making legal decisions, unless researchers can help inform the courts and other relevant parties of the most recent correlates of the disorder. Therefore, in this chapter, we offer an alternative method for discussing psychopathic characteristics. Undoubtedly, much work remains to be conducted and many issues need to be addressed with respect to the potential usefulness of the psychopathy concept as applied to children and adolescents. In light of these concerns we suggest the following in assessing and guiding clinicians in ethical practice.

Using the Term Psychopathy: *Time for a New Nomenclature?*

A new nomenclature might be indicated until we are more certain about the adolescent psychopathy classification. We propose the following as one example that might be used. This proposal is virtually identical to our earlier proposal (see Salekin & Debus, 2008) and also builds on the current DSM-5 conduct disorder diagnosis and limited prosocial emotion specifier, thereby offering a more thorough accounting of psychopathy-like characteristics that were noted to be lacking as overviewed in the section on DBD criteria in the opening pages of this chapter. Of course, clinicians could use *psychopathic features* or *psychopathic-like characteristics* if they deem appropriate so long as they update judges and other relevant personnel on the correlates of the disorder, but some may find it even more beneficial to reduce the confusion further and specify the traits more clearly and also to tie those traits to CD as was done with the LPE specifier and as suggested by Salekin and Debus (2008). We propose the following labels as an option that could fit well with the DSM and ICD CD criteria:

Conduct Disorder – Grandiose-manipulative specifier
Conduct Disorder – Callous-unemotional specifier
Conduct Disorder – Daring-impulsive specifier
Conduct Disorder – Combined specifier – specifying the "specifiers" that apply.

These specific specifics should be examined further particularly regarding interaction with CD.

Forensic Evaluation: Conduct Comprehensive Assessments

While psychopathy represents an important construct at the adult level, and is gaining some momentum with adolescents and children, if the goal is to make predictions about risk for future offending then researchers may want to examine a broader range of factors that might impact the likelihood that a youth is at risk for offending. This might include using measures specifically designed for risk assessment such as the Risk-Sophistication-Treatment-Inventory (RSTI; Salekin, 2004). Kazdin (1997) suggested that the or the Structured Assessment of Violence Risk in Youth (SAVRY; Borum, Bartel, & Forth, 2006), which examines risk and protective factors or the Youth Level of Service/Case Management Inventory (YLS/CMI), which also examines risk and treatment needs. Given the moderate level of stability in psychopathy scores, there are likely many factors that protect against the development of psychopathy and an assessment of protective factors also seems essential. Psychologists should also consult guides for general juvenile assessment (see Salekin, 2015).

Psychological Reports Should Be Relevant Research-Based and Inform Treatment

Diagnostic labels were never intended to harm people, only to help. As such, we recommend that clinicians use the terms or descriptors of psychopathy in youth to inform treatment of CD youth. All reports should include information that highlights the lack of evidence to support conclusions that psychopathic features are untreatable (Caldwell et al., 2006; Hawes, Price, & Dadds, 2014; Salekin, 2002; Skeem et al., 2002) and should highlight the research that is showing treatment effects (Salekin et al., 2012). Also, and relatedly, theories that exist to offer accounts of the origins of psychopathy remain thin. No prospective studies have tested core developmental hypotheses exhaustively. For example, although several theories predict maladaptive transactions with the environment, few have thoroughly examined such exchanges. This important point should also be highlighted in reports. Information should be clearly overviewed in cases in which psychopathy is used in forensic evaluations (Salekin, 2015). A court case published recently (*The People of the State of Illinois v. Deonta Johnson*, 2013) provides optimism that these recommendations can have an effect on the courts. In *The People of the State of Illinois v. Deonta Johnson* (2013) case, a 14-year-old defendant charged with first-degree murder and attempted first-degree murder was evaluated by a psychiatrist regarding his potential for rehabilitation. The psychiatrist indicated that the defendant had "incipient antisocial personality disorder," but that "Children or adolescents who engage in psychopathic behavior in adolescence can develop insight and accountability regarding their actions at a later age" (*The People of the State of Illinois v. Deonta*

Johnson, 2013, para. 16). The court cited the psychiatrist's recommendations in deciding that the trial court "could not effectively determine 'there were no advantages to treatment within the juvenile system'" and the transfer order was reversed, and the defendant was remanded to juvenile court.

Case Study

Gerald, a 16-year-old boy, was brought into juvenile court for violating his parole in a theft and assault charge. Gerald was attempting to steal fuel for his high-performance street car from city vehicles located on a city lot, when a security guard noticed Gerald and approached him. Gerald was surprised and struck the security guard, knocking him to the ground, and then ran away with his fuel container. The security guard called the police, who picked Gerald up and charged him with theft and assault. Gerald had two previous convictions for theft (attempts for fuel), a charge for dangerous driving (drag racing), and a conviction for vandalism. Gerald received the vandalism charge because he and some friends were painting graffiti on a building and were also caught breaking windows in an abandoned building. He also had several suspensions for teasing (bullying) and occasionally fighting with his schoolmates. Despite these behavioral problems, Gerald was very much liked by many people at his school and he was otherwise considered a good student by teachers (he completed homework assignments, performed well on tests, and earned good grades). Occasionally, he would "entertain" one or two classmates who sat close to him, but mostly was reported to be well-behaved. Gerald definitely ran in the "cool" circles according to collateral sources. In fact, he was considered a leader at his school. He was confident, articulate, and likable. Although there were kids who were afraid of him because he was socially powerful, he did have friends that he was responsive with, and to whom he was considered generous. However, if Gerald decided to tease a peer, all he had to do was recruit a few other schoolmates and the mocking and bullying would begin. Recipients of this bullying reported that it was virtually unbearable. Given Gerald's history of repeated thefts and the recent assault, a juvenile court judge requested that he undertake a series of assessments in an attempt to understand his delinquent behavior. Especially given that Gerald was an "A" student at school, the judge was concerned that he might miss important opportunities due to his delinquency. A psychologist administered a battery of tests to Gerald, including a measure of psychopathic features. Through a semi-structured interview, the psychologist discovered that Gerald had a history of behavioral problems, but these typically occurred immediately after school. He currently participated in many risky activities as well as theft and bullying. He was also markedly active with the girls at his school. His past girlfriends reported often being unsure of his intentions. Even though Gerald was quite popular and respected by his teachers, he was considered manipulative and deceitful by a number of friends and he did operate with a bit of a "life's a game" strategy. Gerald had an elevated score on a number of items used to assess psychopathy, including a large number of interpersonal items such as superficial charm, grandiosity, manipulation, and deceit, and a few affective features such as lack of remorse and lack of empathy for his actions, as well as some daring behaviors. The psychologist, after completing her evaluation, recommended that Gerald receive psychological therapy. It was also recommended that his parents be included in the treatment efforts and that they attend classes on appropriate parenting practices. The psychologist further recommended that Gerald become involved in an extracurricular activity of interest to him. It was believed that such activities would incorporate positive activities into his life and provide exposure to more non-deviant peers. The psychologist noted that there were a number of negative life circumstances for Gerald, but was optimistic regarding his potential for gains in psychotherapy. The psychologist also noted that significant change would require regular treatment sessions over the course of several months in order to notice any marked improvements.

Notes

1 Originally, the DSM incorporated personality and affective features of the disorder but later the behavioral model for antisocial personality disorder and CD emerged and reduced the criteria to primarily behavioral characteristics. It was thought that by reducing the criteria to be primarily behavioral characteristics that the disorder (also thought to be sociopathy) could be more reliably assessed (Robins, 1966; Cloninger, 1978). The DSM-5 now has included some affective characteristics (APA, 2013).

2 CD captures a wide variety of youth—those who experiment with delinquency, those who have conduct problems secondary to depression, those who exhibit conduct problems as a temporary expression of extreme play, those who have conduct problems stemming from impulsivity or sensation seeking (Quay, 1965), those who have CDs stemming from callousness, etc.

3 Although theory and clinical lore has suggested that psychopathy is an untreatable syndrome, there is little empirical evidence to back this contention (see Rogers, Jackson, Sewell, & Johansen, 2004; Salekin, 2002; Salekin, Worley, & Grimes, 2010).

References

Achenbach, T. M. (1991). The derivation of taxonomic constructs: A necessary stage in the development of developmental psychopathology. In D. Cicchetti & S. L. Toth (Eds.), *Rochester symposium on developmental psychopathology, Vol. 3: Models and integrations* (pp. 43–74). Rochester, NY: University of Rochester Press.

Achenbach, T. M. (1995). Diagnosis, assessment, and comorbidity in psychological treatment research. *Journal of Abnormal Psychology, 23*, 45–65. doi. 10.1007/BF01447044

American Psychiatric Association. (2013). *Diagnostic and statistical manual of mental disorders* (5th ed.). Arlington, VA: American Psychiatric Publishing.

Andershed, H., Kerr, M., Stattin, H., & Levander, S. (2002). Psychopathic traits in non-referred youths: A new assessment tool. In E. Blaauw & L. Sheridan (Eds.), *Psychopaths: Current international perspectives* (pp. 131–158). The Hague: Elsevier.

Assary, E., Salekin, R. T., & Barker, E. D. (2015). Big-five and callous-unemotional traits in preschoolers. *Journal of Psychopathology and Behavioral Assessment, 37*, 371–379.

Asscher, J. J., van Vugt, E. S., Stams, G. J. J. M., Dekovia, M., Eichelsheim, V. I., & Yousfi, S. (2011). The relationship between juvenile psychopathic traits, delinquency and (violent) recidivism: A meta-analysis. *Journal of Child Psychology and Psychiatry, 52*, 1134–1143.

Barker, E. D., & Salekin, R. T. (2012). Irritable oppositional defiance and callous unemotional traits: Is the association partially explained by peer victimization? *Journal of Child Psychology and Psychiatry, 53*, 1167–1175.

Barrett, K. C., & Campos, J. J. (1987). Perspectives on emotional development II: A functionalist approach to emotions. In J. D. Osofsky (Ed.), *Handbook of infant development* (pp. 555–578). Oxford, England: Wiley.

Barry, T. D., Barry, C. T., Deming, A. M., & Lochman, J. E. (2008). Stability of psychopathic characteristics in childhood: The influence of social relationships. *Criminal Justice and Behavior, 35*, 243–262.

Bauer, D., & Kosson, D. S. (2000, March). *Psychopathy in incarcerated females: Prevalence rates and individual differences in cognition, personality and behavior.* Paper presented at the American Psychology-Law Society, New Orleans, LA.

Bauer, D., Whitman, L. A., & Kosson, D. S. (2011). Reliability and construct validity of psychopathy checklist: Youth version scores among incarcerated adolescent girls. *Criminal Justice and Behavior, 38*, 965–987. doi:10.1177/0093854811418048

Berg, J. M., Lilienfeld, S. O., Reddy, S. D., Latzman, R. D., Roose, A., Craighead, L. W., & . . . Raison, C. L. (2013). The Inventory of Callous and Unemotional Traits: A construct-validational analysis in an at-risk sample. *Assessment, 20*, 532–544. doi:10.1177/1073191112474338

Biederman, J., Newcorn, J., & Sprich, S. (1991). Comorbidity of attention-deficit hyperactivity disorder with conduct, depressive, anxiety, and other disorders. *American Journal of Psychiatry, 148*, 564–577.

Bijttebier, P., & Decoene, S. (2009). Assessment of psychopathic traits in children and adolescents: Further validation of the Antisocial Process Screening Device and the Childhood Psychopathy Scale. *European Journal of Psychological Assessment, 25*, 157–163. doi:10.1027/1015–5759.25.3.157

Blair, R.J.R. (1995). A cognitive developmental approach to morality: Investigating the psychopath. *Cognition, 57*, 1–29. doi:10.1016/0010–0277(95)00676-P

Blair, R.J.R. (1999). Responsiveness to distress cues in the child with psychopathic tendencies. *Personality and Individual Differences, 27*, 135–145. doi:10.1016/S0191–8869(98)00231–1

Blair, R.J.R., & Coles, M. (2000). Expression recognition and behavioural problems in early adolescence. *Cognitive Development, 15*, 421–434. doi:10.1016/S0885–2014(01)00039–9

Blair, R.J.R., Colledge, E., Mitchell, D.G.V. (2001). Somatic markers and response reversal: Is there orbitofrontal cortex dysfunction in boys with psychopathic tendencies? *Journal of Abnormal Child Psychology, 29*, 499–511. doi:10.1023/A:1012277125119

Block, J. (1993). Studying personality the long way. In D. Funder, R. Parke, C. Tomlinson-Keasy, & K. Widaman (Eds.), *Studying lives through time: Personality and development* (pp. 9–41). Washington, DC: American Psychological Association. doi:10.1037/10127–018

Blonigen, D.M., Carlson, M.D., Hicks, B.M., Krueger, R.F., & Iacono, W.G. (2008). Stability and change in personality traits from late adolescence to early adulthood: A longitudinal twin study. *Journal of Personality, 76*, 229–266. doi:10.1111/j.1467–6494.2007.00485.x

Borum, R., Bartel, P., & Forth, A. (2006). *Structured Assessment of Violence Risk in Youth (SAVRY)*. Odessa, FL: Psychological Assessment Resources.

Brandt, J.R., Kennedy, W.A., Patrick, C.J., & Curtin, J.J. (1997). Assessment of psychopathy in a population of incarcerated adolescent offenders. *Psychological Assessment, 9*, 429–435. doi:10.1037/1040–3590.9.4.429

Brinkley, C.A., Newman, J.P., Widiger, T.A., & Lynam, D.R. (2004). Two approaches to parsing the heterogeneity of psychopathy. *Clinical Psychology: Science and Practice, 11*, 69–94. doi:10.1093/clipsy/bph054

Brown, M.M. (2006, February 21). Packed courtroom hears day one of Cody Posey sentencing. *Alamogordo Daily-News*.

Burke, J.D., Loeber, R., & Lahey, B.B. (2007). Adolescent conduct disorder and interpersonal callousness as predictors of psychopathy in young adults. *Journal of Clinical Child and Adolescent Psychology, 36*, 334-346.

Caldwell, M.F., Skeem, J.L., Salekin, R.T., & Van Rybroeck, G. (2006). Treatment response of adolescent offenders with psychopathy features: A two year follow-up. *Criminal Justice and Behavior*. doi:10.1177/0093854806288176

Campbell, M., Doucette, N.L., & French, S. (2009). Validity and stability of the Youth Psychopathic Traits Inventory in a nonforensic sample of young adults. *Journal of Personality Assessment, 91*, 584–592. doi:10.1080/00223890903228679

Campbell, M.A., Porter, S., & Santor, D. (2004). Psychopathic traits in adolescent offenders: An evaluation of criminal history, clinical, and psychosocial correlates. *Behavioral Sciences and the Law, 22*, 23–47. doi:10.1002/bsl.572

Caron, C., & Rutter, M. (1991). Comorbidity in child psychopathology: Concepts, issues, and research strategies. *Journal of Child Psychology and Psychiatry, 32*, 1063–1080. doi:10.1111/j.1469–7610.1991.tb00350.x

Caspi, A., Block, J., Block, J.H., Klopp, B., Lynam, D., Moffitt, T.E., & Stouthamer-Loeber, M. (1992). A 'common-language' version of the California Child Q-Set for personality assessment. *Psychological Assessment, 4*, 512–523. doi:10.1037/1040–3590.4.4.512

Catchpole, R.E.H. & Gretton, H.M. (2003). The predictive validity of risk assessment with violent young offenders. *Criminal Justice and Behavior, 30*, 688–708. doi:10.1177/0093854803256455

Cleckley, H. (1941/1976). *The mask of sanity*. St Louis, MO: Mosby.

Cloninger, C.R. (1978). The antisocial personality. *Hospital Practice, 13*, 97–106.

Cooke, D.J., & Michie, C.M. (2001). Refining the construct of psychopathy: Towards a hierarchical model. *Psychological Assessment, 13*, 171–188. doi:10.1037/1040–3590.13.2.171

Corrado, R., Vincent, G., Hart, S., & Cohen, I. (2004). Predictive validity of the Psychopathy Checklist: Youth Version for general and violent recidivism. *Behavioral Sciences and Law, 22*, 5–22. doi:10.1002/bsl.574

Costa, P.T., Herbst, J.H., McCrae, R.R., & Siegler, I.C. (2000). Personality at midlife: Stability, intrinsic maturation, and response to life events. *Assessment, 7*, 365–378. doi:10.1177/107319110000700405

Costa, P.T., & McCrae, R.R. (1988). Personality in adulthood: A six-year longitudinal of self-reports and spouse ratings on the NEO Personality Inventory. *Journal of Personality and Social Psychology, 54*, 853–863. doi:10.1037/0022–3514.54.5.853

Costa, P. T., & McCrae, R. R. (1989). *The NEO-PI/NEO-FFI manual supplement.* Odessa, FL: Psychological Assessment Resources.

Costa, P. T., & McCrae, R. R. (1994). Set like plaster? Evidence for the stability of adult personality. In T. Heatherton & J. L. Weinberger (Eds.), *Can personality change?* (pp. 21–40). Washington, DC: American Psychological Association. doi:10.1037/10143–002

Derefinko, K. J., & Lynam, D. R. (2006). Using the FFM to conceptualize psychopathy: A test using a drug abusing sample. *Journal of Personality Disorders, 21,* 638–656.

Dillard, C. L., Salekin, R. T., Barker, E. D., & Grimes, R. D. (2013). Psychopathy in adolescent offenders: An item response investigation of the Antisocial Process Screening Device Self Report and the Psychopathy Checklist: Youth Version. *Personality Disorders: Theory Research and Treatment, 4,* 101–120. doi:10.1037/a0028439

Dolan, M. C., & Rennie, C. E. (2006). Reliability and validity of the Psychopathy Checklist: Youth Version in a UK sample of conduct disordered boys. *Personality and Individual Differences, 40,* 65–75. doi:10.1016/j.paid.2005.07.001

Dunn, J. (1987). The beginnings of moral understanding: Development in the second year. In J. Kagan & S. Lamb (Eds.), *The emergence of morality in young children* (pp. 91–112). Chicago: University of Chicago Press.

Eisenberg, N., & Mussen, P. A. (1989). *The roots of prosocial behavior in children.* New York: Cambridge University Press. doi:10.1017/CBO9780511571121

Emde, R. N., Biringen, Z., Clyman, R. B., & Oppenheim, D. (1991). The moral self of infancy: Affective core and procedural knowledge. *Developmental Review, 11,* 251–270. doi:10.1016/0273–2297(91)90013-E

Epstein, M., Douglas, K., Poythress, N., Spain, S., & Falkenbach, D. (2002, March). *A discriminant study of juvenile psychopathy and mental disorders.* Paper presented at the conference of the American Psychology-Law Society, Austin, TX.

Falkenbach, D. M., Poythress, N. G., & Heide, K. M. (2003). Psychopathic features in a juvenile diversion population: reliability and predictive validity of two self-report measures. *Behavioral Sciences and the Law, 21,* 787–805. doi:10.1002/bsl.562

Fisher, L., & Blair, R.J.R. (1998). Cognitive impairment and its relationship to psychopathic tendencies in children with emotional and behavioral difficulties. *Journal of Abnormal Psychology, 26,* 511–519. doi:10.1023/A:1022655919743

Forsman, M., Lichtenstein, P., Andershed, H., & Larsson, H. (2008). Genetic effects explains the stability of psychopathic personality from mid- to late adolescence. *Journal of Abnormal Psychology, 117,* 606-617.

Forth, A. (1995). *Psychopathy and young offenders: Prevalence, family background, and violence.* Canada: Ministry of the Solicitor General of Canada.

Forth, A. E., & Burke, H. C. (1998). Psychopathy in adolescence: Assessment, family background, and violence. In D. J. Cooke, A. E. Forth, & R. D. Hare (Eds.), *Psychopathy: Theory, research and implications for society* (pp. 205–229). Boston, MA: Kluwer.

Forth, A. E., Hart, S. D., Hare, R. D. (1990). Assessment of psychopathy in male young offenders. *Psychological Assessment, 2,* 342–344. doi:10.1037/1040–3590.2.3.342

Forth, A. E., Kosson, D. S., & Hare, R. D. (1996/2003). *The Psychopathy Checklist: Youth Version.* Toronto, ON: Multi-Health Systems.

Frick, P. J. (1998). Callous-unemotional traits and conduct problems: Applying the two-factor model of psychopathy to children. In D. J. Cooke, A. E. Forth, & R. D. Hare (Eds.), *Psychopathy: Theory, research and implications for society* (pp. 161–187). Boston, MA: Kluwer.

Frick, P. J. (2002). Juvenile psychopathy from a developmental perspective: Implications for construct development and use in forensic assessments. *Law and Human Behavior, 26,* 247–253. doi:10.1023/A:1014600311758

Frick, P. J. (2004). *Inventory of callous-unemotional traits.* Unpublished rating scale, University of New Orleans, New Orleans, LA.

Frick, P. J., Bodin, S. D., & Barry, C. T. (2000). Psychopathic traits and conduct problems in community and clinic-referred samples of children: Further development of the Psychopathy Screening Device. *Psychological Assessment, 12,* 382–393. doi:10.1037/1040–3590.12.4.382

Frick, P. J., & Hare, R. D. (2001). *Antisocial process screening device.* Toronto, ON: Multi-Health Systems.

Frick, P.J., Kimonis, E.R., Dandreaux, D.M., Farrell, J.M. (2003). The 4 year stability of psychopathic traits in non-referred youth. *Behavioral Sciences and the Law, 21*, 713–736. doi:10.1002/bsl.568

Frick, P.J., & Marsee, M.A. (2006). Psychopathy and developmental pathways to antisocial behavior in youth. In C.J. Patrick (Ed.), *Handbook of psychopathy* (pp. 353–374). New York: Guilford Press.

Frick, P.J., O'Brien, B.S., Wootton, J.M., & McBurnett, K. (1994). Psychopathy and conduct problems in children. *Journal of Abnormal Psychology, 103*, 700–707. doi:10.1037/0021–843X.103.4.700

Gao, Y., Raine, A., Venables, P.H., Dawson, M.E., & Mednick, S.A. (2010). Association of poor childhood fear conditioning and adult crime. *American Journal of Psychiatry, 167*, 56–60. doi:10.1176/appi.ajp.2009.09040499

Gretton, H.M., McBride, M., Hare, R.D., O'Shaughnessy, R., & Kumka, G. (2001). Psychopathy and recidivism in adolescent sex offenders. *Criminal Justice and Behavior, 28*, 427–449. doi:10.1177/009385480102800403

Grinberg, E. (2006, February 2). A teenage psychopath? *Court TV News.*

Guy, L.S., Edens, J.F., Anthony, C., & Douglas, K.S. (2005). Does psychopathy predict institutional misconduct among adults? A meta-analytic investigation. *Journal of Consulting and Clinical Psychology, 73*, 1056–1064. doi:10.1037/0022–006X.73.6.1056

Haan, N., Aerts, E., & Cooper, B.A. (1987). *On moral grounds.* New York: New York University Press.

Hare, R.D. (1991/2003). *The Hare Psychopathy Checklist–Revised* (2nd ed.). Toronto: Multi-Health Systems.

Hare, R.D. (1993). *Without conscience: The disturbing world of the psychopaths among us.* New York: Pocket Books.

Hare, R.D., & McPherson, L.M. (1984). Psychopathy and perceptual asymmetry during verbal dichotic listening. *Journal of Abnormal Psychology, 93*, 141–149. doi:10.1037/0021–843X.93.2.141

Harpur, T.J., & Hare, R.D. (1994). Assessment of psychopathy as a function of age. *Journal of Abnormal Psychology, 103*, 604–609. doi:10.1037/0021–843X.103.4.604

Harpur, T.J., Hare, R.D., & Hakstian, A.R. (1989). Two-factor conceptualization of psychopathy: Construct validity and assessment implications. *Psychological Assessment, 1*, 6–17. doi:10.1037/1040–3590.1.1.6

Harris, G.T., & Rice, M.E. (2006). Treatment of psychopathy: A review of empirical findings. In C.J. Patrick (Ed.), *Handbook of psychopathy* (pp. 555–572). New York: Guilford Press.

Hart, S.D., & Hare, R.D. (1994). Psychopathy and the Big 5: Correlations between observers' ratings of normal and pathological personality. *Journal of Personality Disorders, 8*, 32–40. doi:10.1521/pedi.1994.8.1.32

Hart, S.D., Watt, K.A., & Vincent, G.M. (2002). Commentary on Seagrave and Grisso: Impressions of the state of the art. *Law and Human Behavior, 26*, 241–245. doi:10.1023/A:1014648227688

Hawes, D., Price, & Dadds, M. (2014). Callous-unemotional traits and the treatment of conduct problems in childhood and adolescence: A comprehensive review. *Clinical Child and Family Psychology Review, 17*, 248–267.

Hinshaw, S.P., Lahey, B.B., & Hart, E.L. (1993). Issues of taxonomy and co-morbidity in the development of conduct disorder. *Development and Psychopathology, 5*, 31–50. doi:10.1017/S0954579400004247

Hinshaw, S.P., & Zupan, B.A. (1997). Assessment of antisocial behavior in children and adolescents. In E.J. Mash & R.A. Barkley (Eds.), *Child psychopathology* (pp. 36–50). New York: Guilford.

In re Harold W., a Minor (The People of the State of Illinois, Petitioner-Appellee, v. Harold W., Respondent-Appellant), 2014 IL App (2d) 121235-U (2014).

Izard, C.E. (1977). *Human emotions.* New York: Plenum.

Izard, C.E., & Harris, P. (1995). Emotional development and developmental psychopathology. In D. Cicchetti & D.J. Cohen (Eds.), *Developmental psychopathology, Vol. 2: Risk, disorder, and adaption* (pp. 467–503). New York: Wiley.

Jang, K., McCrae, R.R., Angleitner, A., Riemann, R., & Livesley, W.J. (1998). Heritability of facet-level traits in a cross-cultural twin sample: Support for a hierarchical model of personality. *Journal of Personality and Social Psychology, 74*, 1556–1565. doi:10.1037/0022–3514.74.6.1556

Johnstone, L., & Cooke, D.J. (2004). Psychopathic-like traits in childhood: Conceptual and measurement concerns. *Behavioral Sciences and the Law, 22*, 103–125. doi:10.1002/bsl.577

Jones, S., Cauffman, E., Miller, J.D., & Mulvey, E. (2006). Investigating different factor structures of the Psychopathy Checklist: Youth Version: Confirmatory factor analytic findings. *Psychological Assessment, 18*, 33–48. doi:10.1037/1040–3590.18.1.33

Karpman, B. B. (1949). The psychopathic delinquent child. *American Journal of Orthopsychiatry, 20*, 223–265.

Kazdin, A. E. (1997). Conduct disorders across the life-span. In S. S. Luthar, J. A. Burack, D. Cicchetti, & J. R. Weisz (Eds.), *Developmental psychopathology: Perspectives on adjustment, risk, and disorder* (pp. 248–272). New York: Cambridge University Press.

Kimonis, E. R., Frick, P. J., & Barry, C. T. (2004). Callous-unemotional traits and delinquent peer affiliation. *Journal of Consulting and Clinical Psychology, 72*, 956–966. doi:10.1037/0022–006X.72.6.956

Klaver, J. R. (2006). *Age of onset of psychopathic traits in adolescent offenders*. Unpublished doctoral dissertation, Simon Fraser University, Burnaby, BC, Canada.

Kochanska, G. (1991). Socialization and temperament in the development of guilt and conscience. *Child Development, 62*, 1379–1392. doi:10.2307/1130813

Kochanska, G. (1993). Toward a synthesis of parental socialization and child temperament in early development of conscience. *Child Development, 64*, 325–347. doi:10.2307/1131254

Kosson, D. S., Cyterski, T. D., Steuerwald, B. L., Neumann, C. S., & Walker-Matthews, S. (2002). The reliability and validity of the Psychopathy Checklist: Youth Version (PCL:YV) in nonincarcerated adolescent males. *Psychological Assessment, 14*, 97–109. doi:10.1037/1040–3590.14.1.97

Kosson, D. S., Neumann, C. S., Forth, A. E., Salekin, R. T., Hare, R. D., Krischer, M. K., & Sevecke, K. (2013). Factor structure of the Hare Psychopathy Checklist: Youth Version (PCL: YV) in adolescent females. *Psychological Assessment, 25*, 71–83. doi:10.1037/a0028986

Kotler, J. S., & McMahon, R. J. (2005). Child psychopathy: Theories, measurement, and relations with the development and persistence of conduct problems. *Clinical Child and Family Psychology Review, 8*, 291–325. doi:10.1007/s10567–005–8810–5

Kotler, J. S., & McMahon, R. J. (2010). Assessment of child and adolescent psychopathy. In R. T. Salekin & D. R. Lynam (Eds.), *Handbook of child and adolescent psychopathy* (pp. 79–109). New York: Guilford Press.

Lahey, B. B., Loeber, R., Burke, J., Rathouz, P. J., & McBurnett, K. (2002). Waxing and waning in concert: Comorbidity of conduct disorder with other disruptive and emotional problems over 7 years among clinic referred boys. *Journal of Abnormal Psychology, 111*, 556–567. doi:10.1037/0021–843X. 111.4.556

Larsson, H., Andershed, H., & Lichtenstein, P. (2006). A genetic factor explains most of the variation in the psychopathic personality. *Journal of Abnormal Psychology, 115*, 221–230. doi:10.1037/0021–843X.115.2.221

Latzman, R. D., Lilienfeld, S. O., Latzman, N. E., & Clark, L. A. (2013). Exploring callous and unemotional traits in youth via general personality traits: An eye toward DSM-5. *Personality Disorders: Theory, Research, and Treatment, 4*, 191–201.

Lee, Z., Vincent, G. M., Hart, S. D., & Corrado, R. R. (2003). The validity of the Antisocial Process Screening Device as a self-report measure of psychopathy in adolescent offenders. *Behavioral Sciences and the Law, 21*, 771–786. doi:10.1002/bsl.561

Leistico, A. R., Salekin, R. T., DeCoster, J., & Rogers, R. (2008). A large-scale meta-analysis relating the Hare measures of psychopathy to antisocial conduct. *Law and Human Behavior, 32*, 28–45. doi:10.1007/s10979–007–9096–6

Loeber, R., Pardini, D., Hipwell, A. E., Stouthamer-Loeber, M., Keenan, K. & Sembower, M. (2009). Are there stable factors in preadolescent girls' externalizing behaviors? *Journal of Abnormal Child Psychology, 37*, 777-792.

Loeber, R, & Stouthamer-Loeber, M. (1986). Family factors as correlates and predictors of juvenile conduct problems and delinquency. In M. Tonry & N. Morris (Eds.), *Crime and justice, Vol. 7: An annual review of research*. Chicago: University of Chicago Press

Loney, B. R., Frick, P. J., Clements, C. B., Ellis, M. L., & Kerlin, K. (2003). Callous-Unemotional traits, impulsivity, and emotional processing in adolescents with antisocial behavior problems. *Journal of Clinical Child and Adolescent Psychology, 32*, 66–80. doi:10.1207/15374420360533077

Loney, B. R., Frick, P. J., Ellis, M. L., & McCoy, M. G. (1998). Intelligence, psychopathy, and antisocial behavior. *Journal of Psychopathology and Behavioral Assessment, 20*, 231–247.

Lorenz, A. R., & Newman, J. P. (2002a). Deficient response modulation and emotion processing in low anxious Caucasian psychopathic offenders: Results from a lexical decision task. *Emotion, 2*, 91–104. doi:10.1037/1528–3542.2.2.91

Lorenz, A.R., & Newman, J.P. (2002b). Utilization of emotion cues in male and female offenders with antisocial personality disorder: Results from a lexical decision task. *Journal of Abnormal Psychology, 111,* 513–516. doi:10.1037/0021–843X.111.3.513

Lykken, D.T. (1995). *The antisocial personalities.* Hillsdale, NJ: Erlbaum.

Lynam, D.R. (1997). Pursuing the psychopath: Capturing the fledgling psychopath in a nomological net. *Journal of Abnormal Psychology, 106,* 425–438. doi:10.1037/0021–843X.106.3.425

Lynam, D.R. (1998). Early identification of the fledgling psychopath: Locating the psychopathic child in the current nomenclature. *Journal of Abnormal Psychology, 107,* 566–575. doi:10.1037/0021–843X.107.4.566

Lynam, D.R. (2002a). Fledgling psychopathy: A view from personality theory. *Law and Human Behavior, 26,* 255–259. doi:10.1023/A:1014652328596

Lynam, D.R. (2002b). Psychopathy from the perspective of the five-factor model. In P.T. Costa & T.A. Widiger (Eds.), *Personality disorders and the five-factor model* (2nd ed.). Washington, DC: American Psychological Association. doi:10.1037/10423–020

Lynam, D.R., Caspi, A., Moffitt, T.E., Loeber, R., & Stouthamer-Loeber, M. (2007). Longitudinal evidence that psychopathy scores in early adolescence predict adult psychopathy. *Journal of Abnormal Psychology, 116,* 155–165. doi:10.1037/0021–843X.116.1.155

Lynam, D.R., Caspi, A., Moffitt, T.E., Raine, A., Loeber, R., & Stouthamer-Loeber, M. (2005). Adolescent psychopathy and the Big Five: Results from two samples. *Journal of Abnormal Child Psychology, 33,* 431–443. doi:10.1007/s10648–005–5724–0

Lynam, D.R., & Gudonis, L. (2005). The development of psychopathy. *Annual Review of Clinical Psychology, 1,* 381–407. doi:10.1146/annurev.clinpsy.1.102803.144019

Lynam, D.R., Whiteside, S., & Jones, S. (1999). Self-reported psychopathy: A validation study. *Journal of Personality Assessment, 73,* 110–132. doi:10.1207/S15327752JPA730108

Marsh, A.A., & Cardinale, E.M. (2014). When psychopathy impairs moral judgments: Neural responses during judgments about causing fear. *Social Cognitive and Affective Neuroscience, 9,* 3–11. doi:10.1093/scan/nss097

Marsh, A.A., Finger, E.C., Fowler, K.A., Adalio, C.J., Jurkowitz, I.N., Schechter, J.C., & . . . Blair, R.R. (2013). Empathic responsiveness in amygdala and anterior cingulate cortex in youths with psychopathic traits. *Journal Of Child Psychology And Psychiatry, 54*(8), 900–910. doi:10.1111/jcpp.12063

McCord, W., & McCord, J. (1964). *The psychopath: An essay on the criminal mind.* Oxford, England: D. Van Nostrand.

McCrae, R.R., & Costa, P.T. (1990). *Personality in adulthood.* New York: Guilford Press.

Miller, J.D., Lynam, D.R., Widiger, T.A., & Leukefeld, C. (2001). Personality disorders as extreme variants of common personality dimensions: Can the Five-Factor model adequately represent psychopathy? *Journal of Personality, 69,* 253–276. doi:10.1111/1467–6494.00144

Millon, T. (1993). *Millon Adolescent Clinical Inventory.* Minneapolis, MN: National Computer Systems.

Mitchell, D.G.V., Colledge, E., Leonard, A., & Blair, R.J.R. (2002). Risky decisions and response reversal: Is there evidence of orbital cortex dysfunction in psychopathic individuals? *Neuropsychologia, 40,* 2013–2022.

Moffitt, T.E. (2003). Life course persistent and adolescent limited antisocial behavior: A ten year research review and a research agenda. In B.B. Lahey, T.E. Moffitt, & A. Caspi (Eds.), *Causes of conduct disorder and juvenile delinquency* (pp. 49–75). New York: Guilford Press.

Munoz, L.C., & Frick, P.J. (2007). The reliability, stability, and predictive utility of the self-report version of the Antisocial Process Screening Device. *Scandinavian Journal of Psychology, 48,* 299-312.

Murrie, D.C., & Cornell, D.G. (2002). Psychopathy screening of incarcerated juveniles: A comparison of measures. *Psychological Assessment, 14,* 390–396. doi:10.1037/1040–3590.14.4.390

Murrie, D.C., Cornell, D.G., Kaplan, S., McConville, D., & Levy-Elkon, A. (2004). Psychopathy scores and violence among juvenile offenders: A multi-measure study. *Behavioral Sciences and the Law, 22,* 49–67. doi:10.1002/bsl.573

Myers, W.C., Burket, R.C., & Harris, H.E. (1995). Adolescent psychopathy in relation to delinquent behaviors, conduct disorder, and personality disorders. *Journal of Forensic Sciences, 40,* 436–440.

Neumann, C.S., Kosson, D.S., Forth, A.E., & Hare, R.D. (2006). Factor structure of the Hare Psychopathy Checklist: Youth Version (PCL:YV) in incarcerated adolescents. *Psychological Assessment, 18,* 142–154. doi:10.1037/1040–3590.18.2.142

Newman, J.P., Patterson, C.M., & Kosson, D.S. (1987). Response perseveration in psychopaths. *Journal of Abnormal Psychology, 96,* 145–148. doi:10.1037/0021–843X.96.2.145

Obradovic, J., Pardini, D., Long, J. D., & Loeber, R. (2007). Measuring interpersonal callousness in boys from childhood to adolescence: An examination of longitudinal invariance and temporal stability. *Journal of Clinical Child and Adolescent Psychology, 36*, 276-292.

O'Brien, B. S., & Frick, P. J. (1996). Reward dominance: Associations with anxiety, conduct problems, and psychopathy in children. *Journal of Abnormal Child Psychology, 24*, 223–240. doi:10.1007/BF01441486

Olver, M., & Stockdale, K. (2010). Psychopathy and youth violence: Research, controversies, and clinical utility. *British Journal of Forensic Practice, 12*, 3–13. doi:10.5042/bjfp.2010.0181

O'Neill, M. L., Lidz, V., & Heilbrun, K. (2003). Adolescents with psychopathic characteristics in a substance abusing cohort: Treatment process and outcome. *Law and Human Behavior, 27*, 299–313. doi:10.1023/A:1023435924569

Pardini, D. A., Lochman, J. E., & Frick, P. J. (2003). Callous/Unemotional traits and social-cognitive processes in adjudicated youths. *Journal of the American Academy of Child and Adolescent Psychiatry, 42*, 364–371. doi:10.1097/00004583–200303000–00018

Pardini, D. A., Lochman, J. E., Powell, N. (2007). Shared or unique developmental pathways to callous-unemotional traits and antisocial behavior in children? *Journal of Clinical Child and Adolescent Psychology, 36*, 319-333.

Patrick, C. J. (2010). Conceptualizing the psychopathic personality: Disinhibited, bold, . . . Or just plain mean? In R. T. Salekin & D. R. Lynam (Eds.), *Handbook of child and adolescent psychopathy* (pp. 15–48). New York: Guilford Press.

Patrick, C. J., Durbin, C., & Moser, J. S. (2012). Reconceptualizing antisocial deviance in neurobehavioral terms. *Development and Psychopathology, 24*, 1047–1071. doi:10.1017/S0954579412000533

Patterson, G. R. (1976). The aggressive child: Victim and architect of a coercive system. In: E. J. Mash, L. A. Hamerlynck, & L. C. Handy (Eds.), *Behavior modification and families* (pp. 267–316). New York, NY: Brunner/Mazel.

Plomin, R., & Caspi, A. (1999). Behavioral genetics and personality. In L. A. Pervin & O. P. John (Eds.), *Handbook of personality: Theory and research* (pp. 251–276). New York: Guilford.

Plutchik, R. (1980). *Emotion: A psychoevolutionary synthesis*. New York: Harper & Row.

Poythress, N. G., Dembo, R., Wareham, J., & Greenbaum, P. E. (2006). Construct validity of the Youth Psychopathic traits Inventory (YPI) and the Antisocial Process Screening Device (APSD) with justice-involved adolescents. *Criminal Justice and Behavior, 33*, 26–55. doi:10.1177/0093854805282518

Poythress, N. G., Douglas, K. S., Falkenbach, D., Cruise, K., Lee, Z., Murrie, D. C., & Vitacco, M. (2006). Internal consistency reliability of the self-report Antisocial Process Screening Device. *Assessment, 13*, 107–113. doi:10.1177/1073191105284279

Quay, H. C. (1964). Dimensions of personality in delinquent boys as inferred from factor analysis of case history data. *Child Development, 35*, 479–484.

Quay, H. C. (1965). Psychopathic personality as pathological stimulation seeking. *American Journal of Psychiatry, 122*, 180–183.

Quay, H. C. (1986). A critical analysis of DSM-III as a taxonomy of psychopathology in childhood and adolescence. In T. K. Millon & L. Gerald (Eds.), *Contemporary directions in psychopathology: Toward the DSM-IV* (pp. 151–165). New York: Guilford Press.

Quay, H. C. (1987). Patterns of delinquent behavior. In H. C. Quay (Ed.), *Handbook of juvenile delinquency* (pp. 118–138). New York: Wiley.

Radke-Yarrow, M., & Zahn-Waxler, C. (1984). Roots, motives and patterns in children's prosocial behavior. In E. Staub, J. Bar-Tal, J. Karylowski, & J. Reykowski (Eds.), *Development and maintenance of prosocial behavior: International perspectives on positive behavior* (pp. 81–99). New York: Plenum. doi 10.1007/978–1–4613–2645–8_6

Raine, A., O'Brien, M., Smiley, N., Scerbo, A., & Chan, C. J. (1990). Reduced lateralization in verbal dichotic listening in adolescent psychopaths. *Journal of Abnormal Psychology, 99*, 272–277.

Reynolds, C. R. (1998). *Adolescent Psychopathology Scale*. Lutz, FL: Psychological Assessment Resources.

Roberts, B. W., & DelVecchio, W. F. (2000). The rank-order consistency of personality traits from childhood to old age: A quantitative review of longitudinal studies. *Psychological Bulletin, 126*, 3–25. doi:10.1037/0033–2909.126.1.3

Robins, L. N. (1966). *Deviant children grown up: A sociological and psychiatric study of sociopathic personality*. Baltimore, MD: Williams & Wilkins.

Robins, L. N. (1978). Sturdy childhood predictors of adult antisocial behavior: Replications from longitudinal studies. *Psychological Medicine, 8*, 611–622.

Rogers, R., Jackson, R. L., Sewell, K. W., & Johansen, J. (2004). Predictors of treatment outcome in dually-diagnosed antisocial youth: An initial study of forensic inpatients. *Behavioral Sciences and the Law, 22*, 215–222. doi:10.1002/bsl.558

Rutherford, M. J., Cacciola, J. S., Alterman, A. I., McKay, J. R., & Cook, T. G. (1999). Two-year test-retest reliability of the Psychopathy Checklist-Revised in methadone patients. *Assessment, 6*, 285–291. doi:10.1177/107319119900600308

Salekin, R. T. (2002). Psychopathy and therapeutic pessimism: Clinical lore or clinical reality? *Clinical Psychology Review, 22*, 79–112. doi:10.1016/S0272–7358(01)00083–6

Salekin, R. T. (2004). *Risk-Sophistication-Treatment Inventory: Professional manual.* Lutz, FL: Psychological Assessment Resources.

Salekin, R. T. (2006). Psychopathy in children and adolescents: Key issues in conceptualization and assessment. In C. J. Patrick (Eds.), *Handbook of psychopathy* (pp. 389–414). New York: Guilford.

Salekin, R. T. (2014). Some new directions for publication in the Journal of Psychopathology and Behavioral Assessment: New constructs, physiological assessment, worldwide contribution, and economics. *Journal of Psychopathology and Behavioral Assessment, 36*, 1–3.

Salekin, R. T. (2015). *Forensic evaluation and treatment of juveniles: Innovation and best practice.* Washington, D.C.: American Psychological Association.

Salekin, R. T. (in press). Psychopathy in childhood: Toward better informing the DSM-5 and ICD-11 Conduct Disorder specifiers. *Personality Disorders: Theory, Research, and Treatment.*

Salekin, R. T., Brannen, D. A., Zalot, A. A., Leistico, A. R., & Neumann, C. S. (2006). Factor structure of psychopathy in youth: Testing the new four-factor model. *Criminal Justice and Behavior, 33*, 135–157. doi:10.1177/0093854805284416

Salekin, R. T., & Debus, S. A. (2008). Assessing child and adolescent psychopathy. In R. Jackson (Ed.), *Learning Forensic Evaluations* (pp. 347–383). New York: Routledge.

Salekin, R. T., Debus, S. A., & Barker, E. D. (2010). Adolescent psychopathy and the five-factor model: Domain and facet analysis. *Journal of Psychopathology and Behavioral Assessment, 32*, 501–514.

Salekin, R. T., & Frick, P. J. (2005). Psychopathy in children and adolescents: The need for a developmental perspective. *Journal of Abnormal Child Psychology, 33*, 403–409. doi:10.1007/s10802–005–5722–2

Salekin, R. T., Leistico, A. R., Trobst, K. K., Schrum, C. L., & Lochman, J. E. (2005). Adolescent psychopathy and personality theory, the interpersonal circumplex: Expanding evidence of a nomological net. *Journal of Abnormal Child Psychology, 33*, 445–460. doi:10.1007/s10802–005–5726–Y

Salekin, R. T. & Lynam, D. R. (2010). *The handbook of child and adolescent psychopathy.* New York: Guilford.

Salekin, R. T., Neumann, C. S., Leistico, A. R., DiCicco, T., & Duros, R. (2004). Psychopathy and comorbidity in a young offender sample: Taking a closer look at psychopathy's potential importance over disruptive behavior disorders. *Journal of Abnormal Psychology, 113*, 416–427. doi:10.1037/0021–843X.113.3.416

Salekin, R. T., Neumann, C. S., Leistico, A. R., & Zalot, A. A. (2004). Psychopathy in youth and intelligence: An investigation of Cleckley's Hypothesis. *Journal of Clinical Child and Adolescent Psychology, 33*, 731–742. doi:10.1207/s15374424jccp3304_8

Salekin, R. T., Rogers, R., & Machin, D. (2001). Psychopathy in youth: Pursuing diagnostic clarity. *Journal of Youth and Adolescence, 30*, 173–195. doi:10.1023/A:1010393708227

Salekin, R. T., Rogers, R., & Sewell, K. W. (1996). A review and meta-analysis of the Psychopathy Checklist and Psychopathy Checklist–Reviewed: Predictive validity of dangerousness. *Clinical Psychology: Science and Practice, 3*, 203–215. doi:10.1111/j.1468–2850.1996.tb00071.x

Salekin, R. T., Tippey, J. G., & Allen, A. D. (2012). Treatment of conduct problem youth with interpersonal callous traits using mental models: Measurement of risk and change. *Behavioral Sciences and the Law, 30*, 470–486. doi:10.1002/bsl.2025

Salekin, R. T., Trobst, K. K., & Krioukova, M. (2001). Construct validity of psychopathy in a community sample: A nomological net approach. *Journal of Personality Disorders, 15*, 425–441. doi:10.1521/pedi.15.5.425.19196

Salekin, R. T., Worley, C., & Grimes, R. D. (2010). Treatment of psychopathy: A review and brief introduction to the mental models approach for psychopathy. *Behavioral Sciences and the Law, 28*, 235–266. doi:10.1002/bsl.928

Salekin, R. T., Ziegler, T. A., Larrea, M. A., Anthony, V. L., & Bennett, A. D. (2003). Predicting psychopathy with two Millon Adolescent psychopathy scales: The importance of egocentric and callous traits. *Journal of Personality Assessment, 80*, 154–163. doi:10.1207/S15327752JPA8002_04

Schroeder, M. L., Schroeder, K. G., & Hare, R. D. (1983). Generalizability of a checklist for the assessment of psychopathy. *Journal of Consulting and Clinical Psychology, 51*, 511–516. doi:10.1037/0022–006X.51.4.511

Schrum, C. L., & Salekin, R. T. (2006). Psychopathy in adolescent female offenders: An item response theory analysis of the Psychopathy Checklist: Youth Version. *Behavioral Sciences and the Law, 24*, 39–63. doi:10.1002/bsl.679

Seagrave, D., & Grisso, T. (2002). Adolescent development and the measurement of juvenile psychopathy. *Law and Human Behavior, 26*, 219–239. doi:10.1023/A:1014696110850

Skeem, J. L., & Cauffman, E. (2003). Views of the downward extension: Comparing the youth version of the Psychopathy Checklist with the Youth Psychopathic Traits Inventory. *Behavioral Sciences and the Law, 21*, 737–770. doi:10.1002/bsl.563

Skeem, J. L., Monahan, J., & Mulvey, E. P. (2002). Psychopathy, treatment involvement, and subsequent violence among civil psychiatric patients. *Law and Human Behavior, 26*, 577–603. doi:10.1023/A:1020993916404

Spain, S. E., Douglas, K. S., Poythress, N. G., & Epstein, M. (2004). The relationship between psychopathic features, violence, and treatment outcome: The comparison of three youth measures of psychopathic features. *Behavioral Sciences and the Law, 22*, 85–102. doi:10.1002/bsl.576

Stevens, D., Charman, T., & Blair, R.J.R. (2001). Recognition of emotion in facial expressions and vocal tones in children with psychopathic tendencies. *The Journal of Genetic Psychology, 162*, 201–211. doi:10.1080/00221320109597961

Stouthamer-Loeber, M. (1986). Lying as a problem behavior in children: A review. *Clinical Psychology Review, 6*, 267–289. doi:10.1016/0272–7358(86)90002–4

The People of the State of Illinois v. Deonta Johnson, IL App (4th) 111007-U (2013).

The People of the State of Illinois v. Rickie T. Nichols, 964 N.E.2d 1190 (2012).

United States v. Doe #3, 113F. Supp. 604 (SDNY 2000).

Van Baardewijk, Y., Vermeiren, R., Stegge, H., & Doreleijers, T. (2011). Self-reported psychopathic traits in children: Their stability and concurrent and prospective association with conduct problems and aggression. *Journal of Psychopathology and Behavioral Assessment, 33*, 236-245.

Viding, E., Blair, R.J.R., Moffitt, T. E., & Plomin, R. (2004). Evidence for substantial genetic risk for psychopathy in 7-year-olds. *Journal of Child Psychology and Psychiatry, 45*, 1–6. doi:10.1111/j.1469–7610.2004.00393.x

Vincent, G. M. (2006). Psychopathy and violence risk assessment in youth. *Child and Adolescent Psychiatric Clinics of North America, 15*, 407–428. doi:10.1016/j.chc.2005.12.001

Vincent, G. M., & Hart, S. D. (2002). Psychopathy in childhood and adolescence: Implications for the assessment and management of multi problem youths. In R. R. Corrado, R. Roesch, S. D. Hart, & J. K. Gierowski (Eds.), *Multi-problem violent youth: A foundation for comparative research on needs, interventions and outcomes* (pp. 150–163). Amsterdam: IOS Press.

Vincent, G. M., Vitacco, M. J., Grisso, T., & Corrado, R. R. (2003). Subtypes of adolescent offenders: Affective traits and antisocial behavior patterns. *Behavioral Sciences and the Law, 21*, 695–712. doi:10.1002/bsl.556

Vitacco, M.J., Rogers, R., & Neumann, C.S. (2003). The Antisocial Process Screening Device: An examination of its construct and criterion-related validity. *Assessment, 10*, 143–150. doi:10.1177/1073191103010002005

Vitacco, M.J., & Salekin, R.T. (2013). Adolescent psychopathy and the law. In K.A. Kiehl & W.P. Sinnott-Armstrong (Eds.), *Handbook on psychopathy and law* (pp. 78–89). New York: Oxford University Press.

Vitacco, M., Salekin, R.T., & Rogers, R. (2010). Forensic issues for child and adolescent psychopathy. In R. T. Salekin & D. R. Lynam (Eds.), *Handbook of child and adolescent psychopathy* (pp. 374–397). New York: Guilford Press.

Vitale, J. E., Newman, J. P., Bates, J. E., Goodnight, J., Dodge, K. A., & Pettit, G. S. (2005). Deficient behavioral inhibition and anomalous selective attention in a community sample of adolescents with psychopathic traits and low-anxiety traits. *Journal of Abnormal Child Psychology, 33*, 461–470. doi:10.1007/s10802–005–5727-X

Walsh, T., & Walsh, Z. (2006). The evidentiary introduction of Psychopathy Checklist–Revised assessed psychopathy in U.S. courts: Extent and appropriateness. *Law and Human Behavior, 30*, 493–507. doi:10.1007/s10979–006–9042-z

White, S. F., Brislin, S., Sinclair, S., Fowler, K. A., Pope, K., & Blair, R. R. (2013). The relationship between large cavum septum pellucidum and antisocial behavior, callous-unemotional traits and psychopathy in adolescents. *Journal of Child Psychology and Psychiatry, 54*, 575–581. doi:10.1111/j.1469–7610.2012.02603.x

Widiger, T. A., & Lynam, D. R. (1998). Psychopathy as a variant of common personality traits: Implications for diagnosis, etiology, and pathology. In T. Millon (Ed.), *Psychopathy: Antisocial, criminal, and violent behavior* (pp. 171–187). New York: Guilford Press.

Williamson, S., Harpur, T. J., & Hare, R. D. (1991). Abnormal processing of affective words by psychopaths. *Psychophysiology, 28*, 260–273. doi:10.1111/j.1469–8986.1991.tb02192.x

Wong, S., & Hare, R. D. (2005). *Guidelines for a psychopathy treatment program.* Toronto, ON: Multi Health Systems.

Zahn-Waxler, C., & Radke-Yarrow, M. (1990). The origins of empathic concern. *Motivation and Emotion, 14*, 107–130. doi:10.1007/BF00991639

Zahn-Waxler, C., Radke-Yarrow, M., Wagner, E., & Chapman, M. (1992). Development of concern for others. *Developmental Psychology, 28*, 126–136. doi:10.1037/0012–1649.28.1.126

15 Assessing Risk for Violence and Offending in Adolescents

Jodi L. Viljoen, Andrew L. Gray, and Carmelina Barone

Violence risk assessments are among the most common types of assessments that adolescent forensic psychologists are asked to conduct (Viljoen, McLachlan, & Vincent, 2010). Courts use these assessments to guide decision making on issues such as whether to transfer an adolescent to adult court, detain a youth at pretrial or following adjudication, or release a youth from custody. In addition, courts and other agencies (e.g., forensic hospitals, probation offices) use risk assessments to help match youth to appropriate interventions (e.g., substance use treatment, intensive supervision).

Initially, research on *adolescent* risk assessment lagged behind the field of risk assessment with adult populations. Adolescent risk assessment tools were not developed until five to ten years after the first adult risk assessment tools. Furthermore, when the field of juvenile risk assessment first emerged, scholars raised questions about whether it may be challenging to assess adolescents' *long-term* risk. For instance, in an amicus curiae brief to the courts, the American Psychological Association (2004) wrote that "mental health professionals' ability to reliably distinguish between the relatively few adolescents who will continue as career criminals and the vast majority of adolescents who will, as adults, 'repudiate their reckless experimentation' is limited" (p. 19). Concerns were also expressed about labeling youth as high risk or "psychopathic," as such labels may follow youth for life (Seagrave & Grisso, 2002).

Since the early 2000s, the field of adolescent risk assessment has made significant strides. In 2000, fewer than 10 research studies had been published on adolescent risk assessment tools; this figure has since grown to over 100 studies.[1] Research shows that leading adolescent risk assessment tools achieve moderate predictive validity in predicting violence and offending in average follow-ups of two to three years (Olver, Stockdale, & Wormith, 2009), and have gained widespread use over a short period of time (Viljoen et al., 2010). Despite this progress, much remains to be learned.

This chapter reviews current best practices in assessing violence risk in youth. We start by discussing developmental issues and how these issues inform adolescent risk assessments. Following this, we review common risk assessment tools for adolescents and provide a case example to illustrate the different perspectives that various tools bring. The chapter ends with a set of practice recommendations for professionals as well as suggested directions for future research. Given that risk assessments often include attention to psychopathy, we mention psychopathy in this chapter, but only briefly. For information on the assessment of psychopathic features in adolescents, see Salekin, Debus, MacDougall, and Clark (Chapter 14 in this volume).

Developmental Considerations in Assessing Adolescent Risk

The assessment of risk in adolescents is, in many ways, similar to the assessment of risk in adults. As with adult risk assessments, it is essential to utilize the best available approaches (e.g., validated tools) and gather information from multiple sources (e.g., justice records, interviews with adolescents and collaterals). Beyond basic similarities, some differences arise however. Firstly, to meaningfully assess and interpret "risk" in adolescents, one must understand adolescent development, and how developmental factors may impact risk.

Understanding Developmental Trajectories and Developmental Factors

Despite public perceptions, youth violence and offending is *not* "on the rise" but in fact has shown decreases from the 1990s to 2011 (Butts & Evans, 2014). That said, adolescents and young adults are more likely than any other age group to engage in violence and offending; this age-crime curve has been observed across many countries and for many decades (Farrington, Loeber, & Jolliffe, 2008). In fact, some theories suggest that adolescent offending is so common it can be considered "normative" (see Moffitt, 1993). Although estimates vary, the International Self-Report Delinquency Study estimated that approximately 20–30% of adolescents engage in some form of delinquent behavior *each year* (e.g., underage drinking, graffiti, skipping school, reckless driving, schoolyard fights; Enzmann et al., 2010). Most of these delinquent behaviors are relatively minor; serious offenses (e.g., robbery, assault with a weapon, shootings) are rare among adolescents (and adults).

The spike in antisocial behavior that occurs during adolescence can, in part, be traced to developmental factors (Sweeten, Piquero, & Steinberg, 2013). Compared to adults, adolescents (particularly those in early to middle adolescence) have a greater susceptibility to negative peer influence (Monahan, Steinberg, Cauffman, & Mulvey, 2009, 2013; Steinberg & Monahan, 2007). Thus, peer factors (e.g., peer delinquency) are especially strong predictors of offending in adolescents (Lipsey & Derzon, 1998). Compared to adults, adolescents also show greater sensitivity to rewards, meaning that they are oriented to focus on the potential rewards of delinquent behaviors (e.g., thrill and excitement, opportunity to impress peers) rather than the potential costs (e.g., punishment; Monahan et al., 2009, 2013; Steinberg et al., 2008). At the same time, they have greater difficulty controlling their impulses.

This pattern has been linked to brain development; in early adolescence, dopaminergic activity in the prefrontal brain increases, resulting in a heightened sensitivity to rewards (Casey, Getz, & Galvan, 2008; Steinberg, 2010). In contrast, the regions of the brain that are responsible for executive functions (e.g., planning and controlling behaviors) continue to develop until at least the mid-20s. Thus, arousal and reward sensitivity heighten at a time when adolescents do not yet have the cognitive capacities to control their behaviors. As such, adolescence is described as akin to "starting the engines with an unskilled driver" (Dahl, 2001, p. 69).

Besides specifying how these maturational issues contribute to adolescent offending, developmental research highlights the different developmental trajectories or pathways that can lead to offending. Moffitt (1993, 2006), for instance, differentiates between "life-course persistent offenders" (which are rare) and "adolescent-limited" offenders (which are thought to comprise the majority of adolescent offenders). Life-course persistent offenders typically begin offending during childhood as a result of a combination of neuropsychological limitations and harsh family environments. In comparison, adolescent-limited offenders begin offending during adolescence as a result of negative peer influence and a desire to appear more mature. These adolescent-limited offenders often show declines in offending as they mature (Monahan et al., 2009, 2013; Piquero, 2008). That said, they do not necessarily magically desist from offending at age 18; some become ensnared and continue to offend into adulthood (Moffitt, Caspi, Harrington, & Milne, 2002; Roisman, Monahan, Campbell, Steinberg, & Cauffman, 2010).

What implications does this developmental research have for the field of violence risk assessment? Given that different pathways to violence and offending exist, assessors should pay attention to the mechanisms that underlie a particular youth's offending. For instance, during adolescence, adolescent-onset and life-course persistent offenders may, on the surface, appear quite similar, but the underlying cause of their behavior varies substantially, as does their future prognosis or risks. As described next, the fact that adolescents are still developing also means that it is critical to think about risk in a *dynamic* fashion, recognizing that a sizable proportion of adolescents (but not all) show decreased offending as they transition into adulthood (Vincent, Terry, & Maney, 2009).

Adopt a "Dynamic" Approach to Risk Assessment

Even if an adolescent is currently high risk for violence and offending, it does not mean that he or she will remain so perpetually. Evidence-based interventions (e.g., multisystemic therapy, functional family therapy, multidimensional treatment foster care, and cognitive behavioral therapy) can decrease risk and reduce reoffense rates by 25% (Lipsey & Landenberger, 2005) to as much as 80% (Henggeler & Sheidow, 2012). In other cases, youths' risk may increase due to life events (e.g., becoming entrenched in a gang, victimization). As an example, one study found that adolescents who were treated in an emergency room after being the victim of assault were at elevated risk of engaging in retaliatory violence, especially in the first four weeks after the hospital visit (Wiebe, Blackstone, Mollen, Culyba, & Fein, 2011).

In other words, adolescents are "moving targets" (Borum, 2003; Grisso, 1998). This is not to say that change is not important to adult populations. However, the specific sources of change may differ between adolescents and adults. For instance, adults' risks might change as a result of life events that occur during *adulthood*, such as marriage (King, Massoglia, & Macmillan, 2007). In comparison, changes in adolescents' risk may stem from life experiences that typically occur during *adolescence*. As an example, a youth's risk for offending and violence may increase in early adolescence as he or she gains more unsupervised time away from his or her parents, and is exposed to more drugs and delinquent peers (see Lacourse, Nagin, Tremblay, Vitaro, & Claes, 2003). A young man might also engage in violence as a means to impress peers, especially as aggression has been found to confer increased social status for adolescent males (Cillessen & Rose, 2005).

Though research is scarce, several studies illustrate the importance of examining changes in adolescents' risk over time. A prospective study of youth on probation found that a high proportion of youth, 40%, were rated as showing changes in violence risk level over a three-month period; 18% showed an increase in risk (e.g., moving from moderate to high risk), and 22% showed a decrease in risk (e.g., moving from moderate to low risk; Viljoen et al., 2012). Estimated rates of change were lower when reliable change indices were calculated (these indices help account for measurement error), but were still meaningful. A study of sexually abusive adolescents reported that risk ratings on the Estimate of Risk of Adolescent Sexual Offense Recidivism (ERASOR; Worling & Curwen, 2001) achieved higher levels of predictive validity in predicting short-term sexual reoffending rather than longer-term reoffending (Worling, Bookalam, & Litteljohn, 2012).

Together, these findings provide initial support for the importance of regular reassessment. Ongoing assessments should include attention to not only adolescents' history (e.g., number of past offenses, age of onset of violence) but also their current functioning on modifiable or dynamic factors (e.g., current peer group, substance use). By dynamic factors we mean those factors "that, when changed, are associated with changes in recidivism" (e.g., antisocial attitudes; Andrews, Bonta, & Hoge, 1990, p. 31); such factors are commonly referred to as *criminogenic needs*. Many professionals appear to be attuned to the importance of a dynamic approach to risk assessment. A survey of forensic psychologists, for instance, found that juvenile risk assessment reports were more likely than adult risk assessment reports to include recommendations to routinely reassess risk (Viljoen et al., 2010).

Communicate Findings in a Careful and Balanced Manner

Courts often seek out and consider risk assessments in guiding important legal decisions, such as whether to incarcerate an adolescent or transfer him or her to adult court (Urquhart & Viljoen, 2014). Prior to *Roper v. Simmons* (2005), which overturned the juvenile death penalty in the United States, risk assessments could even be used to inform decisions about whether an adolescent should be sentenced to *death*. Thus, given the potentially significant role of risk assessments, it is imperative to communicate assessments with caution.

As emphasized by the *Specialty Guidelines for Forensic Psychology* (American Psychological Association, 2013), assessors should explain the rationale for their conclusions and state any limitations (e.g., such as noting if they were unable to obtain certain records). They should avoid "overselling" or exaggerating the predictive accuracy of risk assessments; even the leading tools offer only moderate predictive validity and should not be used as a sole basis for high-stakes decision making (e.g., preventative detention; Olver et al., 2009; Viljoen, Mordell, & Beneteau, 2012; see also Yang, Wong, & Coid, 2010). In addition, assessors should be vigilant to avoid biases. For instance, recent studies have found that professionals are more likely to rate individuals as higher risk if they are working for the prosecution than if they are rated for the defense and vice versa, suggesting that some assessors are swayed by a desire to please or to appear loyal to the party that hires them (Murrie et al., 2009; Murrie, Boccaccini, Guarnera, & Rufino, 2013).

In juvenile risk assessments, it is important to use particular caution in communicating findings regarding psychopathy. Psychopathic features (such as callous and unemotional traits) are a well-established predictor of offending and violence in adolescents (Frick, Ray, Thornton, & Kahn, 2014). Not surprisingly, *many* forensic psychologists (approximately 80% according to one study) assess psychopathy as part of adolescent risk assessments (Viljoen et al., 2010). Although such assessments can be useful for treatment planning (Frick et al., 2014), there is wide consensus that adolescents should not be referred to or labeled as psychopathic (Forth, Kosson, & Hare, 2003; Viljoen et al., 2010). Personality is still developing during adolescence and many adolescents with psychopathic features do not go on to exhibit psychopathic personality disorder as adults (Lynam, Caspi, Moffitt, Loeber, & Stouthamer-Loeber, 2007).

Notably, other common diagnostic terms that are used to describe antisocial behavior (e.g., conduct disorder) can also lead to stigma, although perhaps to a lesser extent than the term *psychopath* (Boccaccini, Murrie, Clark, & Cornell, 2008; Murrie, Boccaccini, McCoy, & Cornell, 2007). In part, this is because antisocial behavior is inherently negative and cannot be made to sound otherwise. However, stigma also arises from misunderstandings, such as an incorrect assumption that youth with such behaviors are "untreatable" (Salekin, Worley, & Grimes, 2010); thus, assessors should work to correct these beliefs through their reports and testimony.

To provide a balanced approach, professionals must attend to protective factors (i.e., factors that may buffer or directly reduce risk of violence and offending) as well as risk factors (de Ruiter & Nicholls, 2011). Simply listing youths' risk factors, without examining the "other side of the coin," provides an incomplete picture of a youth, and may lead to excessive pessimism regarding a youth's future risk (Rogers, 2000). According to research, some measures of protective factors—for example, the Structured Assessment of Violence Risk in Youth (SAVRY; Borum, Bartel, & Forth, 2006)—can significantly predict which youth are more likely to desist from offending, and may even add incremental validity above and beyond common risk factors (Lodewijks, de Ruiter, & Doreleijers, 2010). However, prediction is not the only purpose for which to assess protective factors. Perhaps most significantly, protective factors can generate ideas and directions for planning treatment.

Use Risk Assessments to Guide Intervention Planning and Risk Reduction Efforts

Some experts differentiate between risk assessments that occur for the purpose of predicting risk, and those that are intended primarily to guide risk management and interventions (Quinsey,

Harris, Rice, & Cormier, 2006). Other experts view risk management and intervention planning as the primary goal of *all* risk assessments. As Douglas, Cox, and Webster (1999) write, "prediction surely is required, but so too is action that stems from the prediction" (p. 154). As Hart and Logan (2011) observe, "In clinical contexts, evaluators need to know what to do with a patient or offender. . . . Similarly, in legal contexts, we can think of no issue that concerns *only* the probability of violence" (p. 91).

Similarly, we find it difficult to imagine a situation in the field of adolescent risk assessment in which prediction, rather than intervention or prevention, serves as the ultimate goal. Adolescent risk assessments may be even more intervention-oriented than adult risk assessments; for instance, a survey reported that juvenile risk assessments were more likely than adult assessments to routinely include treatment recommendations (90% vs. 66% respectively, Viljoen et al., 2010). This relative emphasis on intervention may reflect the more rehabilitative focus of the juvenile justice system (Scott & Steinberg, 2008). When the juvenile justice system was first developed, its stated intention was "not so much to punish as to reform, not to degrade but to uplift, not to crush but to develop, not to make [the adolescent] a criminal but a worthy citizen" (Mack, 1909, p. 107). While this emphasis on intervention has eroded somewhat, it remains a central tenet. Even the American public, who are portrayed as notoriously punishment-oriented, reported a preference that their tax dollars go towards rehabilitating juvenile offenders rather than simply incarcerating them (Piquero & Steinberg, 2010).

Although risk assessment aims to assist in intervention planning (such as by matching youth to appropriate services), assessments often fall short of this goal. Even when risk assessments help to identify a youth's needs, these needs, once identified, often remain unaddressed (e.g., Flores, Travis, & Latessa, 2003; Vieira, Skilling, & Peterson-Badali, 2009; Singh et al., 2014). One reason for this is that research has provided little guidance regarding how to *use* risk assessments to inform intervention planning (Viljoen, Brodersen, Shaffer, & McMahon, in press). Recently, several initiatives have aimed to help address this limitation. Some experts have provided a framework for *case formulation* and *scenario planning* (e.g., Douglas, Hart, Webster, & Belfrage, 2013; Hart et al., 2003; Hart, Sturmey, Logan, & McMurran, 2011) in order to help professionals hone in on priorities for interventions. In another type of initiative, Bonta and colleagues developed a training program, Strategic Training in Community Intervention, which teaches probation officers principles and strategies to reduce risk (Bonta, Bourgon, Rugge, Scott, Yessine, & Li, 2010). In our own work (Viljoen, Brodersen, Shaffer, Muir, & ARROW Advisory Team, 2014), we have developed a risk reduction and treatment-planning guide called the *Adolescent Risk Reduction and Resilient Outcomes Work-Plan*; this guide compiles evidence-based strategies for each modifiable risk and protective factor included in the SAVRY.

In order to meaningfully use risk assessments to guide interventions, assessors should provide detailed, evidence-based recommendations in their reports and testimony, such as referrals to empirically supported services that are locally available (e.g., cognitive behavior therapy, functional family therapy). They can also recommend strategies to enhance supervision (e.g., developing incentives for the adolescent to engage in positive behaviors), build the adolescent's motivation to change (e.g., using motivational interviewing approaches), and leverage a youth's existing protective factors (e.g., arranging for the adolescent to spend time with existing prosocial supports; Viljoen et al., in press). At an agency level, administrators should develop policies and provide staff training to link risk assessments to risk management. When such efforts are in place, risk assessments may, indeed, improve service matching (Luong & Wormith, 2011; Vincent, Guy, Gershenson, & McCabe, 2012).

Risk Assessment Tools

Prior to the late 1990s and early 2000s, formal risk assessment tools or standardized assessments for adolescents generally did not exist. Thus, assessors who conducted risk assessments had to rely on their unstructured clinical judgment, personality or psychological testing that was not designed for this particular purpose, and/or adult tools. Nowadays, however, a number of well-validated risk tools exist. Some measures are formally published and distributed through test centers (e.g., SAVRY). Other measures are "in-house" measures that were developed by specific youth justice agencies (e.g., North Carolina Assessment of Risk; see Schwalbe, Fraser, Day, & Arnold, 2004).

Models of Risk Assessment

Although all tools provide a preestablished set of factors and some criteria for rating these factors, they differ in terms of how they combine the data (Skeem & Monahan, 2011). Some tools use an actuarial approach to combining data, such as adding up scores on risk factors and using cutoffs to estimate the probability of reoffending. Other tools use a structured professional judgment (SPJ) approach; in this approach, professionals do not add up scores. Instead, they draw from the data collected via the risk assessment and their professional expertise to make a judgment of whether an individual is low, moderate, or high risk. The SPJ approach allows assessors to individualize the assessment to some degree; professionals may, for instance, consider "case-specific factors" that are not included in the tool but that might nonetheless be important (such as if the youth has threatened to kill someone).

Significant debates have waged regarding the merits of actuarial and SPJ approaches. Both methods have pros and cons, and both types of tools have research support (see Yang et al., 2010). In conducting juvenile risk assessments, most forensic psychologists (60%) believe both approaches are acceptable (Viljoen et al., 2010). Some report a preference for SPJ approaches (31%); a smaller proportion report a preference for actuarial approaches (7%). At the current time, most adolescent risk assessment tools are based on an SPJ model or adjusted actuarial models that do not generate probabilistic estimates.

Growing Obligations to Use Tools

Given that structured risk assessment tools (including both SPJ tools and actuarial tools) outperform unstructured judgments (Ægisdóttir et al., 2006; Hilterman, Nicholls, & van Nieuwenhuizen, 2014; Lidz, Mulvey, & Gardner, 1993), professionals who rely on unstructured clinical judgments have faced criticisms in both legal and scholarly contexts (Urquhart & Viljoen, 2014). For instance, in *Coble v. Texas* (2011), a forensic psychiatrist relied on unstructured clinical judgment in assessing violence risk in an adult offender who was facing the death penalty (American Psychological Association, 2011). In the appeal, the American Psychological Association wrote an amicus curiae brief to the court, strongly criticizing this clinician's failure to use a tool.

Adolescent risk assessment tools, though they were developed only a relatively short time ago, are widely used. Most states in the United States use standardized risk assessment tools at some stage in legal proceedings (National Center for Juvenile Justice, 2012), as do almost all provinces in Canada (Hannah-Moffat & Maurutto, 2004). In a survey by Viljoen et al. (2010), over 97% of forensic psychologists who were members of forensic specialty organizations (e.g., American Psychology-Law Society, International Association of Forensic Mental Health) reported that they use adolescent risk assessment tools at least once in a while when conducting assessments of adolescents' risk. Thus, although some assessors continue to rely on unstructured clinical judgment, this choice has become much harder to justify. The decision for most assessors and agencies is not *whether* to use a tool, but instead, what *particular* tool to use.

What Tool Should I Use?

In selecting a risk assessment tool, it is important to consider the validity of the tool (e.g., Does the tool adequately predict violence or offending?) and its reliability (e.g., Does this tool provide sufficient guidance that multiple assessors who use it would arrive at consistent conclusions about a particular youth's risk?). Many studies have examined these questions. Agencies and assessors often, however, grapple with other considerations, such as: Is this tool user friendly and practical? Are staff members willing to use it? Does the tool provide a balanced focus on protective factors? Does it allow for an examination of changes in risk? Does it improve service planning and treatment matching? Although research in these areas is scarce, there have been some important recent initiatives (most notably, Vincent, Guy, Gershenson, & McCabe, 2012). In addition, implementation science, the study of methods by which to integrate research into applied practice, provides a valuable framework for examining many of these issues (e.g., adherence; Proctor et al., 2011).

Recognizing that many considerations are at play when selecting a tool, the following literature review describes standard psychometric outcomes (e.g., predictive validity), implementation outcomes (e.g., acceptability of a tool to professionals, feasibility of implementing it in practice, adherence to the tool), and service outcomes (e.g., the tool's utility for treatment matching). We focus primarily on tools that are commonly used and widely researched (Archer, Buffington-Vollum, Stredny, & Handel, 2006; Viljoen et al., 2010), and tools to assess violence and general reoffense risk, as well as those designed to assess sexual reoffense risk. In addition, we mention the Short-Term Assessment of Risk and Treatability: Adolescent Version (START:AV; Viljoen, Nicholls, Cruise, Desmarais, & Webster, 2014), a new tool that is designed to assess multiple outcomes (e.g., violence, offending, suicide, victimization). We encourage professionals to monitor research, as there are several emerging tools that appear promising (e.g., Violence Risk Scale–Youth Version, Wong, Lewis, Stockdale, & Gordon, 2011; see Stockdale, Olver, & Wong, 2014).

Risk Assessment Tools for Violence and General Offending

SAVRY

The SAVRY (Borum et al., 2006) was designed to assess violence risk in male and female adolescents. It includes 24 risk factors and six protective factors. The risk factors on the SAVRY are each rated as Low, Moderate, or High, and fall into one of three domains: *Historical* (e.g., history of violence, childhood history of maltreatment, poor school achievement), *Social/Contextual* (e.g., peer delinquency, peer rejection, poor parental management), and *Individual/Clinical* (e.g., risk-taking and impulsivity, substance use, anger management problems). The *Protective Factors* section includes factors such as prosocial involvement, strong attachments and bonds, and resilient personality traits; these factors are rated as Present or Absent.

The SAVRY is based on an SPJ model, such that risk factors are not summed and compared to norms. Instead, evaluators make a summary risk rating of Low, Moderate, or High regarding a youth's risk for violence (Borum, Lodewijks, Bartel, & Forth, 2010). Although the SAVRY was originally developed to assess risk of violence, it is also frequently used to assess risk for nonviolent offending. Thus, a separate summary risk rating for nonviolent offending was recently introduced (e.g., Childs, Frick, Ryals Jr., Lingonblad, & Villio, 2014).

Interrater reliability. The interrater reliability (IRR) of the SAVRY risk total and summary risk rating has consistently been found to be good to excellent. Specifically, intraclass correlation coefficients (ICC) for the SAVRY risk total scores range from .67 to .97 across studies. ICCs for summary risk ratings are quite similar, ranging from .72 to .95 (Borum et al., 2010; Chu, Daffern, Thomas, & Lim, 2012; Hilterman et al., 2014; Lodewijks et al., 2010; Penney, Lee, & Moretti, 2010). Although most studies have focused on IRR in research settings (e.g., when rated by research assistants), Vincent, Guy, Fusco, and Gershenson (2012) examined the field IRR of juvenile probation officers. Excellent IRR was attained for the SAVRY total score (ICC = .86), whereas the summary risk rating achieved good IRR (ICC = .71). Of the 24 SAVRY risk factors, 15 items displayed good to excellent IRR, while 9 items (e.g., parental/caregiver criminality, risk taking/impulsivity) were more problematic (ICC < .60). The IRR for protective factors ranged from moderate to excellent.

Internal consistency. Risk assessment tools are not intended to measure an underlying psychological construct. Thus, high internal consistency as measured by Cronbach's α may be unnecessary (Douglas, Skeem, & Nicholson, 2011). Nevertheless, studies have found high internal consistency for the SAVRY risk total score (α = .82 to .90; Borum et al., 2010; Gammelgård, Weizmann-Henelius, Koivisto, Eronen, & Kaltiala-Heino, 2012; Hilterman et al., 2014).

Convergent validity. Support for the convergent validity of the SAVRY has been demonstrated through significant correlation coefficients between the SAVRY risk total and total scores (.58 to .89) on the Youth Level of Service/Case Management Inventory (YLS/CMI; Hoge & Andrews, 2002) and PCL:YV total score (.66 to .71; Borum et al., 2006; Dolan & Rennie, 2008; Hilterman et al., 2014; Welsh, Schmidt, McKinnon, Chattha, & Meyers, 2008).

Predictive validity. In their 2009 meta-analytic review of nine SAVRY studies, Olver and colleagues (2009) found the SAVRY risk total to be a moderate predictor of general (weighted r [r_w] = .33), violent (r_w = .31), and nonviolent recidivism (r_w = .38). Likewise, Singh, Grann, and Fazel (2011) examined the predictive validity of the SAVRY based on the results of nine studies and found a median AUC (area under the curve of the receiver operating characteristic; see Hanley & McNeil, 1982) value of .71 for the SAVRY in predicting serious recidivism and a diagnostic odds ratio of 6.93 (based on binning strategies of high vs. low/moderate risk). Moreover, the SAVRY ranked highest among the nine risk assessment measures (developed for adults or adolescents) with respect to predictive validity.

Subsequent to these meta-analyses, several studies have provided further evidence for the predictive validity of the SAVRY in predicting community and institutional violence across a broad array of adolescent samples (e.g., specialized school youth, youth offenders, forensic/psychiatric youth, etc.; Gammelgård, Koivisto, Eronen, & Kaltiala-Heino, 2008; Hilterman et al., 2014; McGowan, Horn, & Mellott, 2011; Penney et al., 2010). While most studies were conducted within a research context, to date, two studies have revealed that the SAVRY also has moderate predictive validity in field settings when rated by trained youth justice personnel (Vincent, Chapman, & Cook, 2011; Vincent, Guy, Gershenson, & McCabe, 2012). Studies have reported somewhat mixed results on the SAVRY's ability to predict sexual recidivism; one study found nonsignificant results (Viljoen et al., 2008), whereas another reported high predictive accuracy (AUC = .87 for total score; Schmidt, Campbell, & Houlding, 2011).

Incremental validity. Incremental validity refers to the extent to which a tool outperforms other tools or factors. Several studies have found evidence for the incremental validity of the SAVRY relative to the YLS/CMI and PCL:YV (Dolan & Rennie, 2008; Welsh et al., 2008). Other studies, however, have found that the SAVRY does not outperform other tools in predicting violence and offending, but instead has comparable predictive validity (Hilterman et al., 2014; Schmidt et al., 2011).

Gender. Presently, the bulk of studies suggest that the predictive accuracy of the SAVRY among male and female adolescents is similar, rather than being lower among females (e.g., Gammelgård et al., 2008; Penney et al., 2010). For instance, Lodewijks, de Ruiter, and Doreleijers (2008) found higher AUCs for the total risk score among females (AUC = .84) than males (AUC = .76). In contrast however, Schmidt and colleagues (2011) found higher predictive validity for the SAVRY in predicting violence among male adolescents in comparison to female adolescents (AUC = .78 and .57, respectively for males and females).

Ethnicity. Although the SAVRY has been validated on a diverse range of samples, only a single study has directly tested the impact of race-ethnicity on predictive validity (Vincent et al., 2011). In that study, validity for SAVRY summary risk ratings was generally larger among White and Black adolescents than among Hispanic adolescents. Although race-ethnicity did not moderate the association between the SAVRY total score and *violent* recidivism, there was evidence of moderation for *nonviolent* recidivism (i.e., the SAVRY total score significantly predicted nonviolent recidivism among White adolescents, but not among Black or Hispanic adolescents).

Protective factors. In a meta-analysis of 15 SAVRY studies, Guy (2008) found that SAVRY protective factors yielded moderate to large mean weighted effect sizes for the prediction of *non*-reoffending, including *absence* of general ($AUC_w = .68$), violent ($AUC_w = .73$), and non-violent reoffenses ($AUC_w = .67$). Several more recent studies have also found that protective factors predict non-reoffending (i.e., absence of violence; Lodewijks et al., 2010; McGowan et al., 2011; Vincent, Guy, Gershenson, & McCabe, 2012). In contrast, however, Penney and colleagues (2010) failed to find a significant association between the protective factors and violent recidivism. Also, several studies reported mixed results (e.g., that protective factors were associated with nonviolent recidivism but neither violent nor general recidivism; Vincent et al., 2011; see also Dolan & Rennie, 2008). To date, few studies have tested whether SAVRY protective factors add predictive power beyond that of the SAVRY risk factors. Lodewijks et al. (2010) found that protective factors added incrementally to the prediction of violence relative to the SAVRY dynamic items. However, other research has not demonstrated incremental validity (Schmidt et al., 2011) or has reported mixed results (i.e., incremental validity for general but not for violent recidivism; Dolan & Rennie, 2008).

Changes on dynamic factors. To our knowledge there are no published multiwave empirical investigations examining changes in dynamic risk on the SAVRY and/or the association between intra-individual change and recidivism. The SAVRY authors recommend "regular" reassessment (Borum et al., 2006), but do not list a specific timeframe.

Implementation outcomes (e.g., acceptability to users, adoption, feasibility). Vincent, Guy, Gershenson, and McCabe (2012) examined the implementation of the SAVRY by juvenile probation officers in Louisiana, United States. Results indicated high levels of adherence: juvenile probation officers completed SAVRY assessment for 95% ($n = 195$) of the eligible youth. Guy, Fusco, Hilterman, and Vincent (2011) surveyed attitudes toward the SAVRY following implementation in Louisiana as well as in another implementation in Catalonia, Spain. They found that among both samples there was a high level of endorsement (above 90%) for the usefulness of the SAVRY in aiding case decision making. The main barrier that respondents identified was the amount of time required when completing the assessment; however, such a concern can be raised regarding any comprehensive assessment procedure. A court case review found that the SAVRY (and YLS/CMI) have met tests for legal admissibility and that judges sometimes draw from these assessments in guiding their decisions (Urquhart & Viljoen, 2014).

Impact on intervention planning and services. Following SAVRY implementation, Vincent, Guy, Gershenson, and McCabe (2012) found a *decrease* in the number of youths given dispositions of detention (8% vs. 20%) and state commitment (4% vs. 10%), and an *increase* in the number of youths placed on probation in the community (85% vs. 67%), suggesting a reduced reliance on over-incarceration. Also, following the implementation, the match between risk level and placement decisions improved. Specifically, prior to the implementation of the SAVRY, placement decisions were not associated with adolescents' risk level. However, after the SAVRY was implemented, youth rated as lower risk were at decreased likelihood of being placed (and/or receiving maximum levels of community supervision) compared to youth who were rated as higher risk. Additionally, following the SAVRY implementation, there was a significant increase in the number of service referrals made by juvenile probation officers, with high-risk youth receiving significantly more service referrals in comparison to moderate- and low-risk youth. That said, the SAVRY implementation did not lead to reductions in reoffending per se. This finding might be due to improved tracking of the youth while on probation and/or limitations in the types of evidence-based intervention strategies that were locally available. Overall, the important results found by Vincent et al. (2012) suggest that the SAVRY has the potential to improve the allocation of resources and match youth to appropriate levels of supervision and services.

YLS/CMI 2.0

The Youth Level of Service/Case Management Inventory, Second Edition (YLS/CMI 2.0; Hoge & Andrews, 2011) is an inventory developed to evaluate juvenile offenders' general recidivism risk and to assist in case management planning. The YLS/CMI is based on an *adjusted actuarial model*. Although it provides cutoff scores, assessors may adjust these ratings. The YLS/CMI 2.0 was adapted from the Level of Service Inventory–Revised (LSI-R; Andrews & Bonta, 1995), a well-researched tool designed for adults.

Part I of the YLS/CMI 2.0 includes 42 risk/needs items (rated as Present or Absent), which are divided into eight subscales: *Prior and Current Offenses, Family Circumstances/Parenting, Education/Employment, Peer Associations, Substance Abuse, Leisure/Recreation, Personality/Behavior*, and *Attitudes/Orientation*). On all of the subscales (except for Prior and Current Offenses), strengths can also be identified. In Part II, evaluators add up scores and then classify a youth into risk categories (Low, Moderate, High, or Very High) based on cutoff scores. Part III includes 53 "other needs and special considerations" that may impact a youth's responsiveness to interventions; these include items that pertain to Family/Parents (e.g., abusive parents, significant family trauma) and Youth (e.g., depressed, fetal alcohol spectrum disorder, gang involvement). In Part IV, assessors can adjust their original risk rating; this is called the *professional override* option. In Parts V through VII, evaluators offer recommendations regarding level of supervision and case management.

The YLS/CMI 2.0 is similar to the earlier YLS/CMI (Hoge & Andrews, 2002) in that it includes the same items and same general rating criteria. However, it includes updated norms (including separate norms for male and female youth that are in custody and in the community). It also added guidelines for rating strengths and the responsivity items in Part III. Besides the test manual, only one published study has used the YLS/CMI 2.0 thus far, and that study did not examine its validity (Zeng, Chu, Koh, & Teoh, 2014). However, given that the YLS/CMI 2.0 is very similar to the YLS/CMI, it is likely that research on the YLS/CMI can be generalized to the 2.0 version (Hoge & Andrews, 2011). As such, we present research findings on the YLS/CMI where findings on the YLS/CMI 2.0 are not yet available.

Interrater reliability. Studies have indicated that the YLS/CMI 2.0 (Hoge & Andrews, 2011; Zeng et al., 2014) and YLS/CMI (Catchpole & Gretton, 2003; Hoge, 2005; Poluchowicz, Jung, & Rawana, 2000; Marczyk, Heilbrun, Lander, & Dematteo, 2005; Schmidt, Hoge, & Gomes, 2005; Welsh et al., 2008; Vieira, Skilling, & Peterson-Badali, 2009; Viljoen, Elkovitch, Scalora, & Ullman, 2009) have adequate interrater agreement at both a total score and subscale level. ICCs for total scores have ranged from .76 to .98, whereas the subscales have displayed more variability with ICCs ranging from .43 to 1.00.

Internal consistency. The YLS/CMI 2.0 has excellent internal consistency at a total score level, with Cronbach's α falling around .88 and .90 (Hoge & Andrews, 2011).

Convergent validity. YLS/CMI total scores have been found to correlate significantly with the SAVRY risk ratings and total score ($r = .57$ to .64 and $r = .72$, respectively; Catchpole & Gretton, 2003; Chu, Ng, Fong, & Teoh, 2012; Hilterman et al., 2014), the PCL:YV callous/deceitful traits and conduct problems (Welsh et al., 2008) and total score ($r = .48$ to .82; Hoge & Andrews, 2011), and youth and parental measures of externalizing and internalizing problems and delinquent behavior (Schmidt et al., 2005). Moderate to large associations have been found between the YLS/CMI and measures of risk for sexual recidivism such as the Juvenile Sex Offender Assessment Protocol-II ([J-SOAP-II] Prentky & Righthand, 2003; $r = .71$; Chu, Ng et al., 2012) and ERASOR ($r = .48$ to .91; Chu, Ng et al., 2012; Righthand et al., 2005; Viljoen et al, 2009).

Predictive validity. The YLS/CMI has demonstrated predictive validity for recidivism in youth offenders (Olver et al., 2009; Olver, Stockdale, & Wormith, 2014; Schwalbe, 2007, 2008). In their meta-analysis, Olver et al. (2009) found that across studies, the YLS/CMI significantly predicted general offending ($r_w = .32$), nonviolent offending ($r_w = .31$), violent offending

(r_w = .29), and sexual offending (r_w = .19). Recently, Olver et al. (2014) conducted a large-scale meta-analysis examining the predictive validity of all of the Level of Service measures (including the YLS/CMI). Based on 30 and 13 effect sizes, respectively, the YLS/CMI was found to be a significant predictor of general (fixed-effect r_w = .25; random-effects r_w = .28) and violent recidivism (fixed-effect r_w = .22; random-effects r_w = .23). In line with the results of their previous meta-analysis (Olver et al., 2009), when the effect sizes for the YLS/CMI were broken down by geographic region, effect sizes originating from Canada were found to be larger when compared to those originating from the U.S. and outside North America. In addition, higher scores on the YLS/CMI have been linked with faster rates of reoffending and increased rates of incarceration and technical probation violations (Flores et al., 2003; Schmidt et al., 2005).

Incremental validity. In general, studies have found the YLS/CMI to have similar levels of predictive validity in comparison to other tools, such as the SAVRY and PCL:YV (see Hilterman et al., 2014). However, two studies have found that the SAVRY demonstrated incremental validity relative to the YLS/CMI (Schmidt et al., 2011; Welsh et al., 2008). Moreover, the J-SOAP-II has been found to be a significantly better predictor of sexual and nonsexual recidivism in comparison to the YLS/CMI in a sample of adolescent sex offenders (Chu, Ng et al., 2012).

Gender. Olver et al. (2009) meta-analytically compared the predictive accuracy of the YLS/CMI among male and female youth and found the results to be comparable for the prediction of general and violent recidivism in both males (general recidivism: r_w = .33; violent recidivism r_w = .23) and females (general recidivism: r_w = .36; violent recidivism r_w = .24). Several other studies have found similar predictive accuracy for both male and female adolescent offenders (e.g., Andrews et al., 2012; Schwalbe, 2008; Thompson & McGrath, 2012). In contrast, other studies have demonstrated superior predictive validity for male offenders compared to female offenders (e.g., Bechtel, Lowenkamp, & Latessa, 2007; Marshall, Egan, English, & Jones, 2006; Schmidt et al., 2011). However, the small sample size of females relative to males in these studies may play a role in these findings. Given that tools such as the YLS/CMI were originally developed using male samples, the YLS/CMI 2.0 version included a larger normative sample of female youth, and provides separate cutoff scores for female offenders (Hoge & Andrews, 2011). Moreover, several additional female-informed responsivity factors were incorporated (e.g., victimization, pregnancy, sexual abuse).

Ethnicity. The YLS/CMI has been found to predict general and violent recidivism across various ethnic groups such as Australian Indigenous, African American, and Japanese youth (Shepherd, Luebbers, & Dolan, 2013; Takahashi, Mori, & Kroner, 2013). Furthermore, Olver, Stockdale, and Wong (2012) have found the YLS/CMI total score to be a strong predictor of general, nonviolent, and violent recidivism (up to seven years postassessment) among Aboriginal youth in Saskatchewan, Canada. Upon closer inspection, the predictive validity of the YLS/CMI was found to be somewhat higher among the Aboriginal youth in comparison to the non-Aboriginal youth.

Strengths. Thus far, no published studies have examined YLS/CMI Strengths ratings. A conference presentation reported that relatively few youth were identified as having a Strength on the YLS/CMI (21%), and that the presence of Strengths did not significantly predict reoffending (Viljoen et al., 2012, April). Further research is needed however.

Changes on dynamic factors. To our knowledge, no published studies have examined changes in YLS/CMI factors across multiple time points.

Implementation outcomes (e.g., acceptability to users, adoption, feasibility). Flores et al. (2003) surveyed practitioners at three juvenile justice correctional agencies that had implemented the YLS/CMI. Respondents reported that it took an average of 65 minutes to complete the YLS/CMI. Approximately 86% of practitioners indicated they used the overall YLS/CMI risk score to determine supervision level and 80% reported using the measure for completing case plans. In contrast, only 57% of practitioners indicated that they used the needs score to identify treatment goals, and 80% reported that their agency did not reassess youth using the YLS/CMI to determine any change in criminogenic needs. A fair number of respondents indicated that they found the YLS/CMI challenging to use, and did not feel it was necessary for youth placements or for identifying treatment needs (ratings were 4.9, 5.2, and 5.5, respectively on a 10-point scale with 10 representing the most favorable response). However, further research is needed, as practitioners' views may differ considerably depending on agency readiness to implement a risk assessment tool, as well as the particular approaches, training, and policies that are used to implement a tool.

Impact on intervention planning and services. The YLS/CMI 2.0 is based on the risk-need-responsivity (RNR) model (Andrews & Bonta, 2010; Andrews et al., 1990). This model states that services should be matched to a youth's risk level (e.g., more intensive services for individuals who are high risk versus those who are low risk), and target a youth's specific criminogenic needs. It also asserts that interventions should use cognitive behavioral approaches and be tailored to individual characteristics (e.g., accommodations for youth with learning disabilities).

Consistent with this model, Luong and Wormith (2011) found that youth rated as higher risk on an adaptation of the YLS/CMI, the Level of Service Inventory–Saskatchewan Youth Edition (LSI-SK; Andrews, Bonta, & Wormith, 2001) received more intensive supervision from probation officers than youth rated lower on the measure. Additionally, except in some domains (e.g., antisocial patterns), youth received treatment matching of their identified needs on most LSI-SK subscales. Similarly, Vincent, Paiva-Salisbury, Cook, Guy, and Perrault (2012) found that the implementation of the YLS/CMI and SAVRY (results were combined) resulted in greater reported adherence to the RNR principles. Alternatively, studies at some sites have reported less promising results. For example, Flores et al. (2003) found that only 43% of probation officers used YLS/CMI ratings to inform treatment. Furthermore, the treatment provided generally did not match the youths' needs, except in the case of identified substance use leading to substance use treatment. Similarly, Vieira et al. (2009) found that only 35% of youths' identified needs (as identified by the YLS/CMI) were addressed in treatment. However, when youth were matched to services that addressed their specific needs this was associated with decreased reoffending.

Risk Assessment Tools for Sexual Offending

Sexual offending shares many of the same risk factors as general offending (e.g., antisocial attitudes and orientation; McCann & Lussier, 2008). At the same time, some adolescents who sexually offend possess unique risk factors (e.g., deviant sexual interests). As a result, several tools have been developed specifically to assess risk for sexual offending.

J-SOAP-II

The J-SOAP-II (Prentky & Righthand, 2003) is a 28-item checklist designed to aid in assessing risk for sexual violence and general delinquency. It is intended to be used with adolescents, aged 12 to 18, who have a history of sexually coercive behavior. The J-SOAP-II has two subscales that are conceptualized as static or historical risk factors: the *Sexual Drive/Preoccupation Subscale* (e.g., prior sexual offense charges, male child victims, sexual victimization), and the *Impulsive/Antisocial Behavior Subscale* (e.g., pervasive anger, school behavior problems, charges or arrests prior to age 16). It also includes two subscales that focus on dynamic or modifiable risk factors: the *Intervention Subscale* (e.g., internal motivation for change, understands risk factors, empathy), and the *Community Stability/Adjustment Subscale* (e.g., management of sexual urges, stability of current living situation, positive support systems). Items on the J-SOAP-II are rated on a three-point scale (Absent, Possibly Present, Clearly Present), with a higher score representing greater risk.

Total scores are obtained by summing the items on the four scales. At the present time, the J-SOAP-II does not have any cutoff scores to classify youth into different risk categories.

However, the authors described that they plan to develop this in the future so that it can be used in an actuarial manner (Prentky & Righthand, 2003).

Interrater reliability. Seven studies have assessed the interrater reliability of the J-SOAP-II using ICCs or Pearson correlations (Aebi, Plattner, Steinhausen, & Bessler, 2011; Caldwell & Dickinson, 2009; Caldwell, Ziemke, & Vitacco, 2008; Martinez, Florez, & Rosenfeld, 2007; Parks & Bard, 2006; Rajlic & Gretton, 2010). On the Sexual Drive/Preoccupation, Impulsive/ Antisocial Behavior, and Intervention subscales, ICCs have generally fallen in the excellent range (i.e., >.75; Cicchetti & Sparrow, 1981) or in the good range (i.e., .60-.74). The Community Stability/Adjustment subscale has yielded mixed (but acceptable) results, with two studies demonstrating excellent interrater reliability, and two studies indicating fair reliability.

Internal consistency. Studies indicate that internal consistency of total J-SOAP-II scores falls in the good range, as does the internal consistency of the Impulsive/Antisocial Behavior and Intervention subscales (Aebi et al., 2011; Martinez et al., 2007; Parks & Bard, 2006). In comparison, the Sexual Drive/Preoccupation subscale has shown good internal consistency in two studies, and poor internal consistency in another. The Community Stability/Adjustment subscale demonstrated good internal consistency in one study, and acceptable internal consistency in another.

Convergent validity. Total scores on the J-SOAP-II are positively correlated with measures of general offending (e.g., SAVRY), and measures of sexual reoffending such as the Juvenile Sexual Offense Recidivism Risk Assessment Tool–II (J-SORRAT-II; Epperson, Ralston, Fowers, DeWitt, & Gore, 2006), thus providing support for its convergent validity (Caldwell et al., 2008; Viljoen et al., 2008).

Predictive validity. Studies examining predictive validity of the J-SOAP-II have somewhat mixed results, with some studies finding significant results (e.g., Aebi et al., 2011; Martinez et al., 2007; Prentky et al., 2010; Rajlic & Gretton 2010) but others reporting null findings (e.g., Caldwell et al., 2008; Chu, Ng et al., 2012; Viljoen et al., 2008). However, a meta-analysis found that, when these findings are aggregated, the overall predictive validity of the J-SOAP-II total scores falls in the moderate range for predictions of sexual reoffending (AUC = .67) and for nonsexual reoffending (AUC = .66; Viljoen, Mordell, & Beneteau, 2012). At a subscale level, the Community Stability/Adjustment subscale showed the strongest predictive validity for sexual reoffending (AUC =.70). With respect to predicting general offending, the Impulsive/ Antisocial subscale demonstrated the strongest predictive validity (AUC = .66), whereas the Sexual Drive/Preoccupation subscale predicted no better than chance (AUC = .49). Although Viljoen et al. (2008) found that the J-SOAP-II was less effective in predicting violent reoffending in younger youth (15 and under) compared to older youth, other studies have not replicated this finding (Prentky et al., 2010). Furthermore, Prentky et al. (2010) found that the J-SOAP-II predicts sexually abusive behaviors in not only adolescents but also preadolescents (i.e., age 11 or younger).

Gender. The J-SOAP-II was not designed to assess risk for sexual offending in females and thus, validation studies have only been carried out with male offenders.

Ethnicity. Although several studies have utilized samples comprised of adolescents from diverse ethnic groups (e.g., Martinez et al., 2007; Fanniff & Letourneau, 2012), no studies (to our knowledge) have directly tested whether ethnicity moderates the predictive validity of the J-SOAP-II. Chu, Ng, and colleagues (2012) examined the predictive validity of the J-SOAP-II in a cross-cultural context, with Singaporean male youth who had committed a sexual offense. They found that the J-SOAP-II total score did not predict sexual recidivism in their sample of youth (AUC = .51); however, it was strongly predictive of general recidivism (AUC = .81).

Protective factors. The J-SOAP-II does not include protective factors.

Changes on dynamic factors. Rehfuss et al. (2013) examined whether youth in a sex offender treatment program showed change in their scores on the J-SOAP-II dynamic factors (i.e., combined scores on the Intervention and Community Stability/Adjustment subscales).

Results indicated that those at moderate risk of reoffending demonstrated a significantly greater decrease in J-SOAP-II dynamic scores following treatment than those in either the low or high risk groups.

Implementation outcomes (e.g., acceptability to users, adoption, feasibility). To our knowledge, no studies have examined the implementation of the J-SOAP-II in real-world settings nor examined other issues such as user satisfaction. Despite this, the J-SOAP-II has been widely adopted. For example, a 2009 survey found that the J-SOAP-II was used in 61% of U.S. community programs, 58% of U.S. residential programs, and 27% of Canadian community programs for adolescent sexual offenders (McGrath, Cumming, Burchard, Zeoli, & Ellerby, 2010). In addition, use of the J-SOAP-II in these settings has approximately doubled since 2002.

Impact on intervention planning and services. Research examining the utility of the J-SOAP-II in informing risk management and treatment remains to be completed.

ERASOR

The ERASOR (Worling & Curwen, 2001) is a checklist of risk factors developed specifically for assessing risk of *sexual violence* among adolescents aged 12 to 18 who have committed a prior sexual assault. Like the SAVRY, it is based on the SPJ model. It consists of 25 items, which fall into the following five categories: *Sexual Interests, Attitudes, and Behaviors* (e.g., deviant sexual interests, attitudes supportive of sexual offending), *Historical Sexual Assaults* (e.g., past sexual assault of a child, diverse sexual-assault behaviors), *Psychosocial Functioning* (e.g., lack of intimate peer relationships, poor self-regulation abilities), *Family/Environmental Functioning* (e.g., high-stress family environment, problematic parent-offender relationship), *Treatment* (e.g., incomplete sexual-offense-specific treatment). With the exception of the items relating to Historical Sexual Assaults, the other items are all dynamic factors that should be rated every six months. Risk factors are rated as Present, Possibly or Partially Present, Not Present, or Unknown.

Interrater reliability. Research examining the psychometric properties of the ERASOR has found good to excellent levels of interrater reliability both within a research and clinical context for the ERASOR total score and summary risk rating (ICC = .76 to .94 and .64 to .87, respectively; Morton, 2003; Nelson, 2011; Rajlic & Gretton, 2010; Skowron, 2005; Viljoen et al., 2009; Worling, 2004; Worling et al., 2012). However, Chu, Ng et al. (2012) found only fair interrater agreement for the ERASOR total score and summary risk rating (ICC = .49 and .43, respectively).

Internal consistency. The ERASOR has displayed adequate internal consistency, with α values ranging from .74 to .87 (Hersant, 2006; Morton, 2003; Worling, 2004; Worling et al., 2012).

Convergent validity. Several studies have found support for the convergent validity of the ERASOR as evidenced by significantly large associations with other adolescent risk measures for sexual recidivism. For instance, the J-SOAP-II (Prentky & Righthand, 2003), has been found to correlate highly with the ERASOR total score (r = .70 to .79; Chu, Ng et al., 2012; Rajlic & Gretton, 2010). However, the ERASOR has displayed somewhat lower levels of association with the Static-99 (Hanson & Thornton, 1999), an adult measure of risk for sexual recidivism (r = .32 to .50; Morton, 2003; Viljoen et al., 2009). Moreover, several studies have found moderate to large correlation coefficients between the ERASOR and measures of general antisociality. For instance, correlations between the ERASOR total score and the YLS/CMI have ranged from .48 to .73 (Chu, Ng et al., 2012; Morton, 2003; Skowron, 2005; Viljoen et al., 2009). Likewise, the ERASOR total score has correlated strongly with the PCL:YV (r = .63; Viljoen et al., 2009).

Predictive validity. Within their systematic review, Hempel, Buck, Cima, and van Marle (2013) identified six studies examining the predictive validity of the ERASOR. They found AUC values ranging from small to large for the ERASOR in predicting sexual recidivism (AUC = .50

to .74), small to large for nonsexual violent recidivism (AUC = .56 to .71), and small to moderate for general recidivism (AUC = .53 to .67). In a meta-analytic investigation, Viljoen, Mordell, and Beneteau (2012) aggregated data from 10 studies, and found the ERASOR to be a significant predictor of sexual recidivism with moderate effect sizes for the total score (weighted AUC = .66) and summary risk rating (AUC = .66). However, modest predictive accuracy was found for the ERASOR total score (AUC = .59) and summary risk rating (AUC = .59) in predicting general recidivism.

Incremental validity. Although Chu, Ng et al. (2012) found the ERASOR to be a significantly better predictor of sexual recidivism in comparison to the YLS/CMI and J-SOAP-II, they did not directly test the incremental validity of the ERASOR over these tools as neither the YLS/CMI nor the J-SOAP-II were significantly associated with sexual recidivism. In their meta-analytic review, Viljoen, Mordell, and Beneteau (2012) examined studies that compared risk assessment measures and found nonsignificant differences between the ERASOR and J-SOAP-II (AUC = .68 vs. .62, respectively) and between the ERASOR and Static-99 in predicting sexual recidivism (AUC = .56 vs. .63, respectively).

Gender. To date, no empirical investigations have been conducted that examine the reliability or validity of the ERASOR among female adolescent sex offenders given the low rate of female adolescent sexual offending.

Ethnicity. The majority of studies conducted with the ERASOR have utilized samples primarily consisting of Caucasian youth. Although Chu, Ng et al. (2012) found strong empirical support for the ERASOR among a Singaporean sample comprised of Chinese, Malay, and Indian youth, no studies (to our knowledge) have directly compared the reliability and validity of the ERASOR across various ethnic groups.

Protective Factors. The ERASOR does not include protective factors. However, Worling (2013) has recently developed the Desistence for Adolescents Who Sexually Harm (DASH-13) a 13-item checklist of protective factors related to desistence in adolescent sexual offenders. Still within the experimental phase, the DASH-13 consists of seven items relating to future sexual health (e.g., prosocial sexual arousal, hope for a healthy sexual future, prosocial sexual attitudes) and six items relating to generalized prosocial functioning (e.g., compassion for others, positive problem-solving skills). Although no psychometric data currently exist for the measure, research is under way.

Changes on dynamic factors. The authors state that ERASOR assessments should focus on an adolescent's *short-term* risk, which they define as one year at most, given the rapid development that occurs during adolescence and the fact that most of the risk factors on the ERASOR are dynamic and subject to change (Worling, 2004; Worling & Curwen, 2001). Worling and colleagues (2012) prospectively examined the field validity of the ERASOR as completed by clinicians and found significantly higher predictive accuracy for the ERASOR total score and summary risk rating in predicting sexual recidivism (AUC = .93 and .82, respectively) over a mean follow-up period of 1.4 years in comparison to a longer mean follow-up period of 3.66 years (AUC = .72 and .61, respectively). This study highlights the potential value of reassessment.

Implementation outcomes (e.g., acceptability to users, adoption, feasibility). Although no study (to our knowledge) has examined issues such as user satisfaction for the ERASOR, McGrath and colleagues (2010) found the ERASOR to be among the most commonly used measures of adolescent risk for sexual recidivism in the United States and Canada. Furthermore, there was a significant increase in the percentage of programs administering the ERASOR between 2002 and 2009 in community (21% vs. 53%, respectively) and residential treatment programs (21% vs. 44%, respectively) within the United States.

Impact on intervention planning and services. To our knowledge, no studies examining the impact of the ERASOR on intervention planning or services have been conducted to date (such as whether the ERASOR impacts resource allocation or improves service matching).

Risk Assessment for Multiple Adverse Outcomes
(e.g., Violence, Victimization, Suicide)

Mental health professionals face legal and ethical obligations not only to assess risk of violence in adolescents but also to assess adolescents' own risks of experiencing harm (e.g., suicide, victimization; Werth, Welfel, & Benjamin, 2009). Rates of these other outcomes are high among justice-involved youth and they are often interrelated with violence, sharing many of the same risk factors (e.g., impulsivity, substance use; Viljoen et al. (in progress)). As such, the START:AV was developed to assess multiple adverse outcomes.

START:AV

The START:AV (Viljoen et al., 2014) is an SPJ tool for male and female adolescents in mental health and/or justice settings. It assesses risk for violence as well as other adverse outcomes such as suicide attempts, self-injury, and victimization and was adapted from an adult measure, the Short-Term Assessment of Risk and Treatability (START; Webster, Nicholls, Martin, Desmarais, & Brink, 2006). In developing the START:AV three studies were conducted on a pilot version of the tool (Nicholls, Viljoen, Cruise, Desmarais, & Webster, 2010), including a prospective research study in Canada (Viljoen, Beneteau et al., 2012), a juvenile justice implementation study in the United States (Desmarais, Nicholls, Wilson, & Brink, 2012), and an implementation study in forensic and psychiatric hospital units in the United Kingdom (Sher et al., 2013). Numerous studies (> 20) have researched the adult version of the tool from which the START:AV was developed (for a review see O'Shea & Dickens, 2014).

The START:AV includes 25 items that fall into three clusters: *Individual Adolescent* (e.g., school and work, substance use, coping, emotional state), *Relationships and Environment* (e.g., relationships with caregivers and other adults, parenting, peers), and *Responses to Intervention* (e.g., insight, plans, treatability). Assessors may also consider additional case-specific factors (e.g., culture, sexual orientation). All of the items on the START:AV are modifiable (i.e., dynamic) and are rated as Low, Moderate, or High for both Strengths and Vulnerabilities. It is possible for an adolescent to show both Strengths and Vulnerabilities on a single item. For instance, an adolescent may have some prosocial and positive friends (rated as a Strength) and some antisocial friends (rated as a Vulnerability).

After rating items, assessors evaluate an adolescent's *history* of and *future risk* for adverse outcomes. The START:AV includes nine adverse outcomes that fall into two categories: *Harm to Others and Rule Violations* (i.e., violence, nonviolent offenses, substance abuse, unauthorized absences such as running away, school drop out, and probation violations) and *Harm to the Adolescent* (i.e., suicide, nonsuicidal self-injury, victimization, and health neglect). Assessors can also identify if an imminent threat of harm exists. The final step is to compile this information to develop a case formulation, identify risk-related scenarios that may occur, and develop intervention plans to reduce risks. The START:AV is designed to be administered regularly (e.g., every three months) so as to measure progress and refine intervention strategies.

Interrater reliability. One study reported that the interrater reliability for the Strengths and Vulnerabilities total scores fell within the excellent range for single raters (ICCs = .92 and .86 respectively; Viljoen, Beneteau et al., 2012). Half of the risk estimates for adverse outcomes (e.g., violence) fell in the excellent range (> .75) and half were within the good range (.60–.74).

Internal consistency. Two studies found the Strengths and Vulnerabilities total scores to have high internal consistency (α > .89; Desmarais et al., 2012; Viljoen et al., 2012). Desmarais et al. (2012) found good item homogeneity (mean inter-item correlations of .37 and .26 for Strengths and Vulnerabilities, respectively), and good item-total correlations (.48 and .58 for Strengths and Vulnerabilities).

Concurrent validity. Viljoen et al. (2012) found large positive correlations (> .67) between Vulnerabilities total scores and SAVRY risk ratings and total scores. Similarly, correlations between START:AV Strengths total scores, SAVRY protective factors scores, and asset scores on the Developmental Assets Profile (Search Institute, 2004) were large.

Predictive validity. A three-month prospective study (Viljoen et al., 2012) demonstrated that the START:AV Vulnerabilities total scores were significantly associated with scores on scales of self-reported aggression and offending, victimization, suicide ideation, and alcohol and drug use. Also, the Vulnerabilities total scores significantly predicted arrests for violence and other offenses, as measured through justice records (AUC = .70 and .70). In this same study, START:AV Strengths total scores were negatively associated with self-reported aggression and offending, arrests for violence or other offenses, and use of street drugs. However, Strengths total scores did not predict reduced scores on measures of suicidal ideation, victimization, or alcohol and drug use. Finally, START:AV risk estimates (i.e., SPJ ratings of low, moderate, high risk) were all correlated with scores on relevant outcome scales (e.g., the risk estimate for victimization significantly predicted victimization scores), although it did not predict some dichotomous outcomes (e.g., the AUC for the self-injury risk estimate was .67, $p > .05$).

The Viljoen, Beneteau et al. (2012) findings were drawn from a research study in which the START:AV was rated by trained research assistants. In addition, several implementation studies have examined START:AV assessment completed by professionals in the field. In an implementation study at a secure residential forensic and psychiatric service, total Vulnerabilities scores were significantly correlated with verbal aggression, property damage, and physical aggression (Sher et al., 2013). An implementation study in juvenile justice facilities found that youth who were rated as high risk for violence by case managers were more likely to engage in any violence, physical violence, and nonsexual violence than those rated as low risk (Johnson, Desmarais, Rajagopalan, Sellers, & Singh, 2014). In contrast, total Strengths scores were not associated with adverse outcomes, and higher total Vulnerabilities scores were only associated with unauthorized absences.

Gender. The START:AV was designed to include attention to outcomes, such as sexual victimization, which are elevated in girls. Also, in developing the START:AV, the authors conducted a literature review, which supported the relevance of items for girls as well as boys (Viljoen et al., in progress). Viljoen et al. (2012) tested whether gender moderated the predictive validity of the START:AV in a sample of 28 girls and 62 boys; they did not find evidence of a moderator effect, suggesting that the START:AV functions similarly for girls and boys. Conversely, Sher et al. (2013) found the START:AV did not significantly predict outcomes in a sample of 35 adolescent girls. Notably, the sample size of girls was small in both of these studies. Thus, further research is needed, especially as these studies likely had limited power to adequately test validity across gender.

Ethnicity. To date, no studies have compared the predictive validity of the START:AV across racial and ethnic groups. The START:AV User Guide (Viljoen et al., 2014) includes a case-specific item that focuses on culture (e.g., cultural connectedness, experiences of discrimination); this item aims to assist in intervention planning among youth from minority groups (e.g., identifying youths' interest in culturally tailored services).

Protective factors. Desmarais et al. (2012) and Viljoen et al. (2012) reported that Strengths total scores had a good dispersion (ranging from 4 to 42 and from 7 to 40 respectively). A study comparing the START:AV Strengths section to other measures of protective factors found that all of the adolescents were identified as having at least one strength on the START:AV as compared to 57% of adolescents on the SAVRY and 21% on the YLS/CMI (Viljoen et al., 2012). Also, the START:AV Strengths total score showed incremental validity over SAVRY protective factors and YLS/CMI strengths in the prediction of self-reported violent, property, and total offending.

Changes on dynamic factors. Viljoen et al. (2012) examined change in risk among 65 adolescents over a three-month period; 92% of participants were rated to have changed in at least one risk domain during a three-month period, and approximately half changed in two or more domains (i.e., based on risk estimates). Given that some changes could stem from random fluctuations or measurement error, they also calculated Reliable Change Indices (RCIs) for the Strengths and

Vulnerabilities total scores. Based on RCIs, 16% of the sample showed reliable change when a 95% CI was applied, and 27% showed reliable change when a 90% CI was applied. Sellers et al. (2012) examined dynamic changes in START:AV assessments for 53 adolescents from initial assessment to the follow-up assessment period (mean follow-up length = 104 days); 92% of adolescents showed some change (of one point or more) in their Vulnerabilities total score, and 82% in their Strengths total score.

Implementation outcomes (e.g., acceptability to users, adoption, feasibility). Sher and Gralton (in press) surveyed START:AV users who worked in a forensic and psychiatric service in the United Kingdom (e.g., psychologists, nurses, psychiatrists, social workers, occupational therapists, and teachers). The majority of respondents (> 86%) felt that the information gathered from the START:AV assessment, such as specific risk estimates and ratings of Strengths and Vulnerabilities, was useful for assessing risks in their patients. In addition, 93% of respondents indicated that the START:AV was a clinically useful measure. The main concern expressed was that the START:AV ratings required considerable time to complete (an average of 27 minutes). Feasibility of implementing the START:AV with a youth offender population was examined by Desmarais, Sellers, Viljoen, Cruise, Nicholls, and Dvoskin (2012). In the initial phases of the project, case managers left blank (on each assessment) an average of one Vulnerabilities item, one Strengths item, and three Risk Estimates. Further training and discussion decreased the number of missing risk estimates, emphasizing the importance of ongoing monitoring and training.

Impact on intervention planning and services. A recent study by Singh et al. (2014), found that externalizing behaviors (e.g., violence, offending) were less likely to occur *if* adolescents' Critical Vulnerabilities (as identified with the START:AV) were addressed in their treatment plans. Matching strength-based interventions to youths' Key Strengths on the START:AV was also associated with reduced reoffending. This suggests that using the START:AV may have value for intervention planning. However, similar to studies with other tools (e.g., Flores et al., 2003), needs that were identified with the START:AV often remained unaddressed (Singh et al., 2014). Specifically, case managers addressed Critical Vulnerabilities in approximately only half of the youths' intervention plans. Key Strengths were addressed less often (i.e., a quarter of cases). To help improve adherence and bridge the START:AV to intervention planning, the recently published START:AV User Guide (Viljoen et al., 2014) includes a focus on case formulation, scenario planning, and intervention planning (drawing from the work of Douglas, Hart, Webster, & Belfrage, 2013; Hart et al., 2003). As with other tools, proper implementation is essential, and the effectiveness of a risk assessment is only as good as the documentation, communication, and treatment that results from it.

Summary of Risk Assessment Tools

Each of the adolescent risk assessment tools reviewed in this chapter has some support. Consistent with the criteria proposed by Vincent et al. (2009) they each have a manual or guide, include evidence-based risk factors, have evidence to support their interrater reliability and internal consistency, and have achieved significant predictive validity in at least two studies (including at least one study by independent investigators). In general, the predictive validity of many of these tools appears fairly similar (e.g., SAVRY and YLS/CMI; J-SOAP-II and ERASOR); correlations and AUCs generally fall in the moderate range (or what has been referred to as the "sound barrier" or "ceiling" of risk assessment tools; Skeem & Monahan, 2011). Although some studies suggest that certain tools may outperform others, findings are scarce and inconsistent at best. Indeed, as experts note, risk assessment tools are fairly indistinguishable on the basis of *predictive validity* alone (Kroner, Mills, & Reddon, 2005; Skeem & Monahan, 2011; Yang et al., 2010).

That said, adolescent risk assessment tools differ in other respects. For instance, tools vary in terms of the quantity and type of research support they have. For most tools, studies have focused on to what extent the tool *predicts* reoffending; for other tools, some initial research has also started to examine the extent to which the tool *improves* service matching (especially research on the SAVRY and YLS/CMI). Tools adopt varying degrees of emphasis on the assessment of protective factors; for instance, the SAVRY assesses six protective factors (using criteria of Present or Absent), the YLS/CMI 2.0 evaluates strengths in seven domains (using criteria of Present or Absent), and the START:AV rates Strengths on 25 items (using criteria of Low, Moderate, or High). Tools also differ in terms of their approach to intervention planning: for example, the YLS/CMI 2.0 draws from the RNR principles, whereas the START:AV includes attention to case formulation, scenario planning, and the RNR principles.

Next, we provide a case example to illustrate the similarities and differences between risk assessment tools (i.e., the SAVRY, YLS/CMI 2.0, and START:AV). Due to space constraints we focus only on the risk assessment rather than the resulting case management and intervention plans. This case does not contain any identifying information about a real-life youth.

Case Example

Sebastian is a 15-year-old Caucasian male. During gym class, Sebastian assaulted three male classmates with a baseball bat, causing substantial injuries to the victims (e.g., bruising, one of them had a broken rib). He was found guilty of Assault Causing Bodily Harm; this is his first charge. Sebastian explained that these classmates had been "laughing" at him about his appearance (which is "goth-like"; he has dyed black hair, and wears black clothing and black eyeliner). He stated that they "had it coming." Sebastian has been in approximately four to five fights with "bullies" when he was 12 and 13 years old. He has never committed any nonviolent offenses.

Family and Peer Environment

Sebastian resides in a middle-class neighborhood in suburbia with his biological parents and his two older brothers (aged 17 and 19). Sebastian's family is well off; his father owns a car dealership and his mother is a homemaker. According to his parents, Sebastian has never fit in with his peers. His mother described him as "reclusive" and "different," and noted that he has always been picked on by other children. Her two other sons are very popular and are "star athletes" on the high school football team.

Sebastian describes his parents as having never really tried to understand him, stating that they are disappointed that he is not a "dumb jock" like his older brothers. When he is at home, he stays in his room with the door closed. Sebastian reported that he does not have many friends at school; however, he has several friends that he met online. According to his teachers, Sebastian sometimes alienates his peers because he engages in behaviors that make them uncomfortable (e.g., during biology class, he made a dead frog dance on the textbook of a female classmate). However, Sebastian has recently started to develop a friendship with a new transfer student, Erik, with whom he has a number of shared interests (e.g., gaming).

Current and Past Functioning

Sebastian has never failed a grade or a class. During elementary and middle school, he received straight As. His grades have fallen somewhat in the past year but he is still passing his courses (he has been obtaining grades of Bs and Cs with very little effort). According to prior psychological testing, his IQ falls within the Superior range. Sebastian reported that he generally finds school "boring." However, he described his biology teacher as "cool" and said that he sometimes gives him extra readings that he thinks Sebastian would enjoy. Sebastian is also very talented at drawing and computer graphics.

Sebastian stated that his parents have sent him to see many counselors to "fix him." He said the counselors he saw were "useless," and that he does not need therapy. According to his prior therapist, Sebastian is very sensitive to perceived rejection, despite his bravado. He experiences intense anger in response to bullying and has difficulty coping with his ongoing experiences of being victimized by peers (e.g., he isolates from and avoids others). Sebastian has never tried alcohol or drugs.

SAVRY: On the SAVRY, Sebastian was rated as a Moderate Risk for future violence (i.e., assaults in response to peer bullying), and Low Risk for *nonviolent* offending. With respect to historical risk factors, Sebastian was rated high on history of violence and moderate on early initiation of violence (e.g., fights with bullies, starting at an early age). On social-contextual risk factors, he was noted to have experienced high levels of peer rejection and lack of support. Finally, with respect to individual and clinical factors, he was rated as high on anger management difficulties. Sebastian did not meet the threshold for any of the SAVRY protective factors at the time of the assessment. However, the assessor wrote in "intelligence" as a case-specific protective factor.

YLS/CMI 2.0: On the YLS/CMI 2.0, Sebastian was rated as Moderate risk for reoffending. The assessor judged this to be a fair assessment of Sebastian's risk and thus did not use the option to professionally override this risk rating. Sebastian's risk/need level was low in a couple of domains (prior and current offenses/disposition and substance use), moderate in most domains (family circumstances, education/employment, peer relations, personality/behavior, attitude/orientation), and high in one domain (i.e., leisure and recreation; Sebastian spends most of his time alone playing computer games in his room and does not participate in any structured activities).

START:AV: On the START:AV, Sebastian was rated as Moderate Risk for engaging in violence during the next three months (i.e., assaults in response to provocation by peers) and Moderate Risk for experiencing *victimization* (i.e., bullying or potential assaults by peers). He was rated as Low Risk for committing nonviolent offenses. With respect to his recent functioning over the past three months, Sebastian was identified as showing high vulnerabilities in emotional state (e.g., irritability, anger, depression), social skills (e.g., misreads social cues), and coping (e.g., avoids talking about or seeking help for peer difficulties). However, he showed strengths in mental/cognitive state (e.g., is bright and able to learn quickly).

In terms of relationship and environmental factors, Sebastian showed moderate vulnerabilities in his relationships with both his peers and his parents (e.g., feels rejected by parents, has very few friends). However, at the same time, he was also noted to have some moderate strengths in social supports (e.g., has recently developed a new friendship, feels a strong connection with his biology teacher). Finally, with respect to response to interventions, Sebastian was identified as having high vulnerabilities in his level of insight (e.g., he has limited motivation to engage in treatment). Nonetheless, he had some long-term prosocial plans (e.g., he hopes to become a successful computer programmer to prove to his parents and peers that he is "worth more" than they give him credit for); these prosocial plans may potentially buffer his risks.

Conclusions: As shown, the SAVRY, YLS/CMI, and START:AV assessments generated similar conclusions about Sebastian's level of risk for violence and offending. Yet, at the same time, these tools brought a somewhat different perspective to the case. The YLS/CMI 2.0 focused on general offending, whereas the SAVRY and START:AV differentiated between violent offending (for which Sebastian was judged to be Moderate risk) and nonviolent offending (for which Sebastian was judged to be Low risk). The START:AV also drew attention to Sebastian's own risks for victimization. Compared to the other tools, the START:AV identified a larger set of strengths in this case (because it assesses a larger number of potential strengths), and focused on risk in the next three months, at which time a reassessment occurred. In this particular case, Sebastian showed increased risk at three months, as he was very angry at classmate who made a Facebook© posting about him. He vaguely alluded to having plans to retaliate. Thus, the assessor gathered more information (e.g., interviews with teachers, caregivers, etc.) to determine the extent to which this threat was real, enactable, and acute. We now turn to describing threat assessment and how it is distinct from, yet related to risk assessment.

Threat Assessment

Whereas violence risk assessment focuses on an adolescent's general risks of offending and violence (i.e., without specifying a particular target), threat assessment focuses on risk of violence that is directed towards a specific individual or group of individuals (e.g., school shooting, assassination of a political leader, terrorism; Borum, Fein, Vossekuil, & Berglund, 1999; Meloy, Hoffmann, Guldimann, & James, 2012). Compared to violence risk assessment, threat assessment is generally conducted by frontline law enforcement or school staff (in the case of threats in a school setting) rather than by health, justice, and social service professionals, and consists of a "hot" or rapid process that is ongoing rather than a "cold" or slow process with a specified start and end date (Meloy, Hart, & Hoffmann, 2014). Moreover, protection of victim(s) is its primary goal rather than management of perpetrator(s).

An important concept to threat assessment is the focus on the individual's "pathway toward violent action" (Reddy et al., 2001, p. 168). Thus, threat assessment aims to examine the progression of behavior of the individual over time, and case-specific factors rather than general nomothetic risk factors such as demographic and psychological characteristics (Borum et al., 1999; Borum, Bartel, & Forth, 2005). Specifically, factors considered during a threat assessment could include things such as the underlying motivation for the behavior, whether the youth has experienced recent losses such as those relating to status, evidence for an increased interest in targeted violence, and whether the youth has obtained weapons and/or the means of committing the targeted violence (for more information see Reddy et al., 2001). Importantly, not all who threaten will engage in targeted violence (Borum et al., 1999; Reddy et al., 2001); research indicates that most threats that adolescents make in school contexts (approximately 70%) are transient threats that can easily be resolved rather than substantive threats (Cornell et al., 2004). At the same time, not all who engage in targeted violence will threaten their victim beforehand. Therefore, "while all threats should be taken seriously, they are not the most reliable indicator of risk and therefore should not be a necessary condition to initiate an inquiry or preliminary evaluation" (Reddy et al., 2001, p. 168). As noted by Meloy and colleagues (2012) warning behaviors include those relating to not only the directly communicated threat, but also pathway (e.g., evidence of planning the attack), fixation (e.g., perseveration regarding the situation), identification (e.g., idolizing aggressors, such as school shooters), novel aggression (e.g., trying out aggression in another context), energy burst (e.g., increase in activities), leakage (e.g., telling a third party about the plan), and last resort (e.g., forcing a situation in which violence seems to be the only alternative).

The Virginia Student Threat Assessment Guidelines (V-STAG; Cornell & Sheras, 2006) are a set of comprehensive guidelines designed to aid school administrators in evaluating and responding to threatened school violence. It incorporates a seven-step decision tree (see Cornell, 2013; Cornell & Allen, 2011). A comparison of public high schools using the V-STAG (*n* = 95), some other threat assessment model (*n* = 131), or no threat assessment model (*n* = 54) found reduced bullying, greater willingness of students to seek help, and improved perceptions of school climate in schools adopting the V-STAG (Cornell, Sheras, Gregory, & Fan, 2009). They also found fewer long-term suspensions in schools adopting the V-STAG. Another pre-post implementation study with 49 schools (26 of which had adopted the V-STAG) found a 52% reduction in long-term suspensions and 79% reduction in bullying infractions in schools using the V-STAG. More recently, Cornell, Allen, and Fan (2012) conducted a randomized controlled trial and found significant reductions in the use of long-term suspension and alternative school placement and significant increases in the use of mental health counseling and school parent conferences among schools that had received training and subsequently implemented the V-STAG in comparison to schools assigned to the control condition. Moreover, school personnel have expressed positive attitudes toward the V-STAG and displayed increases in pre-post knowledge of threat assessment and decreases in concerns of school-related homicide (Allen, Cornell, Lorek, & Sheras, 2008).

Conclusions

In sum, the field of adolescent risk assessment has advanced considerably, as has the related field of threat assessment. The following are key recommendations from the literature:

1. When assessing risk of violence and offending, use risk assessment tools rather than relying on unstructured judgments (e.g., Hilterman et al., 2014). This approach offers greater guidance, has better validity, and is more defensible in legal settings (e.g., American Psychological Association, 2013). Similarly, when conducting threat assessments draw from standardized guidelines, such as the V-STAG.
2. Select tools carefully; choose measures that have adequate psychometric properties (Vincent et al., 2009) and which are appropriate for the particular population (e.g., sexually abusive adolescents) and purpose of your evaluation (e.g., screening or comprehensive assessment). Monitor research and new developments in tools.
3. Base risk assessments on multiple sources of information (e.g., interviews with youth and collaterals, and review of justice, mental health, school, and social service records; American Psychological Association, 2013). Interview caregivers whenever possible; they add unique perspectives (De Los Reyes & Kazdin, 2005).
4. Be knowledgeable about developmental factors that may contribute to adolescent offending. For instance, adolescents are less able to resist peer influence and control impulses, and they are oriented to focus on the rewards of behaviors and not the costs (Monahan et al., 2009, 2013). Make active efforts to educate courts about these issues.
5. Develop competence by honing knowledge and skills related to both risk assessment and adolescent psychology (see American Psychological Association, 2013). Psychologists who work primarily with adults are sometimes asked to conduct *adolescent* assessments; in these cases, enhance skills by taking relevant workshops and/or seeking additional clinical supervision.
6. Approach risk assessment as an ongoing process rather than a "one time" event; reassess risk at least every six months if possible, attending to modifiable factors (Vincent, Guy, & Grisso, 2012). An adolescent's risk may change even over relatively short periods of time.
7. Present a balanced perspective of a youth that attends to both risk factors but also protective factors and strengths. This helps to communicate both sides of the coin, and may also generate ideas for interventions (de Ruiter & Nicholls, 2011).
8. Present your findings objectively (e.g., avoid swaying results to satisfy the party that has requested the risk assessment; see Murrie et al., 2013). Also, disclose the limitations of assessments (e.g., no tool can predict with perfect accuracy—see American Psychological Association, 2013).
9. Though it can be useful to assess callous and unemotional features (Frick et al., 2014), avoid labeling youth as "psychopathic" and work to correct misperceptions (e.g., such as the belief that youth with these features are untreatable; Forth et al., 2003).
10. Use your risk assessments to develop clear, precise, and evidence-based intervention plans (Grisso, 2013; Viljoen et al., in press). Remain up-to-date on best practices (e.g., empirically supported interventions) and on services that are locally available.

To advance guidelines for clinical practice, researchers must now move outside the existing "comfort zone" of research questions. Although the ultimate purpose of most risk assessment tools is not only to predict but also to help guide interventions and risk reduction efforts, the vast majority of studies focus on *predictive validity* only. Such studies remain useful, particularly studies that use improved methodologies (e.g., studies that are truly prospective and conducted in real-world contexts). However, beyond this, we need knowledge on topics such as:

- Dynamic changes in risk (e.g., How rapidly does adolescents' risk change and what drives these changes? What is the shelf-life of adolescent risk assessments?)
- Protective factors (e.g., Beyond the protective factors that are included in well-established tools, what other factors can protect against risk? Can protective factors aid risk communication and treatment planning, and if so, how?)
- Implementation outcomes (e.g., Given that even the best tools cannot work if agencies and professionals do not "buy-in" and adhere to them, what training strategies, policies, and other efforts can improve implementation success? How can tools be designed so as to increase their usability?)
- Intervention planning (e.g., To what extent do risk assessments improve service and intervention plans for youth? What strategies can professionals use to further bridge risk assessments to effective risk reduction efforts?)

Providing empirically informed answers to these questions may help the field move forward and ultimately improve the services and interventions that adolescents receive.

Note

1   This estimate is based on PsycInfo searches of studies on risk assessment tools.

References

Aebi, M., Plattner, B., Steinhausen, H.-C., & Bessler, C. (2011). Predicting sexual and nonsexual recidivism in a consecutive sample of juveniles convicted of sexual offences. *Sexual Abuse: Journal of Research and Treatment, 23*, 456–473. doi:10.1177/1079063210384634

Allen, K., Cornell, D., Lorek, E., & Sheras, P. (2008). Response of school personnel to student threat assessment training. *School Effectiveness and School Improvement, 19*, 319–332. doi: 10.1080/09243450802332184

American Psychological Association. (2004, July 19). Amicus brief in *Roper v. Simmons*, 543 U.S. 551 (2005). Retrieved from www.apa.org/about/offices/ogc/amicus/roper.pdf.

American Psychological Association. (2011). Amicus brief in *Coble v. Texas*. Retrieved from www.apa.org/about/offices/ogc/amicus/coble.pdf.

American Psychological Association. (2013). Specialty guidelines for forensic psychology. *American Psychologist, 68*, 7–19. doi:10.1037/a0029889

Andrews, D. A., & Bonta, J. (1995). *The Level of Service Inventory–Revised*. Toronto, ON: Multi-Health Systems.

Andrews, D. A., & Bonta, J. (2010). *The psychology of criminal conduct* (5th ed.). New Providence, NJ: LexisNexis.

Andrews, D. A., Bonta, J., & Hoge, R. D. (1990). Classification for effective rehabilitation: Rediscovering Psychology. *Criminal Justice and Behavior, 17*, 19–52. doi:10.1177/0093854890017001004

Andrews, D. A., Bonta, J., & Wormith, J. S. (2001). *Level of Service Inventory–Saskatchewan Youth Edition*. Toronto, ON: Multi-Health Systems.

Andrews, D. A., Guzzo, L., Raynor, P., Rowe, R. C., Rettinger, L. J., Brews, A., & Wormith, J. S. (2012). Are the major risk/need factors predictive of both female and male reoffending? A test with the eight domains of the Level of Service/Case Management Inventory. *International Journal of Offender Therapy and Comparative Criminology, 56*, 113–133. doi:10.1177/0306624X10395716

Archer, R. P., Buffington-Vollum, J. K., Stredny, R., & Handel, R. W. (2006). A survey of psychological test use patterns among forensic psychologists. *Journal of Personality Assessment, 87*, 84–94. doi:10.1207/s15327752jpa8701_07

Bechtel, K., Lowenkamp, C. T., & Latessa, E. (2007). Assessing the risk of re-offending for juvenile offenders using the Youth Level of Service/Case Management Inventory. *Journal of Offender Rehabilitation, 45*, 85–108. doi:10.1300/J076v45n03_04

Boccaccini, M. T., Murrie, D. C., Clark, J. W., & Cornell, D. G. (2008). Describing, diagnosing, and naming psychopathy: How do youth psychopathy labels influence jurors? *Behavioral Sciences & the Law, 26*, 487–510. doi:10.1002/bsl.821

Bonta, J., Bourgon, G., Rugge, T., Scott, T.L., Yessine, A.K., Gutierrez, L., & Li, J. (2010). *The strategic training initiative in community supervision: Risk–need–responsivity in the real world.* Ottawa, ON: Public Safety Canada. Retrieved from www.publicsafety.gc.ca/.

Borum, R. (2003). Managing at-risk juvenile offenders in the community: Putting evidence-based principles into practice. *Journal of Contemporary Criminal Justice, 19,* 114–137. doi:10.1177/1043986202239745

Borum, R., Bartel, P.A., & Forth, A.E. (2005). Structured assessment of violence risk in youth. In T. Grisso, G. Vincent, & D. Seagrave (Eds.), *Mental health screening and assessment in juvenile justice* (pp. 311–323). New York: Guilford Press.

Borum, R., Bartel, P., & Forth, A. (2006). *Manual for the Structured Assessment for Violence Risk in Youth (SAVRY).* Odessa, FL: Psychological Assessment Resources.

Borum, R., Fein, R., Vossekuil, B., & Berglund, J. (1999). Threat assessment: Defining an approach for evaluating risk of targeted violence. *Behavioral Sciences and the Law, 17,* 323–337. doi:10.1002/(SICI)1099–0798(199907/09)17:3<323::AID-BSL349>3.0.CO;2-G

Borum, R., Lodewijks, H., Bartel, P.A., & Forth, A.E. (2010). Structured Assessment of Violence Risk in Youth (SAVRY). In K. Douglas & R. Otto (Eds.), *Handbook of violence risk assessment* (pp. 63–80). New York: Routledge.

Butts, J.A., & Evans, D.N. (2014). The second American crime drop: Trends in juvenile and youth violence. In W.T. Church II, D. Springer, & A.R. Roberts (Eds.), *Juvenile justice sourcebook* (2nd ed., pp. 61–77). New York: Oxford University Press.

Caldwell, M.F., & Dickinson, C. (2009). Sex offender registration and recidivism in juvenile sexual offenders. *Behavioral Sciences & the Law, 27,* 941–956. doi:10.1002/bsl.907

Caldwell, M.F., Ziemke, M.H., & Vitacco, M.J. (2008). An examination of the sex offender registration and notification act as applied to juveniles: Evaluating the ability to predict sexual recidivism. *Psychology, Public Policy, and Law, 14,* 89–114. doi:10.1037/a0013241

Casey, B.J., Getz, S., & Galvan, A. (2008). The adolescent brain. *Developmental Review, 28,* 62–77. doi:10.1016/j.dr.2007.08.003

Catchpole, R.E.H., & Gretton, H.M., (2003). The predictive validity of risk assessment with violent young offenders: A 1 year examination of criminal outcome. *Criminal Justice & Behavior, 30,* 688–708. doi:10.1177/0093854803256455

Childs, K., Frick, P.J., Ryals, J.S., Jr., Lingonbald, A., & Villio, M.J. (2014). A comparison of empirically based and structured professional judgment estimation of risk using the Structured Assessment of Violence Risk in Youth. *Youth Violence and Juvenile Justice, 12,* 40–57. doi:10.1177/1541204013480368

Chu, C.M., Daffern, M., Thomas, S., & Lim, J.Y. (2012). Violence risk and gang affiliation in youth offenders: A recidivism study. *Psychology, Crime & Law, 18,* 299–315. doi:10.1080/1068316X.2010.481626

Chu, C.M., Ng, K., Fong, J., & Teoh, J. (2012). Assessing youth who sexually offended: The predictive validity of the ERASOR, J-SOAP-II, and YLS/CMI in a non-western context. *Sexual Abuse: A Journal of Research and Treatment, 24,* 153–174. doi:10.1177/1079063211404250

Cicchetti, D.V., & Sparrow, S.A. (1981). Developing criteria for establishing interrater reliability of specific items: Applications to assessment of adaptive behavior. *American Journal of Mental Deficiency, 86,* 127–137.

Cillessen, A.N., & Rose, A.J. (2005). Understanding popularity in the peer system. *Current Directions in Psychological Science, 14,* 102–105. doi:10.1111/j.0963–7214.2005.00343.x

Coble v. Texas, 131 S. Ct. 3030 (2011).

Cornell, D. (2013). The Virginia Student Threat Assessment Guidelines: An empirically supported violence prevention strategy. In N. Böckler, T. Seeger, P. Sitzer, & W. Heitmeyer (Eds.), *School shootings: International research, case studies, and concepts for prevention* (pp. 379–400). New York: Springer.

Cornell, D., & Allen, K. (2011). Development, evaluation, and future directions of the Virginia Student Threat Assessment Guidelines. *Journal of School Violence, 10,* 88–106. doi:10.1080/15388220.2010 .519432

Cornell, D.G., Allen, K., & Fan, X. (2012). A randomized controlled study of the Virginia Student Threat Assessment Guidelines in kindergarten through grade 12. *School Psychology Review, 41,* 100–115.

Cornell, D., & Sheras, P. (2006). *Guidelines for responding to student threats of violence.* Longmont, CO: Sopris West.

Cornell, D., Sheras, P., Gregory, A., & Fan, X. (2009). A retrospective study of school safety conditions in high schools using the Virginia Threat Assessment Guidelines versus alternative approaches. *School Psychology Quarterly, 24*, 119–129. doi:10.1037/a0016182

Cornell, D., G., Sheras, P.L., Kaplan, S., McConville, D., Douglass, J., Elkon, A., . . . Cole, J. (2004). Guidelines for student threat assessment: Field-test findings. *School Psychology review, 33*, 527–546.

Dahl, R. (2001). Affect regulation, brain development, and behavioral/emotional health in adolescence. *CNS Spectrums, 6*, 60–72.

De Los Reyes, A., & Kazdin, A.E. (2005). Informant discrepancies in the assessment of childhood psychopathology: A critical review, theoretical framework, and recommendations for further study. *Psychological Bulletin, 131*, 483–509. doi:10.1037/0033–2909.131.4.483

de Ruiter, C., & Nicholls, T.L. (2011). Protective factors in forensic mental health: A new frontier. *The International Journal of Forensic Mental Health, 10*, 160–170. doi:10.1080/14999013.2011.600602

Desmarais, S.L., Nicholls, T.L., Wilson, C.M., & Brink, J. (2012). Using dynamic risk and protective factors to predict inpatient aggression: Reliability and validity of START assessments. *Psychological Assessment, 24*, 685–700. doi:10.1037/a0026668

Desmarais, S.L., Sellers, B.G., Viljoen, J.L., Cruise, K.R., Nicholls, T.L., & Dvoskin, J.A. (2012). Pilot implementation and preliminary evaluation of START:AV assessments in secure juvenile correctional facilities. *International Journal of Forensic Mental Health, 11*, 150–164. doi:10.1080/14999013.2012.737405

Dolan, M.C., & Rennie, C.E. (2008). The Structured Assessment of Violence Risk in Youth as a predictor of recidivism in a UK cohort of adolescent offenders with conduct disorder. *Psychological Assessment, 20*, 35–46. doi:10.1037/1040–3590.20.1.35

Douglas, K.S., Cox, D.N., & Webster, C.D. (1999). Violence risk assessment: Science and practice. *Legal and Criminological Psychology, 4*, 149–184. doi:10.1348/135532599167824

Douglas, K.S., Hart, S.D., Webster, C.D., & Belfrage, H. (2013). *Historical, Clinical, Risk Management (Version 3): Professional guidelines for evaluating risk of violence.* Burnaby, BC: Mental Health, Law, and Policy Institute.

Douglas, K.S., Skeem, J.L., & Nicholson, E. (2011). Research methods in violence risk assessment. In B. Rosenfeld, & S.D. Penrod (Eds.), *Research methods in forensic psychology* (pp. 325–346). Hoboken, NJ: John Wiley & Sons.

Ægisdóttir, S., White, M.J., Spengler, P.M., Maugherman, A.S., Anderson, L.A., Cook, R.S., . . . Rush, J.D. (2006). The meta-analysis of clinical judgment project: Fifty-six years of accumulated research on clinical versus statistical prediction. *The Counseling Psychologist, 34*, 341–382. doi:10.1177/0011000005285875

Enzmann, D., Marshall, I.H., Killias, M., Junger-Tas, J., Steketee, M., & Gruszczynska, B. (2010). Self-reported youth delinquency in Europe and beyond: First results of the Second International Self-Report Delinquency Study in the context of police and victimization data. *European Journal of Criminology, 7*, 159–183. doi:10.1177/1477370809358018

Epperson, D.L., Ralston, C.A., Fowers, D., DeWitt, J., & Gore, K.S. (2006). Actuarial risk assessment with juveniles who sexually offend: Development of the Juvenile Sexual Offense Recidivism Risk Assessment Tool-II (JSORRAT-II). In D.S. Prescott (Ed.), *Risk assessment of youth who have sexually abused* (pp. 118–169). Oklahoma City, OK: Wood 'N' Barnes.

Fanniff, A.M., & Letourneau, E.J. (2012). Another piece of the puzzle: Psychometric properties of the J-SOAP-II. *Sexual Abuse: A Journal of Research and Treatment, 24*, 378–408. doi:10.1177/1079063211431842

Farrington, D.P., Loeber, R., & Jolliffe, D. (2008). The age-crime curve in reported offending. In R. Loeber, D.P. Farrington, M. Stouthamer-Loeber, & H. White (Eds.), *Violence and serious theft: Development and prediction from childhood to adulthood* (pp. 77–104). New York: Routledge/Taylor & Francis Group.

Flores, A.W., Travis, L.F., & Latessa, E.J. (2003). *Case classification for juvenile corrections: An assessment of the Youth Level of Service/Case Management Inventory (YLS/CMI): Final report.* Washington, DC: National Institute of Justice.

Forth, A.E., Kosson, D.S., & Hare, R.D. (2003). *Hare Psychopathy Checklist: Youth Version.* Toronto, ON: Multi-Health Systems.

Frick, P.J., Ray, J.V., Thornton, L.C., & Kahn, R.E. (2014). Can callous-unemotional traits enhance the understanding, diagnosis, and treatment of serious conduct problems in children and adolescents? A comprehensive review. *Psychological Bulletin, 140*, 1–57. doi:10.1037/a0033076

Gammelgård, M., Koivisto, A., Eronen, M., & Kaltiala-Heino, R. (2008). The predictive validity of the Structured Assessment of Violence Risk in Youth (SAVRY) among institutionalised adolescents. *Journal of Forensic Psychiatry & Psychology*, *19*(3), 352–370. doi:10.1080/14789940802114475

Gammelgård, M., Weizmann-Henelius, G., Koivisto, A. M., Eronen, M., & Kaltiala-Heino, R. (2012). Gender differences in violence risk profiles. *The Journal of Forensic Psychiatry & Psychology*, *23*, 76–94. doi:10.1080/14789949.2011.639898

Grisso, T. (1998). *Forensic evaluation of juveniles*. Sarasota, FL: Professional Resource Press/Professional Resource Exchange.

Grisso, T. (2013). *Forensic evaluation of juveniles* (2nd ed.). Sarasota, FL: Professional Resource Press/Professional Resource Exchange.

Guy, L. S. (2008). *Performance indicators of the structured professional judgment approach for assessing risk for violence to others: A meta-analytic survey*. Doctoral dissertation. Simon Fraser University, Burnaby, BC. Retrieved from ProQuest Dissertations and Theses database (UMI No. NR58733).

Guy, L. S., Fusco, S., Hilterman, E., & Vincent, G. (2011). *Experiences using the SAVRY in the field: A comparison of Spanish clinicians and American probation officers*. Paper presented at the annual conference of the International Association of Forensic Mental Health Services, Barcelona, Spain.

Hanley, J., & McNeil, B. (1982). The meaning and use of the area under a receiver operating characteristic (ROC) curve. *Radiology*, *143*(1), 29–36.

Hannah-Moffat, K., & Maurutto, P. (2004) *Youth risk/needs assessment: An overview of issues and practices*. Ottawa, ON: Department of Justice.

Hanson, R. K., & Thornton, D. (1999). *Static–99: Improving actuarial risk assessments for sex offenders* (User Rep. No. 1999–02). Ottawa, ON: Department of the Solicitor General of Canada.

Hart, S. D., Kropp, P. R., Laws, D. R., Klaver, J., Logan, C., & Watt, K. A. (2003). *The Risk for Sexual Violence Protocol (RSVP): Structured professional guidelines for assessing risk of sexual violence*. Burnaby, BC: Mental Health, Law, and Policy Institute, Simon Fraser University.

Hart, S. D., & Logan, C. (2011). Formulation of violence risk using evidence-based assessments: The structured professional judgment approach. In P. Sturmey & M. McMurran (Eds.), *Forensic case formulation* (pp. 83–106). Chichester, UK: Wiley-Blackwell.

Hart, S., Sturmey, P., Logan, C., & McMurran, M. (2011). Forensic case formulation. *The International Journal of Forensic Mental Health*, *10*, 118–126. doi:10.1080/14999013.2011.577137

Hempel, I., Buck, N., Cima, M., & van Marle, H. (2013). Review of risk assessment instruments for juvenile sex offenders: What is next? *International Journal of Offender Therapy and Comparative Criminology*, *57*, 208–228. doi:10.1177/0306624X11428315

Henggeler, S. W., & Sheidow, A. J. (2012). Empirically supported family-based treatments for conduct disorder and delinquency in adolescents. *Journal of Marital and Family Therapy*, *38*, 30–58. doi:10.1111/j.1752–0606.2011.00244.x

Hersant, J. L. (2006). *Risk assessment of juvenile sex offender reoffense*. Doctoral dissertation. Southern Illinois University, Carbondale. Retrieved from ProQuest Dissertations and Theses database (UMI No. 3229832).

Hilterman, E. L. B., Nicholls, T. L., & van Nieuwenhuizen, C. (2014). Predictive validity of the risk assessments in juvenile offenders: Comparing the SAVRY, PCL:YV, and YLS/CMI with unstructured clinical assessments. *Assessment*, *21*(3), 324-339. doi:10.1177/1073191113498113

Hoge, R. D. (2005). Youth Level of Services/Case Management Inventory. In T. Grisso, G. Vincent, & D. Seagrave (Eds.), *Mental health screening and assessment in juvenile justice* (pp. 283–294). New York: Guildford Press.

Hoge, R. D., & Andrews, D. A. (2002). *The Youth Level of Service/Case Management Inventory manual and scoring key*. Toronto, ON: Multi-Health Systems.

Hoge, R. D., & Andrews, D. A. (2011). *Youth Level of Service/Case Management Inventory 2.0 (YLS/CMI 2.0): User's Manual*. Toronto, ON: Multi-Health Systems.

Johnson, K. L., Desmarais, S. L., Rajagopalan, R., Sellers, B. G., & Singh, J. P. (2014, March). *Validity of START:AV assessments in predicting adverse outcomes in incarcerated youth*. Poster presented at the American Psychology-Law Society Conference, New Orleans, Louisiana.

King, R. D., Massoglia, M., & Macmillan, R. (2007). The context of marriage and crime: Gender, the propensity to marry, and offending in early adulthood. *Criminology: An Interdisciplinary Journal*, *45*, 33–65. doi:10.1111/j.1745–9125.2007.00071.x

Kroner, D. G., Mills, J. F., & Reddon, J. R. (2005). A coffee can, factor analysis, and prediction of antisocial behavior: The structure of criminal risk. *International Journal of Law and Psychiatry, 28*, 360–374. doi:10.1016/j.ijlp.2004.01.011

Lacourse, E., Nagin, D., Tremblay, R. E., Vitaro, F., & Claes, M. (2003). Developmental trajectories of boys' delinquent group membership and facilitation of violent behaviors during adolescence. *Development and Psychopathology, 15*, 183–197. doi:10.1017/S0954579403000105

Lidz, C. W., Mulvey, E. P., & Gardner, W. (1993). The accuracy of predictions of violence to others. *JAMA: The Journal of the American Medical Association, 269*, 1007–1011. doi:10.1001/jama.1993.03500080055032

Lipsey, M. W., & Derzon, J. H. (1998). Predictors of violent or serious delinquency in adolescence and early adulthood: A synthesis of longitudinal research. In R. Loeber & D. P. Farrington (Eds.), *Serious & violent juvenile offenders: Risk factors and successful interventions* (pp. 86–105). Thousand Oaks, CA: Sage.

Lipsey, M. W. & Landenberger, N. A. (2005). Cognitive behavioral interventions: A meta-analysis of randomized controlled studies. In B.C. Welsh & D. P. Farrington (Eds.), *Preventing crime: What works for children, offenders, victims, and places*. Berlin, Heidelberg, & New York: Springer

Lodewijks, H.P.B., de Ruiter, C., & Doreleijers, T.A.H. (2008). Gender differences in violent outcome and risk assessment in adolescent offenders after residential treatment. *International Journal of Forensic Mental Health, 7*, 133–146. doi:10.1080/14999013.2008.9914410

Lodewijks, H.P.B., de Ruiter, C., & Doreleijers, T.A.H. (2010). The impact of protective factors in desistance from violent reoffending: A study in three samples of adolescent offenders. *Journal of Interpersonal Violence, 25*, 568–587. doi:10.1177/0886260509334403

Luong, D., & Wormith, J. S. (2011). Applying risk/need assessment to probation practice and its impact on the recidivism of young offenders. *Criminal Justice and Behavior, 38*, 1177–1199. doi:10.1177/0093854811421596

Lynam, D. R., Caspi, A., Moffitt, T. E., Loeber, R., & Stouthamer-Loeber, M. (2007). Longitudinal evidence that psychopathy scores in early adolescence predict adult psychopathy. *Journal of Abnormal Psychology, 116*, 155–165. doi:10.1037/0021–843X.116.1.155

Mack, J. W. (1909). The juvenile court. *Harvard Law Review, 23*, 104–122. Retrieved from http://heinonline.org.

Marczyk, G. R., Heilbrun, K., Lander, T., Dematteo, D. (2005). Juvenile decertification: Developing a model for classification and prediction. *Criminal Justice and Behavior, 32*, 278–301. doi:10.1177/0093854804274371

Marshall, J., Egan, V., English, M., & Jones, R. M. (2006). The relative validity of psychopathy versus risk/needs-based assessments in the prediction of adolescent offending behaviour. *Legal and Criminological Psychology, 11*, 197–210. doi:10.1348/135532505X68719

Martinez, R., Flores, J., & Rosenfeld, B. (2007). Validity of the Juvenile Sex Offender Assessment Protocol-II (J-SOAP-II) in a sample of urban minority youth. *Criminal Justice and Behavior, 34*, 1284–1295. doi:10.1177/0093854807301791

McCann, K., & Lussier, P. (2008). Antisociality, sexual deviance, and sexual reoffending in juvenile sex offenders: A meta-analytical investigation. *Youth Violence and Juvenile Justice, 6*, 363–385. doi:10.1177/1541204008320260

McGowan, M. R., Horn, R. A., & Mellott, R. N. (2011). The predictive validity of the Structured Assessment of Violence Risk in Youth in secondary educational settings. *Psychological Assessment, 23*, 478–486. doi:10.1037/a0022304

McGrath, R. J., Cumming, G. F., Burchard, B. L., Zeoli, S., & Ellerby, L. (2010). *Current practices and emerging trends in sexual abuser management: The Safer Society 2009 North American Survey*. Brandon, VT: Safer Society Press.

Meloy, J. R., Hart, S. D., & Hoffmann, J. (2014). Threat assessment and threat management. In J. R. Meloy & J. Hoffmann (Eds.), *International handbook of threat assessment* (pp. 3–17). New York: Oxford University Press.

Meloy, J. R., Hoffmann, J., Guldimann, A., & James, D. (2012). The role of warning behaviors in threat assessment: An exploration and suggested typology. *Behavioral Sciences and the Law, 30*, 256–279. doi:10.1002/bsl.999

Moffitt, T. E. (1993). Adolescence-limited and life-course persistent antisocial behavior: A developmental taxonomy. *Psychological Review, 100*, 674–701. doi:10.1037/0033–295X.100.4.674

Moffitt, T.E. (2006). Life-course persistent and adolescent-limited antisocial behavior. In D. Cic-chetti & D.J. Cohen (Eds.), *Developmental psychopathology, Vol. 3: Risk, disorder, and adaptation* (pp. 570–598). New York: Wiley.

Moffitt, T.E., Caspi, A., Harrington, H., & Milne, B.J. (2002). Males on the life-course-persistent and adolescence-limited antisocial pathways: Follow-up at age 26 years. *Development and Psychopathology, 14*, 179–207. doi:10.1017/S0954579402001104

Monahan, K.C., Steinberg, L., Cauffman, E., & Mulvey, E.P. (2009). Trajectories of antisocial behavior and psychosocial maturity from adolescence to young adulthood. *Developmental Psychology, 45*, 1654–1668. doi:10.1037/a0015862

Monahan, K.C., Steinberg, L., Cauffman, E., & Mulvey, E.P. (2013). Psychosocial (im)maturity from adolescence to early adulthood: Distinguishing between adolescence-limited and persisting antisocial behavior. *Development and Psychopathology, 25*, 1093–1105. doi:10.1017/S0954579413000394

Morton, K.E. (2003). *Psychometric properties of four risk assessment measures with male adolescent sexual offenders*. Master's thesis. Carleton University, Ottawa, ON. Retrieved from ProQuest Dissertations and Theses database (UMI No. MQ79677).

Murrie, D.C., Boccaccini, M.T., Guarnera, L.A., & Rufino, K.A. (2013). Are forensic experts biased by the side that retained them? *Psychological Science, 24*, 1889–1897. doi:10.1177/09567976 13481812

Murrie, D.C., Boccaccini, M.T., McCoy, W., & Cornell, D.G. (2007). Diagnostic labeling in juvenile court: How do descriptions of psychopathy and conduct disorder influence judges? *Journal of Clinical Child and Adolescent Psychology, 36*, 228–241. doi:10.1080/15374410701279602

Murrie, D.C., Boccaccini, M.T., Turner, D.B., Meeks, M., Woods, C., & Tussey, C. (2009). Rater (dis) agreement on risk assessment measures in sexually violent predator proceedings: Evidence of adversarial allegiance in forensic evaluation? *Psychology, Public Policy, and Law, 15*, 19–53. doi:10.1037/a0014897

National Center for Juvenile Justice (2012). State juvenile justice profiles, 2005. Retrieved from www.ncjj. org/Publication/State-Juvenile-Justice-Profiles-2005.aspx.

Nelson, R. (2011). *Predicting recidivism among juvenile sex offenders: The validity of the ERASOR*. Master's thesis. Roger Williams University, Bristol, RI. Retrieved from http://docs.rwu.edu/cgi/viewcontent. cgi?article=1012&context=psych_thesis.

Nicholls, T.L., Viljoen, J.L., Cruise, K.R., Desmarais, S.L., & Webster, C.D. (2010). *Short-Term Assessment of Risk and Treatability: Adolescent Version (START:AV) (abbreviated manual)*. Coquitlam: BC Mental Health and Addiction Services.

Olver, M.E., Stockdale, K.C., & Wormith, J.S. (2009). Risk assessment with young offenders: A meta-analysis of three assessment measures. *Criminal Justice and Behavior, 36*, 329–353. doi:10.1177/0093854809331457

Olver, M.E., Stockdale, K.C., & Wormith, J.S. (2014). Thirty years of research on the Level of Service scales: A meta-analytic examination of predictive accuracy and sources of variability. *Psychological Assessment, 26*, 156–176. doi:10.1037/a0035080

Olver, M.E., Stockdale, K.C., & Wong, S.C.P. (2012). Short and long-term prediction of recidivism using the Youth Level of Service/Case Management Inventory in a sample of serious young offenders. *Law and Human Behavior, 36*, 331–344. doi:10.1037/h0093927

O'Shea, L.E., & Dickens, G.L. (2014). Short-Term Assessment of Risk and Treatability (START): Systematic review and meta-analysis. *Psychological Assessment, 26*(3), 990–1002. doi:10.1037/a0036794

Parks, G.A., & Bard, D.E. (2006). Risk factors for adolescent sex offender recidivism: Evaluation of predictive factors and comparison of three groups based upon victim type. *Sexual Abuse: A Journal of Research and Treatment, 18*, 319–342. doi:10.1007/s11194–006–9028-x

Penney, S.R., Lee, Z., & Moretti, M.M. (2010). Gender differences in risk factors for violence: An examination of the predictive validity of the Structured Assessment of Violence Risk in Youth. *Aggressive Behavior, 36*, 390–404. doi:10.1002/ab.20352

Piquero, A.R. (2008). Taking stock of developmental trajectories on criminal activity over the life course. In A. Liberman (Ed.), *The long view of crime: A synthesis of longitudinal research*. New York: Springer.

Piquero, A.R., & Steinberg, L. (2010). Public preferences for rehabilitation versus incarceration of juvenile offenders. *Journal of Criminal Justice, 38*, 1–6. doi:10.1016/j.jcrimjus.2009.11.001

Poluchowicz, S., Jung, S., & Rawana, E.P. (2000). *The interrater reliability of the Ministry Risk/Need Assessment form for juvenile offenders*. Paper presented at the annual conference of the Canadian Psychological Association, Montreal, Quebec.

Prentky, R.A., Li, N., Righthand, S., Schuler, A., Cavanaugh, D., & Lee, A.F. (2010). Assessing risk of sexually abusive behavior among youth in a child welfare sample. *Behavioral Sciences & the Law, 28*, 24–45. doi:10.1002/bsl.920

Prentky, R. A., & Righthand, S. (2003). *Juvenile Sex Offender Assessment Protocol II (J-SOAP-II) Manual.* Washington, DC: U.S. Department of Justice, Office of Justice Programs, Office of Juvenile Justice and Delinquency Prevention.

Proctor, E., Silmere, H., Raghavan, R., Hovmand, P., Aarons, G., Bunger, A., & . . . Hensley, M. (2011). Outcomes for implementation research: Conceptual distinctions, measurement challenges, and research agenda. *Administration and Policy in Mental Health and Mental Health Services Research, 38*, 65–76. doi:10.1007/s10488–010–0319–7

Quinsey, V.L., Harris, G.T., Rice, M.E., & Cormier, C.A. (2006). *Violent offenders: Appraising and managing risk* (2nd ed.). Washington, DC: American Psychological Association.

Rajlic, G., & Gretton, H.M. (2010). An examination of two sexual recidivism risk measures in adolescent offenders: The moderating effect of offender type. *Criminal Justice and Behavior, 37*, 1066–1085. doi:10.1177/0093854810376354

Reddy, M., Borum, R., Berglund, J., Vossekuil, B., Fein, R., & Modzeleski, W. (2001). Evaluating risk for targeted violence in schools: Comparing risk assessment, threat assessment, and other approaches. *Psychology in the Schools, 38*, 157–172. doi:10.1002/pits.1007

Rehfuss, M.C., Underwood, L.A., Enright, M., Hill, S., Marshall, R., Tipton, P., . . . Warren, K. (2013). Treatment impact of an integrated sex offender program as measured by J-SOAP-II. *Journal of Correctional Health Care, 19*, 113–123. doi:10.1177/1078345812474641

Righthand, S., Prentky, R., Knight, R., Carpenter, E., Hecker, J.E., & Nangle, D. (2005). Factor structure and validation of the Juvenile Sex Offender Assessment Protocol (J-SOAP). *Sexual Abuse: A Journal of Research and Treatment, 17*, 13–30. doi:10.1007/s11194–005–1207–7

Rogers, R. (2000). The uncritical acceptance of risk assessment in forensic practice. *Law and Human Behavior, 24*, 595–605. doi:10.1023/A:1005575113507

Roisman, G.I., Monahan, K.C., Campbell, S.B., Steinberg, L., & Cauffman, E., & the National Institute of Child Health and Human Development Early Child Care Research Network (2010). Is adolescence-onset antisocial behavior developmentally normative? *Development and Psychopathology, 22*, 295–311. doi:10.1017/S0954579410000076

Roper v. Simmons, 543 U.S. 551 (2005).

Salekin, R.T., Worley, C., & Grimes, R.D. (2010). Treatment of psychopathy: A review and brief introduction to the mental model approach for psychopathy. *Behavioral Sciences & the Law, 28*, 235–266. doi:10.1002/bsl.928

Schmidt, F., Campbell, M.A., & Houlding, C. (2011). Comparative analyses of the YLS/CMI, SAVRY, and PCL:YV in adolescent offenders: A 10-year follow-up into adulthood. *Youth Violence and Juvenile Justice, 9*, 23–42. doi:10.1177/1541204010371793

Schmidt, F., Hoge, R.D., & Gomes, L. (2005). Reliability and validity analyses of the Youth Level of Service/Case Management Inventory. *Criminal Justice and Behavior, 32*, 329–344. doi:10.1177/0093854804274373

Schwalbe, C.S. (2007). Risk assessment for juvenile justice: A meta-analysis. *Law and Human Behavior, 31*, 449–462. doi:10.1007/s10979–006–9071–7

Schwalbe, C.S. (2008). A meta-analysis of juvenile justice risk assessment instruments: Predictive validity by gender. *Criminal Justice and Behavior, 35*, 1367–1381. doi:10.1177/0093854808324377

Schwalbe, C.S., Fraser, M.W., Day, S.H., & Arnold, E. (2004). North Carolina Assessment of Risk (NCAR): Reliability and predictive validity with juvenile offenders. *Journal of Offender Rehabilitation, 40*, 1–22. doi:10.1300/J076v40n01_01

Scott, E.S., & Steinberg, L. (2008). Adolescent development and the regulation of youth crime. *Future of Children, 18*, 15–33. doi:10.1353/foc.0.0011

Seagrave, D., & Grisso, T. (2002). Adolescent development and the measurement of juvenile psychopathy. *Law and Human Behavior, 26*, 219–239. doi:10.1023/A:1014696110850

Search Institute (2004). *Developmental Assets Profile: Preliminary user manual.* Minneapolis, MN: Author.

Sellers, B., Desmarais, S., Dvoskin, J., Viljoen, J.L., Cruise, K., & Nicholls, T. (2012, March). *Change in dynamic items and risk estimates over time: Findings from a pilot implementation of the START-AV.* Poster presented at the American Psychology-Law Society Conference, San Juan, Puerto Rico.

Shepherd, S.M., Luebbers, S., & Dolan, M. (2013). Gender and ethnicity in juvenile risk assessment. *Criminal Justice and Behavior, 40*, 388–408. doi:10.1177/0093854812456776

Sher, M., & Gralton, E. (in press). Implementation of the START:AV in a secure adolescent service. *Journal of Forensic Practice*.

Sher, M., McLean, A., Rowe, K., Warner, L., Gralton, E., Nicholls, T., Viljoen, J.L., & Cruise, K. (2013). *The Short-Term Assessment of Risk and Treatability (START) for Adolescents: A prospective validation study in a forensic psychiatric adolescent sample*. Paper presented at the International Association of Forensic Mental Health Services Conference, Maastrict, The Netherlands.

Singh, J.P., Desmarais, S.L., Sellers, B.G., Hylton, T., Tirotti, M., & Van Dorn, R.A. (2014). From risk assessment to risk management: Matching interventions to adolescent offenders' strengths and vulnerabilities. *Children and Youth Services Review, 47*(Part 1), 1–9. doi:10.1016/j.childyouth.2013.09.015

Singh, J.P., Grann, M., & Fazel, S. (2011). A comparative study of violence risk assessment tools: A systematic review and metaregression analysis of 68 studies involving 25,980 participants. *Clinical Psychology Review, 31*, 499–513. doi:10.1016/j.cpr.2010.11.009

Skeem, J.L., & Monahan, J. (2011). Current directions in violence risk assessment. *Current Directions in Psychological Science, 20*, 38–42. doi:10.1177/0963721410397271

Skowron, C. (2005). *Differentiation and predictive factors in adolescent sexual offending*. Doctoral dissertation. Carleton University, Ottawa, ON. Retrieved from ProQuest Dissertations and Theses database (UMI No. NR00807).

Steinberg, L. (2010). Commentary: A behavioral scientist looks at the science of adolescent brain development. *Brain and Cognition, 72*, 160–164. doi:10.1016/j.bandc.2009.11.003.

Steinberg, L., Albert, D., Cauffman, E., Banich, M., Graham, S., & Woolard, J. (2008). Age differences in sensation seeking and impulsivity as indexed by behavior and self-report: Evidence for a dual systems model. *Developmental Psychology, 44*, 1764–1778. doi:10.1037/a0012955

Steinberg, L., & Monahan, K.C. (2007). Age differences in resistance to peer influence. *Developmental Psychology, 43*, 1531–1543. doi:10.1037/0012-1649.43.6.1531

Stockdale, K.C., Olver, M.E., & Wong, S.P. (2014). The validity and reliability of the Violence Risk Scale–Youth Version in a diverse sample of violent young offenders. *Criminal Justice And Behavior, 41*(1), 114–138.

Sweeten, G., Piquero, A.R., & Steinberg, L. (2013). Age and the explanation of crime, revisited. *Journal of Youth and Adolescence, 42*, 921–938. doi:10.1007/s10964-013-9926-4

Takahashi, M., Mori, T., & Kroner, D.G. (2013). A cross-validation of the Youth Level of Service/Case Management Inventory (YLS/CMI) among Japanese juvenile offenders. *Law and Human Behavior, 37*, 389–400. doi:10.1037/1hb0000029

Thompson, A.P., & McGrath, A. (2012). Subgroup differences and implications for contemporary risk-need assessment with juvenile offenders. *Law and Human Behavior, 36*, 345–355. doi:10.1037/h0093930

Urquhart, T.A., & Viljoen, J.L. (2014). The use of the SAVRY and YLS/CMI in adolescent court proceedings: A case law review. *International Journal of Forensic Mental Health, 13*, 47–61. doi:10.1080/14999013.2014.885470

Vieira, T.A., Skilling, T.A., & Peterson-Badali, M. (2009). Matching court-ordered services with treatment needs: Predicting treatment success with young offenders. *Criminal Justice and Behavior, 36*, 385–401. doi:10.1177/0093854808331249

Viljoen, J.L. (2014). *Adolescent risk reduction and resilient outcomes work-plan*. Unpublished guide. Simon Fraser University, Burnaby, BC.

Viljoen, J., Beneteau, J., Brodersen, E., Gulbransen, E., Cruise, K., Nicholls, T. . . . & Douglas, K. (2012, April). *Assessing protective factors in adolescent offenders: A comparison of the SAVRY, YLS/CMI, and START:AV*. Paper presented at the International Association of Forensic Mental Health Services Conference, Miami, FL.

Viljoen, J.L., Beneteau, J.L., Gulbransen, E., Brodersen, E., Desmarais, S.L., Nicholls, T.L., & Cruise, K.R. (2012). Assessment of multiple risk outcomes, strengths, and change with the START:AV: A short-term prospective study with adolescent offenders. *International Journal of Forensic Mental Health, 11*, 165–180. doi:10.1080/14999013.2012.737407

Viljoen, J.L., Brodersen, E., Shaffer, C., & McMahon, R.J. (in press). Risk reduction interventions for adolescent offenders. In K. Heilbrun, D. DeMatteo, & N. Goldstein (Eds.), *APA handbook of psychology and juvenile justice*.

Viljoen, J. L., Brodersen, E., Shaffer, C., Muir, N., & ARROW Advisory Team. (2014). *Adolescent Risk Reduction and Resilient Outcomes Work-Plan*. Burnaby, BC: Simon Fraser University.

Viljoen, J. L., Cruise, K. R., Nicholls, T. L., Desmarais, S. L., & Webster, C. D. with contributions by Beneteau, J. L., Petersen, K. Barone, C. & Fusco-Morin, S. (in progress). *Short-Term Assessment of Risk and Treatability: Adolescent Version, Knowledge Guide.*

Viljoen, J. L., Elkovitch, N., Scalora, M. J., & Ullman, D. (2009). Assessment of reoffense risk in adolescents who have committed sexual offenses: Predictive validity of the ERASOR, PCL:YV, YLS/CMI, and Static-99. *Criminal Justice and Behavior, 36*, 981–1000. doi:10.1177/0093854809340991

Viljoen, J. L., McLachlan, K., & Vincent, G. M. (2010). Assessing violence risk and psychopathy in juvenile and adult offenders: A survey of clinical practices. *Assessment, 17*, 377–395. doi:10.1177/1073191109359587

Viljoen, J. L., Mordell, S., & Beneteau, J. L. (2012). Prediction of adolescent sexual reoffending: A meta-analysis of the J-SOAP-II, ERASOR, J-SORRAT-II, and Static-99. *Law and Human Behavior, 36*, 423–438. doi:10.1037/h0093938

Viljoen, J. L., Nicholls, T. L., Cruise, K. R., Desmarais, S. L., & Webster, C. D. with contributions by Douglas-Beneteau, J. (2014). *Short-Term Assessment of Risk and Treatability: Adolescent Version (START:AV)—User Guide.* Burnaby, BC: Mental Health, Law, and Policy Institute.

Viljoen, J. L., Scalora, M., Cuadra, L., Bader, S., Chávez, Ullman, D., & Lawrence, L. (2008). Assessing risk for violence in adolescents who have sexually offended: A comparison of the J-SOAP-II, J-SORRAT-II, and SAVRY. *Criminal Justice and Behavior, 35*, 5–23. doi:10.1177/0093854807307521

Vincent, G. M., Chapman, J., & Cook, N. E. (2011). Risk-needs assessment in juvenile justice: Predictive validity of the SAVRY, racial differences, and contribution of need factors. *Criminal Justice and Behavior, 38*, 42–62. doi:10.1177/0093854810386000

Vincent, G. M., Guy, L. S., Fusco, S. L., Gershenson, B. G. (2012). Field reliability of the SAVRY with juvenile probation officers: Implications for training. *Law and Human Behavior, 36*, 225–236. doi:10.1037/h0093974

Vincent, G. M., Guy, L. S., Gershenson, B. G., & McCabe, P. (2012). Does risk assessment make a difference? Results of implementing the SAVRY in juvenile probation. *Behavioral Sciences in the Law, 30*, 384–405. doi:10.1002/bsl.2014

Vincent, G. M., Guy, L. S., Grisso, T. (2012). *Risk assessment in juvenile justice: A guidebook for implementation.* Chicago: John D. and Catherine T. MacArthur Foundation.

Vincent, G. M., Paiva-Salisbury, M. L., Cook, N. E., Guy, L. S., & Perrault, R. T. (2012). Impact of risk/needs assessment on juvenile probation officers' decision making: Importance of implementation. *Psychology, Public Policy, and Law, 18*, 549–576. doi:10.1037/a0027186

Vincent, G. M., Terry, A. M., & Maney, S. M. (2009). Risk/needs tools for antisocial behavior and violence among youthful populations. In J. T. Andrade (Ed.), *Handbook of violence risk assessment and treatment: New approaches for mental health professionals* (pp. 337–424). New York: Springer.

Webster, C. D., Nicholls, T. L., Martin, M.-L., Desmarais, S. L., & Brink, J. (2006). Short-Term Assessment of Risk and Treatability (START): The case for a new structured professional judgment scheme. *Behavioral Sciences & the Law, 24*, 747–766. doi:10.1002/bsl.737

Welsh, J. L., Schmidt, F., McKinnon, L., Cattha, H. K., & Meyers, J. R. (2008). A comparative study of adolescent risk assessment instruments: Predictive and incremental validity. *Assessment, 15*, 104–115. doi:10.1177/1073191107307966

Werth, J. L., Welfel, E., & Benjamin, G. H. (2009). *The duty to protect: Ethical, legal, and professional considerations for mental health professionals.* Washington, DC: American Psychological Association. doi:10.1037/11866-000

Wiebe, D. J., Blackstone, M. M., Mollen, C. J., Culyba, A. J., & Fein, J. A. (2011). Self-reported violence-related outcomes for adolescents within eight weeks of emergency department treatment for assault injury. *Journal of Adolescent Health, 49*, 440–442. doi:10.1016/j.jadohealth.2011.01.009

Wong, S., Lewis, K., Stockdale, K., & Gordon, A. (2011). *The Violence Risk Scale-Youth Version.* Unpublished manuscript. University of Saskatchewan, Saskatoon.

Worling, J. R. (2004). The Estimate of Risk of Adolescent Sexual Offense Recidivism (ERASOR): Preliminary psychometric data. *Sexual Abuse: A Journal of Research and Treatment, 16*, 235–254. doi:10.1023/B:SEBU.0000029135.53374.0d

Worling, J. R. (2013). *Desistence for Adolescents Who Sexually Harm (DASH-13).* Unpublished document. Sexual Abuse: Family Education and Treatment Program, Toronto, ON.

Worling, J. R., Bookalam, D., & Litteljohn, A. (2012). Prospective validity of the Estimate of Risk of Adolescent Sexual Offense Recidivism (ERASOR). *Sexual Abuse: A Journal of Research and Treatment, 24*, 203–223. doi:10.1177/1079063211407080

Worling, J. R., & Curwen, T. (2001). *Estimate of Risk of Adolescent Sexual Offense Recidivism, Version 2.0.* Toronto, ON: Ontario Ministry of Community and Social Services.

Yang, M., Wong, S. P., & Coid, J. (2010). The efficacy of violence prediction: A meta-analytic comparison of nine risk assessment tools. *Psychological Bulletin, 136,* 740–767. doi:10.1037/a0020473

Zeng, G., Chu, C. M., Koh, L. L., & Teoh, J. (2014). Risk and criminogenic needs of youth who sexually offended in Singapore: An examination of two typologies. *Sexual Abuse: A Journal of Research and Treatment.* Advance online publication. doi:10.1177/1079063213520044

Part IV
Civil Forensic Assessment

16 Child Custody Evaluations

Robert A. Zibbell and Geri Fuhrmann

Separation and divorce are all-too-frequent experiences in modern life. Recent national surveys indicate that between 40% and 50% of first marriages will end in divorce within 20 years (U.S. Department of Health and Human Services, 2012). Second marriages and cohabiting couples have higher rates of separations or divorce than first marriages (U.S. Department of Health and Human Services, 2002). When parents with minor children end their relationships, they must decide issues related to the children's care, including residence, parenting plan, financial support, and which parent has decision-making authority. These are challenging decisions for anyone, but particularly when the parental relationship is acrimonious. Most parents, however, are able to negotiate the details of their separation, including child-pertinent issues, often with the help of mediators and/or attorneys (Maccoby & Mnookin, 1992). While most parents settle their disputes without trial (Melton, Petrilla, Poythress, & Slobogin, 2007), a small percentage is unable to do so and proceed to trial. If there are child-related issues (e.g., parenting time or decision-making authority), the Court may order an evaluation by a forensic mental health professional to provide psychological expertise on issues relevant to child custody. This chapter concerns the nature of that evaluation, popularly called a *child custody evaluation*. It is a type of forensic mental health assessment in the legal context of parental separation and divorce (when parents are married) or in the context of a paternity proceeding (when parents never married). After parental separation, the children will most likely spend time with each parent according to a parenting schedule, whether that is self-determined by the parents or ordered by the Court. To start, we will briefly review some of the historical social and legal changes with respect to divorce law and child custody and consider a systematic way to conceptualize a forensic mental health assessment in the context of child custody disputes in the 21st century.

Historical Context

Postrevolutionary America had an agrarian-based economy. As such, family members were involved in the maintenance of the farm and children were an economic asset, as well as a responsibility. Carrying over the English Common Law tradition, fathers had exclusive authority over children and property (DiFonzo, 2014). Divorce was infrequent and resulted in the father having the care and responsibility for his children, even if he had exhibited moral failings (Mason, 1994). As industrialization and urbanization increased during the late 19th century, work became more independent of family life. Fathers became "marketplace earners," and mothers assumed greater domestic caregiving responsibilities (DiFonzo, 2014). Statutes and case law reflected these social changes, as mothers came to be seen as "instinctive custodians for both young children and those with disabilities" (DiFonzo, 2014, p. 214). The *tender years presumption*, closely related to *maternal preference*, refers to the notion that young children require the care of their mothers, absent evidence of moral laxity. The belief that mothers are uniquely capable of caring for young children was widely held. It dominated legal practice until the 1960s and resulted in mothers obtaining custody of children following divorce (Grossberg, 1985).

The glorification of motherhood continued through the first two-thirds of the 20th century, when converging social-cultural changes began a shift in thinking about gender-related roles in society. More women moved into the paid labor force. There was a steady increase in the divorce rate (Weitzman, 1985), and, along with that, divorced/separated fathers began to demand greater equity in the raising of their children (Crowley, 2008). These changing domestic values are reflected in *Watts v. Watts* (1973), in which a New York Court opined, "The simple fact of being a mother does not, by itself, indicate a capacity or a willingness to render a quality of care different from that which the father can provide" (p. 181).

Law reflects changes in the society at large. By 2010, all state legislatures had enacted laws allowing no-fault divorce, which enabled either parent to unilaterally seek a divorce without needing to prove that the other spouse was responsible for the failure of the marriage or requiring both parties to agree that the relationship was irretrievably broken. Legislatures modified their domestic relations statutes to recognize the need for both parents to be regularly involved in the lives of their children. The law evolved from the "rule of one" (Difonzo, 2014) wherein one parent had sole legal authority over the children (i.e., sole decision making), to a sharing of this authority, that is shared legal decision making and shared parenting. At the present time, all 50 states and the District of Columbia allow courts to order joint legal and/or physical custody, while a majority of states (36) have shared decision making (joint legal custody), "either by presumption, preference, or by adopting statutory language in support of cooperative parenting" (DiFonzo, 2014, p. 216). While there is wide variation in the allocation of parenting time or physical custody, most statutes include the concept "frequent and continuing contact" in regards to allowed parenting time between nonresidential parents and their children (Difonzo, 2014).

Custody determinations are currently based on the *Best Interests of the Child* (BIC) standard. What factors constitute children's best interests has been the subject of considerable scholarly debate. To provide greater guidance about this vaguely defined standard, states have increasingly adopted or modified the Uniform Marriage and Divorce Act (National Conference of Commissioners on Uniform State Laws, 1970). This act notes that a court should consider "all relevant factors," but specifies five issues to be addressed:

1. Wishes of the child's parent or parents;
2. Wishes of the child;
3. Interaction and interrelationship of the child with parents or siblings and any other person who may significantly affect the child's best interest;
4. Child's adjustment to home, school, and community; and
5. Mental and physical health of all individuals involved.

The Uniform Marriage and Divorce Act also notes that the Court should consider relevant in its custody decision only conduct of a proposed custodian that affects his or her parenting of the child.

The BIC standard became the nationwide statutory guide for judicial decisions on child custody and parenting time, with the lone exception of West Virginia.[1] The BIC standard has been criticized for its vagueness and for increasing inconsistency in custody decisions, leading to more divorce litigation (Kohm, 2008). States have defined the BIC standard by specifying specific factors that judges should consider. The number of these factors varies from as few as two (Massachusetts General Laws, Ch. 208 §31) to as many as 19 (Florida Statutes, Title VI, Chapter 61 § 13 [7][d][2][c][3][a-r]). Even when multiple factors have been defined in law, there is no guidance to judges as to how to weigh some factors more than others (Scott, 2014). Such indeterminacy can lead to inconsistency in custody decisions, potential subjectivity through personal judicial bias, and the previously mentioned increase in the possibility of litigation (Mnookin, 1975; Scott, 2014).

Legal Process in Child Custody Cases

The legal process typically begins when one party seeking a divorce files a complaint or petition in the domestic relations court in the county in which the parents resided. In the case of a paternity issue, the initial complaint requires establishment of paternity, unless both parties agree that the putative father is the biological one. Once paternity is established, the case may appear similar to a divorce filing, as the parties will have to consider issues of custody, child support, and a schedule by which each parent may have care of the child (i.e., visitation schedule or a parenting plan). Once the action has been filed at the Court, parties will be encouraged to negotiate the terms of settlement. Several states[2] have crafted model parenting plans that parents can use as guides to fashion arrangements that meet their unique circumstances.

After a final judgment, the terms of the court order remain in effect unless either parent succeeds in obtaining a *modification*. The moving party files a motion requesting a change in the prior legal decision and must demonstrate a *substantial change of circumstances* that supports a reconsideration of the order. For example, one party's loss of job may trigger a request for a change in child support; or a remarriage or a chance for a better job in another state may underlie a request to relocate the children's residence. Frequently, modification requests are filed by parents who want to restructure their parenting plans to reflect the changing needs and desires of older children. As in most child custody disputes, the BIC standard guides the Court in making its decision.

There are several possible entry points in the legal process for a forensic mental health assessment pertinent to child custody. A judge, attorney, or parent may propose a child custody evaluation early in the legal process, if behavioral health concerns are significant factors in the case. A forensic mental health assessment may be ordered in any case in which the Court determines that relevant psychological expertise might improve judicial decision making. At any time during the pendency of a legal matter, a legal professional or parent may raise concerns about a parent or child relevant to a dispute that can result in a request for a forensic mental health assessment. Common reasons for referral include the impact of a parent's mental health or substance use disorder on parenting; the impact on the children if allowed to move out of state with their residential parent; the parenting plan needs of a special-needs child; or the effect of domestic abuse on children in the family.

Roles for Forensic Mental Health Professionals

There are four ways for forensic mental health professionals to become involved in the legal process: as a court-appointed child custody evaluator, an evaluator retained by one side, a science or educational expert, or a consultant to one side.

1. *The court-appointed evaluator* is a professional whose role is that of a neutral examiner for the Court. Appointment may be directly from the Court or through a guardian *ad litem* or special master who is authorized by the Court to obtain a mental health assessment. The evaluator has the Court as the client and performs a forensic mental health evaluation, addressing the questions posed by the Court, such as custody or a parenting plan, and the forensic mental health constructs relevant to those questions.
2. *Evaluator retained by one side.* Attorneys may retain experts to assess their respective clients or to review documents. For example, an allegation that a parent abuses substances or is mentally ill might prompt that parent's attorney to retain a mental health professional to assess the validity of those allegations and whether parenting is negatively impacted. The resultant assessment belongs to the hiring attorney, who may call his or her expert to testify at trial. This evaluator retained by one side offers opinions about those whom he or she has assessed (American Psychological Association, 2010, § 9.01 [b]) and interviews children only when both parents consent. Unless the evaluator assessed

both parents, which is unlikely when hired by one side, she or he should not opine on the issue of custody, as that requires a comparative analysis of parents and of each parent's relationship with the children. In summary, evaluators in the child custody arena may be retained as an expert on one side but must be cognizant of the ethical and clinical limitations of that role.

3. *Educational or science expert retained by one side.* In this role, the forensic professional, who has specialized knowledge or experience in a particular field, serves to educate the attorney and, if he or she testifies, inform the Court about what is known about an issue within that field. The information provided reflects existing knowledge about a topic. A couple of typical examples include:

    a.   The expert is retained to testify about the current literature and practice with respect to parenting plans for very young children, including impact on attachment.

    b.   The expert is retained to testify about the psychological risks and benefits of allowing children of different developmental ages to relocate to another state with a parent.

4. *Consultant retained by one side.* A forensic mental health professional may be retained by one side to assist in trial preparation. He or she might review psychological evaluations or mental health records and help the attorney prepare for deposition or testimony of the evaluating or treating professionals. The consultant may review a child custody report with the attorney to highlight its strengths and weaknesses and suggest questions in preparation for examination at trial (Association of Family and Conciliation Courts, 2011).

Forensic mental health professionals can take on any of the four roles in a case. Care must be taken not to mix roles or take on a dual role in the same case (APA, 2010, §3.06).

Recent Developments in the Field

There have been significant developments in the field of forensic mental health in general and in child custody in particular since the first edition of this book. The 19-volume series, *Best Practices in Forensic Mental Health Assessments*, provides forensic clinicians with comprehensive guidelines for conducting forensic mental health assessments in 18 specific areas. The first volume of the series is a foundation text that provides a useful overview of the principles, ethics, and background common to all forensic mental health assessments (Heilbrun, Grisso, & Goldstein, 2009). Each volume, including *Evaluations for Child Custody* (Fuhrmann & Zibbell, 2012), covers a specific area of practice and includes foundation knowledge and application. Important new or revised professional guidelines have also been published since the first edition of *Learning Forensic Assessment* (Jackson, 2008), including *Guidelines for Child Custody Evaluations in Family Law Proceedings* (American Psychological Association, 2009); *Model Standards of Practice for Child Custody Evaluations* (Association of Family and Conciliation Courts, 2006); *Guidelines for Brief Focused Assessments* (Association of Family and Conciliation Courts, 2009); and *Specialty Guidelines for Forensic Psychology* (American Psychological Association, 2009, 2013). A growing body of research in various areas relevant to child custody continues to inform practice (see references in section on Empirical Foundation and Limits) and books have been published in recent years that are of interest to child-custody evaluators (Galatzer-Levy, Kraus, & Galatzer-Levy, 2009; Gould & Martindale, 2007; Rohrbaugh, 2008; Stahl, 2011; Tolle & O'Donahue, 2012).

In the area of evaluation practice, a shortened variant of a custody evaluation, the Brief Focused Assessment (BFA), has emerged. BFAs have been increasingly used to address limited and specific referral questions in child custody matters. They are less costly and provide a more timely report to the Court than comprehensive evaluations. As noted previously, Association of Family and Conciliation Courts' *Guidelines for Brief Focused Assessments* addresses "the assessment of narrowly defined, issue-specific questions that arise in family court settings" (Association of Family and Conciliation Courts, 2009, p. 1).

Behavioral Health Areas Relevant to Custody Evaluations

What Is a Forensic Mental Health Assessment?

As noted earlier, a child custody evaluation is a type of forensic mental health assessment, an evaluation performed "with the intention of being used in a legal proceeding" (Heilbrun et al., 2009, p. 11). It "assists the legal decision-maker or one of the litigants in using relevant clinical and scientific data" (Heilbrun, 2001, p. 3). Generally, judges are guided by state statutes and case law that specify factors to be considered or addressed in reaching legal decisions. The forensic mental health evaluator's understanding of what the Court relies upon enables him or her to choose which behaviors, capacities, or other psychological attributes to assess in order to better inform judicial decision making. In child custody cases, the primary legal question is "What outcome is in the best interest of the child?" which, by itself, does not provide guidance to the evaluator as to specific factors or behaviors to address. Fortunately, some states provide greater guidance by defining component factors of best interests, although, as noted earlier, no preferential weight is assigned to specific factors. In addition, relevant professional guidelines support the idea that best practice in forensic assessment of custody consists of a multisource, multimethod evaluation of parents and children, interview of collateral contacts, and review of relevant documents (Association of Family and Conciliation Courts, 2006; American Psychological Association, 2013).

What Psycholegal Constructs Are Relevant to the Legal Question or Standard?

Ellis (2008) pointed out that, in earlier years of child custody evaluations, forensic evaluators used traditional clinical assessments and depended on their own clinical judgment to address "best interest" issues. This resulted in inconsistencies in evaluation methods among mental health evaluations, the proverbial "wild west" of assessment practice. Since the promulgation of the American Psychological Association (2009), Association of Family and Conciliation Courts (2006), and American Academy of Child and Adolescent Psychiatry (1997, currently under revision) standards, a more uniform set of behavioral or forensic mental health constructs for child custody evaluations have evolved. These constructs reflect the factors that exist in statutes or case laws (Fuhrmann & Zibbell, 2012), the findings of research on children and divorcing families (Kelly & Emery, 2003), and what judges and lawyers expect from forensic mental health assessments (Bow & Quinnell, 2004; Bow, Gottlieb, & Gould-Saltman, 2011). These constructs fall into four conceptual categories, which are the areas to be assessed in child custody evaluations:

1. Parenting attributes (i.e., strengths and weaknesses of each parent).
2. Developmental needs and abilities of each child.
3. The "fit" between each parent's attributes and the child's needs and abilities.
4. The interparental relationship.

Parenting attributes consist of "functional capacities," or "what the caregiver understands, believes, knows, does, and is capable of doing related to child rearing" (Grisso, 1986, p. 201). Parenting skills often assessed in child custody evaluations include, among others, parenting warmth and support, age-appropriate and clear communication with the child, adequate monitoring, provision of safety, effective discipline, and the ability to support the child's relationship with the other parent (Rohrbaugh, 2008).

The *developmental needs and abilities of each child* refers to his or her cognitive abilities and emotional needs and expression, an ability to communicate his or her needs, the closeness and security he or she has with each parent, the understanding of time and routine, the understanding of the separation/divorce, and perceptions of each parent (Rohrbaugh, 2008). Other relevant factors may include the child's temperament (Chess & Thomas, 1984), special needs (Schutz, Dixon, Lindenburger, & Ruther, 1989), quality of peer relationships (Coolahan, Fantuzzo, Mendez, & McDermott, 2000), and the child's wishes (Larson & McGill, 2010).

The fit between each parent's abilities or deficits and each child's needs is a concept derived from Chess and Thomas' studies of early childhood (Chess & Thomas, 1984). They pioneered the idea that a child's innate temperament interacted with his or her parent's capacities in a bidirectional manner to affect both parenting and individual development. This interaction was conceived of as the "goodness of fit." In child custody evaluations, fit refers to match between what the child needs from a parent and what parenting skills and deficits a particular parent has. Consequently, an evaluator might consider the match between the child's temperament and each of the parents (Caspi, Henry, McGee, Moffitt, & Silva, 1995), the ability of a parent to understand and provide for a child's special needs or talents (Bray, 1991), or each parent's expectations vis-à-vis the child's abilities and developmental level (Thomas & Chess, 1977). Strengths or weaknesses in diverse parenting skills can be valued differently depending on the needs of the particular child, parental expectations, and cultural and social factors (Otto, Buffington-Vollum, & Edens, 2003).

The capacity of each parent to cooperate with the other as a construct derives from the robust research finding that interparental conflict is most strongly correlated with poor adjustment in children of divorce. Intense interparental conflict is a frequent factor in cases referred for child custody evaluations (Kelly, 2012; Maccoby & Mnookin, 1992). The ability of the parents to cooperate, and its corollary—the willingness to support a relationship of the child with the other parent—is an important factor for the Court to consider in custody decisions (Fuhrmann & Zibbell, 2012).

In addition to the four areas of assessment, child custody evaluators are typically asked to address *case-specific questions*. These questions reflect the particular issues within the case being heard and may be unique to the Court making the referral. As each case is fact-specific, the order of appointment may include requests that focus on particular kinds of information, such as the nature of the parent-child relationships, any special needs of any of the children, or any evidence of one parent sabotaging the relationship of the children with the other parent, among other issues. If there are specific factors delineated in the statutes or case law in one's own state, for instance, children of sufficient maturity may decide with whom to live, then those factors are also addressed in the assessment.

As there is no scientific way to differentially weigh many of the factors considered to be important in custody decisions (Scott, 2014; Tippins & Wittman, 2005), the calculus that is necessary in any formulation or analysis of the family is a qualitative one. Peer-reviewed research can clarify or support an opinion (Gould & Martindale, 2013; Kuehnle & Drozd, 2012), but the evaluator is aware that, to be useful, there must be sufficient similarity between the family being evaluated and the research population studied. Because of the great variety in individual family dynamics, one must be cautious in applying findings from research to a specific case (Scott, 2014). The next section summarizes the research on the most frequent issues in child custody disputes.

Empirical Foundation and Limits

The research and academic literature on separation and divorce informs forensic evaluators about what issues to consider in their assessments and is an aid in interpreting the findings in the individual case. The literature in the field informs the evaluation process and content and provides important knowledge that aids opinion formation in cases. There is a substantial body of knowledge about child adjustment to parental separation and developmentally appropriate parenting plans. In addition, there is a literature regarding complex issues encountered in forensic mental health assessment, such as mental illness, substance abuse, child maltreatment, intimate partner violence (IPV), and parental alienation. There is also an emerging literature relevant to relocation cases, that is, when a parent requests to move the child to a distant place.

Children's Adjustment to Divorce

This literature that is essential knowledge for child custody evaluators consists of how children of different ages adjust to parental separation or divorce. Current knowledge about this area is summarized in a recent and detailed review (Kelly, 2012). The essence of hundreds of studies over 30 years indicates that, while the vast majority of children of divorce fall within the average range of adjustment within a few years of divorce, many are still at greater risk for social, emotional, and academic problems than those from continuously married families. Research on the age of a child at divorce shows mixed results, suggesting that the impact of divorce affects the mastery of developmental tasks. In contrast to earlier findings and speculation, children's gender does not significantly predict adjustment to divorce, while economic hardships and stress affect parenting, which then has an impact on child adjustment. Consistent contact with both parents and fewer life disruptions, such as moves and shifts in family composition, have been shown to be a protective factor for children of divorce (Kelly, 2012).

A robust and consistent finding is that conflict—both preseparation and postseparation—has the most significant impact on child adjustment, although children whose parents protect them from witnessing or participating in the conflict are less negatively impacted than children who are directly exposed to their parents' conflict. Conflict that involves IPV that children have witnessed or of which they are aware is a significant risk factor (Kelly & Johnson, 2008). Having a positive and supportive relationship with at least one parent, parental warmth, and sibling support are also correlated with fewer negative outcomes for children of divorce (Kelly, 2012).

Parenting Plans

Evaluators are often ordered to assess a family and recommend an appropriate parenting plan. "Parenting plan" has largely replaced the more antiquated "visitation schedule" to describe time periods when each parent has caretaking responsibility. Many states require litigants to submit a parenting plan proposal as part of their divorce proceeding (Elrod & Dale, 2008; see Note 2 for references to state-sponsored model parenting plans). Parenting plans delineate the times that the children are in the care of each parent, including regular school or day care periods, vacations and holidays during the academic year, and summer vacation periods. "Caretaking responsibilities" (American Law Institute, 2000) for children during allocated times is part of parents' physical custody. In addition, the parenting plan describes the authority each parent has over major decisions in child rearing, such as "residential placement, health and mental health care, and religious upbringing" (Gould & Martindale, 2013, p. 106).

Parental Mental Illness

Most research in this area has been with mothers, as they are more likely to be primary caretakers of children (Nicholson, Biebel, Hinden, Henry, & Steir, 2001). Having a psychiatric illness increases the chances of losing custody of a child, especially if severe in nature (Joseph, Joshi, Lewin, & Abrams, 1999), but social or family support decreases that risk (Benjet, Azar, & Kuersten-Hogan, 2003). While single parenthood is an additional stressor for someone with a mental disorder (Zemenchuk, Rogush, & Mowbray, 1998), the parental role can also motivate one to seek community support and maintain treatment compliance (Oyserman, Mowbray, & Zemenchuk, 1994). Multiple hospitalizations and the concomitant absence of a parent are often more stressful for children than the symptoms of the illness itself (Jenuwine & Cohler, 2009). Other factors frequently associated with mental illness that impact child adjustment include diminished family resources, fewer social supports, impaired parenting skills, increased family stress, and disrupted parent-child relationship (Tebes, Kaufman, Adnopoz, & Racusin, 2001; Rohrbaugh, 2008). The key issue for evaluators is not the presence of a mental disorder, or which mental disorder, but the "documented functional significance of (the impact of) the disorder for the child" (Benjet et al., 2003, p. 241), or the "nexus/link between the disorder and parenting ability" (Fuhrmann & Zibbell, 2012, p. 78).

Parental Substance Abuse

Children who live with a substance abusing parent are at increased risk for externalizing (acting out) and internalizing (anxiety/depression) behaviors (McMahon & Giannini, 2003), academic and school problems (Harden & Pihl, 1995), and problematic substance use in adolescence or young adulthood (Rohrbaugh, 2008). Parents who abuse substances are more likely to demonstrate impairment in caretaking abilities such as inconsistent discipline, inadequate attention to a child's daily living needs, or a lack of attunement to a child's emotional needs (Rohrbaugh, 2008). The added presence of psychiatric disorder or environmental stressors (such as unstable employment and poverty) increase the risk of parenting deficits and negative impact on children (Suchman & Luthar, 2000). As with psychiatric disorders, family and community support, and availability of treatment for adult substance users are predictive of recovery and provide a critical protective factor for children. Adults with a co-occurring psychiatric disorder have a lesser chance of successful recovery than those with a substance use disorder alone (Goldstein, 2003).

Child Maltreatment

Child maltreatment refers to physical, sexual, emotional abuse, or neglect (Center for Disease Control and Prevention, 2014b) of a child under the age of 18 by a parent, caregiver, or another person in a custodial role (e.g., clergy, coach, or teacher). The lifetime childhood prevalence of maltreatment varies from 10.6% for emotional abuse to 28.3% for physical abuse; 14.8% for emotional neglect and 9.9% for physical neglect. Children who experience neglect, abuse, or other forms of family violence can manifest significant psychological difficulties, with greater vulnerability if they experience multiple forms of maltreatment. The psychological sequelae of such abuse can include posttraumatic stress disorder, with the potential of altering brain function or changing brain structure. Maltreated children are more likely to have emotional or behavioral problems, including persistent emotional dysregulation and functional difficulties in biological, cognitive, emotional, and social domains (Kuehnle, Coulter, & Firestone, 2000). Maltreatment in childhood has also been reported to increase risk for long-term health consequences in adulthood (Felitti et al., 1998).

The reported incidence of child sexual abuse in custody disputes is between 1% and 2% (Bala & Schuman, 1999). Families referred for custody evaluations report a higher incidence of child maltreatment (25%–33%) than those not referred, suggesting that an allegation of child maltreatment is likely to result in a child custody evaluation (Johnson, Lee, Walters, & Oleson, 2005). These allegations are confirmed at about the same rate as those in reports of child maltreatment in noncustodial cases (McGleughlin, Meyer, & Baker, 1999), while allegations against fathers as perpetrators are substantiated about 60% more often than allegations against mothers (Johnson et al., 2005) in child custody disputes.

Intimate Partner Violence

Intimate Partner Violence (IPV) is defined as "physical, sexual, or psychological harm caused by a current or former partner or spouse" (Center for Disease Control and Prevention, 2014a). IPV has different subtypes including coercive-controlling violence, conflict-oriented violence, violent resistance, and separation-instigated violence. The most severe form of domestic abuse is coercive-controlling violence, which is characterized by a high degree of relationship control, intimidation, threats, and intrusiveness, and frequently includes physical violence (Jaffe, 2014). Coercive-controlling violence during the relationship is a risk factor for partner aggression to continue after separation (Hardesty, Haselschwerdt, & Johnson, 2012). Conflict-oriented violence, also known as situational couple violence, is the most common form of IPV (Strauss & Gelles, 1988); it is more reactive and related to partner conflict. Additionally, violent resistance consists of acts committed in self-defense and separation-instigated violence refers to aggression that occurs in the context of separation and is not characteristic of the couple relationship (Kelly & Johnson, 2008). The different subtypes of domestic violence call for different parenting plans that consider child and parent safety. The amount and type of contact between the perpetrating parent and child will vary with the nature and severity of the domestic abuse (Hardesty et al., 2012).

Psychological aggression, also called *emotional* or *verbal abuse*, may be a precursor to physical abuse (O'Leary & Slep, 2006), but even in the absence of physical violence, it can be emotionally traumatic (Murphy & Cascardi, 1999). Allegations of IPV are frequent in child-related disputes (Johnson et al., 2005) and 46 states require its consideration in child custody cases by statute or case law. Twenty-six states have a statutory, rebuttable presumption against joint legal custody (i.e., shared decision making) in the context of a legal finding of IPV (Austin & Drozd, 2013). For children, witnessing interparental psychological abuse is associated with increased anxiety, distractibility, and acting-out behaviors (Cummings, Davies, & Campbell, 2002). In addition, the long-term psychological effects of coercive control with or without physical violence can severely impede the ability of parents to collaborate after separation (Jaffe, 2014).

Reviews of child custody reports show between 37% and 72% of cases referred for evaluation contain allegations of IPV. Where the type of IPV was noted, 16% were of the severe type and 33% were moderate in nature (Bow & Boxer, 2003). Witnessing IPV has significant emotional and behavioral impact on children, including effects on mood, behavior, health, and cognitive/academic performance (Kelly & Johnson, 2008). Severity and frequency of domestic violence correlates with severity of behavior problems and mood disturbance in exposed children (Hardesty et al., 2012). Witnessing physical or psychological abuse between parents can be as deleterious as being the victim of child maltreatment (Ayoub, Deutsch, & Maranganore, 1999). Children who are raised in homes in which domestic violence occurs are more likely to be abused, especially if coercive-controlling violence is the main pattern of aggression in the household (Jouriles, McDonald, Smith-Slep, Heyman, & Garrido, 2008).

Parental Alienation

An issue surrounded by professional controversy and debate, parental alienation is one of the most common accusations made by high-conflict parents in child-related family disputes. Gardner (1992) first described this phenomenon, which he called *Parental Alienation Syndrome*. He described alienation as a child's resistance or refusal to see one parent in the absence of aversive parenting. He emphasized the child's absolute negative conviction about and antipathy for the disfavored parent in the context of the favored parent's subtle or overt support of this behavior in the child. Kelly and Johnston (2001) described alienation as existing when a child expresses, freely and persistently, unreasonably negative feelings and beliefs (such as anger, hatred, rejection, and/or fear) toward a parent that are significantly disproportionate to the child's actual experience with that parent. Warshak (2011) later termed this *irrational* or *pathological* alienation, as the child's reaction is far out of proportion to the disfavored or "target" parent's actual behavior.

The child custody evaluator is aware of the literature on parental alienation and assesses the factors contributing to a child's refusal to spend time with a disfavored parent. While alienation includes behaviors by the favored parent that undermine the parent-child relationship, *estrangement* describes a situation in which the child's resistance or refusal to see a parent is related to clear deficiencies in the target parent, which threatens the security of the child while in the care of that parent. This might include any of the special issues noted earlier, such as mental illness, substance abuse, or domestic violence, as well as poor parenting skills or judgment. It is not alienation when a favored parent acts to prevent parenting time with the other parent because of legitimate safety concerns about the target parent's care of the child. Kelly and Johnston (2001) describe alienation as a continuum of behaviors reflecting closeness/distance in the child's relationship with each parent. These include *affinity*, or a natural affection for or attachment to one parent (without rejection of the other), to *alignment*, or a strong preference for one parent and ambivalence about the other, but without rejection, to *alienation*, as defined earlier. Simply labeling one parent as "alienating" risks oversimplification and possible misuse in litigation. The current understanding of and preferred approach to this issue involves a systemic strategy, taking into account and assessing the feelings, behaviors, and experiences of all the relevant parties—both parents and child—but also the contributions of influential actors in the family system, such as friends, extended family, and even therapists on occasion (Friedhandler & Walters, 2010). A summary and review of empirical findings are available by Saini, Johnston, Fidler, and Bala (2012).

Relocation

The United States is a mobile society, with about 11.7% of adults moving each year; divorced/separated adults move about 40% more than those who are married (Schachter, 2004). Most moves are of short distances and within the same county. About one-fifth of the movers shift to another part of the state (Ihrke, 2014). Relocation disputes arise when one parent wishes to move with the child(ren) to a different state, or to a different (but more remote) part of the current state, or to a different country. These cases, also called *move-away* or *removal* cases, are among the thorniest in domestic relations law, as each party to the dispute has significant interests in the outcome, whether those be economic, social, or emotional (Atkinson, 2010). Case law emphasizes the dominance of the BIC standard in guiding these decisions. For example, in the case of *In re Tropea* (1996), the Court wrote of the need to account for "all the relevant facts and circumstances with predominant emphasis being placed on what outcome is most likely to serve the best interests of the child" (p. 739). In 2009, 37 states had relocation statutes (Atkinson, 2010). Statutory and case law typically list factors the Court should consider in making relocation decisions. These often include the motives of the relocating parent, motives of the opposed parent, nature of the relationship between the child and both parents and the frequency of parenting time, history of domestic abuse, likely impact of the move on the child's quality of life, likely impact of the move on the relocating parent's quality of life and degree to which that may benefit the child, the degree to which the parenting schedule can be rearranged to preserve the child's relationship with the other parent, whether the other parent can also relocate to the same community as the moving parent and child, and whether the parent seeking to move would go without the child.

Austin (2008a, b; 2012) developed a risk assessment model for relocation cases. Recognizing that relocation puts children of divorce at greater risk of negative outcomes, Austin suggests a number of risk and protective factors that require consideration in relocation cases. The major risk factor is the level of prior conflict between parents, while the primary protective factor is a good relationship between the child and the primary residential parent (Austin, 2008b). The task of the evaluator is to provide a detailed balance sheet of risk and protective factors for the court, with an analysis of likely outcomes for the child with the possible proposed parenting plans. As described in the case reported at the end of this chapter, many of the issues summarized so far commonly occur in child custody disputes. With that in mind, we turn to a discussion of the mechanics of the evaluation itself.

Performing the Evaluation

Child custody evaluations are inherently complex due to the multiple diverse factors to be assessed as well as the emotional intensity of the dispute. Parents are faced with the possible loss of their most valued relationships—time with and control of their children's lives. For some, their relationship with their child is, to paraphrase Robin Williams in *Mrs. Doubtfire*, akin to the air they breathe. It is important for the evaluator to be mindful of this as he or she moves with them through the process. With the goal of addressing the child's best interests, the forensic evaluator assesses each parent and each child. In addition the evaluator typically seeks out non-professional and professional collateral contacts, who may have information relevant to the child custody evaluation. Useful collateral contacts may include extended family, significant others, neighbors, doctors, educators and/or therapists (Association of Family and Conciliation Courts, 2006, §5.7). Furthermore, the evaluator uses a wide-angle lens with which to assess the dynamics of each caretaker's functional abilities and weaknesses as it affects parenting of each child, and each parent's capacity to cooperate with the other. Child custody evaluators require specialized skills in interviewing adults and children, an understanding of child/adolescent development and family dynamics, current knowledge of research in areas relevant to the questions asked by the court, and familiarity with the relevant family law statutes and cases in the jurisdiction in which they practice. The *Model Standards* is a good source for understanding the forensic nature of the process and the types of skills necessary to perform these assessments (Association of Family and Conciliation Courts, 2006).

The evaluator should also acknowledge when issues arise that are outside his or her level of competence. For example, sexual abuse allegations or evaluation of developmental disorders require training and experience that some child custody evaluators may lack. If these issues of competence deficiency are evident from the court order, the evaluator declines the appointment (APA, 2002, §2.01). If they arise during the evaluation itself, the evaluator seeks consultation and may ask the court for permission to refer part of the assessment to a specialist. Evaluators are also aware of the guidelines or standards promulgated by their own professional organizations (e.g., American Psychological Association guidelines) as well as any developed by the courts in their practice jurisdiction (e.g., Massachusetts, California). Lastly, knowledge of professional ethics in one's own field and in forensic mental health (e.g., American Academy of Psychiatry and the Law, 2005; American Psychological Association, 2013) is essential as part of the foundation for performing this work (Fuhrmann & Zibbell, 2012).

The Order of Appointment and Practice Memoranda

The forensic evaluator usually starts the assessment upon receipt of a court order of appointment. The court order orients the evaluator to the questions for which the Court seeks information and defines the scope of the evaluator's authority. If the order is vague, the evaluator should seek clarification from the Court or from the attorneys who can provide additional information and relevant documents. The evaluator must remember that he or she is working for the Court and is cognizant of any appearance of bias. For example, evaluators avoid substantive communications with attorneys unless both participate in the conversation. The court order may prescribe time limits, methods, or payment for the evaluation, and the evaluator has to decide before accepting the appointment whether he or she can work within those parameters. Consistent with the *Model Standards* (§4.1)(Association of Family and Conciliation Courts, 2006), it is preferable for evaluators to have written policies or practice memoranda about critical issues in an evaluation, such as confidentiality, costs, time frames, and testimony.

Confidentiality

Confidentiality is much more limited in child custody evaluations than in clinical practice. Practically speaking, interview and observation notes, psychological testing, documents, and collateral data are available with the appropriate permissions to all parties to the litigation. The evaluator's report will likely be read by the parties, the attorneys, and the judge. All information, including the forensic evaluator's notes, are "discoverable," a legal term for each side having the right through subpoena to review everything the evaluator utilized or created in his or her assessment (American Psychological Association, 2010, §12.07) Evaluators explain the limits of confidentiality to participants in the evaluation. Children are also informed in language appropriate to their level of comprehension.

Interviewing/Assessing the Parties

Parents are usually anxious about being evaluated, are aware of the high stakes, and have invested considerable financial resources in the process. They are concerned about having their views heard and understood. They typically want enough time to explain themselves, including their parenting strengths and the other parent's deficits, and to have opportunity to respond to the criticisms/complaints of the other parent. The forensic evaluator maintains balance in the order of interviewing parents, the time spent with each, the number and types of collaterals each parent provides. He or she strives to be as even-handed as possible with respect to the kinds of services/assessments performed as part of the overall evaluation, such as psychological testing or home visits (Association of Family and Conciliation Courts, 2006, §5.5).

Typically, the forensic evaluator will alternate several individual interviews with the parents, ideally using a structured interview format to acquire information about their individual and family backgrounds, education, work and social history, relationships, marriage, and separation or divorce (if the dispute is postdivorce). The evaluator asks each party about the same issues in the same sequence, assuring consistent and thorough assessments, and enhancing the perception of fairness and neutrality. Some evaluators will ask parents to complete a detailed questionnaire covering many of the relevant areas of inquiry, to augment the individual interviews (Schutz et al., 1989). It is important to obtain detailed information from each parent about each child and any special needs or abilities/talents each may have. It is essential to gather information about each adult as a parent to each child and hearing his or her criticisms of and concerns about the other parent. Focusing on the various "hands-on," direct caretaking activities each performed for each child over the years is necessary, as well as eliciting information on the indirect parenting responsibilities that involve planning activities and other administrative tasks of family life. Eliciting each parent's self-appraisal of parenting skills as well as perceptions of the other parent's skills is useful. The information gathered will likely suggest parental deficits, for which corroboration or disconfirmation can be sought by other means (e.g., observation, collateral contact information). Lastly, asking parents what their desired outcomes are can reveal how much each values the presence of the other parent in the children's lives, each one's perception and willingness to cooperate with the other parent in raising the children, and how realistic either one is about resolution of the case, and how able one is to prioritize the needs of their children. Some sources with further information on interview topics and methods include Schutz et al. (1989), Gould and Martindale (2007), Rohrbaugh (2008), Stahl (2011), and Fuhrmann and Zibbell (2012).

Parent-Child Observations

As part of the requirement to assess parent-child relationships (Association of Family and Conciliation Courts, 2006, §5.9), it is essential to observe each parent with the children (APA, 2009, §10; Association of Family and Conciliation Courts, 2006, §10.2 (b)). This can be done in the office or in each parent's residence. In either case, the evaluator takes care to assure that the observations are performed under comparable circumstances. Many, but not all, evaluators include home visits as part of their evaluations. The decision is often based on the factors in a particular case: e.g., safety or disorganization of a home; young or special needs child for whom an observation in a familiar environment is preferable. When a home visit is done, each home is visited around the same time of day for about the same amount of time to allow comparisons to be made and to treat each parent similarly. If the observation occurs in the evaluator's office, the setting and materials used should be similar, as should any tasks the evaluator asks of the children and parent. There are no standardized observational protocols (Lampl, 2009). In practice, some evaluators perform unstructured or semi-structured office observations (Rohrbaugh, 2008), while others ask each parent to engage with their children in specific challenges or games (Lampl, 2009; Schutz et al., 1989). Gould and Martindale (2007) remind evaluators to be careful to write descriptive and not interpretive notes about observations, to clearly state the conditions of the observation, and to clarify whether the evaluator merely observed or actively participated in the family interaction. Rohrbaugh (2008) provides recommendations on methods and questions for observational purposes, as well as items to assess during a home visit/observation. Lampl describes a semi-structured assessment instrument, the *Home Observation for Measurement of the Environment* (HOME), which can provide an assessment of the quality of the family environment, although it can be time consuming (Lampl, 2009, p. 79).

Interviewing/Assessing Children

Each child whose caretaking is at issue needs to be seen by the evaluator (Association of Family and Conciliation Courts, 2006, §5.8). As with other facets of the evaluation, balance and fairness require the forensic evaluator to have each parent alternate transporting the children for interviews. The parent's presence with the child for a short time eases the child into the interview office and provides permission for the child to speak to the evaluator. The evaluator's clinical skills and experience help to develop rapport with the child and engage him or her in the interview. Saywitz, Camparo, and Romanoff (2010) provide an overview of the issues in child interviewing in a variety of legal situations, with 10 recommendations for assessing children in custody cases. They stress providing a child-friendly environment with few distractions, using age-appropriate language, and utilizing a nonjudgmental, open-minded approach to the child (Saywitz et al., 2010). A comprehensive list of areas to consider in a child interviews is available in Rohrbaugh (2008, pp. 285–287) and sample questions to ask can be reviewed in Fuhrmann & Zibbell (2012, pp. 154–155). In addition to assessing the developmental status of the children (Gould & Martindale, 2007) and their relationships with each parent, the sibling relationships within the family should be addressed (Association of Family and Conciliation Courts, 2006, §5.8 [b]). Many states require strong consideration of a child's stated preference, if the child is of sufficient age and/or maturity. If a child expresses a preference, the evaluator assesses the manner in which it was conveyed, considers developmental and situational factors in understanding the stated preferences, and is explicit about the weight he or she gave the statement in the report (Association of Family and Conciliation Courts, 2006, §5.8 [a]).

Psychological Testing of Parents

Periodic surveys of psychologists have demonstrated increasing use of psychological tests in custody evaluations over the years (Ackerman & Ackerman, 1997; Keilin & Bloom, 1986; Quinnell & Bow, 2001). Some tests, such as the Minnesota Multiphasic Personality Test-2 (MMPI-2) are used frequently by psychologists. Gould and Martindale (2013) have a succinct discussion of the value of administering such instruments to custody litigants as well as the limitations to their use. There is an increasing use of normative databases of custody litigants for certain tests (Bathhurst, Gottfried, & Gottfried, 1997; McCann et al., 2001). This permits comparison of individual custody litigants' scores on certain tests (e.g., MMPI-2, Millon Clinical Multiaxial Inventory–III) with those of collected samples of custody litigants. There are demand characteristics of custody evaluations that can skew litigants' responses in a "best foot forward" manner, so that these databases allow evaluators to draw more objective comparisons of test results and try to account for this common response bias. In using these instruments, the evaluator considers the nature of the issue or hypothesis to be addressed, the ability to collect the data from other sources in a more cost-efficient and timely manner, the availability of specific instruments to deal with the identified issues, and the financial resources of the parties responsible for the additional expense (Fuhrmann & Zibbell, 2012). If testing is indicated to help answer a referral question, the forensic evaluator selects appropriate instruments that are reliable and valid for the situation. Instruments should be commercially available and have a detailed manual. Lastly, the evaluator should be qualified to administer the test and interpret the results (Gould & Martindale, 2013; Otto et al., 2003; Association of Family and Conciliation Courts, 2006, §6.1–6.6;). Some evaluators prefer to administer and interpret the tests themselves, while others refer the client out for an independent psychological assessment.

Interviewing Collaterals

Gathering information from collateral contacts familiar with the parents and children is one cornerstone of a forensic mental health assessment (Association of Family and Conciliation Courts, 2006 §11.1–11.2; APA, 2009 §10) and has become a customary practice of forensic evaluators (Bow & Quinnell, 2002; Kirkland, McMillan, & Kirkland, 2006). Evaluators typically select the most relevant sources from lists provided by parents or attorneys. Those who have the least interest in the outcome are likely to have more reliable and unbiased information (Austin, 2002). Professionals who deal with parents and children comprise this group, including educators, pediatric and adult physicians, and child or family therapists. Like the parable of the blind men and the elephant, each professional may have only selected information about his or her client (e.g., child, parent), so it may be necessary to contact many sources to get an integrated and balanced view of the family. Nonprofessional, nonfamily members, such as neighbors, friends, coaches, etc., make up a second group of collaterals, although these may favor the party who offers them as informants. A third group consists of extended family members or significant others, who may be the most biased, but they may also be able to offer observations of particular incidents or information otherwise unavailable (Fuhrmann & Zibbell, 2012).

Reviewing Documents

While custody evaluators typically review relevant documents—such as legal pleadings, medical, mental health, and/or educational records, etc. (Bow and Quinnell, 2002)—modern communication technology has made this fundamental part (Association of Family and Conciliation

Courts, 2006, §11.1; APA, 2009, §10) of a custody evaluation more complex. Parties may submit written histories of their marriage or copies of diaries/journals from the recent separation to details reaching back years into the relationship. Increasingly, however, electronically based communications such as e-mails, texts, images, or social media interactions are offered as evidence of misbehavior or poor judgment by one party or the other (American Association of Matrimonial Lawyers, 2010). The possibilities of documentary evidence seem limited only by the imagination, motivations, and resources of either party.

Once the usually voluminous amount of data from parents, children, observations, collaterals, and documents has been collected, it is the task of the evaluator to analyze the relevant information in a manner that addresses the psycholegal questions and the specific issues raised by the Court. In the following section, we briefly consider such a task.

Interpretation

It is incumbent on the forensic evaluator to organize the relevant information in a coherent manner, so that it has meaning for the consumer of the report. There are several conceptual schemas available to analyze or interpret the information. Drozd, Olesen, and Saini (2013) provide a useful blueprint for organizing data and creating working hypotheses, as well as a matrix for sorting that data into the statutory, research-based, or case specific factors. Fuhrmann and Zibbell (2012) offer a second model, conceptually similar to Drozd et al. (2013). It constructs a matrix that takes relevant data from multiple sources and integrates it into the psycholegal (or behavioral) concepts derived from research, statutes, and specific court-order-directed issues (see prior section, "Behavioral Health Areas Relevant to Custody Evaluations"). That matrix, with one addition (i.e., specific court questions), is reproduced in the Table 16.1.

As one proceeds through the multisourced data collection process (horizontal axis), multiple hypotheses about the family are generated. Drozd et al. (2013) define a hypothesis as a "tentative explanation for what is observed" (p. 20), or a "formal statement of the proposed relationship between two or more variables" (p. 20) that are relevant to the issues to be addressed. Where data from one source (e.g., a parent) corroborates information from another source (e.g., a teacher), that convergence strengthens one's conclusions (and the relevant hypothesis) drawn from that data. It is important to clearly state one's hypotheses and supporting/disconfirming data, so that the consumer can evaluate the data collection process and the reasoning of the evaluator in forming conclusions. Conversely, the evaluator is obliged to consider alternative explanations for the same data (Association of Family and Conciliation Courts, 2006, §5.3; Drozd et al., 2013; Pickar & Kaufman, 2013). The chart in Table 16.1 organizes the data to clarify which hypotheses

Table 16.1 Model for interpretation

	Interview/ Psychological Testing	*Observations*	*Collateral Sources*	*Record Review*
Parent A: Strengths & weaknesses				
Parent B: Strengths & weaknesses				
Children's needs and abilities				
Fit between each child and each parent				
Level and type of coparent cooperation/conflict				
Court-ordered questions				

Note: Chart reproduced by permission of Oxford University Press (Fuhrmann & Zibbell, 2012, p. 164).

generate more support than others. An alternative approach may be more relevant to states that, by statute, list a series of factors the court must consider. In this case, the evaluator can organize his or her report by listing the relevant factors (e.g., child relationship with parents, child current functioning) with the data and conclusion about each.

Report Writing

As Pickar and Kaufman (2013) have noted, little attention has been given to report writing, despite all the literature available on custody evaluations. The forensic report documents the scope and focus of the assessment as well as the data obtained relevant to the reason for referral. The report organizes the data in understandable form and interprets that data with respect to its meaning for the psycholegal constructs and the issues the Court wishes to address. It should be structured with headings for different sections, appear professional, and avoid typographical errors. That is, it should give the impression that the evaluator took care in writing it as befits the importance of court proceedings where potentially life-changing decisions are being made. The conclusions should follow logically and clearly from the data, and any recommendations should follow from the conclusions and be specific and practical. The links amongst data, conclusions, and recommendations should be transparent and understandable to all the consumers of the report (Fuhrmann & Zibbell, 2012).

A child custody report has at least three audiences. The first audience is the Court that ordered the evaluation and will make the legal decision if a settlement is not reached. The second audience is the attorney for each client; each of them will go over it with the proverbial "fine-tooth comb," seeking support for their respective client's position. Often attorneys use the information in a report to settle a case without going to trial. If the case proceeds to trial, one attorney may seek ways to impeach the testimony of the evaluator to mitigate the impact of an evaluation unfavorable to his or her client. The third audience is each party, who will want to know if he or she had been heard, if her or his collateral contacts had been interviewed, if he or she had been treated fairly, and if the recommendations support his or her desired outcome.

A fourth audience—the children—typically are not given access to the custody report, although the results may affect them in significant ways. Their welfare is the focus of the work: the report should stress their needs and reflect their experience in the divorce. It should reflect their expressed wishes and place them in context, even if the recommendations do not support those wishes. While there are different perspectives as to the purpose of a report (e.g., consideration of settlement v. legal case resolution; Pickar & Kaufman, 2013), in the end, it should state the facts dispassionately, avoid inflammatory descriptions of one parent by another, and assume a respectful tone about all involved. The evaluator is mindful that after the litigation is over, the parties likely will continue to have a relationship as parents. Consistent with the American Psychological Association ethical code to "strive to benefit those with whom they work and take care to do no harm" (2010, §A), the report and the significant amount of work it represents hopefully benefits the children of high-conflict parents.

Case Example

The case that follows is an example of the complex issues a forensic evaluator may be asked to address in a child custody dispute. Joan and Jim Vitelli have been married for 15 years and have three children: Jennifer (13), Sarah (11), and Jimmy (8). When they married, they moved near the city where Jim lived, as job opportunities were plentiful there. Joan was raised in a small town 100 miles away. Each of them is employed outside of the home. Jim works as an engineer and Joan works as a nurse at a local hospital. The children are healthy, but the youngest has some special education needs and a diagnosis of attention deficit disorder, for which he takes medication. Both parents were regularly involved with the children's care. Jim was home for dinner each night and coached the girls in soccer and softball. He also took care of the children while Joan worked one weekend of each month. Both parents reported that over the last five years, the marriage had declined and their relationship was marked by anger and hostility. Parents reported that there were frequent arguments, shouting, and some physical altercations including pushing, shoving, throwing/breaking things (Jim), and slapping (Joan). Joan claimed her husband was the primary instigator of this aggression and alleged that he was also occasionally verbally abusive toward the children. Jim claimed that Joan often yelled at the children and that the physical aggression was mutual. After Joan discovered that he was engaged in suggestive communications with other women on social media and had posted his profile on an online dating site, they separated. The separation followed a heated argument during dinner in which Jim allegedly threw a plate at Joan, barely missing their son.

Following the separation, Jim left the marital home and rented an apartment with adequate space and beds to accommodate his children when they were in his care. He and Joan agreed to a temporary parenting plan for the children. While Jimmy went with his father readily, the girls expressed anxiety about being away from their mother and home, and increasingly resisted seeing Jim during his scheduled parenting time. Jim reported that Joan was encouraging the girls' resistance and interfering with his relationship with them, in effect, alienating the girls from him. In addition, as part of her divorce complaint, Joan asked the Court for permission to move back to her hometown, where she had friends and family who could support her and help with the children. In her complaint, Joan requested sole decision-making responsibility, as she did not think she could safely co-parent with Jim in light of his alleged physical violence. She also wanted the girls to be allowed to choose when and for how long they were in their father's care. In contrast, Jim asked the Court for an equal share of the parenting time and decision-making authority, claiming that both were involved parents and capable of caring for the children. He opposed letting the children move 100 miles away, stating that it would significantly disrupt his relationship with the children. In the course of early divorce proceedings, the Court appointed a forensic evaluator to assess the family and their allegations, to file a report and make recommendations on legal custody (decision making), physical custody (a parenting plan), and relocation. The Court also asked specific questions for the evaluator to address, including the nature of the alleged domestic abuse and the effect of any recommendations on the child with special educational needs.

The forensic mental health evaluator conducted a thorough assessment, including interviews of each parent and each child, observation of each parent with the children, collateral contacts, and review of record. The resultant report described parenting strengths and weaknesses, the children's needs and abilities, and the interparental conflict, and it offered well-supported opinions as requested by the Court. As occurs with the majority of cases, the balanced report of the neutral evaluator was instrumental in moving the parties to settle the dispute without going to trial. The report noted that the disadvantages of the move to the children outweighed the advantages to them and to Joan. When it was clear that the children's best interests were served by continuing regular and consistent contact with their father, the parents reached an agreement with the assistance of their attorneys.

Notes

1   West Virginia uses the *Approximation Standard*, the American Law Institute's proposal for postdivorce family structure. In short, it suggests that the pattern of child care and decision-making authority (i.e., physical and legal custody) should reflect that which the parents chose before they separated (American Law Institute, 2000).

2   For sample parenting plans see Arizona (www.azcourts.gov/Portals/31/ParentingTime/PPWguidelines. pdf); Indiana (http://www.in.gov/judiciary/rules/parenting/); Massachusetts (http://www.mass.gov/courts/ docs/courts-and-judges/courts/probate-and-family-court/parentingplan.pdf); Oregon (http://courts.oregon. gov/OJD/OSCA/cpsd/courtimprovement/familylaw/Pages/parentingplan.aspx)

References

Ackerman, M., & Ackerman, M. (1997). Custody evaluation practices: A survey of experienced professionals (revisited). *Professional Psychology: Research and Practice, 28*, 137–145.

American Academy of Child and Adolescent Psychiatry (1997). Practice parameters for child custody evaluations. *Journal of the American academy of child and adolescent psychiatry, 36* (10), Sup.

American Academy of Psychiatry and the Law. (2005). *Ethics guidelines for the practice of forensic psychiatry.* Bloomfield, CT: Author.

American Association of Matrimonial Lawyers. (2010, February 10). Big surge in social networking evidence says survey of nation's top lawyers. Retrieved on November 5, 2014 from www.aaml.org/about-the-academy/press/press-releases/e-discovery/big-surge-social-networking-evidence-says-survey-

American Law Institute (2000). *Principles of the law of family dissolution: Analysis and recommendations.* Washington, D.C.: Author.

American Psychological Association (2002). Ethical principles of psychologists and code of conduct. *American Psychologist, 57*, 1060-1073

American Psychological Association. (2009). *Guidelines for child custody evaluations in family law proceedings.* Retrieved on September 2, 2014 from www.apa.org/practice/guidelines/child-custody.aspx.

American Psychological Association (2010). Ethical Principles of Psychologists and Code of Conduct, Including 2010 Amendments. Retrieved on October 3, 2014 at http://www.apa.org/ethics/code/index.aspx

American Psychological Association. (2013). *Specialty guidelines for forensic psychology.* Retrieved on September 2, 2014 from www.apa.org/practice/guidelines/forensic-psychology.aspx.

Association of Family and Conciliation Courts. (2006). *Model standards of practice for child custody evaluations.* Madison, WI: Author.

Association of Family and Conciliation Courts. (2009). *Guidelines for brief focused assessments.* Retrieved on September 2, 2014 from www.afccnet.org/Portals/0/PublicDocuments/Guidelines/BFATF2009final.pdf

Association of Family and Conciliation Courts. (2011). Mental health consultants and child custody evaluations: A discussion paper. *Family Court Review, 49*, 723–736. doi: 10.1111/j.1744–1617.2011.01409.x

Atkinson, J. (2010). The law of relocation of children. *Behavioral Sciences and the Law, 28*, 563–579.

Austin, W. (2002). Guidelines for utilizing collateral sources of information in child custody evaluations. *Family Court Review, 40*, 177–184. doi: 10.1111/j.174–1617.2002.tb00828.x

Austin, W. (2008a). Relocation research, and forensic evaluation: Part I: Effects of residential mobility on children of divorce. *Family Court Review, 46*, 137–150. doi: 10.1111/j.1744–1617.2007.00188.x

Austin, W. (2008b). Relocation research, and forensic evaluation: Part II: Research in support of the relocation risk assessment model. *Family Court Review, 46*, 347–365. doi: 10.1111/j.1744–1617.2008.00205.x

Austin, W. (2012). Relocation, research, and child custody disputes. In K. Kuehnle & L. Drozd (Eds.), *Parenting plan evaluations: Applied research for the family court* (pp. 540–563). New York: Oxford University Press.

Austin, W., & Drozd, L. (2013). Judge's bench book for application of the integrated framework for the assessment of intimate partner violence in child custody disputes. *Journal of Child Custody, 10*, 99–119. doi: 10.1080/15379418.2013.796850

Ayoub, C., Deutsch, R., & Maranganore, A. (1999). Emotional distress in children of high-conflict divorce. *Family and Conciliation Courts Review, 37*, 297–314. doi: 10.1111/j.174–1617.1999.tb01307.x

Bala, N., & Schuman, J. (1999). Allegations of sexual abuse when parents have separated. *Canadian Family Law Quarterly, 17*, 191–243.

Bathhurst, K., Gottfried, A., & Gottfried, A. (1997). Normative data for the MMPI-2 in child custody litigation. *Psychological Assessment, 9*, 205–211. doi: 10.1037/1040–3590.9.3.205

Benjet, C., Azar, S., & Kuersten-Hogan, R. (2003). Evaluating the parental fitness of psychiatrically diagnosed individuals: Advocating a functional-contextual analysis of parenting. *Journal of Family Psychology, 17*, 238–251. doi: 10.1037/1040–3590.9.3.205

Bow, J., & Boxer, P. (2003). Assessing allegations of domestic violence in child custody evaluations. *Journal of Interpersonal Violence, 18*, 1394–1410. doi: 10.1177/0886260503258031

Bow, J., Gottlieb, M., & Gould-Saltman, D. (2011). Attorneys' beliefs and opinions about child custody evaluations. *Family Court Review, 49*, 301–312. doi: 10.1111/j.1744–1617.2011.01372.x

Bow, J., & Quinnell, F. (2002). A critical review of child custody evaluation reports. *Family Court Review, 40*, 164–176. doi: 10.1111/j.174–1617.2002.tb00827.x

Bow, J., & Quinnell, F. (2004). Critique of child custody evaluations by the legal profession. *Family Court Review, 40*, 164-176.

Bray, J. (1991). Psychosocial factors affecting custodial and visitation arrangements. *Behavioral Sciences and the Law, 9*, 419–437. doi: 10.1002/bsl.2370090406

Caspi, A., Henry, B., McGee, R., Moffitt, T., & Silva, P. (1995). Temperamental origins of child and adolescent behavior problems: From age 3 to age 15. *Child Development, 66*, 55–68. doi: 10.2307/1131190

Center for Disease Control and Prevention (2014a). Understanding intimate partner violence. Fact sheet. Retrieved on October 1, 2014 from www.cdc.gov/violenceprevention/intimatepartnerviolence/index.html.

Center for Disease Control and Prevention (2014b). Child maltreatment prevention. Retrieved on October 1, 2014 from www.cdc.gov/violenceprevention/childmaltreatment/index.html.

Chess, S., & Thomas A. (1984). *Origins and evolution of behavior disorders*. Cambridge, MA: Harvard University Press.

Coolahan, K., Fantuzzo, J., Mendez, J., & McDermott, P. (2000). Preschool peer interaction and readiness to learn: Relationships between classroom peer play and learning behaviors and conduct. *Journal of Educational Psychology, 92*, 458–465. doi: 10.1037/0022–0663.92.3.458

Crowley, J. (2008). *Defiant dads: Fathers' rights activists in America*. Ithaca, NY: Cornell University Press.

Cummings, E., Davies, P., & Campbell, S. (2002). Developmental psychopathology and family process: Theory, research, and clinical implications. *Journal of the American Academy of Child And Adolescent Psychiatry, 41*, 886. doi: 10.1097/00004583–200207000–00024

DiFonzo, J. (2014). From the rule of one to shared overnight parenting: Custody presumptions in law and policy. *Family Court Review, 52*, 213–239. doi: 10.1111/fcre.12086

Drozd, L., Olesen, N., & Saini, M. (2013). *Parenting plan evaluations: Using decision trees to increase evaluator competence and avoid preventable errors*. Sarasota, FL: Professional Resources Press.

Ellis, E. (2008). Child custody evaluations. In Jackson, R. (ed.) *Learning forensic assessments* (pp. 417–448). New York: Routledge.

Elrod, L., & Dale, M. (2008). Paradigm shifts and pendulum swings in child custody: The interests of children in the balance. *Family Law Quarterly, 43*, 381–418.

Felitti, V., Anda, R., Nordenberg, D., Williamson, D., Spitz, A., Koss, M., & Marks, J. (1998). Relationship of childhood abuse and household dysfunction to many of the leading causes of death in adults: The adverse childhood experiences (ACE) study. *American Journal of Preventive Medicine, 14*, 245–258. doi: 10.1016/S0749–3797(98)00017–8

Friedhandler, S., & Walters, M. (2010). When a child rejects a parent: Tailoring the intervention to fit the problem. *Family Court Review, 48*, 98–111. doi: 10.1111/j.1744–1617.2009.01291.x

Fuhrmann, G., & Zibbell, R. (2012). *Best practices in forensic mental health assessments: Evaluations for child custody*. New York: Oxford University Press.

Galatzer-Levy, R., Kraus, L., & Galatzer-Levy, J. (Eds.). (2009). *The scientific basis of child custody decisions* (2nd ed.). Hoboken, NJ: Wiley.

Gardner, R., (1992). *The parental alienation syndrome: A guide for mental health and legal professionals*. Cresskill, NJ: Creative Therapeutics.

Goldstein, M. (2003). Parenting and substance abuse: A longitudinal analysis. *Dissertation Abstracts International: Section B: The Sciences and Engineering, 63* (11-B), 5515.

Gould, J., & Martindale, D. (2007). *The art and science of child custody evaluations*. New York: Guilford.

Gould, J., & Martindale, D. (2013). Child custody evaluations: Current literature and practical applications. In R. Otto (Ed.), *Handbook of psychology, Vol. 11: Forensic psychology* (pp. 101–138). New York: Wiley.

Grisso, T. (1986). *Evaluating competencies: Forensic assessments and instruments*. New York: Plenum.

Grossberg, M. (1985). *Governing the hearth: Law and the family in nineteenth-century America*. Chapel Hill: University of North Carolina Press.

Harden, P., & Pihl, R. (1995). Cognitive functioning, cardiovascular activity, and behavior of boys at high risk for alcoholism. *Journal of Abnormal Psychology, 104*, 94–103. doi: 10.1037/0021–843X.104.1.94

Hardesty, J., Haselschwerdt, M., & Johnson, M. (2012). Domestic violence and child custody. In K. Kuehnle & L. Drozd (Eds.), *Parenting plan evaluations: Applied research for the family court* (pp. 442–475). New York: Oxford University Press.

Heilbrun, K. (2001). *Principles of forensic mental health assessment*. New York: Kluwer Academic.

Heilbrun, K., Grisso, T., & Goldstein, A. (2009) *Best practices in forensic mental health assessments, Vol. 1: Foundations of forensic mental health assessment*. New York: Oxford University Press

Ihrke, D. (2014). Reason for moving: 2012 to 2013. *Current population reports*, P20–574. Washington, DC: U.S. Census Bureau.

In re Tropea, 87 N.Y. 2d 727; 665 N.E. 2d 145 (1996).

Jackson, R. (Ed.). (2008). *Learning forensic assessment*. New York: Routledge

Jaffe, P. (2014). A presumption against shared parenting for family court litigants. *Family Court Review, 52*, 187–192. doi: 10.1111/fcre.12081

Jenuwine, M., & Cohler, B. (2009) Child custody evaluations of parents with major psychiatric disorders. In R. Galatzer-Levy., L. Kraus, & J. Galatzer-Levy (Eds.), *The scientific basis of child custody decisions* (2nd ed., pp. 307–352). New York: Wiley.

Johnson, J., Lee, M., Walters, M., & Oleson, N. (2005). Is it alienating parenting, role reversal, or child abuse? A study of children's rejection of a parent in child custody disputes. *Journal of Emotional Abuse, 4*, 191–218. doi: 10.1300/J135v05n04_02

Joseph, J., Joshi, S., Lewin, A., & Abrams, M. (1999). Characteristics and perceived needs of mothers with serious mental illness. *Psychiatric Services, 50*, 1357–1359.

Jouriles, E., McDonald, R., Smith-Slep, A., Heyman, R., & Garrido, E. (2008). Child abuse in the context of domestic violence: Prevalence, explanations, and practice implications. *Violence and Victims, 23*, 221–235. doi: 10.1891/0886–6708.23.2.221

Keilin, W., & Bloom, L. (1986). Child custody evaluation practices: A survey of experienced professionals. *Professional Psychology: Research and Practice, 17*, 338–346. doi: 10.1037/0735–7028.17.4.338

Kelly, J. (2012). Risk and protective factors associated with child and adolescent adjustment following separation and divorce: Social science applications. In K. Kuehnle & L. Drozd (Eds.), *Parenting plan evaluations: Applied research for the family court* (pp. 49–84). New York: Oxford University Press.

Kelly, J., & Emery, R. (2003). Children's adjustment after divorce: Risk and resilience perspectives. *Family Relations, 52*, 352–362. doi: 10.1111/j.1741–3729.2003.00352.x

Kelly, J., & Johnson, M. (2008). Differentiation among types of intimate partner violence: Research update and implications for interventions. *Family Law Review, 46*, 476–499. doi: 10.1111/j.1744–1617.2008.00215.x

Kelly, J., & Johnston, J. (2001). The alienated child: A reformulation of parental alienation syndrome. *Family Court Review, 46*, 476–499. doi: 10.1111/j.1744–1617.2008.00215.x

Kirkland, K., McMillan, E., & Kirkland, K. (2006). Use of collateral contacts in child custody evaluations. *Journal of Child Custody, 2*, 95-109. doi: 10.1111/j.1744-1617.2008.00215.x

Kohm, L. (2008). Tracing the foundations of the best interests of the child standard in American jurisprudence. *Journal of Law and Family Studies, 10*, 337–376.

Kuehnle, K., Coulter, M., & Firestone, G. (2000). Child protection evaluations: The forensic stepchild. *Family Court Review, 38*, 368–391.

Kuehnle, K., & Drozd, L. (2012). Evidence-based practice. In K. Kuehnle & L. Drozd (Eds.), *Parenting plan evaluations: Applied research for the family court* (pp. 587–582). New York: Oxford University Press.

Lampl, A. (2009). Observations of parents, caretakers, and children for child custody assessment. In R. Galatzer-Levy., L. Kraus, & J. Galatzer-Levy (Eds.), *The scientific basis of child custody decisions* (2nd ed., pp. 71–83). New York: Wiley.

Larson, K., & McGill, J. (2010). Adolescent input into custody decisions: Evaluating decision-making capacities. *Journal of Forensic Psychology Practice, 10*, 133–144. doi: 10.1080/15228930903446708

Maccoby, E., & Mnookin, R. (1992). *Dividing the child: The social and legal dilemmas of custody*. Cambridge, MA: Harvard University Press.

Mason, M. (1994). *From father's property to children's rights: The history of child custody in the United States*. New York: Columbia University Press.

Massachusetts General Laws, Ch. 208 §31.

McCann J., Flens, J., Campagna, V., Collman, P., Lazzaro, T., & Connor, C. (2001). The MCMI-III in child custody evaluations: A normative study. *Journal of Forensic Psychology Practice, 1*, 27–44. doi: 10.1300/J158v01n02_02

McGleughlin, J., Meyer, S., & Baker, J. (1999). Assessing child abuse allegations in divorce custody and visitation disputes. In R. Galatzer-Levy & L. Kraus. (Eds.), *The scientific basis of child custody decisions* (pp. 357–388). New York: Wiley.

McMahon, T., & Giannini, F. (2003). Substance abusing fathers in family court: Moving from popular stereotypes to therapeutic jurisprudence. *Family Court Review, 41*, 337–353. doi: 10.1177/1531244503041003006

Melton, G., Petrila, J., Poythress, N., & Slobogin, C. (2007). *Psychological evaluations for the courts* (3rd ed.). New York: Guilford.

Mnookin, R. (1975). Child custody adjudication and judicial function in the face of indeterminacy. *Law and Contemporary Problems, 39*, 226–293. doi: 10.2307/1191273

Murphy, C., & Cascardi, M. (1999). Psychological abuse in marriage and dating relationships. In R. Hampton (Ed.), *Family violence prevention and treatment* (2nd ed., pp. 198–226). Beverly Hills, CA: Sage. doi: 10.4135/9781452231983.n8

National Conference of Commissioners on Uniform State Laws. (1970). Uniform Marriage and Divorce Act. Chicago, IL.

Nicholson, J., Biebel, K., Hinden, B., Henry, A., & Stier, L. (2001). *Critical issues for parents with mental illness and their families*. Rockville, MD: Center for Mental Health Services, Substance Abuse and Mental Health Services Administration Office of Policy, Planning and Administration. Psychiatry Publications and Presentations. Paper 142. http://escholarship.umassmed.edu/psych_pp/142

O'Leary, S., & Slep, S. (2006). Precipitants of partner aggression. *Journal of Family Psychology, 20*, 344–347. doi: 10.1037/0893–3200.20.2.344

Otto, R., Buffington-Vollum, J., & Edens, J. (2003). Child custody evaluations. In I. Goldstein & I. Weiner (Eds.), *Handbook of psychology, Vol. 11: Forensic psychology* (pp. 179–207). New York: Wiley.

Oyserman, D., Mowbray, C., & Zemenchuk, J. (1994). Resources and support for mothers with severe mental illness. *Health and Social Work, 19*, 132–142.

Pickar, D., & Kaufman, (2013). The child custody evaluation report: Toward an integrated model of practice. *Journal of Child Custody, 10*, 17–53. doi: 10.1080/15379418.2013.778702

Quinnell, F., & Bow, J. (2001). Psychological tests used in child custody evaluations. *Behavioral Sciences and the Law, 19*, 491–501. doi: 10.1002/bsl.452

Rohrbaugh, J. (2008). *A comprehensive guide to child custody evaluations: Mental health and legal perspectives*. New York: Springer.

Saini, M., Johnston, J., Fidler, M., & Bala, N. (2012). Empirical studies of alienation. In K. Kuehnle & L. Drozd (Eds.), *Parenting plan evaluations: Applied research for the family court* (pp. 399–441). New York: Oxford University Press.

Saywitz, K., Camparo, L., & Romanoff, A. (2010). Interviewing children in custody cases: implications of research and policy for practice. *Behavioral Science and the Law, 28*, 542–562,

Schachter, J. P. (2004, March). Geographical mobility: 2002 to 2003. (U.S. Census Bureau, No. P20–549). Washington, DC: U.S. Department of Commerce

Schutz, B., Dixon, E., Lindenberger, J., & Ruther, N. (1989). *Solomon's sword: A practical guide to conducting child custody evaluations*. San Francisco: Jossey Bass.

Scott, E. (2014). Planning for children and resolving custodial disputes: A comment on the think tank report. *Family Law Review, 52*, 200–206. doi: 10.1111/fcre.12084

Stahl, P. (2011). *Conducting child custody evaluations*. Thousand Oaks, CA: Sage

Strauss, M., & Gelles, R. (1988). *Intimate violence in families*. New York: Simon and Shuster.

Suchman, N., & Luthar, S. (2000). Maternal addiction, child maladjustment, and sociodemographic context: Implications for parenting. *Addiction, 95*, 1417–1428. doi: 10.1046/j.1360–0443.2000.959141711.x

Tebes, J., Kaufman, J., Adnopoz, J., & Racusin, G. (2001). Resilience and family psychosocial processes among children with parents with serious mental disorders. *Journal of Child and Family Studies, 10*, 115–136. doi: 10.1023/A:1016685618455

Thomas, A., & Chess, S. (1977). *Temperament and development*. New York: Bruner/Mazel.

Tippins, T., & Wittman, J. (2005). Empirical and ethical problems with custody recommendations: A call for clinical humility and judicial vigilance. *Family Court Review, 43*, 266–269. doi: 10.1111/j.1744–1617.2005.00019.x

Tolle, L., & O'Donahue, W. (2012). *Improving the quality of child custody evaluations: A systematic model*. New York: Springer. doi: 10.1007/978–1–4614–3405–4

U.S. Department of Health and Human Services (2012). First Marriages in the United States: Data from the 2006–2010 National Survey of Family Growth. *National Health Statistics Reports, 49.* Retrieved on June 19, 2015 from www.cdc.gov/nchs/data/nhsr/nhsr049.pdf#x2013;2010%20National%20Survey%20of%20Family%20Growth%20[PDF%20-%20419%20KB%3C/a%3E

U.S. Department of Health and Human Services, Centers for Disease Control and Prevention, National Center for Health Statistics (2002). Cohabitation, Marriage, Divorce, and Remarriage in the United States. Data from the National Survey of Family Growth. *Vital and Health Statistics, 23 (#22).*

Warshak, R. (2011, April). *Parental alienation: Not just another custody case.* Presentation at annual conference of Massachusetts Association of Guardians ad Litem, Weston, MA.

Watts v. Watts, 77 Misc.2d 178 (1973).

Weitzman, L. (1985). *The divorce revolution: The unexpected social and economic consequences for women and children in America.* New York: The Free Press.

Zemenchuk, J., Rogosh, F., & Mowbray, C. (1998). The seriously mentally ill woman in the role of parent: Characteristics, parenting, sensitivity, and needs. *Psychosocial Rehabilitation Journal, 15*, 95-99.

17 Evaluations of Individuals for Disability in Insurance and Social Security Contexts

William E. Foote

This chapter considers the psychological evaluation of individuals who have filed claims for disability benefits under two different systems. The first system is one in which a person or his or her employer has purchased a disability insurance policy. The second system involves the Social Security system when a claimant files for Social Security benefits under one of several relevant Social Security programs. In the first case, an insurance carrier requests the evaluation. In the second, either the Social Security Administration (SSA), the claimant, or the claimant's lawyer requests the evaluation. These two systems are considered together in this chapter because both center on the issue of defining parameters of impairment of function. These definitions are not unlike those encountered in evaluations conducted in the context of Americans With Disabilities Act evaluations (Foote, 2013) in that the implications of impairment upon work is the essential focus of the evaluation.

In order to understand disability evaluations, it is critical to understand what *disability* means. As Gold (2013) has observed, the concept of disability rests upon the related concepts of diagnosis and impairment. *Diagnosis* is the definition of a condition using a diagnostic nosology such as the *Diagnostic and Statistical Manual of Mental Disorders*, fifth edition (DSM-5; American Psychiatric Association, 2013). This simply provides a way of communicating the nature and severity of the symptoms that the claimant reports or demonstrates in the evaluation. An accurate diagnosis is a critical part of a disability evaluation because most disability systems require a diagnosis to begin the analysis for disability.

One researcher in the area (Pryor, 1997) defines *impairment* as "organ level abnormalities or restrictions (such as episodes of panic in an anxiety disorder)" (p. 155). Gold (2013) observes that "Impairment constitutes an observational description that should be measurable in some way and related to a health condition" (p. 7).

Disability is impairment in context. For example, a woman with an impairment in walking from a lower-limb amputation may experience disability in tasks requiring significant ambulation, but no disability at all in sedentary work. A child with frontal lobe impairment may experience considerable disability in situations with little external structure, but function with less disability in contexts where such structure is present. A man experiencing impairment from depression may not be able to do work that requires self-initiation, sustained activity, or long work days, but may function much better in tasks when he is closely supervised and does not have to work a full eight-hour day.

The exact definition of disability is usually dependent upon the legal system in which impairment is assessed. In some legal situations the context is all the work for which the person is otherwise qualified. This is a broad context indeed, and one that allows for greater impairment in the absence of a finding of disability. In contrast, other legal systems may define the context as the work the person was doing at the time of the onset of the disability, a much narrower range of potential activities within which an impaired person may function. In both systems addressed in this chapter, the referral source, such as an insurance carrier, or the funding agency, such as the SSA, defines the specific context of disability.

In this chapter, I will bring together a series of topics to address disability evaluations. First, I will explore ethical issues related to these evaluations. Second, I will provide information about the demands that insurance carriers make upon professionals who conduct Independent Medical Evaluations (IMEs).[1] In the course of this discussion, I will lay out procedures that may be followed for most disability evaluations. Third, I will provide information about the SSA system for the evaluation of disability, and then I will provide some concluding remarks.

Ethical Issues

In SSA evaluations and in IMEs, the evaluator encounters ethical issues, much as in other forensic evaluations (American Psychological Association, 2002; American Psychological Association, 2013; Martindale & Gould, 2013; Weissman & DeBow, 2003). Vore (2006) reminds the IME examiner that each evaluation should be treated as though it will be a basis for court testimony, because the insured[2] may file suit against the carrier for bad faith or some other tort, and the evaluation may be the centerpiece of the legal controversy. This means that the examiner should assume that the standards should be equivalent to those of any court-related forensic assessment. Even with this adherence to high standards, in the IME and SSA settings, several issues are of special importance.

The examiner must be clear about defining who is the client (Martindale & Gould, 2013). In the IME, the client is almost always the insurance company. The disability carrier is requesting the evaluation, setting the parameters for the assessment, defining the scope of the report, and paying the examiner for professional time. In the SSA evaluation, the evaluation may be done at the request of the SSA, the claimant, or the claimant's lawyer. In the first case, the SSA provides the parameters for the evaluation, including forms to be completed at the end of the evaluation process or the elements to be covered in a report. In this case the SSA is paying the fee for the evaluation. When the claimant pays for the professional's time, the professional's final product must provide sufficient information for the SSA to adjudicate a claim. From an ethical perspective, the job of the examiner is no different in any of these cases. The examiner is expected to conduct a fair and accurate assessment of the claimant or insured, without bias based upon the source of the referral or payment.

Informed consent is sometimes complicated in forensic assessment (see Foote & Shuman, 2006), but in cases of the SSA or IME evaluation, informed consent is especially important because of the sometimes high stakes riding on the outcome of these assessments (Vanderpool, 2013). The informed consent process should be one of the first things that occurs when the professional meets with the examinee, before any forms are completed and any assessment procedures begun. In all cases, it is recommended that the examiner use a written informed consent, which is read by the examinee and reviewed with the examinee prior to the onset of the evaluation. Any questions should be answered and ambiguities clarified before the examinee signs the consent form.

In some IME contexts, it may be necessary for the insured to sign additional forms that the insurer provides. In both IME and SSA cases, the examiner should include a form with which the examinee provides permission to the examiner to conduct telephone interviews with collaterals. Because these evaluations are done for an insurer or the SSA, the examiner should include a release of information for the evaluation results to the insurance carrier or the SSA as part of the preevaluation consents.

It is critical for the examiner to make his or her role clear to the examinee (Piechowski, 2011). For example, in the IME, the examiner should make it clear that the disability insurance carrier is requesting the evaluation, but that the examiner is not an employee of the insurer. In the SSA evaluation, the examiner should inform the examinee about the examiner's role. The examiner should advise the examinee that he or she may choose to terminate the evaluation at any time, and offer some general idea of the consequences that may follow if the examinee makes that choice. The examiner should tell the examinee that he or she may choose to not answer all questions, but that the examiner will have to make a notation concerning this refusal in the final report. The examiner should provide information to the examinee outlining the procedures to be followed, including testing, interview, and collateral interviews.

In addition, the examiner should disclose who will have access to the report. A special circumstance of some IMEs is that the examiner will be allowed to release the results of the evaluation only to the referring carrier. This means that the examiner may not honor requests for copies of the report from the insured's psychotherapist or physicians. In addition, in most IME contexts, the examiner will not be able to discuss the results of the evaluation with the insured. This is contrary to practice in most assessments (American Psychological Association, 2002), which indicates that the examinee normally should be able to review the results of the examination. For some individuals, not being able to have access to the final report is a "deal breaker," and will result in their withdrawal from the evaluation process.

Independent Medical (Psychological) Evaluations

Private disability insurance preceded the development of Social Security disability insurance in the United States. Before the early part of the twentieth century, the few existing disability policies could be cancelled by the carrier if the person became disabled. In 1916, the first noncancellable policy was sold (First Financial Group, 2006). Early policies narrowly defined disability in terms of permanent and complete disability. After both World Wars, the number and range of disability policies increased. Today, the market for disability policies is competitive, with insurance carriers offering a broad array of policies.

The legal framework of the IME has been largely formed through a series of federal appeals courts decisions. The nuances of this framework require significant elaboration that is not possible within the space confines of this chapter. The interested reader is referred to Gold and Vanderpool (2013) and Piechowski (2011), who have comprehensively covered the case law in this area.

The IME is usually conducted at the request of the insurance carrier. Most commonly, the evaluation is conducted in relation to a claim made by the insured on a disability insurance policy, which may have been purchased by the insured or by his or her employer. The carrier usually requests an evaluation to determine if, in fact, the person is disabled according to the terms of the policy. In this case, the terms of the disability policy are the critical element in this equation, as the insurance policy determines the scope and nature of the IME. The carrier defines, either generally or specifically, the questions to be answered by the evaluation. In addition, the carrier may impose other parameters, such as tests to be administered in the evaluation process.

In the process of the IME, a number of different definitions of disability are used (Anfang & Wall, 2013; Vore, 2006). For example, some policies define disability in relation to "any occupation." These any-occupation policies provide for disability benefits for workers who are unable to perform any occupation for which the worker is reasonably qualified by training, experience, and education. This is similar to the definition for disability under the SSA and may be a very high standard to meet. For example, a well-educated individual like a neurosurgeon may be qualified to perform many other occupations for which he or she is "reasonably qualified." However, some any-occupation policies may require that the job that the disabled insured is still capable of performing will provide the same level of support or income that the worker received in the previous occupation.

"Own occupation" policies may provide benefits for workers who are unable to perform the principal duties of their occupation at the time the individual became disabled. Own-occupation policies provide benefits even though the insured is able to perform the duties of other occupations for which the insured is trained and educated, and for which the insured has appropriate experience. In this situation, the person may be able to be employed full time, yet still receive full disability insurance benefits.

Some insurance policies involve a hybrid of the any-occupation and own-occupation provisions. In many cases, the terms of the insurance policy may not be known to the examiner, but may be inferred from the questions asked by the referring carrier.

Some policies provide for payment for partial as opposed to total disability. Partial disability policies allow benefits in situations in which the insured is unable to perform the critical duties of the occupation, but is able to perform other aspects related to the position. These benefits are usually limited in duration, often to six or nine months (Gold, 2013; Vore, 2006). However, total disability policies usually provide benefits through age 65 and thus may have a very long duration.

Two dates are important in the analysis of these policies: The first is the date of issue. This is the date when the policy becomes effective for that particular worker. The second is the date of claim, when the worker files the claim and states that the disability began. The date of the claim usually must be verified by a medical authority if there is not a particular event, such as an accident, that would provide a temporal anchor for the onset of the disability. Some policies may impose a delay between the date of issue and the date of claim. Although the examiner is unaware of the policy provisions, the insurer may ask for an estimation of when the disabling condition actually began, especially if there is evidence that it began before the date of claim.

Referral

The insurance carrier usually contacts the psychologist and asks to schedule the evaluation. In the interval between the referral and scheduled appointment, the carrier provides a referral letter, which includes the referral questions. These questions may be very particular and may be framed in the language of the insured's insurance policy (Anfang & Wall, 2013).

The psychologist then reviews material provided by the carrier in preparation for the evaluation. In some cases, these materials may include relevant medical and psychological records and reports. Financial records may also be of interest (Black, Serowik, Ablondi, & Rosen, 2013) in order to determine the presence of disabling conditions in the person's history. In many cases, the carrier provides materials that are not as extensive or complete as may be provided to a psychologist conducting an evaluation in other settings, such as those done in the context of a tort claim or an employment discrimination claim (Foote, 2002, 2013; Foote & Goodman-Delahunty, 2005; Foote & LaRue, 2013; Goodman-Delahunty & Foote, 2011; Goodman-Delahunty & Foote, 2013; Goodman-Delahunty, Saunders, & Foote, 2012; Kane & Dvoskin, 2011). In the IME, psychologists are limited in what records they may review, and the opinions of the psychologists may be limited based upon available documented medical history. The psychologist should note any deficiencies in the database, especially if the missing records would illuminate an important aspect of the case.

As noted earlier, before the beginning of the evaluation, the psychologist should prepare an informed consent for the signature of the client. In addition, the psychologist should prepare testing and interview materials so as to be ready to conduct the evaluation expeditiously.

Assessment Procedures

The use of psychological testing is an essential part of the disability evaluation (Heilbrun, DeMatteo, Marczyk, & Goldstein, 2008; Piechowski, 2011, 2013; Stejskal, 2013). The examiner administers or supervises the administration of psychological testing. This usually should be done before any interview is conducted, because the results of the testing may inform the examiner about issues to address in the interview. For example, if the insured endorsed "critical items" on the Minnesota Multiphasic Personality Inventory-2 (MMPI-2), these should be the focus of some questions during the interview to ensure that the examiner understands why the insured endorsed those items.

In line with concerns of researchers (Heilbrun, Rogers, & Otto, 2002), the tests used ought to have appropriate validity, reliability, and norms, and should be administered by qualified individuals who are appropriately licensed to perform the assessment. In addition to the scores from the tests, the testing procedure provides the examiner with an opportunity to observe the insured in a structured setting. These clinical observations may supplement those done in the balance of the evaluation. Two kinds of assessment tools may be used: tests of intelligence/ability, and tests of personality and emotional functioning.

Intellectual assessment may be conducted with the insured to measure overall intellectual capacity, and to identify problems in cognition, memory, attention, and concentration. Formal cognitive testing may be used. In most contexts, because these are limited-duration evaluations, it may be necessary to use a short-form cognitive assessment such as the Wechsler Abbreviated Scale of Intelligence (WASI; The Psychology Corporation, 1999) to determine if the claimant suffers impaired cognitive processing abilities. The examiner should be aware that not all of these short forms yield scores that are psychometrically equivalent to the full Wechsler Adult Intelligence Scale–IV (WAIS-IV; Hays & Shaw, 2003; Wechsler, 2008).

In other situations, more extensive testing, such as the WAIS-IV (Wechsler, 2008) may be appropriate, especially if the insured is complaining of problems in attention, concentration, or memory, or in the case of depression, which may reduce motor speed on timed tasks. Measures of achievement or ability such as the Wide Range Achievement Test–4 (Wilkinson & Robertson, 2006), may be used to determine the level of performance in job-related activities that the insured may be expected to achieve. In addition to these measures, the cognitive assessment should include measures of effort, such as the Test of Memory Malingering (Tombough, 1997), or Validity Indicator Profile (Frederick, 1997) to determine if the examinee performed as well as possible on the cognitive measures.

Personality measures may be used to determine the nature of emotional disorders and the presence of personality or character traits that may relate to work performance. At the least these should include the Personality Assessment Inventory (PAI; Morey, 1991) and the MMPI-2 (Greene, 2011; Pope, Butcher, & Seelen, 2000). These measures provide an assessment of ongoing psychopathology and other disability-related problems. The psychologist may also consider providing a work-related measure such as the Hilson Life Adjustment Profile (Inwald & Resko, 1995). This work-related measure provides an insight into attitudes concerning work and feelings about the work situation, which may be critical to determine whether the individual is, in fact, disabled from functioning in work contexts. The examiner also may wish to employ measures to assess personality disorders, such as the Millon Clinical Multiaxial Inventory–III (MCMI-III; Millon, 1994) to assess long-standing predispositions or pathology that may be comorbid conditions with other disabling conditions, or may themselves constitute disabling conditions. However, some sources (Rogers, 2008; Stejskal, 2013) discourage the use of the MCMI-III in such settings because of limited diagnostic accuracy and concerns about the MCMI-III's tendency to over-diagnose psychiatric disorders.

In general the examiner uses the testing to both generate and confirm hypotheses. That is, the purpose of testing is to provide areas of exploration for the interview and other data gathering techniques. In addition, the testing may confirm hypotheses generated through the interview and allow the examiner to be more certain about conclusions, as they will be based upon more than one source of information. In no case, except perhaps for pegging an IQ score, should the testing be the sole basis for a conclusion.

Interview

On the date of the evaluation, the examiner conducts a clinical interview that should begin with a formal Mental Status Examination (MSE; Gold, 2013; McKenna, 2010; Vore, 2006). The MSE should include an observation of the person's appearance and grooming, and an assessment of orientation according to person, place, time, and situation. The psychologist should assess the client's psychomotor activity, as well as the client's behavior and attitude. The examiner may note the person's affect in terms of his or her flatness or lability and the presence of anxiety symptoms. The MSE should include the insured's mood and its expression in the course of the evaluation. The psychologist may assess the person's ability to engage in reasoning through particular techniques such as the use of proverbs, or reference to formal intellectual assessment. The examiner should observe and analyze the insured's speech in terms of rate, tone, and speed. An evaluation of the person's thought processes to determine the presence of ideas of reference, poverty of thought, thought insertion, circumstantiality, or tangentiality would be appropriate. Assessment of the person's judgment is also essential during this part of this exercise. The psychologist should also assess the client's insight into his or her own problems and how they are affecting the individual. The individual's attention and concentration would be appropriately assessed, as would short-term memory and long-term memory. The psychologist may obtain a rough estimate of the person's intelligence in the course of the MSE, although this would be unnecessary if the evaluation includes cognitive assessment. Overall, the MSE should provide the psychologist's assessment of the individual's current status based upon observations at the time of the evaluation process. In this sense, it is a snapshot of the person's functioning, and may be subject to change over time.

Next, the psychologist should gather the client history (Gold, 2013; Piechowski, 2011) The degree of detail necessary in the client history may vary according to the disability setting. For example, in contexts in which the examiner must determine causation, such as worker's compensation cases (Drukteinis, 2013), causation may be more important than in Social Security evaluations (Williams, 2013). In those cases, the delineation of causation is often a critical part of the evaluation. However, the most central task of the IME is to determine the nature of the deficits related to the mental disorder, not usually the origins of the disorder itself.

In the IME, the history includes exploration of a number of aspects of the insured's history. The psychologist should inquire about the nature of the examinee's family of origin, along with a relationship history. The examinee's family status bears discussion, including a listing of who is living in the examinee's household, including children. Medical history, including hospitalizations and chronic medical conditions such as diabetes or epilepsy, is an important area of inquiry. A mental health history is critical to determine when the condition for which the person is claiming disability began. A history of trauma may also be relevant to mental disabilities, as such a history may magnify the impact of later stressors (Campbell, Greeson, Bybee, & Raja, 2008; Ford & Kidd, 1998; Resnick, Kilpatrick, Dansky, Saunders, & Best, 1993; Roesler & McKenzie, 1994; Wilson, Calhoun, & Bernat, 1999; Zasler & Martelli, 2003). Substance abuse history is critical, as many psychological disabilities have as comorbid conditions problems with drugs or alcohol (Acierno, Kilpatrick, & Resnick, 1999; Kessler, Chiu, Dealer, & Walters, 2005).

The examinee's educational history is an important aspect of the disability evaluation interview, as this is one of the parameters for defining disability. Particular emphasis should be placed upon practical work experiences, such as internships and work-study placements. Employment history provides parameters of experience that play an important role for defining the work that a person is capable of doing. In this regard, the examiner should explore the nature of job duties and responsibilities. Whether the job responsibilities changed over time, especially if the insured was promoted or was given greater responsibilities over time, may be important. The psychologist is also interested in whether merit pay increases were provided, and how the person fared with performance reviews. The nature of the individual's termination of employment may provide important information about work attitudes. If the person left the job without another position waiting, the question of whether the job termination was entirely voluntary should be discussed. The examiner may examine how the individual got along with supervisors and coworkers. Any history of disability in the context of prior employment may provide a basis for a pattern in which the insured repeatedly experienced periods of disability.

In addition to these elements, the interview should focus extensively on the work the person was doing at the time the disability began. Job duties, hours, and compensation are central to this discussion. The nature of the social matrix of the job should be discussed. Who were the coworkers, and supervisors? How did the insured get along with people in the workplace? Were there job duties that the insured disliked, and those that the insured favored? Did the insured experience on-the-job stressors like schedule changes or involuntary layoffs that may have resulted in a loss of coworkers and an increase in duties? Those aspects of the work that were stressful should be explored, as well as how the examinee dealt with those stressors.

If the disability was caused by an accident, the accident itself should be discussed in order to determine the nature of the traumatic aspects of the accident, and the extent to which those may contribute to subsequent disability. If the condition was slowly developing, as in the case of some anxiety disorders or pain syndromes, a discussion of the course of the development of the condition is an essential topic of the interview.

Once the history of the disabling condition is explored, a history of the treatment process for the underlying condition is next to be examined. Who provided the treatment, and the extent to which the treatment was successful, is an important topic. The treatment regime at the time of the evaluation is next for discussion, including medications and ongoing therapy, especially psychotherapy or physical therapy.

The interview then turns to the examinee's current condition. This may begin with questions that elicit the examinee's daily activities from waking to bedtime (see Table 17.1), commonly called Activities of Daily Living. This includes a discussion of the Activities of Daily Living that the examinee is able to do, such as mowing the yard, vacuuming the floor, washing dishes, changing oil in the family auto, etc. The nature and extent of social activities—such as entertaining friends, and going to parties and family gatherings—is part of the current life space that bears exploration. Hobbies and other leisure activities may provide some measure of work-like activities that the examinee may still perform.

The interview should generate a clear picture of the insured's current situation. What is the family context? Who lives in the home with the insured? Are there people within the insured's circle for whom the insured is responsible? For many women, the circle of responsibility extends widely, and may include parents as well as children. If the insured is a professional, what is the

Table 17.1 Activities of Daily Living

Personal hygiene
Household chores
Reading activities
Use of electronic equipment
Social activities
Family responsibilities
Community/religious activities
Exercise regimen
Vacations
Sleep/wake cycle
Eating habits, with any weight gain or loss
Recreational activities, especially as restricted or changed
Driving activities
Financial management
Doctor's visits
Work or work-related activities
Academic pursuits

Note: The material in Table 17.1 was developed from Vore (2006). The original workshop outline was developed in collaboration with Lori Cohen, PhD; material used with Dr. Vore's permission.

status of the insured's current professional license? Is there ongoing litigation concerning some issue? For example, is an insured physician facing malpractice action for acts or omissions during the pre-disability period? A discussion of financial stressors is appropriate. Is the insured in debt? Has the insured filed for bankruptcy?

Throughout the interview, the examiner should be sure that information concerning the examinee's functional limitations is gathered. For example, if the examinee is claiming disability based upon depression, the nature of the problems related to sleep impairment, reduced energy, fatigability, and impaired concentration must be discussed. Even if these impairments do not directly affect work activities, it is important to determine how the impairment affects different aspects of the individual's life activities. Questioning about impairments and their impact should be specific, eliciting details about the duration of time that a person may perform a specific activity, the amount of material that may be read in one sitting, or the number of people that the insured can tolerate at the same time.

Assessment of Malingering or Deception

Most forensic assessments include the evaluation of response set or malingering (Heilbrun et al., 2002; Rogers, 2008). Because of the stakes of disability evaluations, the insured may be tempted to present an inaccurate picture or his or her emotional, physical, or cognitive status (Chavetz & Underhill, 2013; Scott & McDermott, 2013). In this context, as in other forensic assessments, the insured may have a specific goal in this inaccurate presentation (Rogers & Bender, 2003).

The insured may choose to *exaggerate or embellish* the severity of symptoms. In this presentation, the insured begins with symptoms that are real, such as low back pain, and then makes the severity or consequences of the symptoms appear worse than they are. This exaggeration is sometimes difficult to assess, because the symptom may be based in a real injury or illness. A review of psychometric testing, such as the MMPI-2 or the PAI, will provide some indication of exaggeration of emotional symptoms, such as depression or anxiety. However, these measures may not shed much light on exaggeration of physical symptoms, such as pain or limitations in movement.

Frank *malingering* may also be an element of the insured's presentation. In this case, the examinee presents symptoms that do not really exist. In most cases, this presentation involves some clues that the insured is lying. For example, the symptom pattern may include symptoms that are rare, overly specific, or rarely occur in combination. The use of psychometric testing or a specialized instrument, such as the Structured Interview of Reported Symptoms–2 (Rogers, Sewell, & Gillard, 2010) may facilitate detection of malingering.

In some contexts, the insured may be *defensive*. This is the polar opposite of malingering and refers to the conscious denial or gross minimization of physical and/or psychological symptoms. Although this would not be expected in the context of an IME, some insureds may be defensive about some aspects of their presentation, especially those who present with chronic pain problems. In this case the individual may have a stake in convincing the examiner that the pain is real, and not a product of an emotional disorder.

Issues of *secondary gain* are also important, and almost ubiquitous in IMEs. Although some (Rogers & Bender, 2003) argue that this term from psychoanalysis is dated and should not be used, it is still prominent in referrals from insurance carriers and deserves exploration. In disability insurance cases, the insured usually has a financial motive to appear disabled. However, in some cases, the insured has other motives for disability. For example, in the individual's family situation, the disability may garner attention and concern from family members who heretofore had been relying upon the individual as primary wage earner. The disability may allow the individual to avoid activities such as housework or other undesired labor. The worker may use the disability to "get back" at an employer whom the employee has always felt to be unfair. All of these motives are a basis for exaggeration or frank malingering, and should probably be assumed under one of those rubrics. All of these goals and motives may be considered "secondary gain" by the insurance carrier.

In addition to the patterns noted previously, hybrid responding may be evident. This may be a combination of exaggeration and defensiveness. As noted earlier, the pain patient may exaggerate the degree of disability attendant to pain, but may be defensive about the existence of emotional problems. The discovery of one kind of response set giving rise to an inaccurate evaluation does not stop the inquiry. Paying attention to the subtleties of the presentation will increase the quality and accuracy of the assessment.

Collateral Interviews

Conducting interviews with individuals other than the examinee has become an integral part of a comprehensive forensic evaluation (Heilbrun, Rosenfeld, Warren, & Collins, 1994; Heilbrun, Warren, & Picarello, 2003). However, some sources have raised concern about the accuracy of information gathered from collaterals, in that they may be inclined to bias their reports to enhance or decrease the insured's level of disability (Scott & McDermott, 2013).

In the IME, the use of collaterals can also be quite valuable in validating the insured's complaints and determining the impact of disabling conditions (Gold, 2013; Piechowski, 2011; Scott & McDermott, 2013). The ability of the examiner to conduct these additional interviews may be limited by the practices of and the referral from the insurance carrier. In addition, the insured may not provide the names of potential collaterals or permission to contact them. If allowed, however, the interviews may be done with two groups of people.

The first group would be those whom the examinee identifies, which would include friends and family. Disinterested but informed parties such as clergy and neighbors may also be useful sources of information. It is usually important to obtain the permission of the examinee to talk with these individuals, because the examinee will be asked to contact the collateral sources before the examiner does to advise them of the purpose of the examiner's call and enlist their assistance in this task. Permission to contact collaterals is also important in order to protect the privacy of the insured. For example, the proposed collateral may not be aware that the insured is seeking disability insurance benefits, or the nature of the insured's disability. Given the stigma associated with both of these, the insured may not desire to have those issues disclosed through the mechanism of the collateral interview. It is also appropriate for the examiner to discuss the parameters of the interview with the collateral, including who the examiner is, why the examiner is contacting the collateral, and the nature of the information to be gathered in the interview and the purposes to which that information will be put. In this context it is critical to advise the collateral that the information gathered in the interview may be repeated in a written report or in legal proceedings so that the collateral will understand that what they say about the examinee may be repeated to the examinee at some later date.

The second group of individuals to be interviewed is from the insured's former workplace. If the retaining party is associated with the employer, these interviews may be arranged through the carrier and may take place at the insured's former work site. In this case, it is probably not necessary to obtain permission from the insured for these conversations. In contrast, if the retaining party has no connection with the former employer, it is probably necessary to treat these conversations as one would interviews with friends, family, neighbors, or clergy, and obtain permission from the insured and to request that the insured contact the collateral before the examiner does. Once the interviews and testing have been completed, the psychologist prepares a report.

Report Preparation

The psychologist should remember to answer only the questions that the referral source posed. Although a number of other issues may arise in the course of a thorough interview and testing, this is a very specialized examination in which the examiner is required only to provide answers to specific questions that are usually framed in the context of the individual's disability policy.

In the course of the evaluation, the psychologist will usually determine the insured's diagnosis. In most cases, the diagnosis itself is not the critical issue, but the impairments that arise from the mental or emotional problems that the individual claims constitute his or her disability. It is not the examiner's job to determine if the insured's definition of disability is met, but only to describe the nature and extent of the claimant's impairments.

In discussing impairment, the person's functional capacity is the main focus (Vore, 2006; Gold, 2013). Functional capacity (or in SSA terms, Residual Functional Capacity) focuses on what the person is still able to do in spite of his or her impairments. Impairments that would affect work are especially important. For example, if the individual has impairment of social skills that would interfere with that individual functioning in a job that requires contact with the public, a notation concerning that impairment would be very important as part of the disability evaluation. To the extent possible, the examiner should discuss functional capacities in terms of concrete limitations on activities. For example, if the insured is limited in the duration of sustained concentration, a description of that limitation in hours is most helpful.

In order to provide appropriate context, the psychologist should also discuss other factors that may not relate to the disability itself, but have an impact on whether the individual wants to work (Gold, 2013). For example, a woman claiming disability may be five years younger than her husband, who just retired. She may want to spend more time with him, and the choice of her retirement may be attractive on that basis alone. If the individual is experiencing a pain problem, the psychologist must ask if there are identifiable psychological factors that exacerbate or ameliorate the experience of pain.

The insurance carrier may want an assessment of treatment issues. For example, is the current treatment appropriate for the claimed impairments? What are the insured's current treatment needs? What would the optimal treatment plan include? Would adjunctive psychotropic medication or psychotherapy improve the prognosis? If optimal treatment is provided, what is the probability that the insured will return to work? Does the insured have the motivation to engage in treatment and follow treatment recommendations? Under conditions of maximum motivation on the part of the insured and optimal treatment, would the worker be able to return to work?

Depending on the language of the insured's disability policy, the carrier may be interested in an opinion about the insured's ability to return to the former job. Alternatively, the insurer may describe a range of jobs and ask for opinions concerning the insured's fitness for those occupations. To be able to offer opinions about these issues, the psychologist should be certain that sufficient information is available about the nature of the duties of those jobs and other parameters of the insured's condition (e.g., medical limitations) that may limit work capacities.

The report should conclude with a summary section that brings together the insured's strength and impairments as they relate to work contexts. To the extent that the impairments are evident in non-work contexts, discussion may be more complete. By the end of the report, the reader should have a complete and balanced picture of the individual.

Psychological Evaluations in the Social Security System

President Franklin Delano Roosevelt signed the Social Security Act on June 8, 1934 as part of a number of legislative initiatives designed to pull the United States out of the Great Depression (Social Security Administration, 2014b). The original legislation provided for retirement income for older Americans through both grants to states for elderly people and a federal government–administered benefit program that we now know as Social Security. In 1956, the Social Security Act was amended to provide benefits for disabled workers aged 50–64 and to disabled children. President Eisenhower signed a bill in 1960 to extend benefits to disabled workers of any age. After the initial development of Social Security, a number of state-run programs for short-term disability were developed, but they differ widely in criteria for qualifications, benefits, and the efficiency with which those programs were run. In 1972, the federal government brought these programs together under the SSA because the SSA had an established an efficient system for evaluating disability and disbursing benefits (Social Security Administration. 2014b).

The Social Security system developed two programs that provide benefits: Supplemental Security Income (SSI) and Social Security Disability Insurance (SSDI; Kodimer, 1988). These programs differ in terms of who is qualified, the nature of the benefits provided, and other factors, but disability evaluation for both programs is essentially the same.

SSDI is designed to provide benefits for workers who are disabled. In order to qualify for SSDI, the worker must have earned benefits by paying Federal Insurance Contributions Act (FICA) tax contributions for a minimum of 20 quarter-years in a 40-quarter period (e.g., 5 years out of a 10-year period), which ends at the time the worker applies for benefits. The quarter-year (now called "credits") system allows for those quarter-years to be worked in noncontiguous periods. In addition, the worker cannot have reached the age for retirement, and must wait for a five-month delay period (Social Security Administration, 2010). The criteria for receiving SSDI are as follows: (a) the worker must be unable to engage in any substantial gainful activity because of a physical or mental impairment; (b) the worker must not only be unable to do his or her previous work, but also any other type of work, considering the worker's age, education, and work experience; (c) the worker's impairment must be established by objective medical evidence; (d) the worker's impairment will either result in death or last for at least 12 months in a row; and (e) the worker must meet the nonmedical criteria required for insurance by the program.

SSI is "designed to help aged, blind, and disabled people, who have little or no income and provides cash to meet basic needs for food, clothing, and shelter" (Social Security Administration, 2015). In order to receive SSI, the individual must first meet income criteria, which limit the income that a person may earn and still receive SSI. The program also limits the resources that the person may have, although the person's home, auto, and other assets are usually eliminated from this accounting (Social Security Administration, 2015). Unlike SSDI, the SSI program does not require the worker to have paid into the system through FICA. An individual may receive SSDI and SSI at the same time, if he or she meets the criteria for both programs and if his or her level of qualification for SSDI does not provide full benefits.

Application and Appeals Procedures

Although these programs differ, the qualifications and procedures for disability determination are similar (Brandt, Houtenville, Huynh, Chan, & Rasch, 2011; Kodimer, 1988). The individual must first go to a local SSA office and put in an application. Then, the SSA office gathers information about the individual. This information includes medical records, which provide data about the nature of the person's medical condition and the limits that the condition places upon the person's ability to function in the workplace. On the basis of this information, the SSA begins to determine if the individual meets the criteria for disability under the SSA system. First, the individual must have a medically determinable impairment. The applicant must list the medical history related to the disability, and the SSA will review the available information to determine if the individual qualifies. A physician or psychologist is usually involved in this review process. Although the SSA may take into account information gathered from a medical or mental health professional, the determination of disability is still made by the SSA, not the professional (Kodimer, 1988).

The most recent statistics for how well the application and appeals process functions may be found in a review of the final outcome of disabled worker evaluations between 2002 and 2010 (Social Security Administration, 2012a). In the first stage of the process, 23% of the claims are successful. If this stage fails, the applicant has only 60 days in which to request reconsideration. This is not likely to result in a favorable decision, as the success rate for this stage adds only 2%

to the rate of successful applications. The hearing process provides a major increase in those found disabled, as it adds an additional 9% to the number found disabled. Between 2002 and 2010, the rate of eventual approval dropped from 51% to 41%. This decrease in percentage of applicants who finally received benefits occurred during a dramatic rise in applications. In the period between 2002 and 2010, the number of successful applications rose from 5,539,597 to 8,203,951, an increase of about 33%. Although applicants may file suit in federal court to appeal the Appeals Board determination, this has historically been rarely done, but is increasing because of administrative denials.

The delays encountered in following through on these procedures are significant. Although current figures are not available, the historic average interval between the initial determination and reconsideration has been about five months, between reconsideration and appeal to the Administrative Law Judge (ALJ) is two months, between this stage and the Appeals Board, some three months (Benitez-Silva, Buchinsky, Chan, Rust, & Sheidvasse, 1999). If the applicant is successful, however, these intervals usually encompass the required five-month delay for receipt of benefits, so that benefits usually begin shortly after a successful determination.

Through this process, the SSA may request more thorough direct evaluations of the claimant, especially if evidence from various sources is contradictory or inadequate for a complete adjudication. Specialist consultants may be brought in to assist in evaluating data, or may be asked to conduct evaluations with the claimant to determine if the claimant meets the criteria for disability under existing rules.

Criteria for Establishing Disability

The definition for disability under Social Security is: "the inability to engage in any substantial gainful activity by reason of any medically determinable physical or mental impairment(s) which can be expected to result in death or which has lasted or can be expected to last for a continuous period of not less than 12 months" (Social Security Administration, 2012b).

To unpack this definition, the meaning of "substantial gainful activity" is straightforward. As of 2012, if one earns over $1,010 a month in a job, that person is said to be engaging in "substantial gainful activity." This figure is linked to the Cost of Living Index (often referred to as *COLI*), and changes periodically. The meaning of "medically determinable impairment" is: "A medically determinable *physical or mental impairment* is an impairment that results from anatomical, physiological, or psychological abnormalities that can be shown by medically acceptable clinical and laboratory diagnostic techniques. An impairment must be established by medical evidence consisting of signs, symptoms, and laboratory findings" (Social Security Administration, 2012b).

If the individual is unable to return to the work that he or she was doing at the time of the disability, the SSA then considers Residual Functional Capacity. This is what the person is still able to do despite limitations that mental and physical impairments impose. These impairments may include pain, or mental or emotional symptoms that may cause limitations or restrictions in the person's capacity to do work-related physical or mental activities. This Residual Functional Capacity is determined by evaluating the person's maximum remaining ability to engage in sustained work activities in an ordinary work setting over an ordinary work week. The person must be able to engage in work activities on a regular and continuing basis, which means eight hours a day for five days a week, or an equivalent schedule.

Role of the Psychologist

It is within the parameters of these definitions that the SSA reviews available medical documentation to determine the extent to which a person is unable to work. This determination takes into account both physical and mental disabilities. If limitations imposed by physical disabilities do not result in a finding of disability, then mental disabilities may be taken into account. If both mental and physical disabilities result in an inability to engage in substantial gainful activity, then a finding of "disabled" is appropriate.

The psychologist evaluating these issues may be the treating psychotherapist (Levin, 2013) or behavioral manager, or may be an evaluating expert. Although most psychologists now recognize that these roles should be separated (Greenberg & Shuman, 1997), the SSA may require the psychotherapist to comment upon these issues if the therapy record provides sufficient basis for answering the disability-related questions. SSA often prefers to gain information from the treatment provider because of the longitudinal quality of the data gathered in treatment (Williams, 2013). The treating professional will be required to review the claimant's capacity according to SSA guidelines.

The psychologist must follow the same guidelines when conducting an independent psychological evaluation of the claimant. In the Social Security system, this examiner is called a Consultative Mental Health Examiner (Chafetz, 2011). As Williams (2013) notes, psychologists may receive referrals for these consultative examinations (CEs) through three routes. In the first route, a local Disability Determination Service (DDS; the state-run agency tasked with processing disability applications) may ask a mental health professional to conduct a CE as a basis for determining disability if insufficient information exists in the applicant's file. These are reimbursed at a level set for that particular state, and may require only a file review. The second kind of evaluation occurs at a later stage in the process, when the ALJ who is reviewing a file may request a CE in order to have sufficient evidence as a basis for a decision. In a third context, the attorney representing an applicant may request that the DDS order a CE to document the applicant's disability. In any CE, or for a therapist completing the SSA forms, the definition of disability is not in the hands of the psychologist. Rather, the mental health professional must make the effort to learn and follow the SSA guidelines in order to produce a product that is useful to the SSA system. Reference to the SSA *Criteria for Mental Disorders and Impairments* is essential (Noblitt & Noblitt, 2012).

The Assessment Process

The SSA evaluation consists of two parts. The first part is a discussion of the clinical findings that establishes whether the person has a diagnosable mental or physical condition. This part of the evaluation makes reference to the SSA listings (Social Security Administration, 2014b), which are the criteria that the SSA uses for purposes of diagnosis. They do not necessarily match the more familiar diagnostic criteria contained in the DSM-5, but correspond in general ways with the standard nomenclature. The criteria are arranged in nine diagnostic categories: organic mental disorders, schizophrenic, paranoid, and other psychotic disorders, affective disorders, intellectual disability, anxiety-related disorders, somatoform disorders, personality disorders, substance addiction disorders, and autistic disorder and other pervasive developmental disorders (Social Security Administration, 2014b). As an example, Table 17.2 contains the criteria for schizophrenic, paranoid, and other psychotic disorders (Social Security Administration, 2014a). Please note that the initial part of the listings are the positive and negative symptoms commonly associated with schizophrenia.

In Table 17.2, also note how the SSA discusses the second part of the criteria. Part B provides a metric of the degree to which the symptoms of schizophrenia actually constitute a disability. In this case, the illness must adversely affect two of these four elements: (1) Activities of Daily Living, (2) social functioning, (3) aspects of work-related behavior that contribute to focusing on the job and doing it in a timely way (e.g., maintaining concentration, persistence, or pace), or (4) being unable to work because of recurrent exacerbations of symptoms evident in psychotic decompensation.

The severity of impairment must be *marked*, which the SSA defines rather vaguely as "more than moderate but less than extreme. A marked limitation may arise when several activities or

Table 17.2 Schizophrenic, paranoid, and other psychotic disorders characterized by the onset of psychotic features with deterioration from a previous level of functioning

The required level of severity for these disorders is met when the requirements in both A and B are satisfied, or when the requirements in C are satisfied.

A. Medically documented persistence, either continuous or intermittent, of one or more of the following:
  1. Delusions or hallucinations; or
  2. Catatonic or other grossly disorganized behavior; or
  3. Incoherence, loosening of associations, illogical thinking, or poverty of content of speech if associated with one of the following:
    a. Blunt affect; or
    b. Flat affect; or
    c. Inappropriate affect;
  OR
  4. Emotional withdrawal and/or isolation;
  AND
B. Resulting in at least two of the following:
  1. Marked restriction of activities of daily living; or
  2. Marked difficulties in maintaining social functioning; or
  3. Marked difficulties in maintaining concentration, persistence, or pace; or
  4. Repeated episodes of decompensation, each of extended duration;
  OR
C. Medically documented history of a chronic schizophrenic, paranoid, or other psychotic disorder of at least two years' duration that has caused more than a minimal limitation of ability to do basic work activities, with symptoms or signs currently attenuated by medication or psychosocial support, and one of the following:
  1. Repeated episodes of decompensation, each of extended duration; or
  2. A residual disease process that has resulted in such marginal adjustment that even a minimal increase in mental demands or change in the environment would be predicted to cause the individual to decompensate; or
  3. Current history of one or more years' inability to function outside a highly supportive living arrangement, with an indication of continued need for such an arrangement.

functions are impaired, or even when only one is impaired, as long as the degree of limitation is such as to interfere seriously with ability to function independently, appropriately, effectively, and on a sustained basis" (Social Security Administration, 2014b).

In SSA parlance, Activities of Daily Living refer to those things people do every day in order to live their lives (see earlier discussion and Table 17.1). For example, these would include shopping, cooking, cleaning, using public transportation, paying bills, maintaining appropriate grooming and hygiene, maintaining a residence, etc. Activities of Daily Living (also known as ADLs) would be examined in terms of how independent the person was in performing these essential functions, whether the person did the appropriate thing at the appropriate time, whether the person was effective at performing the action, and whether the person could sustain the activity over time. For example, even if a person could explain how to pay a bill, if that person fails to pay their bills on a sustained basis because of a mental illness–imposed disability, then the impairment could be considered *marked*.

Social functioning refers to the claimant's "capacity to interact independently, appropriately, effectively, and on a sustained basis with other individuals" (Social Security Administration, 2014a). This criterion relates to the ability of the person to develop and maintain social relationships, and to get along with essential people in their lives, such as family members, neighbors, friends, grocery clerks, bus drivers, or landlords. Impaired social functioning may be evident in a history of evictions, firings, and altercations with family members and friends. The absence of relationships may also be important: avoidance of social contacts and social isolation would be evidence of impaired social functioning. An understanding of social customs and implicit social rules is important, as well as an awareness of others' feelings and an ability to work cooperatively with others. Determination of whether any of these impairments are *marked* focuses on the degree and persistence of the problem and the extent to which it may impair critical functions, such as maintaining consistent work performance.

Concentration, persistence, or pace "refers to the ability to sustain focused attention and concentration sufficiently long to permit the timely and appropriate completion of tasks commonly found in work settings" (Social Security Administration, 2014b). Work settings are the most common places where these problems become evident, although other settings may also reflect impairments in this area. The insured's self-report, psychological testing, and observation all may be used to determine the extent of impairment in this area. For example, tasks measuring short-term memory or clerical tasks may be used. However, even data from these measures should be supplemented by confirmation of those impairments from other sources. A work evaluation may allow for assessment of concentration, persistence, or pace by examining the claimant's ability to sustain work at appropriate production standards in either a real or simulated work task such as assembling objects, sorting materials, filing cards, or looking up phone numbers. The measures in these tasks may pertain to the extent to which the claimant is able to work consistently until the task is completed or to repeat a sequence of actions.

The examiner must keep in mind that an assessment of these capacities in the context of a psychological evaluation may lack validity when applied to an actual work situation, with the most common errors in the overestimation of the claimant's abilities. The latter often includes time pressures, a lack of structure, or a low level of support. The timely completion of a simple task may not determine if the claimant is able to sustain attention for a complex one. Even if the claimant is able to complete a sequence of tasks, the claimant may require significant supervision or support, or may be unable to perform the task in accordance with commonly accepted competitive accuracy standards. Too many breaks, or a high number of distractions or interruptions, may also signal impairment related to this criterion.

Episodes of decompensation are periods in which the claimant is experiencing increases in symptoms in conjunction with a loss of adaptive functioning, usually measured by a reduction in capacity to perform Activities of Daily Living, impaired social functioning, or reductions in concentration, persistence, or pace. A review of the claimant's medical records may reveal periodic exacerbations of symptoms that result in hospitalization, provision of medication, and withdrawal from usual social and work-related activities. In most cases, these periods of decompensation require placement in a more structured setting and increased intensity of treatment, sometimes with the use of psychotropic medication. For these periods of decompensation to be considered "of extended duration" the record must show three such episodes within a one-year period, or an average of one every four months, with each episode lasting two weeks. Less frequent episodes of shorter duration may also be considered if these episodes cause a significant functional impact upon the ability of the claimant to work.

Documentation

As Williams (2013) notes, "Examiners should bear in mind that the examination is requested because someone involved in the disability determination process, either the DDS or the claimant, has determined that more information than the treating mental health clinician has already provided is required to fully evaluate the disability claim" (p. 202). Documentation is required to provide sufficient evidence to "(1) establish the presence of a medically determinable mental impairment(s), (2) assess the degree of functional limitation the impairment(s) imposes, and (3) project the probable duration of the impairment(s)" (Social Security Administration, 2014b). This documentation may come from appropriate sources such as a medical history, records of mental status examinations, psychological testing, and records related to treatment, including hospitalizations. These records should reflect the issues noted earlier, such as concentration and persistence.

In addition to documentary sources, the claimant can also be a source of important data. The claimant can usually accurately discuss limitations that the disabling condition places upon activities. Of course, for the psychologist conducting the evaluation, these descriptions should also be verified through other sources, such as documentation and psychological testing. The psychologist may also want to gain information directly from other sources, such as interviews with treating physicians, nurses, aides, and physical therapists. As noted in the earlier discussion of collateral interviews, nonmedical sources, such as family members or neighbors, may also provide valuable data.

The SSA Assessment

The data from these sources should reflect the natural history of the claimed impairment. In other words, the longitudinal course of the impairments should be evident through the various data sources, as it may reflect how the underlying disorder and its effect on functioning vary over time. A one-time assessment may not adequately assess the severity of the impairment.

If the claimant attempted to work, these work attempts may provide invaluable data about the severity of the impairments. What the claimant was hired to do, how well the claimant performed the duties, and what led to the termination of the work period are all important. The presence or absence of work supports—such as those provided in supported or sheltered employment settings—may provide some idea of the deficits to be remedied (see Foote, 2013).

An MSE is a necessary part of the Social Security Administration evaluation. It may be assessed as a natural part of the clinical interview and history, and will include the common elements associated with this review. Please see the discussion on the Interview earlier in this chapter.

Psychological testing is a common and necessary part of SSA psychological examinations. Please see the section on testing in the Assessment section of this chapter for details concerning the use of testing in disability evaluations. Specifically in the context of the SSA evaluation, intelligence testing is critical for the assessment of intellectual disability, brain injury, or learning disability. In cases in which intellectual disability is the issue, intelligence testing must be done and may be the most important basis for adjudication. The Wechsler scales (the WAIS-IV and the Wechsler Intelligence Scale for Children–IV) are considered the gold standard for intelligence testing because of their well-accepted definitions for IQ and their long history in the field. The current standards for intellectual disability use the results of obsolete versions of the Wechsler Adult Intelligence Scale such as the WAIS-III (Wechsler, 1997), consisting of the Verbal IQ, Performance IQ, and Full-Scale IQ. The current measure, the WAIS-IV (Wechsler 2008) produces scores with a rough equivalence: the Verbal Index Score, the Performance Index Score, and the Full-Scale IQ. The SSA uses the lowest of those to determine whether the claimant meets the listings for intellectual disability. In situations in which the Wechsler scales may be biased—such as the assessment of a person whose first language is not English, or one from a markedly different cultural setting—other measures such as the Test of Nonverbal Intelligence (TONI; Brown Sherbenou, & Johnsen, 1997) may be employed.

Personality assessment measures may also be used much in the same way as discussed in the Assessment section of this chapter. In this case, these instruments may be used to assist in arriving at a DSM-5 diagnosis necessary for the completion of the evaluation related forms.

The SSA CE report

A CE report must include specific elements: the claimant's major or chief complaint(s); a detailed description, within the area of specialty of the examination, of the history of the major complaint(s); a description, and disposition, of pertinent positive and negative detailed findings based on the history, examination, and laboratory tests related to the major complaint(s), and any other abnormalities or lack thereof reported or found during examination or laboratory testing; results of laboratory and other tests (for example, X-rays) performed according to the requirements stated in the Listing of Impairments; the diagnosis and prognosis for the claimant's impairment(s); and a statement about what the claimant can still do despite his or her impairment(s), unless the claim is based on statutory blindness. If the claimant is an adult of age 18 or over, this statement should describe the opinion of the consultant about the claimant's ability, despite his or her impairment(s), to do work-related activities, such as sitting, standing, walking, lifting, carrying, handling objects, hearing, speaking, and traveling. In adult cases involving mental impairment(s) or mental functional limitations, this statement should also describe the opinion of the consultant about the claimant's capacity to understand, to carry out and remember instructions, and to respond appropriately to supervision, coworkers, and work pressures in a work setting. If the claimant is a child under age 18, this statement should describe the opinion of the consultant about the child's functional limitations compared to children his or her age who do not have impairments in acquiring and using information, attending and completing tasks, interacting and relating with others, moving about and manipulating objects, caring for him- or herself, and health and physical well-being. The statement should also include the consultant's consideration, and some explanation or comment on, the claimant's major complaint(s) and any other abnormalities found during the history and examination or reported from the laboratory tests. The history, examination, evaluation of laboratory test results, and the conclusions will represent the information provided by the consultant who signs the report (Social Security Administration, 2014c).

The SSA requires more particular attention to some issues in the assessment of mental disorders. The evaluation report should go beyond a description of the claimant's signs, symptoms, psychological test results, and diagnosis. It should include the effect of the mental or emotional disorder upon the claimant's ability to function in personal, social, and occupational spheres. It should also include general observations of how the claimant came to the evaluation—whether the person was alone or accompanied, how far the claimant traveled to get to the evaluation, and if an auto was used, who drove. The examiner should comment upon the claimant's general appearance, including dress and grooming, along with observations of the claimant's general attitude and degree of cooperation, and of his or her posture, gait, and general motor behavior, including involuntary movements.

If an informant or collateral source is utilized, the psychologist should identify the person providing the history, and should attempt to estimate the reliability of the history. The claimant's chief complaint, and the history of the present illness is the next area for exploration. This should include: (1) date and circumstances of onset of the condition; (2) date the claimant reported that the condition began to interfere with work, and how it interfered; (3) date the claimant reported inability to work because of the condition and the circumstances; and (4) attempts to return to work and the results.

The report should include an account of outpatient evaluations and treatment for mental or emotional problems, including the names of treating sources, dates of treatment, types of treatment (names and dosages of medications, if prescribed), and response to treatment. Hospitalizations should also be addressed, including the names of the hospitals, the dates of hospitalization, the treatment received, and the response to that treatment.

The SSA provides additional guidance for reports concerning particular mental disorders. For example, for schizophrenic disorders, the SSA requires information about (1) periods of residence in structured settings such as halfway houses and group homes, (2) frequency and duration of episodes of illness and periods of remission, and (3) side effects of medications (Social Security Administration, 2014c).

It should be noted that the narrative that would be normally classified under the Summary and Conclusion section is very important for the SSA adjudicator. This will allow the examiner to bring together all the information about the functional limitations and residual capacities of the claimant. It is also a chance for a practical discussion of real-life limitations that the individual faces, to whatever extent they exist (see Williams, 2013 for an excellent SSA CE report outline).

Conclusion

IME and SSA evaluations bring together a system for providing benefits and an individual seeking those benefits. Both kinds of evaluations have their own "culture" and requirements, and they provide for the psychologist an opportunity to examine the current status of an individual in light of that person's capabilities and deficits. To whatever extent the examiner's interaction with the insured or claimant generates emotional reactions, the job of the examiner does not change. For example, if the SSA claimant has suffered a series of reversals in life culminating in the development of a claimed emotional disability, the examiner's job is to review the records, interview and test the claimant, and write a report about the claimant's capacities in light of the listings. In this case, the examiner's compassionate reaction to the claimant's distress is best channeled into a rather dry recitation of the claimant's capabilities and deficits. This professional attitude and the precision it brings to the task will best serve not only the claimant, but the disability system as well.

Notes

1   In this chapter, the phrase *Independent Medical Evaluation* is used, even though these assessments are technically independent psychological evaluations. The term is generic and refers to all evaluations conducted by health professionals to assess disability in relation to insurance claims.
2   Throughout the chapter, the term *insured* will be used to designate the examinee in the IME. In SSA cases the term *claimant* is used. Both terms are in preference to the term *client*, as the client in these evaluations is the insurance carrier, or may be the SSA.

References

Acierno, R., Kilpatrick, D. G., & Resnick, H. S. (1999). Posttraumatic stress disorder in adults relative to criminal victimization: Prevalence, risk factors, and comorbidity. In P. A. Saigh & J. D. Bremner (Eds.), *Posttraumatic stress disorder: A comprehensive text* (pp. 44–68). Boston, MA: Allyn & Bacon.

American Psychiatric Association. (2013). *Diagnostic and statistical manual of mental disorders* (5th ed.). Arlington, VA: American Psychiatric Publishing.

American Psychological Association. (2002). Ethical principles of psychologists and code of conduct. *American Psychologist, 57,* 1060–1073. doi: 10.1037/0003–066X.57.12.1060

American Psychological Association. (2013). Specialty guidelines for forensic psychology. *American Psychologist, 68,* 7–19. doi: dx.doi.org/10.1037/a0029889

Anfang, S. A., & Wall, B. W. (2013). Long-term disability evaluations for private insurers. In L. H. Gold & D. L. Vanderpool (Eds.), *Clinical guide to mental disability evaluations* (pp. 241–257). New York: Springer.

Benitez-Silva, H., Buchinsky, M., Chan, H. M., Rust, J., & Sheidvasser, S. (1999). An empirical analysis of the Social Security disability application, appeal, and award process. *Labour Economics, 6,* 147–178.

Black, A. C., Serowik, K. L., Ablondi, K. M., & Rosen, M. I. (2013). Timeline historical review of income and financial transactions: A reliable assessment of personal finances. *Journal of Nervous and Mental Disease, 201,* 56–59.

Brandt, D. E., Houtenville, A. J., Huynh, M. T., Chan, L., & Rasch, E. K. (2011). Connecting contemporary paradigms to the Social Security Administration's disability evaluation process. *Journal of Disability Policy Studies, 22,* 116–128.

Brown, L., Sherbenou, R. J., & Johnsen, S. K. (1997). *Test of nonverbal intelligence: A language-free measure of cognitive ability* (3rd ed.). Austin, TX: PRO-ED.

Campbell, R., Greeson, M. R., Bybee, D., & Raja, S. (2008). The co-occurrence of childhood sexual abuse, adult sexual assault, intimate partner violence, and sexual harassment: A mediational model of posttraumatic stress disorder and physical health outcomes. *Journal of Consulting and Clinical Psychology, 76,* 194–207

Chafetz, M. D. (2011). The psychological consultative examination for social security disability. *Psychological Injury and Law*, *4*, 235–244.

Chafetz, M., & Underhill, J. (2013). Estimated costs of malingered disability. *Archives of Clinical Neuropsychology*, *28*, 633–639.

Drukteinis, A. M. (2013). Workers' compensation evaluations. In L. H. Gold & D. L. Vanderpool (Eds.), *Clinical guide to mental disability evaluations* (pp. 215–239). New York: Springer.

First Financial Group. (2006). The history of disability insurance. Retrieved on September 10, 2006, from www.disability-insurance.com/disability-history/.

Foote, W. E. (2002). The clinical assessment of people with disabilities. In R. B. Ekstrom & D. K. Smith (Eds.), *Assessing individuals with disabilities in educational, employment, and counseling settings* (pp. 103–120). Washington, DC: American Psychological Association. doi:10.1037/10471–007

Foote, W. E. (2013). Forensic evaluation in Americans With Disabilities Act cases. In R. Otto & I. B. Weiner (Eds.), *Comprehensive handbook of forensic psychology, Vol. 11: Forensic psychology* (2nd ed.). New York: Wiley.

Foote, W. E., & Goodman-Delahunty, J. (2005). *Evaluating sexual harassment: Psychological, social, and legal considerations in forensic examinations*. Washington, DC: American Psychological Association Press.

Foote, W. E., & Larue, C. R. (2013), Psychological damages in personal injury cases. In R. Otto & I. B. Weiner (Eds.), *Comprehensive handbook of forensic psychology, Vol. 11: Forensic psychology* (2nd ed.) New York: Wiley.

Foote, W. E., & Shuman, D. W. (2006). Consent, disclosure, and waiver for the forensic psychological evaluation: Rethinking the roles of psychologist and lawyer. *Professional Psychology: Research and Practice*, *37*, 437–445. doi:10.1037/0735–7028.37.5.437

Ford, J. D., & Kidd, P. (1998). Early childhood trauma and disorders of extreme stress as predictors of treatment outcome with chronic posttraumatic stress disorder. *Journal of Traumatic Stress, 11*, 743–761.

Frederick, R. (1997). *The Validity Indicator Profile manual*. Minneapolis, MN: National Computer Systems.

Gold, L. H. (2013). Mental health disability: A model for assessment. In L. H. Gold & D. L. Vanderpool (Eds.), Clinical guide to mental disability evaluations (pp. 3–35). New York: Springer.

Gold, L. H., & Vanderpool, D. L. (Eds.). (2013). *Clinical guide to mental disability evaluations*. New York: Springer.

Goodman-Delahunty, J. & Foote, W. E. (2011) *Workplace discrimination and harassment*. London: Oxford University Press.

Goodman-Delahunty, J., & Foote, W. E. (2013). Using a five-stage model to evaluate workplace discrimination injuries. *Psychological Injury and Law*, *6*, 92–98.

Goodman-Delahunty, J., Saunders, P., & Foote, W. (2012) Evaluating claims for workplace discrimination: A five-stage model. *Proceedings of the 2011 APS Forensic Psychology Conference*. Sydney: The Australian Psychological Society Ltd (APS).

Greenberg, S. A., & Shuman, D. W. (1997). Irreconcilable conflict between therapeutic and forensic roles. *Professional Psychology: Research and Practice, 50*, 28–39.

Greene, R., (2011). *The MMPI-2/MMPI-RF: An interpretive manual*. New York: Allyn & Bacon.

Hays, J. R., & Shaw, J. B. (2003). WASI profile variability in a sample of psychiatric inpatients. *Psychological Reports, 92*, 164–166.

Heilbrun, K., DeMatteo, D., Marczyk, G., & Goldstein, A.M. (2008). Standards of practice and care in forensic mental health assessment: Legal, professional, and principles-based consideration. *Psychology, Public Policy, and Law, 14*, 1–26.

Heilbrun, K., Rogers, R., & Otto, R. (2002). Forensic assessment: Current status and future directions. In J. R. P. Ogloff (Ed.), *Taking psychology and law into the twenty-first century* (pp. 119–146). New York: Kluwer Academic/Plenum.

Heilbrun, K., Rosenfeld, B., Warren, J. I., & Collins, S. (1994). The use of third-party information in forensic assessments: A two state comparison. *Bulletin of the American Academy of Psychiatry & Law, 22*, 399–406.

Heilbrun, K., Warren, J., & Picarello, K. (2003). Third party information in forensic assessment. In A. M. Goldstein (Ed.), *Handbook of psychology: Forensic psychology, Vol. 11* (pp. 69–86). Hoboken, NJ: Wiley.

Inwald, R. E., & Resko, J. A. (1995). Preemployment screening for public safety personnel. In L. Van-deCreek, S. Knapp, & T. L. Jackson (Eds.), *Innovations in clinical practice: A source book, Vol. 14.* (pp. 365–382). Sarasota, FL: Professional Resource Press/Professional Resource Exchange.

Kane, A. W., & Dvoskin, J. A. (2011). *Best practices in forensic mental health assessment: Evaluation for personal injury claims.* New York: Oxford University Press.

Kessler, R. C., Chiu, W. T., Dealer, O., & Walters, E. E. (2005). Prevalence, severity, and comorbidity of 12-month DSM-IV Disorders in the National Comorbidity Survey Replication. *Archives of General Psychiatry, 62,* 617-627.

Kodimer, C. (1988). Neuropsychological assessment and Social Security disability: Writing meaningful reports and documentation. *Journal of Head Trauma Rehabilitation, 3,* 77–85.

Levin, A. P. (2013). What should I do? When patients seek disability documentation. In L. H. Gold & D. L. Vanderpool (Eds.), *Clinical guide to mental disability evaluations* (pp. 75–94). New York: Springer.

Martindale, D. A., & Gould, J. W. (2013). Ethics in forensic practice. In R. K. Otto & I. B. Weiner (Eds.), *Handbook of psychology, Vol. 11: Forensic psychology* (2nd ed., pp. 37–61). Hoboken, NJ: Wiley.

McKenna, M. C. (2010). Completing Social Security disability assessments. In S. Walfish (Ed.), *Earning a living outside of managed mental health care: 50 ways to expand your practice* (pp. 106–109).Washington, DC: American Psychological Association.

Millon, T. (1994). *Millon Clinical Multiaxial Inventory-III: Manual.* Minneapolis, MN: Pearson Assessments.

Morey, L. C. (1991). *Personality Assessment Inventory Professional Manual.* Odessa, FL: Psychological Assessment Resources.

Noblitt, R., & Noblitt, P. (2012). Social security disability criteria and substance dependence. *Professional Psychology: Research and Practice, 43,* 94–99.

Piechowski, L. D. (2011). *Best practices in forensic mental health assessment. Evaluation of workplace disability.* New York: Oxford University Press.

Piechowski, L. D. (2013). Disability and worker's compensation. In R. K. Otto & I. B. Weiner (Eds.), *Handbook of psychology, Vol. 11: Forensic psychology* (2nd ed., pp. 201–224). Hoboken, NJ: Wiley.

Pope, K. S., Butcher, J. N., & Seelen, J. (2000). The MMPI, MMPI-2, and MMPI-A in court testimony. In *The MMPI, MMPI-2 & MMPI-A in court: A practical guide for expert witnesses and attorneys* (2nd ed.; pp. 9–49). Washington, DC: American Psychological Association.

Pryor, E. S. (1997). Mental disabilities and the disability fabric. In R. J. Bonnie & J. Monahan (Eds.), *Mental disorder, work disability, and the law* (pp. 153–198). Chicago: University of Chicago Press.

Psychology Corporation. (1999). *Wechsler Abbreviated Scale of Intelligence manual.* Dallas, Texas: Author.

Resnick, H. S., Kilpatrick, D. G., Dansky, B. S., Saunders, B. E., & Best, C. L. (1993). Prevalence of civilian trauma and posttraumatic stress disorder in a representative national sample of women. *Journal of Consulting and Clinical Psychology, 61,* 984–991.

Roesler, T. A., & McKenzie, N. (1994). Effects of childhood trauma on psychological functioning in adults sexually abused as children. *The Journal of Nervous and Mental Disease, 182,* 145–150.

Rogers, R. (2008). *Clinical assessment of malingering and deception* (3rd ed.). New York: Guilford Press.

Rogers, R., & Bender, S. D. (2003). Evaluation of malingering and deception. In A. M. Goldstein (Eds.), *Handbook of psychology, Vol. 11: Forensic psychology* (pp. 109–129). Hoboken, NJ: Wiley.

Rogers, R. Sewell, K. W., & Gillard, N. D. (2010). *SIRS-2: Structured Interview of Reported Symptoms: Professional manual.* Odessa, FL: Psychological Assessment Resources.

Scott, C. L., & McDermott, B. (2013). Malingering and mental health disability evaluations. In L. H. Gold & D. L. Vanderpool (Eds.), *Clinical guide to mental disability evaluations* (pp. 155–182). New York: Springer. doi:10.1007/978-1-4614-5447-2_6

Social Security Administration. (2010). Definition of disability for disabled worker's benefits. Retrieved May 1, 2014 from www.ssa.gov/OP_Home/handbook/handbook.05/handbook-0507.html.

Social Security Administration. (2012a). Outcomes of applications for disability benefits. Retrieved May 1, 2014 from www.ssa.gov/policy/docs/statcomps/di_asr/2012/sect04.pdf.

Social Security Administration. (2012b). Annual statistical report on the Social Security Disability Insurance Program, 2012. Retrieved May 5, 2014 from www.ssa.gov/policy/docs/statcomps/di_asr/2012/di_asr12.pdf.

Social Security Administration. (2014a). Disability evaluation under Social Security: Mental disorders, adult. Retrieved May 5, 2014 from www.ssa.gov/disability/professionals/bluebook/12.00-MentalDisorders-Adult.htm.

Social Security Administration. (2014b). Historical background and development of social security. Retrieved May 1, 2014 from www.ssa.gov/history/briefhistory3.html.

Social Security Administration. (2014c). Social Security handbook. Retrieved May 1, 2014 from http://socialsecuritybenefitshandbook.com/

Social Security Administration. (2015) Supplemental Security Income Home Page—2015 Edition. Retrieved May 1, 2015 from www.ssa.gov/ssi/.

Stejskal, W. J. (2013). Psychological testing in workplace disability evaluations. In L. H. Gold & D. L. Vanderpool (Eds.), *Clinical guide to mental disability evaluations* (pp. 127–154). New York: Springer.

Tombough, T. M. (1997). The Test of Memory Malingering (TOMM): Normative data from cognitively intact and cognitively impaired individuals. *Psychological Assessment, 9*, 260–268.

Vanderpool, D. L. (2013). Legal and ethical issues in providing mental health disability evaluations. In L. H. Gold & D. L. Vanderpool (Eds.), *Clinical guide to mental disability evaluations* (pp. 37–74). New York: Springer.

Vore, D. (2006). The disability psychological independent medical evaluation: Case law, ethical issues and procedures. In A. Goldstein (Ed.), *Forensic psychology: Emerging topics and expanding roles* (pp. 489–510). Hoboken, NJ: Wiley.

Wechsler, D., (1997). *Wechsler Adult Intelligence Scale—Third Edition Administration and Scoring Manual*. San Antonio, TX: The Psychological Corporation.

Wechsler, D. (2008). *WAIS-IV administration and scoring manual*. San Antonio, TX: Pearson

Weissman, H. N., & DeBow, D. M. (2003). Ethical principles and professional competencies. In A.M. Goldstein (Ed.), *Handbook of psychology, Vol. 11: Forensic psychology* (pp. 33–53). Hoboken, NJ: Wiley.

Wilkinson, G. S., & Robertson, G. J. (2006). *WRAT4 Professional Manual*. Lutz, FL: Psychological Assessment Resources.

Williams, C. D. (2013). Social Security disability income claims: Treating mental health clinicians and consultative mental health examiners. In L. H. Gold & D. L. Vanderpool (Eds.), *Clinical guide to mental disability evaluations* (pp. 185–213). New York: Springer.

Wilson, A. E., Calhoun, K. S., & Bernat, J. A. (1999). Risk recognition and trauma-related symptoms among sexually revictimized women. *Journal of Consulting and Clinical Psychology, 67*, 705–710.

Zasler, N. D., & Martelli, M. F. (2003). Mild traumatic brain injury: Impairment and disability assessment caveats. *Neuropsychological Rehabilitation, 13*, 31–41.

Acknowledgments

The author expresses his appreciation to David Vore for his assistance in preparing the IME material. The books and chapters by Lisa Piechowski and Lisa Gold (see References) are excellent detailed resources for those desiring to include disability evaluations in their psychology practice, and the author recommends them to your attention. In addition, the author appreciates the work of Terry Hipkiss in preparing the manuscript, and the sharp eye of his favorite editor, Cheryl Foote.

18 Personal Injury Evaluations

Christmas N. Covell and Jennifer G. Wheeler

Historically, legal disputes involving injury or harm that one person or organization may cause another, specifically addressed by tort laws, have centered around physical injury. However, the 19th century brought recognition of the psychological effects of injuries associated with railway accidents and injuries sustained during war (Koch, Douglas, Nicholls, & O'Neill, 2006). With the recognition of psychological harm, the legal system has increasingly developed and refined its "receptivity to, conception of, and mechanisms for addressing psychological injuries" (Koch et al., 2006, p.16) under tort laws. At this same time, the mental health disciplines (psychiatry and psychology) have also continued to develop their methodology, knowledge, and practices in understanding mental phenomena and its application to legal processes and decision making, resulting in expanding roles for researchers and practitioners in the area of personal injury litigation. Mental health experts are now involved in many areas of tort law related to psychological injury and mental distress, including accidents, disability and workplace injuries, medical malpractice, discrimination, harassment and hostile work environments, criminal activity or intentional mistreatment, and defamation (i.e., slander and libel).

This chapter focuses on evaluations of psychological injury under tort law. The first portion of this chapter is devoted to a brief discussion of tort law and procedure, to improve understanding of the psycholegal context of forensic assessment in this area. Relevant case law exemplifying the evolution of the legal conceptualization and treatment of psychological injury over time and the admissibility of psychological evidence and expert testimony is presented next. This chapter will also outline the assessment process for evaluations of psychological injury, including identification of relevant referral questions, data collection, and communication of findings. Finally, ethical issues and a case example are presented.

Tort Law: A Brief Overview

A tort is a wrongful act that causes someone harm or injury. This wrong, whether intentional or accidental, can result in legal liability for the person who committed the wrongful act (or *tortfeasor*). Tort laws allow for injured parties to seek compensation for their injuries or losses, and are also used to deter others from committing similar wrongful acts or causing harm. Psychological evaluations in personal injury claims typically occur in intentional and negligent tort actions.

Torts are addressed under civil law; they differ from crimes, which are dealt with under criminal law. A tort is a wrong against an individual or violation of a private duty to another, while a crime is a wrong against society or violation of public duty. Though some similarities exist between the interests of tort and criminal laws in punishing/deterring wrongdoers, tort laws are primarily concerned with damages and compensation, and they are started by an individual or private party; while criminal laws are focused on protecting public welfare and are initiated by the government (American Law Institute, 2013; Edwards, Edwards, & Wells, 2011). However, a crime can also be considered a tort. For instance, an assault can result in both criminal charges and sanctions against the perpetrator, as well as a civil suit or tort claim for injuries or harm caused by the perpetrator.

Types of Torts

There are three major categories of torts: intentional, negligent, and strict liability (American Law Institute, 2013):

1. *Intentional* torts essentially involve wrongful acts committed on purpose, which result in harm or injury caused to another. To be considered intentional, it must be established that the tortfeasor (or wrongdoer/liable party) was aware that injury or harm would result from the act (Edwards et al., 2011). Intentional torts are also often crimes, and typically include assault, battery, false imprisonment, fraud, libel, slander, trespass to property (land or chattel), and intentional infliction of emotional distress.
2. By contrast, *negligent* torts typically involve injury or harm resulting from carelessness, or failure to exercise the care or caution expected of a "reasonably prudent person" in a similar situation or circumstances (American Law Institute, 2013).
3. *Strict liability* torts hold parties responsible for injury or harm occurring in certain situations or activities regardless of their behavior (i.e., intentional or negligent) or any precautions that may have been taken. Strict liability often arises in product liability cases to provide recourse for harm caused by defective products. Increasingly, strict liability also involves cases where using, storing, or moving materials or objects considered inherently or abnormally dangerous, such as explosives, weapons or toxic chemicals, or possessing or keeping certain animals results in injury or harm to another (American Law Institute, 2013; Edwards et al., 2011).

Elements of a Tort

Intentional and negligent tort claims involve establishing several important factors or elements, which the plaintiffs (individual[s] or group initiating the lawsuit) must prove to be successful in their claim. The degree or level of proof required for civil cases is lower than for criminal cases, which are typically seen as involving more serious penalties (such as loss of liberty). For civil cases, plaintiffs must typically prove their cases based on a preponderance of the evidence, often equated to a "more likely than not" standard (Young & Shore, 2007).

To be successful in a tort claim, a plaintiff must establish each of the following elements: (1) *Duty*, that the defendant (individual or group accused of a civil wrong, or defending against a lawsuit) was legally obligated or had a duty to behave in a particular way; (2) *breach of duty*, that the defendant engaged in behavior that violated or failed to conform to that duty; (3) *causation*, that the defendant's behavior caused injury to the plaintiff; and (4) *damages*, that the plaintiff suffered legally recognizable harm, injury, or loss as a result of the negligent behavior. Establishing these elements will support a tort claim based on negligence, however, plaintiffs with intentional tort claims must also demonstrate that the defendant acted intentionally or purposefully.

Duty, or Duty of Care. A *duty of care* is essentially a legal obligation to take reasonable care or precaution to avoid harm to others. In general, a reasonable person is expected to act with care and prudence, consider the possibility that others may be harmed by his or her actions, and take appropriate precautions or choose available alternative courses of action to avoid "creating an unreasonable risk of harm" (American Law Institute, 2013. p. 58). Duty of care also considers "special" classes of people and imposes the appropriate expectation—such as a duty that might be expected of a "reasonable doctor" in malpractice cases (Edwards et al., 2011; American Law Institute, 2013)—and considers the appropriate standard of care or duty required depending on the relationship between the parties and the situation (e.g., Does an emergency room physician owe a duty to an injured person in the emergency room where the physician is employed? Or at the scene of an accident on the road?). In addition, establishing a duty for children and persons with emotional or cognitive limitations involves considering what obligation might be expected of children of a similar "age, intelligence, and experience" (American Law Institute, 2013, p. 77) or of persons with a similar disability under the same circumstances (Edwards et al., 2011; Zelig, 2013).

Breach of Duty. The second element of a tort involves establishing *breach of duty*, or assuming a duty exists, whether the defendant then failed to meet his or her legal obligation to take reasonable care and precaution or his or her behavior fell below the expected standard of care or typical practice (American Law Institute, 2013). Determinations of breach of duty often employ an objective test or standard, by consideration of whether a "reasonable person" would have behaved similarly to the defendant in a comparable situation (Edwards et al., 2011). Cases that consider the behavior of a professional, child, or certain classes of disabled individuals would involve use of a "subjective" standard and consideration of how "reasonable" persons in a similar category as the defendant (rather than a layperson or typical adult) would behave under the circumstance presented in the negligence case (American Law Institute, 2013; Edwards et al., 2011; Zelig, 2013). For instance, in malpractice cases, the standard applied is whether a "reasonable person" of the same profession would have acted in a similar fashion under the same circumstances (Kane & Dvoskin, 2011), while a "violation" of duty may be "excused" if it is "reasonable in light of the actor's childhood, physical disability, or physical incapacitation" (American Law Institute, 2013, p. 93).

Causation. To satisfy the third element of a tort claim, the plaintiff must establish that the actions of the defendant caused his or her injuries. Causation involves consideration of both factual and proximate cause. Factual cause is often referred to as "but-for" causation, in which the injury would not have occurred *but for* the defendant's actions. Proximate cause considers whether, given a particular act and its context, the harm caused was reasonably foreseeable. Proximate cause also requires that the negligent act of the defendant immediately precede or occur temporally near the resultant injury, without any additional "superseding or intervening forces" that might also account for or materially contribute to the injury (Shuman & Hardy, 2007). This aspect of proximate causation seeks to limit the extent or scope of liability to that which is considered legally reasonable. These elements of proximate causation are now referred to as "scope of liability" in the Third Restatement of Torts (American Law Institute, 2013).

Issues of general and specific causation may also arise in tort cases involving psychological injury (Kane, 2007a; Shuman & Hardy, 2007). General causation is concerned with whether a particular event can cause emotional harm (e.g., Can abruptly terminating therapy result in psychological trauma?), while specific causation is concerned with whether a specific event resulted in an injury for a specific person (e.g., Did Dr. A's sudden termination of therapy with Patient B cause her to develop panic disorder?).

Some individuals are more vulnerable to experiencing injury or a greater degree of harm than others, by virtue of their history or general psychological makeup. The law recognizes these differences under "eggshell personality" doctrines (Koch et al., 2006) and as relevant to determinations of causation and damages. Also known as "thin skull" or "eggshell skull" plaintiffs, this concept applies to persons whose preexisting sensitivity or predisposition contributes to the psychological injury, as well as persons who have existing emotional issues or conditions that are exacerbated by the index event (Kane, 2006). In such cases, defendants may be considered liable for injuries caused to such persons, even if a typical person would not have experienced the same injury or level of harm (Kane, 2007c). Such laws expect, in essence, that defendants take such individuals as they find them (Shuman & Hardy, 2007; Young & Shore, 2007). Jurisdictional treatment of this issue may vary, and some courts assign liability only to negligent acts resulting in injury to a "normally consisted person" (Koch et al., 2006), particularly in claims related to negligent infliction of emotional distress.

Identifying Damage and Damages. This element of a tort claim requires that a plaintiff prove he or she has suffered actual loss or harm (i.e., injury) as a result of the defendant's behavior, and this injury is compensable. This can encompass two concepts: (1) that of *damage* or the degree and extent of harm (to include establishing legal thresholds that a particular harm occurred that is verifiable and/or "serious or severe," such as in cases of pure emotional injury or distress); and (2) that of *damages*, or remuneration or compensation for established losses or the impact of the injury or harm (American Law Institute, 2013; Foote & Lareau, 2013). These concepts are based on the idea that some degree of psychological distress is an expected part of the normal human experiences and that hurt feelings, embarrassment, or otherwise transitory emotional reactions are not necessarily consistent with a legal concept of injury. In addition, damages can be sought by a plaintiff to compensate for pecuniary losses and costs, such as medical bills, lost earnings or earning capacity, and damaged/lost property, and to compensate for nonpecuniary damages such as pain and suffering (known as *compensatory damages*), and/or to punish the defendant for his or her actions (known as *punitive damages*). In cases where a plaintiff cannot establish that he or she has experienced significant harm or loss but the defendant is found liable for causing an injury, nominal damages (such as one dollar) may be awarded (Foote & Lareau, 2013).

The notion of "eggshell skull" or "thin/crumbling skull" plaintiffs also applies to determinations of damages, as preexisting psychological distress, functional limitations or conditions may impact the degree to which defendants are responsible for damages in cases where liability is established (Greenberg & Wheeler, 2004; Koch et al., 2006). Compensation may be reduced by the extent to which preexisting difficulties are thought to account for the plaintiff's current degree of distress and difficulty (Kane, 2007c). In addition, the defendant's responsibility for damages may be reduced in cases in which preexisting conditions/distress or functional limits can be established, as laws in some jurisdictions or circumstances require that defendants be responsible only for returning plaintiffs to their condition prior to the negligent or intentional act, not restoring them to full health (Koch et al., 2006).

Infliction of Emotional Distress

Personal injury cases can also be based on nonphysical injuries sustained as a result of negligent or intentionally harmful behavior. Emotional harm is defined as "impairment or injury to a person's emotional tranquility" in the Third Restatement of Torts and can include "a variety of emotional states. . . and a host of other detrimental—from mildly unpleasant to disabling—mental conditions" (American Law Institute, 2013, p. 229). Civil laws governing emotional distress torts allow for plaintiffs to recover for emotional injury or distress that is "serious" or "severe" and more than "routine, every day distress that is part of life in modern society" (American Law Institute, 2013, p. 242). Though the legal criteria or definition of "serious" or "severe" emotional harm is somewhat vague, emotional reactions that persist for significant periods of time, are extreme or profound, and/or result in significant functional impairments or physical manifestations of mental distress (e.g., ulcers) are more likely to be seen as "severe" (Koch et al., 2006).

To establish a tort based on negligent infliction of emotional distress, plaintiffs must prove the elements of a negligent tort (see previous), *and* that they experienced damage consistent with *serious* emotional harm (American Law Institute, 2013; Edwards et al., 2011). For intentional infliction of emotional distress claims, a plaintiff must establish the basic elements of an intentional tort, *and* the defendant either intentionally or recklessly engaged in extreme or outrageous conduct that subjected the plaintiff to *severe* emotional distress (Edwards et al., 2011). To establish intentionality, it must be proved that the defendant intended to cause emotional harm or was "substantially certain" that severe emotional distress was likely to occur as a result of his or her actions (American Law Institute, 2013). In addition, defendants can also be found liable if they were aware (or should have been aware) that their behavior created a substantial risk of emotional harm, but deliberately disregarded that risk (e.g., recklessness). A plaintiff must also establish that the defendant's conduct was extreme and outrageous, or conduct that is "considered intolerable by a civilized society and is characterized as exceeding all possible bounds of decency" (Edwards et al., 2011, p. 35). Otherwise ordinary offensive behavior or insults can be considered "extreme or outrageous" if a repeated or prolonged pattern of behavior can be established, if the defendant is aware that the plaintiff is particularly vulnerable to emotional distress due to a physical or mental condition or symptom, or because the defendant was in a position of authority or power over the plaintiff (American Law Institute, 2013, p. 232).

Tort Procedure: A Brief Summary

A tort suit involves several procedural steps, initiated by the plaintiff filing a *complaint*. A complaint outlines the court of jurisdiction (or the court that has authority over the matter and/or parties), the parties involved in the suit (i.e., plaintiff and defendant), summary of each element of the case (such as the duty, breach of duty, causation, etc.), and compensation sought by the plaintiff (also termed *prayer for relief*; Edwards et al., 2011). A copy of the complaint detailing this information (called a *summons*) must be provided to the defendant, and typically must be formally served to the defendant. Additional requirements may occur (such as where and how defendants can be served) and can vary by jurisdiction (federal or each state), covered under their respective Rules of Civil Procedure (Edwards, Edwards, & Wells, 2011). A properly served summons allows the identified court authority (or jurisdiction) over the legal matter and the defendant(s).

After the defendant has been notified of the tort claim, he or she can respond by filing an *answer* (Greenberg, 2003). In the answer, a defendant can acknowledge or deny the allegations in the complaint, file a cross or counter claim against other parties that may be involved in the suit, and raise any defenses (such as the defendant contributed to his or her injury; also termed contributory or comparative negligence). The defendant also has the option to file motions for dismissal or seek summary judgment (or determination without trial). If a defendant fails or chooses not to respond to a complaint, a default judgment may be entered, which essentially results in an outcome in the plaintiff's favor.

Tort claims may be resolved by a legal agreement between parties and not proceed through trial. In a settlement, the plaintiff agrees not to pursue any further legal action associated with his or her claim in return for compensation (typically monetary) or certain actions by the defendant (such as changing or stopping a particular practice). The settlement is outlined in a legal contract enforced by the court.

If cases are not dismissed, nor reach settlement, the process will likely proceed to the *discovery* phase, where the plaintiff and defendant obtain information from one another to establish facts in their respective cases to be presented at trial.

At *trial*, the defendant and plaintiff each present their version of the facts of the case and present evidence in support of their claims (Edwards et al., 2011). After each side has presented their case, the trier of fact (judge or jury) determines, based on a preponderance of the evidence, whether the defendant is liable for the plaintiff's injuries, and if so, to what extent (considering comparative negligence/responsibility and damages). This final decision, or *verdict*, is announced in court and placed formally on record.

Evaluations of Psychological Injury: Legal Context

Kane and Dvoskin (2011) postulate that "the purpose of a psychological evaluation in a personal injury case is to ascertain *whether an individual has been psychologically injured by a traumatic event, and if so, to what extent"* (p. 39, emphasis in original). In this context however, psychological injury is not purely a mental health construct nor one that is synonymous with a diagnosable condition. Litigation surrounding personal injury claims with psychological components are concerned not with *any* mental health symptom or condition, but primarily those that may have been caused by the defendant, result in impairment, and are consequently compensable. Therefore, psychological injury is better understood as a psycholegal construct, including elements of both mental health condition and functioning, and legal concepts, particularly causation (Koch, et al., 2006).

Though society has a long history of interest in protection from and compensation for physical injury, the concept of psychological injury is relatively more recent. Historically, psychological injuries have largely been recognized within the legal system only by their connection to or as a consequence of a physical injury (e.g., parasitic damages; Edwards et al., 2011; Koch et al, 2006; Vallano, 2013). Recognition of distinct psychological injury or emotional distress has been more difficult, as is apparent in the variability of methods of addressing emotional distress claims by various jurisdictions over the years. This difficulty is particularly evident in treatment of claims for negligent infliction of emotional distress, as courts have been reluctant to consider pure psychological claims due to fears of opening the floodgates for frivolous and fraudulent claims, as well as difficulty setting reasonable limitations on liability for damages for defendants (American Law Institute, 2013). Many of these concerns are related to perceptions of psychological injury as murky, intangible, and subjective, and therefore not objectively verifiable (Vallano, 2013). This perception has raised concerns of fabrication or malingering (American Law Institute, 2013; Edwards, Edwards & Wells, 2011; Melton et al., 2007; Spector, 1982) as well as practical difficulty determining whether mental health symptoms stem or result from the actions of another (causation), and understanding their impact on functioning or quantifying damages (compensability) associated with relatively limited scientific knowledge or understanding of mental health issues historically (Koch et al., 2006). Various jurisdictions have therefore utilized different methods of considering claims of emotional distress to address these concerns, often requiring some connection to physical symptoms or injury. Specifically, recovery for emotional distress has been restricted to cases in which either actual physical contact or injury occurred, where there was a direct risk of injury or harm to the plaintiff, or when serious harm or death of a relative is witnessed. Even when plaintiffs can demonstrate that they meet the various jurisdictional rules to establish a claim involving a mental injury, some jurisdictions have required that they must also demonstrate physical manifestation of symptoms of emotional distress (Edwards et al., 2011; Spector, 1982). These manifestations of symptoms need not be severe themselves (e.g., headaches, nausea, etc.), but merely present to offer some evidence of observable and presumed "objective" phenomena. The evolution and reasoning behind these treatments of emotional harm in personal injury litigation are reviewed below.

In jurisdictions applying the Impact Rule, plaintiffs were not permitted to recover for emotional damages unless these could be connected to a physical impact or some form of actual contact as a result of the defendant's negligence. This conceptualization had its roots in the science of the time, in which psychological symptoms were thought to have physical origins, as well as concerns that allowing for claims based purely on mental health symptoms would leave the legal system vulnerable to large numbers of fraudulent claims that were difficult to disprove or establish reasonable compensable damages. These issues are exemplified in the case of *Mitchell v. Rochester Railway Company* (1896), in which Mitchell alleged that a horse-drawn car operated by the defendant came so close to her that she suffered "fright and excitement," resulting in her miscarriage. Her claim for negligence resulting in a psychological injury was rejected by the New York appellate court, which held that Mitchell cannot recover for injuries caused by "mere fright," as causation could not be established without a physical injury. The Court also held that:

If the right of recovery in this class of cases should be once established, it would naturally result in a flood of litigation in cases where the injury complained of may be easily feigned without detection, and where the damages must rest upon mere conjecture or speculation . . . To establish such a doctrine would be contrary to principles of public policy. (*Mitchell v. Rochester Railway Co.*, 1896, pp. 354–355)

Over time, considerations of psychological injury claims have expanded beyond impact to include circumstances in which the plaintiff is in close enough proximity to a dangerous situation created by negligent action of the defendant as to fear or be at risk of physical harm. This concept is exemplified in the case of *Palsgraf v. Long Island Railroad* (1928), which established the Zone of Danger rule and the concept of proximate causation. In this case, a man carrying a package was running across a railroad platform to catch a departing train. When two railroad employees assisted the passenger in boarding the moving train, he dropped the package. Unbeknownst to the railroad employees, the package contained fireworks, which exploded when the package hit the rails. The resulting explosion caused a large scale at the other end of the platform to fall, striking Helen Palsgraf, who suffered both physical injuries and developed "shock-related" symptoms several days later. She then sued the railroad company for her injuries. Though Ms. Palsgraf originally prevailed, the decision was overturned on appeal. The majority opinion of the Court, lead by Judge Cardozo, held that the railroad employees could not have reasonably anticipated the possibility Ms. Palsgraf would be injured under the circumstances of the case, and therefore did not owe a duty to her. The "Cardozo approach" therefore generally establishes that a person owes a duty only to those for whom risk of injury is reasonably foreseeable; to be reasonably foreseeable, a person must be within a zone of danger created by a defendant's negligent acts. The dissenting opinion, lead by Judge Andrews (and known as the "Andrews approach"), held alternatively that a duty did exist, as "everyone owes to the world at large the duty of refraining from those acts that may unreasonably threaten the safety of others" (*Palsgraf v. Long Island Railroad Company*, 1928, para. 15). Thus a negligent party is subject to liability to all people proximately harmed by it, regardless of whether the risk of harm was immediately foreseeable to the reasonable person (i.e., "but for" the railroad's employee's negligent action, Ms. Palsgraf would not have been harmed). The Andrews opinion also identified that this liability is not infinite and limited the scope of liability to those injuries that can be immediately traced back to a defendant's negligent actions without other intervening or superseding events causing harm to the plaintiff (Edwards et al., 2011; Young & Shore, 2007).

More recently, courts have given increasing consideration to psychological injury in the absence of physical harm or the personal threat of physical harm.

The California Supreme Court case *Dillon v. Legg* (1968) addresses multiple important issues in psychological injury litigation, including expansion of the scope of duty and the use of the Zone of Danger rule, as well as further recognizing emotional trauma, in the absence of direct personal physical injury or risk of harm, as a basis for a tort claim (Spector, 1982; Zelig, 2013). In this case, a mother witnessed a car run over and kill her daughter while crossing the street, though she was not at physical risk of harm herself. Ms. Dillon sued the driver of the vehicle for emotional distress of witnessing her daughter's death. The trial court held that under the existing Zone of Danger rule, Ms. Dillon was not in physical proximity of or physically at risk of being struck by the automobile, and therefore the driver did not owe her a duty of care. The decision was reversed on appeal, with the Court holding that the negligent driver did owe Ms. Dillon a duty of care, as the potential for emotional harm was foreseeable given the circumstances of the accident. Known as the Bystander Rule, the court established specifically that emotional harm is foreseeable when the plaintiff is physically near the accident scene, actually witnessed the accident, and has a close relationship with the victim of the accident.

Rodrigues v. State (1970) has been recognized as the first case to allow for *full recovery* and recognize a psychological injury claim in the absence of witnessing or experiencing a physical injury or threat of injury, or the manifestation of physical injury. In *Rodrigues*, the Hawaii Supreme Court held that a plaintiff could recover in a claim of negligent infliction of emotional distress as a result of neglect acts by the state highway department that resulted in flood damage to the family home. Further, the Court in *Rodrigues* established an objective standard for defining the severity of psychological injury requiring such claims in opining: "serious mental distress may be found where a reasonable man, normally constituted, would be unable to cope with the mental stress engendered by the circumstances of the case" (*Rodrigues v. State*, 1970, section IV, para. 13). Subsequently, *Molien v. Kaiser Foundation Hospitals* (1980) established the right of recovery for emotional distress alone, in the absence of any parasitic claim (either physical or property damage), and is the first case "in which the emotional distress claim truly was an independent cause of action" (Spector, 1982, p. 130). In *Molien*, the plaintiff's wife was mistakenly informed by her doctors that she had contracted syphilis, resulting in her suspecting the plaintiff of an extra-marital affair and the breakup of their marriage. The Court rejected previous limitations that connections to physical harm were necessary to establishing emotional distress, as "arbitrary and artificial" (Spector, 1982, p. 132) and in their opinion noted that "the requirement of physical injury . . . encourages extravagant pleading and distorted testimony" (*Molien v. Kaiser Foundation Hospitals*, 1980, section B, para. 16).

In sum, the legal system has a long history of difficulty accepting emotional distress as a basis for tort claims, with much greater consideration of recovery for emotional distress in the form of damages parasitic to another claim (such as physical injury or property damage). Even so, there has been increasing criticism for the various methods used by the system to limit recovery for emotional distress in recent years, as the prevailing mechanisms (such as requirements of a zone of danger or physical manifestation of symptoms) are considered arbitrary and there is increased appreciation of experiences of "pure emotional harm" in certain circumstances, particularly when this harm significantly impairs day-to-day functioning (American Law Institute, 2013). In the concise *Restatement of Torts*, it is observed that courts appear increasingly comfortable with considering claims based purely on emotional distress (American Law Institute, 2013). In the expanded treatment of the topic, it also recognizes "pure or stand alone emotional harm" that "can occur without . . . [physical] trauma" and that has an "existence and severity" that is "ordinarily dependent on self-reporting" and subjective experience (American Law Institute, 2013, p. 229). As such, applications of psychological science and roles for mental health experts are likely to continue to grow with the Court's expanded acceptance of emotional distress as a basis for tort claims and the development of associated legal procedures for evaluating the veracity, actionability, and compensability of these claims.

Admissibility of Expert Testimony in Personal Injury Matters

Courts have long accepted that mental health professionals have specialized knowledge on psychological matters that can assist them in making legal decisions, and that such testimony may be more valuable or relevant in some contexts than others. Prior to 1993, the prevailing standard for evaluating and introducing expert testimony was based on the 1923 case of *Frye v. United States* (Kane & Dvoskin, 2011; Melton, Petrilla, Poythress, & Slobogin, 1997). Under the *Frye* rule, the Court allowed expert testimony that was "generally accepted" in its respective field. Concerns regarding the application of the *Frye* standard included exclusion of novel clinical evidence and testimony that was still valid and reliable (but not yet "generally accepted" in the field), while allowing testimony that lacked adequate scientific support, but had achieved general acceptance by the field (Melton et al., 1997). In the 1990s, several landmark cases expanded the basis for admitting expert testimony beyond the "general acceptance" standard in *Frye*. In a series of court decisions, the courts established new guidelines or criteria for admitting expert testimony under the Federal Rules of Evidence (*Daubert v. Merrell Dow Pharmaceuticals, Inc.*, 1993, 1995), determined that expert testimony could be excluded when there is insufficient basis or scientific reasoning to support the opinions offered (*General Electric Co. v. Joiner*, 1997), and expanded the definition of expert to include persons with any "specialized" or "technical" knowledge and experience while identifying specific criteria for district court judges to consider in their role as gatekeepers for the admission of all expert evidence (*Kumho Tire Co. v. Carmichael*, 1999).

The decisions in *Daubert, Joiner*, and *Kumho* resulted in an amendment to Rule 702 of the Federal Rules of Evidence governing admissibility of expert testimony in 2000. Rule 702, "Testimony by Expert Witnesses," was again revised in 2011 and now reads as follows:

> A witness who is qualified as an expert by knowledge, skill, experience, training, or education may testify in the form of an opinion or otherwise if:
>
> (a) the expert's scientific, technical, or other specialized knowledge will help the trier of fact to understand the evidence or to determine a fact in issue;
> (b) the testimony is based on sufficient facts or data;
> (c) the testimony is the product of reliable principles and methods; and
> (d) the expert has reliably applied the principles and methods to the facts of the case. (Federal Evidence Review, 2015, p. 30)

Ultimately, the *Daubert* standards (and subsequent refinement with the *Joiner* and *Kumho* decisions), emphasize the obligation of mental health experts involved in personal injury litigation to attend to the quality of the methodology and data on which they base their opinions and to be prepared to demonstrate that the information they present is valid, reliable, and relevant to the issues before the court (Koch et al., 2006). In addition to ensuring adequate methodology and relevance, Kane (2007a) emphasized the importance of experts remaining current with the relevant literature in the field and staying abreast of the latest research to avoid having their work and opinions be excluded. Kane (2007a) also explored typical reasons psychological testimony or opinions are excluded by courts, which can be summarized as: failure to establish the relevance of their opinion(s); insufficient data on plaintiff's premorbid functioning to establish any changes in postevent functioning; failure to establish sufficient data to support opinion or to connect hypothesis to case facts; and poor scientific bases for their opinions, including unreliable methodology, failure to identify error rates, inappropriate application/use of psychological tests, and failure to cite relevant research in support of opinions or hypotheses (p. 276).

Though the standards outlined in the *Daubert, Joiner*, and *Kumho* decisions, and now codified in the Federal Rules of Evidence, are required in federal courts, state courts are not bound by these same rules. Although a majority of states utilize the *Daubert* standard in some form, many states also continue to apply the *Frye* standard. Mental health experts are expected to be familiar with the evidentiary standard in their jurisdiction of practice to ensure that their work product and testimony are consistent with these standards.

Performing Psychological Evaluations of Personal Injury

Psychological evaluations of personal injury are centered on addressing fundamental issues relevant to tort claims, namely whether a mental injury has occurred, and if so, the cause of the injury and its impact on functioning (Greenberg, 2003; Kane & Dvoskin, 2011; Melton et al, 1997). Inherent in these issues is a comparison of a person's premorbid (or preinjury) functioning with his or her current functioning. Assessing these issues requires the development of a comprehensive, chronological history based on a variety of sources of data, including relevant records (e.g., medical, education, employment, etc.), collateral informants/observations, standardized testing, individual statements in interviews, and formal legal documentation. This information is crucial to establishing a time line, or sequencing of events and functioning over time, allowing for determinations of the nature and degree of any changes and precipitants or influences of those changes relevant to the purpose of personal injury evaluations (Kane & Dvoskin, 2011; Zelig, 2013). In addition, multi-trait, multimethod data collection methods are essential to performance of forensic mental health assessments, including evaluations of psychological injury. Collecting and integrating information derived from various methods and various sources is essential to corroborating self-report information (Melton et al., 1997), enhancing consistent and accurate assessments of "any given trait, behavior, or symptom" (including response style, see Heilbrun, 2001, p. 104), and developing a comprehensive understanding of an individual's presenting difficulty and functioning, longitudinally and across a variety of contexts in personal injury evaluations (Koch et al., 2006).

Mental Health Diagnosis: Challenges and Limitations for Tort Cases

In clinical practice, psychiatric diagnosis serves the important functions of facilitating communication between professionals and informing treatment, and is therefore one of the primary objectives of clinical assessment. In contrast, perspectives on the use of diagnosis in forensic evaluations of psychological injury range from "not required" (Goldstein, 2003, p. 5) to "distracting at best and misleading or prejudicial at worst" (Greenberg & Wheeler, 2004, p. 81). Instead, the primary objective is ascertaining the nature and degree of functional impairment, and the relationship of this impairment to a legally relevant event in order to inform legal decisions (such as establishing damages and causation). To that end, establishing whether a plaintiff meets specific criteria for a psychiatric diagnosis is less relevant, and therefore less helpful, in informing legal issues before the trier of fact (judge or jury): a particular diagnosis says very little about a plaintiff's actual functioning or any relationship it may have to the defendant's alleged negligence. As previously noted, *psychological injury* is a psycholegal term, encompassing both psychological and legal constructs; a particular diagnosis is therefore not synonymous with the legal definition of psychological injury. Further, two individuals meeting criteria for the same diagnosis may present with significantly different degrees of functional impairment and relationships to the defendant's alleged negligence, allowing one to meet the legal threshold for showing causation and damages (and therefore a compensable psychological injury), while the other does not. Similarly, individuals who do not meet formal diagnostic criteria for a particular disorder (e.g., subsyndromal conditions) may nonetheless demonstrate severe impairment entitling them to compensation (Foote & Lareau, 2013; Koch et al., 2006).

Despite the importance of function over diagnosis in the evaluation of psychological injury, determining and providing psychiatric diagnoses continue to be considered a relevant component of work in this area. The most common diagnoses/diagnostic categories occurring in relation to psychological injuries are posttraumatic stress disorder (PTSD), major depression, neurocognitive disorders, and pain-related disorders (Koch et al., 2006; Miller, Sadoff, & Datillio, 2011; Young & Kane, 2007). Various editions of the *Diagnostic and Statistical Manual of Mental Disorders* (DSM), published by the American Psychiatric Association, remain the most widely utilized diagnostic system in the United States in practice (Kane & Dvoskin, 2011), including in the arena of forensic assessment. Until recently, practitioners relied on the criteria laid out in the revised fourth edition of the DSM (hereafter referenced as DSM-IV-TR; American Psychiatric Association, 2000) to establish diagnoses. Difficulty with the forensic applications of the DSM-IV-TR includes the limited relevance of clinical conceptualizations and criteria to legal constructs, with the American Psychiatric Association explicitly identifying this limitation in the manual's introduction (2000, p. xxvii). Further, the DSM-IV-TR has been criticized for insufficient scientific rigor in establishing diagnostic constructs and criteria, notably arrived at by "consensus" of purportedly knowledgeable mental health professionals (Gordon & Cosgrove, 2013). Finally, difficulty with the reliability of some diagnoses has routinely been identified (Gordon & Cosgrove, 2013) particularly for clinicians diagnosing PTSD (Koch, O'Neill, & Douglas, 2005; Koch, Nader, & Haring, 2009), as well as difficulty with low validity for cognitive disorder diagnoses (Schultz, 2013).

In May of 2013, the American Psychiatric Association published the fifth edition of the DSM (known as the DSM-5). This publication brought changes to diagnostic criteria and conceptualization of PTSD, [Neuro]Cognitive Disorders, and Somatoform Disorders (now Somatic Symptom and Related Disorders), as well as overall structural changes, such as the removal of the multiaxial system and "reordering and regrouping the existing disorders" (American Psychiatric Association, 2013, p. 10). Despite these changes, many of the criticisms resulting in limited applicability of the DSM-IV-TR to forensic settings continue to apply to the DSM-5—and further, "the newly revised changes to the DSM-5 diagnostic criteria may in some cases circumvent legal determinations about what constitutes psychological injury in claims for compensation" (Thomas, 2013, p. 325). Anticipated challenges in the application of the DSM-5 conceptualization of PTSD diagnoses to evaluations of psychological injury include expanded (and more vague) language around what qualifies as a stressor or traumatic event for the purposes of a diagnosis of PTSD; greater emphasis on behavioral (versus intrapsychic) symptoms, as well as the addition of dissociative specifiers potentially allowing for increased opportunity for exaggeration/malingering of these symptoms; and criteria including distorted cognitions and attributions of self-blame regarding a traumatic event being confused with actual legal culpability (or comparative negligence/responsibility; Zoellner, Bedard-Gilligan, Jun, Marks, & Garcia, 2013). Schultz (2013) notes that many of the difficulties with forensic application of the cognitive disorders as described in the DSM-IV-TR persist, despite changes in the DSM-5. Moreover, Schultz (2013) highlights new concerns related to classification of cognitive difficulty as either mild or major neurocognitive disorder, forcing those who actually demonstrate deficits in the "moderate" range into the mild disorder diagnostic category. When faced with these diagnoses, decision makers in legal contexts may minimize or fail to appreciate the actual level of functional impairment experienced by individuals falling in this range. Similarly, concerns that a circumscribed functional assessment limited to activities of daily living (now a diagnostic criteria), with the exclusion of consideration of other domains of functioning in assessing severity of neurocognitive impairment for diagnostic purposes, may also minimize plaintiffs' ability to demonstrate or reduce legal decision makers' appreciation of functional impairments relevant to this legal context (Schultz, 2013). Finally, changes to diagnoses for chronic pain—now subsumed as a specifier for Somatic Symptom Disorder (SSD)—and the low threshold for diagnoses of SSD are anticipated to contribute to "pathologizing the normal" and over diagnosis, while failing to capture the degree of suffering and impairment of "genuine pain patients" (Young, 2013a, p. 312). Moreover, Young (2013a) anticipates that these difficulties will lead to reduced credibility of experts and increased confusion for legal decision makers in psychological injury claims.

In sum, difficulty with the application of DSM diagnostic formulations to evaluations of psychological injury persist in the DSM-5, and the utility and relevance of these diagnoses in this forensic context remain limited, requiring that professionals exercise care in their application of diagnostic practices and concepts to their work (Young, 2013b). As previously suggested by Greenberg and Wheeler (2004), and reiterated by Thomas (2013): "the prudent psychologist will . . . focus on the functional implication of the evaluee's situation—not just a DSM diagnosis" (Thomas, 2013, p. 328).

Malingering and Symptom Exaggeration

The nature and context of psychological injury evaluations creates incentives for exaggeration and malingering (i.e., intentional fabrication for financial gain) of mental health symptoms and dysfunction. Given a legal context that is already quite skeptical of psychological injury, examiners in this area are expected to assess for and be prepared to respond to inquiries regarding the response style of the individuals they evaluate (Melton et al., 1997; Miller et al., 2011).

However, assessments in this area can be complex, due to difficulty clearly distinguishing malingering from other forms of symptom magnification and the potential for significant negative consequences for persons identified as malingerers (such as loss of benefits, loss of credibility, unfavorable legal outcomes, etc.; Foote & Lareau, 2013; Nicholson & Martelli, 2007). This is particularly problematic as malingering and genuine psychiatric disorder and dysfunction are not mutually exclusive. Malingering is typically understood as a conscious, intentional effort to fabricate or grossly exaggerate psychiatric symptoms and/or dysfunction for external gain (American Psychiatric Association, 2013). This is conceptually distinct from some forms of symptom magnification that are seen as less extreme in presentation and are motivated by other factors besides external incentives such as avoiding criminal prosecution or culpability or monetary gain; instead, symptom magnification may be associated with efforts to express or receive validation for one's subjective level of distress or difficulty, or unconscious efforts to obtain support from others (particularly in contexts where support persons inadvertently reinforce a "sick role" for plaintiffs). Stress from the litigation process, as well as repeated rehearsal of the index event and experience of symptoms in response to repeated inquires from multiple sources (e.g., opposing counsel, multiple experts, etc.), can also lead to inflated symptom presentation or even exacerbation of symptoms (Young & Kane, 2007).

Further, genuine clinical presentation of psychopathology and functional difficulty can also be misconstrued as symptom exaggeration or malingering. For instance, individuals presenting with symptoms of major depression may demonstrate low or suboptimal effort on cognitive assessments or screening instruments; however, such a presentation is also consistent with overall poor motivation characteristic of depression. In addition, intentional fabrication of symptoms motivated by assuming a "sick role" are the essential features of factitious disorder and assuming such a role is not considered related to external incentive, nor a conscious and deliberate effort to deceive; persons exhibiting symptoms of this disorder are typically not considered to be malingering. Accordingly, thorough assessments of malingering include use of standardized methods, consideration of multiple sources of data, and exploration of alternative hypotheses or explanations for a plaintiff's presentation or behavior that might otherwise suggest malingering (Kane & Dvoskin, 2011; Miller et al., 2011; Rogers & Shuman, 2005).

Components of Evaluations of Psychological Injury

Referral Questions

Evaluations begin with understanding the referral question(s), or the purpose of the evaluation and the psycholegal questions to be addressed in order to inform a third-party decision. The referral question helps to shape and focus the evaluation, including selection of areas of inquiry and assessment methods, and ensures that the evaluation is relevant to the legal process (also a component of the *Daubert* criteria).

There are a number of basic referral questions that are relevant to the psycholegal issues in personal injury evaluations. Greenberg and Wheeler (2004) and Zelig (2013), each identify several such questions (paraphrased here), as well as their relevance to the legal issues at hand (in parentheses):

- What was the plaintiff's level of functioning or "baseline" state before the injury? (*Damages, compensation, thin/crumbling skull, normally constituted person*)
- Did the plaintiff suffer a psychological injury? (*Damages)*
- What is the likely cause of the injury? Was the injury caused by the defendant? (*Causation*)
- What is the nature and extent of any significant impairment to the plaintiff's functioning and/or damages experienced because of the injury? (*Damages, compensation, severe emotional distress*)
- What must the defendant do to restore the plaintiff to his or her preinjury state or level of functioning? (*Compensation*)

Further, questions pertaining to causation are critical to evaluations of psychological injury, though they can be quite complex. In cases where a psychological injury has been established, Kane (2007b, pp. 293–295) offers further refinement of this central question of causation by identifying five major hypotheses to be explored with regard to causation while conducting the evaluation, considering the index event as: (1) the sole cause of the injury, (2) the major or proximate cause of the injury, (3) a material or significant contributor to the injury, (4) a minor contributor that may have aggravated a preexisting condition, and (5) not significantly related to the injury.

The referral source (typically the retaining attorney) may also have additional case-specific questions be addressed in the evaluation. Finally, experts are expected to confirm their understanding of relevant legal statutes and provisions (e.g., evidentiary standards, controlling case law, etc.) that govern personal injury evaluations in their jurisdiction with the attorney at the time of referral, as these may have implications for understanding and/or addressing the relevant psycholegal issues in a particular case.

Informed Consent

Participating in a forensic psychological evaluation is a daunting process for most individuals, requiring disclosure of information that is deeply personal and typically private within the adversarial climate of the legal process. Such persons are likely to be distracted and vulnerable due to these circumstances, and they may fail to appreciate the potential personal and legal consequences of their behavior and disclosures in an evaluation. For these reasons, forensic evaluators have ethical standards and guidelines (e.g., Ethical Principles of Psychologists and Code of Conduct [EPPCC], American Psychological Association, 2010, Standards 3.10 and 9.03; Specialty Guidelines for Forensic Psychology [SGFP], American Psychological Association, 2013, Guideline 6.03), and sometimes legal mandates, that require they disclose certain information or make an effort to inform participants about the evaluation process and unless court-ordered to do otherwise, to obtain their consent before proceeding (Kalmbach & Lyons, 2006; American Psychological Association, 2010, 2013).

Informed consent and disclosure processes should include information on the nature and purpose of the evaluation, the process of the evaluation and what is expected of participants, the type of information that will be requested and the methods of collecting that information, the role of the expert as an independent examiner and one that is distinct from that of a therapist, whether individuals can decline to participate or answer questions and any consequences for doing so, the limits of confidentiality (including to whom and under what circumstances results of the evaluation will be disclosed, e.g., provision of report to attorney, live testimony before the court, etc.), and any mandated reporting requirements (American Psychological Association, 2013; Kalmbach & Lyons, 2006; Melton et al., 1997).

Practitioners are also expected to make efforts to ensure participants understand the information given and provide opportunities for questions and clarifying explanations (Kane, 2007b). If, despite these efforts, a participant does not understand this information (e.g., due to psychosis or severe cognitive impairment) and is therefore unable to competently consent, practitioners are expected to consult with the examinee's attorney or a "legally authorized person" before proceeding (EPPCC Standards 3.10, 9.03; SGFP Guideline 6.03.03). For mandated or court-ordered cases in which consent is not required, a participant's inability to fully comprehend information provided in the disclosure process must be noted in the final report, along with any potential implications for the conclusions (Kalmbach & Lyons, 2006; Kane, 2007b).

Collateral Information

Review of records is critical to informing an expert's understanding of a plaintiff's functioning. In fact, Melton et al., 1997 observed that "archival and third party information is particularly important in reconstructive evaluations . . . [such as] psychological conditions preexisting an accident . . . where the focus is the client's mental state at a remote point in the past" (p. 51). Therefore, the scope of the records review should include information from prior to the index event or alleged injury through the current period to allow for comparisons of preevent versus postevent functioning. Kane (2007b) recommends that records be reviewed three to five years prior to the index event "to form a substantial baseline of pre-trauma functioning" (p. 295). However, seeking more remote records is essential for plaintiffs with personal histories of significant events or circumstances prior to that time frame that may have relevance for the current evaluation, such as histories of significant trauma (e.g., assault, childhood sexual abuse), brain insults (e.g., traumatic brain injury), or psychiatric episodes involving hospitalization (Kane, 2007b; Kane & Dvoskin, 2011). Experts would also benefit from making a concerted effort to seek multiple sources of documentation, covering a wide variety of domains to ensure they have gathered a comprehensive foundation for evaluating an individual's functioning in multiple life domains, to the extent possible. Sources of documentation include medical and mental health, pharmacy/medication, military, educational, employment, personnel, and arrest and incarceration records (federal and local jurisdictions). Prior mental health assessment and cognitive or neuropsychological testing are also important sources for assessing prior functioning, as well as informing the current evaluation (e.g., avoid repeating test batteries). Financial records, including tax returns, credit card and bank statements, may also provide important information as to "lifestyle changes," including changes to activities, and financial planning and management (Greenberg, 2003; Kane & Dvoskin, 2011; Zelig, 2013). Review of legal documentation for the current matter (e.g., complaint, depositions, etc.), documented interviews with or statements from third-party information, and prior legal or administrative claims (including worker's compensation and disability) is also relevant. Finally, review of relevant personal materials and records is also recommended where available (Greenberg, 2003; Zelig, 2013) including photographs, videos, letters, e-mails, text messages and online blogging and posting activity, hobby projects, awards, diaries and journals, calendars, and appointment books. In addition to informing a time line of important events and functioning over time (Miller et al., 2011), comprehensive review of collateral documentation and records also further informs hypotheses and areas of inquiry to be addressed as the evaluation progresses, provides a means of corroborating information provided by the plaintiff or other sources (Melton et al., 1997), and can assist with identifying patterns amongst various sources of data (such as records, collateral informants, testing, etc.) to strengthen support for an expert's opinions and conclusions. Finally, lack of adequate record review may result in provision of expert services that is below the standard of care (Kane & Dvoskin, 2011) and demonstrates inadequate methodology and lack of adequate foundation for an expert's report and opinions (e.g., failure to meet *Daubert* standard), barring admission of related psychological evidence to a legal proceeding.

Interview data from persons who have significant contacts with, and therefore firsthand knowledge and observations of, the individual being evaluated in other contexts can also provide valuable, relevant information to inform an assessment of personal injury. Collateral informants can include individuals who are familiar with and have had regular contact with the plaintiff or who have "had the opportunity to observe a particularly relevant behavior" (Heilbrun, 2001, p. 99). Possible individuals to consider for collateral interviews include professional service providers, employers, employees and coworkers, witnesses to the index event, neighbors, roommates, family members, and friends (Greenberg, 2003). Information provided by collateral informants is essential to a multisource, multimethod assessment model to augment information in written records (particularly in the case of professional informants) and to inform retrospective assessments of functioning, assessments of response style, and evaluations of current functioning.

Review of Relevant Research

Scientific knowledge, both in the field of mental health in general, and that specific to evaluations of psychological injury, continues to advance exponentially. Experts are expected to remain abreast of these changes and their relevance to the individual cases on which they work, to ensure that they maintain adequate scientific rigor in the methods and tools they employ to conduct their evaluations, and on which they base their options both as an ethical principle (e.g., EPPCC Standard 9.02; SGFP Guideline 10.02) and to ensure admissibility (by either *Frye* or *Daubert* standards). Available research can be applied to improving experts' understanding of presentations of various symptoms and disorders, and the prevalence with which these present in the community; ensuring the appropriate application of various assessment tools and techniques to a particular issue, context, or client; informing prognosis of various conditions and difficulties, as well as their application to a particular client in a particular context; and understanding the limitations of the knowledge in the field in particular areas or in relationship to an individual case (Kane, 2007c). For example, assessment techniques and tools are continually being developed and refined; however, it often takes significant time for these tools to be adequately applied to various populations, circumstances, and conditions to demonstrate adequate validity and reliability for general use, and often more time for specific application to forensic populations and contexts. An expert is expected to remain aware of the developing research regarding an assessment tool to ensure the new tool has sufficient psychometric properties to support its use both in the context of evaluation of psychological injury and its applicability to the specific individual being assessed (e.g., adequately represented in the normative sample).

Interview

An individual interview of the plaintiff is an essential component of a psychological injury evaluation, in order to integrate and contextualize information gathered from various data sources (Kane & Dvoskin, 2011). In addition to the plaintiff's statements, the interview is also an important source of behavioral observation for the evaluator, and it is important for evaluating "signs" of clinical psychopathology, as well as understanding the nature and degree of reported difficulty and related coping ability (Miller et al., 2011). Indeed, observational data can be key to developing a better understanding of a plaintiff's symptoms and level of distress (e.g., displays of visible trembling with expressions of anxiety), functioning (e.g., demonstrating panic symptoms in response to unexposed loud noises), resiliency and management of distress (e.g., displays of explosive verbal anger when pushed for information), and congruency between reported level of distress and difficulty and behavior (e.g., reporting severe levels of depressed mood and poor motivation while presenting as well dressed and groomed, and laughing, smiling, and joking with the examiner).

Miller and colleagues (2011), as well as Kane and Dvoskin (2011) observed that the primary purposes of interviewing the plaintiff are to evaluate the effect of the index event on the plaintiff, and to gather information to assist with formulating and evaluating hypotheses in key psycholegal issues to be further considered in conjunction with other data from various sources. Particularly relevant to evaluations of psychological injury, the interview is a key source of information regarding the plaintiff's perception of his or her injury and its impact (Kane & Dvoskin, 2011), which speaks to the psycholegal construct of damages.

The importance of conducting an individual interview is also emphasized in the ethics code for psychologists (EPPCC Standard 9.01) and the specialty guidelines for forensic psychology (SGFP Guideline 9.03), associated with concerns that providing conclusions and opinions in the absence of interview data substantially weakens the foundations on which they are based and is inconsistent with the standard of care (and therefore may also fail to meet admissibility criteria for jurisdiction with *Frye* and *Daubert* standards). Evaluators who must provide evaluations in the absence of interview data, or with insufficient interview data due to the circumstances (e.g., mandated evaluation; noncooperative or incapacitated examinee, etc.), are expected to identify the limitations of their assessment and related conclusions accordingly (American Psychological Association, 2013; Kane & Dvoskin, 2011).

Methods of conducting interviews in personal injury evaluations vary across practitioners, and can include structured, semi-structured, or unstructured interview formats (as well as some combination therein). Topics addressed in the interview typically include clinical symptoms and functioning, personal history and background information, perspectives on the index event and alleged injury, as well as the perceived impact of that injury, efforts and relative success of any efforts to ameliorate symptoms and distress associated with the injury, clarification of data from other sources (including psychological testing), and address of inconsistencies from and between other data sources.

Psychological Testing

Psychological tests provide examiners with a means of measuring and observing an individual's behavior in a specific domain. This information can be used to describe various characteristics of an individual, such as his or her intellectual ability or perceptions of social support, and to generate or inform existing hypotheses regarding an individual's condition, functioning, attitudes, or behaviors and the ways in which these features interact (Kane, 2007b) as well as to support or disconfirm hypothesis generated from other types of data (Foote & Lareau, 2013). As there are no psychological tests or measures that were developed specifically for use in evaluations of psychological injury, evaluators must select instruments designed for other purposes but are applicable in this context (Kane & Dvoskin, 2011). In choosing psychological tests for use in a psychological injury evaluation, Zelig (2013) suggests that examiners base their choices on the functional capacities to be assessed, strengths and weaknesses of the test in the context of the evaluation, standards for admissibility of expert evidence (e.g., *Daubert* criteria), ability to preserve test security, and ability to address response bias.

Consideration of reliability and relevance (Heilbrun, 2001), as well as contextual strengths and weaknesses of a particular psychological test (Zelig, 2013) speak to the importance of understanding its psychometric properties. Correctly administered test instruments with empirically demonstrated patterns of consistently and accurately measuring what they purport to measure (i.e., reliability and validity) are most likely to meet these expectations. Kane (2007b) and Heilbrun (2001) also emphasize that examiners be present and personally administer testing to ensure adherence to standardized test procedures as well as to allow for behavioral observations during testing that may be relevant to the examination or interpretation of test results. Adequate and ethical interpretation of test results requires knowledge of literature regarding interpretation of findings for instruments utilized, idiographic application of nomothetic data, consideration/integration of information from other sources of data and the context of the evaluation, and avoiding reliance on (or worse) inclusion of verbatim text from computerized interpretations of testing (Heilbrun, 2001; Kane & Dvoskin, 2011).

Evaluators may employ a variety of testing instruments in personal injury evaluations. Most commonly, forensic clinicians specializing in evaluations of psychological injury select tests assessing the areas of personality and psychopathology, PTSD, pain/somatization, cognition, and malingering/exaggeration (Kane, 2007b; Kane & Dvoskin, 2011; Koch et al., 2006). These instruments vary in the degree to which they assess or address nosological and conceptual features of some disorders or symptom patterns with the publication of the DSM-5, as well as their psychometric properties; both issues may have implications for relevance and reliability expectations for admissibility. Detailed reviews of individual instruments in each of these domains are beyond the scope of this chapter. A brief overview of types of tests, with a listing of some more common tests employed in psychological injury evaluations in each domain appears next.

Measures of Personality and Psychopathology provide information on major symptoms of clinical psychopathology and maladaptive personality characteristics. *Objective tests* are standardized instruments with structured questions and limited response options (such as true/false) and standardized scoring procedures independent of the examiner's bias or beliefs. These instruments also include scales assessing test validity and response bias. Objective tests of personality include the Millon Clinical Multiaxial Inventory-III (MCMI-III), the Minnesota Multiphasic Personality Inventory-2 (MMPI-2, MMPI-2-RF), and the Personality Assessment Inventory (PAI). *Projective measures* require responses to ambiguous test stimuli, which are thought to compel an individual to "project" their interpretation of the stimuli onto it and reflect unconscious motivations, thoughts, and perceptions. Projective measures include the Rorschach test and the Thematic Apperception Test. *Structured clinical interviews* consist of highly standardized, detailed inquiries regarding symptoms of psychopathology that conform closely to diagnostic categories and are designed to be administered by a clinician in an oral format. Structured clinical interview measures include the Diagnostic Interview Schedule for DSM-IV (DIS), the Mini International Neuropsychiatric Interview (MINI), and the various Structured Clinical Interview(s) for DSM Disorders (SCID-I, SCID-II, SCID-D, SCID-5-CV).

PTSD Measures specifically assess symptoms associated with trauma- and stressor-related pathology. *Objective tests* include the PTSD Checklist for DSM-5 (PCL-5), Life Events Checklist for DSM-5 (LEC-5), Impact of Event Scale–Revised (IES-R), Detailed Assessment of Posttraumatic Stress (DAPS), Posttraumatic Diagnostic Scale (PDS), and the Trauma Symptom Inventory (TSI-2). *Structured clinical interview* measures include the Clinician-Administered PTSD Scale for DSM-5 (CAPS-5), and sections of the SCID, MINI, and DIS assessing PTSD and/or trauma- or stressor-related symptomology.

Pain and Somatization Measures specifically assess features of chronic pain. *Self-report* measures include the Multidimensional Pain Inventory, which also assesses the impact of pain on functioning, and the Pain Patient Profile (P3), which includes impact of related constructs of depression, anxiety, and somatization.

Cognitive Tests inform evaluations of an individual's cognitive status in various domains, including intellectual ability, memory, attention, problem solving, language, visuospatial, processing speed, and motor skills. Commonly used tests include the Wechsler Adult Intelligence Scale–IV (WAIS-IV), the Wechsler Memory Scale–IV (WMS-IV), California Verbal Learning Test (CVLT), Trail Making Test (TMT), and the Halstead-Reitan Neuropsychological Battery (HRNB).

Malingering and Exaggeration Measures assess response styles and patterns consistent with symptom exaggeration, low effort, and/or malingering. *Self-Report* instruments and screening tools include the Structured Inventory of Malingered Symptoms (SIMS), Victoria Symptom Validity Test (VSVT), Validity Indicatory Profile (VIP), and validity scales on the MMPI-2, MMPI-2-RF, and PAI. *Clinician Administered* instruments and screening tools include the Miller Forensic Assessment of Symptoms Test (M-FAST), Structured Interview of Reported Symptoms (SIRS), and Test of Memory Malingering (TOMM).

Communicating Findings

Most evaluations of psychological injury culminate in a written report (Kane & Dvoskin, 2011). Consistent with forensic mental health assessments in general, these reports: (1) provide a written record establishing that an evaluation has occurred, detailing the nature, methods, data sources, and findings of that evaluation; (2) require that evaluators organize their conceptualization of the case, consider and reconsider hypotheses, and identify weaknesses; (3) assist with organization of case information, the evaluation process, and findings in preparation for oral testimony; and (4) can be used to settle or dispose of cases without further legal proceedings (Heilbrun, 2001; Melton et al., 1997). The written style of the evaluation must be consistent and jargon free, checked for grammatical and spelling errors, with use of objective language to allow for readability, clear communication of findings, maintenance of creditability, and attention to detail and accuracy, and to avoid the appearance of bias (Heilbrun, 2001; Kane & Dvoskin, 2011; Melton et al., 1997). The content areas of the report typically include information on the specific referral questions, informed consent procedures, dates and types of clinical contact, sources of data relied upon, any relevant personal history information, clinical observations, results from psychological testing, and information on the evaluee's current mental status and functioning. Incorporation of relevant research to support assessment methodology and conclusions, as well as an identification of the weaknesses of any diagnoses provided and an emphasis on describing functioning, is also recommended for personal injury evaluations (Zelig, 2013). The forensic formulation, or application of psychological data to the psycholegal issues, typically follows the model utilized in conducting the evaluation (see Miller & Gagliardi, Chapter 20 in this volume, for examples); for personal injury evaluations, such models include address of relevant psycholegal issues recommended by Greenberg and Wheeler (2004), Kane (2007b), and/or Zelig (2013) and discussed previously in this chapter.

Importantly, the conclusions and opinions in the forensic formulation should be clearly grounded in and supported by the data gathered during the assessment, and connected to or relevant to the psycholegal issues before the trier of fact (Heilbrun, 2001). Kane and Dvoskin (2011) also recommend that evaluators include weaknesses and limitation of their conclusions, and identify any areas in which they were unable to come to a conclusion or develop an opinion.

Finally, creation of a written time line outlining the facts and relevant events of the case, with associated references to support/establish these facts, assists with conceptualization of the case and organization of (typically significant amounts of) collateral information, as well as facilitates provision of testimony (Kane & Dvoskin, 2011; Zelig, 2013).

Ethical Issues

Consistent with ethical principles for conducting forensic mental health assessments in general, experts involved in personal injury litigation have an obligation to avoid engaging in dual or multiple roles with a plaintiff. Other ethical issues that may arise in psychological evaluations of personal injury involve third-party observers, and the release of test data and materials to nonprofessionals.

Provision of competent and ethical treatment requires that mental health practitioners establish a supportive, accepting, and helping relationship with the client to develop a context for change and to assist him or her in achieving personal goals for treatment and foster well-being; which is in marked contrast to the objective detachment that must be employed by forensic experts, whose "client" is not the person being evaluated, but the attorney or court who retained their services in order to help inform a psycholegal matter to be decided by a third party. By their nature, these roles are irreconcilable or mutually exclusive, and efforts to serve both roles can result in significant harm (for a thorough review of this topic, see Greenberg & Shuman, 1997, 2007). In addition, forensic experts may be retained in personal injury matters as either consultants or forensic examiners (i.e., expert witness). Serving as both a consultative and expert witness may also involve inherent role conflicts, as the consultative expert's role involves advocacy (i.e., to take a particular side or to benefit or assist the retaining attorney with winning their case) while an expert witness is ethically bound to maintain objectivity and to help inform the psycholegal matter before the Court, regardless of its potential benefit or harm to the case of either the plaintiff or defendant (Heilbrun, 2001; Kane & Dvoskin, 2011). For these reasons, mental health professionals are obliged to be cautious and endeavor to avoid or minimize the impact of dual- or multiple-role scenarios.

Next, as part of the legal proceeding, attorneys may demand to review testing protocols, administration and scoring manuals, and examinee responses or raw data generated as part of the evaluation. In addition to violating copyright contracts a practitioner may have with the test developer/publisher, this request conflicts with the ethical obligations that psychologists have to maintain test security and avoid misrepresentation and issue of test data (EPPCC Standards 9.04, 9.11). Psychologists faced with demands to release test data and materials are expected to limit such disclosures, including: releasing such information to another psychologist or professionals with training in psychological assessment, seeking protective court orders requiring in-camera (or nonpublic) review, precluding or restricted copying of this information, and/or sealing of legal records including such information against public disclosure (Committee on Legal Issues, American Psychological Association, 2006).

Forensic practitioners may also face ethical dilemmas resulting from requests for a third party to observe or record the evaluation and/or testing procedures as part of the litigation process (distinct from issues related to third-party participation necessary to reduce barriers to assessments, such as interpreters). However, such third-party observers violate procedures for standardized testing, and can have a negative impact on an evaluee's performance and responses to psychological tests, which has been consistently noted in empirical investigation (Committee on Psychological Tests and Assessment, American Psychological Association, 2007; Eastvold, Belanger, & Rodney, 2012; Kane & Dvoskin, 2011). Psychologists also have ethical obligations to maintain standardized testing conditions or justify deviations from such conditions, explicating threats to validity and the limited interpretability and application of any findings under these conditions (EPPCC Standards 9.02, 9.06). Third-party observers, who are not typically trained as psychologists or in psychological assessment, may also represent a threat to test security, and may misinterpret or misuse observed test behavior and responses, resulting in ethical concerns similar to those identified earlier. Finally, the impact of third-party presence on interviews is more ambiguous, though alterations in the behavior of both the evaluee and the examiner are likely, affecting the nature and potential reliability and quality of the data stemming from the interview (Committee on Psychological Tests and Assessment, American Psychological Association, 2007). Overall, the prevailing stance of the field, as well as available research data, does not support the presence of third-party observers during testing and interview procedures, suggesting experts must make an effort to avoid or limit their presence wherever possible (National Academy of Neuropsychology Policy and Planning Committee, 2000). Experts may receive support for this stance in some jurisdictions; other jurisdictions maintain an individual's right to have a third party present during the evaluation (Kane & Dvoskin, 2011). In the latter case, forensic evaluators have an obligation to assess and describe the impact of the third party on their individual case as well as on the results of any testing procedures and related limitations with regard to conclusions and opinions (American Psychological Association, 2010; Committee on Psychological Tests and Assessment, American Psychological Association, 2007).

Case Example

Referral

Mr. Joe Laesus was referred for a forensic psychological evaluation by his attorney in the context of a personal injury lawsuit against the ABC Construction Company and Green Pastures Real Estate Developers. The purpose of this evaluation is to assess and review Mr. Laesus's psychological functioning over time, identify the nature and degree of psychological distress (if any) as well as its functional impact, identify possible sources of or factors contributing to that distress, and make recommendations for relieving this distress and improving functioning.

Sources of information for this evaluation included several hours of clinical interviews with Mr. Laesus on two separate dates in addition to psychological testing (PAI, P3, MINI, TSI, and LEC-5). Medical, legal, employment, and financial records were reviewed, and collateral interviews with Mr. Laesus's mother, employment supervisor, daughter, ex-wife, girlfriend, and close friend were conducted.

Case Formulation

Baseline assessment of functioning (prior to the alleged traumatic event): Mr. Laesus is a 41-year-old, divorced, Caucasian male. He achieved developmental milestones at the anticipated times and had no history of developmental or learning difficulty, and his report is consistent with information provided in collateral interviews with Mr. Laesus's mother. No academic or medical records from Mr. Laesus's childhood were available for review. There are also no known severe childhood illnesses/injuries or mental health conditions or services, though his mother noted difficulty with recurring general illnesses, to which Mr. Laesus seemed particularly susceptible as a child (e.g., colds, flu, etc.).

Mr. Laesus dropped out of high school in the twelfth grade to work full time in an auto-repair shop. He obtained a GED shortly thereafter and completed training with a welding certification the following year. He has subsequently maintained steady employment in industrial welding, primarily with local shipyards and companies fabricating parts for aircrafts. At the time of the events in the current matter, Mr. Laesus had maintained full-time employment with QAC Industries for the past nine years. Personnel records indicated no history of performance issues/complaints or disciplinary actions, though Mr. Laesus maximized his use of sick leave each year. Collateral interviews with Mr. Laesus's supervisor of 5 years also did not identify performance concerns or interpersonal difficulties at work, though did note that Mr. Laesus was very health conscious and routinely admonished coworkers for coming to work ill and potentially spreading illness to others.

Mr. Laesus married at the age of 30. He and his wife did not have children, though they did raise his daughter, born of a prior relationship and of whom he maintained joint physical custody throughout her formative years. He continued to maintain a close relationship with his daughter, now aged 20, after she married and moved away from home.

Mr. Laesus denied a history of illicit drug use, marijuana use, or abuse of inhalants or prescription medication. He reported a period of excessive, "binge" drinking in his early 20s, ending when he received a DUI and completed court-ordered classes. Collateral contacts indicated that they were unaware of current or historical difficulty with substance use, and legal records indicated a DUI conviction, with deferred sentencing upon completion of a court-ordered evaluation and treatment. Employment records did not reveal any positive findings as a result of random drug urinalysis. One driving infraction for speeding was noted; Mr. Laesus otherwise has no other history of contact with law enforcement.

Mr. Laesus disclosed a history of undergoing a tonsillectomy and appendectomy in childhood, consistent with his mother's report. He maintained that he was in excellent health prior to the accident, exercising regularly and monitoring his diet, with no significant medical conditions. Review of records indicated generally routine care visits for the three years preceding his injury, with several visits per year in which Mr. Laesus presented with vague symptoms (such as headaches, gastrointestinal upset, dizziness, etc.) and expressed concerns regarding onset of a serious or unusual illness (e.g., swine flu, brain tumor, and once, leukemia), though tests for serious conditions were negative. Medical records note that Mr. Laesus has high blood pressure, with recommendations for dietary changes, and they report a sedentary lifestyle. Collateral informants indicated that Mr. Laesus engaged in fishing, though no other formal sporting activities or regular exercise regimen, though was conscious of maintaining a low-salt, low-fat diet.

Mr. Laesus has no history of psychiatric hospitalization, or participation in therapy or mental health counseling. There are no complaints of psychological distress in medical records covering the period prior to his alleged injury, and depression screens were negative.

Alleged traumatic event(s): Approximately 18 months prior to the evaluation, Mr. Laesus was visiting a friend who had purchased a home in a recently completed housing development. While watching the ongoing construction of a nearby residence, Mr. Laesus came in proximity of heavy machinery and was struck in the head, chest, and groin area, resulting in a concussion, several rib fractures and lacerations, and partial torsion and tearing and detachment (or degloving) of his scrotum. Mr. Laesus also sustained a mild concussion, cervical strain, and superficial abrasions to his scalp though no obvious trauma to the brain was identified in a CT scan. No cognitive deficits were identified on initial screen. Mr. Laesus was hospitalized for two days and underwent surgical repair to his scrotum, suturing of deep lacerations, and setting/stabilization of rib and pelvic fractures.

After six weeks of convalescence at home, no complications related to Mr. Laesus's experience of fractures or surgical repair of his scrotum were noted in follow-up appointments, and his injuries were noted to have healed well, with scarring noted for several deep lacerations requiring sutures on his torso. Follow-up neurological screens, imaging, and consultation with a neurologist did not identify any cognitive impairment. Mr. Laesus initiated physical therapy to resume strength and mobility in his torso and hips, though he experienced extreme pain with these efforts and the therapy was terminated after several weeks. Despite repeated visits to medical specialists and his general practitioner over the next year, he continued to report chronic, severe pain and limited mobility, erectile dysfunction and painful intercourse, and difficulty with confusion and memory functioning. At that time, Mr. Laesus initiated litigation against the real estate developer and construction company building the homes.

Claimed Psychological Damage/Harm as a Result of These Events

Occupational functioning: Mr. Laesus had taken a three-month leave of absence while initially recuperating from his injuries, which was extended an additional three months; at that time, he quit his position, indicating that he did not feel he was capable of returning to work due to difficulty tolerating standing positions, chronic pain with use of pain medications that might affect his work performance and safety, poor confidence in his ability to recall details of work-related tasks, and anxiety in industrial settings and around machinery.

Marital, Sexual, and Social functioning: Mr. Laesus relayed that he began experiencing marital difficulty following his injury, noting that his wife became unsupportive, often prodding him to go to work or participate in household chores and repair tasks, and increasingly suggesting that he was lazy or simply unwilling to engage in these tasks. In collateral contacts, Mr. Laesus's wife indicated that he became withdrawn, irritable, and disinterested in her and most of the activities he once enjoyed; he ceased socializing with their mutual friends or attending family gatherings. She noted the he increasingly complained of pain, headaches, limited mobility, and gastrointestinal distress, and she had difficulty meeting his increasing demands for caretaking, such as assistance dressing, bathing, transportation, and repeated requests for assistance in getting comfortable or for special meals that would not cause gastrointestinal distress. She also noted that he was reluctant to pursue physical intimacy and eventually avoided sexual contact altogether due to reported pain. She reported that these difficulties appeared to increase, despite her perception that his doctor and care providers suggested that he had healed from his injuries and were uncertain as to the source of his limitations. She also had to take on a second job to meet their expenses, and had difficulty with the financial strain. She noted that these issues ultimately became overwhelming for her and she filed for divorce, which became final six months ago.

Mental Health/Emotional Functioning: At interviews, Mr. Laesus presented as somatically preoccupied, with recurring expressions of physical complaints and associated impact, regardless of the topic under discussion. He also presented with significant pain behaviors, frequently demonstrating facial grimacing and expression of pain, shifting in his chair, complaining of discomfort, nausea, dizziness, or headaches, and utilizing heat and ice packs he brought with him during interviews, indicating that participating in such interviews for several hours would be intolerable without them. Mr. Laesus also endorsed significant symptoms of depression, including sad mood, fatigue, amotivation, feelings of worthlessness and shame, and poor sleep. He noted hopelessness that his situation (particularly his physical condition) would improve and endorsed vague suicidal ideation. However, he denied planning or intending to end his life, as well as any history of suicide attempts. His experience of symptoms has gradually worsened over the past year, and he denied improvement with medication use. He attributed his symptoms to losses and lifestyle changes he had incurred over the past 18 months. Mr. Laesus also endorsed posttraumatic symptoms, including intrusive recollections, reactivity to diesel fumes, "whining, buzzing" and "beeping" sounds he associates with heavy machinery or large vehicles backing up, and hypervigilance and significant "jumpiness" in response to loud noises, crowded public settings, and sudden movement. He noted that he is withdrawn and isolates himself from family and friends, which he related to shame regarding changes in his functioning, feeling misunderstood (particularly with his level of perceived pain and incapacity), and irritability, noting that he tended to be easily annoyed and "snap at" these persons. He noted that he has difficulty "focusing," experiences his thoughts as "drifting," routinely forgets what he was doing or was about to do (recalling these a few moments later with effort), and also has difficulty recalling appointments, now relying on a calendar that he checks daily. Mr. Laesus reported that he no longer engages in hobbies or leisure interests outside watching television and utilizing the Internet, and he relies on assistance from others for transportation, shopping for basic needs (such as food and hygiene items), meal preparation outside consumption of ready-made snacks, financial support, attendance to hygiene and grooming tasks, and completion of typical household chores. He did note feeling supported by his girlfriend, whom he had met six months ago at the doctor's office. He noted that she appears fairly understanding of his pain issues and limitations, has not expressed dissatisfaction with their lack of physical intimacy, and encouraged him to move in with her several months ago, providing significant practical support (e.g., providing transportation, preparing meals, filling his prescriptions, assisting him with changing and bathing).

Mr. Laesus completed several self-report psychological measures, including the PAI, P3, TSI, and the LEC, and participated in a structured diagnostic interview of clinical symptoms (MINI). Mr. Laesus's responses on these measures were notable for preoccupation with bodily function, and pain and health-related concerns seen as quite disruptive to his life, endorsement of physical, cognitive, and affective symptoms of depression, report of experience of a traumatic event and anxious arousal (e.g., sweating, shortness of breath, dizziness, etc.), low self-esteem, perception of social isolation and lack of support, and pessimism that symptoms and difficulty would improve, with associated low interest in counseling interventions. Review of validity indices on three self-report measures revealed no efforts at exaggeration on two of the instruments (P3 and TSI), though there were indications of overendorsement of symptoms and/or their degree on the third (PAI); assessment of his response pattern on this instrument indicates that his endorsement may be better accounted for by significant negativity and high levels of distress rather than conscious efforts at misrepresentation. Mr. Laesus was also referred for a neuropsychological evaluation, which indicated generally average functioning, with above-average performance on assessments of perceptual reasoning and working memory, despite indications of suboptimal effort and observed preoccupation with pain during the assessment. There were no findings of notable deficits or declines from an estimated prior level of functioning.

Information from collateral informants revealed that Mr. Laesus tends to avoid social events and family functions, is slow to return calls or e-mails, appears uncomfortable and preoccupied with pain and physical limits, often appears "helpless" and rejects suggestions or advice for making improvements, no longer engages in known hobbies of fishing and working on restoring an old car, often appears fatigued and to have lost weight, and appears "shaky and fearful" when family and freinds have made efforts to "get him out of the house." He was also noted to spend a fair amount of time on the Internet looking for support groups/blogs and herbal remedies to relieve symptoms, and researching diagnostic techniques and interventions for various conditions, a practice his girlfriend reported she attempts to discourage as he appears to become increasingly distressed and fearful after doing so.

Extensive medical records are available documenting Mr. Laesus's experience of physical injury at the construction site, as well as Mr. Laesus's friend's report of witnessing the accident, as recorded by emergency responders. Progressive complaints of depressive symptoms are noted in medical records following his experience of physical injury. Records indicate that Mr. Laesus was prescribed an antidepressant six months following his experience of injury to address reported difficulty with chronic pain, and noted mild elevations of depressive symptoms on Patient Health Questionnaire (PHQ) screens. Two months later, he was also prescribed a non-anxiolytic agent to address complaints of anxiety (particularly complaints of fearfulness, discomfort in public settings, and feeling nervous and jumpy). Mr. Laesus denied any impact on his experience of pain, anxiety, or depressive symptoms with use of pharmacological intervention, though he has consistently persisted in taking the same antidepressant medication at the same dose as prescribed. Mr. Laesus's prescription for antianxiety medication was discontinued after two months without reported effect, and without changes to the dose or type of medication. In addition, Mr. Laesus's reported symptoms of depression worsened following his divorce, with PHQ scores now entering the moderate range for depressive symptoms and ongoing complaints of anxiety noted. No significant changes in his report of depression or anxiety symptoms were noted following his initiation of legal proceedings in this matter (roughly three months before the assessment). Mr. Laesus was also noted to complain of increasing pain and physical limitations, and to demonstrate considerable guarded behaviors and reluctance to attempt movement or recommended physical therapy exercises. He did report some relief from use of ice and heat packs, as well as hot baths, though he indicated that such relief was short lived. He also noted that pain medications made his experience tolerable, though he continued to experience significant pain in his torso and groin area, along with regular headaches and reported regular nausea, headaches, light-headedness, and loose stools, which he attributed to medication use. Medical records were notable for identification of positive Waddell's signs, difficulty identifying medical sources of explanations for his report of pain, restricted range of movement, and sexual dysfunction (including lack of findings on nerve conduction and vascular studies and ultrasounds), with concerns identified for "psychogenic" origin for pain and motion complaints. Records do not suggest that Mr. Laesus was referred for counseling related to these difficulties.

In sum, Mr. Laesus currently describes intrusive and distressing recollections of this experience, particularly in response to environmental cues (e.g., smell of diesel fuel), subsequent difficulty with negative cognitions, and increased arousal and reactivity consistent with irritable outbursts, hypervigilance, and an exaggerated startle response. He also reports difficulty with depressed mood, poor motivation, fatigue, sleep disturbances, and feelings of worthlessness. In addition, he presents prominent concern regarding his health. He describes his life as one that is significantly impacted by pain and physical limitations, with substantial associated time and energy devoted to medical appointments and care, as well as a perception of his difficulties as complex and treatment resistant. Mr. Laesus did not demonstrate significant cognitive or memory limitations, and his complaints of difficulty with concentration and memory are likely best accounted for by anxiety and depressive symptoms, as well as preoccupation with pain.

Observations and presentation of functional difficulty, as well as complaints of somatic dysfunction, anxiety, and depression are consistent across records and close collateral informants (specifically, Mr. Laesus's ex-wife, friend, daughter, and girlfriend), and in his report to medical care providers and in the current assessment (both in interviews and as suggested by test findings). In review of the various validity and effort measures employed in this assessment, Mr. Laesus's responses overall suggest an effort to provide valid responses and adequate efforts on test protocols. There are indications that the interplay of his psychological symptoms may serve to amplify his expressed level of distress. For instance, Mr. Laesus's difficulty with depression and anxiety appear to continue to increase in his sensitivity to, as well as his descriptions of, more intense and prolonged difficulty with pain and physical limitations (with a tendency to express psychological distress through physical symptoms), and he describes sensitivity to lack of validation/expressed understanding of his difficulties by providers and support persons that likely also serve to magnify his perception of the intensity, maintenance/persistence, and expression of his depressive and anxiety symptoms.

Taken together, information from multiple sources over time support diagnoses of major depressive disorder, PTSD, and undifferentiated somatoform disorder.

Conceptualization Regarding "Cause" of Alleged Psychological Harm/Damage

As previously noted, Mr. Laesus has no prior history of mental health diagnosis or treatment preceding his involvement in the accident at the construction site. Indications of some focus on bodily processes and concerns regarding his health and physical functioning are evident prior to his experience of injury, though substantial interference or associated functional issues are not evident; specifically, he has no history of discipline, loss of employment, or demotions, no disruption to social functioning or relationships, and there is no indication that significant amounts of time or expense were utilized in seeking medical attention related to his concerns in review of medical records, financial records, employment records, and discussion with his most recent supervisor (of five years) or personal collateral informants familiar with Mr. Laesus at that time. Development of severe symptoms and functional declines are demonstrated following the accident (as detailed earlier), and there are no indications of prior traumatic experiences. There are indications that Mr. Laesus's experience of depressive and somatization symptoms worsened with his divorce, loss of work, and financial distress (with loss of his home), though these events appear to be related to his symptoms and difficulties following the accident. There are no indications that prior to the accident Mr. Laesus's employment, finances, or marriage were in distress, or that he was experiencing significant difficulty in these areas. Mr. Laesus continues to experience significant symptoms of depression, traumatic anxiety, and somatization, and associated disrupted functioning in his activities of daily living, recreational/leisure activities, social engagement and interaction, employment, and finances 18 months following the accident. Taken together, Mr. Laesus's symptoms and functional declines cannot be accounted for by conditions or events that predated the accident, and there are no other events or circumstances that can be identified that would significantly account for his demonstrated conditions and limitations. There are also no indications of other significant events following the accident that may have precipitated these losses or otherwise have significantly contributed to his experience of symptoms.

Prognostic Formulation

Mr. Laesus demonstrates significant somatic preoccupation and moderate symptoms of depression and trauma-related anxiety that have markedly limited his functioning in multiple life domains for an extended period of time. He appears to have achieved little benefit from medication management, though efforts to individualize and develop a medication regimen specific to Mr. Laesus's presenting complaints and difficulties appear limited. Further, he lacks any significant exposure to nonpharmacological interventions. Given the prominence of psychological factors in his experience of pain and physical limitation, he may benefit from participation in a coordinated medical-psychotherapy program that focuses on the integration of psychological and physical techniques (e.g., biofeedback, mindfulness training, etc., and particularly in a multidisciplinary clinic or treatment setting that specializes in somatoform and pain disorders) to assist him in exploring the cognitive, emotional, and interpersonal facets of his symptoms, and to improve his cognitive skills and emotional resources for coping with depression, anxiety, and chronic pain symptoms. Specific participation in focused interventions to address trauma-related symptoms will also be essential. Intensive participation in such programming may result in mild, gradual improvements over time. However, given the nature, severity, and chronicity of Mr. Laesus's symptoms, the interplay of his experience of depression, traumatic, and somatization symptoms, as well as his resistance to acknowledging the role of psychological features (rather than physical conditions) in his experience of physical pain and limitations likely complicating treatment efforts and exacerbating his somatic symptoms, the ultimate success of these interventions is highly questionable, and would minimally require a substantial amount of time, effort, and resources, delivered consistently over several years to result in the significant improvements necessary for Mr. Laesus to return to his level of functioning prior to the accident.

References

American Law Institute. (2013). *A concise restatement of torts* (3rd ed.). St. Paul, MN: American Law Institute Publishers.

American Psychiatric Association. (2000). *Diagnostic and statistical manual of mental disorders* (4th ed., text rev.). Washington, DC: Author.

American Psychiatric Association. (2013). *Diagnostic and statistical manual of mental disorders* (5th ed.). Arlington, VA: Author.

American Psychological Association. (2010). *Ethical principles of psychologists and code of conduct.* Retrieved from www.apa.org/ethics/code/principles.pdf.

American Psychological Association. (2013). Specialty guidelines for forensic psychology. *American Psychologist, 68,*7–19. doi: 10.1037/a0029889

Committee on Legal Issues, American Psychological Association. (2006). Strategies for private practitioners coping with subpoenas or compelled testimony for client records or test data. *Professional Psychology: Research and Practice, 37,* 215–222. doi:10.1037/0735–7028.37.2.215

Daubert v. Merrell Dow Pharmaceuticals, Inc. 509 U.S. 579, 113 S.Ct. 2786, 125 L.Ed. 2d 469 (1993).

Daubert v. Merrell Dow Pharmaceuticals, 43 F.3d 1311 (9th Cir. 1995).

Dillon v. Legg, 68 Cal.2d 728, 441 P.2d 912, 69 Cal. Rptr. 72, 29 A.L.R.3d 1316 (1968).

Eastvold, A.D., Belanger, H.G. & Vanderploeg, R.D. (2012). Does a third party observer affect neuropsychological test performance? It depends. *The Clinical Neuropsychologist, 26,* 520–541. doi: 10.1080/13854046.2012.663000

Edwards, L.L., Edwards, J.S., & Wells, P.K. (2011). *Tort law* (5th ed.). Clifton Park, NY: Delmar Cengage Learning.

Federal Evidence Review. (2015). Federal rules of evidence. Retrieved June 21, 2015 from http://federalevidence.com/downloads/rules.of.evidence.pdf.

Foote, W.E. & Lareau, C.R. (2013). Psychological evaluation of emotional damages in tort claims. In I. B. Weiner (Series Ed.) & R. Otto (Vol. Ed.), *Handbook of psychology, Vol. 11: Forensic psychology* (2nd ed., pp. 172–200). Hoboken, NJ: Wiley.

Frye v. United States, 293 F. 1013, 34 ALR 145 (D.C. Cir. 1923).

General Electric Company v. Joiner, 522 U.S. 136. (Sup. Ct. 1997).

Goldstein, A. (2003). Overview of forensic psychology. In I. B. Weiner (Series Ed.) & A. M. Goldstein (Vol. Ed.), *Handbook of psychology, Vol. 11: Forensic psychology* (pp. 3–20). Hoboken, NJ: Wiley.

Gordon, R.M., & Cosgrove, L. (2013). Ethical considerations in the development and application of mental and behavioral nosologies: Lessons from DSM-5. *Psychological Injury and Law, 6,* 330–335. doi:10.1007/s12207–013–9172–9

Greenberg, S.A. (2003). Personal injury examinations in torts for emotional distress. In I.B. Weiner (Series Ed.) & A.M. Goldstein (Vol. Ed.), *Handbook of psychology, Vol. 11: Forensic psychology* (pp. 233–257). Hoboken, NJ: Wiley.

Greenberg, S.A., & Shuman, D.W. (1997). Irreconcilable conflict between therapeutic and forensic roles. *Professional Psychology: Research and Practice, 28,* 50–57. doi: 10.1037/0735–7028.28.1.50

Greenberg, S.A., & Shuman, D.W. (2007). When worlds collide: Therapeutic and forensic roles. *Professional Psychology: Research and Practice, 38,*129–132. doi: 10.1037/0735–7028.38.2.129

Greenberg, S.A., & Wheeler, J.G. (2004). Forensic psychological examinations in personal injury cases: Empirical haves and have nots. *Journal of Forensic Psychology Practice, 4,* 79–95. doi: 10.1300/J158v04n01_06

Heilbrun, K.H. (2001). *Principles of forensic mental health assessment.* New York: Kluwer Academic/Plenum.

Kalmbach, K. C. & Lyons, P. M. (2006). Ethical issues in conducting forensic evaluations. *Applied Psychology in Criminal Justice*, 2, 261–290.

Kane, A. W. (2006). Psychology, causality, and court. In G. Young, A. W. Kane, & K. Nicholson (Eds.), *Psychological knowledge in court: PTSD, pain and TBI* (pp. 13–51). New York: Springer SBM.

Kane, A. W. (2007a). Basic concepts in psychology and law. In G. Young, A. W. Kane, & K. Nicholson (Eds.), *Causality of psychological injury: Presenting evidence in court* (pp. 261–292). New York: Springer SBM.

Kane, A. W. (2007b). Conducting a psychological assessment. In G. Young, A. W. Kane, & K. Nicholson (Eds.), *Causality of psychological injury: Presenting evidence in court* (pp. 293–323). New York: Springer SBM.

Kane, A. W. (2007c). Other psycho-legal issues. In G. Young, A. W. Kane, & K. Nicholson (Eds.), *Causality of psychological injury: Presenting evidence in court* (pp. 325–367). New York: Springer SBM.

Kane, A. W., & Dvoskin, J. A. (2011). *Evaluation for personal injury claims*. New York: Oxford University Press.

Koch, W. J., Douglas, K. S., Nicholls, T. L, & O'Neill, M. L. (2006). *Psychological injuries: Forensic assessment, treatment and law*. New York: Oxford University Press.

Koch, W. J., Nader, R. & Haring, M. (2009). The science and pseudoscience of assessing psychological injuries. In J. Skeem, K. Douglas, & S. Lilienfeld (Eds.), *Psychological science in the courtroom: Consensus and controversy* (pp. 263–283). New York: Guilford.

Koch, W. J., O'Neill, M. L., & Douglas, K. S. (2005). Empirical limits for the forensic assessment of PTSD litigants. *Law and Human Behavior*, 29, 12–149. doi: 10.1007/s10979–005–1401–7

Kumho Tire Co. v. Carmichael, 526 U.S. 137. (Sup. Ct. 1999)

Melton, G. B., Petrilla, J., Poythress, N. G., & Slobogin, C. (1997). *Psychological evaluations for the courts* (2nd ed.). New York: Guilford.

Melton, G. B., Petrilla, J., Poythress, N. G., & Slobogin, C. (2007). Psychological evaluations for the courts: A handbook for mental health professionals and lawyers (3rd ed.). New York: Guilford.

Miller, L., Sadoff, R. L., & Dattilio, F. M. (2011). Personal injury: The independent medical examination in psychology and psychiatry. In E. Drogin, F. Dattilio, R. Sadoff, & T. Gutheil (Eds.), *Handbook of forensic assessment: Psychological and psychiatric perspectives* (pp. 277–301). Hoboken, NJ: Wiley.

Mitchell v. Rochester Railway Co., 151 N.Y. 107, 45, N.E. 354 (1896).

Molien v. Kaiser Foundation Hospitals, 27 Cal.3d 916 (1980).

National Academy of Neuropsychology Policy and Planning Committee. (2000). Presence of third party observers during neuropsychological testing: Official statement of the National Academy of Neuropsychology. *Archives of Clinical Neuropsychology*, 15, 379–380.

National Academy of Neuropsychology Policy and Planning Committee. (2003). Test security: An update. Official statement of the National Academy of Neuropsychology. Retrieved from www.nanonline.org/docs/PAIC/PDFs/NANTestSecurityUpdate.pdf.

Nicholson, K., & Martelli, M. (2007). Malingering: Overview and basic concepts. In G. Young, A. W. Kane, & K. Nicholson (Eds.), *Causality of psychological injury: Presenting evidence in court* (pp. 375–409). New York: Springer SBM.

Palsgraf v. Long Island Railroad Company, 248 NY 339. (NY 1928).

Rodrigues v. State. 472 P. 2d 509 (Hawaii 1970).

Rogers, R., & Shuman, D. W. (2005). *Fundamentals of forensic practice: Mental health and criminal law*. New York: Springer SBM.

Schultz, I. Z. (2013). DSM-5 neurocognitive disorders: Validity, reliability, fairness, and utility in forensic applications. *Psychological Injury and Law*, 6, 299–306. doi: 10.1007/s12207–013–9174–7

Shuman, D. W. & Hardy, J. L. (2007). Causation, psychology, and law. In G. Young, A. W. Kane, & K. Nicholson (Eds.), *Causality of psychological injury: Presenting evidence in court* (pp. 517–548). New York: Springer SBM.

Spector, C. J. (1982). Negligent infliction of emotional distress absent physical impact or subsequent physical injury: Molien v. Kaiser Foundation hospitals. *Missouri Law Review*, 47, 124–132.

Thomas, L. C. (2013). The DSM-5 and forensic relationship status; It's complicated. *Psychological Injury and Law*, 6, 324–329. doi: 10.1007/s12207–013–9179–2

Vallano, J. P. (2013). Psychological injuries and legal decision making in civil cases: What we know and what we do not know. *Psychological Injury and Law*, 6, 99–112. doi: 10.1007/s12207–013–9153–z

Young, G. (2007). Causality: Concepts, issues, and recommendations. In G. Young, A. W. Kane, & K. Nicholson (Eds.), Causality *of psychological injury: Presenting evidence in court* (pp. 49–86) New York: Springer SBM.

Young, G. (2013a). Breaking bad: DSM-5 description, criticisms, and recommendations. *Psychological Injury and Law*, *6*, 345–348. doi: 10.1007/s12207–013–9181–8

Young, G. (2013b). Ill-treatment of pain in the DSM-5. *Psychological Injury and Law*, *6* (4), 307–313. doi: 10.1007/s12207–013–9178–3

Young, G., & Kane, A. W. (2007). Causality in psychology and law. In G. Young, A. W. Kane, & K. Nicholson (Eds.), *Causality of psychological injury: Presenting evidence in court* (pp. 13–47). New York: Springer SBM.

Zelig, M. (2013, September). *Personal injury evaluations: Ethics, case law, and practice*. Workshop materials presented at American Academy of Forensic Psychology continuing education workshops. Arlington, Virginia.

Zoellner, L. A., Bedard-Gilligan, M. A., Jun, J. J., Marks, L. H., & Garcia, N. M. (2013). The evolving construct of posttraumatic stress disorder (PTSD): DSM-5 criteria changes and legal implications. *Psychological Injury and Law*, *6*, 277–289. doi: 10.1007/s12207–013–9175–6

19 Civil Forensic Assessment

Current Practice and Suggestions for the Future

Eric Strachan

Imagine a man named John. John has had his share of problems since graduating from high school. Despite a great deal of promise up until graduation, he has since been in and out of psychiatric hospitals with limited benefit. When John is in the hospital he receives basic care consisting of psychiatric medications to which he often objects initially and ultimately discontinues. The meds have been of modest—but certainly never complete—benefit in terms of positive psychiatric symptoms but have led to a variety of physical problems and troubling side effects (weight gain, metabolic syndrome, involuntary motor movements, and avolition). They have done little to improve other sources of John's problems such as unemployment, unstable housing, lack of social support, and a life that alternates between boredom and intense anxiety and fear. He acknowledges that he has a diagnosis of schizophrenia but does not think schizophrenia is his major problem.

John currently lives in an apartment, paid for by his parents, that he keeps "secure from the microwave beams" by coating every wall and window with aluminum foil. He often (but not always) believes there is a chip in his gut that detects the beam and causes him great pain in punishment for his sins. John's landlord is not amused by the aluminum foil wallpaper and John's parents are constantly dealing with threats from the landlord to evict John. They know from experience that John will not live at home (no protection from the beams) but also that he is in danger of serious harm on the streets from people and from the elements. From time to time John is able to work in supported settings and access services at a local community mental health center. But because John's problems are episodic, access to work and services is episodic as well.

Psychologists who provide forensic evaluation services in civil cases are likely to see people who present with a set of problems similar to John's. There is evidence that the content of John's thoughts is unusual with important (i.e., behaviorally relevant) components that are almost certainly untrue. There is also evidence that John's belief in the validity of those thoughts changes, based on a variety of factors (some known, some unknown). John has a history of age-appropriate functioning and educational achievement that changed suddenly in early adulthood. His parents give him as much support as he allows them to, but the relationship is strained. The treatment that John receives is somewhat helpful, but somewhat unpleasant and unlikely to address important sources of John's disability. In addition, John typically does not want to take psychiatric medications because of side effects but has little access to other forms of rehabilitation and recovery.

At one point or another in John's life he may require evaluation for civil commitment, guardianship proceedings, PADs, and treatment refusals or other issues related to informed consent (e.g., research). In this chapter, I intend to describe the "world as it currently is" regarding such civil mental health proceedings and then to challenge that status quo in ways that, I believe, could improve the science and practice of civil forensic assessment. I think that evaluators-to-be will find that doing civil forensic assessments with an eye to a more psychologically sophisticated future will not detract from their ability to complete current clinical, ethical, and legal obligations while demanding more from courts, legal decision makers, and psycholegal researchers.

Setting the Scene

There are a number of contextual concepts that should be clarified before diving any deeper into the specifics of civil forensic assessment. To begin, I have already outlined a standard list of civil legal proceedings that are likely to involve professional evaluation or expert testimony (involuntary civil commitment, guardianship, PADs, treatment decision making, and research-informed consent), and each of these has different legal bases and different rules that vary (at least somewhat) from state to state. The first concept, then, is that most (all, actually, for the purposes of this chapter) civil mental health law is established at the state level and handled in state courts. Therefore, competent civil forensic evaluators need to be intimately familiar with the laws (legislation, case law, and administrative rules and regulations) of their particular state. In addition, the reality of practice "on the ground" is likely to reflect political and economic pressures that dictate how the laws are actually carried out. For example, a shortage of publicly funded inpatient psychiatric hospital beds may lead affected jurisdictions toward de facto restrictions of involuntary civil commitments.

Given that introduction, the task at hand begins with three questions. The first is, Where does government power to intervene in matters of mental health come from? Following that, What needs to be done in a competent civil forensic assessment? The final question combines the first two into something like, Does what we do follow coherently from what we should be doing, based on the source of government power to intervene in the private lives of its citizens? The answer to the final question will then open the door to further discussion of changing the system for the benefit of those targeted by mental health interventions as well as treatment and rehabilitation providers, lawyers and judges, and the general public.

The Role of the Government: *Parens Patriae* and Police Powers

The power of a democratic government to interfere in the private lives of its citizens is meant to be limited. However, governments are established, in part, for the dual purposes of protecting the safety and welfare of citizens and protecting or caring for those who are unable to protect or care for themselves. The former is typically referred to as the state's police power, whereas the latter is referred to as the state's *parens patriae* authority/obligation (which translates something like "parent of last resort for all citizens"; see, e.g., Schopp, 2001; and Zanni & Stavis, 2007 for a fuller description of these powers). Criminal statutes and systems of punishment are rooted in police power and maintain their moral authority through strict procedural protections for those accused of wrongdoing (to prevent the conviction of innocent people). Involuntary treatment and other forms of intrusion into normally self-regarding matters are rooted in the *parens patriae* obligation, which historically has not included the same level of procedural protection. When people have demonstrated that they are a threat to society—by committing a crime, for example—the state relies on its police power to rein in that behavior and retrospectively punish it. To prevent abuses of that power, however, the state has to follow strict rules (e.g., reading the *Miranda* rights at arrest, providing adequate counsel, avoiding cruel and unusual punishments) and standards of proof ("beyond a reasonable doubt" for criminal offenses) in order to intervene. When, however, people are considered dangerous because of mental disorders, the State relies on its *parens patriae* authority to justify providing care and assistance even if the person, in his or her presumably incapacitated state, does not choose such care and assistance. In those cases, the procedural protections are less salient and the standard of proof is lower (typically, either a "preponderance of the evidence" or "clear and convincing evidence"; the latter is theoretically stricter than the former). Plus, the intervention is often prospective (i.e., preventing exposure to risk rather than punishing a crime already committed).

As just one example, contemporary mental health law reflects the fact that involuntary civil commitment—regarded by the U.S. Supreme Court as a "massive curtailment of liberty" (*Humphrey v. Cady*, 1972, p. 509)—is an intolerable intrusion unless it is supported by a finding that the person to be committed is mentally ill and dangerous. This formula attempts to reinforce the idea that while individual liberty is central to American political morality, liberties can be revoked in the face of a sufficiently compelling societal (or governmental) interest (Morris, 1999; Schopp, 2001; Winick, 1997). In other words, according to the standard account, the decision to deprive an individual of freedom should not be made lightly, but theoretically there are ways in which such action can be justified without sacrificing important political ideals.

The mental illness predicate in current civil commitment law, then, is thought to aid legal decision makers in deciding who is eligible for commitment (i.e., justifying the special treatment), and the dangerousness predicate is thought to provide procedural protection for potential detainees (i.e., preventing commitment for people who are merely odd or disagreeable). On one hand, within this system there are some who believe that many mentally ill adults are prevented from receiving the care they "require"—but do not want—because the procedural bar is too high (Torrey, 1995, 2012). On the other hand, there are some who believe that the system does not do enough to protect the interests of patients from the will of clinicians practicing an imprecise craft with questionable outcomes (Morse, 1987; Zanni & Stavis, 2007). The controversies behind the conventional wisdom are the subject of voluminous debate that will not be repeated in detail here (a sampling of relevant readings would include Morris, 1999; Janus, 1996, 1997, 2000; Schopp, 2001; Torrey, 2012; Winick, 1997). What is true, however, is that forensic evaluators in civil commitment proceedings are going to be asked their opinion regarding the extent to which a defendant is mentally ill and dangerous and, depending on the jurisdiction, whether the dangerousness is meaningfully connected to the mental illness.

At this point it is worth mentioning that involuntary civil commitment is different from other forms of civil mental health interventions in ways that make it vulnerable to the kind of "procedural protections" versus "right-to-treatment" arguments that plague civil commitment law. As I have already noted, involuntary civil commitment in all U.S. jurisdictions is going to be allowed only when the person in question is both mentally ill (defined in various ways) and dangerous to self or others. Dangerousness to others is basically self-explanatory, although it should be noted that the dangerousness is supposed to be imminent rather than at some hypothetical point in the future. Dangerousness to self, however, can be either suicidality (the classic form of dangerousness to self but, again, with the imminent qualifier) or grave disability. Grave disability has not undergone the kind of empirical and legal analysis that dangerousness to others and suicidality has (Brooks, 2006; Turkheimer & Parry, 1992), and it may be more commonly misunderstood than other aspects of dangerousness (Kaufman & Way, 2010), but the general idea is that persons are so disabled as a consequence of their mental illnesses that they are likely to decompensate clinically and come to significant harm if left alone.

The reliance on vaguely defined notions of mental illness and dangerousness is what differentiates involuntary civil commitment from criteria for guardianship, PADs, and other treatment decisions. In each of the latter cases, the question focuses on competent decision making in specific contexts without reference to clinical concepts of mental illness or dangerousness per se. That is not to say that information about mental illness and dangerousness are left out of those equations, but legal findings on those questions are not required. Instead, the basic question is, Does this person have the capacity to make competent decisions in self-regarding matters?[1]

In the case of guardianship, legal decision makers are asked to decide whether a person has the capacity to make competent self-regarding decisions either broadly or in specific contexts (e.g., finances, health care, contracts). It is possible for a court to rule that a person is incompetent and therefore in need of a guardian, accountable to the court, to make important decisions. The decisions that guardians make on behalf of their wards are supposed to be some combination of what the person would choose if he or she were competent and, if that is not immediately ascertainable, in his or her best interest. The same basic notion underlies treatment decision making (informed consent). It is important to keep in mind that "under ordinary conditions, competent adults have a right to refuse health care, including life-sustaining care" (Schopp, 2001, p. 19). Thus, for treatment decision making (see Winick, 1997, for a comprehensive overview of the right to refuse treatment), the questions are, Does this person have the capacity to make competent decisions in health-care related matters? If not, a substitute decision maker will be appointed or a predetermined course of treatment (typically medications) will be implemented. An additional factor that is relevant to treatment refusals is whether the person is refusing without posing a threat or is both refusing and posing a threat. In the latter case, courts have determined that the police power allows psychiatrists to take steps which "in the exercise of professional judgment . . . (are) deemed necessary to prevent the patient from endangering himself or others" (*Rennie v. Klein*, 1982, p. 269). Under the *parens patriae* authority—that is, when the person is not a threat to others—psychiatrists also have the ability to involuntarily administer some treatments (e.g., psychotropic medications but not lobotomies; see *Aden v. Younger*, 1976) but only for patients who have been deemed incompetent to participate in treatment decisions.

Even that, however, can sometimes be undermined by poorly conceived statutes. In Nebraska, for example, the civil commitment statute specifically states that "A subject in custody or receiving treatment under the Nebraska Mental Health Commitment Act . . . has the right . . . (1) To be considered legally competent for all purposes unless he or she has been declared legally incompetent" (Neb. Rev.St. §71–959). However, in a subsequent section of the statute, it is established that a civilly committed individual has the right "(3) To refuse treatment medication, except (b) following a hearing and order of a mental health board, such treatment medication as will substantially improve his or her mental illness" (Neb.Rev.St. §71–959). This is a de facto judgment of incompetence for the purpose of health-care decision making because the civilly committed person is only allowed to refuse treatments that the "mental health board" does not think will "substantially improve" the mental illness. Assuming, then, that the mental health board is not inclined toward malfeasance (e.g., deliberately prescribing unwanted and unnecessary treatments) the person is only allowed to refuse treatments that would not be offered in the first place.

Psychiatric advance directives (PADs) follow the same line of reasoning as guardianship and treatment refusals but have a particular spin attached. PADs are designed to allow mental health consumers to identify—in advance of a period of incompetence related to psychiatric symptom exacerbation—their competently chosen treatment preferences (Nicaise, Soto, Dubois, & Lorant, 2014; Srebnik, Appelbaum, & Russo, 2004). PADs can also include a Durable Power of Attorney specification giving decision-making authority to a specific person for specific purposes (similar to guardianship but done voluntarily and in advance). Not all states have PAD statutes (the National Resource Center on Psychiatric Advance Directives has up-to-date information at www.nrc-pad.org/) and even those that do cannot always accommodate them because some forms of treatment are not going to be available. This leaves aside the question of whether PADs can or should be used to express a desire for no treatment whatsoever (as some mental health consumers might choose). In any case, the legal relevance is establishing that the person is competent to make such treatment choices at the time he or she creates the PAD and is then incompetent at the time of its deployment.

Conducting Civil Forensic Evaluations

Based on the discussion just completed, I would like to divide civil forensic evaluations into two kinds. The first is evaluations for involuntary civil commitment. The second is evaluations related to competent decision making. This second category includes treatment decision making, PADs, and guardianship.

Evaluations for Involuntary Civil Commitment

Understanding and Assessing Mental Illness

Despite nuances in different jurisdictions, the basic criteria for involuntary civil commitment are mental illness and dangerousness to self or others. Sometimes grave disability is carved out specifically, sometimes it is implicit in dangerousness to self, and sometimes it does not qualify as a criterion. Again, it is imperative for forensic evaluators to be intimately familiar with the statutes, case law, administrative rules, and practical realities of their region. In Washington State, for example, involuntary civil commitment is allowed if a person, as a result of a mental disorder, presents a likely risk of serious harm or is gravely disabled (Revised Code of Washington [RCW] 71.05.150). For the purposes of this statute, *mental disorder* is defined as "any organic, mental, or emotional impairment which has substantial adverse effects on a person's cognitive or volitional functions" (RWC 71.05.020). The first thing that many commentators note at this point is that the legal definition of mental disorder makes no specific reference to current clinical diagnostic categories and thus the clinical and legal definitions of mental illness are different. This well-intentioned attention to detail, however, washes out somewhat when we ask the question that immediately follows: If the legal definition of mental illness or disorder does not refer to diagnostic categories, what, exactly, does it refer to? Are there other ways to evaluate "organic, mental, or emotional impairments" that are commonly used in clinical practice besides DSM-5 categories (American Psychiatric Association, 2013)? As Schopp (1998) has written,

> Although the courts [have] denied that the clinical meaning of mental illness controls for statutory purposes, they [have] relied heavily on expert testimony by clinicians and on the current diagnostic manual. A reasonable reading of these cases would support the interpretation that individuals fulfill mental illness, mental abnormality, personality disorder, or analogous statutory requirements just in case clinical expert witnesses testify that they do. (p. 327; Schopp's use of the phrase "just in case" can be understood as "whenever")

To be clear, Schopp (1998) is not advocating for the use of DSM categories in mental health statutes. But for the purposes of current civil forensic evaluation, he recognizes that most evaluators conduct a clinical interview with the purpose of establishing a DSM diagnosis, whether or not such diagnoses are part of the statutory definition of mental illness/disorder/abnormality. Following that step, some consideration is typically given to whether the diagnosis in question can be linked to cognitive or behavioral dysfunction of the kind relevant to the case at hand. It is worth noting, though, that in Washington (as in several other states), there is specific mention that the "likely risk of serious harm" is the "result of a mental disorder." In other words, it cannot merely be the case a person is coincidentally mentally disordered and dangerous without a connection between the two.

Imagine, for example, a person who has a diagnosis of schizophrenia based on hearing distressing voices and who is at risk of serious harm and even death because he refuses treatment and lives on the street, where he has been assaulted numerous times (including the night before he is being evaluated for involuntary civil commitment). Imagine further that the person is refusing treatment not because of his voices but because he is a Christian Scientist and was raised by strict Christian Science parents who support his refusal of psychiatric intervention. According to the black letter of the Washington statute, this person might not be eligible for involuntary treatment because his dangerousness (refusing treatment and thus leaving himself vulnerable) is not a result of his mental illness. If, however, he is refusing treatment because he believes he will receive the blood of the devil and be cast down into hell for all eternity, a court might be more sympathetic to involuntary civil commitment. Problems with de facto reliance on DSM categories in invoking legal mental illness will be discussed in greater detail later.

Because of the problems associated with imposing DSM categories on statutory systems that do not reference them, momentum is growing for functional assessments of mental illness that are better related to the legal questions in civil commitment cases (Banner, 2012; Grisso & Appelbaum, 1998; Grisso, Appelbaum, & Hill-Fotouhi, 1997; Morse, 1987; Schopp, 2001). The most prominent example of functional assessments would be the MacArthur instruments and their offspring (discussed later) that have been developed to assess competence in treatment decision making, research informed consent, and PADs, among others. Those instruments focus on the legally established criteria for competent decision making: understanding, appreciation, rationality, and expression of a choice. Because civil commitment does not reference (and has no direct legal bearing on) decisional competence, such instruments are not of specific utility in civil commitment proceedings. However, their general approach provides a good framework for conducting a functional assessment of mental illness that could be useful in civil commitment proceedings. I would characterize a reasonable functional approach as consisting of:

1. Understanding the referral question and history (i.e., Why is civil commitment potentially indicated in this case?) and the clinical claims made about the person;
2. Assessing additional relevant clinical constructs, especially neuropsychological functioning;
3. Assessing the link between the clinical picture and the person's explanation of his or her situation (including specifics about the person's justification for his or her hesitance in seeking voluntary treatment);
4. Making a statement describing the clinical picture, whether it reflects impairment, and whether the impairment exposes the person or the public to the kind of danger that is relevant to civil commitment proceedings (aka writing the report).

Let's take each of these in turn.

Understanding the Referral Question, History, and Clinical Claims

Although developing a clear understanding of why someone is being evaluated for civil commitment may sound self-evident, it bears mentioning, given that civil commitment is possible based on two or three different legal findings—dangerousness to self, dangerousness to others, and possibly grave disability—in addition to the mental illness finding and other contextual variables. This is essentially an information gathering stage that will precede a clinical interview and inform the dialogue with the person. Where this information comes from will vary by jurisdiction and situation, but in general this stage would include review of medical records and any documentation regarding the reasons for referral and possible civil commitment. Specifically, as an evaluator, one is looking for evidence that the person's clinical presentation can be linked to the dangerousness that is being claimed (and that the dangerousness being claimed meets the statutory definitions—typically, recent behaviors). Recall that the person cannot merely be mentally ill without evidence of exposing him- or herself to risk of harm or clinical decompensation. Nor can the person merely be dangerous without any evidence of mental illness.

The information gathered should be useful in querying the person during the subsequent interview assessing the link between the clinical picture and the refusal to seek voluntary treatment. Thus, the evaluator might look for history of diagnosis, treatment, and treatment response; recent dangerous behaviors that seem linked to some mental, emotional, or cognitive problem; and some sense that the person is either denying obvious behavioral and cognitive problems or explaining those problems in ways that fail a test of basic rationality (more on that later). It will be helpful if the evaluator gathers the information with an eye to how he or she might turn the information into the kinds of questions outlined in the "Assessing the Link" section. That is, the evaluator will want to be able to ask questions about the person's understanding of his or her diagnosis, the kinds of behaviors that others are concerned about, how the person explains those behaviors, and how the person justifies not seeking help.

Assessing Relevant Clinical Constructs

It is my assertion that a brief neuropsychological screening can be of value in civil commitment evaluations regardless of the ultimate disposition. Realistically speaking, however, many forensic evaluators do not have the time to include such a battery, especially during the early stages of civil commitment proceedings. Even so, a brief mental status exam such as the Folstein Mini Mental Status Exam (MMSE) can be informative, particularly if the results show notable impairment. Better than the MMSE would be a brief but multidimensional screening such as the Repeatable Battery for the Assessment of Neuropsychological Status (RBANS; Randolph, 1997). The RBANS measures a number of basic cognitive abilities—immediate and delayed memory, attention, language skills, visuospatial/constructional ability—relevant to understanding how a person takes in, manipulates, and uses information. An additional benefit of using the RBANS is that the scoring is standardized with reference groups that include both the general population and specific diagnostic groups (including schizophrenia). Some measure of executive functioning, such as the Wisconsin Card Sorting Task (Grant & Berg, 2005), would also be valuable. Serious impairments in any of these areas might help explain how and why a person is behaving in ways that suggest the need for involuntary treatment.

One example of how neuropsychological data might inform an evaluation is when the data suggest impairment in memory, language skills, and executive functioning. Having obtained these results, the evaluator would be able to include some text in the final report suggesting that the person being evaluated (let's imagine a man, in this case) is likely to have difficulty in retaining information related to his circumstances and the various options available to him. This lack of understanding may be distressing in and of itself, or it may cause the person to revert back (time and again) to some unhelpful or false explanation of what is happening to him. In addition (based on the particular executive functioning outcomes), it may be that the person has a difficult time initiating goal-oriented behavior, changing course when such change is required, or staying focused on one particular course as long as is necessary. Finally, the person may have some difficulty understanding or generating the relevant language to make sound decisions in cooperation with his treatment team. Any one of these findings would be relevant to the question of mental disorder resulting in dangerousness. Plus, there is value beyond the evaluation because the data may help future providers build empathy and develop a better, more comprehensive treatment plan.

Assessing the Link Between Clinical Presentation and Personal Explanations and Writing the Report

This is the crux of the evaluation. At this point the evaluator is asking the person about his or her understanding and explanation of the current situation, following a complete description of the purpose and structure of the interview. Because these evaluations will typically have some legal mandate, they do not necessarily require informed consent per se. All the same, better rapport is likely to generate better results. If the person refuses the interview, it is of central importance to document the attempt and the refusal, and to qualify the report accordingly (see Phenix & Jackson, Chapter 8 in this volume).

In terms of information that is valuable at this point, Saks (1991) and Slobogin (1996) have presented a compelling case for using a "basic rationality" standard to assess whether a decision is being made competently. Although they are talking about decisional competence—which, again, is not the question in current civil commitment jurisprudence—an evaluation of basic rationality can be informative in a civil commitment evaluation. The standard of basic rationality as described by Saks and advocated by Slobogin is simple: First, does the person understand the relevant facts of the case? Second, does the person have any patently false beliefs about those facts? If the answer to the first question is "yes" and the answer to the second questions is "no," that might argue against the appropriateness of civil commitment. If the reverse is true, however, civil commitment might be indicated. Along these lines, it is of central importance for evaluators to seek out information that might disconfirm either the mental illness or dangerousness predicates in addition to seeking out information that confirms it. Thus, if the person being evaluated makes a statement such as "I won't go to the hospital because they're trying to poison me," it is important to gain a full understanding of the meaning of that statement. Does the person really believe the intention of hospitalization is fatal poisoning (a patently false belief)? Or is the person telling the evaluator in shorthand that the side effects of the medications are troublesome (likely an accurate reflection of treatment history)?

During this phase of the evaluation, the evaluator is armed with a social and psychiatric history, a clear understanding of the referral question and relevant clinical claims, and perhaps even some basic neuropsychological data. This allows the evaluator to ask questions of the person being evaluated that are specific to his circumstances and the relevant legal criteria. In Washington, as in many states, the evaluator would want to structure questions in order to tell a story that runs "This person believes (or experiences) the following things (e.g., a particular set of delusions or a particular set of distressing voices) and exhibits the following functional impairments (if RBANS or other such data are available). Such phenomena are often associated with a diagnosis of (fill in the blank) and that diagnosis is warranted in this case. Because of this person's beliefs (or hallucinations, or negative affect, or social withdrawal, etc.), the person has in the recent past engaged in the following dangerous behaviors (again, fill in the blank). The person explains the symptoms and behaviors in the following way. In my opinion, these behaviors are the result of the mental illness and functional impairments described above." Note that the evaluator is not making a judgment about the appropriateness of civil commitment (which is a legal, not clinical, decision).

The question of "least restrictive alternative" (LRA) may also arise in the course of civil commitment evaluations. Although consistent with the ideal that any deprivation of liberty should be restricted to absolute necessity, the practical reality is that LRA depends heavily on whether there are resources in the community that allow for a viable alternative to inpatient hospitalization (e.g., Lin, 2003). LRA also raises issues that may be difficult to objectively assess. For example, it may be less restrictive from the perspective of the state to release a person detained for mental illness into the community with a prescription and a plan for maximizing adherence. However, from the perspective of the person detained, it may be less restrictive to be admitted to a hospital until such time as he or she stabilizes without the use of medications. Practically speaking, the best contribution that a clinical evaluator can make to the question of LRA is to evaluate treatment history with an eye toward what strategies have generated the longest periods of recovery at the highest level of independence. Acute awareness of the actual, current options in the community will serve evaluators well in this regard as it does little good to propose an LRA that does not actually exist.

A final point is to make the report complete and comprehensive but succinct. It is of little use to anyone involved to write a report so long that no one will read it thoroughly.

Understanding and Assessing Dangerousness

This assessment will take place as part of the functional assessment described earlier. However, because there are several issues specific to assessing dangerousness, I have separated it out.

In the state of Washington, "likelihood of serious harm" is defined as,

> A substantial risk that: (i) physical harm will be inflicted by a person upon his or her own person, as evidenced by threats or attempts to commit suicide or inflict physical harm on oneself; (ii) physical harm will be inflicted by a person upon another, as evidenced by behavior which has caused such harm or which places another person or persons in reasonable fear of sustaining such harm; or (iii) physical harm will be inflicted by a person upon the property of others, as evidenced by behavior which has caused substantial loss or damage to the property of others; or (b) The person has threatened the physical safety of another and has a history of one or more violent acts. (RCW 71.05.020)

As opposed to other forms of dangerousness assessment, particularly those that attempt to predict future dangerous behavior, civil commitment statutes require current behavioral evidence of risk (*Lessard v. Schmidt*, 1972, established the behavioral evidence requirement that has been adopted in civil commitment law). Thus, the use of predictive tools is not necessary for involuntary civil commitment assessments. In Washington, a competent evaluation would require specific detailing of behaviors (including threats) that have occurred in reasonable proximity to the evaluation itself (i.e., the behaviors cannot be old or unrelated to the current context). Again, there would need to be some meaningful connection between the mental illness and the dangerousness. If we take the case that began this chapter as an example, we might imagine that John has been evicted from his apartment and is living on the streets, where he has been the victim of assault and robbery and is also exposed to the elements without adequate protection. If on one hand it is the case that John simply could not or did not pay the rent, his current situation might not be cause for involuntary treatment. If, on the other hand, it could be shown that John's homelessness and decompensation were the result of his psychotic experiences, he might be eligible for involuntary treatment.

It bears mentioning at this point that the language of involuntary civil commitment statutes such as Washington's leaves important questions unanswered. Recall from the mental illness section that the statute requires a finding of some "organic, mental, or emotional impairment which has substantial adverse effects on a person's cognitive or volitional functions." The problem with this definition is that "impairment," "substantial," "adverse," "effects," and "functions" are not further defined.

Although lacking a definition of each of these is problematic, not having a clear sense of what is meant by "substantial" is particularly so. The key for forensic evaluators is not to get drawn into disputes as to what constitutes substantial impairment. Professional evaluations and expert testimony should fulfill a particular purpose in legal proceedings, and that purpose is to exercise relevant professional judgment in the domain of professional expertise (Schopp, 2001). That domain, of course, is clinical and not legal. Making a judgment as to what constitutes "substantial" impairment is a legal decision (not clinical) because "substantial" in this case refers to the notion that the impairment is substantial enough (i.e., sufficient) to warrant involuntary treatment based on principles of American liberal democracy. Clinical evaluators can and should offer every piece of information that serves the purpose of adequately describing, and drawing warranted inferences about, the defendant in involuntary civil commitment hearings. They should not, however, be tempted to offer, or be drawn into offering, legal opinions.

The same idea, then, applies to the "dangerousness" component of involuntary civil commitment statutes. The Washington statute uses the phrase "likelihood of serious harm" which, in many legal settings, would be taken to mean "more likely than not." Such a definition would be extremely problematic because violence (to self or others) is a low-base-rate event, even if one accepts the premise that some persons classified under certain diagnostic categories under certain conditions have an increased risk of violence compared to other persons not similarly classified (e.g., Torrey, Stanley, Monahan, Steadman, & MacArthur Study Group, 2008; Treatment Advocacy Center, 2003). In other words, to minimize the number of errors based exclusively on probabilities, it would be necessary to estimate that no one would engage in violence. In case the reasoning for that is not clear, let me explain. Let us assume that 1 out of 10 persons diagnosed with paranoid schizophrenia with a history of assault will engage in additional aggressive behavior compared to a rate in the general population of 1 out of 20 (these number are made up to illustrate the point). In other words, twice as many people diagnosed with paranoid schizophrenia are going to commit an act of violence compared to the group of people without such a diagnosis. Even given that, however, it is very unlikely that any individual in either group will engage in violence (1/10 = 10% for the schizophrenia group; 1/20 = 5% for the general population). Thus, estimating that no person in the schizophrenia group is going to be violent would mean being right 90% of the time whereas estimating that all persons are going to be violent would mean being wrong 90% of the time. Trying to figure out which one out of the 10 is going to be violent could mean being wrong 99% of the time (10% actual base rate of persons who will commit a violent act × 10% arbitrarily classified as being the person who will commit a violent act = 1% likelihood of classifying the right person).

But that potential assessment fiasco is not even the main problem with dangerousness assessment in comparison to the realization that dangerousness is not (or at least should not be) a prediction of harmful conduct in the future (this is discussed at length by Schopp, 2001, pp. 215–229). This goes rather strongly against the conventional wisdom in civil commitment legal debates that tend to go back and forth on the validity of predictions of dangerousness. As Schopp (2001) notes, however, "according to the statutes and ordinary language, a dangerous person is one who currently has the property of exposing himself or others to risk or peril of harm or injury" (p. 216). It may make sense to predict that the person will continue to expose him or herself or others to risk or peril of harm or injury, but it is not necessary to predict actual harm or injury in the future. Think back to the hypothetical risk percentages presented. It may be the case that the citizens of Washington or another state decide that a 10% risk of violence for persons diagnosed with schizophrenia is too great compared to a population risk of 5%. This may be true even though an evaluator would not predict that the person is likely to be violent (the evaluator would, in fact, predict the opposite). Instead, the citizens of the hypothetical state are legitimately declaring that the person is too dangerous because their risk of violence (10%) exceeds a threshold (5%) that has been defined as legally meaningful (assuming that such a definition has taken place). Thus, assessing dangerousness is not about predicting violence but rather assessing the factors that expose an individual or others around that individual to unacceptable levels of risk of harm or injury.

A person's actual history of violent acts or threats while (and as a result of being) psychotic or depressed should be the relevant evidence, then, without predictions of violent behavior at some vague point in the future. That is, the evidence should be in the form of "Person A recently engaged in these behaviors while responding to his beliefs/hallucinations/negative emotions and those beliefs/hallucinations/emotions are still present in the person." The evidence should not be in the form of "Person A has the characteristics of Group X in which 15 out of 100 members committed an act of violence within 6 months of evaluation." Schopp (2001) points out that attributing the characteristics of a group to individual members of that group embodies the fallacy of division. As an example of that fallacy, it seems absurd to say that my friends from high school went to 10 different colleges and universities, Damian is a friend of mine from high school, therefore Damian went to more than 10 different colleges and universities. But that is the type of inference sometimes drawn by forensic evaluators in civil proceedings.

None of this, of course, yet answers the question of what constitutes "substantial risk." Again, this is a question that clinical evaluators should not be answering in legal proceedings. Clinical experts should provide expertise on clinical matters, including how much impairment a person demonstrates, and leave the normative judgments, including how much impairment justifies involuntary treatment, to the lawyers (who, in turn, should be practicing law that reflects the will of the citizenry; see Schopp, 2001, pp. 249–267).

To summarize, then, an effective evaluation for involuntary civil commitment will include a functional assessment of mental illness such as the one described earlier. It is then necessary to show behavioral evidence of dangerousness and, in many jurisdictions, a connection between the dangerousness and the mental illness. A structured risk assessment battery such as the Short-Term Assessment of Risk and Treatability (START; Nicholls, Brink, Desmarais, Webster, & Martin, 2006) may be of value in these assessments. The START takes only about 30 minutes to complete and guides clinicians toward an integrated, balanced opinion regarding risk in seven domains: violence, suicide, self-harm, self-neglect, unauthorized absence, substance use, and victimization. The intent of instruments such as START is to inform clinical interventions and assist in treatment and risk management plans. The dangerousness evaluation, however, will not be a prediction of future harm, but a description of risk that will serve the legal decision maker in determining whether that level of risk is sufficient for involuntary treatment. In no case should the clinical expert be providing opinions as to whether the mental illness meets the legal criteria for sufficient impairment or whether the level of risk is sufficient for a person to be considered dangerous for statutory purposes.

Evaluation Relevant to Decisional Capacity

The reason for dividing out guardianship, treatment decision making, and PADs from involuntary civil commitment—despite their differences from each in terms of context—is that they all share the characteristic of requiring evidence of decisional incompetence in order for a legal determination to be made. As noted earlier, involuntary civil commitment in places such as Nebraska does not allow the inference that a person is an incompetent decision maker. Unlike the definition of mental illness or impairment in involuntary civil commitment, there has been extensive consideration of the requisite criteria for mental impairment in decisional competence cases. This is not to say that the question of what constitutes a competent decision has been satisfactorily answered from an empirical psychology perspective, but there are legal criteria that refer to certain (at least pseudo-) psychological capacities that are necessary for competent decision making.

Briefly stated, a competent decision is one that reflects understanding, rationality, and appreciation, along with the capacity to express a choice (Grisso & Appelbaum, 1998; Grisso et al., 1997; Saks & Behnke, 1999; Vollmann, Bauer, Danker-Hopfe, & Helmchen, 2003). Taking each of those separately, the "understanding" criterion refers to the capacity to understand the information relevant to making an informed decision. "Rationality" refers to the capacity to manipulate that information rationally (i.e., to reason about it). "Appreciation" refers to the capacity to relate the information to one's own circumstances. Finally, "expressing a choice" refers to the capacity to indicate a preferred course of action and stick to it absent relevant changes in the context of the decision (i.e., not arbitrarily changing the decision). In guardianship and treatment decision making, the criteria directly reflect the legal question at hand. In the case of PADs, it is important to establish that the person is competent at the time of completing the PAD because concerns about decisional competence "may cast doubt on the validity of PADs and reduce the likelihood that they will be honored" (Srebnik et al., 2004, p. 240).

Although it is certainly possible to develop one's own operationalization of each of the legal criteria, there are three standardized assessment instruments that were developed to address questions of treatment competence: the MacArthur Competence Assessment Tool for Treatment (MacCAT-T; Grisso & Appelbaum, 1998; Grisso et al., 1997), the MacArthur Competence Assessment Tool for Clinical Research (MacCAT-CR; Appelbaum & Grisso, 2002), and competence to develop a PAD (the Competence Assessment Tool for Psychiatric Advance Directives;

CAT-PAD; Srebnik et al., 2004). Each of these tools was developed to reflect the understanding, appreciation, rationality, and expressing-a-choice criteria.

The MacCAT-T is a proprietary instrument that was built from a longer set of research instruments with clinical realities in mind (e.g., it needed to be relatively quick to administer). In assessing "understanding" of disorders, treatment, and treatment disclosures, the MacCAT-T provides a framework for relating information generally relevant to a psychiatric diagnosis, and its treatment then can be tailored to an individual. That is, the evaluator establishes the diagnosis, features of the diagnosis specific to the person, and prognosis. The evaluator then asks the person to "explain in [his or her] own words what [the evaluator has] said about" the diagnosis, treatment options, and risks and benefits. A score of 0, 1, or 2 is then generated based on the ability of the person to recall and discuss the information (generally, 0 for no understanding, 1 for some, and 2 for complete). "Reasoning" is assessed using questions focused on why the person might choose one treatment over another, the consequences of the choice, and the general logical consistency of the choice. "Appreciation" is measured by the extent to which a person agrees with various assessments made about them such as diagnosis, severity, and symptoms. In each of the latter cases, a 0–2 scale is used, with 2 reflecting good reasoning or appreciation and 0 reflecting poor reasoning or appreciation. There is no cut-off score for a competent versus incompetent decision, of course, given that such a determination is a legal one, but these data could add to a good functional description of the overall clinical picture.

Saks and Behnke (1999) have provided an excellent review of the materials and their development, and I will not reproduce their entire effort here. I do, however, want to mention their general concerns about the instrument because it applies to other attempts at assessing competent decisions. Those concerns boil down, first, to the empirical question of whether the cognitive capacities that are assessed are actually necessary (or even commonly used) for competent decision making, and, second, to the question of whether rejecting what doctors believe is tantamount to incompetence. The former is a call for more consideration of, and research regarding, a psychologically sophisticated understanding of decision making that may or may not comport with established legal criteria (which, of course, were not developed based on psychological research). The latter is a more complicated question that, in its extreme, runs into the question of how well mental health, mental illness, and mental health treatments are understood by professionals of any ilk (see also Charland, 2001).

The CAT-PAD (Srebnik et al., 2004) is a close cousin to the MacCAT-T but it differs in at least two ways. First, the CAT-PAD takes a two-stage approach. That is, people have to demonstrate that they understand, appreciate, and can reason about whether to complete a PAD. Then they have to demonstrate that they understand, appreciate, can reason about, and can express a choice regarding their particular treatment decisions. Second, there are some differences in items, especially regarding generating consequences for everyday life of the particular treatment decisions. Again, such a standardized instrument is useful is assessing competence but, given its heritage, is likely to embody the same set of concerns developed by Saks and Behnke (1999; their review preceded development of the CAT-PAD). There have also been notable problems in uptake of PADs, resulting in limited implementation despite their initial promise (Nicaise et al., 2014).

In summary, each of the legal questions in this section is related to understanding information, appreciating that information in one's own current circumstances, being able to make reasoned judgments about the information, and being able to express a choice. There are no hard-and-fast rules for assessing these criteria, but there are some standardized instruments that are gaining popularity. Concerns exist regarding the ultimate validity of these instruments, and perhaps even the validity of our current understanding of competent decision making. But specifying measurable legal criteria is actually an advance in these areas compared to assessment for involuntary civil commitment. I turn, now, to a discussion of bringing these areas closer together, conceptually and practically.

An Alternative Approach to Involuntary Mental Health Interventions

Psychiatry has always been bound up with state control of social deviance (Boyle, 2002: Foucault, 1971; Szasz, 1974), but state control of social deviance has a history much longer than psychiatry. In 16th-century Paris, for example, beggars were arrested and forced to work in the city sewers while chained in pairs (Foucault, 1971). But beggars were not the only victims of this forced labor. Poor scholars, unemployed workers, and impoverished students were also among the sewer chain gangs. During approximately the same period in England, poor citizens and vagrants were punished for their misfortune and often kept in "houses of correction." Within and among these groups were persons who most certainly would have qualified as "mentally ill" had such a concept existed at time. But pre-Enlightenment, no such distinctions were made among the social deviants (Stavis, 2000). Whether one was unemployed, physically disabled, insane (in the colloquial use of the term), or bent toward public drunkenness, it was assumed by many that corruption of the soul, demonic possession, or other magical interlocutors (e.g., a curse) were to blame (Foucault, 1971).[2]

Summing up his view on this process of putting social deviance in the hands of medical professionals, Stavis (2000) noted that "It was the Enlightenment, and philosophers and scientists of that age postulated that mental illness was a disease and therefore those suffering with it were properly deserving of government assistance. It was a political innovation for government policy to accept the new science and develop policy and funding to ameliorate mental illness" (p. 162).

That account of the transformation from social deviance as moral weakness to mental illness, however, is somewhat oversimplified. Stavis captures the idea that governments were establishing a relatively new obligation to care for those who could not or would not care for themselves, but he takes for granted the notion that medicine (with its disease-based understanding of dysfunction) was necessarily relevant to that process. As Scull (1979) has convincingly demonstrated, the growth of the asylum system and the medicalization of madness should not be seen as "twin processes in a progression towards more humane and scientific treatment of the 'mentally ill' " (Boyle, 2002, p. 18). There were important reasons that the medical model came to dominate the debate on madness that had little to do with humane treatment and science.

Boyle (2002) has provided additional details that help explain the shift in perceptions about madness during and since the Enlightenment and the growth of the medical model of mental illness. According to Boyle (see also Foucault, 1971), conceiving madness as disease was the final (but still largely unsuccessful) maneuver in the attempt to solve the practical problems faced by "poor relief" programs developed in the spirit of the Enlightenment. That is, poor relief programs were often laxly administered, which tended to encourage poverty and idleness—at least for those already on the borderline—rather than relieving it. As the costs of such programs began to increase there was a general call for some reliable method to discriminate those who actually needed assistance from those who were malingering. Before the disease idea took hold, however, separating the needy from the freeloader was accomplished by making poor relief somewhat unattractive. As Boyle (2002) notes,

> Institutions, in the form of workhouses, came to be seen as the ideal solution. Their unattractiveness would deter the able bodied, while a disciplined regime within them would prepare those not so deterred for a life of industrial labour. If this was clearly out of the question, then the discipline would do no harm. (p. 19)

During that period, there was little interest in further discriminating the needy into groups ("segmenting deviants" as Boyle puts it; p. 20). In part, this was due to the fact that the population within the workhouses was fairly small and the only criterion of real interest was deserving versus undeserving. However, as the workhouses grew and the staff attempted to be more efficient at separating out the able bodied from the non–able bodied, insanity started to stand out from "the previous inchoate mass of deviant behaviours so that it was seen as a distinct problem requiring specialized treatment in an institution of its own" (Scull, 1979, p. 36). Boyle (2002) writes,

> This transition, however, involved much more than the compulsory construction of state asylums. It was accompanied by the transformation of the term "insanity" from a "vague, culturally defined phenomenon afflicting an unknown but probably small, proportion of the population into a condition which could only be authoritatively diagnosed, certified and dealt with by a group of legalised experts." The segregation of those labeled insane from society in general and other deviants in particular was therefore contemporaneous with the growth of medical influence over this population and with the emergence of the new specialty of psychiatry. (pp. 17–18; citations omitted)

Despite the growing trend toward isolating the insane, medical dominance in the world of madness was by no means a certainty in the mid-18th century. For example, in England, the 1744 Vagrancy Act was the first to specifically single out those "who by lunacy or otherwise are so far disordered in their Senses that they may be dangerous to be permitted to go Abroad." However, the power to detain a suspicious vagrant was given to any citizen, who then would turn the person over to two justices of the peace. Those justices would determine the fate of the detainee (including possible institutionalization) without any input from the medical community at all. In other words, "lunacy" at that time was seen as a legitimate reason to detain suspicious people, but it was not seen as a medical issue.

Ultimately, the reasons that physicians came to be seen as experts on insanity are many and complex. One glaring omission in the list of reasons, however, was scientific achievement. In this section, I argue that categorical classification of human behavior has done little to illuminate the mystery of disturbed (or disturbing) behavior and that a new approach is very much needed. I agree with Pilgrim's contention that "psychiatrists have claimed a special knowledge about madness without providing, to this day, a single shred of evidence to support the assertion that 'insanity is purely a disease of the brain' " (1990, p. 229). The victory of medicine in the madhouse was one of political influence much more than scientific advancement. In fact, as recently as 2010, Thomas Insel, Director of the National Institute of Mental Health, wrote that "After a century of studying schizophrenia, the cause of the disorder remains unknown . . . [and] there is little evidence that treatments have substantially improved outcomes" (Insel, 2010, p. 187; see also Whitaker, 2001, 2010).

It is worth noting that although it is typical to associate the medical model with biological theories of pathology and treatment, biological perspectives are not a necessary part of the model. As Spaulding, Sullivan, and Poland (2003) point out, the medical model has survived dominance by psychoanalysis as well as biological psychiatry. By challenging the credibility of the medical model of mental illness, then, I do not intend to dispute the notion that biology and physiology play a significant role in the production of behavior (both normal and abnormal). As one group of researchers has noted, "acknowledgment of the biological components of mental illness does not imply that mental illness sorts itself into the categories of medical model nomenclature or that services should be provided by medical professionals in medical treatment settings" (Spaulding, Poland, Elbogen, & Ritchie, 2000, p. 139). In fact, acknowledging that behavior is the product of biology does not even mean that abnormal behavior is the product of abnormal biology. A brain that is functioning as it should may still, for any number of reasons, fail to generate behaviors that are adaptive in a given situation.

What makes the medical model distinct from other approaches, then, is not biology, but rather the idea that insane behavior sorts itself into discrete categories (e.g., schizophrenia and depression) that reflect naturally co-occurring patterns of signs and symptoms (e.g., hallucinations and delusion for schizophrenia; sad mood and low energy for depression). In addition, medical model practitioners assume that each set of signs and symptoms arises from some common underlying cause (e.g. "chemical imbalances") but that different sets have different underlying causes. Of course, when biological processes are emphasized, these naturally occurring patterns are assumed to be caused by diseased brains (i.e., brains that have discrete structural or functional abnormalities). Thus, to criticize the validity and applicability of the medical model is to criticize the validity of its method of classifying and explaining behavior (Boyle, 2002; Caplan, 1996). If it is true that the medical model is untrue, unscientific, or even just unproven as of yet, the practical implication is that the categories it relies on cannot and should not be used as explanatory mechanisms. Thus, to the extent that the medical model is invalid, it is circular at best (incoherent at worst) to say that "John believes his feet are being electrocuted because he has schizophrenia" or that "Jane's decision-making ability is impaired because of her bipolar disorder."

Among other reasons, medical dominion over madness and social deviance was influenced by the nature of the competition. Among all the relevant players—laypersons, physicians, philosophers, theologians, and others—who were either pursuing the financially lucrative business of running madhouses or pursuing an academic understanding of madness, the outcome was skewed in favor of physicians because of the natural co-occurrence of disturbing behavior and bodily disease (Boyle, 2002). Despite the fact that many such co-occurrences were merely by chance, the traditional role of physicians as helpers gave them an advantage that was again independent of any particular madness-related expertise. As an example, both proponents and opponents of medical model-based mental illness cite the discovery of T. pallidum (the bacterium responsible for syphilis) as critical in the rise of modern medical theories of abnormal behavior. Because tertiary syphilis was often associated with dementia and behavioral symptoms that landed victims in asylums, and because syphilis could be successfully treated in its earlier stages with somatic therapies, psychopathology researchers began to hypothesize that all abnormal thoughts and behaviors might be the product of diseased brains amenable to medical treatment (hence the citation by proponents of the medical model).

Opponents of the medical model, however, cite the case as the exception, not the rule. While conceding that tertiary syphilis is an example of mental illness caused by a diseased brain, they indicate that further successes have been few and far between in over 100 years of intensive research on a variety of disorders (Claridge, 1990; Heinrichs, 1993; McGuire & Troisi, 1998; Pilgrim, 1990; Whitaker, 2010). Nevertheless, with very few scientific victories in hand, 19th-century physicians parlayed their professional status and personal influence into legislation granting them "a mandate from the State to define and manage certain forms of deviance as illness" (Pilgrim, 1990, p. 211). Whatever one thinks of the current state of biological psychiatry, it is clear that the reins of power in managing social deviance were passed to psychiatry long before there was any scientific evidence to justify that decision.

The lack of repeatable scientific discovery in medical model psychopathology remains a problem to this day despite the general impression in the lay population (and some scientific and clinical communities) that the medical model is the correct lens through which to view the domain of bizarre and disturbing behavior. As one experienced neuroscientist (who spent his 40-year career investigating the biological roots of behavior) has written, "contrary to what is often claimed, no biochemical, anatomical, or functional signs have been found that reliably distinguish the brains of mental patients" (Valenstein, 2002). Unfortunately, even a brief summary of all the critiques of the medical model and the research it has generated would be difficult. I will address some of the specific critiques here, but space precludes consideration of many other valuable insights gained by medical model critics (see Boyle, 2002 for a rigorous and comprehensive critique of schizophrenia research; Breggin, 1995 for a general, if somewhat emotional, critique of biological psychiatry; Caplan, 1996 for a critique of the current diagnostic manual and the methods used to develop it; Heinrichs, 1993 for a critical review of the premises behind "a neuropsychology of madness"; Kirsch, 2009 and Kirsch & Lynn, 1999 for a review of the placebo effect in antidepressant medication; Kutchins & Kirk, 1997 for a critique of the process behind categorical classification of deviant behavior; McGuire & Troisi, 1998 for a discussion of the problems generated by conceptual pluralism in psychiatry; Nylund, 2000, for a critique of current ADD/ADHD research; Whitaker, 2010, for a critique of psychopharmaceutical science).

To summarize this section, the relevance of the medical model of mental illness to the exercise of mental health interventions is tenuous scientifically but firmly entrenched practically. As I have attempted to lay out, state control of social deviance shifted from punishment to assistance in the wake of the Enlightenment (i.e., there was a shift from using the police power to control social deviance to using *parens patriae* authority). The result of this shift was, as William Blackstone (1765) wrote, a new view that the government should serve as "the general guardian of all infants, idiots, and lunatics," and as the superintendent of "all charitable uses in the kingdom" (p. 47). The shift in social control methods was accomplished in part by creating institutions for the express purpose of providing relief to the poor and disadvantaged while discouraging the abuse of freeloaders. To prevent dramatic expansion of the poor-relief systems, however, administrators began to require finer distinctions between the deserving and undeserving and between the able bodied and not–able bodied. This created many questions about the nature and causes of human behavior, and those questions were debated among a variety of scholars from different disciplines. In the end, however, the growing field of medicine and its physician practitioners declared madness to be a disease and won the political mandate to manage some forms of deviance as illness. Unfortunately, at the time (and even today) there was little reason to believe that physicians had any special insight into the problem of madness as one form of social deviance. However, the scientific weaknesses of medical model concepts of mental illness do not mean that no concept of mental illness will adequately inform a cohesive system of *parens patriae*–based interventions.

The purpose of spending time examining the medical model of mental illness is to provide ammunition for changing the focus of the debate in police power and *parens patriae*–based mental health interventions, especially civil commitment. Currently, the civil commitment debate centers around how to deal with mentally ill individuals who do not wish to receive the treatment that clinical "experts," families, or the state believe a person needs. Evidence of this focus can be found in the vast literature dedicated to fleshing out the relationship between involuntary psychiatric treatment and the informed consent doctrine that typically precludes involuntary medical treatment (Janus, 1997; Schopp, 2001; Winick, 1997). In discussing the fact that those with physical illnesses typically cannot be treated against their will, Winick (1996) has noted,

> The differential approach that those with mental illness are subjected to appears largely to be based on the assumption that the effects of mental illness impair decision-making capacity in ways that prevent those with mental illness (but not others) from satisfying the requirements for informed consent. This assumption reflects 19th-century thinking about mental illness, which was based on the belief that mental illness destroys decision-making capacity. Under this conception, those with mental illness were regarded as globally incompetent—cognitively impaired in every area of functioning—in a way that was durable, probably lasting a lifetime. One of the most significant contributions of [recent empirical research] is that [the] findings directly refute these assumptions. (p. 140)

In other words, the medical model understanding of mental illness and treatment need—which is long out-of-date but still heavily entrenched in the legal setting—may not have the kind of substantive meaning behind it that is required to sustain a useful system of involuntary interventions. More important, the focus on medical-model notions of mental illness may actually be preventing the development of alternative lines of research and policy with greater long-term promise (Poland, Von Eckardt, & Spaulding, 1994).

Going back to Winick (1996), though, the assumption on the part of those seeking involuntary treatment for another is that the potential patient (let's imagine a woman), because of her mental illness, lacks the capacity to make reasonable choices about her mental health care (and perhaps her life in general), and therefore the choices should be made for her. The treatment recommendations, of course, are almost invariably based on the medical model approach to mental illness. Thus, the current system seems to be structured around the question of whether some individual has a mental illness, as that term is currently defined by medical model practitioners. There is also some consideration of whether the person is taking sufficiently good care of herself (e.g., Is she suicidal? Does she have a safe place to live and enough to eat?), but there is a bias toward assuming that whatever problems the person is experiencing are attributable to her mental illness. It is taken for granted that medical model interventions are going to be helpful across the board.

Poland et al. (1994) propose that classification of atypical functioning and social deviance into discrete categories of disease (viz the DSM-5) is an irremediably flawed method because the phenomena are simply not discrete categories. Stated briefly, these authors contend that

> DSM constitutes a faulty conceptualization of the domain of psychopathology and . . . interferes with optimal pursuit of clinical and scientific purposes. Indeed, there has been a decade of widespread complaint regarding DSM, but such complaint has been largely ineffective in stemming the impact of the approach. One reason for this ineffectiveness is the absence of a well-developed alternative that can play the roles currently served by DSM. (p. 235)

According to Poland et al. (1994), a psychopathology classification scheme ought to accomplish two major goals: enhancing clinical effectiveness and promoting scientific research programs (both basic and applied). One way clinical effectiveness is enhanced is by reducing clinical uncertainty (i.e., by answering questions such as what is wrong, what treatment is required, and what the prognosis is). To promote scientific research, a relevant classification scheme ought to spur productive and acceptable research. According to these authors, however, DSM accomplishes none of these purposes. They develop a coherent argument that the diagnostic categories are uninformative and irrelevant with respect to the problems that clinicians face, that the research programs based on it are unacceptable because the diagnostic criteria are unquantified, protoscientific, and massively heterogeneous, and that productive research is hindered because the signs and symptoms identified by DSM are not nomologically related to etiological and pathological processes.

This last point emphasizes the notion that DSM categories are not "syndromes with unity" and that such syndromes may not exist to be discovered (i.e., the classification scheme is irremediably flawed). Hence, this is an unpropitious method for studying and treating psychopathology. Poland et al. (1994) conclude:

> As we see it, there is a need for an alternative approach to classification that embodies a better model of scientific rigor and a more accurate theory of the domain of psychopathology. Such an alternative needs to place less emphasis on clinical phenomenology in classification and give more balanced attention to processes at all levels of analysis. And it needs to get a handle on the massive interindividual variation with respect to attributes and functioning, as well as their evident context sensitivity. Furthermore, it is especially important that an alternative be based on a more intimate relationship with basic science than is DSM. (p. 255)

This is only a brief summary of the arguments that Poland et al. (1994) develop. The relevance to the present chapter, though, is this: The domain of psychopathology is unlikely to be fully (or even partially) explained using a DSM-based approach to classification because the clinical phenomenology probably does not exist as "syndromes with unity" (or "natural kinds," in the language of philosophers). Thus, any work (including legislation and judicial proceedings) based on DSM-derived conceptions of psychopathology is likely to be substantially and irremediably flawed. But as Poland et al. note, a well-developed alternative is required if DSM (and other artifacts of the medical model of mental illness) are to be replaced.

Replacing Medical Model Involuntary Interventions

The question, then, is, What might an alternative be and how might a revised system be structured? Because of its dependence on medical model notions of mental illness, and based on the arguments advanced by Schopp (2001), I argue that the institution of civil commitment could be done away with in favor of a system of interventions that focus on whether or not individuals are competent to make self-regarding decisions. Such a system would be structured much like the current system of guardianship in most states, in which a court "may appoint a guardian if it is satisfied by clear and convincing evidence that the person for whom a guardian is sought is incapacitated" (Neb.Rev.St § 30–2620). The central question of such a system would not be whether a person has a clinically defined mental illness and therefore needs medical model treatment, but rather whether the difficulties that a person is facing are due to the inability to make reasonable decisions in important settings.

The Question of Criteria

As I have already mentioned, the history of involuntary interventions—and especially inpatient civil commitment—reflects a tension between paternalistic and libertarian concerns, with everyone basically accepting the medical model of mental illness as a given. On the side of paternalism is the feeling that adults disabled by serious mental illness have a right to treatment even if they cannot grasp the need for it in their own (presumably diseased) minds. On the libertarian side is the feeling that individual liberty is too precious a right to be left in the hands of clinicians practicing an imprecise science based on constructs with dubious reliability and validity. As a result of the push and pull of these forces, civil commitment in all U.S. jurisdictions requires that the potential committee be mentally ill and dangerous to self or others.

On the surface this appears to be a sensible arrangement. We do not want to interfere in the lives of people simply because they are odd or disagreeable. Candidates for civil commitment must have a bona fide mental illness (or at least a bona fide mental problem) and must—in addition to the mental illness—be a threat to the health and safety of the public or of themselves. The criteria for civil commitment fail, however, because the statutory definitions of mental illness do not inform us as to what specific impairments must exist, how a court is to know that they exist, and how much of an impairment is necessary to justify intervention. The problem, in other words, is that civil commitment statutes do not help legal decision makers reliably discriminate between those eligible for civil commitment and those not, especially in the hard cases. According to Schopp (2001), part of the solution to this problem rests in grounding the criteria for any involuntary intervention in the justification that is used to support such an intervention.

Parens patriae interventions, by definition, are justified by reference to the state's power to care for those who are unable to care for themselves. Schopp (2001) writes,

> The justification for *parens patriae* intervention rests on the state's responsibility to protect and promote the well-being of those who lack the capacities needed to make and communicate reasoned decisions regarding their own interests. Incompetence provides the central justification for such intervention because the individual lacks the capacities of practical reasoning that would enable him to direct self-regarding decisions through the exercise of minimally adequate comprehension and reasoning and qualify him for sovereign discretion in the nonpublic jurisdiction. (p. 11)

The logical conclusion is that the criteria for *parens patriae* interventions should reference impairments in one's capacity to make reasonable decisions in self-regarding matters and the disposition should include surrogate decision making.

Other commitments are justified by reference to the State's police power, which obligates the government to take reasonable steps to protect the safety and welfare of the general public. Regarding those interventions, Schopp (2001) writes that,

> The justification for [involuntary civil commitment] through the mental health system under the police power requires evidence that the individual lacks the capacity to participate in the public jurisdiction as a responsible subject of the criminal justice system and that he poses a risk to others sufficient to justify coercive intervention. The appropriate form of intervention is that which is likely to prevent such a severely impaired individual from harming others. (p. 25)

Thus, a police power–based mental health intervention would be justified to the extent that the person involved is impaired in the ability to conform his or her behavior to the demands of civil life. This is similar to, but again more specific than, the current notion of dangerousness to others.

To supplement his discussion of justifications, Schopp (2001) introduces a useful framework for understanding how definitions of legal mental illness (LMI) might optimally be constructed based on his analysis. According to Schopp, persons are not eligible for a particular legal status if and only if: (1) they suffer impairment of psychological capacities (2) rendering them unable to competently perform (3) the psychological operations necessary for that legal status.

In this framework of LMI, the legal status in question is phrased positively; an example would be "competent to make self-regarding decisions." Clause 1, then, is a specification of the kind of impairment that is necessary to negate eligibility for the legal status. Ideally, the psychological capacities would be stated in terms that are more specific and (hopefully) more meaningful than "mental disease" or "mental illness" (i.e., the current language). Clause 3 refers to the particular psychological operations that form the basis for the legal status (i.e., the criteria of eligibility for that status). In between is Clause 2, which establishes that the Clause 1 impairment must hinder the Clause 3 operations such that they fall below "some threshold of competence established by lawmakers and evaluated by legal decision makers" (Schopp, 2001, p. 46).

In the realm of *parens patriae* involuntary interventions, then, a policy regarding involuntary treatment might start with a declaration such as this: Individuals are to be deemed incompetent if and only if: (1) They suffer impairment of the capacity to understand, reason, appreciate, and express a choice, (2) rendering them unable to competently (3) make decisions about their own life.

Having found that all three of these obtain, the court would then order a substitute decision maker to be appointed and would lay out the scope of the decision maker's authority. Some decision makers might be given authority over all self-regarding decisions, whereas others might have a very limited decision making role. Although the content of Clauses 1 and 3 would be different for police power interventions, and hence the ideal disposition might also be different, the basic principles are the same.

My argument, then, is that Schopp's (2001) framework for understanding legal mental illness and for implementing involuntary interventions is better than the existing system in its specification of criteria that are rooted in the underlying justification for the intervention itself. I would also argue that Schopp's framework allows for the maximization of paternalistic and libertarian interests in a way that the current system (and the current debate) does not because it allows for the inclusion of criteria based on scientifically valid psychological constructs that are or could be objectively assessed. This forces the realization, however, that such a system cannot practically be implemented until we do away with a good deal of baggage from the history of mental health interventions and adopt a new agenda of research and policymaking that asks and answers a new set of questions.

First, a system structured to be consistent within this framework would require a change from the current implicit reliance of legal decision makers on psychiatric categories of mental illness to inform the legal question of mental illness. I believe it is basically uncontroversial to suggest that everyone involved in mental health care would like to see adequate care made available for those who avoid and refuse care but who do so incompetently. Nothing about psychiatric diagnosis, however, informs the question of competence. Some argue, for example, that at least 40% of persons diagnosed with bipolar disorder and schizophrenia may lack insight into their illness and therefore might be making incompetent decisions regarding treatment. In addition, persons diagnosed with schizophrenia tend, again as a class, to demonstrate generalized cognitive deficits. But to speak about persons diagnosed with schizophrenia or bipolar disorder as a class does nothing to inform the question of whether a particular person diagnosed with schizophrenia is making an incompetent decision. To know whether a particular person is incompetent in his or her decision making means understanding generally what is meant by the term and then engaging in idiographic assessment to discover the particular person's capacities. In other words, it means engaging in exactly the process that Schopp recommends and that was described in the assessment section.

The second piece of baggage that would need to go is the one that contains outdated psychological constructs. In the case of *parens patriae* interventions, for example, we would need to discard empirically unsustainable notions about decision making, such as that human beings are utility-maximizing rational agents. Whether or not utility-maximizing decision making is a norm toward which we should strive as a species, it is demonstrably the case that human beings do not (as a class) make decisions based on such principles in most situations (Hastie & Dawes, 2001, for a discussion of both sides of the issue). Instead, psychological assessments might focus on the components of decision making such as attention, working memory capacity, executive functioning, reaction time, perception, etc. If these capacities are impaired, and if evidence exists of a history of poor decision making, a court may be justified in inferring that a person's decision making ability is impaired. In the case of police power interventions, evidence of abnormal responding to contingencies might help inform the question of retributive competence.

Whatever the particulars might be, the net effect would be a major shift in the way involuntary treatment statutes are written. This has the potential, I believe, to shift the focus of attention away from unproductive lines of research and practice (such as searching for objective markers of diagnoses that have little established validity) toward approaches to behaviors that have a better chance of bearing fruit. In addition, such a system would bring together the various sides of the debate: patients would be granted self-determination to the extent that they have the capacity for it, clinicians could rest assured that no one who needed treatment was failing to get it (as a product of the structure of the legal system at least), clinical researchers could focus their efforts on understanding important psychological constructs, and legal decision makers could feel confident in the science behind the law. The good news is, a shift toward involuntary treatment decisions being made only in the context of decisional incapacity seems both possible and highly relevant given that the vast majority of civil commitments are based on findings of grave disability (i.e., the inability to care for oneself), both with and without dangerousness, rather than dangerousness alone (Turkheimer & Parry, 1992).

Case Example

Taking all of this into account, let us go back to the case of John that started this chapter. John was arrested in a grocery store when he refused to stop opening boxes of aluminum foil and wrapping the contents around his arms, legs, and torso. He did not make any overt threats but the store employees indicated that he would not respond to anything they said to him and reported that he "seemed kind of menacing." The police officers took him directly to the county hospital, rather than jail, and he was admitted to the psychiatric unit for observation and evaluation. As the initial observation period drew to a close, the attending psychiatrist requested an evaluation for possible civil commitment based on the notion that he was gravely disabled. The evaluator reviewed his medical chart (which had records from three previous stays along with some follow-up information) and briefly discussed the case with the psychiatrist.

One of the important findings from that review was that on two occasions John had been committed, spent several weeks in an inpatient facility, and was eventually able to return to his apartment with access to services from the local community mental health center. Those two hospitalizations were more than two years apart. On the other occasion, however (which preceded the two just mentioned), John was released from the hospital without further care, continued to decompensate, and was found lying under a bridge suffering from malnutrition, dehydration, exposure to the elements, and injuries that appeared to be from a fight. To the evaluator, this suggested that John may decompensate without further care. This was further bolstered when the evaluator learned that John had been homeless for three days prior to the store incident.

During the interview itself, the evaluator had a chance to administer the RBANS and noted deficits in immediate memory, delayed memory, and attention. When John was asked how he lost his apartment, he responded with the belief that his "landlord was part of the conspiracy to punish [him] for [his] sins." When asked for more information on the conspiracy, John merely replied, "the writing is on the wall and through the wall, and I can't cover it up." In response to a question about how he was living on the streets, John stated that he tried to stay safe but that the beams could find him unless he was "shielded." In terms of his thoughts about his hospital stay so far, John indicated that the "pills are part of the conspiracy." When gently pressed for more information, he said "I know the pills are part of it because I can't feel my heart, and my soul is long and outside itself. And then the beams don't come anymore, but the punishment keeps coming." When asked why he was being punished, John, in a fairly lucid non sequitur, mentioned that he knew that his parents were worried about him and that he wished he did not have "this pain because there was a time when the future looked so bright. I was going to be someone. A doctor, maybe, like the doctors here. They look out for me." He was unable to reconcile that statement, though, with his concerns about the pills except for stating that "doctors don't always know what goes into their pills." He also became somewhat agitated when asked to put those differing thoughts together. When asked why he did not want to go to the hospital voluntarily, John merely replied, "I already told you why." John's final response came to the question of what he thought would happen to him if he left the hospital without further care. He said, "I'm not the one in control, because my control is love and compassion."

In the report, then, the evaluator described all of relevant data in such a way as to suggest that John presented with symptoms (i.e., beliefs) of sufficient duration, intensity, and connection with impairment to warrant a diagnosis of schizophrenia, paranoid type. She also indicated that the beliefs were related to behaviors that put him at risk for further decompensation and disability (i.e., they were gravely disabling) because they generated resistance to both mental health care and the services that are critical to recovery from serious mental illness (e.g., housing, work, recreation). She went on to describe his functional cognitive impairments and the role such impairments might play in making it difficult for John to understand, appreciate, and reason about his situation. Knowing that competency is not the issue in civil commitment evaluations, this latter material was presented in support of a potential finding of grave disability. At no point did the evaluator give an opinion as to legal question of whether John was sufficiently impaired to warrant civil commitment, but that, ultimately, is what happened.

A Postscript on Gun Legislation and Forensic Assessment

Since the first edition of this volume was published, the United States and other countries have been deeply affected by mass shootings committed by individuals with a history of mental health problems. Although the shooting of 26 people, including 20 elementary school–age children in Newtown, Connecticut, was perhaps the most shocking, the deadliest was the day that Seung-Hui Cho killed 32 people in two locations at Virginia Tech and then killed himself. Predictably, these mass killings have "triggered calls for doing something to keep guns away from the mentally ill" (Nocera, 2014). Thus it may surprise many people to learn that most states and the federal government already have legislation in place to regulate access to firearms by people with a history of mental illness and particularly with a history of civil commitment or other finding of incapacity. 18 U.S.C. Section 922(g), for example, makes is unlawful to sell a gun or ammunition to any person who "has been adjudicated as a mental defective or has been committed to any mental institution." In 44 states and the District of Columbia, laws are in place that regulate access to guns or permits to carry guns based on a history of either diagnosis with certain conditions (usually psychosis-spectrum, dementia, and psychopathy) or a history of involuntary commitment.

I raise this issue not to take a position on whether mental health should be relevant to gun control (it already is) but instead to point out that no matter what the civil commitment statutes and other legislation might say, and what mental health advocates might aspire to, the provision of effective, empirically supported, and diverse treatment approaches is critical to the success of any public health approach to mental illness. If involuntary treatment programs included treatments with excellent efficacy, it seems unlikely that so many people would object to their use. If housing, job support, access to recreation, and other critical community-based services were readily available in the same place where people receive medications and psychological treatments, then decompensation to the point of dangerousness to self or others might be less common. Civil forensic assessment exists not in a vacuum but in a living, breathing society that must make choices about the provisioning of resources and the acceptability of intrusions into private lives. Striving for objective assessments based on sound psychological and political principles to provide care to people who need it in contexts that are acceptable and effective should be the ultimate goal for people undertaking the difficult task of evaluating people in civil forensic settings.

Notes

1   Although *capacity* and *competence* are often used interchangeably, I will use capacity to refer to the kinds of cognitive and behavioral abilities thought to underlie decision making and execution. Competence refers to having sufficient capacity for some decision making and execution purpose.
2   It should be noted that biological, supernatural, psychological, and psychosocial theories of madness have coexisted throughout history, with different adherents at different times. It would be inaccurate to suggest that there has been a simple progression from supernatural theories to modern bio-medical theories or that any of the theories has unequivocal support (see McGuire & Troisi, 1998)

References

Aden v. Younger, 157 Cal.App.3d 662, 129 Cal.Rptr. 535 (Ct. App. 1976).

American Psychiatric Association. (2013). *The diagnostic and statistical manual of mental disorders* (5th ed.). Washington, DC: Author.

Appelbaum P.S., & Grisso T. (2002). *The MacArthur competence assessment tool for clinical research (MacCAT-CR)*. Sarasota, FL: Professional Resource Press.

Banner, N.F. (2012). Unreasonable reasons: Normative judgements in the assessment of mental capacity. *Journal of Evaluation in Clinical Practice, 18*, 1038–1044. http://dx.doi.org/10.1111/j.1365–2753.2012.01914.x

Blackstone, W. (1765). *Commentaries on the laws of England*. Oxford: Clarendon Press.

Boyle, M. (2002). *Schizophrenia: A scientific delusion?* (2nd ed.). Worcester, UK: Routledge.

Breggin, P. (1995). *Toxic psychiatry*. New York: St. Martin's Press.

Brooks, R. A. (2006). U.S. psychiatrists' beliefs and wants about involuntary civil commitment grounds. *International Journal of Law and Psychiatry, 29*, 13–21. http://dx.doi.org/10.1016/j.ijlp.2005.04.004

Caplan. P. J. (1996). *They say you're crazy: How the world's most powerful psychiatrists decide who's normal.* Cambridge, MA: Perseus Publishing.

Charland, L. C. (2001). Mental competence and value: The problem of normativity in the assessment of decision-making capacity. *Psychiatry, Psychology, and Law, 8*, 135–145. http://dx.doi.org/10.1080/13218710109525013

Claridge, G. (1990). Can a disease model of schizophrenia survive? In R. P. Bentall (Ed.), *Reconstructing schizophrenia* (pp. 157–183). Worcester, UK: Routledge.

Foucault, M. (1971). *Madness and civilisation: A history of insanity in the age of reason.* London: Tavistock.

Grant, D. A., & Berg, E. A. (2005). *Wisconsin Card Sorting Task* (WCST). Lutz, FL: PAR

Grisso, G., & Appelbaum, P. S. (1998). *Assessing competence to consent to treatment: A guide for physicians and other health professionals.* New York: Oxford University Press.

Grisso, G., Appelbaum, P. S., & Hill-Fotouhi, C. (1997). The MAC-CAT-T: A clinical tool to assess patients' capacities to make treatment decisions. *Psychiatric Services, 48*, 1415–1419.

Hastie, R., & Dawes, R. M. (2001). *Rational choice in an uncertain world.* Thousand Oaks, CA: Sage.

Heinrichs, R. W. (1993). Schizophrenia and the brain: Conditions for a neuropsychology of madness. *American Psychologist, 48*, 221–233. http://dx.doi.org/10.1037/0003–066X.48.3.221

Humphrey v. Cady, 405 U.S. 504 (1972).

Insel, T. (2010). Rethinking schizophrenia. *Nature, 468*, 187–193. http://dx.doi.org/10.1038/nature09552

Janus, E. S. (1996). Preventing sexual violence: Setting principled Constitutional boundaries on sex offender commitments. *Indiana Law Review, 72*, 157–214.

Janus, E. S. (1997). Toward a conceptual framework for assessing police power commitment legislation: A critique of Schopp's and Winick's explications of legal mental illness. *Nebraska Law Review, 76*, 1–50.

Janus, E. S. (2000). Sexual predator commitment laws: Lessons for law and the behavioral sciences. *Behavioral Sciences and the Law, 18*, 5–21. http://dx.doi.org/10.1002/(SICI)1099–0798(200001/02)18:1<5::AID-BSL374>3.0.CO;2-C

Kaufman, A. R., & Way, B. (2010). North Carolina resident psychiatrists knowledge of the commitment statutes: Do they stray from the legal standard in the hypothetical application of involuntary commitment criteria? *Psychiatric Quarterly, 81*, 363–367. http://dx.doi.org/10.1007/s11126–010–9144–0

Kirsch, I. (2009). *The Emperor's new drugs.* New York: Random House.

Kirsch, I., & Lynn, S. J. (1999). Automaticity in clinical psychology. *American Psychologist, 54*, 504–515. http://dx.doi.org/10.1037/0003–066X.54.7.504

Kutchins, H., & Kirk, S. A. (1997). *Making us crazy.* New York: The Free Press.

Lessard v. Schmidt, 349 F. Supp. 1078 (E.D. Wis. 1972).

Lin, C-Y. (2003). Ethical exploration of the least restrictive alternative. *Psychiatric Services, 54*, 866–870. http://dx.doi.org/10.1176/appi.ps.54.6.866

McGuire, M., & Troisi, A. (1998). *Darwinian psychiatry.* New York: Oxford University Press.

Morris, G. H. (1999). Defining dangerousness: Risking a dangerous definition. *Journal of Contemporary Legal Issues, 61*, 61–101.

Morse, S. J. (1987). Treating crazy people less specially. *West Virginia Law Review, 90*, 353–385.

Nicaise, P., Soto, V. E., Dubois, V., & Lorant, V. (2014). Users' and health professionals' values in relation to a psychiatric intervention: The case of psychiatric advance directives. *Administration and Policy in Mental Health*, 05 August 2014 [epub].

Nicholls, T. L., Brink, J., Desmarais, S. L., Webster, C. D., & Martin, M-L. (2006). The Short-Term Assessment of Risk and Treatability (START): A prospective validation study in a forensic psychiatric sample. *Assessment, 13*, 313–327.

Nocera, J. (2014, June 3). Guns and mental illness. *The New York Times*, p. A23.

Nylund, D. (2000). *Treating Huckleberry Finn: A new narrative approach to working with kids diagnosed ADD/ADHD.* New York: Jossey-Bass.

Pilgrim, D. (1990). Competing histories of madness: Some implications for modern psychiatry. In R. P. Bentall (Ed.), *Reconstructing schizophrenia* (pp. 211–233). Worcester, UK: Routledge.

Poland, J., Von Eckardt, B., & Spaulding, W. (1994). Problems with the DSM approach to classifying psychopathology. In G. Graham & G. L. Stephens (Eds.), *Philosophical psychopathology* (pp. 235–260). Cambridge, MA: The MIT Press.

Rennie v. Klein, 462 F. Supp. 1131 (D.N.J. 1978), aff'd in part, modified in part, and remanded, 653 F.2d 836 (3d Cir. 1980) (en banc), vacated and remanded, 458 U.S. 1119 (1982), on remand, 720 F.2d 266 (3d Cir. 1983) (en banc).

Randolph, C. (1997). *Repeatable battery for the assessment of neuropsychological status (RBANS): Manual*. San Antonio, TX: The Psychological Corporation.

Saks, E.R., & Behnke, S.H. (1999). Competency to decide on treatment and research: MacArthur and beyond. *Journal of Contemporary Legal Issues, 10*, 103–129.

Saks, M.J. (1991). Comment on "A modest proposal: Psychotherapists with knowledge of danger." *Ethics & Behavior, 1*, 212-215.

Schopp, R.F. (1998). Civil commitment and sexual predators: Competence and condemnation. *Psychology, Public Policy, and Law, 4*, 323–376. http://dx.doi.org/10.1037/1076–8971.4.1–2.323

Schopp, R.F. (2001). *Competence, condemnation, and commitment: An integrated theory of mental health law*. Washington, DC: American Psychological Association.

Scull, A. (1979). *Museums of madness: The social organization of insanity in nineteenth century England*. London: Allen Lane: New York: St. Martin's Press.

Slobogin, C. (1996). "Appreciation" as a measure of competency: Some thoughts about the MacArthur group's approach. *Psychology, Public Policy, & Law, 2*, 18–30. http://dx.doi.org/10.1037/1076–8971.2.1.18

Spaulding, W., Poland, J., Elbogen, E., & Ritchie, A. J. (2000). Applications of therapeutic jurisprudence in rehabilitation for people with severe and disabling mental illness. *Thomas M. Cooley Law Review, 17*, 135–170.

Spaulding, W.S., Sullivan, M.E., & Poland, J.S. (2003). *Treatment and rehabilitation for severe mental illness*. New York: Guilford.

Srebnik, D., Appelbaum, P.S., & Russo, J. (2004). Assessing competence to complete psychiatric advance directives with the Competence Assessment Tool for Psychiatric Advance Directives. *Comprehensive Psychiatry, 45*, 239–245. http://dx.doi.org/10.1016/j.comppsych.2004.03.004

Stavis, P.F. (2000). Why prisons are brim-full of the mentally ill: Is their incarceration a solution or a sign of failure? *George Mason University Civil Rights Law Journal, 11*, 157–202.

Szasz, T.S. (1974). *The myth of mental illness*. New York: Harper & Row.

Torrey, E.F. (1995). *Surviving schizophrenia*. New York: Harper Colophon Books.

Torrey, E.F. (2012). *The insanity offense: How America's failure to treat the seriously mentally ill endangers its citizens*. New York: W. W. Norton.

Torrey, E.F., Stanley, J., Monahan, J., Steadman, H.J., & MacArthur Study Group. (2008). The MacArthur Violence Risk Assessment Study revisited: Two views ten years after its initial publication. *Psychiatric Services, 59*, 147–152. http://dx.doi.org/10.1176/appi.ps.59.2.147

Treatment Advocacy Center. (2003). Violent behavior: One of the consequences of failing to treat severe mental illnesses. Retrieved on June 19, 2015 from www.treatmentadvocacycenter.org/resources/consequences-of-lack-of-treatment/violence/1381.

Turkheimer, E., & Parry, C.D.H. (1992). Why the gap? Practice and policy in civil commitment hearings. *American Psychologist, 47*, 646–655. http://dx.doi.org/10.1037/0003–066X.47.5.646

Whitaker, R. (2001). *Mad in America*. New York: Basic Books.

Whitaker, R. (2010). *Anatomy of an epidemic*. New York: Random House.

Valenstein, E. (2002). *Blaming the brain: The truth about drugs and mental health*. New York: Free Press.

Vollmann, J., Bauer, A., Danker-Hopfe, H., & Helmchen, H. (2003). Competence of mentally ill patients: A comparative empirical study. *Psychological Medicine, 33*, 1463–1471. http://dx.doi.org/10.1017/S0033291703008389

Winick, B.J. (1996). The MacArthur treatment compliance study: Legal and therapeutic implications. *Psychology, Public Policy, & Law, 2*, 137–166. http://dx.doi.org/10.1037/1076–8971.2.1.137

Winick, B.J. (1997). *The right to refuse mental health treatment*. Washington, DC: American Psychological Association. http://dx.doi.org/10.1037/10264–000

Zanni, G.R., & Stavis, P.F. (2007). The effectiveness and ethical justification of psychiatric outpatient commitment. *The American Journal of Bioethics, 7*, 31–41. http://dx.doi.org/10.1080/15265160701638678

Part V
Communicating Your Findings

20 Writing Forensic Psychological Reports

Audrey K. Miller and Gregg J. Gagliardi

An entire course in clinical-forensic psychology could be taught using report writing as a vehicle. Everything of importance to forensic psychological assessment culminates in the written report. The purpose of this chapter is a practical one. The reader will find little theory here and just a brief summary of the published empirical literature on forensic mental health report writing. Instead, our aim is to help the beginning forensic report writer start and complete respectable forensic psychological reports and, importantly, develop sufficient confidence and enthusiasm to write more reports.

Our coverage is organized around five themes: types or varieties of forensic report, overarching principles that guide forensic psychological report writing, the structure or anatomy of the forensic report, summary of the empirical literature on forensic mental health report writing, and practical tips to help report writers overcome common problems in report writing.

Varieties of Forensic Psychological Report

Every communication a psychologist makes to a party connected with a case is a forensic report. Although the present chapter focuses on the traditional written forensic report, much of what is said is applicable to these "other" kinds of forensic reports.

Written forensic reports vary in length and content depending on multiple factors, including the (a) referring party (e.g., plaintiff, defense, judge, commissioner), (b) venue (criminal, civil, or administrative), (c) jurisdiction (federal or state), (d) geography, and (e) referral question(s). It is therefore impossible to provide a single set of guidelines that will work in every situation.

Some contexts (e.g., civil) may require that the report include ancillary documents, such as the professional's publications, list of other cases in which the expert has been deposed or has testified, list of continuing professional education courses taken, and the fee for professional services rendered to the referring attorney. Other contexts (e.g., involuntary civil commitment) may require only that an examining expert file a petition that the respondent (patient in a civil commitment hearing) needs to be civilly committed and fill out a form (affidavit) in support of that petition.

For narrow referral questions, such as competency to stand trial, short reports are customary, whereas for custody evaluations or sexually violent predator evaluations, a brief report would be inadequate. In some parts of the country, local standards or customs may affect the length and content of the report; such practices have changed over several decades and may continue to change.

In the end, it is most important that the report writer know which legal and professional standards, and customary practices, apply for a particular report. The referring attorney can be of some help, but ultimately the writer bears responsibility for knowing the relevant statutory law, pertinent case law, specialty practice guidelines, and local professional standards that apply.

Several resources provide additional guidance on standards and styles for forensic psychological reports. For example, a special series of the *Journal of Clinical Psychology* on psychological report writing, edited by Groth-Marnat (2006), includes an article by Ackerman on forensic report writing. The first handbook to address forensic psychological reports was Melton, Petrila, Poythress, and Slobogin's classic, *Psychological Evaluations for the Courts: A Handbook for Mental Health Professionals and Lawyers* (1987); its third edition was published in 2007. This source discusses the special role of the report in legal proceedings and includes sample reports, and commentary, covering a variety of criminal and civil psycholegal issues. Heilbrun, DeMatteo, Holliday, and LaDuke's (2014) casebook of sample reports covers 24 distinct psycholegal issues and demonstrates cardinal principles of forensic psychological assessment. Striking among the aforementioned sample reports is the rich diversity of structure and format. The American Psychological Association published Karson and Nadkarni's (2013) *Principles of Forensic Report Writing*, which includes a chapter on culturally competent report writing. Finally, books contained in Grisso, Goldstein, and Heilbrun's *Best Practices in Forensic Mental Health Assessment* series (2008–2012) each contain a section on report writing about respective psycholegal issues (e.g., competence to stand trial, criminal responsibility, violence risk, personal injury).

Overarching Principles That Guide Forensic Psychological Report Writing

Clinical-Therapeutic Versus Clinical-Forensic Reports

Table 20.1, adapted after the work of Greenberg and Shuman (1997), identifies ten key differences between clinical-therapeutic and clinical-forensic reports. The most telling difference is the identity of the writer's client. Whereas the clinical-therapeutic report writer usually works on behalf of the patient (evaluee), the forensic report writer works for an attorney or other third party/institution.[1] Most clinicians are unaccustomed to regarding the attorney as the client, which can grate against deeply held patient-centered clinical values.

The fact that in a forensic evaluation the attorney, not the evaluee, is the writer's client has obvious impact on the report. First, the attorney, not the evaluee, pays for the report if one is written. Second, although the report is about the evaluee, it is written to assist the attorney and, more generally, the court. Also, it should be borne in mind that attorneys may request forensic psychological evaluations for decidedly nonclinical purposes, including safeguarding their own professional interests (e.g., avoiding a malpractice lawsuit filed against them by a disgruntled client, avoiding an ethics complaint, or avoiding an appeal based on ineffective assistance of counsel).

Table 20.1 Differences between clinical-therapeutic and clinical-forensic reports

	Therapeutic	*Forensic*
Who is the client?	Patient	Attorney/third party
Operative privilege	Therapist-client	Attorney-client or attorney-work product
Rule governing report disclosure	HIPAA	Statute/case law
Sources of interview data	Mostly client report	Multiple collateral sources
Informed consent recipient(s)	Patient or guardian	Attorney and evaluee
Purpose of the report	Help the patient	Assist the attorney
Report writer's attitude/tone	Empathic, supportive	Impartial, objective
Advocacy	For the patient	For the expert opinion
Focus	Presenting problem(s)	Psycholegal question(s)
Expertise required	Clinical	Clinical + forensic

The fact that the attorney is the evaluator's client likewise affects the operative privilege, a special legal right, exemption, or immunity that controls the disclosure of information (e.g., psychological reports) to third parties. For the therapist, the applicable privilege is *therapist-client* privilege. The evaluee owns that privilege, and the Health Insurance Portability and Accountability Act of 1996 (HIPAA) controls the disclosure of most patient information to third parties. For the forensic evaluator, the applicable privilege may be *attorney-client privilege* or *attorney work-product privilege*, and information disclosures usually are governed by discovery rules.[2]

Because the ground rules for forensic evaluations differ markedly from those guiding other clinical assessments, obtaining informed consent is doubly important. Forensic evaluees often believe that evaluators are advocates working for *them*, to help resolve *their* problems, including their legal problems. Most do not understand the limited legal purposes of the evaluation report, what it may entail, or which rules govern the disclosure of report findings to third parties. Consequently, forensic evaluators should ensure that evaluees are thoroughly informed of the purpose(s) and nature of the evaluation, their rights with respect to the evaluation (e.g., nonparticipation, declining to answer questions, having an attorney present), the role of the evaluator, foreseeable uses of information, intended report recipients, relevant limitations to privacy, confidentiality, or privilege, and preclusion of feedback. If the evaluee is responsible for the cost of the evaluation, the anticipated cost should be described. The evaluee should have ample opportunity to ask questions about all these matters. Further, the informed consent procedure should be described in the written report. When the evaluation is court ordered and, therefore, the evaluator may proceed without consent, objections and other remarkable behaviors should be documented in the report. When the evaluee is presumed by law to lack capacity to consent, the evaluator nevertheless should provide and document explanations and memorialize in the report both the evaluee's assent and the legal representative's consent.

Several important qualities of a genuinely helpful report are readily apparent if we place ourselves as writers in the attorneys' shoes. First, a high-quality report should focus on the psycholegal questions before the court and not peripheral matters. The evaluator must know well these technical questions and their legal contours in order to address them in a report. An otherwise rich clinical report that fails to adequately address the crux psycholegal questions is unhelpful at best and harmful at worst. Finding and reading psycholegal definitions and standards is a fairly easy task, but merely ascertaining them is not enough to apply them or write about them in a report. The keywords contained within these standards are legal terms of art that cannot be properly applied without first acquiring a foundational understanding of the legal doctrines that give rise to them and the manner in which relevant higher courts have interpreted them. This foundational knowledge is usually acquired in specialized clinical training programs such as forensic tracks in clinical psychology graduate programs or postdoctoral fellowships in clinical-forensic psychology.

Although the referring attorney can be a helpful guide and educator, attorneys frequently have strong differences of opinion—and obvious partisan biases—about how to apply psycholegal standards. The report writer needs to be cautious about accepting advice on psycholegal standards that comes from the retaining attorney. The best source of information about how to apply a psycholegal standard is the applicable statutory or decisional law. The West Publishing Corporation provides excellent resources for conducting this kind of inquiry. Although few evaluators have sufficient legal training to practice law, every evaluator needs to learn how the law has applied critical psycholegal standards, develop an appreciation of the nature and dimensions of legal controversies raised by the application of those standards, and know how those standards are applied in the jurisdiction(s) in which the evaluator practices.

Best Evidence Model of Report Writing

At the conclusion of a forensic evaluation, the writer is faced with a mountain of data that vary in relevance to resolving the psycholegal issues of the case. Some data are essential and must be included to answer the psycholegal question(s); other data are partially relevant and their inclusion in a report may provide a background that promotes understanding; still other data are untrustworthy or frankly irrelevant and must be discarded to reduce distraction and prevent misunderstanding. Somehow the evaluator must sift through this pile of information and decide what to include in the written report—but how?

Here, it is helpful to consider that a forensic evaluation conceptually parallels another fact-finding process, a trial. The court wants a jury to consider only trustworthy, relevant information in reaching its decision. This legal doctrine is known as the *best evidence rule*. The law relies on evidence rules for screening out inaccurate, unfairly prejudicial, and irrelevant data from that information ultimately presented to a jury. Generally, the best evidence for a jury in deciding a psycholegal question is also the best evidence for both the evaluator to report and the consumer of the forensic report to read.

Following the structural analogy between the forensic evaluation and a trial further, the forensic report writer needs a screening process (rules) for including or excluding (admitting or not admitting) a statement or fact (evidence) before offering it up in a report to support an opinion (finding). This is especially the case for psychologists and other mental health care providers who have been conditioned to regard, and report as "facts," fragmentary, distorted, and/or biased information from unverified records and oral reports. The first step in writing a forensic report is to separate the information wheat from the chaff, a quality-control process. After this step is complete, the information load is greatly reduced, enhancing the accuracy of clinical judgment, simplifying the integration of findings into an opinion, and promoting a brief, well-organized report.

One model for the evaluator to consider in screening facts is that embodied in the Federal Rules of Evidence and their state counterparts. Learning even a small set of these evidence rules and employing them as a flexible guide is a good investment, as doing so can help determine which information to include in a report and which to discard.[3] Using this method, statements of fact would not be included unless they first pass a reasonably fair series of tests used by U.S. courts to screen evidence.

Although at first blush this may appear to be a daunting recommendation, applying evidence rules to forensic report writing does not require becoming a legal expert on evidence or an attorney. It is a learning task that is well within the reach of the clinical-forensic specialist. In practice, the idea is quite simple. It is most effectively applied as an editing tool after the first draft of the report has been written. As you review the first draft, imagine you are a trial judge tasked with ruling on the admissibility of each factual statement in your forensic report. Are there any objections to entering the statement into evidence? If so, which side objects, and on what grounds (i.e., according to what evidence rule)? Balancing the rights and interests of both sides of the litigation, would you as a neutral party, interested only in furthering accuracy, fairness, justice, and efficiency admit *that statement* into evidence, i.e., include it in your report?[4]

Accuracy

The report writer's first responsibility to the reader is to accurately reflect the state of knowledge in the field of psychology. This is a tall order, since it demands a candid, up-to-date appraisal of what the field actually has to offer about the factual matters at issue in a case. The honest writer will inevitably recognize that for any given psycholegal issue, science and clinical knowledge provide only a partial or approximate answer to the question. The expert's findings more often inform the fact finder's quest for the answer than provide the answer itself. It is therefore important that the report acknowledge deficiencies in the state of the science and in the state of clinical practice, where and when these arise, sometimes requiring a footnote or appendix to explain.

It is likewise important that the report writer acknowledge and disclose the properties, purposes, and limitations of various assessment methods. Strong training and supervised experience in psychometrics and psychological assessment enables evaluators to make appropriate test-based inferences that are sensitive to the design, intended purpose(s), and standardization of an instrument (e.g., measuring response styles, detecting the presence and nature of current psychopathology), and avoid reaching beyond an instrument's established utility. Careful consideration of reliability and validity is warranted when utilizing any assessment method, including third-party interviews and records.

Facts vs. Inferences

It is essential that the writer clarify whether a statement is a fact, inference, or professional opinion. Failure to distinguish among these can result in needless confusion, misunderstanding, and unproductive legal wrangling.

At one end of the fact–inference continuum are concrete matters the writer assumes to be facts, such as the evaluee's age, what the evaluee said during an interview, or the evaluee's score on a psychological test. At the other end of the continuum are inferences, which are synthetic conclusions drawn in trying to make sense out of the facts. For the forensic psychologist, a common example of an inference is the evaluee's subjective mental state (e.g., intent) or mental capacity at a legally relevant point in time.

An ordinary clinical example helps clarify the distinction between fact and inference. An evaluee's self-reported auditory hallucination is not a fact for anyone but the evaluee. For everyone else it is an inference. What *is* a fact is that the evaluee reported the experience of the hallucination to the evaluator.

In general, the law distinguishes expert opinions from lay opinions by requiring that the subject matter of the opinion be beyond the "ken of the jury." An expert opinion is, therefore, a special kind of inference that the law reserves for persons qualified as experts. Several kinds of expert opinion are routinely found in forensic reports, the most common of which are diagnoses and psycholegal opinions. Clinical formulations (e.g., evaluee's personality traits, abilities, knowledge, intrapsychic dynamics, future dangerousness, social and occupational functioning, etc.) also are inferences—that is, they are matters of professional opinion, not facts.

One reason for delineating between facts and inferences is a duty to help readers understand and use information in the report. If an attorney wishes to appraise an expert's opinion, this is best done by looking at the verity of the underlying facts upon which it is based, evaluating the expert's reasoning, scrutinizing the expert's knowledge, and considering the state of knowledge in the expert's field of expertise. However, if an attorney wishes to examine a factual assertion made by the expert, this may instead direct an inquiry into the credibility of the source of the fact (e.g., witness who made the statement, document that contained the statement) and/or the method by which the fact was acquired (e.g., the reliability and validity of a psychological test, interview technique, or clinical observation).

Communication

Thomas Edison is alleged to have said that if you cannot explain something to your paperboy you probably do not understand it yourself. This colorful remark speaks volumes about communicating with the audience of your forensic report, most often attorneys or judges unfamiliar with psychological science, clinical psychology, and clinical-forensic psychology. It is important to remember that most attorneys were undergraduate majors in subjects emphasizing verbal abilities and skills such as political science, history, etc. Law school also emphasizes the development of verbal abilities, not scientific thinking, quantitative reasoning or analysis, or clinical skills. Unless an attorney specializes in mental health law or practices in an area of litigation that routinely involves mental health testimony, it is unlikely the attorney has had much experience working with mental health experts.

The level of technical difficulty in a forensic report should be no greater than that in an average newspaper article. In fact, writing the report *as if* it were a newspaper article, not a clinical report, is close to an ideal frame of reference. Jargon (e.g., "The evaluee adopted a *passive-aggressive* stance during the interview") should be avoided. When technical or clinical terms are necessary, they should be defined briefly in context or in footnotes. If this is not feasible, or if technical terms are frequent, the writer should consider adding terms and their definitions to a glossary appended to the end of the report.

The report should ordinarily be as short as possible. The writer must keep in mind the reader's limited attention span, motivation, and memory. The longer the report, the more likely the reader will skim it instead of reading it. More than one young report writer has been dismayed after spending hours writing a 30-page forensic psychological masterpiece to watch attorneys jump to the last page and hurriedly read the conclusions or wait as a judge takes a "5 minute recess to read the expert's report."

A longer report also will more likely contain inapt or unclear language that opposing counsel can use to "spin" the meaning of the writer's statements. A concise report, however, is like a bullet or a spear. It is far more powerful and much more difficult to attack—and it is far more likely that readers will understand it.

It is usually more difficult to write a short report than a long report. Most good short reports begin as longer first drafts that are trimmed and edited before assuming their final polished form. This is as it should be, as the goal of the first draft is to err on the side of overinclusion, to leave out nothing of importance. Using the best evidence model as an editing tool can go a long way toward making the final report no longer than it needs to be.

Unfortunately, forensic report writers rarely get feedback from consumers about the quality of their reports. Without such feedback, learning proceeds slowly, if at all, and it is easy for a writer to acquire an inflated sense of report writing skill. Extant research provides general information about what forensic experts value in reports, but studies rarely provide feedback about writers' work and the way others appraise it. One solution to this problem on an individual level is to request feedback from the consumers of your reports. This is easily accomplished by enclosing a prepaid postcard evaluation form with the report to the referring party.

Anatomy of a Generic Clinical-Forensic Report

Although a variety of styles and formats exist, forensic psychological reports usually include certain basic sections. We discuss these here, drawing attention to their most important features and to stylistic variations.

Opening

Forensic reports are customarily printed on professional or institutional letterhead. The first page contains key identifying information, most commonly the legal case number(s), evaluator file number, date(s) of evaluation, date of the report, and the evaluee's name, date of birth, social security number, and hospital number. The salutation and opening tone usually take one of two forms. For attorney-referred cases, the salutation follows that adopted in ordinary business correspondence. The tone is appropriately warm and friendly. If the evaluee has been referred by the court or by an institution, a more official salutation (e.g., "Your Honor") is preferred, and the tone is appropriately respectful.

Warnings

Warnings state the legally authorized, intended recipients of the report, often in a typeface that offsets this section from the remaining text (e.g., bold or italic). Warnings appear most commonly in reports sent to courts or institutions wherein a danger exists that the report or its contents could be inappropriately released to a third party. If the evaluator is concerned about the potentially harmful impact of a report on an evaluee or another person, this concern can be included in the warning.

Reason for Referral

This section of the report serves a simple, pragmatic function. It identifies *how, when,* and *why* a case was referred for evaluation. It therefore sets the stage for everything else that follows. It need not be long, but it does need to be clear, chronologically accurate, and legally precise. It is best to enumerate each referral question and state it as precisely as the law permits (e.g., "Attorney Jones referred the evaluee for an assessment of his competency to stand trial under RCW 10.77.060 pursuant to court order no. xx-xxx.xx.")

Synopsis

Although it is an uncommon practice, the writer may report next a synopsis of the evaluation's main findings. Reporting the bottom line first, known in journalism as the *inverted pyramid* style of reporting, confers advantages. Immediately disclosing the conclusions gratifies the reader's need to know the bottom line and may provide dramatic relief. Once the conclusions are known, the reader can settle down and learn how and why the evaluator reached the conclusions. It also conveys an attitude of forthrightness that portrays the writer as an honest, frank professional who takes full responsibility for opinions and who is willing to get straight to the point rather than beat around the bush or soft peddle the findings. On the negative side, reporting the conclusions early may tempt hasty readers to stop reading the report. However, these may be the same readers who would otherwise skim the report for the conclusions or read the final page of the report first. Alternately, a summary of the findings and opinions can be placed at the end of the report where it is usually found.

Informed Consent Procedures

Informed consent procedures are so important to clinical-forensic evaluation that they warrant a special section in the report. The informed consent section may run only a few sentences, or it may occupy a whole paragraph or more depending on the circumstances. It is important that the writer disclose procedural details and the evaluee's response to them. If the procedure required the evaluee to sign a consent form, this should be reported so that the reader knows if a signed form is on file. In some cases, attorneys may demand to inspect the form to gain a better understanding of what the evaluee consented to when the form was signed.

It is especially important to document in the report any problems with the informed consent procedure, such as evidence that the evaluee did not (or could not) understand it, and steps taken by the evaluator to manage this problem.

Database/Missing Information/Caveats

Full disclosure is a key feature of the database section of a forensic report. The database describes what information the evaluator considered (and did not consider) in forming opinions. Many different kinds of data are potentially important to addressing a psycholegal question, but most of the time only a subset of that data is available to the evaluator. Some records may no longer exist (e.g., childhood school records). Others may take too long to obtain (e.g., a veteran's service records or combat records). Third parties may be reluctant or slow to release medical records. Collateral witnesses may refuse or perpetually avoid being interviewed. It may not be possible to perform valid psychological testing if norms do not exist for the evaluee's culture (e.g., sensory impaired, non-English speaking) or if the evaluee's educational level or reading ability is too low.

Most forensic evaluators simply list the data upon which they relied. This can be done in a long, messy paragraph, but, if sources are numerous, it is preferable to organize them as a bulleted list. Listed items should clearly identify the written source or, in the case of oral interviews, the name of the interviewee, the date, and the time spent during the interview. References to psychological testing need to state the full name of the test, not its abbreviation, and briefly explain the test's purpose. References to research need to contain the full citation, along with an explanatory remark about the relevance of the research to the evaluation.

It is equally important for the report writer to list sources of information that were sought but unavailable and, hence, omitted from consideration. These also should be formatted in a list. The potential importance of the missing information to the evaluation, what was done to try to obtain it, and the reason it was not obtained briefly should be described. In fairness to the referring attorney, the evaluator should strive to make information needs known at every step of the evaluation and notify the attorney when there are problems obtaining important data, especially that which, passively or actively, has been blocked.

Finally, the writer should report any problems or concerns with the validity of the information sources, including psychological test findings and any parties interviewed by the evaluator whose adverse reporting styles (e.g., malingering, deception, denial) could skew or otherwise degrade the accuracy of evaluation findings. This is best reported in a summary paragraph that appraises the overall quality of the database. The importance of this caveat paragraph cannot be overemphasized. Evaluators work with the data available to them. Unlike attorneys or judges, they have no standing to issue subpoenas. They rely on the cooperation and honesty of others to obtain information, and frequently access to information that could alter the evaluator's opinions is denied. It is better to proactively identify missing data in the report than attempt to explain its absence later in deposition or cross-examination.

Relevant History

In a forensic psychological report, the only history that really matters is that which is relevant to answering the psycholegal questions before the court. What to include and discard is largely a matter of professional judgment. Evaluees often have colorful histories, which (although interesting) contain information that is distracting, unfairly prejudicial, and potentially biased. Here again, the report writer is reminded of the importance of screening data using a method like the best evidence model.

There are several ways to structure the history section of a report, and the decision about how to do it may change with circumstances. Commonly, the history section is divided into subcomponents (e.g., family history, early childhood history, school history, relationship history, occupational history, military history, criminal history, medical history, substance use history, psychiatric history). The primary advantage of this method is that the report is organized by topic and, thus, affords greater ease in locating details and responding to questions about specific categories of information. It is sometimes preferable to report a biographical chronology that integrates various aspects of history into a narrative or story. This is especially true for situations in which there is a marked change in the evaluee's life trajectory following one or more major events or a complex interplay among aspects of the history. Examples of such include mental illness that predisposes the evaluee to substance abuse, or vice versa; a tragic loss that produces an abrupt change in life course; and recurrent patterns or cycles of maladaptive social functioning that demonstrate personality dysfunction, a cyclic mental disorder, or a recurrent substance abuse problem. Reconstruction of past mental states or functional capacities (Simon & Shuman, 2002), and comparison of past states with present and forecasted future states or capacities, comprises such a critical class of questions for forensic psychological evaluation that a temporal structure demarcating *before/after* or *past, present, and future* may be most appropriate.

Finally, it is essential to identify the source(s) of historical data and to present contradictory data, if it exists. Again, there are at least two methods for accomplishing this. One method, which attorneys often prefer, is to report the evaluee's history from each source separately. This has the advantage of identifying the sources as separate deposits of evidence and, in the case of person sources, distinguishing them as potential fact witnesses. A second method is to integrate the historical information, comparing, contrasting, and reconciling if possible the information from different sources along the way, as a historian might attempt to balance accounts of a historical controversy.

Clinical Formulation

The clinical formulation section—which may include the mental status examination (MSE), test results, and diagnostic formulations—often is troublesome for forensically inexperienced writers. Care should be taken to avoid technical language and to define clinical terms where use is necessary. The writer should clarify that the MSE describes a static state of affairs and functions to provide a snapshot of the evaluee at the time the evaluation was performed. It is occasionally helpful to report a series of MSEs to track notable changes in the evaluee's mental condition across time.

When reporting test results, the evaluee's test-taking response style should be described. Numerical test findings, if they are reported at all, should be reported in a way that will not mislead the reader. Error bands, which represent confidence intervals, should be included to indicate that any numerical score is merely a best estimate of the evaluee's standing on the relevant construct. The writer also needs to consider on which scale to report the score. Nonpsychologists often are best able to understand percentile ranks, and it is easier for the reader to compare the evaluee's relative standing on different tests using percentile ranks.

The relative importance of clinical diagnoses varies markedly from one kind of forensic setting and jurisdiction to the next. Some kinds of evaluations (e.g., disability evaluations) require an official diagnosis if the evaluee is to be awarded disability funds. In other settings, a diagnosis may be a necessary condition for a legal disposition (e.g., the diagnosis of a paraphilia to satisfy the definition of sexually violent predator, the diagnosis of a mental disease or defect to satisfy the definition of insanity). For other settings (e.g., personal injury evaluations), the parties may want a diagnosis but obliging them might enable needless confusion and distraction from the crux psycholegal issue, which is whether the evaluee's biopsychosocial functioning has declined following an injury that the defendant is allegedly legally liable for causing.

When a diagnosis is reported, it is imperative to (a) explain the diagnosis, (b) document how the evaluee satisfied diagnostic criteria, and (c) establish the relevance of the diagnosis in informing the crux psycholegal issues. Generally, a comprehensive functional assessment of the evaluee is far more helpful than a diagnosis. A diagnosis is never a legitimate substitute for a functional assessment—which means that when a diagnosis is reported, the writer *still* has an obligation to report the impact of the diagnosis on the evaluee's capacities, abilities, and traits.

Forensic Analyses and Opinions

The section containing forensic psychological analyses and opinions is introduced by citing the applicable psycholegal standards or definitions (with statutory code number and source) or, if no concise statutory standard is available, the basic psycholegal questions. This informs the reader what psycholegal standards or definitions the writer applied in forming expert opinion(s).

Psychologists rely on multiple kinds of data to form their psycholegal opinions, including interviews of the evaluee, testing, and third-party information (e.g., documents, records, interviews of persons other than the evaluee). It is common for the writer to report findings separately for each source. For example, if three individuals were interviewed concerning observations of the evaluee at some critical point in time, each interviewee's report might be summarized in a separate paragraph. Key test findings might be reported the same way, one test after another. Interviews of the evaluee likewise might be reported serially.

Ideally, all sources converge in telling a similar story but from different perspectives. However, sources sometimes tell different, even contradictory, stories, and in such cases it is necessary to include a summary section that integrates the data and resolves discrepancies. If factual discrepancies are not too numerous, this also can be accomplished as each controverted fact is introduced.

The natural structure of the psycholegal question(s) often serve as a template for organizing the forensic analyses and opinions section of the report. Two examples help illustrate this concept. Once the basic idea is understood, it is readily generalized to other psycholegal questions.

Consider the following question about sanity: Was the evaluee *unable to know the nature and quality of the act committed* or *unable to know whether the act was wrong* as the result of a *mental disease or defect?* Because there are three key prongs to the question, the forensic section of the report conveniently can be divided into three parts, one to address each component of the legal test. Data from interviews of the evaluee, test results, and third-party information can be presented in turn to address each component. A summary paragraph or two then integrates—and reconciles if possible—data from different sources into an overall opinion. Following is an outline demonstrating this method.

I.   Statement of the statutory psycholegal standard
    A)   Mental disease or defect
        1.   Third-party data
        2.   Test data
        3.   Interview data
    B)   Ability to know the nature and quality of the act
        1.   Third-party data
        2.   Test data
        3.   Interview data
    C)   Ability to know whether the act was wrong
        1.   Third-party data
        2.   Test data
        3.   Interview data
II.   Summary: Integrates data and provides the expert opinion.

Next, consider a personal injury evaluation. Here, the primary question might be: What, if anything, has the plaintiff lost due to a legally liable defendant's injury to the plaintiff? It is apparent from the question that two detailed functional assessments of the plaintiff are required, one before the injury and a second following the injury; thus, a *before/after* format may be adopted in the forensic analyses section of the report. The writer will want to report a fairly detailed longitudinal account of the plaintiff's life in its many aspects (e.g., employment, education, relationships, physical health, mental health, social life, avocations/hobbies) before the injury as well as a detailed assessment of changes in these domains after the injury. Both assessments will likely include data from third-party sources, interviews of the plaintiff, and testing. Following is an outline demonstrating this method.

I.   Plaintiff's functioning (adjustment) before the alleged injury
    A)   Life area I (third-party data, interviews, test results)
    B)   Life area II (third-party data, interviews, test results)
    C)   Life area *n* (third-party data, interviews, test results)

II. Plaintiff's functioning (adjustment) following the alleged injury
    A) Life area I (third-party data, interviews, test results)
    B) Life area II (third-party data, interviews, test results)
    C) Life area *n* (third-party data, interviews, test results)
III. Comparison of preinjury and postinjury functioning (adjustment).

Summary of Findings

Writers may include a section summarizing their findings. It is best to keep such a summary brief and focused, rather like an abstract for a journal article or paper presentation. A bulleted summary containing the main points may be helpful.

Recommendations

Recommendations about the evaluee's future treatment or other dispositions are usually not an issue until a case has reached a particular stage (e.g., after a defendant has been found incompetent to stand trial, at the sentencing stage of criminal proceedings). Consequently, the inclusion of a recommendations section depends on the psycholegal questions posed and the stage of the legal proceedings.

In some situations, such as custody evaluations, specific recommendations (e.g., parenting plans) are arguably the most important part of the report, whereas in cases such as personal injury evaluations rendering an opinion about an evaluee's future treatment may be premature. In other cases, such as competency to stand trial evaluations, sanity evaluations, or determinations of release from an institution, this section of the report might contain "what if" or contingency recommendations for professional intervention should the court make certain rulings (e.g., find the defendant insane, release the defendant to a less restrictive setting).

Miscellany

If the writer cites research, it is appropriate for the sources to be included in an appendix. Also, tables and diagrams may help organize and explain findings, and these too may be included in appendices. When the report must make reference to technical terms, an appendix should contain a glossary of these terms. It is also common for writers to precede certain sections of a report with disclaimers (e.g., paragraphs that warn the reader about the limitations of psychological testing or predictions of future dangerousness). Finally, writers may precede their signatures with a declaration or oath affirming the authenticity and truthfulness of the proffered professional opinions.

Empirical Literature on Forensic Mental Health Reports

In this section, we briefly summarize the empirical literature on forensic mental health reports. Even though this literature is relatively sparse and far from definitive, we include this summary to encourage readers to consider the notion of empirically based forensic report writing practices, learn what we know and do not know about forensic mental health report writing, and acquire the habit of following this literature for future developments. Notable results that have emerged from this small body of studies are summarized in Table 20.2.

Wettstein (2005) reviewed the empirical literature on the quality of the forensic mental health evaluation, including its primary product, the report (many of Wettstein's references are contained in Table 20.2). In addition to highlighting limitations of the research itself (e.g., problems with generalizability, including nonrandom selection of reports and evaluators), this review described apparent weaknesses of forensic report writing in practice as revealed by the research.

Table 20.2 Summary of the empirical literature on forensic mental health reports

Study	Method	Results
Borum & Grisso (1996)	• Surveyed national sample of forensic psychologists and psychiatrists regarding beliefs about necessary CST ($n = 102$) and CR ($n = 96$) report content	• "Essential": defendant identification, evaluation methods, clinical data, elements specific to each forensic question • Lack of consensus: offering "ultimate issue" opinions
Bow & Quinnell (2001)	• Surveyed national sample of psychologists ($n = 198$) regarding child custody report practices	• Average report length = 21 pages, range = 4–80 pages • 94% made explicit custody/visitation decisions • 88% administered Minnesota Multiphasic Personality Inventory to parents
Bow & Quinnell (2002)	• In national sample of child custody reports ($n = 52$), examined (a) report content, (b) content relative to that recommended in survey data, and (c) communication of results	• Average report length = 24 pages, range = 5–63 pages • Report format and content varied • Evaluation procedures generally were consistent with those recommended in survey research and guidelines • Problems included failure to identify information such as evaluation procedures and referral question(s)
Budd & Springman (2011)	• Examined recommendations for parents in reports submitted for use in child abuse and neglect proceedings in Chicago ($n = 204$)	• For narrow, statute-based issues, direct recommendations always were offered • For other issues, community-based evaluators offered more direct recommendations than court-based evaluators (who rather discussed risks and protective factors)
Christy, Douglas, Otto, & Petrila (2004)	• Examined report content for private evaluations of juveniles adjudicated incompetent to proceed in Florida ($n = 1,357$)	• Reports frequently failed to address legal issues (e.g., cause of incapacity, commitment eligibility) • Reports incompletely described evaluation methods, examinees, and examinees' capacities • Consent to participate was documented in only 59.3% of reports
Doyle, Ogloff, & Thomas (2011)	• Examined reports assessing risk of sex offending for preventive detention proceedings ($n = 86$)	• Minority of reports stated various limitations of Static-99 (3.8%–45.6%) and general risk assessment (2.3%–33.7%) • Most reports included final opinion of risk (91.9%)
Fuger, Acklin, Nguyen, Ignacio, & Gowensmith (2014)	• Assessed quality of CR reports in Hawaii ($n = 150$) according to 44-item report quality measure	• Reports were of "mediocre" quality (e.g., few reported history or testing data)
Hecker & Steinberg (2002)	• Rated evaluators' explanations for disposition recommendations in Pennsylvania juvenile predisposition reports ($n = 172$)	• Only 7% of reports included disposition recommendations rated "sufficient" or better
Heilbrun & Collins (1995)	• Compared content of CST and CR reports written in the hospital ($n = 167$) and community ($n = 110$) in Florida	• Overall mean length = 3.9 pages • Reviewed prior evaluations: 80% hospital, 30% community • Reviewed arrest reports: 95% hospital, 48% community • Addressed CST legal criteria: 95% hospital, 61% community • Offered "ultimate issue" opinion: 95% hospital, 99% community

LaFortune & Nicholson (1995)	• Surveyed Oklahoma judges and attorneys ($n = 110$) regarding adequacy of submitted CST reports	• Outpatient reports were judged higher quality than inpatient reports • Desired more information regarding relevant functional capacities
Lander & Heilbrun (2009)	• Assessed correspondence between CST report content ($n = 125$) and forensic mental health assessment principles (Heilbrun, 2001) and relation between adherence to principles and experts' ratings of relevance, helpfulness, and overall quality	• Majority of reports failed to correspond to principles (e.g., did not cite information sources, did not reference prior records, did not address all psycholegal domains • Most reports (83.4%) offered an "ultimate issue" opinion • Adherence to principles correlated with expert ratings of relevance, helpfulness, and quality
Nguyen, Acklin, Fuger, Gowensmith, & Ignacio (2011)	• Assessed quality of conditional release reports in Hawaii ($n = 150$) according to 44-item report quality measure	• Reports were of "mediocre" quality (e.g., few reported history or testing data; many failed to document informed consent, describe nexus between psychiatric condition and legal issues, or provide complete rationale for psycholegal opinions)
Owens, Rosner, & Harmon (1985, 1987)	• Surveyed New York judges ($n = 22$, $n = 20$) regarding pertinent CST report content and satisfaction	• Judges adhered to strict CST definitions • Judges used CST information for advice on other issues (e.g., dangerousness) • Judges were eager for, and satisfied with, psychiatric input (e.g., clinical data)
Petrella & Poythress (1983)	• Compared quality of CST ($n = 120$) and CR ($n = 80$) reports written by psychiatrists to those written by psychologists and social workers in Michigan	• Psychologists used more collateral data sources than did psychiatrists • Psychologists' reports were blindly rated as relatively higher quality
Robbins, Waters, & Herbert (1997)	• Assessed quality of actual CST reports in New Jersey and Nebraska ($n = 66$) by comparing to Grisso's (1988) model	• 39% included defendant interview only (no test or third-party data) • 94% included psychiatric diagnosis, but only 27% stated how diagnosis affected functional ability • 94% offered "ultimate issue" opinion • Reports often contained extraneous information
Robinson & Acklin (2010)	• Assessed quality of CST reports in Hawaii ($n = 150$) according to 38-item report quality measure	• Reports exhibited "pervasive mediocrity" (e.g., few reported history or testing data, few documented that evaluee was informed of confidentiality limits)
Ryba, Cooper, & Zapf (2003)	• Surveyed national sample of psychologists ($n = 82$) regarding essential juvenile CST report content	• "Essential": clinical data, data specific to forensic question(s) • Lack of consensus: offering "ultimate issue" opinions

(Continued)

Table 20.2 Continued

Study	Method	Results
Skeem, Golding, Cohn, & Berge (1998)	• Experts rated expressed CST conceptualizations and nexus between psychopathology and CST impairments in Utah community CST reports (n = 100)	• Collateral data inconsistently were reviewed (police report = 63%, mental health records = 37%) • Few (5%) described requested, but unavailable, records • Foundational CST abilities consistently were addressed but decisional abilities were not • Rarely (10%) expressed specific reasoning about nexus between psychopathology and CST impairments
Viljoen, Wingrove, & Ryba (2008)	• Surveyed juvenile and criminal court judges from seven states (n = 166) regarding preferred content in adjudicative competence reports	• "Ultimate issue" opinions, with penultimate opinions about mental illness and legal deficits, were considered most essential • More than 70% of judges considered testing essential or recommended • Opinions about maturity were considered important in juvenile evaluations
Warren, Murrie, Chauhan, Dietz, & Morris (2004)	• Examined clinical, criminal, and demographic attributes of defendants described in Virginia sanity reports (n = 5,175) and their relations to opinions of insanity	• Database often did not include statements by the defendant, defendant's criminal history, psychiatric/medical records, and witness statements
Zapf, Hubbard, Cooper, Wheeles, & Ronan (2004)	• Examined CST report quality in terms of Alabama statute (n = 53)	• In all but one case the court accepted the expert's opinion • Reports frequently omitted relevant CST functional areas (e.g., 22% did not address the defendant's understanding of the nature of the proceedings)

Note: CST = competency to stand trial; CR = criminal responsibility

Prominent weaknesses described in Wettstein's review, which have been corroborated by subsequent research, include:

1. Variable use and reporting of data sources (e.g., collateral information, psychological testing) (e.g., Fuger et al., 2014; Lander & Heilbrun, 2009; Nguyen et al., 2011; Robbins et al., 1997; Skeem et al., 1998; Warren et al., 2004), particularly in evaluations conducted in the community (e.g., Heilbrun & Collins, 1995);
2. Failure to describe psycholegal functional capacities and the linkages among psychopathology, psycholegal functioning, and forensic opinions (e.g., Christy et al., 2004; Lander & Heilbrun, 2009; Nguyen et al., 2011; Robbins et al., 1997; Skeem et al., 1998; Zapf et al., 2004); and,
3. Failure to acknowledge evaluation limitations (e.g., Doyle et al., 2011).

Also, although some scholars have cautioned against the practice (Allnutt & Chaplow, 2000; Heilbrun, 2001; Melton et al., 2007), forensic reports frequently contain "ultimate issue" opinions (Bow & Quinnell, 2001; Budd & Springman, 2011; Heilbrun & Collins, 1995; Robbins et al., 1997; Skeem et al., 1998), and courts rely heavily on these opinions (e.g., Viljoen et al., 2008; Zapf et al., 2004).

The *Specialty Guidelines for Forensic Psychology*, updated by the American Psychological Association in 2013, speak to the importance of forensic evaluators relying on multiple data sources (Guideline 9.02), and appropriately disclosing these sources (Guideline 11.03), addressing the psycholegal issues at hand (e.g., evaluating functional capacities) (Guidelines 10.01, 11.02), and describing both strengths *and limitations* of their work (Guidelines 9.02, 9.03, 10.02, 10.03). Also, forensic evaluators are encouraged to describe in their reports the data and reasoning that are the bases for their opinions (Guideline 11.04)—this may be especially important where "ultimate issue" opinions are offered. To the extent that findings garnered from the extant empirical literature suggest a gap between forensic report writing in practice and the aspirations of these guidelines, more widespread training in clinical-forensic evaluation and report writing appears warranted (Robinson & Acklin, 2010).

Practical Tips for the Apprehensive Report Writer

We assume at this point that the report writer has conducted a competent forensic evaluation and has done a fair, accurate job of organizing data, sifting, and separating probative, relevant facts from irrelevant, unfairly prejudicial chaff. If not, an attempt to write likely will fail and the writer will need to go back and complete these preliminary steps before proceeding. We also need to make a distinction between *what* the evaluator says in the report (content) and *how* the writer says it (process). Ensuring quality report content, a prerequisite for effective report writing, requires attention to data organization, synthesis, and reasoning. No amount of writing skill can ever compensate for inadequate facts, lack of integration, or poorly reasoned conclusions.

The way the evaluator chooses to write is a creative process. Creative processes consist of three basic elements: a creator, a medium, and inspiration. Michelangelo (1475–1564) is alleged to have said, "Every block of stone has a statue inside it, and it is the task of the sculptor to discover it." One thing to learn from this remark is the crucial role that the creator's recursive interaction with the medium plays in creation and, most importantly, how inspiration arises from this active struggle. The creator begins by attempting to produce a change in the medium; the medium then undergoes a change, but not necessarily the one intended; the creator perceives the result, and this opens up possibilities for the creator's next operation on the medium; and, so on and so forth. Slowly, a shape begins to emerge, and at some point this embryonic form suggests to the creator what it can become and what must be done next to accomplish this result. This implies that the forensic evaluator must put words on a page before truly beginning to write, using language itself to generate language. Not until we begin to *interact* with what we have written does the real writing begin. It is in this sense that all good writing is really just good editing.

Beginning writing is typically the most difficult step. A blank computer screen can be a lonely, intimidating, if not paralyzing, experience. It is easy to make excuses to avoid writing in favor of other professional activities that provide more instant gratification. The initial struggle to overcome procrastination can be difficult, especially if the writer experiences report writing as an arduous task. One common obstacle to starting or continuing to write is perfectionism, the irrational belief that the right word or idea will come to mind if we persist long enough in looking for it, that we should be able to write one clear, coherent sentence after another, that we should not move on to the next paragraph until the last one is written well, or that we should start at the beginning of the report and rigidly follow the report outline until the final sentence is written. A related problem is the belief that we have to be in a special, inspired mood or mental state to write well. This latter belief can cause the writer to wait passively for the muse to appear, which may be long past the report deadline.

Table 20.3 lists problems that commonly plague report writers (e.g., procrastination), along with potential remedies. One way to remedy perfectionism is to encourage the opposite, writing whatever comes to mind in whatever order it appears. Abandon grammar and rules. Just write. If necessary, write by hand, draw circles around key words and link them together with lines, arrows, or other structural representations. This is more like play than work, and it establishes a mental set conducive to both organization and enjoyment.

It is possible that, owing to years of conditioning, you may experience difficulty writing with reckless abandon. If so, try dictating your report. Turn on a voice recorder and start talking. If this does not work, get up from your desk, look out the window, or walk about your office, dictating while you walk or pace. Once you have generated verbal output, ideas about how to further organize often appear. If not, go for a walk. Bring your voice recorder or notepad because there is a good chance that once you escape the confines of your office, and you continue to mull over what you have been trying to write, ideas will begin to pop into consciousness. Remember too that there is a place for perfectionism. This talent, which many psychologists possess in surplus, is most helpful in editing and polishing the report.

Lack of direction can be another obstacle to report writing. Adopting a report outline—any outline—is one solution to this malady. If the adopted outline later proves to be a poor structural fit for the report, it can be rearranged to improve the fit. In the meantime, the template has served a useful temporary purpose in helping the writer compose the lion's share of the report.

Table 20.3 Common report writing problems and potential remedies

Problem	Remedies
Information overload	Start by creating the database section. Sort database into categories. Summarize main findings into list of bullet points.
Difficulty beginning/ procrastination	Begin anywhere, even in the middle of the report. Dictate instead of typing the report. Carry a voice recorder and record ideas in any order. Pick an easy first writing task (e.g., social history).
Lack of direction	Follow someone else's outline or template. Write conclusions first, then work backward. Turn your report into a PowerPoint presentation.
Perfectionism	Speed type or dictate the report, in any order. Reserve perfectionism for editing the report.
Anxiety	Monitor body sensations as you write. Check your posture and muscle tension. Monitor your feelings and imagery. Ask "for whom am I writing this report?" Consult self-help resources for writers. Seek professional help.

Another means to facilitate getting going on the report is to write the synopsis or conclusions section first. Or, you might imagine that your report is a Microsoft PowerPoint presentation. A PowerPoint outline forces us to think, prioritize what we wish to say, and say it succinctly. Also, if you follow this advice literally, you may find the slide show useful in presenting your findings on the witness stand.

Evaluators who find report writing a difficult, unpleasant chore often have acquired a learned negative emotional response to the task. A sure sign this has occurred is heightened anxiety or dread when thinking about or writing reports. Increased body tension and awkward or uncomfortable body postures while writing are also telltale signs of traumatic learning associated with writing. Although the origins of this unproductive state vary, it may be perpetuated through negative self-talk, negative imagery, and unpleasant affect. Introspection may reveal that the distraught writer is more preoccupied with favorably impressing—or, alternately, is worried about displeasing—an inner audience of critics than on the practical task of communicating with the intended reader. The first step toward becoming more aware of such influences is to consciously monitor body sensations, emotions, thoughts, and fantasies while writing. This takes some practice and dedication but is well worth the effort. Waking up to these influences changes the writer's relationship to them and promotes freedom from them or at least learning how to write despite them. For some, it may be advisable to take courses on writing, seek self-help resources for writers, or even seek professional help for deeper issues that adversely may influence writing.

Conclusion

In this chapter, we have introduced the reader to forensic psychological report writing. Although no shortage of aspiration and conjecture exist regarding how to write forensic reports, little reliable empirical research is available to guide the evaluator in performing this critical task. If readers have reexamined fundamental assumptions and beliefs about how to write a forensic report, we have accomplished a major goal. If we also have helped the reader develop a more positive attitude toward forensic report writing, or a greater sense of confidence in taking on the task, so much the better.

It should be clear by now that forensic psychological report writing begins long before we type or dictate. It begins with a high-quality forensic evaluation, which cannot be conducted unless the evaluator has acquired skill in the methods of clinical and forensic assessment, mastered the pertinent psycholegal standards, and gathered sufficient reliable data to address the psycholegal questions. Assuming a good evaluation has been completed, the evaluator must next critically evaluate the quality of obtained data, decide what data are relevant to answering the psycholegal question(s), and then answer those questions only to the extent the data permit. Although veteran forensic practitioners and specialty organizations can be invaluable sources of wisdom about how to write forensic reports, the evaluator must ultimately follow his or her own light and proceed with self-honesty and courage throughout the entire evaluation and report writing process. If "the only way to become a better writer is to become a better person" (Ueland, 1938/1987, p. 129), perhaps the best way to become a better forensic report writer is to become a better forensic evaluator.

Notes

1   Hereinafter, we use the word *attorney* to represent the retaining party, which could be a judge, social service agency, forensic hospital, correctional agency such as a jail or prison, or other third party.

2   See Borkosky, Pellett, and Thomas (2014) and Connell and Koocher (2003) concerning the unsettled matter of whether forensic work is regulated by HIPAA and whether this issue is moot because forensic practitioners exceed HIPAA standards in regard to individuals' privacy.

3   For further reading, see Graham's *Federal Rules of Evidence in a Nutshell* (2015). Start with the following basic set of Federal Rules of Evidence (FRE): 401, 403, 702, 703, 704, 705, 803 (4), 803 (6),

and 803 (18). Additional evidence rules will be relevant for civil and criminal cases involving sexual misconduct (FRE 412, 413, 414, and 415). Although most jurisdictions have adopted evidence rules that parallel federal rules quite closely, there are also important jurisdictional differences that the report writer should follow.

4   See Federal Rule of Evidence 102. For an entire book devoted to an exposition of that rule as it applies to expert testimony, see Sales and Shuman (2005).

References

Ackerman, M. J. (2006). Forensic report writing. *Journal of Clinical Psychology, 62,* 59–72. doi:10.1002/jclp.20200

Allnutt, S. H., & Chaplow, D. (2000). General principles of forensic report writing. *Australian and New Zealand Journal of Psychiatry, 34,* 980–987.

American Psychological Association. (2013). Specialty guidelines for forensic psychology. *American Psychologist, 68,* 7–19. doi:10.1037/a0029889

Borkosky, B. G., Pellett, J. M., & Thomas, M. S. (2014). Are forensic evaluations "health care" and are they regulated by HIPAA? *Psychological Injury and Law, 7,* 1–8. doi:10.1007/s12207–013–9158–7

Borum, R., & Grisso, T. (1996). Establishing standards for criminal forensic reports: An empirical analysis. *Bulletin of the American Academy of Psychiatry and the Law, 24,* 297–317.

Bow, J. N., & Quinnell, F. A. (2001). Psychologists' current practices and procedures in child custody evaluations: Five years after American Psychological Association guidelines. *Professional Psychology: Research and Practice, 32,* 261–268. doi:10.1037/0735–7028.32.3.261

Bow, J. N., & Quinnell, F. A. (2002). A critical review of child custody evaluation reports. *Family Court Review, 40,* 164–176.

Budd, K. S., & Springman, R. E. (2011). Empirical analysis of referral issues and "ultimate issue" recommendations for parents in child protection cases. *Family Court Review, 49,* 34–45. doi:10.1111/j.1744–1617.2010.01351.x

Christy, A., Douglas, K. S., Otto, R. K., & Petrila, J. (2004). Juveniles evaluated incompetent to proceed: Characteristics and quality of mental health professionals' evaluations. *Professional Psychology: Research and Practice, 35,* 380–388. doi:10.1037/0735–7028.35.4.380

Connell, M., & Koocher, G. (2003). HIPAA & forensic practice. *American Psychology-Law Society News, 23,* 16–19.

Doyle, D. J., Ogloff, J. R. P., & Thomas, S. D. M. (2011). An analysis of dangerous sexual offender assessment reports: Recommendations for best practice. *Psychiatry, Psychology and Law, 18,* 537–556. doi:10.1080/13218719.2010.499159

Fuger, K. D., Acklin, M. W., Nguyen, A. H., Ignacio, L. A., & Gowensmith, W. N. (2014). Quality of criminal responsibility reports submitted to the Hawaii judiciary. *International Journal of Law and Psychiatry, 37,* 272–280. doi:10.1016/j.ijlp.2013.11.020

Graham, M. H. (2015). *Federal Rules of Evidence in a nutshell* (9th ed.). St. Paul, MN: West Academic Publishing.

Greenberg, S. A., & Shuman, D. W. (1997). Irreconcilable conflict between therapeutic and forensic roles. *Professional Psychology: Research and Practice, 28,* 50–57.

Grisso, T. (1988). *Competency to stand trial evaluations: A manual for practice.* Sarasota, FL: Professional Resource Exchange.

Grisso, T., Goldstein, A. M., & Heilbrun, K. (Eds.). (2008–2012). *Best practices in forensic mental health assessment* (Vols. 1–19). New York, NY: Oxford University Press. https://global.oup.com/academic/content/series/b/best-practices-for-forensic-mental-health-assessments-gbp/?cc=us&lang=en&

Groth-Marnat, G. (2006). Introduction to the special series on psychological reports. *Journal of Clinical Psychology, 62,* 1–4. doi:10.1002/jclp.20195

Hecker, T., & Steinberg, L. (2002). Psychological evaluation at juvenile court disposition. *Professional Psychology: Research and Practice, 33,* 300–306. doi:10.1037//0735–7028.33.3.300

Heilbrun, K. (2001). *Principles of forensic mental health assessment.* New York, NY: Kluwer Academic/Plenum.

Heilbrun, K., & Collins, S. (1995). Evaluations of trial competency and mental state at the time of offense: Report characteristics. *Professional Psychology: Research and Practice, 26,* 61–67. doi:10.1037/0735–7028.26.1.61

Heilbrun, K., DeMatteo, D., Holliday, S. B., & LaDuke, C. (2014). *Forensic mental health assessment: A casebook* (2nd ed.). New York, NY: Oxford University Press.

Karson, M., & Nadkarni, L. (2013). *Principles of forensic report writing.* Washington, DC: American Psychological Association.

LaFortune, K. A., & Nicholson, R. A. (1995). How adequate are Oklahoma's mental health evaluations for determining competency in criminal proceedings? The bench and the bar respond. *Journal of Psychiatry and Law, 23,* 231–262.

Lander, T. D., & Heilbrun, K. (2009). The content and quality of forensic mental health assessment: Validation of a principles-based approach. *International Journal of Forensic Mental Health, 8,* 115–121. doi:10.1080/14999010903199324

Melton, G. B., Petrila, J., Poythress, N. G., & Slobogin, C. (2007). *Psychological evaluations for the courts: A handbook for mental health professionals and lawyers* (3rd ed.). New York, NY: Guilford.

Nguyen, A. H., Acklin, M. W., Fuger, K., Gowensmith, W. N., & Ignacio, L. A. (2011). Freedom in paradise: Quality of conditional release reports submitted to the Hawaii judiciary. *International Journal of Law and Psychiatry, 34,* 341–348. doi:10.1016/j.ijlp.2011.08.006

Owens, H., Rosner, R., & Harmon, R. B. (1985). The judge's view of competency evaluations. *Bulletin of the American Academy of Psychiatry and the Law, 13,* 389–397.

Owens, H., Rosner, R., & Harmon, R. B. (1987). The judge's view of competency evaluations: II. *Bulletin of the American Academy of Psychiatry and the Law, 15,* 381–389.

Petrella, R. C., & Poythress, N. G. (1983). The quality of forensic evaluations: An interdisciplinary study. *Journal of Consulting and Clinical Psychology, 51,* 76–85.

Robbins, E., Waters, J., & Herbert, P. (1997). Competency to stand trial evaluations: A study of actual practice in two states. *Journal of the American Academy of Psychiatry and the Law, 25,* 469–483.

Robinson, R., & Acklin, M. W. (2010). Fitness in paradise: Quality of forensic reports submitted to the Hawaii judiciary. *International Journal of Law and Psychiatry, 33,* 131–137. doi:10.1016/j.ijlp.2010.03.001

Ryba, N. L., Cooper, V. G., & Zapf, P. A. (2003). Juvenile competence to stand trial evaluations: A survey of current practices and test usage among psychologists. *Professional Psychology: Research and Practice, 34,* 499–507. doi:10.1037/0735–7028.34.5.499

Sales, B. D., & Shuman, D. W. (2005). *Experts in court: Reconciling law, science and professional knowledge.* Washington, DC: American Psychological Association.

Simon, R. I., & Shuman, D. W. (Eds.). (2002). *Retrospective assessment of mental states in litigation: Predicting the past.* Washington, DC: American Psychiatric.

Skeem, J. L., Golding, S. L., Cohn, N. B., & Berge, G. (1998). Logic and reliability of evaluations of competence to stand trial. *Law and Human Behavior, 22,* 519–547.

Ueland, B. (1938/1987). *If you want to write: A book about art, independence and spirit.* St. Paul, MN: Graywolf.

Viljoen, J. L., Wingrove, T., & Ryba, N. L. (2008). Adjudicative competence evaluations of juvenile and adult defendants: Judges' views regarding essential components of competence reports. *International Journal of Forensic Mental Health, 7,* 107–119. doi:10.1080/14999013.2008.9914408

Warren, J. I., Murrie, D. C., Chauhan, P., Dietz, P. E., & Morris, J. (2004). Opinion formation in evaluating sanity at the time of the offense: An examination of 5175 pre-trial evaluations. *Behavioral Sciences and the Law, 22,* 171–186. doi:10.1002/bsl.559

Wettstein, R. M. (2005). Quality and quality improvement in forensic mental health evaluations. *The Journal of the American Academy of Psychiatry and Law, 33,* 158–175.

Zapf, P. A., Hubbard, K. L., Cooper, V. G., Wheeles, M. C., & Ronan, K. A. (2004). Have the courts abdicated their responsibility for determination of competency to stand trial to clinicians? *Journal of Forensic Psychology Practice, 4,* 27–44. doi:10.1300/J158v04n01_02

21 Testifying in Court

Evidence-Based Recommendations for Expert-Witness Testimony

Marcus T. Boccaccini, Phylissa P. Kwartner, and Paige B. Harris

Psychologists who testify in court should strive to provide accurate, objective, and educative testimony. The goal for the expert witness is to provide this testimony in a way that will be useful to the decision maker, whether the decision maker is a judge or a jury. The goal for this chapter is to use findings from empirical expert-witness research to identify evidence-based recommendations for providing effective testimony.

Psychologists and all other potential expert witnesses must be recognized, or qualified, as experts before they can testify during a trial. Because potential expert witnesses cannot testify about their opinions unless they are first recognized as experts, this chapter begins with an overview of the most common standards used to qualify potential experts and research about how judges make decisions about the admissibility of expert-witness testimony. The second section identifies principles for providing effective testimony once the mental health professional has been recognized as an expert. Psychologists who are preparing to testify in court must be ready to be persuasive in establishing their status as an expert and in communicating their opinions to the trier of fact.

Qualification as an Expert Witness

Federal Rules of Evidence

The criteria used to qualify a mental health professional as an expert vary by jurisdiction, although a number of states have adopted criteria similar to those followed in Federal courts. According to Federal Rule of Evidence 702, an expert witness is someone who, through knowledge, skill, experience, training, or education, has attained sufficient expertise in her area to satisfy the court that her opinion will be helpful in assisting the trier of fact.

> *FRE Rule 702*: If scientific, technical, or otherwise specialized knowledge will assist the trier of fact to understand the evidence or determine a fact in issue, a witness qualified as an expert by knowledge, skill, experience, training, or education may testify thereto in the form of an opinion or otherwise.

Whether or not a potential witness qualifies as an expert is at the judge's discretion. Judges may qualify potential experts based on a combination of factors including, but not limited to: education, professional credentials, board certification, publication in peer reviewed journals, and previous experiences as an expert witness (Blau, 1998; Groscup, 2004). Psychologists, for example, do not automatically qualify as expert witnesses on the basis that they hold a doctoral degree and limit their practice to psychology (Wilkinson, 1997). Decisions about the admissibility of expert testimony are often made before trial, based on testimony provided in a pretrial hearing.

The **Daubert** *Standard and Scientific Merit*

In *Daubert v. Merrell Dow Pharmaceuticals* (1993) the Supreme Court addressed the issue of how judges in Federal courts should interpret the Federal Rules of Evidence (FRE) and make decisions about the admissibility of expert evidence. The Court held that the decision about whether a potential witness qualifies as an expert should be based on the scientific merit of the expert's methods and theories underlying his or her conclusions. The Court suggested that judges consider several factors when determining scientific merit, including (a) whether the expert's conclusions are based on testable hypotheses, (b) the known error rate associated with the expert's procedures, (c) whether the procedures have been subject to peer review, and (d) whether the methods are generally accepted in the relevant scientific community.

Although the *Daubert* decision addressed the issue of how judges should make determinations about the admissibility of "scientific" evidence, it was initially unclear whether the same standards should be applied to "technical, or other specialized knowledge," upon which expert opinions can also be based (FRE 702). Many of the clinical and forensic activities about which mental health professionals might testify can be conceptualized as falling at least partly under the domains of technical or otherwise specialized knowledge, areas not addressed in the *Daubert* decision. However, the Supreme Court ruled in *Kumho Tire Co. v. Carmichael* (1999) that the *Daubert* decision applied to all types of expert evidence and that there was no bright line distinction that could be made between scientific and other types of expert evidence. This clarification is important for psychologists, because research suggests that judges tend to view expert testimony based on clinical inference as being based on technical or specialized knowledge, not science. For example, 60% of judges in one post-*Daubert* study identified "psychological testimony derived from clinical inference" as being based on technical specialized knowledge (Gatowski et al., 2001, p. 449). Only 38% of the judges identified this type of psychological testimony as based on scientific knowledge.

After the *Daubert* decision, most states adopted *Daubert*-based admissibility standards (see Greiffenstein & Kaufmann, 2012; Parry, 2004), although some continue to use the older *Frye* standard (*Frye v. United States*, 1923), which focuses solely on the general acceptance of the expert's methods and theories in the scientific community.

Factors Associated With Judges' Admissibility Decisions

The *Daubert* decision prompted a series of empirical studies examining the impact of the decision on judges' admissibility decisions. One line of research has focused on reviewing appellate court decisions that addressed the issue of expert admissibility (Dixon & Gill, 2002; Groscup, 2004; Groscup, Penrod, Studebaker, Huss, & O'Neil, 2002). Findings from these studies have suggested that the *Daubert* decision led to an increase in the amount of attention paid to factors for admissibility discussed in FRE 702, such as the expert's experience, training, credentials, and the relevance and potential prejudicial impact of the expert's testimony. Although the *Daubert* decision focused on identifying the characteristics of valid science, FRE 702 begins with a statement clarifying that an expert witness is someone who is qualified by knowledge, skill, experience, training, or education. Thus, research suggests that judges tend to focus on the characteristics of the experts—as opposed to the expert's methods—even in the post-*Daubert* era.

The four scientific merit criteria discussed by the Supreme Court in the *Daubert* decision appear to have had less of an impact on admissibility decisions. Indeed, after reviewing cases in which the admissibility of expert testimony from a behavioral science expert was challenged, researchers concluded that "courts pay lip service" to *Daubert* criteria, but base their decisions on whether the methods and conclusions being offered were generally accepted in the scientific community (Fradella, Fogarty, & O'Neill, 2003, p. 443). Other researchers reported an increase in discussion of these criteria in cases that were appealed immediately following the *Daubert* decision, but noted that this pattern decreased over time, with only peer review and general acceptance continuing to be discussed more frequently than they had before *Daubert* (Dixon & Gill, 2002). There is, however, some evidence that this trend is changing for some types of experts. Indeed, findings from one recent study suggest that judges are more likely to consider the four *Daubert* criteria when experts include quantitative information (e.g., test results, research) in their testimony (Merlino, Murray, & Richardson, 2008).

Another line of research has examined judges' reports of the factors they consider when making admissibility decisions and their understanding of the scientific merit criteria outlined in the *Daubert* decision (Dahir et al., 2005; Gatowski et al., 2001; Kovera & McAuliff, 2000). Findings from this line of research are consistent with those from the appellate court decision reviews in several ways. First, Dahir et al. (2005) found that issues relating to FRE 702, such as the expert's credentials, were the most frequently considered piece of information by judges for making determinations about the admissibility of psychological syndrome evidence. Few of these judges reported considering the *Daubert* scientific merit criteria when making admissibility decisions in these cases. Those who did mention one of the *Daubert* criteria were most likely to mention general acceptance (25%), with relatively few mentioning peer review (7%), and fewer than 1% mentioning falsifiability or error rates. One possible reason for this pattern of findings is that judges are more familiar with the concepts of general acceptance and peer review than the other scientific merit criteria. Indeed, research with this same sample of judges revealed that many judges were able to provide adequate descriptions of general acceptance and peer review, but few were able to adequately describe error rates and falsifiability (Gatowski et al., 2001).

Recommendations for Admissibility Hearings

The findings from admissibility research present somewhat of a conundrum for experts preparing to testify in court. Although the *Daubert* decision asks judges to address the scientific merit of an expert's potential testimony, these factors appear to have little bearing on judges' determinations of admissibility. Does this mean that experts should not be prepared to respond to *Daubert* related questions? Of course not. Responsible experts recognize that the extent to which their methods and conclusions are challenged can vary widely from case to case, but that they should always be prepared for stringent challenges. What the findings from admissibility research do clearly indicate is that mental health professionals preparing to testify in court should pay particular attention to demonstrating that their experience and training merits their recognition as an expert and that they can make clear arguments that will convince the judge that testimony "fits with the case, thus providing assistance to the trier of fact" (Groscup, 2004, p. 65).

But experts should always be prepared to address questions relating to the scientific merit underlying their methods or conclusions (see Otto, DeMier, & Boccaccini, 2014). The best-prepared experts are those who think through issues before conducting an evaluation, choosing to adopt methods and procedures that (a) can be tested, (b) have been tested, (c) have empirical support from that testing, and (d) have been published in peer-reviewed outlets (see Faust, Grimm, Ahern, & Sokolik, 2010).

Evidence-Based Principles of Effective Testimony

Once a mental health professional is sure that she or he meets the criteria to assume the expert role, she or he may wonder what factors lead to the most useful testimony. One recent focus of psychology-law research has been to identify the characteristics of expert witnesses and their testimony that will influence judges' and jurors' decisions. The remaining portions of this chapter describe findings from empirical expert-witness research to provide evidence-based principles for effective courtroom testimony.

The evidence-based principles for providing effective testimony that are described in this chapter are based on the findings from more than 75 expert-witness research studies (see Kwartner, 2007; Kwartner & Boccaccini, 2008; Otto et al., 2014). We included studies from mental health professionals and all other types of expert witnesses in our review because principles of effective testimony should generalize across professions, fields, and types of experts. Most of the studies examined the effect of an experimental manipulation in expert-witness characteristics or testimony on judge or juror decision making, but we also reviewed findings from several correlational studies and surveys that asked jurors or potential jurors about expert witness issues.

The Four Cs of Effective Expert Testimony

Our review of expert-witness research studies revealed four evidence-based principles of effective testimony. We refer to these principles as the four Cs: credibility, clarity, clinical knowledge, and certainty. We identified these principles in the first edition of this book (Kwartner & Boccaccini, 2008) and present a revised version here, based on an updated review and reconceptualization (see Otto et al., 2014).

Principle 1: Credibility

The first evidence-based principle of effective testimony is that highly credible experts are more effective than less credible experts. Highly credible experts are confident, likeable, trustworthy, and knowledgeable (Brodsky, Griffin, & Cramer, 2010). One research team recently developed a 20-item Witness Credibility Scale (WCS) to assess these credibility dimensions (Brodsky et al., 2010). According to their measure, knowledgeable experts are those who receive high ratings on items such as being educated, scientific, and informed. Trustworthy experts receive high ratings on items such as being honest, dependable, and reliable. Confident experts receive high ratings on items such as being poised, relaxed, and well-spoken. Likeable experts receive high ratings on items such as being kind, friendly, and respectful.

Research with the WCS has found that jurors who rate experts highly on the WCS tend to render verdicts and sentences that are consistent with the experts' testimony (Cramer, DeCoster, Harris, Fletcher, & Brodsky, 2011). Some experts may be surprised to hear that appearing kind and friendly (i.e., likeable) may be as important to jurors as appearing educated and honest. In one study, this same research team experimentally manipulated the warmth and competence of a psychologist testifying as an expert witness in a death penalty case (Neal, Guadagno, Eno, & Brodsky, 2012). The high warmth expert used personal references when speaking (e.g., defendant name), maintained moderate levels of smiling, and used a self-effacing presentation style, whereas the low warmth expert did not smile, used formal references (e.g., "the defendant"), and had a narcissistic presentation style. The expert competence manipulation focused on the expert's credentials (e.g., degree, years of experience) and the quality of the evaluation (e.g., how many times met with the defendant). The researchers found that jurors' perceptions of expert warmth better explained their perceptions of expert credibility than their perceptions of expert confidence.

There is some evidence that jurors perceive experts who testify frequently—especially for one side—or those with high fees as less credible than other experts. In one study of more than 400 jury-eligible citizens, participants were provided with several scenarios and asked to identify which mental health professional they found most credible when offering expert testimony. Only 5% identified an expert who spent much of his or her time involved in forensic matters to be the most credible, whereas 82% identified an expert who spent most of his or her time working with patients to be the most credible. Most participants also reported that they would prefer testimony from an expert who had previously testified for both the prosecution and defense (57%)

or had never testified (30%), than an expert who had testified for only one side in prior cases (4%). Finally, these participants perceived lower-paid experts as more credible than higher-paid experts. In fact, most participants (76%) reported that they would be most likely to believe an expert who was paid nothing for his or her testimony.

Other research examining expert witness credibility suggests that experts will be viewed as most credible when they make eye contact with the jury about 80% of the time, as opposed to 50% or 10% of the time (Neal & Brodsky, 2008). There may, however, be drawbacks to making too much eye contact. Boccaccini and Brodsky (2002) asked potential jurors about the amount of eye contact they expected from a believable expert witness. The most common response was that a believable expert would look at the jury some of the time and at the attorney some of the time (41% of jurors). Very few reported that they would most likely believe an expert who mostly looked at the jury (7% of jurors). Others reported that they would most likely believe an expert looking at the jury occasionally and mostly at the attorney (24%), or looking always at the attorney (20%).

Together, these credibility findings suggest that experts should do all they can to increase the likelihood that jurors will perceive them as being highly credible, perhaps using the WCS (Brodsky et al., 2010) items as a guide (e.g., informed, educated, honest, dependable, well-spoken, confident, relaxed, kind, friendly, well-mannered, respectful). Although experts may not be able to control some factors associated with perceived credibility, such as the frequency with which they are called to testify for one side or the prestige of their graduate institution, they can work to improve traits associated with perceived likeability and warmth (e.g., eye contact, kindness, friendliness), which appear to play an important role in perceptions of expert credibility.

Principle 2: Clarity

The second evidence-based principle of effective testimony is that *experts should communicate in a clear and comprehensible manner*. The primary goal of expert testimony is to assist the trier of fact to understand evidence and issues that may be relevant to the case (FRE 702). To achieve this goal, the expert needs to be able to explain his or her methods and conclusions in a way that allows the decision maker to understand the information and its relevance to the trial. Indeed, a survey of 167 former jurors across three states revealed that the ability to convey information in a nontechnical fashion was the characteristic jurors most frequently associated with expert credibility (Shuman, Whitaker, & Champagne, 1994). A sample of 85 experts who testified in the trials heard by these same jurors also identified the ability to convey technical information in a nontechnical manner as the most important factor for establishing their credibility. Using jargon-free testimony that is clear and easy to understand is one of the most common recommendations found in how-to guides for expert witnesses (see Blau, 1998; Brodsky & Anderer, 1999; Chappelle & Rosengren, 2001; Gutheil, 2000; Lubet, 1998). Brodsky and Robey (1972) include the presentation of clear, jargon-free testimony as a key characteristic of an effective courtroom-oriented witness. Similarly, Harris, Varela, Boccaccini, and Turner (2014) found that jurors who had listened to expert testimony in real trials identified testimony style (e.g., clarity) as being one of the most important aspects of exert testimony, second only to the expert's description of the evaluation and outcome.

The influence of testimony clarity on judge and juror decision making was evident across a series of experimental studies examining how the use of technical and complex language can affect jurors' decisions. Researchers have manipulated complexity and technicality of testimony in these studies by changing the amount of psychological or medical jargon the expert uses while testifying. Many studies in this area have focused on testimony from physicians, demonstrating that jurors prefer experts who use terms such as "cancer of the breast" compared to those who testify about "infiltrating ductal carcinoma" (Bourgeois, Horowitz, & ForsterLee, 1993). With a few caveats, findings from this line of research suggest that an expert's ability to communicate clearly is crucial for ensuring that the trier of fact understands the testimony and can apply it when making decisions.

Risk communication research provides an example of how testimony complexity may influence legal decision making. Researchers in these studies have compared how judges and jurors respond to risk messages from experts that convey assessment results in either a quantitative (e.g., 29% probability) or categorical (e.g., low-risk) format. In other words, these studies have examined whether judges and jurors prefer more complex (quantitative) or less complex (categorical) risk assessment testimony. Findings from these studies converge to suggest that judges and jurors better understand and are more persuaded by categorical (less complex) testimony. For example, judges rate categorical messages as higher in probative value than quantitative messages (Kwartner, Lyons, & Boccaccini, 2006), and jurors appear to be better able to differentiate between high-risk and low-risk offenders when experts use categorical risk communication messages (Varela, Boccaccini, Cuervo, Murrie, & Clark, 2014).

PROBLEMS WITH HIGHLY TECHNICAL TESTIMONY

Horowitz and colleagues have conducted a series of studies in which they manipulated the technicality of expert-witness testimony. In an early study by this research team, jurors' verdicts in a medical malpractice case were found to be consistent with the weight of the evidence when an expert's audiotaped testimony was not highly technical, but inconsistent with the weight of the evidence when the expert's testimony was highly technical (Bourgeois et al. 1993). However, when jurors were given access to transcripts of the highly technical testimony, their verdicts were more consistent with the evidence, implying that they were only able to accurately process the technical evidence when it was given to them in writing.

Horowitz and colleagues used a videotape of a simulated trial in a series of three studies examining the impact of testimony complexity on jurors' decisions in a toxic tort case (ForsterLee, Horowitz, & Bourgeois, 1993; Horowitz, Bordens, Victor, Bourgeois, & ForsterLee, 2001; Horowitz, ForsterLee, & Brolly, 1996). ForsterLee et al. (1993) found that jurors were unable to differentially compensate four plaintiffs with varying levels of injury severity when an immunologist's expert testimony was highly technical, but they were able to do so when the testimony was moderately technical. This result was replicated and extended by Horowitz et al. (1996) using a toxic tort trial with multiple witnesses, including engineers, an environmentalist, and a clinical psychologist. Again, less complex language allowed jurors to make distinctions about liability between the different plaintiffs. This effect was stronger when jurors participated in a low information–load condition in which they heard testimony from the four plaintiffs for whom they needed to make determinations, as opposed to a high information–load condition in which they also heard testimony from four additional plaintiffs. Therefore, the jurors were better equipped to differentially assign liability when they had less evidence to process and it was presented in a comprehensible manner.

GETTING AWAY WITH HIGHLY TECHNICAL TESTIMONY

Several studies suggest that there are certain situations in which highly technical testimony may be as desirable, or possibly even more desirable, than less complex testimony. Specifically, more complex testimony may be persuasive when jurors expect complex testimony, such as when an expert comes from a highly technical field or has prestigious credentials.

Horowitz et al. (2001) found that jurors were more likely to vote in favor of a plaintiff when the experts clearly supporting the plaintiff spoke in a highly technical manner. The authors explained this result in terms of juror expectations of the primary experts in the case: engineers, biologists, and physicians. Jurors likely expect such professionals to use jargon, whereas they may not expect technical terminology from mental health professionals (who played a relatively small role in this case).

Cooper, Bennett, and Sukel (1996) varied the complexity of testimony from an expert for the plaintiff in a civil tort case. High-complexity testimony was characterized by technical jargon, while low-complexity testimony included less scientific terminology and language that could be more easily understood by laypersons. Participants voted with the plaintiff after hearing high-complexity testimony, but only when the expert was described as an accomplished researcher, from a prestigious university, who served as editor-in-chief of a biology journal. A similar study, which also included a manipulation of expert pay, found an interaction between complexity and pay (Cooper & Neuhaus, 2000). In the high complexity condition, verdicts consistent with the expert's testimony decreased as the expert's pay increased from $200 to $350 to $750 per hour. Jurors who viewed the low-complexity testimony voted for the plaintiff about 50% of the time, regardless of the expert's pay schedule. Overall, the expert was most persuasive when his testimony was presented in clear, easy to understand language, regardless of how much he was being paid. However, when the testimony was complex, mock jurors used the expert's credentials and pay scale as the basis for their judgments.

Although these findings could be interpreted to suggest that experts who want to be persuasive should charge smaller fees or should increase the complexity of their testimony if they are highly qualified, a more professionally responsible interpretation is that experts should work to reduce the complexity of their testimony. Jurors may be willing to tolerate complex information in some situations, but purposefully giving technically complex testimony is at best a high-risk gambit that could ultimately backfire and harm the parties involved in the case.

Principle 3: Clinical Knowledge

The third evidence-based principle of effective testimony is that mental health experts will be more persuasive when they include information about clinical experience and knowledge in their testimony. Mental health experts provide opinions to the court about a variety of issues, and the basis for their opinions can range from purely experience-based to purely research-based, with many combinations in between. In the mental health professions, experience-based knowledge is often referred to as *clinical knowledge*, and we use these terms interchangeably in this chapter. Because most clinical methods have at least some empirical basis or scientific support, experts have some flexibility in choosing whether to emphasize the clinical or empirical basis for their opinions.

Survey research with judges and potential jurors suggests that testimony about clinical knowledge and involvement in clinical practice may be especially important to triers of fact. Redding, Floyd, and Hawk (2001) asked 59 judges in Virginia to rank the importance of various types of expert evidence in insanity cases. Of the eight potential pieces of evidence, clinical diagnoses and mental illness were ranked first and second, while information about diagnostic reliability and statistics about the relation between crime and diagnoses were ranked fifth and eighth, respectively. Boccaccini and Brodsky (2002) surveyed 488 jury-eligible community members about the types of witnesses they would be most likely to believe and found that 82% reported that they would be most likely to believe an expert who spends most of his or her time seeing patients, as opposed to experts who focused on teaching or other scholarly work.

The most common framework for studying the influence of clinically based testimony is to compare it to actuarially based testimony. Findings from these studies suggest that judges and jurors do indeed prefer clinically based testimony.

ACTUARIAL VS. CLINICALLY BASED TESTIMONY

Actuarial judgments are sometimes referred to as being made mechanically, because they require the use of a computer or a formula. Experts typically describe actuarial assessment results using a probability or percentage. In contrast, they explain that clinical judgment testimony is based on their professional experience and firsthand knowledge of the issue being debated in court. Despite the clear research support for actuarial methods (Grove et al., 2000; Hanson & Morton-Bourgon, 2009), most clinicians still rely on clinical judgment. Most forensic evaluations require evaluators to form judgments about functioning with respect to a legal criterion, and actuarial models are not available for many of these types of evaluations. Moreover, many actuarial models used by mental health professionals require information that is based, in part, on clinical judgment. For example, actuarial models used to predict risk for future violence often require information about psychopathy. The most frequently used and research supported psychopathy measure, the Psychopathy Checklist–Revised (PCL-R; Hare, 2003), requires evaluators to make a series of structured clinical judgments that are made based on the evaluator's training and experience with the instrument.

THE PREFERENCE FOR CLINICALLY BASED TESTIMONY

A number of studies have compared the effects of actuarial- and clinically based expert-witness testimony. These studies have compared testimony based on anecdotal case histories to testimony based on empirical data in a variety of contexts, including violence risk assessment in a civil commitment case, dangerousness in a capital sentencing trial, and personal injury trials.

Findings from mock jury studies tend to show that experts who base their conclusions about violence risk on actuarial test results are less persuasive than those who do not use such tools (Krauss & Sales, 2001; McCabe, Krauss, & Lieberman, 2010). Field research with jurors who made actual civil commitment decisions after hearing experts testify about reoffense risk also indicates that jurors prefer clinically based to scientifically based testimony (Turner, 2011; Turner, Boccaccini, Murrie, & Harris, 2015). These jurors viewed experts who based opinions about risk for reoffending on meeting with and interviewing an offender as much more credible than experts who based their opinions on results from actuarial risk assessment instruments (Meeks, Boccaccini, & Turner, 2009). They also reported that actuarial risk assessment instrument results had significantly less influence on their civil commitment decisions than more clinically based information, such as the examinee's reported diagnosis, level of remorse, and motivation for treatment (Turner et al., 2015).

Researchers have reported similar effects for other types of expert-witness testimony. Bornstein (2004) conducted two experiments in which jurors read a summary of a personal injury suit that contained experts for the plaintiff (statistician) and defense (scientist vs. medical doctor). The defense expert's testimony was based on either three case histories or a lab experiment. Mock jurors in both studies showed a preference for the clinically based testimony. The results from both experiments converged on a finding that jurors who read testimony from the defense expert about experimental evidence were more likely to find the defendant liable than those who read testimony about the anecdotal case histories. This result was especially likely when the plaintiff's expert described that the incidence of the condition (arthritis) was high as opposed to low. Similar findings have also been reported by Gelinas and Alain (1993), who found that clinically based findings were considered more useful than statistical findings and that an expert presenting clinically based findings was considered more competent and professional than an expert presenting statistical findings.

THE POTENTIAL BENEFITS OF COMBINING CLINICAL AND ACTUARIAL TESTIMONY

Bornstein's (2004) second study manipulated the presence or absence of both experimental and anecdotal testimonies, so that it was possible for a juror to read a defense expert's presentation of experimental data, anecdotal information, neither, or both. Overall, results from this second study again suggested that jurors preferred clinically based testimony. Mock jurors were less likely to find the defendant liable when the expert presented anecdotal evidence than when it was absent. However, findings from this second study also indicated that the defense expert received higher credibility ratings when presenting both anecdotal and experimental testimony than when presenting experimental testimony only. Therefore, the addition of anecdotal evidence to experimental testimony increased jurors' perceptions of the expert's credibility.

Findings from a recent study examining judges' preferences for testimony about risk for future violence also suggest that combining clinical and actuarial information during testimony may be perceived as especially useful by triers of fact. Kwartner et al. (2006) examined judges' preferences for risk communication messages in a hypothetical civil commitment case. Judges preferred a categorical message (high risk) over probabilistic (76% likelihood) or frequency (76 out of every 100 people with similar features will commit a violent act towards others) messages. Of the 110 judges participating in the study, 62 (56%) reported that they would prefer testimony containing both categorical and numerical (probabilistic or frequency) formats. Only 16 (14%) expressed a preference for purely numerical testimony. Although the categorical testimony format used in this study was not directly tied to either clinically based or actuarially based information, the findings clearly indicated that judges did not prefer the two types of risk communication messages that were clearly based on actuarial methods.

For those who testify about risk assessment, using a structured professional judgment (SPJ) measure may allow experts to present results using an assessment model that clearly integrates scientifically and clinically based data (Otto & Douglas, 2010). SPJ measures provide clinicians with a list of empirically supported risk factors and ask evaluators to assign scores to each factor based on the extent to which the risk factors are present for the offender. But these measures do not require evaluators to base their conclusions on a particular score or the results of a mathematical model. Instead, they give the evaluator leeway in determining which factors are important for each specific offender or patient. Findings from one recent mock jury study suggest that this approach may resonate with jurors (Gamache, Platania, & Zaitchik, 2013). These researchers presented jurors with testimony from a mental health expert who reached a decision that an offender was at a moderate risk for reoffending. Some jurors heard testimony indicating that the expert's opinion was based on the results an actuarial risk assessment instrument (Static-2002), while others heard that the opinion was based on the results of a SPJ tool (the Sexual Violence Risk-20-R), or based on unguided clinical judgment. The jurors' perceptions of offender dangerousness were more strongly influenced by the expert using an SPJ tool or unguided clinical judgment than an actuarial measure. Although experts should not base their clinical practices on the preferences of jurors, it may make sense to use and testify about the results of an SPJ measure—either alone or in combination with other methods—if an empirically supported SPJ exists for the referral issue.

Principle 4: Certainty

The fourth evidence-based principle of effective testimony is that *persuasive experts express a high level of confidence in their opinions but do not express absolute confidence.* Experts who testify in court are often asked to express the degree of confidence they have in their opinions, and research with real jurors, experts, and attorneys suggests that expert certainty is an important component of effective testimony. Experts can demonstrate confidence in many ways, including explicitly stating levels of confidence, implying levels of confidence through strongly worded testimony, and by expressing opinions about an ultimate legal issue.

Shuman and his colleagues have conducted two surveys of experts, attorneys, and jurors from real cases and asked them to identify characteristics of effective expert witnesses (Champagne et al., 1991; Shuman et al., 1994). Findings from both studies were consistent in showing that all parties believed that an expert's "willingness to draw firm conclusions" was the second most important component of expert testimony, with the most important characteristic being the ability to convey technical information. In addition, attorneys identified being tentative as the most problematic expert-witness characteristic (Champagne et al., 1991).

Experts give ultimate-issue testimony when they provide an opinion about the decision that the trier of fact must make. For example, an expert who states that a defendant is "competent to stand trial" would be giving an opinion about the ultimate legal issue. Forensic psychologists are divided in their preferences for ultimate opinion testimony (an opinion about the ultimate legal issue). Some believe that it is inappropriate to testify to the ultimate legal issue (Tillbrook, Mumley, & Grisso, 2003), whereas others are opposed to limiting the scope of expert testimony by prohibiting ultimate opinions (Rogers & Ewing, 2003).[1] The Federal Rules of Evidence were changed after the insanity acquittal of John Hinkley Jr. to bar experts from providing ultimate-issue testimony about insanity (FRE 704 b). However, some states require ultimate issue opinions in certain types of cases (e.g., Florida and Texas require an ultimate opinion about competence to stand trial) and the courts often expect ultimate-issue testimony (Redding et al., 2001). Perhaps consistent with these expectations, studies of forensic evaluation reports (Heilbrun & Collins, 1995) and clinical practices (Borum & Grisso, 1996) suggest that forensic evaluators often provide ultimate issue opinions.

Although few studies have examined the impact of expressed confidence or ultimate-issue testimony from experts, findings from these studies seem to converge in suggesting that the most persuasive expert is one who expresses confidence in his or her opinion without appearing overconfident..

Rogers, Bagby, Crouch, and Cutler (1990) found no statistically significant effects for the presence or absence of ultimate opinion testimony on mock jurors' perceptions of insanity. However, there was a significant interaction: Jurors who read testimony about diagnosis and impairment that suggested that the defendant was insane judged the defendant to be more insane at the time of the crime than jurors who heard testimony suggesting or stating that the defendant was sane. Thus, the diagnostic and impairment testimony arguing for insanity was more influential than ultimate-issue testimony stating that the defendant was insane.

In a follow-up study, Rogers, Bagby, and Chow (1992) failed to find any effects for the presence of ultimate opinion testimony. Interestingly, there was an interaction between the content of the expert's testimony and the expert's expressed confidence. An expert who was 80% confident in his or her sanity opinion exerted significantly more influence on juror perceptions of insanity than experts who were 60% or 100% confident in their opinions. Although the authors did not find significant differences in ratings of clarity and believability for experts who did and did not give an ultimate opinion, jurors' evaluations of expert clarity increased in relation to the level of confidence expressed by the expert. Ratings of expert believability were highest when the expert expressed high confidence in his or her opinion (80% or 100%). Studies examining confidence among experts offering risk opinions have reported similar findings (Cramer, Brodsky, & DeCoster, 2009).

Fulero and Finkel (1991) examined differences in the influence of ultimate issue and penultimate-issue testimony on mock jurors' perceptions of insanity. An expert giving penultimate-issue testimony speaks directly to the criteria that the trier of fact should consider when making decisions, but does not offer an ultimate issue opinion. For example, penultimate-issue testimony in an insanity case might speak to whether or not the defendant knew what he or she was doing and, if so, knew what he or she was doing was wrong. Although Fulero and Finkel (1991) found no statistically significant differences between penultimate and ultimate opinion testimony, their study was underpowered ($n < 25$ in several conditions) for detecting differences in the three case outcomes available to jurors (insanity, first degree murder, and manslaughter). Nevertheless, their findings were clear in showing the ultimate-issue testimony from the prosecution; a combination of ultimate-issue testimony from both the defense and prosecution had little impact on jurors' decisions. However, 51% of the jurors who heard uncontested penultimate-issue testimony from the defense arguing that the defendant was insane found that the defendant was insane. Only 30% of those who heard uncontested ultimate-issue testimony from the defense found that the defendant was insane. The effect-size for this difference is moderate in size ($\Phi = .21$) and is consistent with Rogers et al.'s (1990, 1992) findings in suggesting that jurors may be most influenced by testimony that clearly and strongly speaks to the decisions they have to make, but leaves some room for them to exercise their own judgment.

SLANTED AND STRONGLY WORDED TESTIMONY

Another way in which researchers have studied expert certainty is to manipulate the extent to which the expert's conclusions are unambiguous in favoring one side of the case, or are more cautious or balanced in acknowledging possible limitations. The two studies that have manipulated this aspect of certainty indicate that jurors prefer unambiguous testimony that is strongly worded. For example, Brekke, Enko, Clavet, and Seelau (1991) manipulated whether the testimony was slanted in favor of the prosecution or balanced. In the balanced conditions, the expert discussed limitations of the evidence. Results indicated that, as expected, the slanted testimony yielded the highest conviction rates for defendants in both the prosecution and court-appointed expert conditions. The slanted testimony was also rated as being more useful and of higher quality than more balanced testimony that acknowledged the presence of some shortcomings. Rudy (1996) manipulated the strength of the expert's testimony in a sexual abuse case. There were no significant differences in verdict between jurors hearing a high-certainty expert statement and more neutral testimony. However, mock jurors rated the high-certainty testimony as more credible than neutral testimony.

From Principles to Practice

Together, findings from existing research suggest that the most influential testimony is testimony that is easy to understand, based on clinical knowledge, and stated with a high degree of certainty. The most influential experts are those who present as both competent and likeable. The four evidence-based principles for effective testimony we have identified in this chapter are clearly interrelated. Testimony based on clinical knowledge may be influential because it is usually more clear and case-specific than research-based testimony. Experts who express a high degree of certainty in their opinions may be more persuasive because their testimony is clearer and easier to understand than balanced testimony.

The extent to which experts can and should apply the four principles in the courtroom will depend on a number of factors. First, the format of courtroom testimony requires that experts provide information by responding to attorney questions. The information that the attorney attempts to elicit from the expert may not necessarily be the information that the expert feels is most relevant or persuasive. For example, an attorney may choose to ask hypothetical questions instead of case-specific questions to limit the scope of the questions that can be asked about the client during cross-examination. Many experts insist on pretrial discussions with the attorneys who are calling them to testify. The purpose of pretrial discussions is for the expert to ensure that the attorney is aware of the information that the expert will be able to provide, and that the expert is aware of the information that the attorney would like the expert to provide. Pretrial discussions between the expert and attorney can prevent awkward situations in the courtroom in which the expert is unprepared to answer the attorney's questions and the attorney is unprepared to ask questions about the expert's opinions.

Second, experts are bound by their professional ethical principles and must not violate these principles to improve the persuasiveness of their testimony. For example, the American

Psychological Association's *Ethical Principles and Code of Conduct* (American Psychological Association, 2002) maintain that psychologists have a responsibility to communicate their conclusions using language that is understandable and "do not make false, misleading, or fraudulent statements"(p. 1067). Likewise, the American Psychological Association's *Specialty Guidelines for Forensic Psychologists* (2013) require that "forensic practitioners do not distort or withhold relevant evidence or opinion in reports or testimony" (p. 16). If psychologists blindly followed our evidence-based principles for effective testimony without adherence to their professional ethical code they might give false testimony by overstating their confidence in an opinion or purposefully use highly complex testimony to improve their persuasiveness (if they have prestigious credentials).

Third, case characteristics should drive the expert's testimony more than the principles identified in this chapter and will place limits on what the expert can and cannot say in the courtroom. For example, forensic cases vary in complexity and in the information available for completing evaluations. The complexity of an expert's testimony and the relevance of clinical and research knowledge will be driven by the characteristics of the case, and the expert will usually only have a limited amount of leeway in testifying about these issues.

Other Resources for Experts

There are many useful and popular "how-to" books available for clinicians interested in providing effective testimony (e.g., Otto et al., 2014). These guides for expert witnesses provide practical suggestions for witness preparation and extensive recommendations for effective courtroom presentation. Stan Brodsky's series of books on testifying in court (Brodsky, 1991, 1999, 2004, 2013) are highly readable and an invaluable resource for expert witnesses. Experts may also find it useful to review books designed to provide attorneys with information and techniques for discrediting or impeaching mental health experts during cross-examination (e.g., Faust, 2012). Mental health professionals may consult with these texts in an effort to prepare for the rigors of cross-examination. Finally, beginning experts should consult books by Barsky and Gould (2002) and Otto et al. (2014), which provide useful information about a variety of issues related to testifying, including the trial process, rules of testifying, preparing affidavits, and responding to subpoenas and court orders.

Note

1   See Roesch and Viljoen (Chapter 12 in this volume) for a discussion of ultimate opinion testimony in the context of competency to stand trial assessments.

References

American Psychological Association. (2002). Ethical principles of psychologists and code of conduct. *American Psychologist, 57*, 1060–1073. doi: 10.1037/0003–066X.57.12.1060

American Psychological Association. (2013). Specialty guidelines for forensic psychologists. *American Psychologist, 68*, 7–19. doi: 10.1037/a0029889

Barsky, A. E., & Gould, J. W. (2002). *Clinicians in court: A guide to subpoenas, depositions, testifying, and everything else you need to know*. New York: Guilford.

Blau, T. H. (1998). *The psychologist as expert witness* (2nd ed.) New York: Wiley.

Boccaccini, M. T. & Brodsky, S. L. (2002). Believability of expert and lay witnesses: Implications for trial consultation. *Professional Psychology: Research and Practice, 33*, 384–388. doi: 10.1037/0735–7028.33.4.384.

Bornstein, B. H. (2004). The impact of different types of expert scientific testimony on mock jurors' liability verdicts. *Psychology, Crime, and Law, 10*, 429–446. doi: 10.1080/1068316030001629292

Borum, R., & Grisso, T. (1996). Establishing standards for criminal forensic reports: An empirical analysis. *Bulletin of the American Academy of Psychiatry and Law, 24*, 297–317.

Bourgeois, M.J., Horowitz, I.A., & ForsterLee, L. (1993). Effects of technicality and access to trial transcripts on verdicts and information processing in a civil trial. *Personality and Social Psychology Bulletin, 19,* 220–227. doi: 10.1177/0146167293192012

Brekke, N.J., Enko, P.J., Clavet, G., & Seelau, E. (1991). Of juries and court-appointed experts. *Law and Human Behavior, 15,* 451–475. doi: 10.1037/h0093997

Brodsky, S.L. (1991). *Testifying in court: Guidelines and maxims for the expert.* Washington, DC: American Psychological Association.

Brodsky, S.L. (1999). *Expert expert witness: More maxims and guidelines for testifying in court.* Washington, DC: American Psychological Association.

Brodsky, S.L. (2004). *Coping with cross-examination and other pathways to effective testimony.* Washington, DC: American Psychological Association.

Brodsky, S.L. (2013) *Testifying in court: Guidelines and maxims for the expert witnesses* (2nd ed.). Washington, DC: American Psychological Association.

Brodsky, S.L. & Anderer, S.J. (1999). Serving as an expert witness: Evaluations, subpoenas, and testimony. In F. W. Kaslow (Ed.), *Handbook of couple and family forensics: A sourcebook for mental health and legal professionals* (pp. 475–490). New York: Wiley.

Brodsky, S.L., Griffin, M.P., & Cramer, R.J. (2010). The Witness Credibility Scale: An outcome measure for expert witness research. *Behavioral Sciences and the Law, 28,* 892–907. doi: 10.1002/bsl.917

Brodsky, S.L. & Robey, A. (1972). On becoming an expert witness: Issues of orientation and effectiveness. *Professional Psychology, 3,* 173–176. doi: 10.1037/h0034505

Champagne, A., Shuman, D., & Whitaker, E. (1991). An empirical examination of the use of expert witnesses in American courts. *Jurimetrics Journal, 31,* 375–392.

Chappelle, W., & Rosengren, K. (2001). Maintaining composure and credibility as an expert witness during cross-examination. *Journal of Forensic Psychology Practice, 1,* 51–67. doi: 10.1300/J158v01n03_03

Cooper, J., Bennett, E.A., & Sukel, H.L. (1996). Complex scientific testimony: How do jurors make decisions? *Law and Human Behavior, 20,* 379–394. doi: 10.1007/BF01498976

Cooper, J., & Neuhaus, I.M. (2000). The "hired gun" effect: Assessing the effect of pay, frequency of testifying, and credentials on the perception of expert testimony. *Law and Human Behavior, 24,* 149–171. doi: 10.1023/A:1005476618435

Cramer, R.J., Brodsky, S.L., & DeCoster, J. (2009). Expert witness confidence and juror personality: Their impact on credibility and persuasion in the courtroom. *Journal of the American Academy of Psychiatry and the Law, 37,* 63–74.

Cramer, R.J., DeCoster, J., Harris, P.B., Fletcher, L., & Brodsky, S.L. (2011). A confidence-credibility model of expert witness persuasion: Mediating effects and implications for trial consultation. *Consulting Psychology Journal: Practice and Research, 63,* 129–137. doi: 10.1037/a0024591

Dahir, V.B., Richardson, J.T., Ginsburg, G.P., Gatowski, S.I., Dobbin, S.A., & Merlino, M.M. (2005). Judicial application of *Daubert* to psychological syndrome and profile evidence: A research note. *Psychology, Public Policy, and Law, 11,* 62–82. doi: 10.1037/1076–8971.11.1.62

Daubert v. Merrell Dow Pharmaceuticals, 509 US 579 (1993).

Dixon, L., & Gill, B. (2002). Changes in standards for admitting expert evidence in federal civil cases since the *Daubert* decision. *Psychology, Public Policy, and Law, 8,* 251–308. doi: 10.1037/1076–8971.8.3.251

Faust, D., Grimm, P.W., Ahern, DC, & Sokolik, M. (2010). The admissibility of behavioral science evidence in the courtroom: The translation of legal to scientific concepts and back. *Annual Review of Clinical Psychology, 6,* 49–77. doi: 10.1146/annurev.clinpsy.3.022806.091523

Faust, D. (2012). *Coping with psychiatric and psychological testimony* (6th ed.). New York: Oxford University Press.

Federal Rules of Evidence, Rule 702.

ForsterLee, L., Horowitz, I.A., & Bourgeois, M.J. (1993). Juror competence in civil trials: Effects of preinstruction and evidence technicality. *Journal of Applied Psychology, 78,* 14–21. doi: 10.1037/0021–9010.78.1.14

Fradella, H.F., Fogarty, A., & O'Neill, L. (2003). The impact of Daubert on the admissibility of behavioral science testimony. *Pepperdine Law Review, 30,* 403–444.

Frye v. United States, 293 F.1013 (DC Cir. 1923).

Fulero, S.M., & Finkel, N.J. (1991). Barring ultimate-issue testimony: An "insane" rule? *Law and Human Behavior, 15,* 495–507. doi: 10.1007/BF01650291

Gamache, K., Platania, J., & Zaitchik, M. (2013). Evaluating future dangerousness and need for treatment: The roles of expert testimony, attributional complexity, and victim type. *Open Access Journal of Forensic Psychology, 5*, 53–80.

Gatowski, S. I., Dobbin, S. A., Richardson, J. T., Ginsburg, G. P., Merlino, M. L., & Dahir, V. (2001). Asking the gatekeepers: A national survey of judges on judging expert evidence in a post-*Daubert* world. *Law and Human Behavior, 25*, 433–458. doi: 10.1023/A:1012899030937

Gelinas, L., & Alain, M. (1993). Expertise psycho-juridique: Une evaluation de deux types de rapports et de leur influence sur la perception de jures potentiels. *Canadian Journal of Behavioural Sciences, 25*, 175–192. doi: 10.1037/h0078806

Greiffenstein, M. F., & Kaufmann, P. J. (2012). Neuropsychology and the law: Principles of productive attorney-neuropsychologist relations. In G. J. Larrabee (Ed.), *Forensic neuropsychology: A scientific approach* (2nd ed., pp. 75–98). New York: Oxford University Press.

Groscup, J. L. (2004). Judicial decision making about expert testimony in the aftermath of *Daubert* and *Kumho. Journal of Forensic Psychology Practice, 4*, 57–67.

Groscup, J. L., Penrod, S. D., Studebaker, C. A., Huss, M. T., & O'Neil, K. M. (2002). The effects of *Daubert* on admissibility of expert testimony in state and federal criminal cases. *Psychology, Public Policy, and Law, 8*, 339–372. doi: 10.1300/J158v04n02_03

Grove, W. M., Zald, D. H., Lebow, B. S., Snitz, B. E., & Nelson, C. (2000). Clinical versus mechanical prediction: A meta-analysis. *Psychological Assessment, 12*, 19–30. doi: 10.1037/1040–3590.12.1.19

Gutheil, T. G. (2000). The presentation of forensic psychiatric evidence in court. *Israel Journal of Psychiatry and Related Science, 37*, 137–144.

Hanson, R. K., & Morton-Bourgon, K. E. (2009). The accuracy of recidivism risk assessments for sexual offenders: A meta-analysis of 118 prediction studies. *Psychological Assessment, 21*, 1–21. doi: 10.1037/a0014421

Hare, R. D. (2003). *The Hare Psychopathy Checklist–Revised manual* (2nd ed.). North Tonawanda, NY: Multi-Health Systems.

Harris, P. B., Varela, J. G., Boccaccini, M. T., & Turner, D. B. (2014, March). *Responses of real jurors in SVP trials regarding helpfulness of expert witness testimony*. Poster presented at the meeting of the American Psychology-Law Society, New Orleans, LA.

Heilbrun, K., & Collins, S. (1995). Evaluations of trial competency and mental state at the time of the offense: Report characteristics. *Professional Psychology: Research and Practice, 26*, 61–67. doi: 10.1037/0735–7028.26.1.61

Horowitz, I. A., Bordens, K. S., Victor, E., Bourgeois, M. J., & ForsterLee, L. (2001). The effects of complexity on jurors' verdicts and construction of evidence. *Journal of Applied Psychology, 86*, 641–652. doi: 10.1037/0021–9010.86.4.641

Horowitz, I. A., ForsterLee, l., & Brolly, I. (1996). Effects of trial complexity on decision making. *Journal of Applied Psychology, 81*, 757–768. doi: 10.1037/0021–9010.81.6.757

Kovera, M. B., & McAuliff, B. D. (2000). The effects of peer review and evidence quality on judge evaluations of psychological science: Are judges effective gatekeepers? *Journal of Applied Psychology, 85*, 574–586. doi: 10.1037/0021–9010.85.4.574

Krauss, D. A., & Sales, B. D. (2001). The effects of clinical and scientific expert testimony on juror decision making in capital sentencing. *Psychology, Public Policy, and Law, 7*, 267–310. doi: 10.1037/1076–8971.7.2.267

Kumho Tire Co. v. Carmichael, 526 U.S. 137 (1999).

Kwartner, P. P. (2007). *The impact of educative and evaluative expert witness testimony on trial outcome: A meta-analytic review* (Doctoral dissertation). Available from ProQuest dissertations and theses database. (UMI No. AAI3278733).

Kwartner, P. P., & Boccaccini, M. T. (2008). Testifying in court: Evidence-based recommendations for expert-witness testimony. In R. Jackson (Ed.), *Learning forensic assessment* (pp. 565–588). New York: Routledge.

Kwartner, P. P., Lyons, P. M., & Boccaccini, M. T. (2006). Judges' risk communication preferences in risk for future violence cases. *International Journal of Forensic Mental Health, 5*, 185–194. doi: 10.1080/14999013.2006.10471242

Lubet, S. (1998). *Expert testimony: A guide for expert witnesses and the lawyers who examine them*. Notre Dame, IN: NITA.

McCabe, J., Krauss, D., & Lieberman, J. (2010). Reality check: A comparison of college students and community samples of mock jurors in a simulated sexual violent predator civil commitment. *Behavioral Sciences and the Law, 28*, 730–750. doi: 10.1002/bsl.902

Meeks, M., Boccaccini, M. T., & Turner, D. (2009, March). Evidence or experts?: SVP jurors beliefs about influences in their trial decisions. In D. Krauss (Chair), *Expert witness testimony in sexually violent predator trials*. Symposium presented at the meeting of the American Psychology-Law Society, San Antonio, Texas.

Merlino, M. L., Murray, C. I., & Richardson, J. T. (2008). Judicial gatekeeping and the social construction of the admissibility of expert testimony. *Behavioral Sciences and the Law, 26*, 187–206. doi: 10.1002/bsl.806

Neal, T.M.S., & Brodsky, S. L. (2008). Expert witness credibility as a function of eye contact behavior and gender. *Criminal Justice and Behavior, 35*, 1515–1526. doi: 10.1177/0093854808325405

Neal, T.M.S., Guadagno, R. E., Eno, C., & Brodsky, S. L. (2012). Warmth and competence on the witness stand: Implications for the credibility of male and female expert witnesses. *Journal of the American Academy of Psychiatry and the Law, 40*, 488–497.

Otto, R. K., DeMier, R. L., & Boccaccini, M. T. (2014). *Forensic reports and testimony: A guide to effective communication for psychologists and psychiatrists*. Hoboken, NJ: Wiley.

Otto, R. K., & Douglas, K. (Eds.). (2010). *Handbook of violent risk assessment*. New York: Routledge.

Parry, J. W. (2004). Expert evidence and testimony: Daubert vs. Frye. *Mental and Physical Disability Law Reporter, 28*, 136–140.

Redding, R. E., Floyd, M. Y., & Hawk, G. L. (2001). What judges and lawyers think about the testimony of mental health experts: A survey of the courts and bar. *Behavioral Sciences and the Law, 19*, 583–594. doi: 10.1002/bsl.455

Rogers, R., Bagby, R. M., & Chow, M. K. (1992). Psychiatrists and the parameters of expert testimony. *International Journal of Law and Psychiatry, 15*, 387–396. doi: 10.1016/0160–2527(92)90019-W

Rogers, R., Bagby, R. M., Crouch, M., & Cutler, B. (1990). Effects of ultimate opinion on juror perceptions of insanity. *International Journal of Law and Psychiatry, 13*, 225–232. doi: 10.1016/0160–2527(90)90018-X

Rogers, R., & Ewing, C. P. (2003). The prohibition of ultimate opinions: A misguided enterprise. *Journal of Forensic Psychology Practice, 3*, 65–75. doi: 10.1300/J158v03n03_04

Rudy, L.A. (1996). Custody and expert opinion as factors in sexual abuse cases. Doctoral dissertation, Ohio State University, 1996. *Dissertation Abstracts International*, 57, 3422.

Shuman, D., Whitaker, E., & Champagne, A. (1994). An empirical examination of the use of expert witnesses in the courts. Part II: A three-city study. *Jurimetrics Journal, 34*, 193–208.

Tillbrook, C., Mumley, D., & Grisso, T. (2003). Avoiding expert opinions on the ultimate legal question: The case for integrity. *Journal of Forensic Psychology Practice, 3*, 77–87. doi: 10.1300/J158v03n03_05

Turner, D. B. (2011). Juror perceptions of the influence of expert witness testimony in Texas sexually violent predator civil commitment hearings. Doctoral dissertation. Sam Houston State University, Huntsville, Texas. Available from ProQuest dissertations and theses database (UMI No. 3484779).

Turner, D. B., Boccaccini, M. T., Murrie, D. C., & Harris, P. B. (2015). Jurors report that risk scores matter in SVP trials, but that other factors matter more. *Behavioral Sciences and the Law, 33*, 56-73. doi: 10.1002/bsl.2154

Varela, J. G., Boccaccini, M. T., Cuervo, V. A., Murrie, DC, & Clark, J. W. (2014). Same score, different message: Jurors' perceptions of offender risk depend on Static-99R risk communication format. *Law and Human Behavior. 38*, 418-427. doi: 10.1037/lhb0000073

Wilkinson, A. P. (1997). Forensic psychiatry: The making and breaking of expert opinion testimony. *The Journal of Psychiatry and Law, 25*, 51–112.

Index

Note: Italicized page numbers indicate a figure. Page numbers in bold indicate a table.

Date Due

APR 0 3 2019			

BRODART, CO.   Cat. No. 23-233   Printed in U.S.A.